Contents

righter Thinking

A Level Mathematics for OCR A

Student Book 2 (Year 2)

Vesna Kadelburg, Ben Woolley, Paul Fannon and Stephen Ward

CAMBRIDGE
UNIVERSITY PRESS

University Printing House, Cambridge CB2 8BS, United Kingdom

One Liberty Plaza, 20th Floor, New York, NY 10006, USA

477 Williamstown Road, Port Melbourne, VIC 3207, Australia

314–321, 3rd Floor, Plot 3, Splendor Forum, Jasola District Centre, New Delhi – 110025, India

79 Anson Road, #06–04/06, Singapore 079906

Cambridge University Press is part of the University of Cambridge.

It furthers the University's mission by disseminating knowledge in the pursuit of education, learning and research at the highest international levels of excellence.

www.cambridge.org
Information on this title: www.cambridge.org/9781316644300 (Paperback)
www.cambridge.org/9781316644676 (Paperback with Cambridge Elevate edition)

First published 2017

20 19 18 17 16 15 14 13 12 11 10 9 8 7 6 5 4 3

Printed in the United Kingdom by Latimer Trend

A catalogue record for this publication is available from the British Library

ISBN 978-1-316-64430-0 Paperback
ISBN 978-1-316-64467-6 Paperback with Cambridge Elevate edition

Additional resources for this publication at www.cambridge.org/education

Introduction

You have probably been told that mathematics is very useful, yet it can often seem like a lot of techniques that just have to be learnt to answer examination questions. You are now getting to the point where you will start to see where some of these techniques can be applied in solving real problems. However, as well as seeing how maths can be useful we hope that anyone working through this book will realise that it can also be incredibly frustrating, surprising and ultimately beautiful.

The book is woven around three key themes from the new curriculum:

Proof

Maths is valued because it trains you to think logically and communicate precisely. At a high level, maths is far less concerned about answers and more about the clear communication of ideas. It is not about being neat – although that might help! It is about creating a coherent argument that other people can easily follow but find difficult to refute. Have you ever tried looking at your own work? If you cannot follow it yourself it is unlikely anybody else will be able to understand it. In maths we communicate using a variety of means – feel free to use combinations of diagrams, words and algebra to aid your argument. And once you have attempted a proof, try presenting it to your peers. Look critically (but positively) at some other people's attempts. It is only through having your own attempts evaluated and trying to find flaws in other proofs that you will develop sophisticated mathematical thinking. This is why we have included lots of common errors in our 'work it out' boxes – just in case your friends don't make any mistakes!

Problem solving

Maths is valued because it trains you to look at situations in unusual, creative ways, to persevere and to evaluate solutions along the way. We have been heavily influenced by a great mathematician and maths educator, George Polya, who believed that students were not just born with problem solving skills – they were developed by seeing problems being solved and reflecting on their solutions before trying similar problems. You may not realise it but good mathematicians spend most of their time being stuck. You need to spend some time on problems you can't do, trying out different possibilities. If after a while you have not cracked it then look at the solution and try a similar problem. Don't be disheartened if you cannot get it immediately – in fact, the longer you spend puzzling over a problem the more you will learn from the solution. You may never need to integrate a rational function in future, but we firmly believe that the problem solving skills you will develop by trying it can be applied to many other situations.

Modelling

Maths is valued because it helps us solve real-world problems. However, maths describes ideal situations and the real world is messy! Modelling is about deciding on the important features needed to describe the essence of a situation and turning that into a mathematical form, then using it to make predictions, compare to reality and possibly improve the model. In many situations the technical maths is actually the easy part – especially with modern technology. Deciding which features of reality to include or ignore and anticipating the consequences of these decisions is the hard part. Yet it is amazing how some fairly drastic assumptions – such as pretending a car is a single point or that people's votes are independent – can result in models that are surprisingly accurate.

More than anything else, this book is about making links. Links between the different chapters, the topics covered and the themes above, links to other subjects and links to the real world. We hope that you will grow to see maths as one great complex but beautiful web of interlinking ideas.

Maths is about so much more than examinations, but we hope that if you take on board these ideas (and do plenty of practice!) you will find maths examinations a much more approachable and possibly even enjoyable experience. However, always remember that the results of what you write down in a few hours by yourself in silence under exam conditions is not the only measure you should consider when judging your mathematical ability – it is only one variable in a much more complicated mathematical model!

How to use this book

Throughout this book you will notice particular features that are designed to aid your learning. This section provides a brief overview of these features.

In this chapter you will:

- review proof by deduction, proof by exhaustion and disproof by counter example
- learn a new method of proof called proof by contradiction
- practise criticising proofs.

Learning objectives
A short summary of the content that you will learn in each chapter.

Before you start…

Student Book 1, Chapter 1	You should be able to use logical connectors.	1 Insert either ⇒, ⇐ or ⇔ in the places marked A and B: $x^2-1=8$ A $x^2=9$ B $x=3$
Student Book 1, Chapter 1	You should be able to use disproof by counter example.	2 Disprove the statement 'apart from 1 there are no other integers that can be written as both n^2 and n^3'.

Before you start
Points you should know from your previous learning and questions to check that you're ready to start the chapter.

WORKED EXAMPLE

The left-hand side shows you how to set out your working. The right-hand side explains the more difficult steps and helps you understand why a particular method was chosen.

Key point

A summary of the most important methods, facts and formulae.

PROOF

Step-by-step walkthroughs of standard proofs and methods of proof.

Explore

Ideas for activities and investigations to extend your understanding of the topic.

WORK IT OUT

Can you identify the correct solution and find the mistakes in the two incorrect solutions?

Tip

Useful guidance, including on ways of calculating or checking answers and using technology.

Each chapter ends with a **Checklist of learning and understanding** and a **Mixed practice exercise**, which includes **past paper questions** marked with the icon .

In between chapters, you will find extra sections that bring together topics in a more synoptic way.

Focus on …

Unique sections relating to the preceding chapters that develop your skills in proof, problem solving and modelling.

CROSS-TOPIC REVIEW EXERCISE

Questions covering topics from across the preceding chapters, testing your ability to apply what you have learnt.

You will find **Paper 1, Paper 2 and Paper 3 practice questions** towards the end of the book, as well as a glossary of key terms (picked out in colour within the chapters), and **answers** to all questions. Fully **worked solutions** can be found on the Cambridge Elevate digital platform, along with other essential resources such as a **digital version** of this Student Book.

Maths is all about making links, which is why throughout this book you will find signposts emphasising connections between different topics, applications and suggestions for further research.

Rewind

Reminders of where to find useful information from earlier in your study.

Focus on ...

Links to problem solving, modelling or proof exercises that relate to the topic currently being studied.

Fast forward

Links to topics that you may cover in greater detail later in your study.

Did you know?

Interesting or historical information and links with other subjects to improve your awareness about how mathematics contributes to society.

Some of the links point to the material available only through the **Cambridge Elevate** digital platform.

Elevate

A support sheet for each chapter contains further worked examples and exercises on the most common question types. Extension sheets provide further challenge for the more ambitious.

Gateway to A Level

GCSE transition material that provides a summary of facts and methods you need to know before you start a new topic, with worked examples and practice questions.

Colour-coding of exercises

The questions in the exercises are designed to provide careful progression, ranging from basic fluency to practice questions. They are uniquely colour-coded, as shown below.

1. A sequence is defined by $u_n = 2 \times 3^{n-1}$. Use the principle of mathematical induction to prove that $u_1 + u_2 + \ldots + u_n = 3^n - 1$.
2. Show that $1^2 + 2^2 + \ldots + n^2 = \frac{n(n+1)(2n+1)}{6}$
3. Show that $1^3 + 2^3 + \ldots + n^3 = \frac{n^2(n+1)^2}{4}$
4. Prove by induction that $\frac{1}{1\times 2} + \frac{1}{2\times 3} + \frac{1}{3\times 4} + \ldots + \frac{1}{n(n+1)} = \frac{n}{n+1}$
5. Prove by induction that $\frac{1}{1\times 3} + \frac{1}{3\times 5} + \frac{1}{5\times 7} + \ldots + \frac{1}{(2n-1)\times(2n+1)} = \frac{n}{2n+1}$
6. Prove that $1 \times 1! + 2 \times + 3 \times 3! \ldots + n \times n! = (n+1)! - 1$
7. Use the principle of mathematical induction to show that $1^2 - 2^2 + 3^2 - 4^2 + \ldots + (-1)^{n-1} n^2 = (-1)^{n-1}\frac{n(n+1)}{2}$.
8. Prove that $(n+1) + (n+2) + (n+3) + \ldots + (2n) = \frac{1}{2}n(3n+1)$
9. Prove using induction that $\sin\theta + \sin 3\theta + \ldots + \sin(2n-1)\theta = \frac{\sin^2 n\theta}{\sin\theta},\ n \in \mathbb{Z}^+$
10. Prove that $\sum_{k=1}^{n} k\, 2^k = (n-1)2^{n+1} + 2$

Black – drill questions. These come in several parts, each with subparts **i** and **ii**. You only need attempt subpart **i** at first; subpart **ii** is essentially the same question, which you can use for further practice if you got part **i** wrong, for homework, or when you revisit the exercise during revision.

Green – practice questions at a basic level.

Blue – practice questions at an intermediate level.

Red – practice questions at an advanced level.

Yellow – designed to encourage reflection and discussion.

Working with the large data set

As part of your course you are expected to work with the large data set covering different methods of transport and age distributions in different parts of the country and in different years. This large data set is an opportunity to explore statistics in real life. As well as supporting the ideas introduced in Chapters 16 and 18 we shall be using the large data set to guide you through four key themes. All of these themes will be explored with examples and questions in the large data set section in the Cambridge Elevate edition. You will not have to work with the full data set in the final examination, but familiarity with it will help you as many examination questions will be set in the context of this data set.

Practical difficulties with data

Unlike most textbook or examination problems, the real world is messy. Often there are difficulties with being overwhelmed by too much data, or perhaps there are errors, missing items or labels which are ambiguous. For example, how do you deal with the fact that in 2001 Cornwall was made up of separate districts that were later combined into a single unitary authority, if you want to compare areas over time? If you are grouping data for a histogram, how big a difference does it make where you choose to put the class boundaries?

Using technology

Modern statistics is heavily based on familiarity with technology. We will be encouraging you to use spreadsheets and graphing packages, looking at the common tools available to help simplify calculations and present data effectively.

One important technique we can employ with modern technology is simulation. We will try to gain a better understanding of hypothesis testing by using the data set to simulate the effect of sampling on making inferences about the population.

Thinking critically about statistics

Why might someone want to use a pie chart rather than a histogram? Whenever statistics are calculated or data sets are represented graphically, some information is lost and some information is highlighted. An important part of modern statistics is to ask critical questions about the way evidence provided by statistics is used to support arguments.

One important part of this is the idea of validating statistics. For example, with the information presented it is not clear which category or categories a person would be included in if they travel to work by bicycle on some days and take the bus on others. We will look at ways in which we can interrogate the data to try to understand it more.

Statistical problem solving

Technology can often do calculations for us. However the art of modern statistics is deciding what calculations to do on what data. One of the big difficulties is that we rarely have exactly the data we want, so we have to make indirect inferences from the data we have. For example, you will probably not see newspaper headlines saying 'the correlation coefficient between median age and percentage of people cycling to work is 0.64', but you might see something saying 'Pensioners promote pedalling!' Deciding on an appropriate statistical technique to determine whether older people are more likely to use a bicycle and then interpreting results is the type of thing which is hard to examine but very valuable in real-world statistics.

There are lots of decisions to be made. Should you use the total number of cyclists in an area? Or the percentage of people who cycle? Or the percentage of people who travel to work who cycle? We shall see how the answer to your main question depends on decisions like these.

1 Proof and mathematical communication

In this chapter you will:

- review proof by deduction, proof by exhaustion and disproof by counter example
- learn a new method of proof called proof by contradiction
- practise criticising proofs.

Before you start…

Student Book 1, Chapter 1	You should be able to use logical connectors.	1 Insert either $\Rightarrow$, $\Leftarrow$ or $\Leftrightarrow$ in the places marked A and B: $x^2-1=8$ A $x^2=9$ B $x=3$
Student Book 1, Chapter 1	You should be able to use disproof by counter example.	2 Disprove the statement 'apart from 1 there are no other integers that can be written as both n^2 and n^3'.
Student Book 1, Chapter 1	You should be able to use proof by deduction.	3 Prove that the sum of any two odd numbers is always even.
Student Book 1, Chapter 1	You should be able to use proof by exhaustion.	4 Use proof by exhaustion to prove that 17 is a prime number.

Developing proof

One of the purposes of this chapter is to act as revision of the material from Student Book 1. It draws on all chapters from that book but, in particular, it builds on the fundamental ideas of proof from Chapter 1. This chapter introduces a new and very powerful method of proof that mathematicians often rely on: proof by contradiction.

Section 1: A reminder of methods of proof

In Student Book 1 you met proof by deduction, proof by exhaustion and disproof by counter example. The following questions show how these methods can be used in topics from throughout Student Book 1.

EXERCISE 1A

1. Use proof by exhaustion to prove that 17 is a prime number.

2. Prove by exhaustion that all square numbers end in 0, 1, 4, 5, 6 or 9.

3. The velocity of a particle after time t is given by $v = t^2 + 3$. Prove that the particle never returns to its original position.

4. **a** Prove from first principles that if $y = x^2$ then $\frac{dy}{dx} = 2x$.

   b Use a counter example to show that if $\frac{dy}{dx} = 2x$, then it is not necessarily true that $y = x^2$.

5. Use a counter example to show that the following statement is not true:

$$\sin 2x = 1 \Rightarrow x = 45°$$

6. Prove that $\binom{n}{1} = n$.

7. A set of data has mean A, mode B and median C. Consider the following statement: $B < A \Rightarrow C < A$.

   Prove this statement or use a counter example to disprove it.

8. The diagram shows triangle OAB, where AB lies on the circle with centre O. M is the midpoint of AB.

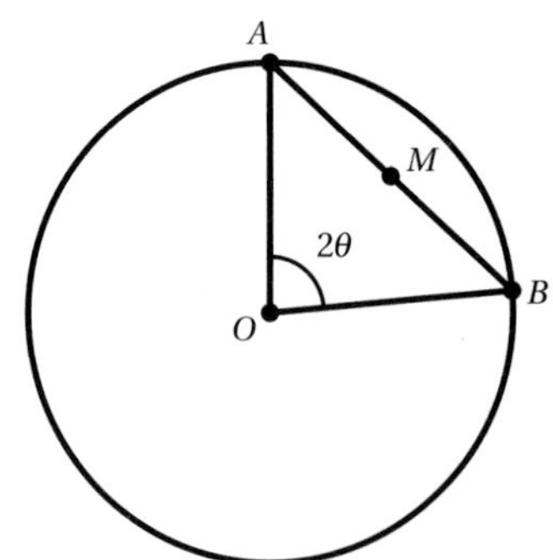

   a Use the cosine rule to prove that $AB = \sqrt{2r^2 - 2r^2 \cos(2\theta)}$.

   b Show that $AM = r \sin\theta$.

   c Hence, prove that $\cos 2\theta = 1 - 2\sin^2\theta$.

9. In quadrilateral $OABC$, O is the origin and **a**, **b**, **c** are the position vectors of points A, B, and C. P is the midpoint of OA, Q is the midpoint of AB, R is the midpoint of BC and S is the midpoint of OC.

   a Show that $PQ = \frac{1}{2}\mathbf{b}$.

   b Hence, prove that $PQRS$ is a parallelogram.

   c If $PQRS$ is a rectangle, what can be said about the quadrilateral $OABC$?

10. **a** Use a counter example to disprove the statement $\ln(x + y) \equiv \ln x + \ln y$.

    b Prove that if $\ln(x + y) \equiv \ln x + \ln y$, then $y = \frac{x}{x-1}$.

    c If $y = \frac{x}{x-1}$, does it follow that $\ln(x + y) \equiv \ln x + \ln y$?

11. **a** Show that $a^3 + 1 \equiv (a + 1)[a^2 + ka + 1]$, where k is a constant to be determined.

    b Hence, prove that $a^3 + 1$ is prime if and only if $a = 1$.

12. Prove algebraically that if $X \sim B(n, p)$, then the sum of the probabilities of the different values X can take is 1.

Section 2: Proof by contradiction

Proof by contradiction starts from the opposite of the statement you are trying to prove, and shows that this results in an impossible conclusion.

WORKED EXAMPLE 1.1

Use proof by contradiction to prove that there are an infinite number of prime numbers.

Assume that there is a largest prime number, P.

Proof by contradiction always starts by assuming the opposite of what you want to prove.

Construct another number, N, that is the product of all the prime numbers up to and including P.

Now set about trying to find a larger prime than P.

Consider $N+1$. This is 1 greater than a number divisible by all the primes up to and including P, so it cannot be divisible by any of the primes up to and including P.

Therefore, $N+1$ is either itself prime, or is divisible by primes larger than P.

Either way, you have shown that there must be a prime larger than P. This contradicts the premise that there is a largest prime number.

Here, the contradiction to the original assumption (that there is a largest prime) occurs.

Therefore, there are an infinite number of prime numbers.

Did you know?

A variation on the previous proof can be found in Euclid's masterpiece *The Elements*, a textbook written in approximately 300 BCE but still in use in many schools in the first half of the twentieth century!

WORKED EXAMPLE 1.2

Prove that $\sqrt{2}$ is irrational. You may use the fact that if a^2 is even, so is a.

Assume that $\sqrt{2} = \frac{p}{q}$,

To use proof by contradiction, you start from the opposite statement: that $\sqrt{2}$ is rational. This means that it can be written as a fraction.

where p and q are integers with no common factors.

Every fraction can be cancelled down to its lowest terms.

Squaring both sides gives:

$$2 = \frac{p^2}{q^2}$$

$$\Leftrightarrow p^2 = 2q^2 \ (*)$$

This means that p^2 is even so p must also be even.

Using the fact given.

You can then write that $p = 2k$, for some integer k, so $p^2 = 4k^2$.

Substituting this into the equation marked (*) gives:

$$4k^2 = 2q^2$$

$$\Leftrightarrow 2k^2 = q^2$$

This means that q^2 is even, so q must be even.

Using the given fact again.

But you have shown that both p and q are even, so they share a factor of 2. This contradicts the original assertion (that p and q are integers with no common factors), so it must be incorrect.

Here, the contradiction (to the fact that p and q share no common factors) arises.

Therefore, $\sqrt{2}$ is irrational and cannot be written as $\frac{p}{q}$.

EXERCISE 1B

1 Prove that if n^2 is even, then n is also even.

2 Prove that $\sqrt{3}$ is irrational.

3 Prove that there are infinitely many even numbers.

4 Prove that the sum of a rational and irrational number is irrational.

5 Prove that if ab is even with a, b integers, then at least one of them is even.

6 Prove that $\sqrt[3]{2}$ is irrational.

7 Prove that $\log_2 3$ is irrational.

Elevate

See Support sheet 1 for an example of the same type as Question 7 and further practice questions on proof by contradiction.

8 Suppose that n is a composite integer. Prove that n has a prime factor less than or equal to $\sqrt{n}$.

9 Prove that if any 25 different dates are chosen, some 3 must be within the same month.

10 Prove that the value of $a^2 - 4b^2$ is never 2 if a and b are whole numbers.

11 **a** Show that if $x = \frac{p}{q}$ is a solution to the equation $x^3 + x + 1 = 0$, then $p^3 + pq^2 + q^3 = 0$.

b Explain why there is no solution to this equation if p is odd or q is odd.

c Prove that there are no rational solutions to $x^3 + x + 1 = 0$.

12 Prove that if a triangle has sides a, b and c such that $a^2 + b^2 = c^2$, then it is a right-angled triangle.

Section 3: Criticising proofs

In Student Book 1 you were introduced to the notation used in logic:

$A \Leftrightarrow B$ means that statements A and B are equivalent.

$A \Rightarrow B$ means if A is true, then so is B.

$A \Leftarrow B$ means if B is true, then so is A.

When checking a proof (including solving equations, which is a type of proof!) you have probably looked out for errors in things like arithmetic or algebra. You now need to also look out for errors in logic.

WORKED EXAMPLE 1.3

Yas was solving the equation $2\log_{10} x = 4$. Find the errors in her working.

1 $\quad 2\log_{10} x = 4$

2 $\Leftrightarrow \log_{10}(x^2) = 4$

3 $\Rightarrow x^2 = 10^4 = 10\,000$

4 $\Leftrightarrow x = \pm 1000$

On line 2, the symbol should be $\Rightarrow$: if x is negative, line 2 could be correct but line 1 is not possible.

This is an error in logic.

In line 3 the symbol should be $\Leftrightarrow$: if $x^2 = 10^4$, then $\log_{10}(x^2) = 4$.

This is an error in logic.

In line 4 the positive square root of 10 000 should be 100.

This is an arithmetic error.

Because one of the implications goes only one way, the final solutions might not work in the original equation. They should be checked.

This is an error in logic. Even if Yas had not made the arithmetic error, she would still need to state that $x = -100$ is not a valid solution, because a negative number cannot be substituted into the original equation.

EXERCISE 1C

1. Lambert was asked to solve the equation $x=\sqrt{3x+4}$. Here is his working:

   1 $\quad x=\sqrt{3x+4}$

   2 $\Leftrightarrow x^2=3x+4$

   3 $\Leftrightarrow x^2-3x-4=0$

   4 $\Leftrightarrow (x-4)(x+1)=0$

   5 $\Leftrightarrow x=4$ or $x=-1$

   a By checking his working, find the correct solution.

   b In which line of working is his mistake?

2. Craig was asked to solve the equation $x^2=3x$. Here is his solution:

   1 $\quad x^2=3x$

   2 $\Leftrightarrow x=3$

   a Show that $x=0$ is also a solution to the original equation.

   b What logical symbol should Craig have used in the second line?

3. Freja was asked to solve the equation $x-\dfrac{1}{x-3}=1+\dfrac{5-2x}{x-3}$. Here is her working:

   1 $\quad x-\dfrac{1}{x-3}=1+\dfrac{5-2x}{x-3}$

   2 $\Leftrightarrow x-1=\dfrac{6-2x}{x-3}$

   3 $\Leftrightarrow (x-1)(x-3)=6-2x$

   4 $\Leftrightarrow x^2-4x+3=6-2x$

   5 $\Leftrightarrow x^2-2x-3=0$

   6 $\Leftrightarrow (x-3)(x+1)=0$

   7 $\Leftrightarrow x=3$ or $x=-1$

   a By checking her working, find the correct solution.

   b In which line of working is her mistake?

4. Jamie was asked to solve $\log_2(-x)+\log_2(2-x)=3$. Here is her working:

   1 $\quad \log_2(-x)+\log_2(2-x)=3$

   2 $\Leftrightarrow \log_2(-x(2-x))=3$

   3 $\Leftrightarrow \log_2(x^2-2x)=3$

   4 $\Leftrightarrow x^2-2x=2^3$

   5 $\Leftrightarrow x^2-2x-8=0$

   6 $\Leftrightarrow (x-4)(x+2)=0$

   7 $\Leftrightarrow x=4$ or $x=-2$

   In which line of working did Jamie make a mistake?

5 Andrew was asked to prove the following statement:

The function $y = x^3 - 3x$ has a minimum at $x = 1$. His working is shown below.

1 $\frac{dy}{dx} = 3x^2 - 3 = 0$

2 $x^2 = 1$

3 $x = 1$

4 $\frac{d^2y}{dx^2} = \frac{d}{dx}\left(\frac{dy}{dx}\right)$

5 $= \frac{d}{dx}(0)$

6 $= 0$

7 So it is a minimum.

Describe the errors in this proof.

6 Criticise the following proof of the statement:

If $x + q$ is a factor of $x^3 + px + q$, then the other factor is $x^2 - qx + 1$.

If $x + q$ is a factor of $x^3 + px + q$, then you can write:

1 $x^3 + px + q \equiv (x + q)(x^2 + bx + 1)$

2 $\equiv x^3 + x^2(b + q) + x(bq + 1) + q$

3 Comparing coefficients of x^2: $0 = b + q$

4 Therefore, the remaining factor is $x^2 - qx + 1$.

7 Find the error in the following proof that $\sqrt{16}$ is irrational.

1 Assume that $\sqrt{16} = \frac{p}{q}$, where p and q are integers with no common factors.

2 Squaring both sides gives $16 = \frac{p^2}{q^2}$.

3 So $p^2 = 16q^2$ (*).

4 This means that p^2 is even, so p must also be even.

5 You can then write that $p = 2k$, so $p^2 = 4k^2$.

6 Substituting this into the equation marked (*) gives $4k^2 = 16q^2$.

7 So $k^2 = 4q^2$.

8 This means that q^2 is even, so q must be even.

9 But you have shown that both p and q are even, so they share a factor of 2.

10 This contradicts the original assertion, so it must be incorrect. This means that $\sqrt{16}$ cannot be written as $\frac{p}{q}$.

Checklist of learning and understanding

- You should be able to apply counter examples, proof by exhaustion and proof by deduction to material from Student Book 1.
- Proof by contradiction is a method of proof that works by showing that assuming the opposite of the required statement leads to an impossible situation.
- When criticising proofs, look out for flaws in logic as well as mistakes in algebra or arithmetic.

Mixed practice 1

1. Prove that $n^2 - n$ is always even.

2. Prove that $\sqrt{5}$ is irrational.

3. Prove that there are infinitely many square numbers.

4. Find the error(s) in the following working to solve $\tan x = 2\sin x$ for $0° \leqslant x < 360°$:

   1 $\frac{\sin x}{\cos x} = 2\sin x$

   2 $\Leftrightarrow \sin x = 2\sin x \cos x$

   3 $\Leftrightarrow 1 = 2\cos x$

   4 $\Leftrightarrow 0.5 = \cos x$

   5 $\Leftrightarrow x = 60°$

5. Choosing from options **A** to **D**, which symbol should be used to replace ? in the working below?

   A $\Rightarrow$ **B** $\Leftrightarrow$ **C** $\Leftarrow$ **D** $\equiv$

   1 $x^2 = 8x$

   2 ? $x = 8$

6. Prove that $\log_2 5$ is irrational.

7. *OABC* is a parallelogram with *O* at the origin, and **a**, **b**, **c** are the position vectors of points *A*, *B*, and *C*. *P* is the midpoint of *BC* and *Q* is the point on *OB* such that *OQ* : *QB* is 2 : 1.

   Prove that *AQP* is a straight line.

8. Prove that if a and b are whole numbers, then $a^2 - b^2$ is either odd or a multiple of 4.

9. **a** Prove that if f(x) is a polynomial of finite order with integer coefficients and n is an integer, then f(n) is an integer.

   b Use a counter example to show that the following statement is not always correct:

   If f(x) is a polynomial, where f(n) is an integer whenever n is an integer, then f(x) must have integer coefficients.

10. Consider the following working to solve $x + \frac{4x}{x-2} = \frac{8}{x-2}$:

    1 $x + \frac{4x}{x-2} = \frac{8}{x-2}$

    2 $\Leftrightarrow x(x-2) + 4x = 8$

    3 $\Leftrightarrow x^2 - 2x + 4x = 8$

    4 $\Leftrightarrow x^2 + 2x = 8$

    5 $\Leftrightarrow (x+1)^2 = 9$

    6 $\Leftrightarrow x + 1 = 3$

    7 $\Leftrightarrow x = 2$

    a In which lines are there mistakes?

    b Rewrite the solution correctly, making appropriate use of logical connectors.

11 Fermat said that if x is prime then $2x+1$ is prime. Find the smallest value of x that provides a counter example to this statement.

12 The proof below is trying to demonstrate that there are an arbitrary number of consecutive composite (non-prime) numbers.

A Consider $n!$ for $n \geqslant r \geqslant 1$.

B $n!+r$ is divisible by r.

C So the numbers $n!+1$, $n!+2$ ... $n!+n$ are not prime.

D This is a list of n consecutive composite numbers.

Which is the first line to contain an error?

13 Prove that if a, b and c are integers such that $a^2+b^2=c^2$, then either a or b is even.

14 **a** By considering a right-angled triangle, prove that if A is an acute angle, then $\tan(90° - A) = \dfrac{1}{\tan A}$.

b Hence, prove that $\tan 10° \times \tan 20° \times \tan 30° \ldots \times \tan 80°$ is a rational number.

15 Prove that for x between 90° and 180°, $\sin x - \cos x \geqslant 1$.

Elevate

See Extension sheet 1 to complete the details of a couple of famous proofs.

2 Functions

In this chapter you will learn:

- about the difference between mappings and functions
- about one-one and many-one functions
- about the domain and range of a function
- how to find composite functions
- how to find the inverse of a function.

Before you start…

Student Book 1, Chapter 1	You should be able to interpret function notation.	1 Given that $f(x) = 2 - x$, evaluate: a $f(3)$ b $f(-4)$
Student Book 1, Chapter 1	You should be able to use set notation and interval notation.	2 Write the following sets using the interval notation. a $\{x: x > 3 \text{ and } x \leqslant 6\}$ b $\{x: x < 3 \text{ or } x \geqslant 6\}$
Student Book 1, Chapter 3	You should be able to complete the square.	3 a Express $f(x) = x^2 + 5x + 3$ in the form $(x+a)^2 + b$. b Hence, state the coordinates of the turning point of $f(x)$.
Student Book 1, Chapter 3	You should be able to solve quadratic inequalities.	4 Solve the inequality $x^2 - 4x - 5 > 0$.
Student Book 1, Chapter 7	You should be able to rearrange exponential and log expressions.	5 Make x the subject of the following. a $y = e^{2x-1}$ b $y = \ln(3x+4)$
Student Book 1, Chapter 13	You should be able to establish where a function is increasing/decreasing.	6 Find the range of x values for which $f(x) = x^{\frac{3}{2}} - 2x$ is an increasing function.

Why study functions?

Doubling, adding 5, finding the largest prime factor – these are all instructions that can be applied to numbers to produce a numerical result. This idea comes up a lot in mathematics. The formal study of it leads to the concept of a function.

Functions can be used whenever you need to express how one quantity changes with another, whether it is how the strength of the gravitational force varies with distance, or how the amount of paint needed depends on the area of a wall.

In this chapter we will focus on developing the theory of functions. You have already seen many examples of modelling with linear, quadratic and exponential functions in Student Book 1. In Chapter 7 of this book you will meet further models using trigonometric functions.

Section 1: Mappings and functions

A **mapping** takes numbers from a given set (inputs) and assigns to each of them one or more output values, using a mapping rule. For example:

- $x \mapsto x^2 + 3, x \in \mathbb{R}$ maps 4 to 19, 0 to 3, and –2.1 to 7.41.
- $x \mapsto \pm 3x, x \in \mathbb{Z}$ maps 2 to 6 and –6, –4 to 12 and –12, and 0 to 0.
- $x \mapsto$ a factor of $x, x \in \{1, 2, 3, 4, 5, 6\}$ maps 1 to 1, 5 to 1 and 5, and 6 to 1, 2, 3 and 6.

We can represent a mapping using the arrow notation, as shown above, or we can give a name to the output value and write, for example, $y = x^2 + 3, x \in \mathbb{R}$. We can also use a mapping diagram:

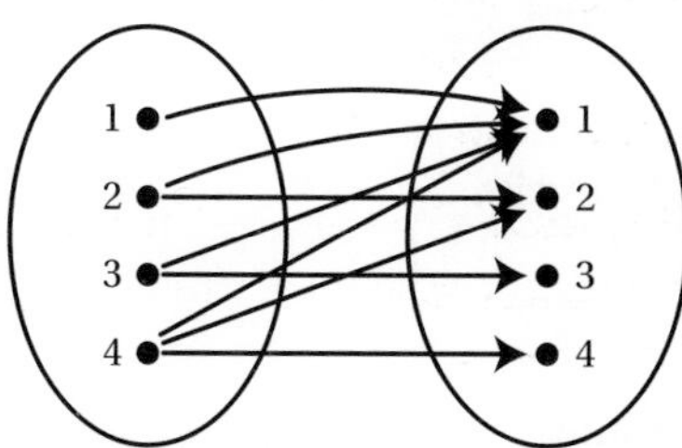

$x \longmapsto$ a factor of x, for $x \in \{1, 2, 3, 4\}$.

Another useful representation is on a graph, where the input values are shown on the horizontal axis and the output values on the vertical axis.

You should remember that, to fully define a mapping, you need to state the set of the input values as well as the mapping rule. This set of all possible input values is called the **domain** of the mapping. For example, the mapping $x \mapsto \pm 3x, x \in \{-1, 0, 1, 2\}$ is different from the mapping $x \mapsto \pm 3x, x \in \mathbb{R}$, as can be seen from their graphs:

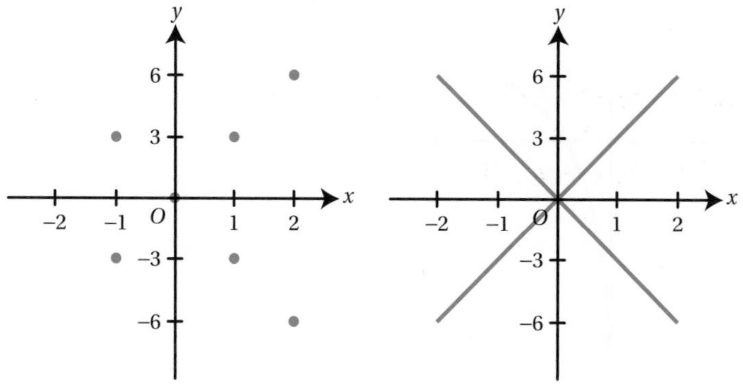

Did you know?

There is a more general way to describe a relationship between two sets, called a *relation*, where the output does not need to be written explicitly in terms of the input. For example, a relation could be given by $\{(x, y): x^2 + y^2 = 4\}$; you already know that the graph of this relation is a circle. Although you will not study relations in much detail, you will learn how to find gradients of some curves defined by relations (see Chapter 10, Section 4).

Fast forward

You will learn more about domains in Section 2.

A mapping rule can assign more than one output to each input. A special type of mapping, where each input value has only one output, is called a **function**. Of the three mappings given previously, only $x \mapsto x^2 + 3, x \in \mathbb{R}$ is a function.

When a mapping is given by its graph, the easiest way to decide whether or not it is a function is to carry out a **vertical line test**:

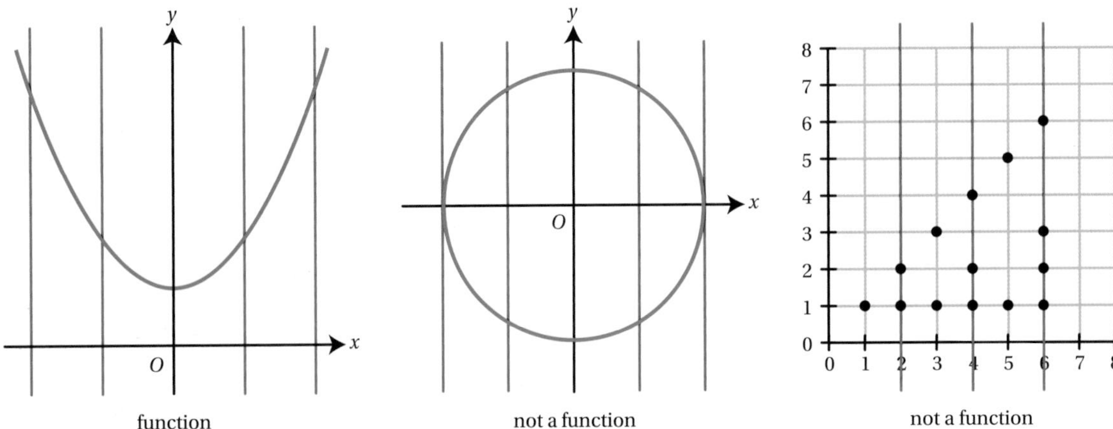

Key point 2.1

- A mapping is a function if every input value maps to a single output value.
- Vertical line test: if a mapping is a function, any vertical line will meet its graph at most once.

Functions are often named with letters, such as f or g. For example, $\text{f}: x \mapsto x^2 + 3, x \in \mathbb{R}$. You can also use the function notation $\text{f}(x) = x^2 + 3, x \in \mathbb{R}$. Then $\text{f}(1) = 4$, $\text{f}(0) = 3$ and $\text{f}(-2.1) = 7.41$; we say that 7.41 is the **image** of -2.1.

Having decided that a mapping is a function, you can ask whether each output comes from just one input. To check this, you can apply the **horizontal line test**:

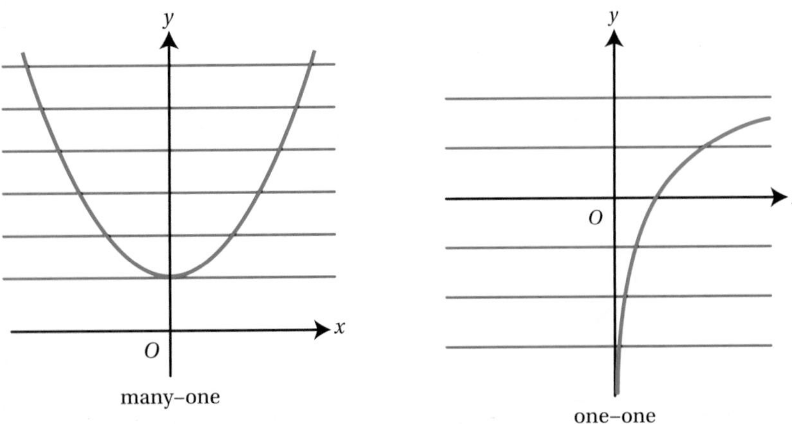

Key point 2.2

A function is:

- **one–one** if every y value corresponds to only one x value.
- **many–one** if there is at least one y value that comes from more than one x value.

Horizontal line test: if a function is one–one, any horizontal line will meet the graph at most once.

A mapping where a single input corresponds to more than one output (so is not a function) is called **one–many**.

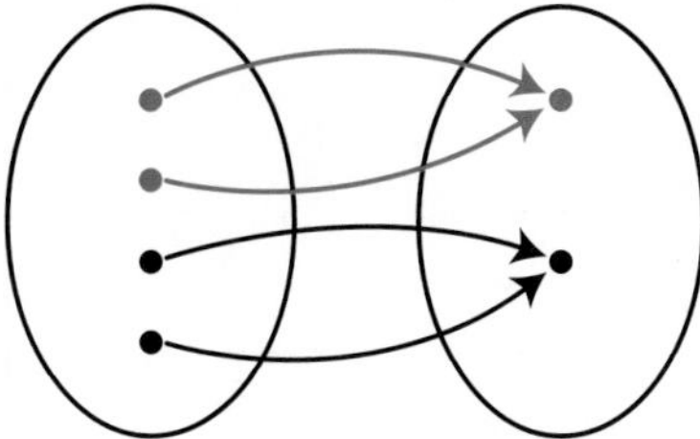

Many–one function

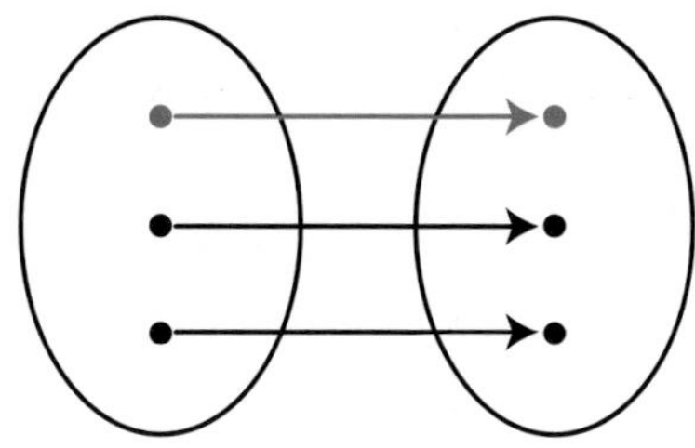

One–one function

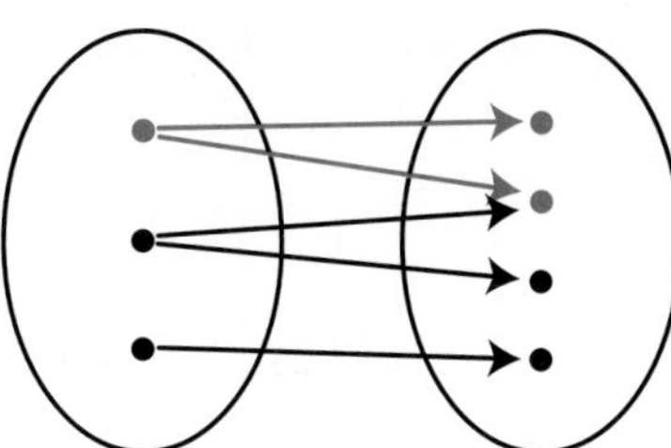

One–many mapping
(not a function)

WORKED EXAMPLE 2.1

Which of the graphs below could represent functions? For those that could be functions, classify them as one–one or many–one.

a

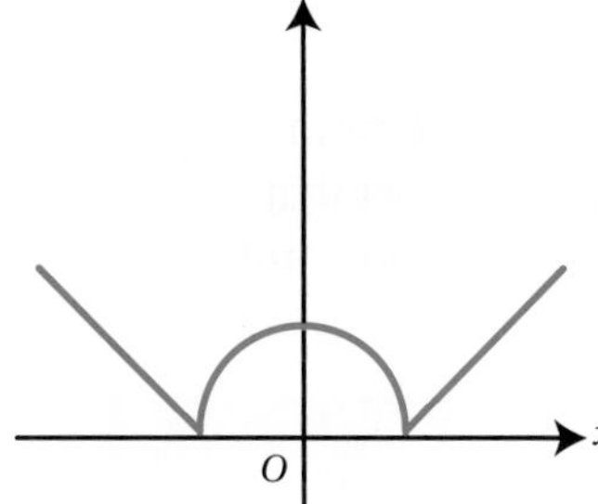

b

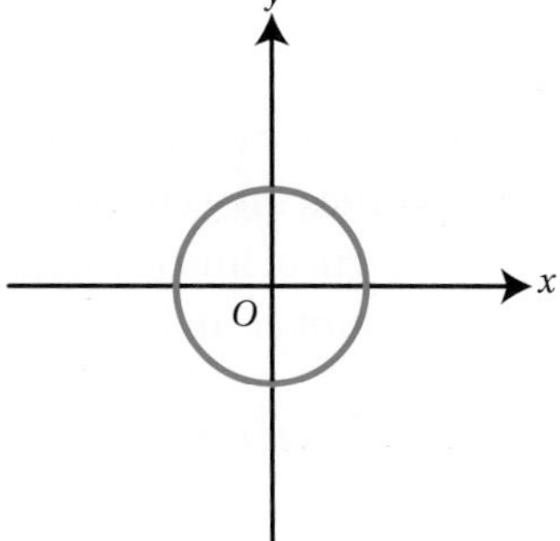

c

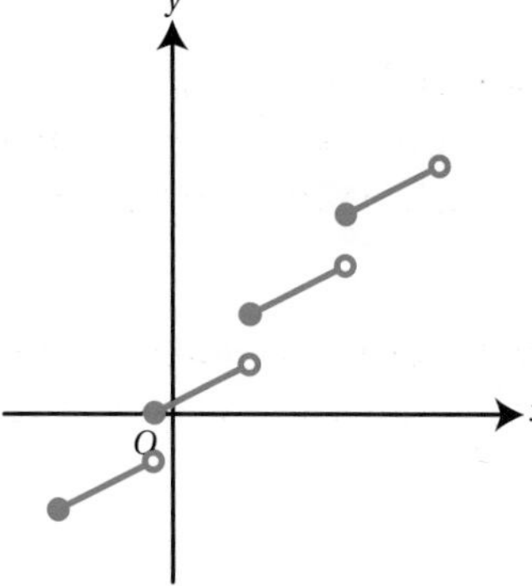

a

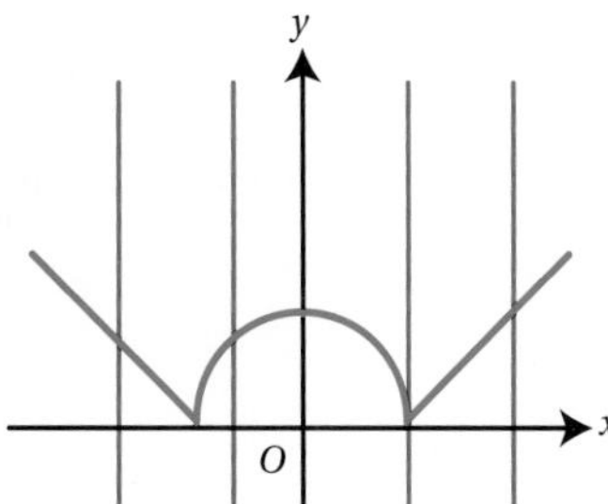

Draw several vertical lines and see how many times they cross the graph.

Any vertical line meets the graph at most once; therefore it could be a function.

Continues on next page ...

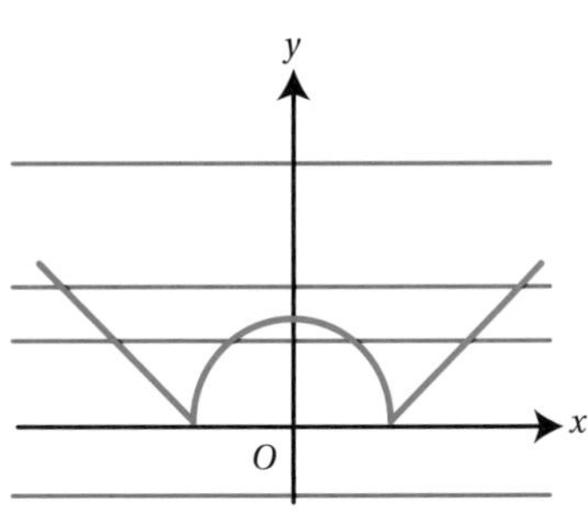

Draw several horizontal lines and see how many times they cross the graph.

At least one of the horizontal lines meets the graph at more than one point; therefore it could be a many-one function.

b

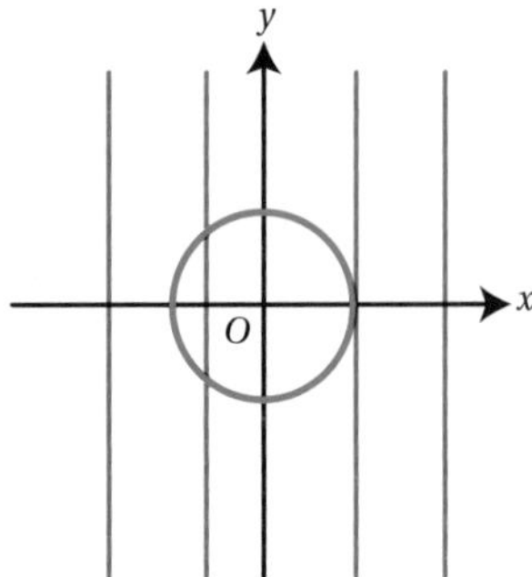

Draw several vertical lines and see how many times they cross the graph.

At least one of the vertical lines meets the graph more than once; therefore it is not a function.

c

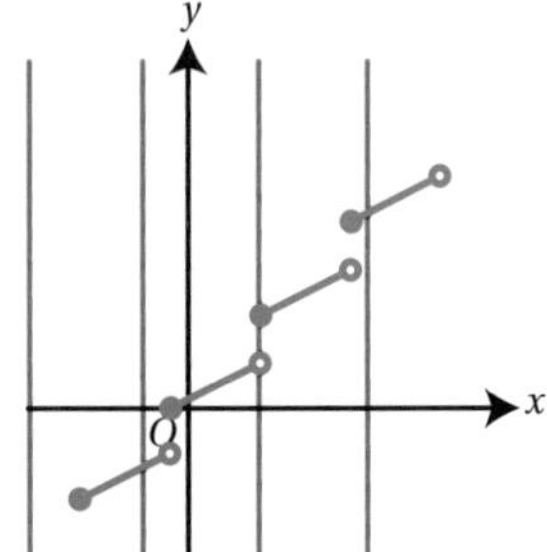

Draw several vertical lines and see how many times they cross the graph. Remember that a vertical line through an open circle does not count as an intersection.

Any vertical line meets the graph at most once; therefore it could be a function.

Tip

An open circle on a graph means that that point is not a part of the graph, and a closed circle means that it is.

Continues on next page ...

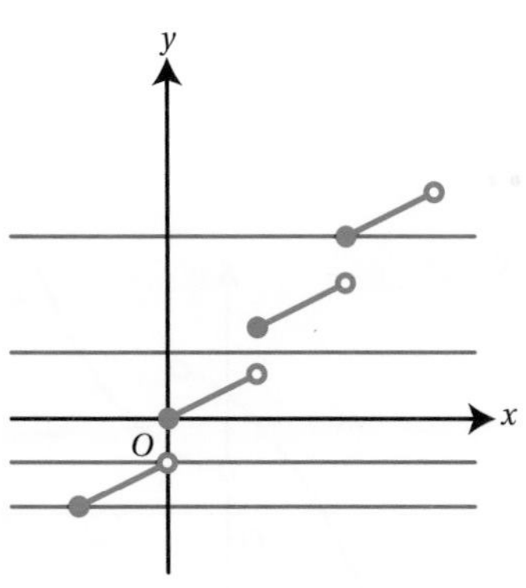

Draw several horizontal lines and see how many times they cross the graph.

Any horizontal line meets the graph at most once; therefore it could be a one–one function.

When you are given a rule for a function, rather than its graph, it can be more difficult to decide whether the function is one–one. If a function is not one–one, you need to find only one example of an output value with two corresponding input values. To prove that a function is one–one, you need to rearrange the equation $y = f(x)$ and show that each y comes from only one x.

You should remember that whether a function is one–one depends on its domain, as well as the function rule.

WORKED EXAMPLE 2.2

a The function f is defined for all real numbers x and has the rule $f(x) = x^2 + 3$. Show that f is not a one–one function.

b The function g also has the rule $g(x) = x^2 + 3$ but its domain is $x > 0$. Show that g is a one–one function.

a $f(-1) = f(1) = 4$

Two inputs have the same output, hence f is not a one–one function.

Look for two input values that have the same output. In this case, you know that squaring a number gives the same result as squaring its negative.

b Let $y = g(x)$. Then:

$$y = x^2 + 3$$

$$\Leftrightarrow x^2 = y - 3$$

$$\Leftrightarrow x = \pm\sqrt{y-3}$$

You need to show that each possible y comes from only one x. One way to do this is to find x in terms of y.

However, $x > 0$ so $x = \sqrt{y-3}$.

Each y value comes from just one x value, so g is a one–one function.

This equation appears to give two x values for each y value. However, the domain of g is $x > 0$, so x must be positive.

EXERCISE 2A

1 Which of these graphs could **not** represent functions? For each one that could represent a function, state if it is one-one or many-one.

a

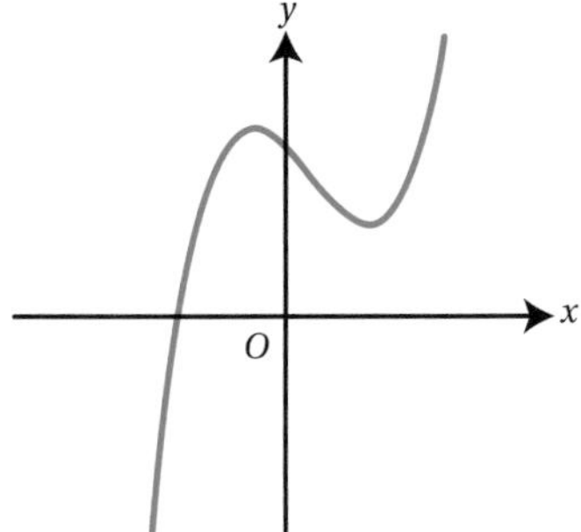

b

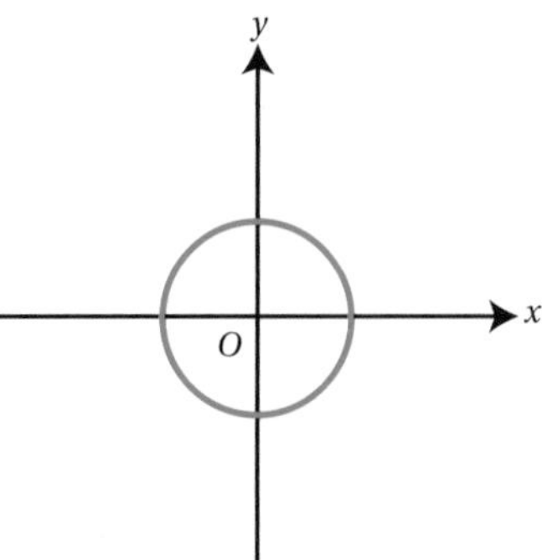

c

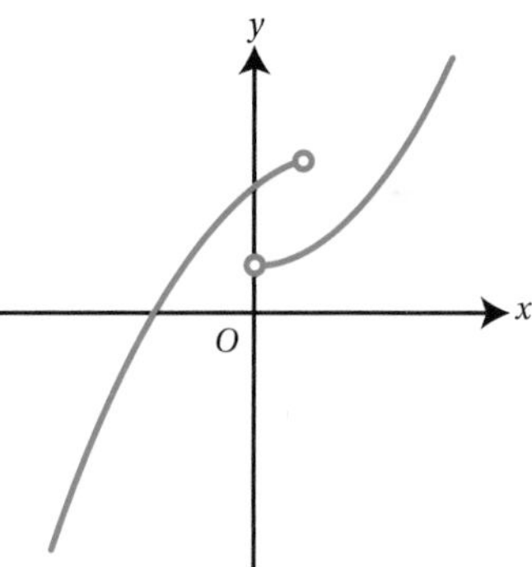

d

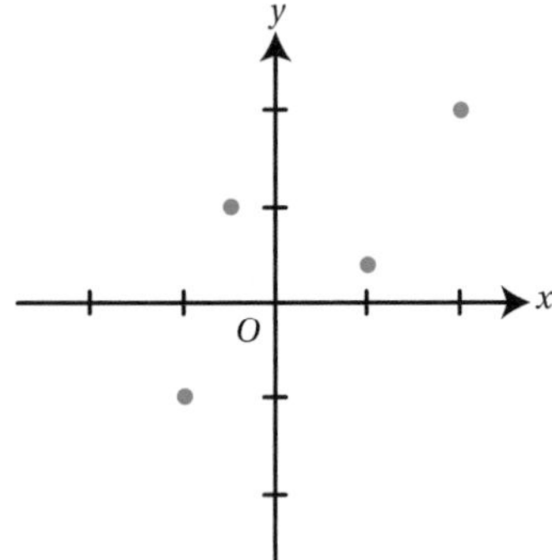

e

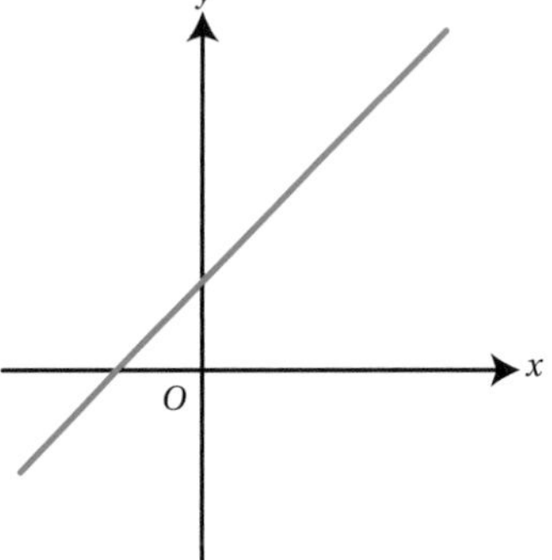

f

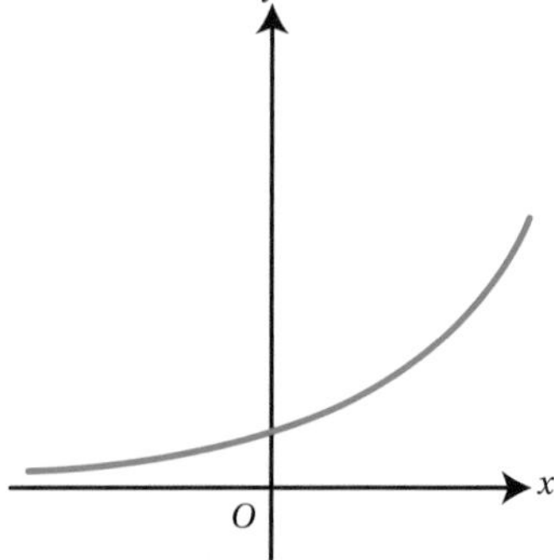

2 Determine whether each of the following functions is one-one.

a **i** $f(x) = x^2 - 2, x < 3$ **ii** $f(x) = x^2 + 5, x > -2$

b **i** $g(x) = x^2 - 3, x \leqslant -2$ **ii** $g(x) = x^2 + 1, x \geqslant 3$

c **i** $h(x) = x^3 + 5, x > 1$ **ii** $h(x) = x^3 - 2, x \leqslant 0$

Section 2: Domain and range

The previous section mentioned that, in order to fully define a function, you must specify both the set of allowed inputs and the rule that tells you what to do with each input.

Key point 2.3

The set of allowed input values is called the **domain** of the function.

WORKED EXAMPLE 2.3

Sketch the graph of $f(x) = x + 1$ over the domain:

a $x \in \mathbb{R}, x > 2$ **b** $x \in \mathbb{Z}$

Continues on next page ...

Tip

Remember that $\mathbb{R}$ stands for the set of all real numbers and $\mathbb{Z}$ for the set of whole numbers.

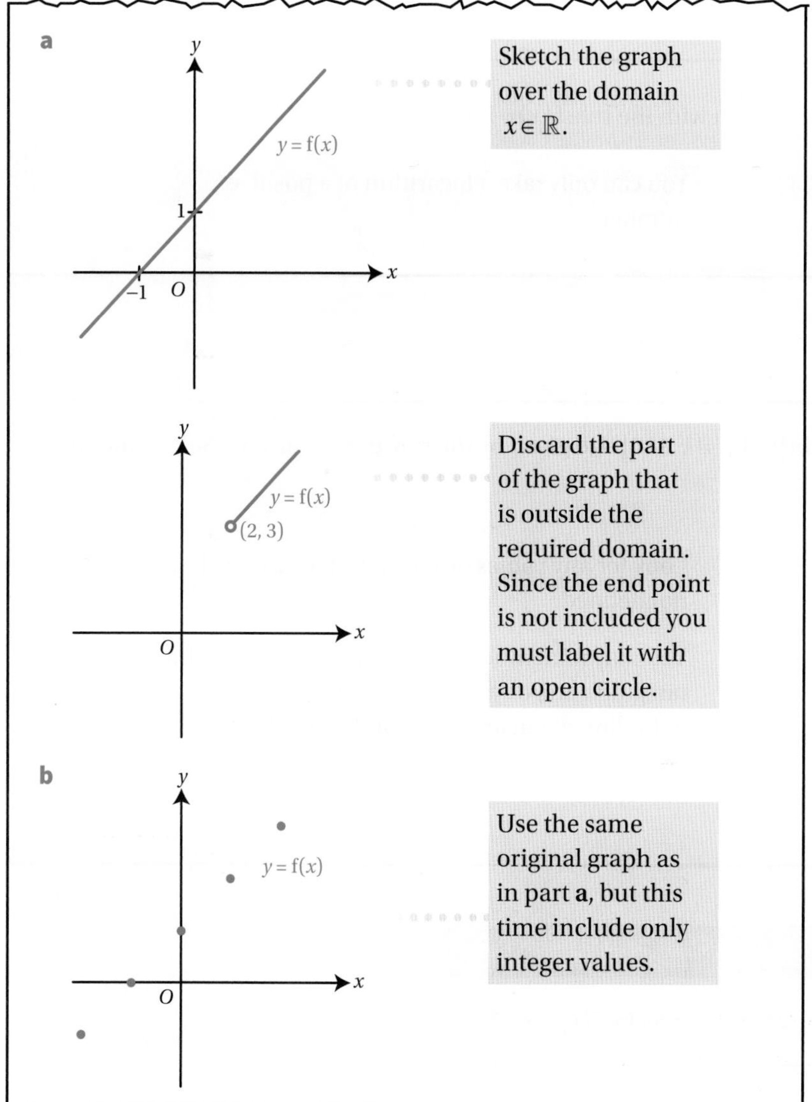

If no domain is explicitly mentioned, you can assume that the domain is the largest possible set of real numbers for which the values are defined. You may wonder why you would ever need any other domain. There are two main reasons.

1 You may be modelling a physical situation where the variables can take only particular values; for example, if the variable is age of humans, you would not want it to be negative or much beyond 120.

2 The mathematical operation you are using may not be able to handle certain types of numbers. For example, if you are looking for the largest prime factor of a number, you would normally only be looking at positive integers. When working with real numbers, the four most common reasons to restrict the domain are:

- You cannot divide by zero.
- You cannot take a square root of a negative number.
- You cannot take the logarithm of a non-positive number.
- You cannot find the tan or cot of certain angles (for example, $\tan 90$ or $\cot \theta$).

Tip

Unless told otherwise, you can assume that the domain is a subset of real numbers. For example, $x > 2$ in fact means $x \in \mathbb{R}$ and $x > 2$.

WORKED EXAMPLE 2.4

Find the largest possible domain of a function with the rule $f(x) = \ln(4 - 2x)$.

You need $4 - 2x > 0$.

You can only take a logarithm of a positive number.

So the largest possible domain is $x < 2$.

WORKED EXAMPLE 2.5

A function, g, is defined on the domain $[0, k) \cup (k, 180]$ and given by the rule $g: x \mapsto \tan((x - 30)°)$. Find the value of k.

$\tan((x-30)°) = \dfrac{\sin((x-30)°)}{\cos((x-30)°)}$

Look for any values of x for which $\tan(x - 30)°$ is not defined.

Not defined when $\cos((x-30)°) = 0$.

This is when $x - 30 = 90$,

so $x = 120$.

You may remember where the asymptotes of the tan graph are, or you may need to use the definition of tan and look for division by zero.

Hence, $k = 120$.

Tip

Remember that $f: x \mapsto x + 3$ is just an alternative notation for $f(x) = x + 3$.

WORKED EXAMPLE 2.6

What is the largest possible domain of a function with the rule $h: x \mapsto \dfrac{1}{x-2} + \sqrt{x+3}$? Write your answer using interval notation.

There will be division by zero when $x - 2 = 0$.

Look for division by zero.

There will be a square root of a negative number when $x + 3 < 0$.

Look for a square root of a negative number.

The largest possible domain is: $x \geqslant -3$ and $x \neq 2$

Decide what can therefore be allowed into the function.

Hence, $x \in [-3, 2) \cup (2, \infty)$.

This describes two intervals: from –3 to 2 and from 2 to infinity, excluding 2.

As well as knowing the set of inputs for a function (the domain), it is useful to identify the set of possible outputs.

Tip

Be aware that the range will depend upon the domain.

Key point 2.4

The set of all possible outputs of a function is called the **range**.

Tip

Graph-plotting software or graphical calculators can be useful when investigating the domain and range of functions.

The easiest way of finding the range is to sketch the graph.

WORKED EXAMPLE 2.7

A function, f, is given by the rule $f(x) = x^2 + 3$. Find its range if the domain is:

a $x \in \mathbb{R}$ **b** $x > 2$

a

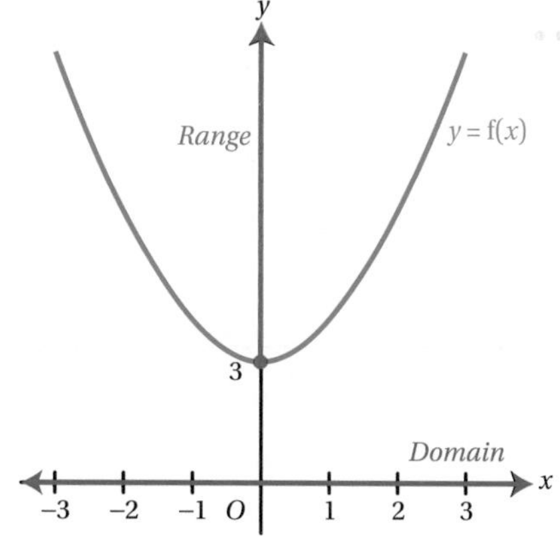

Sketch the graph $y = f(x)$.

Range: $f(x) \geqslant 3$

Use the graph to state which y values can occur.

b

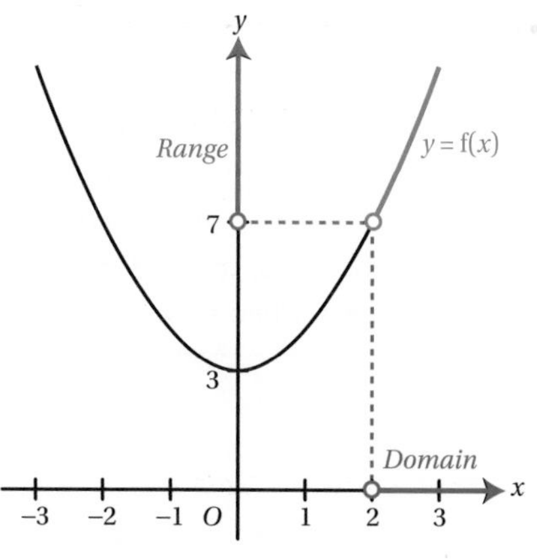

Sketch the graph $y = f(x)$.

Range: $f(x) > 7$

Use the graph to state which y values can occur.

EXERCISE 2B

In this exercise, unless otherwise stated, x is a real number.

1 Find the largest possible domain, and the corresponding range, of the functions with the following rules.

a **i** $f(x)=2^x$ **ii** $f(x)=a^x,\ a>0$

b **i** $f(x)=\log_{10} x$ **ii** $f(x)=\log_b x,\ b>1$

2 Find the largest possible domain of the functions with the following rules.

a **i** $f(x)=\dfrac{1}{x+2}$ **ii** $f(x)=\dfrac{5}{x-7}$

b **i** $f(x)=\dfrac{3}{(x-2)(x+4)}$ **ii** $g(x)=\dfrac{x}{x^2-9}$

c **i** $r(y)=\sqrt{y^3-1}$ **ii** $h(x)=\sqrt{x+3}$

d **i** $f(a)=\dfrac{1}{\sqrt{a-1}}$ **ii** $f(x)=\dfrac{5x}{\sqrt{2-5x}}$

e **i** $a(x)=\dfrac{1}{x}+\dfrac{2}{x+1}$ **ii** $f(x)=\sqrt{x+1}+\dfrac{1}{x+2}$

f **i** $f(x)=\sqrt{x}+\dfrac{1}{x+7}-x^3+5$ **ii** $f(x)=e^x+\sqrt{2x+3}-\dfrac{1}{x^2+4}-2$

3 Find the range of the following functions.

a **i** $f(x)=7-x^2,\ x\in\mathbb{R}$ **ii** $f(x)=x^2+3, x\in\mathbb{R}$

b **i** $g(x)=x^2+3,\ x\geqslant 3$ **ii** $g(x)=x^2-1, x<-3$

c **i** $h(x)=x-2, x<5, x\in\mathbb{Z}$ **ii** $h(x)=x+1, x>3, x\in\mathbb{Z}$

d **i** $d(x)=\frac{1}{x}, x\geqslant -1, x\neq 0$ **ii** $q(x)=3\sqrt{x}, x>0$

4 Find the largest possible domain and the corresponding range of the functions with the following rules.

a **i** $f(x)=x^2-4x-1$ **ii** $f(x)=x^2+2x+5$

b **i** $g: x\mapsto 5-x^2$ **ii** $g: x\mapsto 3-2x^2$

c **i** $f(x)=\sqrt{x^2-5}$ **ii** $f(x)=\sqrt{9-x^2}$

d **i** $f: x\mapsto 2\sqrt{x^2-6x+8}$ **ii** $f: x\mapsto 4\sqrt{x^2+2x-3}$

5 **a** Write $2x^2+6x-3$ in the form $a(x+p)^2+q$.

b Hence, state the range of the function $f: x\rightarrow 2x^2+6x-3, x\in\mathbb{R}$.

6 Find the largest possible domain and the corresponding range of the function with the rule $g(x)=\ln(6+4x)$.

7 The function f has the rule $f(x)=\sqrt{\ln(x-4)}$. Find the largest possible domain of this function.

8 Find the largest possible domain of the function with the rule

$$f(x)=\frac{4^{\sqrt{x-1}}}{x+2}-\frac{1}{x^2-5x+6}+x^2+1.$$

Rewind

Exponential and logarithm functions were covered in Student Book 1, Chapter 7.

Rewind

Some of these questions require completing the square and the solution of quadratic inequalities, covered in Student Book 1, Chapter 3.

9 a Sketch the graph of $y = 6 - x - 2x^2$.

b Hence, find the largest possible domain of the function with the rule $f: x \to \sqrt{6 - x - 2x^2}$.

10 Find the largest possible domain of the function with the rule $g(x) = \ln(x^2 + 3x + 2)$.

11 Find the largest set of real values of x such that the function f with the rule $f(x) = \sqrt{\frac{8x-4}{x-12}}$ takes real values.

12 a State the largest possible domain of the function with the rule $f(x) = \sqrt{x-a} + \ln(b-x)$ if:

i $a < b$ ii $a \geqslant b$

b Find f(a) in each of the two cases.

Section 3: Composite functions

After applying a function to a number it is possible to apply another function to the image. The resulting rule is called a **composite function**.

Tip

Whichever notation is being used, remember the correct order: the function nearest to x acts first!

Key point 2.5

Applying the function g to x and then the function f to the result is written:

$$f(g(x)) \quad \text{or} \quad fg(x) \quad \text{or} \quad f \circ g(x)$$

It can be useful to refer to g(x) as the *inner function* and f(x) as the *outer function*.

WORKED EXAMPLE 2.8

If $f(x) = x^2$ and $g(x) = x - 3$, find:

a $f \circ g(1)$ b $fg(x)$ c $gf(x)$

a $g(1) = 1 - 3 = -2$

$f(-2) = (-2)^2 = 4$

$\therefore f(g(1)) = 4$

Evaluate g(1) and then apply f to the result.

Note that you don't need to work out the general expression for $f \circ g(x)$.

b $f(g(x)) = f(x-3)$

$= (x-3)^2 = x^2 - 6x + 9$

Replace x in f(x) with the expression for g(x).

c $g(f(x)) = g(x^2) = x^2 - 3$

Replace x in g(x) with the expression for f(x).

Tip

Be careful: f(g(x)) and g(f(x)) are not the same function.

WORK IT OUT 2.1

Two functions are defined for all real numbers by $f(x) = 3x - 2$ and $g(x) = x^2 - 1$. Find $f \circ g\,(5)$.

Which of the following solutions is correct? Identify the mistake in the other two.

Solution 1	Solution 2	Solution 3
$f(5) = 15 - 2 = 13$ $g(5) = 25 - 1 = 24$ $f(5)g(5) = 312$	$g(5) = 25 - 1 = 24$ $f(24) = 72 - 2 = 70$	$f(5) = 15 - 2 = 13$ $f \circ g\,(5) = 13^2 - 1 = 168$

You can also compose a function with itself.

Key point 2.6

$f \circ f\,(x)$ can also be written as $f^2\,(x)$.

WORKED EXAMPLE 2.9

Given that $f(x) = \frac{2}{x-3}$, find and simplify an expression for $f^2(x)$.

$$f^2(x) = f(f(x))$$

$f^2(x)$ means do $f(x)$, then do f to the result.

$$= \frac{2}{\frac{2}{x-3} - 3}$$

$$= \frac{2(x-3)}{2-3(x-3)}$$

Multiply top and bottom of the fraction by $(x-3)$ to simplify the denominator.

$$= \frac{2x-6}{11-3x}$$

For the composite function fg to exist, the range of g must lie entirely within the domain of f, otherwise you would be trying to put values into f that it cannot take.

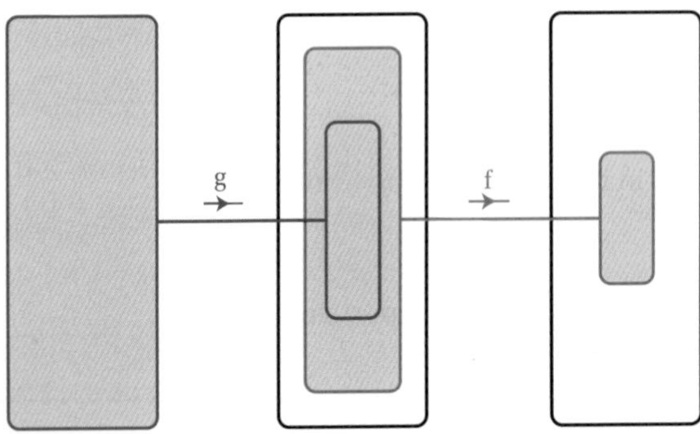

In the diagram above, the large blue rectangle represents the domain of g. Its image (which is the range of g) is represented by the smaller blue rectangle. The larger red rectangle represents the domain of f.

WORKED EXAMPLE 2.10

The functions f and g are defined by $f: x \mapsto x^2 - 5, x \in \mathbb{R}$ and $g: x \mapsto \sqrt{x+3}, x \geqslant -3$.

a Explain why the composite function g f is not defined.

b Find the largest possible domain for which g f is defined. In this case, state the range of g f.

Working	Explanation
a You need $f(x) \geqslant -3$.	Check whether the output from f is within the domain of g.
But, for example, $f(0) = -5$, and this is not in the domain of g.	It is enough to find one counter example to show that $f(x) \geqslant -3$ is not true for all x.
b $x^2 - 5 \geqslant -3$ $\Leftrightarrow x^2 \geqslant 2$	You need $f(x) \geqslant -3$.
$\Leftrightarrow x \leqslant -\sqrt{2}$ or $x \geqslant \sqrt{2}$	This is a quadratic inequality; the solution consists of two separate intervals.
The range of g f is $g\,f(x) \geqslant 0$.	With the domain above, $f(x)$ takes all real values $\geqslant -3$, so $g(f(x)) = \sqrt{(f(x)+3)}$ can be any non-negative real number.

A more complex problem is to recover one of the original functions when you have a composite function. A good way to do this is to use a substitution.

WORKED EXAMPLE 2.11

If $f(x+1) = 4x^2 + x$, find the expression for $f(x)$ in the form $ax^2 + bx + c$.

Working	Explanation
$y = x + 1$	Substitute y for the inner function.
$x = y - 1$	Rearrange to get $x = \ldots$.
$f(y) = 4(y-1)^2 + (y-1)$ $= 4y^2 - 8y + 4 + y - 1$ $= 4y^2 - 7y + 3$	Replace all instances of x.
$f(x) = 4x^2 - 7x + 3$	Write the answer in terms of x.

EXERCISE 2C

In this exercise, functions are defined with their largest possible real domain, unless specified otherwise.

1 Given that $f(x) = x^2 + 1$ and $g(x) = 3x + 2$, find:

a **i** $g(f(0))$ **ii** $fg(1)$

b **i** $f \circ g(-2)$ **ii** $g(f(3))$

2 Given that $f(x) = x^2 + 1$ and $g(x) = 3x + 2$, find:

a **i** $g(f(x))$ **ii** $f^2(x)$

b **i** $gg(x)$ **ii** $f \circ g(x)$

3 **a** Given that $f(x) = x^2 + 1$ and $g(x) = 3x + 2$, find:

i $g^2\left(\sqrt{a}+1\right)$ **ii** $f^2(y-1)$

b Given that $f(x) = 4 - x$ and $g(x) = x^2$, find:

i $fg(x-2)$ **ii** $gf(3-x)$

4 Given that $f(x) = x^2 + 1$ and $g(x) = 3x + 2$, find:

a $ggf(y)$ **b** $gfg(z)$

5 Find $f(x)$, given the following conditions.

a **i** $f(2a) = 4a^2$ **ii** $f\left(\frac{b}{3}\right) = \frac{b^3}{27}$

b **i** $f(x+1) = 3x - 2$ **ii** $f(x-2) = x^2 + x$

c **i** $f(1-y) = 5 - y$ **ii** $f(y^3) = y^2$

d **i** $f(e^k) = \ln k$ **ii** $f(3n+2) = \ln(n+1)$

6 Given that $f(x) = x^2 + 1$ and $g(x) = 3x + 2$, solve the equation $fg(x) = gf(x)$.

7 Given that $f(x) = 3x + 1$ and $g(x) = \frac{x}{x^2+25}$, solve the equation $gf(x) = 0$.

8 The function f is defined by $f: x \mapsto x^3$. Find an expression for $g(x)$ in terms of x in each of the following cases.

a $(f \circ g)(x) = 2x + 3$ **b** $(g \circ f)(x) = 2x + 3$

9 Let f and g be two functions. Given that $(f \circ g)(x) = \frac{x+2}{3}$ and $g(x) = 2x + 5$, find an expression for $f(x-1)$.

Section 4: Inverse functions

Functions transform an input into an output, but sometimes you want to reverse this process: to be able to say which input produced a given output. When this is possible, it is done by finding the **inverse function**, usually labelled f^{-1}.

For example, if $f(x) = 3x$, then $f^{-1}(12)$ is a number that, when put into f, produces output 12. In other words, you are looking for a number x such that $f(x) = 12$. Hence, $f^{-1}(12) = 4$.

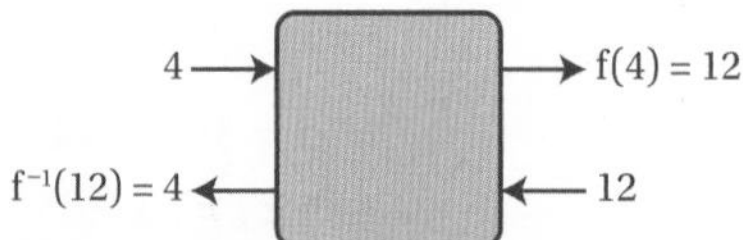

Tip

Make sure you don't get confused about this notation. With numbers, the superscript '–1' denotes reciprocal; for example, $x^{-1} = \frac{1}{x}$, $3^{-1} = \frac{1}{3}$. With functions, f^{-1} denotes the inverse function of f.

Finding the inverse function

To find the inverse function you must rearrange the formula to find the input (x) in terms of the output (y).

Tip

Finding the domain of the inverse function can be difficult; this will be discussed in the next subsection.

Key point 2.7

To find the expression for inverse function $f^{-1}(x)$, given an expression for $f(x)$:

1. Start with $y = f(x)$.
2. Rearrange to get x (the input) in terms of y (the output).
3. Give $f^{-1}(x)$ by replacing every instance of y with x.

WORKED EXAMPLE 2.12

The function f is defined for $x > -4$ by the rule $f(x) = 3\ln(x + 4)$. Find an expression for $f^{-1}(x)$.

$y = 3\ln(x + 4)$ — Start with $y = f(x)$.

$\Leftrightarrow \frac{y}{3} = \ln(x + 4)$ — Rearrange to make x the subject.

$\Leftrightarrow x + 4 = e^{\frac{y}{3}}$ — Taking e to the power of both sides removes the logarithm.

$\Leftrightarrow x = e^{\frac{y}{3}} - 4$

$f^{-1}(x) = e^{\frac{x}{3}} - 4$ — Write the resulting function in terms of x.

WORK IT OUT 2.2

Find the rule for the inverse function of $f(x)=\frac{3x-1}{x+4}, x \neq 4$.

Which of the following solutions is correct? Identify the mistake in the other two.

Solution 1	Solution 2	Solution 3
$y=\frac{3x-1}{x+4}$ $\Rightarrow xy+4y=3x-1$ $\Rightarrow x(y-3)=-1-4y$ $\Rightarrow x=\frac{4y+1}{3-y}$ $\therefore f^{-1}(x)=\frac{4x+1}{3-x}$	$f(x)=\frac{3x-1}{x+4}$ $\Rightarrow f^{-1}(x)=\frac{x+4}{3x-1}$	$y=\frac{3x-1}{x+4}$ $\Rightarrow xy+4y=3x-1$ $\Rightarrow xy=3x-1-4y$ $\Rightarrow x=3x-1-4$ $\therefore f^{-1}(x)=3x-5$

The relationship between f and f^{-1}

Once you know how to find inverse functions, there are a couple of very important facts you need to know about them.

When you are finding the inverse function you switch the inputs and the outputs, so on the graph you switch the x- and y-axes:

Key point 2.8

The graph of $y=f^{-1}(x)$ is a reflection of the graph of $y=f(x)$ in the line $y=x$.

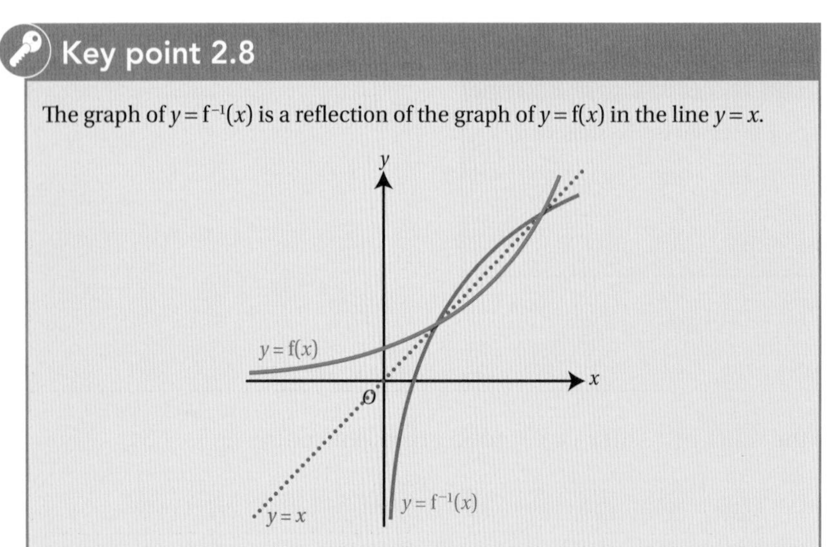

When you do and undo a function, you get back to where you started.

Key point 2.9

$$f(f^{-1}(x))=f^{-1}(f(x))=x$$

WORKED EXAMPLE 2.13

The graph of $y = \mathrm{h}(x)$ is shown below. Sketch the graphs of:

a $y = \mathrm{h}^{-1}(x)$ **b** $y = \mathrm{h} \circ \mathrm{h}^{-1}(x)$

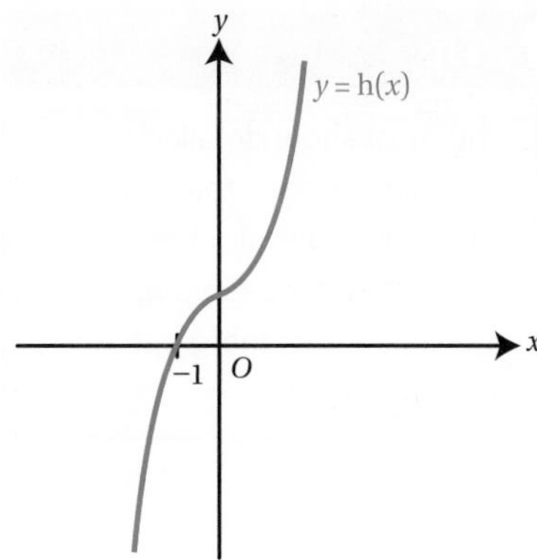

a

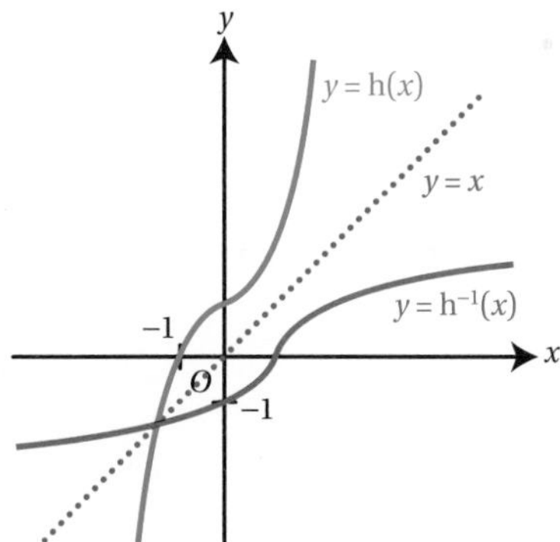

The graph of $y = \mathrm{h}^{-1}(x)$ is a reflection in the line $y = x$ of $y = \mathrm{h}(x)$.

b

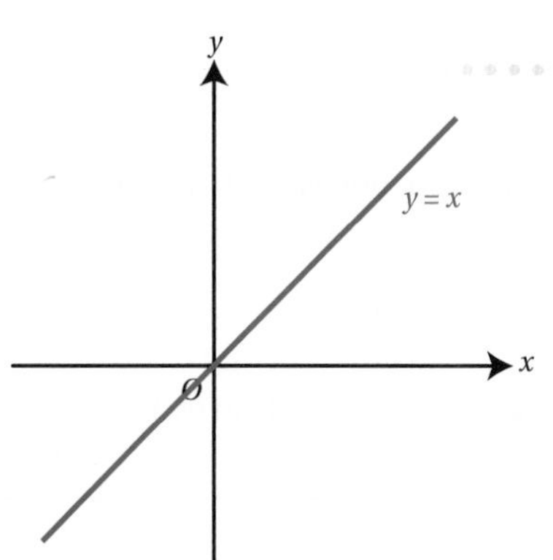

Simplify $y = \mathrm{h} \circ \mathrm{h}^{-1}(x)$ to $y = x$.

The fact that the graphs of f and f^{-1} are reflections of each other gives you a very useful trick to solve some equations that would otherwise involve complicated (or impossible) algebra.

WORKED EXAMPLE 2.14

In this question you must show detailed reasoning.

This diagram shows a part of the graph of function $f(x) = \frac{1}{27}x^3 + x - 8$, $x \in \mathbb{R}$.

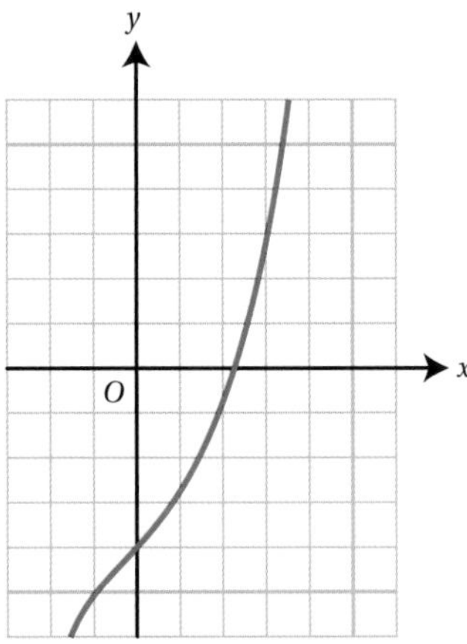

> **Tip**
>
> 'You must show detailed reasoning' means that you must solve equations algebraically rather than, for example, using intersections of the graph on your calculator.

a On the same axes, sketch the graph of $y = f^{-1}(x)$.

b Solve the equation $f(x) = f^{-1}(x)$.

a

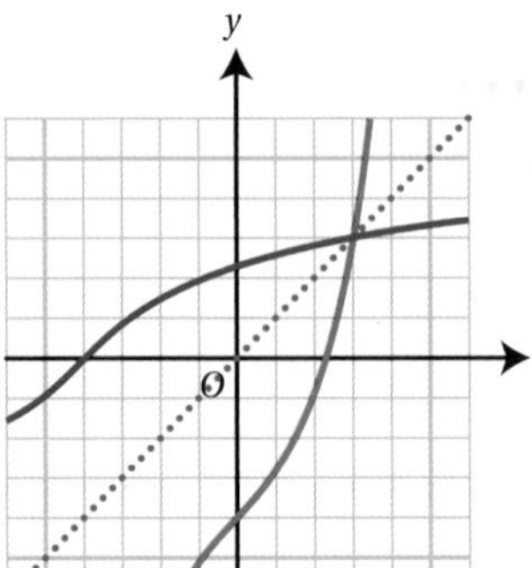

The graph of $f^{-1}(x)$ is the reflection of the graph of $y = f(x)$ in the line $y = x$.

b

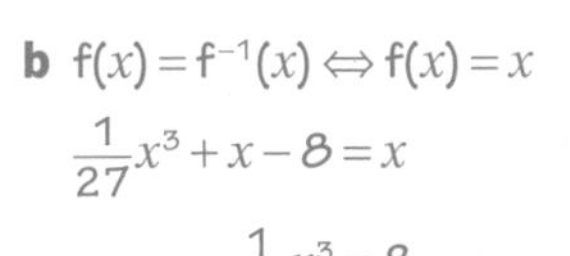

$f(x) = f^{-1}(x) \Leftrightarrow f(x) = x$

$\frac{1}{27}x^3 + x - 8 = x$

$\frac{1}{27}x^3 = 8$

$x^3 = 8 \times 27$

$x = 2 \times 3 = 6$

Finding the equation for the inverse function would involve solving a cubic equation, and you don't know how to do that.

Luckily, you can see from the graph that the graphs of f and f^{-1} intersect on the line $y = x$. This means that solving the equation $f = f^{-1}$ is equivalent to solving the equation $f(x) = x$.

The reflection in the line $y = x$ swaps the domain and the range of a function (because it swaps x and y coordinates).

Key point 2.10

- The domain of $f^{-1}(x)$ is the same as the range of $f(x)$.
- The range of $f^{-1}(x)$ is the same as the domain of $f(x)$.

WORKED EXAMPLE 2.15

The function f is defined by $f(x)=\dfrac{1+x}{3-x}$ for $x \neq 3$.

a Find an expression for $f^{-1}(x)$ and state its domain and range.

b State the range of f.

a $y=\dfrac{1+x}{3-x}$ — Set $y = f(x)$.

$y(3-x)=1+x$
$3y-yx=1+x$
$3y-1=x+xy$
$3y-1=x(1+y)$
$x=\dfrac{3y-1}{1+y}$

Make x the subject.

$f^{-1}(x)=\dfrac{3x-1}{1+x}$ — Replace y with x.

The domain of f^{-1} is $x \neq -1$. — In the expression for f^{-1}, the denominator cannot be zero.

The range of f^{-1} is $f^{-1}(x) \neq 3$. — The range of f^{-1} is the same as the domain of f, which is given in the question.

b The range of f is $f(x) \neq -1$. — The range of f is the same as the domain of f^{-1}, which you have just found.

EXERCISE 2D

1 Find an expression for $f^{-1}(x)$ if:

a i $f(x)=3x+1$ ii $f(x)=7x-3$

b i $f(x)=\dfrac{2x}{3x-2},\ x\neq\dfrac{2}{3}$ ii $f(x)=\dfrac{x}{2x+1}$

c i $f(x)=\dfrac{x-a}{x-b},\ x\neq b$ ii $f(x)=\dfrac{ax-1}{bx-1},\ x\neq\dfrac{1}{b}$

d i $f(a)=1-a$ ii $f(y)=3y+2$

e i $f(x)=\sqrt{3x-2},\ x\geqslant\dfrac{2}{3}$ ii $f(x)=\sqrt{2-5x},\ x\leqslant\dfrac{2}{5}$

f i $f(x)=\ln(1-5x),\ x<0.2$ ii $f(x)=\ln(2x+2),\ x>-1$

g i $f(x)=7e^{\frac{x}{2}}$ ii $f(x)=9e^{10x}$

h i $f(x)=x^2-10x+6,\ x>5$ ii $f(x)=x^2+6x-1,\ x>0$

2 Sketch the inverses of the following functions.

a

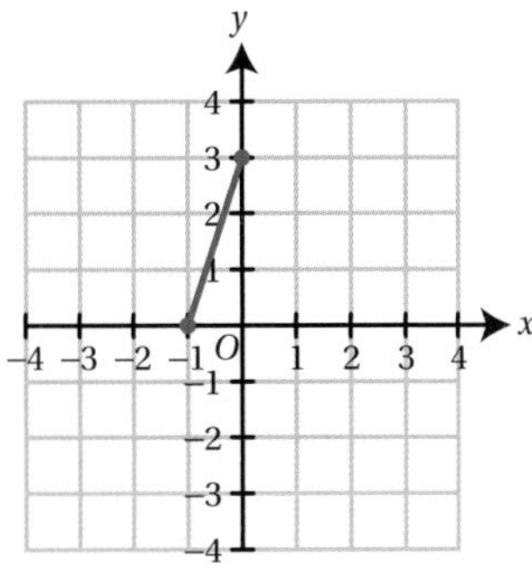

b

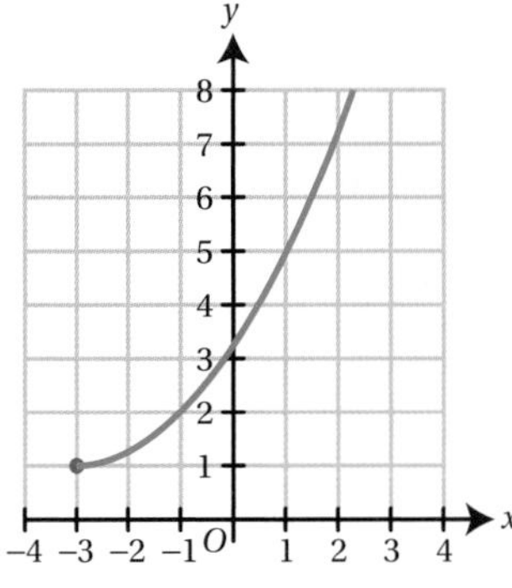

c

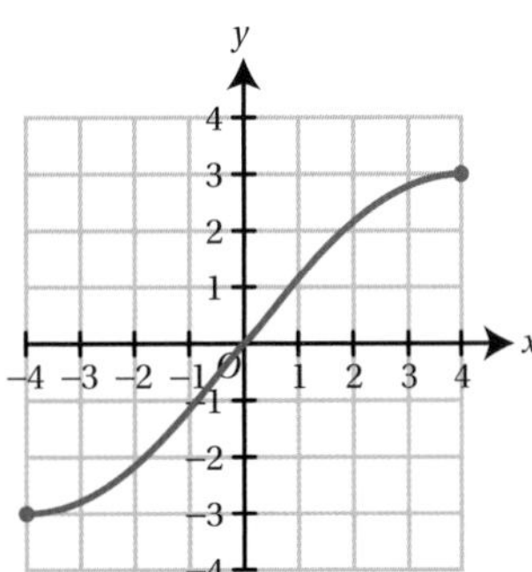

d

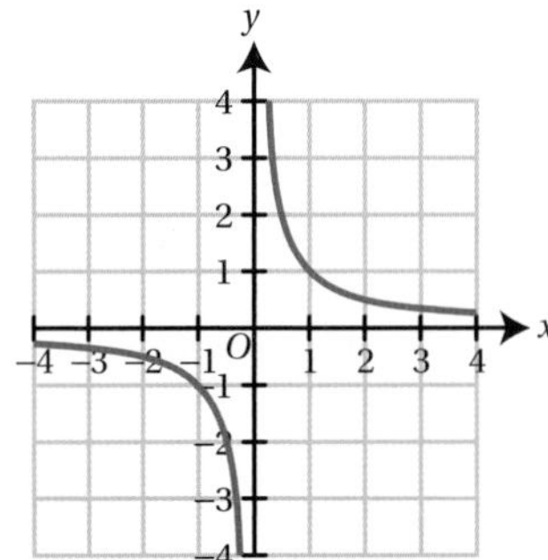

3 Each of the following functions is defined on the largest possible real domain such that the inverse function exists. Find the expression for f^{-1} in each case. State the domain and range for both f and f^{-1}.

a **i** $f(x)=\frac{3x-1}{x+2}$ **ii** $f(x)=\frac{2x+3}{x-2}$

b **i** $f(x)=2-3\sqrt{3x-1}$ **ii** $f(x)=\frac{1}{2}\sqrt{4-x}+1$

c **i** $f(x)=3+\ln(4x-3)$ **ii** $f(x)=2\ln(x+3)-1$

d **i** $f(x)=3-2e^{x-2}$ **ii** $f(x)=3e^{5-2x}+1$

4 Below is a table giving selected values of the one-one function f(x).

x	−1	0	1	2	3	4
f(x)	−4	−1	3	0	7	2

a Evaluate f f (2). **b** Evaluate $f^{-1}(3)$.

5 **In this question you must show detailed reasoning.**

The function f is defined by $f: x \mapsto \sqrt{3-2x}$ for $x \leqslant \frac{3}{2}$.

Evaluate $f^{-1}(7)$.

6 Given that $f(x) = 3e^{2x}$:

a Find the inverse function $f^{-1}(x)$.

b State the domain and range of f^{-1}.

7 Given functions $f: x \mapsto 2x+3$ and $g: x \mapsto x^3$, find the function $(f \circ g)^{-1}$.

Elevate

See Support sheet 2 for a further example of finding inverse functions and their domains, and for more practice questions.

8 Let f and g be two functions such that $f \circ g$ is defined, and suppose that both f^{-1} and g^{-1} exist.
Let $h(x) = f \circ g\,(x)$. Prove that $h^{-1}(x) = g^{-1} \circ f^{-1}(x)$.

9 The diagram shows the graph of $y = f(x)$. The lines $y = -9$ and $y = 9$ are the asymptotes of the graph.

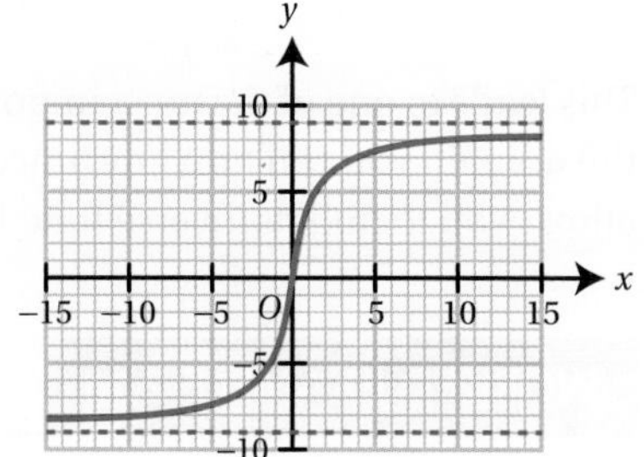

a Copy the graph and, on the same axes, sketch the graph of $y = f^{-1}(x)$.

b State the domain and range of f^{-1}.

c Write down the solutions to the equation $f(x) = f^{-1}(x)$.

10 The functions f and g are defined by $f: x \mapsto e^{2x}$ and $g: x \mapsto x + 1$.

a Calculate $f^{-1}(3) \times g^{-1}(3)$.

b Show that $(f \circ g)^{-1}(3) = \ln\sqrt{3} - 1$.

11 The function f is defined for $x \leqslant 0$ by $f(x) = \frac{x^2 - 4}{x^2 + 9}$. Find an expression for $f^{-1}(x)$.

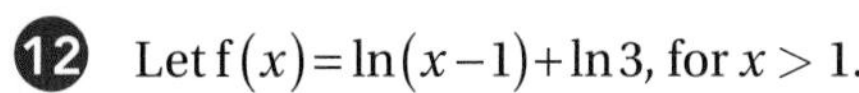

12 Let $f(x) = \ln(x - 1) + \ln 3$, for $x > 1$.

a Find $f^{-1}(x)$.

Let $g(x) = e^x$ for $x \in \mathbb{R}$.

b Find $(g \circ f)(x)$, giving your answer in the form $ax + b$, where $a, b \in \mathbb{Z}$. Find the domain and range of $g \circ f$.

13 **In this question you must show detailed reasoning.**

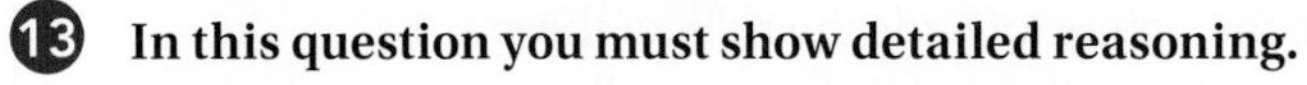

The function f is defined by $f(x) = \sqrt[3]{x^3 + 30x - 45}$ for $x \in \mathbb{R}$.
The graph of $y = f(x)$ is shown in the diagram.

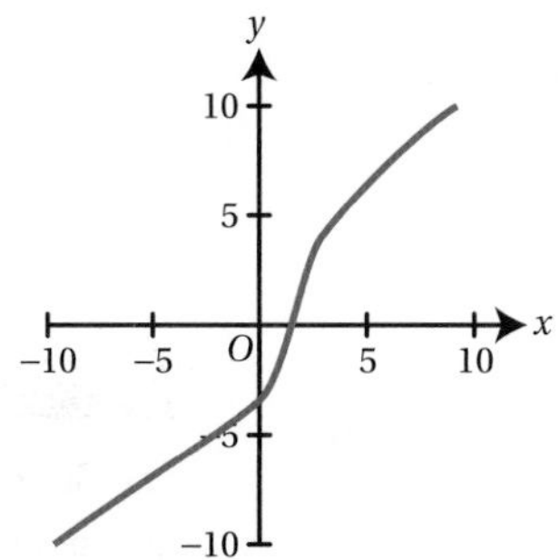

a On the same set of axes, sketch the graph of $y = f^{-1}(x)$.

b Solve the equation $f(x) = f^{-1}(x)$.

When does the inverse function exist?

All functions have inverse mappings, but these inverse mappings are not necessarily themselves functions. Since an inverse function is a reflection in the line $y = x$, for the result to pass the vertical line test the original function must pass the horizontal line test. But, as you saw in Section 1, this means it must be a one-one function.

Fast forward

You will apply this idea in Chapter 7 when you define inverses of trigonometric functions.

Key point 2.11

Only one-one functions have inverse functions.

This leads to one of the most important uses of domains. By restricting the domain you can turn any function into a one-one function, which allows you to find its inverse function.

WORKED EXAMPLE 2.16

a Find the largest value of k such that the function $f(x) = (x - 3)^2$, $x \leqslant k$ is one-one.
b For this value of k, find $f^{-1}(x)$ and state its range.

a

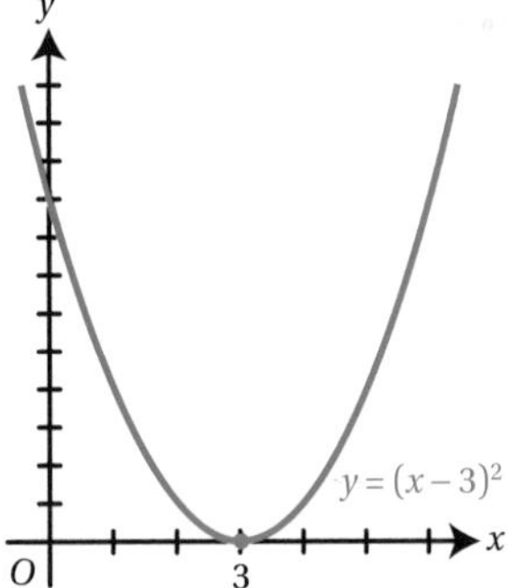

Sketch the graph of $y=(x-3)^2$, $x \in \mathbb{R}$.

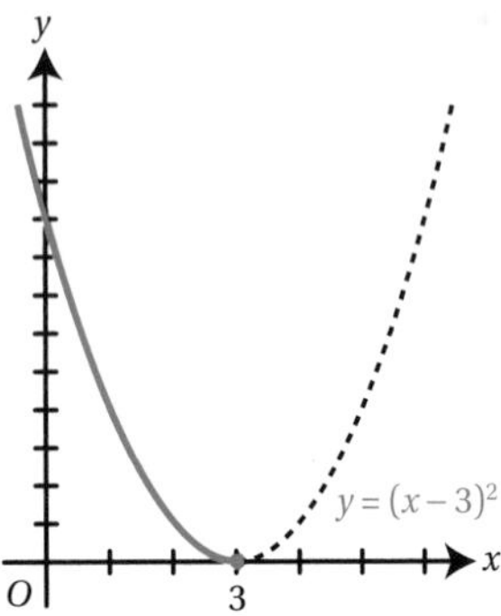

Eliminate the points towards the right of the graph which cause the horizontal line test to fail.

$k=3$

Decide which section remains.

b $y=(x-3)^2$

$\pm\sqrt{y}=x-3$

$x=3\pm\sqrt{y}$

Follow standard procedure for finding inverse functions.

Since $x \leqslant 3$, $x=3-\sqrt{y}$.

Use the fact that $x \leqslant 3$ to decide which root to take.

$f^{-1}(x)=3-\sqrt{x}$

Write $f^{-1}(x)$.

The range of f^{-1} is $f^{-1}(x) \leqslant 3$.

The range of f^{-1} is the domain of f.

WORK IT OUT 2.3

What is the inverse function of $f(x) = x^2 - 3, x \in \mathbb{R}$?

Which of the following solutions is correct? Identify the mistake in the other two.

Solution 1	Solution 2	Solution 3
$y = x^2 - 3$ $\Rightarrow x^2 = y + 3$ $\Rightarrow x = \pm\sqrt{y+3}$ $\therefore f^{-1}(x) = \pm\sqrt{x+3}$	$y = x^2 - 3$ $\Rightarrow x^2 = y + 3$ $\Rightarrow x = \sqrt{y+3}$ $\therefore f^{-1}(x) = \sqrt{x+3}$	It doesn't exist.

It should be clear from the horizontal line test that if a function, either increases or decreases throughout its domain, then it is one-one. As soon as there is a turning point, the function is no longer one-one (and therefore has no inverse).

WORKED EXAMPLE 2.17

In this question you must show detailed reasoning.

If $f(x) = x^2 - 8x^{\frac{3}{2}} + 18x$, for $x \geqslant 0$, prove that f has an inverse function.

$f'(x) = 2x - 12x^{\frac{1}{2}} + 18$

$= 2(x - 6x^{\frac{1}{2}} + 9)$

If the function is either increasing or decreasing, then it will have an inverse, so this is a good thing to check first.

$= 2(x^{\frac{1}{2}} - 3)^2 \geqslant 0$

for all $x \geqslant 0$.

Complete the square. Note that this is a common way of showing that a function is non-negative.

$\therefore$ f is an increasing function for all $x \geqslant 0$.

Although $f'(9) = 0$, the gradient is never negative. Since f has no turning points or asymptotes, this means that it is increasing.

Hence, f is one-one and so has an inverse function.

There are two things to notice in problems about one-one functions. First of all, in Worked Example 2.17 , the fact that the gradient is $\geqslant 0$ allowed you to conclude that the function is always increasing. This may not be true if its graph has asymptotes or other breaks, as illustrated by the two diagrams below. The graphs have positive gradients but are not always increasing.

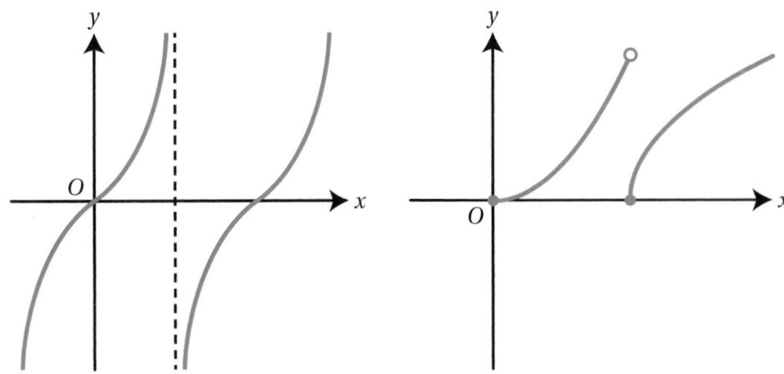

Secondly, although a function increasing (or decreasing) implies that it is one–one, the converse is not true: a one–one function can have both increasing and decreasing sections. The diagram below shows the graph of the function

$$f(x)=\begin{cases} x, & 0\leqslant x<1 \\ 3-x, & 1\leqslant x\leqslant 2 \end{cases}$$

You can use the horizontal line test to show that this function is one–one, and therefore has an inverse function.

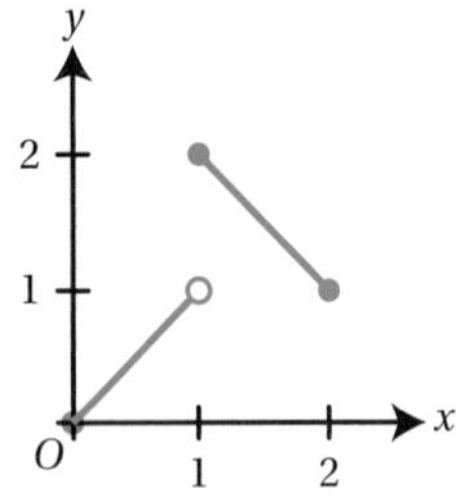

Most functions you will meet in this course will not require you to consider these issues, but it is useful to be aware of them.

EXERCISE 2E

1 In the following situations, find the value of k that gives the largest possible domain such that the inverse function exists. For this domain, find the inverse function.

a $y=x^2, x\leqslant k$ **b** $y=(x+1)^2+2, x>k$

c $y=5+2x-x^2, x\leqslant k$ **d** $y=x^2+4x+3, x>k$

2 For each function shown in the diagrams below, determine a possible domain of the given form for which the inverse function exists.

a Domain: $x\leqslant k$

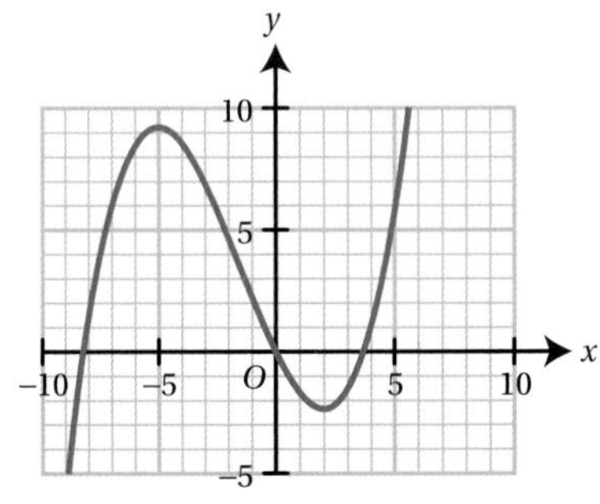

b Domain: $x \in [a, b]$

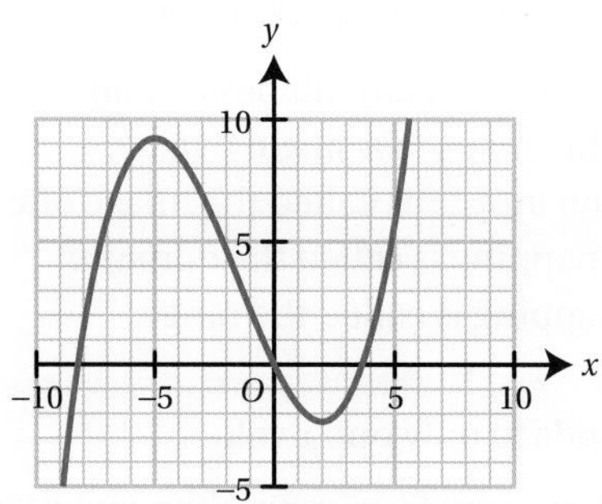

c Domain: $a \leqslant x < b$

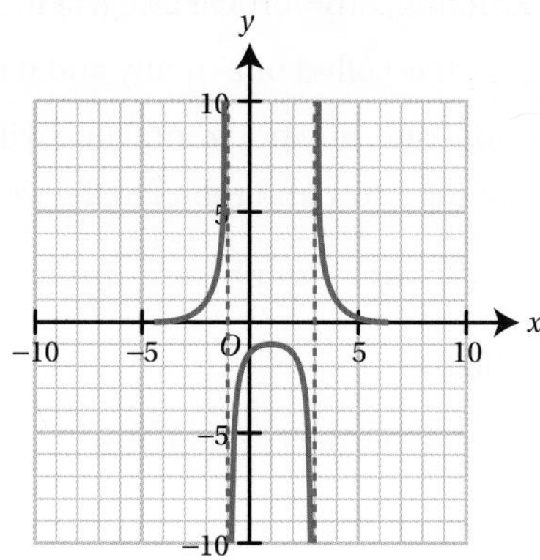

3 Given that $f(x) = e^x - 3x$ for $x \in \mathbb{R}$:

a Find $f'(x)$.

b Explain why $f^{-1}(x)$ does not exist.

The domain of f is changed to $x \leqslant k$ so that f^{-1} now exists.

c Find the largest possible value of k.

4 A function is called *self-inverse* if $f(x) = f^{-1}(x)$ for all x in the domain. Find the value of the constant k so that $g(x) = \dfrac{3x-5}{x+k}$ is a self-inverse function.

5 A function is defined by $f(x) = x^3 + 3ax^2 + 3ax + 1$, where a is a constant. Find the set of values of a for which $f^{-1}(x)$ exists for all x.

Checklist of learning and understanding

- A mapping takes input values from a given set and maps each one of them to one or more output values.
- A mapping is a function if every x value maps to a single y value.
- The output value corresponding to the input x is called the image of x.
- The set of allowed input values of a mapping is called the domain.
- The set of all possible outputs of a mapping is called the range.
- A function is:
  - one-one if every y value corresponds to only one x value.
  - many-one if at least one y value that come from more than one x value.
- The vertical and horizontal line tests can be applied to graphs of mappings.
  - Vertical line test: if a mapping is a function, any vertical line will meet its graph at most once.
    - If a mapping fails a vertical line test, it is called one-many and it is not a function.
  - Horizontal line test: if a function is one-one, any horizontal line will meet the graph at most once.
- The composite function formed by applying g to x and then f to the result is written as:

$$\mathrm{f}(\mathrm{g}(x)) \quad \text{or} \quad \mathrm{fg}(x) \quad \text{or} \quad \mathrm{f} \circ \mathrm{g}(x)$$

- The inverse, f^{-1}, of a function f is such that:

$$\mathrm{f}\left(\mathrm{f}^{-1}(x)\right) = \mathrm{f}^{-1}\left(\mathrm{f}(x)\right) = x$$

- To find the expression for the inverse function $\mathrm{f}^{-1}(x)$, given an expression for $\mathrm{f}(x)$:
  - Start with $y = \mathrm{f}(x)$.
  - Rearrange to get x (the input) in terms of y (the output).
  - Obtain $\mathrm{f}^{-1}(x)$ by replacing every instance of y with x.
- Only one-one functions have inverse functions.
- The graph of $y = \mathrm{f}^{-1}(x)$ is a reflection of the graph of $y = \mathrm{f}(x)$ in the line $y = x$.
  - The domain of f^{-1} is the same as the range of f.
  - The range of f^{-1} is the same as the domain of f.

Mixed practice 2

In this exercise, if a domain of a function is not stated, you may assume that it is all real numbers.

1 Find the inverse of the following functions.

a $f(x)=\log_3(x+3), x>-3$

b $f(x)=3e^{x^3-1}, x\in\mathbb{R}$

2 The diagram shows three graphs.

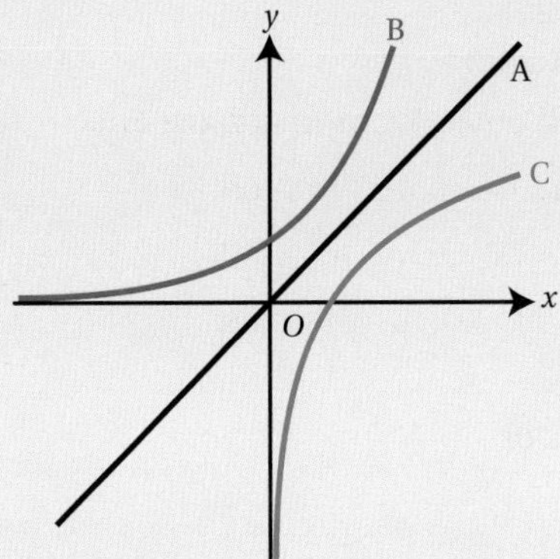

A is part of the graph of $y=x$.

B is part of the graph of $y=2^x$.

C is the reflection of graph B in line A.

Write down:

a the equation of C in the form $y=f(x)$

b the coordinates of the point where C cuts the x-axis.

3 Let $f(x)=\sqrt{x}$, and $g(x)=2^x$, where both functions are defined on their largest possible real domain. Solve the equation $(f^{-1}\circ g)(x)=0.25$.

4 Let and $f(x)=x^2+1, x\geqslant 3$ and $g(x)=5-x$.

a Evaluate f(3).

b Find and simplify an expression for g f(x).

c State the geometric relationship between the graphs of $y=f(x)$ and $y=f^{-1}(x)$.

d **i** Find an expression for $f^{-1}(x)$.

ii Find the range of $f^{-1}(x)$.

iii Find the domain of $f^{-1}(x)$.

e Explain why the equation $f(x)=g(3x)$ has no solutions.

5 Functions f and g are defined for all real values of x by

$f(x)=x^3+4$ and $g(x)=2x-5$.

Evaluate,

i fg(1),

ii $f^{-1}(12)$

6 The function f is given by $f(x)=x^2-6x+10$, for $x\geqslant 3$.

a Write f(x) in the form $(x-p)^2+q$.

b Find the inverse function $f^{-1}(x)$, stating its domain.

Tip

Whenever you find a function, you should always state its domain.

7 Let $f(x)=2x+1$, $x\in\mathbb{R}$ and $g(x)=\dfrac{x+3}{x-1}$, $x\neq 1$.

a Find and simplify:

i f(7)

ii the range of f(x)

iii f(z)

iv f g(x)

v f f(x)

b Explain why g f(x) does not exist.

c **i** Find the form of $g^{-1}(x)$.

ii State the geometric relationship between the graphs of $y=g(x)$ and $y=g^{-1}(x)$.

iii State the domain of $g^{-1}(x)$.

iv State the range of $g^{-1}(x)$.

8 **In this question you must show detailed reasoning.**

The functions f and g are defined over the domain of all real numbers by $f(x)=x^2+4x+9$ and $g(x)=e^x$.

a Write $f(x)=x^2+4x+9$, $x\in\mathbb{R}$ in the form $f(x)=(x+p)^2+q$.

b Hence, sketch the graph of $y=x^2+4x+9$, labelling all axes intercepts and the coordinates of the turning point.

c State the range of f(x) and g(x).

d Hence, or otherwise, find the range of $h(x)=e^{2x}+4e^x+9$.

9 The functions f and g are defined for all real values of x by
$f(x)=4x^2-12x$ and $g(x)=ax+b$,
where a and b are non-zero constants.

i Find the range of f.

ii Explain why the function f has no inverse.

iii Given that $g^{-1}(x)=g(x)$ for all values of x, show that $a=-1$.

iv Given further that $gf(x)<5$ for all values of x, find the set of possible values of b.

© OCR, GCE Mathematics, Paper 4723, June 2010

10 Let $h(x) = x^2 - 6x + 2$.

a Write $h(x)$ in the form $(x - p)^2 + q$.

b Hence, or otherwise, find the range of h when its domain is all real numbers.

c Another function g is now defined with the same rule as h, but with the largest possible domain of the form $x \geqslant k$, for which it has an inverse function. Find an expression for $g^{-1}(x)$.

11 **a** Show that if $g(x) = \frac{1}{x}$, then $gg(x) = x$.

b A function satisfies the identity $f(x) + 2f\left(\frac{1}{x}\right) = 2x + 1$.

By replacing all instances of x with $\frac{1}{x}$, find another identity satisfied by $f(x)$.

c By solving these two identities simultaneously, express $f(x)$ in terms of x.

12 **In this question you must show detailed reasoning.**

The functions $f(x)$ and $g(x)$ are given by $f(x) = \sqrt{x-2}$ and $g(x) = x^2 + x$. The function $(f \circ g)(x)$ is defined for $x \in \mathbb{R}$, except for the interval $a < x < b$.

a Calculate the value of a and of b.

b Find the range of $f \circ g$.

13 An odd function is any function $f(x)$ that satisfies $f(x) = -f(-x)$.

a Show that $f(x) = x^3$ is an odd function.

b What type of symmetry must the graph of any odd function have?

c Given any function $g(x)$, show that $g(x) - g(-x)$ is an odd function.

An even function is any function that satisfies $f(x) = f(-x)$.

d Show that $f(x) = x^4$ is an even function.

e What type of symmetry must the graph of any even function have?

f Given any function $g(x)$, show that $g(x) + g(-x)$ is an even function.

g Hence, or otherwise, show that any function can be written as the sum of an even function and an odd function.

See Extension sheet 2 for a selection of more challenging problems.

3 Further transformations of graphs

In this chapter you will learn how to:

- draw a graph after two (or more) transformations
- find the equation of a graph after a combination of transformations
- sketch graphs of functions involving the modulus (absolute value)
- use modulus graphs to solve equations and inequalities.

Before you start…

Student Book 1, Chapter 5	You should be able to recognise a graph transformation from the equation.	1 The graph of $y = \mathrm{f}(x)$ is shown in the diagram. Sketch the graph of: a $y = \mathrm{f}(x+2)$ b $y = -\mathrm{f}(x)$
Student Book 1, Chapter 5	You should be able to change the equation of a graph to achieve a given transformation.	2 A graph has equation $y = x^2 - 3x$. Find the equation of the graph after: a a translation of 5 units in the positive y direction b a horizontal stretch with scale factor 2.
Student Book 1, Chapter 1	You should be able to use interval notation to express solution of inequalities.	3 In this question, write the solution using interval notation. a Solve the inequality $3x - 2 \geqslant 7$. b Solve the system of inequalities $2x + 5 > 1$ and $3 - 2x > 1$.

Combining transformations

In this chapter you'll take the transformations you met in Student Book 1, Chapter 5, and combine them to produce a sequence of transformations of the original graph.

You'll also meet the modulus function, which is used in many contexts where a quantity needs to be positive. For example, the total distance travelled by a particle must be the sum of positive quantities even though it may change direction. You've also seen this idea used to find the area between a curve and the x-axis when the enclosed region is below the axis.

Section 1: Combined transformations

In this section we look at what happens when you apply two transformations to a graph. An important question to consider is: does the order in which the two transformations are done affect the outcome? To investigate this question, let us first consider transformations of a single point.

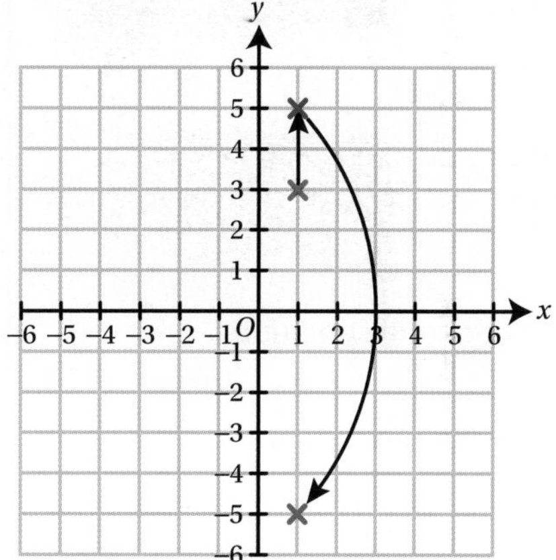

The point $(1, 3)$ is translated 2 units up and then reflected in the x-axis. The new point is $(1, -5)$.

The point $(1, 3)$ is reflected in the x-axis first and then translated 2 units up. The new point is $(1, -1)$.

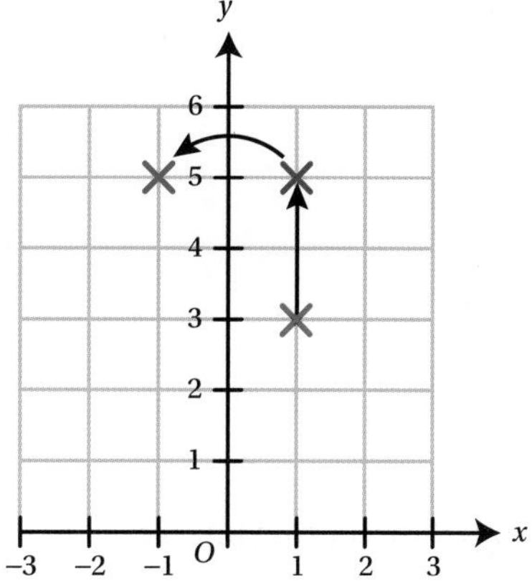

The point $(1, 3)$ is translated 2 units up and then reflected in the y-axis. The new point is $(-1, 5)$.

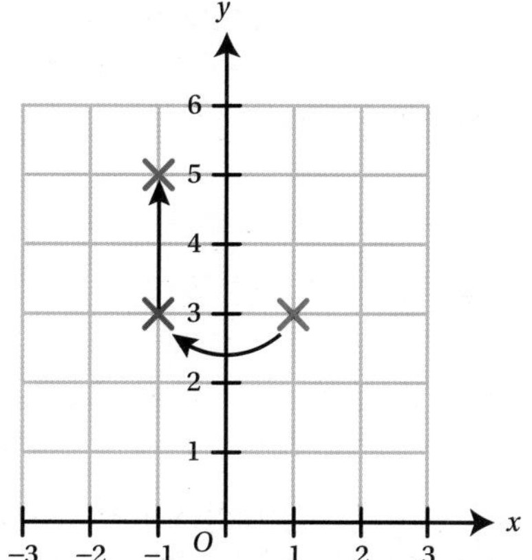

The point $(1, 3)$ is reflected in the y-axis first and then translated 2 units up. The new point is $(-1, 5)$.

These examples suggest the following rules for combining transformations.

Key point 3.1

When two vertical transformations or two horizontal transformations are combined, changing the order may affect the outcome.

When one vertical and one horizontal transformation are combined, the outcome does not depend on the order.

Explore

In advanced mathematics, algebra is much more than using letters to represent numbers. Unknowns can include transformations, as well as many other things.

As demonstrated in this section, the rules for transformations are different from the rules for numbers, but there are certain similarities, too. The study of this more general form of algebra includes group theory, which has many applications, from particle physics to painting polyhedra.

Combining one vertical and one horizontal transformation

WORKED EXAMPLE 3.1

The diagram shows the graph of the function $y = \mathrm{f}(x)$.

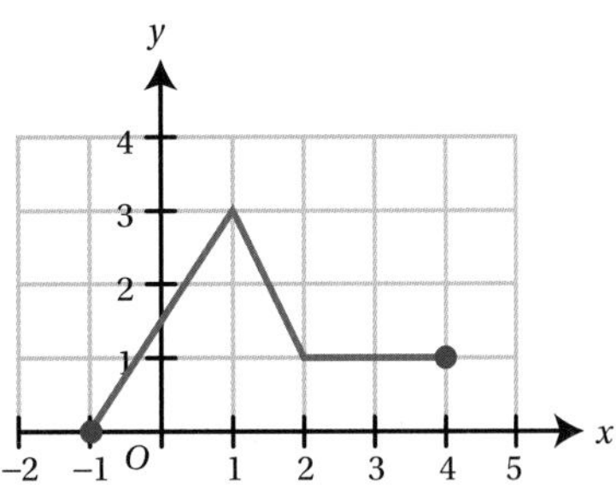

On separate diagrams, draw the graphs of:

a $y = 2\mathrm{f}(x+3)$ **b** $y = -\mathrm{f}\left(\frac{x}{2}\right)$

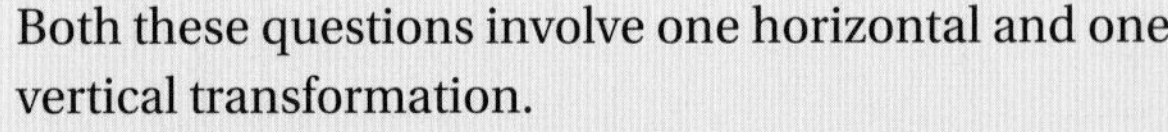
Both these questions involve one horizontal and one vertical transformation.

Since the order doesn't matter, you can carry out the transformation in brackets first.

a $y = \mathrm{f}(x+3)$: translate 3 units to the left.

x is replaced by $x + 3$, so the graph is translated to the left.

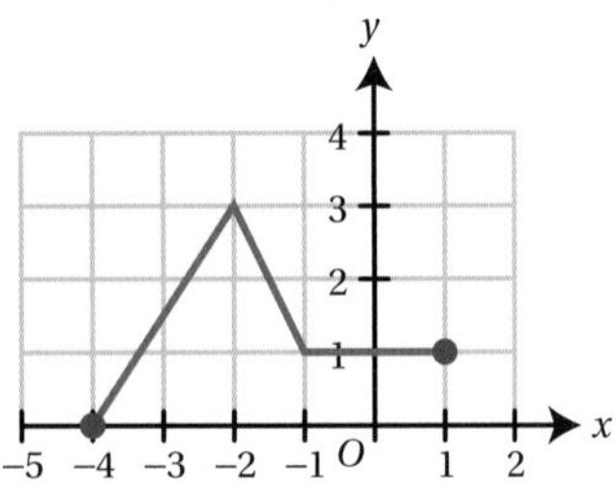

$y = 2\,\mathrm{f}(x+3)$: vertical stretch with scale factor 2.

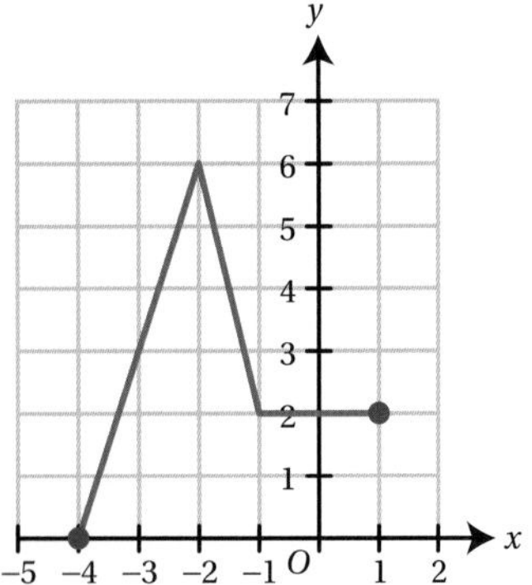

Continues on next page ...

b $x = f\left(\frac{x}{2}\right)$: horizontal stretch with scale factor 2

x is replaced by $\frac{x}{2}$, so the graph is stretched horizontally.

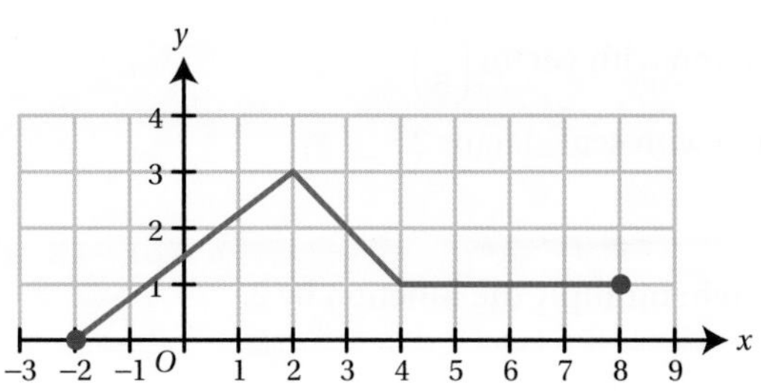

$y = -f\left(\frac{x}{2}\right)$: reflection in the x-axis

Making the y-coordinate negative results in a reflection in the x-axis.

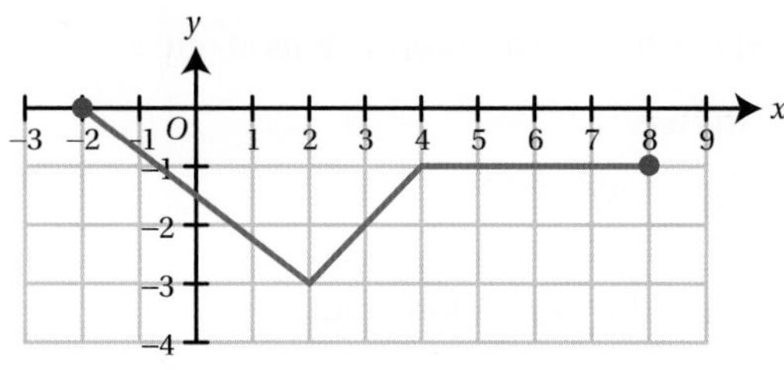

Combining two vertical transformations

To transform the graph of $y = f(x)$ into the graph of:

$$y = p\,f(x) + c$$

you first multiply $f(x)$ by p and then add c. The flow chart shows the order of operations and the corresponding transformations:

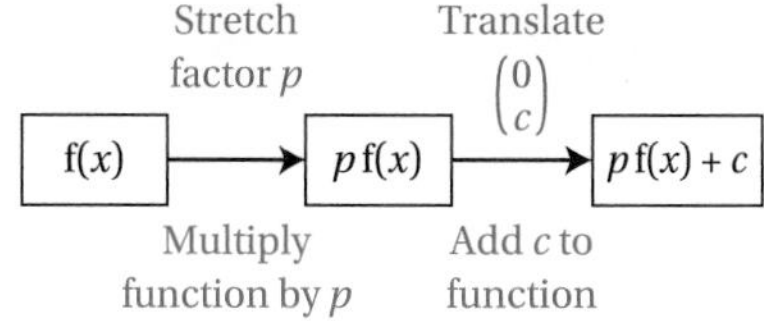

Notice that this follows the normal order of operations: multiplication is done before addition.

WORKED EXAMPLE 3.2

A graph has equation $y = x^2 - 3$. Find the equation of the graph after the following transformations.

a a vertical stretch with scale factor 2 followed by a translation with vector $\begin{pmatrix} 0 \\ 5 \end{pmatrix}$

b a translation with vector $\begin{pmatrix} 0 \\ 5 \end{pmatrix}$ followed by a vertical stretch with scale factor 2.

a Vertical stretch:
$y = x^2 - 3$ becomes
$y = 2x^2 - 6$.

Vertical stretch: multiply the function by 2.

Vertical translation:
$y = 2x^2 - 6$ becomes
$y = 2x^2 - 1$.

Vertical translation: add 5 to the whole expression.

The final equation is
$y = 2x^2 - 1$.

You could perform the two transformations in one go:
The new equation is
$y = 2\mathrm{f}(x) + 5 = 2(x^2 - 3) + 5 = 2x^2 - 1$

b Vertical translation:
$y = x^2 - 3$ becomes $y = x^2 + 2$.

This time, add 5 to the expression first...

Vertical stretch:
$y = x^2 + 2$ becomes $y = 2x^2 + 4$.

... then multiply the whole expression by 2.

The final equation is $y = 2x^2 + 4$.

Again, we can write this in one go:
$y = (\mathrm{f}(x) + 5) \times 2 = 2(x^2 - 3 + 5) = 2x^2 + 4$

Combining two horizontal transformations

If we combine two horizontal transformations, we can transform the graph of $y = \mathrm{f}(x)$ into the graph of

$$y = \mathrm{f}(qx + d)$$

We can achieve this by first replacing x with $x + d$ and then replacing *all* occurrences of x by qx. The flow chart shows the resulting order of transformations.

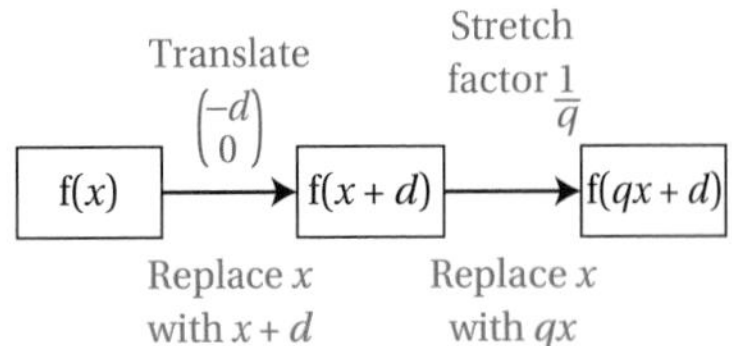

Notice that the transformations are in the 'wrong' order: the translation, which corresponds to addition, is done first.

WORKED EXAMPLE 3.3

The following graph shows $y = f(x)$. Sketch the graph of:

a $y = f(2x + 1)$ **b** $y = f(2(x + 1))$

a

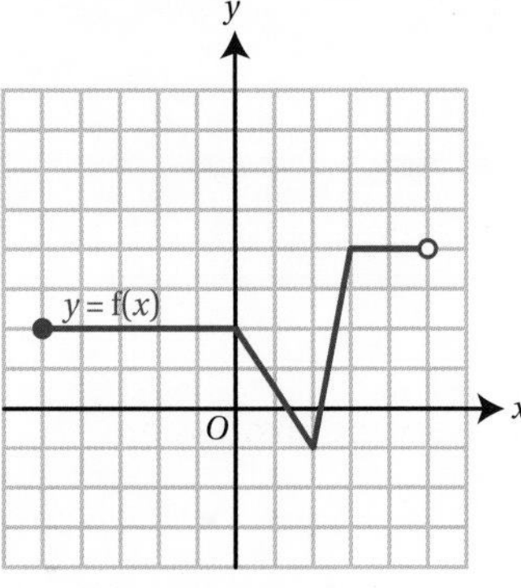

a $y = f(2x + 1)$

There are two transformations:

① x is replaced by $x + 1$.

② x is replaced by $2x$.

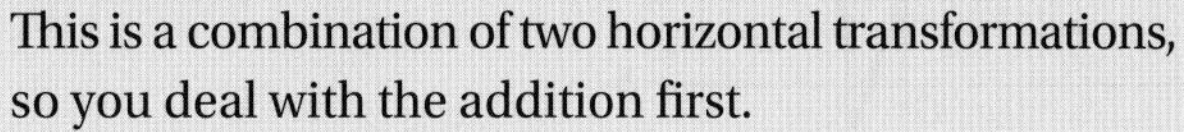

This is a combination of two horizontal transformations, so you deal with the addition first.

① x is replaced by $x + 1 \rightarrow$ horizontal translation $\begin{pmatrix} -1 \\ 0 \end{pmatrix}$.

Replace x with $x + 1$.

Change $y = f(x)$ to $y = f(x + 1)$

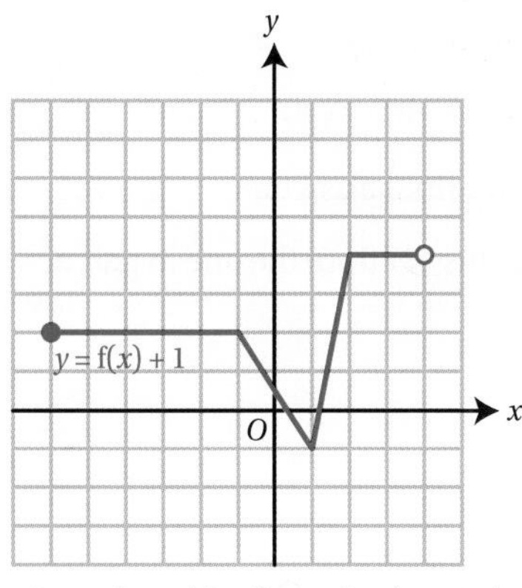

② x is replaced by $2x \rightarrow$ horizontal stretch, scale factor $\frac{1}{2}$.

Replace x with $2x$.

Change $y = f(x + 1)$ to $y = f(2x + 1)$.

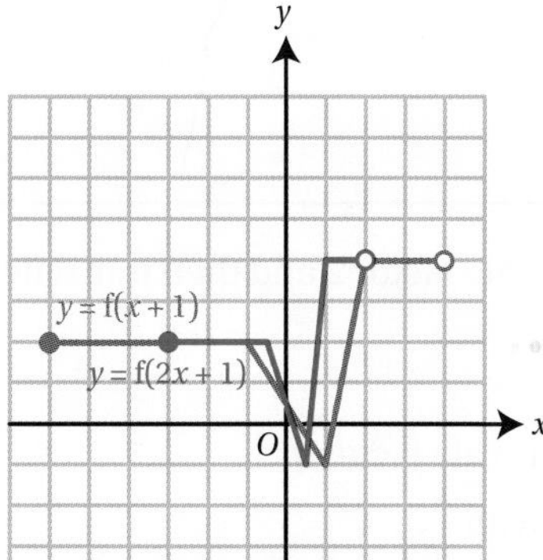

The red graph shows the final answer.

Continues on next page ...

b $y = \mathrm{f}(2(x+1))$

The two transformations are:

① x is replaced by $2x$.

② x is replaced by $x+1$.

The presence of brackets means that now we deal with the multiplication first.

① x is replaced by $2x \rightarrow$ stretch, scale factor $\frac{1}{2}$.

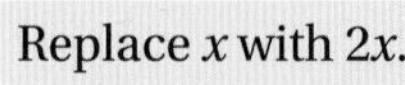

Replace x with $2x$.

Change $y = \mathrm{f}(x)$ to $y = \mathrm{f}(2x)$.

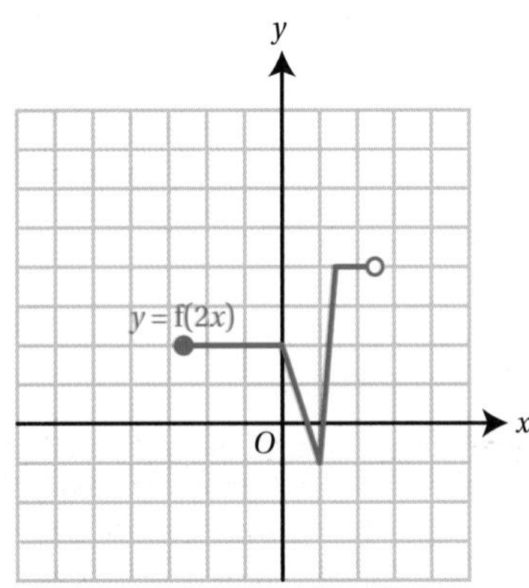

② x is replaced by $x+1 \rightarrow$ horizontal translation $\begin{pmatrix} -1 \\ 0 \end{pmatrix}$.

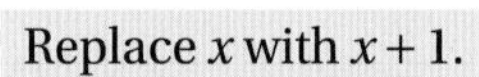

Replace x with $x+1$.

Change $y = \mathrm{f}(2x)$ to $y = \mathrm{f}(2(x+1))$.

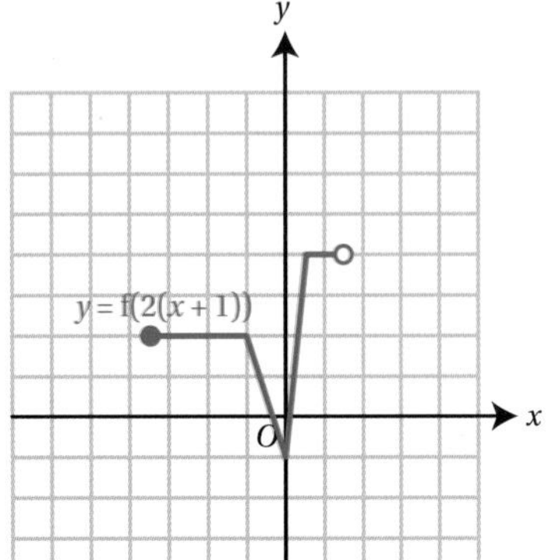

The green graph shows the final answer.

Note that this is a different answer from the one in part **a**.

As illustrated in Worked Example 3.3, if you want to perform a horizontal stretch before a translation you need to use brackets correctly in the equation.

WORKED EXAMPLE 3.4

The graph of $y = \sin(x)$ is transformed using a horizontal stretch with scale factor 2 and then translated 3 units to the right. Find the equation of the resulting graph.

① Replace x by $\frac{x}{2}$:

$y = \sin(x)$ is changed to $y = \sin\left(\frac{x}{2}\right)$.

A horizontal stretch with scale factor q is achieved by replacing x with $\frac{x}{q}$.

Continues on next page ...

② Replace x by $x-3$:

$y=\sin\left(\frac{x}{2}\right)$ is changed to $y=\sin\left(\frac{x-3}{2}\right)$.

A horizontal translation by d units is achieved by replacing x with $x-d$.

The final equation is $y=\sin\left(\frac{x}{2}-\frac{3}{2}\right)$.

Notice that if we had performed the translation before the stretch, the resulting equation would have been $y=\sin\left(\frac{x}{2}-3\right)$.

WORK IT OUT 3.1

Describe the sequence of two transformations that transform the graph of $y=f(x)$ to the graph of $y=f(2x+4)$.

Which of the following solutions is correct? Identify any mistakes in the other two.

Solution 1	Solution 2	Solution 3
1 Add 4 to x; this is a horizontal translation 4 units to the left. 2 Replace x by $2x$; this is a horizontal stretch with scale factor $\frac{1}{2}$.	1 Replace x by $2x$; this is a horizontal stretch with scale factor $\frac{1}{2}$. 2 Add 4 to x; this is a horizontal translation 4 units to the left.	1 Add 4 to x; this is a horizontal translation 4 units to the left. 2 Replace x by $2x$; this is a horizontal stretch with scale factor 2.

EXERCISE 3A

1 The following graphs show $y=f(x)$ and $y=g(x)$.

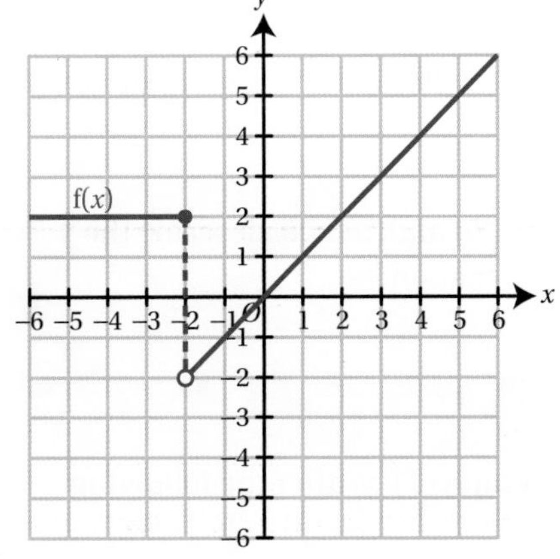

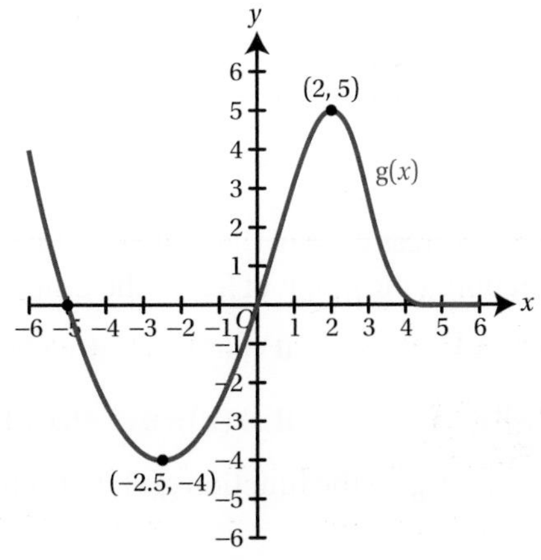

Sketch the graphs of:

a **i** $y=2f(x)-1$ **ii** $y=\frac{1}{2}g(x)+3$

b **i** $y=4-f(x)$ **ii** $y=2-2g(x)$

c **i** $y = 3(\mathrm{f}(x)-2)$ **ii** $y = \frac{1-\mathrm{g}(x)}{2}$

d **i** $y = \mathrm{f}\left(\frac{x}{2}-1\right)$ **ii** $y = \mathrm{g}(2x+3)$

e **i** $y = \mathrm{f}\left(\frac{4-x}{5}\right)$ **ii** $y = \mathrm{g}\left(\frac{x-3}{2}\right)$

2 Given that $\mathrm{f}(x)=x^2$, express each of the following functions as $a\,\mathrm{f}(x)+b$ and, hence, describe the sequence of transformations mapping the graph of f(x) to the graph of the given function.

a **i** $\mathrm{k}(x)=2x^2-6$ **ii** $\mathrm{k}(x)=5x^2+4$

b **i** $\mathrm{h}(x)=5-3x^2$ **ii** $\mathrm{h}(x)=4-8x^2$

3 Given that $\mathrm{f}(x)=2x^2-4$, give the function g(x) that represents the graph of f(x) after the following transformations.

a **i** Translation $\begin{pmatrix}0\\2\end{pmatrix}$ followed by a vertical stretch of scale factor 3.

ii Translation $\begin{pmatrix}0\\6\end{pmatrix}$ followed by a vertical stretch of scale factor $\frac{1}{2}$.

b **i** Vertical stretch of scale factor $\frac{1}{2}$ followed by a translation $\begin{pmatrix}0\\6\end{pmatrix}$.

ii Vertical stretch of scale factor $\frac{7}{2}$ followed by a translation $\begin{pmatrix}0\\10\end{pmatrix}$.

c **i** Reflection in the horizontal axis followed by a translation $\begin{pmatrix}0\\-1\end{pmatrix}$.

ii Reflection in the horizontal axis followed by a translation $\begin{pmatrix}0\\2\end{pmatrix}$.

d **i** Reflection in the horizontal axis, followed by a vertical stretch of scale factor $\frac{1}{2}$, followed by a translation $\begin{pmatrix}0\\3\end{pmatrix}$.

ii Reflection in the horizontal axis, followed by a translation $\begin{pmatrix}0\\-6\end{pmatrix}$, followed by a vertical stretch of, scale factor $\frac{3}{2}$.

4 Given that $\mathrm{f}(x)=x^2$, express each of the following functions as $\mathrm{f}(ax+b)$ and, hence, describe the transformation mapping the graph of f(x) to the graph of the given function.

a **i** $\mathrm{g}(x)=x^2+2x+1$ **ii** $\mathrm{g}(x)=x^2-6x+9$

b **i** $\mathrm{k}(x)=4x^2+8x+4$ **ii** $\mathrm{k}(x)=9x^2-6x+1$

5 Given that $\mathrm{f}(x)=2x^2-4$, give the function g(x) that represents the graph of f(x) after the following transformations.

a **i** Translation $\begin{pmatrix}1\\0\end{pmatrix}$ followed by a horizontal stretch of scale factor $\frac{1}{4}$.

ii Translation $\begin{pmatrix}-2\\0\end{pmatrix}$ followed by a horizontal stretch of scale factor $\frac{1}{2}$.

b **i** Horizontal stretch of scale factor $\frac{1}{2}$ followed by a translation $\begin{pmatrix} -4 \\ 0 \end{pmatrix}$.

ii Horizontal stretch of scale factor $\frac{2}{3}$ followed by a translation $\begin{pmatrix} 1 \\ 0 \end{pmatrix}$.

c **i** Translation $\begin{pmatrix} -3 \\ 0 \end{pmatrix}$ followed by a reflection in the y-axis.

ii Reflection in the vertical axis followed by a translation $\begin{pmatrix} -3 \\ 0 \end{pmatrix}$.

6 Find the resulting equation after the graph of $y = \sin(x)$ is transformed using each sequence of transformations.

a A vertical translation c units up, then a vertical stretch with scale factor p.

b A vertical stretch with scale factor p followed by a vertical translation c units up.

c A horizontal stretch with scale factor q, then a horizontal translation d units to the left.

d A horizontal translation d units to the left followed by a horizontal stretch with scale factor q.

7 **a** The graph of $y = x^2$ is transformed using a horizontal stretch with scale factor 2 followed by a vertical stretch with scale factor 4. Find the equation of the resulting graph. Can you explain why this is the case?

b The graph of $y = e^x$ is transformed using a horizontal translation 2 units to the left followed by a vertical stretch with scale factor q. The equation of the resulting graph is again $y = e^x$. Find the value of q.

c The graph of $y = \ln(x)$ is translated 2 units up. What transformation (other than a translation 2 units down) will return the graph to its original position?

Use technology to sketch the graphs and see why this is the case.

8 The diagram shows the graph of $y = f(x)$.

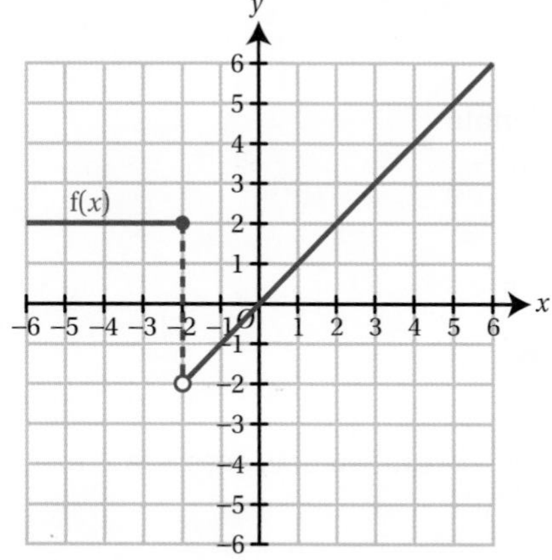

On separate axes, sketch the graphs of:

a $y = f(2x) - 3$ **b** $y = 1 - 3f(x)$

9 Sketch the following graphs.

a $y = \ln x$ **b** $y = 3\ln(x+2)$ **c** $y = \ln(2x-1)$

In each case, indicate clearly the positions of the vertical asymptote and the x-intercept.

10 The graph of $y=x^2-3x$ is translated 2 units to the right and then reflected in the x-axis. Find the equation of the resulting graph, in the form $y=ax^2+bx+c$.

11 The graph of $y=ax+b$ is transformed by the following sequence:

- translation by $\begin{pmatrix}1\\2\end{pmatrix}$
- reflection in $y=0$
- horizontal stretch with scale factor $\frac{1}{3}$.

The resulting graph has equation $y=1-15x$. Find the values of a and b.

12 The graph of $y=ax^2+bx+c$ is transformed by the following sequence:

- reflection in $x=0$
- translation by $\begin{pmatrix}-1\\3\end{pmatrix}$
- horizontal stretch with scale factor 2.

The resulting graph has equation $y=\frac{1}{2}x^2+\frac{1}{2}x-3$. Find the values of a, b and c.

13 Given that $f(x)=2^x+x$, give in simplest terms the formula for $h(x)$, which is obtained by transforming $f(x)$ by the following sequence of transformations:

- vertical stretch, scale factor 8
- translation by $\begin{pmatrix}1\\4\end{pmatrix}$
- horizontal stretch, scale factor $\frac{1}{2}$.

Section 2: Modulus function

The **modulus** (or **absolute value**) is a function that leaves non-negative numbers alone but reverses the sign of negative numbers. We use $|x|$ to denote the modulus of number x; for example, $|5|=5$ and $|-3|=3$. Note that $|0|=0$.

You can define the modulus function by this equation:

Key point 3.2

$$|x|=\begin{cases}x & x\geqslant 0\\ -x & x<0\end{cases}$$

Did you know?

You can think of the modulus function as giving the distance of a number from zero on the number line. You applied a similar idea to vectors in Student Book 1. But the distance between two objects is not always easy to define. For example, what length gives the 'distance' between two points on the surface of the Earth? This question leads to the idea of a *metric*. You may want to find out about the *Minkowski Metric* for finding the distance between two points in space–time in the theory of relativity.

The graph of $y=|x|$ is shown. It will be useful to call the red branch the *reflected branch* (as it is the reflection of a part of the graph $y=x$ in the x-axis) and the blue branch the *unreflected branch*.

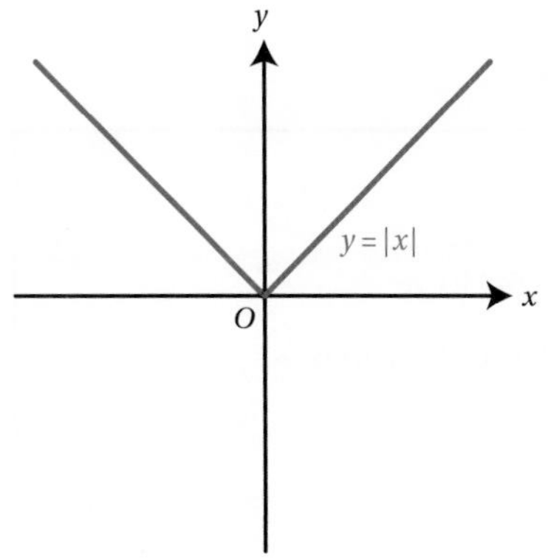

The domain of $|x|$ is all real numbers, whereas the range is all positive numbers and zero.

You can combine this with the rules for transforming graphs to sketch some other functions involving the modulus.

WORKED EXAMPLE 3.5

Sketch the graphs of:

a $y=|x-3|$ **b** $y=|x+2|-5$

In each case, find the y-intercept of the graph.

a y-intercept: $|0-3|=|-3|=3$

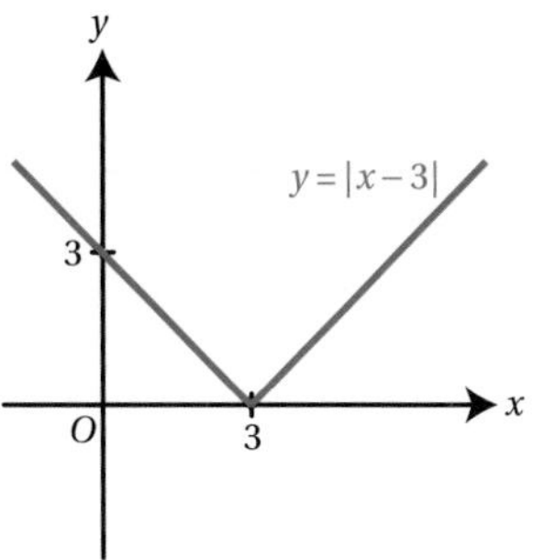

x has been replaced by $x-3$, so the graph is shifted 3 units to the right.

The y-intercept is when $x=0$.

b y-intercept: $|0+2|-5=2-5=-3$

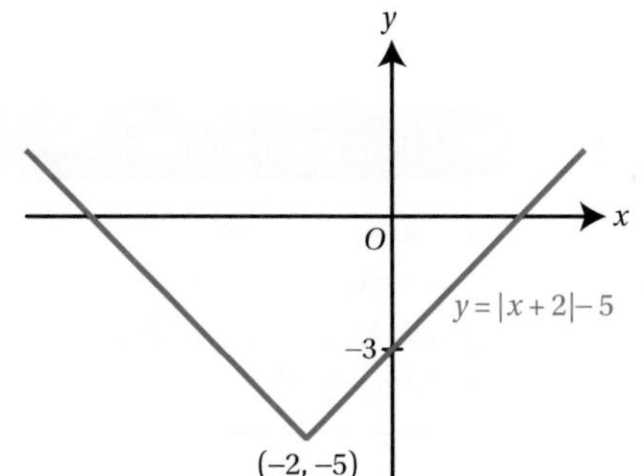

x has been replaced by $x+2$, so the graph is shifted 2 units to the left.

Subtracting 5 shifts the graph 5 units down.

You can also think about applying the modulus function to the graph of the function 'inside' the modulus. Any parts of the 'original' graph that are below the x-axis will have their y values changed from negative to positive; so those parts of the graph will be reflected in the x-axis.

WORKED EXAMPLE 3.6

Sketch the graph of $y = |5 - 2x|$, indicating the intercepts with the coordinate axes.

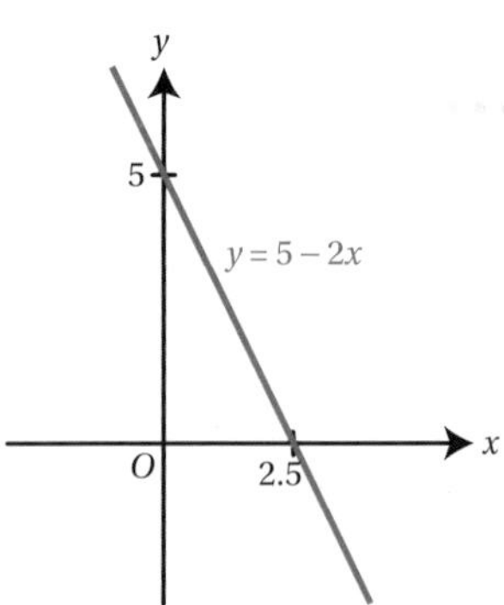

Start by drawing the graph of $y = 5 - 2x$.

This crosses the x-axis at (2.5, 0) and the y-axis at (0, 5).

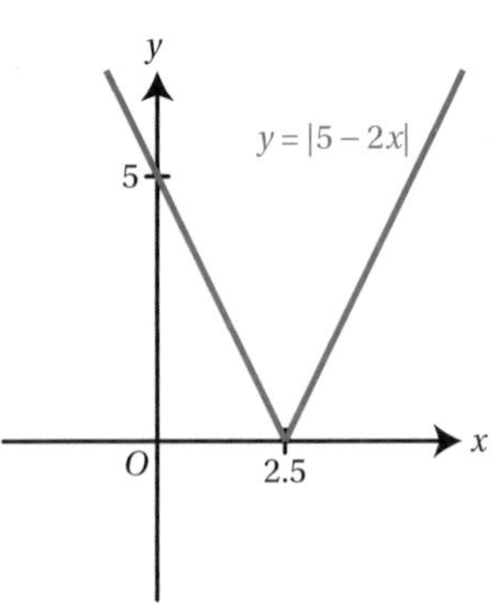

The part of the graph to the right of the x-intercept has negative y values; taking the modulus will make those positive, so this part of the graph needs to be reflected in the x-axis.

Key point 3.3

To sketch the graph of $y = |f(x)|$, start with the graph of $y = f(x)$ and reflect any parts that are below the x-axis.

In particular, the graph of $y = |ax + b|$ has a V-shape with the vertex at $\left(-\frac{b}{a}, 0\right)$ and y-intercept $(0, b)$.

Using modulus notation in inequalities

You often meet inequalities where the variable is between a number and its negative; for example, if $x^2 < 9$ then $-3 < x < 3$. You can write this more concisely using modulus notation: $|x| < 3$.

It is possible to extend this notation to write other inequalities that represent a single interval. For example, what does $|x - 5| < 3$ mean? If we replace $x - 5$ by y then, as in the previous example, $|y| < 3$ means that $-3 < y < 3$. So $-3 < x - 5 < 3$, which can be rearranged into $2 < x < 8$.

Fast forward

You will use inequalities of this form with sequences (Chapter 4) and binomial expansion (Chapter 6).

There is a nice interpretation of this inequality on the number line:

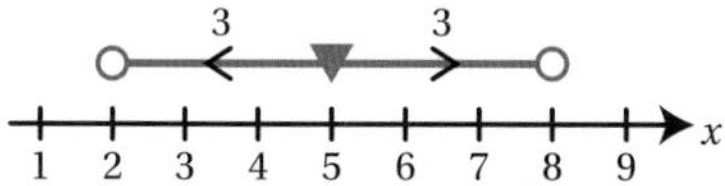

The number 5 is in the middle of the interval (2, 8), 3 units away from each end. So the inequality $|x-5|<3$ can be read as: 'the distance between x and 5 is less than 3.'

Key point 3.4

The modulus inequality $|x-a|<b$ is equivalent to $a-b<x<a+b$.

Fast forward

If you study Further Mathematics, in Student Book 1, you will extend the modulus notation to measure distances between points in the complex plane.

Rewind

You already use the modulus of a vector to represent the distance between two points.

WORKED EXAMPLE 3.7

a Write the inequality $|x+4|<6$ in the form $p<x<q$.

b Write the interval $[-3, 7]$ using an inequality of the form $|x-a| \leqslant b$.

a $-4-6<x<-4+6$

So $-10<x<2$.

Use the result from Key point 3.4:

$|x-a|<b \Leftrightarrow a-b<x<a+b$

In this example, $a=-4$ and $b=6$.

Alternatively, you can think of $|x+4|<6$ as saying that x is at most 6 units on either side of -4.

b $a=\dfrac{(-3)+7}{2}=2$

a is the number in the middle of the interval.

$b=7-2=5$

b is the distance from the middle of the interval to one end.

So $|x-2| \leqslant 5$.

The end points of the interval are included.

EXERCISE 3B

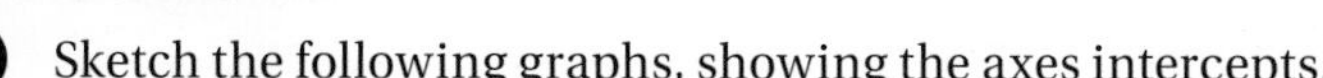

1 Sketch the following graphs, showing the axes intercepts.

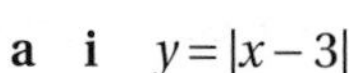

a	**i** $y=\vert x-3\vert$	**ii**	$y=\vert x+5\vert$
b	**i** $y=\vert 3x+5\vert$	**ii**	$y=\vert 2x-1\vert$
c	**i** $y=\vert 4-2x\vert$	**ii**	$y=\vert -3x+2\vert$
d	**i** $y=\vert x\vert+1$	**ii**	$y=\vert x\vert-2$

2 Write the equation of each graph in the form $y = |ax + b|$.

a **i**

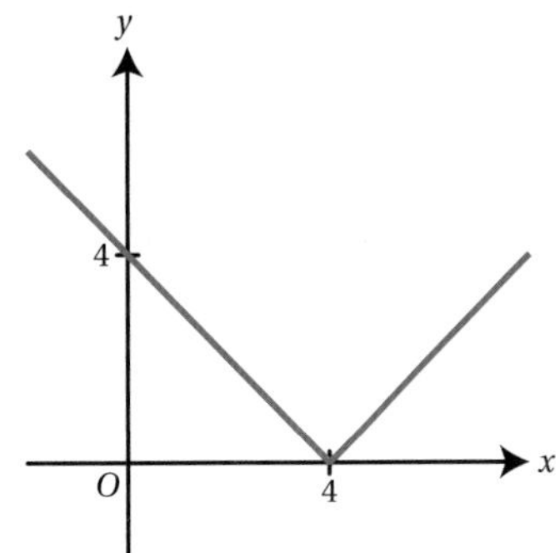

ii

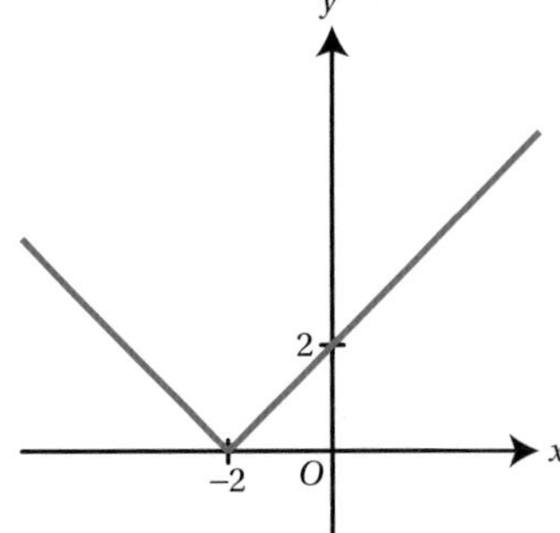

b **i**

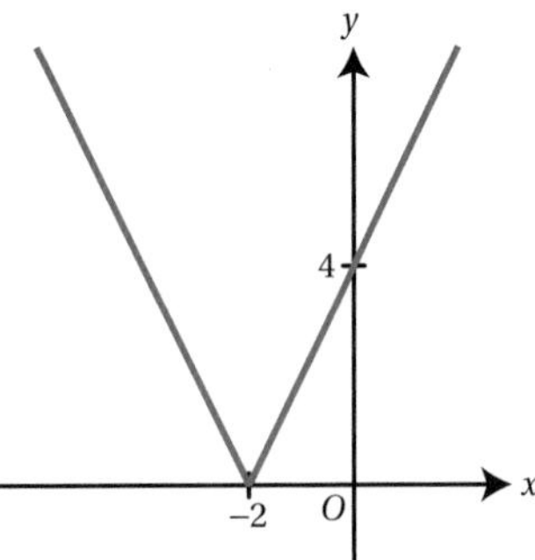

ii

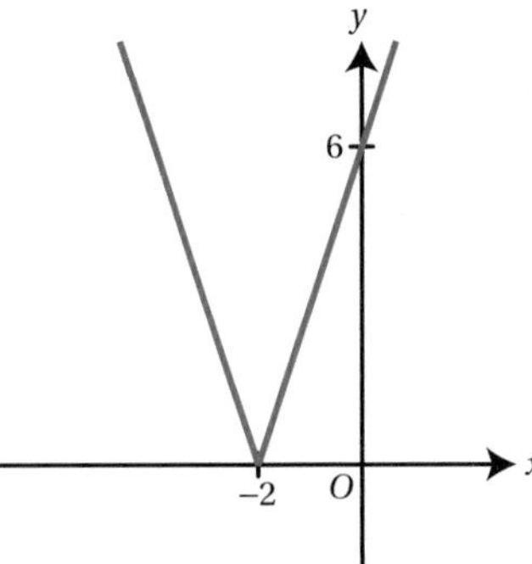

c **i**

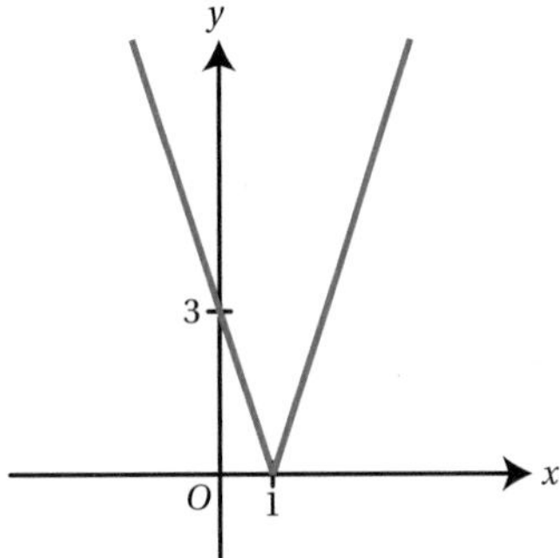

ii

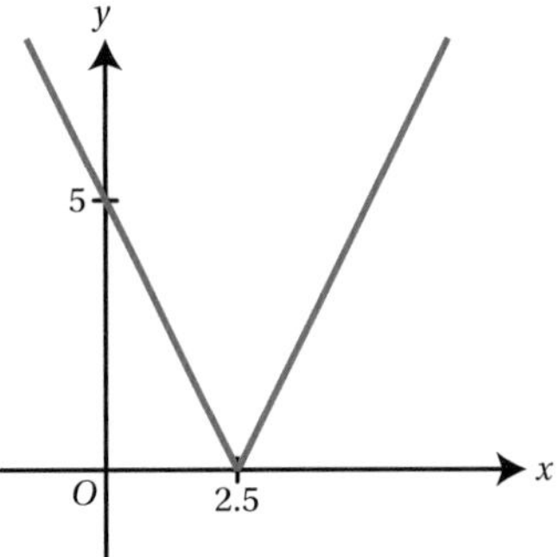

3 Write the following inequalities in the form $a < x < b$.

a **i** $|x - 5| < 8$ **ii** $|x - 2| < 9$

b **ii** $|x + 1| < 5$ **ii** $|x + 6| < 3$

4 Write the following statements in the form $|x - a| \leqslant b$.

a **i** $x \in [5, 13]$ **ii** $x \in [11, 25]$

b **i** $x \in [-14, 10]$ **ii** $x \in [-16, 2]$

c **i** $x \in [3, 10]$ **ii** $x \in [5, 20]$

5 Sketch the graphs of the following, showing the coordinates of the y-intercept and the vertex.

a $y = |x - 2|$ **b** $y = |x - 2| + 3$

6 Sketch the graph of $y=|2x+3|$, labelling the intercepts with the coordinate axes.

7 Sketch the graph of $y=5-|x-2|$. Give the coordinates of the points where the graph crosses the y-axis.

8 Sketch the graph of $y=x|x|$.

Section 3: Modulus equations and inequalities

You can use graphs to solve equations and inequalities involving the modulus function.

Key point 3.5

When solving an equation involving a modulus function, sketch the graph.

You need to use the graph to decide whether the intersection is on the reflected or the unreflected part of the graph. If it is on the unreflected part, you can rewrite the equation without the modulus sign. If it is on the reflected part, you need to replace the modulus sign by a minus sign.

WORKED EXAMPLE 3.8

Solve the equation $\frac{x}{2}=|x-1|$.

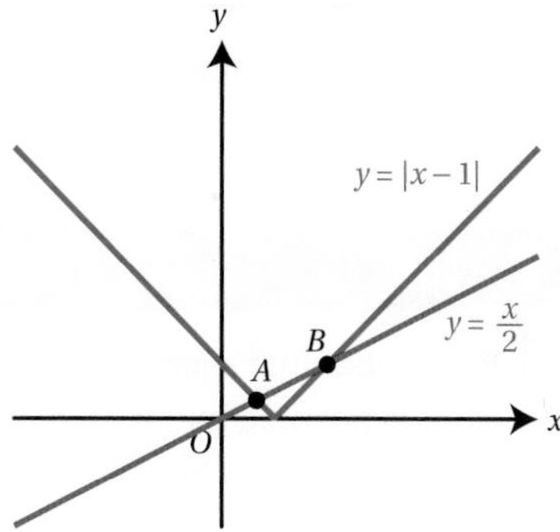

Sketch the graphs of $y=\frac{x}{2}$ and $y=|x-1|$.

There are two intersection points:

A the blue graph intersects the reflected part of the red graph.

B the blue line intersects the unreflected part of the red graph.

You need to write a separate equation for each.

A $\frac{x}{2}=-(x-1)$

$\frac{3x}{2}=1$

$x=\frac{2}{3}$

For the reflected part, replace the modulus sign with brackets and a minus sign.

B $\frac{x}{2}=x-1$

$-\frac{x}{2}=-1$

$x=2$

For the unreflected part, just remove the modulus sign.

So the solution is:

$x=\frac{2}{3}$ or 2

You can also intersect two modulus graphs.

WORKED EXAMPLE 3.9

Solve the equation $|x+1|=|2x-1|$.

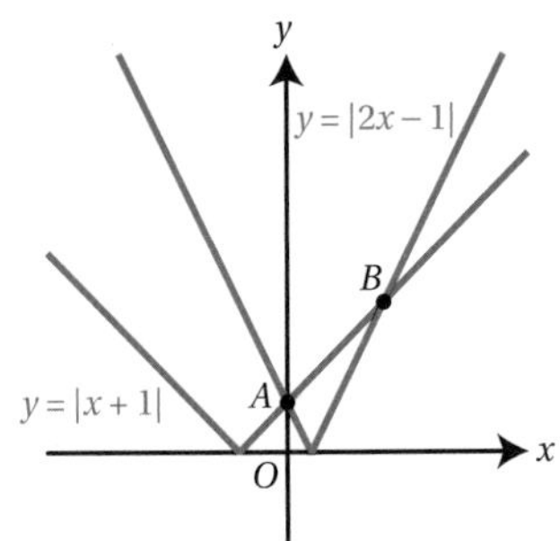

Sketch the graphs of $y=|x+1|$ and $y=|2x-1|$.

There are two intersections:

A the unreflected blue line and the reflected red line.

B the unreflected blue line and the unreflected red line.

A $x+1=-(2x-1)$

$x+1=-2x+1$

$3x=0$

$x=0$

You need the reflected part of the red graph, so replace the modulus sign with brackets and a minus sign.

B $x+1=2x-1$

$x=2$

You need the unreflected parts for both graphs, so remove the modulus signs.

The solution is: $x=0$ or 2.

There is an alternative method that can be used to solve an equation where both sides are inside a modulus. You then know that both sides of the equation are non-negative, so you can square both sides.

Key point 3.6

$$|a|=|b| \Leftrightarrow a^2=b^2$$

Tip

Remember that squaring both sides is possible only if both sides are inside a modulus. For example, $|a|=b$ is not equivalent to $a^2=b^2$, as b could be negative.

We illustrate this with the equation from Worked Example 3.9. See which method you prefer.

WORKED EXAMPLE 3.10

Solve the equation $|x+1|=|2x-1|$.

$(x+1)^2=(2x-1)^2$

Both sides are positive so can be squared.

$\Leftrightarrow x^2+2x+1=4x^2-4x+1$

$\Leftrightarrow 3x^2-6x=0$

$\Leftrightarrow 3x(x-2)=0$

$\Leftrightarrow x=0$ or 2

Write as a quadratic equation with the x^2 terms positive.

WORK IT OUT 3.2

Solve the equation $|2x-1|=|3-x|$.

Which of the following solutions is correct? Identify the mistake in the other two.

Solution 1	Solution 2	Solution 3
$2x-1=3-x$ or $2x-1=-3+x$	$2x-1=3-x$ or $-(2x-1)=-(3-x)$	$2x-1=3-x$ or $2x-1=3+x$
$3x=4$ or $x=-2$	$3x=4$ or $-3x=-4$	$x=-2$ or $x=4$
Solution: $x=\frac{4}{3}$ or -2	Solution: $x=\frac{4}{3}$	Solution: $x=-2$ or 4

To solve inequalities, first sketch the graphs and find their intersections. You can then decide on which parts of the graph the inequality is satisfied.

Rewind

This is the same method as you use to solve quadratic inequalities – see Student Book 1, Chapter 3.

WORKED EXAMPLE 3.11

Solve $|2x-3|>x+4$.

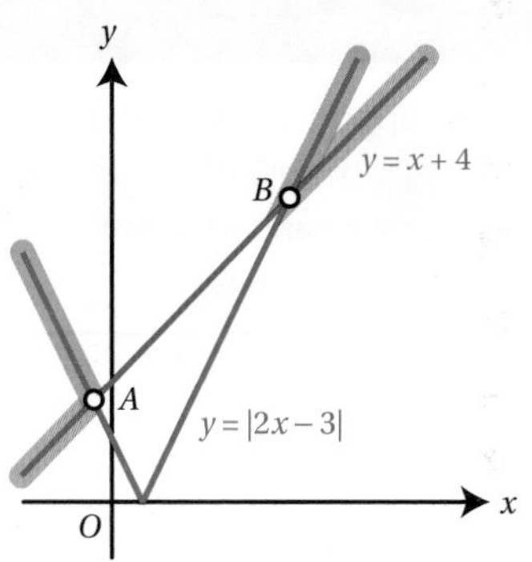

Sketch the graphs of $y=|2x-3|$ and $y=x+4$, highlighting where the inequality is satisfied.

A $x+4=-(2x-3)$

$3x=-1$

$x=-\frac{1}{3}$

Find the intersection points:

A is on the reflected part of the red line.

B $x+4=2x-3$

$x=7$

B is on the unreflected part of the red line.

$x\in\left(-\infty,-\frac{1}{3}\right)\cup(7,\infty)$

Describe the highlighted region in terms of x. Remember that you can use either the inequality notation or the interval notation to do this.

EXERCISE 3C

1 Solve the following equations.

a **i** $|x| = 4$ **ii** $|x| = 18$

b **i** $|2x - 4| = 4$ **ii** $|3x + 1| = 2$

c **i** $|2x + 4| = 4 - x$ **ii** $|5 - 2x| = x + 3$

d **i** $|3x - 4| = 8 - x$ **ii** $|5 + 2x| = 3 - 2x$

e **i** $|3 - 2x| = |x + 1|$ **ii** $|4 + x| = |5 - 3x|$

f **i** $|6 - x| = |5 + x|$ **ii** $|4 + 3x| = |x|$

2 Solve the following inequalities. Write your answer using the stated notation.

a Use interval notation.

i $|x| > 5$ **ii** $|x| > 2$

b Use inequality notation.

i $|x| < 3$ **ii** $|x| < 10$

c Use interval notation.

i $|2x + 1| \geqslant 4$ **ii** $|3x - 2| \leqslant 3$

d Use inequality notation.

i $|2x - 5| < x + 1$ **ii** $|5 - 3x| > 2x$

e Use interval notation.

i $|2x + 1| > |x + 4|$ **ii** $|3x - 4| > |2x + 1|$

f Use inequality notation.

i $|x + 4| \geqslant |2x|$ **ii** $|1 + 3x| \leqslant |x + 3|$

3 **a** Solve the equation $|4x + 1| = x + 3$.

b Solve the inequality $|4x + 1| < x + 3$.

4 **a** Solve the equation $|2x - 5| = |x + 2|$.

b Solve the inequality $|2x - 5| \leqslant |x + 2|$. Write your answer using the interval notation.

5 **a** Sketch the graph of $y = |3x - 7|$.

b Hence, solve the inequality $|3x - 7| < 1 - x$.

6 Solve the inequality $|3x + 1| > 2x$.

7 Given that $k > 0$, find in terms of k the solution of the inequality $|x - k| \leqslant |2x - k|$.

8 Solve the equation $|x + k| = |x| + k$, where $k > 0$.

Elevate

See Support sheet 3 for a further example of modulus inequalities and for more practice questions.

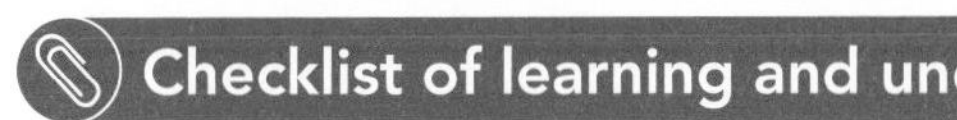

Checklist of learning and understanding

- You can combine any two (or more) transformations of graphs: translations, stretches and reflections (both horizontal and vertical).
- The order in which transformations occur may affect the outcome.
  - One horizontal and one vertical transformation can be done in either order.
  - Changing the order of two horizontal or two vertical transformations may affect the outcome.
  - For a function of the form $y = p\,\mathrm{f}(x) + c$, the stretch is performed before the translation.
  - For a function of the form $y = \mathrm{f}(qx + d)$, the translation is performed before the stretch.
- The modulus function can be used to reflect the part of the graph below the x-axis so that the whole graph is on or above it.
  - The graph of $y = |mx + c|$ has a V-shape with the vertex at $\left(-\frac{c}{m}, 0\right)$.
- To solve equations and inequalities involving the modulus function, always use graphs. You need to decide whether the solutions are on the reflected or unreflected part of the graph.
- You can solve some modulus equations by squaring both sides, using $|a| = |b| \Leftrightarrow a^2 = b^2$.
- You can use modulus notation to express some inequalities. In particular, $|x - a| < b \Leftrightarrow a - b < x < a + b$.

Mixed practice 3

1 The graph of $y = f(x)$ is shown.

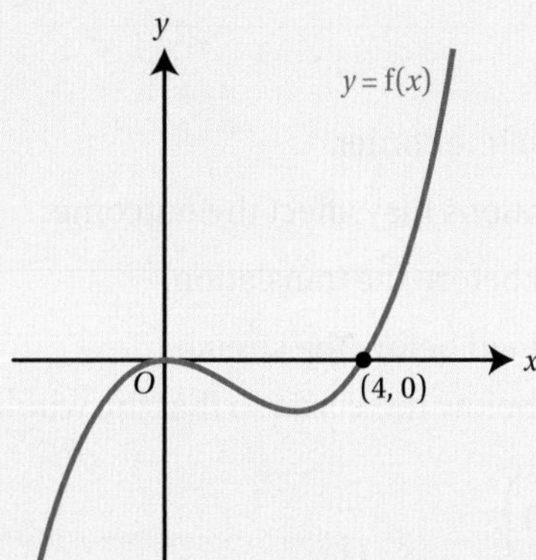

On separate diagrams, sketch the graphs of:

a $y = 3\,f(x-2)$ **b** $y = 3 - f(2x)$

2 The graph of $y = x^3 - 1$ is transformed by applying a translation with vector $\begin{pmatrix} 2 \\ 0 \end{pmatrix}$, followed by a vertical stretch with scale factor 2. Find the equation of the resulting graph in the form $y = ax^3 + bx^2 + cx + d$.

3 **a** On the same set of axes, sketch the graphs of $y = x$ and $y = |2x - 1|$.

b Hence, solve the inequality $|2x - 1| < x$.

4 **a** Describe two transformations that transform the graph of $y = x^2$ to the graph of $y = 3x^2 - 12x + 12$.

b Describe two transformations that transform the graph of $y = x^2 + 6x - 1$ to the graph of $y = x^2$.

c Hence, describe a sequence of transformations that transform the graph of $y = x^2 + 6x - 1$ to the graph of $y = 3x^2 - 12x + 12$.

5 The transformations R, S and T are defined as follows:

R : reflection in the x-axis

S : stretch in the x direction with scale factor 3

T : translation in the positive x direction by 4 units.

i The curve $y = \ln x$ is transformed by R followed by T. Find the equation of the resulting curve.

ii Find, in terms of S and T, a sequence of transformations that transforms the curve $y = x^3$ to the curve $y = \left(\frac{1}{9}x - 4\right)^3$. You should make clear the order of the transformations.

6 Find two transformations whose composition transforms the graph of $y=(x-1)^2$ to the graph of $y=3(x+2)^2$.

7 Solve the inequality $|2x-1|>|x-6|$.

8 **a** Describe two transformations whose composition transforms the graph of $y=\mathrm{f}(x)$ to the graph of $y=3\,\mathrm{f}\left(\frac{x}{2}\right)$.

b Sketch the graph of $y=3\ln\left(\frac{x}{2}\right)$.

c Sketch the graph of $y=3\ln\left(\frac{x}{2}+1\right)$, marking clearly the positions of any asymptotes and x-intercepts.

9 **a** State the sequence of three transformations that transform the graph of $y=|x|$ to the graph of $y=5-3|x|$. Hence, sketch the graph of $y=5-3|x|$.

b Solve the equation $|2x-1|=5-3|x|$.

c Write down the solution of the inequality $|2x-1|\leqslant 5-3|x|$.

10 **a** Describe a transformation that transforms the graph of $y=\mathrm{f}(x)$ to the graph of $y=\mathrm{f}(x+2)$.

b On the same diagram, sketch the graphs of:

i $y=\ln(x+2)$

ii $y=3-\ln(x+2)$

Mark clearly any asymptotes and x-intercepts on your sketches.

c The graph of the function $y=\mathrm{g}(x)$ has been translated and then reflected in the x-axis to produce the graph of $y=\mathrm{h}(x)$.

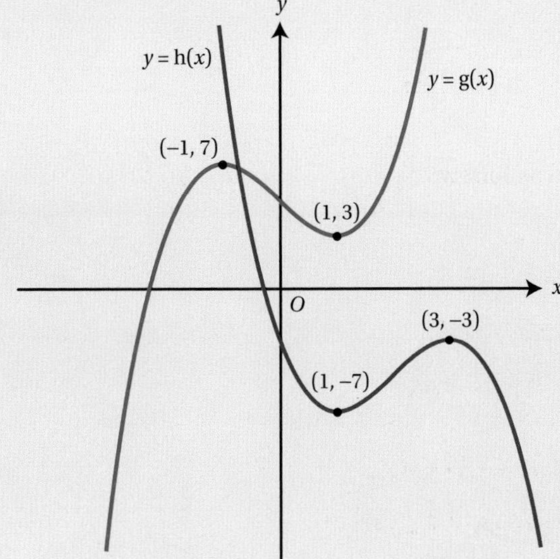

i State the translation vector.

ii If $\mathrm{g}(x) = x^3 - 3x + 5$, find constants a, b, c, d such that $\mathrm{h}(x) = ax^3 + bx^2 + cx + d$.

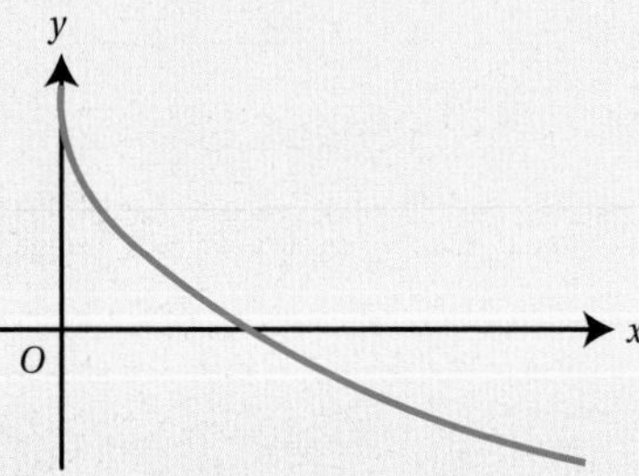

The function f is defined by $\mathrm{f}(x) = 2 - \sqrt{x}$ for $x \geqslant 0$. The graph of $y = \mathrm{f}(x)$ is shown above.

i State the range of f.

ii Find the value of ff(4).

iii Given that the equation $|\mathrm{f}(x)| = k$ has two distinct roots, determine the possible values of the constant k.

12 Solve the equation $x|x| = x^2$.

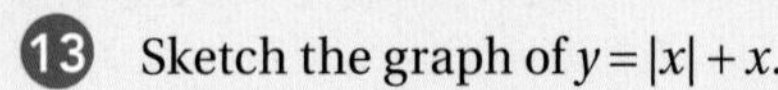

13 Sketch the graph of $y = |x| + x$.

Elevate

See Extension sheet 3 for more challenging questions on modulus graphs and equations.

4 Sequences and series

In this chapter you will learn:

- how to determine the behaviour of some sequences
- how to use sigma notation for series
- about sequences with a constant difference between terms
- about finite series with a constant difference between terms
- about sequences with a constant ratio between terms
- about finite and infinite series with a constant ratio between terms
- how to apply sequences to real-life problems.

Before you start…

GCSE	You should be able to find the formula for the nth term of a linear sequence.	1 Find the formula for the nth term of the following sequences. a 2, 5, 8, 11, … b 15, 11, 7, 3, …
GCSE	You should be able to use term-to-term rules to generate sequences.	2 Find the second and third terms of the sequence defined by $u_{n+1} = 3u_n - 2, \quad u_1 = 4$
Student Book 1, Chapter 3	You should be able to solve quadratic equations and inequalities.	3 Find the smallest positive integer that satisfies the inequality $3x^2 + 7x > 163$.
Student Book 1, Chapter 7	You should be able to solve exponential equations and inequalities.	4 Find the smallest integer value of n such that $3.5 \times 1.2^n > 75$.
GCSE	You should be able to solve linear simultaneous equations.	5 Solve: $a + 4b = 8$ $3a + 5b = 3$
Student Book 2, Chapter 3	You should be able to use modulus notation.	6 List all integers r that satisfy $\left\|\frac{3r}{5}\right\| < 2$.

Modelling with sequences

If you drop a ball, it will hit the ground and bounce but the new height that it reaches will be a little lower on each subsequent bounce. The heights the ball reaches after each bounce form a sequence. Although the idea of a sequence may just seem to be about abstract number patterns, it has a remarkable number of applications in the real world – from calculating mortgages to estimating harvests on farms.

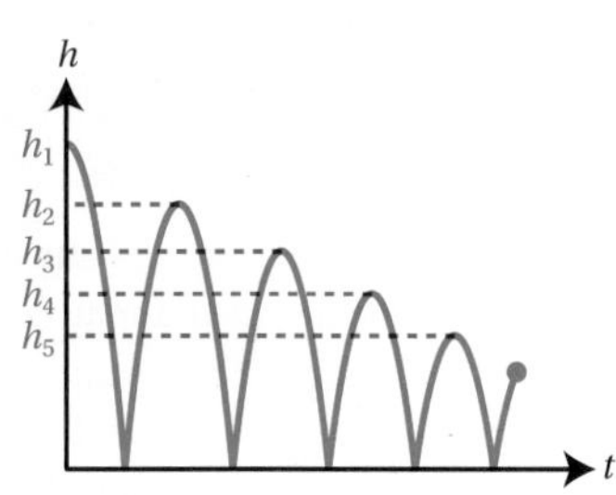

Section 1: General sequences

A sequence is a list of numbers in a specific order, and can be finite or infinite. A **finite sequence** has a finite number of terms. For example, the sequence 31, 28, 31, 30, 31, 30, 31, 31, 30, 31, 30, 31 (the number of days in each month) has 12 terms. Such a sequence can be described by simply listing all terms, as we have done here. An **infinite sequence** continues forever, so it is not possible to list all the terms. Instead, we need to give a rule, either describing how to find each term, or how to get from one term to the next.

For example, the sequence

$$2, 5, 8, 11, 14, \ldots$$

can be described in two different ways:

- by a **term-to-term rule**: $u_1 = 2, \quad u_{n+1} = u_n + 3$
- by a **position-to-term rule** (also called 'the formula for the nth term'): $u_n = 3n - 1$

Tip

u_n is the standard notation for the nth term of a sequence. So in the sequence 2, 5, 8, 11, 14, ..., $u_1 = 2, u_2 = 5, u_3 = 8$ etc.

Gateway to A Level

For a reminder of how these two types of rules work, see Gateway to A Level Section X. There is also further practice at the beginning of Exercise 4A.

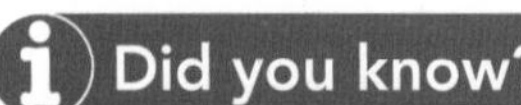

Term-to-term rules can involve more than one previous term. You may already know the example of the famous Fibonacci Sequence, $u_{n+2} = u_{n+1} + u_n$ with $u_1 = u_2 = 1$. Based on a model Leonardo Fibonacci made for the breeding of rabbits, this has found many applications from patterns on pine cones to a proof of the infinity of prime numbers. There is also a beautiful link to the golden ratio, $\frac{1 \pm \sqrt{5}}{2}$.

Increasing, decreasing and periodic sequences

Sequences can behave in many different ways but you need to be aware of three possibilities:

Key point 4.1

- An **increasing sequence** is one where each term is larger than the previous one: $u_{n+1} > u_n$ for all n.
- A **decreasing sequence** is one where each term is smaller than the previous one: $u_{n+1} < u_n$ for all n.
- A **periodic sequence** is one where the terms start repeating after a while: $u_{n+k} = u_n$ for some number k (the period of the sequence).

Tip

When asked to comment on the behaviour of the sequence, you can use your calculator to generate terms, and investigate whether the sequence is increasing, decreasing or periodic.

WORKED EXAMPLE 4.1

Find the first five terms of each sequence, and describe the behaviour of the sequence.

a $x_{n+1} = 5x_n - 1, x_1 = 2$

b $u_n = \frac{32}{2^n}$

c $a_{n+1} = \frac{1}{a_n}, a_1 = 3$

a $x_1 = 2$

$x_2 = 10 - 1 = 9$

$x_3 = 45 - 1 = 44$

$x_4 = 220 - 1 = 219$

$x_5 = 1095 - 1 = 1094$

Substitute each term into the formula to get the next term.

The sequence is increasing.

The terms are getting larger.

b $u_1 = \frac{16}{2^1} = 16$

Substitute $n = 1, 2, 3...$ to calculate the terms.

$u_2 = \frac{16}{2^2} = 4$

$u_3 = \frac{16}{2^3} = 2$

$u_4 = \frac{16}{2^4} = 1$

$u_5 = \frac{16}{2^5} = \frac{1}{2}$

The sequence is decreasing.

The terms are getting smaller.

c $a_1 = 3$

Substitute each term into the formula to get the next term.

$a_2 = \frac{1}{3}$

$a_3 = \frac{1}{\frac{1}{3}} = 3$

$a_4 = \frac{1}{3}$

$a_5 = 3$

The sequence starts to repeat after two terms: $u_3 = u_1$

The sequence is periodic, with period 2.

Focus on ...

Focus on ... Problem solving 1 looks further at the technique of using small cases to establish patterns in sequences.

The limit of a sequence

In Worked Example 4.1, the sequence in part **b** decreases but the terms remain positive although they get closer and closer to zero. The sequence **converges** to zero. By contrast, the sequence in part **a** **diverges** – the terms increase without a limit.

You can use your calculator to investigate long-term behaviour of sequences by generating a large number of terms until you can see what is going on. But you can also find the limit of a convergent sequence by solving an equation.

Tip

Use the table function if the sequence is given by the formula, or the ANS button if you have a term-to-term rule.

Key point 4.2

To find the limit, L, of a convergent sequence defined by a term-to-term rule, set $u_{n+1} = u_n = L$ and solve for L.

Fast forward

You will see in Chapter 14 how you can use convergent sequences to solve some equations.

WORKED EXAMPLE 4.2

A convergent sequence is defined by $u_{n+1} = \frac{2}{3}u_n + 5$, $u_1 = 6$.

By setting up and solving an equation, find the limit of the sequence.

Let $u_{n+1} = u_n = L$ — Replace u_{n+1} and u_n by L.

$L = \frac{2}{3}L + 5$ — Solve the equation for L.

$\frac{1}{3}L = 5$

$L = 15$

The limit is 15.

Explore

It is important to remember that the method in Worked Example 4.2 can be applied only if you know that a sequence converges. For example, trying to use it with $u_1 = 1$, $u_{n+1} = 3u_{n+2}$ gives $L = -1$, but the sequence (1, 5, 17, 53, ...) clearly does not converge. Find out about different methods for proving convergence of a sequence.

EXERCISE 4A

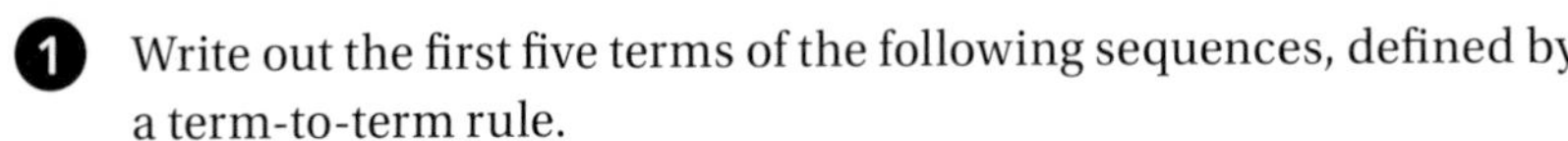

1 Write out the first five terms of the following sequences, defined by a term-to-term rule.

a i	$u_{n+1} = u_n + 5,\ u_1 = 3.1$	**ii**	$u_{n+1} = u_n - 3.8,\ u_1 = 10$
b i	$u_{n+1} = 3u_n + 1,\ u_1 = 0$	**ii**	$u_{n+1} = 9u_n - 10,\ u_1 = 1$
c i	$u_{n+1} = \frac{u_n + 2}{u_n},\ u_1 = 1$	**ii**	$u_{n+1} = -\frac{3}{u_n},\ u_1 = 3$
d i	$u_{n+1} = u_n + 4,\ u_4 = 12$	**ii**	$u_{n+1} = u_n - 2,\ u_6 = 3$

2 Write out the first four terms of the following sequences, each defined by an nth term formula.

a **i** $u_n = 3n+2$ **ii** $u_n = 1.5n-6$

b **i** $u_n = n^3 - 1$ **ii** $u_n = 5n^2$

c **i** $u_n = 3^n$ **ii** $u_n = 8\times(0.5)^n$

d **i** $u_n = n^n$ **ii** $u_n = \sin(90n°)$

3 Suggest a possible formula for the nth term of each sequence.

a **i** 4, 5, 6, 7, 8, … **ii** 3, 6, 9, 12, …

b **i** 2, 5, 10, 17, 26, … **ii** 4, 9, 16, 25, 36, …

c **i** 2, 4, 8, 16, 32, … **ii** $\frac{1}{3}, \frac{1}{9}, \frac{1}{27}, \frac{1}{81}, \ldots$

d **i** $\frac{1}{2}, \frac{2}{3}, \frac{3}{4}, \frac{4}{5}, \ldots$ **ii** $\frac{3}{1}, \frac{4}{2}, \frac{5}{3}, \frac{6}{4}, \frac{7}{5}, \ldots$

4 Using your calculator, determine the behaviour of these sequences.

a **i** $x_{n+1} = 0.8x_n + 2$, $x_1 = 5$ **ii** $x_{n+1} = 1.6x_n - 4$, $x_1 = 5$

b **i** $u_{n+1} = -\frac{4}{u_n}$, $u_1 = 2$ **ii** $u_{n+1} = 10 - u_n$, $u_1 = 3$

5 A sequence is defined by $u_n = n\times 2^n$.

a Write down u_1 and u_2.

b Show that $\frac{u_{n+1}}{u_n} = a + \frac{a}{n}$ for a constant a.

6 A sequence is defined by $x_{n+1} = \frac{x_n + 6}{x_n}$, with $x_1 = 2$.

a Find the fifth term of the sequence.

b Describe the long-term behaviour of the sequence.

7 A sequence is defined by $u_{n+1} = ku_n + 9$, $u_1 = 5$, where k is a constant. The limit of the sequence is 15. Find the value of k.

8 **a** A sequence is defined by $x_1 = 1$, $x_{n+1} = ax_n + x_n^2$, where a is a constant. Show that $x_3 = 2a^2 + 3a + 1$.

b Given that $x_3 = 3$ and that the sequence is increasing, find the value of a.

9 A sequence is defined by $u_{n+1} = \frac{6u_n + 2}{4 - 13u_n}$, $u_1 = 0$.

a Find u_2, u_3, u_4, u_5 and u_6. **b** State the value of u_{102}.

10 A sequence is defined by $u_{n+1} = \frac{u_n^2 + 1}{2}$, $u_1 = 2$.

a Find u_2 and u_3.

b Determine, explaining your reasoning fully, whether the sequence converges. If it does, state the limit.

Elevate

See Extension sheet 4 for some more challenging questions on the long-term behaviour of sequences and series.

Section 2: General series and sigma notation

When savings in a bank account earns 5% interest each year, these interest payments form a sequence. While it may be useful to know how much interest is paid in each year, you may be even more interested to know how much will be paid altogether.

This is one of many examples of a situation where you may want to add up the terms of a sequence. The sum of a sequence up to a certain point is called a **series**. Use the symbol S_n to denote the sum of the first n terms of a sequence, that is

$$S_n = u_1 + u_2 + u_3 + \ldots + u_n$$

Instead of writing $S_n = u_1 + u_2 + u_3 + \ldots + u_n$, you will often see exactly the same thing in a shorter form using **sigma notation**:

Key point 4.3

Sigma notation is a shorthand way to describe a series.

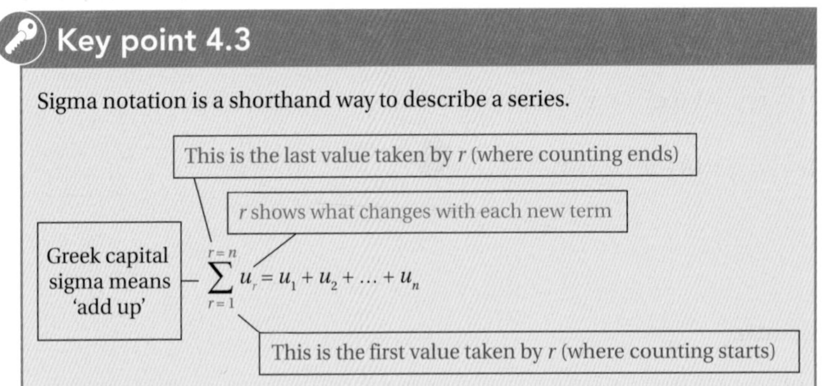

Tip

Don't be intimidated by this notation. If you are in doubt, try writing out the first few terms and the last term.

There is nothing special about the letter r here; any letter could be used but r and k are the most usual. You may also see the r or k being missed out above and below the sigma.

WORKED EXAMPLE 4.3

$$S_n = \sum_{r=2}^{n} r^2$$

Find the value of S_4.

$S_4 = 2^2 + 3^2 + 4^2$

Put the starting value, $r = 2$, into the expression to be summed, r^2.

You've not reached the end value, so put in $r = 3$.

You've still not reached the end value, so put in $r = 4$.

$= 4 + 9 + 16$

$= 29$

You've reached the end value, so stop and evaluate.

WORKED EXAMPLE 4.4

Write the series $\frac{1}{2}+\frac{1}{3}+\frac{1}{4}+\frac{1}{5}+\frac{1}{6}$ in sigma notation.

General term $=\frac{1}{r}$ — Describe each term of the series using a general term in the variable *r*.

Starts at $r=2$. — Note the first value of *r*.

Ends at $r=6$. — Note the final value of *r*.

$\frac{1}{2}+\frac{1}{3}+\frac{1}{4}+\frac{1}{5}+\frac{1}{6}=\sum_{r=2}^{6}\frac{1}{r}$ — Summarise in sigma notation.

Notice that there is more than one possible answer to the question in Worked Example 4.4. For example, we could write the sum as $\sum_{r=1}^{5}\frac{1}{r+1}$.

EXERCISE 4B

1 Evaluate the following expressions.

a **i** $\sum_{r=2}^{4}3r$ **ii** $\sum_{r=5}^{7}(2r+1)$ **b** **i** $\sum_{r=3}^{6}2^r-1$ **ii** $\sum_{r=-1}^{4}1.5^r$

c **i** $\sum_{a=1}^{a=4}b(a+1)$ **ii** $\sum_{q=-3}^{q=2}pq^2$

2 Write the following expressions in sigma notation. Be aware that there is more than one correct answer.

a **i** $2+3+4+\ldots+43$ **ii** $6+8+10+\ldots+60$

b **i** $\frac{1}{4}+\frac{1}{8}+\frac{1}{16}+\ldots+\frac{1}{128}$ **ii** $2+\frac{2}{3}+\frac{2}{9}+\ldots+\frac{2}{243}$

c **i** $14a+21a+28a+\ldots+70a$ **ii** $0+1+2^b+3^b+\ldots+19^b$

3 A sequence is defined by

$u_1=1,$

$u_{n+1}=u_n{}^2-2u_n+3$

Find $\sum_{r=1}^{5}u_r$.

4 A sequence is defined by

$u_1=k,$

$u_{n+1}=3u_n-2$

where *k* is a constant.

a Show that $u_3=9k-8$.

b Given that $\sum_{r=1}^{4}u_r=24$, find the value of *k*.

5 Find the exact value of $\sum_{k=1}^{5} \ln(3^k)$, giving your answer in the form $a \ln 3$.

6 **a** Find the exact value of $\sum_{k=1}^{6} \sin(60k°)$.

b Hence, find the exact value of $\sum_{k=1}^{92} \sin(60k°)$.

Section 3: Arithmetic sequences

Arithmetic sequences have a **common difference** between each term: to get from one term to the next you add the common difference (which may be negative). For example:

- 1, 5, 9, 13, 17, … (add 4 to each term)
- 20, 17, 14, 11, … (add −3 to each term)

In general, if the first term is a and the common difference is d, then you have:

1st term	2nd term	3rd term	4th term	5th term
a	$a+d$	$a+2d$	$a+3d$	$a+4d$

From this you can see how to form the nth term of an arithmetic sequence.

Key point 4.4

The nth term of an arithmetic sequence with first term a and common difference d is

$$u_n = a+(n-1)d$$

Tip

An arithmetic sequence is sometimes also called an arithmetic progression.

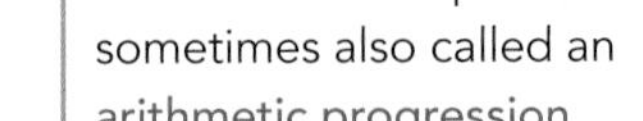

For practise at identifying arithmetic sequences and finding their nth term, see Gateway to A Level Section Y.

Tip

The formula for the nth term involves $(n-1)d$ and not nd. So, for example, $u_8 = a+7d$ and not $u_9 = a+8d$.

WORKED EXAMPLE 4.5

An arithmetic sequence has first term 5 and common difference 7.

Find the term with the value 355.

$u_n = a+(n-1)d$

$355 = 5+7(n-1)$

You need to find n when $u_n = 355$.

Use $u_n = a+(n-1)d$ with $a=5$ and $d=7$.

$350 = 7(n-1)$

$50 = n-1$

$n = 51$

Solve the equation.

So 355 is the 51st term.

You will often need to set up simultaneous equations to find a and d.

WORKED EXAMPLE 4.6

The fifth term of an arithmetic progression is 7 and the eighth term is 16.

a Find the first term, a, and common difference, d.
b Hence, find the 100th term.

$u_5 = a + (5-1)d$ — Use $u_n = a + (n-1)d$ with $n = 5$.

$7 = a + 4d \quad (1)$ — But you know that $u_5 = 7$.

$u_8 = a + 7d$
$16 = a + 7d \quad (2)$ — Repeat for the eighth term.

(2) − (1):
$9 = 3d$
$d = 3$
$\therefore a = -5$
— Solve the simultaneous equations (1) and (2) using elimination (substitution would also work).

$u_n = a + (n-1)d$
$= -5 + (n-1) \times 3$
— Now form the nth term formula. Note that you could tidy up by expanding the brackets and simplifying: $u_n = 3n - 8$. However, there is no need to, as you are not asked to state the formula at all.

$u_{100} = -5 + (100-1) \times 3$
$= 292$
— Substitute $n = 100$.

Elevate

See Support sheet 4 for a further example of using simultaneous equations to find a and d.

WORKED EXAMPLE 4.7

The first three terms of an arithmetic sequence are 12, x^2 and $5x$.

Find the possible values of x.

$u_3 - u_2 = u_2 - u_1$ — The difference between terms must be constant (i.e. d).

$5x - x^2 = x^2 - 12$

$2x^2 - 5x - 12 = 0$
$(2x+3)(x-4) = 0$
$x = -\frac{3}{2}$ or 4
— Rearrange and solve the quadratic equation.

EXERCISE 4C

1 Find the formula for the nth term for the arithmetic sequence, given the following conditions.

a **i** first term 9, common difference 3

ii first term 57, common difference 0.2

b **i** first term 12, common difference -1

ii first term 18, common difference $-\frac{1}{2}$

c **i** first term 1, second term 4

ii first term 9, second term 19

d **i** first term 4, second term 0

ii first term 27, second term 20

e **i** third term 5, eighth term 60

ii fifth term 8, eighth term 38

2 How many terms are there in the following sequences?

a **i** 1, 3, 5, …, 65

ii 18, 13, 8, …, -122

b **i** first term 8, common difference 9, last term 899

ii first term 0, ninth term 16, last term 450

3 An arithmetic sequence has 5 and 13 as its first two terms, respectively.

a Write down, in terms of n, an expression for the nth term, u_n.

b Find the number of terms of the sequence that are less than 400.

4 The 10th term of an arithmetic sequence is 61 and the 13th term is 79. Find the value of the 20th term.

5 The 8th term of an arithmetic sequence is 74 and the 15th term is 137. Which term has the value 227?

6 The height of the rungs in a ladder forms an arithmetic sequence. The third rung is 70 cm above the ground and the tenth rung is 210 cm above the ground. If the top rung is 350 cm above the ground, how many rungs does the ladder have?

7 The first four terms of an arithmetic progression are 2, $a-b$, $2a+b+7$ and $a-3b$, where a and b are constants. Find a and b.

8 A book starts at page 1 and has a page number on every page.

a Show that the first eleven page numbers contain thirteen digits in total.

b The total number of digits used for all the page numbers is 1260. How many pages are in the book?

Section 4: Arithmetic series

When you add up terms of an arithmetic sequence you get an **arithmetic series**. Just as it was useful to have a formula for the nth term, so it is useful to have a formula that will find the sum of the first n terms.

There are two different versions of this.

Key point 4.5

For an arithmetic series with first term a, common difference d and nth term L, the sum of the first n terms is

$$S_n = \frac{n}{2}[2a+(n-1)d]$$

$$S_n = \frac{n}{2}(a+L)$$

These formulae are given in your formula book.

Focus on ...

The first formula is proved in Focus on ... Proof 1.

The second formula follows immediately from the first, since the last term, L, equals $a+(n-1)d$.

PROOF 1

Starting from the formula $S_n = \frac{n}{2}[2a+(n-1)d]$, prove that $S_n = \frac{n}{2}(a+L)$.

$S_n = \frac{n}{2}[2a+(n-1)d]$ — Start from the formula given.

$= \frac{n}{2}[a+a+(n-1)d]$ — You want to introduce L, which is the nth term: $L = a+(n-1)d$

$= \frac{n}{2}[a+L]$

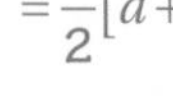

Tip

You will need the first formula when you know or want d, and the second when you know or want L.

WORKED EXAMPLE 4.8

a Find the sum of the first 30 terms of an arithmetic progression with first term 8 and common difference 0.5.

b The first term of an arithmetic sequence is 12 and the 50th term is 525. Find the sum of all 50 terms.

a $S_{30} = \frac{30}{2}[2\times 8+(30-1)0.5]$
$= 457.5$ — Use $S_n = \frac{n}{2}[2a+(n-1)d]$, with $n=30, a=8, d=0.5$.

b $S_{50} = \frac{50}{2}(12+525)$
$= 14175$ — Use $S_n = \frac{n}{2}[a+L]$, with $n=50$, $a=12$ and $L=525$.

You must be able to work backwards too, and find how many terms there are in a series when given the sum of the series. Remember that the number of terms can only be a positive integer.

WORKED EXAMPLE 4.9

An arithmetic sequence has first term 5 and common difference 10. The sum of the first n terms is 720. Find the value of n.

$S_n = \frac{n}{2}[2a+(n-1)d]$

$720 = \frac{n}{2}[2\times5+(n-1)\times10]$

Use $S_n = \frac{n}{2}[2a+(n-1)d]$, with $S_n = 720, a = 5, d = 10$.

$720 = \frac{n}{2}(10+10n-10)$

$720 = 5n^2$

$n^2 = 144$

$n = \pm12$

Simplify and then solve the equation.

$\therefore n = 12$

n must be positive.

Sometimes you have to interpret the question carefully to see that it is about an arithmetic series.

WORKED EXAMPLE 4.10

Find the sum of all the multiples of 3 between 100 and 1000.

$S = 102 + 105 + 108 + \ldots + 999$

This is an arithmetic series with

$a = 102$ and $a = 3$.

Write out the first few terms and the last term to see what is happening.

$u_n = a+(n-1)d$

$999 = 102+3(n-1)$

$897 = 3(n-1)$

$n = 300$

You need to know how many terms there are in this series, so set $u_n = 999$ in the formula $u_n = a+(n-1)d$ and solve for n.

$S_{300} = \frac{300}{2}(102+999)$

$= 165\,150$

Now use $S_n = \frac{n}{2}(a+L)$, with $n = 300$, $a = 102$, $L = 999$.

EXERCISE 4D

1 Find the sum of the following arithmetic sequences.

a **i** 12, 33, 54, … (17 terms) **ii** −100, −85, −70, … (23 terms)

b **i** 3, 15, …, 459 **ii** 2, 11, …, 650

c **i** 28, 23, …, −52 **ii** 100, 97, …, 40

d **i** 15, 15.5, …, 29.5 **ii** $\frac{1}{12}, \frac{1}{6}, \ldots, 1.5$

2 An arithmetic sequence has first term 4 and common difference 8. How many terms are required to get a sum of each of the following?

a i 676 ii 4096

b i x^2, for some positive even number x ii $100x$, for some square number x

3 For the arithmetic series $2+5+8+\ldots$, find the value of n for which $S_n = 1365$.

4 The sum of the first n terms of a series is given by $S_n = 2n^2 - n$, where $n \in \mathbb{Z}^+$.

a Find the first three terms of the series.

b Find an expression for the nth term of the series.

5 The second term of an arithmetic sequence is 7. The sum of the first four terms is 12. Find the first term, a, and the common difference, d, of the sequence.

6 The fourth term of an arithmetic sequence is 17. The sum of the first 20 terms is 990. Find the first term, a, and the common difference, d, of the sequence.

7 The sum of the first three terms of an arithmetic progression is -12, and the sum of the first 12 terms is 114. Find the first term, a, and common difference, d.

8 Prove that the sum of the first n odd numbers is n^2.

9 Find the largest possible value of the sum of the arithmetic sequence 85, 78, 71, ….

10 Find the least number of terms so that the sum of the series $-6+1+8+15+\ldots$ is greater than 10 000.

11 The sum of the first n terms of an arithmetic sequence is $S_n = 3n^2 - 2n$. Find the nth term u_n.

12 A circular disc is cut into 12 sectors whose areas are in an arithmetic sequence. The angle of the largest sector is twice the angle of the smallest sector. Find the size of the angle of the smallest sector.

13 a Find the sum of all multiples of 7 between 1 and 1000.

b Hence, find the sum of all integers between 1 and 1000 that are not divisible by 7.

14 The ratio of the fifth term to the twelfth term of a sequence in an arithmetic progression is $\frac{6}{13}$. If each term of this sequence is positive, and the product of the first term and the third term is 32, find the sum of the first 100 terms of this sequence.

15 a Find an expression for the sum of the first 20 terms of the series $S_{20} = \ln x + \ln x^4 + \ln x^7 + \ln x^{10} + \ldots$.

b Hence, find the exact value of x for which $S_{20} = 2950$.

16 Find the sum of all three digit numbers that are multiples of 14 but not 21.

Section 5: Geometric sequences

A **geometric sequence** (or **geometric progression**) has a **common ratio** between each term: to get from one term to the next you multiply by the common ratio. For example:

- 1, 2, 4, 8, 16, … ($2 \times$ previous term)
- 100, 50, 25, 12.5, 6.25, … ($\frac{1}{2} \times$ previous term)
- 1, –3, 27, –81, … ($-3 \times$ previous term)

In general, if the first term is a and the common ratio is r, then you have

1st term	2nd term	3rd term	4th term	5th term
a	ar	ar^2	ar^3	ar^4

From this you can see how to form the nth term of a geometric sequence.

Key point 4.6

The nth term of a geometric sequence with first term a and common ratio r is

$$u_n = ar^{n-1}$$

Tip

The formula for the nth term involves r^{n-1} and not r^n. So, for example, $u_8 = ar^7$ and not $u_8 = ar^8$.

WORKED EXAMPLE 4.11

For the geometric sequence 324, −108, 36, −12, …:

a Find a formula for the nth term.

b Hence, find the 10th term of the sequence.

a $a = 324$

$r = \frac{-108}{324} = -\frac{1}{3}$ — If the common ratio isn't obvious, divide the second term by the first term (or u_3 by u_2, etc.) to find it.

$\therefore u_n = 324\left(-\frac{1}{3}\right)^{n-1}$ — Now use $u_n = ar^{n-1}$.

b $u_{10} = 324\left(-\frac{1}{3}\right)^{10-1}$ — Substitute $n = 10$.

$= 324\left(-\frac{1}{3}\right)^{9}$

$= -\frac{4}{243}$

As with arithmetic sequences, you will often need to set up simultaneous equations.

Elevate

See Support sheet 4 for a further example of using simultaneous equations to find a and r.

WORKED EXAMPLE 4.12

The 7th term of a geometric sequence is 13. The 9th term is 52. Find the possible values of the common ratio.

$u_7 = ar^6$ — Use $u_n = ar^{n-1}$, with $n = 7$.

$13 = ar^6 \quad (1)$ — But you know that $u_7 = 13$.

$52 = ar^8 \quad (2)$ — Repeat for the ninth term.

Continues on next page …

(2) ÷ (1) gives:

$\frac{52}{13} = \frac{ar^8}{ar^6}$

$4 = r^2$

$r = \pm 2$

Solve simultaneously. Note that dividing the equations is a quick way of eliminating *a* and solving for *r*.

Tip

Notice that the question asked for values rather than a value, so you should expect to give at least two answers.

WORKED EXAMPLE 4.13

Three consecutive terms of a geometric sequence with common ratio $r \neq 0$ are $x-2$, $x+2$, $5x-2$.

a Find the possible values of x.

b For each value of x, find the common ratio of the sequence.

a $\frac{x+2}{x-2} = \frac{5x-2}{x+2}$

The ratio between terms must be constant (i.e. r).

$(x+2)(x+2) = (5x-2)(x-2)$

$x^2 + 4x + 4 = 5x^2 - 12x + 4$

$4x^2 - 16x = 0$

$x(x-4) = 0$

$x = 0$ or 4

Rearrange and solve the quadratic.

b When $x = 0$,

$r = \frac{x+2}{x-2} = \frac{2}{-2} = -1$

When $x = 4$,

$r = \frac{4+2}{4-2} = \frac{6}{2} = 3$

Find the ratio of the first two terms for each value of x in turn.

When you are asked which term satisfies a particular condition, you normally need to use logarithms.

WORKED EXAMPLE 4.14

A geometric sequence has first term 10 and common ratio $\frac{1}{3}$. What is the term number of the first term that is less than 10^{-6}?

$u_n < 10^{-6}$

Express the condition for the nth term to be less than 10^{-6} as an inequality.

Continues on next page ...

$$10\times\left(\frac{1}{3}\right)^{n-1}<10^{-6}$$

Use $u_n = ar^{n-1}$ with $a = 10$ and $r = \frac{1}{3}$.

$$\left(\frac{1}{3}\right)^{n-1}<(10^{-7})$$

The unknown is in the power so solve using logarithms.

$$\log\left(\frac{1}{3}\right)^{n-1}<\log(10^{-7})$$

$$(n-1)\log\left(\frac{1}{3}\right)<\log(10^{-7})$$

$$(n-1)>\frac{\log 10^{-7}}{\log\left(\frac{1}{3}\right)}$$

$\log\left(\frac{1}{3}\right)$ is negative, so when you divide by it you must remember to change the inequality sign.

$$n-1>14.67$$

$$n>15.67$$

$$\therefore n=16$$

n is an integer, so we need the first integer greater than 15.7.

Rewind

See Student Book 1, Chapter 7, if you need a reminder of how to solve exponential equations.

EXERCISE 4E

1 Find an expression for the nth term of the following geometric sequences.

a **i** 6, 12, 24, … **ii** 12, 18, 27, …

b **i** 20, 5, 1.25, … **ii** $1, \frac{1}{2}, \frac{1}{4}, \ldots$

c **i** 1, −2, 4, … **ii** 5, −5, 5, …

d **i** $2, 2\sqrt{3}, 6, 6\sqrt{3}, \ldots$ **ii** $4, \frac{4}{\sqrt{2}}, 2, \frac{2}{\sqrt{2}}, \ldots$

e **i** $a, ax, ax^2, \ldots$ **ii** $3, 6x, 12x^2, \ldots$

2 How many terms are there in the following geometric sequences?

a **i** 6, 12, 24, …, 24 576 **ii** 20, 50, …, 4882.8125

b **i** 1, −3, …, −19 683 **ii** 2, −4, 8, …, −1024

c **i** $\frac{1}{2}, \frac{1}{4}, \ldots, \frac{1}{1024}$ **ii** $3, 2, \frac{4}{3}, \ldots, \frac{128}{729}$

3 The second term of a geometric sequence is 6 and the fifth term is 162.

a Find a formula for the nth term of the sequence.

b Hence, find the tenth term.

4 The third term of a geometric progression is 12 and the fifth term is 48.

a Find the possible values of the first term and the common ratio.

b Hence, find the two possible values of the eighth term.

Tip

'Progression' is just another word for 'sequence'.

5 The first three terms of a geometric sequence are a, $a + 4$ and $9a$.

a Find the possible values of a.

b In each case, find the tenth term of the sequence.

6 The third term of a geometric sequence is 112 and the sixth term is 7168. Which term takes the value 1 835 008?

7 A geometric sequence has first term 2 and common ratio -3. For a particular value of n, $u_n = -4374$.

a Show that $(n-1)\ln 3 = \ln 2187$.

b Hence, find the value of n.

8 Which is the first term of the sequence $\frac{2}{5}, \frac{4}{25}, \frac{8}{125}, \ldots$ to be less than 10^{-9}?

9 The difference between the fourth and the third terms $(u_4 - u_3)$ of a geometric progression equals one-quarter of the second term. Find two possible values of the common ratio.

10 The three terms a, 1, b are in arithmetic progression. The three terms 1, a, b are in geometric progression. Find the value of a and b given that $a \neq b$.

11 The sum of the first n terms of an arithmetic sequence is given by the formula $S_n = 4n^2 - 2n$. Three terms of this sequence, u_2, u_m and u_{32}, are consecutive terms in a geometric sequence. Find m.

Section 6: Geometric series

When you add up the terms of a geometric sequence you get a **geometric series**. Just as for arithmetic series, there is a formula for the sum of the first n terms of a geometric sequence.

Key point 4.7

The sum of the first n terms of a geometric series with first term a and common ratio r is

$$S_n = \frac{a(1-r^n)}{1-r}$$

or equivalently:

$$S_n = \frac{a(r^n-1)}{r-1}$$

This formula is given in your formula book.

Focus on …

This formula is proved in Focus on … Proof 1.

Tip

In general, use the first of these formulae when the common ratio is less than 1 and the second when the common ratio is greater than 1. This avoids having to work with negative numbers.

WORKED EXAMPLE 4.15

Find the exact value of the sum of the first six terms of the geometric sequence with first term 8 and common difference $\frac{1}{2}$.

$$S_6 = \frac{8\left(1-\left(\frac{1}{2}\right)^6\right)}{1-\frac{1}{2}}$$

$a=8, r=\frac{1}{2}$ and $n=6$. Use the first sum formula as $r<1$.

$$= \frac{8\left(1-\frac{1}{64}\right)}{\frac{1}{2}}$$

$$=16\left(\frac{63}{64}\right)$$

$$=\frac{63}{4}$$

You will need to use logarithms if you are asked to find the term number or the number of terms.

WORKED EXAMPLE 4.16

How many terms are needed for the sum of the geometric series $3+6+12+24+\ldots$ to exceed 100 000?

$a=3$

$r=2$

You need n, but you know a and r.

$$S_n > 100\,000$$

$$\frac{3(2^n-1)}{2-1} > 100\,000$$

Use the second sum formula ($r>1$) and express the condition as an inequality.

$$3(2^n-1) > 100\,000$$

$$2^n > \frac{100\,003}{3}$$

$$\log 2^n > \log\left(\frac{100\,003}{3}\right)$$

The unknown is in the power, so use logarithms to solve the inequality.

$$n\log 2 > \log\left(\frac{100\,003}{3}\right)$$

$$n > \frac{\log\left(\frac{100\,003}{3}\right)}{\log 2}$$

$$n > 15.02$$

But n is a whole number, so 16 terms are needed.

EXERCISE 4F

1 Find the sums of the following geometric series. (There may be more than one possible answer!)

a **i** 7, 35, 175, … (10 terms) **ii** 1152, 576, 288, … (12 terms)

b **i** 16, 24, 36, …, 182.25 **ii** 1, 1.1, 1.21, …, 1.771561

c **i** first term 8, common ratio –3, last term 52 488

ii first term –6, common ratio –3, last term 13 122

d **i** third term 24, fifth term 6, 12 terms

ii ninth term 50, 13th term 0.08, last term 0.0032

2 Find the possible values of the common ratio if:

a **i** first term is 11, sum of the first two terms is 12.65

ii first term is 1, sum of the first two terms is 3.7.

b **i** first term is 12, sum of the first three terms is 16.68

ii first term is 10, sum of the first three terms is 1.5.

3 The nth term, u_n, of a geometric sequence is given by $u_n = 3\times 5^{n+2}, n \in \mathbb{Z}^+$.

a Find the common ratio r.

b Hence, or otherwise, find an expression for S_n the sum of the first n terms of this sequence.

4 The first term of a geometric sequence is 6 and the sum of the first three terms is 29. Find the common ratio.

5 The sum of the first two terms of a geometric sequence is $23\frac{3}{4}$ and the sum of the first four terms is $40\frac{5}{8}$. Find the first term and the common ratio.

6 The sum of the first four terms of a geometric sequence is 520, the sum of the first five terms is 844, and the sum of the first six terms is 1330.

a Find the common ratio.

b Find the sum of the first two terms.

7 **a** What is the sum of the first four terms of the geometric sequence with first term 1 and common ratio x?

b Factorise $x^6 - 1$ into a linear factor and a polynomial of order 5.

Section 7: Infinite geometric series

If you keep adding together terms of any arithmetic sequence, the sum increases (or decreases if d it is negative) without limit. This can happen with geometric series too, but there is also a possibility that the sum will **converge**.

Tip

Remember that *converge* means that the numbers are approaching a limit (without necessarily reaching it).

For example, consider adding the numbers $\frac{1}{2}, \frac{1}{4}, \frac{1}{8}, \ldots$ (this is a geometric sequence with common ratio $\frac{1}{2}$). Using your calculator you can see that, as you add more and more terms of the sequence, the sum gets closer and closer to 1. You can try some more sequences, with different common ratios; some have sums that grow without a limit, whereas others seem to converge.

Tip

Here we are talking about the *sum* of the sequence converging to 1. The example sequence itself also converges, but its limit is 0.

Looking at the formula for the sum of a geometric sequence,

$$S_n = \frac{a(1-r^n)}{1-r}$$

you can see that the only part that is affected by making n bigger is r^n. When you raise most numbers to a large power the result gets bigger and bigger. The exception is when r is a number between -1 and 1; in this case, r^n gets smaller in magnitude as n increases – in fact it tends towards zero. Thus, we have:

Key point 4.8

As n increases the sum of a geometric series converges to

$$S_\infty = \frac{a}{1-r} \text{ if } |r|<1.$$

This is called the **sum to infinity** of the series.

If $|r| > 1$ the series **diverges** (has an infinite sum).

This formula is given in your formula book.

Tip

The condition that $|r| < 1$ is just as important as the formula itself.

WORKED EXAMPLE 4.17

For the geometric series $16-4+1-\frac{1}{4}+\ldots$, find:

a the sum of the first 4 terms

b the sum of the first 10 terms, correct to 6 decimal places

c the sum to infinity.

$a=16, r=-\frac{1}{4}$

To find the common ratio, divide the second term by the first term.

a $16-4+1-\frac{1}{4}=\frac{51}{4}$ $(=12.75)$

b $S_{10} = \dfrac{16\left(1-\left(-\frac{1}{4}\right)^{10}\right)}{1-\left(-\frac{1}{4}\right)}$

$\geqslant 12.799998$

Use $S_n = \frac{a(1-r^n)}{1-r}$. Be careful: r is negative.

c $S_\infty = \dfrac{16}{1-\left(-\frac{1}{4}\right)} = \dfrac{64}{5}$ $(=12.8)$

Use $S_\infty = \frac{a}{1-r}$. This is valid since $|[-\frac{1}{4}]| < 1$.

WORKED EXAMPLE 4.18

The sum to infinity of a geometric series is 5 and the second term is $-\frac{6}{5}$. Find the common ratio.

$5=\frac{a}{1-r}$ (1) — Use $S_\infty=\frac{a}{1-r}$, with $S_\infty=5$.

$-\frac{6}{5}=ar$ (2) — Use $u_2=ar$, with $u_2=-\frac{6}{5}$.

From (2): — Solve simultaneously.

$a=-\frac{6}{5r}$

Substituting into (1):

$$-\frac{6}{5r(1-r)}=5$$

$$-6=25(r-r^2)$$

$$0=25r^2-25r-6$$

$$0=(5r-6)(5r+1)$$

$r=\frac{6}{5}$ or $-\frac{1}{5}$

But since the sum to infinity exists,

$-1<r<1$ — Check that the series actually converges for the values of r found.

$\therefore r=-\frac{1}{5}$

Remember that some questions may focus on the condition for the sequence to converge, as well as the value that it converges to.

WORKED EXAMPLE 4.19

The geometric series $(2-x)+(2-x)^2+(2-x)^3+\ldots$ converges. Find the range of possible values of x.

$r=(2-x)$ — Identify r.

Since the series converges: — Use the fact that the series converges.

$-1<2-x<1$

$-3<-x<-1$ — Solve the inequality.

$1<x<3$

EXERCISE 4G

1. Find the value of the following infinite geometric series, or state that they are divergent.

   a **i** $9+3+1+\frac{1}{3}+\ldots$ **ii** $56+8+1\frac{1}{7}+\ldots$

   b **i** $0.3+0.03+0.003+\ldots$ **ii** $0.78+0.0078+0.000078+\ldots$

   c **i** $0.01+0.02+0.04+\ldots$ **ii** $\frac{19}{10000}+\frac{19}{1000}+\frac{19}{100}+\ldots$

   d **i** $10-2+0.4-\ldots$ **ii** $6-4+\frac{8}{3}-\ldots$

   e **i** $10-40+160-\ldots$ **ii** $4.2-3.36+2.688-\ldots$

2. Find the values of x that allow the following geometric series to converge.

   a **i** $9+9x+9x^2+\ldots$ **ii** $-2-2x-2x^2-\ldots$

   b **i** $1+3x+9x^2+\ldots$ **ii** $1+10x+100x^2+\ldots$

   c **i** $-2-10x-50x^2-\ldots$ **ii** $8+24x+72x^2+\ldots$

   d **i** $40+10x+2.5x^2+\ldots$ **ii** $144+12x+x^2+\ldots$

   e **i** $243-81x+27x^2-\ldots$ **ii** $1-\frac{5}{4}x+\frac{25}{16}x^2-\ldots$

   f **i** $3-\frac{6}{x}+\frac{12}{x^2}-\ldots$ **ii** $18-\frac{9}{x}+\frac{9}{2x^2}-\ldots$

   g **i** $5+5(3-2x)+5(3-2x)^2+\ldots$ **ii** $7+\frac{7(2-x)}{2}+\frac{7(2-x)^2}{4}+\ldots$

   h **i** $1+\left(3-\frac{2}{x}\right)+\left(3-\frac{2}{x}\right)^2+\ldots$ **ii** $1+\frac{1+x}{x}+\frac{(1+x)^2}{x^2}+\ldots$

   i **i** $7+7x^2+7x^4+\ldots$ **ii** $12-48x^3+192x^6-\ldots$

3. Find the sum to infinity of the geometric sequence $-18, 12, -8, \ldots$.

4. The first and fourth terms of a geometric series are 18 and $-\frac{2}{3}$, respectively. Find:

   a the sum of the first n terms of the series

   b the sum to infinity of the series.

5. A geometric sequence has all positive terms. The sum of the first two terms is 15 and the sum to infinity is 27. Find the value of:

   a the common ratio

   b the first term.

6. The sum to infinity of a geometric series is 32. The sum of the first four terms is 30 and all the terms are positive. Find the difference between the sum to infinity and the sum of the first eight terms.

7. Consider the infinite geometric series $1+\left(\frac{2x}{3}\right)+\left(\frac{2x}{3}\right)^2+\ldots$.

   a For what values of x does the series converge?

   b Find the sum of the series if $x=1.2$.

8. The sum of an infinite geometric progression is 13.5, and the sum of the first three terms is 13. Find the first term.

9 An infinite geometric series is given by $\sum_{k=1}^{\infty} 2(4-3x)^k$.

a Find the values of x for which the series has a finite sum.

b When $x = 1.2$, find the minimum number of terms needed to give a sum that is greater than 1.328.

10 The common ratio of the terms in a geometric series is 2^x.

a State the set of values of x for which the sum to infinity of the series exists.

b If the first term of the series is 35, find the value of x for which the sum to infinity is 40.

11 $f(x) = 1 + 2x + 4x^2 + 8x^3 + \ldots$ is an infinite series. Evaluate where possible:

a $f\left(\frac{1}{3}\right)$ **b** $f\left(\frac{2}{3}\right)$

Section 8: Using sequences and series to solve problems

In this section you will see how to model various situations using sequences and series. If the sequence in question is arithmetic or geometric, you can use the formulae from previous sections to calculate individual terms and sums of terms. If a sequence is not either of those two types, you can use your calculator to investigate its behaviour.

When dealing with sequences and series problems, you usually need to:

- Identify whether it is a geometric or an arithmetic sequence (or neither).
- Identify whether it is asking for a term in the sequence or the sum of terms in the sequence.
- Translate the information given in the question into equations.

WORKED EXAMPLE 4.20

A savings account pays 2.4% annual compound interest, added at the end of each year. If £200 is paid into the account at the start of the first year, how much will there be in the account at the start of the seventh year?

For a 2.4% increase, multiply by $1 + \frac{2.4}{100} = 1.024$

The balance of the account at the beginning of:

Year 1: 200

Year 2: 200×1.024

Year 3: 200×1.024^2

This is a geometric sequence with $a = 200$ and $r = 1.024$.

Each year the balance of the account is increased by the same percentage, so this gives a geometric sequence. It is a good idea to write out the first few terms in questions like this, to make sure you know what is happening.

$u_7 = ar^6$

$= 200 \times 1.024^6$

$= £230.58$

The balance at the start of the seventh year is u_7.

A common example of sequences and series is to calculations involving mortgages and other types of loans. In a typical example, the amount owed is increased by a fixed percentage, and a fixed amount is paid off at regular intervals (such as annually or monthly).

Tip

A spreadsheet is a very useful tool to investigate loans and mortgages. You can also use an iterative function on your calculator to generate the sequence.

WORKED EXAMPLE 4.21

Sam borrows £8000 to buy a car. At the end of each year (including the first) she pays back £1000 (or the amount still owed if less than £1000). At the start of each year (starting from the second) 4% interest is added.

a Show that at the end of the third year, before the interest has been added, she will still owe £5531.

b Let $£L_n$ be the amount Sam will owe at the end of year n. Find an expression for L_{n+1} in terms of L_n.

c Hence, find how many years it will take for Sam to pay off the loan.

a End of first year: $8000 - 1000 = £7000$

End of second year: $7000 \times 1.04 - 1000 = £6280$

End of third year: $6280 \times 1.04 - 1000 = £5531$

The interest is not added until the start of the second year.

b $L_{n+1} = 1.04L_n - 1000$

Each year, the amount owed is increased by 4% and then decreased by £7000.

c $L_1 = 7000$

$L_2 = 6280$

...

$L_9 = 366$

$L_{10} = -620$

Use your calculator to generate the terms of the sequence with the formula from part **b**.

Show the first few and the last few terms.

Sam will pay off the loan at the end of the 10th year.

When the terms become negative, the debt has been paid off.

WORK IT OUT 4.1

A job advert isement states that the starting salary is £18 500 with an annual increase of £350. How much would you earn in total by the start of the fifth year?

Which of the following is correct? Identify the mistake in the other two.

Solution 1	Solution 2	Solution 3
Arithmetic sequence, $a = 18\,500$, $d = 350$ You need the sum of the first five terms: $S_5 = \frac{5}{2}(2\times18500 + 4\times350)$ $= £96\,000$	Arithmetic sequence, $a = 18\,500$, $d = 350$ The fifth term is: $u_5 = 18\,500 + 4\times350$ $= £19\,900$	Arithmetic sequence, $a = 18\,500$, $d = 350$ The sum of the first four terms is: $S_4 = \frac{4}{2}(2\times18500 + 3\times350)$ $= £76\,100$

EXERCISE 4H

1 Philippa invests £1000 for 6 years, earning 3% compound interest each year.

- **a** How much interest does she earn in the 6th year?
- **b** What is the total amount of her investment at the end of 6 years?

2 Lars starts a job on an annual salary of £32 000 and is promised an annual increase of £1500.

- **a** What will be his 20th year's salary?
- **b** After how many complete years will Lars have earned a total of £1 million?

3 A sum of £5000 is invested, earning 6.3% per annum compound interest.

- **a** Write down an expression for the value of the investment after n full years.
- **b** What will be the value of the investment at the end of 5 years?
- **c** Given that the value of the investment will exceed £10 000 after n full years:
  - **i** Write an inequality to represent this information.
  - **ii** Calculate the minimum value of n.

4 A florist orders 60 bunches of flowers. By the end of the day he has sold 20% of his flowers. He orders 10 more bunches for the next day. The same happens on each day afterwards:

- **a** Let f_n be the number of bunches of flowers in the florist's shop at the end of the nth day. Write down an expression for f_{n+1} in terms of f_n.
- **b** Describe the behaviour of the sequence f_n. How many bunches of flowers will be in the shop in the long term?

5 A sum of £100 is invested.

a If the interest is compounded annually at a rate of 5% per year, find the total value, V, of the investment after 20 years.

b If the interest is compounded monthly at a rate of $\frac{5}{12}$% per month, find the minimum number of months for the value of the investment to exceed V.

6 A marathon is a 26-mile race. In a training regimen for a marathon, a runner runs 1 mile on her first day of training and each day increases her distance by $\frac{1}{4}$ of a mile.

a After how many days has she run for a total of 26 miles?

b On which day does she first run over 26 miles?

7 Aaron and Blake each keep some money in a safe. Aaron deposits £100 in the first month and then increases his deposits by £10 each month. Blake deposits £50 in the first month and then increases his deposits by 20% each month. After how many months will Blake have more money in his safe than Aaron?

8 A ball is dropped vertically from 2 metres in the air. With each bounce, it bounces only up to a height of 80% of its previous height.

a What height does it reach after the fourth bounce?

b How far has it travelled when it hits the ground for the ninth time?

c Give one reason why this model is unlikely to be accurate after 20 bounces.

9 Miriam deposits £1000 into a bank account at the beginning of each year, starting in 2010. At the end of each year 4% interest is added to the account.

a Show that at the beginning of 2012 there is $1000+1000\times1.04+1000\times(1.04)^2$ in the account.

b Find an expression for the amount in the account at the beginning of the year.

c When Miriam has a total of at least £50 000 in her account at the beginning of a year, she will start looking to buy a house. In which year will this happen?

10 Each row of seats in a theatre has 20 more seats than the row in front of it. There are 50 seats in the front row and the designer wants the capacity to be at least 2500.

a How many rows are required?

b Assuming the rows are equally spread, what percentage of people are seated in the front half of the theatre?

11 Dineth takes out a mortgage to buy a house. He borrows £70 000 at an annual interest rate of 2%. The interest is added at the end of each year, after which Dineth pays back £5 000.

a Show that at the start at the third year, Dineth owes about £62 700.

b Let M_n be the amount Dineth owes at the start of year n (so that $M_1 = 70\,000$ and $M_3 = 62\,700$). Express M_{n+1} in terms of M_n.

c Hence find long it will take for Dineth to pay off his mortgage.

Checklist of learning and understanding

- A sequence can be defined by a formula for the nth term (a position-to-term rule) or by a rule that generates the next term of a sequence from the previous term or terms (a term-to-term rule).
- Behaviour of a sequence:
  - an increasing sequence is one where each term is larger than the previous one: $u_{n+1} > u_n$, and a decreasing sequence is one where each term is smaller than the previous one: $u_{n+1} < u_n$.
  - a periodic sequence is one where the terms start repeating after a while: $u_{n+k} = u_n$ for some number k (the period of the sequence).
  - a convergent sequence is one where the terms approach a limit as n increases, and a divergent sequence is one where they increase/decrease without a limit.
- A series is a sum of terms in a sequence and it can be described succinctly using sigma notation:

$$\sum_{r=1}^{n} \mathrm{f}(r) = \mathrm{f}(1) + \mathrm{f}(2) + \ldots + \mathrm{f}(n)$$

- Arithmetic sequences have a constant difference, d, between terms.
  - If you know the first term (a), the general term is:

$$u_n = a + (n-1)d$$

  - If you know the first term (a) and last term (L), the sum of all terms in the sequence is:

$$S_n = \frac{n}{2}(a + L)$$

  - If you know the first term (a) and the common difference (d):

$$S_n = \frac{n}{2}\left[2a + (n-1)d\right]$$

- Geometric sequences have a constant ratio, r, between terms.
  - If you know the first term (a), the general term is:

$$u_n = ar^{n-1}$$

  - The sum of the first n terms is:

$$S_n = \frac{a(1-r^n)}{1-r}$$

    or equivalently

$$S_n = \frac{a(r^n - 1)}{r-1}$$

  - If $|r| < 1$, the series converges and the sum to infinity is given by:

$$S_\infty = \frac{a}{1-r}$$

Mixed practice 4

1. The third term of an arithmetic sequence is 4 and the sum of the first 20 terms is -445. Find the first term and the common difference.

2. The fourth term of an arithmetic progression is 9.6 and the ninth term is 15.6. Find the sum of the first nine terms.

3. The third term of a geometric sequence is 192 and the sixth term is 3.

   a Find the first term and the common ratio.

   b Find the sum to infinity.

4. The nth term of a geometric progression is $u_n = r^n$. The sum to infinity is 5. Find the value of r.

5. The fifth term of an arithmetic sequence is three times the second term. Find the ratio:

$$\frac{\text{Common difference}}{\text{First term}}$$

6. A sequence, S, has terms $u_1, u_2, u_3, \ldots$ defined by
$u_n = 3n - 1$, for $n \geqslant 1$.

   i Write down the values of u_1, u_2 and u_3, and state what type of sequence S is.

   ii Evaluate $\sum_{n=1}^{100} u_n$.

7. Which is the first term of the sequence $\frac{1}{3}, \frac{1}{9}, \ldots, \frac{1}{3^n}$ less than 10^{-6}?

8. The sum of the first three terms of a geometric progression is 19. The sum to infinity is 27. Find the common ratio, r.

9. Find the exact value of $\sum_{r=0}^{\infty} \frac{\sqrt{2}}{4^r}$.

10. Ben builds a pyramid out of toy bricks. The top row contains one brick, the second row contains three bricks and each row after that contains two more bricks than the previous row.

    a How many bricks are in the nth row?

    b If a total of 36 bricks are used, how many rows are there?

    c In Ben's largest ever pyramid, he noticed that the total number of bricks was four more than four times the number of bricks in the last row. What is the total number of bricks?

11. Kalinda is offered two investment plans, each requiring an initial investment of \$10,000:

    Plan A offers a fixed return of \$800 per year.

    Plan B offers a return of 5% each year, reinvested in the plan.

    Over what period of time is plan A better than plan B?

12. The first three terms of a geometric sequence are $2x + 4$, $x + 5$ and $x + 1$.

    a Find the two possible values of x.

    b Given that it exists, find the sum to infinity of the series.

13 Evaluate $\sum_{n=0}^{\infty} \frac{(2^n + 4^n)}{6^n}$.

14 Find the sum of all the integers between 300 and 600 that are divisible by 7.

15 A sequence is defined by $u_{n+1} = ku_n - 3$, $u_1 = 2$.

a If $u_3 \geqslant -1$, find the range of possible values of the constant k.

b Given that $k = -\frac{1}{4}$, find the limit of the sequence as n tends to infinity.

16 i John aims to pay a certain amount of money each month into a pension fund. He plans to pay £100 in the first month, and then to increase the amount paid by £5 each month; that is, paying £105 in the second month, £110 in the third month etc.

If John continues making payments according to this plan for 240 months, calculate

a how much he will pay in the final month,

b how much he will pay altogether over the whole period.

ii Rachel also plans to pay money monthly into a pension fund over a period of 240 months, starting with £100 in the first month. Her monthly payments will form a geometric progression, and she will pay £1500 in the final month.

Calculate how much Rachel will pay altogether over the whole period.

© OCR, GCE Mathematics, Paper 4722, June 2006

17 A geometric progression has first term a and common ratio r, and the terms are all different. The first, second and fourth terms of the geometric progression form the first three terms of an arithmetic progression.

i Show that $r^3 - 2r + 1 = 0$.

ii Given that the geometric progression converges, find the exact value of r.

iii Given also that the sum to infinity of this geometric progression is $3 + \sqrt{5}$, find the value of the integer a.

© OCR, GCE Mathematics, Paper 4722, June 2010

18 A geometric sequence and an arithmetic sequence both start with a first term of 1. The third term of the arithmetic sequence is the same as the second term of the geometric sequence. The fourth term of the arithmetic sequence is the same as the third term of the geometric sequence. Find the possible values of the common difference of the arithmetic sequence.

19 The first, second and fourth terms of a geometric sequence form consecutive terms of an arithmetic sequence. Given that the sum to infinity of the geometric sequence exists, find the exact value of the common ratio.

20 Find an expression for the sum of the first 23 terms of the series

$$\ln\frac{a^3}{\sqrt{b}} + \ln\frac{a^3}{b} + \ln\frac{a^3}{b\sqrt{b}} + \ln\frac{a^3}{b^2} + \ldots$$

giving your answer in the form $\ln\frac{a^m}{b^n}$, where $m, n \in \mathbb{Z}$.

21 A student writes '1' on the first line of a page, then the next two integers '2, 3' on the second line of the page and then the next three integers '4, 5, 6' on the third line. He continues this pattern.

a How many integers are on the nth line?

b What is the last integer on the nth line?

c What is the first integer on the nth line?

d Show that the sum of all the integers on the nth line is $\frac{n}{2}(n^2+1)$.

e The sum of all the integers on the last line of the page is 16 400. How many lines are on the page?

22 Suresh has a mortgage of £150 000. At the end of each year 6% interest is added, then Suresh pays £10 000.

a Show that at the end of the third year the amount owing (£) is:

$$150000\times(1.06)^3-10000\times(1.06)^2-10000\times1.06-10000$$

b Find an expression for how much is owing at the end of the nth year.

c After how many years will the mortgage be paid off?

5 Rational functions and partial fractions

In this chapter, you will learn how to:

- manipulate rational functions, including by polynomial division with remainders
- decompose rational functions into a sum of algebraic fractions when the denominator contains distinct linear factors
- decompose rational functions into a sum of algebraic fractions when the denominator contains repeated linear factors.

Before you start...

GCSE	Factorise quadratic expressions.	1 Factorise $6x^2 + 7x + 2$.
GCSE	Add algebraic fractions.	2 Simplify this expression into one fraction: $\frac{1}{x}+\frac{1}{2+x}$
Student Book 1, Chapter 4	Carry out polynomial division.	3 Simplify $(x^3 + 8) \div (x + 2)$.
Student Book 1, Chapter 4	Use the factor theorem.	4 Find a linear factor of $x^3 + x^2 + 5x - 7$.

What are rational functions?

In Student Book 1 you studied polynomials. A **rational function** is a fraction where both the denominator and numerator are polynomials. These functions have a wide range of real–world applications, from economics to medicine. For example, the function $\frac{t}{t^2+1}$ is often used to model the amount of anaesthetic in a patient after a time, t. In this chapter you will focus on applying algebraic techniques to change rational functions into forms that will allow more advanced manipulations later in the course. To do this you shall start by reviewing a very important theorem about polynomials – the factor theorem.

Focus on ...

Focus on ... Modelling 1 compares models, using rational functions to exponential models.

Section 1: Review of the factor theorem

In Student Book 1 you met the factor theorem as a way of checking if a polynomial had a particular factor.

Key point 5.1

If $f\left(\frac{b}{a}\right)=0$, then $(ax-b)$ is a factor of $f(x)$.

Once you have established that a polynomial has a particular factor, you can then factorise the whole polynomial. One major use of this is to solve equations.

WORKED EXAMPLE 5.1

a Show that $2x-1$ is a factor of $f(x)=2x^3-5x^2-14x+8$.
b Hence, solve $2x^3-5x^2-14x+8=0$.

a $f\left(\frac{1}{2}\right)=2\times\frac{1}{8}-5\times\frac{1}{4}-14\times\frac{1}{2}+8$

$=\frac{1}{4}-\frac{5}{4}-7+8$

$=0$

By the factor theorem, $(2x-1)$ is a factor of $f(x)$.

The factor theorem says that $2x-1$ is a factor if and only if $f\left(\frac{1}{2}\right)=0$. You need to show enough working to convincingly demonstrate that $f\left(\frac{1}{2}\right)=0$.

b

$$
\begin{array}{r}
x^2-2x-8\\
(2x-1)\overline{)2x^3-5x^2-14x+8}\\
\underline{2x^3-x^2}\\
-4x^2-14x+8\\
\underline{-4x^2+2x}\\
-16x+8\\
\underline{-16x+8}\\
0
\end{array}
$$

You can use polynomial division to find the remaining factor.

$x^2-2x-8=(x-4)(x+2)$

You can factorise the quadratic expression.

So $2x^3-5x^2-14x+8$

$=(2x-1)(x-4)(x+2)$

Writing the expression in the factorised form allows you to find where it equals zero.

When $(2x-1)(x-4)(x+2)=0$,

$x=\frac{1}{2}$, 4 or -2.

Tip

Remember: if you do not like long division you can also write $2x^3-5x^2-14x+8$ as $(2x-1)(ax^2+bx+c)$, then multiply out and compare coefficients.

Rewind

You first met polynomial division in Student Book 1, Chapter 4.

The factor theorem also works in reverse, so if you know that $(ax - b)$ is a factor, then $f\left(\frac{b}{a}\right) = 0$.

WORKED EXAMPLE 5.2

Given that $3x + 2$ is a factor of $3x^3 - 10x^2 + 4x + a$, find the value of a.

$$3\left(-\frac{2}{3}\right)^3 - 10\left(-\frac{2}{3}\right)^2 + 4\left(-\frac{2}{3}\right) + a = 0$$

$3x + 2$ can be written as $3x - (-2)$, so the factor theorem says that $f\left(-\frac{2}{3}\right) = 0$.

$$-8 + a = 0$$

$$a = 8$$

EXERCISE 5A

1 Show that the following expressions have the given factor and, hence, factorise completely.

a **i** $2x^3 - 9x^2 + 7x + 6$ has factor $(2x + 1)$

ii $3x^3 - 7x^2 + 5x - 1$ has factor $(3x - 1)$

b **i** $2x^3 + 7x^2 - 3x - 18$ has factor $(2x - 3)$

ii $3x^3 + 5x^2 - 48x - 80$ has factor $(3x + 5)$

2 Show that $2x + 5$ is a factor of $4x^3 - 31x - 15$. Hence, factorise it completely.

3 $5x - 2$ is a factor of $20x^3 + 22x^2 + ax - 4$. Find the value of a.

4 **a** $3x + 1$ is a factor of $f(x) = 12x^3 - 2x^2 + ax - 2$. Find the value of a.

b Hence, factorise $f(x)$.

5 **a** Show that $2x - a$ is a factor of $2x^3 - 5ax^2 + 4a^2x - a^3$.

b Hence, factorise $2x^3 - 5ax^2 + 4a^2x - a^3$.

6 Show that $x - a$ is a factor of $f(x) = x^3 - 6ax^2 + 11a^2x - 6a^3$. Hence, solve $f(x) = 0$.

7 Prove that if $ax + b$ is a factor of $ax^2 + bx + c$, then $c = 0$.

8 If $ax + b$ is a factor of $x^2 + bx + a$, find an expression for b in terms of a.

9 **a** $2x + 1$ and $3x + 1$ are factors of $f(x) = 30x^4 + 67x^3 + 4x^2 + ax + b$. Find the values of a and b.

b Hence, solve $f(x) = 0$.

10 Show that $4x^2 - 1$ is a factor of $f(x) = 4x^4 + 4x^3 - 25x^2 - x + 6$ and, hence, solve $f(x) = 0$.

Section 2: Simplifying rational expressions

You need to be able to simplify and manipulate rational functions using your knowledge of algebra. In particular, always look to factorise expressions and simplify.

WORKED EXAMPLE 5.3

Simplify:

$$\frac{x+1}{x^2-1} \div \frac{2}{x^2-3x+2}$$

$$\frac{x+1}{x^2-1} \div \frac{2}{x^2-3x+2} \equiv \frac{x+1}{(x-1)(x+1)} \div \frac{2}{(x-2)(x-1)}$$

Always try to simplify first. You can do this by factorising and looking for common factors. Always look out for the difference of two squares!

$$\equiv \frac{1}{x-1} \div \frac{2}{(x-2)(x-1)}$$

You can divide the top and bottom of the first fraction by the factor of $x + 1$.

$$\equiv \frac{1}{x-1} \times \frac{(x-2)(x-1)}{2}$$

To divide, you flip the second fraction and multiply. Remember that you do not need a common denominator.

$$\equiv \frac{1}{1} \times \frac{x-2}{2}$$

$$\equiv \frac{x-2}{2}$$

There is a factor of $x - 1$ in the denominator of the first fraction and the denominator of the second fraction. You can 'cancel' these when the fractions are being multiplied.

You can use polynomial division to simplify rational functions when the degree of the numerator is at least the degree of the denominator. This turns the rational function into the sum of a polynomial and a simpler rational function, called the remainder term.

Tip

In the previous example you used an identity symbol to emphasise that all the expressions are equivalent.

Key point 5.2

If $P(x)$ is a polynomial then

$$\frac{P(x)}{ax+b} \equiv Q(x) + \frac{r}{ax+b}$$

In the previous expression, $Q(x)$ is also a polynomial, called the **quotient**, and r is called the **remainder**.

Fast forward

This is used in calculus (see Chapter 12), the binomial expansion (see Chapter 6) or partial fractions (see Section 5.3).

WORKED EXAMPLE 5.4

Write $\frac{2x^2+5x+1}{2x-3}$ in the form $Ax+B+\frac{C}{2x-3}$.

$$\begin{array}{r} x+4 \\ 2x-3\overline{)2x^2+5x+1} \\ 2x^2-3x \\ \hline 8x+1 \\ 8x-12 \\ \hline 13 \end{array}$$

You can use polynomial division.

So $\frac{2x^2+5x+1}{2x-3}=x+4+\frac{13}{2x-3}$

The remainder found in polynomial division forms the numerator of the rational expression.

WORK IT OUT 5.1

Simplify $\frac{x^2-1}{x-1}$.

Which of the following solutions is correct? Identify the mistakes in the other two.

Solution 1	Solution 2	Solution 3
$\frac{x^2-1}{x-1}\equiv\frac{(x-1)^2}{x-1}\equiv\frac{x-1}{1}\equiv x-1$	$\frac{x^2-1}{x-1}\equiv\frac{(x-1)(x+1)}{x-1}\equiv\frac{x+1}{1}=x+1$	Cancelling -1 from top and bottom: $\frac{x^2-1}{x-1}=\frac{x^2}{x}=x$

EXERCISE 5B

1 Simplify the following expressions.

a **i** $\frac{6x+9}{3}$ **ii** $\frac{10x+20}{5}$

b **i** $\frac{x-4}{2x-8}$ **ii** $\frac{x+3}{5x+15}$

c **i** $\frac{3x^2+4x}{x}$ **ii** $\frac{5x^2-7x}{x}$

d **i** $\frac{1-x}{x-1}$ **ii** $\frac{7-2x}{2x-7}$

e **i** $\frac{2x+4}{x^2-4}$ **ii** $\frac{4x+12}{x^2+6x+9}$

f **i** $\frac{x^2+2x+1}{x^2+5x+4}$ **ii** $\frac{x^2+5x+6}{x^2+7x+12}$

g **i** $\frac{6x^2+5x+1}{8x^2+6x+1}$ **ii** $\frac{12x^2-7x-10}{9x^2-4}$

2 Simplify the following expressions.

a i $4x \times \frac{1}{2}$ ii $12x \times \frac{1}{4}$

b i $\frac{x^2}{4} \times \frac{2}{x}$ ii $\frac{x^3}{3} \times \frac{15}{x}$

c i $\frac{1}{x^2} \times \frac{x}{2} \times \frac{x}{3}$ ii $\frac{x^2}{4} \times 2x \times \frac{5}{x^3}$

d i $\frac{2x+4}{5x} \times \frac{10x^2}{x+2}$ ii $\frac{2x+8}{x} \times \frac{3x^2}{3x+12}$

e i $\frac{x^2+7x+12}{x^2+2x+3} \times \frac{x+1}{x+4}$ ii $\frac{x^2-10x+21}{x^2-6x+5} \times \frac{x-5}{x-7}$

3 Simplify the following expressions.

a i $\frac{x}{2} \div \frac{x}{4}$ ii $\frac{3x}{4} \div \frac{9x}{20}$

b i $\frac{x}{x+1} \div \frac{x}{2}$ ii $\frac{3x}{x-2} \div \frac{5}{x-2}$

c i $\frac{(x^2-x)}{3x+6} \div \frac{x-1}{x+2}$ ii $\frac{x^2+5x}{5x+5} \div \frac{x}{5}$

d i $\frac{x^2+3x}{3x+2} \div (x+3)$ ii $\frac{5x}{7x-2} \div x$

4 Write the following expressions in the form $ax+b+\frac{r}{px+q}$.

a i $\frac{x^2}{2x+1}$ ii $\frac{x^2}{2x+3}$

b i $\frac{2x^2+3x+4}{2x+1}$ ii $\frac{5x^2+3x+4}{5x+3}$

5 Simplify $\frac{1}{x^2+7x+12} \div \frac{1}{x^2+8x+15}$.

6 Simplify $\left(\frac{1}{x-3} - \frac{1}{x}\right) \div \frac{6x}{x^2-9}$.

7 a Simplify $\frac{x^2+5x+6}{x+3}$.

b Hence, or otherwise, solve the equation $\frac{x^2+5x+6}{x+3} = x^2+4x+4$.

8 Solve the equation $\frac{x}{x+3} \div \frac{9}{2x+6} = \frac{8}{x}$.

9 Find the quotient and remainder when $4x + 15$ is divided by $2x - 5$.

10 Find the quotient and remainder when $2x^2 - 3x + 4$ is divided by $2x - 1$.

11 Write $\frac{2x^2-x-28}{x^2-2x-8}$ in the form $A+\frac{B}{x+C}$.

12 Show that $5x - 2$ is a factor of $5x^3 + 18x^2 + 7x - 6$ and, hence, simplify $\frac{5x^3+18x^2+7x-6}{5x^2+13x-6}$.

13 a Show that $2x + a$ is a factor of $2x^3 + ax^2 - 2a^2x - a^3$.

b Hence, simplify $\frac{(2x^3+ax^2-2a^2x-a^3)}{2x^2+3ax+a^2}$.

14 The remainder when $x^2 + ax + 3$ is divided by $x - 2$ is 5. Find the value of a and then find the quotient.

15 When the polynomial $f(x)$ is divided by $x - 2$, the quotient is the same as the remainder. Prove that $f(x)$ is divisible by $x - 1$.

16 **a** A car travels at speed a km h^{-1} for 10 km, then at speed b km h^{-1} for 20 km. Find and simplify an expression for the average speed during this journey.

b If the average speed equals the arithmetic mean of the two speeds, show that either the speeds in the two sections of the journey are equal or the speed in the second section is twice that of the first section.

Section 3: Partial fractions with distinct factors

You know that you can write a sum of two algebraic fractions as a single fraction:

$$\frac{1}{x+1}+\frac{1}{x+2}\equiv\frac{2x+3}{(x+1)(x+2)}$$

However, there are situations when you need to reverse this process. The method for doing this is called **partial fractions**.

To do this you need to know the form the partial fractions will take:

Fast forward

You will see that you need to do this with binomial expansions in Chapter 6 and integration in Chapter 11. You can also use it to help sum some series if you study Further Mathematics, in Student Book 2.

Key point 5.3

$\frac{mx+n}{(x+p)(x+q)}$ decomposes into $\frac{A}{x+p}+\frac{B}{x+q}$.

$\frac{mx+n}{(x+p)(x+q)(x+r)}$ decomposes into $\frac{A}{x+p}+\frac{B}{x+q}+\frac{C}{x+r}$.

Rewind

Comparing coefficients was discussed in Student Book 1, Chapter 1.

Once you know the form you are aiming for, you write it as an identity and multiply both sides by the denominator of the original fraction. You can then either compare coefficients or substitute convenient values to find the values of A and B.

WORKED EXAMPLE 5.5

Write $\frac{2x+3}{(x+1)(x+2)}$ in partial fractions.

$$\frac{2x+3}{(x+1)(x+2)}\equiv\frac{A}{x+1}+\frac{B}{x+2}$$

Write your expression in the form suggested in Key point 5.3.

$$2x+3\equiv A(x+2)+B(x+1)$$

Multiply both sides by $(x + 1)(x + 2)$ to eliminate fractions.

Continues on next page ...

When $x = -1$:

$-2 + 3 \equiv A \times 1 + B \times 0$

$1 \equiv A$

You are working with an identity so choose a convenient value of x to work with. When $x = -1$ the coefficient of B is zero, so you can find out about A.

When $x = -2$

$-4 + 3 \equiv A \times 0 + B \times -1$

$-1 \equiv -B$

$1 \equiv B$

When $x = -2$ the coefficient of A is zero, so you can find out about B.

So $\frac{2x+3}{(x+1)(x+2)} \equiv \frac{1}{x+1} + \frac{1}{x+2}$

This method only works when the degree of the numerator is less than the degree of the denominator. If this is not the case, you need to use polynomial division to turn it into the required form.

WORKED EXAMPLE 5.6

a Show that $\frac{x^4 - x^2 + 2}{x^3 - x}$ can be written in the form $x + \frac{R}{x^3 - x}$.

b Hence, write $\frac{x^4 - x^2 + 2}{x^3 - x}$ in partial fractions.

a $\frac{x^4 - x^2 + 2}{x^3 - x} = \frac{x(x^3 - x) + 2}{x^3 - x}$

You need to make a link between the top and the bottom.

$= \frac{x(x^3 - x)}{x^3 - x} + \frac{2}{x^3 - x}$

You can then split the top into two fractions.

$= x + \frac{2}{x^3 - x}$

This is the required form.

b $\frac{2}{x^3 - x} = \frac{2}{x(x-1)(x+1)}$

You will first work with the fraction from part a. If you want to use partial fractions, you must factorise the denominator, using the difference of two squares.

$\frac{2}{x(x-1)(x+1)} = \frac{A}{x} + \frac{B}{x-1} + \frac{C}{x+1}$

You need to use the form suggested in Key point 5.3.

$2 = A(x-1)(x+1) + Bx(x+1) + Cx(x-1)$

Multiply by the denominator to eliminate fractions.

When $x = 0$:

$2 = A \times -1 \times 1 + B \times 0 + C \times 0$

$A = -2$

Try to find values of x that make lots of the brackets equal to zero.

Continues on next page ...

When $x = 1$:

$2 = A \times 0 + B \times 1 \times 2 + C \times 0$

$B = 1$

When $x = -1$:

$2 = A \times 0 + B \times 0 + C \times -1 \times -2$

$C = 1$

Therefore

$$\frac{2}{x(x-1)(x+1)} = -\frac{2}{x} + \frac{1}{x-1} + \frac{1}{x+1}$$

So $\frac{x^4 - x^2 + 2}{x^3 - x} = x - \frac{2}{x} + \frac{1}{x-1} + \frac{1}{x+1}$

EXERCISE 5C

1 Write the following expressions in terms of partial fractions.

a **i** $\frac{2x+2}{x(x+2)}$ **ii** $\frac{3}{x(x-3)}$

b **i** $\frac{3x+4}{(x+1)(x+2)}$ **ii** $\frac{5x+1}{(x-1)(x+2)}$

c **i** $\frac{10-x}{x^2+x-12}$ **ii** $\frac{27-x}{x^2+x-30}$

2 Write the following expressions in terms of partial fractions.

a **i** $\frac{6-4x}{x(x-3)(x-2)}$ **ii** $\frac{3x+4}{x(x+1)(x+2)}$

b **i** $\frac{13x+17}{(x-1)(x+1)(x+2)}$ **ii** $\frac{19x+55}{(x-3)(x+4)(x+1)}$

3 Given that $\frac{A}{2x+5} + \frac{B}{5x+2} = \frac{1}{(2x+5)(5x+2)}$, find the values of A and B.

4 Express $\frac{1}{4x^2-1}$ in terms of partial fractions.

5 Simplify $\frac{3x+2}{x^3+3x^2+2x}$.

6 Decompose $\frac{2}{27x^3-3x}$ into partial fractions.

7 Write $\frac{1}{x^4-5x^2+4}$ in partial fractions.

8 **a** Show that $\frac{x^2-3x+5}{x-1} = x - 2 + \frac{3}{x-1}$.

b Hence, write $\frac{x^2-3x+5}{(x-1)(x-2)}$ in terms of partial fractions.

9 Write in partial fractions $\frac{a}{x(x-a)}$, where a is a constant.

10 Write in partial fractions $\frac{2x-3a}{x^2-3ax+2a^2}$, where a is a constant.

11 a Show that $\frac{x^2+7x+7}{x^2+7x+6}$ can be written in the form $1+\frac{R}{x^2+7x+6}$, where R is a constant to be determined.

b Hence, write $\frac{x^2+7x+7}{x^2+7x+6}$ in terms of partial fractions.

12 Check what happens if you try to write $\frac{x^2}{(x-1)(x-2)}$ in the form $\frac{A}{x-1}+\frac{B}{x-2}$.

Section 4: Partial fractions with a repeated factor

If there is a repeated factor in the denominator, you need to use an alternative expression for the partial fractions.

Key point 5.4

$\frac{mx+n}{(x+p)(x+q)^2}$ decomposes into $\frac{A}{x+p}+\frac{B}{x+q}+\frac{C}{(x+q)^2}$.

WORKED EXAMPLE 5.7

Express $\frac{3x+5}{(x+1)^2(x+2)}$ as partial fractions.

$\frac{3x+5}{(x+1)^2(x+2)}=\frac{A}{x+1}+\frac{B}{(x+1)^2}+\frac{C}{x+2}$

Write out the expression using the form given in Key point 5.4.

$3x+5=A(x+1)(x+2)+B(x+2)+C(x+1)^2$

Multiply both sides by $(x+1)^2(x+2)$ to eliminate fractions.

When $x=-1$:

$2=A\times 0+B\times 1+C\times 0$

$B=2$

You can choose convenient values for x. When $x=-1$ the coefficient of A and C is zero, so you can find out about A.

When $x=-2$:

$-1=A\times 0+B\times 0+C\times(-1)^2$

$C=-1$

When $x=-2$ the coefficient of A and B is zero, so you can find out about C.

When $x=0$:

$5=2A+2B+C$

There is no value of x that can make the coefficients of B and C zero, so you have to choose another simple alternative. In such a case, $x=0$ often makes the arithmetic simple.

$5=2A+4-1$

$A=1$

You can substitute the values of B and C found previously.

So

$\frac{3x+5}{(x+1)^2(x+2)}=\frac{1}{x+1}+\frac{2}{(x+1)^2}-\frac{1}{x+2}$

EXERCISE 5D

1 Express the following in terms of partial fractions.

a **i** $\dfrac{x}{(x+1)^2}$ **ii** $\dfrac{x}{(x-2)^2}$

b **i** $\dfrac{16}{x^2(x+4)}$ **ii** $\dfrac{1}{x^2(x-1)}$

c **i** $\dfrac{9x+9}{(x-1)(x+2)^2}$ **ii** $\dfrac{9x}{(x+1)(x-2)^2}$

2 Split $\dfrac{4}{x^2(x-2)}$ into partial fractions.

3 Express $\dfrac{5x+1}{x^3+x^2}$ as partial fractions.

4 Write $\dfrac{1}{(x^2-4)(x-2)}$ in terms of partial fractions.

5 **a** Use the factor theorem to show that $2x-1$ is a factor of $2x^3+3x^2-1$.

b Hence, factorise $2x^3+3x^2-1$.

c Write $\dfrac{9x}{2x^3+3x^2-1}$ in partial fractions.

6 **a** Write $\dfrac{x^4+5x^3+6x^2+2}{x^3+3x^2}$ in the form $Ax+B+\dfrac{C}{x^3+3x^2}$.

b Hence, write $\dfrac{x^4+5x^3+6x^2+2}{x^3+3x^2}$ in partial fractions.

7 **a** Prove that if a function can be written as $\dfrac{A}{x-p}+\dfrac{B}{(x-p)^2}$, it can also be written as $\dfrac{Cx+D}{(x-p)^2}$.

b Write $\dfrac{1}{(x-1)(x-2)^2}$ in the form $\dfrac{A}{x-1}+\dfrac{Bx+C}{(x-2)^2}$.

8 Write $\dfrac{x(a+1)-a^2}{x(x-a)^2}$ in terms of partial fractions.

Elevate

See Support sheet 5 for a further example of partial fractions with a repeated factor and for more practice questions.

Checklist of learning and understanding

- A rational function is a fraction where both the denominator and numerator are polynomials. In arithmetic they follow all the same rules as normal fractions.
- If the degree of the numerator is equal or greater than the degree of the denominator, you can use polynomial division to simplify the function:

$$\frac{P(x)}{ax+b} \equiv Q(x)+\frac{r}{ax+b}$$

  Here, $Q(x)$ is called the quotient and r the remainder.

- If the rational function has a numerator with a degree less than the denominator, it can be decomposed into partial fractions:

$$\frac{mx+n}{(x+p)(x+q)} \text{ decomposes into } \frac{A}{x+p}+\frac{B}{x+q}.$$

$$\frac{mx+n}{(x+p)(x+q)(x+r)} \text{ decomposes into } \frac{A}{x+p}+\frac{B}{x+q}+\frac{C}{x+r}.$$

$$\frac{mx+n}{(x+p)(x+q)^2} \text{ decomposes into } \frac{A}{x+p}+\frac{B}{x+q}+\frac{C}{(x+q)^2}.$$

Mixed practice 5

1 **a** Use polynomial division to simplify $\dfrac{x^3+1}{x+1}$.

b Hence, find the prime factors of 1001.

2 **a** Show that $2x + 3$ is a factor of $6x^3 + 27x^2 + 3x - 36$.

b Factorise $6x^3 + 27x^2 + 3x - 36$.

c Solve $6x^3 + 27x^2 + 3x - 36 = 0$.

d Simplify $\dfrac{6x^3+27x^2+3x-36}{4x^2+22x+24}$.

3 Write $\dfrac{5}{x^2-x-6}$ in partial fractions.

4 Express $\dfrac{9x-9}{x^3-9x}$ in partial fractions.

5 Write $\dfrac{x}{18x^2-8}$ in terms of partial fractions.

6 Write $\dfrac{1}{x(x+2)^2}$ in partial fractions.

7 Find the derivative of $\dfrac{6x^3+13x^2+27x+14}{3x+2}$.

Rewind

Differentiation is covered in Student Book 1, Chapter 13.

8 Decompose $\dfrac{20}{x^2-10}$ into partial fractions.

9 It is given that

$$\mathrm{f}(x) \neq \frac{x^2+2x-24}{x^2-4x} \text{ for } x \neq 0,\ x \neq 4.$$

Express $\mathrm{f}(x)$ in its simplest form.

10 Express $\dfrac{x^2}{(x-1)^2(x-2)}$ in partial fractions.

11 **a** Simplify $\mathrm{f}(x) = \dfrac{3x+3}{6x^2+13x+6} \times \dfrac{3x+2}{x^2+3x+2}$.

b Hence, write $\mathrm{f}(x)$ in terms of partial fractions.

12 **a** Use the factor theorem to show that $3x + 1$ is a factor of $9x^3 - 3x^2 - 5x - 1$.

b Hence, factorise $9x^3 - 3x^2 - 5x - 1$.

c Solve $9x^3 - 3x^2 - 5x = 1$.

d Write $\dfrac{4x+4}{9x^3-3x^2-5x-1}$ in partial fractions.

13 **a** Show that $2x+1$ is a factor of $\mathrm{f}(x) = 4x^3+4x^2-x-1$.

b Solve $\mathrm{f}(x) = 0$.

c Write $\dfrac{4x+1}{4x^3+4x^2-x-1}$ in partial fractions.

14 **a** Write $f(x) = \dfrac{2x^3 + 11x^2 + 20x + 13}{x^2 + 5x + 6}$ in the form $Ax + B + \dfrac{Cx + D}{x^2 + 5x + 6}$.

b Hence, write f(x) in partial fractions.

15 Find the quotient and remainder when $3x^3 + 5x - 9$ is divided by $3x - 1$.

16 **a** $f(x) = 6x^4 + 35x^3 + 62x^2 + ax + b$ is divisible by $2x + 1$ and by $x + 2$. Find the values of a and b.

b Fully factorise f(x).

c Solve f(x) = 0.

17 **a** Write $\dfrac{4}{(x+1)(x+5)}$ in terms of partial fractions.

b Hence, write $\dfrac{16}{(x+1)^2(x+5)^2}$ in terms of partial fractions.

18 **a** Use polynomial division to simplify $\dfrac{u+4}{u-4}$.

b Hence, or otherwise, write $\dfrac{x^2+4}{x^2-4}$ in partial fractions.

19 Write $\dfrac{3x^2 - a^2}{x^2(x-a)}$ in terms of partial fractions.

20 $\dfrac{2x^2 + 3x + k}{2x - 1}$ can be written as $Ax + B + \dfrac{5}{2x-1}$. Find the value of A, B and k.

21 The remainder when $x^2 + 5ax + b$ is divided by $x - a$ is $4a^2$. Write b in terms of a.

22 The remainder when a polynomial, f(x), is divided by $x - 1$ is the same as the quotient. Find the value of f(0).

23 Given that $\dfrac{A}{x+a} + \dfrac{B}{x+b} + \dfrac{C}{x+c} = \dfrac{f(x)}{(x+a)(x+b)(x+c)}$, prove that if f($x$) is linear, then $A + B + C = 0$.

24 If two resistors with resistance R_1 and R_2 are connected in parallel, the combined system has resistance R_T. These are related by the equation $\dfrac{1}{R_T} = \dfrac{1}{R_1} + \dfrac{1}{R_2}$.

a Find and simplify an expression for R_T in terms of R_1 and R_2.

b Hence, prove that $R_T < R_1$.

Elevate

See Extension sheet 5 for questions on continued fractions.

6 General binomial expansion

In this chapter you will learn how to:

- expand $(a + bx)^n$, where n is any rational power
- decide when a binomial expansion will converge
- use partial fractions to write expressions in the form required for the binomial expansion
- use binomial expansions to approximate functions.

Before you start…

GCSE	You should be able to simplify expressions with exponents.	1 Simplify $\left(8x^6\right)^{\frac{1}{3}}$.
Student Book 1, Chapter 9	You should be able to use binomial expansions for positive integer powers.	2 Expand $(3 - 2x)^4$.
Chapter 5	You should be able to write an expression in partial fractions.	3 Write $\dfrac{4-x}{x(x-2)}$ in the form $\dfrac{A}{x-2}+\dfrac{B}{x}$.
Chapter 3	You should be able to write inequalities using the modulus function.	4 Write $\lvert x-2\rvert < 3$ in the form $a < x < b$.

Extending the binomial theorem

In Student Book 1 the binomial expansion was simply a quick way to expand brackets. You will see in this chapter that it can be extended to allow us to approximate many other functions by polynomials.

Section 1: General binomial expansion

In Student Book 1 you met the binomial expansion when raising a sum to a positive integer power. For example:

$$(1+x)^n = \binom{n}{0} + \binom{n}{1}x + \binom{n}{2}x^2 + \binom{n}{3}x^3 + \ldots + \binom{n}{n}x^n$$

The binomial coefficients can be expanded:

$$\binom{n}{0} = 1, \quad \binom{n}{1} = n, \quad \binom{n}{2} = \frac{n(n-1)}{2!}, \quad \binom{n}{3} = \frac{n(n-1)(n-2)}{3!}$$

Although difficult to prove, it turns out that this formula also works for any rational power n.

Tip

Remember that  $\binom{n}{r}$ is another way of writing ${}^nC_r$.

Key point 6.1

If $|x| < 1$:

$$(1+x)^n \equiv 1 + nx + \frac{n(n-1)}{2!}x^2 + \frac{n(n-1)(n-2)}{3!}x^3 + \ldots, \text{ for any rational value of } n.$$

This formula will appear in your formula book.

Notice that if n is not a positive whole number, this is an infinite series.

You can always create the series on the right–hand side but it will only converge if $|x| < 1$. If the expression in the bracket on the left is different, for example $(1 + 3x)$, then the interval of convergence might be different, in this case $|3x| < 1$ or $|x| < \frac{1}{3}$.

Rewind

The idea of a convergent series was covered in Chapter 4.

WORKED EXAMPLE 6.1

Find the first four terms in ascending powers of y in the binomial expansion of $\frac{1}{1-y}$ if $-1 < y < 1$.

$$\frac{1}{1-y} = (1-y)^{-1}$$

You need to rewrite the fraction in the form $(1 + x)^n$.

$$= 1 + (-1)(-y) + \frac{(-1)(-1-1)}{2}(-y)^2 + \frac{(-1)(-1-1)(-1-2)}{6}(-y)^3 + \ldots$$

Susbstitute $n = -1$ and $x = -y$ into the formula presented in Key point 6.1.

$$= 1 + y + y^2 + y^3 + \ldots$$

The formula in Key point 6.1 only works if the first number in the bracket is 1. If it is something else, then you have to factorise the expression to turn the first number into 1. The interval over which the expansion converges might also then change.

Tip

Saying that 'the expansion is valid' is the same as saying that it converges.

WORKED EXAMPLE 6.2

a Find the first three terms in ascending powers of y in the binomial expansion of $\sqrt{4+y}$.

b Find the values of y for which this expansion is valid.

a $\sqrt{4+y} = (4+y)^{\frac{1}{2}}$

You need to rewrite the square root as a power.

$$= \left(4\left(1+\frac{y}{4}\right)\right)^{\frac{1}{2}}$$

Take out a factor of 4 inside the bracket to leave $(1 + \ldots)^n$.

$$= 4^{\frac{1}{2}}\left(1+\frac{y}{4}\right)^{\frac{1}{2}}$$

Use the rules of exponents to separate out the numerical factor.

Continues on next page ...

$$=2\left(1+\left(\frac{1}{2}\right)\left(\frac{y}{4}\right)+\frac{\frac{1}{2}\left(\frac{1}{2}-1\right)}{2}\left(\frac{y}{4}\right)^2+\ldots\right)$$

Substitute $n=\frac{1}{2}$ and $x=\frac{y}{4}$ into the formula presented in Key point 6.1.

$$=2\left(1+\frac{y}{8}-\frac{1}{128}y^2+\ldots\right)$$

$$=2+\frac{y}{4}-\frac{1}{64}y^2+\ldots$$

Finally, multiply out the bracket.

b $\left|\frac{y}{4}\right|<1$

The expansion is valid when $|x|<1$, and you have used $x=\frac{y}{4}$.

$|y|<4$

Multiplying through by 4.
You could also write $-4<y<4$.

You can generalise the method from Worked Example 6.2 to find the binomial expansion of any expression of the form $(a+bx)^n$.

Key point 6.2

The binomial expansion of $(a+bx)^n=a^n\left(1+\frac{bx}{a}\right)^n$ is valid for $\left|\frac{bx}{a}\right|<1$.

Binomial expansions such as these produce infinite series, so you might wonder how they can be useful. If x is small then very large powers of x are extremely small, so they can be neglected. You can use the first few terms of the binomial expansion to *approximate* the original expression.

WORKED EXAMPLE 6.3

Use the first two terms of the binomial expansion of $(9+4x)^{0.5}$ to approximate $\sqrt{9.4}$, to 3 decimal places.

a $\sqrt{9+4x}=(9+4x)^{\frac{1}{2}}$

You need to rewrite the square root in the form $(a+x)^n$.

$$=\left(9\left(1+\frac{4x}{9}\right)\right)^{\frac{1}{2}}$$

Take out a factor of 9 inside the bracket to leave (1 + something).

$$=9^{\frac{1}{2}}\left(1+\frac{4x}{9}\right)^{\frac{1}{2}}$$

Use the rules of exponents to separate out the numerical factor.

$$=3\left(1+\left(\frac{1}{2}\right)\left(\frac{4x}{9}\right)+\ldots\right)$$

Substitute $n=\frac{1}{2}$ and 'x' $=\frac{4x}{9}$ into the formula presented in Key point 6.1.

$$=3\left(1+\frac{2}{9}x+\ldots\right)$$

$$=3+\frac{2x}{3}+\ldots$$

Multiply out the bracket.

Continues on next page ...

b You need x such that $\sqrt{9+4x}=\sqrt{9.4}$.

Find the value of x that will give $\sqrt{9.4}$.

$$9+4x=9.4$$
$$4x=0.4$$
$$x=0.1$$

$$\therefore \sqrt{9.4}=3+\frac{2\times 0.1}{3}+\ldots$$
$$\approx 3.066$$

Substitute $x=0.1$ into $\sqrt{9+4x}=3+\frac{2x}{3}+\ldots$.
The terms after the second term will be so small that they won't affect the first 3 decimal places. (You can check that the next term is 0.0000823.)

Did you know?

Calculators use a method similar to binomial expansion, called Taylor series, to find values of functions such as $\sin x$ or $\tan^{-1} x$.

You can also use the approximate binomial expression in solving equations, differentiation or integration.

WORKED EXAMPLE 6.4

a Find the first three non-zero terms in the binomial expansion of $\frac{1}{4+x^2}$ and state the range of values for which the expansion is valid.
b Use your expansion to find an approximate value of $\int_0^1 \frac{1}{4+x^2}\,dx$.

a
$$\frac{1}{4+x^2}=(4+x^2)^{-1}$$

You need to write the expression in the form $(a+y)^n$ and then take out a factor of 4.

$$=4^{-1}\left(1+\frac{x^2}{4}\right)^{-1}$$

$$=\frac{1}{4}\left(1+(-1)\left(\frac{x^2}{4}\right)+\frac{(-1)(-2)}{2}\left(\frac{x^2}{4}\right)^2+\ldots\right)$$

Substitute $n=-1$ and 'x' $=\frac{x^2}{4}$ into Key Point 6.1.

$$=\frac{1}{4}\left(1-\frac{x^2}{4}+\frac{x^4}{16}+\ldots\right)$$

Expand all brackets and simplify.

$$=\frac{1}{4}-\frac{1}{6}x^2+\frac{1}{64}x^4+\ldots$$

The expansion is valid when $\left|\frac{x^2}{4}\right|<1\Leftrightarrow |x|<2$

You used $\frac{x^2}{4}$ in place of 'x'.

b
$$\int_0^1 \frac{1}{x^2+4}\,dx\approx\int_0^1 \frac{1}{4}-\frac{1}{6}x^2+\frac{1}{64}x^4\,dx$$
$$=\left[\frac{1}{4}x-\frac{1}{18}x^3+\frac{1}{320}x^5\right]_0^1$$
$$\approx 0.198\ (3\text{ s.f.})$$

Replace the expression you want to integrate by its approximate expansion. Note that you can do this only when the expansion is valid within the limits of integration.

Fast forward

If you study Further Mathematics, in Pure Core Student Book 2, you will learn how to integrate this function exactly. The actual value of the integral in Worked Example 6.4 is 0.232 (3 s.f.).

EXERCISE 6A

1 Find the first three terms of the binomial expansion of each of the following expressions, stating the range of convergence.

a **i** $(1+x)^{-2}$ **ii** $(1+x)^{-3}$ **b** **i** $(1+x)^{\frac{1}{3}}$ **ii** $(1+x)^{\frac{1}{4}}$

c **i** $\sqrt{1-2x}$ **ii** $\sqrt{1-3x}$ **d** **i** $\dfrac{1}{4-x}$ **ii** $\dfrac{1}{5-x}$

2 Find the expansion of $\dfrac{1}{\left(1-\frac{1}{3}x\right)^3}$ in ascending powers of x, up to and including the term in x^2.

3 Find the expansion of $\dfrac{1}{\sqrt[3]{8+x}}$ in ascending powers of x, up to and including the term in x^3.

4 **a** Find the first three terms in the expansion of $\dfrac{1}{(4x^2+4x+1)}$.

b Find the values of x over which this expansion is valid.

5 **a** Use the binomial expansion to show that

$$\sqrt{1+\frac{x}{9}}=1+\frac{x}{18}-\frac{x^2}{648}+\ldots$$

b State the range of values for which this expansion converges.

c Deduce the first three terms of the binomial expansion of:

i $\sqrt{1-\dfrac{x}{9}}$ **ii** $\sqrt{1+\left(\dfrac{x}{3}\right)^2}$ **iii** $\sqrt{9+x}$

d Use the first three terms of the expansion to find an approximation for $\sqrt{10}$, to 4 decimal places.

6 **a** Find the first four terms of $\sqrt{1-4x}$ in ascending powers of x.

b State the range of values for which this expansion is valid.

c Hence, approximate $\sqrt{96}$, to 5 decimal places.

d Hence, approximate $\sqrt{6}$, to 4 decimal places.

7 The cubic term in the expansion of $(1+ax)^{-2}$ is $-256x^3$. Find the value of a.

8 **a** Find the first three non-zero terms of the binomial expansion of $\sqrt[3]{8+x^2}$ and state the range of values of x for which the expansion is valid.

b Use your expansion to find an approximate value of $\int_{-1}^{1}\sqrt[3]{8+x^2}\,dx$.

Elevate

See Support sheet 6 for a further example of an expansion when the constant term isn't 1, and for more practice questions.

9 **a** Find the first three non-zero terms, in ascending powers of x, in the binomial expansion of $\frac{1}{81+x^4}$

Consider the definite integrals $I=\int_{-1}^{2}\frac{1}{81+x^4}\mathrm{d}x$ and $J=\int_{0}^{4}\frac{1}{81+x^4}\mathrm{d}x$.

b The expansion from part **a** can be used to find and approximate value of only one of those integrals. State, with a reason, which one it is and find its approximate value.

10 Given that the expansion of $(1+ax)^n$ is $1-12x+90x^2+bx^3+\ldots$, find the value of b.

11 Given that the expansion of $(1+ax)^n$ is $1-x-\frac{x^2}{2}+bx^3+\ldots$, find the value of b.

12 Assume that $\sqrt{1+x}=a_0+a_1x+a_2x^2+\ldots$.

By squaring both sides and comparing coefficients, find the values of a_0, a_1 and a_2. Does this agree with the binomial expansion of $\sqrt{1+x}$?

Section 2: Binomial expansions of compound expressions

Binomial expansions can be part of a larger expression.

WORKED EXAMPLE 6.5

Find the quadratic term in the binomial expansion of $\sqrt{\frac{1+x}{1-x}}$ if $|x|<1$.

$$\sqrt{\frac{1+x}{1-x}}=(1+x)^{\frac{1}{2}}(1-x)^{-\frac{1}{2}}$$

Use the laws of indices to create expressions of the form $(1+x)^n$.

$$=\left(1+\frac{1}{2}x+\frac{\left(\frac{1}{2}\right)\left(\frac{1}{2}-1\right)}{2}x^2+\ldots\right)\left(1+\left(-\frac{1}{2}\right)(-x)+\frac{\left(-\frac{1}{2}\right)\left(-\frac{1}{2}-1\right)}{2}(-x)^2+\ldots\right)$$

Expand both brackets, identifying $n=\frac{1}{2}$, 'x' $=x$ for the first bracket and $n=-\frac{1}{2}$, 'x' $=-x$ for the second.

$$=\left(1+\frac{1}{2}x-\frac{1}{8}x^2+\ldots\right)\left(1+\frac{1}{2}x+\frac{3}{8}x^2+\ldots\right)$$

It is worth tidying up the expressions before you continue.

Quadratic term:

$$1\times\frac{3}{8}x^2+\frac{1}{2}x\times\frac{1}{2}x+-\frac{1}{8}x^2\times 1$$
$$=\frac{3}{8}x^2+\frac{1}{4}x^2-\frac{1}{8}x^2$$
$$=\frac{1}{2}x^2$$

You only need terms that result in x^2. You can get this from the constant in the first bracket multiplied by the quadratic in the second, the two linear terms multiplied together or the quadratic in the first bracket multiplied by the constant in the second bracket.

Sometimes you have to use partial fractions to write an expression in a form where binomial expansion is possible.

Rewind

Partial fractions were covered in Chapter 5.

WORKED EXAMPLE 6.6

a Find the first two terms in the expansion of $\frac{12x+5}{(2x+1)(3x+1)}$.

b State the range of values for which this expansion converges.

a $\frac{12x+5}{(2x+1)(3x+1)} \equiv \frac{A}{2x+1} + \frac{B}{3x+1}$

You can write the expression using the standard partial fraction decomposition.

$12x+5 \equiv A(3x+1)+B(2x+1)$

Substituting $x = -\frac{1}{2}$:

$-1 = -\frac{1}{2}A$

So $A = 2$.

Substituting $x = -\frac{1}{3}$:

$1 = \frac{1}{3}B$

So $B = 3$.

Therefore

$\frac{12x+5}{(2x+1)(3x+1)} \equiv \frac{2}{2x+1} + \frac{3}{3x+1}$

The first term is

$2\times(1+2x)^{-1} = 2(1+(-1)(2x)+\ldots)$

$= 2-4x+\ldots$

Write the first term in the required form and identify $n=-1$ and 'x' $= 2x$.

The second term is

$3\times(1+3x)^{-1} = 3(1+(-1)(3x)+\ldots)$

$= 3-9x+\ldots$

Write the second term in the required form and identify $n=-1$ and 'x' $= 3x$.

So $\frac{12x+5}{(2x+1)(3x+1)} = 5-13x+\ldots$

Combine the two expansions together.

b The first expansion converges if $|2x| < 1$ so $|x| < \frac{1}{2}$.

Consider the range of convergence of each expansion separately.

The second expansion converges if $|3x| < 1$ so $|x| < \frac{1}{3}$.

Therefore, both will converge if $|x| < \frac{1}{3}$.

You need both inequalities to be satisfied.

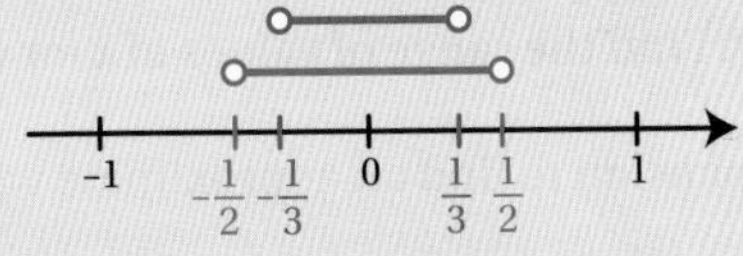

WORK IT OUT 6.1

Find the first three non–zero terms, in ascending powers of x, in the binomial expansion of $f(x)=\frac{1}{2+x}$.

Which of the following solutions is correct? Identify the mistake in the other two.

Solution 1	Solution 2	Solution 3
Set $u=1+x$. Then you need the expansion of $\frac{1}{1+u}=(1+u)^{-1}$. The expansion is $1+(-1)(u)+\frac{(-1)(-1-1)}{2}(u)^2+\dots$ $=1-u+u^2+\dots$ Substituting back for x: $f(x)=1-(1+x)+(1+x)^2+\dots$ $=1-1-x+1+2x+x^2+\dots$ $=1+x+x^2+\dots$	$f(x)=(2+x)^{-1}$ $=\left(2\left(1+\frac{x}{2}\right)\right)^{-1}=\frac{1}{2}\left(1+\frac{x}{2}\right)^{-1}$ $=\frac{1}{2}\left(1+(-1)\left(\frac{x}{2}\right)+\frac{(-1)(-2)}{2}\left(\frac{x}{2}\right)^2+\dots\right)$ $=\frac{1}{2}\left(1-\frac{x}{2}+\frac{x^2}{4}\right)+\dots$ $=\frac{1}{2}-\frac{x}{4}+\frac{x^2}{8}+\dots$	$f(x)=2\left(1+\frac{x}{2}\right)^{-1}$ $=2\left(1-\frac{x}{2}+\frac{(-1)(-2)}{2}\frac{x^2}{2}+\dots\right)$ $=2-x+x^2+\dots$

EXERCISE 6B

1. Find the first three terms, in ascending powers of x, in the expansion of $x(1-x)^{-2}$ for $|x|<1$.
2. Find the first three terms of the expansion of $\sqrt{x^2+2x^3}$ in ascending powers of x, stating the range over which the expansion converges.
3. Find the first three terms in the expansion of $\frac{1+x}{1-x}$.
4. Find the first three terms in the expansion of $\left(\frac{1+x}{1+2x}\right)^2$.
5. a Decompose $\frac{3x+2}{(x+1)(2x+1)}$ into partial fractions.

   b Hence, find the first three terms in the binomial expansion of $\frac{3x+2}{(x+1)(2x+1)}$.

   c Write down the set of values for which this expansion is valid.
6. a Express $\frac{5x+8}{(2-x)(x+1)^2}$ as partial fractions.

   b Find the first three terms, in ascending powers of x, in the binomial expansion of $\frac{5x+8}{(2-x)(x+1)^2}$.

   c Find the values of x for which this expansion converges.
7. Find the first three terms of the binomial expansion for $\frac{1}{(1+2x)(1+x)}$.
8. a Write $\frac{1}{(x-2)(x+1)^2}$ in partial fractions.

   b Find the first three non-zero terms, in ascending powers of x, in the binomial expansion of $\frac{1}{(x-2)(x+1)^2}$. Find the range of values of x for which the expansion converges.

   c Use your expansion to find an approximate value of $\int_0^{\frac{1}{2}} \frac{1}{(x-2)(x+1)^2}\,dx$.

9 **a** By first expressing it in partial fractions find the first two terms, in ascending powers of x, in the expansion of $\frac{64x-356}{(x-8)^2(x+5)}$.

b Let m be the largest integer for which the expansion from part **a** can be used to approximate the value of $\int_{-m}^{m} \frac{64x-356}{(x-8)^2(x+5)}\,dx$. State the value of m and find the approximate value of the integral in this case.

10 **a** Find the first two terms, in ascending powers of x, in the expansion of $\sqrt{\frac{1+5x}{1+12x}}$.

b Over what range of values is the expansion valid?

c By substituting $x = 0.01$, find an approximation to $\sqrt{15}$, to 2 decimal places.

11 The first three non–zero terms of the expansion of $(1-x)(1+ax)^n$ are $1+x^2+bx^3$. Find the value of b.

12 Is it possible to find a binomial expansion for $\sqrt{x-1}$?

Checklist of learning and understanding

- For any rational value of n, the binomial expansion $(1+x)^n \equiv 1+nx+\frac{n(n-1)}{2!}x^2+\frac{n(n-1)(n-2)}{3!}x^3+\ldots$ is valid for $|x| < 1$.
- To find the binomial expansion of $(a+bx)^n$, write it as $a^n\left(1+\frac{bx}{a}\right)^n$. This expansion is valid for $\left|\frac{bx}{a}\right|<1$.
- A rational function may need to be written in partial fractions before using the binomial expansion.
- You can use the first few terms of a binomial expansion to approximate the expression for small values of x.

Mixed practice 6

1. Find the first four terms, in ascending powers of x, in the expansion of $\frac{1}{(1-2x)^2}$, stating the range of x for which the expansion converges.

2. Find the first three non–zero terms, in ascending powers of x, in the expansion of $\frac{1}{\sqrt{4+x}}$, stating the range of x for which this is valid.

3. Find the first four terms in the expansion of $\frac{1}{1+2x+x^2}$.

4. Find the first three non–zero terms in ascending order in the expansion of $\sqrt{1-x}\sqrt{1+x}$.

5. **i** Expand $(1+x)^{\frac{1}{3}}$ in ascending powers of x, up to and including the term in x^2.

   ii a Hence, or otherwise, expand $(8+16x)^{\frac{1}{3}}$ in ascending powers of x, up to and including the term in x^2.

   b State the set of values of x for which the expansion in part **ii a** is valid.

   © OCR, GCE Mathematics, Paper 4724, January 2010

6. **a** Find the first three terms of the binomial expansion of $\sqrt[3]{8+x}$.

   b Hence, find an approximation for $\sqrt[3]{8100}$, to 2 decimal places, showing your reasoning.

7. **a** Write $\frac{3x+16}{(3-x)(x+2)^2}$ in partial fractions.

   b Hence, find the first three terms in the expansion of $\frac{3x+16}{(3-x)(x+2)^2}$.

   c Write down the set of x values for which this expansion is valid.

8. Find the first three terms in the binomial expansion of $\frac{1-x}{x^2-5x+6}$, stating the range of values for which it is valid.

9. The first three terms in the binomial expansion of $\frac{1}{(1+ax)^b}+\frac{1}{(1+bx)^a}$ are $2-6x+15x^2$. Find the values of a and b.

10. **i** Show that $\sqrt{\frac{1-x}{1+x}} \approx 1-x+\frac{1}{2}x^2$, for $|x|<1$.

    ii By taking $x=\frac{2}{7}$, show that $\sqrt{5} \approx \frac{111}{49}$.

    © OCR, GCE Mathematics, Paper 4724, June 2008

11. **a** Find the first three non–zero terms of the binomial expansion of $\sqrt[3]{\frac{1+2x}{1-x}}$.

    b By setting $x=0.4$, find an approximation for $\sqrt[3]{3}$, to 5 decimal places.

12. Given that the expansion of $(1+ax)^n$ is $1-9x+54x^2+bx^3$, find the value of b.

13. Find the first three terms of the expansion of $\frac{1}{1+x+x^2}$.

14. **a** $f(x)=\frac{x}{1+x}$ can be written in the form $Ax+Bx^2+Cx^3+\dots$. Find the values of A, B and C, and state the set of values of x for which this converges.

    b Show that f(x) can be written in the form $\frac{1}{1+\frac{1}{x}}$.

    c f(x) can be written in the form $P+\frac{Q}{x}+\frac{R}{x^2}+\dots$. Find the values of P, Q and R, and state the set of values of x for which this converges.

d Use an appropriate expansion to approximate $\frac{100}{101}$ to 4 decimal places, showing your reasoning.

e Use an appropriate expansion to approximate $\frac{1}{51}$ to 5 significant figures, showing your reasoning.

15 In special relativity the energy of an object with mass m and speed v is given by $E = \frac{mc^2}{\sqrt{1-\frac{v^2}{c^2}}}$, where $c \approx 3 \times 10^8\ \text{m s}^{-1}$ is the speed of light.

a Find the first three non–zero terms of the binomial expansion in increasing powers of v, stating the range over which it is valid.

Let E_2 be the expansion containing two terms and let E_3 be the expansion containing three terms.

b By what percentage is E_3 bigger than E_2 if v is:

i 10% of the speed of light?

ii 90% of the speed of light?

c Prove that $E > E_3 > E_2$.

Elevate

See Extension sheet 6 for a look at Babylonian multiplication.

FOCUS ON ... PROOF 1

Sums of series

Arithmetic series

You are going to demonstrate that, for an arithmetic series with first term a and common difference d, the sum of the first n terms is

$$S_n = \frac{n}{2}[2a+(n-1)d]$$

PROOF 2

Parts of this proof have been omitted. They are indicated by numbers in dark blue angled brackets. Work out what should be written there before turning to the answer.

$$S_n = \underbrace{a+[a+d]+\ldots+[a+(n-2)d]+[a+(n-1)d]}_{n \text{ terms}}$$

Write the first couple of terms of the series and the last couple of terms.

$$S_n = \underbrace{[<1>]+[<2>]+\ldots+[a+d]+a}_{n \text{ terms}}$$

Writing these terms in the opposite order has no effect on the outcome.

$$2S_n = \underbrace{[2a+(n-1)d]+[<3>]+\ldots+[<4>]}_{n \text{ terms}}$$

Adding the two expressions gives n identical terms.

$$2S_n = <5>(2a+(n-1)d)$$

Collect like terms.

$$S_n = \frac{n}{2}(2a+(n-1)d)$$

<6>

Did you know?

Carl Friedrich Gauss (1777–1855)

Carl Gauss was among the most eminent mathematicians of the 19th century. His many contributions to mathematics include great strides in number theory, statistics and physics. He was a child prodigy and there is a famous legend about a lesson where his teacher was hoping to keep him quiet by asking him to add together all the numbers from 1 to 100. The teacher was somewhat disappointed when he replied with the correct answer within seconds. It is believed that he applied a procedure similar to the one used in this proof.

Geometric series

You are going to demonstrate that for a geometric series with first term a and common ratio r, the sum of the first n terms is

$$S_n = \frac{a(1-r^n)}{1-r}$$

PROOF 3

Parts of this proof have been omitted. They are indicated by numbers in blue angled brackets. Work out what should be written there before turning to the answer.

$S_n = a + ar + ar^2 + \ldots + ar^{n-2} + ar^{n-1}$	Write the first few terms and the last few terms of the sum.
$rS_n = ar + ar^2 + ar^3 + \ldots + ar^{n-1} + ar^n$	<1>
$S_n - rS_n = <2> - <3>$	By subtracting you can remove all the terms in common between the two series.
$S_n(<4>) = a(<5>)$	Factorise both sides.
$S_n = \frac{a(1-r^n)}{1-r}$	Divide by $1 - r$.

Questions

1. This proof does not work when $r = 1$. At which stage does it break down? What is the formula for S_n when $r = 1$?

2. This proof appeals to the very important mathematical idea of self-similarity – looking to get similar structures in two different ways so that things cancel out. Use this idea to evaluate:

   a $\sqrt{1+\sqrt{1+\sqrt{1+\ldots}}}$

   b $\dfrac{1}{1+\dfrac{2}{1+\dfrac{2}{1+\ldots}}}$

Elevate

See Extension sheet 5 for more examples of continued fractions.

FOCUS ON ... PROBLEM SOLVING 1

Trying small cases

In this section you will look at solving problems about sequences, but the ideas apply in other contexts, too. In addition to thinking about trying small cases to spot patterns in sequences, you should also remember several other problem solving ideas. In particular:

- introduce letters to represent unknowns
- look for things that stay the same
- persevere.

WORKED EXAMPLE

The terms of a sequence of positive integers $u_1, u_2, u_3, \dots$ follow the rule $u_n = \frac{1+u_{n-1}}{u_{n-2}}$ for $n \geqslant 3$. Find $u_{2020} - u_{2000}$.

Let $u_1 = a$ and $u_2 = b$.

Then

$$u_3 = \frac{1+b}{a}$$

First thoughts are that 2020 is a very large number and you should avoid simply working out all the numbers on the way up to it. Also you are not told what the first few terms are, so maybe it doesn't matter. You'll need to give them names to work with them though.

$$u_4 = \frac{1+\left(\frac{1+b}{a}\right)}{b} = \frac{a+1+b}{ab}$$

Let's keep working out some more cases and hope you see something useful! It's worth simplifying these expressions to help anything useful stand out.

$$u_5 = \frac{1+\left(\frac{a+1+b}{ab}\right)}{\frac{1+b}{a}} = \frac{ab+a+b+1}{ab} \times \frac{a}{1+b} = \frac{(a+1)(b+1)}{ab} \times \frac{a}{1+b} = \frac{(a+1)}{b}$$

Persevere...

$$u_6 = \frac{1+\left(\frac{a+1}{b}\right)}{\frac{a+1+b}{ab}} = \frac{b+a+1}{b} \times \frac{ab}{a+1+b} = a$$

The algebra gets messy, but it works out quite nicely in the end!

$$u_7 = \frac{1+a}{\left(\frac{a+1}{b}\right)} = (1+a) \times \frac{b}{a+1} = b$$

This is nice - you've got back to a followed by b.

Continues on next page ...

Importantly,

$u_{2000} = u_{2005} = u_{2010} = u_{2015} = u_{2020}$

So $u_{2020} - u_{2000} = 0$

Since $u_1 = u_6$ and $u_2 = u_7$ and the sequence depends only on the previous two terms, it will continue to repeat every five terms.

Questions

1. The sequence of integers $u_0, u_1, u_2, \ldots$ satisfies $u_0 = 1$ and $u_{n+1} = \frac{ku_n}{u_{n-1}}$ for $n \geqslant 1$, where k is a positive constant. Given that $u_{2024} = 2025$, find the value of k.
2. Find a formula for the sum of the first n odd numbers.
3. An expression for the sum of the first n terms of an arithmetic sequence is given by $S_n = n^2 + 6n$. Find an expression for the nth term of the sequence.
4. Rebecca can walk upstairs one at a time or two at a time. For example, to go up 5 stairs she might go 1, 2, 1, 1 or 2, 1, 2.

   Her house has stairs with 10 steps. How many different ways can she go up the stairs?

Modelling with rational functions

You are already familiar with exponential models, where the rate of change of a quantity is proportional to the quantity itself. In Student Book 1 you used them to model situations like chemical reactions, population growth and cooling of a liquid. Here are some graphs resulting from exponential models.

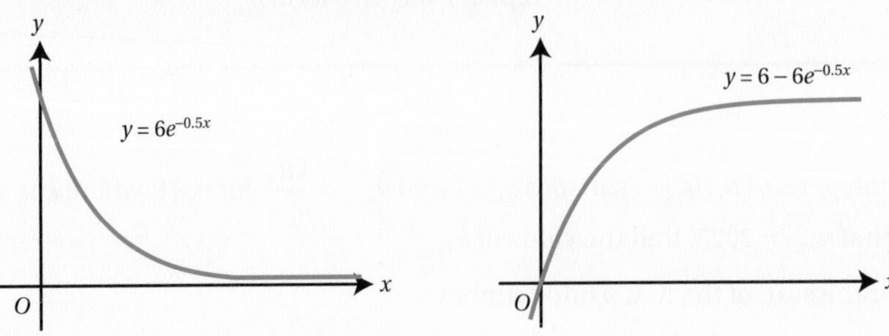

But exponential equations are not the only ones that result in graphs of this shape. Here are the graphs of some rational functions:

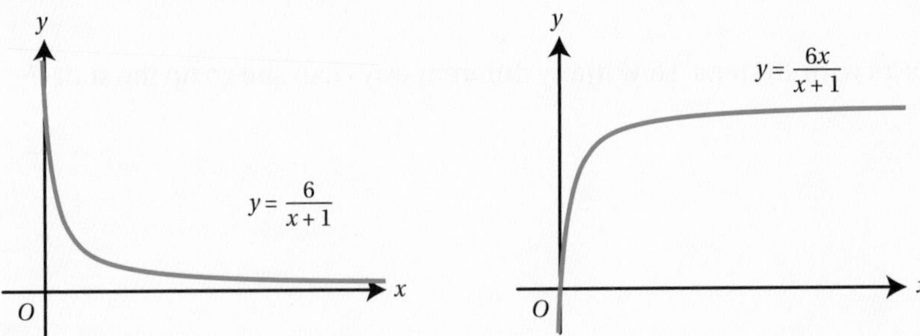

Notice that for a simple rational function, the rate of change is proportional to the *square* of its value. For example, if $y = \frac{3}{x}$ then $\frac{dy}{dx} = -\frac{3}{x^2} = -\frac{1}{3}y^2$.

In this section you will meet an example of a model using a rational function and then learn a technique that allows you decide whether an exponential or a rational model is a better fit for given data.

Questions

1 In biochemistry, the Michaelis–Menten model for the rate of enzymatic reaction relates the reaction rate, v, to the concentration of the substrate, S:

$$v = \frac{v_0 S}{k + S}$$

In this formula v_0 and k are constants which depend on the substances involved in the reaction.

a Given that $k = 8000$ and $v_0 = 0.6$ (in suitable units):

i Find the rate of reaction when the concentration is 10 000.

ii Find the concentration for which the rate of reaction is 0.3.

iii Sketch the graph of v against S.

b What does v_0 represent?

In Student Book 1, Chapter 8, you learnt a method for determining the parameters in an exponential model by using logarithms to turn it into an equation of a straight line: If $y = Ae^{kx}$, then $\ln y = kx + \ln A$.

You can use a similar idea for a rational function of the form like the Michaelis–Menten model. If $y = \frac{bx}{x+c}$ then:

$$\frac{1}{y} = \frac{x+c}{bx} = \frac{1}{b} + \frac{c}{b}\frac{1}{x}$$

Hence, the graph of $\frac{1}{y}$ against $\frac{1}{x}$ is a straight line, with gradient $\frac{c}{b}$ and vertical axis intercept $\frac{1}{b}$.

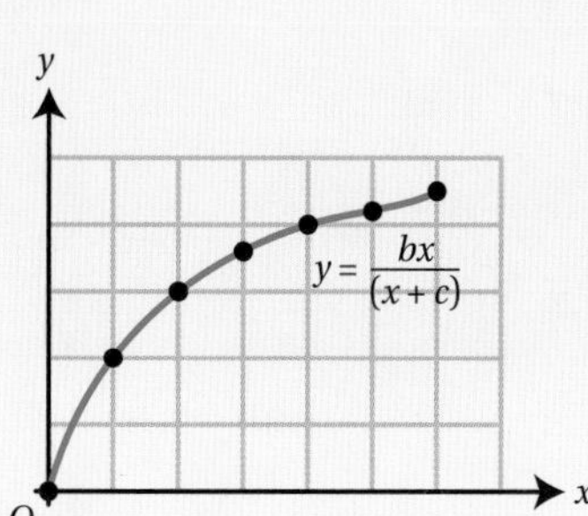

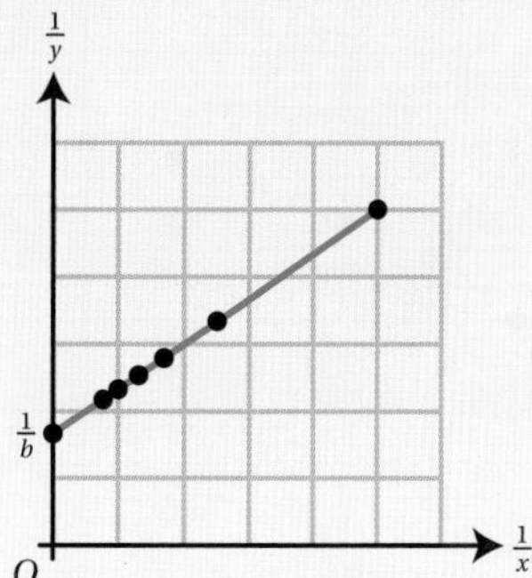

2 The data in the table can be modelled by the equation of the form $y = \frac{bx}{x+c}$.

x	y
0	0.0
1	1.0
2	1.3
3	1.5
4	1.6
5	1.7

Draw the graph of $\frac{1}{y}$ against $\frac{1}{x}$. Hence, determine the values of the constants b and c.

The technique of transforming a graph into a straight line can also be used to decide whether a rational or an exponential function is a better model for a set of data.

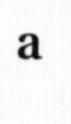 Each graph shows a set of experimental data. Plot $\ln y$ against x, and $\frac{1}{y}$ against $\frac{1}{x}$. Hence, decide whether an exponential or a rational function is a better model for the data.

a

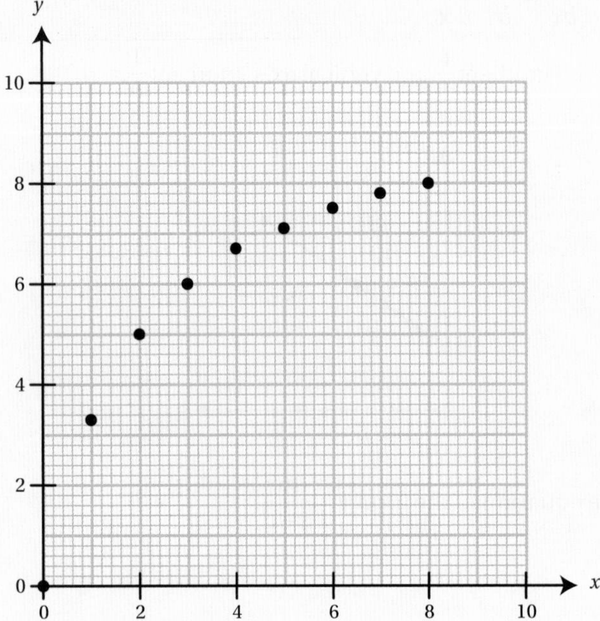

b Hint: consider $9 - y$.

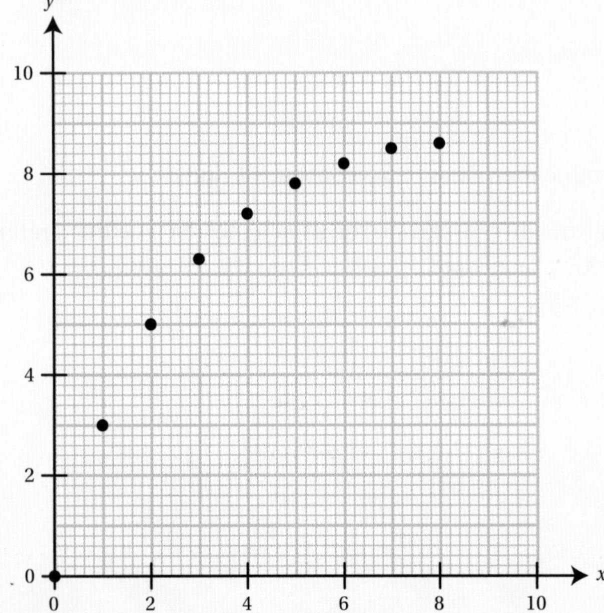

CROSS-TOPIC REVIEW EXERCISE 1

1 a Sketch the graph of $y = |9 - 3x|$.

b Solve the equation $|9 - 3x| = 6$.

c Solve the inequality $|9 - 3x| > 6$.

2 The sum of the first n terms of an arithmetic sequence is given by $S_n = 3n + 2n^2$. Find the common difference of the sequence.

3 If $f(x) = |x|$, sketch $f'(x)$ for $-2 \leqslant x \leqslant 2$, $x \neq 0$.

4 Find an expression for the mean value of the first n terms of a geometric series with first term a and common ratio r.

5 The function f is defined by $f(x) = (x-1)^2 + 3$, and the function g is defined by $g(x) = ax + b$, where a and b are constants. Given that $f(g(x)) = 16x^2 - 16x + 7$, find the possible values of a and the corresponding values of b.

6 The polynomial $f(x)$ is defined by $f(x) = 9x^3 - 19x + 10$.

a i Find $f(1)$.

ii Show that $(3x + 5)$ is a factor of $f(x)$.

b Simplify $\dfrac{12x^2 - 8x}{f(x)}$, giving your answer in a fully factorised form.

7

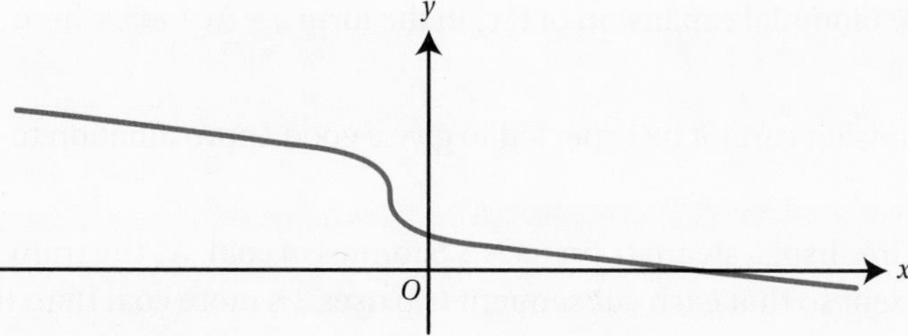

The function f is defined for all real values of x by

$$f(x) = 2 - \sqrt[3]{x+1}.$$

The diagram shows the graph of $y = f(x)$.

i Evaluate $ff(-126)$.

ii Find the set of values of x for which $f(x) = |f(x)|$.

iii Find an expression for $f^{-1}(x)$.

iv State how the graphs of $y = f(x)$ and $y = f^{-1}(x)$ are related geometrically.

© OCR, GCE Mathematics, Paper 4723, January 2010

8 a Find the range of the function $f(x) = 2x^2 - 12x + 25$.

b Prove that there is no real value of x such that $x^2 + 10$, $6x$ and $x^2 + 15$ are consecutive terms of an arithmetic sequence.

9 The sequence u_n is defined by $u_n = 0.5^n$.

a Find the exact value of $\sum_{0}^{10} u_r$.

b Find the exact value of $\sum_{0}^{10} \ln(u_r)$.

10 The functions f and g are defined by $f(x)=3x+1$ and $g(x)=ax^2-x+5$. Find the value of a such that $f(g(x))=0$ has equal roots.

11 For what values of x is the series $x^2-x+(x^2-x)^2+(x^2-x)^3+\ldots$ convergent?

12 Functions g and h are defined by $g(x)=\sqrt{x}$ and $h(x)=\frac{2x-3}{x+1}$ $(x \neq -1)$.

a Find constants A and B such that $h(x)=A+\frac{B}{x+1}$.

b Using transformations, or otherwise, sketch the graph of $y=h(x)$. Label the axes intercepts and state the range of h.

c Find the domain and range of $g \circ h$.

13 It is given that $f(x)=\frac{4+3x}{(1+2x)(2-x)}$.

a Express $f(x)$ in the form $\frac{A}{2-x}+\frac{B}{1+2x}$, where A and B are integers.

b i Find the first three terms of the binomial expansion of $f(x)$ in the form $a+bx+cx^2$, where a, b and c are rational numbers.

ii Explain why the binomial expansion cannot be expected to give a good approximation to $f(-0.5)$.

14 On its first trip between Malby and Grenlish, a steam train uses 1.5 tonnes of coal. As the train does more trips, it becomes less efficient so that each subsequent trip uses 2% more coal than the previous trip.

i Show that the amount of coal used on the fifth trip is 1.624 tonnes, correct to 4 significant figures.

ii There are 39 tonnes of coal available. An engineer wishes to calculate N, the total number of trips possible. Show that N satisfies the inequality

$$1.02^N \leqslant 1.52.$$

iii Hence, by using logarithms, find the greatest number of trips possible.

© OCR, GCE Mathematics, Paper 4722, January 2007

15 In the special theory of relativity, the energy of a particle with mass m and speed v is given by the formula $E=\frac{mc^2}{\sqrt{1-\frac{v^2}{c^2}}}$, where c is the speed of light. Find the first three non-zero terms in the binomial expansion, in ascending powers of v, and comment on the result.

16 If $\sum_{r=1}^{n} \ln\left(\frac{r+1}{r}\right)=8$, find the exact value of n.

17 The following table shows the values and gradient of $f(x)$ at various points.

x	0	1	2	3	4
$f(x)$	4	2	3	4	6
$f'(x)$	7	9	-3	4	2

a Is $f(x)$ a one-to-one function?

b Evaluate $f \circ f(3)$.

c The graph $y = g(x)$ is formed by translating the graph of $y = f(x)$ by a vector $\begin{pmatrix} 2 \\ 3 \end{pmatrix}$ and then reflecting it in the x-axis. Find $g'(2)$.

18 **a** Find the coordinates of the image of $P(x, y)$ after a reflection in the line $y = x$, followed by a reflection in the y-axis.

b $f(x)$ is a one-to-one function. The graph of $f(x)$ is rotated $90°$ anticlockwise. Find the equation of the resulting graph.

19 **a** If the polynomial $f(x)$ is divided by $(x-a)^2$ the remainder is a linear function. Explain why this statement can be written as $f(x) = (x-a)^2 g(x) + mx + c$, where $g(x)$ is a polynomial.

b Find an expression for $f'(x)$ in terms of $g(x)$ and $g'(x)$.

c Hence, show that the remainder is $f(a) + f'(a)(x-a)$ when $f(x)$ is divided by $(x-a)^2$.

d State the condition that must be satisfied if $(x-a)^2$ is to be a factor of $f(x)$.

7 Radian measure

In this chapter you will learn:

- about different units for measuring angles, called radians
- how to calculate certain special values of trigonometric functions in radians
- how to use trigonometric functions in modelling real-life situations
- how to solve geometric problems involving circles
- that trigonometric functions can be approximated by polynomials.

You will also revise solving trigonometric equations.

Before you start…

Student Book 1, Chapter 10	You should be able to define trigonometric functions beyond acute angles, including exact values.	1 What is the exact value of $\sin 120°$?
Student Book 1, Chapter 10	You should be able to solve trigonometric equations.	2 Solve $\cos 2x = \frac{1}{2}$ for $0° < x < 360°$.
Chapter 3	You should be able to identify transformations of graphs.	3 The graph of $y = \cos x$ is translated $30°$ in the positive x direction and stretched vertically with a scale factor of 2. Find the equation of the new graph.
Student Book 1, Chapter 11	You should be able to use the sine and cosine rules.	4 Find the smallest angle in a triangle with sides 3, 4 and 6.
Chapter 6	You should be able to use the binomial expansion for negative and fractional powers.	5 Find the first three non-zero terms in the expansion of $\frac{2}{1-3x^2}$, in ascending powers of x.

What are radians?

Measuring angles is related to measuring lengths around the perimeter of the circle. This observation leads to the introduction of a new unit for measuring angles, the radian, which will be a more useful unit of measurement in advanced mathematics.

Section 1: Introducing radian measure

An angle measures the amount of rotation between two straight lines. You are already familiar with measuring angles in degrees, where a full turn measures $360°$.

The measure of 360° for a full turn may seem a little arbitrary. There are many other ways of measuring sizes of angles. In advanced mathematics, the most useful unit for measuring angles is the **radian**. This measure relates the size of the angle to the distance moved by a point around a circle.

Consider a circle with centre O and radius 1 (this is called the **unit circle**), and two points, A and B, on its circumference.

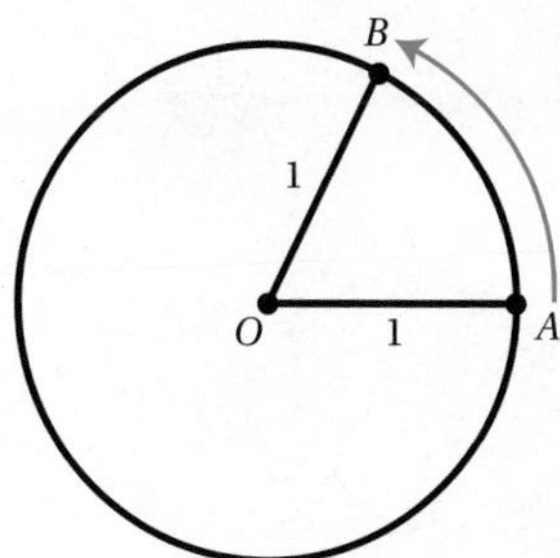

As the line OA rotates into position OB, point A moves a distance equal to the length of the arc AB. The measure of the angle AOB in radians is simply this arc length.

If point A makes a full rotation around the circle, it will cover a distance equal to the length of the circumference of the circle. As the radius of the circle is 1, the length of the circumference is 2π. Hence, a full turn measures 2π radians. You can then deduce the sizes of other common angles in radians; for example, a right angle is one-quarter of a full turn, so it measures $\frac{2\pi}{4} = \frac{\pi}{2}$ radians. Although sizes of common angles measured in radians are often expressed as fractions of π, you can also use decimal approximations. Thus, a right angle measures approximately 1.57 radians.

WORKED EXAMPLE 7.1

a Convert 75° to radians.

b Convert 2.5 radians to degrees.

a $\frac{75}{360} = \frac{5}{24}$ — What fraction of a full turn is 75°?

$\frac{5}{24} \times 2\pi = \frac{5\pi}{12}$ — Calculate the same fraction of 2π.

$\therefore 75° = \frac{5\pi}{12}$ radians — This is the *exact answer*. You can also find the decimal equivalent, to 3 significant figures.

$75° = 1.31$ radians (3 s.f.)

b $\frac{2.5}{2\pi} (\approx 0.3979)$ — What fraction of a full rotation is 2.5 radians?

$\frac{2.5}{2\pi} \times 360 = 143.24$ — Calculate the same fraction of 360°.

2.5 radians $= 143°$ (3 s.f.)

Key point 7.1

Full turn $= 360° = 2\pi$ radians

To convert from degrees to radians, divide by 180 and multiply by π.

To convert from radians to degrees, divide by π and multiply by 180.

Did you know?

There are many different measures of angle. One historical attempt was gradians, which split a right angle into 100 units.

It is conventional to draw the unit circle with the centre at the origin and measure angles anticlockwise from the positive x-axis.

WORKED EXAMPLE 7.2

Mark on the unit circle the points corresponding to the following angles, measured in radians.

$A: \pi$ $\quad B: -\frac{\pi}{2}$ $\quad C: \frac{5\pi}{2}$ $\quad D: \frac{13\pi}{3}$

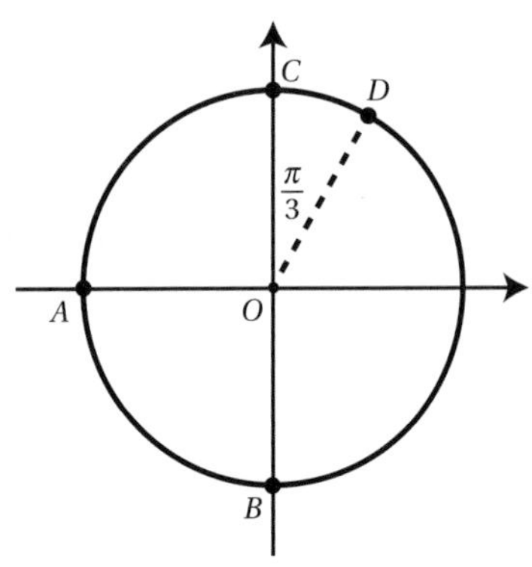

π radians is one-half of a full turn, so point A represents half a turn around the circle.

$\frac{\pi}{2}$ is one-quarter of the full turn and the '–' sign represents clockwise rotation; so point B represents a quarter of a turn in the clockwise direction.

$\frac{5\pi}{2} = 2\pi + \frac{\pi}{2}$, so point C represents a full turn followed by another quarter of a turn.

$\frac{13\pi}{3} = 4\pi + \frac{\pi}{3}$, so point D represents two full turns followed by another $\frac{1}{6}$th of a turn.

You can still find the values of trigonometric functions in radians, just as you could in degrees, but you'll need to make sure you change your calculator to radian mode.

However, as well as getting values of trigonometric functions from your calculator, you also need to recognise a few special angles for which you can find exact values. The method relies on properties of special right-angled triangles.

Gateway to A Level

See Gateway to A Level Section Z for revision of working with exact values in degrees.

WORKED EXAMPLE 7.3

Find the exact values of $\sin\frac{\pi}{6}$, $\cos\frac{\pi}{6}$ and $\tan\frac{\pi}{6}$.

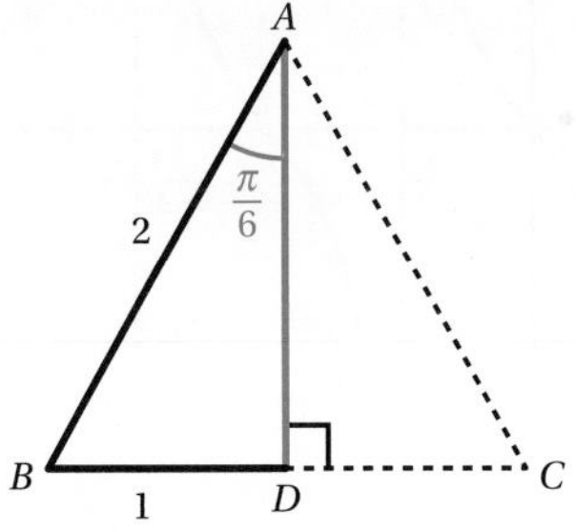

If a right-angled triangle has a $\frac{\pi}{6}$ angle then the third angle is $\frac{\pi}{3}$, so this is half of an equilateral triangle.

You can choose any length for the side of the equilateral triangle. Let $AB = 2$; then $BD = 1$.

$AD^2 = 2^2 - 1^2 = 3$

$\therefore AD = \sqrt{3}$

To find AD, use Pythagoras' theorem.

$\sin\frac{\pi}{6} = \frac{\text{opp}}{\text{hyp}} = \frac{1}{2}$

$\cos\frac{\pi}{6} = \frac{\text{adj}}{\text{hyp}} = \frac{\sqrt{3}}{2}$

$\tan\frac{\pi}{6} = \frac{\text{opp}}{\text{adj}} = \frac{1}{\sqrt{3}}$

You can now use the definitions of sin, cos and tan in right-angled triangles.

The results for other values follow similarly and are summarised in the table.

Key point 7.2

Radians	0	$\frac{\pi}{6}$	$\frac{\pi}{4}$	$\frac{\pi}{3}$	$\frac{\pi}{2}$	π
Degrees	0°	30°	45°	60°	90°	180°
$\sin\theta$	0	$\frac{1}{2}$	$\frac{\sqrt{2}}{2}$	$\frac{\sqrt{3}}{2}$	1	0
$\cos\theta$	1	$\frac{\sqrt{3}}{2}$	$\frac{\sqrt{2}}{2}$	$\frac{1}{2}$	0	−1
$\tan\theta$	0	$\frac{1}{\sqrt{3}}$	1	$\sqrt{3}$	not defined	0

Tip

You should make sure you know how to change your calculator between degree and radian modes.

You can extend this table to include multiples of these angles and derive other properties, using symmetries of the trigonometric graphs. You therefore need to recognise x-intercepts and turning points of these graphs in radians.

Key point 7.3

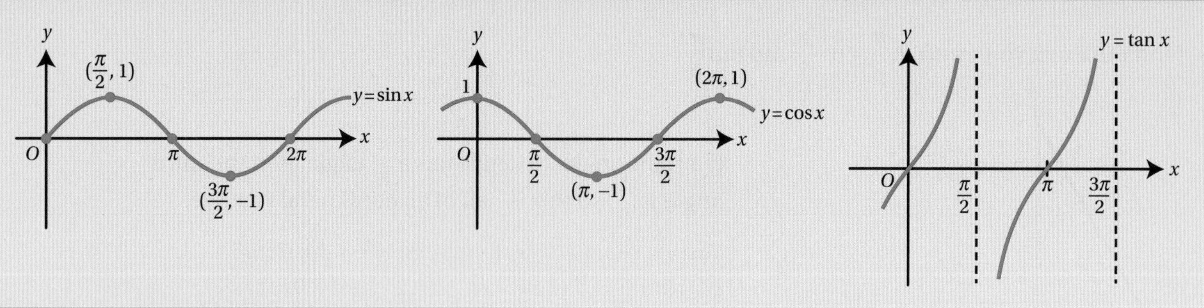

WORKED EXAMPLE 7.4

Given that $\sin\theta = 0.6$, find the values of:

a $\sin(\pi - \theta)$

b $\sin(\pi + \theta)$

a

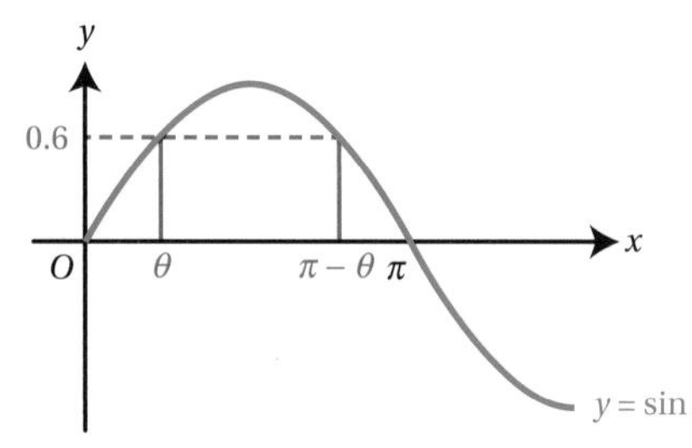

Label θ and $\pi - \theta$ on the horizontal axis.

The graph shows that $\sin(\pi - \theta) = 0.6$.

The graph has the same height at the two points.

b

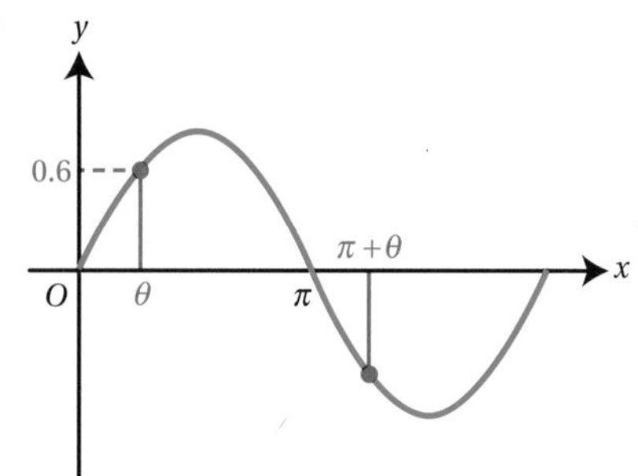

Label θ and $\pi + \theta$ on the horizontal axis.

The graph shows that $\sin(\pi + \theta) = -0.6$.

WORK IT OUT 7.1

Given that $\cos\theta = 0.2$, find the value of $\cos(\pi + \theta)$.

Which of the following solutions is correct? Identify the mistake in the other two.

Solution 1	Solution 2	Solution 3
$\cos(\pi + \theta) = \cos\pi + \cos\theta$ $= -1 + 0.2$ $= -0.8$	From the graph, $\cos(\pi + \theta) = -\cos\theta$ $= -0.2$	$\theta = \cos^{-1} 0.2 = 1.37$ So: $\cos(\pi + \theta) = \cos(4.51)$ $= -0.202$

EXERCISE 7A

In this exercise, all angles are measured in radians unless stated otherwise.

1 Draw a unit circle for each part and mark the points corresponding to the following angles.

a **i** $\frac{\pi}{4}$ **ii** $\frac{\pi}{3}$ **b** **i** $\frac{4\pi}{3}$ **ii** $\frac{3\pi}{4}$

c **i** $-\frac{\pi}{3}$ **ii** $-\frac{\pi}{6}$ **d** **i** -2π **ii** -4π

2 Express the following angles in radians, giving your answer in terms of π.

a **i** $135°$ **ii** $45°$ **b** **i** $90°$ **ii** $270°$

c **i** $120°$ **ii** $150°$ **d** **i** $50°$ **ii** $80°$

3 Express the following angles in radians, correct to 3 decimal places.

a **i** $320°$ **ii** $20°$ **b** **i** $270°$ **ii** $90°$

c **i** $65°$ **ii** $145°$ **d** **i** $100°$ **ii** $83°$

4 Express the following angles in degrees.

a **i** $\frac{\pi}{3}$ **ii** $\frac{\pi}{4}$ **b** **i** $\frac{5\pi}{6}$ **ii** $\frac{2\pi}{3}$

c **i** $\frac{3\pi}{2}$ **ii** $\frac{5\pi}{3}$ **d** **i** 1.22 **ii** 4.63

5 Sketch the graph of:

a **i** $y = \sin x$ for $-\frac{\pi}{2} \leqslant x \leqslant \frac{\pi}{2}$ **ii** $y = \sin x$ for $-\pi \leqslant x \leqslant 2\pi$

b **i** $y = \cos x$ for $\frac{\pi}{2} \leqslant x \leqslant \frac{3\pi}{2}$ **ii** $y = \cos x$ for $-\pi \leqslant x \leqslant 2\pi$

Solve questions 6 to 10 without using a calculator.

6 Given that $\sin\frac{\pi}{7} = 0.434$, find the value of:

a $\sin\frac{6\pi}{7}$ **b** $\sin\frac{29\pi}{7}$

c $\sin\frac{8\pi}{7}$ **d** $\sin\frac{13\pi}{7}$

7 Given that $\cos\frac{\pi}{5} = 0.809$, find the value of:

a $\cos\frac{4\pi}{5}$ **b** $\cos\frac{21\pi}{5}$

c $\cos\frac{9\pi}{5}$ **d** $\cos\frac{6\pi}{5}$

8 Given that $\tan\frac{\pi}{8} = 0.414$, find the value of:

a $\tan\frac{9\pi}{8}$ **b** $\tan\frac{7\pi}{8}$

c $\tan\frac{25\pi}{8}$ **d** $\tan\frac{15\pi}{8}$

9 Find the exact values of:

a **i** $\cos\frac{3\pi}{4}$ **ii** $\cos\frac{5\pi}{4}$

b **i** $\sin\left(-\frac{\pi}{6}\right)$ **ii** $\sin\left(-\frac{\pi}{3}\right)$

c **i** $\tan\frac{3\pi}{4}$ **ii** $\tan\left(-\frac{\pi}{4}\right)$

10 Evaluate the following, simplifying as far as possible.

a $1-\sin^2\left(\frac{\pi}{6}\right)$ **b** $\sin\left(\frac{\pi}{4}\right)+\sin\left(\frac{\pi}{3}\right)$ **c** $\cos\frac{\pi}{3}-\cos\frac{\pi}{6}$

11 Show that $\cos^2\left(\frac{\pi}{6}\right)-\sin^2\left(\frac{\pi}{6}\right)\equiv\cos\left(\frac{\pi}{3}\right)$.

12 Show that $\left(1+\tan\frac{\pi}{3}\right)^2 \equiv 4+2\sqrt{3}$.

13 Simplify $\cos(\pi+x)+\cos(\pi-x)$.

14 Simplify the following expression.

$$\sin x+\sin\left(x+\frac{\pi}{2}\right)+\sin(x+\pi)+\sin\left(x+\frac{3\pi}{2}\right)+\sin(x+2\pi)$$

Section 2: Inverse trigonometric functions and solving trigonometric equations

When solving trigonometric equations in Student Book 1, Chapter 10, you used $\sin^{-1} k$ to solve equations of the form $\sin x = k$. Based on the work in Chapter 2 of this book, you can see that this is an example of an **inverse trigonometric function**.

> **Rewind**
>
> You met inverse functions in Chapter 2, Section 4.

Not every function has an inverse function; we need the original function to be *one-one*. Looking at the graph of the sine function, it is clear that it is not one-one. So how can you define inverse sine?

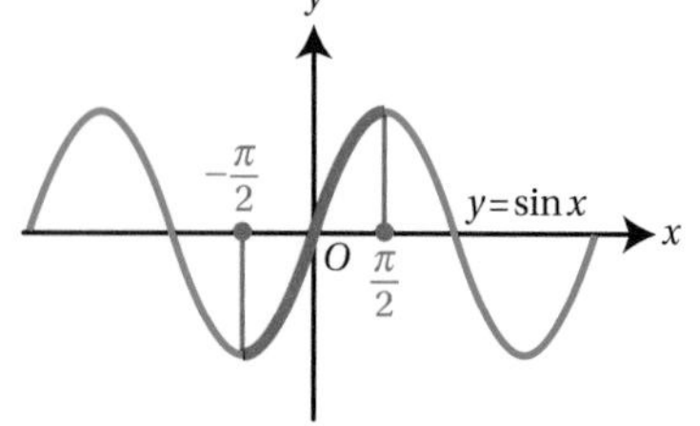

You need to consider the sine function on a restricted domain on which the function is one-one. From the graph on the previous page, a suitable domain is $-\frac{\pi}{2} \leqslant x \leqslant \frac{\pi}{2}$. (There are other options but this is chosen by convention.) It is now possible to define the inverse function. The graph of the inverse function is the reflection of the graph of the original function in the line $y = x$. From the graph you can see the domain and range of the inverse function.

Key point 7.4

The inverse function of $f(x) = \sin x$ is $f^{-1}(x) = \arcsin x$.

Its domain is $[-1,1]$ and its range $\left[-\frac{\pi}{2}, \frac{\pi}{2}\right]$ (or $[-90°, 90°]$).

Tip

You need to know the ranges of inverse trigonometric functions in both radians and degrees.

You can carry out similar analysis for cosine and tangent functions to identify the domains on which their inverse functions are defined. The results are as follows.

Tip

As with the inverse sine function, it is possible to use a different restricted domain for cos when defining the inverse function (e.g. $[\pi, 2\pi]$ is another possibility). However, unless told otherwise, you should assume the standard restricted domain $[0, \pi]$.

Key point 7.5

The inverse function of $f(x) = \cos x$ is $f^{-1}(x) = \arccos x$.

Its domain is $[-1, 1]$ and its range $[0, \pi]$ (or $[0°, 180°]$).

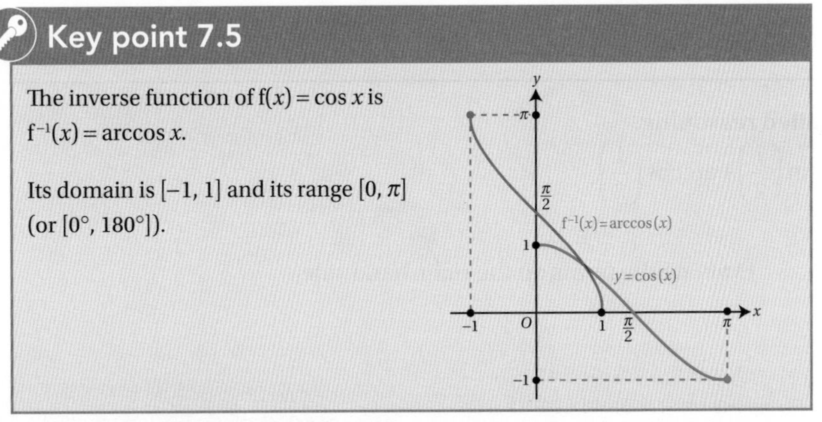

Key point 7.6

The inverse function of $f(x) = \tan x$ is $f^{-1}(x) = \arctan x$.

Its domain is $\mathbb{R}$ and its range is $\left[-\frac{\pi}{2}, \frac{\pi}{2}\right]$ (or $[-90°, 90°]$).

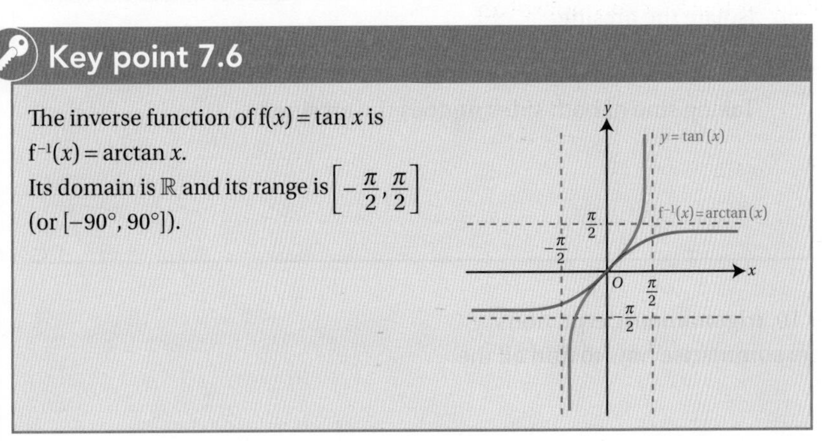

You should remember what happens when you compose a function with its inverse: $f\left(f^{-1}(x)\right)=x$. Applying this to inverse trigonometric functions, you get

$$\sin(\arcsin x)=x, \quad \cos(\arccos x)=x, \quad \tan(\arctan x)=x.$$

You need to be a little more careful when composing the other way around. For example, $\arcsin(\sin x)=x$ only when x is in the restricted domain you used to define the arcsin function (so $x\in\left[-\frac{\pi}{2},\frac{\pi}{2}\right]$).
For example, $\arcsin\left(\sin\frac{5\pi}{6}\right)=\arcsin\left(\frac{1}{2}\right)=\frac{\pi}{6}$.

WORK IT OUT 7.2

Evaluate $\arctan(1)$.

Which of the following solutions are valid? What errors have been made in the solution(s) that are not correct?

Solution 1	Solution 2	Solution 3
$\arctan(1)=\frac{\pi}{4}$	$\arctan(1)=\frac{1}{\tan(1)}\approx 0.642$	$\arctan(1)=\frac{\arcsin(1)}{\arccos(1)}$ This is undefined because $\arccos(1)=0$.

WORKED EXAMPLE 7.5

In this question you must show detailed reasoning.

Solve the equation $3\arcsin(3x)=\arcsin\left(\frac{1}{2}\right)+\arccos\left(\frac{1}{2}\right)$.

$$3\arcsin(3x)=\arcsin\left(\frac{1}{2}\right)+\arccos\left(\frac{1}{2}\right)$$

Evaluate the terms on the right-hand side.

$$=\frac{\pi}{6}+\frac{\pi}{3}$$
$$=\frac{\pi}{2}$$

$$\arcsin(3x)=\frac{\pi}{6}$$

Isolate the arcsine.

$$\sin(\arcsin(3x))=\sin\left(\frac{\pi}{6}\right)$$

Taking sine of both sides undoes the arcsine.

$$3x=\frac{1}{2}$$
$$x=\frac{1}{6}$$

As you learnt in Student Book 1, Chapter 10, trigonometric equations can have more than one solution. Here we summarise how to find all the solutions when working in radians.

Key point 7.7

Equation	First solution, θ_1	Second solution, θ_2	Further solutions
$\sin\theta = k$	$\arcsin k$	$\pi - \theta_1$	Add or subtract multiples of 2π
$\cos\theta = k$	$\arccos k$	$-\theta_1$	Add or subtract multiples of 2π
$\tan\theta = k$	$\arctan k$		Add or subtract multiples of π

WORKED EXAMPLE 7.6

Find the values of x between $-\pi$ and 2π for which $\cos x = \frac{\sqrt{2}}{2}$.

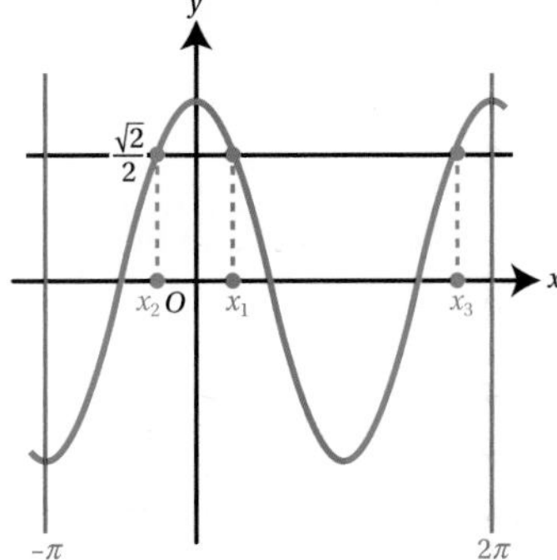

Sketch the graph.

Three solutions.

Note how many solutions.

$x_1 = \arccos\frac{\sqrt{2}}{2} = \frac{\pi}{4}$

Use inverse cos to find the first solution.

$x_2 = -\frac{\pi}{4}$

$x_3 = 2\pi - \frac{\pi}{4}$

$= \frac{7\pi}{4}$

Use the symmetry of the graph to find the other solutions.

WORK IT OUT 7.3

Solve $\tan 3x = \sqrt{3}$ for $0 < x < \frac{\pi}{2}$.

Which of the following solutions are valid? What errors have been made in the solution(s) that are not correct?

Solution 1	Solution 2	Solution 3
$\tan x = \frac{\sqrt{3}}{3} = \frac{1}{\sqrt{3}}$ So $x = \arctan\frac{1}{\sqrt{3}}$ $= \frac{\pi}{6}$	$3x_0 = \arctan\left(\sqrt{3}\right) = \frac{\pi}{3}$ $x_0 = \frac{\pi}{9}$ Adding π would take you outside of the required region, so this is the only solution.	$3x_0 = \arctan\left(\sqrt{3}\right) = \frac{\pi}{3}$ $3x = \frac{\pi}{3}, \frac{4\pi}{3}, \frac{7\pi}{3}, \ldots$ $x = \frac{\pi}{9}, \frac{4\pi}{9}$ are the only solutions in the required range.

EXERCISE 7B

1 Use your calculator to evaluate the following in radians, correct to 3 significant figures.

a **i** $\arccos(0.6)$ **ii** $\arcsin(0.2)$

b **i** $\arctan(-3)$ **ii** $\arcsin(-0.8)$

In questions 2 to 5 you must show detailed reasoning.

2 Find the exact value of the following, in radians.

a **i** $\arcsin\left(\frac{1}{2}\right)$ **ii** $\arccos\left(\frac{\sqrt{3}}{2}\right)$

b **i** $\arctan\left(-\sqrt{3}\right)$ **ii** $\arccos\left(-\frac{1}{\sqrt{2}}\right)$

c **i** $\arcsin(-1)$ **ii** $\arctan(1)$

3 Find the exact value of:

a **i** $\arcsin\left(\sin\left(\frac{\pi}{3}\right)\right)$ **ii** $\arccos\left(\cos\left(\frac{5\pi}{6}\right)\right)$

b **i** $\arcsin\left(\sin\left(\frac{2\pi}{3}\right)\right)$ **ii** $\arccos(\cos(-3\pi))$

c **i** $\arccos\left(\cos\left(\frac{5\pi}{3}\right)\right)$ **ii** $\arcsin\left(\sin\left(\frac{7\pi}{4}\right)\right)$

d **i** $\arctan\left(\tan\frac{7\pi}{4}\right)$ **ii** $\arctan\left(\tan\frac{11\pi}{6}\right)$

4 Solve the following equations.

a $\arcsin x = \frac{\pi}{3}$

b $\arccos 2x = \frac{5\pi}{6}$

c $\arctan(3x-1) = -\frac{\pi}{6}$

5 Find the values of x between 0 and 2π for which:

a **i** $\cos x = \frac{\sqrt{3}}{2}$ **ii** $\cos x = \frac{\sqrt{2}}{2}$

b **i** $\cos x = -\frac{1}{2}$ **ii** $\cos x = -\frac{\sqrt{3}}{2}$

c **i** $\sin x = \frac{\sqrt{2}}{2}$ **ii** $\sin x = \frac{\sqrt{3}}{2}$

d **i** $\tan x = \frac{1}{\sqrt{3}}$ **ii** $\tan x = -1$

6 Solve these equations in the given interval, giving your answers to 3 significant figures. Do not use equation solver or graphs on the calculator.

a **i** $\cos t = \frac{4}{5}$ for $t \in [0, 4\pi]$ **ii** $\cos t = \frac{2}{3}$ for $t \in [0, 4\pi]$

b **i** $\sin\theta = -0.8$ for $\theta \in [-2\pi, 2\pi]$ **ii** $\sin\theta = -0.35$ for $\theta \in [-2\pi, 2\pi]$

c **i** $\tan\theta = -\frac{2}{3}$ for $-\pi \leqslant \theta \leqslant \pi$ **ii** $\tan\theta = -3$ for $-\pi \leqslant \theta \leqslant \pi$

d **i** $\cos\theta = 1$ for $\theta \in [0, 4\pi]$ **ii** $\cos\theta = 0$ for $\theta \in [0, 4\pi]$

7 Find the exact values of $x \in (-\pi, \pi)$ for which $2\sin x + 1 = 0$.

8 Sketch the graph of $y = 3\arcsin x$ for $-1 \leqslant x \leqslant 1$.

Tip

Remember that 'show detailed reasoning' means you must use known values and algebra rather than solving with a calculator.

Elevate

See Support sheet 7 for a further example of solving equations in radians and for more practice questions.

9 Find the exact solutions to $\tan 4x = \sqrt{3}$ for $0 \leqslant x \leqslant \pi$.

10 **a** If $3\cos x = \tan x$, show that $\sin x = \dfrac{-1+\sqrt{37}}{6}$.

b Find all solutions to $3\cos x = \tan x$ for $0 < x < 2\pi$.

11 Find the exact solutions of the equation $2\cos\theta \tan\theta = \tan\theta$ for $\theta \in [0, \pi]$.

12 Leo says that $\arccos(\cos x) = x$ for all x. Prove by counter example that this statement is false.

13 Find the exact solutions of the equation $\sin(x^2) = \dfrac{1}{2}$ for $-\pi < x < \pi$.

14 **a** Prove by a counter example that $\arctan x \not\equiv \dfrac{\arcsin x}{\arccos x}$.

b Express $\arcsin x$ in terms of $\arccos x$.

c Solve the equation $2\arctan x = \arcsin x + \arccos x$.

Section 3: Modelling with trigonometric functions

Trigonometric functions can be used to model real-life situations that show periodic behaviour; for example, the height of the tide, or the motion of a point on a Ferris wheel. To do this, you need to consider trigonometric functions with different periods and amplitudes.

You can use your knowledge of transformations of graphs, from Chapter 3, to change the amplitude or the period of a function. Remember that the **amplitude** of an oscillating function is the vertical distance between the central line and the extreme values. This can be changed by applying a vertical stretch.

For example, the function $y = 2\sin x$ has amplitude 2, while the period is unchanged.

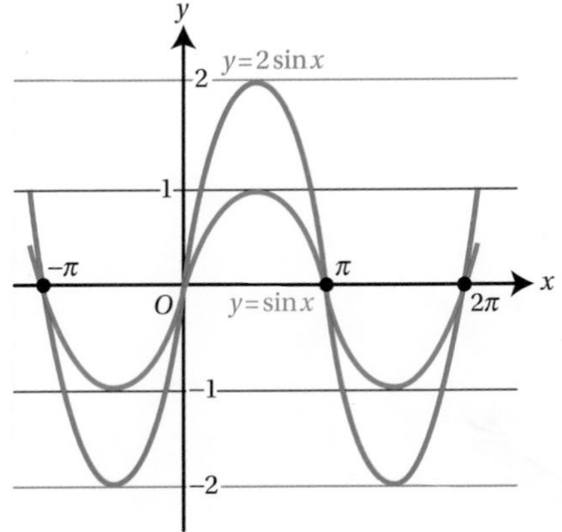

The **period** is the horizontal distance until the graph repeats. You can change it by applying a horizontal stretch to the graph. For example, the equation $y = \sin 2x$ is of the form $y = f(2x)$, so you need to apply a horizontal stretch with scale factor $\dfrac{1}{2}$ to the graph of $y = \sin x$.

Tip

$\sin 2x$ is not the same as $2\sin x$.

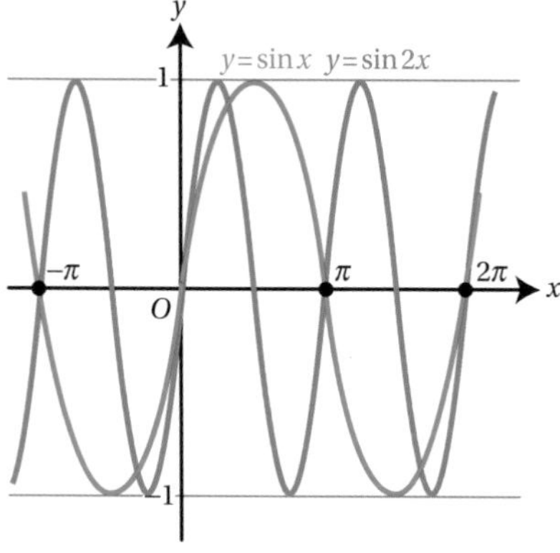

You can see that the amplitude of the function is still 1, but the period is halved to π.

The two types of transformation can be combined to change both the amplitude and the period of the function. The same transformations can also be applied to the graph of the cosine function.

Key point 7.8

The functions $y = a\sin(bx)$ and $y = a\cos(bx)$ have amplitude a and period $\frac{2\pi}{|b|}$.

WORKED EXAMPLE 7.7

a Sketch the graph of $y = 4\cos\left(\frac{x}{3}\right)$ for $0 \leqslant x \leqslant 6\pi$.

b Write down the amplitude and the period of the function.

Vertical stretch with scale factor 4.

Horizontal stretch with scale factor 3.

You start with the graph of $y = \cos x$ and think what transformations to apply to it.

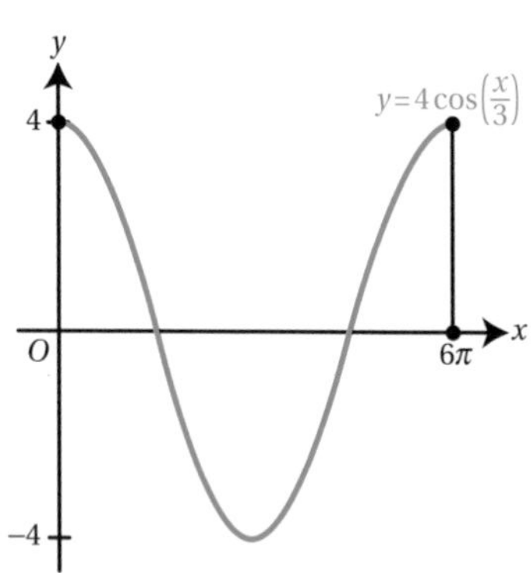

Hence, amplitude $= 4$ and period $= \frac{2\pi}{(1/3)} = 6\pi$.

As well as vertical and horizontal stretches, you can also apply translations to graphs. They will leave the period and the amplitude unchanged, but will change the positions of maximum and minimum points and the axes intercepts.

WORKED EXAMPLE 7.8

a Sketch the graph of $y=\sin\left(x-\frac{\pi}{3}\right)+2$ for $x\in[0,2\pi]$.

b Find the coordinates of the maximum and the minimum points on the graph.

a

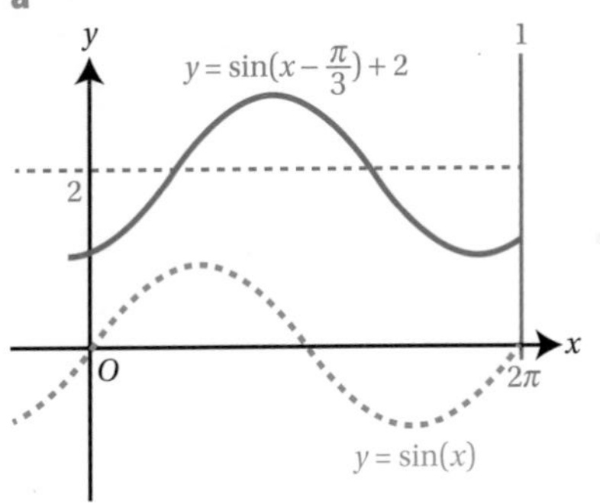

The equation is of the form $y=f\left(x-\frac{\pi}{3}\right)+2$. This represents a translation of $\frac{\pi}{3}$ units to the right and 2 units up.

b Maximum point:

$x=\frac{\pi}{2}+\frac{\pi}{3}=\frac{5\pi}{6}$

$y=1+2=3$

So the maximum point is $\left(\frac{5\pi}{6},3\right)$.

Minimum point:

$x=\frac{3\pi}{2}+\frac{\pi}{3}=\frac{11\pi}{6}$

$y=-1+2=1$

So the minimum point is $\left(\frac{11\pi}{6},1\right)$

The maximum and minimum points of $\sin x$ are $\left(\frac{\pi}{2},1\right)$ and $\left(\frac{3\pi}{2},-1\right)$. You need to apply the translation to these points.

The result of combining all four transformations can be summarised as follows.

Key point 7.9

The functions $y=a\sin b(x+c)+d$ and $y=a\cos b(x+c)+d$ have:

- amplitude $|a|$
- central value d
- minimum value $d-|a|$ and maximum value $d+|a|$
- period $\frac{2\pi}{|b|}$

You can use your knowledge of transformations of graphs to find an equation of a function when given its graph.

WORKED EXAMPLE 7.9

The graph shown has the equation $y = a\sin(bx) + d$.

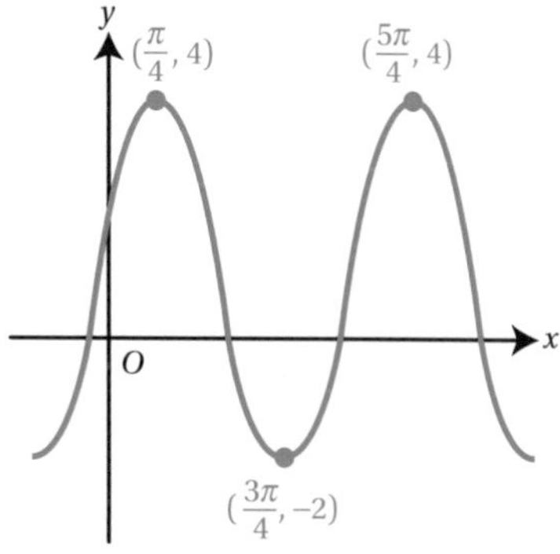

Find the values of a, b and d.

Amplitude $= \frac{4-(-2)}{2} = 3$

$\therefore a = 3$

a is the amplitude, which is half the difference between the minimum and maximum values.

Period $= \frac{5\pi}{4} - \frac{\pi}{4} = \pi$

$\pi = \frac{2\pi}{b}$

$\therefore b = 2$

b is related to the period, which is the distance between the two consecutive maximum points. The formula is period $= \frac{2\pi}{b}$.

$d = \frac{4+(-2)}{2}$

$\therefore d = 1$

d represents the vertical translation of the graph. It is the value halfway between the minimum and the maximum values.

You can now use these ideas to create mathematical models of periodic motion, such as motion around a circle, oscillation of a particle attached to the end of a spring, water waves, or heights of tides. In practice, you would collect experimental data to sketch a graph and then use your knowledge of trigonometric functions to find its equation. You can then use the equation to do further calculations.

WORKED EXAMPLE 7.10

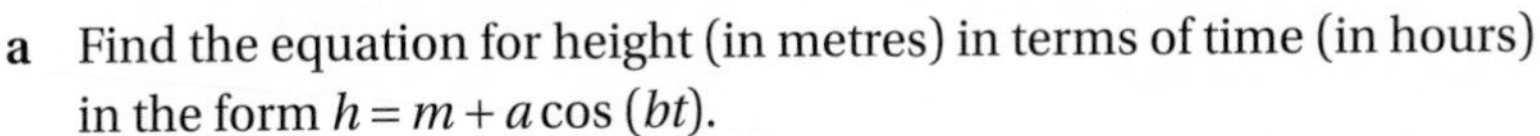

The height of water in the harbour is 16 metres at high tide, and 10 metres at low tide 12 hours later. The graph at right shows how the height of water changes with time over 24 hours.

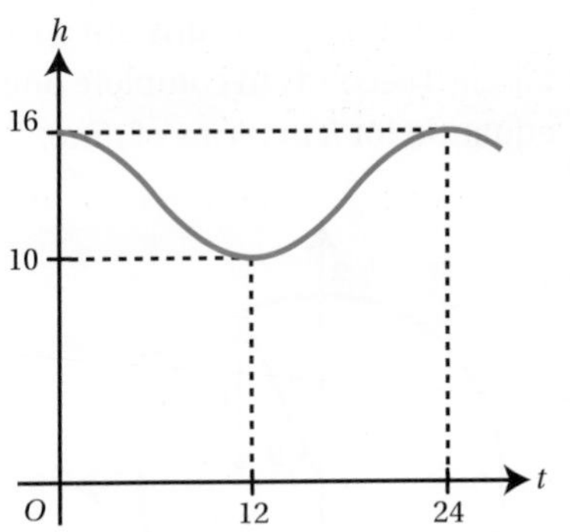

a Find the equation for height (in metres) in terms of time (in hours) in the form $h = m + a\cos(bt)$.

b Find the first two times after the high tide when the height of water is 12 metres.

a $m = \frac{16+10}{2} = 13$ — m is the 'central value', halfway between the minimum and maximum values.

Amplitude $= \frac{16-10}{2} = 3$ — a is the amplitude, which is half the distance between the minimum and maximum values.

$\therefore a = 3$

Period $= 24$ — The period is $\frac{2\pi}{b}$.

$24 = \frac{2\pi}{b}$

$\therefore b = \frac{\pi}{12}$

So $h = 13 + 3\cos\left(\frac{\pi}{12}t\right)$ — Write an equation that says that $h = 12$.

b $13 + 3\cos\left(\frac{\pi}{12}t\right) = 12$

$\Leftrightarrow \cos\left(\frac{\pi}{12}t\right) = -\frac{1}{3}$ — Rearrange the equation into the form $\cos(A) = k$.

$\frac{\pi}{12}t = \arccos\left(-\frac{1}{3}\right) = 1.91$

or $2\pi - 1.91 = 4.37$ — The high tide is when $t = 0$, so you want the first two answers with $t > 0$. Find two possible values of $\frac{\pi}{12}t$.

To find t:

$t_1 = \frac{1.91 \times 12}{\pi} = 7.30$ (3 s.f.) — Solve for t.

$t_2 = \frac{4.37 \times 12}{\pi} = 16.7$ (3 s.f.)

The height of the water will be 12 m 7.30 h and 16.7 h after the high tide.

WORKED EXAMPLE 7.11

A point moves with constant speed around a circle of radius 2 cm, starting from the positive x-axis and taking 3 seconds to complete one full rotation. Let h be the height of the point above the x-axis. Find an equation for h in terms of time.

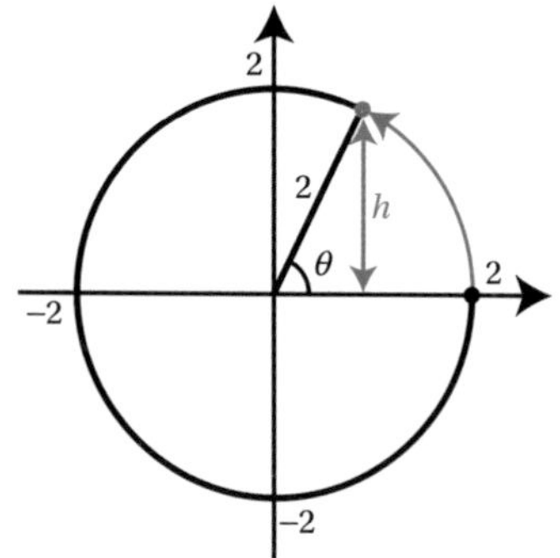

Draw a diagram; you can see that $h = 2\sin\theta$, where θ is the angle between the radius and the x-axis.

You now need to find how θ depends on time.

From the diagram: $h = 2\sin\theta$

Let t be the time, measured in seconds.

$\theta = 0$ when $t = 0$

$\theta = 2\pi$ and $t = 3$

You have information about the values of θ at the start and 3 seconds later.

So $\theta = \frac{2\pi}{3}t$.

As the point moves with constant speed, θ is directly proportional to t.

Hence, $h = 2\sin\left(\frac{2\pi}{3}t\right)$.

EXERCISE 7C

1 State the amplitude and the period of the following functions, where x is in radians.

a $f(x) = 3\sin 4x$ **b** $f(x) = \cos\left(\frac{x}{2}\right)$ **c** $f(x) = \cos 3x$ **d** $f(x) = 2\sin \pi x$

2 Sketch the following graphs, giving coordinates of maximum and minimum points.

a i $y = 2\cos\left(x - \frac{\pi}{3}\right)$ for $0 \leqslant x \leqslant 2\pi$ **ii** $y = 3\sin\left(x + \frac{\pi}{2}\right)$ for $0 \leqslant x \leqslant 2\pi$

b i $y = \sin 2x$ for $-\pi \leqslant x \leqslant \pi$ **ii** $y = \cos 3x$ for $0 \leqslant x \leqslant \pi$

c i $y = \tan\left(x - \frac{\pi}{2}\right)$ for $0 \leqslant x \leqslant \pi$ **ii** $y = \tan\left(x + \frac{\pi}{3}\right)$ for $0 \leqslant x \leqslant \pi$

d i $y = 3\cos x - 2$ for $0 \leqslant x \leqslant 4\pi$ **ii** $y = 2\sin x + 1$ for $-\pi \leqslant x \leqslant \pi$

3 The depth of water in a harbour varies during the day and is given by the equation $d = 16 + 7\sin\left(\frac{\pi}{12}t\right)$, where d is measured in metres and t in hours after midnight.

a Find the depth of the water at low and high tide.

b At what times does high tide occur?

4 A small ball is attached to one end of an elastic spring, and the other end is fixed to the ceiling. The ball is pulled down and released, and starts to oscillate vertically. The graph shows how the length of the spring, x cm, varies with time, t seconds. The equation of the graph is $x = L + A\cos(5\pi t)$.

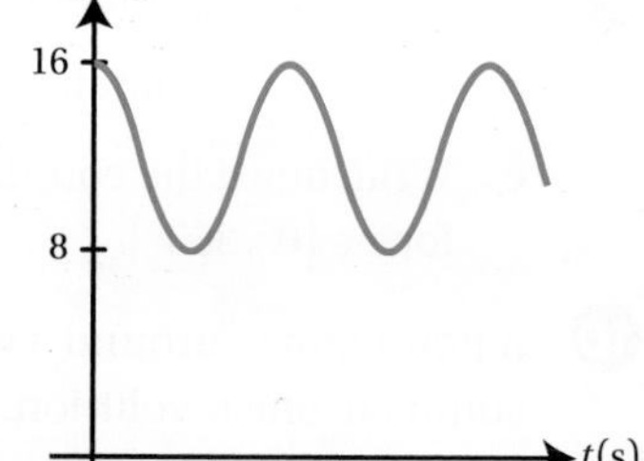

a Write down the amplitude of the oscillation.

b How long does it take for the ball to perform five complete oscillations?

c State one assumption that was made in this model.

> **Tip**
>
> Remember that modelling assumptions are about aspects of the real situation which are not taken into account by the equation you are using.

5 The following graph has equation $y = p\sin(qx)$ for $0 \leqslant x \leqslant 2\pi$. Find the values of p and q.

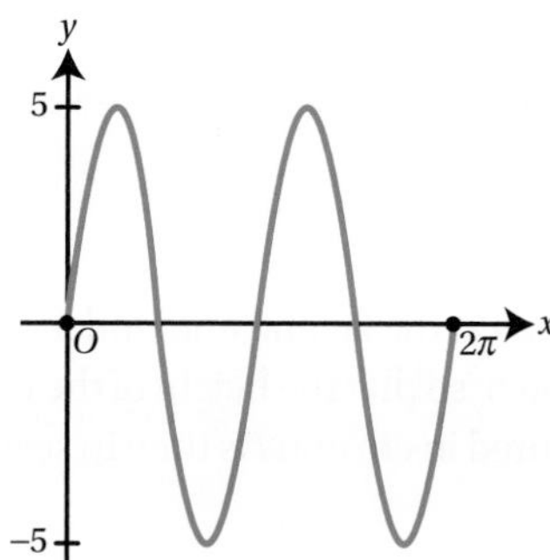

6 The following graph has equation $y = a\cos(x - b)$ for $0° \leqslant x \leqslant 720°$. Find the values of a and b.

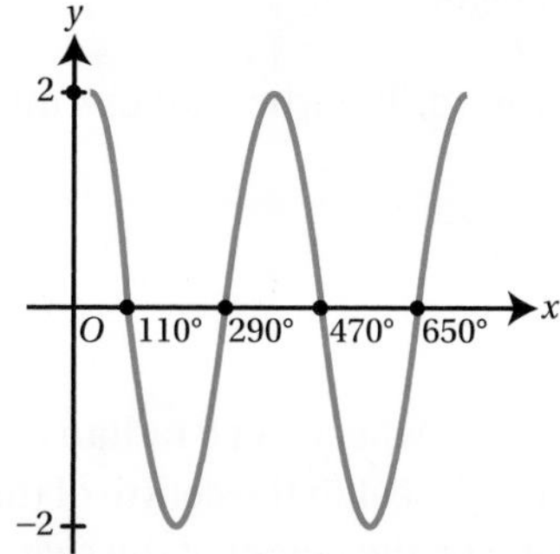

7 **a** On the same set of axes sketch the graphs of $y = 1 + \sin 2x$ and $y = 2\cos x$ for $0 \leqslant x \leqslant 2\pi$.

b Hence, state the number of solutions of the equation $1 + \sin 2x = 2\cos x$ for $0 \leqslant x \leqslant 2\pi$.

c Write down the number of solutions of the equation $1 + \sin 2x = 2\cos x$ for $-2\pi \leqslant x \leqslant 6\pi$.

8 The graph shows the height of water below the level of a walkway as a function of time. The equation of the graph is of the form $y = a\cos(bt) + m$. Find the values of a, b and m.

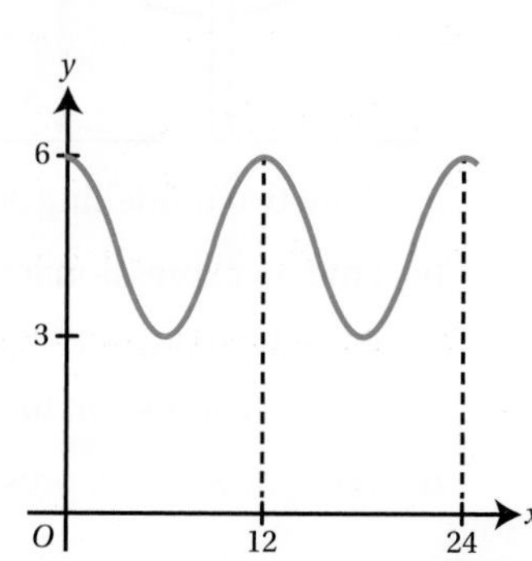

9 a Sketch the graph of $y = 2\cos(x + 60°)$ for $x \in [0°, 360°]$.

b Find the coordinates of the maximum and minimum points on the graph.

c Write down the coordinates of the maximum and minimum points on the graph of $y = 2\cos(x + 60°) - 1$ for $x \in [0°, 360°]$.

10 A point moves around a vertical circle of radius 5 cm, as shown in the diagram. It takes 10 seconds to complete one revolution.

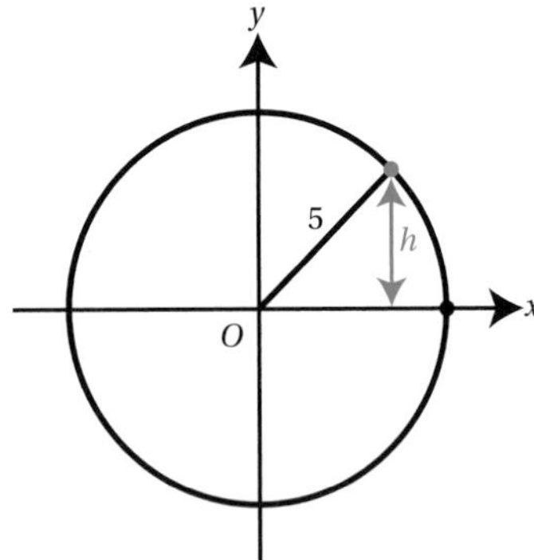

a The height of the point above the x-axis is given by $h = a\sin(kt)$, where t is time, measured in seconds. Find the values of a and k.

b Find the time during the first revolution when the point is 5 cm below the x-axis.

11 A ball is attached at its top and bottom to elastic strings, with each string attached at the far end and under tension. When the ball is pulled down and released, it starts moving up and down, so that the height of the ball above the ground is given by the equation $h = 120 - 10\cos 10t$, where h is measured in cm and t is time in seconds.

a Find the least and greatest height of the ball above the ground.

b Find the time required to complete one full oscillation.

c Find the first time after the ball is released when it reaches the greatest height.

12 A Ferris wheel has radius 12 m and the centre of the wheel is 14 m above ground. The wheel takes 4 min to complete a full rotation.

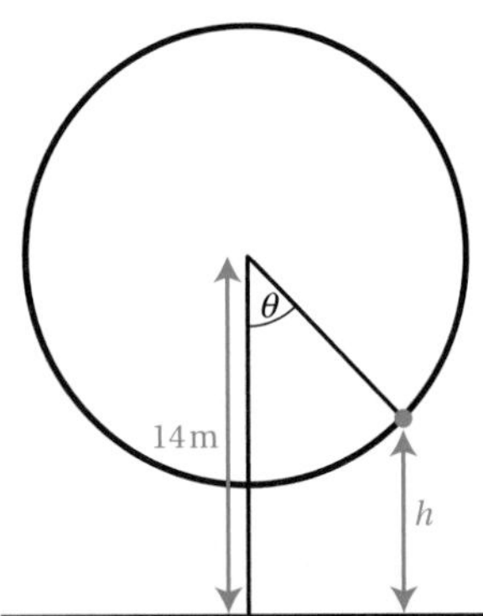

Seats are attached to the circumference of the wheel. Let θ radians be the angle between the radius connecting a seat to the centre of the wheel and the downward vertical, and let h be the height of the seat above ground.

a State two modelling assumptions, relating to the seat, that have been made in the above diagram.

b Find an expression for h in terms of θ.

c Initially, the seat is at the lowest point on the wheel. Assuming that the wheel rotates at constant speed, find an expression for θ in terms of t, where t is the time, measured in minutes.

d Write down an expression for h in terms of t. For how long is the seat more than 20 m above ground?

Section 4: Arcs and sectors

The following diagram shows a circle with centre O and radius r, and points A and B on its circumference. The part of the circumference between points A and B is called an **arc** of a circle.

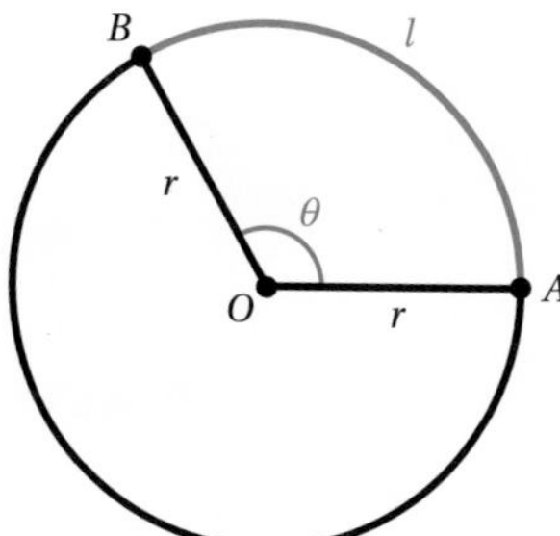

You can see that there are in fact two such parts; the shorter one is called the **minor arc**, and the longer one the **major arc**. The minor arc AB **subtends** an angle θ at the centre of the circle.

The ratio of the length of the arc to the circumference of the whole circle is the same as the ratio of angle θ to the angle measuring a full turn. If l is the length of the arc, and angle θ is measured in radians, this means that $\frac{l}{2\pi r}=\frac{\theta}{2\pi}$. Rearranging this equation gives the formula for the length of an arc.

Key point 7.10

The length of an arc is given by

$$l=r\theta$$

where r is the radius of the circle and θ is the angle subtended at the centre, measured in radians.

WORKED EXAMPLE 7.12

Arc AB of a circle with radius 5 cm subtends an angle of 0.6 at the centre, as shown on the diagram.

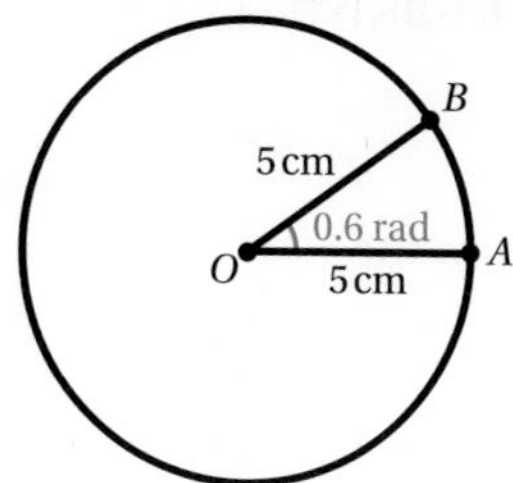

a Find the length of the minor arc AB.

b Find the length of the major arc AB.

a $l=r\theta$
$=5\times0.6$
$=3\text{ cm}$

You know the formula for the length of an arc.

b $\theta_1=2\pi-0.6$
$=5.683\ldots$

$l=r\theta_1$
$=5\times5.683\ldots$
$\approx28.4\text{ cm (3 s.f.)}$

The angle subtended by the major arc is equal to a full turn minus the smaller angle. Full turn is 2π radians.

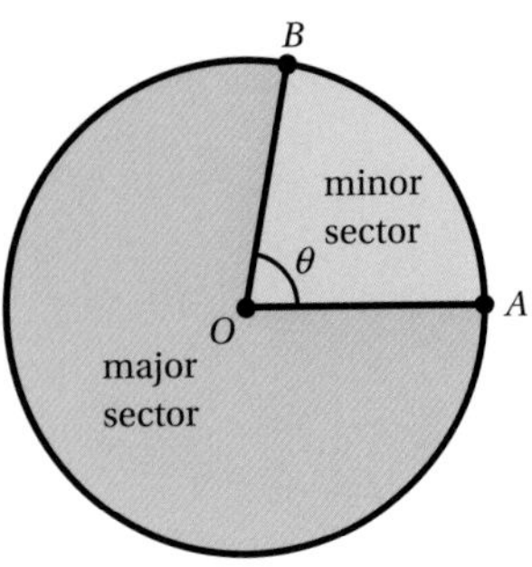

A **sector** is a part of a circle bounded by two radii and an arc. As with arcs, we distinguish between a **minor sector** and a **major sector**.

The ratio of the area of the sector to the area of the whole circle is the same as the ratio of angle θ to the angle measuring a full turn. If A is the area of the sector, and angle θ is measured in radians, this means that $\frac{A}{\pi r^2}=\frac{\theta}{2\pi}$. Rearranging this equation gives the formula for the area of the sector.

Key point 7.11

The area of a sector of a circle is

$$A=\frac{1}{2}r^2\theta$$

where r is the radius of the circle and θ is the angle subtended at the centre, measured in radians.

Tip

You can only use the formulae for arc length and area of sector given in Key points 7.10 and 7.11 when the angle is in radians.

WORKED EXAMPLE 7.13

A sector of a circle has perimeter $p=12$ cm and its angle at the centre $\theta=0.87$ radians. Find the area of the sector.

$A=\frac{1}{2}r^2\theta$

$\theta=0.87,\ r=?$

You want to use the formula for the area, which is $A=\frac{1}{2}r^2\theta$. You need to find r.

$p=r\theta+2r$

You are given the perimeter, and you know the formula for it. You can use this to find r.

$12=0.87r+2r=2.87r$

$r=\frac{12}{2.87}=4.181\ldots$

$A=\frac{1}{2}(4.181)^2(0.87)$

$A\approx7.60\text{ cm}^2$ (3 s.f.)

EXERCISE 7D

1 Calculate the length of the minor arc subtending an angle of θ radians at the centre of the circle of radius r cm, when:

a $\theta = 1.2, r = 6.5$ **b** $\theta = 0.4, r = 4.5$

2 Points A and B lie on the circumference of a circle with centre O and radius r cm. Angle AOB is θ radians. Calculate the length of the major arc AB, when:

a $r = 15, \theta = 0.8$ **b** $r = 1.4, \theta = 1.4$

3 Points M and N lie on the circumference of a circle with centre O and radius r cm, and angle $MON = \alpha$. Calculate the area of the minor sector MON, when:

a $r = 5, \alpha = 1.3$ **b** $r = 0.4, \alpha = 0.9$

4 Points A and B lie on the circumference of a circle with centre C and radius r cm. The size of the angle ACB is θ radians. Calculate the area of the major sector ACB, when:

a $r = 13, \theta = 0.8$ **b** $r = 1.4, \theta = 1.4$

5 Calculate the length of the minor arc AB in the diagram.

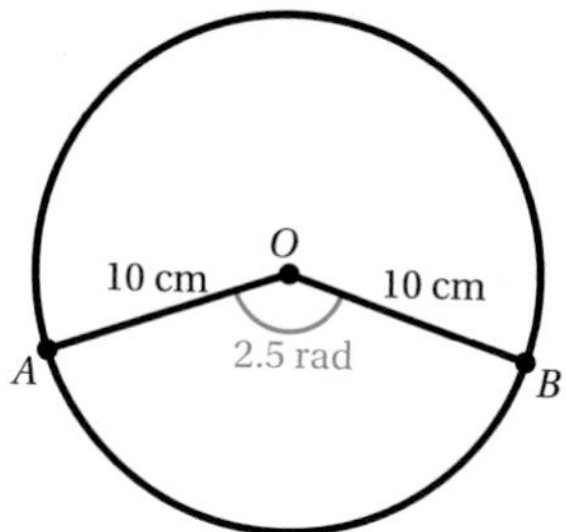

6 In the following diagram the radius of the circle is 8 cm and the length of the minor arc AB is 7.5 cm. Calculate the size of the angle AOB:

a in radians **b** in degrees.

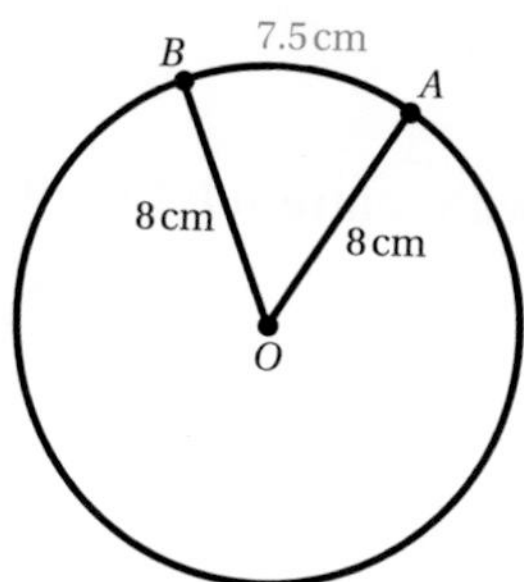

7 Points M and N lie on the circumference of a circle with centre C and radius 4 cm. The length of the *major* arc MN is 15 cm. Calculate the size of the *smaller* angle MCN.

8 Points P and Q lie on the circumference of the circle with centre O. The length of the minor arc PQ is 12 cm and angle $POQ = 1.6$ radians. Find the radius of the circle.

9 A circle has centre O and radius 10 cm. Points A and B lie on the circumference of the circle so that the area of the minor sector AOB is 40 cm^2. Calculate the size of the angle AOB.

10 Points P and Q lie on the circumference of a circle with radius 21 cm. The area of the *major* sector POQ is 744 cm^2. Find the size of the smaller angle POQ, in degrees.

11 In the diagram, the length of the major arc XY is 28 cm. Find the radius of the circle.

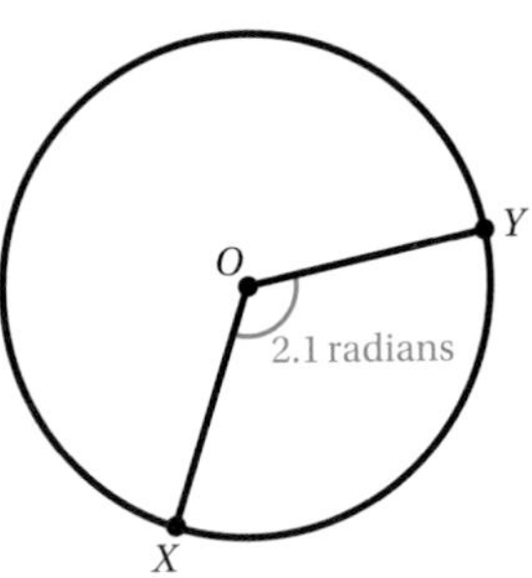

12 A sector of a circle with angle 1.2 radians has area 54 cm^2. Find the radius of the circle.

13 The perimeter of the sector shown in the diagram is 28 cm. Find its area.

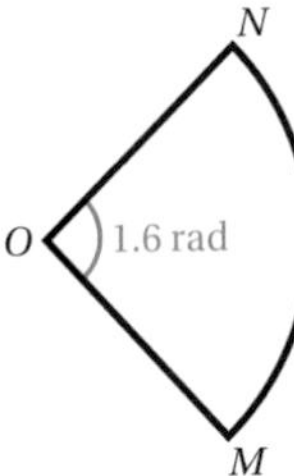

14 The figure in the diagram shows an equilateral triangle ABC with side 5 cm, and three arcs of circles with centres at the vertices of the triangle. Calculate the perimeter of the figure.

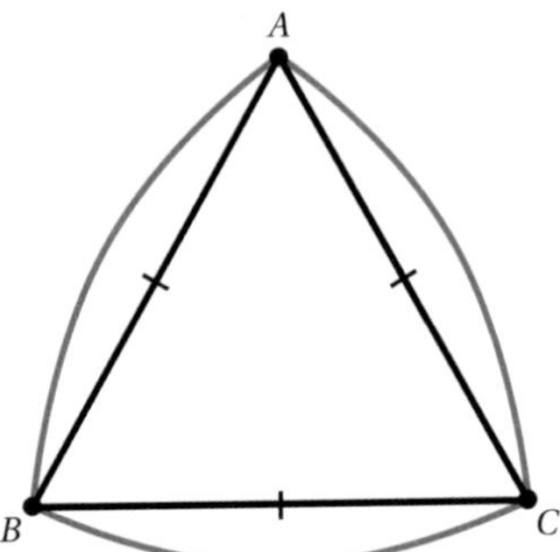

15 The figure shown in the diagram consists of a rectangle and an arc of a circle with centre at P. Calculate the perimeter of the figure.

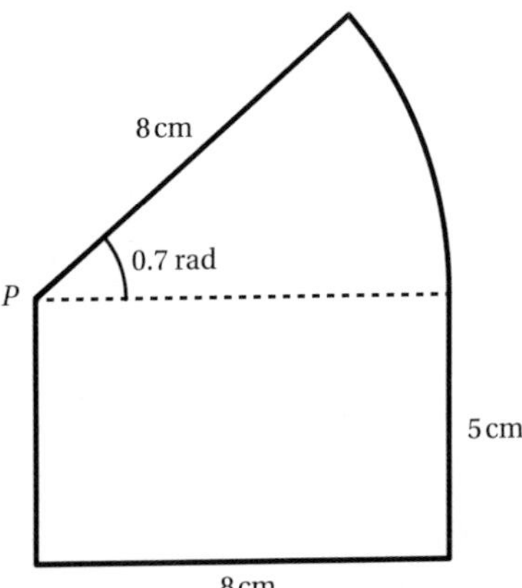

16 A sector of a circle with angle 162° has area 180 cm^2. Find the radius of the circle.

17 The diagram shows a triangle and the segment of a circle. The centre of the circle is at point A. Find the exact perimeter of the figure.

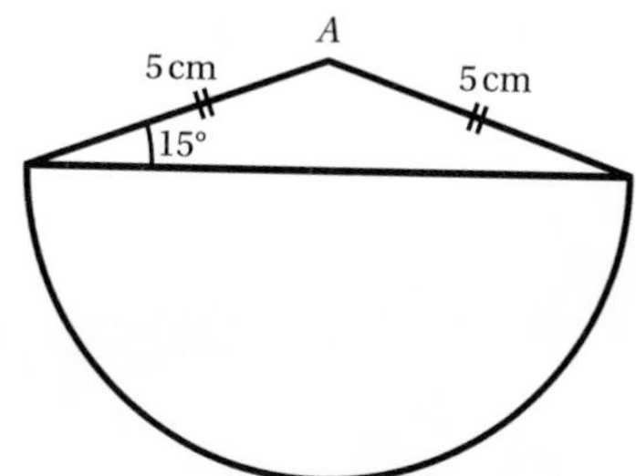

18 A sector of a circle has perimeter $p = 12$ cm and its angle at the centre $\theta = 0.4$. Find the radius of the circle.

19 The diagram shows a sector of a circle with radius 6 cm. Find the area of the shaded region.

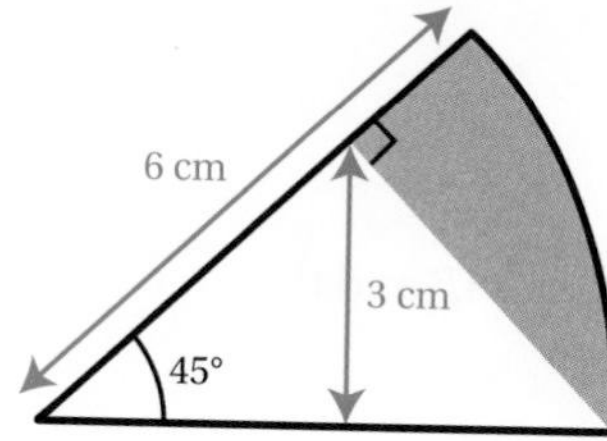

20 A sector of a circle has perimeter 7 cm and area 3 cm^2. Find the possible values of the radius of the circle.

21 Points P and Q lie on the circumference of a circle with centre O and radius 5 cm. The difference between the areas of the major sector POQ and the minor sector POQ is 15 cm^2. Find the size of the angle POQ.

22 A cone is made by rolling a piece of paper, as shown in the diagram.

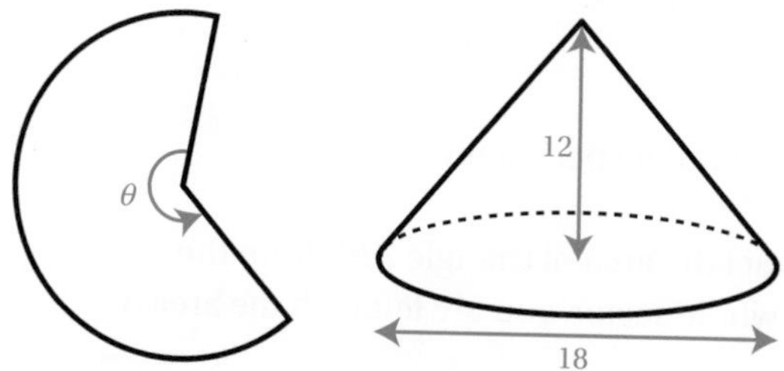

If the cone is to have height 12 cm and base diameter 18 cm, find the size of the angle marked θ.

Section 5: Triangles and circles

In this section we look at two other important parts of circles: **chords** and **segments**. You will need to combine the results about arcs and sectors with the formulae for lengths and angles in triangles.

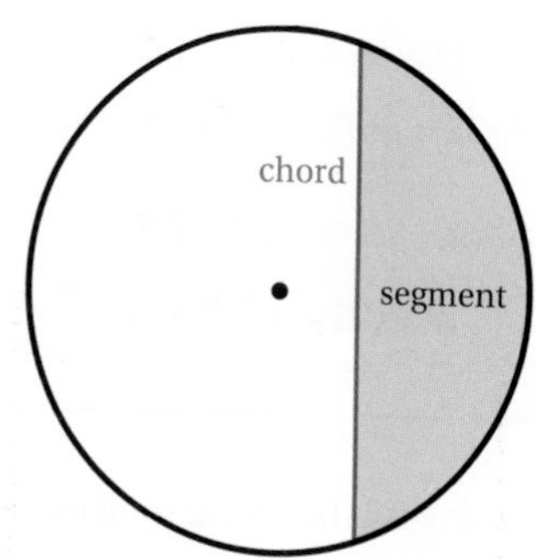

Rewind

See Student Book 1, Chapter 11 if you need a reminder of the cosine rule and the formula for the area of a triangle.

WORKED EXAMPLE 7.14

The diagram shows a sector of a circle of radius 7 cm and its angle at the centre $\theta = 0.8$ radians. For the shaded region shown, find:

a the perimeter
b the area.

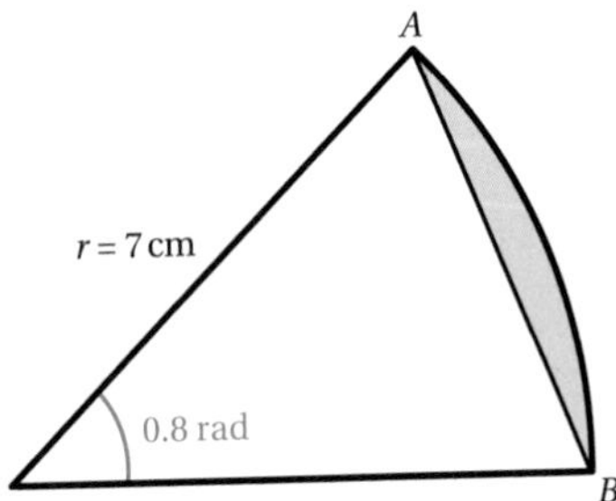

a For the arc:

The perimeter is made up of the arc AB and the chord AB.

$l = 7 \times 0.8 = 5.6\,\text{cm}$

The formula for the length of the arc is $l = r\theta$.

For the chord:
Cosine rule:

$AB^2 = 7^2 + 7^2 - 2 \times 7 \times 7\cos 0.8$

$AB^2 = 29.72\ldots$

$AB = \sqrt{29.72} = 5.45\,\text{cm (3 s.f.)}$

The chord AB is the third side of the triangle ABC. As you know two sides and the angle between them, you can use the cosine rule. Remember that the angle is in radians.

$\therefore P = 5.6 + 5.45 = 11.1\,\text{cm (3 s.f.)}$

You can now find the perimeter.

b For the sector:

If you subtract the area of triangle ABC from the area of the whole sector, you are left with the area of the sector.

$\text{Area} = \frac{1}{2}(7^2 \times 0.8) = 19.6\,\text{cm}^2$

Area of a sector $= \frac{1}{2}r^2\theta$.

For the triangle:
$\text{Area} = \frac{1}{2}(7 \times 7)\sin 0.8 = 17.575\,\text{cm}^2$

Area of a triangle $= \frac{1}{2}ab\sin C$.

$\therefore \text{Area} = 19.6 - 17.575\ldots$

$\approx 2.02\,\text{cm}^2\text{ (3 s.f.)}$

You can now find the area of the segment.

You can follow the same method to derive general formulae for the length of a chord and area of a segment.

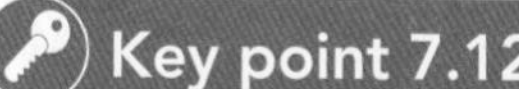

Key point 7.12

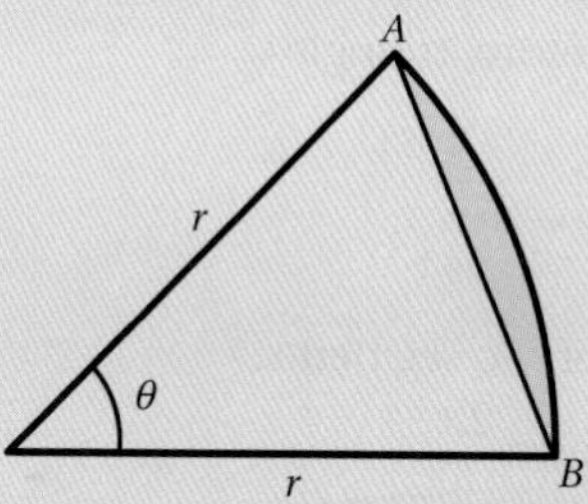

The length of a chord of a circle is given by

$$AB = r\sqrt{2(1-\cos\theta)}$$

and the area of the shaded segment is

$$\frac{1}{2}r^2(\theta - \sin\theta)$$

where angle θ is measured in radians.

The next example shows how you can solve more complex geometry problems by splitting up the figure into basic shapes, such as triangles and sectors.

WORKED EXAMPLE 7.15

The diagram shows two equal circles of radius 12 such that the centre of one circle is on the circumference of the other.

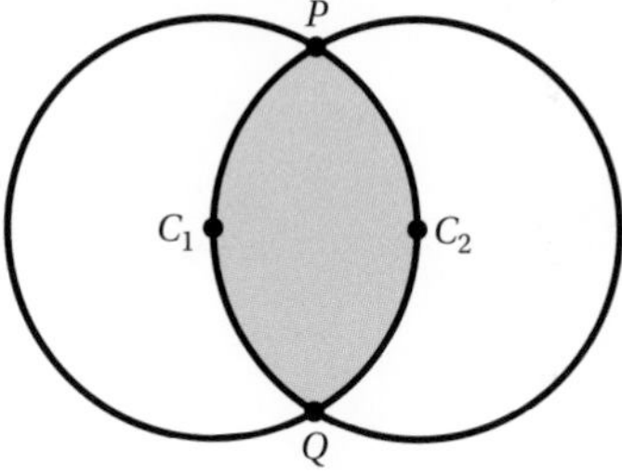

a Find the exact size of angle PC_1Q, in radians.

b Calculate the exact area of the shaded region.

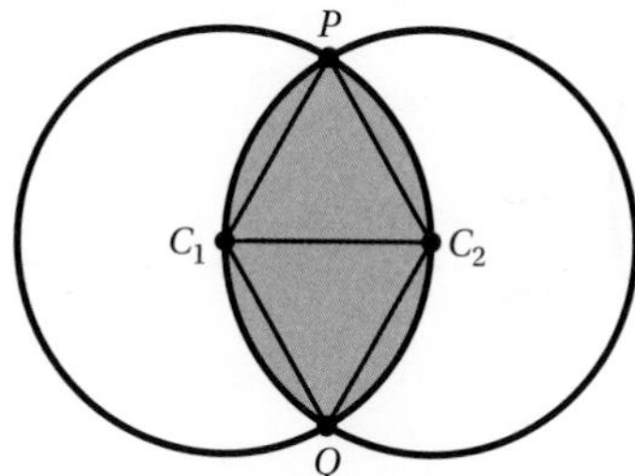

a The only thing you know is the radius of the circle, so draw all the lengths that are equal to the radius.

Continues on next page ...

$PC_1C_2 = \frac{\pi}{3}$

$\therefore PC_1Q = \frac{2\pi}{3}$

The lengths C_1P, C_2P and C_1C_2 are all equal to the radius of the circle. Therefore, triangle PC_1C_2 is equilateral.

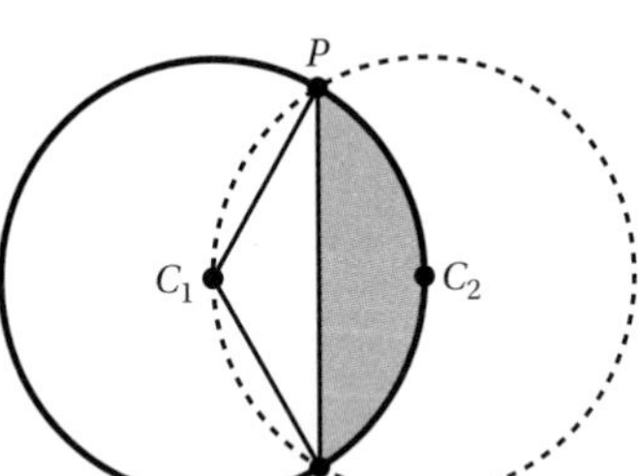

b The shaded area is made up of two segments, each with an angle at the centre $\frac{2\pi}{3}$.

$$\text{Area of one segment} = \frac{1}{2}(12^2)\left(\frac{2\pi}{3} - \sin\left(\frac{2\pi}{3}\right)\right)$$
$$= 72\left(\frac{2\pi}{3} - \frac{\sqrt{3}}{2}\right)$$
$$= 48\pi - 36\sqrt{3}$$

You can find the area of one segment using the formula. Remember to use the exact value of $\sin\left(\frac{2\pi}{3}\right)$.

$$\therefore \text{Shaded area} = 96\pi - 72\sqrt{3}$$

The shaded area consists of two equal segments.

EXERCISE 7E

1 Find the length of the chord AB in each of the following.

a **i**

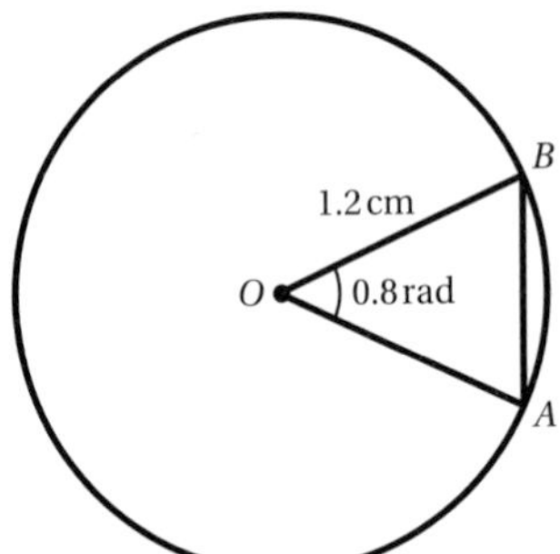

ii

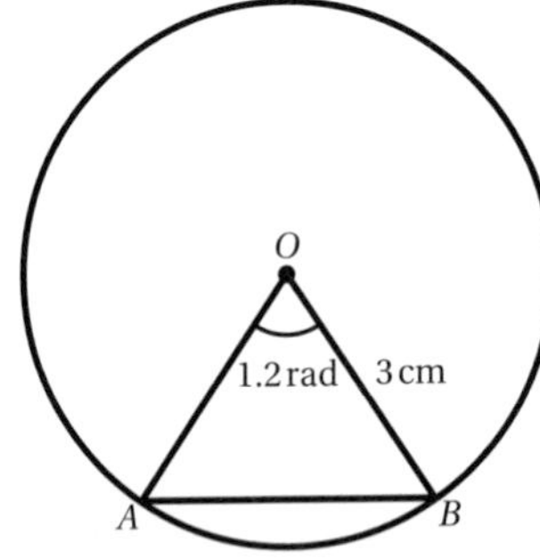

b **i**

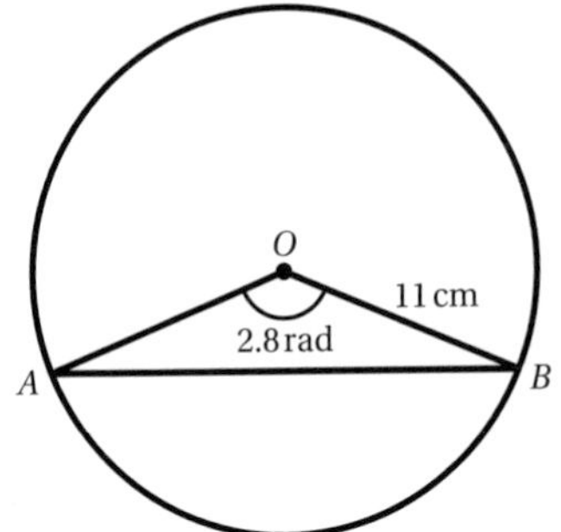

ii

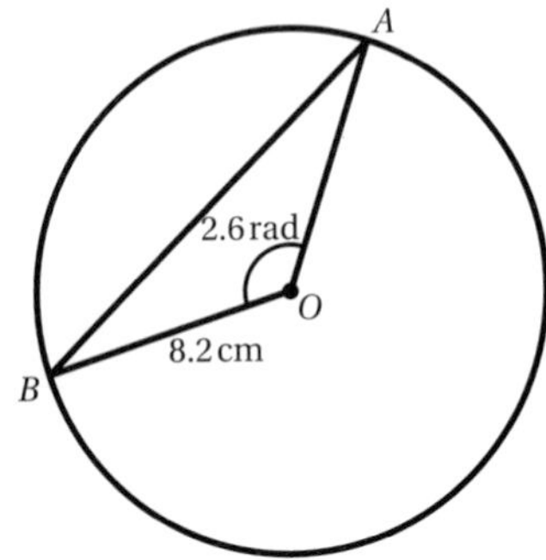

2 Find the perimeters of the minor segments from question 1.

3 Find the areas of the minor segments from question 1.

4 A circle has centre O and radius 5 cm. Chord PQ subtends angle θ at the centre of the circle. Given that the area of the minor segment is 15 cm², show that $\sin\theta = \theta - 1.2$.

5 Two circles, with centres A and B, intersect at P and Q. The radii of the circles are 6 cm and 4 cm, and $PAQ = 45°$.

a Show that $PQ = 6\sqrt{2-\sqrt{2}}$.

b Find the size of angle PBQ.

c Find the area of the shaded region.

Elevate

See Extension sheet 7 for some more challenging questions of this type.

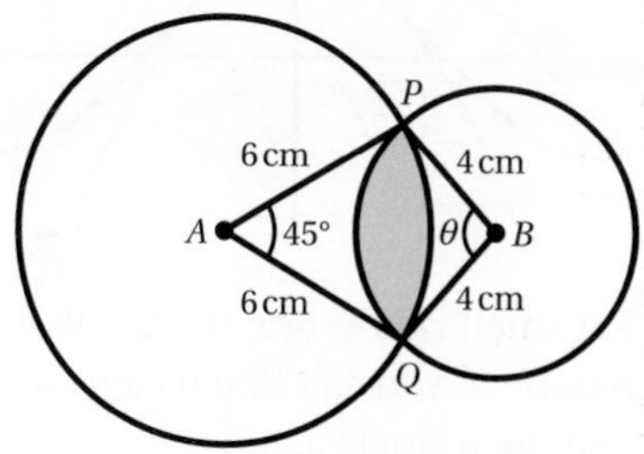

Section 6: Small angle approximations

The following diagram shows the graphs of $y=\sin x$ and $y=x$, where x is in radians. As you can see, near the origin, the two graphs are very close to each other. This means that $\sin x \approx x$ for x close to zero.

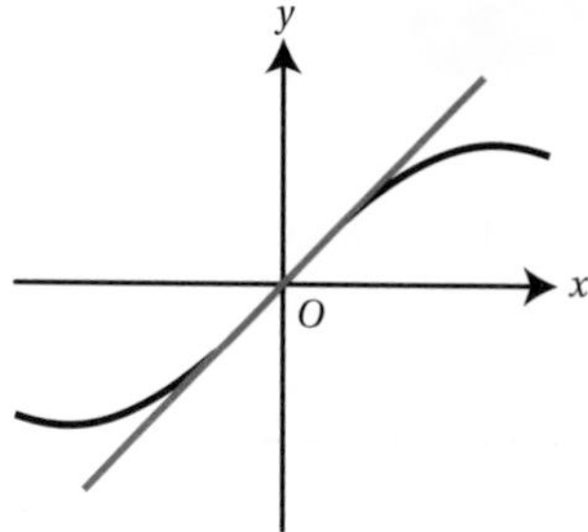

PROOF 4

By considering the diagram, prove that, for small values of θ (measured in radians), $\sin\theta \approx \theta$.

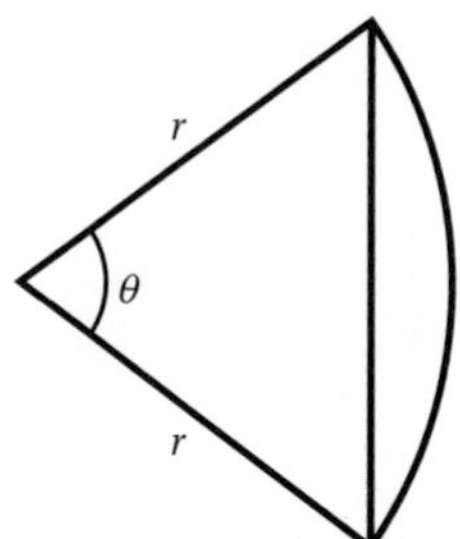

If the angle of the sector is θ radians, then its area is $\frac{1}{2}r^2\theta$.

The area of the triangle is $\frac{1}{2}r^2\sin\theta$.

When θ is small, the sector and the triangle have nearly the same area. Hence,

$$\frac{1}{2}r^2\sin\theta \approx \frac{1}{2}r^2\theta$$
$$\Rightarrow \sin\theta \approx \theta$$

For small values of θ, the sector and the triangle have approximately equal areas. So write down the expression for each.

You can try to find a similar approximation for the cosine graph.

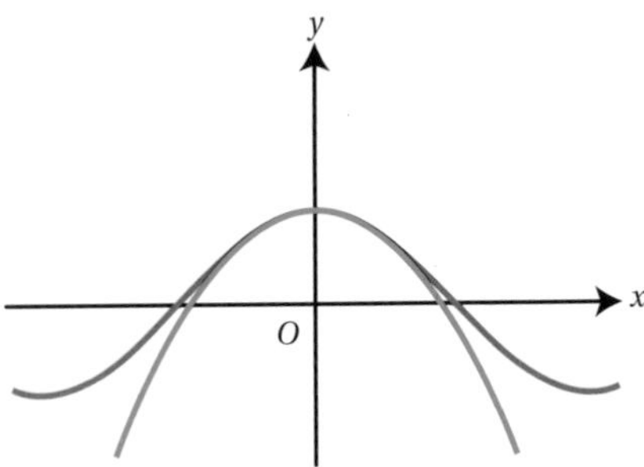

For small values of x, the graph of $y = \cos x$ looks like a (negative) parabola. You can find its approximate equation by looking at the sector and the triangle again.

PROOF 5

Prove that, for small values of θ, $\cos\theta \approx 1 - \frac{1}{2}\theta^2$ when θ is measured in radians.

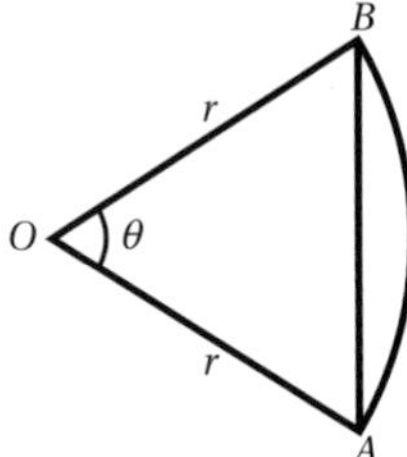

$\cos\theta$ appears in the cosine rule, so compare the length of the arc and the straight line AB.

The length of the arc AB is $r\theta$.

The length of the line is

$AB^2 = r^2 + r^2 - 2r^2\cos\theta$

When θ is small:

$2r^2 - 2r^2\cos\theta \approx (r\theta)^2$

$\Rightarrow \cos\theta \approx 1 - \frac{1}{2}\theta^2$

For small values of θ, the arc and the line have approximately equal lengths.

It is possible to derive a similar approximation for $\tan\theta$. All three results, called the **small angle approximations**, are summarised in Key point 7.13.

Key point 7.13

For small values of θ, measured in radians:

$\sin\theta \approx \theta$

$\cos\theta \approx 1 - \frac{1}{2}\theta^2$

$\tan\theta \approx \theta$

These results can be used to find approximate values of trigonometric functions.

Rewind

This is similar to using the binomial expansion to find approximate values of powers, as you learnt to do in Student Book 1, Chapter 9.

WORKED EXAMPLE 7.16

a Use a small angle approximation to estimate the value of $\cos 0.4$.
b Find the percentage error in your estimate.

a $\cos 0.4 \approx 1-\frac{1}{2}(0.4^2)$
$=1-\frac{0.16}{2}$
$=0.92$

Using $\cos\theta \approx 1-\frac{1}{2}\theta^2$, as 0.4 is close to 0.

b Percentage error $=\frac{|\cos 0.4-0.92|}{\cos 0.4}\times 100$
$=0.115\%$

You need to use a calculator to find the actual value.

Fast forward

The 'exact' value of cos(0.4) you get from the calculator is in fact also an approximation. It is obtained from a generalisation of small angle approximations, called the Maclaurin series, which you will study if you take the Further Mathematics course, in Pure Core Student Book 2.

Just as with the binomial expansion, you can replace θ by another function, such as 3θ or x^2. You can also multiply two expansions together.

WORKED EXAMPLE 7.17

Assuming that x is sufficiently small that terms in x^3 and higher can be ignored, find an approximate expression for:

a $\cos 3x$
b $\cos 3x(1+\sin 5x)$

a $\cos 3x \approx 1-\frac{1}{2}(3x)^2$
$\approx 1-\frac{9}{2}x^2$

Replace θ by $3x$ in $\cos\theta \approx 1-\frac{1}{2}\theta^2$.

b $\cos 3x(1+\sin 5x) \approx \left(1-\frac{9}{2}x^2\right)(1+5x)$

Use the result from part **a** and $\sin\theta \approx \theta$.

$\approx 1+5x-\frac{9}{2}x^2$

Expand the brackets, but only keep the terms up to x^2.

You need to be a little more careful when dividing two approximate expressions, you may need to turn the quotient into a product and then use the binomial expansion.

Rewind

See Chapter 6 for a reminder of binomial expansion with negative powers.

WORKED EXAMPLE 7.18

Find an approximate expression for $\frac{\sin 4\theta}{1+\cos\theta}$, given that θ is small enough to neglect the terms in θ^3 and above.

$$\frac{\sin 4\theta}{1+\cos\theta} \approx \frac{4\theta}{1+\left(1-\frac{1}{2}\theta^2\right)}$$

Replace $\sin 4\theta$ and $\cos\theta$ with their small angle approximations.

$$= \frac{8\theta}{4-\theta^2}$$

$$= 8\theta(4-\theta^2)^{-1}$$

To complete the expansion, you need to rewrite the expression.

$$= 8\theta \times 4^{-1}\left(1-\frac{\theta^2}{4}\right)^{-1}$$

Now do the binomial expansion. Remember that the bracket needs to be in the form $(1+x)^{-1}$.

$$\approx 2\theta\left(1+\frac{\theta^2}{4}+\ldots\right)$$

$$\approx 2\theta$$

Expand the bracket and ignore any terms in θ^3 or higher.

EXERCISE 7F

1 Find the approximate value of:

a **i** $\sin(0.2)$ **ii** $\sin(-0.14)$ **b** **i** $\cos(-0.3)$ **ii** $\cos(0.2)$

c **i** $\tan(0.12)$ **ii** $\tan(-0.2)$

2 Find the small angle approximation for:

a **i** $\sin(2\theta)$ **ii** $\sin(-3x)$ **b** **i** $\cos(3x)$ **ii** $\cos(-5\theta)$

c **i** $\tan(x^2)$ **ii** $\tan\left(\frac{\theta^2}{2}\right)$

3 Assuming θ is sufficiently small so that terms in θ^3 and above can be ignored, find an approximate expression for each of the following.

a **i** $\cos(2\theta)\cos(3\theta)$ **ii** $\cos\left(\frac{\theta}{2}\right)\cos(4\theta)$

b **i** $(1+2\sin\theta)\cos(2\theta)$ **ii** $\cos\theta(1-\sin(2\theta))$

c **i** $(2+\sin\theta)(1-\tan(2\theta))$ **ii** $(3+\tan\theta)(\sin(3\theta)-1)$

4 **a** Find a small angle approximation for $(1 - \sin(2\theta))(1 + 3\tan\theta)$.

b Hence, find an approximate value of $(1 - \sin(0.4))(1 + 3\tan(0.2))$.

5 **a** Given that θ is sufficiently small, write down an approximate expression for $\cos\theta$ in the form $a + b\theta + c\theta^2$.

b Use your expression with $\theta = \frac{\pi}{6}$ to find an approximate value of π.

6 **a** Find an approximate expression for $(1 + \sin(2x))^3$ when x is sufficiently small so that the terms in x^3 and higher can be ignored.

b Find the percentage error when this approximation is used to estimate the value of:

i $(1 + \sin(0.4))^3$

ii $(1 + \sin(1.4))^3$

7 **a** For each of the three small angle approximations, find the largest value of θ for which the approximation error is less than 1%.

b Show that using the small angle approximation for $\sin\theta$ and the identity $\cos\theta = \sqrt{1 - \sin^2\theta}$ gives the correct small angle approximation for $\cos\theta$. Why is it not appropriate to use $\pm$ in front of the square root?

8 Given that θ is close to zero, find an approximate expression for $\frac{\cos\theta}{1 - \sin(3\theta)}$, ignoring powers of θ higher than 2.

9 Find an approximate expression for $\frac{\cos(2\theta)}{1 + \tan 3\theta}$ when θ is close to zero.

10 Let θ be a small angle, measured in *degrees*. Use small angle approximations to find an approximate expression for $\sin\theta$ and $\cos\theta$.

11 **a** Find an approximate expression for $\sqrt{1 + \tan\theta}$ for small values of θ, including terms up and including θ^2.

b Hence, find an approximate value of $\int_0^{\pi/10} \sqrt{1 + \tan\theta}\, d\theta$.

12 Given that x is close to zero, find an approximate expression for $\frac{3 + \sin 2x}{(3 + \tan x)^2}$.

13 Find an approximate expression for $\frac{4 + \sin\theta}{\sqrt{3 + \cos\theta}}$ when θ is sufficiently small to ignore the terms in θ^3 or higher.

Checklist of learning and understanding

- The radian is defined in terms of the distance travelled around the unit circle, so that a full turn $= 2\pi$ radians.
  - To convert from degrees to radians, divide by 180 and multiply by π.
  - To convert from radians to degrees, divide by π and multiply by 180.
- For some real numbers the three main trigonometric functions have exact values, which should be learnt:

Radians	0	$\frac{\pi}{6}$	$\frac{\pi}{4}$	$\frac{\pi}{3}$	$\frac{\pi}{2}$
Degrees	0°	30°	45°	60°	90°
Sin	0	$\frac{1}{2}$	$\frac{\sqrt{2}}{2}$	$\frac{\sqrt{3}}{2}$	1
Cos	1	$\frac{\sqrt{3}}{2}$	$\frac{\sqrt{2}}{2}$	$\frac{1}{2}$	0
Tan	0	$\frac{\sqrt{3}}{3}$	1	$\sqrt{3}$	undefined

- The functions $y = a\sin b(x+c)+d$ and $y = a\cos b(x+c)+d$ have:
  - amplitude $|a|$
  - central value d
  - minimum value $d-|a|$ and maximum value $d+|a|$
  - period $\frac{2\pi}{|b|}$
- Properties of inverse trigonometric functions:

Inverse function	Domain	Range
$\arcsin x$	$[-1,1]$	$\left[-\frac{\pi}{2},\frac{\pi}{2}\right]$ or $[-90°, 90°]$
$\arccos x$	$[-1,1]$	$[0,\pi]$ or $[0°, 180°]$
$\arctan x$	$\mathbb{R}$	$\left(-\frac{\pi}{2},\frac{\pi}{2}\right)$ or $[-90°, 90°]$

- Trigonometric equations can be solved in radians:

Equation	First solution, θ_1	Second solution, θ_2	Further solutions
$\sin\theta = k$	$\sin^{-1} k$	$\pi-\theta_1$	Add or subtract multiples of 2π
$\cos\theta = k$	$\cos^{-1} k$	$-\theta_1$	Add or subtract multiples of 2π
$\tan\theta = k$	$\tan^{-1} k$		Add or subtract multiples of π

- If r is the radius of a circle and θ is the angle subtended at the centre, measured in radians, then the length of an arc is $l = r\theta$ and the area of a sector is $A = \frac{1}{2}r^2\theta$.
- For small θ, measured in radians:

$$\sin\theta \approx \theta, \quad \cos\theta \approx 1-\frac{1}{2}\theta^2, \quad \tan\theta \approx \theta$$

Mixed practice 7

1 **a** The height of a wave, in metres, at a distance x metres from a buoy is modelled by the function $f(x)=1.4\sin(3x-0.1)-0.6$. State the amplitude of the wave.

b Find the distance between consecutive peaks of the wave.

2 Solve the equation $5\sin^2\theta = 4\cos^2\theta$ for $-\pi \leqslant \theta \leqslant \pi$.

3 In the diagram, $OABC$ is a rectangle with sides 7 cm and 2 cm. PQ is a straight line. AP and CQ are circular arcs, with centre O and angle $AOP = \frac{\pi}{6}$.

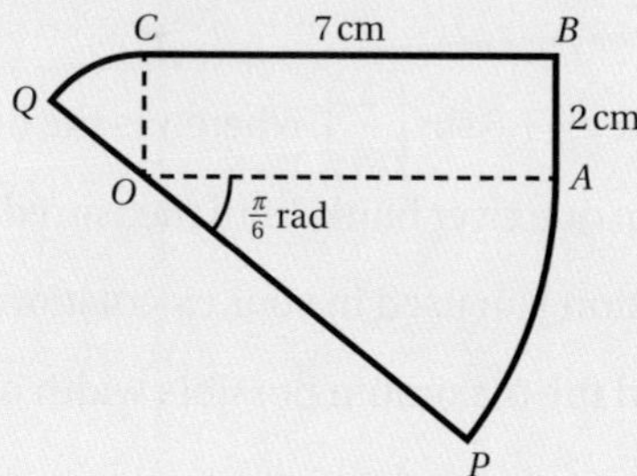

a Write down the size of angle COQ.

b Find the area of the whole shape.

c Find the perimeter of the whole shape.

4 A sector has perimeter 36 cm and radius 10 cm. Find its area.

5 Use small angle approximations to estimate the value of $(1-\sin(0.2))(1+\cos(0.3))$.

6 The diagram shows a circle with centre O and radius $r = 7$ cm. The chord PQ subtends angle $\theta = 1.4$ radians at the centre of the circle.

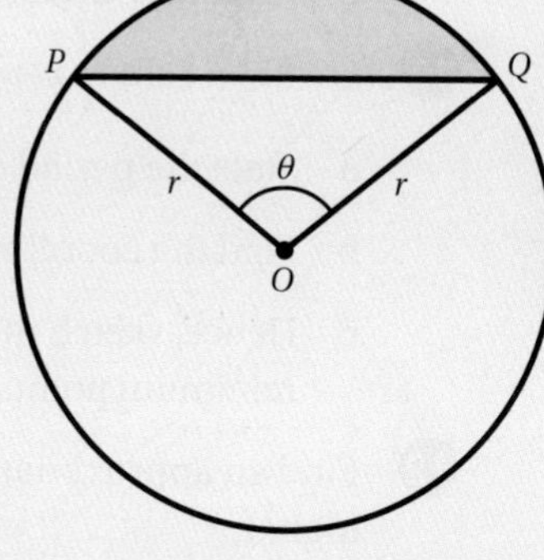

Find:

a the area of the shaded region

b the perimeter of the shaded region.

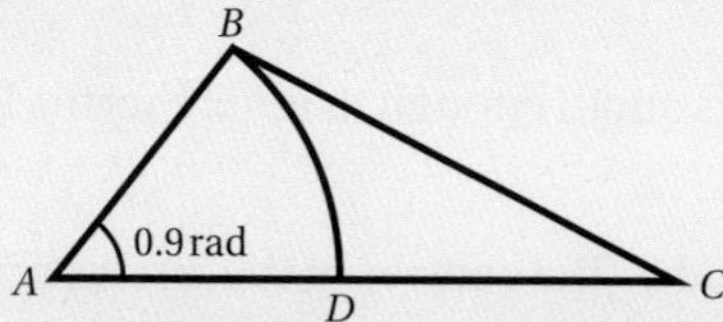

The diagram shows a triangle, ABC, where angle BAC is 0.9 radians. BAD is a sector of the circle with centre A and radius AB.

i The area of the sector BAD is 16.2 cm². Show that the length of AB is 6 cm.

ii The area of triangle ABC is twice the area of sector BAD. Find the length of AC.

iii Find the perimeter of the region BCD.

© OCR, GCE Mathematics, Paper 4722, June 2007

8 The diagram shows the graph of the function $f(x)=a\sin(bx)$. Find the values of a and b.

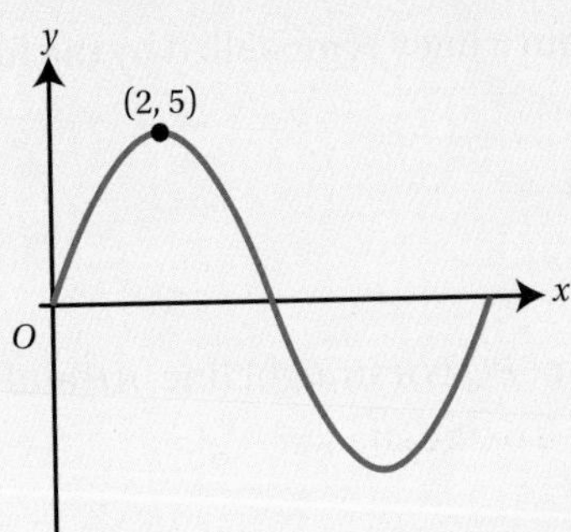

9 The shape of a small bridge can be modelled by the equation $y=1.8\sin\left(\frac{x}{3}\right)$, where y is the height of the bridge above water, and x is the horizontal distance from one river bank, both measured in metres.

a Find the width of the river. State one modelling assumption you used in your calculation.

b A barge has height 1.2 metres above the water level. Find the maximum possible width of the barge so it can pass under the bridge.

c Another barge has width 3.5 metres. What is the maximum possible height of the barge so it can pass under the bridge?

10 A runner is jogging at a constant speed around a level circular track. His distance north of the centre of the track, in metres, is given by $60\cos 0.08t$, where t is measured in seconds.

a How long does is take the runner to complete one lap?

b What is the length of the track?

c At what speed is the runner jogging?

11 Let $f(x)=3\sin 2\left(x-\frac{\pi}{3}\right)$.

a State the period of the function.

b Find the coordinates of the points where the graph of $y=f(x)$, for $x\in[0,2\pi]$, crosses the x-axis.

c Hence, sketch the graph of $y=f(x)$ for $x\in[0,2\pi]$, showing the coordinates of the maximum and minimum points.

12 Find an approximate expression for $\frac{\cos\theta}{1+\tan\theta}$, assuming θ is small enough to ignore terms in θ^3 and higher.

13 Two circles have equal radius r and intersect at points S and T. The centres of the circles are A and B, and angle $ASB=90°$.

a Explain why SAT is also $90°$.

b Find the length AB in terms of r.

c Find the area of the sector AST.

d Find the area of the overlap of the two circles.

14 **In this question you must show detailed reasoning.**
Find the exact values of $x\in[-\pi,\pi]$ satisfying the equation $2\cos\left(2x+\frac{\pi}{3}\right)=\sqrt{2}$.

15 In the following diagram, O is the centre of the circle and AT is the tangent to the circle at T.

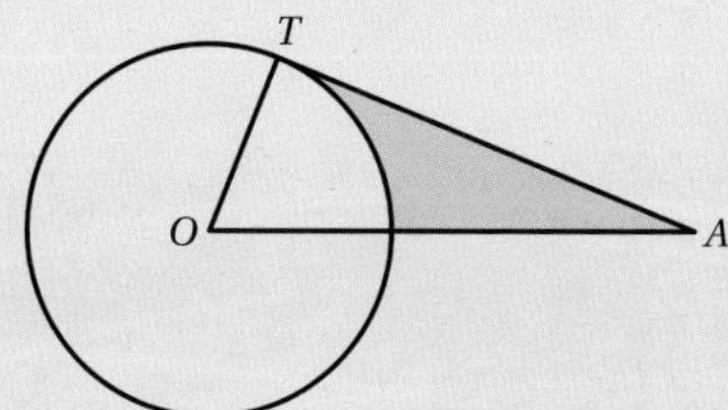

If $OA = 8$ cm, and the circle has a radius of 4 cm, find the area of the shaded region.

16 **i** Sketch the graph of $y = \tan\left(\frac{1}{2}x\right)$ for $-2\pi \leqslant x \leqslant 2\pi$.

On the same axes, sketch the graphs of $y = 3\cos\left(\frac{1}{2}x\right)$ for $-2\pi \leqslant x \leqslant 2\pi$, indicating the point of intersection with the y-axis.

ii Show that the equation $\tan\left(\frac{1}{2}x\right) = 3\cos\left(\frac{1}{2}x\right)$ can be expressed in the form

$$3\sin^2\left(\frac{1}{2}x\right) + \sin\left(\frac{1}{2}x\right) - 3 = 0.$$

Hence, solve the equation $\tan\left(\frac{1}{2}x\right) = 3\cos\left(\frac{1}{2}x\right)$ for $-2\pi \leqslant x \leqslant 2\pi$.

© OCR, GCE Mathematics, Paper 4722, January 2012 [Abridged]

17 **a** Given that x is small enough so that the terms in x^3 and higher can be neglected, find an approximate expression for $\sqrt{4 + \sin 3x}$.

b Hence, find an estimate for $\int_0^{\pi/8} \sqrt{4 + \sin 3x}\, dx$.

18 Find the exact solutions to the equation $\cos\theta - 2\sin^2\theta + 2 = 0$ for $\theta \in [0, 2\pi]$.

19 Two circular cogs are connected by a chain, as shown in the first diagram. The radii of the cogs are 3 cm and 8 cm, and the distance between their centres is 25 cm.

The second diagram shows the quadrilateral O_1ABO_2. Line O_2P is drawn parallel to AB.

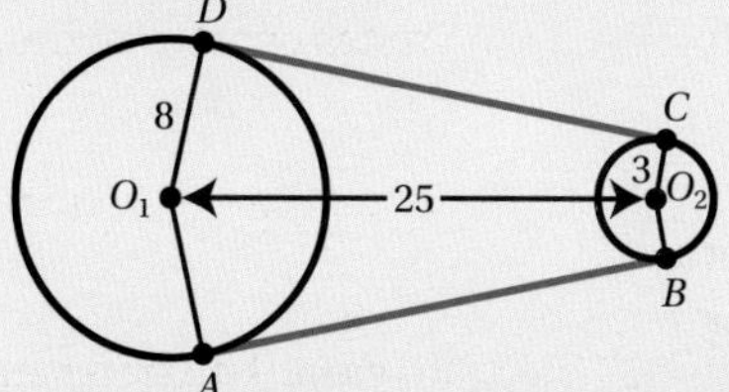

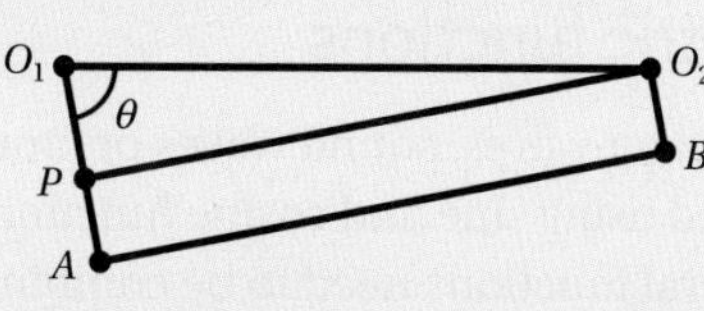

a Write down the size of O_1AB in radians, giving a reason for your answer.

b Explain why $PO_2 = AB$.

c Hence, find the length of AB.

d Find the size of the angle marked θ, giving your answer in radians, correct to.

e Calculate the length of the chain $ABCD$.

20 **a** Write down an expression for $\sin(\arcsin x)$.

b Show that $\sin(\arccos x) \equiv \sqrt{1 - x^2}$.

c Hence, solve the equation $\arcsin x = \arccos x$ for $0 \leqslant x \leqslant 1$.

8 Further trigonometry

In this chapter you will learn:

- how to find trigonometric functions of sums and differences of two angles (e.g. $\sin(A+B)$)
- a useful method for working with sums of trigonometric functions (e.g. $3\sin A + 5\cos B$)
- about some new trigonometric functions.

Before you start...

Student Book 1, Chapter 10	You should be able to use the identities $\sin^2 x + \cos^2 x \equiv 1$ and $\tan x \equiv \frac{\sin x}{\cos x}$.	1 Given that x is an acute angle with $\cos x = \frac{1}{3}$, find the exact value of: a $\sin x$ b $\tan x$
Chapter 7 and Student Book 1, Chapter 10	You should know and use graphs of trigonometric functions, in degrees and radians.	2 State the coordinates of the minimum point on the graph of $y = 1 - 3\sin(2-x)$, for $x \in \left[0, \frac{\pi}{2}\right]$.
Chapter 7 and Student Book 1, Chapter 10	You should be able to solve trigonometric equations in degrees and radians.	3 Solve the following equations. a $\sin(3x) = 2\cos(3x)$ for $0° \leqslant x \leqslant 90°$ b $2\cos^2\theta - \sin\theta = 1$ for $\theta \in [-\pi, \pi]$.

Combining trigonometric functions

Periodic phenomena, such as water waves, sound waves or motion around a circle, can be modelled using sine and cosine functions. There are many situations where several functions need to be combined. For example, you can model the interference of two waves by adding the functions that describe their shapes. Some fairground rides, such as the 'waltzer', have groups of seats arranged in a circle, which rotates on top of a larger rotating platform.

In this chapter you will learn how to simplify expressions involving some sums and products of trigonometric functions. This will enable you to, for example, sketch graphs such as $y = 3\sin x + 5\cos x$.

Section 1: Compound angle identities

Working in radians, use your calculator to find:

$$\sin 1.2, \sin 0.3 \text{ and } \sin 1.5$$
$$\cos 1.2, \cos 0.3 \text{ and } \cos 1.5$$

There seems to be no obvious connection between the values of, for example, $\sin A$, $\sin B$ and $\sin(A+B)$. In fact, there are formulae, called **compound angle identities**, to express $\sin(A+B)$ in terms of the functions of the individual angles. The derivations are given in the Focus on ... Proof 2, and the results are:

Focus on ...

The proofs of the results from this section are given in Focus on ... Proof 2.

Key point 8.1

$\sin(A+B) \equiv \sin A\cos B + \cos A\sin B$

$\sin(A-B) \equiv \sin A\cos B - \cos A\sin B$

$\cos(A+B) \equiv \cos A\cos B - \sin A\sin B$

$\cos(A-B) \equiv \cos A\cos B + \sin A\sin B$

This will appear in your formula book.

Tip

Notice the signs in the cosine identities: in the identity for the sum you use the minus sign, and in the identity for the difference you use the plus sign.

In fact, you need to prove only the identities for $\sin(A+B)$ and $\cos(A+B)$. They can then be used to prove the identities with $A-B$.

PROOF 6

Use the identity $\cos(A+B) \equiv \cos A\cos B - \sin A\sin B$ to prove that $\cos(A-B) \equiv \cos A\cos B + \sin A\sin B$.

Replace B by $-B$ in the first identity:

$\cos(A+(-B)) \equiv \cos A\cos(-B) - \sin A\sin(-B)$

The only difference between the two expressions on the left-hand side is the sign of B, so see what happens when you replace B with $-B$.

$\Leftrightarrow \cos(A-B) \equiv \cos A\cos B - \sin A(-\sin B)$

Now use the symmetries of the sine and cosine graphs:

$$\cos(-B) = \cos B \text{ and } \sin(-B) = -\sin B.$$

$\Leftrightarrow \cos(A-B) \equiv \cos A\cos B + \sin A\sin B$, as required.

One of the simplest applications of these identities is to calculate exact values of trigonometric functions.

Rewind

You met exact values of trigonometric functions in Chapter 7, Section 1.

WORKED EXAMPLE 8.1

Find the exact values of:

a $\sin 75°$ **b** $\cos 15°$

a $\sin 75° = \sin(30° + 45°)$

$= \sin 30° \cos 45° + \cos 30° \sin 45°$

$= \frac{1}{2}\frac{\sqrt{2}}{2} + \frac{\sqrt{3}}{2}\frac{\sqrt{2}}{2}$

$= \frac{\sqrt{2}+\sqrt{6}}{4}$

You only know the exact values of sine for a few angles: 0°, 30°, 45°, 60°, 90°. You can write 75° as a sum of two of those.

b $\cos 15° = \cos(45° - 30°)$

$= \cos 45° \cos 30° + \sin 45° \sin 30°$

$= \frac{\sqrt{2}}{2}\frac{\sqrt{3}}{2} + \frac{\sqrt{2}}{2}\frac{1}{2}$

$= \frac{\sqrt{6}+\sqrt{2}}{4}$

Look for a way to make 15° from the special angles.

Notice that the answers to parts **a** and **b** are the same. This is because $\cos(90° - x) = \sin(x)$.

Did you know?

A sum of square roots can sometimes also be shown as a nested root.

For example, an alternative representation for worked example 8.1 would be:

$\sin 75° = \frac{1}{2}\sqrt{2+\sqrt{3}}$

You can now use the sine and cosine compound angle identities to derive new ones. In particular:

Key point 8.2

$$\tan(A+B) \equiv \frac{\tan A + \tan B}{1 - \tan A \tan B}$$

WORKED EXAMPLE 8.2

Prove that $\tan(A+B) \equiv \frac{\tan A + \tan B}{1 - \tan A \tan B}$.

$\tan(A+B) \equiv \frac{\sin(A+B)}{\cos(A+B)}$

If you can't think of any relevant identity for tan, you can always express it in terms of sin and cos.

$\equiv \frac{\sin A \cos B + \cos A \sin B}{\cos A \cos B - \sin A \sin B}$

$\equiv \frac{\frac{\sin A}{\cos A} + \frac{\sin B}{\cos B}}{1 - \frac{\sin A}{\cos A}\frac{\sin B}{\cos B}}$

You want to express this in terms of tan. Looking at the top of the fraction, if you divide by $\cos A$ you will get $\tan A$ in the first term, and if you divide by $\cos B$ you will get $\tan B$ in the second term. So divide top and bottom by $\cos A \cos B$.

$\tan(A+B) \equiv \frac{\tan A + \tan B}{1 - \tan A \tan B}$

EXERCISE 8A

1 Express the following in the form $A\sin x + B\cos x$, giving exact values of A and B.

a $\sin\left(x+\frac{\pi}{3}\right)$ **b** $\sin\left(x-\frac{\pi}{4}\right)$

c $\cos\left(x+\frac{3\pi}{4}\right)$ **d** $\cos\left(x-\frac{3\pi}{2}\right)$

2 Find the exact value of the following.

a $\cos 75°$ **b** $\sin\left(\frac{7\pi}{12}\right)$ **c** $\tan 105°$

3 Find the exact value of $\cos(A-B)$ for angles shown in these diagrams.

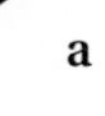

a

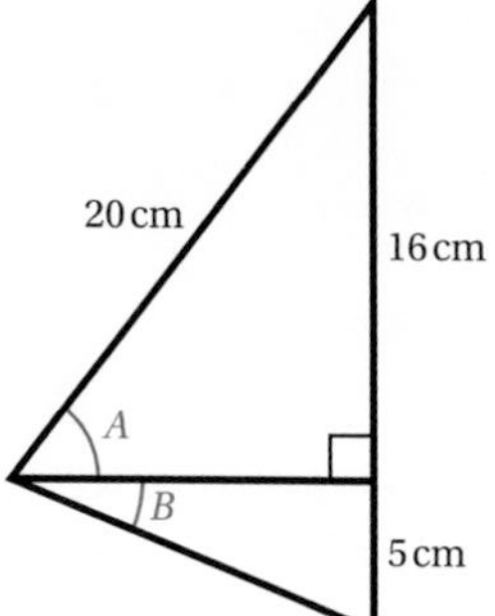

b

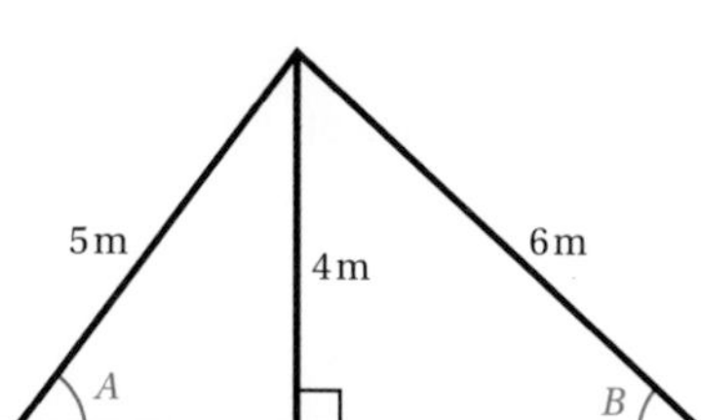

4 **a** Show that $\sin\left(x+\frac{\pi}{3}\right)+\sin\left(x-\frac{\pi}{3}\right)=\sin x$.

b Simplify $\sin\left(x+\frac{\pi}{4}\right)+\cos\left(x+\frac{\pi}{4}\right)$.

5 **a** Express $\tan\left(\theta-\frac{\pi}{4}\right)$ in terms of $\tan\theta$.

b Given that $\tan\left(\theta-\frac{\pi}{4}\right)=6\tan\theta$, find two possible values of $\tan\theta$.

c Hence, solve the equation $\tan\left(\theta-\frac{\pi}{4}\right)=6\tan\theta$ for $0<\theta<\pi$.

6 Write each of the following as a single trigonometric function. Hence, find the maximum value of each expression, and the smallest positive value of x for which it occurs.

a $\sin x\cos\frac{\pi}{4}+\cos x\sin\frac{\pi}{4}$

b $2\cos x\cos 25°+2\sin x\sin 25°$

7 Assuming x is small enough so that the terms in x^3 and higher can be ignored, find an approximate expression for $\sin\left(\frac{\pi}{3}+x\right)$ in terms of non-negative powers of x.

8 **a** Show that $\sin(A+B)+\sin(A-B)=2\sin A\cos B$.

b Hence, solve the equation $\sin\left(x+\frac{\pi}{6}\right)+\sin\left(x-\frac{\pi}{6}\right)=3\cos x$ for $0\leqslant\theta\leqslant\pi$.

9 **a** Show that $\cos(x+y)+\cos(x-y)=2\cos x\cos y$.

b Hence, solve the equation $\cos 3x+\cos x=3\cos 2x$ for $x\in[0,2\pi]$.

Section 2: Double angle identities

If you set $A = B$ in the compound angle identities, you get the **double angle identities**.

Key point 8.3

$$\sin 2A \equiv 2 \sin A \cos A$$

$$\cos 2A \equiv \begin{cases} 2\cos^2 A - 1 \\ 1 - 2\sin^2 A \\ \cos^2 A - \sin^2 A \end{cases}$$

$$\tan 2A \equiv \frac{2 \tan A}{1 - \tan^2 A}$$

Tip

You can derive these identities from those given in the formula book; however, you will need them so often that it is a good idea to learn them.

You can convert between the three different forms of the cos $2A$ identity by using $\sin^2 A + \cos^2 A \equiv 1$.

A useful application of these identities is finding exact values of half-angles.

WORKED EXAMPLE 8.3

Using the exact value of $\cos 30°$, show that $\sin 15° = \sqrt{\frac{2-\sqrt{3}}{4}}$.

Using $\cos 2A \equiv 1 - \sin^2 A$:

$\cos(2 \times 15°) = 1 - 2\sin^2 15°$

$\cos 30° = 1 - 2\sin^2 15°$

You know that $\cos 30° = \frac{\sqrt{3}}{2}$, so you can use a double angle formula to relate this to $\sin 15°$.

$\frac{\sqrt{3}}{2} = 1 - 2\sin^2 15°$

But you know that $\cos 30° = \frac{\sqrt{3}}{2}$.

$\sqrt{3} = 2 - 4\sin^2 15°$

$4\sin^2 15° = 2 - \sqrt{3}$

$\sin^2 15° = \frac{2-\sqrt{3}}{4}$

$\sin 15° = \sqrt{\frac{2-\sqrt{3}}{4}}$ (as $\sin 15° > 0$)

You have to choose between the positive and negative square root here. As $\sin 15° > 0$, take the positive square root.

Recognising the form of double angle formulae can be useful in solving trigonometric equations.

WORKED EXAMPLE 8.4

Solve the equation $6\sin x\cos x = 1$ for $-\pi < x < \pi$.

$6\sin x\cos x = 1$

$2\sin x\cos x = \frac{1}{3}$

$\sin 2x = \frac{1}{3}$ (as $2\sin x\cos x = \sin 2x$)

Write the left-hand side in terms of only one trigonometric function.

The LHS is similar to $2\sin x\cos x$, which equals $\sin 2x$.

Substitute $A = 2x$

Since $-\pi < x < \pi$, $-2\pi < 2x < 2\pi$

Follow the standard procedure and look at the graph to find that there are four solutions in the given domain.

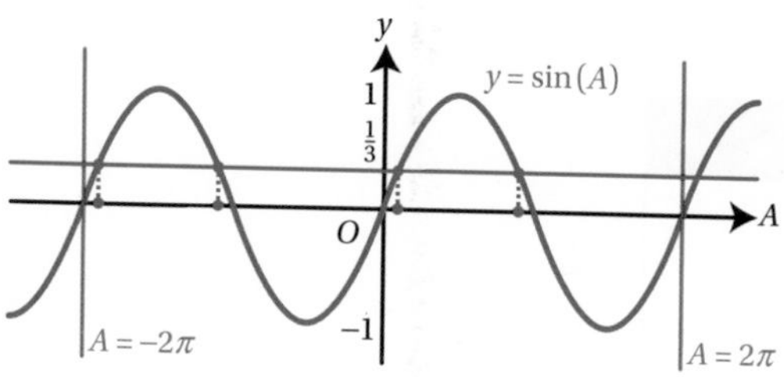

$\arcsin\left(\frac{1}{3}\right) = 0.3398$

$A = 0.3398, 2.802, -5.943, -3.481$

$x \approx 0.170, 1.40, -2.97, -1.74$ (3 s.f.)

If an equation contains both $\cos 2\theta$ and $\cos\theta$, you can use identities to turn it into an equation involving only $\cos\theta$.

WORKED EXAMPLE 8.5

Showing detailed reasoning, find exact solutions of the equation $\cos 2x = \cos x$ for $0° \leqslant x \leqslant 360°$.

$\cos 2x = \cos x$

$\Leftrightarrow 2\cos^2 x - 1 = \cos x$

(as $\cos 2x = 2\cos^2 x - 1$)

As before, you need to write the equation in terms of only one trigonometric function. (Note that $\cos 2x$ and $\cos x$ are not the same function!)

The LHS involves a double angle, so choose the $\cos 2x$ identity involving just $\cos x$.

$\Leftrightarrow 2\cos^2 x - \cos x - 1 = 0$

$\Leftrightarrow (2\cos x + 1)(\cos x - 1) = 0$

$\Leftrightarrow \cos x = -\frac{1}{2}$ or $\cos x = 1$

This is a quadratic in $\cos x$, so make one side equal to zero and try to factorise.

Continues on next page ...

When $\cos x = -\frac{1}{2}$:

$x = 120°$ or $360 - 120 = 240°$

Solve each equation separately.

When $\cos x = 1$:

$x = 0°$ or $360°$

$\therefore x = 0°, 120°, 240°, 360°$

Remember to list all the solutions at the end.

Although they are called the double angle identities, they can also be used with higher multiples.

Fast forward

In Chapter 11 you will use double angle identities to integrate some trigonometric functions.

WORKED EXAMPLE 8.6

Find an expression for $\cos 4x$ in terms of:

a $\cos 2x$ **b** $\cos x$

a Using $\cos 2x = 2\cos^2 x - 1$

$\cos 2 \times 2x = 2\cos^2 2x - 1$

$\cos 4x = 2\cos^2 2x - 1$

$4x = 2 \times 2x$ and so use one of the cosine double angle identities.

Since you want an expression involving only cosine, it has to be $\cos 2x \equiv 2\cos^2 x - 1$.

b From part a:

$\cos 4x = 2\cos^2 2x - 1$

$= 2(2\cos^2 x - 1)^2 - 1$

$(\text{as } \cos 2x = 2\cos^2 x - 1)$

It is always a good idea to try using the answer from the previous part of the question.

Use a double angle formula again to replace $\cos 2x$ in the answer in part **a**.

A combination of double angle and compound angle identities can be used to derive 'triple-angle identities'.

WORKED EXAMPLE 8.7

a Show that $\sin 3A \equiv 3\sin A - 4\sin^3 A$.

b Solve the equation $\sin 3x = \sin x$ for $x \in [0, 2\pi]$.

a $\sin 3A = \sin(2A + A)$

$= \sin 2A \cos A + \cos 2A \sin A$

If you write $3A = 2A + A$, you can use a compound angle identity.

$= (2\sin A \cos A)\cos A$

$+ (1 - 2\sin^2 A)\sin A$

(as $\sin 2A = 2\sin A \cos A$ and

$\cos 2A = 1 - 2\sin^2 A$)

You need an expression involving only single angles so you now use the double angle identities.

Since the answer only involves sine, use $\cos 2x \equiv 1 - 2\sin^2 x$.

$= 2\sin A \cos^2 A + \sin A - 2\sin^3 A$

$= 2\sin A(1 - \sin^2 A)$

$+ \sin A - 2\sin^3 A$

(as $\cos^2 x - 1 - \sin^2 x$)

You want only sine in the expression so replace $\cos^2 x$ with $1 - \sin^2 x$.

$= 2\sin A - 2\sin^3 A + \sin A - 2\sin^3 A$

$\sin 3A = 3\sin A - 4\sin^3 A$

b $\sin(3x) = \sin x$

$3\sin x - 4\sin^3 x = \sin x$

You need an equation in only one trigonometric function, which can be achieved by using the result in part **a**.

$2\sin x - 4\sin^3 x = 0$

$2\sin x(1 - 2\sin^2 x) = 0$

This is a cubic in $\sin x$, so rearrange to make the RHS = 0 and then factorise.

$\sin x = 0$ or $\sin^2 x = \frac{1}{2}$

When $\sin x = 0$:

$x = 0, \pi, 2\pi$

When $\sin^2 x = \frac{1}{2}$:

$\sin x = \frac{1}{\sqrt{2}}$ or $-\frac{1}{\sqrt{2}}$

$x = \frac{\pi}{4}, \frac{3\pi}{4}, \frac{5\pi}{4}, \frac{7\pi}{4}$

The double angle formulae allow you to simplify some complex and awkward expressions involving functions and inverse functions.

WORKED EXAMPLE 8.8

Let $x \in [-1, 1]$. Find an expression in terms of x for:

a $\cos(2\arccos x)$ **b** $\sin(2\arccos x)$

a Using $\cos 2\theta = 2\cos^2\theta - 1$:

$\cos(2\arccos x) = 2\cos^2(\arccos x) - 1$

$= 2(\cos(\arccos x))^2 - 1$

$\cos(2\arccos x) = 2x^2 - 1$

You know that $\cos(\arccos x) = x$ but this doesn't help you in dealing with $\cos(2\arccos x)$.

However, you do have a double angle here, so use the identity involving only cos (as you have no interest in introducing sin here).

b Using $\sin 2\theta = 2\sin\theta\cos\theta$:

Use the sine double angle identity this time.

$\sin(2\arccos x) = 2\sin(\arccos x)$
$\cos(\arccos x)$(*)

Using $\sin^2\theta = 1 - \cos^2\theta$:

You can't do anything with $\sin(\arccos x)$ but you can work with $\cos(\arccos x)$.

$\sin^2(\arccos x) = 1 - \cos^2(\arccos x)$

$= 1 - x^2$

$\arccos x \in [0, \pi]$, so $\sin(\arccos x) > 0$

When you take the square root, there could be two possible answers.

$\sin(\arccos x) = \sqrt{1 - x^2}$

Substituting into (*)

$\sin(2\arccos x) = 2x\sqrt{1 - x^2}$

EXERCISE 8B

1 **a** **i** Given that $\cos\theta = -\frac{1}{4}$, find the exact value of $\cos 2\theta$.

ii Given that $\sin A = -\frac{2}{3}$, find the exact value of $\cos 2A$.

b **i** Given that $\sin x = \frac{1}{3}$ and $0 < x < \frac{\pi}{2}$, find the exact value of $\cos x$.

ii Given that $\sin x = \frac{3}{5}$ and $0 < x < \frac{\pi}{2}$, find the exact value of $\cos x$.

c **i** Given that $\sin x = \frac{1}{3}$ and $0 < x < \frac{\pi}{2}$, find the exact value of $\sin 2x$.

ii Given that $\sin x = \frac{3}{5}$ and $0 < x < \frac{\pi}{2}$, find the exact value of $\sin 2x$.

2 Find the exact value of:

a $\sin^2 22.5°$ **b** $\cos^2 75°$ **c** $\cos^2\left(\frac{\pi}{12}\right)$

3 Find the exact value of $\tan 22.5°$.

4 Simplify using a double angle identity:

a $2\cos^2(3A)-1$ b $4\sin 5x\cos 5x$

c $3-6\sin^2\left(\frac{b}{2}\right)$ d $5\sin\left(\frac{x}{3}\right)\cos\left(\frac{x}{3}\right)$

5 Use double angle identities to solve the following equations.

a $\sin 2x = 3\sin x$ for $x\in[0, 2\pi]$ b $\cos 2x - \sin^2 x = -2$ for $0° \leqslant x \leqslant 180°$

c $5\sin 2x = 3\cos x$ for $-\pi < x < \pi$ d $\tan 2x - \tan x = 0$ for $0° \leqslant x \leqslant 360°$

6 Prove these identities:

a $(\sin x + \cos x)^2 \equiv 1 + \sin 2x$ b $\cos^4\theta - \sin^4\theta \equiv \cos 2\theta$

c $\tan 2A - \tan A \equiv \dfrac{\tan A}{\cos 2A}$ d $\tan\alpha - \dfrac{1}{\tan\alpha} \equiv -\dfrac{2}{\tan 2\alpha}$

7 Find all the values of $\theta\in[-\pi, \pi]$ that satisfy the equation $\cos^2\theta + \cos 2\theta = 0$.

8 Show that $\dfrac{1-\cos 2\theta}{1+\cos 2\theta} \equiv \tan^2\theta$.

9 a Given that $\tan\alpha\tan 2\alpha = 6$, find the possible values of $\tan\alpha$.

b Solve the equation $\tan\alpha\tan 2\alpha = 1$ for $\alpha\in(0, \pi)$, giving your answer in terms of π.

10 a Express $\cos 3A$ in terms of $\cos A$.

b Express $\tan 3A$ in terms of $\tan A$.

11 Express $\cos 4\theta$ in terms of:

a $\cos\theta$ b $\sin\theta$

12 a Show that:

i $\cos^2\left(\frac{1}{2}x\right) = \frac{1}{2}(1+\cos x)$ ii $\sin^2\left(\frac{1}{2}x\right) = \frac{1}{2}(1-\cos x)$

b Express $\tan^2\left(\frac{1}{2}x\right)$ in terms of $\cos x$.

13 Given that $a\sin 4x = b\sin 2x$ and $0 < x < \frac{\pi}{2}$, express $\sin^2 x$ in terms of a and b.

14 Without using your calculator, find the exact value of:

a $\tan(\arctan(1.2) + \arctan(0.5))$

b $\tan\left(2\arctan\left(\frac{1}{3}\right)\right)$

15 a Show that $\cos^2\left(\frac{1}{2}A\right) = \frac{1}{2}(1+\cos A)$.

b Hence, show that $\cos\left(\frac{1}{2}\arccos x\right) = \sqrt{\frac{1}{2}(1+x)}$ for $-1 \leqslant x \leqslant 1$.

Section 3: Expressions of the form $a\sin x + b\cos x$

In this section you look at a useful method for dealing with sums of trigonometric functions. Suppose you are trying to solve the equation $3\sin x + 4\cos x = 2$. You know that you need to try to write everything in terms of one trigonometric function, so start by considering the identities met so far.

You cannot just replace $\sin x$ with a function of $\cos x$ (or $\cos x$ with a function of $\sin x$), because the only identity you have linking these is $\sin^2 x + \cos^2 x = 1$ and you have neither $\sin^2 x$ or $\cos^2 x$ in the equation. So instead look for an identity involving both $\sin x$ and $\cos x$. From the list of compound angle identities there are several options. Try one with the understanding that if it does not work you will just try another.

Tip

Notice that $\cos(x - y) = \cos x \cos y + \sin x \sin y$ would work here as well as it also has a + sign.

So consider the first one you met:

$$\sin(x + y) \equiv \sin x \cos y + \cos x \sin y$$
$$\equiv \cos y \sin x + \sin y \cos x$$

Now, compare this with the equation:

$$3\sin x + 4\cos x = 2$$

You can see that the LHS of the equation would be the same as the compound angle expression if you could find y so that $\cos y = 3$ and $\sin y = 4$. This is not possible, because $\sin y$ and $\cos y$ cannot be greater than 1. However, you can adjust the original identity by multiplying by a constant, R:

$$R\sin(x + y) \equiv (R\cos y)\sin x + (R\sin y)\cos x$$

Now you have:

$$R\cos y = 3 \quad \text{and} \quad R\sin y = 4$$

which constitutes a pair of simultaneous equations in two unknowns (R and y).

To find R, you can use $\sin^2\theta + \cos^2\theta \equiv 1$:

$$(R\sin y)^2 + (R\cos y)^2 = 4^2 + 3^2 \Leftrightarrow R^2(\sin^2 y + \cos^2 y) = 16 + 9$$
$$\Leftrightarrow R^2 = 25$$
$$\therefore R = 5 \text{ (by convention } R > 0)$$

To find y you can eliminate R by dividing one equation by the other:

$$\frac{R\sin y}{R\cos y} = \frac{4}{3} \Leftrightarrow \tan y = \frac{4}{3}$$
$$\therefore y = \arctan\left(\frac{4}{3}\right) = 0.927 \text{ (3 s.f.)}$$

Tip

There are other possible values of y that satisfy $\tan y = \frac{4}{3}$, but here we need to find only one such value.

So, you have shown that $3 \sin x + 4 \cos x$ can be written as $5 \sin(x + 0.927)$, which allows you to rewrite the equation as:

$$5 \sin(x + 0.927) = 2$$

This is now a type of equation that you know how to solve.

Although this whole procedure looks rather long and complicated, with practice you will find that you can complete it quite quickly. In the next example, you will see that you can express the same function in terms of cosine rather than sine, following the same procedure, and then continue to solve the equation.

WORKED EXAMPLE 8.9

a Write $3\sin x + 4\cos x$ in the form $R\cos(x-\alpha)$.
b Solve $3\sin x + 4\cos x = 2$ for $x \in [0, 2\pi]$.

a $R\cos(x-\alpha) \equiv R(\cos x\cos\alpha + \sin x\sin\alpha)$

$\equiv (R\cos\alpha)\cos x + (R\sin\alpha)\sin x$

$\equiv (R\sin\alpha)\sin x + (R\cos\alpha)\cos x$

You are told to use $R\cos(x-\alpha)$, so you first expand this using the compound angle identity.

Comparing this with $3\sin x + 4\cos x$ we have
$R\sin\alpha = 3$, $R\cos\alpha = 4$

$R^2(\cos^2\alpha + \sin^2\alpha) = 4^2 + 3^2 = 25$

$R = 5$

R can now be found using $\sin^2\alpha + \cos^2\alpha \equiv 1$...

$\frac{R\sin\alpha}{R\cos\alpha} = \frac{3}{4}$

... and α can be found using $\frac{\sin\alpha}{\cos\alpha} \equiv \tan\alpha$.

$\tan\alpha = \frac{3}{4}$

$\alpha = \tan^{-1}\left(\frac{3}{4}\right) = 0.644$ (3 s.f.)

$\therefore 3\sin x + 4\cos x = 5\cos(x - 0.644)$

b $3\sin x + 4\cos x = 2$

You can use the answer from the previous part.

$5\cos(x - 0.644) = 2$

$\cos(x - 0.644) = \frac{2}{5}$

Let $A = x - 0.644$.

You have met this type of equation before, so follow the standard procedure.

Since $0 < x < 2\pi$, $-0.644 < A < 2\pi - 0.644$

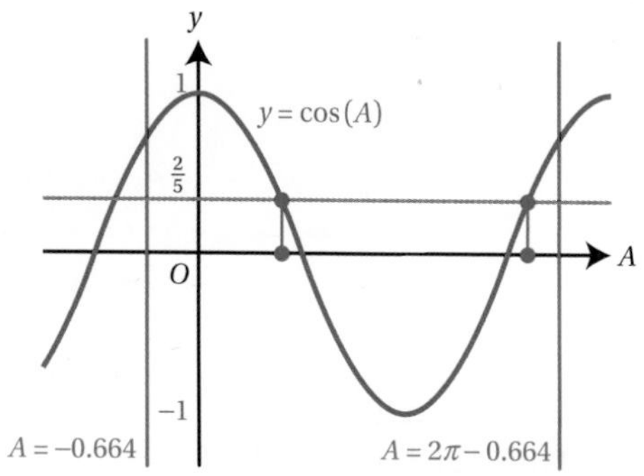

$\arccos\left(\frac{2}{5}\right) = 1.159$

$A = 1.159, 5.124$

$x \approx 1.80, 5.77$ (3 s.f.)

The procedure can be summarised as follows.

Key point 8.4

To write $a \sin x \pm b \cos x$ in the form $R \sin(x \pm \alpha)$ or $R \cos(x \pm \alpha)$:

- Expand the brackets using compound angle identities.
- Equate coefficients of $\sin x$ and $\cos x$ to get equations for $R \sin \alpha$ and $R \cos \alpha$.
- Use $R^2 = a^2 + b^2$.
- To get $\tan \alpha$, divide the $\sin \alpha$ equation by the $\cos \alpha$ equation.

The next example illustrates the method with a difference of two trigonometric functions.

WORKED EXAMPLE 8.10

a Write $4\sin x - 6\cos x$ in the form $R\sin(x-\theta)$, where $R > 0$ and $\theta \in \left[0, \frac{\pi}{2}\right]$.

b Hence, find the maximum value of $4 \sin x - 6 \cos x$ and the smallest positive value of x for which it occurs.

c Sketch the graph of $4 \sin x - 6 \cos x$ for $x \in [-2\pi, 2\pi]$.

a $R\sin(x-\theta) \equiv R(\sin x \cos\theta - \cos x \sin\theta)$

$\equiv (R\cos\theta)\sin x - (R\sin\theta)\cos x$

You can now follow the standard procedure for this type of question.

So, start by expanding $R\sin(x-\theta)$.

Comparing this with $4\sin x - 6\cos x$ you have

$R\cos\theta = 4$, $R\sin\theta = 6$

$R^2 = 4^2 + 6^2 = 52$

$R = \sqrt{52} = 2\sqrt{13}$

$\tan\theta = \frac{R\sin\theta}{R\cos\theta} = \frac{6}{4} = \frac{3}{2}$

$\theta = \arctan\left(\frac{3}{2}\right) = 0.983$ (3 s.f.)

$\therefore 4\sin x - 6\cos x = 2\sqrt{13}\sin(x - 0.983)$

b Maximum value $= 2\sqrt{13} \approx 7.21$

Since sine has a maximum value of 1, the maximum value of this function must be R.

This value occurs when $\sin(x - 0.983) = 1$.

For the smallest positive value of x:

The maximum value of $\sin y$ occurs when $y = \frac{\pi}{2}$.

$x - 0.983 = \frac{\pi}{2}$

$\Leftrightarrow x = 0.983 + \frac{\pi}{2} = 2.55$ (3 s.f.)

c $y = 7.21\sin(x - 0.983)$

This is the graph of $y = \sin x$, translated 0.983 units to the right and stretched vertically with scale factor 7.21.

x-intercepts: $-5.30, -2.16, 0.98, 4.12$
y-intercept: -6

The x-intercepts of $y = \sin x$ are $-2\pi, -\pi, 0, \pi$; add 0.983 to these values.

Maximum points: $(-3.73, 7.21)$ and $(2.55, 7.21)$

You found one of the maximum points in part **b**. Subtract 2π to find the other one.

Minimum points: $(-0.59, -7.21)$ and $(5.70, -7.21)$

Add and subtract π to find the minimum points.

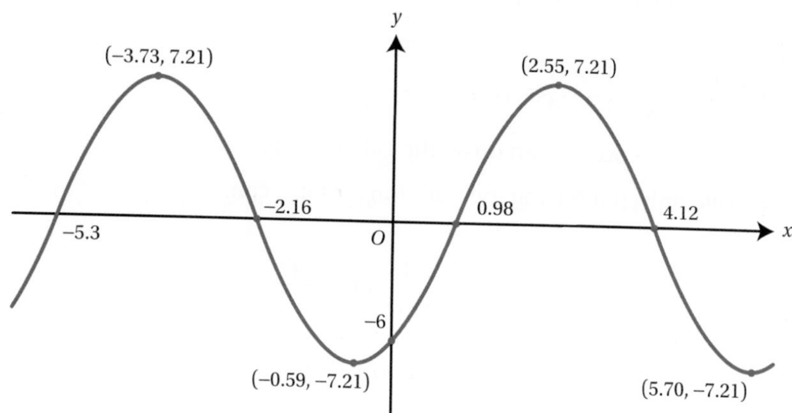

EXERCISE 8C

1 Express the following in the form $R\sin(x + \alpha)$, where $R > 0$ and $0 < \alpha < \frac{\pi}{2}$:

a $4\sin x + 6\cos x$ **b** $\cos x + 3\sin x$

2 Express in the form $r\sin(\theta - a)$, where $r > 0$ and $0° < a < 90°$:

a $2\sin\theta - 2\cos\theta$ **b** $\sin\theta - \sqrt{3}\cos\theta$

3 Express in the form $r\cos(x + \theta)$, where $r > 0$ and $0 < \theta < \frac{\pi}{2}$:

a $\sqrt{6}\cos x - \sqrt{2}\sin x$ **b** $5\cos x - 5\sin x$

4 Express in the form $R\cos(x - \theta)$, where $R > 0$ and $0° < \theta < 90°$:

a $6\sin x + 7\cos x$ **b** $5\sin x + 12\cos x$

5 **a** Express $5\sin x + 12\cos x$ in the form $R\sin(x + \theta)$.

b Hence, give details of two successive transformations that transform the graph of $y = \sin x$ into the graph of $y = 5\sin x + 12\cos x$.

6 **a** Express $3\sin x - 7\cos x$ in the form $R\sin(x - \theta)$.

b Hence, find the range of the function $f(x) = 3\sin x - 7\cos x$.

7 **a** Express $4\cos x - 5\sin x$ in the form $R\cos(x+\alpha)$.

b Hence, find the smallest positive value of x for which $4\cos x - 5\sin x = 0$.

8 **a** Express $\sqrt{3}\sin x + \cos x$ in the form $R\cos(x-\theta)$.

b Hence, find the coordinates of the minimum and maximum points on the graph of $y=\sqrt{3}\sin x + \cos x$ for $x \in [0, 2\pi]$.

9 Find, to 3 significant figures, all values of x in the interval $[0, 2\pi]$ for which $2\sin x - \cos x = 2$.

10 By expressing $\sin 2x + \cos 2x$ in the form $R\sin(2x+a)$, solve the equation $\sin 2x + \cos 2x = 1$ for $-\pi \leqslant x \leqslant \pi$.

Elevate

See Support sheet 8 for a further example of solving equations of the form $a\sin x + b\cos x$ and for more practice questions.

Section 4: Reciprocal trigonometric functions

You already know that $\tan x \equiv \dfrac{\sin x}{\cos x}$, so you can do all the calculations you need with sine and cosine only, but having the notation for tan x can simplify many expressions.

Similarly, since expressions of the form $\dfrac{\cos x}{\sin x}\left(\equiv \dfrac{1}{\tan x}\right)$, $\dfrac{1}{\sin x}$ and $\dfrac{1}{\cos x}$ often occur, it seems sensible to have notations for these as well. This is part of the motive for introducing three additional trigonometric functions.

Key point 8.5

The secant function: $\sec x \equiv \dfrac{1}{\cos x}$ for $x \neq \left(k+\dfrac{1}{2}\right)\pi$

The cosecant function: $\operatorname{cosec} x \equiv \dfrac{1}{\sin x}$ for $x \neq k\pi$

The cotangent function: $\cot x \equiv \dfrac{1}{\tan x} \equiv \dfrac{\cos x}{\sin x}$ for $x \neq k\pi$

for any integer k

Using the graphs of sine, cosine and tangent you can draw the graphs of $y = \sec x$, $y = \operatorname{cosec} x$ and $y = \cot x$. For example, the graph of $y = \sec x$ will have vertical asymptotes at the values of x where $\cos x = 0$ (because you can't divide by zero). As cos x increases in magnitude, sec x will decrease, and vice versa. When cos x is positive, sec x is also positive. Finally, when $\cos x = 1$ or -1, sec x has the same value. A similar analysis can be applied to cosec x and cot x as well.

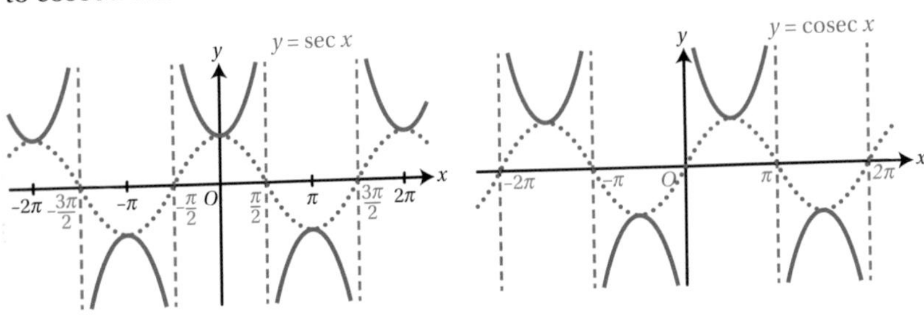

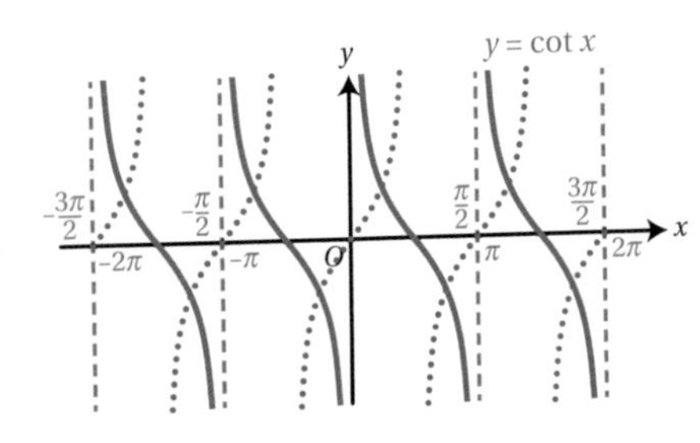

The graphs show the domains and ranges of the reciprocal trigonometric functions.

Key point 8.6

Function	Domain	Range
sec	$x \neq \left(k+\frac{1}{2}\right)\pi$	$\sec x \in (-\infty, -1] \cup [1, \infty)$
cosec	$x \neq k\pi$	$\operatorname{cosec} x \in (-\infty, -1] \cup [1, \infty)$
cot	$x \neq k\pi$	$\cot x \in \mathbb{R}$

In each domain, k is an integer

The following identities can be deduced from the familiar $\sin^2 x + \cos^2 x = 1$ by dividing through by $\cos^2 x$ and $\sin^2 x$, respectively.

Key point 8.7

$\sec^2 x \equiv 1 + \tan^2 x$

$\operatorname{cosec}^2 x \equiv 1 + \cot^2 x$

Tip

The reciprocal trigonometric functions follow the same conventions as the normal trigonometric functions, so $\sec^2 x$ means $(\sec x)^2$.

WORKED EXAMPLE 8.11

Solve the equation $2\tan^2 x + \dfrac{3}{\cos x} = 0$ for $-\pi < x < \pi$.

$$2\tan^2 x + \frac{3}{\cos x} = 0$$

$\dfrac{1}{\cos x} \equiv \sec x$ and therefore $\dfrac{3}{\cos x} = 3\sec x$.

$$2\tan^2 x + 3\sec x = 0$$

$$2(\sec^2 x - 1) + 3 = 0$$

(since $\tan^2 x = \sec^2 x - 1$)

As always, you require the equation to contain only one trigonometric function, so you use an identity to replace $\tan^2 x$ with a function of $\sec^2 x$.

$$2\sec^2 x + 3\sec x - 2 = 0$$

$$(2\sec x - 1)(\sec x + 2) = 0$$

$$\sec x = \frac{1}{2} \text{ or } \sec x = -2$$

$$\cos x = 2 \text{ or } \cos x = -\frac{1}{2}$$

You don't know how to find inverse sec, so express $\sec x$ in terms of $\cos x$.

When $\cos x = 2$:

Finally, you solve each equation separately.

Reject since $-1 \leqslant \cos x \leqslant 1$.

When $\cos x = -\frac{1}{2}$:

$$\arccos\left(-\frac{1}{2}\right) = \frac{2\pi}{3}$$

$$x = \frac{2\pi}{3} \text{ or } -\frac{2\pi}{3}$$

WORKED EXAMPLE 8.12

Show that $\sec 2\theta \equiv \frac{\sec^2\theta}{2-\sec^2\theta}$.

$\sec 2\theta \equiv \frac{1}{\cos 2\theta}$

You have a formula for $\cos 2\theta$, so start by introducing cos.

$\equiv \frac{1}{2\cos^2\theta - 1} \quad (\text{as } \cos(2\theta) \equiv 2\cos^2\theta - 1)$

$\equiv \frac{1}{\frac{2}{\sec^2\theta} - 1} \quad \left(\text{as } \cos\theta \equiv \frac{1}{\sec\theta}\right)$

You need $\sec\theta$ in the answer so you change back from $\cos\theta$.

$\sec 2\theta \equiv \frac{\sec^2\theta}{2-\sec^2\theta}$

Finally, you can simplify by multiplying top and bottom of the fraction by $\sec^2\theta$.

EXERCISE 8D

In this exercise, all arguments of trigonometric functions are given in radians, unless specified otherwise.

1 Giving your answers to 4 significant figures, find the value of:

a **i** $\sec(1.2)$ **ii** $\operatorname{cosec} 2.4$

b **i** $\cot(-3.5)$ **ii** $\sec(-0.6)$

c **i** $\operatorname{cosec}\left(\frac{2\pi}{5}\right)$ **ii** $\cot\left(\frac{4\pi}{3}\right)$

2 Find the exact value of:

a **i** $\operatorname{cosec}\left(\frac{\pi}{3}\right)$ **ii** $\operatorname{cosec}\left(\frac{\pi}{4}\right)$

b **i** $\sec\left(\frac{3\pi}{4}\right)$ **ii** $\sec\left(\frac{5\pi}{6}\right)$

c **i** $\cot\left(-\frac{\pi}{4}\right)$ **ii** $\cot\left(-\frac{2\pi}{3}\right)$

d **i** $\operatorname{cosec}\left(\frac{3\pi}{2}\right)$ **ii** $\cot\left(\frac{\pi}{2}\right)$

3 Find the values of $\operatorname{cosec} A$ and $\sec B$ in the following diagram.

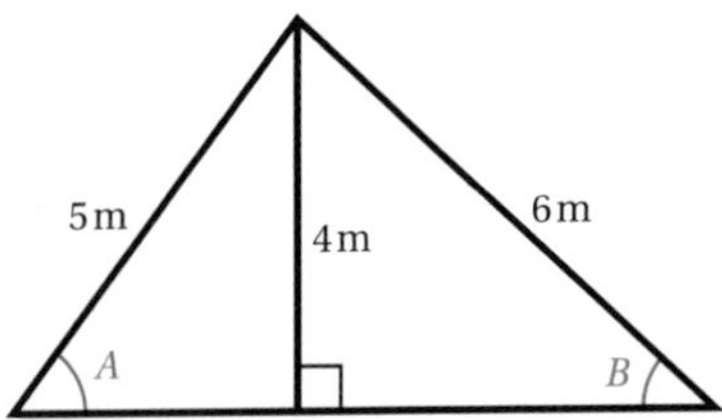

4 Solve the following equations for $x \in [0, 2\pi]$, giving your answers to 3 s.f.

a **i** $\sec x = 2$ **ii** $\sec x = 3$

b **i** $\operatorname{cosec} x = 1.5$ **ii** $\operatorname{cosec} x = 2.7$

c **i** $\cot x = 5$ **ii** $\cot x = 0.5$

d **i** $\sec 2x = 3$ **ii** $\operatorname{cosec} 2x = 4$

5 Find the exact solution of the following equations for $-\pi \leqslant \theta \leqslant \pi$.

a **i** $\operatorname{cosec}\theta = -2$ **ii** $\operatorname{cosec}\theta = -1$

b **i** $\cot\theta = \sqrt{3}$ **ii** $\cot\theta = 1$

c **i** $\sec\theta = 1$ **ii** $\sec\theta = -\frac{2}{\sqrt{3}}$

d **i** $\cot\theta = 0$ **ii** $\cot\theta = -1$

6 **a** **i** Given that $\tan\theta = \frac{4}{3}$ and $0° < \theta < 90°$, find the exact value of $\sec\theta$.

ii Given that $\tan\theta = \frac{2}{5}$ and $0° < \theta < 90°$, find the exact value of $\sec\theta$.

b **i** Given that $\operatorname{cosec}\theta = 5$ and $\theta \in \left[0, \frac{\pi}{2}\right]$ find the exact value of $\cot\theta$.

ii Given that $\operatorname{cosec}\theta = 3$ and $\theta \in \left[0, \frac{\pi}{2}\right]$ find the exact value of $\cot\theta$.

c **i** Given that $\cot\theta = 3$ and $\pi < \theta < \frac{3\pi}{2}$, find the exact value of $\sin\theta$.

ii Given that $\cot\theta = \frac{1}{2}$ and $\pi < \theta < \frac{3\pi}{2}$, find the exact value of $\sin\theta$.

d **i** Given that $\sin\theta = \frac{\sqrt{2}}{3}$, find the possible values of $\sec\theta$.

ii Given that $\sin\theta = -\frac{1}{2}$, find the possible values of $\sec\theta$.

7 Show that $\tan x + \cot x \equiv \sec x \operatorname{cosec} x$.

8 Prove that $\sin^2\theta + \cot^2\theta \sin^2\theta \equiv 1$.

9 Prove that $\frac{\sin\theta}{1-\cos\theta} - \frac{\sin\theta}{1+\cos\theta} \equiv 2\cot\theta$.

10 **a** Given that $\sec^2 x - 3\tan x + 1 = 0$, show that $\tan^2 x - 3\tan x + 2 = 0$.

b Find the possible values of $\tan x$.

c Hence, solve the equation $\sec^2 x - 3\tan x + 1 = 0$ for $x \in [0, 2\pi]$.

11 Prove that $\operatorname{cosec} 2x \equiv \frac{\sec x \operatorname{cosec} x}{2}$.

12 Prove that $\cot 2x \equiv \frac{\cot^2 x - 1}{2\cot x}$.

13 Given that θ is small enough to neglect the terms in θ^3 and above, find an approximate expression for $\sec(3\theta)$ in ascending powers of θ.

14 Find the inverse function of $\sec x$ in terms of the arccos function.

Checklist of learning and understanding

- Double angle identities and compound angle identities (Be careful to get the signs right!):

$$\sin(A \pm B) \equiv \sin A \cos B \pm \cos A \sin B$$
$$\cos(A \pm B) \equiv \cos A \cos B \mp \sin A \sin B$$
$$\tan(A \pm B) \equiv \frac{\tan A \pm \tan B}{1 \mp \tan A \tan B}$$
$$\sin 2\theta \equiv 2\sin\theta\cos\theta$$
$$\cos 2\theta \equiv \begin{cases} 2\cos^2\theta - 1 \\ 1 - 2\sin^2\theta \\ \cos^2\theta - \sin^2\theta \end{cases}$$
$$\tan 2\theta \equiv \frac{2\tan\theta}{1-\tan^2\theta}$$

- One particular application of these identities is to write $a\sin x \pm b\cos x$ in the form $R\sin(x \pm \alpha)$ or $R\cos(x \pm \alpha)$:
  - Expand the brackets using compound angle identities.
  - Equate coefficients of $\sin x$ and $\cos x$ to get equations for $R\sin\alpha$ and $R\cos\alpha$.
  - Find R: $R^2 = a^2 + b^2$.
  - To get $\tan\alpha$, divide the $\sin\alpha$ equation by the $\cos\alpha$ equation.
- Reciprocal trigonometric functions are defined by:

  $\sec x \equiv \frac{1}{\cos x}$ for $x \neq \left(k + \frac{1}{2}\right)\pi$

  $\operatorname{cosec} x \equiv \frac{1}{\sin x}$ for $x \neq k\pi$

  $\cot x \equiv \frac{1}{\tan x} \equiv \frac{\cos x}{\sin x}$ for $x \neq k\pi$ where k is an integer
- Two identities for reciprocal trigonometric functions can be derived from the Pythagorean identity:

  $\sec^2 x \equiv 1 + \tan^2 x$

  $\operatorname{cosec}^2 x \equiv 1 + \cot^2 x$

Mixed practice 8

1 **a** Use the identity for $\cos(A+B)$ to prove that $\cos 2\theta \equiv 1-2\sin^2\theta$.

b Find the exact solutions of the equation $\cos 2\theta = \sin\theta$ for $0 \leqslant \theta \leqslant 2\pi$.

2 **a** Write $\cos\left(x+\frac{\pi}{3}\right)$ in the form $a\cos x + b\sin x$.

b Hence, find the exact value of $x \in [-2\pi, 2\pi]$ for which $\cos\left(x+\frac{\pi}{3}\right) = \cos\left(x-\frac{\pi}{3}\right)$.

3 The circle shown in the diagram has centre O and radius r. AC is the diameter of the circle.

a Write down the lengths of AB and BC in terms of r and θ.

b Write down an expression for the area of the triangle ABC.

c Write down an expression for the area of the triangle OBC.

d Hence, find the ratio of the two areas in the form

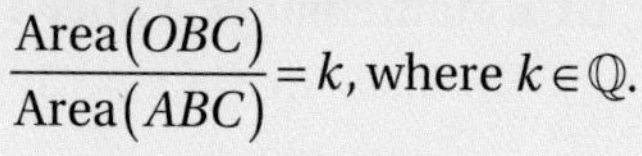

$$\frac{\text{Area}(OBC)}{\text{Area}(ABC)} = k, \text{ where } k \in \mathbb{Q}.$$

4 **a** Use the identity for $\tan(A+B)$ to show that $\tan 2A \equiv \dfrac{2\tan A}{1-\tan^2 A}$.

b Write down the value of $\tan 135°$.

c Hence, find the exact value of $\tan 67.5°$.

5 A water wave has the profile shown in the graph, where y represents the height of the wave, in metres, and x is the horizontal distance, also in metres.

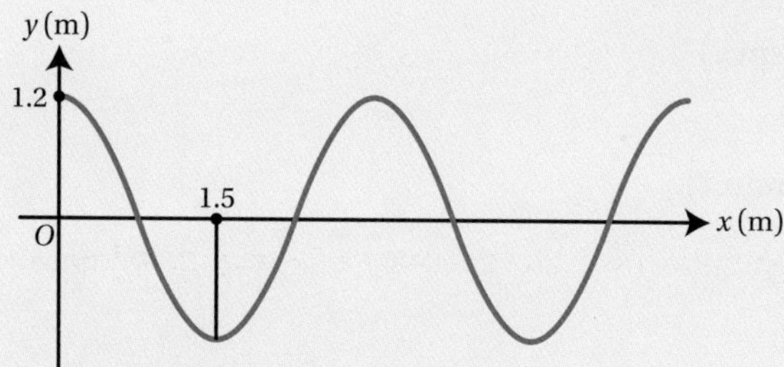

a Given that the equation of the wave can be written as $y_1 = a\cos(px)$, find the values of a and p.

b A second wave has the profile given by the equation $y_2 = 0.9\sin\left(\frac{2\pi}{3}x\right)$. Write down the amplitude and the period of the second wave.

When the two waves combine a new wave is formed, with the profile given by $y = y_1 + y_2$.

c Write the equation for y in the form $R\sin(x+\alpha)$ for a suitable value of α, where $R > 0$ and $0 < \alpha < \frac{\pi}{2}$.

d State the amplitude and the period of the combined wave.

e Find the smallest positive value of x for which the height of the combined wave is zero.

f Find the first two positive values of x for which the height of the combined wave is 1.3 metres.

6 **i** Sketch the graph of $y = \sec x$ for $0 \leqslant x \leqslant 2\pi$.

ii Solve the equation $\sec x = 3$ for $0 \leqslant x \leqslant 2\pi$, giving the roots correct to 3 significant figures.

iii Solve the equation $\sec\theta = 5\,\text{cosec}\,\theta$ for $0 \leqslant \theta \leqslant 2\pi$, giving the roots correct to 3 significant figures.

7 **a** Use the identity for $\cos(A+B)$ to show that $\cos 2\theta \equiv 2\cos^2\theta - 1$.

b Hence, solve the equation $\dfrac{\sin\theta}{1+\cos\theta} = 3\cot\dfrac{\theta}{2}$ for $\theta \in (0, 2\pi)$.

8 **a** Write $t^3 - 3t^2 - 3t + 1$ as a product of a linear and a quadratic factor.

b Show that $\tan 3A = \dfrac{3\tan A - \tan^3 A}{1 - 3\tan^2 A}$.

c Write down the exact value of $\tan 45°$.

d Hence, find the exact value of $\tan 15°$ and $\tan 75°$.

9 **i** Express $3\cos x + 3\sin x$ in the form $R\cos(x - \alpha)$, where $R > 0$ and $0 < \alpha < \frac{1}{2}\pi$.

ii The expression $\mathrm{T}(x)$ is defined by $\mathrm{T}(x) = \dfrac{8}{3\cos x + 3\sin}$.

a Determine a value of x for which $\mathrm{T}(x)$ is not defined.

b Find the smallest positive value of x satisfying $\mathrm{T}(3x) = \frac{8}{9}\sqrt{6}$, giving your answer in an exact form.

10 **a** Express $\sqrt{15}\sin(2x) + \sqrt{5}\cos(2x)$ in the form $R\sin(2x + \alpha)$.

b The function f is defined by $\mathrm{f}(x) = \dfrac{2}{5 + \sqrt{15}\sin(2x) + \sqrt{5}\cos(2x)}$.

Using your answer to part **a**, find

i the maximum value of $\mathrm{f}(x)$, giving your answer in the form $p + q\sqrt{5}$ where $p, q \in \mathbb{Q}$;

ii the smallest value of x for which this maximum occurs, giving your answer exactly, in terms of π.

11 In this question, $x \in [-1, 1]$

a Write down an expression for $\sin(\arcsin x)$.

b Show that $\cos(\arcsin x) = \sqrt{1 - x^2}$.

c Hence, find an expression for $\sin(2\arcsin x)$.

12 **a** **i** Expand $\left(x - \sqrt{10}\right)^2$.

ii Hence, show that $x^2 + 10 \geqslant 2\sqrt{10}\,x$.

iii State the value of x for which the equality holds.

A picture of height 3 m hangs on the wall. An observer stands at a distance d m from the wall with the lower end of the picture 2 m above their eye-level. The angle between the lines from the observer's eyes to the top and bottom of the picture is θ, as shown in the diagram.

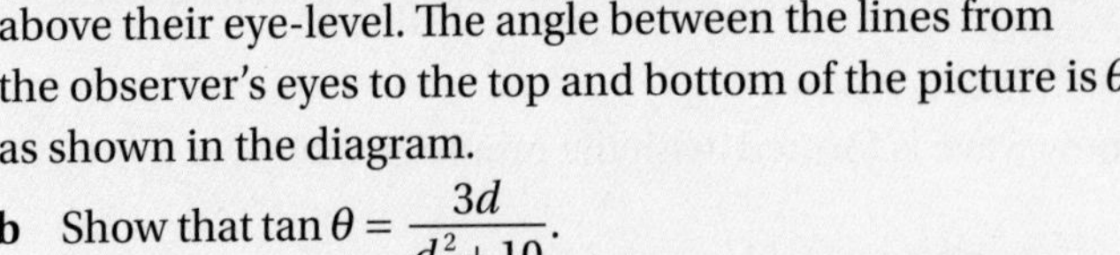

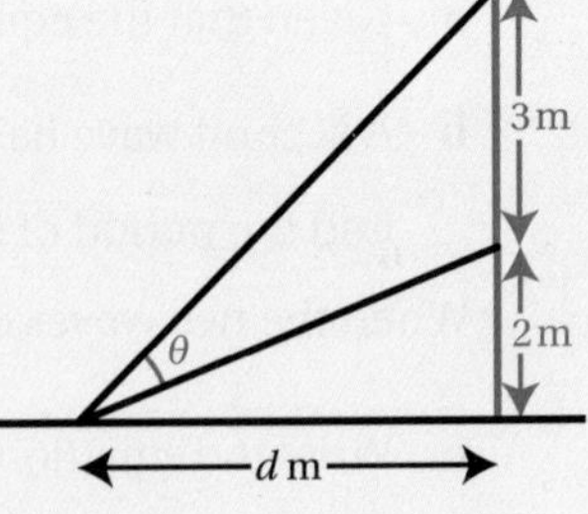

b Show that $\tan\theta = \dfrac{3d}{d^2 + 10}$.

c Use the answer to part **a** to show that $\tan\theta \leqslant \frac{3}{20}\sqrt{10}$.

d Hence, find the value of d that gives the largest possible value of $\tan\theta$.

e Find the largest possible value of angle θ.

Elevate

See Extension sheet 8 for a selection of more challenging problems.

9 Calculus of exponential and trigonometric functions

In this chapter you will:

- learn how to differentiate e^x, $\ln x$, $\sin x$, $\cos x$ and $\tan x$
- learn how to integrate e^x, $\frac{1}{x}$, $\sin x$ and $\cos x$
- review applications of differentiation to find tangents, normals and stationary points
- review applications of integration to find the equation of a curve and areas.

Before you start…

Student Book 1, Chapters 2 and 7	You should be able to use rules of indices and logarithms.	1 Write $\ln(3x^4)$ in the form $A + B\ln x$.
Student Book 1, Chapter 13	You should be able to differentiate x^n.	2 Differentiate $y = \left(3x - \frac{1}{x}\right)\left(x + \frac{2}{3x}\right)$.
Student Book 1, Chapter 14	You should be able to integrate x^n for $n \neq -1$.	3 Find the exact value of $\int_1^2 \frac{x^3+3}{2x^2}\,dx$.
Chapters 7 and 8	You should be able to use compound angle formulae and small angle approximations.	4 Use small angle approximations to find the approximate value of $\cos\left(\frac{\pi}{3} + \frac{\pi}{100}\right)$.

Extending differentiation and integration

You have already seen many situations that can be modelled using trigonometric, exponential and logarithm functions. For example, in Chapter 8 of Student Book 1 you studied exponential models for population growth, and in Chapters 7 and 8 of this book you saw an example of modelling water waves using sine and cosine functions.

We are often interested in the rate of change of quantities in such models; for example, at what rate is the population increasing after 3 years? Finding rates of change involves differentiation. Integration reverses this process; when given the rate of change you can find the equation for the original quantity.

So far you have learnt how to differentiate and integrate functions of the form ax^n. In this section you will extend rules of differentiation and integration to include a wider variety of functions.

Section 1: Differentiation

You already know from Student Book 1, Chapter 8 that the rate of growth of an exponential function is proportional to the value of the function.

Rewind

You learnt about inverse functions and their graphs in Chapter 2, Section 4.

In particular, for $y = e^x$ the rate of growth, which is the same as the derivative, equals the y value.

The derivative of the natural logarithm function is perhaps surprising, but you will see how it follows from the fact that $y = \ln x$ is the inverse function of $y = e^x$.

Key point 9.1

- If $y = e^x$, then $\frac{dy}{dx} = e^x$.
- If $y = \ln x$, then $\frac{dy}{dx} = \frac{1}{x}$.

PROOF 7

Let point A on the graph of $y = e^x$ have y-coordinate a.

Let point B be the point on the graph of $y = \ln x$, which is the reflection of A in the line $y = x$.

The reflection swaps x- and y-coordinates, so B has x-coordinate a.

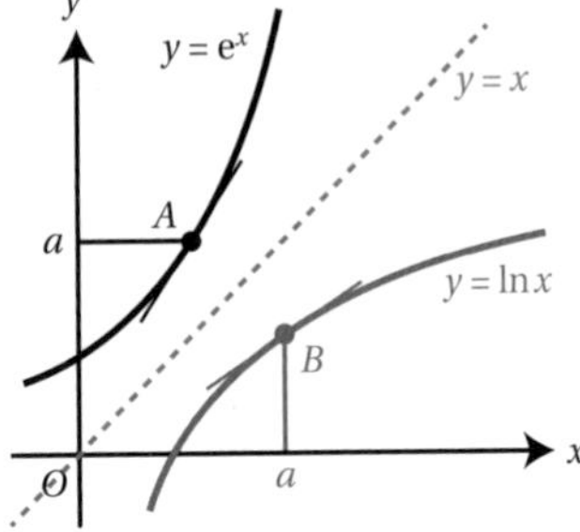

You know how to differentiate $y = e^x$, and how the graphs of $y = e^x$ and $y = \ln x$ are related. So you can use the gradient of the first graph to find the gradient of the second graph.

The gradient of $y = e^x$ at A is a.

You know that the gradient of $y = e^x$ at A equals the y value.

To see what happens to the gradient on reflection in $y = x$, consider reflecting a right-angled triangle.

gradient $\frac{a}{1} = a$

gradient $\frac{1}{a}$

This shows that, if a line with gradient a is reflected in $y = x$, the gradient of the reflected line is $\frac{1}{a}$.

So the gradient of the reflected line at B is $\frac{1}{a}$.

The gradient of the graph $y = \ln x$ at B is $\frac{1}{a}$.

So the gradient of $y = \ln x$ is $\frac{1}{x}$.

The rules for differentiating sums and constant multiples of expressions still apply. Sometimes an expression needs to be simplified before it can be differentiated.

WORKED EXAMPLE 9.1

Differentiate $y = e^{x+3} - 3\ln(4x^2)$.

$y = e^3 e^x - 3(\ln 4 + 2\ln x)$

$= e^3 e^x - 3\ln 4 - 6\ln x$

You can differentiate only e^x and $\ln x$, so you need to simplify the expression using rules of indices and logarithms.

$\frac{dy}{dx} = e^3 e^x - \frac{6}{x}$

$= e^{x+3} - \frac{6}{x}$

e^x is multiplied by a constant (e^3).
3 ln 4 is a constant, so its derivative is 0.
The derivative of $6\ln x$ is $6 \times \frac{1}{x}$.

To find out how to differentiate $\sin x$ and $\cos x$ you need to remember differentiation from first principles (Student Book 1, Chapter 13). You also need to use compound angle formulae from Chapter 8, Section 1 and small angle approximations from Chapter 7, Section 6.

Tip

Once you have derived the rules, as summarised in Key Point 9.2, on the next page you can use them without proof.

WORKED EXAMPLE 9.2

Use differentiation from first principles to prove that the derivative of $\sin x$ is $\cos x$, where x is measured in radians.

Let $f(x) = \sin x$

$f'(x) = \lim_{h \to 0}\left\{\frac{\sin(x+h) - \sin x}{h}\right\}$

$f'(x) = \lim_{h \to 0}\left\{\frac{f(x+h) - f(x)}{h}\right\}$

$= \lim_{h \to 0}\left\{\frac{\sin x \cos h + \sin h \cos x - \sin x}{h}\right\}$

Use $\sin(A + B) = \sin A \cos B + \sin B \cos A$.

$= \lim_{h \to 0}\left\{\frac{\sin x\left(1 - \frac{1}{2}h^2\right) + (h)\cos x - \sin x}{h}\right\}$

Use small angle approximations:
$\cos h \approx 1 - \frac{1}{2}h^2$
$\sin h \approx h$

$= \lim_{h \to 0}\left\{\frac{-\frac{1}{2}h^2 \sin x + h\cos x}{h}\right\}$

$= \lim_{h \to 0}\left\{-\frac{1}{2}h\sin x + \cos x\right\}$

$= \cos x$

Let h tend to 0.

Differentiating $\cos x$ follows the same method. The result for $\tan x$ can also be proved in this way, as well as by the quotient rule, which you will meet in Chapter 10, Section 3.

Key point 9.2

- If $y = \sin x$, then $\frac{dy}{dx} = \cos x$.
- If $y = \cos x$, then $\frac{dy}{dx} = -\sin x$.
- If $y = \tan x$, then $\frac{dy}{dx} = \sec^2 x$.

Tip

These formulae apply only if x is in radians.

The following two examples should help you remember two applications of differentiation: finding equations of tangents and normals, and finding stationary points.

WORKED EXAMPLE 9.3

Find the equations of the tangent and the normal to the graph of the function $f(x) = \cos x + e^x$ at the point where $x = 0$. Give your answer in the form $ax + by + c = 0$, where a, b, c are integers.

$f'(x) = -\sin x + e^x$

$\therefore f'(0) = -\sin 0 + e^0 = 1$

You need the gradient, which is $f'(0)$.

When $x = 0$:

$y = f(0)$
$= \cos 0 + e^0$
$= 1 + 1$
$= 2$

To find the equation of a straight line, you also need coordinates of one point.

The tangent passes through the point on the graph where $x = 0$. Its y-coordinate is $f(0)$.

Tangent:

$y - y_1 = m(x - x_1)$
$y - 2 = 1(x - 0)$
$y = x + 2$
$y - x - 2 = 0$

Put all the information into the equation of a line.

Normal:

$y - 2 = -1(x - 0)$
$y = -x + 2$
$y + x - 2 = 0$

The gradient of the normal is $-\frac{1}{m}$ and it passes through the same point.

WORKED EXAMPLE 9.4

Find the coordinates of the stationary point on the graph of $y = \ln x + \frac{1}{x^2}$ and determine its nature.

$\frac{dy}{dx} = \frac{1}{x} - 2x^{-3}$

You need to find where the gradient equals 0.
Write $\frac{1}{x^2}$ as x^{-2}.

$\frac{1}{x} - \frac{2}{x^3} = 0$

$x^2 - 2 = 0$

$x > 0$, so $x = \sqrt{2}$.

$\ln x$ is only defined for $x > 0$.

$y = \ln\sqrt{2} + \frac{1}{2}$

The stationary point is $\left(\sqrt{2}, \frac{1}{2}\ln 2 + \frac{1}{2}\right)$.

Use rules of logs to rewrite the y-coordinate.

$\frac{d^2y}{dx^2} = -\frac{1}{x^2} + 6x^{-4}$

$= -\frac{1}{\left(\sqrt{2}\right)^2} + \frac{6}{\left(\sqrt{2}\right)^4}$

$= -\frac{1}{2} + \frac{6}{4} = 1 > 0$

To determine the nature of the stationary point, you need to evaluate the second derivative at $x = \sqrt{2}$.

The stationary point is a minimum.

EXERCISE 9A

1 Differentiate the following.

a i $y = 3e^x$ ii $y = \frac{2e^x}{5}$

b i $y = -2\ln x$ ii $y = \frac{1}{3}\ln x$

c i $y = \frac{\ln x}{5} - 3x + 4e^x$ ii $y = 4 - \frac{e^x}{2} + 3\ln x$

d i $y = 3\sin x$ ii $y = 2\cos x$

e i $y = 2x - 5\cos x$ ii $y = \tan x + 5$

f i $y = \frac{\sin x + 2\cos x}{5}$ ii $y = \frac{1}{2}\tan x - \frac{1}{3}\sin x$

2 Differentiate after simplifying first:

a i $y = \ln x^3$ ii $y = 2\ln x^5$

b i $y = 3\ln 2x$ ii $y = \ln 5x$

c i $y = e^{x+3}$ ii $y = e^{x-3}$

d i $y = e^{2\ln x}$ ii $y = e^{3\ln x + 2}$

e i $y = \frac{3\sin x - \cos x}{\cos x}$ ii $y = \frac{2\cos x + 4\sin x}{\cos x}$

f i $y = \frac{e^{2x} - 2e^x}{e^x}$ ii $y = \frac{4e^x - e^{2x}}{2e^x}$

3. Find the exact value of the gradient of the graph of $f(x)=\frac{1}{2}e^x-7\ln x$ at the point $x=\ln 4$.
4. Find the exact value of the gradient of the graph $f(x)=e^x-\frac{\ln x}{2}$ when $x=\ln 3$.
5. Find the value of x where the gradient of $f(x)=5-2e^x$ is -6.
6. Find the value of x where the gradient of $g(x)=x^2-12\ln x$ is 2.
7. Find the rate of change of $f(x)=\sin x+x^2$ at the point $x=\frac{\pi}{2}$.
8. Find the rate of change of $g(x)=\frac{1}{4}\tan x-3\cos x-x^3$ at the point $x=\frac{\pi}{6}$.
9. Find the equation of the tangent to the curve $y=e^x+x$ that is parallel to $y=3x$.
10. Find the equation of the tangent to the curve $y=5\sin x$ that is parallel to $2x-y=6$.
11. Given that $h(x)=\sin x+\cos x, 0\leqslant x<2\pi$, find the values of x for which $h'(x)=0$.
12. Find the equations of the tangent and the normal to the graph of $y=3\tan x-2\sqrt{2}\sin x$ at $x=\frac{\pi}{4}$. Give all the coefficients in an exact form.
13. Given that $y=\frac{1}{4}\tan x+\frac{1}{x^2}$ for $0<x\leqslant 2\pi$, solve the equation $\frac{dy}{dx}=1-\frac{2}{x^3}$.
14. Find and classify the stationary points on the curve $y=\sin x+4\cos x$ in the interval $0<x<2\pi$.
15. Show that the function $f(x)=\ln x+\frac{1}{x^k}$ has a stationary point with y-coordinate $\frac{\ln k+1}{k}$.
16. Find the range of the function $f: x\mapsto e^x-4x+2, x\in\mathbb{R}$.
17. Find and classify the stationary points of:

    a $y=\ln x-\sqrt{x}$ **b** $y=2e^x-5x$
18. The volume of water (V), in millions of litres, in a tidal lake is modelled by $V=60\cos t+100$, where t is the time, in days, after a hydroelectric plant is switched on.

    a What is the smallest volume of the lake?

    b The hydroelectric plant produces an amount of electricity proportional to the rate of flow of water (measured as volume per unit time) through a tidal dam. Assuming all flow is through the dam, find the time, in the first 6 days, when the plant is producing maximum electricity.

Section 2: Integration

You can reverse all the differentiation results from the previous section to integrate several new functions.

Key point 9.3

- $\int e^x\, dx=e^x+c$
- $\int \frac{1}{x}\, dx=\ln|x|+c$
- $\int \sin x\, dx=-\cos x+c$
- $\int \cos x\, dx=\sin x+c$

Note the modulus sign in $\int \frac{1}{x}\,\mathrm{d}x = \ln|x| + c$. $\ln(x)$ is not defined for negative x. However, you can see from the diagram that the area between the x-axis and the negative part of the graph of $\frac{1}{x}$ is the same as the corresponding area between the x-axis and the positive part of the graph.

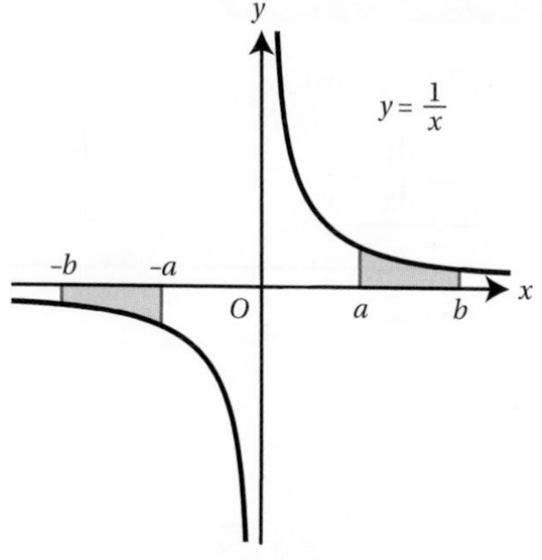

Explore

Is it possible to find the shaded area between the graph of $y = \frac{1}{x}$ and the x-axis? Using definite integration gives $\int_{-2}^{6} \frac{1}{x}\,\mathrm{d}x = \ln|6| - \ln|-2| = \ln 3$. However, splitting the area in two doesn't give the same answer: $\int_{-2}^{0} \frac{1}{x}\,\mathrm{d}x + \int_{0}^{6} \frac{1}{x}\,\mathrm{d}x$ has no value, since $\ln(0)$ is undefined. It turns out that the shaded area does not have a finite value.

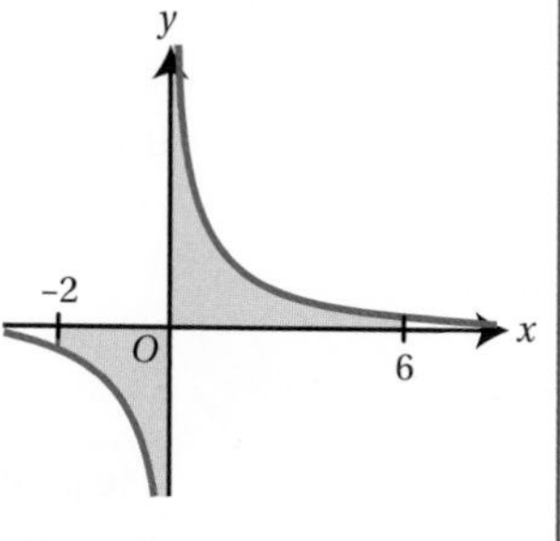

However, some graphs with asymptotes can still enclose a finite area; find out about improper integrals.

You can combine these facts with rules of integration you already know. Sometimes an expression needs to be rewritten in a different form before integrating.

WORKED EXAMPLE 9.5

Find $\int \frac{5x - 3x^3}{2x^2}\,\mathrm{d}x$.

$$\int \frac{5x - 3x^3}{2x^2}\,\mathrm{d}x = \int \frac{5}{2x} - \frac{3}{2}x\,\mathrm{d}x$$

You don't know how to integrate a quotient, but you can split the fraction and integrate each term separately.

$$= \frac{5}{2}\ln x - \frac{3}{4}x^2 + c$$

WORK IT OUT 9.1

Which of the following statements is correct? Identify the mistake in the other three.

Statement 1	Statement 2	Statement 3	Statement 4
$y=\frac{1}{x}$ $\Rightarrow \frac{dy}{dx}=\ln x$	$\int \frac{1}{x^2}\,dx=\ln(x^2)+c$	$y=\ln(3x)$ $\Rightarrow \frac{dy}{dx}=\frac{1}{3x}$	$y=\ln(3x)$ $\Rightarrow \frac{dy}{dx}=\frac{1}{x}$

Remember that integration is the reverse of differentiation, so if you know the derivative of a function you can use integration to find the function itself.

WORKED EXAMPLE 9.6

A curve passes through the point $(-1, 3)$ and its gradient is given by $\frac{dy}{dx}=3e^x-1$. Find the equation of the curve.

$$y=\int 3e^x-1\,dx$$
$$=3e^x-x+c$$

Integrate $\frac{dy}{dx}$ to get y.
Don't forget the constant of integration.

Using $x=-1, y=3$:

$$3=3e^{-1}-(-1)+c$$
$$\Rightarrow c=2-\frac{3}{e}$$

Use given values of x and y to find the constant of integration.

$$\therefore y=3e^x-x+2-\frac{3}{e}$$

You can also use integration to find the area between the curve and the x-axis. This involves evaluating **definite integrals**. It is always a good idea to draw a diagram to make sure you are finding the correct area.

Rewind

You know from Student Book 1, Chapter 15 that when a curve is below the x-axis the integral is negative.

WORKED EXAMPLE 9.7

Find the exact area enclosed between the x-axis, the curve $y = \sin x$ and the lines $x = 0$ and $x = \frac{\pi}{3}$.

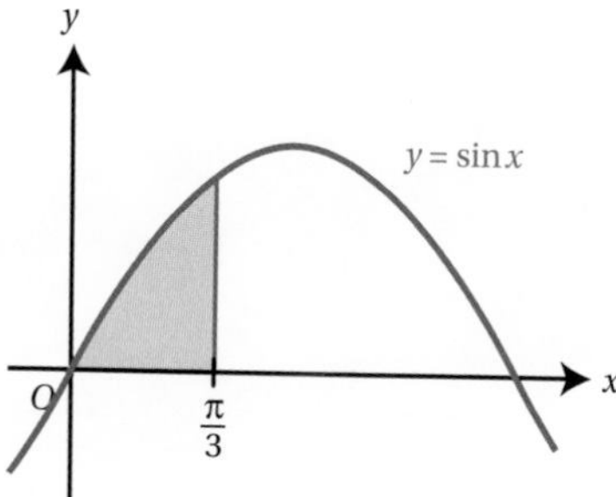

Sketch the graph and identify the required area.

$$A = \int_0^{\pi/3} \sin x \, dx = \left[-\cos x\right]_0^{\pi/3}$$

Integrate and write in square brackets.

$$= \left(-\cos\frac{\pi}{3}\right) - (-\cos 0)$$

$$= \left(-\frac{1}{2}\right) - (-1) = \frac{1}{2}$$

Evaluate the integrated expression at the upper and lower limits, and subtract the lower from the upper.

EXERCISE 9B

1 Find the following integrals.

a i $\int 5e^x \, dx$ ii $\int 9e^x \, dx$

b i $\int \frac{2e^x}{5} \, dx$ ii $\int \frac{7e^x}{11} \, dx$

c i $\int \frac{(e^x + 3x)}{2} \, dx$ ii $\int \frac{(e^x + x^3)}{5} \, dx$

d i $\int 3\cos x \, dx$ ii $\int 4\sin x \, dx$

e i $\int \frac{\sin x - 2\cos x}{2} \, dx$ ii $\int \frac{2\cos x - \sin x}{3} \, dx$

f i $\int \sqrt{x} + \sin x \, dx$ ii $\int \cos x - \frac{1}{\sqrt{x}} \, dx$

2 Find the following integrals.

a i $\int \frac{2}{x} \, dx$ ii $\int \frac{3}{x} \, dx$

b i $\int \frac{1}{2x} \, dx$ ii $\int \frac{1}{3x} \, dx$

c i $\int \frac{5}{2x} \, dx$ ii $\int \frac{2}{3x} \, dx$

d **i** $\int \frac{x^2-1}{x}\,dx$ **ii** $\int \frac{x^3+5}{x}\,dx$

e **i** $\int \frac{3x+2}{x^2}\,dx$ **ii** $\int \frac{3x-5x^2}{x^3}\,dx$

f **i** $\int \frac{2\sqrt{x}+3x}{x\sqrt{x}}\,dx$ **ii** $\int \frac{x^2-4\sqrt{x}}{x\sqrt{x}}\,dx$

3 Find the exact value of these definite integrals.

a **i** $\int_0^2 3e^x\,dx$ **ii** $\int_1^3 2e^x\,dx$

b **i** $\int_0^{\ln 3} e^x\,dx$ **ii** $\int_0^{\ln 5} 2e^x\,dx$

c **i** $\int_1^{\ln 2} (3e^x+2)\,dx$ **ii** $\int_1^{\ln 3} (4-3e^x)\,dx$

d **i** $\int_1^3 \frac{3}{2x}\,dx$ **ii** $\int_2^5 \frac{4}{3x}\,dx$

e **i** $\int_e^{e^2} \frac{2}{x}\,dx$ **ii** $\int_1^{e^3} \frac{3}{2x}\,dx$

f **i** $\int_0^{\pi/2} \cos x\,dx$ **ii** $\int_\pi^{2\pi} \sin x\,dx$

g **i** $\int_{-\pi}^{\pi} 3\sin x - 4\cos x\,dx$ **ii** $\int_0^{2\pi} 2\cos x - \sin x\,dx$

4 Find the exact value of the area enclosed by the curve $y=\frac{2}{3x}$, the x-axis and the lines $x=2$ and $x=6$. Give your answer in the form $a \ln b$.

5 Find the area enclosed by the curve $y=3\sin x$, the x-axis, and the line $x=\frac{\pi}{3}$.

6 Find the exact value of $\int_0^{\frac{\pi}{3}} (\sin x + 2\cos x)\,dx$.

7 Find the exact value of $\int_1^{e^5} \frac{3}{x}\,dx$.

8 **a** Evaluate $\int_{-9}^{-3} \frac{2}{x}\,dx$.

b State the value of the area between the graph of $y=\frac{1}{x}$, the x-axis and the lines $x=-9$ and $x=-3$.

9 Find the equation of the curve given that $\frac{dy}{dx}=\cos x+\sin x$ and the curve passes through the point $(\pi, 1)$.

10 Find $\int \frac{\sin x+\cos x}{2\cos x}\,dx$.

11 The derivative of the function $f(x)$ is $\frac{1}{2x}$.

a Find an expression for all possible functions $f(x)$.

b If the curve $y=f(x)$ passes through the point (2, 7), find the equation of the curve.

Elevate

See Support sheet 9 for a further example of finding the equation of a curve and for more practice questions.

12 The diagram shows part of the curve $y = e^x - 5\sin x$.

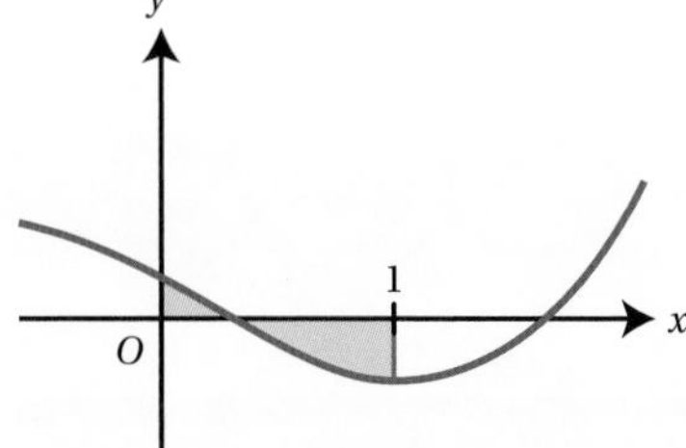

a Use your calculator to find the x-intercept of the graph.

b Find the shaded area enclosed between the curve, the x-axis and the lines $x = 0$ and $x = 1$.

> **Tip**
>
> The equation $e^x - 5\sin x = 0$ cannot be solved exactly. You can use the solver function on your calculator. Note that the answer for the area is only an approximation.

13 The diagram shows a part of the curve with equation $y = \frac{4}{x} + x - 5$.

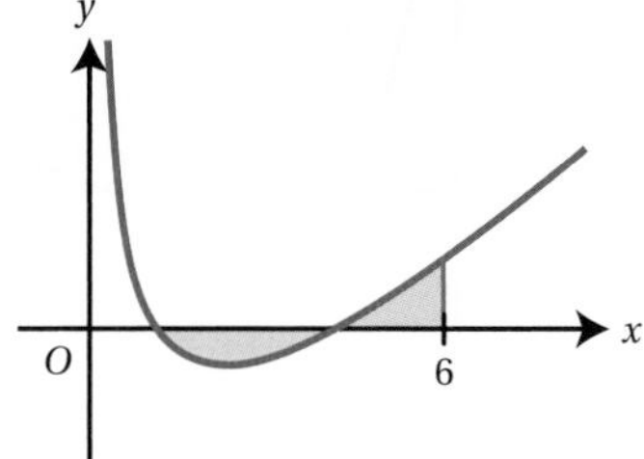

a Show that the curve crosses the x-axis at $x = 1$ and $x = 4$.

b Find the exact value of the shaded area. Give your answer in the form $p - 4\ln q$, where p and q are rational numbers.

> **Fast forward**
>
> Areas of regions that are partly above and partly below the x-axis are discussed in more detail in Chapter 12, Section 4.

14 Show that the value of the integral $\int_k^{2k} \frac{1}{x}\, dx$ is independent of k.

15 The gradient of the normal to a curve at any point is equal to the x-coordinate at that point. If the curve passes through the point $(e^2, 3)$, find the equation of the curve in the form $y = \ln|g(x)|$ where $g(x)$ is a rational function.

Checklist of learning and understanding

- You can now differentiate basic trigonometric, exponential and logarithm functions:
  $\frac{d}{dx}(\sin x) = \cos x$, $\frac{d}{dx}(\cos x) = -\sin x$, $\frac{d}{dx}(\tan x) = \sec^2 x$, $\frac{d}{dx}(e^x) = e^x$, $\frac{d}{dx}(\ln x) = \frac{1}{x}$
- The results for $\sin x$ and $\cos x$ can be derived using differentiation from first principles.
- You can also integrate some new functions:
  $\int \sin x\, dx = -\cos x + c$, $\int \cos x\, dx = \sin x + c$, $\int e^x\, dx = e^x + c$, $\int \frac{1}{x}\, dx = \ln|x| + c$
- You can combine these with the rules of differentiation and integration you already know, to find:
  - Rates of change
  - Equations of tangents and normals
  - Stationary points
  - Equation of a curve with a given gradient
  - Area between a curve and the x-axis.

Mixed practice 9

1. Find the equation of the tangent to the curve $y = e^x + 2\sin x$ at the point where $x = \frac{\pi}{2}$.

2. If $f'(x) = \sin x$ and $f\left(\frac{\pi}{3}\right) = 0$, find f(x).

3. Find the exact value of the gradient of the graph $f(x) = 3e^x - \frac{\ln x}{2}$ when $x = \ln 4$.

4. Find the exact value of the integral $\int_0^{\pi} e^x + \sin x + 1\,dx$.

5. The diagram shows the curve with equation $y = x - 7 + \frac{10}{x}$, which crosses the x-axis at 2 and 5.

   Find the exact value of the shaded area.

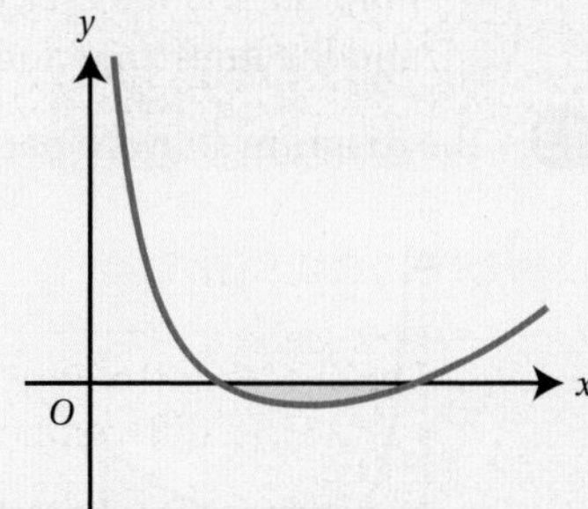

6. Find the indefinite integral $\int \frac{1 + x^2\sqrt{x}}{x}\,dx$.

7. Find and classify the stationary points on the curve $y = \sin x + 4\cos x$ in the interval $0 < x < 2\pi$.

8. Find and classify the stationary points on the curve $y = \tan x - \frac{4x}{3}$ for $-\pi < x < \pi$. Give only the x-coordinates, and leave your answers in terms of π.

9. Find the equation of the normal to the curve $y = 3e^x$ at the point $x = \ln 3$. Give your answer in the form $x + ky = p + \ln q$, where k, p and q are integers.

10. The population of bacteria (P), in thousands, at a time t, in hours, is modelled by $P = 10 + e^t - 3t, t \geqslant 0$.

    a **i** Find the initial population of bacteria.

    ii At what time does the number of bacteria reach 14 million? (Hint: use a solver function on your calculator.)

    b **i** Find $\frac{dP}{dt}$.

    ii Find the time at which the bacteria are growing at a rate of 6 million per hour.

    c **i** Find $\frac{d^2P}{dt^2}$ and explain the physical significance of this quantity.

    ii Find the minimum number of bacteria, justifying that it is a minimum.

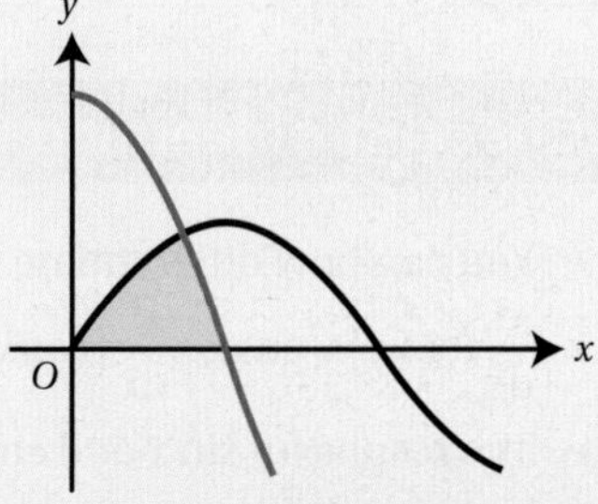

11. The diagram at right shows the graphs of $y = \sin x$ and $y = \sqrt{3}\cos x$. Find the exact value of the shaded area.

12. Find $\int \frac{\cos 2x}{\cos x - \sin x}\,dx$.

Elevate

See Extension sheet 9 for a selection of more challenging problems.

10 Further differentiation

In this chapter you will learn:

- how to differentiate composite functions using the chain rule
- how to differentiate products and quotients of functions
- about implicit functions and their derivatives
- how to differentiate inverse functions.

Before you start…

Student Book 1, Chapter 13 and Student Book 2, Chapter 9	You should be able to differentiate the following functions. x^n, $\sin x$, $\cos x$, $\tan x$, e^x, $\ln x$	1 Differentiate: a $2x^3 - 3\sqrt{x}$ b $5\ln x + \dfrac{1}{3x^3}$ c $5\mathrm{e}^x$ d $4\sin x - 3\cos x + 2\tan x$
Student Book 1, Chapter 14	You should be able to use differentiation to find the equations of tangents and normals, and stationary points.	2 A curve has equation $y = x - 2\ln x$. a Find the equations of the tangent and the normal at the point where $x = 1$. b Find the coordinates of the stationary point and show that it is a minimum point.
Student Book 1, Chapter 10	You should know basic trigonometric identities.	3 Simplify: a $3\sin^2 x + 3\cos^2 x$ b $\dfrac{3\sin x}{4\cos x}$
Chapter 8	You should know the definitions of reciprocal trigonometric functions.	4 Write in terms of $\sin x$ and $\cos x$: a $\sec x \tan x$ b $\dfrac{\operatorname{cosec} x}{\cot x}$
Student Book 1, Chapter 2 and Student Book 2, Chapter 5	You should be able to simplify expressions involving fractions and surds.	5 Simplify: a $\dfrac{x - \dfrac{1}{x+1}}{\dfrac{2}{x+1} - 3}$ b $\dfrac{\sqrt{x-1} + \dfrac{1}{\sqrt{x-1}}}{x-1}$
GCSE and Student Book 1, Chapter 7	You should be able to change the subject of a formula.	6 Make y the subject of the formula: a $x = \mathrm{e}^{2y-1}$ b $2x + 3xy = (x-2)y$

Differentiating more complex functions

In Chapter 9 you learnt how to differentiate a variety of functions. You can also differentiate sums, differences and constant multiples of those functions; for example, $y=3\sin x+e^x-3x^2$.

How can you differentiate products and quotients of functions such as $y=x^2 e^x$ or $y=\frac{\sin x}{x}$?

You know from Student Book 1, Chapter 12 that you can't just differentiate the separate components of a product (or quotient) and then multiply (or divide) the results, so you need a new rule for these situations.

Before looking at products and quotients you will learn how to differentiate composite functions, such as $\sin 3x$ or e^{x^2}. You will also learn how to differentiate equations such as $x^2+y^2=5$ without making y the subject, and apply this method to differentiate inverse functions.

Section 1: The chain rule

If you were asked to differentiate $y=(3x^2+5x+2)^2$ you could expand the brackets and differentiate term by term. But in most situations this is either too difficult or not possible; for example, $\sqrt{3x^2+5x+2}$ cannot be 'expanded' and $(3x^2+5x+2)^7$ would lead to a very long expression.

And what about functions such as $y=\sin 3x$ or $y=e^{x^2}$? While you can differentiate $y=\sin x$ and $y=e^x$, you have no rules so far telling you what to do when x is replaced by $3x$ or x^2.

These functions may seem quite different but they do have something in common – they are all composite functions:

- $y=(3x^2+5x+2)^7$ $\quad y=u^7$, where $u(x)=3x^2+5x+2$.
- $y=\sin 3x$ $\quad y=\sin u$, where $u(x)=3x$.
- $y=e^{x^2}$ $\quad y=e^u$, where $u(x)=x^2$.

To differentiate a composite function you can think about how a change in x affects the change in y. If x changes by Δx this causes u to change by Δu, which, in turn, causes y to change by Δy. If you multiply the two rates of change you see that:

$$\frac{\Delta y}{\Delta u}\times\frac{\Delta u}{\Delta x}=\frac{\Delta y}{\Delta x}$$

This leads to the rule for differentiating composite functions:

Key point 10.1

Chain rule:

If $y=f(u)$, where $u=g(x)$, then

$$\frac{dy}{dx}=\frac{dy}{du}\times\frac{du}{dx}$$

Tip

The chain rule also can be written using function notation:

If $y = f(g(x))$ then

$$\frac{dy}{dx}=\frac{d}{dx}f(g(x)).$$
$$=f'(g(x))g'(x))$$

WORKED EXAMPLE 10.1

Differentiate the following functions.

a $y=(3x^2+5x+2)^7$ **b** $y=\sin(3x)$ **c** $y=e^{x^2}$

a $y=u^7$, where $u=3x^2+5x+2$.

$$\frac{dy}{dx}=\frac{dy}{du}\times\frac{du}{dx}=7u^6\times(6x+5)$$

These are all composite functions, so use the chain rule on each of them.

$$=7(3x^2+5x+2)^6(6x+5)$$

Write the answer in terms of x. There is no need to expand the brackets.

b $y=f(g(x))$, where $f(x)=\sin x$ and $g(x)=3x$.

In this example we use function notation.

$$\frac{dy}{dx}=f'(g(x))g'(x)=\cos(3x)\times(3)$$

$$=3\cos(3x)$$

Write the answer in terms of x and rearrange into the conventional form.

c $y=e^u$, where $u=x^2$.

$$\frac{dy}{dx}=\frac{dy}{du}\times\frac{du}{dx}=e^u\times 2x$$

$$=2xe^{x^2}$$

Write the answer in terms of x in the conventional form.

Part **b** of the previous example illustrates a special case of the chain rule when the 'inside' function is of the form $ax+b$:

Key point 10.2

$$\frac{d}{dx}f(ax+b)=a\,f'(ax+b)$$

For example:

$$\frac{d}{dx}(4x+1)^7=4\times7(4x+1)^6$$

and

$$\frac{d}{dx}\left(e^{3-2x}\right)=-2e^{3-2x}.$$

It is useful to remember this shortcut as it occurs quite commonly; just look for an 'inner function' u.

In particular, you can apply this to the functions you learnt to differentiate in Chapter 9.

Key point 10.3

$$\frac{d}{dx}(e^{kx})=ke^{kx}$$

$$\frac{d}{dx}(\ln kx)=\frac{k}{|kx|}=\frac{1}{|x|}$$

$$\frac{d}{dx}(\sin kx)=k\cos kx$$

$$\frac{d}{dx}(\cos kx)=-k\sin kx$$

$$\frac{d}{dx}(\tan kx)=k\sec^2 kx$$

Tip

Notice that the derivative of $\ln kx$ is the same as the derivative of $\ln x$. This is because $\ln kx=\ln k+\ln x$, and $\ln k$ is a constant which differentiates to zero.

Sometimes you need to apply the chain rule more than once.

WORKED EXAMPLE 10.2

Differentiate $y = \cos^3(\ln 2x)$.

$y = (\cos(\ln 2x))^3$ — Remember that $\cos^3 A$ means $(\cos A)^3$.

$y = u^3$, where $u = \cos v$ and $v = \ln 2x$. — This is a composite of three functions.

$$\frac{dy}{dx} = \frac{dy}{du} \times \frac{du}{dv} \times \frac{dv}{dx}$$

$$= 3u^2 \times (-\sin v) \times 2 \times \frac{1}{2x}$$

Use the chain rule with three derivatives. For ln $2x$ you can use the shortcut from Key point 10.3.

$$= 3(\cos(\ln 2x))^2 \times (-\sin(\ln 2x)) \times \frac{1}{x}$$

$$= -\frac{3}{x}\cos^2(\ln 2x)\sin(\ln 2x)$$

Write everything in terms of x and simplify.

You can now use the chain rule to differentiate reciprocal trigonometric functions.

Rewind

For a reminder of how to differentiate $\sin x$, $\cos x$ and $\tan x$, see Chapter 9, Section 1.

WORKED EXAMPLE 10.3

Show that $\frac{d}{dx}(\sec x) = \sec x \tan x$.

$y = \sec x = (\cos x)^{-1}$ — Express $\sec x$ in terms of $\cos x$ as you know how to differentiate that.

$y = u^{-1}$, where $u = \cos x$. — This is a composite function ...

$$\frac{dy}{dx} = -u^{-2} \times (-\sin x)$$

... so apply the chain rule.

$$= -(\cos x)^{-2}(-\sin x)$$

$$= \frac{\sin x}{\cos^2 x}$$

$$= \frac{1}{\cos x}\frac{\sin x}{\cos x} = \sec x \tan x, \text{ as required}$$

You want the answer to contain $\tan x$, which is $\frac{\sin x}{\cos x}$.

The proofs for the other two reciprocal trigonometric functions follow the same pattern, giving the results in Key point 10.4.

Key point 10.4

$y = \sec x \quad \frac{dy}{dx} = \sec x \tan x$

$y = \operatorname{cosec} x \quad \frac{dy}{dx} = -\operatorname{cosec} x \cot x$

$y = \cot x \quad \frac{dy}{dx} = -\operatorname{cosec}^2 x$

EXERCISE 10A

1 Use the chain rule to differentiate the following expressions with respect to x.

a **i** $(3x+4)^5$ **ii** $(5x+4)^7$

b **i** $\sqrt{3x-2}$ **ii** $\sqrt{x+1}$

c **i** $\frac{1}{3-x}$ **ii** $\frac{1}{(2x+3)^2}$

d **i** e^{10x+1} **ii** e^{4-3x}

e **i** $\sin 4x$ **ii** $\cos(3x+\pi)$

f **i** $\ln(5-x)$ **ii** $\ln(3-2x)$

2 Use the chain rule to differentiate the following expressions with respect to x.

a **i** $(x^2-3x+1)^7$ **ii** $(x^3+1)^5$

b **i** e^{x^2-2x} **ii** e^{4-x^3}

c **i** $(2e^x+1)^{-3}$ **ii** $(2-5e^x)^{-4}$

d **i** $\sin(3x^2+1)$ **ii** $\cos(x^2+2x)$

e **i** $\cos^3 x$ **ii** $\sin^4 x$

f **i** $\ln(2x-5x^3)$ **ii** $\ln(4x^2-1)$

g **i** $(4\ln x-1)^4$ **ii** $(\ln x+3)^{-5}$

h **i** $\sqrt{3x^2+1}$ **ii** $\sqrt{5-2x^2}$

3 Differentiate the following, using the short cut from Key point 10.2.

a **i** $(2x+3)^5$ **ii** $(4x-1)^8$

b **i** $(5-x)^{-4}$ **ii** $(1-x)^{-7}$

c **i** $\cos(1-4x)$ **ii** $\cos(2-x)$

d **i** $\ln(5x+2)$ **ii** $\ln(x-4)$

e **i** $\cot(3x)$ **ii** $\operatorname{cosec}(5x)$

f **i** $\sec(2x+1)$ **ii** $\tan(1-x)$

4 Differentiate the following, using the chain rule twice.

a **i** $\sec^2 3x$ **ii** $\tan^2 2x$

b **i** $e^{\sin^2 3x}$ **ii** $e^{(\ln 2x)^2}$

c **i** $(1-2\sin^2 2x)^2$ **ii** $(4\cos 3x+1)^2$

d **i** $\ln(1-3\cos 2x)$ **ii** $\ln(2-\cos 5x)$

5 Find the equation of the tangent to the graph of $y=(3x+5)^2$ at the point where $x=2$.

6 Find the equation of the normal to the curve $y=\frac{1}{\sqrt{4x^2+1}}$ at the point where $x=\sqrt{2}$.

7 The function f is defined by $f: x \mapsto \ln(x^2-35)$ for $|x| \geqslant 6$. For what values of x does the graph of this function have gradient 1?

8 Find the coordinates of the stationary points on the curve with equation $y=(3x^2-6)^3$.

9 A particle moves in a straight line, with displacement s at time t from O given by $s=6\cos\left(\frac{t}{3}\right)$ m.

At time $t=2\pi$ seconds, find:

a the velocity of the particle

b the acceleration of the particle.

Rewind

You met kinematics in Student Book 1, Chapter 19.

10 Find the coordinates of the stationary points on the graph of $y=(x^3-1)^5$.

11 Find the exact coordinates of stationary points on the curve $y=e^{\sin x}$ for $x \in [0, 2\pi]$.

12 Find the exact coordinates of the stationary point on the curve $y=\frac{4}{x^2-12x}$.

13 A population of bacteria increases exponentially so that the number of bacteria, N, after t minutes is given by $N=45e^{0.4t}$. Find the size of the population at the moment when its rate of increase is 197 bacteria per minute.

14 Given that $f(x)=\operatorname{cosec}^2 x$:

a Find $f'(x)$.

b Solve the equation $f'(x)=2f(x)$ for $-\pi < x < \pi$.

15 A non-uniform chain hangs from two posts. Its height, h, above the ground satisfies the equation for $h=e^x+\frac{1}{e^{2x}}, -1 \leqslant x \leqslant 2$.

The left post is positioned at $x=-1$, and the right post is positioned at $x=2$.

a State, with reasons, which post is taller.

b Show that the minimum height occurs when $x=\frac{1}{3}\ln 2$.

c Find the exact value of the minimum height of the chain.

Did you know?

Many people think that a chain fixed at both ends will hang as a parabola, but it can be proved that it hangs in the shape of the curve in question 15, called a *catenary*. The proof requires techniques from a mathematical area called *differential geometry*.

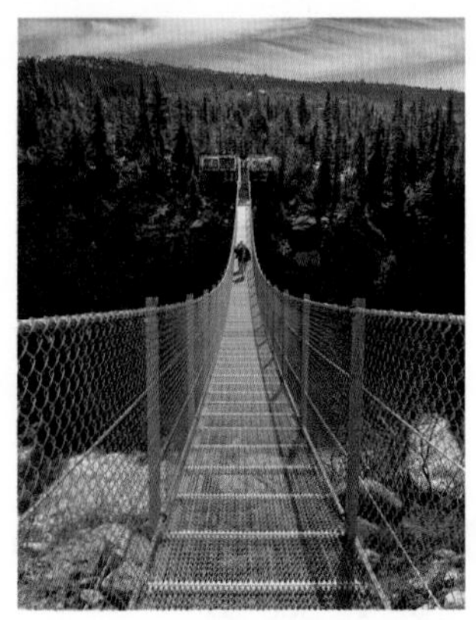

16 **a** Solve the equation $\sin 2x = \sin x$ for $0 \leqslant x \leqslant 2\pi$, giving your answers in terms of π.

b Find the coordinates of the stationary points of the curve $y=\sin 2x - \sin x$ for $0 \leqslant x \leqslant 2\pi$, giving your answers correct to 3 significant figures.

c Hence, sketch the curve $y=\sin 2x-\sin x$ for $0 \leqslant x \leqslant 2\pi$.

Section 2: The product rule

There is also a rule for differentiating products such as $y = x^2 \cos x$ or $y = x \ln x$.

Key point 10.5

Product rule:

If $y = uv$ then

$$\frac{dy}{dx} = v\frac{du}{dx} + u\frac{dv}{dx}$$

Tip

The product rule can also be written in function notation:
If $y = f(x)g(x)$ then
$\frac{dy}{dx} = f'(x)g(x) + f(x)g'(x)$.

WORKED EXAMPLE 10.4

Differentiate:

a $y = x^2 \cos x$

b $y = x \ln x$

a Let $u = x^2$ and $v = \cos x$.

It doesn't matter which function you call u and which v.

Then

$$\frac{du}{dx} = 2x$$

and

$$\frac{dv}{dx} = -\sin x$$

So:

$$\frac{dy}{dx} = v\frac{du}{dx} + u\frac{dv}{dx}$$
$$= (\cos x)2x + x^2(-\sin x)$$
$$= 2x\cos x - x^2 \sin x$$

Applying the product rule.

b Let $f(x) = x$ and $g(x) = \ln x$. Then:

y is a product of two functions, so use the product rule.

$f'(x) = 1$ and $g'(x) = \frac{1}{x}$

So:

$$\frac{dy}{dx} = f'(x)g(x) + f(x)g'(x)$$
$$= (1)(\ln x) + (x)\left(\frac{1}{x}\right)$$
$$= \ln x + 1$$

WORK IT OUT 10.1

Differentiate $y = \sin\left(x^2 + 3x\right)$.

Which of the following solutions is correct? Identify the mistakes in the other two.

Solution 1	Solution 2	Solution 3
$u = \sin,\ v = x^2 + 3x$ $\frac{du}{dx} = \cos x,\ \frac{dv}{dx} = 2x+3$ $\frac{dy}{dx} = \frac{du}{dx}v + u\frac{dv}{dx}$ $= \cos\left(x^2+3x\right) + \sin(2x+3)$	$\frac{dy}{dx} = (2x+3)\cos\left(x^2+3x\right)$	$\frac{dy}{dx} = \cos(2x+3)$

When differentiating a more complicated product, you may need to use the chain rule as well as the product rule. When the function involves powers, the two terms in the product rule often have a common factor.

WORKED EXAMPLE 10.5

Differentiate $y = x^4\left(3x^2-5\right)^5$ and factorise your answer.

Let $u = x^4$ and $v = \left(3x^2-5\right)^5$. Then:

This is a product, so use the product rule.

$$\frac{du}{dx} = 4x^3$$

$$\frac{dv}{dx} = 5\left(3x^2-5\right)^4(6x)$$

v is a composite function, so use the chain rule.

$$= 30x\left(3x^2-5\right)^4$$

$$\frac{dy}{dx} = v\frac{du}{dx} + u\frac{dv}{dx}$$

Now apply the product rule.

$$= \left(3x^2-5\right)^5 4x^3 + x^4 30x\left(3x^2-5\right)^4$$

$$= 2x^3\left(3x^2-5\right)^4\left[2\left(3x^2-5\right)+15x^2\right]$$

You are asked to factorise the answer, so instead of expanding the brackets look for common factors.

$$= 2x^3\left(3x^2-5\right)^4\left(6x^2-10+15x^2\right)$$

$$= 2x^3\left(3x^2-5\right)^4\left(21x^2-10\right)$$

EXERCISE 10B

1 Differentiate the following using the product rule.

a **i** $y = x^2 \cos x$ **ii** $y = x^{-1} \sin x$

b **i** $y = x^{-2} \ln x$ **ii** $y = x \ln x$

c **i** $y = x^3 \sqrt{2x+1}$ **ii** $y = x^{-1} \sqrt{4x}$

d **i** $e^{2x} \tan x$ **ii** $e^{x+1} \sec 3x$

2 Find f′(x) and factorise your answer fully.

a **i** $f(x) = (x+1)^4 (x-2)^5$ **ii** $f(x) = (x-3)^7 (x+5)^4$

b **i** $f(x) = (2x-1)^4 (1-3x)^3$ **ii** $f(x) = (1-x)^5 (4x+1)^2$

3 Differentiate $y = (3x^2 - x + 2)e^{2x}$, giving your answer in the form $P(x)e^{2x}$, where $P(x)$ is a polynomial.

4 Given that $f(x) = x^2 e^{3x}$, find f″(x) in the form $(ax^2 + bx + c)e^{3x}$.

5 Find the x-coordinates of the stationary points on the curve $y = (2x+1)^5 e^{-2x}$.

6 Find the exact values of the x-coordinates of the stationary points on the curve $y = (3x+1)^5 (3-x)^3$.

7 Find the derivative of $\sin(xe^x)$ with respect to x.

8 **a** Given that $f(x) = x \ln x$, find f′(x).

b Hence, find $\int \ln x \, dx$.

9 Find the exact coordinates of the minimum point of the curve $y = e^{-x} \cos x$, $0 \leqslant x \leqslant \pi$.

10 Given that $f(x) = x^2 \sqrt{1+x}$, show that $f'(x) = \frac{x(a+bx)}{2\sqrt{1+x}}$, where a and b are constants to be found.

11 **a** Write $y = x^x$ in the form $y = e^{f(x)}$.

b Hence, or otherwise, find $\frac{dy}{dx}$.

c Find the exact coordinates of the stationary points of the curve $y = x^x$.

12 **a** If $a < b$ and p and q are positive integers, find the x-coordinate of the stationary point of the curve $y = (x-a)^p (x-b)^q$ in the domain $a < x < b$.

b Sketch the graph in the case when $p = 2$ and $q = 3$.

c By considering the graph, or otherwise, identify a condition involving p and/or q to determine when this stationary point is a local minimum.

Section 3: The quotient rule

If you need to differentiate a quotient such as

$$y=\frac{x^2-4x+12}{(x-3)^2}$$

you could start by expressing it as

$$y=(x^2-4x+12)(x-3)^{-2}$$

and use a combination of the chain rule and the product rule.

However, there is a shortcut that allows you to differentiate quotients directly.

Key point 10.6

Quotient rule:

If $y=\frac{u}{v}$ then

$$\frac{dy}{dx}=\frac{v\frac{du}{dx}-u\frac{dv}{dx}}{v^2}$$

WORKED EXAMPLE 10.6

Differentiate $y=\frac{x^2-4x+12}{(x-3)^2}$, using the quotient rule, and simplify as far as possible.

$y=\frac{u}{v}$, $u=x^2-4x+12$, $v=(x-3)^2$

$$\frac{dy}{dx}=\frac{v\frac{du}{dx}-u\frac{dv}{dx}}{v^2}$$

Use the quotient rule, making sure to get u and v the right way around.

$$=\frac{(x-3)^2(2x-4)-(x^2-4x+12)2(x-3)}{\left[(x-3)^2\right]^2}$$

You need the chain rule to differentiate v.

$$=\frac{(2x-4)(x-3)-(x^2-4x+12)2}{(x-3)^3}$$

Notice that you can cancel a factor of $(x-3)$.

$$=\frac{2x^2-10x+12-2x^2+8x-24}{(x-3)^3}$$

$$=\frac{-2x-12}{(x-3)^3}$$

Chapter 9 stated the result that the derivative of $\tan x$ is $\sec^2 x$. You can now use the quotient rule, together with the derivatives of $\sin x$ and $\cos x$, to prove this result.

WORKED EXAMPLE 10.7

Prove that $\frac{d}{dx}(\tan x) = \sec^2 x$.

$y = \tan x = \frac{\sin x}{\cos x}$, $u = \sin x$, $v = \cos x$

You know how to differentiate $\sin x$ and $\cos x$, so use $\tan x \equiv \frac{\sin x}{\cos x}$.

$\frac{dy}{dx} = \frac{v\frac{du}{dx} - u\frac{dv}{dx}}{v^2}$

Use the quotient rule.

$= \frac{\cos x \cos x - \sin x(-\sin x)}{(\cos x)^2}$

$= \frac{\cos^2 x + \sin^2 x}{\cos^2 x}$

Notice that $\sin^2 x + \cos^2 x \equiv 1$.

$= \frac{1}{\cos^2 x}$

$= \sec^2 x$

WORK IT OUT 10.2

In each example, find a quicker method of differentiating the expression.

How many of the solutions are correct? Identify any mistakes.

Example 1	Example 2	Example 3
Differentiate $y = 5\cos x$.	Differentiate $y = \frac{\cos x}{\sin^2 x}$.	Differentiate $y = \frac{3}{\tan^2 x}$.
Solution 1	**Solution 2**	**Solution 3**
Using the product rule: $u = 5$, $v = \cos x$ $\frac{du}{dx} = 0$, $\frac{dv}{dx} = -\sin x$ So, $\frac{dy}{dx} = 5(-\sin x) + 0(\cos x)$ $= -5\sin x$	$y = \frac{\cos x}{\sin^2 x} = \cos x(\sin x)^{-2}$ So use the product rule: $u = \cos x$, $v = (\sin x)^{-2}$ $\frac{du}{dx} = -\sin x$ $\frac{dv}{dx} = -2(\sin x)^{-3}(\cos x)$ So, $\frac{dy}{dx} = -2\cos x(\sin x)^{-3}\cos x + (\sin x)^{-2}(-\sin x)$ $= -2\cos^2 x(\sin x)^{-3} - (\sin x)^{-1}$ $= -\frac{2\cos^2 x}{\sin^3 x} - \frac{1}{\sin x}$	Using the quotient rule: $u = 3$, $v = \tan^2 x$ $\frac{du}{dx} = 0$, $\frac{dv}{dx} = 2\tan x \sec^2 x$ So, $\frac{dy}{dx} = \frac{0(\tan^2 x) - 3(2\tan x \sec^2 x)}{(\tan^2 x)^2}$ $= \frac{-6\tan x \sec^2 x}{(\tan x)^4}$ $= -\frac{6\sec^2 x}{\tan^3 x}$

Tip

You need to use the quotient rule only when differentiating a quotient of two *functions*. If a function is multiplied or divided by a number, you can do it more simply.

Elevate

See Support sheet 10 for a further example of combining the chain rule with the product or quotient rule and some more practice questions.

The quotient rule, just like the product rule, often leads to a long expression. If you are required to simplify it, you may need to work with fractions and roots, as in the following example.

WORKED EXAMPLE 10.8

Differentiate $\frac{x}{\sqrt{x+1}}$, giving your answer in the form $\frac{x+c}{k\sqrt{(x+1)^p}}$, where $c,k,p \in \mathbb{N}$.

$y=\frac{x}{\sqrt{x+1}}, u=x, v=\sqrt{x+1}=(x+1)^{\frac{1}{2}}$

$$\frac{dy}{dx}=\frac{v\frac{du}{dx}-u\frac{dv}{dx}}{v^2}$$

Use the quotient rule.

$$=\frac{(x+1)^{\frac{1}{2}}\times 1-x\times\frac{1}{2}(x+1)^{-\frac{1}{2}}}{\left((x+1)^{\frac{1}{2}}\right)^2}$$

$$=\frac{\sqrt{x+1}-\frac{x}{2\sqrt{x+1}}}{x+1}$$

As you want a square root in the answer, turn the fractional powers back into roots.

$$=\frac{2(x+1)-x}{2(x+1)\sqrt{x+1}}$$

Remove 'fractions within fractions' by multiplying top and bottom by $2\sqrt{x+1}$.

$$=\frac{x+2}{2\sqrt{(x+1)^3}}$$

Notice that $a\sqrt{a}=a^{\frac{3}{2}}=\sqrt{a^3}$.

EXERCISE 10C

1 Differentiate the following using the quotient rule.

a i $y=\frac{x-1}{x+1}$ ii $y=\frac{x+2}{x-3}$

b i $y=\frac{\sqrt{2x+1}}{x}$ ii $y=\frac{x^2}{\sqrt{x-1}}$

c i $y=\frac{1-2x}{x^2+2}$ ii $y=\frac{4-x^2}{1+x}$

d i $y=\frac{\ln 3x}{x}$ ii $y=\frac{\ln 2x}{x^2}$

2 Find the equation of the normal to the curve $y=\frac{\sin x}{x}$ at the point where $x=\frac{\pi}{2}$, giving your answer in the form $y=mx+c$, where m and c are exact.

3 Find the coordinates of the stationary points on the graph of $y=\frac{x^2}{2x-1}$.

4 The graph of $y = \frac{x-a}{x+2}$ has gradient 1 at the point $(a, 0)$ and $a \neq -2$. Find the value of a.

5 Find the exact coordinates of the stationary point on the curve $y = \frac{\ln x}{x}$ and determine its nature.

6 Find the range of values of x for which the function $f(x) = \frac{x^2}{1-x}$ is increasing.

7 Given that $y = \frac{x^2}{\sqrt{x+1}}$, show that $\frac{dy}{dx} = \frac{x(ax+b)}{2(x+1)^p}$, stating clearly the value of the constants a, b and p.

8 Show that if the curve $y = f(x)$ has a maximum stationary point at $x = a$, then the curve $y = \frac{1}{f(x)}$ has a minimum stationary point at $x = a$ as long as $f(a) \neq 0$.

Section 4: Implicit differentiation

The functions you have differentiated so far have always been of the form $y = f(x)$. From time to time, you will come across equations of curves that are written differently. For example, the equation of the circle shown in the diagram is $x^2 + y^2 = 16$. Such equations are said to be **implicit**, whereas those in the form $y = f(x)$ are said to be **explicit**.

Tip

Any equation that describes a relationship between x and y is called a *relation*. Mappings are a special type of relation (where the equation gives y explicitly in terms of x) and functions are a special type of mapping (where each x corresponds to just one y).

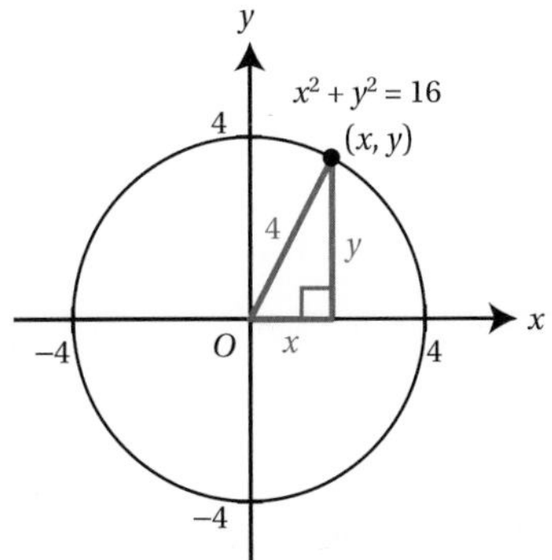

Explore

Strictly speaking the equation $x^2 + y^2 = 16$ does not define a function, but instead a **relation**. Explore the difference between functions and relations.

The gradient of the tangent at any point on the circle is still given by $\frac{dy}{dx}$.

Rather than attempting to rearrange the equation to make it explicit, you can just differentiate term by term with respect to x:

$$\frac{d}{dx}(x^2) + \frac{d}{dx}(y^2) = \frac{d}{dx}(16)$$

Some care needs to be taken when you come to y^2, as it is not expressed explicitly in terms of x; here, you will need the chain rule:

$$\frac{d(y^2)}{dx} = \frac{d(y^2)}{dy} \times \frac{dy}{dx} = 2y\frac{dy}{dx}$$

This will generally be the case when differentiating terms involving y.

Key point 10.7

When differentiating implicitly, you need to use

$$\frac{d}{dx}[f(y)] = f'(y) \times \frac{dy}{dx}$$

WORKED EXAMPLE 10.9

Find an expression for $\frac{dy}{dx}$ for the circle $x^2 + y^2 = 16$.

$\frac{d}{dx}(x^2)+\frac{d}{dx}(y^2)=\frac{d}{dx}(16)$ — Differentiate each term.

$\Rightarrow 2x+2y\frac{dy}{dx}=0$ — Use the chain rule on the term involving y.

Remember that a constant (16) differentiates to zero.

$\Rightarrow 2y\frac{dy}{dx}=-2x$

$\Rightarrow \frac{dy}{dx}=-\frac{x}{y}$ — You now need to rearrange the equation to find $\frac{dy}{dx}$.

Notice that the expression for $\frac{dy}{dx}$ will often be in terms of both x and y.

Sometimes you may need to use the product rule as well as the chain rule in the process of implicit differentiation.

WORKED EXAMPLE 10.10

Find an expression for $\frac{dy}{dx}$ if $e^x + x\sin y = \cos 2y$.

$\frac{d}{dx}(e^x)+\frac{d}{dx}(x\sin y)=\frac{d}{dx}(\cos 2y)$ — Differentiate term by term, using the chain rule on all terms involving y.

$e^x+\left(x\times\cos y\frac{dy}{dx}+\sin y\times 1\right)=-2\sin 2y\frac{dy}{dx}$ — $x\sin y$ is a product, so you need to use the product rule together with the chain rule on all terms involving y.

$x\cos y\frac{dy}{dx}+2\sin 2y\frac{dy}{dx}=-e^x-\sin y$ — Group the terms involving $\frac{dy}{dx}$.

$(x\cos y+2\sin 2y)\frac{dy}{dx}=-e^x-\sin y$

$\frac{dy}{dx}=\frac{-e^x-\sin y}{x\cos y+2\sin 2y}$

If you are interested only in the gradient at a particular point, or you are given the gradient and need to find the x- and y-coordinates, you can substitute the given value into the differentiated equation without rearranging it.

WORKED EXAMPLE 10.11

For the curve with equation $x^2+y^2-xy=3$:

a Find the gradient at the point (1, 2).

b Find the coordinates of the point where the gradient is 1.

$$\frac{d}{dx}(x^2)+\frac{d}{dx}(y^2)-\frac{d}{dx}(xy)=\frac{d}{dx}(3)$$

Differentiate each term with respect to x. The term xy will require the product rule.

$$2x+2y\frac{dy}{dx}-\left(x\times\frac{dy}{dx}+y\times 1\right)=0$$

Use the chain rule on terms involving y.

$$(2y-x)\frac{dy}{dx}+(2x-y)=0$$

Group terms involving $\frac{dy}{dx}$.

a When $x=1$ and $y=2$:

$$(4-1)\frac{dy}{dx}+(2-2)=0$$

Substitute the numbers before rearranging.

$$\frac{dy}{dx}=0$$

b When $\frac{dy}{dx}=1$:

$$(2y-x)(1)+(2x-y)=0$$

Put in the given value of the gradient.

$$x+y=0$$

$$y=-x$$

Substitute into $x^2+y^2-xy=3$:

$$x^2+(-x)^2-x(-x)=3$$

$$3x^2=3$$

$$x=\pm 1$$

This is a second equation relating x and y. You can solve it simultaneously with the original equation.

Using $y=-x$, the coordinates are $(1,-1)$ and $(-1,1)$.

Remember to find both x- and y-coordinates.

The method used in part **b** can also be used to find stationary points.

WORKED EXAMPLE 10.12

Find the coordinates of the turning points on the curve $y^3+3xy^2-x^3=27$.

$$\frac{d}{dx}(y^3)+\frac{d}{dx}(3xy^2)-\frac{d}{dx}(x^3)=\frac{d}{dx}(27)$$

Differentiate each term with respect to x but be aware that the term $3xy^2$ will require the product rule.

Continues on next page ...

$$\Rightarrow 3y^2\frac{dy}{dx}+\left(3x\times 2y\frac{dy}{dx}+y^2\times 3\right)-3x^2=0$$

$$\Rightarrow 3y^2\frac{dy}{dx}+6xy\frac{dy}{dx}+3y^2-3x^2=0$$

Use the chain rule on all terms involving y.

For stationary points, $\frac{dy}{dx}=0$.

$$3y^2-3x^2=0$$
$$(y-x)(y+x)=0$$
$$y=x \text{ or } y=-x$$

You know the value of $\frac{dy}{dx}$.

When $x=y$:

$$x^3+3xx^2-x^3=27$$
$$3x^3=27$$
$$x^3=9$$
$$x=\sqrt[3]{9}$$

You have found a relationship between x and y at the stationary points, but to actually find the points you need to substitute back into the original equation.

$\therefore \left(\sqrt[3]{9},\sqrt[3]{9}\right)$ is a stationary point.

When $x=-y$:

$$(-x)^3+3x(-x)^2-x^3=27$$
$$-x^3+3x^3-x^3=27$$
$$x^3=27$$
$$x=3$$

$\therefore (3,-3)$ is a stationary point.

One application of implicit differentiation is to differentiate exponential functions with base other than e.

WORKED EXAMPLE 10.13

Given that $y=2^x$, show that $\frac{dy}{dx}=2^x\ln 2$.

Let $y=2^x$. Then:

Take ln of both sides.

$$\ln y=x\ln 2$$

$$\Rightarrow \frac{d}{dx}(\ln y)=\frac{d}{dx}(x\ln 2)$$

You can now use implicit differentiation.

$$\Rightarrow \frac{1}{y}\frac{dy}{dx}=\ln 2$$

Remember that $\ln 2$ is a constant.

$$\Rightarrow \frac{dy}{dx}=y\ln 2$$
$$=2^x\ln 2$$

Key point 10.8

$$\frac{d}{dx}(a^x)=a^x \ln a$$

Rewind

This confirms that the gradient of any exponential function is proportional to the y value, as you learnt in Student Book 1, Chapter 8.

EXERCISE 10D

1 Find the gradient of each curve at the given point.

a **i** $x^2+3y^2=7$ at $(2, -1)$ **ii** $2x^3-y^3=-6$ at $(1, 2)$

b **i** $\cos x+\sin y=0$ at $(0, \pi)$ **ii** $\tan x+\tan y=2$ at $\left(\frac{\pi}{4}, \frac{\pi}{4}\right)$

c **i** $x^2+3xy+y^2=20$ at $(2, 2)$ **ii** $3x^2-xy^2+3y=21$ at $(-1, 3)$

d **i** $x\mathrm{e}^y+y\mathrm{e}^x=2\mathrm{e}$ at $(1, 1)$ **ii** $x\ln y-\frac{x}{y}=2$ at $(-1, 1)$

2 Find $\frac{dy}{dx}$ in terms of x and y.

a **i** $3x^2-y^3=15$ **ii** $x^4+3y^2=20$

b **i** $xy^2-4x^2y=6$ **ii** $y^2-xy=7$

c **i** $\frac{x+y}{x-y}=2y$ **ii** $\frac{y^2}{xy+1}=1$

d **i** $x\mathrm{e}^y-4\ln y=x^2$ **ii** $3x\sin y+2\cos y=\sin x$

3 Find the coordinates of stationary points on the curves given by these implicit equations.

a $-x^2+3xy+y^2=13$ **b** $2x^2-xy+y^2=28$

4 Find the exact value of the gradient at the given point.

a **i** $y=3^x$ at $(1, 3)$ **ii** $y=5^x$ at $(2, 25)$

b **i** $y=\left(\frac{1}{2}\right)^x$ when $x=-2$ **ii** $y=\left(\frac{1}{3}\right)^x$ when $x=-1$

c **i** $y=2^{3x}$ when $x=-1$ **ii** $y=4^{2x}$ when $x=\frac{1}{4}$

d **i** $y=3^{3-x}$ when $x=2$ **ii** $y=5^{1-x}$ when $x=2$

5 Find the gradient of the curve $x^2+y^2=5$ at the point $(-2, 1)$.

6 A curve has equation $3x^2+5y^3=22$.

a Show that $\frac{dy}{dx}=-\frac{2x}{5y^2}$.

b Find the equation of the tangent to the curve at the point $(3, -1)$.

7 A curve has equation $3x^2-y^2=8$. Point A has coordinates $(-2, 2)$.

a Show that point A lies on the curve.

b Find the equation of the normal to the curve at A.

8 Find the gradient of the curve with equation $x^2-3xy+y^2+1=0$ at the point $(1, 2)$.

9 Find the equation of the tangent to the curve with equation $3x^2+xy-y^2=-3$ at the point $(2, 5)$.

10 Find the equation of the tangent to the curve with equation $4x^2-3xy-y^2=25$ at the point $(2, -3)$.

11 A curve has implicit equation $x2^y=\ln y$. Find an expression for $\frac{dy}{dx}$ in terms of x and y.

12 Find the coordinates of the stationary point on the curve given by $e^x + ye^{-x} = 2e^2$.

13 The line L is tangent to the curve C, which has the equation $y^2 = x^3$ when $x = 4$ and $y > 0$.

a Find the equation of L.

b Show that L meets C again at the point P with an x-coordinate that satisfies the equation $x^3 - 9x^2 + 24x - 16 = 0$.

c Find the coordinates of the point P.

Section 5: Differentiating inverse functions

Another application of the chain rule is to differentiate inverse functions. If $y = f(x)$ then $x = f^{-1}(y)$. The derivative of f is $\frac{dy}{dx}$ and the derivative of f^{-1} is $\frac{dx}{dy}$. But the chain rule says that

$$\frac{dy}{dx} \times \frac{dx}{dy} = \frac{dy}{dy} = 1$$

and so:

Key point 10.9

The derivative of the inverse function is

$$\frac{dx}{dy} = \frac{1}{\left(\frac{dy}{dx}\right)}$$

You may remember that Chapter 9, Section 1 showed a graphical proof for the result for the derivative of ln x. You can now prove it by using the fact that ln x is the inverse function of e^x.

WORKED EXAMPLE 10.14

Use the derivative of e^x to prove that the derivative of $\ln x$ is $\frac{1}{x}$.

Let $y = \ln x$.

Then $x = e^y$.

You can't use the result you are trying to prove, so cannot differentiate ln x directly. Instead, you can use known properties of its inverse function, e^x.

$\Rightarrow \frac{dx}{dy} = e^y$

Be careful – you are differentiating x with respect to y.

$\Rightarrow \frac{dy}{dx} = \frac{1}{e^y}$

Use the inverse function rule here.

But $e^y = x$, so

$\frac{dy}{dx} = \frac{1}{x}$, as required.

You can use the derivative of the inverse function to solve some integration problems that you could not work out before.

WORKED EXAMPLE 10.15

The deceleration of a parachute is proportional to the square of its velocity, so that $a=\frac{dv}{dt}=-0.05v^2$.

When $t=0$ the velocity is 12 m s^{-1}. Find an expression for the velocity in terms of time.

$$\frac{dv}{dt}=-0.05v^2$$

You can't integrate $-0.05v$ with respect to t, but you can integrate it with respect to v.

$$\Rightarrow \frac{dt}{dv}=-\frac{20}{v^2}$$

So you are trying to find the inverse function, t in terms of v.

$$\Rightarrow t=\int -\frac{20}{v^2}dv$$
$$=\frac{20}{v}+c$$

You can now integrate with respect to v.

When $t=0$, $v=12$:

$$0=\frac{20}{12}+c$$

Use initial conditions to find c.

$$\Rightarrow c=-\frac{5}{3}$$

$$\therefore t=\frac{20}{v}-\frac{5}{3}$$

$$\Leftrightarrow \frac{20}{v}=t+\frac{5}{3}=\frac{3t+5}{3}$$

$$\Leftrightarrow v=\frac{60}{3t+5}$$

You need to express v in terms of t.

Fast forward

In Chapter 12 you will learn how to solve similar problems where the acceleration depends on both t and v.

EXERCISE 10E

1 If you prefer, you can differentiate inverse functions using implicit differentiation. For example, given that $y=\sqrt{x}$:

- **a** Express x in terms of y.
- **b** Use implicit differentiation to find $\frac{dy}{dx}$. Write your answer in terms of x.

2 A population is increasing at a rate proportional to its current size, N. The initial size of the population is 2500 and its initial rate of increase is 45.

- **a** Show that $\frac{dN}{dt}=0.018N$.
- **b** Solve the differential equation and, hence, find the size of the population when $t=22$.

3 A function is defined by $f(x)=x^3+3x+2$.

- **a** By considering $f'(x)$, prove that $f(x)$ has an inverse function.
- **b** Find the gradient of the graph of $y=f^{-1}(x)$ at the point where $x=2$.

4
- **a** Given that $f(x)=\log_a x$, write down an expression for $f^{-1}(x)$.
- **b** Hence, prove that $\frac{d}{dx}(\log_a x)=\frac{1}{x\ln a}$.

5 A spherical balloon is being inflated at a constant rate of $32\text{ cm}^3\text{ s}^{-1}$. The radius at time t seconds is r cm.

a Find an equation for $\frac{\mathrm{d}t}{\mathrm{d}r}$ in terms of r.

b Given that initially the radius is 5 cm, find an expression for the radius in terms of time.

6 A function is defined by $\mathrm{f}(x)=x+\cos x$.

a Prove that f is an increasing function.

b Show that the point $\left(\frac{\pi}{4}, \frac{\pi+2\sqrt{2}}{4}\right)$ lies on the graph of $y=\mathrm{f}(x)$.

c Find the exact value of the gradient of the graph of $y=\mathrm{f}^{-1}(x)$ at the point $x=\frac{\pi+2\sqrt{2}}{4}$.

7 Given that $y=\arcsin x$:

a Find $\frac{\mathrm{d}x}{\mathrm{d}y}$ in terms of y.

b Hence, find $\frac{\mathrm{d}y}{\mathrm{d}x}$ in terms of x.

8 Given that $\mathrm{f}(x)$ is an increasing function, prove that $\mathrm{f}^{-1}(x)$ is also an increasing function.

Checklist of learning and understanding

- The chain rule is used to differentiate composite functions:
  $\frac{dy}{dx}=\frac{dy}{du}\times\frac{du}{dx}$
- The product rule is used to differentiate two functions multiplied together:
  If $y=uv$ then $\frac{\mathrm{d}y}{\mathrm{d}x}=u\frac{\mathrm{d}v}{\mathrm{d}x}+v\frac{\mathrm{d}u}{\mathrm{d}x}$.
- The quotient rule is used to differentiate one function divided by another:
  If $y=\frac{u}{v}$ then $\frac{\mathrm{d}y}{\mathrm{d}x}=\frac{v\frac{\mathrm{d}u}{\mathrm{d}x}-u\frac{\mathrm{d}v}{\mathrm{d}x}}{v^2}$.
- The derivatives of the reciprocal trigonometric functions are:
  - $\frac{\mathrm{d}}{\mathrm{d}x}(\sec x)=\sec x\tan x$, $\frac{\mathrm{d}}{\mathrm{d}x}(\operatorname{cosec} x)=-\operatorname{cosec} x\cot x$, $\frac{\mathrm{d}}{\mathrm{d}x}(\cot x)=-\operatorname{cosec}^2 x$
- You need to know the following standard derivatives:
  $\frac{\mathrm{d}}{\mathrm{d}x}\left(\mathrm{e}^{kx}\right)=k\mathrm{e}^{kx}$
  $\frac{\mathrm{d}}{\mathrm{d}x}\left(a^{kx}\right)=a^{kx}\ln a^k$
  $\frac{\mathrm{d}}{\mathrm{d}x}(\sin kx)=k\cos kx$
  $\frac{\mathrm{d}}{\mathrm{d}x}(\cos kx)=-k\sin kx$
  $\frac{\mathrm{d}}{\mathrm{d}x}(\tan kx)=k\sec^2 kx$
- To differentiate an implicit equation:
  - Differentiate each term.
  - Use the chain rule for any term containing y: $\frac{\mathrm{d}}{\mathrm{d}x}[\mathrm{f}(y)]=\mathrm{f}'(y)\frac{\mathrm{d}y}{\mathrm{d}x}$.
- Differentiation of inverse functions:
  - $\frac{\mathrm{d}x}{\mathrm{d}y}=\frac{1}{\left(\frac{\mathrm{d}y}{\mathrm{d}x}\right)}$

Mixed practice 10

1. Find $\frac{dy}{dx}$ if:

   a $y = e^{5x}$

   b $y = \sqrt{3x+2}$

   c $y = e^{5x}\sqrt{3x+2}$

2. Find the exact value of the gradient of the curve with equation $y = \frac{1}{4-x^2}$ when $x = \frac{1}{2}$.

3. A particle moves in a straight line with velocity given by $v = e^{2t} - 13e^{t} + 15t + 20 \text{ m s}^{-1}$.

   Find the minimum value of the velocity in the particle's motion.

4. A curve has equation $x^2 + 3y^2 - 2xy = 22$.

   a Show that the point $P(1, 3)$ lies on the curve.

   b Find the gradient of the curve at P.

5. The curve C has equation $y = \frac{x}{\sqrt{x^2-5}}$. The tangent to the curve at the point $x = 3$ crosses the coordinate axes at points A and B. Find the area of the triangle AOB.

6. Differentiate each of the following with respect to x.

   i $x^3(x+1)^5$

   ii $\sqrt{3x^4+1}$

7. The graph of $y = xe^{-kx}$ has a stationary point when $x = \frac{2}{5}$. Find the value of k.

8. Find the exact coordinates of the stationary point on the curve with equation $ye^{x} = 3x - 6$.

9. a Find the value of k so that $a^x = e^{kx}$.

   b Hence, show that the derivative of a^x is $a^x \ln a$.

Rewind

Compare this derivation with the one using implicit differentiation in Worked example 10.14.

10. Find the exact value of the gradient of the curve with equation $y = 3^x$ at the point where $x = 2$.

11. At time t seconds, the displacement of a particle from O is $s = 10(t^2 - 3)e^{-t}$ m.

    a Find the value of t when the particle is instantaneously at rest.

    b Find the particle's maximum speed.

12. A curve has equation $y = \frac{x^2}{1-2x}$.

    a Write down the equation of the vertical asymptote of the curve.

    b Use differentiation to find the coordinates of stationary points on the curve.

    c Determine the nature of the stationary points.

    d Sketch the graph of $y = \frac{x^2}{1-2x}$.

13 **a** Prove that the derivative of cosec x is $-\text{cosec}\, x \cot x$.

b Find the equation of the tangent to the graph of $y = \text{cosec}\, x$ at the point where $x = \frac{\pi}{6}$.

14 A function is defined by $g(x) = 3x + \ln 2x$ for $x > 0$.

a Find $g'(x)$ and, hence, prove that $g(x)$ has an inverse function.

b Find the gradient of $g'(x)$ at the point $(3, 1)$.

15 The equation of a curve is $x^3 + y^3 = 6xy$.

i Find $\frac{dy}{dx}$ in terms of x and y.

ii Show that the point $\left(2^{\frac{4}{3}}, 2^{\frac{5}{3}}\right)$ lies on the curve and that $\frac{dy}{dx} = 0$ at this point.

iii The point (a, a), where $a > 0$, lies on the curve. Find the value of a and the gradient of the curve at this point.

16 A curve is given by the implicit equation $x^2 - xy + y^2 = 12$.

a Find the coordinates of the stationary points on the curve.

b Show that, at the stationary points, $(x - 2y)\frac{d^2y}{dx^2} = 2$.

c Hence, determine the nature of the stationary points.

17 **a** Express $\sec^2 x$ in terms of $\tan x$.

b Let $y = \arctan x$. By first expressing x in terms of y, prove that $\frac{dy}{dx} = \frac{1}{1 + x^2}$.

c Find the equation of the normal to the curve $y = \arctan(3x)$ at the point where $x = \frac{1}{\sqrt{3}}$.

18 **a** Given that $y = \frac{x+1}{\sqrt{x+2}}$, find $\frac{dy}{dx}$. Give your answer in the form $\frac{Ax + B}{2(x+2)^{\frac{3}{2}}}$, where A and B are integers.

The diagram shows part of the curve $y = \frac{x}{(x+2)^{\frac{3}{2}}}$.

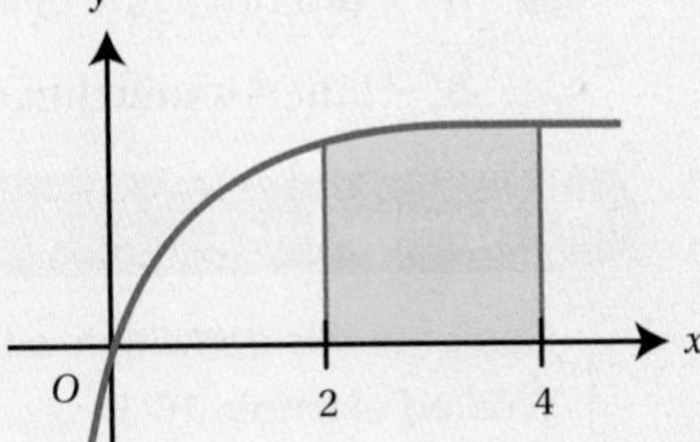

b Find the coordinates of the stationary point on the curve.

c Find the shaded area enclosed by the curve, the x-axis and the lines $x = 2$ and $x = 7$.

Elevate

See Extension sheet 10 for questions on some properties of e that use differentiation.

11 Further integration techniques

In this chapter you will learn how to integrate using:

- known derivatives
- the chain rule in reverse
- a change of variable (substitution)
- the product rule in reverse (integration by parts)
- trigonometric identities
- the separation of a fraction into two fractions.

Before you start…

Chapter 9	You should be able to differentiate and integrate polynomial, exponential and trigonometric functions.	1 Find: a $\int 4x^2 + \frac{3}{x}\,dx$ b $\int 5 \sin x\, dx$
		2 Given that $y = 4e^x$, find: a $\frac{dy}{dx}$ b $\int_0^1 y\, dx$
Chapter 10	You should be able to use the chain rule for differentiation.	3 Differentiate with respect to x: a $\sin 4x$ b $\ln(x^2+1)$
Chapter 8	You should know how to use double angle formulae.	4 Given that $\cos 2A = 0.28$, find the possible values of $\cos A$.
Chapter 5	You should know how to split an expression into partial fractions.	5 Write $\frac{36}{(x-1)(x+2)^2}$ in partial fractions.

Integrating more complex functions

Having extended the range of functions you can differentiate, you now need to do the same for integration. In some cases you will be able to use results from Chapter 11 directly, but in many others you will require new techniques. In this chapter you look at each of these in turn and then face the challenge of selecting the appropriate technique from the not inconsiderable list of options you have built up.

Section 1: Reversing standard derivatives

You already know how to integrate many functions by reversing the corresponding differentiation results:

- $\int x^n\, dx = \frac{1}{n+1}x^{n+1} + c$ when $n \neq -1$

- $\int e^x \, dx = e^x + c$
- $\int \frac{1}{x} \, dx = \ln|x| + c$
- $\int \sin x \, dx = -\cos x + c$
- $\int \cos x \, dx = \sin x + c$

In Chapter 10 you differentiated sec x, cosec x and cot x. You can now reverse these standard derivatives too and add the following results to your list:

- $\int \sec^2 x \, dx = \tan x + c$
- $\int \sec x \tan x \, dx = \sec x + c$
- $\int \operatorname{cosec} x \cot x \, dx = -\operatorname{cosec} x + c$
- $\int \operatorname{cosec}^2 x \, dx = -\cot x + c$

Thinking about reversing the chain rule for differentiation allows you to go one step further and deal with integrals such as $\int \cos 2x \, dx$.

You know that the answer must include sin $2x$ as sin is the integral of cos, but this isn't the final answer.

If you work backwards and differentiate sin $2x$, you get

$$\frac{d}{dx} \sin 2x = 2 \cos 2x.$$

Since you don't want the 2 in front of cos $2x$, you divide by 2 (or multiply by $\frac{1}{2}$) to get:

$$\int \cos 2x \, dx = \frac{1}{2} \sin 2x + c$$

WORKED EXAMPLE 11.1

Find $\int (7x-3)^4 \, dx$.

$$\int (7x-3)^4 \, dx = \frac{1}{7} \times \frac{1}{5}(7x-3)^5$$

$(u)^4$ integrates to $\frac{1}{5}(u)^5$. But differentiating back, the chain rule will also give a factor of 7 (the derivative of $7x-3$). Remove this by multiplying by $\frac{1}{7}$.

$$= \frac{1}{35}(7x-3)^5 + c$$

WORKED EXAMPLE 11.2

$$\int e^{4x+5} dx = \frac{1}{4} \times e^{4x+5} + c$$

If you differentiate $e^{(4x+5)}$, the chain rule will give a factor of 4 (the derivative of $4x+5$). Remove this by multiplying by $\frac{1}{4}$.

You may be noticing a pattern here: you always end up integrating the function and then dividing by the coefficient of x. This is indeed a general rule when the 'inside' function is of the form $(ax+b)$.

Key point 11.1

$$\int f(ax+b)\,dx = \frac{1}{a}F(ax+b)+c$$

where $F(x)$ is the integral of $f(x)$.

Tip

Note that this rule only applies when the 'inside' function is of the form $(ax+b)$.

It is worth remembering three particular examples of this rule:

Key point 11.2

$$\int e^{kx}dx = \frac{1}{k}e^{kx}+c$$

$$\int \sin kx\,dx = -\frac{1}{k}\cos kx + c$$

$$\int \cos kx\,dx = \frac{1}{k}\sin kx + c$$

WORKED EXAMPLE 11.3

Find $\int \frac{1}{5-3x}\,dx$.

$$\int \frac{1}{5-3x}\,dx = \frac{1}{-3}\ln|5-3x|+c$$

Divide by the coefficient of x.

$$= -\frac{1}{3}\ln|5-3x|+c$$

WORK IT OUT 11.1

Find $\int \frac{1}{3x}\,dx$.

Which of the following solutions are correct? (There may be more than one.) Identify the mistakes in those that are not correct.

Solution 1	Solution 2	Solution 3
$\int \frac{1}{3x}dx = \int 3x^{-1}dx$ $= 3\ln\|x\|+c$	$\int \frac{1}{3x}dx = \frac{1}{3}\ln\|3x\|+d$	$\int \frac{1}{3x}dx = \frac{1}{3}\int\frac{1}{x}dx$ $= \frac{1}{3}\ln\|x\|+k$

How can solutions 2 and 3 both be correct? The answer lies in the constant of integration. The answer in Solution 2 can be re-written as follows:

$$\frac{1}{3}\ln|3x|+d=\frac{1}{3}(\ln 3+\ln|x|)+d$$

$$=\frac{1}{3}\ln|x|+\frac{1}{3}\ln 3+d$$

for an arbitrary constant, d.

But $\frac{1}{3}\ln 3$ is simply a number, so $\frac{1}{3}\ln 3+d$ is another arbitrary constant, so the answer in Solution 2 can be written as $\frac{1}{3}\ln|x|+k$ (where $k=\frac{1}{3}\ln 3+d$).

WORKED EXAMPLE 11.4

Find $\int 3\sec^2(5x-2)\,dx$.

$$\int 3\sec^2(5x-2)dx = 3\times\frac{1}{5}\tan(5x-2)+c$$

Integrate $\sec^2(u)$ to $\tan(u)$ and divide by the coefficient of x.

$$=\frac{3}{5}\tan(5x-2)+c$$

EXERCISE 11A

1 Find the following indefinite integrals.

a **i** $\int 5(x+3)^4\,dx$ **ii** $\int (x-2)^5\,dx$

b **i** $\int (4x-5)^7\,dx$ **ii** $\int \left(\frac{1}{8}x+1\right)^3 dx$

c **i** $\int 4\left(3-\frac{1}{2}x\right)^6 dx$ **ii** $\int (4-x)^8\,dx$

d **i** $\int \sqrt{2x-1}\,dx$ **ii** $\int 7(2-5x)^{\frac{3}{4}}\,dx$

e **i** $\int \frac{1}{\sqrt[4]{2+\frac{x}{3}}}\,dx$ **ii** $\int \frac{6}{(4-3x)^2}\,dx$

2 Find the following integrals.

a **i** $\int 3e^{3x}\,dx$ **ii** $\int e^{2x+5}\,dx$

b **i** $\int 4e^{\frac{2x-1}{3}}\,dx$ **ii** $\int e^{\frac{1}{2}x}\,dx$

c **i** $\int -6e^{-3x}\,dx$ **ii** $\int \frac{1}{e^{4x}}\,dx$

d **i** $\int \frac{-2}{e^{\frac{x}{4}}}\,dx$ **ii** $\int e^{-\frac{2}{3}x}\,dx$

3 Find:

a i $\int \frac{1}{x+4}\,dx$ ii $\int \frac{5}{5x-2}\,dx$

b i $\int \frac{2}{3x+4}\,dx$ ii $\int \frac{-8}{2x-5}\,dx$

c i $\int \frac{-3}{1-4x}\,dx$ ii $\int \frac{1}{7-2x}\,dx$

d i $\int 1-\frac{3}{5-x}\,dx$ ii $\int 3+\frac{1}{3-x}\,dx$

4 Integrate the following.

a $\int -\operatorname{cosec} x \cot x\,dx$ b $\int 3\sec^2 3x\,dx$

c $\int \sin(2-3x)\,dx$ d $\int \operatorname{cosec}^2\left(\frac{1}{4}x\right)dx$

e $\int 2\cos 4x\,dx$ f $\int \sec\frac{x}{2}\tan\frac{x}{2}\,dx$

5 Find the exact value of $\int_0^{\frac{\pi}{3}} 2\sin(5x)\,dx$.

6 Find the exact area enclosed by the graph of $y=3e^{-2x}$, the x-axis and the lines $x=1$ and $x=4$.

7 Find the area enclosed by the x-axis and the curve with equation $y=9-(2x-5)^2$.

8 Given that $0<a<1$ and the area between the x-axis, the lines $x=a^2$, $x=a$ and the graph of $y=\frac{1}{1-x}$ is 0.4, find the value of a, correct to 3 significant figures.

Section 2: Integration by substitution

The shortcut for reversing the chain rule from the previous section (Key point 11.1) works only when the derivative of the 'inside' function is a constant. This is because a constant factor can 'move through the integral sign', as shown in the following example.

$$\begin{aligned}\int \cos 2x\,dx &= \int \frac{1}{2}\times 2\cos 2x\,dx\\ &= \frac{1}{2}\int 2\cos 2x\,dx\\ &= \frac{1}{2}\sin 2x + c\end{aligned}$$

This cannot be done with a variable: $\int x\sin x\,dx$ is not the same as $x\int \sin x\,dx$. So you need a different rule for integrating a product of two functions. In some cases this can be achieved by extending the principle of reversing the chain rule, leading to the method of **integration by substitution**.

Fast forward

Another method for integrating products is integration by parts, which is the reverse of the product rule. You will meet it in Section 3.

Reversing the chain rule

When using the chain rule to differentiate a composite function, you differentiate the outer function and multiply this by the derivative of the inner function; for example:

$$\frac{\mathrm{d}}{\mathrm{d}x}\left(\sin\left(x^2+2\right)\right)=\cos\left(x^2+2\right)\times 2x$$

You can think of this as using a substitution $u=x^2+2$, and then $\frac{\mathrm{d}y}{\mathrm{d}x}=\frac{\mathrm{d}y}{\mathrm{d}u}\times\frac{\mathrm{d}u}{\mathrm{d}x}$.

Tip

When making a substitution of this type, only replace the inner function with u. Any other instances of x will cancel out when changing $\mathrm{d}x$ to $\mathrm{d}u$.

Now look at $\int x\cos\left(x^2+2\right)\mathrm{d}x$. Since $\cos(x^2+2)$ is a composite function, you can write it as $\cos u$, where $u=x^2+2$. Thus the integral becomes $\int x\cos u\,\mathrm{d}x$.

You know how to integrate $\cos u$. But you need to be integrating with respect to u, so you should have $\mathrm{d}u$ instead of $\mathrm{d}x$. Those two are not the same thing but they are related because $u=x^2+2$, so $\frac{\mathrm{d}u}{\mathrm{d}x}=2x$.

This can then be rearranged to make x the subject so that it can be replaced in the integral: $x=\left(\frac{1}{2}\frac{\mathrm{d}u}{\mathrm{d}x}\right)$

Substituting all of this into the integral gives

$$\begin{aligned}\int x\cos\left(x^2+2\right)\mathrm{d}x&=\int\frac{1}{2}\frac{\mathrm{d}u}{\mathrm{d}x}\cos(u)\,\mathrm{d}x\\&=\frac{1}{2}\int\cos u\frac{\mathrm{d}u}{\mathrm{d}x}\mathrm{d}x\end{aligned}$$

It follows from the chain rule that $\int\cos u\frac{\mathrm{d}u}{\mathrm{d}x}\mathrm{d}x=\int\cos u\,\mathrm{d}u$ so,

$$\begin{aligned}\int x\cos\left(x^2+2\right)\mathrm{d}x&=\frac{1}{2}\int\cos u\,\mathrm{d}u\\&=\frac{1}{2}\sin u+c\\&=\frac{1}{2}\sin\left(x^2+2\right)+c\end{aligned}$$

Notice that having got an answer in terms of u, it needed to be written back in terms of x.

In practice, this method can be shortened by appreciating that $\frac{\mathrm{d}u}{\mathrm{d}x}$ can be 'split up' just like a fraction, so $\frac{\mathrm{d}u}{\mathrm{d}x}=2x$ gives $\mathrm{d}x=\frac{1}{2x}\mathrm{d}u$.

This is illustrated in the following examples.

WORKED EXAMPLE 11.5

Find the following:

a $\int \sin^5 x \cos x \, dx$

b $\int x^2 e^{x^3+4} \, dx$

a Let $u = \sin x$.

Then $\frac{du}{dx} = \cos x \Rightarrow dx = \frac{1}{\cos x} du$

Think of $\sin^5 x$ as $(\sin x)^5$; therefore, the inner function is $\sin x$.

$$\int (\sin x)^5 \cos x \, dx = \int u^5 \cos x \frac{1}{\cos x} du$$

Make the substitution.

$$= \int u^5 \, du$$

$$= \frac{1}{6} u^6 + c$$

$$= \frac{1}{6} \sin^6 x + c$$

Write the answer in terms of x.

b Let $u = x^3 + 4$.

e^{x^3+4} is a composite function with inner function $x^3 + 4$.

Then $\frac{du}{dx} = 3x^2 \; dx = \frac{1}{3x^2} du$

$$\int x^2 e^{x^3+4} \, dx = \int x^2 e^u \frac{1}{3x^2} du$$

Make the substitution.

$$= \int \frac{1}{3} e^u \, du$$

$$= \frac{1}{3} e^u + c$$

$$= \frac{1}{3} e^{x^3+4} + c$$

Write the answer in terms of x.

When limits are given, you must ensure they are changed, too. In that case there is no need to change back to the original variable at the end.

WORKED EXAMPLE 11.6

Evaluate $\int_0^1 \frac{x-3}{x^2-6x+7} dx$, giving your answer in the form $a \ln p$, where a and p are rational numbers.

Let $u = x^2 - 6x + 7$.

This is of the form something $\times \frac{1}{(x^2-6x+7)}$, so the 'inner' function is $x^2 - 6x + 7$.

Then $\frac{du}{dx} = 2x - 6 \Rightarrow dx = \frac{1}{2x-6} du$

Continues on next page ...

Limits:
$x=0 \Rightarrow u=7,\ x=1 \Rightarrow u=2$

Write the limits in terms of u.

$$\int_0^1 \frac{x-3}{x^2-6x+7}\,dx = \int_7^2 \frac{x-3}{u}\,\frac{1}{2x-6}\,du$$

Make the substitution.

$$= \int_7^2 \frac{1}{2u}\,du$$

Simplify: $2x-6=2(x-3)$.

$$= \left[\frac{1}{2}\ln|u|\right]_7^2$$

$$= \frac{1}{2}(\ln 2 - \ln 7)$$

$$= \frac{1}{2}\ln\left(\frac{2}{7}\right)$$

This particular case of substitution, where the top of the fraction is related to the derivative of the bottom, is definitely worth remembering:

Key point 11.3

$$\int \frac{f'(x)}{f(x)}\,dx = \ln|f(x)|+c$$

You can use this result to integrate some trigonometric functions.

WORKED EXAMPLE 11.7

Show that $\int \tan x\,dx = \ln|\sec x|+c$.

$$\int \tan x\,dx = \int \frac{\sin x}{\cos x}\,dx$$

$$= -\int \frac{-\sin x}{\cos x}\,dx$$

If $f(x)=\cos x$ then $f'(x) = -\sin x$. So you can write the integral in the form $\int \frac{f'(x)}{f(x)}\,dx$.

$$= -\ln|\cos x|+c$$

Using the result of Key point 11.3.

$$= \ln\left|\frac{1}{\cos x}\right|+c$$

$$= \ln|\sec x|+c$$

You want the answer in terms of $\sec x$, so remember that $\sec x = \frac{1}{\cos x}$ and use $-\ln a = \ln(a^{-1})$.

EXERCISE 11B

1 Use either a suitable substitution or the reverse chain rule to find the following integrals.

a i $\int 2x(x^2+3)^3\,\mathrm{d}x$ ii $\int 2x(x^2-1)^5\,\mathrm{d}x$

b i $\int (2x-5)(3x^2-15x+4)^4\,\mathrm{d}x$ ii $\int (x^2+2x)(x^3+3x^2-5)^3\,\mathrm{d}x$

c i $\int \frac{2x}{x^2+3}\,\mathrm{d}x$ ii $\int \frac{3x^2-4}{x^3-4x+5}\,\mathrm{d}x$

d i $\int \frac{x+4}{x^2+8x-3}\,\mathrm{d}x$ ii $\int \frac{x^2+2x-5}{x^3+3x^2-15x+1}\,\mathrm{d}x$

e i $\int \frac{x}{\sqrt{x^2+2}}\,\mathrm{d}x$ ii $\int \frac{x^2}{(x^3-4)^2}\,\mathrm{d}x$

f i $\int 4\cos^5 x\sin x\,\mathrm{d}x$ ii $\int \cos 2x\sin^3 2x\,\mathrm{d}x$

g i $\int \tan^3 x\sec^2 x\,\mathrm{d}x$ ii $\int \cot^4 x\operatorname{cosec}^2 x\,\mathrm{d}x$

h i $\int 3x\,\mathrm{e}^{3x^2-1}\,\mathrm{d}x$ ii $\int 3x\,\mathrm{e}^{x^2}\,\mathrm{d}x$

i i $\int \frac{\mathrm{e}^{2x+3}}{\mathrm{e}^{2x+3}+4}\,\mathrm{d}x$ ii $\int \frac{\cos x}{3+4\sin x}\,\mathrm{d}x$

2 Find $\int \sin x\,\mathrm{e}^{\cos x}\,\mathrm{d}x$.

3 Find the exact value of $\int_0^2 (2x+1)\mathrm{e}^{x^2+x-1}\,\mathrm{d}x$, showing all your working.

4 Show that $\int_2^5 \frac{2x}{x^2-1}\,\mathrm{d}x = \ln k$, where k is an integer to be found.

5 Find $\int \frac{\cos 3x}{\sin^5 3x}\,\mathrm{d}x$.

6 Find $\int \operatorname{cosec}^5 2x\cot 2x\,\mathrm{d}x$.

> **Tip**
>
> You don't have to make a substitution if you can see that the expression is of the form $\int f'(x)[f(x)]^n\,\mathrm{d}x,\ n \neq -1$ i.e. with both a function and its derivative present. You can just go straight to the answer using the reverse chain rule: $\frac{1}{n+1}[f(x)]^{n+1}+c$.

General substitution

In all the examples you have done so far, after making the substitution, the part of the integral that was still in terms of x cancelled with a similar term coming from $\frac{\mathrm{d}u}{\mathrm{d}x}$. This will always happen when one part of the expression to be integrated is an exact multiple of the **derivative** of the **inner function**. You can explain this by looking at the chain rule.

In some cases you will not be able to cancel all terms in x, so you will have to express x in terms of u to obtain a function of u only. The full method of substitution will then be as follows:

Tip

If you are not told which substitution to use, look for a composite function and take u = 'inner' function.

Key point 11.4

1. Select a substitution (if not already given).
2. Differentiate the substitution and write dx in terms of du.
3. Replace dx by the expression above, and replace any obvious occurrences of u.
4. Change the limits from x to u.
5. Simplify as far as possible.
6. If any terms with x remain, write them in terms of u.
7. Do the new integral in terms of u.
8. Write the answer in terms of x.

WORKED EXAMPLE 11.8

Find $\int x\sqrt{4x-1}\ dx$, using the substitution $u=4x-1$.

$$u=4x-1$$

$$\frac{du}{dx}=4$$

Differentiate the substitution and write dx in terms of du (step 2).

$$\therefore dx=\frac{1}{4}du$$

$$\int x\sqrt{4x-1}\,dx=\int x\sqrt{u}\,\frac{1}{4}du$$

Replace those parts that you already have expressions for, and simplify if possible (steps 3 to 5).

$$=\int \frac{1}{4}x\sqrt{u}\,du$$

$$=\int \frac{1}{4}\frac{u+1}{4}u^{1/2}\,du$$

There is still an x remaining, so replace it using $u=4x-1 \Rightarrow x=\frac{u+1}{4}$ (step 6).

$$=\frac{1}{16}\int u^{3/2}+u^{1/2}\,du$$

Now everything is in terms of u so you can integrate (step 7). Remember that $\sqrt{u}=u^{1/2}$.

$$=\frac{1}{16}\left(\frac{2}{5}u^{5/2}+\frac{2}{3}u^{3/2}\right)+c$$

$$=\frac{1}{40}\left(\sqrt{4x-1}\right)^5+\frac{1}{24}\left(\sqrt{4x-1}\right)^3+c$$

Write the answer in terms of x, using $u=4x-1$ (step 8).

A substitution can be given as x in terms of u, rather than u in terms of x.

WORKED EXAMPLE 11.9

Use the substitution $x = u^2$ (with $u > 0$) to evaluate $\int_9^{25} \frac{1}{x - 2\sqrt{x}}\,\mathrm{d}x$.

$\frac{dx}{du} = 2u \Rightarrow dx = 2u\,du$

Differentiate the substitution. Note that now you are finding $\frac{\mathrm{d}x}{\mathrm{d}u}$.

$x = u^2 = 9 \Rightarrow u = 3$

$x = u^2 = 25 \Rightarrow u = 5$

Find limits for u. This involves solving an equation.

$\int_9^{25} \frac{1}{x - 2\sqrt{x}}\,dx = \int_3^5 \frac{1}{u^2 - 2u}\,2u\,du$

Replace $\mathrm{d}x$ by $2u\,\mathrm{d}u$ and x by u^2. Use the fact that $\sqrt{u^2} = u$.

$= \int_3^5 \frac{2}{u - 2}\,du$

Simplify if possible.

$= \left[2\ln|u - 2|\right]_3^5$

$= 2\ln 3 - 2\ln 1$

$= 2\ln 3$

Now everything is in terms of u so you can integrate. Remember the modulus sign with the ln.

EXERCISE 11C

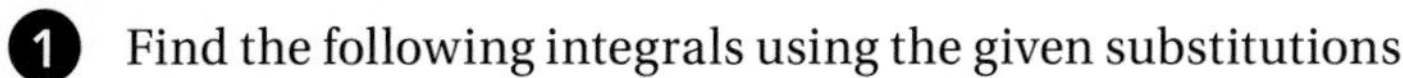

1 Find the following integrals using the given substitutions.

a **i** $\int x\sqrt{x+1}\,\mathrm{d}x, u = x + 1$ **ii** $\int x^2\sqrt{x-2}\,\mathrm{d}x, u = x - 2$

b **i** $\int 2x(x-5)^7\,\mathrm{d}x, u = x - 5$ **ii** $\int x(x+3)^5\,\mathrm{d}x, u = x + 3$

2 Use the given substitutions to find these integrals.

a **i** $\int \frac{1}{x+\sqrt{x}}\,\mathrm{d}x, x = u^2$ **ii** $\int \frac{1}{3\sqrt{x}+4x}\,\mathrm{d}x, x = u^2$

b **i** $\int \frac{1}{x\ln x}\,\mathrm{d}x, x = \mathrm{e}^u$ **ii** $\int \frac{1}{x(\ln x)^3}\,\mathrm{d}x, x = \mathrm{e}^u$

3 Find the following, using appropriate substitutions.

a **i** $\int x(2x-1)^4\,\mathrm{d}x$ **ii** $\int 9x(3x+2)^5\,\mathrm{d}x$

b **i** $\int x\sqrt{x-3}\,\mathrm{d}x$ **ii** $\int (x+1)\sqrt{5x-6}\,\mathrm{d}x$

c **i** $\int \frac{x^2}{\sqrt{x-5}}\,\mathrm{d}x$ **ii** $\int \frac{4(x+5)}{(2x-3)^3}\,\mathrm{d}x$

4 Use the given substitutions to evaluate the following definite integrals.

a **i** $\int_1^3 4x(2x+1)^3\,\mathrm{d}x,\ u=2x+1$ **ii** $\int_0^1 6x(3x-2)^4\,\mathrm{d}x,\ u=3x-2$

b **i** $\int_0^{\frac{\pi}{2}} \cos x\sin^5 x\,\mathrm{d}x,\ u=\sin x$ **ii** $\int_0^{\frac{\pi}{4}} \sec^2 x\tan^2 x\,\mathrm{d}x,\ u=\tan x$

c **i** $\int_2^3 \left(\frac{x}{4-x}\right)^2 \mathrm{d}x,\ u=4-x$ **ii** $\int_1^3 \frac{x^3}{(x+2)^2}\,\mathrm{d}x,\ u=x+2$

5 Use the substitution $u=x-2$ to find $\int \frac{x}{\sqrt{x-2}}\,\mathrm{d}x$.

6 **a** Show that $(x-1)$ is a factor of x^3-1.

b Find $\int \frac{2x^2-x-1}{x^3-1}\,\mathrm{d}x$.

7 Use the substitution $x=\mathrm{e}^u$ to find $\int \frac{\sec^2(\ln(x^2))}{2x}\,\mathrm{d}x$.

8 Show that $\int_1^3 \frac{(2x-3)\sqrt{x^2-3x+3}}{x^2-3x+3}\,\mathrm{d}x = a\sqrt{b}+c$, where a, b and c are integers to be found.

9 Using the substitution $u=\mathrm{e}^x$, find the exact value of $\int_0^{\frac{1}{2}\ln 3} \frac{1}{\mathrm{e}^x+\mathrm{e}^{-x}}\,\mathrm{d}x$.

Section 3: Integration by parts

You have already seen, in Section 2, cases in which you can integrate products of functions by the reverse chain rule or a substitution. But you still can't do integrals such as $\int x\sin x\,\mathrm{d}x$ or $\int x^2\mathrm{e}^x\,\mathrm{d}x$.

To integrate these you need to return to the product rule for differentiation:

$$\frac{\mathrm{d}}{\mathrm{d}x}(uv)=u\frac{\mathrm{d}v}{\mathrm{d}x}+v\frac{\mathrm{d}u}{\mathrm{d}x}$$

Integrating with respect to x we get:

$$uv=\int u\frac{\mathrm{d}v}{\mathrm{d}x}\,\mathrm{d}x+\int v\frac{\mathrm{d}u}{\mathrm{d}x}\,\mathrm{d}x$$

$$\Rightarrow \int u\frac{\mathrm{d}v}{\mathrm{d}x}\,\mathrm{d}x=uv-\int v\frac{\mathrm{d}u}{\mathrm{d}x}\,\mathrm{d}x$$

Key point 11.5

The **integration by parts** formula is:

$$\int u\frac{\mathrm{d}v}{\mathrm{d}x}\,\mathrm{d}x=uv-\int v\frac{\mathrm{d}u}{\mathrm{d}x}\,\mathrm{d}x$$

Tip

This derivation shows that you can think of integration by parts as the 'reverse product rule'. In practice, though, there is no need to write out the product rule every time; you can just use the integration by parts formula.

WORKED EXAMPLE 11.10

Find $\int x \sin x \, dx$.

$u = x$ and $\frac{dv}{dx} = \sin x$

$\Rightarrow \frac{du}{dx} = 1$ and $v = -\cos x$

This is a product to which you can't apply the reverse chain rule, so try integration by parts.

$\int u \frac{dv}{dx} \, dx = uv - \int v \frac{du}{dx} \, dx$

Apply the formula.

$$\int x \sin x \, dx = x(-\cos x) - \int (-\cos x) 1 \, dx$$

$$= -x \cos x + \int \cos x \, dx$$

$$= -x \cos x + \sin x + c$$

In Worked example 11.10, taking u to be x worked well because $\frac{du}{dx}$ is a constant. So after applying the formula, the resulting integral was just $\int \cos x \, dx$. You could do this only because $\frac{dv}{dx} = \sin x$ is easy to integrate, so you could find v. In some examples this is not possible.

WORKED EXAMPLE 11.11

Find $\int x \ln x \, dx$.

$u = \ln x, \quad \frac{dv}{dx} = x$

$\Rightarrow \frac{du}{dx} = \frac{1}{x}, \quad v = \frac{1}{2}x^2$

This is a product, so use integration by parts.

You can't take $u = x$ because you don't know how to integrate $\frac{dv}{dx} = \ln x$. So try choosing them the other way round.

$$\int x \ln x \, dx = \ln x \times \frac{1}{2}x^2 - \int \frac{1}{2}x^2 \frac{1}{x} \, dx$$

Apply the formula.

$$= \frac{1}{2}x^2 \ln x - \int \frac{1}{2}x \, dx$$

Always simplify before integrating.

$$= \frac{1}{2}x^2 \ln x - \frac{1}{4}x^2 + c$$

You can summarise the strategy for choosing which function is u and which is $\frac{dv}{dx}$ as shown in Key point 11.6.

Key point 11.6

When using integration by parts for $\int x^n \, f(x)\,dx$, choose $u = x^n$ in all cases except when $f(x) = \ln x$.

Somewhat surprisingly, this strategy can even be used to integrate $\ln x$ by itself.

WORKED EXAMPLE 11.12

Use integration by parts to find $\int \ln x \, dx$.

$$\int \ln x \, dx = \int 1 \times \ln x \, dx$$

The trick is to write $\ln x$ as a product of $\ln x$ and 1 so that you can use integration by parts.

$$u = \ln x, \quad \frac{dv}{dx} = 1$$

$$\Rightarrow \frac{du}{dx} = \frac{1}{x} \quad \text{and} \quad v = x$$

As suggested in Key point 11.6, let $u = \ln x$.

$$\int u \frac{dv}{dx} dx = uv - \int v \frac{du}{dx} dx$$

$$\int 1 \times \ln x \, dx = (\ln x)x - \int \frac{1}{x} x \, dx$$

$$= x \ln x - \int 1 \, dx$$

$$= x \ln x - x + c$$

Apply the formula.

EXERCISE 11D

1. Find the following using integration by parts.
   - a i $\int x \cos 2x \, dx$ ii $\int x \sin\left(\frac{x}{2}\right) dx$
   - b i $\int 4x \, e^{-2x} \, dx$ ii $\int x \, e^{4x} \, dx$
   - c i $\int 2x \ln 5x \, dx$ ii $\int x \ln x \, dx$
   - d i $\int \frac{x^3}{2} \ln x \, dx$ ii $\int 3x^5 \ln 2x \, dx$
2. Use integration by parts to evaluate $\int_0^{\frac{\pi}{2}} x \sin x \, dx$.
3. Find the exact value of $\int_1^e 3x^2 \ln(2x) \, dx$.

Repeated integration by parts

It may be necessary to use integration by parts more than once.

WORKED EXAMPLE 11.13

Find the exact value of $\int_0^{\ln 2} x^2 e^x \, dx$.

$u = x^2$ and $\frac{dv}{dx} = e^x$

$\Rightarrow \frac{du}{dx} = 2x$ and $v = e^x$

This is a product to which you can't apply the reverse chain rule, so try integration by parts.

Choose u to be the polynomial.

$\int u \frac{dv}{dx} dx = uv - \int v \frac{du}{dx} dx$

$\int_0^{\ln 2} x^2 e^x \, dx = \left[x^2 e^x\right]_0^{\ln 2} - \int_0^{\ln 2} 2x e^x \, dx$

Apply the formula.

Put in the limits on the uv part straight away.

$u = 2x$ and $\frac{dv}{dx} = e^x$

$\frac{du}{dx} = 2$ and $v = e^x$

You have to integrate a product again, so use integration by parts for the second time.

Choose u to be the polynomial again.

(Notice that if you were to now change and choose $u = e^x$ and $\frac{dv}{dx} = 2x$, you would end up back where you started!)

So, $\int_0^{\ln 2} 2x e^x dx = \left[2x e^x\right]_0^{\ln 2} - \int_0^{\ln 2} 2e^x \, dx$

$= \left[2x e^x\right]_0^{\ln 2} - \left[2e^x\right]_0^{\ln 2}$

Apply the formula again and use the limits.

Therefore,

$\int_0^{\ln 2} x^2 e^x dx = \left[x^2 e^x\right]_0^{\ln 2} - \left\{\left[2x e^x\right]_0^{\ln 2} - \left[2e^x\right]_0^{\ln 2}\right\}$

$= ((\ln 2)^2 e^{\ln 2} - 0) - (2\ln 2 e^{\ln 2} - 0)$

$+ (2e^{\ln 2} - 2)$

$= 2(\ln 2)^2 - 4\ln 2 + 2$

Put both integrals together, making sure to keep track of negative signs by using brackets appropriately.

Tip

When doing integration by parts twice, make sure you apply the negative sign in front of the integral to *all* of the second application of the parts formula.

EXERCISE 11E

1 Use integration by parts twice to find the following.

a $\int x^2 \cos 3x \, dx$

b $\int x^2 \sin x \, dx$

c $\int \frac{1}{4}x^2 e^{\frac{x}{4}} \, dx$

d $\int (\ln x)^2 \, dx$

2 Use integration by parts to find.

a $\int 2\ln(3x) \, dx$

b $\int \ln(2x+1) \, dx$

3 Evaluate the following exactly.

a $\int_0^{\frac{\pi}{2}} x \cos x \, dx$

b $\int_1^2 \frac{\ln x}{x^2} \, dx$

4 When using the integration by parts formula, you start with $\frac{dv}{dx}$ and find v. Why do you not include a constant of integration when you do this? Try a few examples, adding $+c$ to v and see what happens.

5 Find $\int 2x e^{-3x} \, dx$.

6 Evaluate $\int_1^e x^5 \ln x \, dx$.

7 a Show that $\int \tan x \, dx = \ln|\sec x| + c$.

b Hence, find $\int \frac{x}{\cos^2 x} \, dx$.

8 Use the substitution $\sqrt{x+1} = u$ to find the exact value of $\int_{-1}^{3} \frac{1}{2} e^{\sqrt{x+1}} \, dx$.

9 Let $I = \int e^x \cos x \, dx$.

a Use integration by parts twice to show that $I = \cos x \, e^x + (\sin x \, e^x - I) + c$.

b Hence, find $\int e^x \cos x \, dx$.

Section 4: Using trigonometric identities in integration

Trigonometric identities are useful for integrating the squares of trigonometric functions.

WORKED EXAMPLE 11.14

Find $\int \tan^2 x \, dx$.

$$\int \tan^2 x \, dx = \int (\sec^2 x - 1) \, dx$$

You can integrate $\sec^2 x$, so use $\tan^2 x + 1 = \sec^2 x$.

$$= \tan x - x + c$$

In Section 2 you integrated expressions such as $\sin^2 x \cos x$ using the substitution $u = \sin x$; the derivative $\frac{du}{dx}$ cancels with the $\cos x$. But if you try to integrate just $\int \sin^2 x \, dx$ the same substitution doesn't work. You could try rewriting it as $\int 1 - \cos^2 x \, dx$, but you don't know how to do this either.

The trick is to notice that $\sin^2 x$ appears in one of the versions of the double angle formulae for $\cos 2x$: $\cos 2x = 1 - 2\sin^2 x$, and you know how to integrate $\cos 2x$.

This leads to a method for integrating both $\sin^2 x$ and $\cos^2 x$.

Rewind

Double angle identities were covered in Chapter 8, Section 2.

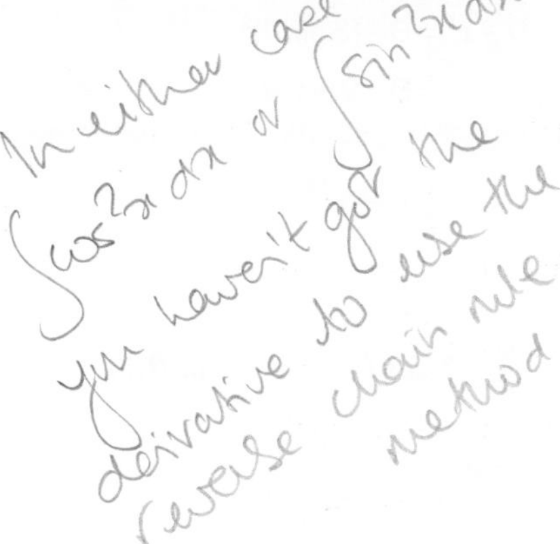

Key point 11.7

To integrate $\sin^2 x$ use $\cos 2x = 1 - 2\sin^2 x$.

To integrate $\cos^2 x$ use $\cos 2x = 2\cos^2 x - 1$.

WORKED EXAMPLE 11.15

Find $\int \sin^2 x \, dx$.

$\cos 2x = 1 - 2\sin^2 x$

$\sin^2 x = \frac{1}{2}(1 - \cos 2x)$

You can find an alternative expression for $\sin^2 x$ by using a double angle identity.

$\therefore \int \sin^2 x \, dx = \int \frac{1}{2}(1 - \cos 2x) \, dx$

$= \int \frac{1}{2} - \frac{1}{2}\cos 2x \, dx$

$= \frac{1}{2}x - \frac{1}{2}\frac{1}{2}\sin 2x + c$

Divide by the coefficient of x when integrating $\cos 2x$.

$= \frac{1}{2}x - \frac{1}{4}\sin 2x + c$

Sometimes trigonometric identities turn out to be useful in integrals that don't appear to involve trigonometry.

WORKED EXAMPLE 11.16

Use the substitution $x = 3\sin\theta$ to find $\int_0^3 \sqrt{9-x^2}\, dx$.

$9 - x^2 = 9 - (3\sin\theta)^2$
$= 9 - 9\sin^2\theta$

Make the substitution. Simplify each part separately first.

$= 9\cos^2\theta$

Use $1 - \sin^2\theta = \cos^2\theta$.

$\frac{dx}{d\theta} = 3\cos\theta \Rightarrow dx = 3\cos\theta\, d\theta$

Differentiate the substitution.

Now we have:

Simplify fully before attempting to integrate.

$\int \sqrt{9-x^2}\, dx = \int \sqrt{9\cos^2\theta} \times 3\cos\theta\, d\theta$
$= \int 3\cos\theta \times 3\cos\theta\, d\theta$
$= \int 9\cos^2\theta\, d\theta$

$= \int \frac{9}{2}(\cos 2\theta + 1)\, d\theta$

Use the method from Key point 11.7:
$\cos 2\theta = 2\cos^2\theta - 1 \Rightarrow \cos^2\theta = \frac{\cos 2\theta + 1}{2}$.

$= \frac{9}{4}\sin 2\theta + \frac{9}{2}\theta + c$

Remember to divide by 2 when integrating $\cos 2\theta$.

Limits: $x = 0 \Rightarrow \sin\theta = 0 \Rightarrow \theta = 0$
$x = 3 \Rightarrow \sin\theta = 1 \Rightarrow \theta = \frac{\pi}{2}$

Find the limits for θ.

$\int_0^3 \sqrt{9-x^2}\, dx = \left[\frac{9}{4}\sin 2\theta + \frac{9}{2}\theta\right]_0^{\pi/2}$
$= \left(\frac{9}{4}\sin\pi + \frac{9\pi}{4}\right) - \left(\frac{9}{4}\sin 0 + 0\right)$
$= \frac{9\pi}{4}$

Apply the limits to the indefinite integral.

In integrals of this type, you may need to use trigonometric identities again to write the answer in terms of x at the end.

Tip

The substitution in Worked example 11.16 is useful in other integrals involving expressions like $\sqrt{a^2 - x^2}$.

WORKED EXAMPLE 11.17

a Show that $\frac{\sec\theta}{\tan^2\theta} = \operatorname{cosec}\theta \cot\theta$.

b Use the substitution $x = \sec\theta$ to find $\int (x^2 - 1)^{-\frac{3}{2}}\,dx$.

a $\frac{\sec\theta}{\tan^2\theta} = \frac{1}{\cos\theta}\frac{1}{\left(\frac{\sin\theta}{\cos\theta}\right)^2}$

There is no obvious identity linking the functions on the left to the ones on the right. So write everything in terms of $\sin\theta$ and $\cos\theta$.

$= \frac{1}{\cos\theta}\frac{\cos^2\theta}{\sin^2\theta}$

$= \frac{1}{\sin\theta}\frac{\cos\theta}{\sin\theta}$

$= \operatorname{cosec}\theta \cot\theta$

b $x = \sec\theta$

$\frac{dx}{d\theta} = \sec\theta\tan\theta$

$dx = \sec\theta\tan\theta\,d\theta$

Differentiate the substitution and express dx in terms of θ.

$\int (x^2 - 1)^{-\frac{3}{2}}\,dx = \int (\sec^2\theta - 1)^{-\frac{3}{2}}\sec\theta\tan\theta\,d\theta$

Replace those parts that you already have expressions for.

$= \int (\tan^2\theta)^{-\frac{3}{2}}\sec\theta\tan\theta\,d\theta$

$= \int (\tan\theta)^{-2}\sec\theta\,d\theta$

There are no instances of x remaining, so you can integrate.

Notice that $\sec^2\theta - 1 = \tan^2\theta$.

$= \int \operatorname{cosec}\theta\cot\theta\,d\theta$

$= -\operatorname{cosec}\theta + c$

Using the result from part **a**, you now have a standard derivative (Section 1).

$x = \sec\theta \Rightarrow \cos\theta = \frac{1}{x}$

To express the answer in terms of x, you need to link $\sin\theta$ to $\cos\theta$.

$\sin\theta = \sqrt{1 - \cos^2\theta}$

$= \sqrt{1 - \frac{1}{x^2}} = \sqrt{\frac{x^2 - 1}{x^2}}$

Notice that, in choosing the substitution $x = \sec\theta$, we can choose θ to be between 0 and π. Then $\sin\theta$ is non-negative, so we can take the positive square root here.

$\operatorname{cosec}\theta = \frac{1}{\sin\theta} = \sqrt{\frac{x^2}{x^2 - 1}}$

$\therefore \int (x^2 - 1)^{-\frac{3}{2}}\,dx = -\sqrt{\frac{x^2}{x^2 - 1}} + c$

WORK IT OUT 11.2

Three students integrate $\cos x \sin x$ in three different ways.

How many of the solutions are correct? Identify any mistakes.

Solution 1	Solution 2	Solution 3
Amara uses reverse chain rule with $u = \sin x$.	Tim uses reverse chain rule with $u = \cos x$.	Carlos uses the double angle formula $\sin 2x = 2\sin x \cos x$.
$\frac{du}{dx} = \cos x$, so $\int \cos x \sin x \, dx = \int u \, du$ $= \frac{1}{2}\sin^2 x + c$	$\frac{du}{dx} = -\sin x$, so $\int \cos x \sin x \, dx = \int -u \, du$ $= -\frac{1}{2}\cos^2 x + c$	$\int \cos x \sin x \, dx = \int \frac{1}{2}\sin 2x \, dx$ $= -\frac{1}{4}\cos 2x + c$

EXERCISE 11F

1 Simplify to get standard integrals, and then integrate the following.

a $\int \frac{\tan 3x}{\cos 3x} \, dx$ **b** $\int \frac{1}{\sin^2 x} \, dx$ **c** $\int \sin 5x \cos x - \cos 5x \sin x \, dx$

d $\int \left(\frac{3 - \cos 2x}{\sin^2 2x}\right) dx$ **e** $\int \frac{\cos 2x}{\cos x + \sin x} \, dx$

2 Use trigonometric identities before using a substitution (or reversing the chain rule) to integrate the following.

a $\int \cos^3 x \sin^2 x \, dx$ **b** $\int \frac{\cos^3 x}{\sin^2 x} \, dx$ **c** $\int \sin x \cos x \, e^{\cos 2x} \, dx$

d $\int \tan^4 3x + \tan^6 3x \, dx$ **e** $\int \frac{\sin 2x \cos 2x}{\sqrt{1 + \cos 4x}} \, dx$

3 Find the following.

a i $\int 2\cos^2 x \, dx$ **ii** $\int \cos^2 3x \, dx$

b i $\int 2\tan^2\left(\frac{x}{2}\right) dx$ **ii** $\int \tan^2 3x \, dx$

4 Find the exact value of the following.

a i $\int_0^{\pi} \sin^2 2x \, dx$ **ii** $\int_{\frac{\pi}{4}}^{\pi} (1 + \cos 2x)^2 \, dx$

b i $\int_0^{\frac{\pi}{4}} (\tan x - 1)^2 \, dx$ **ii** $\int_0^{2\pi} \tan^2\left(\frac{x}{6}\right) dx$

5 Use the given substitutions to find the following.

a i $\int_0^{\frac{\pi}{6}} \frac{1 + \sin\theta}{\cos\theta} \, d\theta, u = \sin\theta$ **ii** $\int_0^{\frac{\pi}{2}} \frac{\sin 2\theta}{1 + \cos\theta} \, d\theta, u = 1 + \cos\theta$

b **i** $\int_0^{1/3} \sqrt{4-9x^2}\,dx,\ x=\frac{2}{3}\sin\theta$ **ii** $\int_2^4 \sqrt{4x^2-1}\,dx,\ x=2\sec\theta$

c **i** $\int \sqrt{1-x^2}\,dx,\ x=\cos\theta$ **ii** $\int \sqrt{36-x^2}\,dx,\ x=6\sin\theta$

6 Find $\int \sin^2\left(\frac{x}{3}\right)dx$.

7 **a** Show that $\tan^3 x=\tan x\sec^2 x-\tan x$.

b Hence, find $\int \tan^3 x\,dx$.

8 Given that $\int_0^{\pi/12} \tan^2(kx)\,dx=\frac{4-\pi}{12}$, where k is positive, find the least value of k that satisfies the equation.

9 **a** Use the formula for $\cos(A+B)$ to show that $\cos 2x=2\cos^2 x-1$.

b Hence, find $\int \cos 2x\sin x\,dx$.

10 Use the substitution $x=\sin^2 u$ to find $\int \frac{1}{\sqrt{x(1-x)}}\,dx$.

11 Use the substitution $x=\tan\theta$ to find $\int \frac{1}{1+x^2}\,dx$.

12 **a** Show that $\sin^3\theta=\sin\theta-\sin\theta\cos^2\theta$.

b Hence, find the exact value of $\int_0^{3\pi} \sin^3\left(\frac{x}{3}\right)dx$.

13 The diagram shows a part of the circle with its centre at the origin and radius 5.

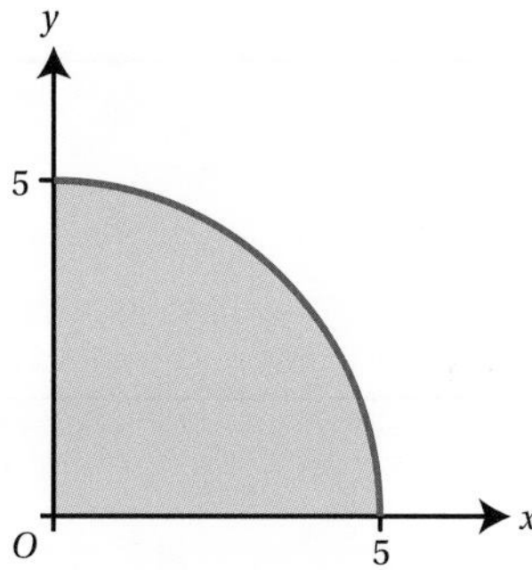

a Write the equation of the curve in the form $y=f(x)$.

b Use integration to prove that the size of the shaded area is $\frac{25\pi}{4}$.

Section 5: Integrating rational functions

You can already use Key point 11.3 to do integrals such as $\int \frac{x}{x^2-1}\,dx$, where the derivative of the denominator is a multiple of the numerator. This can be done with a substitution or directly with the reverse chain rule.

If you change the numerator or the denominator just a little, this may not work any more. For example, using $u=x^2-1$ in $\int \frac{x-2}{x^2-1}\,dx$ gives $\int \frac{1}{u}\times\frac{x-2}{2x}\,du$, so the x terms do not cancel.

An alternative method is to split the fraction into two. You can either do this by splitting the numerator or by using partial fractions. You will look at partial fractions first.

Rewind

See Chapter 5 for a reminder of partial fractions.

WORKED EXAMPLE 11.18

Use partial fractions to find $\int \frac{2}{x^2-1}\,dx$ in the form $\ln(f(x))+c$.

$$\frac{2}{x^2-1}=\frac{A}{x-1}+\frac{B}{x+1}$$

$$\Rightarrow 2=A(x+1)+B(x-1)$$

Solve for A and B using substitution or by comparing coefficients (as shown here).

$$\Rightarrow \begin{cases} A+B=0 \\ A-B=2 \end{cases}$$

$$\Rightarrow A=1,\ B=-1$$

$$\int \frac{2}{x^2-1}\,dx=\int \frac{1}{x-1}-\frac{1}{x+1}\,dx$$

$$=\ln|x-1|-\ln|x+1|+c$$

$$=\ln\left|\frac{x-1}{x+1}\right|+c$$

Use $\ln a-\ln b=\ln\left(\frac{a}{b}\right)$.

Remember that you can also use partial fractions when the denominator has a non-linear factor.

WORKED EXAMPLE 11.19

Find the exact value of $\int_{-1}^{0} \frac{5x+4}{(x-1)(x+2)^2}\,dx$.

$$\frac{5x+4}{(x-1)(x+2)^2}=\frac{A}{x-1}+\frac{B}{x+2}+\frac{C}{(x+2)^2}$$

There are three fractions.

$$\Rightarrow 5x+4=A(x+2)^2+B(x-1)(x+2)+C(x-1)$$

$$x=1: 9=A(9)\Rightarrow A=1$$

$$x=-2: -6=C(-3)\Rightarrow C=2$$

$$x^2 \text{ term}: Ax^2+Bx^2=0\Rightarrow B=-A=-1$$

$$\int_{-1}^{0} \frac{1}{x-1}-\frac{1}{x+2}+\frac{2}{(x+2)^2}\,dx$$

$$=\left[\ln|x-1|-\ln|x+2|-\frac{2}{x+2}\right]_{-1}^{0}$$

Remember the modulus signs when integrating $\frac{1}{x}$.

To integrate $\frac{2}{(x+2)^2}$, write it as $2(x+2)^{-2}$.

$$=[\ln 1-\ln 2-1]-[\ln 2-\ln 1-2]$$

$$=1-2\ln 2$$

Before starting the partial fraction process, it is worth checking whether the fraction can be simplified.

WORKED EXAMPLE 11.20

Find $\int \frac{x+4}{12-5x-2x^2}\,dx$.

$$\int \frac{x+4}{12-5x-2x^2}\,dx = \int \frac{x+4}{(3-2x)(x+4)}\,dx$$

It is generally a good idea to check whether polynomials factorise.

$$= \int \frac{1}{3-2x}\,dx$$

$$= -\frac{1}{2}\ln|3-2x| + c$$

You now have a standard integral. Remember to divide by the coefficient of x.

Improper fractions can be integrated after splitting them into a polynomial plus a proper fraction, either by polynomial division or by splitting a numerator so that one part cancels with the denominator.

 **Rewind**

See division of improper rational functions in Chapter 5.

WORKED EXAMPLE 11.21

Find:

a $\int \frac{x^2+5}{x+2}\,dx$

b $\int \frac{x+2}{x-1}\,dx$

a $\frac{x^2+5}{x+2} = x-2+\frac{9}{x+2}$

Polynomial division gives quotient $x-2$ and remainder 9.

$$\int \frac{x^2+5}{x+2}\,dx = \int x-2+\frac{9}{x+2}\,dx$$

$$= \frac{1}{2}x^2 - 2x + 9\ln|x+2| + c$$

b $\frac{x+2}{x-1} = \frac{(x-1)+3}{x-1}$

$= 1+\frac{3}{x-1}$

In this case, you can perform polynomial division informally by splitting the numerator in a convenient way.

$$\int \frac{x+2}{x-1}\,dx = \int 1+\frac{3}{x-1}\,dx$$

$$= x + 3\ln|x-1| + c$$

EXERCISE 11G

1 State whether each of the following integrals can be done by using a substitution (or reversing the chain rule). For those that can, carry out the integration.

a $\int \frac{3x}{x^2-4}\,dx$ b $\int \frac{4x-6}{x^2-3x+1}\,dx$

c $\int \frac{4}{x^2-4}\,dx$ d $\int \frac{5x}{x^2+1}\,dx$

e $\int \frac{4x^2-12x-18}{x^3-9x}\,dx$ f $\int \frac{x^2-3}{x^3-9x}\,dx$

g $\int \frac{12x^2}{x^3+2}\,dx$

2 By first simplifying, find the following integrals.

a $\int \frac{(4x^2-9)^2}{(2x+3)^2}\,dx$ b $\int \frac{x+3}{6-13x-5x^2}\,dx$

c $\int \frac{x^2}{3x^3-3x^2}\,dx$ d $\int \frac{x^2-3x+2}{x^2-2x}\,dx$

3 Find the following integrals by splitting them into partial fractions.

a i $\int \frac{5x-29}{(x-3)(x-10)}\,dx$ ii $\int \frac{x-7}{(x+1)(x-3)}\,dx$

b i $\int \frac{1}{x^2-1}\,dx$ ii $\int \frac{x}{x^2-1}\,dx$

c i $\int \frac{1-2x}{(x-2)(1-x)}\,dx$ ii $\int \frac{3x-1}{(1-x)(1+x)}\,dx$

d i $\int \frac{3(2x^2+2x+3)}{x^3+3x^2}\,dx$ ii $\int \frac{4x^2-5x+2}{x^3-2x^2}\,dx$

e i $\int \frac{6x+2}{(x-1)^2(x+3)}\,dx$ ii $\int \frac{-(2x+5)}{(x+1)^2(x-2)}\,dx$

4 Find the following integrals by first performing polynomial division (or splitting the numerator).

a i $\int \frac{x+1}{x+2}\,dx$ ii $\int \frac{2x+3}{x-1}\,dx$

b i $\int \frac{x^2+2}{x-3}\,dx$ ii $\int \frac{x^2+2x-1}{x+5}\,dx$

5 Find the remaining integrals from question 1.

6 a Write $\frac{5}{x^2+x-6}$ as a sum of partial fractions.

b Hence, find $\int \frac{5}{x^2+x-6}\,dx$, giving your answer in the form $\ln|f(x)|+c$.

7 Find the exact value of $\int_0^1 \frac{4}{x^2-4}\,dx$.

Elevate

See Support sheet 11 for further examples of integrating rational functions and for more practice questions.

8 Find the exact value of $\int_2^5 \frac{x-1}{x+2}\,dx$.

9 **a** Split $\frac{5-x}{2+x-x^2}$ into partial fractions.

b Given that $\int_0^1 \frac{5-x}{2+x-x^2}\,dx = \ln k$, find the value of k.

10 Find the exact value of $\int_3^4 \frac{8-3x}{x^3-4x^2+4x}\,dx$. Give your answer in the form $\ln p + q$, where p and q are rational numbers.

Checklist of learning and understanding

- When using integration by substitution remember to:
  - Differentiate the substitution and express dx in terms of du.
  - Simplify the resulting expression.
  - Find the limits for u.
- Two special cases of integration by substitution should be remembered:
  - $\int f(ax+b)\,dx = \frac{1}{a}F(ax+b)+c$, where $F(x)$ is the integral of $f(x)$.
  - $\int \frac{f'(x)}{f(x)}\,dx = \ln|f(x)|+c$
- Integration by parts can be used for some products:

$$\int u\frac{dv}{dx}dx = uv - \int v\frac{du}{dx}dx$$

  - In integrals of the form $\int x^n f(x)dx$, take $u = x^n$ unless $f(x) = \ln x$.
  - You may need to do integration by parts more than once.
- Some integrals can be simplified by using a trigonometric identity. The particularly useful ones to remember are:
  - For $\int \sin^2 x\,dx$ and $\int \cos^2 x\,dx$, use a rearrangement of the double angle formula: $\cos 2x = 2\cos^2 x - 1 = 1 - 2\sin^2 x$
  - For $\int \sqrt{a^2 - x^2}\,dx$, use the substitution $x = a\sin\theta$.
- Some rational fractions can be integrated by splitting them into partial fractions.
  - Look out for improper fractions where you may be able to split the numerator.

Mixed practice 11

1 Find the exact value of $\int_0^{\pi} \cos^2(3x)\,dx$.

2 Use integration by parts to find $\int x\cos 2x\,dx$.

3 Given that $\int_0^m \frac{1}{3x+1}\,dx = 1$ calculate, to three significant figures, the value of m.

4 Find the exact value of $\int_0^{\pi/12} \frac{1}{\cos^2 4x}\,dx$.

5 Find the following integrals:

a $\int \frac{1}{1-3x}\,dx$

b $\int \frac{1}{(2x+3)^2}\,dx$

6 Use the substitution $u = 2+\ln t$ to find the exact value of $\int_1^e \frac{1}{t(2+\ln t)^2}\,dt$.

7 Find $\int \ln x\,dx$.

8 a Simplify $\frac{e^{-4x}+3e^{-2x}}{e^{-4x}-9}$.

b Hence find $\int \frac{e^{-4x}+3e^{-2x}}{e^{-4x}-9}\,dx$

9 Use the substitution $x = 2\sin u$ to find $\int \frac{1}{\sqrt{4-x^2}}\,dx$.

10 a Write $\frac{x+5}{(x-1)(x+2)}$ in partial fractions.

b Hence find, in the form $\ln k$, the exact value of $\int_5^7 \frac{x+5}{(x-1)(x+2)}\,dx$.

11 Find $\int \frac{1}{x\ln x}\,dx$.

12 Using the substitution $u = \frac{1}{2}x-1$, or otherwise, find $\int \frac{x}{\sqrt{\frac{1}{2}x-1}}\,dx$.

13 i Use integration by parts to find $\int x\sec^2 x\,dx$.

ii Hence find $\int x\tan^2 x\,dx$.

14 Find $\int \frac{x+3}{(x-2)^2}\,dx$.

15 Given that $\int_{-a}^{a} \frac{2}{1-x^2}\,dx = 2$, find the exact value of a.

16 **a** Use a suitable substitution to find $\int_{-3}^{3} \sqrt{9-x^2}\, dx$.

b The ellipse shown in the diagram has equation $\frac{x^2}{9}+\frac{y^2}{4}=1$.

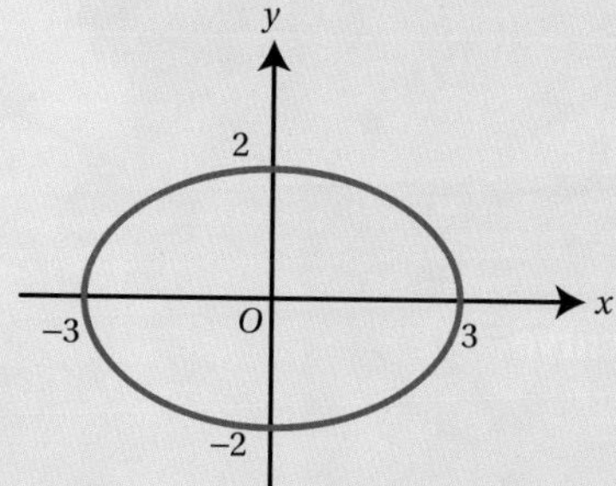

Use integration to prove that the area enclosed by the ellipse is 6π.

17 Let $I=\int \frac{\sin x}{\sin x+\cos x}\, dx$ and $J=\int \frac{\cos x}{\sin x+\cos x}\, dx$.

a Find $I+J$.

b Using the substitution $u=\sin x+\cos x$, find $J-I$.

c Hence, find $\int \frac{\sin x}{\sin x+\cos x}\, dx$.

18 A particle P moves in a straight line with acceleration given by

$$a=\frac{2t+3}{t+1}\ \text{m s}^{-2}$$

When $t=0$, P is at rest.

Find the distance P travels in the first 3 seconds of its motion.

Elevate

See Extension sheet 11 for a selection of more challenging problems.

12 Further applications of calculus

In this chapter you will learn:

- how to use the second derivative to determine the shape of a curve
- about a new way of describing curves, using a parameter
- how to calculate rates of change of related quantities
- how to find the area between two curves, or between a curve and the y-axis.

Before you start…

Chapter 10	You should be able to find the first and second derivatives of various functions, including by using chain, product and quotient rules.	1 Differentiate: a $y=e^{2x}\sin 3x$ b $y=\dfrac{\ln(x^2+1)}{x^2+1}$
Chapter 8	You should be able to use trigonometric identities to simplify expressions and solve equations.	2 Solve the equation $\cos 2x = 3\sin x$ for $0 \leqslant x \leqslant 2\pi$.
Student Book 1, Chapter 10	You should be able to use integration to find the area between a curve and the x-axis.	3 Find the area between the x-axis and the graph of $y = \cos 2x$, between $x = 0$ and $x = \dfrac{\pi}{6}$.
Chapter 11	You should be able to integrate various functions, use substitution and integration by parts.	4 Integrate the following: a $\int \sin^2 x\,dx$ b $\int \dfrac{x}{x^2-2}\,dx$ c $\int x\cos 3x\,dx$

More uses of differentiation and integration

In the previous three chapters you learnt how to differentiate and integrate many different functions. You can now use these techniques to solve problems.

Differentiation can be applied to analyse further properties of curves and to look at rate of change calculations that involve more than one variable. Integration is used to calculate more complex areas between curves.

You will also learn about a new way of describing the equation of a curve, using a parameter, which has applications in mechanics and engineering; for example, to circular motion and projectile motion.

Elevate

See Extension sheet 12 for some uses of differentiation in economics.

Section 1: Properties of curves

You already know that the first derivative tells you whether a function is increasing or decreasing. But an increasing function can have three different shapes:

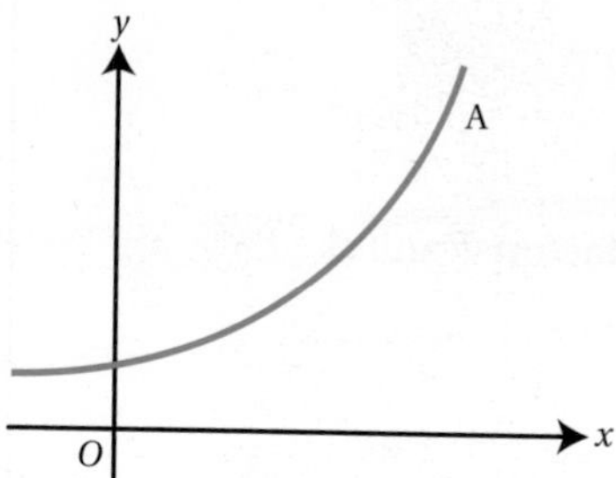

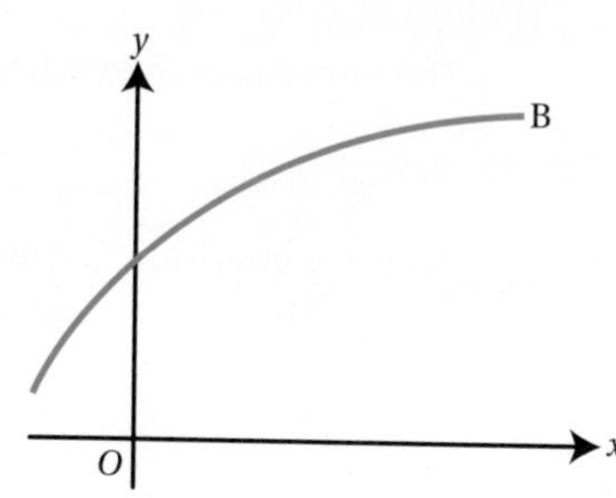

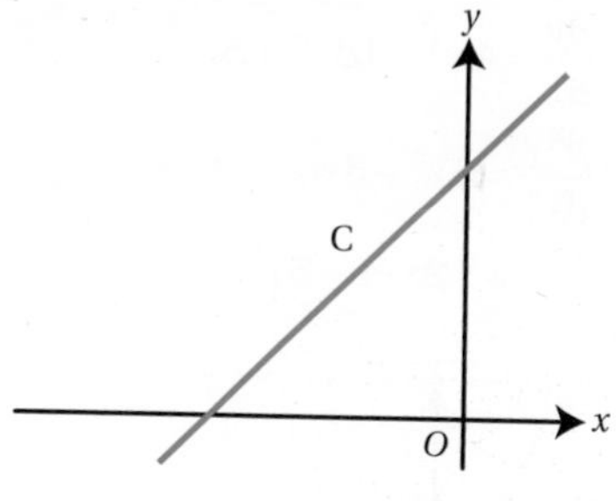

Similarly, a decreasing function can decrease in three ways:

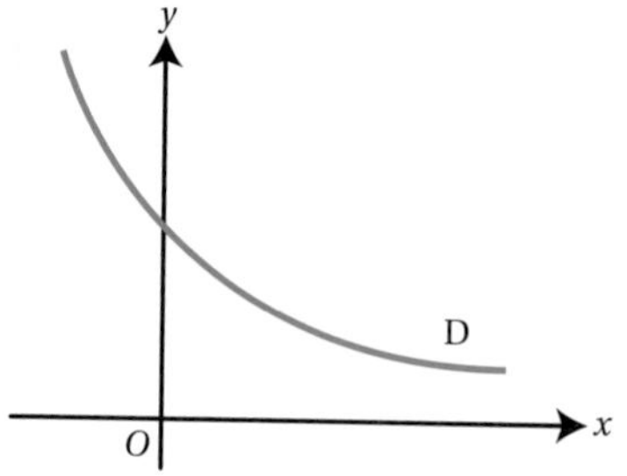

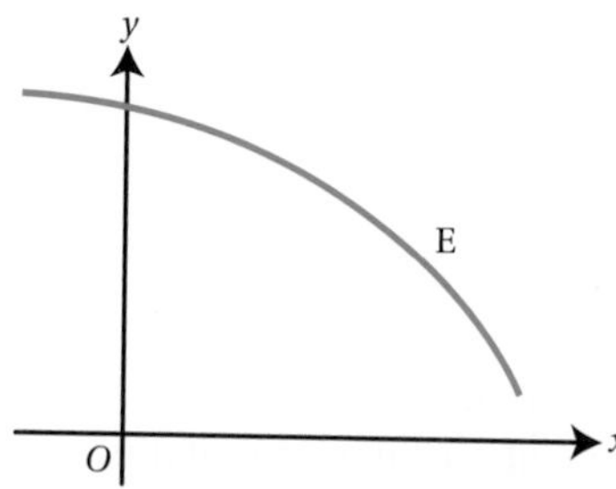

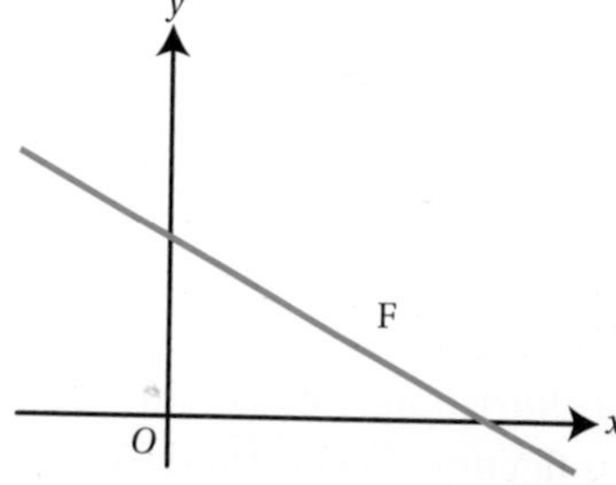

The curves A and D curve upwards; they are called convex curves. The curves B and E, which curve downwards, are called concave curves.

The two convex curves have something in common: their gradients are increasing (curve D has negative gradient, which becomes less negative as we move to the right). So the rate of change of gradient is positive. But this rate of change is measured by the **second derivative**, so $\frac{d^2y}{dx^2} > 0$ for curves A and D. For curves B and E, the second derivative is negative.

Curves C and F have constant gradients, so their second derivatives equal zero.

Key point 12.1

A curve that curves upwards is called **convex** and has $\frac{d^2y}{dx^2} > 0$.

A curve that curves downwards is called **concave** and has $\frac{d^2y}{dx^2} < 0$.

WORKED EXAMPLE 12.1

Find the values of x corresponding to the convex sections of the curve $y = x^4 - 6x^3 + 3x - 2$.

$\frac{dy}{dx} = 4x^3 - 18x^2 + 3$

$\frac{d^2y}{dx^2} = 12x^2 - 36x > 0$ — The curve is convex when $\frac{d^2y}{dx^2} > 0$.

$\Leftrightarrow 12x(x-3) > 0$ — This is a quadratic inequality, so factorise and sketch the graph.

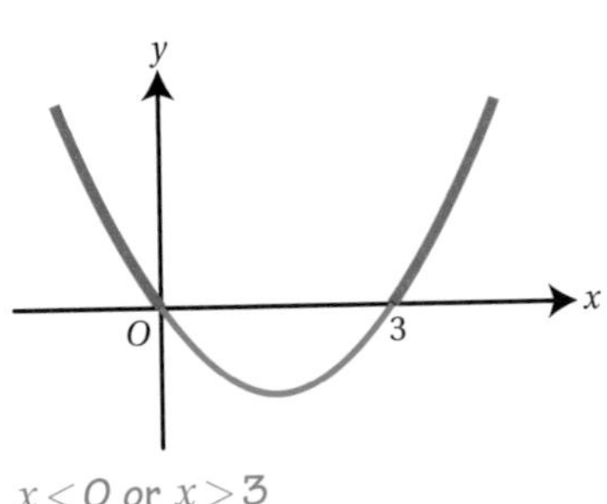

$x < 0$ or $x > 3$

As you can see on the diagrams above, a point of inflection can be horizontal (so it is a stationary point, ie $f'(x) = 0$ here as well) or non-horizontal (ie $f'(x) \neq 0$ here). At a horizontal (stationary) point of inflection, $f'(x) = 0$ and $f''(x) = 0$ but you will see later on that the converse is not necessarily true; if $f'(x) = 0$ and $f''(x) = 0$ at a point then that point is not necessarily a horizontal **point of inflection**.

Tip

Remember that $f''(x)$ is another notation for $\frac{d^2y}{dx^2}$, where $y = f(x)$.

Key point 12.2

At a point of inflection, $f''(x) = 0$ and the curve changes from convex to concave or from concave to convex.

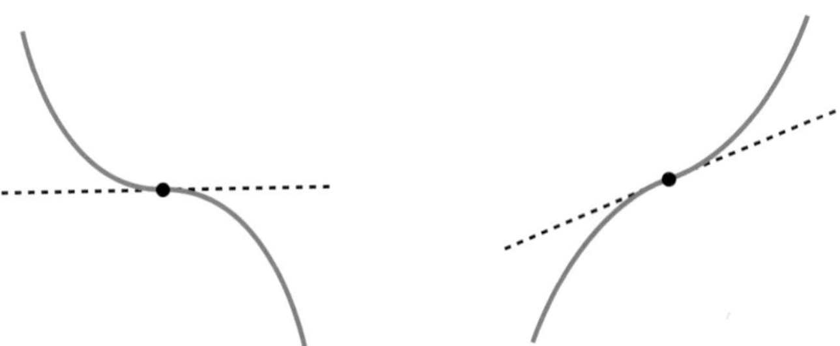

As you can see on the diagrams above, a point of inflection can be horizontal (so it is a stationary point) or non-horizontal. Notice that if you try to draw a tangent at a point of inflection, it will cross the curve at that point.

WORKED EXAMPLE 12.2

The curve $y = 3\cos x - x$ has two points of inflection with $x \in [0, 2\pi]$. Find their coordinates.

$f'(x) = -3\sin x - 1$

$f''(x) = -3\cos x = 0$

$x = \frac{\pi}{2}, \frac{3\pi}{2}$

The points of inflection are

$\left(\frac{\pi}{2}, -\frac{\pi}{2}\right)$ and $\left(\frac{3\pi}{2}, -\frac{3\pi}{2}\right)$.

The points of inflection satisfy $f''(x) = 0$.

Remember to find the y-coordinates as well.

Tip

In Worked examples 12.2 and 12.3 you are told that the curve has two points of inflection, so you just need to find the two points with $f''(x) = 0$. You will see later that not every point with $f''(x) = 0$ is a point of inflection, so you may need to do some additional checks.

WORKED EXAMPLE 12.3

The curve $y = x^3(6 - x)$ has two points of inflection. Find their coordinates and determine whether they are stationary or non-stationary. Hence, sketch the curve.

$y = 6x^3 - x^4$

$f'(x) = 18x^2 - 4x^3$

$f''(x) = 36x - 12x^2$

$= 12x(3 - x)$

$= 0$ when $x = 0$ or 3

Points of inflection have $f''(x) = 0$. However not all points with $f''(x) = 0$ are points of inflection.

$f(0) = 0$ and $f'(0) = 0$.
So $(0, 0)$ is a stationary point of inflection.

Stationary points have $f'(x) = 0$.

$f(3) = 81$ and $f'(3) = 54$.
So $(3, 81)$ is a non-stationary point of inflection.

To sketch the curve:

x-intercepts: $x^3(6 - x) = 0 \Rightarrow x = 0$ or 6

To sketch the curve, you also need the x-intercepts and other stationary points.

Stationary points:

$18x^2 - 4x^3 = 2x^2(9 - 2x) = 0 \Rightarrow x = 0$ or $\frac{9}{2}$

$f''\left(\frac{9}{2}\right) = -81 < 0$, so this is a maximum point.

You already know that $(0, 0)$ is a point of inflection. Use the second derivative to find out about the other stationary point.

Continues on next page ...

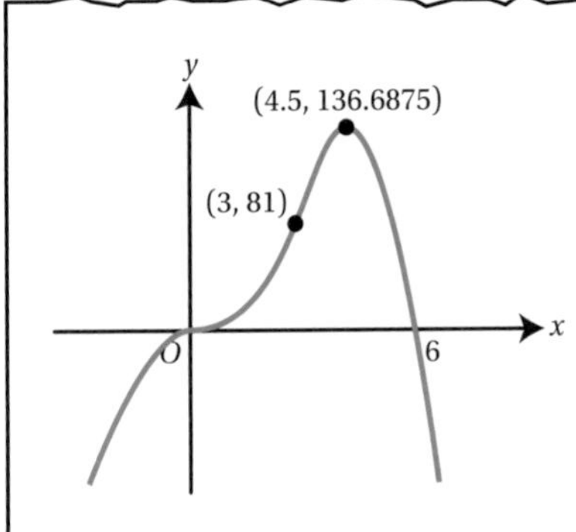

The curve has a point of inflection at the origin and a maximum point. The second point of inflection is between those two, where the curve changes from convex to concave.

A stationary point with $f''(x) = 0$ is not necessarily a point of inflection. For example, consider the graph of $f(x) = x^4$, which has $f'(x) = 4x^3$ and $f''(x) = 12x^2$. Although, at $x = 0$, both $f'(x)$ and $f''(x)$ are 0, the graph has a minimum point there.

Key point 12.3

A point where both $f'(x) = 0$ and $f''(x) = 0$ can be any of the three types of stationary point.

To determine which one it is, you need to look at the gradient on either side of the point.

Explore

Are there any other ways to identify points of inflection? For example, it is possible to use the third derivative, $\frac{d^3y}{dx^3}$.

WORKED EXAMPLE 12.4

Find the x-coordinates of the stationary points on the graph of $y = x^5 - 5x^4$ and determine their nature.

$f'(x) = 5x^4 - 20x^3 = 0$

Stationary points have $\frac{dy}{dx} = 0$.

$5x^3(x - 4) = 0$
$x = 0$ or 4

This equation can be solved by factorising.

$f''(x) = 20x^3 - 60x^2$

The second derivative tells us about the nature of the stationary points.

$f''(4) = 320 > 0$, so this is a minimum point.

If the second derivative is positive, the stationary point is a minimum.

$f''(0) = 0$
Check the gradient on two sides of the point:

$f'(-1) = 25 > 0$
$f'(1) = -15 < 0$

The second derivative equals zero, so you can't tell the nature of the stationary point. You need to check the gradient on either side.

Continues on next page ...

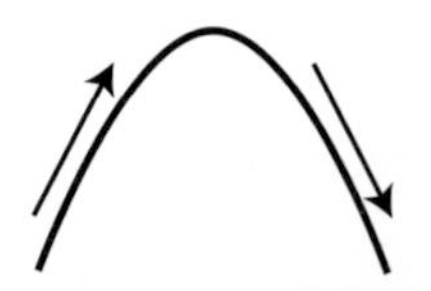

The gradient changes from positive to negative, so the curve goes up then down.

So $x = 0$ is a maximum point.

This table summarises the possible shapes of a curve, depending on the signs of the first and second derivatives:

	$f'(x) < 0$	$f'(x) = 0$	$f'(x) > 0$
$f''(x) < 0$	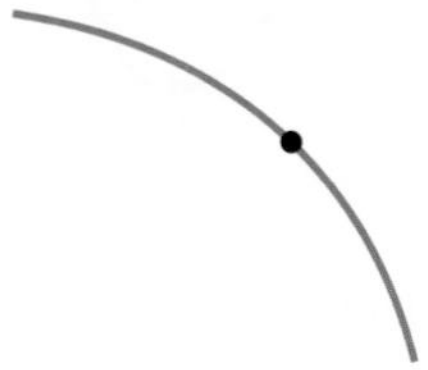		
$f''(x) = 0$			
$f''(x) > 0$			

WORK IT OUT 12.1

Show that the function $f(x) = x^2 \sin x$ has a stationary point at the origin, and determine its nature.

How many of the solutions are correct? Identify any mistakes.

Solution 1	Solution 2	Solution 3
$f'(x) = 2x\sin x + x^2 \cos x$ $f'(0) = 0$, so there is a stationary point at $x = 0$. $f''(x) = 2\sin x + 2x\cos x + 2x\cos x - x^2 \sin x$ $= 2\sin x + 4x\cos x - x^2 \sin x$		
$f''(0) = 0$ So this is a point of inflection.	$f''(0) = 0$ Test the derivative on either side: $f'(-1) = 2.2 > 0$ $f'(1) = 2.2 > 0$ The curve goes from increasing to increasing, so this is a point of inflection.	$f''(0) = 0$ Test the second derivative on either side: $f''(-1) = -3.0 < 0$ $f''(1) = 3.0 > 0$ The curve changes from concave to convex, so this is a point of inflection.

EXERCISE 12A

1 Describe each section of the given curve using one or more of the words ‘increasing’, ‘decreasing’, ‘convex’, ‘concave’.

a **i** A to B **ii** C to E **iii** F to G

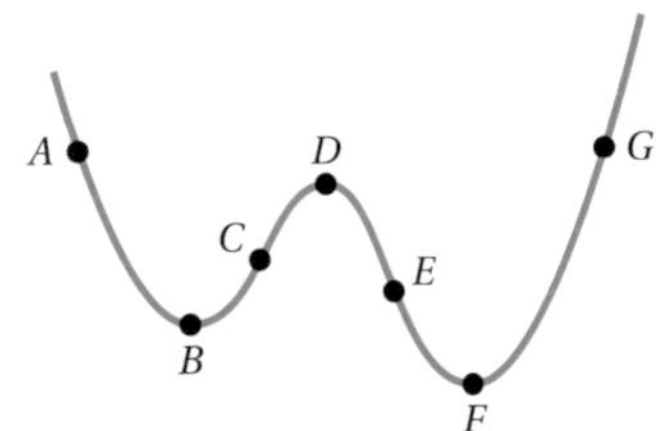

b **i** B to D **ii** C to D **iii** D to E

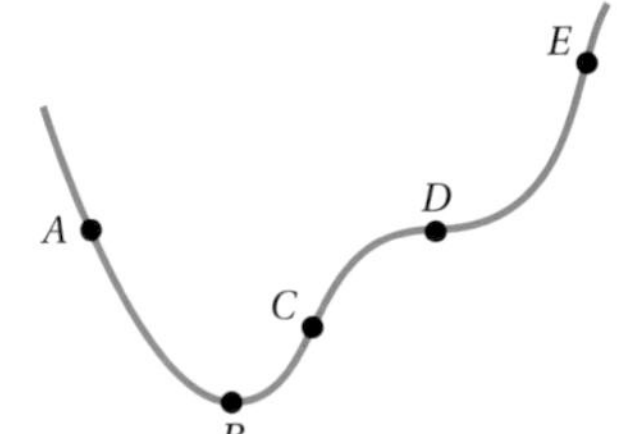

2 Mark the points A, B and C on the given curves.

A Local maximum point

B Stationary point of inflection

C Non-stationary point of inflection

a

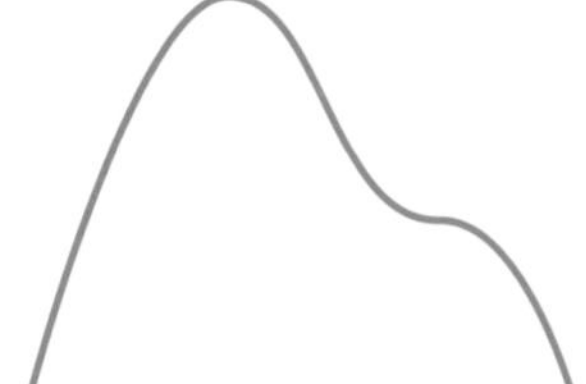

b

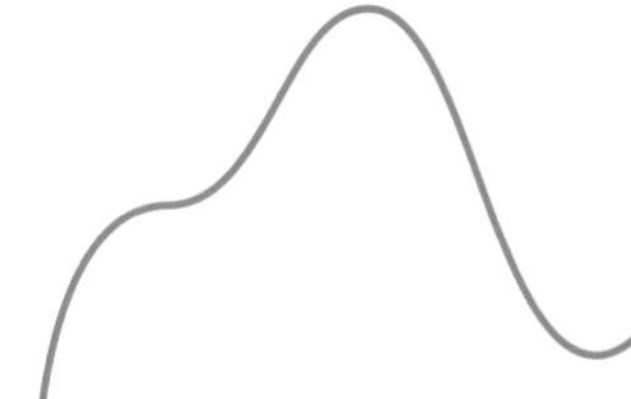

3 Mark one (or more if there is more than one) of each of the points A, B, C, D and E on the curve $y = \mathrm{f}(x)$ that satisfy the given conditions.

A $\mathrm{f}'(x) = 0$ and $\mathrm{f}''(x) > 0$

B $\mathrm{f}'(x) < 0$ and $\mathrm{f}''(x) = 0$

C $\mathrm{f}'(x) = 0$ and $\mathrm{f}''(x) = 0$

D $\mathrm{f}'(x) = 0$ and $\mathrm{f}''(x) < 0$

E $\mathrm{f}'(x) > 0$ and $\mathrm{f}''(x) = 0$

4 Find the coordinates of the point of inflection on the curve $y = \mathrm{e}^x - x^2$.

5 The curve $y = x^4 - 6x^2 + 7x + 2$ has two points of inflection. Find their coordinates.

6 Show that all points of inflection on the curve $y = \sin x$ lie on the x-axis.

7 Find the set of values of x corresponding to the convex sections of the curve $y = x^4 + 2x^3 - 36x^2 + 5$.

8 Find the coordinates of the points of inflection on the curve $y = 2\cos x + x$ for $0 \leqslant x \leqslant 2\pi$. Justify carefully that these are points of inflection.

9 Show that the graph of $y = \tan^3 x$ has only one stationary point for $x \in \left(-\frac{\pi}{2}, \frac{\pi}{2}\right)$, and that this is a point of inflection.

10 Show that the curve with equation $y = x^3 \sin x$ has a stationary point at the origin, and determine its nature.

11 The curve $y = x^3 - ax^2 - bx + c$ has a stationary point of inflection. Show that $a^2 = -3b$.

12 The curve $y = 4x + x^2 - ax^3$ is concave for $x < 3$. Find the value of a.

13 Find the set of values of x corresponding to the concave section of the curve $y = x^2\,\mathrm{e}^{-x}$.

14 The graph shows $y = f'(x)$.

On a copy of the diagram:

a Mark points corresponding to a local minimum of $f(x)$ with an A.

b Mark points corresponding to a local maximum of $f(x)$ with a B.

c Mark points corresponding to a point of inflection of $f(x)$ with a C.

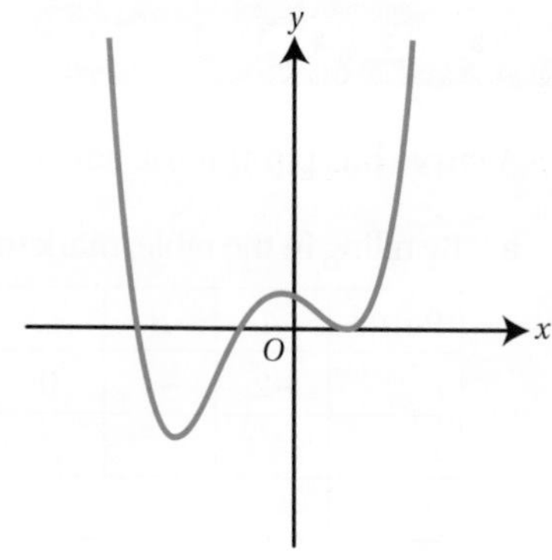

Section 2: Parametric equations

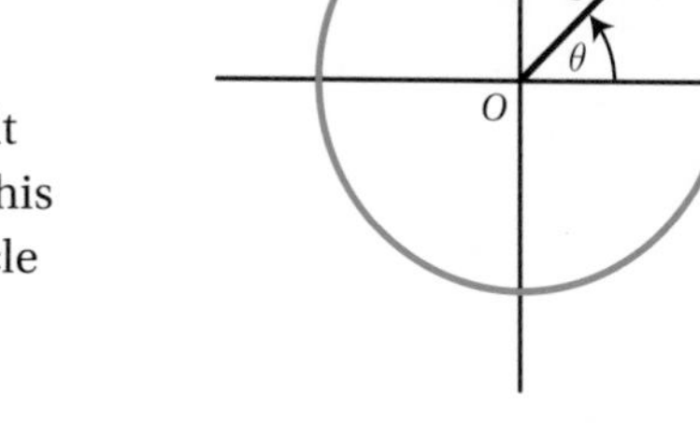

You are by now very familiar with the idea of using equations to represent graphs and using differentiation to find their gradients. In Chapter 10, Section 4 you saw that some curves can't be represented by equations of the form $y = f(x)$.

For example, a circle with radius 5 centred at the origin has an implicit equation $x^2 + y^2 = 25$. But there is another way to describe points on this circle, using the angle from the horizontal. Let P be a point on the circle and let θ be the angle OP makes with the x-axis.

Then the coordinates of P are

$$x = 5\cos\theta, y = 5\sin\theta$$

You have expressed both x and y in terms of a third variable, θ. These are called **parametric equations** and θ is called the **parameter**.

You can check that these coordinates satisfy the original equation of the circle:

$$x^2 + y^2 = 25\cos^2\theta + 25\sin^2\theta$$

$$= 25(\sin^2\theta + \cos^2\theta)$$

$$\Rightarrow x^2 + y^2 = 25$$

Each value of the parameter corresponds to a single point on the curve.

Tip

The last equation, involving just x and y, is called a **Cartesian equation**.

Tip

You can use a calculator or graphing software to plot parametric equations.

WORKED EXAMPLE 12.5

A curve has parametric equations $x=3t^2-9$ and $y=t^3-3t$.

a By filling in the table, mark the points corresponding to the given parameter values. Hence, sketch the curve.

Point	A	B	C	D	E
t	-2	-1	0	1	2
x					
y					

b Find the parameter value(s) at the point:

i $(21.72, 23.168)$

ii $(0, 0)$

a

Point	A	B	C	D	E
t	-2	-1	0	1	2
x	3	-6	-9	-6	3
y	-2	2	0	-2	2

Use the equations to find x and y for each t.

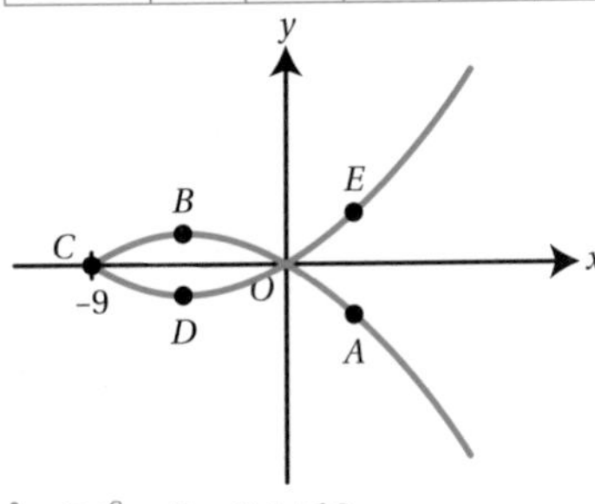

b i $3t^2-9=21.72$

$\Rightarrow t^2=10.24$

$\Rightarrow t=\pm 3.2$

The equation for t is quadratic, so we can solve it.

When $t=-3.2$, $y=-23.168$.

When $t=3.2$, $y=23.168$.

So the value of t is 3.2.

There are two possible values of t, so we need to check which one gives the correct value of y.

ii $3t^2-9=0$

$\Rightarrow t^2=3$

$\Rightarrow t=\pm\sqrt{3}$

When $t=-\sqrt{3}$,

$y=-3\sqrt{3}-3\left(-\sqrt{3}\right)=0$

When $t=\sqrt{3}$, $y=3\sqrt{3}-3\sqrt{3}=0$.

So the possible values of t are $\sqrt{3}$ or $-\sqrt{3}$.

Although each parameter value gives a single point, there can be several parameter values giving the same point. Notice that $y=0$ also when $t=0$, but $x\neq 0$ there.

You can sometimes convert a parametric equation to a Cartesian equation by eliminating the parameter. Two of the most common ways of doing this are by substitution or by using a trigonometric identity.

WORKED EXAMPLE 12.6

Find Cartesian equations of the following curves.

a $x = t^2 - 1, y = t + 2$ for $t \in \mathbb{R}$.

b $x = \tan\theta, y = 2\cos\theta$ for $0 \leqslant \theta \leqslant 2\pi, x \neq \pm\frac{\pi}{2}$.

a $y = t + 2 \Rightarrow t = y - 2$

$x = (y-2)^2 - 1$

$\Leftrightarrow x = y^2 - 4y + 3$

Express t from the y equation and substitute it into the x equation.

b $\cos\theta = \frac{y}{2} \Rightarrow \sec\theta = \frac{2}{y}$

There is a trigonometric identity relating tan and sec, so write $\sec\theta$ in terms of y.

$\sec^2\theta - \tan^2\theta = 1$

$\Rightarrow \left(\frac{2}{y}\right)^2 - x^2 = 1$

$\Rightarrow \frac{4}{y^2} - x^2 = 1$

The Cartesian equation does not need to be in the form $y = f(x)$; any equation containing just x and y is fine.

You can also write a Cartesian equation in parametric form. The simplest way to do this is to write $x = t$. For example, the equation $y = x^2$ can be written in parametric form as $x = t, y = t^2$. But you could choose x to be another function of t. For example, you could take $x = e^t$ and then $y = x^2 = e^{2t}$.

Explore

Parametric equations can be used to describe many interesting curves that don't have simple Cartesian equations. Find out about the cardioid and the cycloid.

WORKED EXAMPLE 12.7

A straight line, l, has the Cartesian equation $3x + 4y = 15$.

a Show that the point A(1, 3) lies on the line.

b Find the parametric equations for l in the form $x = p + 0.8t, y = 3 + qt$, where p and q are constants to be found, and the domain of t is the set of real numbers.

a $3(1) + 4(3) = 15$

So the point (1, 3) lies on the line.

Check that $x = 1$ and $y = 3$ satisfy the equation of the line.

b $3(p + 0.8t) + 4(3 + qt) = 15$

Substitute the given form of x and y into the equation of the line.

$\Rightarrow \begin{cases} 2.4 + 4q = 0 \\ 3p + 12 = 15 \end{cases}$

Compare the coefficients of t and the constant terms.

$\Rightarrow q = -0.6, p = 1$

So the parametric equations are

$x = 1 + 0.8t, y = 3 - 0.6t$

In the example above, the parameter t represents the distance along the line. For example, consider the points $B(5, 0)$, which has $t = 5$, and $C(17, -9)$, which has $t = 20$. The distance from B to C is $\sqrt{12^2 + 9^2} = 15$, which is also the difference between the corresponding parameter values. Usually, the parameter does not have a meaning as such but is simply a construct.

Fast forward

In Section 3 you will see other examples of parametric equations, when you study related rates of change.

Fast forward

If you study Further Mathematics, in Student Book 2, you will see how to use parametric equations of this type to describe lines in three dimensions.

Fast forward

Kinematics in two dimensions and projectiles are covered in more detail in Chapters 19 and 20.

In our first example of parametric equations of a circle, the parameter represented the angle between the radius and the x-axis. In other contexts the parameter can represent time taken to travel between points; sometimes the parameter has no obvious meaning, but in all cases it determines where you are on the curve. One important application of parametric equations is modelling motion in two dimensions.

WORKED EXAMPLE 12.8

A ball is thrown upwards at an angle from the point (0, 0). The x-axis represents the ground level. The coordinates of the ball are given by

$x = 3.2t,\ y = 10.6t - 4.9t^2,$

where t represents the time, in seconds.

a Find the coordinates of the ball 2 seconds after projection.

b Find the two times when the ball is 2.7 m above ground.

c Show that the path of the ball is a parabola, and find its (approximate) Cartesian equation.

a When $t = 2$:

$x = 3.2 \times 2 = 6.4$

$y = 10.6 \times 2 - 4.9 \times 4 = 1.6$

The coordinates are (6.4, 1.6).

b $10.6t - 4.9t^2 = 2.7$

$4.9t^2 - 10.6t + 2.7 = 0$

$t = 0.295$ and 1.87

The two times are 0.295s and 1.87s.

The height is measured by the y-coordinate.

c $x = 3.2t \Rightarrow t = \dfrac{x}{3.2}$

$y = 10.6\left(\dfrac{x}{3.2}\right) - 4.9\left(\dfrac{x}{3.2}\right)^2$

$\Rightarrow y \approx 3.3x - 0.48x^2$

Eliminate t from the first equation and substitute into the second.

EXERCISE 12B

1 By creating a table of values, sketch the curves given by the following parametric equations.

a **i** $x = 2t^2,\ y = 3t$ for $t \in [-2, 2]$

ii $x = t^2,\ y = 5t$ for $t \in [-4, 4]$

b **i** $x = 3 \sin t, y = 5 \cos t$ for $t \in [0, 2\pi]$

ii $x = 4 \cos t, y = 2 \sin t$ for $t \in [0, 2\pi]$

c **i** $x = \sin(2t), y = \sin t$ for $t \in [0, 2\pi]$

ii $x = \cos t, y = \sin(2t)$ for $t \in [0, 2\pi]$

Tip

You can check your answers by using a calculator or graphing software.

2 Find the parameter value at the given point on the curve.

a **i** $x = 3t^2, y = 2t$; point $(3, -2)$

ii $x = 5t^2, y = 2 - t$; point $(20, 0)$

b **i** $x = 2t^2, y = t^3$; point $(8, -8)$

ii $x = 2t^3, y = 5t^2$; point $(-54, 45)$

c **i** $x = 5 \sin\theta, y = 5 \cos\theta$; point $(3, -4)$

ii $x = 2 \cos\theta, y = 6 \sin\theta$; point $(1, 3\sqrt{3})$

3 Find a possible parametric equation of each curve.

a **i** $12x - 5y = 7$ using $x = 5t + 1$

ii $6x + 11y = 12$ using $x = t - 2$

b **i** $y = 4x^2$ using $x = t - 1$

ii $y = 2 - 2x^2$ using $x = t + 1$

c **i** $x^2 + 4y^2 = 9$ using $x = 3 \cos t$

ii $16x^2 + y^2 = 4$ using $y = 2 \sin t$

d **i** $3x - 5y = 14$ in the form $x = 3 + pt, y = q + 3t$

ii $6x + y = 7$ using $x = p + t, y = 1 + qt$

4 Find a Cartesian equation for each of these parametric curves.

a **i** $x = 3t^2, y = 2t$ **ii** $x = 5t^2, y = 2 - t$

b **i** $x = 2t^2, y = t^3$ **ii** $x = 2t^3, y = 5t^2$

c **i** $x = 5 \sin\theta, y = 5 \cos\theta$ **ii** $x = 2 \cos\theta, y = 6 \sin\theta$

d **i** $x = 2 \cos 2\theta, y = \cos\theta$ **ii** $x = \cos 2\theta, y = 3 \sin\theta$

e **i** $x = \tan\theta, y = \sec\theta$ **ii** $x = 3 \sec\theta, y = 2 \tan\theta$

5 A ball is projected from point O on the horizontal ground and moves in the vertical plane. The ball follows a parabolic path with parametric equations $x = 3.5t$, $y = 12t - 4.9t^2$, where t is the time after the projection. The units on the x- and y-axes are metres, and time is measured in seconds.

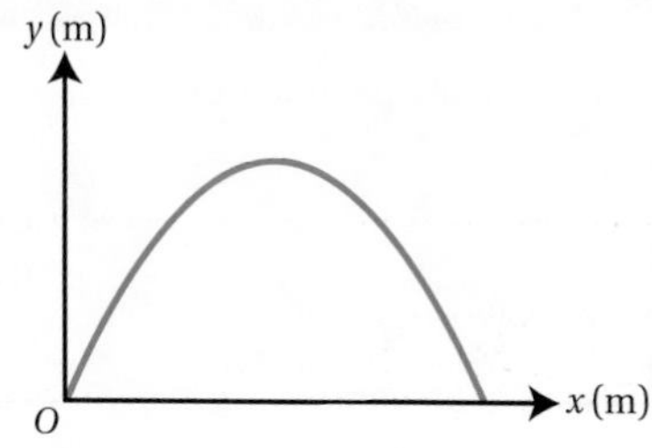

a Find the height of the ball above ground 2 seconds after projection.

b Find the distance from O of the point where the ball hits the ground.

6 A straight line has parametric equations $x = 1 + \frac{\sqrt{3}}{2}t$, $y = 2 + \frac{1}{2}t$.

a Find the y-intercept of the line.

b Find the distance between the points on the line with $t=4$ and $t=6$. What does the parameter t represent?

c Find the Cartesian equation of the line in the form $ax+by=c$.

7 A model for infectious disease (such as a cold) consists of two variables: the number of infected individuals (I thousand) and the number of susceptible individuals (S thousand). The model proposes that, at time t weeks after the start of the infection,

$$I=\frac{125-125\mathrm{e}^{-t}}{\mathrm{e}^{-t}+3} \text{ and } S=\frac{175\mathrm{e}^{-t}+25}{\mathrm{e}^{-t}+3}$$

a Show that $I+S$ is constant. Hence find the values of S and I when they are equal. Find also after how many days this happens.

b Find the values of I and S in the long term.

8 An economist models how the supply (S) and demand (D) for a good depend on the selling price (p). He uses the following equations:

$$S=8p-80 \text{ (for } p>10\text{)}, D=\frac{2400}{p+10}$$

a Find the value of D when $S=150$.

b Find an equation relating S and D.

c The *equilibrium price* is the price of the good for which supply equals demand. Find the equilibrium price predicted by this model.

Differentiating parametric equations

When a curve is given parametrically, we can find its gradient $\frac{\mathrm{d}y}{\mathrm{d}x}$ using the chain rule:

$$\frac{\mathrm{d}y}{\mathrm{d}t}=\frac{\mathrm{d}y}{\mathrm{d}x}\times\frac{\mathrm{d}x}{\mathrm{d}t}$$

Key point 12.4

Gradient of a parametric curve:

$$\frac{\mathrm{d}y}{\mathrm{d}x}=\frac{\left(\frac{\mathrm{d}y}{\mathrm{d}t}\right)}{\left(\frac{\mathrm{d}x}{\mathrm{d}t}\right)}$$

WORKED EXAMPLE 12.9

If a curve has parametric equations $x = \tan t,\ y = \sin 2t$, find the gradient of the curve:

a at the point where $t = \dfrac{\pi}{4}$ **b** at the point $\left(\sqrt{3}, \dfrac{\sqrt{3}}{2}\right)$.

a $\dfrac{dy}{dt} = 2\cos 2t$

$\dfrac{dx}{dt} = \sec^2 t$

$\therefore \dfrac{dy}{dx} = \dfrac{2\cos 2t}{\sec^2 t}$

$= \dfrac{2\cos\frac{\pi}{2}}{\sec^2\frac{\pi}{4}}$

$= 0$

The formula involves $\dfrac{dy}{dt}$ and $\dfrac{dx}{dt}$.

b To find t:

$\tan t = \sqrt{3} \Rightarrow t = \dfrac{\pi}{3}, \dfrac{4\pi}{3}, \ldots$

The formula for the gradient is in terms of t, so we need to find the value of t first.

$\sin 2t = \dfrac{\sqrt{3}}{2} \Rightarrow 2t = \dfrac{\pi}{3}, \dfrac{2\pi}{3}, \ldots$

$\Rightarrow t = \dfrac{\pi}{6}, \dfrac{\pi}{3}, \ldots$

$\therefore t = \dfrac{\pi}{3}$ at this point.

We need the value of t that satisfies both equations.

$\dfrac{dy}{dx} = \dfrac{2\cos\left(\frac{2\pi}{3}\right)}{\sec^2\left(\frac{\pi}{3}\right)}$

$= -\dfrac{1}{4}$

Use the equation from the previous part.

WORK IT OUT 12.2

Find the equation of the tangent to the curve with parametric equations $x = 2t^2, y = t^3$ at the point (18, –27).

Which of the following solutions is correct? Identify the mistakes in the other two.

Solution 1	Solution 2	Solution 3
$\dfrac{dy}{dx} = \dfrac{3t^2}{4t} = \dfrac{3}{4}t$ Equation of the tangent: $y + 54 = \dfrac{3}{4}t(x - 18)$ $\Leftrightarrow y = \dfrac{3}{4}tx - \dfrac{27}{2}t - 54$	$\dfrac{dy}{dx} = \dfrac{3t^2}{4t} = \dfrac{3}{4}t$ When $x = 18$, $t^2 = 9 \Rightarrow t = \pm 3$ But $y = -27$, so $t = -3$ When $t = -3$, $\dfrac{dy}{dx} = -\dfrac{9}{4}$ Tangent: $y + 27 = -\dfrac{9}{4}(x - 18)$ $\Leftrightarrow 9x + 4y = 54$	$\dfrac{dy}{dx} = \dfrac{3t^2}{4t} = \dfrac{3}{4}t$ When $x = 18$, $t^2 = 9$, $t = 3$ Then $\dfrac{dy}{dx} = \dfrac{9}{4}$ Tangent: $y + 27 = \dfrac{9}{4}(x - 18)$ $\Leftrightarrow 9x - 4y = 270$

Curves given by parametric equations often have both horizontal and vertical tangents. You can find them by looking at the values of $\frac{dx}{dt}$ and $\frac{dy}{dt}$.

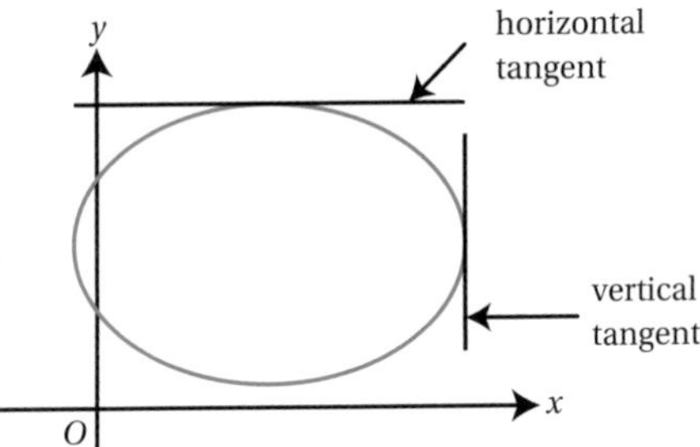

Key point 12.5

At a point where the tangent is parallel to the x-axis, $\frac{dy}{dt} = 0$.

At a point where the tangent is parallel to the y-axis, $\frac{dx}{dt} = 0$.

Tip

Note that these statements are not reversible. So, for example, $\frac{dy}{dt} = 0$ does not necessarily imply that the tangent is parallel to the x-axis.

WORKED EXAMPLE 12.10

A curve has parametric equations $x = 2\sin t$, $y = e^{-2t}$ for $0 \leqslant t \leqslant \pi$.

a Find the equation of the tangent parallel to the y-axis.

b Show that the curve has no tangents parallel to the x-axis.

a $\frac{dx}{dt} = 0$

If a tangent is parallel to the y-axis, then $\frac{dx}{dt} = 0$.

$2\cos t = 0 \Rightarrow t = \frac{\pi}{2}$

$x = 2\sin\frac{\pi}{2} = 2$

The equation of the tangent is $x = 2$.

This tangent is vertical, so it is of the form $x = k$. Check that $\frac{dy}{dt} \neq 0$ at the point where $t = \frac{\pi}{2}$

b $\frac{dy}{dt} = -2e^{-2t}$

If a tangent is parallel to the x-axis, then $\frac{dy}{dt} = 0$.

But $-2e^{-2t} < 0$ for all t.

Hence, $\frac{dy}{dt} \neq 0$, so there are no horizontal tangents.

The exponential function is always positive.

Parametric equations can be used to describe some interesting curves and to prove properties of their tangents and normals. In many of these proofs you need to work with the general value of the parameter.

WORKED EXAMPLE 12.11

A curve has parametric equations $x = 5\cos^3 t$, $y = 5\sin^3 t$, for $0 \leqslant t < 2\pi$. P is a point on the curve.

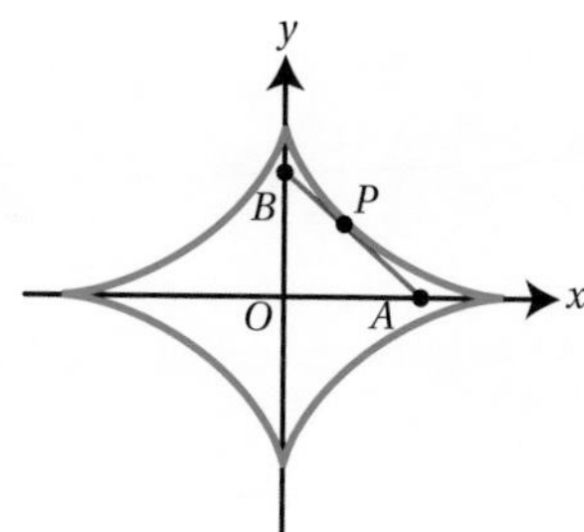

a Find, in terms of t, the equation of the tangent to the curve at P.

The tangent at a point, P, meets the x-axis at A and the y-axis at B.

b Prove that the length of AB does not depend on the position of P on the curve.

a $\frac{dy}{dx} = \frac{\left(\frac{dy}{dt}\right)}{\left(\frac{dx}{dt}\right)}$

The gradient of the tangent is $\frac{dy}{dx}$.

$= \frac{15\sin^2 t\cos t}{-15\cos^2 t\sin t}$

Use the chain rule to differentiate each function.

$= -\tan t$

Equation of the tangent:

$y - 5\sin^3 t = -\tan t\,(x - 5\cos^3 t)$

The equation of the tangent is $y - y_1 = m(x - x_1)$.

At A, $y = 0$:

$\Leftrightarrow -5\sin^3 t = -\tan t\,(x - 5\cos^3 t)$

Set $y = 0$ and $x = 0$ to find axis intercepts.

$\Rightarrow 5\sin^2 t\cos t = x - 5\cos^3 t$

Divide both sides by $-\tan t$.

$\Rightarrow x = 5\sin^2 t\cos t + 5\cos^3 t$

$= 5\cos t\,(\sin^2 t + \cos^2 t)$

You can factorise and use $\sin^2 t + \cos^2 t = 1$.

$= 5\cos t$

At B, $x = 0$:

$y - 5\sin^3 t = -\tan t\,(-5\cos^3 t)$

$\Rightarrow y = 5\sin t\cos^2 t + 5\sin^3 t$

$= 5\sin t(\cos^2 t + \sin^2 t)$

$= 5\cos t$

The distance between $A(5\cos t, 0)$ and $B(0, 5\sin t)$ is:

Now you have the coordinates of A and B, so you can find the distance between them.

$\sqrt{(5\cos t)^2 + (5\sin t)^2} = \sqrt{25} = 5$

This length does not depend on t, so it is the same for every position of P.

Did you know?

The curve in this question is called the astroid. A ladder sliding down a wall is always tangent to a curve of this shape.

EXERCISE 12C

1 Find the expression for $\frac{dy}{dx}$ in terms of t for the following parametric curves.

a i $x = 3t^2, y = 2t$ ii $x = 5t^2, y = 2 - t$

b i $x = 2\cos 2\theta, y = \cos\theta$ ii $x = \cos 2\theta, y = 3\sin\theta$

c i $x = \tan\theta, y = \sec\theta$ ii $x = 3\sec\theta, y = 2\tan\theta$

2 Find the gradient of each curve at the given point. (You need to find the parameter value first.)

a i $x = 3t^2, y = 2t$; point $(3, -2)$

ii $x = 5t^2, y = 2 - t$; point $(20, 0)$

b i $x = 2t^2, y = t^3$; point $(8, -8)$

ii $x = 2t^3, y = 5t^2$; point $(54, 45)$

c i $x = 5\sin\theta, y = 5\cos\theta$; point $(3, -4)$

ii $x = 2\cos\theta, y = 6\sin\theta$; point $(1, 3\sqrt{3})$

3 A curve has parametric equations $x = 3t^2, y = t - 2$. Find the equation of the normal to the curve at the point where $t = 1$.

4 A curve has parametric equations $x = t + \sin t, y = \cos t$. Find the equation of the tangent to the curve at the point where $t = \pi$.

5 The tangent to the curve with parametric equations $x = t^2, y = e^{-t}$ at the point $(1, \frac{1}{e})$ crosses the coordinate axes at the points M and N. Find the exact area of triangle OMN.

6 **a** Find the equation of the normal to the curve with equation $x = 4t, y = \frac{4}{t}$ at the point $(16, 1)$.

b Find the coordinates of the point where the normal crosses the curve again.

7 A parabola has parametric equations $x = 3t^2, y = 6t$. The normal to the parabola at the point where $t = 1$ crosses the parabola again at the point Q. Find the coordinates of Q.

8 Prove that the curve with parametric equations $x = t^3 - 3t^2 + 7t$, $y = 5t^2 + 1$ has no tangents parallel to the y-axis.

9 Let P be the point on the curve $x = t^2, y = \frac{1}{t}$ with coordinates $\left(p^2, \frac{1}{p}\right)$. The tangent to the curve at P meets the x-axis at point A and the y-axis at point B. Prove that $PA = 2PB$.

10 Point $Q\,(aq^2, 2aq)$ lies on the parabola with parametric equations $x = at^2, y = 2at$.

a Let M be the point where the normal to the parabola at Q crosses the x-axis. Find, in terms of a and q, the coordinates of M.

b N is the perpendicular from Q to the x-axis. Prove that the distance $MN = 2a$.

Elevate

See Support sheet 12 for a further example of finding tangents and normals with parametric equations and for more practice questions.

11 A *predator-prey model* describes the population sizes of two species. The number of snakes (S) and the number of rats (R), at time t months, are modelled by the equations:

$$S = 20 + 20e^{-0.1t}\sin\left(\frac{\pi t}{6}\right),\ R = 20 + 20e^{-0.1t}\cos\left(\frac{\pi t}{6}\right)$$

a Find all the times in the first two years when the number of snakes equals the number of rats.

b Between which times in the first year are the numbers of both species increasing?

c Show that $\frac{dR}{dS} = \frac{5\tan\left(\frac{\pi t}{6}\right)+3}{3\tan\left(\frac{\pi t}{6}\right)-5}$. What does this quantity represent.

Integrating parametric equations

When the equation of a curve is given in a parametric form, you can still use integration to find the area between the curve and the x-axis.

Key Point 12.6

The area under the curve $(x(t), y(t))$, between points $x = a$ and $x = b$, is given by

$$\int_{t_1}^{t_2} y\frac{dx}{dt}\,dt$$

where t_1 and t_2 are the parameter values at the points on the curve where $x = a$ and $x = b$.

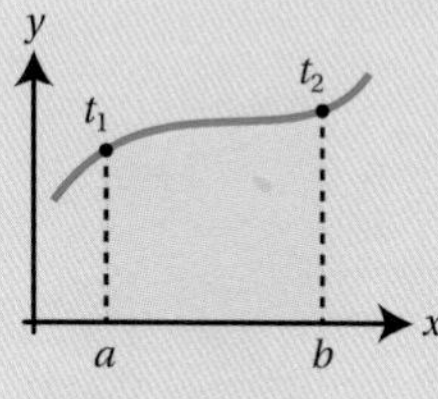

Rewind

This is very much like the idea used in integration by substitution in Chapter 11, Section 2 to change from x to u.

WORKED EXAMPLE 12.12

The diagram shows a part of the curve with parametric equations $x = t^2$, $y = 3 - t$. Points A and B have x-coordinates 0 and 9.

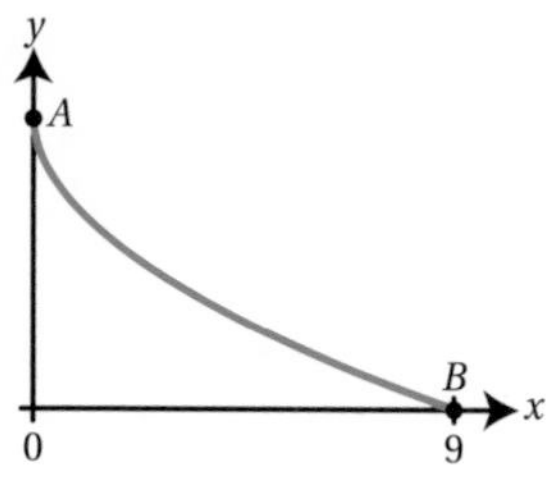

Continues on next page ...

a Find the values of the parameter at A and B.

b Find the area bounded by the curve, the x-axis and the y-axis.

a At A: $x=0 \Rightarrow t=0$

At B: $y=0 \Rightarrow t=3$

Notice that there are two possible values of t that give $x=9$, but only one of them is consistent with $y=0$.

b $\text{Area} = \int_0^3 y\frac{dx}{dt}dt$

$= \int_0^3 (3-t)2t\,dt$

$= \int_0^3 6t - 2t^2 dt$

$= \left[3t^2 - \frac{2}{3}t^3\right]_0^3 = 9$

Use the formula for parametric integration with the parameter values at A and B.

EXERCISE 12D

1 For each curve with the given parametric equations, find the shaded area.

a **i** $x=t^2+2, y=t+3$

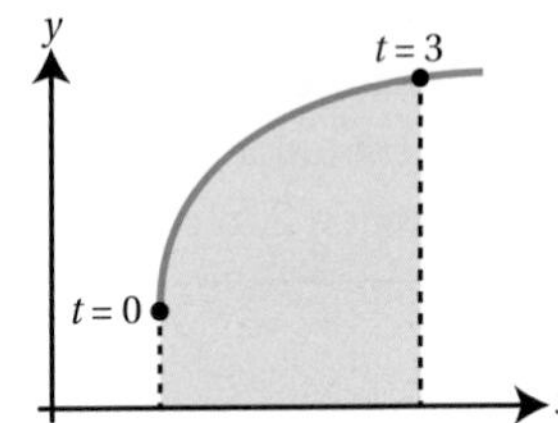

ii $x=t^2, y=t+5$

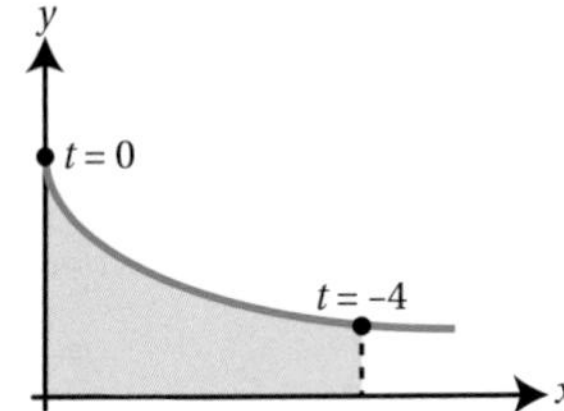

b **i** $x=1+t, y=1-\frac{1}{t}$

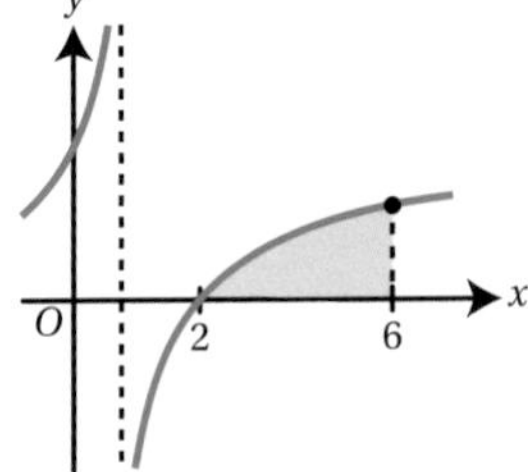

ii $x=2t^2, y=1-\frac{1}{t^2}$

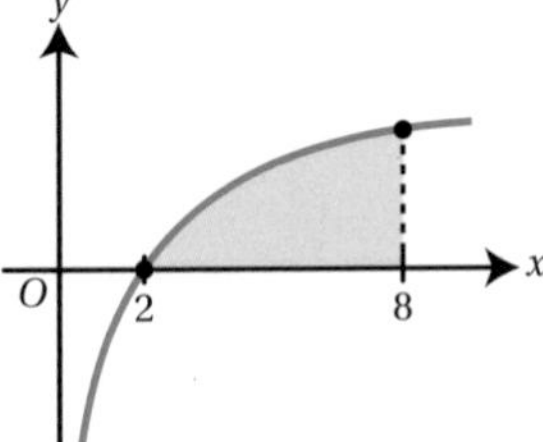

c **i** $x=3t, y=\sin t$

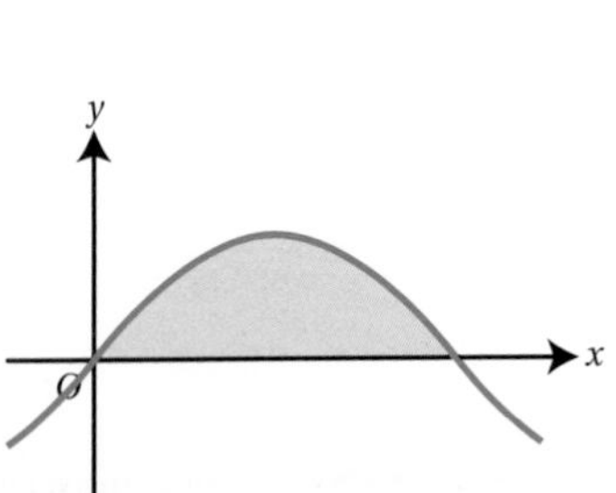

ii $x=4t, y=\sec^2 t-2$

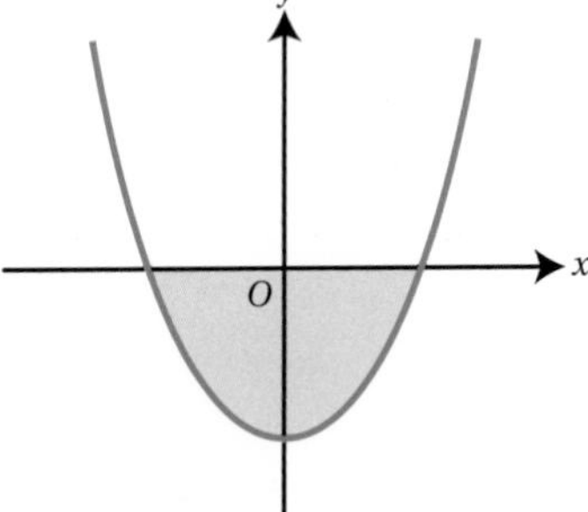

2 **a** Find the coordinates of the points where the curve with parametric equations $x = (t+2)^2$, $y = t^2 - t - 2$ crosses the x-axis.

b Find the area enclosed by the curve and the x-axis.

3 A curve is defined by the parametric equations $x = t + e^{-t}$, $y = 1 - e^{-t}$.

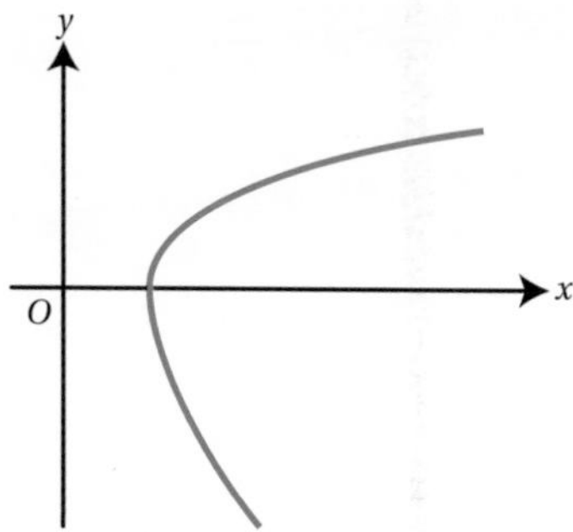

a Find the exact values of t at the points where $y = 0$ and $y = \frac{1}{2}$.

b Find the area bounded by the curve, the x-axis and the line $x = \frac{1}{2} + \ln 2$.

4 Point $C\left(\frac{10}{3}, \frac{8}{3}\right)$ lies on the curve with parametric equations $x = t + \frac{1}{t}$, $y = t - \frac{1}{t}$.

a Find the parameter value at C.

b The diagram shows a part of the curve and the normal at C. Find the shaded area.

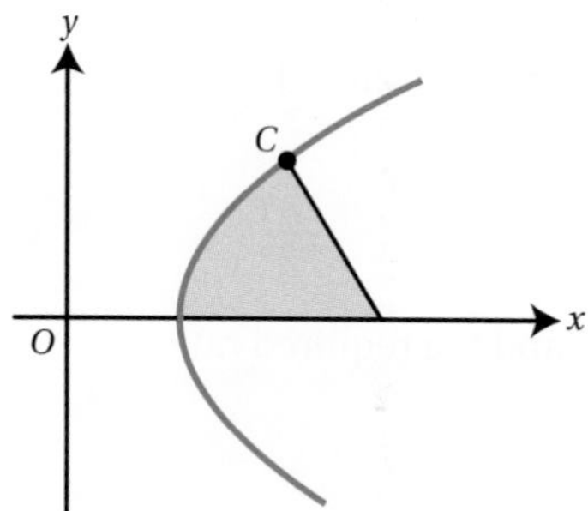

c Find the Cartesian equation of the curve.

Section 3: Related rates of change

In the previous sections you learnt that you can use parametric equations to model situations where two variables both depend on a third one. Here we look at some more contexts where such situations occur, and how to calculate various rates of change in these situations.

Consider, for example, inflating a balloon. Both the amount of gas in the balloon (V) and the radius of the balloon (r) vary with time, but they are also linked to each other. If we plotted a curve to show how V changes with r, then $V(t)$ and $r(t)$ would give parametric equations of that curve.

We can consider three different rates of change:

$\frac{dV}{dr}$ measures how quickly the amount (volume) of gas in the balloon is increasing.

$\frac{dr}{dt}$ measures how quickly the radius is increasing.

$\frac{dV}{dt}$ shows how the volume changes with radius.

You know from the previous section that $\frac{dV}{dr} = \frac{\frac{dV}{dt}}{\frac{dr}{dt}}$. But in this situation, you already know $\frac{dV}{dr}$ (because you know the formula linking the volume to the radius), and you can control the speed at which you inflate the balloon (this is $\frac{dV}{dt}$). You can then combine these two pieces of information to find the rate of change of the radius.

WORKED EXAMPLE 12.13

A spherical balloon is being inflated with air at a rate of 200 cm³ per minute. At what rate is the radius increasing when the radius is 8 cm?

V = volume of air in balloon, in cm^3
r = radius of balloon, in cm
t = time, in minutes

When solving problems in context you should always start by defining variables.

$$\frac{dV}{dt} = 200$$
$$\frac{dr}{dt} = ?$$

Write the given rate of change and the required rate of change.

$$\frac{dV}{dt} = \frac{dV}{dr} \times \frac{dr}{dt}$$

So you need to find $\frac{dV}{dr}$.

Relate these rates of change using the chain rule.

Since the balloon is spherical $V = \frac{4}{3}\pi r^3$, so $\frac{dV}{dr} = 4\pi r^2$.

Use geometric context.

$$\frac{dV}{dt} = 4\pi r^2 \frac{dr}{dt}$$

Substitute into the chain rule.

$$200 = 256\pi \frac{dr}{dt}$$

$$\frac{dr}{dt} = 0.249 \text{ (3 s.f.)}$$

So radius is increasing at about 0.249 cm per minute.

Sometimes the chain rule needs to be combined with the product or the quotient rule.

WORKED EXAMPLE 12.14

The length of a rectangle is increasing at a constant rate of 3 cm per second, and the width is decreasing at a constant rate of 2 cm per second. Find the rate of change of the area of the rectangle at the instant when the length is 18 cm and the width is 10 cm.

Let $x(t)$ be the length, $y(t)$ be the width and $A(t)$ be the area.

Then $\frac{dx}{dt}=3$ and $\frac{dy}{dt}=-2$.

Start by defining variables. The length and the width are both functions of time.

$$A=xy$$

$$\Rightarrow \frac{dA}{dt}=\frac{dx}{dt}y+x\frac{dy}{dt}$$

$$=3y-2x$$

Use the product rule to differentiate A.

When $x=18$ and $y=10$:

$$\frac{dA}{dt}=3(10)-2(18)=-6$$

Use the given values of x and y.

The area is decreasing at the rate of $6\text{ cm}^2\text{ s}^{-1}$.

WORKED EXAMPLE 12.15

As a conical stalactite melts, the rate of decrease of height, h, is 1 cm per hour and the rate of decrease of the radius of the base, r, is 0.1 cm per hour. At what rate is the volume of the stalactite decreasing when the height is 30 cm and the base radius is 4 cm?

$$\frac{dh}{dt}=-1$$

$$\frac{dr}{dt}=-0.$$

$$\frac{dV}{dt}=?$$

Write the given rates of change and the required rates of change.
Remember that decrease means negative derivative.

$$V=\frac{1}{3}\pi r^2 h$$

Use geometric context to relate the variables.

$$\frac{dV}{dt}=\frac{d}{dt}\left(\frac{1}{3}\pi r^2\right)h+\left(\frac{1}{3}\pi r^2\right)\frac{dh}{dt}$$

$$=\frac{2}{3}\pi r\frac{dr}{dt}h+\frac{1}{3}\pi r^2\frac{dh}{dt}$$

Differentiate both sides with respect to t. This requires the product rule and the chain rule.

$$\frac{dV}{dt}=\frac{2}{3}\pi\times4\times(-0.1)\times30+\frac{1}{3}\pi\times4^2\times(-1).$$

$$=-41.9\text{ cm}^3\ h^{-1}$$

Put in given values.

The volume is decreasing at $41.9\text{ cm}^3\ h^{-1}$.

EXERCISE 12E

1 In each of the following cases, find an expression for $\frac{dz}{dx}$ in terms of x.

a i $z = 4y^2, y = 3x^2$

ii $z = y^2, y = x^3 + 1$

b i $z = \cos y, y = 3x^2$

ii $z = \tan y, y = x^2 + 1$

2 a i Given that $z = y^2 + 1$ and $\frac{dy}{dx} = 5$, find $\frac{dz}{dx}$ when $y = 5$.

ii Given that $z = 2y^3$ and $\frac{dy}{dx} = -2$, find $\frac{dz}{dx}$ when $y = 1$.

b i If $w = \sin x$ and $\frac{dw}{dt} = -3$, find $\frac{dx}{dt}$ when $x = \frac{\pi}{3}$.

ii If $P = \tan h$ and $\frac{dP}{dx} = 2$, find $\frac{dh}{dx}$ when $h = \frac{\pi}{4}$.

c i Given that $V = 12r^3$, $\frac{dr}{dt} = 1$ and $\frac{dV}{dt} = 4$, find the possible values of r.

ii Given that $H = 3S^{-2}$, find the value of S for which $\frac{dH}{dx} = 3$ and $\frac{dS}{dx} = 4$.

3 a i Given that $A = xy$, find $\frac{dA}{dt}$ when $x = 4, y = 5, \frac{dx}{dt} = 2$ and $\frac{dy}{dt} = 3$.

ii Given that $S = ab$, find $\frac{dS}{dt}$ when $a = 12, b = 5, \frac{da}{dt} = -2$ and $\frac{db}{dt} = 4$.

b i Given that $V = 3r^2h$, find $\frac{dV}{dt}$ when $r = 3, h = 2, \frac{dr}{dt} = 2$ and $\frac{dh}{dt} = -1$.

ii Given that $N = kx^4$, find $\frac{dN}{dt}$ when $x = 2, k = 5, \frac{dk}{dt} = 1$, and $\frac{dx}{dt} = 1$.

c i Given that $m = \frac{S}{N}$ and that when $S = 100$, $\frac{dS}{dt} = 20$, $N = 50$, and $\frac{dN}{dt} = 4$, find $\frac{dm}{dt}$.

ii Given that $\rho = \frac{m}{V}$ and that when $m = 24$, $\frac{dm}{dt} = 2, V = 120$, and $\frac{dV}{dt} = 6$, find $\frac{d\rho}{dt}$.

4 A circular stain is spreading so that the radius is increasing at the constant rate of 1.5 cm s^{-1}. Find the rate of increase of the area when the radius is 12 cm.

5 The area of a square is increasing at the constant rate of 50 cm^2 s^{-1}. Find the rate of increase of the side of the square when the length of the side is 12.5 cm.

6 A spherical ball is inflated so that its radius increases at the rate of 3 cm per second. Find the rate of change of the volume when the radius is 8 cm.

7 A rectangle has length a and width b. Both the length and the width are increasing at a constant rate of 3 cm per second. Find the rate of increase of the area of the rectangle at the instant when $a = 10$ cm and $b = 15$ cm.

8 The surface area of a closed cylinder is given by $A = 2\pi r^2 + 2\pi rh$, where h is the height and r is the radius of the base. At the time when the surface area is increasing at the rate of 20π cm^2 s^{-1}, the radius is 4 cm, the height is 1 cm and is decreasing at the rate of 2 cm s^{-1}. Find the rate of change of radius at this time.

9 The radius of a cone is increasing at the rate of 0.5 cm s^{-1} and its height is decreasing at the rate of 0.3 cm s^{-1}. Find the rate of change of the volume of the cone at the instant when the radius is 20 cm and the height is 30 cm.

10 A point is moving in the plane so that its coordinates are both functions of time, $(x(t), y(t))$. When the coordinates of the point are (5, 7), the x-coordinate is increasing at the rate of 16 units per second and the y-coordinate is increasing at the rate of 12 units per second. At what rate is the distance of the point from the origin changing at this instant?

Section 4: More complicated areas

In Student Book 1, Chapter 14, you learnt how to use integration to find the area between a curve and the x-axis. In this section you will extend this technique to areas bounded by other lines and curves.

Area between two curves

The area, A, in the diagram is bounded by two curves with equations $y = \text{f}(x)$ and $y = \text{g}(x)$.

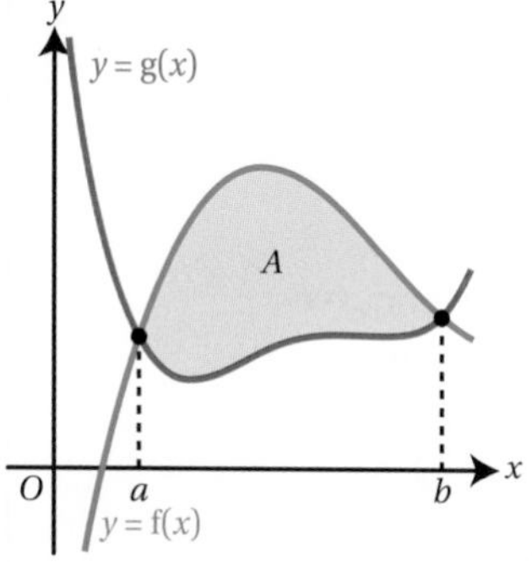

The area can be found by taking the area bounded by f(x) and the x-axis and subtracting the area bounded by g(x) and the x-axis, that is

$$A = \int_a^b \text{f}(x)\,\text{d}x - \int_a^b \text{g}(x)\,\text{d}x$$

You can do the subtraction before integrating so that you have to integrate only one expression instead of two. This gives an alternative formula for the area:

Key point 12.7

The area enclosed by the curves $y = \text{f}(x)$ and $y = \text{g}(x)$ is given by

$$A = \int_a^b \text{f}(x) - \text{g}(x)\,\text{d}x$$

where a and b are the x-coordinates of the intersection points of the two curves.

WORKED EXAMPLE 12.16

Find the exact area enclosed between the curves $y=\frac{1}{2}x+\frac{15}{2}$ and $y=x^2-6x+13$.

For intersection:

$$x^2-6x+13=\frac{1}{2}x+\frac{15}{2}$$
$$\Leftrightarrow 2x^2-12x+26=x+15$$
$$\Leftrightarrow 2x^2-13x+11=0$$
$$\Leftrightarrow (2x-11)(x-1)=0$$
$$\therefore x=\frac{11}{2},1$$

You first need to find the x-coordinates of the intersections.

It may help to do a rough sketch to see the relative positions of the two curves.

$y=x^2-6x+13$, $y=\frac{x+15}{2}$, A, O, 1, $\frac{11}{2}$, x, y

$$A=\int_1^{\frac{11}{2}}\left(\frac{1}{2}x+\frac{15}{2}\right)-\left(x^2-6x+13\right)dx$$
$$=\int_1^{\frac{11}{2}}-x^2+\frac{13}{2}x-\frac{11}{2}\,dx=\left[-\frac{1}{3}x^3+\frac{13}{4}x^2-\frac{11}{2}x\right]_1^{\frac{11}{2}}$$
$$=\left(\frac{605}{48}\right)-\left(-\frac{31}{12}\right)=\frac{243}{16}$$

Subtract the equation of the lower curve from the equation of the higher curve before integrating.

Rewind

Notice that in Student Book 1, Chapter 15 you found an area such as that in Worked example 12.16 by subtracting the area under the curve from the area of a trapezium. However, this new method is more direct.

Subtracting the two equations before integrating is particularly useful when one of the curves is partly below the x-axis. As long as $f(x)$ is always above $g(x)$ then the expression you are integrating, $f(x)-g(x)$, is always positive, so you do not have to worry about the signs of $f(x)$ and $g(x)$ themselves.

WORKED EXAMPLE 12.17

Find the area bounded by the curves $y = e^x - 3$ and $y = 5 - 7e^{-x}$.

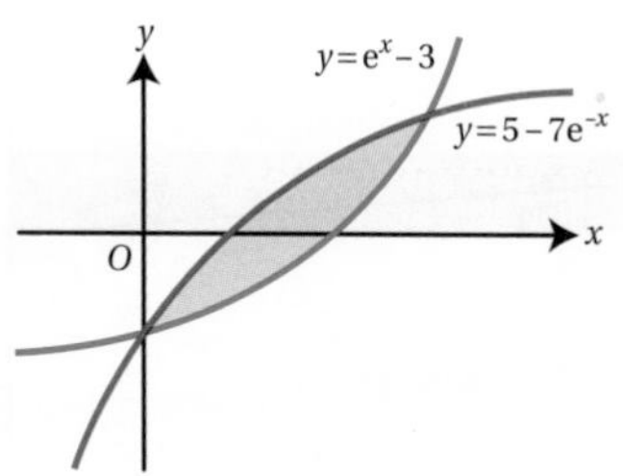

Sketch the graph to see the relative position of two curves.

Intersections:

$$e^x - 3 = 5 - 7e^{-x}$$
$$\Leftrightarrow e^{2x} - 3e^x = 5e^x - 7$$

Find the intersection points; start by multiplying through by e^x.

$$\Leftrightarrow e^{2x} - 8e^x + 7 = 0$$
$$\Leftrightarrow (e^x - 1)(e^x - 7) = 0$$
$$\therefore x = 0 \text{ or } \ln 7$$

This is a disguised quadratic that can be factorised.

$$A = \int_0^{\ln 7} (5 - 7e^{-x}) - (e^x - 3)\,dx$$

Write down the integral representing the area. You can see from the graph that the 'top' curve is $5 - 7e^{-x}$.

$$= \int_0^{\ln 7} 8 - 7e^{-x} - e^x\,dx$$
$$= \left[8x + 7e^{-x} - e^x\right]_0^{\ln 7}$$

Simplify before integrating.

$$= (8\ln 7 + 1 - 7) - (0 + 7 - 1)$$
$$= 8\ln 7 - 12$$

Use $e^{\ln 7} = 7$.

WORK IT OUT 12.3

Find the area enclosed between the line $y = 2x$ and the curve $y = x^2 - 3x$.

Which of the following solutions is correct? Identify the mistake in the other two.

Solution 1

Sketching the graph shows that part of the area is below the x-axis, so you need to split it up into two parts.

$$A = \int_0^3 x^2 - 3x\,dx = \left[\frac{1}{3}x^3 - \frac{3}{2}x^2\right]_0^3 = -4.5$$

$$B = \int_0^5 2x\,dx = \left[x^2\right]_0^5 = 25$$

Total area = 25 + 4.5 = 29.5

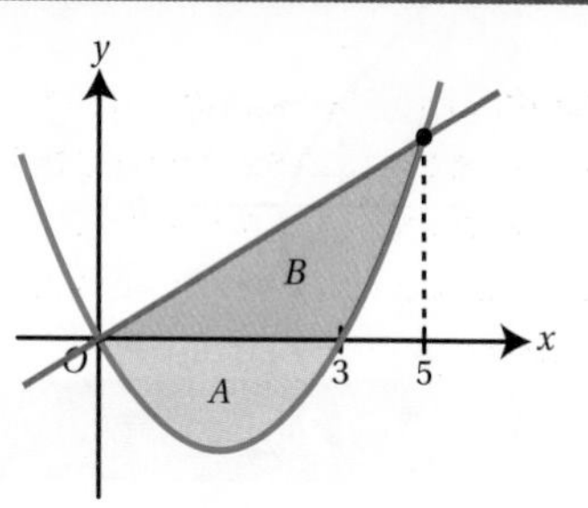

Continues on next page ...

Solution 2

The intersection points are at $x = 0$ and $x = 5$.

$$\int_0^5 x^2 - 3x - 2x\,dx = \left[\frac{1}{3}x^3 - \frac{5}{2}x^2\right]_0^5 = -\frac{125}{6}$$

Solution 3

The intersection points are at $x = 0$ and $x = 5$.

$$\int_0^5 2x - (x^2 - 3x)\,dx = \left[\frac{5x^2}{2} - \frac{x^3}{3}\right]_0^5 = 20.8 \text{ (3 s.f.)}$$

Area between a curve and the y-axis

How can you find the shaded area A in the diagram alongside, bounded by the curve and the y-axis?

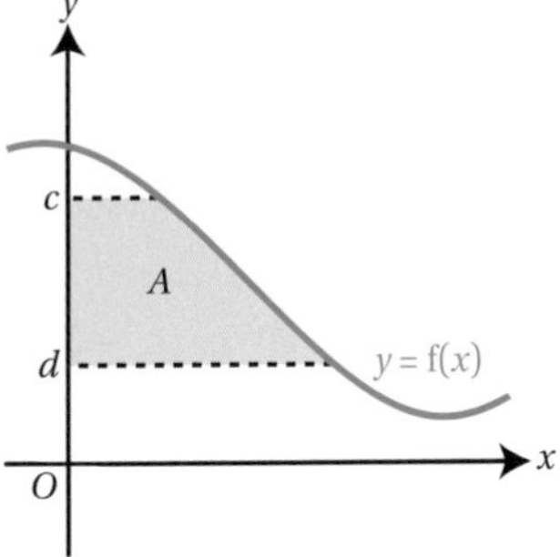

You know how to find the area between the curve and the x-axis, so one possible strategy is to draw vertical lines to create the region labelled A_1. The required area is equal to the area of A_1 minus the orange rectangle plus the blue rectangle.

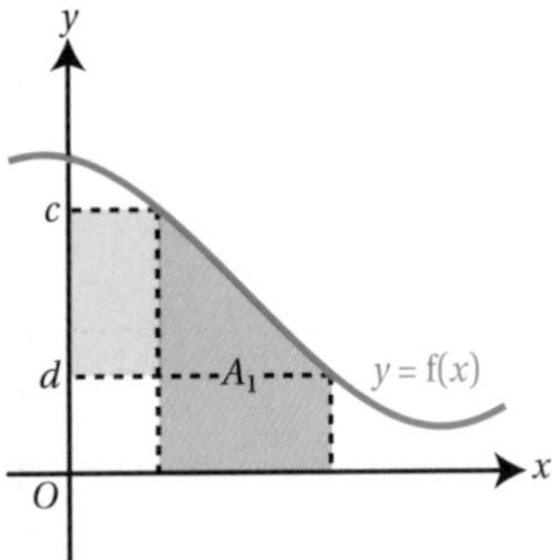

Happily, there is a quicker way: you can treat x as a function of y, effectively reflecting the whole diagram in the line $y = x$.

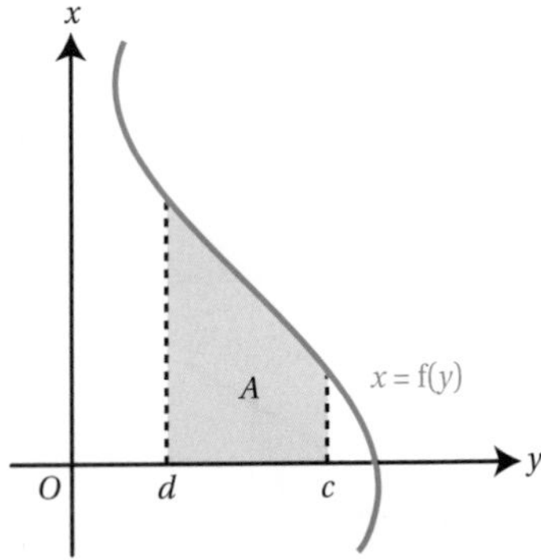

Key point 12.8

The area bounded by the curve $y = \text{f}(x)$, the y-axis and the lines $y = c$ and $y = d$ is given by $\int_c^d \text{g}(y)\,dy$, where $\text{g}(y)$ is the expression for x in terms of y; i.e. $x = \text{g}(y)$.

Rewind

You may have realised that this is related to inverse functions from Chapter 2.

WORKED EXAMPLE 12.18

The curve shown has equation $y = 2\sqrt{x-1}$. Find the shaded area.

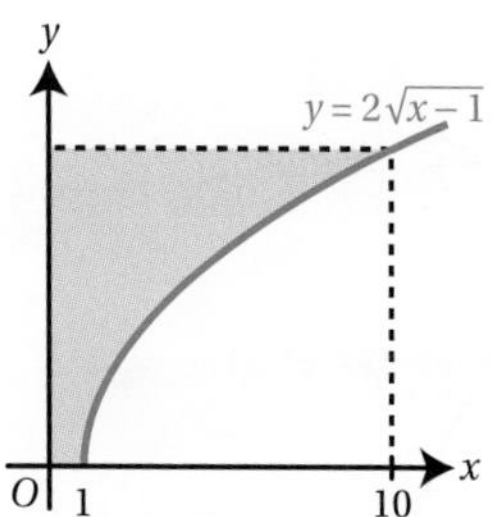

$x - 1 = \left(\frac{y}{2}\right)^2$ — Express x in terms of y.

$\Rightarrow x = \frac{y^2}{4} + 1$

When $x = 1$, $y = 2\sqrt{1-1} = 0$ — Find the limits on the y-axis.

When $x = 10$, $y = 2\sqrt{10-1} = 6$

$$\text{Area} = \int_0^6 \left(\frac{y^2}{4} + 1\right) dx = \left[\frac{y^3}{12} + y\right]_0^6$$

$$= (18 + 6) - (0) = 24$$

WORKED EXAMPLE 12.19

Find the exact area enclosed by the graph of $y = \ln(x+3)$, the y-axis and the line $y = 1$.

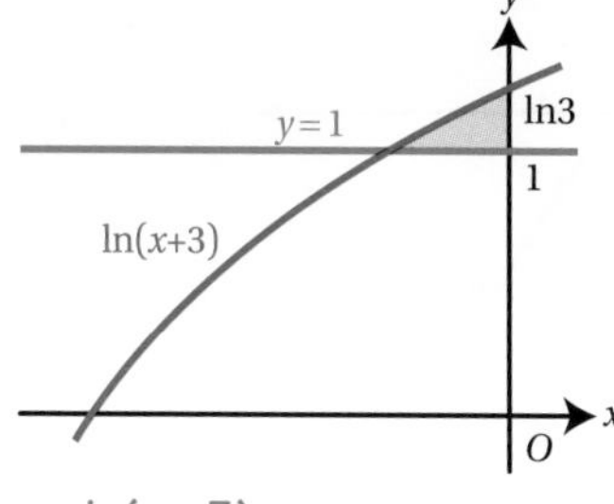

Sketch the graph and identify the area required. The graph crosses the y-axis at $y = \ln(0+3)$.

$y = \ln(x+3)$

$\Leftrightarrow x + 3 = e^y$

$\Leftrightarrow x = e^y - 3$

The area between a curve and the y-axis is given by $\int_a^b x \, dy$, so we need to express x in terms of y...

$$\int_1^{\ln 3} (e^y - 3)\, dy = \left[e^y - 3y\right]_1^{\ln 3}$$

$$= (e^{\ln 3} - 3\ln 3) - (e^1 - 3)$$

... and then evaluate the definite integral.

$$= (3 - 3\ln 3) - (e - 3)$$

$$= 6 - e - 3\ln 3$$

Remember that $e^{\ln k} = k$.

So

Area $= 3\ln 3 + e - 6$

Notice that this value is negative; this is because the shaded area is to the left of the y-axis.

EXERCISE 12F

1 Find the shaded areas below. You need to find the intersection points of the two curves first.

a **i**

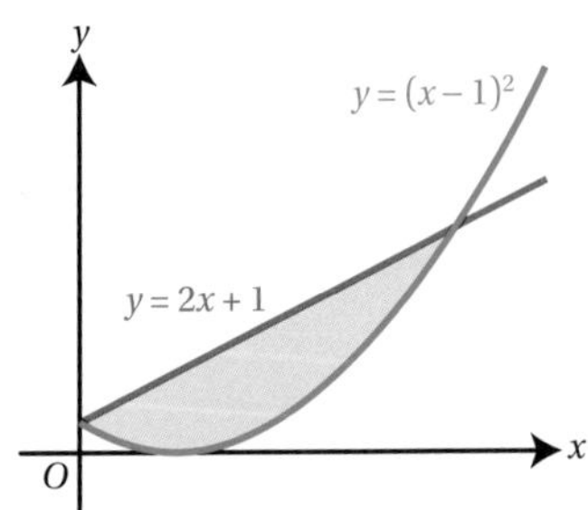

ii

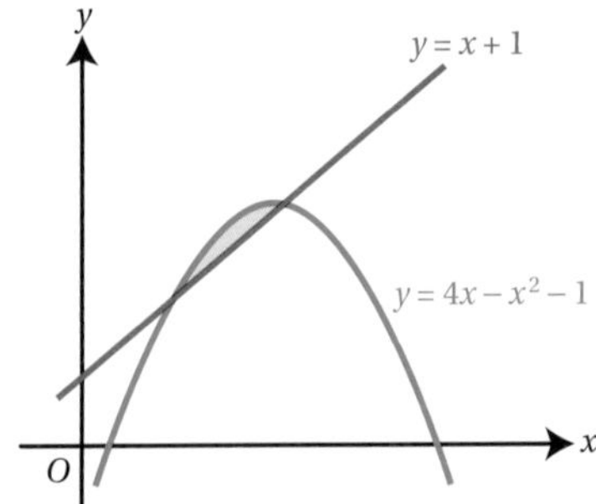

b **i**

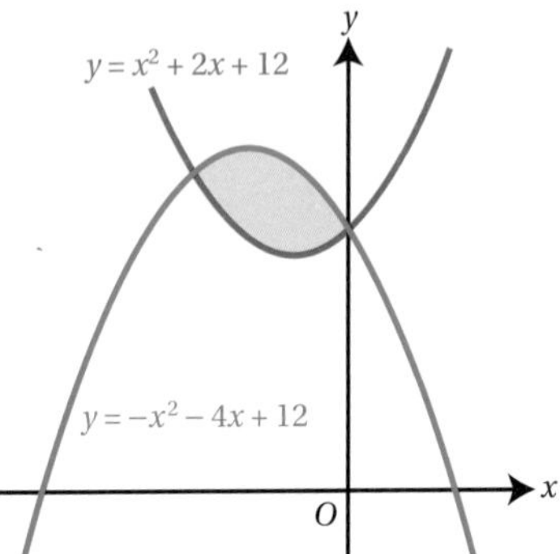

ii

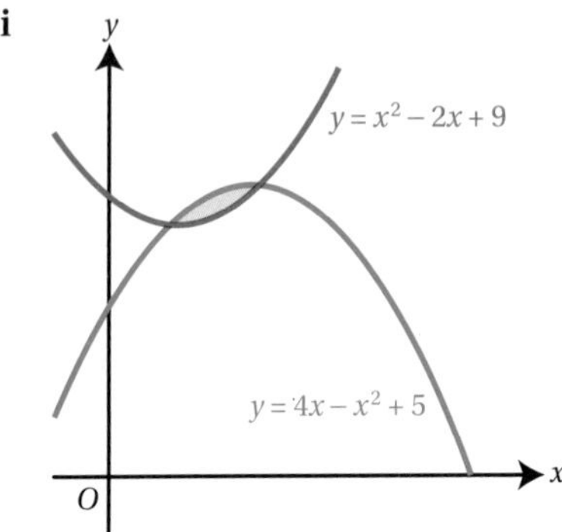

c **i**

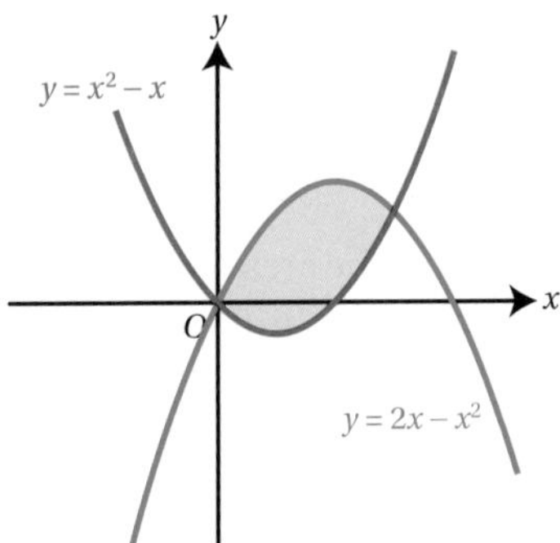

ii

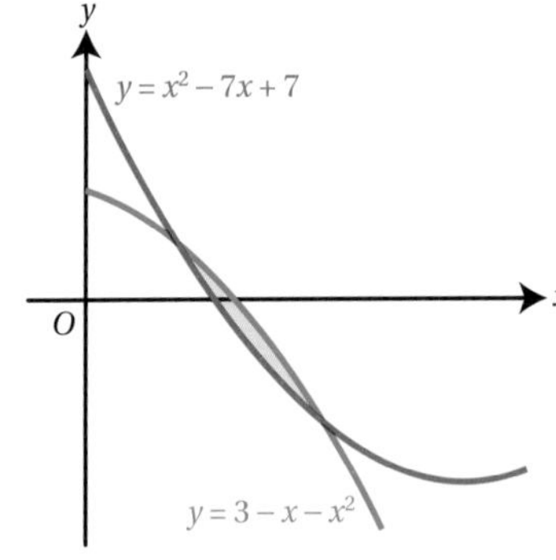

d **i**

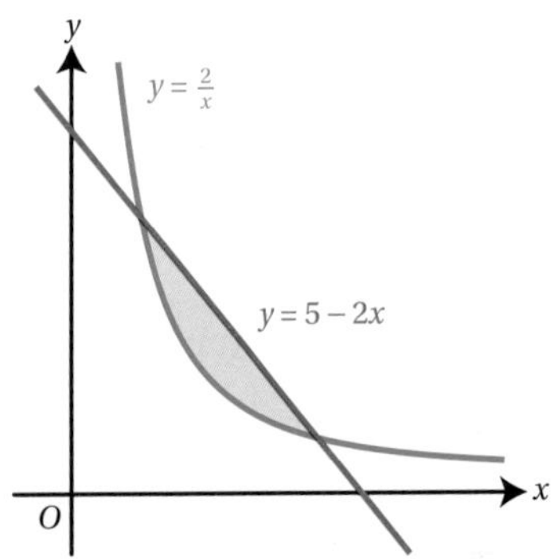

ii

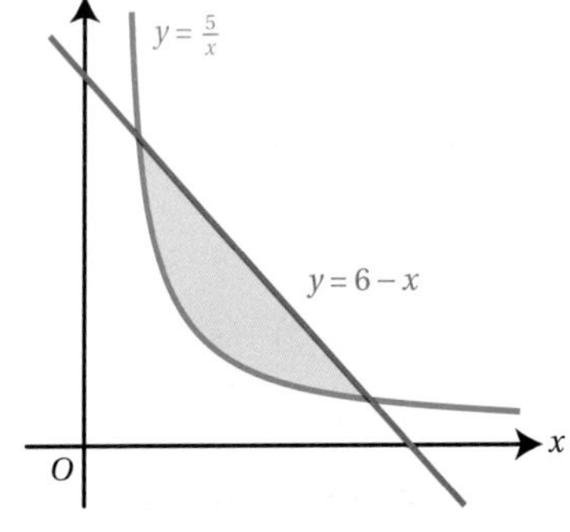

2 Find the shaded areas in the following diagrams.

a **i**

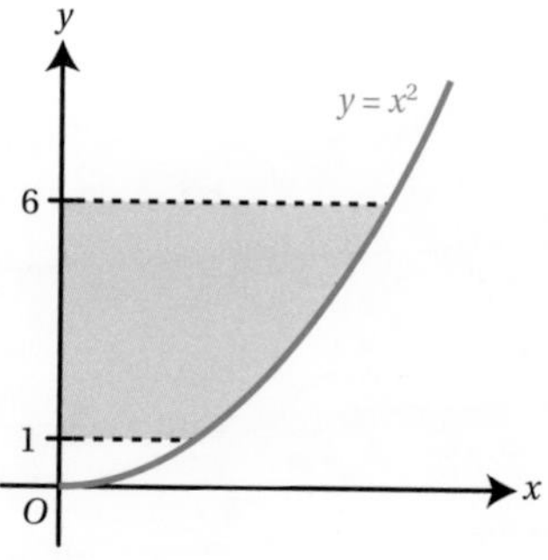

ii

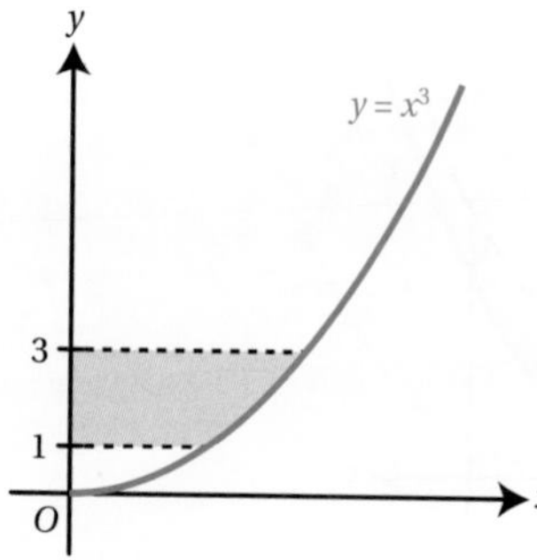

b **i**

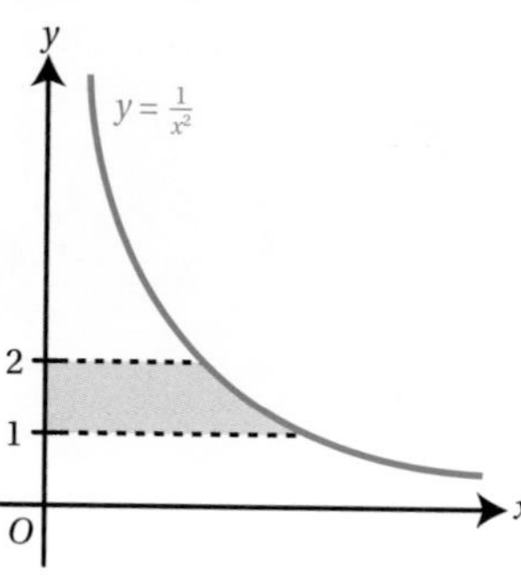

ii

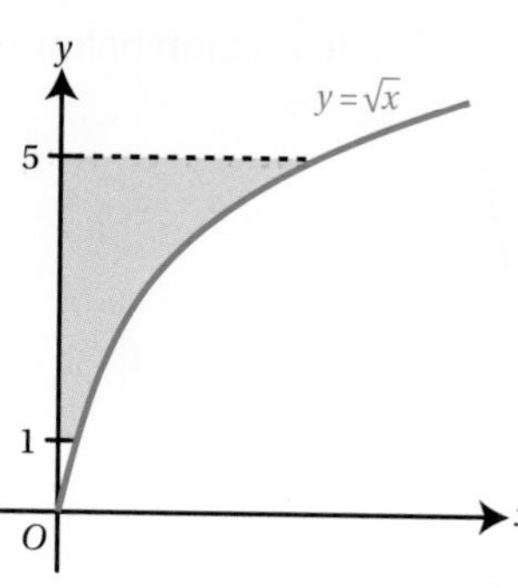

c **i**

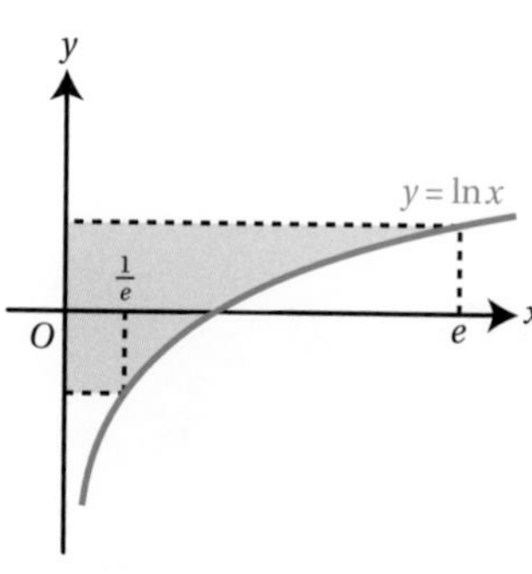

ii

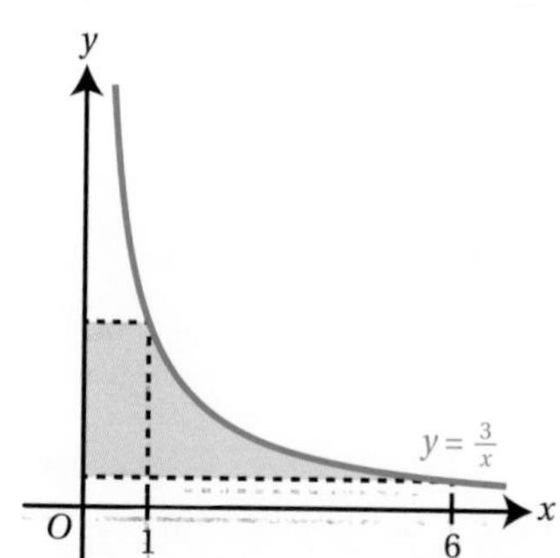

3 A part of the graph of $y = x^2 - 4x + 3$ is shown below. The curve crosses the x-axis at $x = 1$. The shaded region is enclosed by the curve, the x-axis and the lines $x = 0$ and $x = 2$.

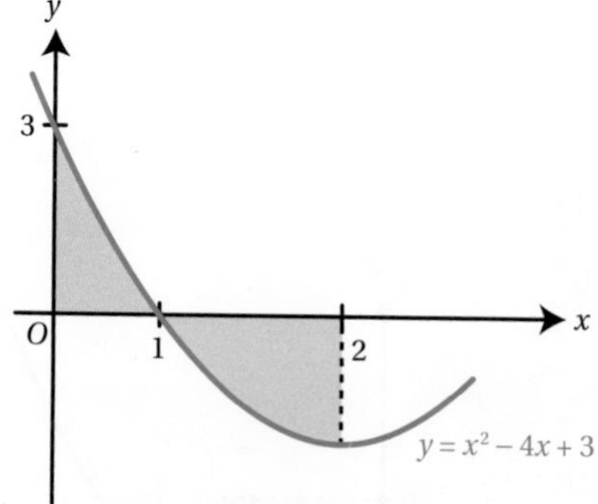

Find the area of the shaded region.

4 Find the area enclosed between the graphs of $y = x^2 + x - 2$ and $y = x + 2$.

5 The diagram shows the graphs of $y = e^x$ and $y = x^2$. Find the exact value of the shaded area.

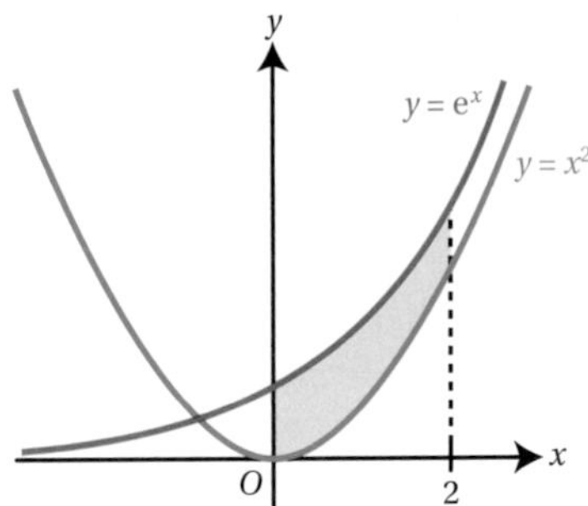

6 Show that the area of the shaded region below is $\frac{9}{2}$.

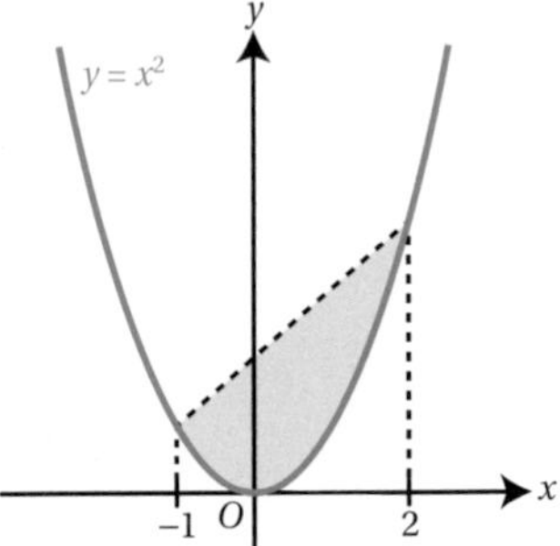

7 The diagram below shows the curve $y = \sqrt{x}$.

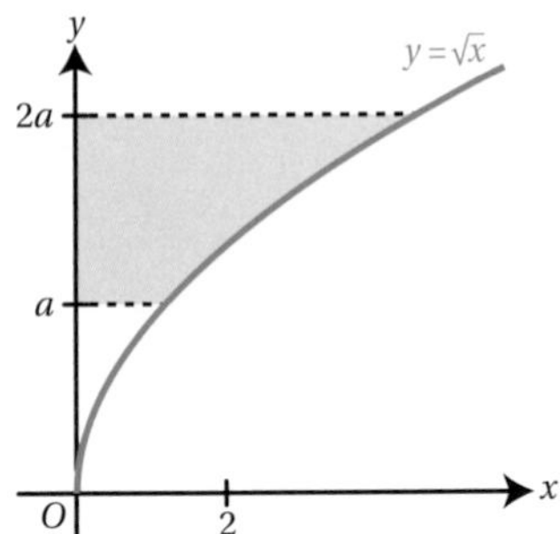

If the shaded area is 504, find the value of a.

8 Find the exact value of the area enclosed by the graph of $y = \ln(x+1)$, the line $y = 2$ and the y-axis.

9 Find the exact value of the area between the graphs of $y = \frac{5}{x}$ and $y = 6 - x$.

10 Find the total area enclosed between the graphs of $y = x(x-4)^2$ and $y = 4x - x^2$.

11 The area enclosed between the curve $y = x^2$ and the line $y = mx$ is $10\frac{2}{3}$. Find the value of m if $m > 0$.

12 The diagram below shows the graph of $y = x^2$.

Prove that the area of the orange region is equal to twice the area of the blue region for all values of a.

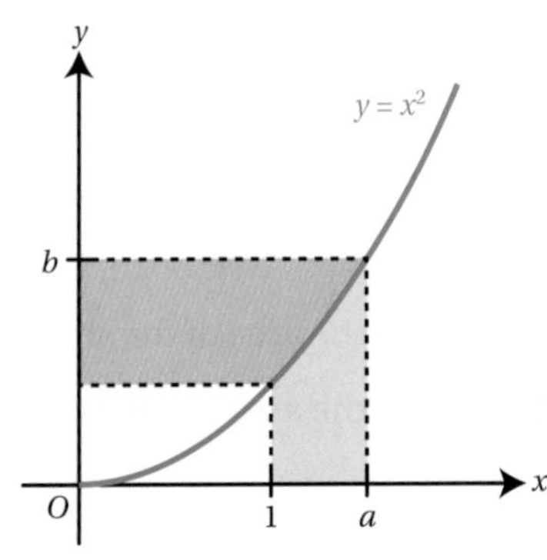

Checklist of learning and understanding

- A convex curve has $\frac{d^2y}{dx^2} > 0$; a concave curve has $\frac{d^2y}{dx^2} < 0$.
- At a point of inflection, $\frac{d^2y}{dx^2} = 0$ and the curve changes from convex to concave, or vice versa.
- Parametric equations are a way of describing a curve where both x- and y-coordinates are given in terms of a parameter (usually called t or θ).
  - Each parameter value corresponds to a single point on the curve.
- The gradient of a curve given in a parametric form is $\frac{dy}{dx} = \frac{\left(\frac{dy}{dt}\right)}{\left(\frac{dx}{dt}\right)}$.
- The area between the x-axis and a part of a curve with parametric equations $(x(t), y(t))$ is given by $\int_{t_1}^{t_2} y\frac{dx}{dt}\,dt$, where t_1 and t_2 are the parameter values at the end points.
- The chain rule can be used to connect rates of change of two related variables. If u depends on t, and y depends on u, then $\frac{dy}{dt} = \frac{dy}{du} \times \frac{du}{dt}$. You often need the geometric context of the question to work out how y depends on u.
- The area enclosed between two curves with equations $y = f(x)$ and $y = g(x)$ is given by $\int_a^b (f(x) - g(x))\,dx$, where a and b are x-coordinates of the intersection points.
- The area between a curve, the y-axis and the lines $y = c$ and $y = d$ is given by $\int_c^d g(y)\,dy$, where $x = g(y)$ is the expression for x in terms of y.

Mixed practice 12

1 Find the coordinates of the point of inflection on the graph of $y=\frac{x^3}{6}-x^2+x$.

2 A curve has parametric equations $x=3t^2$, $y=2t-t^3$.

a Show that the point $P(3, 1)$ lies on the curve, and find the value of t at this point.

b Find the equation of the tangent to the curve at P.

3 The diagram shows the graph of $y=(x-3)^2$ with a horizontal line drawn through its y-intercept. Find the exact value of the shaded area.

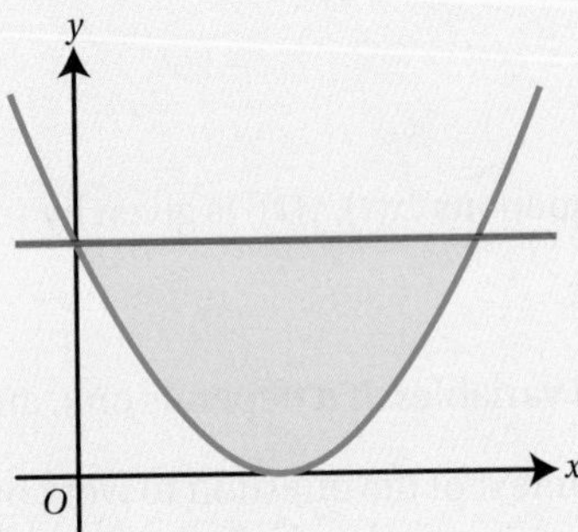

4 **a** Find $\int_0^3 x^2-1\,dx$.

b The graph of $y=x^2-1$ is shown below. The shaded region is bounded by the curve, the x-axis and the lines $x=0$ and $x=3$.

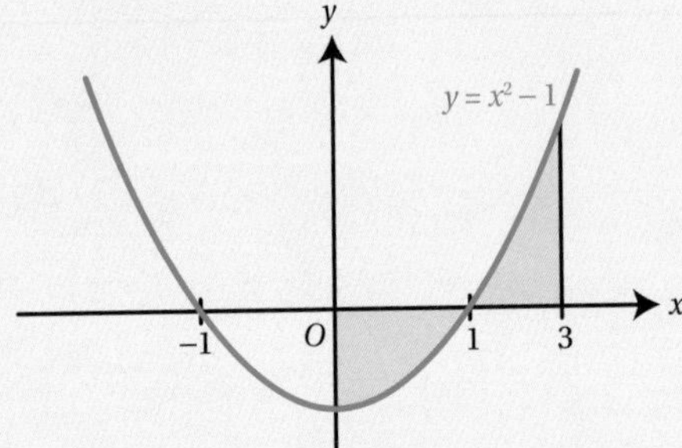

Find the area of the shaded region.

 5

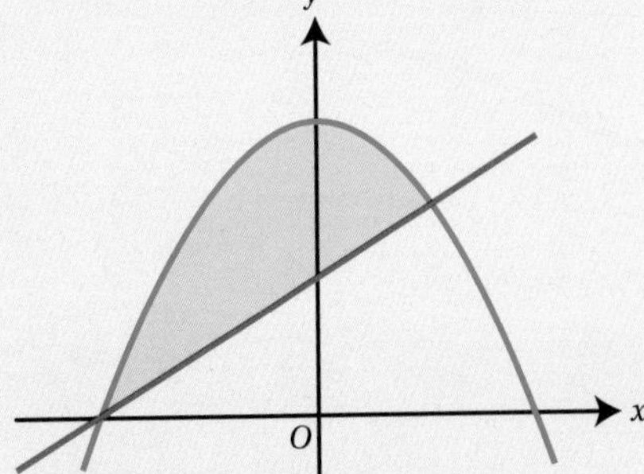

The diagram shows the curve $y=4-x^2$ and the line $y=x+2$.

i Find the x-coordinates of the points of intersection of the curve and the line.

ii Use integration to find the area of the shaded region bounded by the line and the curve.

6 The diagram below shows the graph of $y = \sqrt{x}$.

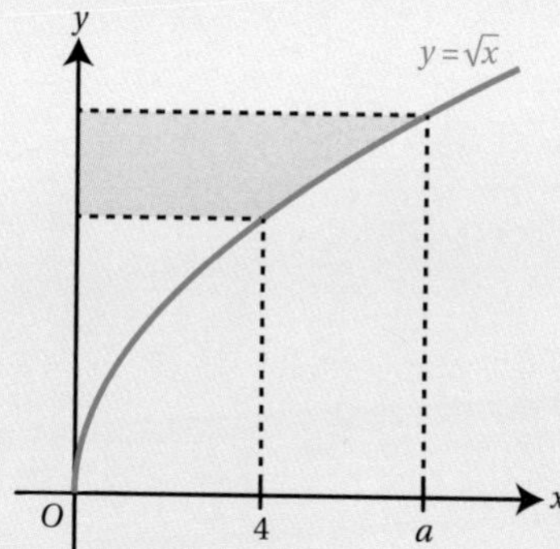

The shaded area is 39 units. Find the value of a.

7 **a** Find the coordinates of the stationary points on the graph of $y = x^4 - x^5$ and determine their nature.

b Prove that the graph has one non-horizontal point of inflection.

8 The curve shown in the diagram has parametric equations $x = 8t^3$, $y = 12t^2$ for $t \geqslant 0$. A tangent to the curve is drawn at the point (64, 48). Find the shaded area enclosed between the curve, the tangent and the y-axis.

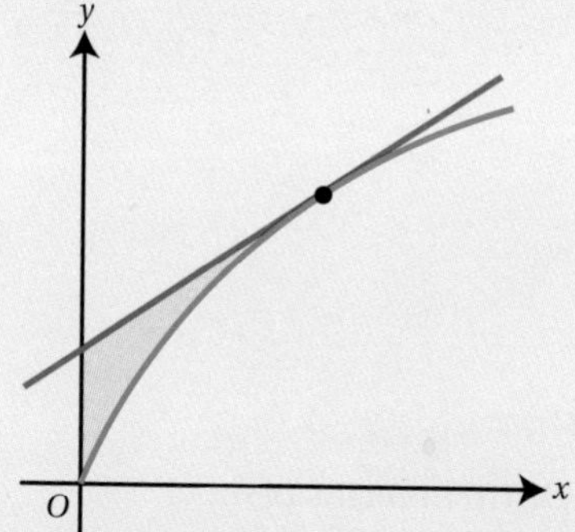

9 **a** Solve the equation $\sin x = \sin 2x$ for $0 \leqslant x \leqslant \pi$.

b The diagram shows the curves $y = \sin x$ and $y = \sin 2x$. Find the exact value of the shaded area.

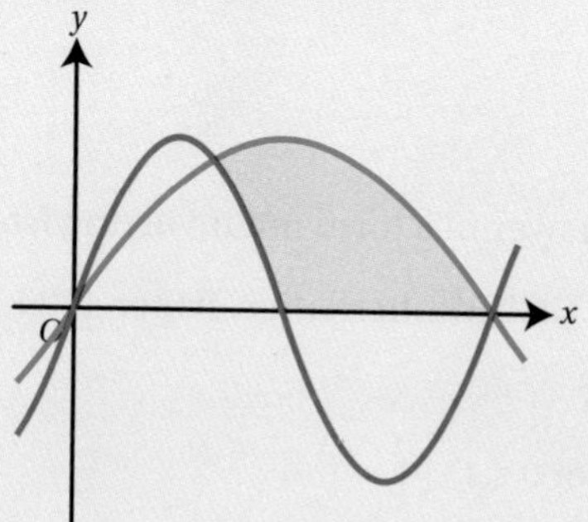

10 Consider the graph of $y = x\sin 2x$ for $x \in [0, 2\pi]$.

a Show that the x-coordinates of the points of inflection satisfy $\tan 2x = \frac{1}{x}$.

b Use graphs to find the number of points of inflection on the graph.

11 The diagram shows a part of the graph of $y = x^n$ for $n > 1$.

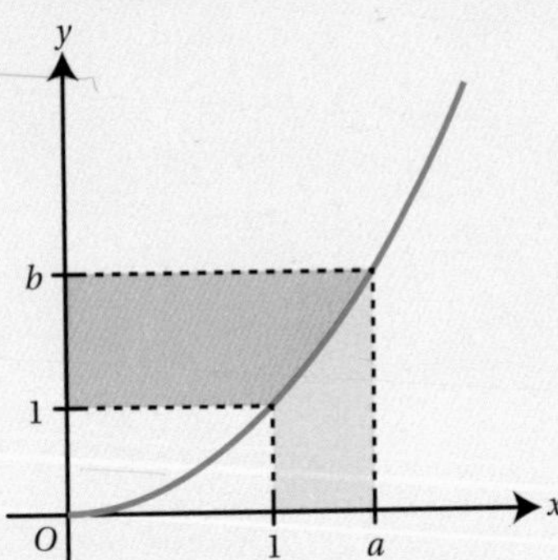

The orange area is three times as large as the blue area. Find the value of n.

12 Prove that the function $f(x) = x^3 \cos x$ has a stationary point of inflection at the origin.

13 The diagram shows an isosceles right-angled triangle of side 100 cm. Point D is moving along the side AB towards point B so that the area of the trapezium $DBCE$ is decreasing at the constant rate of $18\text{ cm}^2\text{ s}^{-1}$.

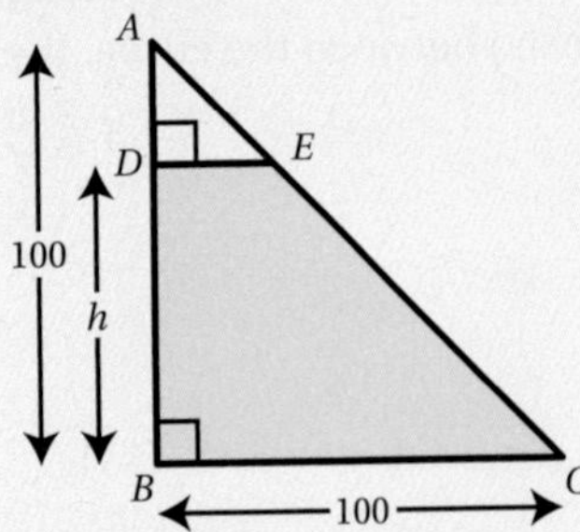

Let $BD = h$.

a Write down an expression for the area of the trapezium $DBCE$ in terms of h.

b Show that $\frac{dh}{dt} = \frac{18}{h-100}$.

Initially point D is at vertex A.

c Given that $h = 100 - k\sqrt{t}$, find the value of k.

14 The parametric equations of a curve are $x = \frac{t+2}{t+1}$, $y = \frac{2}{t+3}$.

i Show that $\frac{dy}{dx} > 0$.

ii Find the cartesian equation of the curve, giving your answer in a form not involving fractions.

15 A particle, P, moves in a straight line with velocity given by

$$v = 3\mathrm{e}^{-t}(\cos t - \sin t)\text{ m s}^{-1} \text{ for } 0 \leqslant t \leqslant 4$$

a Find the times when P is instantaneously at rest.

b Find the total distance travelled in the first π seconds of motion, giving your answer to 3 significant figures.

16 Show that the shaded area in the diagram below is $\frac{9}{2}$.

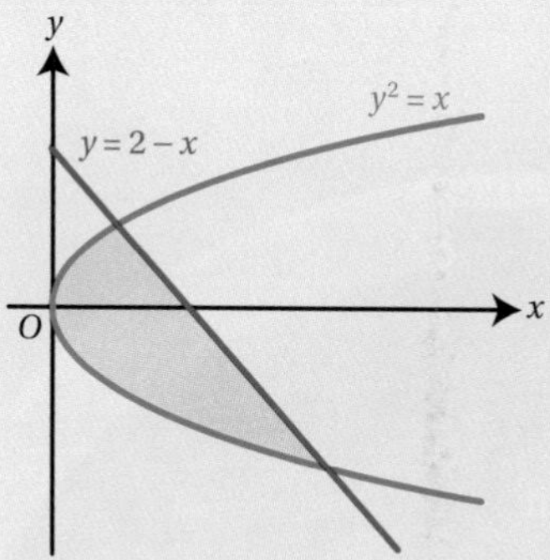

17 The ellipse shown in the diagram has parametric equations $x = 5\cos\theta, y = 2\sin\theta$, with $\theta \in [0, 2\pi]$.

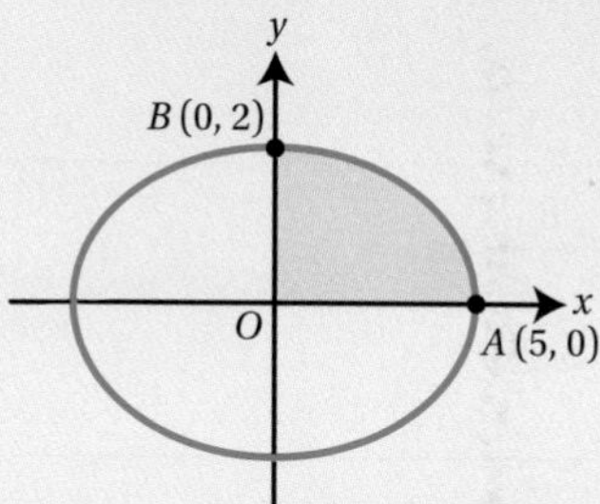

a State the values of θ at the points marked A and B.

b Find the shaded area and, hence, state the total area enclosed by the ellipse.

18 The graph below shows $y = f'(x)$.

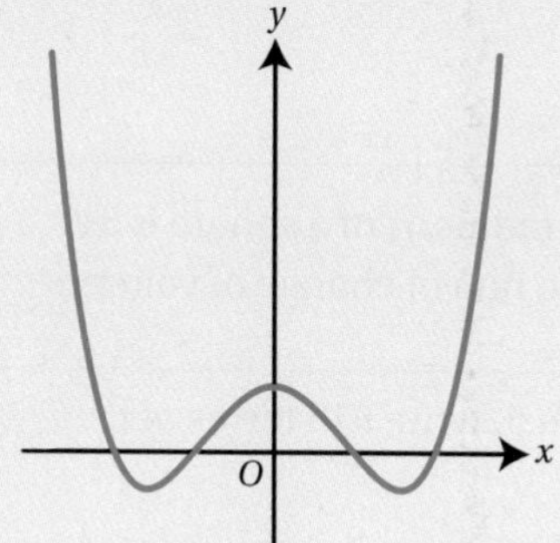

On a sketch of this graph:

a Mark points corresponding to a local minimum of $f(x)$ with an A.

b Mark points corresponding to a local maximum of $f(x)$ with a B.

c Mark points corresponding to a point of inflection of $f(x)$ with a C.

19 **a** Show that $5a^2 + 4ax - x^2 = (5a - x)(x + a)$.

b Find the coordinates of the points of intersection of the graphs $y = 5a^2 + 4ax - x^2$ and $y = x^2 - a^2$.

c Find the area enclosed between these two graphs.

d Show that the fraction of this area above the axis is independent of a and state the value that this fraction takes.

13 Differential equations

In this chapter you will learn:

- how to solve differential equations of the form $\frac{dy}{dx} = f(x)g(y)$
- how to write differential equations in a variety of contexts
- how to interpret a solution of a differential equation and decide whether it is realistic in the given context.

Before you start…

Chapter 11	You should know how to integrate using partial fractions and simplify the answer using log rules.	1 Integrate and simplify $\int \frac{8}{4-x^2}\,dx$.
Chapter 11	You should know how to use integration by substitution and by parts.	2 Integrate: a $\int \frac{4x}{x^2+3}\,dx$ b $\int x^2 \ln x\,dx$
Chapter 11	You should know how to integrate using trigonometric identities.	3 Find $\int \tan^2 2x\,dx$.
Chapter 12	You should know how to write equations involving related rates of change.	4 The rate of change of the radius, r, of a sphere is $5\sqrt{r}$. Find an expression for the rate of change of volume.
Student Book 1, Chapter 7	You should know how to rearrange expressions involving exponents and logarithms.	5 Given that $\ln(v-3) = t + \ln 5$, write v in terms of t.
Student Book 1, Chapter 21	You should know how to draw force diagrams and find net force.	6 An object of weight 35 N falls under gravity. The magnitude of the air resistance is 8 N. Find the net force on the object.

Modelling using differential equations

In Student Book 1, Chapter 19 you looked at problems that involved velocity as the rate of change of displacement, and acceleration as the rate of change of velocity. There are many processes in nature that can be modelled by equations involving the rate of change of some variable, such as population growth and cooling of bodies. In fact Newton's well-known Second Law actually states that force is equal to the rate of change of momentum. To find the underlying variable from these rates of change involves solving differential equations.

In this chapter you look at forming differential equations with emphasis on real-world applications, and at a method for solving a particular type of differential equation.

Section 1: Introduction to differential equations

To solve a **differential equation** means to go from an equation involving derivatives to one without. You have done this already for the case where the equation can be written in the form $\frac{dy}{dx} = f(x)$.

As an example, consider the differential equation $\frac{dy}{dx} = 3x^2$. To solve this differential equation all that is needed is integration: $y = \int 3x^2 \, dx = x^3 + c$. Because of the constant of integration, you find that there is not just one solution to the differential equation; it could be any one of a **family of solutions**:

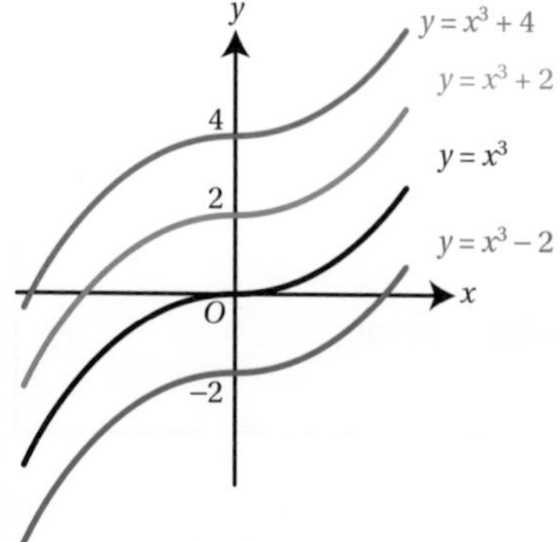

All the curves have the same gradient function, so they have the same shape. The solution $y = x^3 + c$ is called the **general solution** to the differential equation. You may also be told that the curve passes through the point (0, 2). This is called a **boundary condition** or **initial condition** and it allows you to narrow down the general solution to the **particular solution**, in this case $y = x^3 + 2$.

Sometimes it is necessary to rearrange the equation before integrating.

WORKED EXAMPLE 13.1

Find the particular solution of the differential equation

$$\left(x^2 - 2\right)\frac{dy}{dx} = 3x$$

with the boundary condition $y = \ln 2$ when $x = 2$.

Continues on next page ...

$\frac{dy}{dx} = \frac{3x}{x^2 - 2}$ — You need to write the equation in the form $\frac{dy}{dx} = f(x)$.

$y = \int \frac{3x}{x^2 - 2}\,dx$ — Then integrate.

Integration by substitution:

$u = x^2 - 2 \Rightarrow \frac{du}{dx} = 2x$ — Since the numerator is related to the derivative of the denominator, a substitution should work.

$dx = \frac{1}{2x}\,du$

$y = \int \frac{3x}{u}\frac{1}{2x}\,du$ — Make the substitution, and simplify as much as possible.

$= \int \frac{3}{2u}\,du$

$= \frac{3}{2}\ln|u| + c$ — Remember $+c$; this is the general solution.

$= \frac{3}{2}\ln|x^2 - 2| + c$

When $x = 2$, $y = \ln 2$ — Use the boundary condition to find c.

$\frac{3}{2}\ln 2 + c = \ln 2$

$\Rightarrow c = -\frac{1}{2}\ln 2$

So

$y = \frac{3}{2}\ln|x^2 - 2| - \frac{1}{2}\ln 2$ — This value of c gives the particular solution.

EXERCISE 13A

1 Find the general solution of the following differential equations.

a **i** $\frac{dy}{dx} = 3\sin 2x$ **ii** $\frac{dy}{dx} = 4\cos\left(\frac{x}{3}\right)$

b **i** $3\frac{dy}{dx} - 2e^{2x} = 0$ **ii** $4e^{x/2} - \frac{dy}{dx} = 0$

c **i** $\cos^2 x\frac{dy}{dx} = 3$ **ii** $\cot^2 x\frac{dy}{dx} = 1$

d **i** $x^3\frac{dy}{dx} = \ln x$ **ii** $\cos^2 x\frac{dy}{dx} = \sin x$

2 Find the particular solution of the following differential equations.

a **i** $\frac{dy}{dx} = \frac{2}{\sqrt{3x+9}}$, $y = 2$ when $x = 0$ **ii** $\frac{dy}{dx} = \frac{1}{\sqrt{4-x}}$, $y = 1$ when $x = 3$

b **i** $(x^2+1)\frac{dy}{dx} = 2x$, $y = 0$ when $x = 1$ **ii** $2x\frac{dy}{dx} = x^2 + 1$, $y = 1$ when $x = 1$

c **i** $\frac{1}{2}e^{3x}\frac{dy}{dx} = 3$, $y = 0$ when $x = 0$ **ii** $e^{2x-1}\frac{dy}{dx} = 4$, $y = 0$ when $x = \frac{1}{2}$

d **i** $\sec x\frac{dy}{dx} = \sin^3 x$, $y = \frac{13}{64}$ when $x = \frac{\pi}{3}$ **ii** $\cos^3 x\frac{dy}{dx} = \sin x$, $y = 5$ when $x = \frac{\pi}{4}$

Section 2: Separable differential equations

In the previous section you looked at differential equations where $\frac{dy}{dx}$ depends just on x. But there are situations where the gradient depends on y, or on both variables; for example, $\frac{dy}{dx} = x^2 y$.

You can't solve this equation by direct integration as the right-hand side contains y. However, if you divide through by y, the equation becomes $\frac{1}{y}\frac{dy}{dx} = x^2$. You can then integrate both sides of the equation with respect to x.

$$\int \frac{1}{y}\frac{dy}{dx}\,dx = \int x^2\,dx$$

However, $\int \frac{1}{y}\frac{dy}{dx}\,dx = \int \frac{1}{y}\,dy$ so the equation above becomes

$$\int \frac{1}{y}\,dy = \int x^2\,dx \qquad (*)$$

$$\Rightarrow \ln|y| = \frac{x^3}{3} + c$$

$$\Rightarrow y = e^{x^3/3+c} = A\,e^{x^3/3}$$

Tip

On the final line we used $e^{x^3/3+c} = e^c e^{x^3/3} = Ae^{x^3/3}$, where A is a new arbitrary constant.

Just as with integration by substitution, though, you get the same results from just splitting up $\frac{dy}{dx}$ as if it were a fraction when you separate the x terms and y terms to different sides; this leads straight to (*).

This method of solving differential equations is called **separation of variables**. If the equation can be written in the form $\frac{dy}{dx} = f(x)g(y)$, then the procedure is as follows.

Key point 13.1

To solve a differential equation by separation of variables:

- Get all of the x terms on one side and all of the y terms on the other side by multiplication or division.
- Separate $\frac{dy}{dx}$ as if it were a fraction.
- Integrate both sides.

WORKED EXAMPLE 13.2

Solve the equation

$$\frac{dy}{dx} = (1.2 + 0.4x)y$$

given that $y = 32$ when $x = 0$.

$\frac{1}{y}\frac{dy}{dx} = 1.2 + 0.4x$ — Use multiplication or division to get the y term onto the left-hand side.

$\int \frac{1}{y}\,dy = \int (1.2 + 0.4x)\,dx$ — Separate $\frac{dy}{dx}$ and integrate.

Continues on next page ...

$\ln|y| = 1.2x + 0.2x^2 + c$ — Since the difference of two constants is just another constant, you need $+c$ on only one side.

When $x = 0, y = 32$:

$\ln 32 = 0 + 0 + c$ — Use the initial condition to find c.

$\Rightarrow c = \ln 32$

Therefore:

$\ln|y| = 1.2x + 0.2x^2 + \ln 32$

$\Rightarrow y = e^{1.2x+0.2x^2+\ln 32}$ — Since $y > 0$ at $x = 0$, the curve will take positive values for y, so $|y|$ can be written as y.

$= 32e^{1.2x+0.2x^2}$ — Using $e^{\ln 32} = 32$.

Sometimes the equation needs to be factorised first to get it into the correct form.

WORKED EXAMPLE 13.3

Show that the general solution to the differential equation $\frac{dy}{dx} = xy - x$ can be written as $y = 1 + Ae^{0.5x^2}$.

$\frac{dy}{dx} = x(y-1)$ — You can use separation of variables if you can write the equation in the form $\frac{dy}{dx} = f(x)g(y)$.

$\int \frac{1}{y-1}\,dy = \int x\,dx$ — Separate variables: divide by $y - 1$ and multiply by dx. Then integrate.

$\ln|y-1| = 0.5x^2 + c$

$|y-1| = e^{0.5x^2+c}$

But since $y - 1 > 0$:

$y - 1 = e^{0.5x^2+c}$

$= e^{0.5x^2}e^c$ — Since e^c is a constant, re-label it as A.

$= Ae^{0.5x^2}$

$\therefore y = 1 + Ae^{0.5x^2}$

WORK IT OUT 13.1

Find the general solution of the differential equation $\frac{dy}{dx} = xy$.

Which of the following solutions is correct? Identify the mistake in the other two.

Solution 1	Solution 2	Solution 3
$\frac{dy}{dx} = xy$ $\Rightarrow y = \int xy\, dx$ $= y\int x\, dx$ $= y\frac{x^2}{2} + c$ $\Rightarrow y\left(1 - \frac{x^2}{2}\right) = c$ $\Rightarrow y = \frac{c}{1 - \frac{x^2}{2}}$	$\frac{dy}{dx} = xy$ $\Rightarrow \frac{1}{y}\frac{dy}{dx} = x$ $\Rightarrow \int \frac{1}{y}\, dy = \int x\, dx$ $\Rightarrow \ln\lvert y\rvert = \frac{x^2}{2} + c$ $\Rightarrow y = Ae^{\frac{x^2}{2}}$	$\frac{dy}{dx} = xy$ $\Rightarrow \frac{1}{y}\frac{dy}{dx} = x$ $\Rightarrow \int \frac{1}{y}\, dy = \int x\, dx$ $\Rightarrow \ln\lvert y\rvert = \frac{x^2}{2} + c$ $\Rightarrow y = e^{\frac{x^2}{2}} + c$

If $\frac{dy}{dx}$ depends just on y, you can take a slight shortcut, using the fact that $\frac{dx}{dy} = \frac{1}{\left(\frac{dy}{dx}\right)}$.

Key point 13.2

If $\frac{dy}{dx} = f(y)$ then $x = \int \frac{1}{f(y)}\, dy$.

Rewind

$\frac{dx}{dy}$ is the derivative of the inverse function, which you met in Chapter 10, Section 5.

WORKED EXAMPLE 13.4

Newton's law of cooling states that the rate of change of temperature of a cooling body is proportional to the difference between the body's temperature and the surrounding temperature.

A cup of coffee cools in the room where the air temperature is 21 °C. The temperature of the coffee, θ °C, satisfies the differential equation

$$\frac{d\theta}{dt} = -0.054(\theta - 21)$$

where t is the time, measured in minutes.

The initial temperature of the coffee is 94 °C. Find the temperature of the coffee after 6 minutes.

Continues on next page ...

$$\frac{dt}{d\theta}=\frac{1}{-0.054(\theta-21)}$$

Integrate with respect to θ.

So:

$$t=\int\frac{1}{-0.054(\theta-21)}d\theta$$

$$=-\frac{1}{0.054}\ln|\theta-21|+c$$

When $t=0$, $\theta=94$:

Find c using the initial conditions.

$$0=-\frac{1}{0.054}\ln|94-21|+c$$

$$\Rightarrow c=\frac{\ln 73}{0.054}\approx 79.5$$

When $t=6$:

Substitute in the given value of t before rearranging.

$$6=-\frac{1}{0.054}\ln|\theta-21|+79.5$$

$$\Rightarrow \ln(\theta-21)=73.5\times 0.054=3.97$$

Because of the context of the question, you are interested only in the solution in which θ decreases from 94. Hence, $\theta - 21$ is positive, so you can remove the modulus signs.

$$\Rightarrow \theta=21+e^{3.97}$$

$$=73.8\,°C$$

EXERCISE 13B

1 Find the particular solutions of the following differential equations, giving your answer in the form $y=f(x)$, simplified as far as possible.

a **i** $\frac{dy}{dx}=\frac{2x^2}{3y}$, $y=0$ when $x=0$ **ii** $\frac{dy}{dx}=4xy^2$, $y=1$ when $x=0$

b **i** $\frac{dy}{dx}=\frac{4y}{x}$, $y=2$ when $x=1$ **ii** $\frac{dy}{dx}=-3x^2y$, $y=3$ when $x=0$

2 Find the particular solutions of the following differential equations. You do not need to give the equation for y explicitly.

a **i** $\frac{dy}{dx}=\frac{\sin x}{\cos y}$, $y=0$ when $x=\frac{\pi}{3}$ **ii** $\frac{dy}{dx}=\frac{\sec^2 x}{\sec^2 y}$, $y=0$ when $x=\frac{\pi}{3}$

b **i** $\frac{dy}{dx}=x^2y$, $y=1$ when $x=0$ **ii** $\frac{dy}{dx}=\frac{y^2}{x}$, $y=1$ when $x=1$

c **i** $\frac{dy}{dx}=2e^{x+2y}$, $y=0$, when $x=0$ **ii** $\frac{dy}{dx}=e^{x-y}$, $y=2$ when $x=0$

3 Find the general solution of the following differential equations, giving your answer in the form $y=f(x)$ simplified as far as possible.

a **i** $2y\frac{dy}{dx}=3x^2$ **ii** $\frac{1}{y^2}\frac{dy}{dx}=2x$

b **i** $x\frac{dy}{dx}=\sec y$ **ii** $(x-2)\frac{dy}{dx}=\cos^2 y$

c **i** $(x-1)\frac{dy}{dx}=x(y+3)$ **ii** $\frac{(1-x^2)dy}{dx}=xy+y$

Elevate

See Support sheet 13 for a further example of solving a separable differential equation and for more practice questions.

4. Solve the differential equation $\frac{dy}{dx} = 2y(1-x)$, given that when $x = 1$, $y = 1$. Give your answer in the form $y = f(x)$.

5. The function $H(t)$ satisfies the differential equation $t\frac{dH}{dt} = H$. When $t = 1$, $H = 2a$. Find the value of H when $t = 5$.

6. Given that $\frac{dN}{dt} = -kN$, where k is a positive constant, show that $N = Ae^{-kt}$.

7. Find the general solution of the differential equation $x\frac{dy}{dx} + 4 = y^2$, giving your answer in the form $y = f(x)$.

8. Given that $\frac{dy}{dx} = \sqrt{\frac{1-y^2}{1-x^2}}$ and that $y = \frac{\sqrt{3}}{2}$ when $x = \frac{1}{2}$, show that $2y = x\sqrt{k} + \sqrt{1-x^2}$, where k is a constant to be found.

Section 3: Modelling with differential equations

Now that you can solve various differential equations, we look at how such equations arise in a variety of contexts. There are many situations where you know (or it is reasonable to assume) what the rate of change of a quantity depends on. You can then write down and solve a differential equation to find out how the actual quantity behaves.

In many applications, the rate of change is with respect to time. For example, in mechanics, the acceleration is the rate of change of velocity, $a = \frac{dv}{dt}$. But you also know that $F = ma$, so the rate of change of velocity depends on the force acting on the object.

WORKED EXAMPLE 13.5

A skydiver of mass 60 kg jumps out of an aeroplane with zero initial velocity. The air resistance is proportional to velocity and may be modelled as $R = 0.8\,v$. Using $g = 9.8\text{ m s}^{-2}$, write and solve a differential equation to find an expression for the velocity of the skydiver in terms of time.

Forces on the skydiver:

Always start by drawing a force diagram.

The weight acts downwards and the air resistance upwards.

Net force:

$F = ma$

$60g - 0.8v = 60\frac{dv}{dt}$

Write Newton's second law equation, taking the positive direction to be downwards (because that's the direction of motion).

$\frac{dt}{dv} = \frac{60}{588 - 0.8v}$

Since the left-hand side is in terms of v, rewrite the equation in terms of $\frac{dt}{dv}$.

Also use $g = 9.8$.

Continues on next page ...

$t = \int \frac{60}{588 - 0.8v}\,\mathrm{d}v$

$= \frac{60}{-0.8}\ln|588 - 0.8v| + c$ — Integrate with respect to v.

$= -75\ln|588 - 0.8v| + c$

When $t = 0, v = 0$:

$0 = -75\ln 588 + c$ — Now use the initial condition.

$\Rightarrow c = 75\ln 588$

So:

$t = -75\ln|588 - 0.8v| + 75\ln 588$

$\Rightarrow \ln|588 - 0.8v| = \ln 588 - \frac{t}{75}$ — You need to express v in terms of t.

$\Rightarrow 588 - 0.8v = 588e^{-\frac{t}{75}}$

$\Rightarrow v = 735 - 735e^{-\frac{t}{75}}$

If $\ln A = \ln B - C$ then $A = e^{\ln B - C} = Be^{-C}$.

Since you are interested in the solution for which $v = 0$ initially, $588 - 0.8v$ is positive so you can remove the modulus sign.

Notice that in the penultimate line the modulus sign was removed. This is justified only if $588 - 0.8v \geqslant 0$; i.e. $v \leqslant 735$. Since initially $v = 0$, this is certainly true for some initial part of the motion. But you should ask whether eventually v becomes larger than 735; if it does then the equation needs to be changed. Looking at the final solution, $e^{-\frac{t}{75}}$ is always positive, so v is in fact always less than 735 and your solution is valid for all t. Therefore, according to our model, it is impossible for v to breach the 735 m s^{-1} barrier.

Focus on ...

There are a number of examples of modelling real-life situations with differential equations in Focus on ... Modelling 2.

Did you know?

In fact, $e^{-\frac{t}{75}}$ decreases and tends to zero, so v increases towards 735 without ever reaching it.

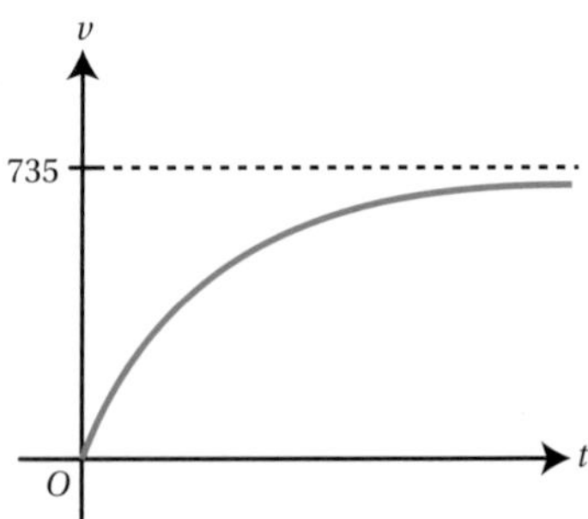

This is called *terminal velocity*. Of course, the object might hit the ground before getting close to terminal velocity.

Often you have a model where some constants are unknown. You can find them using experimental or observational information.

WORKED EXAMPLE 13.6

In a simple model of a population of bacteria, the growth rate is assumed to be proportional to the number of bacteria.

a Let N be the number of bacteria after t minutes. Initially there are 2000 bacteria and this number increases to 10 000 after 12 minutes. Write and solve a differential equation to find the number of bacteria after t minutes.

b Comment on one limitation of this model.

a $\frac{dN}{dt} = kN$

The rate of growth is $\frac{dN}{dt}$.
'Proportional to N' means you can write it as kN for some constant k.

$\frac{dt}{dN} = \frac{1}{kN}$

$\Rightarrow t = \frac{1}{k}\ln N + c$

You have information about t and N but not about $\frac{dN}{dt}$, so you need to solve the differential equation before you can put in the numbers. Since N is positive, you don't need modulus signs in $\ln|N|$.

When $t = 0, N = 2000$:

$0 = \frac{1}{k}\ln 2000 + c$

$\Rightarrow c = -\frac{1}{k}\ln 2000$

To find the constants c and k, use the two given conditions: first use $N = 2000$ initially (i.e. when $t = 0$).

When $t = 12, N = 10000$:

A second equation is needed to find k, so next use the condition that $N = 10\,000$ when $t = 12$.

$12 = \frac{1}{k}\ln 10000 - \frac{1}{k}\ln 2000$

$= \frac{1}{k}\ln 5$

Use $\ln A - \ln B = \ln\left(\frac{A}{B}\right)$.

$k = \frac{\ln 5}{12}$

$\therefore c = -\frac{12\ln 2000}{\ln 5}$

Now put k and c back in and rearrange the equation to get N in terms of t.

Check that you can follow all the steps!

So:

$t = \frac{12}{\ln 5}\ln N - \frac{12\ln 2000}{\ln 5}$

$t\ln 5 = 12\ln N - 12\ln 2000$

$= 12\ln\left(\frac{N}{2000}\right)$

$\Rightarrow \frac{N}{2000} = e^{\frac{t\ln 5}{12}}$

$N = 2000e^{\left(\frac{\ln 5}{12}\right)t}$

b This model predicts unlimited population growth, which is not realistic.

Exponential growth models often work initially, but need to be adapted for longer time periods.

Sometimes a problem has several variables and you need to use the geometric context and related rates of change to produce a single differential equation.

WORKED EXAMPLE 13.7

A cylindrical tank with cross-sectional area 5 m^2 and height 4 m is initially filled with water. The water leaks out of the tank through a small hole at the bottom at the rate of $0.08\sqrt{h}\text{ m}^3\text{s}^{-1}$, where h m is the height of water in the tank after t seconds.

a Find an equation for $\frac{dh}{dt}$ in terms of h.

b Hence, find how long it takes for the tank to empty.

a $V = 5h \Rightarrow \frac{dV}{dt} = \frac{dV}{dh}\frac{dh}{dt}$

$= 5\frac{dh}{dt}$

$\Rightarrow \frac{dh}{dt} = \frac{1}{5}\frac{dV}{dt}$

The given rate of change is for the volume, so you need to relate volume to the height.

You have

$\frac{dV}{dt} = -0.08\sqrt{h}$

so

$\frac{dh}{dt} = -0.016\sqrt{h}$

The rate of change is negative since the volume is decreasing.

b $\frac{dt}{dh} = \frac{1}{-0.016\sqrt{h}} = -62.5h^{-\frac{1}{2}}$

so

$t = -62.5\int h^{-\frac{1}{2}}\,dh$

Solve the equation by integrating $\frac{dt}{dh}$.

$= -125h^{\frac{1}{2}} + c$

When $t = 0$, $h = 4$:

$0 = -125\sqrt{4} + c$

Initially the tank is full.

$\Rightarrow c = 250$

When $h = 0$:

$t = -125\sqrt{h} + 250$

The tank is empty when $h = 0$.

$= 250$

The tank is empty after 250 seconds.

EXERCISE 13C

1 Write differential equations to describe the following situations. You do not need to solve the equations.

a **i** A population increases at the rate equal to 5 times the size of the population (N).

ii The mass of a substance (M) decreases at the rate equal to three times the current mass.

b **i** The rate of change of velocity is directly proportional to the velocity and inversely proportional to the square root of time.

ii The population size increases at a rate proportional to the square root of the population size (N) and to the cube root of time.

c i The area of a circular stain increases at a rate proportional to the square root of the radius. Find an equation for the rate of change of radius with respect to time.

ii The volume of a sphere decreases at a constant rate of $0.8\text{ m}^3\text{s}^{-1}$. Find an equation for the rate of decrease of the radius.

2 In a simple model for a population of bacteria, the rate of growth is proportional to the size of the population. When the population size (N) is 5000 bacteria, the rate of growth is 1000 bacteria/minute.

a Show that $\frac{dN}{dt} = 0.2N$.

Initially there were 700 bacteria.

b Solve the differential equation and predict the number of bacteria after 20 minutes.

3 The mass of a radioactive substance (M g) decays at a rate proportional to the mass. Initially the mass is 12 g and it decays at the rate of 2.4 g s^{-1}.

a Show that $\frac{dM}{dt} = -\frac{1}{5}M$.

b Find the amount of time it takes for the mass to halve.

4 A particle of mass 1.2 kg is moving with speed 8ms^{-1} in a straight line on a horizontal table. A resistance force is applied to the particle in the direction of motion. The magnitude of the force is proportional to the square of the speed, so that $|F| = 0.3v^2$.

a Show that $\frac{dv}{dt} = -0.25v^2$.

b Find an expression for the velocity in terms of time and, hence, find how long it takes for the speed to decrease below 2 ms^{-1}.

5 The population of fish in a lake, N thousand, can be modelled by the differential equation $\frac{dN}{dt} = (0.8 - 0.14t)N$, where t is the time, in years, since the fish were first introduced into the lake. Initially there were 2000 fish.

a Show that the population initially increases and find when it starts to decrease.

b Find the expression for N in terms of t.

c Hence, find the maximum population of fish in the lake.

d What does this model predict about the size of the population in the long term?

6 In Economics, there is a model that shows how the demand for a commodity (Q) depends on its price (P). It states that the rate of change of Q with respect to P is proportional to Q but inversely proportional to P.

a Explain how this model leads to the differential equation $\frac{1}{Q}\frac{dQ}{dP} = \frac{\varepsilon}{P}$, where ε is a negative constant (called *elasticity*).

b Find the general solution of this differential equation.

c Sketch the graph of Q against P, and describe how demand depends on price, in the following cases.

i $\varepsilon = -1$ ii $\varepsilon = 0$

7 Newton's law of cooling states that the rate of change of temperature of a body is proportional to the difference in temperature between the body and its surroundings.

A bottle of milk has a temperature of 5 °C when it is initially taken out of the fridge. It is placed on the table in the kitchen, where the room temperature is 19 °C. Initially, the milk is warming up at a rate of 5.7 °C per minute.

4.2°C

a Show that $\frac{d\theta}{dt} = 0.3(19 - \theta)$, where θ °C is the temperature of the milk and t is the time, in minutes, since the milk was taken out of the fridge.

b Solve the differential equation and, hence, find how long it takes, to the nearest minute, for the temperature of the milk to reach the kitchen temperature, correct to the nearest degree.

8 A particle of mass 3 kg is pulled through liquid using a light inextensible string. The tension in the string is 12 N. The resistance force is proportional to the velocity and equals $2.4\,v$. The particle starts from rest.

a Find an expression for the velocity after time, t.

b Describe the velocity of the particle for large values of t.

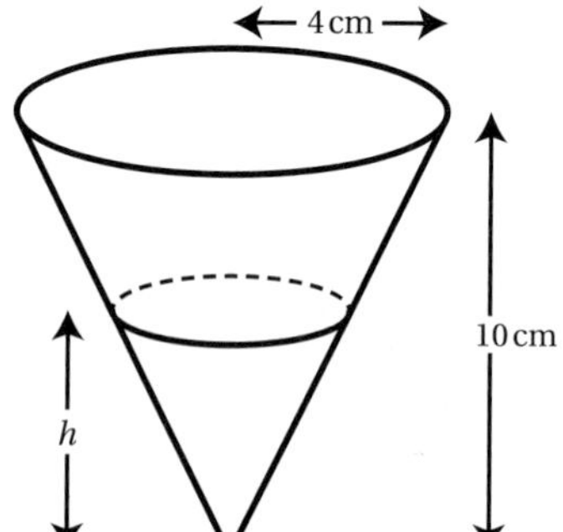

9 An inverted cone has base radius 4 cm and height 10 cm.

The cone is filled with water at a constant rate of $80\,\text{cm}^3\,\text{s}^{-1}$.

a Show that the height of water (h) satisfies the differential equation

$$\pi h^2 \frac{dh}{dt} = 500.$$

b Given that the cone is initially empty, find how long it takes to fill it.

10 A particle of mass 0.4 kg is moving at a speed of 10 m s^{-1} when it enters a viscous liquid at a point, B. Inside the liquid the resistance force is proportional to the velocity, and initially equal to 1.2 N. Apart from the resistance and the weight, no other forces are acting on the particle.

a Show that the velocity of the particle satisfies the differential equation $\frac{dv}{dt} = -0.3\,v$.

b Find an expression for the velocity of the particle t seconds after entering the liquid.

c Find the displacement of the particle from point B, and describe what happens to the displacement for large values of t.

11 A population model for two competing species postulates that their numbers, x and y (in appropriate units), vary with time according to the equations:

$$\frac{dx}{dt} = x - xy, \; \frac{dy}{dt} = -y + xy.$$

a Find the range of values of x and y for which both variables are increasing.

b Find an expression for $\frac{dy}{dx}$.

c Solve this differential equation to show that $ye^{-y} = \frac{A}{x}e^x$ for some constant A.

Checklist of learning and understanding

- A differential equation is an equation for the derivative of a function. To solve a differential equation means to find an expression for the function itself.
- Some differential equations can be solved by separation of variables: Write the equation in the form $g(y)\frac{dy}{dx} = f(x)$ and integrate both sides.
- Initial conditions can be used to find the constant of integration.
- Differential equations often describe the rate of change of a quantity; this is the derivative with respect to time.
- The rate of change is often proportional to one of the variables. You may need to use given information to find the constant of proportionality.
- Sometimes a problem involves more than one variable and you need to use related rates of change to write a differential equation.

Mixed practice 13

1. Solve the differential equation $\frac{dy}{dx} = 2xy - 6x$, given that $y = 4$ when $x = 0$. Give your answer in the form $y = f(x)$.

2. Find the particular solution of the differential equation $\frac{dy}{dx} = \cos x \cos^2 y$ such that $y = \frac{\pi}{4}$ when $x = \frac{\pi}{6}$.

3. In a chemical reaction, the amount of the reactant (M g) follows the differential equation $\frac{dM}{dt} = 3 - 0.5M$.

   Initially there was 2 g of the reactant. Show that $M = A - Be^{-\frac{t}{2}}$, where A and B are constants to be found.

4. **i** Find the general solution of the differential equation

   $$\frac{\sec^2 y}{\cos^2(2x)} \frac{dy}{dx} = 2.$$

   ii For the particular solution in which $y = \frac{1}{4}\pi$ when $x = 0$, find the value of y when $x = \frac{1}{6}\pi$.

   © OCR, GCE Mathematics, Paper 4724, January 2007

5. A population of fish initially contains 250 fish and increases at the rate of 10 fish per month. Let N be the number of fish after t months.
   In a simple model of population growth, the rate of increase is directly proportional to the population size.

   a Show that $\frac{dN}{dt} = 0.04N$.

   b Solve the differential equation and find how long it takes for the number of fish to reach 1000.

   c Comment on the long-term suitability of this model.

   An improved model takes into account seasonal variation:

   $$\frac{dN}{dt} = 0.04N\left(1 + 2.5\cos\left(\frac{\pi t}{6}\right)\right)$$

   d Given that initially there are 250 fish, find an expression for the size of the population after t months.

6. A model for a relationship between the price of a commodity (P) and the demand for the commodity (Q) states that $\frac{dQ}{dP} = \frac{\varepsilon Q}{P}$, where ε is the elasticity.

   a Find the general solution to this differential equation.

   b Describe the relationship between the price and demand when $\varepsilon = -\frac{1}{2}$.

   c For most commodities, $\varepsilon \leqslant 0$. Suggest, with a reason, what sort of commodity might have $\varepsilon > 0$.

7. A cylindrical tank has radius 2 m and height 12 m. The height is being filled with water so that $\frac{dV}{dt} = \frac{\pi}{5}(10 - h)^2$. Initially the tank is empty.

   a Show that $20\frac{dh}{dt} = (10 - h)^2$ and, hence, find an expression for the height of water in the tank at time t.

   b By writing your expression in the form $h = A - \frac{B}{t+2}$, or otherwise, determine whether the tank will ever completely fill with water.

8 A ball of mass 300 g falls vertically downwards. When the velocity of the ball is v m s^{-1} the air resistance has magnitude 1.47 v.

a Show that $\frac{dv}{dt} = 4.9(2 - v)$.

The ball falls from rest.

b Show that $v = C(1 - e^{-kt})$, stating the values of constants C and k.

c Hence, describe the motion of the ball.

9 A liquid is being heated in an oven maintained at a constant temperature of 160 °C. It may be assumed that the rate of increase of the temperature of the liquid at any particular time, t minutes, is proportional to $160 - \theta$, where θ °C is the temperature of the liquid at that time.

i Write down a differential equation connecting θ and t.

When the liquid was placed in the oven, its temperature was 20 °C and 5 minutes later its temperature had risen to 65 °C.

ii Find the temperature of the liquid, correct to the nearest degree, after another 5 minutes.

© OCR, GCE Mathematics, Paper 4724, January 2009

10 Consider the following model of population growth:

$\frac{dN}{dt} = 1.2N - 0.4N^2$, where N thousand is the population size at time t months.

a Suggest what the term $-0.4N^2$ could represent.

b Given that initially $N = 1.5$, solve the differential equation.

c Show that the solution may be written as $N = \frac{3}{1 + e^{-1.2t}}$. Hence, describe what happens to the population in the long term.

11 Variables x and y satisfy the differential equation $\frac{dy}{dx} = e^{x - ey}$.

Given that $y = \frac{1}{e}$ when $x = 0$, show that $x - ey + 1 = 0$.

12 A particle moves in a straight line. Its acceleration depends on the displacement as follows:

$\frac{dv}{dt} = -8e^{-4x}$.

a Find an expression for $\frac{dv}{dx}$ in terms of x and v.

Initially the particle is at the origin and its speed is 2 m s^{-1}. The velocity of the particle remains positive for $t > 0$.

b Show that $v = 2e^{-2x}$.

c Find expressions for the displacement and velocity in terms of time.

Elevate

See Extension sheet 13 for questions on some other types of differential equation.

14 Numerical solution of equations

In this chapter you will learn:

- that some equations cannot be solved by algebraic rearrangement
- how to find an interval that contains a root of an equation, and how to check that a given solution is correct to a specified degree of accuracy (the sign change method)
- that you can approximate a part of the curve by a tangent, and use this to find an improved estimate for a solution (Newton–Raphson method)
- how to create a sequence that converges to a root of an equation (fixed-point iteration)
- how to identify situations in which the methods above fail to find a solution.

Before you start…

Student Book 1, Chapters 4, 7 and 10	You should know how to rearrange equations involving polynomials, fractions, exponentials, logarithms and trigonometric functions.	1 Rearrange each equation into the required form. a $x=3\ln(x+2)$ into $x=\mathrm{e}^{kx}-C$ b $x=2\sqrt{x^2-3}$ into $x=\frac{1}{2}\sqrt{x^2+k}$ c $x\cos x-3\sin x=0$ into $x=\arctan\left(\frac{x}{a}\right)$
Chapter 10	You should know how to differentiate a variety of functions.	2 Differentiate the following. a $y=3x^2\tan x$ b $y=\frac{\ln x}{x^2}$ c $y=\mathrm{e}^{3x^2}-\ln(2x)$
Chapter 4	You should know how to use the term-to-term rule to generate a sequence.	3 Find the first four terms of the sequence defined by $x_{n+1}=5x_n-2x_n^2$, $x_1=1$.

What is a 'numerical solution'?

Throughout your studies of mathematics you have learnt to solve various types of equations: linear, quadratic, exponential, trigonometric … Some equations can be solved by algebraic rearrangement; for example:

$$2x-3=2 \Rightarrow x=\frac{2+3}{2}=2.5$$

Sometimes you can write solutions in an exact form, such as

$$x^2 - 1 = 4 \Rightarrow x = \pm\sqrt{5}$$

or

$$\sin 2x = \frac{1}{2}\ (\text{for } 0 \leqslant x \leqslant \pi) \Rightarrow x = \frac{\pi}{12}, \frac{5\pi}{12}$$

Alternatively, you can use calculator buttons to find approximate solutions; for example:

$$\sin x = \frac{1}{3}\ (\text{for } 0 \leqslant x \leqslant \frac{\pi}{2}) \Rightarrow x = 0.340\ (3\text{ s.f.})$$

Tip

You can write the solution of $\sin x = \frac{1}{3}$ in an exact form as $x = \arcsin\left(\frac{1}{3}\right)$.

But there are some equations that can't be solved by any combination of algebraic rearrangement and using calculator buttons. For example, how would you solve the equation $3\sin x = 2x$? However you try rearranging it, you can't get it into the form 'x = number'. If you have a graphical calculator or graphing software, you can use them to find approximate solutions by drawing the graphs of $y = 3\sin x$ and $y = 2x$ and finding their intersection.

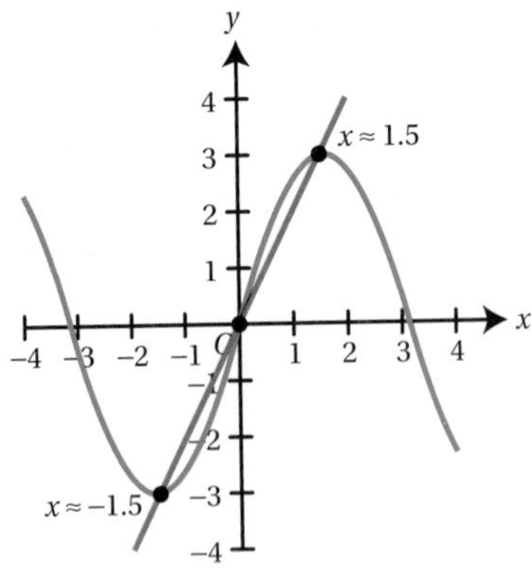

Your calculator may have a 'solver' function that allows it to find approximate solutions without drawing the graph. (In the example of the equation $3\sin x = 2x$ it should give you solutions -1.5, 0 and 1.5; the solution $x = 0$ is exact, but the other two are accurate to 2 s.f.) But how does it do that? Does it try lots of different values for x until it finds one that works? Or is there some clever way to decide which values of x to try?

In this chapter you will learn several different methods for solving equations numerically. (This means that a solution is not found by algebraic manipulation, but by evaluating certain expressions to find increasingly accurate approximations.) You should be aware that these methods can give only approximate solutions, but you can choose the level of accuracy. You will also see that in some situations these methods fail to find an answer and will learn how to recognise such situations.

Section 1: Locating roots of a function

The simplest numerical methods involve finding an interval in which the solution lies, and then improving accuracy by making this interval smaller.

For example, try finding approximate solutions of the equation $3\sin x = 2x$. It is easier to see how the method works if you rearrange the equation into the form 'expression = 0', so look at this equation:

$$3\sin x - 2x = 0$$

Tip

When equations involve trigonometric functions you should work in radians unless told otherwise.

A sensible way to start is to try some values of x, and then see if any of them give an answer close to zero. Here is a table of values:

x	0	1	2	3
$3\sin x - 2x$	0	0.524	−1.27	−5.58

From the table you can see that $x = 0$ is a solution. But you can also see that the value of the expression $3\sin x - 2x$ changes sign between $x = 1$ and $x = 2$: it is positive when $x = 1$ but negative when $x = 2$. The graph is a continuous curve, so this means that it must equal zero somewhere between these two x values.

Tip

'Continuous' is a technical term but, put simply, a function is continuous over an interval if you can draw its graph within that interval without taking your pen from the paper.

You can see this if you draw the graph of $y = 3\sin x - 2x$. If the y-coordinate changes from positive to negative, then the graph must cross the x-axis.

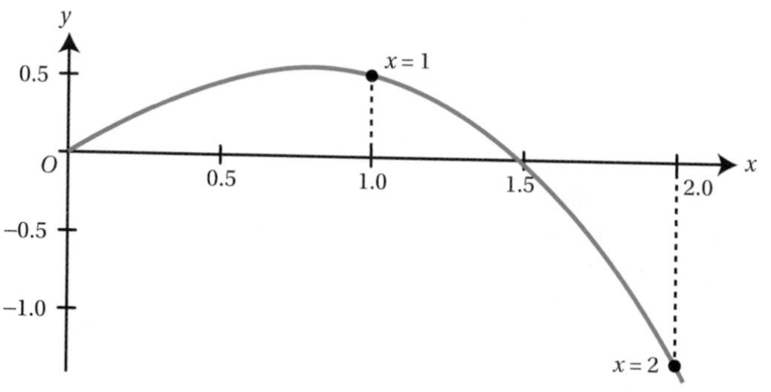

You can try to locate this solution more accurately by looking for a smaller interval. For example:

x	1.0	1.5	2.0
$3\sin x - 2x$	0.524	−0.00752	−1.27

This tells you that the solution is between 1.0 and 1.5. You can continue finding smaller and smaller intervals to find the solution to any degree of accuracy you want.

Explore

Can you use a spreadsheet to find the solution, correct to 3 decimal places?

This method uses the following result:

Key point 14.1

If $f(x)$ is a sufficiently well behaved function and a and b are numbers such that $f(x)$ changes sign between a and b, then the equation $f(x) = 0$ has at least one root (solution) between a and b. However a lack of change of sign does not necessarily imply that there are no roots.

Tip

This method finds only one solution. The previous equation $y = 3\sin x - 2x$ also has a negative solution, between −1.5 and −1.0. In general, with numerical methods, you can never be sure that you have found all the solutions.

Can the change of sign method fail?

In Key point 14.1 we refer to 'sufficiently well behaved' functions. There are several situations in which the change of sign method cannot be used.

If the graph of the function has a vertical asymptote, or another break in its graph, there may be a change of sign even if the graph does not cross the x-axis.

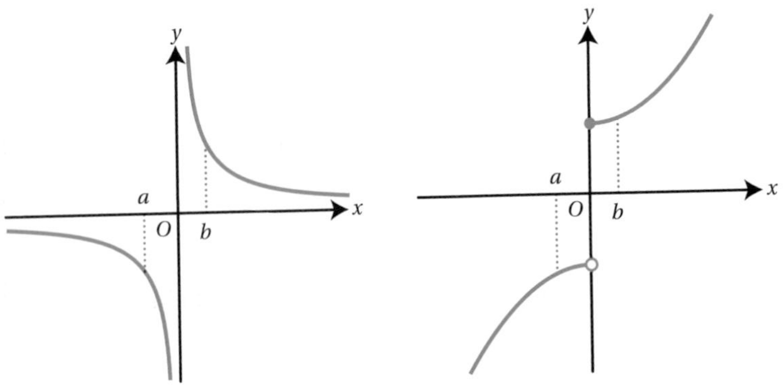

It is also possible that the change of sign method does not detect a root when there is one (or more). This can happen if the graph is tangent to the x-axis, or if it crosses it several times in a small interval.

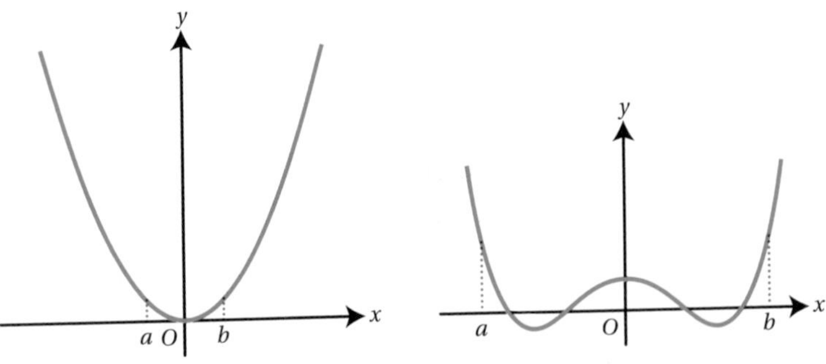

For the second graph above, the change of sign method may work if you picked a different interval. The problem is that, unless we know the approximate location of the roots already, there is no way of knowing how small an interval we need.

You should also note that a change of sign between $x = a$ and $x = b$ implies that there is at least one root between those two values; but it does not tell us whether there is more than one.

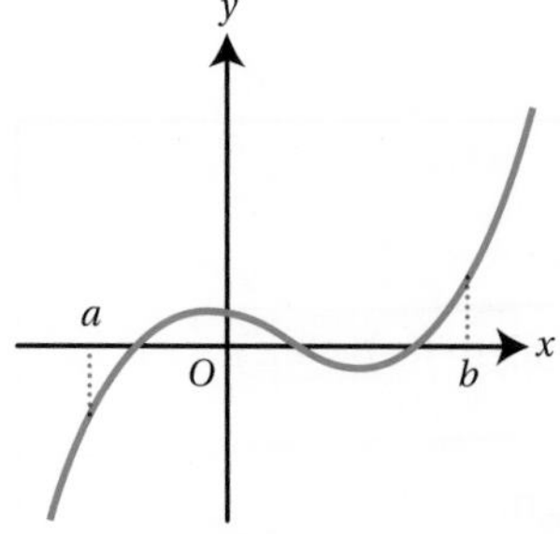

WORKED EXAMPLE 14.1

Let $f(x) = \frac{5}{x} - 2x + x^2$.

a Show that the equation $f(x) = 0$ has a solution between -1 and -2.

b **i** Evaluate $f(-0.5)$ and $f(0.5)$.

ii Explain why, in this case, the change of sign does not imply that $f(x) = 0$ has another solution between -0.5 and 0.5.

a $f(-1) = \frac{5}{-1} - 2(-1) + (-1)^2 = -2 < 0$

Show clearly which values of x you used.

$f(-2) = \frac{5}{-2} - 2(-2) + (-2)^2 = 5.5 > 0$

There is a change of sign, so there is a root between $x = -2$ and $x = -1$.

Note that $f(x)$ is sufficiently well-behaved in the domain $-2 < x < -1$.

b **i** $f(-0.5) = \frac{1}{-0.5} - 2(-0.5) + (-0.5)^2 = -0.75$

$f(0.5) = \frac{1}{0.5} - 2(0.5) + (0.5)^2 = 1.25$

Show clearly which values of x you used.

ii $f(x)$ has a vertical asymptote at $x = 0$, so the change of sign does not imply that the graph crosses the x-axis.

Think about the graph: if it has an asymptote then it does not necessarily cross the x-axis.
$\frac{1}{x}$ is not defined for $x = 0$, so the graph will have an asymptote there.

Checking the accuracy of a solution

In practice, rather than knowing that a solution lies in a particular interval, you want to express it to a specified degree of accuracy, such as 1 decimal place. Consider, as an example, the equation $\ln x = \frac{x}{4}$. By trying some values of x you can find that this equation has a solution around 8.6. But how can you check that this is in fact correct to 1 decimal place?

The solution, when rounded to 1 decimal place, equals 8.6. But the numbers that round to 8.6 are between 8.55 and 8.65, so you should look for a change of sign between those two values.

WORKED EXAMPLE 14.2

Show that the equation $\ln x = \frac{x}{4}$ has a root $x = 8.6$, correct to 1 decimal place.

Let $f(x) = \ln x - \frac{x}{4}$.

First write the equation in the form $f(x) = 0$...

$f(8.55) = \ln 8.55 - \frac{8.55}{4} = 0.00843 > 0$

... then look for a change of sign.

$f(8.65) = \ln 8.65 - \frac{8.65}{4} = -0.00594 < 0$

There is a change of sign, so there is a root between 8.55 and 8.65.

This root equals 8.6, to 1 d.p.

You are looking at the degree of accuracy of the x value here, not the y value. For the equation from Worked example 14.2, $f(8.62) = 0.00091$, which equals 0 to 2 decimal places. However, the root is not equal to 8.62 to 2 d.p. Look at this table of values:

x	8.605	8.615	8.625
$f(x) = \ln x - \frac{x}{4}$	0.00109	−0.000254	−1.27

The change of sign actually occurs between 8.605 and 8.615 so the root is 8.61, correct to 2 d.p.

Focus on ...

Focus on ... Problem Solving 2 compares a numerical and analytical solution to the same problem.

EXERCISE 14A

1 Classify these equations as 'can find exact solutions' or 'can't rearrange algebraically'.

a $x^2 - 4x = 7$

b $e^{-x} = 4x$

c $\sin x = 3\tan x$

d $e^{4x} = 5$

e $\tan x = 3x^2$

f $3\ln(4x) = 4$

g $e^{5x} = 3\ln x$

h $x^3 - 4x - 4 = 0$

Explore

There is, in fact, a formula for solving cubic equations, but you will not learn about it in this course.

2 Each of the following equations has a root between −3 and 3. In each case, find two integers between which the root lies.

a $x^3 - 4x - 4 = 0$

b $2\sin x - 4x + 1 = 0$

c $25\ln x = 3x^2$

d $\cos(3 - x) + x^3 = -5$

3 For each of the following equations, show that there is a root in the given interval.

a **i** $x - 5\ln x = 0$, between 1 and 2

ii $3e^{2x} - 4x^2 = 0$, between -1 and 0

b **i** $\cos 2x = \sqrt{x}$, between 0 and 1

ii $3\tan x = 5x^3$, between -2 and -1

4 For each equation, show that the given root is correct to the stated degree of accuracy.

a **i** $x^5 - 3x^2 + 1 = 0$, $x = 0.6$ (1 d.p.)

ii $x^3 - 3x + 4 = 0$, $x = -2.2$ (1 d.p.)

b **i** $4\sin x - e^{-2x} = 0$, $x = 3.14$ (3 s.f.)

ii $2\ln x - 3\cos x = 0$, $x = 1.36$ (3 s.f.)

c **i** $3\tan x = 5x^3$, $x = 1.31$ (2 d.p.)

ii $2x = e^{-x}$, $x = 0.35$ (2 d.p.)

d **i** $3e^x = x^4$, $x = 6.20$ (3 s.f.)

ii $3\cos x = \ln x$, $x = 5.30$ (3 s.f.)

5 **a** Show that the equation $x^3 - 3x - 1 = 0$ has a solution between 1 and 2.

b Show that this solution equals 1.9, correct to 1 decimal place.

6 The equation $\ln\left(\frac{x}{3}\right) - \frac{x^2}{4} + 2 = 0$ has two solutions.

a Show that one of the solutions equals 0.425, correct to 3 significant figures.

b The other solution lies between positive integers k and $k+1$. Find the value of k.

7 A function is defined by $f(x) = \frac{x^2+2}{2x-5}$.

a Show that the equation $f(x) = 0$ has no solutions.

b **i** Evaluate f(2) and f(3).

ii Alicia says that the change of sign implies that the equation $f(x) = 0$ has a root between 2 and 3. Explain why she is wrong.

8 Let $g(x) = \cos 8x$.

a **i** Sketch the graph of $y = g(x)$ for $0 \leqslant x \leqslant \frac{\pi}{2}$.

ii State the number of solutions of the equation $g(x) = 0$ between 0 and $\frac{\pi}{4}$.

b **i** State the values of g(0) and $g\left(\frac{\pi}{4}\right)$.

ii George says, 'There is no change of sign between 0 and $\frac{\pi}{4}$ so the equation $g(x) = 0$ has no roots in this interval.' Use your graph to explain why George's reasoning is incorrect.

iii Use the change of sign method (without referring to the graph) to show that the equation $g(x) = 0$ has two roots between 0 and $\frac{\pi}{4}$.

Section 2: The Newton–Raphson method

The method of sign change allows you to show that a root of an equation lies in a certain interval, but how do you know which interval to try? In the first example, with $f(x) = 3\sin x - 2x$, a table of integer values of x helped you to find that there is a solution between 1 and 2. You could then look at $x = 1.1, 1.2, \ldots$ to locate the change of sign more accurately:

x	1.0	1.1	1.2	1.3	1.4	1.5
$3\sin x - 2x$	0.524	0.00752	0.396	0.291	0.156	−0.007

This shows that the root is between 1.4 and 1.5. You can continue like this until you make the interval as small as you like.

If you wanted to locate the root to three or four decimal places, this could take quite a long time. In some applications, solutions of equations are required to even higher accuracy, and then this method becomes unfeasible, even with a fast computer.

The numbers in the table above suggest that the root may be much closer to 1.5 than to 1.4, so maybe the next search should not start from 1.41 but from 1.48 or 1.49, but how do you know which one? It would be good to have a method to tell you which number to try next. There are in fact many such methods. In this section you will meet the **Newton–Raphson method**, which uses the tangent to the graph of f(x) to suggest where to look for the root.

The diagram below shows the section of the graph of $y = 3\sin x - 2x$ for $1.3 \leqslant x \leqslant 1.6$ (in red). It crosses the x-axis between 1.4 and 1.5. The diagram also shows the tangent to the graph at $x = 1.4$ (in blue). Near this point, the tangent follows the graph closely, so it will cross the x-axis near the root of the equation.

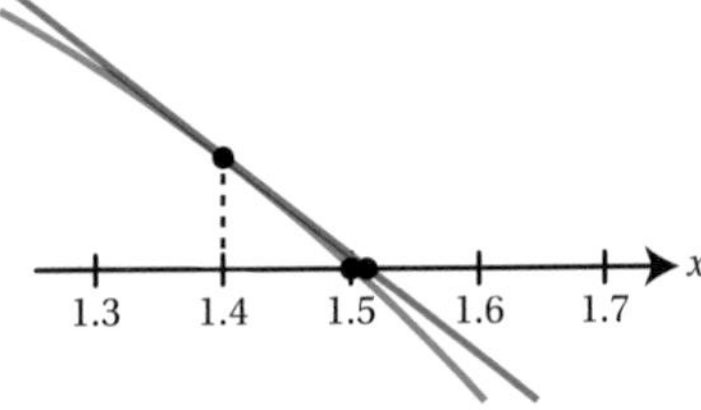

Use a graph plotter to draw the graph and the tangent and find where the tangent crosses the x-axis. You will find that the value is $x = 1.504925\ldots$

You can now repeat the same procedure by drawing a tangent at this new value of x; this new tangent crosses the x-axis at $x = 1.49585\ldots$

You can check that this gives the correct root to three decimal places:

$$\left.\begin{array}{l} f(1.4955) = 0.0004997 > 0 \\ f(1.4965) = -0.001276 < 0 \end{array}\right\} \Rightarrow x = 1.496 \text{ (3 d.p.)}$$

Repeating one more time gives the root correct to seven decimal places. This would have taken a very long time with the sign change method!

So far you have used a graph plotter to draw tangents and find their x-intercepts. But is there a formula to calculate the x-intercept of the tangent without having to rely on the graph? The answer is yes: you can find the equation of a tangent at any given point, and then use this equation to find where the tangent crosses the x-axis.

Key point 14.2

Newton–Raphson method:

Given an approximate root x_n of the equation $f(x) = 0$, a better approximation is

$$x_{n+1} = x_n - \frac{f(x_n)}{f'(x_n)}$$

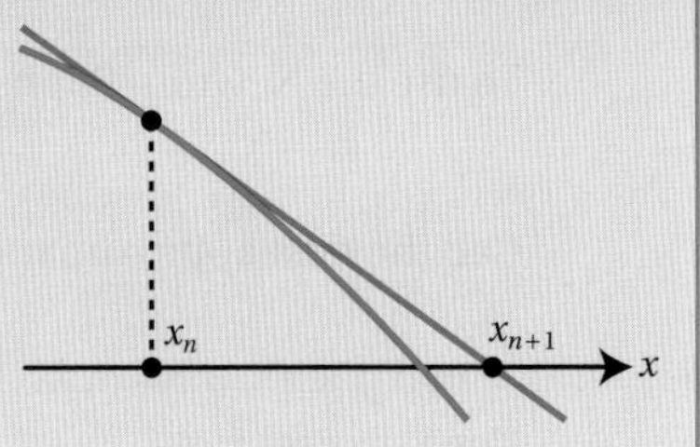

PROOF 8

The tangent to the graph at $x = x_n$ has gradient $m = f'(x_n)$ and it passes through the point (x_n, y_n), where $y_n = f(x_n)$.

Therefore, its equation is

$$y - y_n = m(x - x_n)$$

$$\Leftrightarrow y - f(x_n) = f'(x_n)(x - x_n)$$

To find where this tangent crosses the x-axis, you need to set $y = 0$:

$$0 - f(x_n) = f'(x_n)(x - x_n)$$

$$\Leftrightarrow x - x_n = -\frac{f(x_n)}{f'(x_n)}$$

$$\Leftrightarrow x = x_n - \frac{f(x_n)}{f'(x_n)}$$

Rewind

You met equations of tangents in Student Book 1, Chapter 14.

Repeating the Newton–Raphson procedure, starting with the new value of x each time, gets you closer and closer to the root.

WORKED EXAMPLE 14.3

a Show that the equation $e^{2x} - 10x = 0$ has a root between 1 and 2.

b Starting from $x_0 = 1.5$, use three repetitions of the Newton–Raphson method to find a better approximation for the root.

c Show that this approximation gives the root correct to three decimal places.

Continues on next page ...

a Let $f(x)=e^{2x}-10x$.

$f(1)=e^2-10=-2.61<0$

$f(2)=e^4-20=34.6>0$

There is a change of sign, so there is a root between 1 and 2.

Look for a change of sign between 1 and 2.

b $f'(x)=2e^{2x}-10$

To use the Newton-Raphson formula you need $f'(x)$.

$$x_1=x_0-\frac{e^{2x_0}-10x_0}{2e^{2x_0}-10}=1.33144...$$

Call the next approximation x_1.

$$x_2=x_1-\frac{e^{2x_1}-10x_1}{2e^{2x_1}-10}=1.276655...$$

Use x_1 to find x_2.

$x_3=1.271367....$

Use x_2 to find x_3.

c $f(1.2705)=e^{2\times1.2705}-12.705$
$=-0.0126...<0$

$f(1.2715)=e^{2\times1.2715}-12.715$
$=0.0027...>0$

To show that the root equals 1.271 to 3 d.p., you need to show that it is between 1.2705 and 1.2715.

There is a change of sign, so there is a root between 1.2705 and 1.2715.

Hence, the root equals 1.271 (3 d.p.).

Repeating the Newton-Raphson calculation several times, as in Worked example 14.3, involves using the same formula with different numbers, whereby the number you need to put into the equation is the answer from the previous calculation. Most calculators have an ANS button that can be used to carry out such repetitive calculations. Here is how you could use it for Worked example 14.3, with the keys of a typical calculator.

Start by entering the starting value of x_0 (in this case 1.5) and press the = /EXE button.

Then type in

$$\text{ANS}-\frac{e^{2\text{ANS}}-10\text{ANS}}{2e^{2\text{ANS}}-10}$$

and press the = /EXE button again. The answer is the value of x_1. Pressing the = /EXE button repeatedly gives x_2, x_3 and so on. This way you can quickly generate as many approximations to the root as you like.

Elevate

See Support sheet 14 for a further example of using the Newton–Raphson method and for more practice questions.

Tip

You should familiarise yourself with the equivalent keys on your own calculator, as they may differ to this. You should also ensure that you show evidence of numerical reasoning, for example through writing down iterations.

EXERCISE 14B

1 Each equation below is to be approximately solved using Newton–Raphson method with the given starting value x_0. In each case, use technology to sketch the graph, draw the tangent at x_0 and find the next approximation to the root.

a **i** $x^3 - 2x^2 - 1 = 0,\ x_0 = 2.5$ **ii** $5x - \frac{1}{2}x^4 - 3 = 0,\ x_0 = 1$

b **i** $x^2 - 10\ln x = 0,\ x_0 = 4$ **ii** $x - 2\cos x = 0,\ x_0 = 2$

2 For each equation, use the Newton–Raphson method with the given starting value to find the root correct to three significant figures. Use the change of sign method to show that your root is correct to three significant figures.

a **i** $x^4 - 3x + 1 = 0,\ x_0 = 1.5$ **ii** $3x - x^3 + 1 = 0,\ x_0 = 0$

b **i** $\sin\left(\frac{x}{2}\right) - x + 1 = 0,\ x_0 = 0$ **ii** $e^{0.2x} - 3\sqrt{x} = 0,\ x_0 = 11$

3 The equation $1 - x^2 + 2x^3 = 0$ has a root near -0.5. Using this value as the first approximation, use the Newton–Raphson method to find the next approximation to the root.

4 **a** Show that the equation $2x^2 - 1 = \frac{3}{x}$ can be written as $2x^3 - x - 3 = 0$.

b Given that the equation has a root near 1.5, use the Newton–Raphson method to find the next two approximations.

5 The equation $\sin x = \frac{2}{x}$ has a root near 6.5. Use the Newton–Raphson method to find the next two approximations to the root.

6 **a** Show that the equation $2 - x + \frac{4}{x} = 0$ has a root between 3 and 4.

b Using $x_0 = 3$ as the starting value, use the Newton–Raphson method to find the next approximation to the root. Give your answer correct to two decimal places.

c Show that the approximation from part **b** is correct to one decimal place, but not to two decimal places.

7 **a** Show that the equation $e^{-x} - 0.2x = 0$ has a root between 1 and 2.

b Use the Newton–Raphson method to find this root correct to three decimal places, and show that the root you found is correct to three decimal places.

8 The equation $\cos 3x = \ln(x+1)$ has a root between 0 and 1. Use the Newton–Raphson method to find this root correct to three significant figures, and show that the solution you found is correct to three significant figures.

Section 3: Limitations of the Newton–Raphson method

The Newton–Raphson method can find a root to a high degree of accuracy very quickly, so it seems to be a very good method. Unfortunately, there are some situations when it doesn't work.

For example, try to find a root of the equation $x^3 + x^2 - 0.2 = 0$.
The sign change check confirms that this equation has a root between 0 and 1. The Newton–Raphson iteration formula is:

$$x_{n+1} = x_n - \frac{x_n^3 + x_n^2 - 0.2}{3x_n^2 + 2x_n}$$

If you start from $x_0 = 0$ you get $x_1 = 0 - \frac{-0.2}{0}$. But you can't divide by zero, so it's impossible to find x_1. You could try changing the starting point slightly; for example, $x_0 = 0.1$. Try it! The sequence moves away from the root but then comes back again.

Key point 14.3

The Newton–Raphson method doesn't work if the starting value is a stationary point of $f(x)$.

If the root is close to a stationary point, the sequence may initially (or permanently) move away from the root.

WORKED EXAMPLE 14.4

a Show that the equation $x^4 - 4x^3 - 7.5x^2 + 50x - 55 = 0$ has a root between 2 and 3.

b Explain why $x_0 = 2.5$ is not a suitable starting point for a Newton–Raphson iteration to find this root.

c Use the starting value $x_0 = 2.6$ to find the root correct to three decimal places.

a Let $f(x) = x^4 - 4x^3 - 7.5x^2 + 50x - 55$

Use the sign change method.

Then:

$f(2) = -1 < 0$

$f(3) = 0.5 > 0$

There is a change of sign, so $f(x) = 0$ has a root between 2 and 3.

b $f'(x) = 4x^3 - 12x^2 - 15x + 50$

$f'(2.5) = 0$

The Newton–Raphson method fails when $f'(x_0) = 0$, so find $f'(2.5)$ to check.

So there would be division by zero if the Newton–Raphson formula were used.

c $x_0 = 2.6$

Use the Newton–Raphson formula with $x_0 = 2.6$

$$x_{n+1} = x_n - \frac{x_n^4 - 4x_n^3 - 7.5x_n^2 + 50x_n - 55}{4x_n^3 - 12x_n^2 - 15x_n + 50}$$

The sequence converges to 2.866 (3 d.p.).

Continue the sequence until you can see what the limit is. You are not being asked to write down all the iterations.

Explore

Sketch the graph to see why the sequence initially moves farther away from the root before getting closer again.

Another situation where the Newton–Raphson method can fail is if x_1 falls outside of the domain of the function. This can happen, for example, if the graph of the function has a vertical asymptote.

WORKED EXAMPLE 14.5

a The equation $\frac{\ln x + 0.2}{x} = 0$ has a root between 0.5 and 2. Explain why a Newton–Raphson iteration from $x_0 = 1.5$ fails to find this root.

b Starting from $x_0 = 1$, carry out three iterations of the Newton–Raphson method, showing the values correct to three decimal places.

a $f(x) = \frac{\ln x + 0.2}{x}$

In order to use the Newton–Raphson formula you first need to find $f'(x)$ using the quotient rule.

$$f'(x) = \frac{\frac{1}{x}x - 1(\ln x + 0.2)}{x^2}$$

$$= \frac{0.8 - \ln x}{x^2}$$

$x_0 = 1.5$

Use the formula with $x_0 = 1.5$ to find x_1.

$$x_1 = 1.5 - \frac{f(1.5)}{f'(1.5)}$$

$$= -0.8$$

$$x_2 = -0.8 - \frac{f(-0.8)}{f'(-0.8)}$$

But $f(x)$ is not defined for $x < 0$, so it is not possible to find x_2.

To find x_2 you would need to use the formula with $x_1 = -0.8$. But $f(x)$ has a vertical asymptote at $x = 0$ and is not defined for $x < 0$, so this is impossible.

b $x_0 = 1$

$$x_1 = 1 - \frac{f(1)}{f'(1)} = 0.750$$

$x_2 = 0.810$

$x_3 = 0.819$

You can use graphing software to see that the tangent at $x_0 = 1.5$ crosses the x-axis to the left of the vertical asymptote.

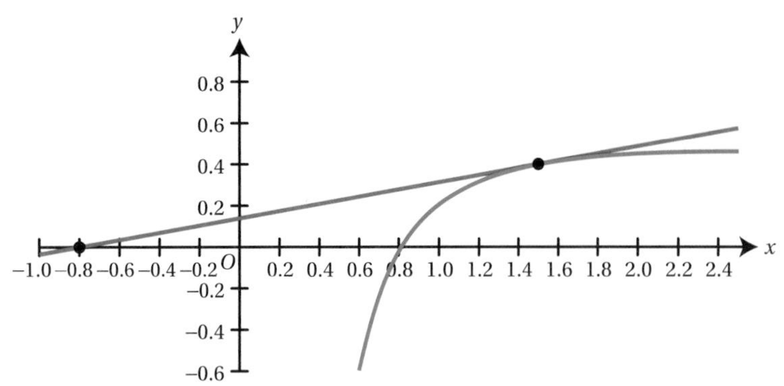

Explore

Try plotting tangents at different values of x_0 to see when the iteration works. (You should find that x_0 needs to be less than about 1.35.)

EXERCISE 14C

1 For each equation below, carry out one iteration of the Newton–Raphson method starting with the given value of x_0. In each case, sketch the graph (using technology) to explain why x_1 is not a better approximation to the root than x_0.

a **i** $2x^3 - 5x + 2 = 0,\ x_0 = 1$ **ii** $\sqrt{x} - 0.2x^3 - 0.5 = 0,\ x_0 = 1$

b **i** $\tan x - x - 1 = 0,\ x_0 = 0.5$ **ii** $\dfrac{\ln 2x + x}{x} = 0,\ x_0 = 1$

2 Let $f(x) = 10x^3 - 5x^2 - 1$.

a Find the x-coordinates of the stationary points of $f(x)$.

b Show that the equation $f(x) = 0$ has a root between $\frac{1}{3}$ and 1.

c The Newton–Raphson formula with $x_0 = 0.35$ is used to find x_1. Explain why x_1 may not be an improved approximation for the root.

3 The diagram shows the curve with equation $f(x) = (x-2)e^{-x} + 1$.

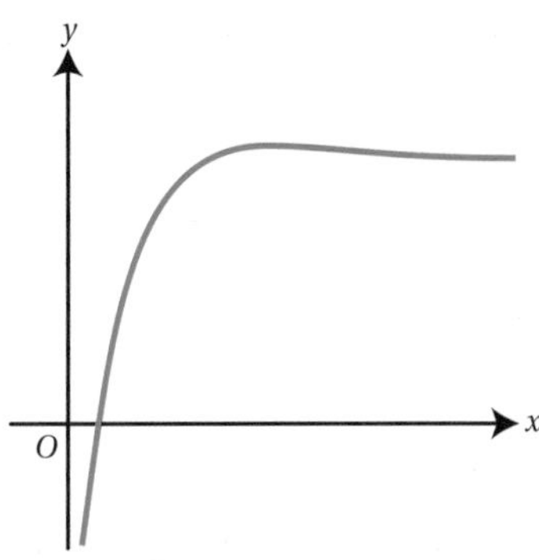

Find the x-coordinate of the stationary point of $f(x)$ and, hence, explain, with an aid of a diagram, why a Newton–Raphson iteration with $x_0 = 3.5$ will not converge to the root of $f(x) = 0$.

4 The diagram shows the curve with equation $f(x)=3x^2-x^3-2$.

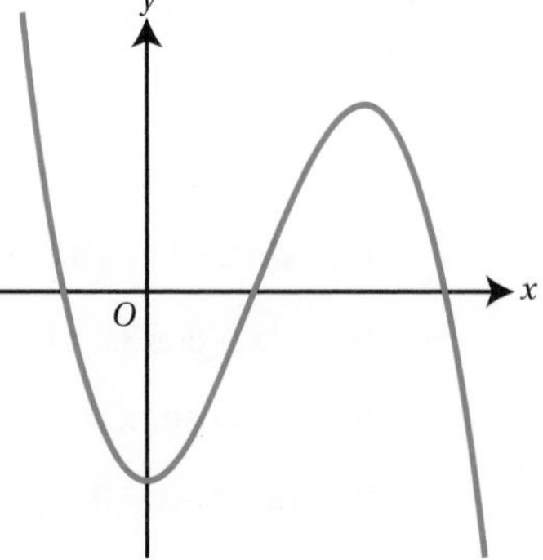

a Find the coordinates of the turning points of $f(x)$.

The curve crosses the x-axis at $x=\alpha$, $x=\beta$ and $x=\gamma$, with $\alpha<\beta<\gamma$.

The Newton–Raphson method is to be used to find the roots of $f(x)=0$, with $x_0=k$.

b To which root, if any, do the successive approximations converge when:

i $k=-1$? ii $k=2$?

c Write down the range of values of k for which the Newton–Raphson iteration converges to γ.

5 Let $f(x)=\ln x-\tan x+2$.

a Write down the values of x between 0 and 10 for which $f(x)$ is not defined.

The equation $f(x)=0$ has a root between 0 and 1.

b Taking $x_0=0.7$, use the Newton–Raphson method to find x_1.

c Explain why the Newton–Raphson iteration cannot be continued to find a better approximation to the root.

6 The function $f(x)=2x^3-6x+1$ has three zeros $(a<b<c)$ between -2 and 2.

a For each of the zeros, find two integers between which it lies.

b Find the exact coordinates of the stationary points of $f(x)$ and sketch its graph.

c Find the coordinates of the point where the tangent to the graph at $x=0.9$ crosses the x-axis.

The Newton–Raphson method is to be used to find the root $x=b$.

d Explain why the iteration with $x_0=0.9$ does not converge to b.

e Use an iteration with $x_0=0.5$ to find b, correct to three significant figures.

7 Let $f(x)=\ln x-0.5x^2+2$.

a Find the coordinates of the stationary point on the graph $y=f(x)$ and show that this is a maximum point.

b Show that $f(x)$ has no points of inflection. Hence, sketch the graph of $y=f(x)$.

The equation $f(x)=0$ has two roots.

c Show that one of the roots is between 0 and 1 and find two integers between which the other root lies.

The Newton–Raphson iteration is to be used to find the roots.

d Explain why the starting value $x_0=0.5$ cannot be used to find the smaller root.

e State the range of values of x_0 for which the Newton–Raphson iteration converges to the larger root.

8 Each of the following equations has a root near the given starting value x_0. In each case:

a Explain why starting with x_0 does not lead to a better approximation to the root.

b Use technology to investigate for which starting values the Newton–Raphson method works.

i $\sin 2x + \cos 3x = 0$, $x_0 = 1.25$ to find the root between 1 and 2.

ii $\sqrt{x} - \cos 3x = 0$, $x_0 = 1$

iii $2 - \operatorname{cosec} x = 0$, $x_0 = 1$ to find the root between 0 and 1.

iv $\tan x - x = 0$, $x_0 = 4$ to find the root between 4 and 5.

9 A function is defined by $f(x) = \dfrac{x^4 - 10x^2 + 25}{x^2 - 1}$ for $x \neq \pm 1$.

a Show that if α is any root of the equation $f(x) = 0$, then $f'(\alpha) = 0$.

The graph of $y = f(x)$ is shown below.

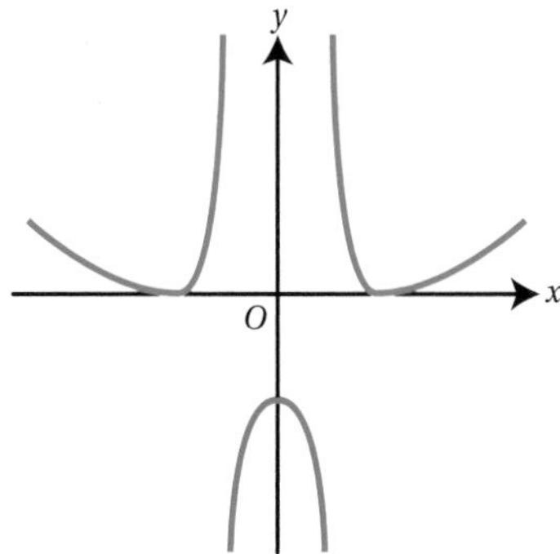

The Newton–Raphson formula with a positive value of x_0 is used to find x_1.

b State the range of positive values of x_0 for which x_1 is closer than x_0 to the positive root of $f(x) = 0$.

c Use a diagram to show that there is a positive value of x_0 such that $x_1 < 0$, but subsequent approximations converge to the positive root of $f(x) = 0$.

10 **a** Sketch the graphs of $y = \tan x$ and $y = 2x$ for $0 < x < \frac{1}{2}\pi$. Hence, show that the equation $\tan x - 2x = 0$ has a solution, α, in that interval.

Consider the Newton–Raphson iteration with the starting value x_0.

b Show that the iteration converges to α when $x_0 = 1.1$ but not when $x_0 = 0.9$.

c There is a value k such that the iteration with $k < x_0 < \frac{1}{2}\pi$ converges to α. Sketch the graph of $y = \tan x - 2x$ for $0 < x < \frac{\pi}{2}$. Show the value k on your sketch and draw the tangent to the curve at $x = k$.

d When $x_0 < k$, the Newton–Raphson iteration may not converge to α. Describe two different cases that can arise.

Section 4: Fixed-point iteration

You saw in the previous section that the Newton–Raphson method doesn't always work. Luckily, there are alternative methods you can use in such situations. In this section you will learn about **fixed-point iteration**, which also involves creating a sequence that gets closer and closer to the root, but in a different way from Newton–Raphson.

To use fixed-point iteration the equation needs to be rearranged into the form $x = \mathrm{g}(x)$. Suppose you have a starting guess of x_1. If $x_1 = \mathrm{g}(x_1)$ you have found a solution of the equation. Otherwise we are looking for an improved guess. Since you want x to equal $\mathrm{g}(x)$, it makes sense to try $x_2 = \mathrm{g}(x_1)$. You can see why this works by looking at the graph.

The solution of the equation $x = \mathrm{g}(x)$ is the intersection of the graphs $y = x$ and $y = \mathrm{g}(x)$. Starting from the point x_1 on the x-axis, you can find x_2 on the y-axis using the graph $y = \mathrm{g}(x)$. To see whether x_2 is closer to the solution than x_1, you need to find x_2 on the x-axis. You can do this by reflecting it in the line $y = x$.

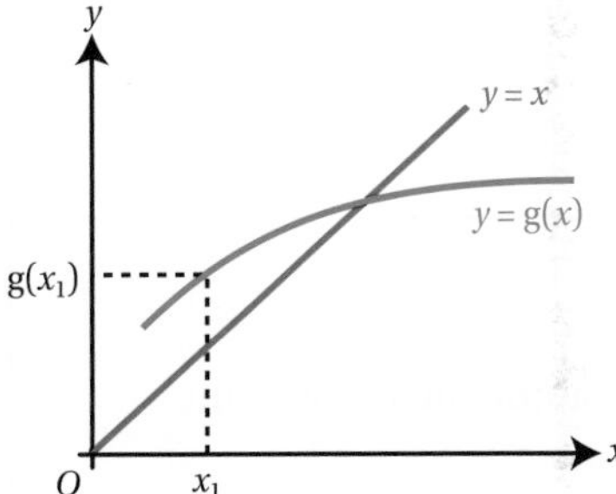

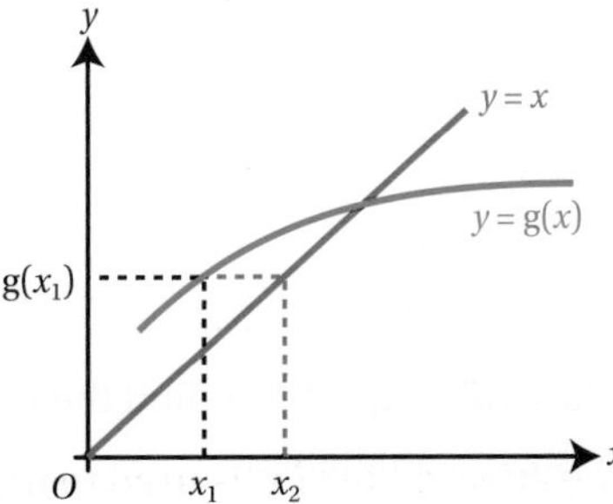

In the example shown in the previous diagram, x_2 is closer to the solution than x_1. If you now repeat the same process you can hope to get closer and closer to the solution. In other words, you create the following sequence:

Start with x_1.

$$x_2 = \mathrm{g}(x_1)$$

$$x_3 = \mathrm{g}(x_2)$$

$$\ldots$$

You can write the general rule for the sequence as $x_{n+1} = \mathrm{g}(x_n)$. This sequence may **converge** to a **limit**, meaning that the terms of the sequence get closer and closer to a certain number, α. If this is the case, both x_n and x_{n+1} will get closer to α, so the sequence equation becomes $\alpha = \mathrm{g}(\alpha)$ and so α is a solution of the equation $x = \mathrm{g}(x)$.

Rewind

Sequence rules and convergence were covered in Chapter 4.

Did you know?

The name 'fixed-point iteration' refers to the fact that the solution is a fixed point of the function g(x). It is the value where the output equals the input.

The procedure can be summarised as follows.

Key point 14.4

Fixed point iteration:

To solve an equation in the form $x = g(x)$:

- Using a starting guess x_1, generate a sequence $x_{n+1} = g(x_n)$.
- If this sequence converges to a limit, then this limit is a solution of the equation.

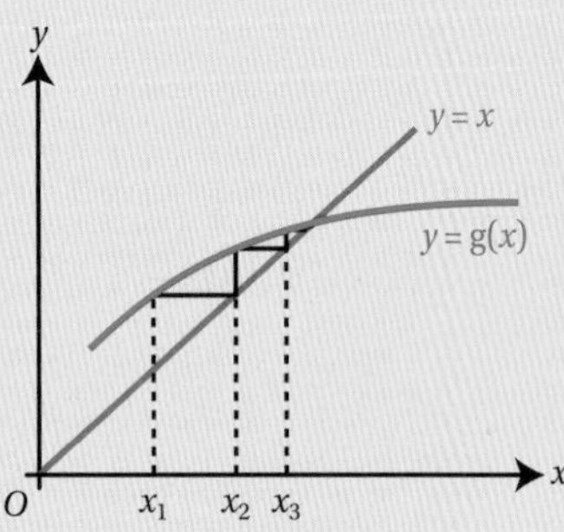

WORKED EXAMPLE 14.6

The equation $x = \ln x + 3$ has a solution between 4 and 5.

a Use fixed-point iteration, with the starting value $x_1 = 4.5$, to find the first five approximations to the solution. Give the values correct to five significant figures.

b Show that this solution is correct to two decimal places.

a Sequence: $x_{n+1} = \ln x_n + 3$

$x_1 = 4.5$

$x_2 = \ln 4.5 + 3 = 4.5041$

$x_3 = 4.5050$

$x_4 = 4.5052$

$x_5 = 4.5052$

Start by entering '4.5' into the calculator and use ln (ANS) + 3 to generate subsequent values.

b The solution is 4.51 (2 d.p.).

$x = \ln x + 3 \Leftrightarrow \ln x + 3 - x = 0$

$\ln(4.505) + 3 - 4.505 = 1.88 \times 10^{-4} > 0$

$\ln(4.515) + 3 - 4.515 = -7.59 \times 10^{-3} < 0$

There is a sign change, so the solution is between 4.505 and 4.515. It equals 4.51 (2 d.p.).

To check that the solution is 4.51 correct to 2 d.p., we need to rearrange the equation into the form $f(x) = 0$ and look for a sign change between 4.505 and 4.515.

In Worked example 14.6 the sequence increased towards the limit. But it is also possible for a sequence to oscillate above and below the limiting value.

WORKED EXAMPLE 14.7

The equation $x = \cos x$ has a root between 0 and 1. The sequence $x_{n+1} = \cos(x_n)$, with $x_1 = 0.5$, is used to find an approximation to this root.

a Draw a graph to illustrate the first three approximations.

b Find the root correct to three decimal places.

a

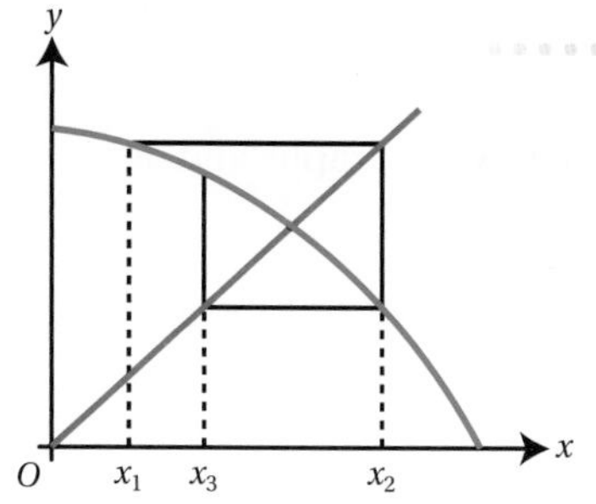

Draw the curve $y = \cos(x)$ and the line $y = x$.

Start with $x_1 = 0.5$ on the x-axis. Find the corresponding point on the curve and reflect it in the line $y = x$ to find x_2.

Repeat to find x_3.

b $x_2 = \cos(0.5) = 0.8776$

$x_3 = \cos(0.8776) = 0.6390$

$x_4 = 0.8027$

...

Start with 0.5. Use cos (ANS) to generate the sequence.

The sequence converges to $x = 0.739$ (3 d.p.).

Continue until the third decimal place stops changing.

Key point 14.5

The graphs showing fixed-point iteration are often called:

- **staircase diagrams** (if successive terms of an iterative sequence are all increasing or all decreasing); or
- **cobweb diagrams** (if successive terms of an iterative sequence oscillate either side of a value to which the sequence is converging).

EXERCISE 14D

1 Use fixed-point iteration with the given starting value to find the first five approximations to the roots of the following equations. Give your answers to three decimal places.

a **i** $x = 2\ln(x+2), x_1 = 3$ **ii** $x = 3 - e^{-x}, x_1 = 4$

b **i** $x = \frac{3}{x+4} - 1, x_1 = -1$ **ii** $x = \cos(2x - 1), x_1 = 1$

c **i** $\ln x - x^2 + 2 = x, x_1 = 0.5$ **ii** $1.5x\sin(x+1) = x, x_1 = 1$

2 Use fixed-point iteration with the given starting value to find an approximate solution, correct to two decimal places.

a **i** $x = e^{-\frac{x}{2}}, x_1 = 0$ **ii** $x = \cos\left(\frac{x}{3}\right), x_1 = 0$

b **i** $x = \ln x + 3, x_1 = 4$ **ii** $x = \tan\left(\frac{x}{2}\right) + 0.2, x_1 = 1$

3 Each of the equations below is to be solved using fixed-point iteration. Draw the graphs and use technology to investigate the following.

a $x = \arctan x + 1$ **b** $x = \sqrt[3]{x+2}$

c $x = \ln(x+2)$ **d** $x = e^{x-2}$

i Does the limit depend on the starting point?

ii Does starting on different sides of the root give a different limit?

iii If there is more than one root, which one does the sequence converge to? Does it matter where you start?

4 The equation $x = \frac{13 - e^{-x}}{5}$ has a root between 2 and 3. Use fixed-point iteration to find this root, correct to two decimal places.

5 Use the iterative formula $x_{n+1} = \cos\left(\frac{x_n}{3}\right)$, with $x_1 = 0.5$, to find x_5. Give your answer correct to four decimal places.

This value of x_5 is an approximation to the root of the equation $f(x) = 0$. Write down an expression for $f(x)$ and suggest the value of the root, correct to two decimal places.

6 The equation $x = \arcsin\left(\frac{x+3}{5}\right)$ has a root between 0 and 1. Use fixed-point iteration to find this root correct to three decimal places. Show the first three approximations, correct to five decimal places.

7 **a** Use the iterative formula $x_{n+1} = \frac{2x_n^3 - 5}{6x_n^2 + 3}$, with $x_0 = 0$, to find x_4 and x_5, correct to four decimal places.

b The sequence $\{x_n\}$ converges to the root of the equation $ax^3 + bx + c = 0$. Find the values of a, b and c.

8 The diagram shows the graphs of $y = x$ and $y = \text{g}(x)$. The iteration $x_{n+1} = \text{g}(x_n)$ converges to the root of the equation $x = \text{g}(x)$. The starting value x_1 is shown on the diagram.

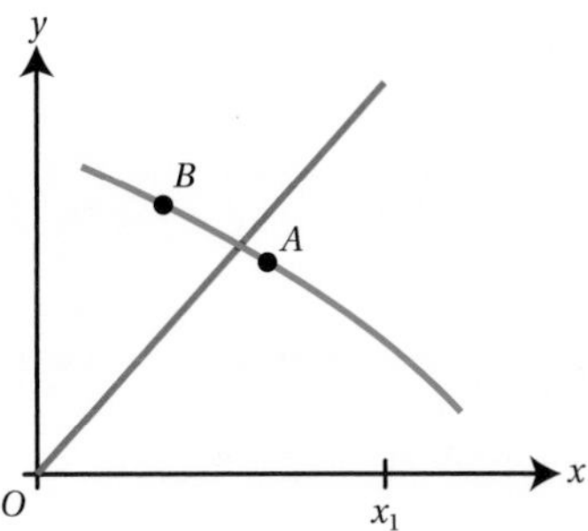

The values of x_2 and x_3 are the x-coordinates of the points marked A and B. Which of the two values corresponds to the point A?

9 **a** Show that the equation $x = \frac{1}{3}\left(x + \frac{5}{x}\right)$ has a root between 1 and 2.

b Use fixed-point iteration with $x_1 = 1.5$ to find next three approximations to the root.

c Show that your value of x_4 gives the root correct to two decimal places.

10 The diagram shows the graphs of $y = x$ and $y = 6 - \frac{4}{x}$.

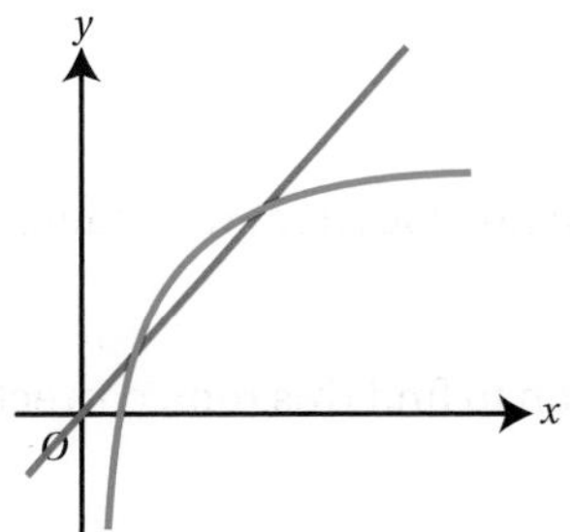

a Use the diagram to show that the iteration $x_{n+1} = 6 - \frac{4}{x_n}$ converges to a root of the equation $x = 6 - \frac{4}{x}$.

b Use the iteration from part **a** to find this root, correct to two decimal places.

c By rewriting the equation in the form $ax^2 + bx + c = 0$, find the exact value of the root. Hence, find the percentage error in your approximation.

11 The diagram shows the graphs of $y = x$ and $y = \frac{1}{2}\left(x + \frac{10}{x}\right)$.

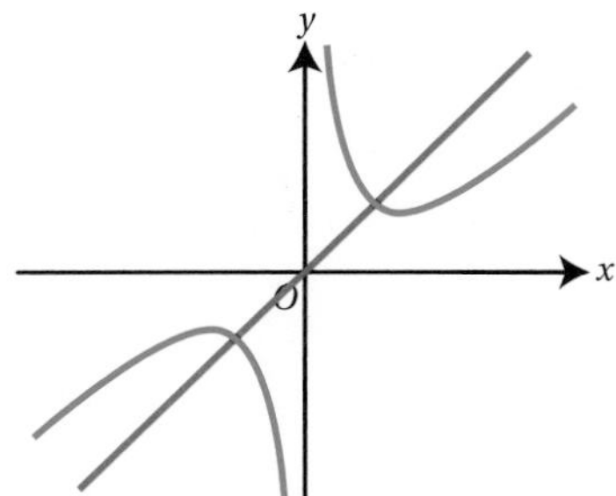

a Show on the diagram that the iteration $x_{n+1} = \frac{1}{2}\left(x_n + \frac{10}{x_n}\right)$, with $x_1 = 2$, converges.

b Prove that the iteration converges to $\sqrt{10}$.

Section 5: Limitations of fixed-point iteration; alternative rearrangements

Fixed-point iteration seems a little easier to implement than the Newton–Raphson method, as there is no need to differentiate any of the expressions. It also works in some situations when the Newton–Raphson method doesn't. However, there are other situations when fixed-point iteration doesn't work because the sequence fails to converge to the root.

For example, let us try solving the equation $x = e^x - 2$ for $x > 0$ by the iterative formula $x_{n+1} = e^{x_n} - 2$. Sketching graphs and trying some integer values of x shows that there is a root between $x = 1$ and $x = 2$.

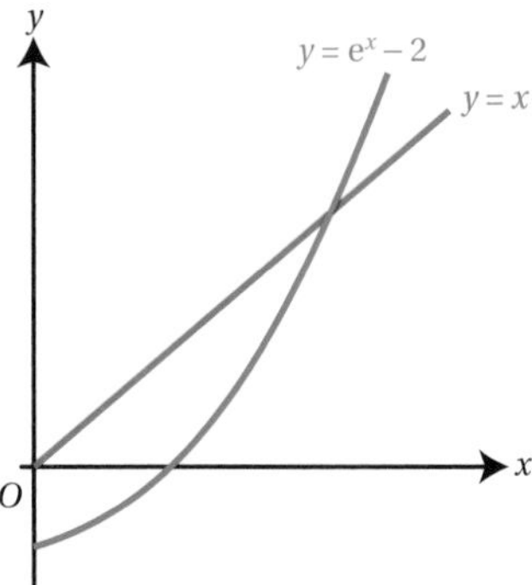

Starting the iteration at $x_1 = 1.5$ gives the following sequence.

$$x_1 = 1.5,\ x_2 = 2.482,\ x_3 = 9.965,\ \ldots$$

The sequence is clearly getting further away from the root; the sequence **diverges**. You can also try starting the sequence below the root, at $x_1 = 1$; the resulting sequence is:

$$x_1 = 1,\ x_2 = 0.718,\ x_3 = 0.0509,\ \ldots$$

Again, the sequence doesn't seem to be approaching the root. You can see this on the graph by drawing the staircase diagram.

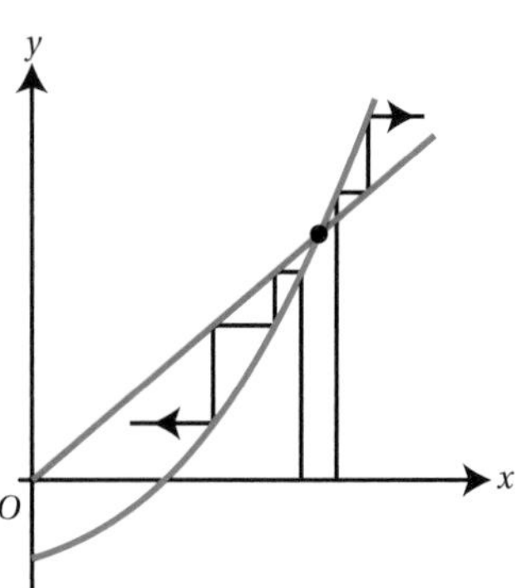

If you continue the second sequence it actually converges to the other root of the equation:

$x_1 = 1,\ x_2 = 0.718,\ x_3 = 0.0509,\ x_4 = -0.9478,\ x_5 = -1.61,\ x_6 = -1.83,$
$x_7 = -1.84,\ x_8 = -1.84, \ldots$

But is there any way you can use fixed-point iteration to find the first root?

The equation $x = e^x - 2$ can be written in a different way:

$$x = e^x - 2$$
$$\Leftrightarrow e^x = x + 2$$
$$\Leftrightarrow x = \ln(x+2)$$

The sequence based on this rearrangement, $x_{n+1} = \ln(x+2)$, starting at $x_1 = 1.5$, is:

$x_1 = 1.5,\ x_2 = 1.25,\ x_3 = 1.18,\ x_4 = 1.16,\ x_5 = 1.15,\ x_6 = 1.15\ldots$

Looking at the graph confirms that this sequence does indeed converge to the root between 1 and 2.

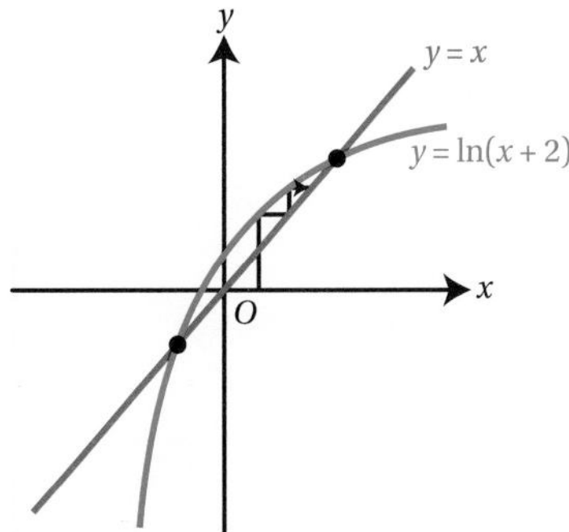

Interestingly, starting this iteration near the other root ($x = -1.84$) leads either to a divergent sequence or to one converging to the positive root. Starting at $x_1 = -1.5$ gives the following sequence.

0.693, 0.268, 0.819, 1.04, 1.11, 1.13, 1.14, 1.15, 1.15 …

Starting with $x_1 = -1.9$ we get $x_2 = -2.30$, and then the sequence cannot be continued further because $\ln(x+2)$ is not defined for $x \leqslant -2$.

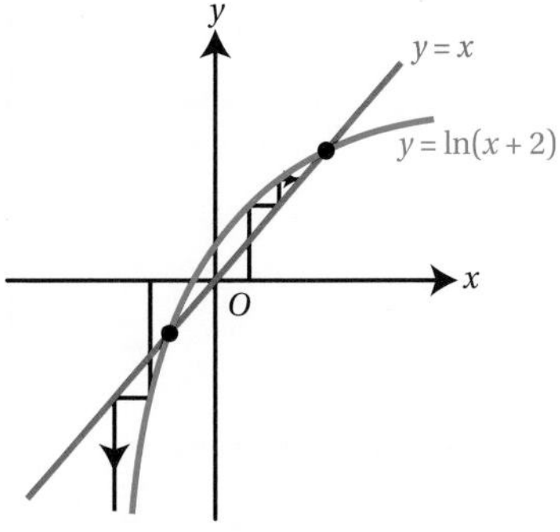

In this investigation you have found the following.

Key point 14.6

- Some rearrangements of the equation lead to **convergent** sequences, and others to **divergent** sequences.
- A divergent sequence does not find the required root.
- If an equation has more than one root, different rearrangements may converge to different roots.

WORKED EXAMPLE 14.8

a Show that the equation $x = 2\cos x$ has a root between 0 and 2.

b Starting with $x_1 = 1$, find the next four terms of the sequence $x_{n+1} = 2\cos x_n$ and describe the behaviour of the sequence.

c Illustrate the behaviour of the sequence using a cobweb diagram.

d Show that the equation $x = 2\cos x$ can be written as $x = \cos^{-1}\left(\frac{x}{2}\right)$. Use this rearrangement to find an approximate solution of the equation, correct to three decimal places.

a Write $f(x) = 2\cos x - x$.

$f(0) = 2 > 0$

$f(2) = -2.83 < 0$

There is a change of sign, so there is a root between 0 and 2.

To use the change of sign method you need to rewrite the equation in the form $f(x) = 0$.

b $x_2 = 2\cos 1 = 1.08$

$x_3 = 2\cos 1.08 = 0.942$

$x_4 = 2\cos 0.942 = 1.18$

$x_5 = 2\cos 1.18 = 0.77$

The sequence seems to diverge.

The terms of the sequence are getting farther away from each other.

c

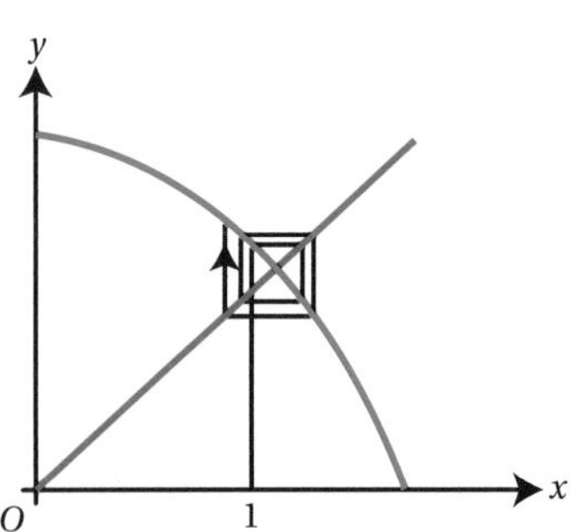

Continues on next page ...

d $x = 2\cos x$

$\Leftrightarrow \cos x = \frac{x}{2}$

$\Leftrightarrow x = \cos^{-1}\left(\frac{x}{2}\right)$

Make sure you show all the steps in a 'show that' type of question.

$x_{n+1} = \cos^{-1}\left(\frac{x_n}{2}\right)$

Use this new arrangement to form a sequence. It makes sense to start at $x_1 = 1$ again.

$x_1 = 1$

$x_2 = 1.047$

$x_3 = 1.020$

$x_4 = 1.036$

...

$x_{12} = 1.029945...$

$x_{13} = 1.02982...$

$x_{14} = 1.02989...$

$\therefore x = 1.030$ (3 d.p.)

You are not asked to show all the approximations, so just keep going until the third decimal place stops changing.

Is there any way you can tell, without actually trying it, whether a sequence from a particular rearrangement would converge? Looking at some staircase diagrams suggests that the answer has something to do with the gradient of the graph of g(x) at the point where it crosses the line $y = x$.

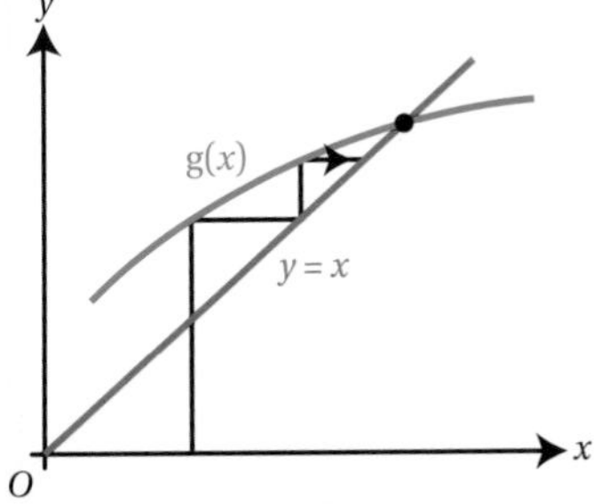

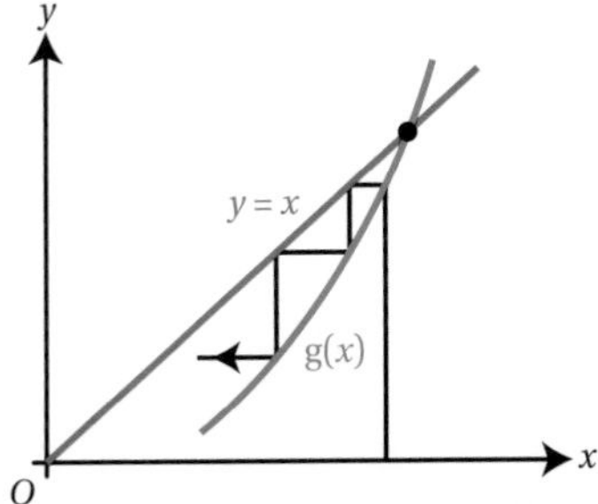

In the first diagram the gradient of the graph of g(x) is smaller than the gradient of $y = x$ and the sequence seems to converge. In the second diagram, where the sequence diverges, the graph of g(x) is steeper than the line $y = x$. This suggests that the sequence converges when the gradient of g(x) is smaller than 1 and diverges when it is greater than 1.

It is less obvious what happens when the gradient of g(x) is negative, so the iteration produces a cobweb diagram. It turns out that it depends on whether the gradient of g(x) is smaller or greater than -1.

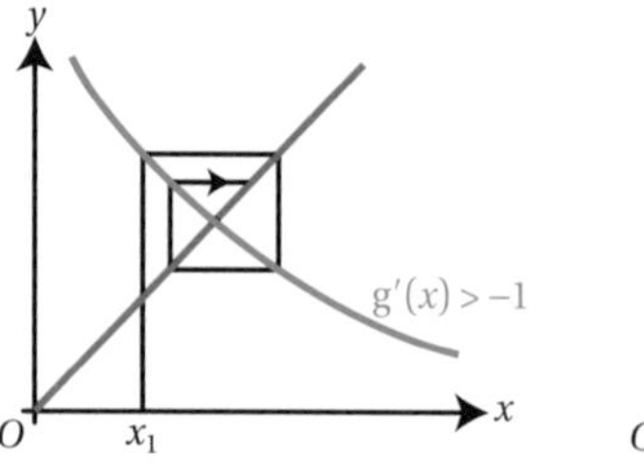

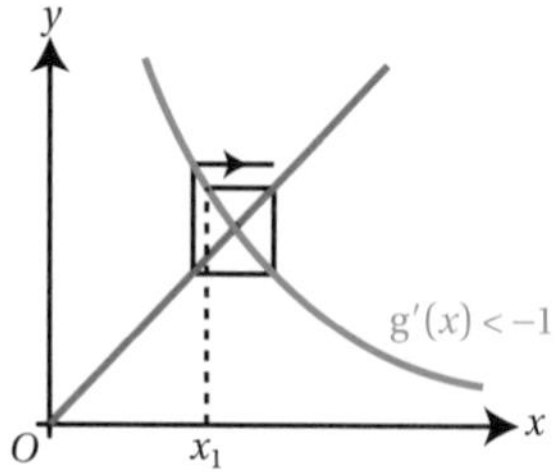

Both cases can be summarised as follows.

Key point 14.7

A fixed-point iteration $x_{n+1} = g(x_n)$:

- converges if $|g'(x)| < 1$ near the root and x_1 is sufficiently close to the root
- diverges if $|g'(x)| > 1$ near the root.

If $g'(x) = 1$ or -1 it is impossible to tell whether the sequence will converge without trying it.

WORKED EXAMPLE 14.9

The equation $x^3 + 2x + 5 = 0$ has a root near -1.3. Two possible rearrangements of this equation are

$$x = -\frac{5}{x^2+2} \text{ and } x = -\sqrt[3]{2x+5}.$$

Determine which rearrangement will produce a sequence that converges to the root.

Write the sequence as $x_{n+1} = g(x_n)$

The iteration converges if $|g'(x)| < 1$ near the root.

When $g(x) = -\frac{5}{x^2+2}$:

$$g'(x) = \frac{10x}{(x^2+2)^2}$$

$$g'(-1.3) = -\frac{13}{3.69^2} < -1$$

The root is near -1.3, so evaluate the derivative at this point.

$|g'(x)| > 1$ near the root, so this iteration will not converge.

When $g(x) = -\sqrt[3]{2x+5}$:

$$g'(x) = -\frac{2}{3}(2x+5)^{-\frac{2}{3}}$$

$$g'(-1.3) = -\frac{2}{3}(2.4)^{-\frac{2}{3}} > -1$$

$|g'(x)| < 1$ near the root, so this iteration will converge.

EXERCISE 14E

1 For each sequence below, find the first five terms, the 20th and the 21st term, and describe the behaviour of the sequence.

a $x_{n+1} = 3x_n^2 - 1, x_1 = 0$

b $x_{n+1} = 5 - \frac{1}{2}x_n^2, x_1 = 1$

c $x_{n+1} = 2 - \frac{x_n^2}{2} + \frac{x_n^3}{5}, x_1 = 0$

d $x_{n+1} = \sin\left(\frac{1}{2}x_n\right) - 0.2, x_1 = 2$

e $x_{n+1} = 3 - x_n, x_1 = 2$

f $x_{n+1} = 3\ln x_n, x_1 = 2$

g $x_{n+1} = 3\ln x_n, x_1 = 1.5$

2 Each diagram below shows the graphs of $y = x$ and $y = g(x)$, and the starting value x_1. Describe what happens to the iteration defined by $x_{n+1} = g(x_n)$.

a

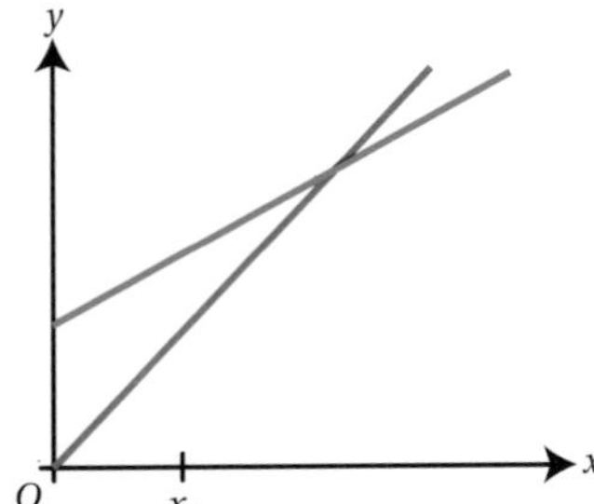

b

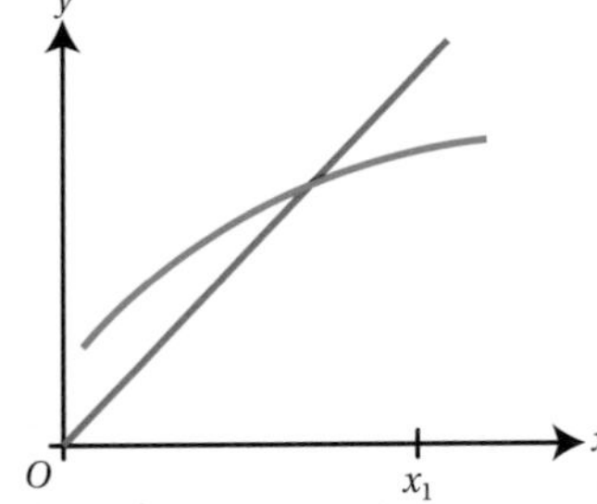

c

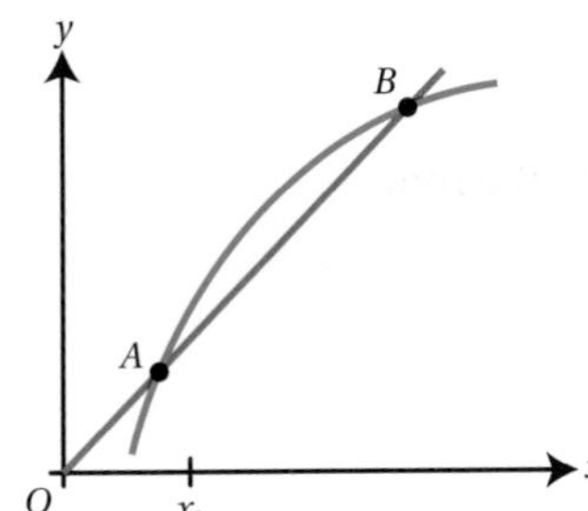

d

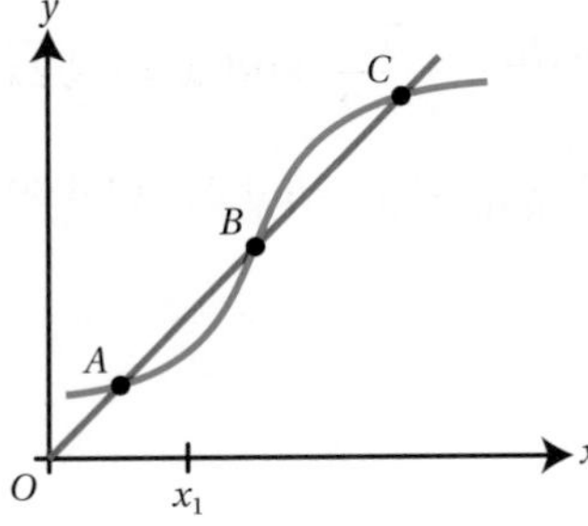

e

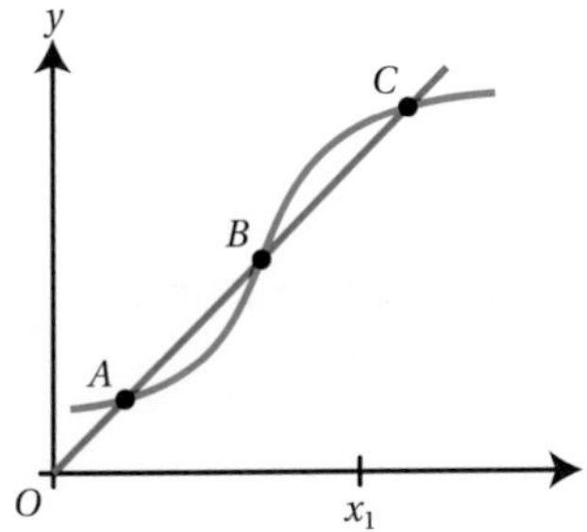

f

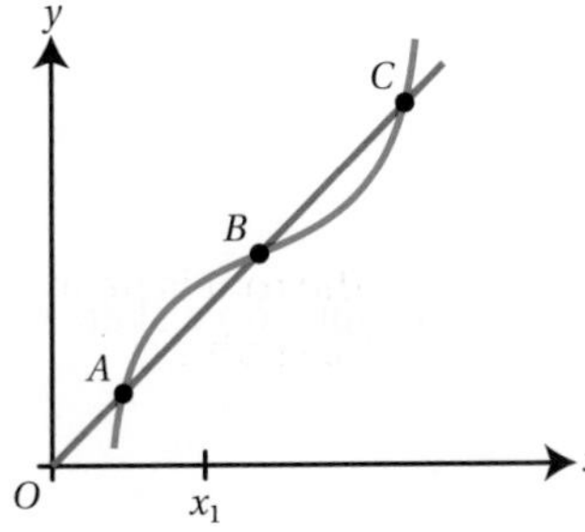

g

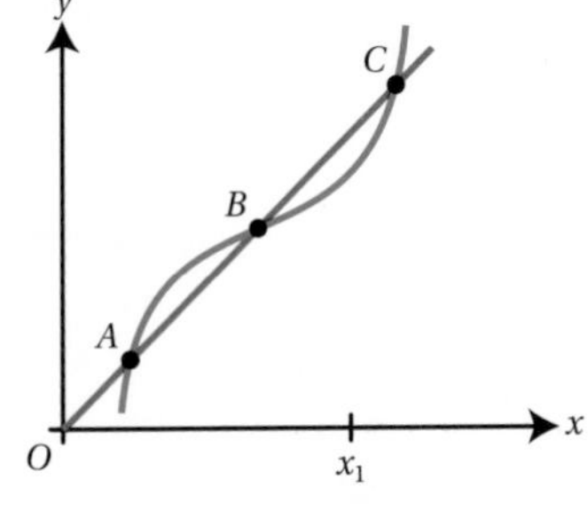

3 Find an alternative rearrangement for each of the following equations.

a **i** $x = 3\sin x$ **ii** $x = 5\tan x$

b **i** $x = \ln(x-3)$ **ii** $x = e^{x-2}$

c **i** $x = 3\sqrt{x-1}$ **ii** $x = 2\sqrt[3]{x+5}$

d **i** $x = 3x^2 - 1$ **ii** $x = \frac{x^2+1}{7}$

4 Find the missing constants to rearrange each of the following equations into the given equivalent form.

a **i** $2x^3 - 4x + 1 = 0 \Leftrightarrow x = \sqrt[3]{ax+b}$

ii $x - \frac{1}{2}x^4 - 3 = 0 \Leftrightarrow x = \sqrt[4]{ax+b}$

b **i** $x^3 + x^2 - 4 = 0 \Leftrightarrow x = \frac{a}{x} - bx^2$

ii $2x^3 - 2x^2 + 1 = 0 \Leftrightarrow x = \frac{ax^3+b}{cx}$

c **i** $2x^3 - x + 5 = 0 \Leftrightarrow x = \sqrt{a + \frac{b}{x}}$

ii $x^2 - 3x^3 + 2 = 0 \Leftrightarrow x = \sqrt{cx + \frac{d}{x}}$

d **i** $x^3 - 3x^2 + 5x + 2 = 0 \Leftrightarrow x = \frac{ax^3+b}{3x-5}$

ii $2x^3 + x^2 - 3x + 1 = 0 \Leftrightarrow x = \frac{2x^3+1}{a-bx}$

5 The equations below each have more than one root. For each root, use technology to find a rearrangement that converges to it.

a $x = 2 + 3\ln(x-2)$

b $3\arctan(x-2) = x - 1$

c $x^3 - 3x^2 - 5x + 3 = 0$

6 The diagram below shows the graph of a function g(x) and the line $y = x$. The equation g(x) $= x$ has three roots, marked, α, β and γ. Which of the roots, if any, does the iteration $x_{n+1} = g(x_n)$ converge to when:

a $x_1 = p$? **b** $x_1 = q$?

Justify your answer by showing several iterations on a sketch copy of the diagram.

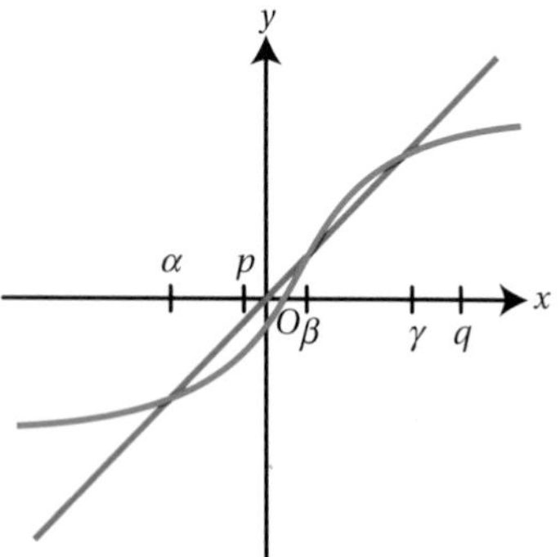

7 The iterative formula $x_{n+1} = \mathrm{f}(x_n)$ is used to find an approximate solution of the equation $x = \mathrm{f}(x)$. The graphs of $y = \mathrm{f}(x)$ and $y = x$ are shown below.

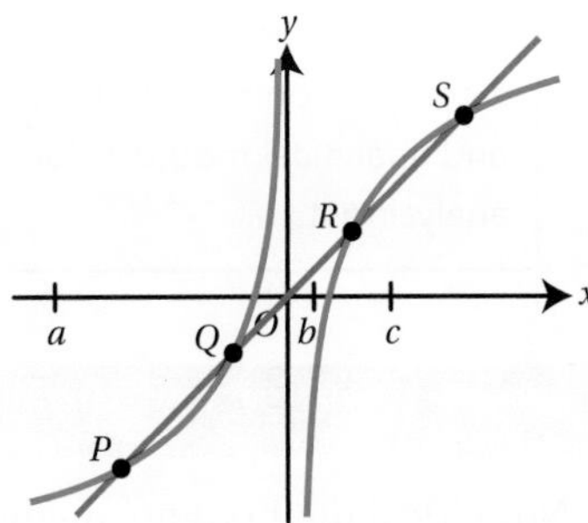

Use the diagram to determine the behaviour of the sequence $\{x_n\}$ when:

a $x_1 = a$ **b** $x_1 = b$ **c** $x_1 = c$

8 The Newton–Raphson iteration for solving $\mathrm{f}(x) = 0$ is $x_{n+1} = x_n - \frac{\mathrm{f}(x_n)}{\mathrm{f}'(x_n)}$. This can also be considered as a fixed-point iteration for solving $x = \mathrm{g}(x)$.

a Express $\mathrm{g}(x)$ in terms of $\mathrm{f}(x)$.

Let a be the solution of the equation, and assume that $\mathrm{f}'(x) \neq 0$ for x near a.

b Find $\mathrm{g}'(x)$, and, hence, prove that the Newton–Raphson method always converges when the starting value is sufficiently close to a.

9 **a** Show that the equation $x = 2 - \mathrm{e}^{-\frac{x}{2}}$ has a root between -4 and -3, and another one between 1 and 2.

b Let $\mathrm{g}(x) = 2 - \mathrm{e}^{-\frac{x}{2}}$ and define the sequence $x_{n+1} = \mathrm{g}(x_n)$ with $x_1 = 0$. Solve the inequality $\mathrm{g}'(x) > 1$ and, hence, determine to which of the two roots the sequence $\{x_n\}$ converges.

10 The function $\mathrm{f}(x)$ is defined by $\mathrm{f}(x) = x^4 + 3x^3 - 15x + 1$. The equation $\mathrm{f}(x) = 0$ has two positive real roots, $\alpha < \beta$.

a Show that α is between 0 and 0.1, and that β is between 1.7 and 1.8.

b The rearrangement $x = \sqrt[3]{\frac{-x^4 + 15x - 1}{3}}$ is used to find an approximate root of the equation $\mathrm{f}(x) = 0$. *Without* carrying out the iteration, determine to which of the two roots the sequence $x_{n+1} = \sqrt[3]{\frac{-x_n^4 + 15x_n - 1}{3}}$ converges.

c Show that an alternative rearrangement is $x = \frac{x^4 + c}{k + mx^2}$, and find the constants c, k and m. Use this rearrangement to find the root α, correct to three decimal places.

11 **a** Find, in terms of k, the roots of the equation $x = kx(1-x)$.
Let $g(x) = kx(1-x)$, where $k > 1$.

b Find $g'(\alpha)$, where α is the non-zero root of the equation $x = g(x)$.

c The iterative formula $x_{n+1} = kx_n(1-x_n)$, with $x_1 = 0.5$, is used to find approximate roots of the equation $x = g(x)$. Find the set of values of k for which the iteration converges to the non-zero root.

Focus on ...

See Focus on ... Problem solving 2 for some applications of this equation, and also for a comparison of numerical and analytical methods for analysing it.

Checklist of learning and understanding

- Some equations can be solved only by finding numerical approximations. Numerical methods are methods that tell you how to find an improved approximation.
- When an equation is written in the form $f(x) = 0$, you can show that it has a root (solution) between $x = a$ and $x = b$ by showing that $f(a)$ and $f(b)$ have different signs.
    - The change of sign method works only for sufficiently well-behaved functions; it can fail if, for example, the graph of $f(x)$ has a vertical asymptote, a break, or touches the x-axis.
    - You can use the change of sign method to check the accuracy of the solution by 'unrounding' the number.
- The methods you met in this chapter involve creating a sequence that converges to the root of the equation. The first term of the sequence needs to be chosen from an interval that contains the root.
- The Newton–Raphson method works by approximating the curve by its tangent. The equation needs to be written in the form $f(x) = 0$. The resulting sequence is given by

$$x_{n+1} = x_n - \frac{f(x_n)}{f'(x_n)}$$

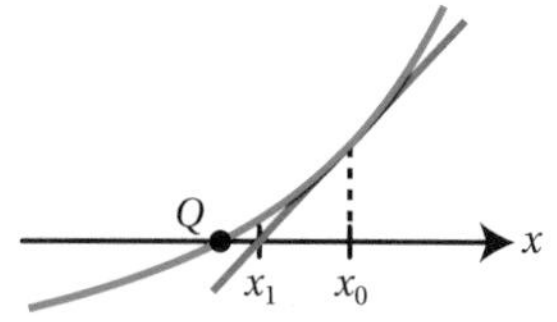

    - The Newton–Raphson method fails to converge if the starting point is close to a stationary point of $f(x)$ (where $f'(x) = 0$).
- Fixed-point iteration requires the equation to be written in the form $x = g(x)$. The iteration sequence is given by

$$x_{n+1} = g(x_n)$$

    - This iteration can be represented graphically as a staircase or a **cobweb** diagram.

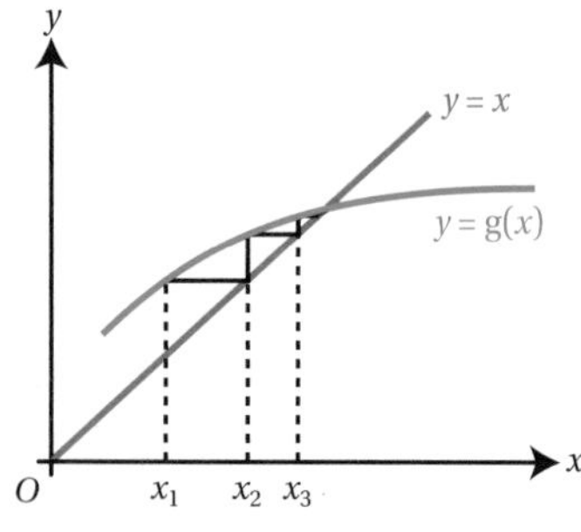

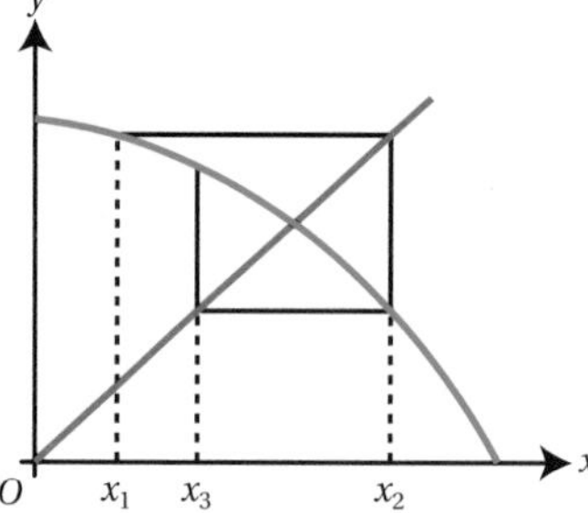

    - Sometimes the sequence diverges, meaning that the terms get farther away from the required root. To get a convergent sequence we may need to rearrange the equation.
    - If the equation has several roots, different rearrangements may converge to different roots.
    - The iteration converges if $|g'(x)| < 1$ near the root and diverges it if $|g'(x)| > 1$.

Mixed practice 14

1 The graph of $y = \sin\left(\frac{x}{2}\right) - x^2$ has a stationary point between 0 and 1.

a Show that the x-coordinate of the stationary point satisfies $x = \frac{1}{4}\cos\left(\frac{x}{2}\right)$.

b Use fixed-point iteration with a suitable starting point to find the x-coordinate of the stationary point, correct to three decimal places.

2 The diagram shows a sector of a circle with radius 5 cm. The angle at the centre is θ. The shaded area equals 30 cm^2.

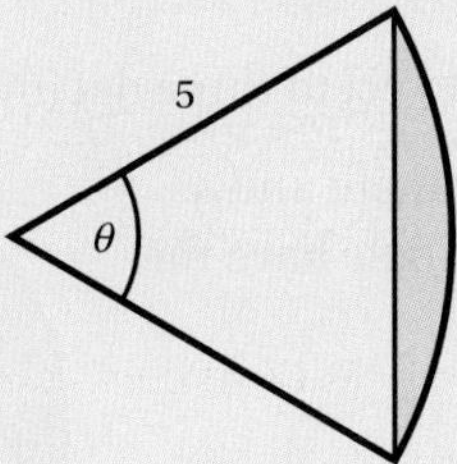

a Show that $\theta - \sin\theta = 2.4$.

b Show that the equation given in part **a** has a root between 2 and 3.

c Use the Newton–Raphson method with a suitable starting point, to find the value of θ, correct to two decimal places.

3 a Sketch the graphs of $y = e^{x-1}$ and $y = \ln(x+2)$ on the same set of axes. State the number of solutions of the equation $e^{x-1} = \ln(x+2)$.

b Show that the equation given in part **a** has a solution between 1 and 2.

c Use an iteration of the form $x_{n+1} = A + \ln(\ln(x_n + B))$ to find this solution, correct to two decimal places.

4 The diagram shows the graph of $y = x^2 + 1$. The shaded area is enclosed by the curve, the coordinate axes and the line $x = a$.

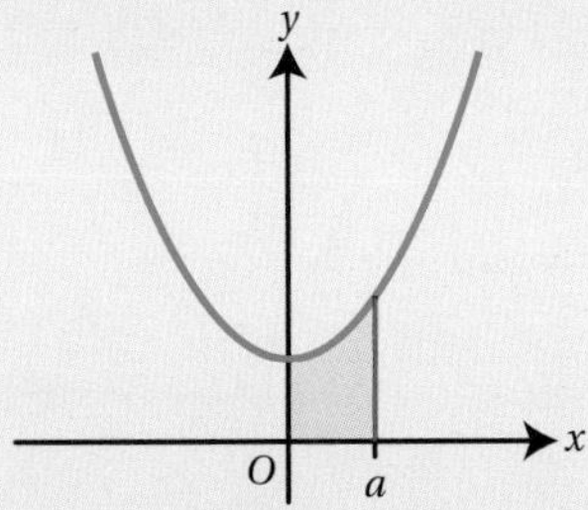

a Given that the shaded area equals 5, show that $a^3 + 3a - 15 = 0$.

b Show that the equation given in part **a** has a root between 2 and 3.

c Use the Newton–Raphson method to find the value of a, correct to14 three decimal places.

5 The sequence defined by

$$x_1 = 3, \qquad x_{n+1} = \sqrt[3]{31 - \frac{5}{2}x_n}$$

converges to the number α.

i Find the value of α correct to 3 decimal places, showing the result of each iteration.

ii Find an equation of the form $ax^3 + bx + c = 0$, where a, b and c are integers, which has α as a root.

© OCR, GCE Mathematics, Paper 4723, January 2008

6 Let $f(x) = \dfrac{x^3 + 4x + 8}{x^3 + 1}$ for $x < -1$.

a Show that the equation $f(x) = 0$ has a root between -2 and -1.

b Starting from $x_0 = -2$, use the Newton–Raphson method to find x_1.

c Explain why this iteration cannot be continued to find the root.

d Use the Newton–Raphson method with $x_0 = -1.5$ to find the root, correct to three decimal places.

7 A sector of a circle, with angle θ radians at the centre, is split into a segment and a triangle. as shown in the diagram. Given that the segment and the triangle have the same area:

a Show that $\theta = 2\sin\theta$.

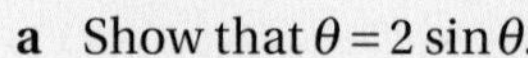

b Use an iterative formula, with the starting value $\theta_0 = \dfrac{\pi}{2}$, to find the value of θ, correct to three decimal places.

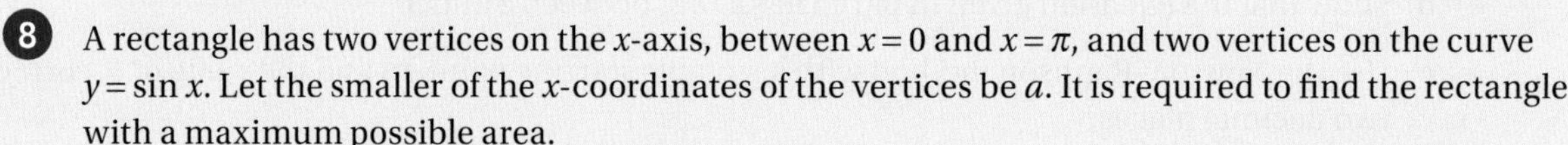

8 A rectangle has two vertices on the x-axis, between $x = 0$ and $x = \pi$, and two vertices on the curve $y = \sin x$. Let the smaller of the x-coordinates of the vertices be a. It is required to find the rectangle with a maximum possible area.

a Show that, for this rectangle, $2\tan a = \pi - 2a$.

b Use the Newton–Raphson method, with the starting value $a_0 = 0$, to find the value of a, correct to four decimal places. Hence, find the maximum possible area of the rectangle.

9 Marek and Anjali each deposit £1000 into their respective bank accounts. Marek's account earns 5% simple interest per year, and Anjali's account earns 3% compound interest per year. Neither of them make withdrawals nor further deposits into their accounts. Using the Newton–Raphson method, find after how many whole years Anjali will first have more money than Marek.

10

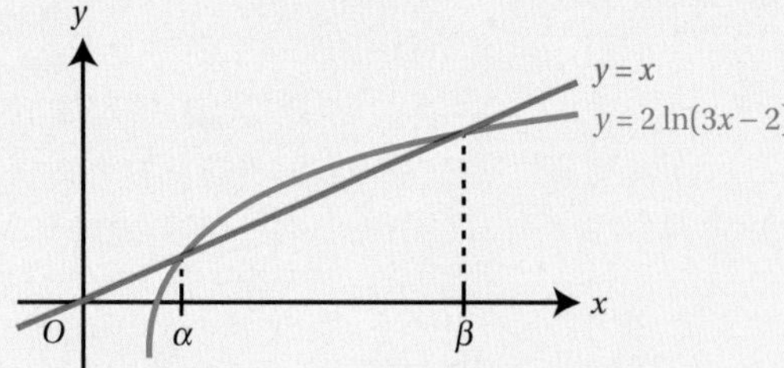

The line $y = x$ and the curve $y = 2\ln(3x - 2)$ meet where $x = \alpha$ and $x = \beta$, as shown in the diagram.

i Use the iteration $x_{n+1} = 2\ln(3x_n - 2)$, with initial value $x_1 = 5.25$, to find the value of β correct to 2 decimal places. Show all your working.

ii With the help of a 'staircase' diagram, explain why this iteration will not converge to α, whatever value of x_1 (other than α) is used.

iii Show that the equation $x = 2\ln(3x - 2)$ can be rewritten as $x = \dfrac{1}{3}\left(e^{\frac{1}{2}x} + 2\right)$. Use the Newton-Raphson method with $f(x) = \dfrac{1}{3}\left(e^{\frac{1}{2}x} + 2\right) - x$ and $x_1 = 1.2$, to find α correct to 2 decimal places. Show all your working.

iv Given that $x_1 = \ln 36$, explain why the Newton–Raphson method would not converge to a root of $f(x) = 0$.

© OCR, GCE Mathematics, Paper 4726, June 2010

11 A curve is defined by $y = \dfrac{\sin x}{x^2}$ for $x > 0$.

a Show that the x-coordinate of any stationary point on the curve satisfies the equation $x = 2\tan x$.

One of the roots of this equation is between 4 and 5.

b By considering the derivative of $2\tan x$, prove that the iteration $x_{n+1} = 2\tan x_n$ does not converge to this root.

c Find an alternative rearrangement of the equation $x = 2\tan x$ and use it to find the x-coordinate of the stationary point on the curve $y = \dfrac{\sin x}{x^2}$ between $x = 4$ and $x = 5$. Give your answer correct to three decimal places.

Elevate

See Extension sheet 14 for a look at Euler's method for finding approximate solutions to differential equations.

15 Numerical integration

In this chapter you will learn:

- why definite integration is connected to the area under a curve
- how to approximate integrals that can't be found exactly
- how to establish whether these approximations are overestimates or underestimates.

Before you start…

GCSE	You should be able to calculate the area of a trapezium.	1 Find the area of this shape. 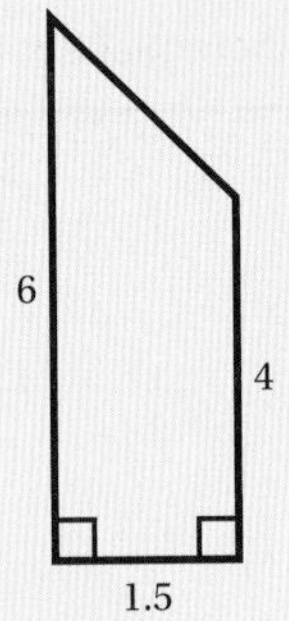
Student Book 1, Chapter 15	You should know that a definite integral represents the area between the curve and the x-axis.	2 Shade the area given by $\int_1^2 \sin x \, dx$. 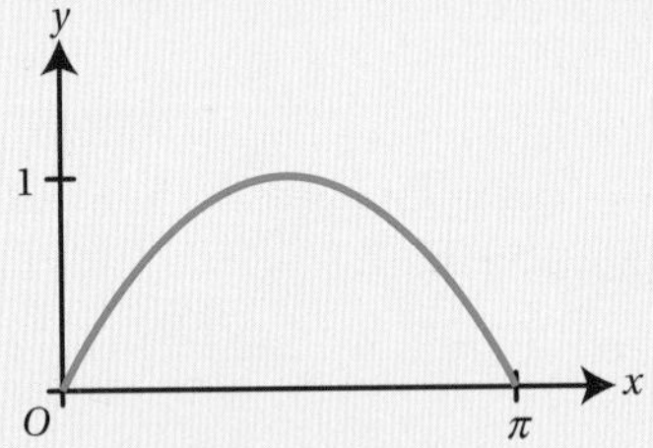
Student Book 1, Chapter 19	You should know how to find distance from a velocity–time graph.	3 Find the total distance travelled in the first 10 seconds. 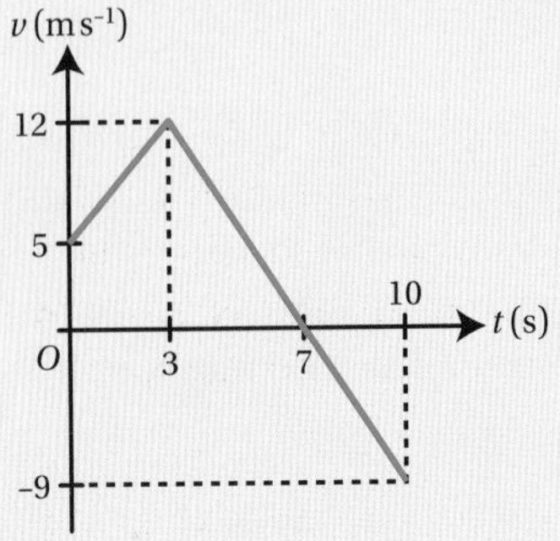

An approximation to definite integration

Using definite integration to find the area between a curve and the x-axis has many applications, for example in Mechanics (finding distance from a velocity-time graph); and Statistics, (where the area under the normal distribution–curve represents probability).

Since you already know many different integration methods, you may think that in most cases the area under the curve can be found exactly. It turns out that in many real-world problems, it is actually not possible to integrate the function exactly (or the integration method is very complicated). In such cases you can find an approximation for the area using one of the methods from this chapter.

Section 1: Integration as the limit of a sum

The simplest way to estimate the value of an area is to split it into rectangles. For example, an approximation to the area under the curve $y = e^{-x^2}$ between $x = 0$ and $x = 1$ is needed because it turns out that it is impossible to find the exact value of the integral $\int_0^1 e^{-x^2}\,dx$.

Fast forward

You will see in Chapter 17 that the function $e^{-0.5x^2}$ is used when finding probabilities from a standard normal distribution so it is important to be able to, find the area under its graph.

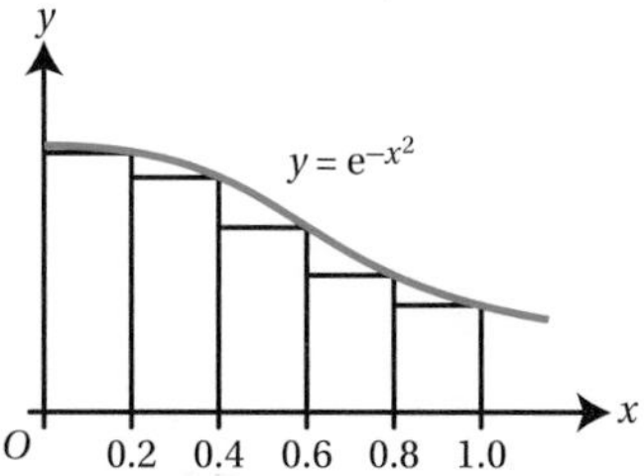

In the previous diagram the required area has been split into five rectangles of equal width, $h = 0.2$. The height of each rectangle is the y-coordinate of its top-right vertex; so the height of the first rectangle is the value of y when $x = 0.2$, which is $e^{-0.2^2}$. You can make a table to show the heights of all five rectangles.

x-coordinate	0.2	0.4	0.6	0.8	1.0
Height $y = e^{-x^2}$	$e^{-0.2^2}$	$e^{-0.4^2}$	$e^{-0.6^2}$	$e^{-0.8^2}$	$e^{-1.0^2}$

The total area of the five rectangles (each of width $h = 0.2$) is

$$0.2\left(e^{-0.2^2} + e^{-0.4^2} + e^{-0.6^2} + e^{-0.8^2} + e^{-1.0^2}\right) = 0.681 \quad (3 \text{ d.p.})$$

and this is an approximate value of the required area. You can see from the diagram that the actual area is a little bit larger; a **lower bound** for the area is 0.681. Unfortunately, this procedure doesn't tell you anything about how good the approximation is. To assess this, it would also be useful to have an **upper bound**, so that you know the area lies between those two values.

To find an upper bound use rectangles with the top edge above the curve. You can draw such rectangles using the left end point of each interval.

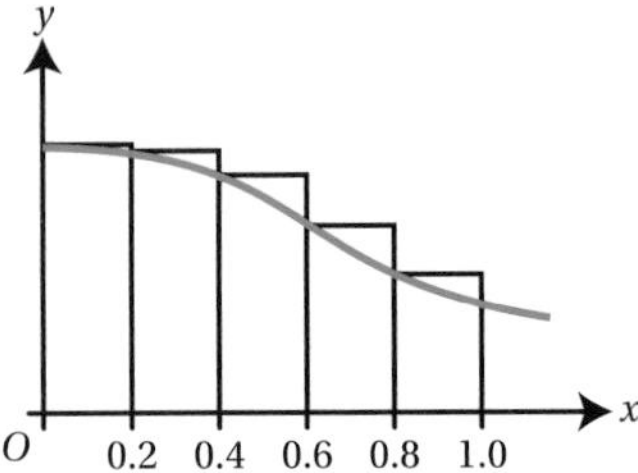

The heights of the five rectangles are:

x-coordinate	0.0	0.2	0.4	0.6	0.8
Height $y=e^{-x^2}$	$e^{-0.0^2}$	$e^{-0.2^2}$	$e^{-0.4^2}$	$e^{-0.6^2}$	$e^{-0.8^2}$

So their total area is

$$0.2\left(e^{-0.0^2}+e^{-0.2^2}+e^{-0.4^2}+e^{-0.6^2}+e^{-0.8^2}\right)=0.808 \text{ (3 d.p.)}$$

You can therefore say that the required area under the curve is certainly between 0.681 and 0.808, and you can write

$$0.681<\int_0^1 e^{-x^2}\,dx<0.808$$

Key point 15.1

You can find **upper and lower bounds** for the area under a curve by using rectangles that lie above and below the curve. The actual area lies between the lower and the upper bound.

WORKED EXAMPLE 15.1

The diagram shows a part of the graph of $y=\cos\left(x^2\right)$.

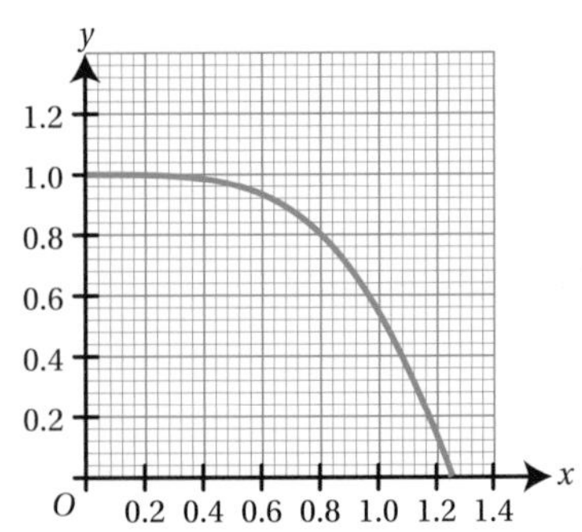

Using six rectangles of equal width, find a lower bound for the value of $\int_0^{1.2}\cos(x^2)\,dx$.

Continues on next page ...

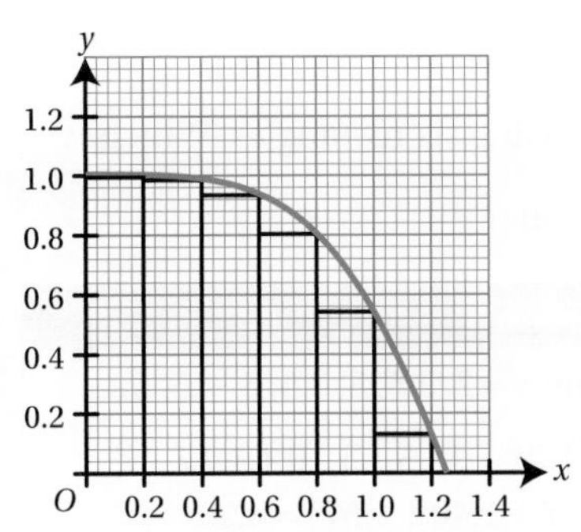

From the graph you can see that for the lower bound (rectangles below the curve) you need to use x-coordinates at the right end point of each interval.

x	0.2	0.4	0.6	0.8	1.0	1.2
y	0.9992	0.9872	0.9368	0.8021	0.5402	0.1304

The width of each rectangle is $\frac{1.2}{6} = 0.2$.

Area $= 0.2(0.9992 + 0.9872 + \ldots + 0.1304) \approx 0.879$ (3 s.f.)

So $\int_0^2 \cos(x^2)\,dx > 0.879$

Each rectangle has width 0.2 and height equal to the y-coordinate.

WORKED EXAMPLE 15.2

A part of the curve with equation $y = \ln(x^2 + 1)$ is shown in the diagram.

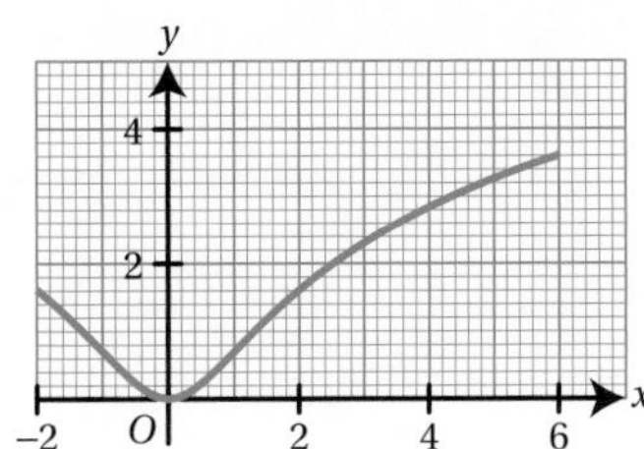

Use four rectangles of equal width to find an upper bound for $\int_2^6 \ln\left(x^2+1\right) dx$.

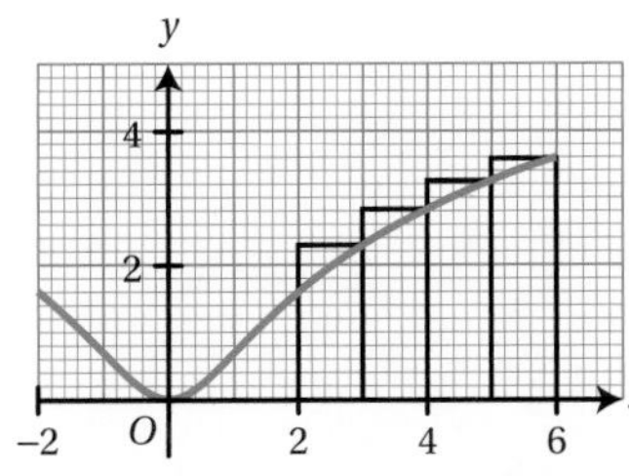

From the graph we can see that for the upper bound we now need to use x-coordinates at the right end point of each interval.

x	3	4	5	6
y	2.303	2.833	3.258	3.611

The width of each rectangle is $\frac{6-2}{4} = 1$.

Area $= 1(2.303 + \ldots + 3.611) = 11.311$ or 11.3 (to 3 s.f.)

So $\int_2^6 \ln(x^2+1)\,dx$ has an upper bound of 11.3 (3 s.f.) < 12

WORK IT OUT 15.1

Three students try to find an upper bound for the value of $\int_2^5 \operatorname{cosec}\sqrt{x+1}\,dx$, using six rectangles. Which is the correct solution? Can you identify the errors made in the incorrect solutions?

Solution 1	Solution 2	Solution 3
Using $x = 2, 2.5, 3, 3.5, 4, 4.5$:	Using $x = 2.5, 3, 3.5, 4, 4.5, 5$:	Using $x = 2, 2.5, 3, 3.5, 4, 4.5, 5$:
$0.5(1.01 + 1.05 + 1.10 + 1.17 + 1.27 + 1.40) = 3.50$	$0.5(1.05 + 1.10 + 1.17 + 1.27 + 1.40 + 1.57) = 3.78$	$0.5(1.01 + 1.05 + 1.10 + 1.17 + 1.27 + 1.40 + 1.57) = 4.29$
So $\int_2^5 \operatorname{cosec}\sqrt{x+1}\,dx < 3.5$	So $\int_2^5 \operatorname{cosec}\sqrt{x+1}\,dx < 3.8$	So $\int_2^5 \operatorname{cosec}\sqrt{x+1}\,dx < 4.3$

To get a more accurate approximation for the area you need to make the upper and lower bounds closer to each other. This can be done using more rectangles of smaller width. For the original example, estimating $\int_0^1 e^{-x^2}\,dx$, you can use a spreadsheet to calculate areas using more and more rectangles. Here are some of the results.

Tip

Always use the graph to decide which rectangles to use.

Number of rectangles	Width	Lower bound	Upper bound
5	0.2	0.681	0.808
10	0.1	0.715	0.778
20	0.05	0.731	0.762
50	0.02	0.740	0.753
100	0.01	0.744	0.750

You can use a graphical calculator or graphing software to check that the actual area is 0.747 (3 d.p.).

Key point 15.2

As the number of rectangles increases, the upper and the lower bounds approach a **limit**, which is the actual value of a definite integral.

EXERCISE 15A

1 Use five rectangles to find upper and lower bounds for the value of each of the following integrals. Use technology to draw the graph first.

a **i** $\int_0^5 e^{-x^2}\,dx$ **ii** $\int_0^2 \frac{1}{x^3+1}\,dx$

b **i** $\int_0^2 \sin(\sqrt{x})\,dx$ **ii** $\int_3^4 \ln(x^3-2)\,dx$

c **i** $\int_0^2 e^{\sqrt{x}} - 1\,dx$ **ii** $\int_0^1 \tan(x^2)\,dx$

2 Use a spreadsheet to find upper and lower bounds for each of the following integrals, using:

i 10 rectangles

ii 20 rectangles

iii 40 rectangles.

In each case, find the difference between the upper and lower bounds.

a $\int_0^{\frac{\pi}{2}} \cos(\sin x)\,dx$ b $\int_2^3 \ln(\sin x)\,dx$

c $\int_0^2 e^{0.1x^3}\,dx$ d $\int_2^5 \frac{1}{\sqrt{x}+1}\,dx$

e How does the difference decrease when the number of rectangles doubles?

3 A part of the curve with equation $y = \sin(\ln x)$ is shown in the diagram.

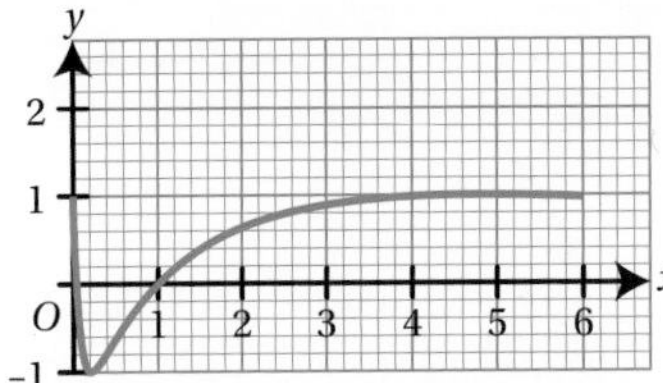

Using six rectangles of equal width, find upper and lower bounds for $\int_1^4 \sin(\ln x)\,dx$.

4 The diagram shows the graph of $y = 3e^{-\sqrt{x}}$.

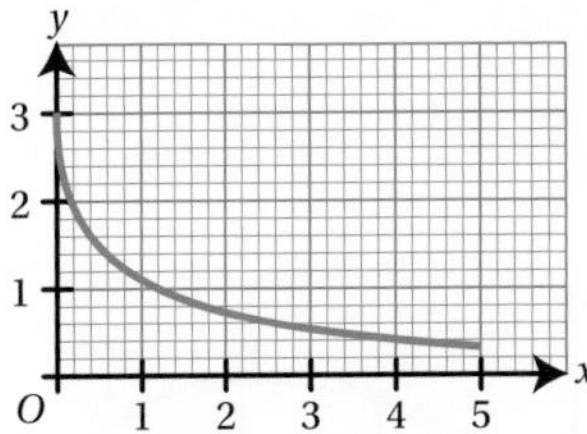

a Use five rectangles of equal width to find the upper and lower bounds for $\int_0^4 3e^{-\sqrt{x}}\,dx$.

b How could the difference between the upper and lower bounds be reduced?

5 a Sketch the graph of $y = \sec x$ for $x \in \left[0, \frac{\pi}{2}\right]$.

b Use four rectangles of equal width to find an upper bound for $\int_0^1 \sec x\,dx$.

c If 20 rectangles are used, will the upper bound increase or decrease?

6 The diagram shows a part of the graph $y = \sqrt{\sin x}$.

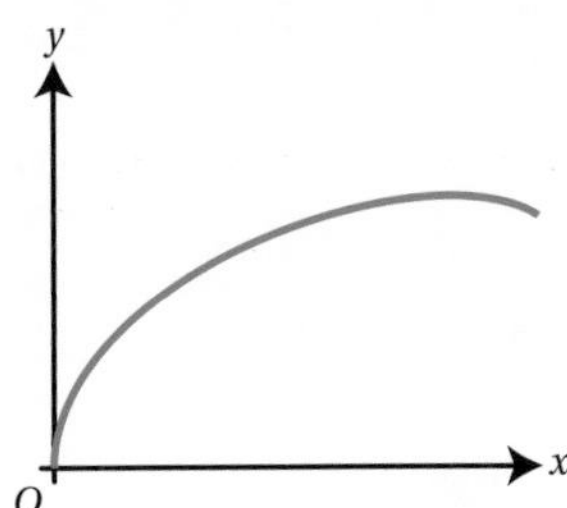

a State the exact coordinates of the maximum point on the curve.

b Use four rectangles of equal width to find a lower bound for $\int_0^{\pi} \sqrt{\sin x}\,dx$.

Section 2: The trapezium rule

You saw in Section 1 that you can approximate a definite integral using sums of areas of rectangles. However, you may need many rectangles to achieve high accuracy. You can improve this method by replacing each rectangle by a trapezium that connects the points on the curve corresponding to the end points of each interval (as shown in red in the diagram below). Each trapezium has an area somewhere between that of the upper and the lower rectangles.

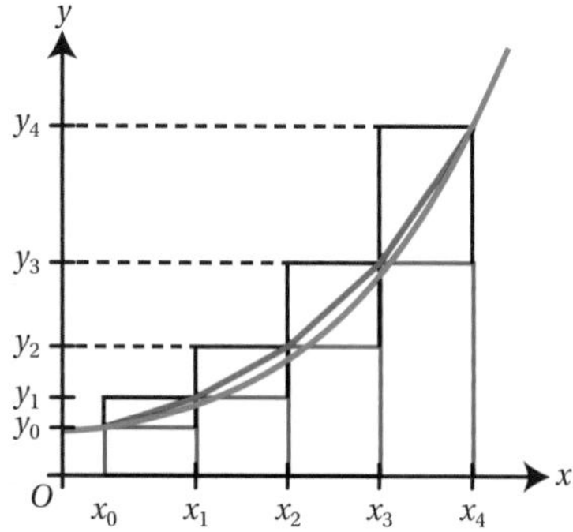

The area of a trapezium is given by $\frac{(a+b)h}{2}$, where a and b are the parallel sides and h is the height (perpendicular distance between the parallel sides). Looking at the first trapezium above, its height is equal to the width of the interval (h) and the parallel sides have lengths equal to the y-coordinates of the end points.

If there are n intervals, you can label the x-coordinates $x_0, x_1, x_2, \ldots, x_n$ and the corresponding y-coordinates $y_0, y_1, y_2, \ldots, y_n$. The areas of each trapezium are then:

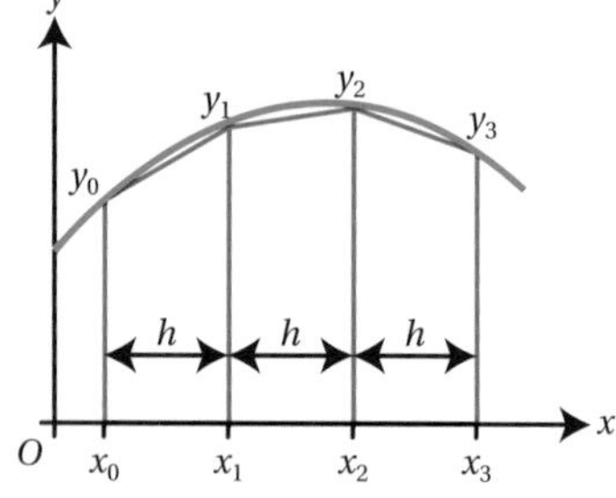

$$\frac{(y_0+y_1)h}{2}, \frac{(y_1+y_2)h}{2}, \ldots, \frac{(y_{n-1}+y_n)h}{2}$$

Adding these together, each y-coordinate appears twice, except the first and the last one. The following expression therefore gives an approximation for the total area under the curve.

Key point 15.3

The **trapezium rule** using n equal intervals with end points $x_0, x_1, \ldots, x_n$:

$$\int_a^b f(x)\,dx \approx \frac{h}{2}\left[y_0 + y_n + 2(y_1 + y_2 + \ldots + y_{n-1})\right]$$

where $y_i = f(x_i)$ and $h = \frac{b-a}{n}$.

Tip

It is a good idea to set out the x and y values in a table. The formula then says '$\frac{h}{2}$ times (first + last + twice the sum of the rest)', where h is the difference between the x-coordinates.

WORKED EXAMPLE 15.3

Use the trapezium rule, with five equal intervals, to find an approximate value of $\int_0^1 e^{-x^2}\,dx$. Give your answer correct to three decimal places.

$h = \frac{1-0}{5} = 0.2$

Divide the interval from 0 to 1 into five equal parts.

x	0	0.2	0.4	0.6	0.8	1.0
y	1	0.9608	0.8521	0.6977	0.5273	0.3679

The x values start from 0 and go up in steps of 0.2 until they reach 1.0.

Note that since there are five intervals, there should be six x values.

The y values are calculated using $y = e^{-x^2}$. Since you want the answer correct to 3 d.p., you should record the y values to 4 d.p. and round at the end.

$$\text{Area} \approx \frac{0.2}{2}\left[1 + 0.3679 + 2\begin{pmatrix}0.9608 + 0.8521 + \\ 0.6977 + 0.5273\end{pmatrix}\right]$$
$$= 0.1(1.3679 + 2(3.0379))$$
$$= 0.74437$$

$$\therefore \int_0^1 e^{-x^2}\,dx \approx 0.744$$

Use the formula. You should show the numbers used in the calculation.

Tip

You may have a TABLE function on your calculator that will produce the table of values. Alternatively, you can save the six numbers in memory to use in the trapezium rule calculation. If the expression for f(x) is short, you can just type in the whole sum; e.g. $e^{-0^2} + e^{-1^2} + 2\left(e^{-0.2^2} + e^{-0.4^2} + e^{-0.6^2} + e^{-0.8^2}\right)$.

The actual value of the integral is 0.747 (3 d.p.), so our approximation is within 0.003 of the correct value. The trapezium rule tends to be generally more efficient than using rectangles.

In this case the approximation is a slight underestimate. Looking at the graph explains why this is the case: most of the trapezia lie below the curve.

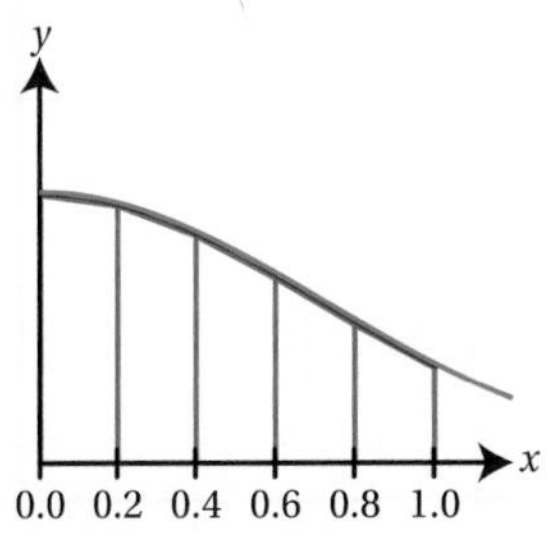

Did you know?

Your calculator may have a function for finding approximate values of definite integrals. It probably uses the trapezium rule.

Rewind

You can see from the graph that the trapezium rule gives an overestimate when the function is convex. See Chapter 12, Section 1 for a definition of a convex function.

Key point 15.4

To determine whether the trapezium rule gives an underestimate or overestimate, you need to look at the shape of the graph.

WORKED EXAMPLE 15.4

The diagram shows the graph of $y = \tan^3 x$.

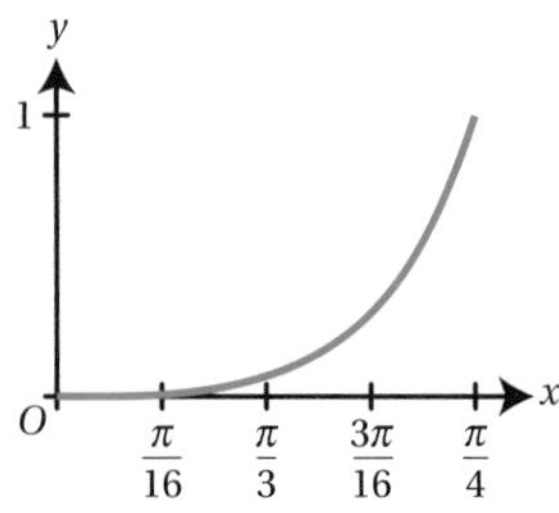

a Use the trapezium rule, with four equal intervals, to estimate the value of $\int_0^{\pi/4} \tan^3 x \, dx$, giving your answer correct to three significant figures.

b Explain whether your answer is an overestimate or an underestimate.

a $h = \frac{\pi}{4} \div 4 = \frac{\pi}{16}$

Divide the interval from 0 to $\frac{\pi}{4}$ into four equal parts.

x	0	$\frac{\pi}{16}$	$\frac{\pi}{8}$	$\frac{3\pi}{16}$	$\frac{\pi}{4}$
y	0	0.00787	0.07107	0.29832	1

The x-coordinates start from 0 and increase in increments of $\frac{\pi}{16}$.

The y-coordinates are found using $y = \tan^3 x$.

$\text{Area} \approx \frac{\pi}{32}[0 + 1 + 2(0.00787 + 0.07107 + 0.29832)]$

Use the trapezium rule.

$= \frac{\pi}{32}(1 + 2(0.37726))$

$= 0.17225$

$\therefore \int_0^{\pi/4} \tan^3 x \, dx \approx 0.172$

b Since the function is convex between $x = 0$ and $x = \frac{\pi}{4}$, the trapezia are above the curve.

The explanation should refer to the shape of the graph.

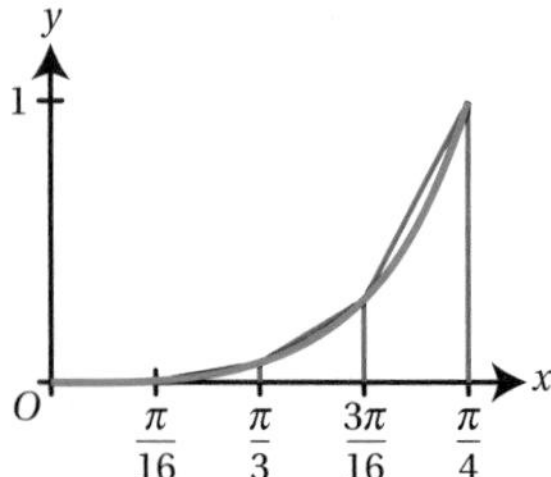

Hence, this approximation is an overestimate.

WORK IT OUT 15.2

Three students are asked to estimate the value of $\int_1^2 (\ln x)^2 \, dx$ using the trapezium rule, with five strips.

Which is the correct solution? Can you identify the errors made in the incorrect solutions?

Solution 1

1.0	1.25	1.5	1.75	2.0
0	0.05	0.16	0.31	0.48

$0.125(0.48 + 2 \times 0.53) = 0.192$

Solution 2

1.0	1.2	1.4	1.6	1.8	2.0
0	0.03	0.11	0.22	0.345	0.48

$0.1(0 + 0.03 + 0.11 + \ldots) = 0.119$

Solution 3

1.0	1.2	1.4	1.6	1.8	2.0
0	0.03	0.11	0.22	0.345	0.48

$0.1(0.48 + 1.43) = 0.191$

EXERCISE 15B

1 Use the trapezium rule, with the given number of intervals, to find the approximate value of each integral. Compare your answer to the upper and lower bounds found in question 1 of Exercise 15A.

a **i** $\int_0^5 e^{-x^2} \, dx$, 5 intervals **ii** $\int_0^2 \frac{1}{x^3+1} \, dx$, 4 intervals

b **i** $\int_0^2 \sin(\sqrt{x}) \, dx$, 5 intervals **ii** $\int_3^4 \ln(x^3 - 2) \, dx$, 4 intervals

c **i** $\int_0^2 e^{\sqrt{x}} - 1 \, dx$, 6 intervals **ii** $\int_0^1 \tan(x^2) \, dx$, 3 intervals

2 For each integral from question 1:

a Use technology to find its value, correct to eight decimal places.

b Use a spreadsheet to calculate trapezium rule approximations using 2, 4, 8 and 16 intervals.

c Find the percentage error in each estimate. How do the percentage errors decrease when you double the number of intervals?

3 For each of the following integrals, either find its exact value where possible, or an approximation using six trapezia.

a $\int_3^6 \ln\sqrt{x-2} \, dx$ **b** $\int_1^4 \frac{1}{\sqrt{x+1}} \, dx$ **c** $\int_0^\pi \sin^2 x \, dx$

d $\int_0^\pi \sin(x^2) \, dx$ **e** $\int_2^3 \ln(x^3) \, dx$ **f** $\int_1^4 \operatorname{cosec}\left(\frac{x}{2}\right) dx$

4 **a** Sketch the graph of $y = 3\ln(x-1)$.

b Use the trapezium rule, with five strips, to estimate the value of $\int_2^4 3\ln(x-1) \, dx$. Give your answer to two decimal places.

c Explain whether your answer is an overestimate or an underestimate.

5 a Use the trapezium rule, with four intervals, to find an approximate value of $\int_4^5 e^{\sqrt{5-x}}\, dx$.

b Describe how you could obtain a more accurate approximation.

6 The diagram shows a part of the graph of $y=\cos\left(x^2\right)$.

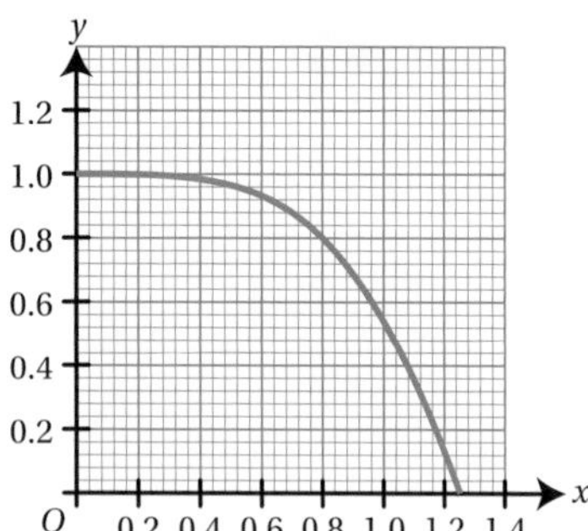

The graph crosses the x-axis at the point where $x=a$.

a Find the exact value of a.

b Use the trapezium rule, with four intervals, to find an approximation for $\int_0^a \cos(x^2)\, dx$.

c Is your approximation an overestimate or an underestimate? Explain your answer.

7 A particle moves in a straight line with velocity given by $v=e^{\sqrt{t}}$, where v is measured in m s^{-1} and t in seconds. Use the trapezium rule, with six strips, to find the approximate distance travelled by the particle in the first 3 seconds.

8 The velocity, v m s^{-1}, of a particle moving in a straight line is given by $v=\sin\left(\sqrt{t}\right)$. The diagram shows the velocity–time graph for the particle.

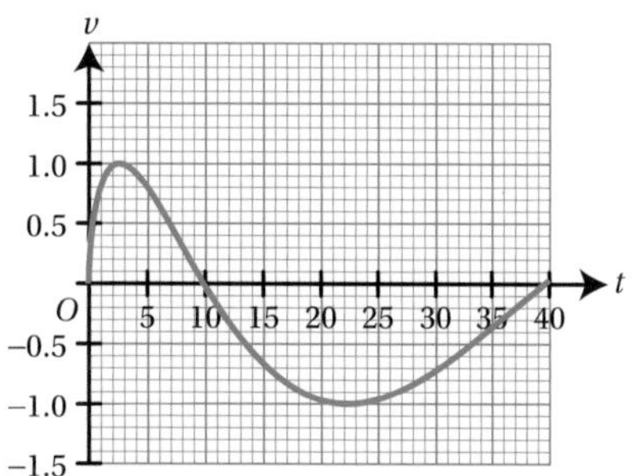

a The particle changes direction when $t=p$ and $t=q$ (with $p<q$). Find the exact values of p and q.

b Use the trapezium rule, with eight equal intervals, to estimate the total distance travelled by the particle during the first q seconds.

Elevate

See Support sheet 15 for a further example of using the trapezium rule and for more practice questions.

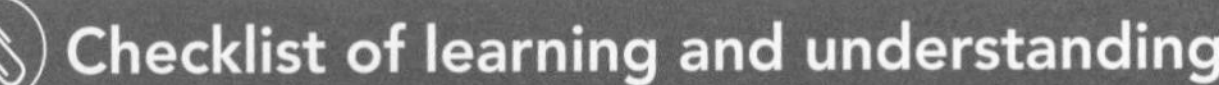

Checklist of learning and understanding

- Some definite integrals cannot be evaluated exactly. In such cases it is possible to use rectangles to find upper and lower bounds.
  - An upper bound for an area is a number that is larger than the area; a lower bound is a number that is smaller than the area.
  - As the rectangles get smaller, the upper and lower bounds get closer to each other. The actual area is the limit of the sum of the rectangles.
- The trapezium rule is a way of estimating the area using trapezia. We need fewer trapezia than rectangles to achieve the same accuracy.
  - Using n equal intervals with end points $x_0, x_1, \ldots, x_n$:

$$\int_a^b \mathrm{f}(x)\,\mathrm{d}x \approx \frac{h}{2}\left[y_0 + y_n + 2\left(y_1 + y_2 + \ldots + y_{n-1}\right)\right]$$

where $y_i = \mathrm{f}(x_i)$ and $h = \dfrac{b-a}{n}$.

Mixed practice 15

1 The diagram shows a part of the graph of $y = \dfrac{5}{\sqrt{x+2}+1}$.

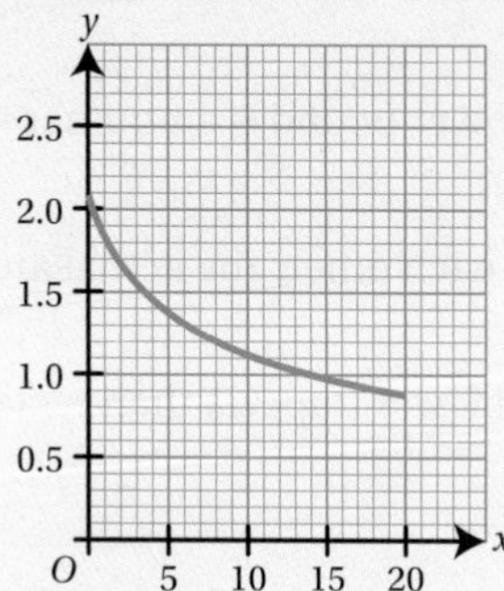

Using five rectangles of equal width, find a lower bound for the value of $\int_0^{15} \dfrac{5}{\sqrt{x+2}+1}\,dx$. Give your answer correct to one decimal place.

2 The diagram shows a part of the curve with equation $y = \ln(x^2+1)$.

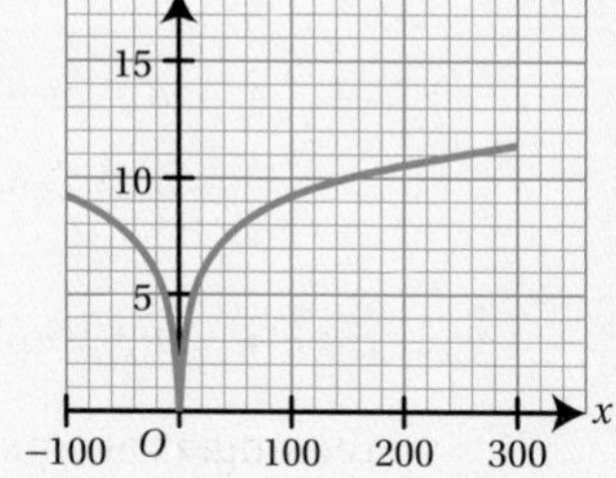

a Use the trapezium rule, with five strips of equal width, to estimate the value of $\int_0^{200} \ln(x^2+1)\,dx$.

b State, with a reason, whether your answer is an underestimate or an overestimate.

c Explain how you could find a more accurate estimate.

3 Use six rectangles of equal width to find the values of L and U such that $L < \int_2^5 (\ln x)^2\,dx < U$.

4

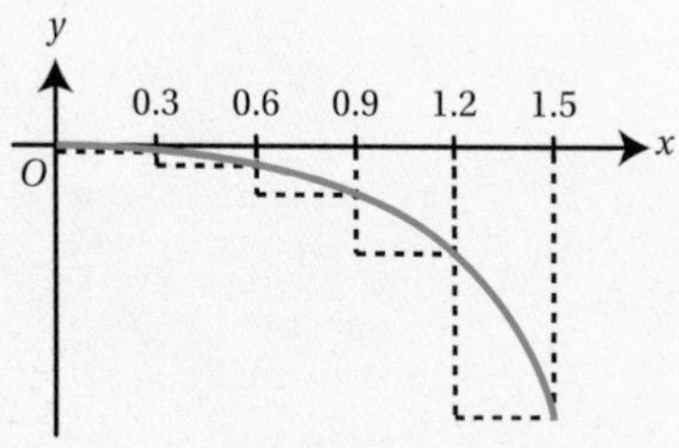

The diagram shows the curve with equation $y = \ln(\cos x)$, for $0 \leqslant x \leqslant 1.5$. The region bounded by the curve, the x-axis and the line $x = 1.5$ has area A. The region is divided into five strips, each of width 0.3.

i By considering the set of rectangles indicated in the diagram, find an upper bound for A. Give the answer correct to 3 decimal places.

ii By considering another set of five suitable rectangles, find a lower bound for A. Give the answer correct to 3 decimal places.

iii How could you reduce the difference between the upper and lower bounds for A?

© OCR, GCE Mathematics, Paper 4726, June 2009

5 Use the trapezium rule, with 3 strips each of width 2, to estimate the value of

$$\int_1^7 \sqrt{x^2+3}\,dx.$$

© OCR, GCE Mathematics, Paper 4722, January 2008

6 The diagram shows a part of the curve with equation $y=\ln(7x-x^2-9)$. Use the trapezium rule, with six strips of equal width, to estimate the area enclosed between the curve and the x-axis.

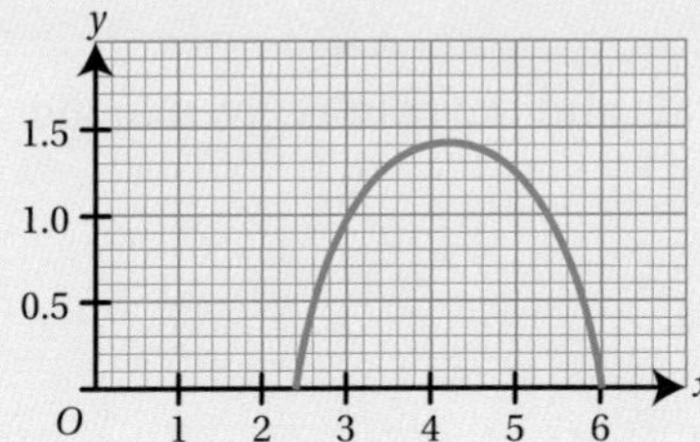

7 A particle moves in a straight line so that its velocity is given by the equation $v=\sin t\sin 3t$.

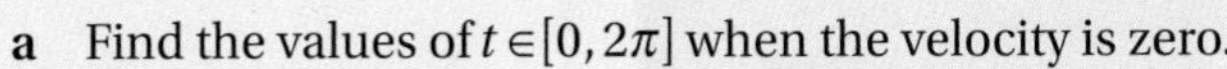

a Find the values of $t\in[0,2\pi]$ when the velocity is zero.

b Use the trapezium rule, with strips of width $\frac{\pi}{6}$, to find an approximate value of the distance travelled by the particle from $t=0$ to $t=\pi$.

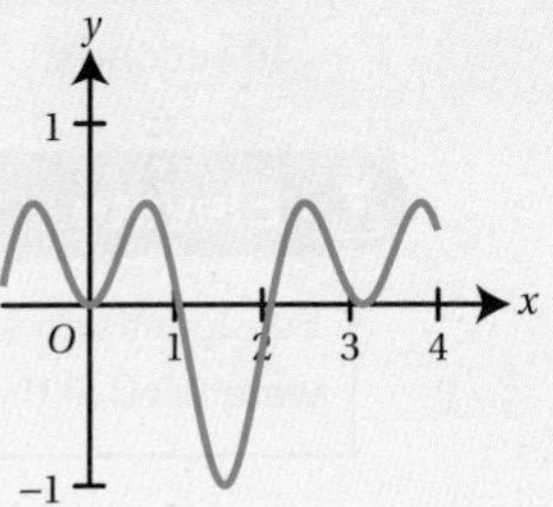

8 A part of the graph of $y=\ln\left(\frac{4x+2}{x+2}\right)$ is shown in the diagram. Use four rectangles of equal width to find a rational number K such that $\int_0^{20}\ln\left(\frac{4x+2}{x+2}\right)dx<\ln K$.

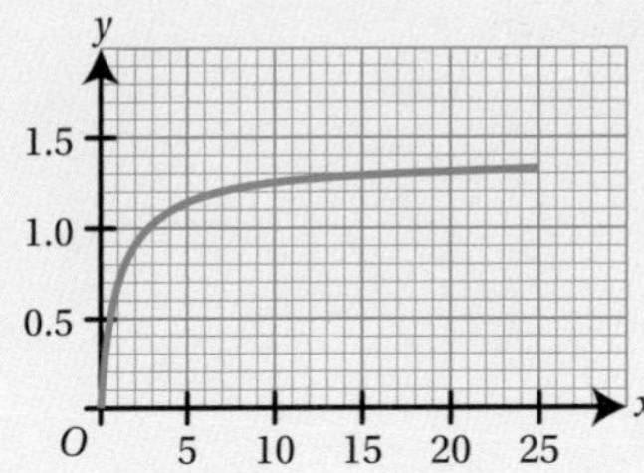

9 A curve has equation $y=\sqrt{x^4+1}$.

a Sketch the curve, showing the coordinates of any stationary points.

b Use four rectangles of equal width to find a lower bound for $\int_{-1}^{1}\sqrt{x^4+1}\,dx$.

10 The diagram shows the velocity–time graph for a particle moving in a straight line.

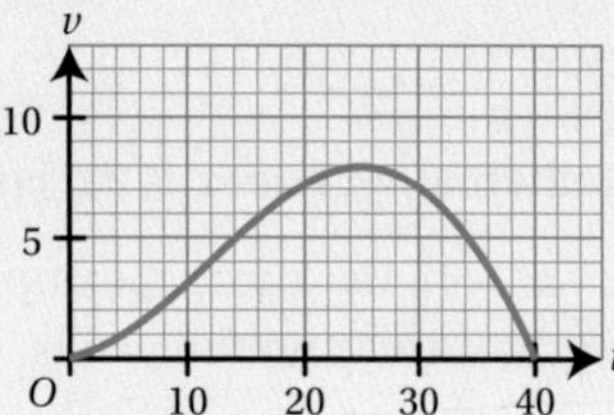

The velocity of the particle is measured at 10 second intervals and the results given in the following table.

t (s)	0	10	20	30	40
v (m s^{-1})	0.0	3.1	7.2	7.1	0.0

Estimate the average speed of the particle during the 40 seconds.

Elevate

See Extension sheet 15 for a look at how approximation methods were used in the development of calculus.

FOCUS ON ... PROOF 2

Deriving the compound angle identities

This proof will demonstrate that:

$\sin(A+B) = \sin A \cos B + \cos A \sin B$

and

$\cos(A-B) = \cos A \cos B + \sin A \sin B$

Rewind

In Student Book 1, Focus on ... Proof 2 used this strategy to prove the sine and cosine rules.

You have already seen trigonometric proofs that use right-angled triangles to prove results about more complicated figures. The same approach works here.

The sine compound angle formula

You'll prove the sine compound angle formula first: $\sin(A+B) = \sin A \cos B + \cos A \sin B$.

PROOF 9

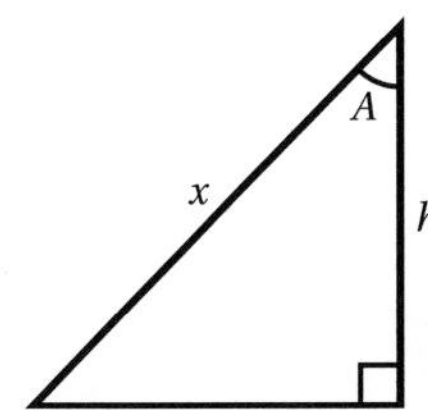

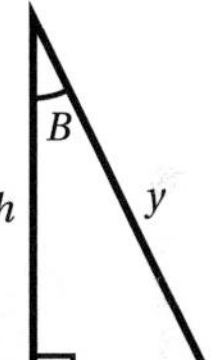

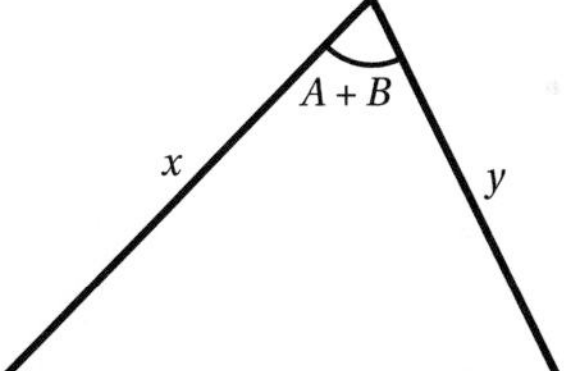

Create a triangle with angle $A+B$ by joining two right-angled triangles with angles A and B.

From the left right-angled triangle:
$h = x\cos A$

Now express all the other lengths in terms of x, y, A and B.

Similarly, from the other right-angled triangle:
$h = y\cos B$

You can write h in two different ways.

The area of the left-hand triangle is:
$\frac{1}{2}x \times (y\cos B) \times \sin A$

Use Area $= \frac{1}{2}ab\sin C$ on each of the triangles individually.

The area of the right-hand triangle is:
$\frac{1}{2}y \times (x\cos A) \times \sin B$

The area of the whole triangle is:
$\frac{1}{2}xy\sin(A+B)$

And then on the triangle as a whole.

Therefore:
$\frac{1}{2}xy\sin(A+B) = \frac{1}{2}xy\cos B\sin A + \frac{1}{2}xy\cos A\sin B$

$\Rightarrow \sin(A+B) = \sin A\cos B + \cos A\sin B$

Dividing by $\frac{1}{2}xy$.

Questions

1. Is it possible to draw two right-angled triangles with the same height for any pair of acute angles A and B?

2. Does the identity still hold when the angles A and B are not acute? Can you prove it?

The cosine compound angle formula

To derive the compound angle identities for $\cos(A+B)$ and $\cos(A-B)$, you could use the same triangles and the cosine rule. However, there is a simpler proof that uses the relationship between sin and cos:

$$\sin\left(\frac{\pi}{2}-\theta\right)=\cos\theta \text{ and } \cos\left(\frac{\pi}{2}-\theta\right)=\sin\theta$$

3. Write $\cos(A-B)=\sin\left(\frac{\pi}{2}-(A-B)\right)=\sin\left(\left(\frac{\pi}{2}-A\right)+B\right)$

   and use the compound angle identity for $\sin(A+B)$ to prove that

$$\cos(A-B)=\cos A\cos B+\sin A\sin B$$

FOCUS ON ... PROBLEM SOLVING 2

Choosing between analytical and numerical methods

Many problems you have encountered in this course can be solved in more than one way. In real-life situations you are free to choose whatever method and approach you prefer. In making your decision you should think about the following.

- How difficult is the method?
- How efficient is it? Does it require lots of detailed or repeated calculations?
- How accurate is it? What level of accuracy do you actually need?
- Can it be easily adapted to solve other similar problems?

For example, when solving an equation you have essentially two options: you can try to rearrange the equation using rules of algebra (an 'analytical solution'), or you can use one of the iterative methods from Chapter 14 (a 'numerical solution'). The former may not always be possible but, when it works, it gives you an exact solution (such as $e^{2\pi}$). However, in many applications you need an answer to only a couple of decimal places, so you should consider whether the effort required to rearrange the equation is justified.

On the other hand, your equation may have a parameter in it (for example, $x^2+3ax+1=0$) and you may want to know how changing the value of the parameter affects the solution; in this case, finding the analytical solution once (in terms of the parameter) may be more efficient than repeating the numerical calculation lots of times.

Here is a problem that can be investigated both analytically and numerically. You can try various approaches and decide for yourself which one suits you best.

The fishing lake problem

The number of fish in a lake can be modelled by the equation

$$x_{n+1} = \alpha x_n - \beta x_n^2 - k$$

In this model, x_n is the number of fish in year n. Each year, due to natural birth and death rates, the population increases by a factor of α. Meanwhile, βx_n^2 die out due to lack of resources, and a constant number (k) of fish are caught and removed.

What is the maximum number of fish that can be removed each year without causing the population to die out?

Questions

1 Use a spreadsheet to investigate how the population changes with the following parameter values.

a $\alpha = 1.4, \beta = 0.0002, x_1 = 1000$ and:

i $k = 150$ **ii** $k = 200$ **iii** $k = 205$

b $\alpha = 1.4, \beta = 0.0002, x_1 = 2000$ and:

i $k = 150$ **ii** $k = 200$ **iii** $k = 205$

c What is the largest number of fish that can be caught each year without causing the population to die out? Does this depend on the initial size of the population?

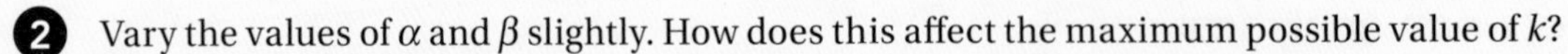

2 Vary the values of α and β slightly. How does this affect the maximum possible value of k?

You need to try many different values of the parameters to find the relationship between k, α and β. Is it possible to solve this problem analytically instead, to find an equation linking the three quantities?

The sequence $x_{n+1} = \alpha x_n - \beta x_n^2 - k$ is not one of the types you are familiar with; in fact, it is not possible to find a general formula for x_n. However, you are only interested in the long-term behaviour of the sequence: does it eventually decrease to zero or not? You know from Chapter 14 that, if a sequence $x_{n+1} = g(x_n)$ has a limit, then this limit is a solution of the equation $x = g(x)$.

3 Consider the case when $\alpha = 1.4$ and $\beta = 0.0002$.

a Solve the equation $x = \alpha x - \beta x^2 - k$ when:

i $k = 150$ **ii** $k = 200$ **iii** $k = 205$

Compare the solution to what you observed in question 1.

b Find the discriminant of the equation $x = 1.4x - 0.0002x^2 - k$ in terms of k. Hence, show that the equation has a solution only when $k \leqslant 200$.

c Use the quadratic formula to write the two solutions in terms of k. Hence, show that, when $0 < k < 200$, both solutions are positive. Could you tell, without doing the spreadsheet investigation, to which of the two solutions the sequence will converge to?

Rewind

In Chapter 14, Section 5, you learnt that the iteration $x_{n+1} = g(x_n)$ converges to a root of $x = g(x)$ if $|g(x)| < 1$ near the root.

4 For the general case of the equation $x = \alpha x - \beta x^2 - k$:

a Find the discriminant in terms of α, β and k.

b Hence, show that the largest number of fish that can be removed without causing the population to die out is $k = \dfrac{(\alpha-1)^2}{4\beta}$.

5 Did you find the theoretical analysis or the spreadsheet investigation easier to follow? Which one do you think gives a more reliable answer? Which helps you understand the problem better?

6 When $\alpha = 1.6$ and $\beta = 0.0007$, the formula we found previously says that the maximum number of fish that can be removed is 128. However, with $k = 130$ and $x_1 = 500$, the spreadsheet shows that there are still 400 fish in the lake after 50 years. So is the additional accuracy you get from using the formula always required?

FOCUS ON ... MODELLING 2

Translating information into equations

The aim of a mathematical model is to describe a real-life situation using equations that can be solved and used to make predictions.

In this section you look at writing differential equations. These are equations involving the rate of change of a quantity. You need to remember the following.

- The rate of change of y with respect to x is $\frac{dy}{dx}$.
- 'y is proportional to x' means that $y = kx$ for some constant k.

When writing differential equations, you usually have some information about particular values of the quantities involved. Sometimes you can use those to find constants in the equation (such as the k in $y = kx$), but sometimes you need to wait until you have solved the equation.

Tip

In many examples, 'rate of change' means change in time; however, look out for examples where this is not the case!

Rewind

Solving some differential equations is covered in Chapter 13. In this section you will not need to solve any equations.

WORKED EXAMPLE 1

The speed of an object decreases at a rate proportional to the square root of its current speed. When the speed is $12\,\text{m}\,\text{s}^{-1}$ it is decreasing at a rate of $1.5\,\text{m}\,\text{s}^{-2}$. Using v for speed and t for time, write an equation to represent this information.

$$\frac{dv}{dt} = -k\sqrt{v}$$

'Rate of change' means the derivative with respect to time.

The speed is decreasing, so you write '$-k$' to emphasise this.

When $v = 12$, $\frac{dv}{dt} = -1.5$:

$$-1.5 = -k\sqrt{12}$$

$$\Rightarrow k = \frac{\sqrt{12}}{1.5} = \frac{4\sqrt{3}}{3}$$

You can use the given information to find k.

So the equation is:

$$\frac{dv}{dt} = -\frac{4\sqrt{3}}{3}\sqrt{v}$$

Remember that the rate of change is negative.

Rewind

You know that the rate of change of velocity is acceleration which is proportional to the force acting on an object. The model in Worked example 1 could therefore be used when there is a resistance force proportional to the square root of the speed, such as air resistance or drag when an object is moving through liquid.

WORKED EXAMPLE 2

In one possible model of population growth, the rate of growth depends on two factors: it is proportional to the current size of the population, and is also proportional to $\cos(30t)$. (The last factor represents seasonal breeding patterns.) When the measurements began the population size was 160. Using N for the size of the population and t for time, measured in months, write a differential equation to represent this information.

$$\frac{dN}{dt} = kN\cos(30t)$$

The two factors need to be multiplied together. Don't forget to include the constant of proportionality.

You only have information about N when $t = 0$, so you can't find k until you have solved the equation.

Questions

Write a differential equation to represent each of the following situations. Where possible, find the values of any constants.

1. A population of a new town (N thousand) increases at a rate proportional to its size. Initially, the size of the population is 3500 and it is increasing at the rate of 120 per year.

2. During the decay of a radioactive substance, the rate at which mass is lost is proportional to the mass present at that instant. Use m for the mass of the substance, in grams, and t for the time, in seconds. Initially there is 24 g of the substance and the mass is decreasing at the rate of $1.2\,\text{g s}^{-1}$.

3. In an electrical circuit, the voltage is decreasing at a rate proportional to the square of the present voltage. When the voltage is 25 volts, it is decreasing at a rate of 2 volts per second.

4. Newton's law of cooling states that the rate at which a body cools is proportional to the difference between its temperature and the temperature of its surroundings. A cup of tea is initially at 100 °C and is cooling at the rate of 2 °C per minute in a room of temperature 24 °C. Use T for the temperature and t for time (in minutes).

5. A metal rod, of length 48 cm, has one of its ends heated. After a while the temperature remains constant in time. However, the temperature changes along the length of the rod, decreasing at a rate proportional to the distance from the hot end. The temperatures at the two ends are 230 °C and 52 °C. Use T for temperature and x for the distance from the hot end (measured in cm).

6. The water pressure in the sea increases with depth. The pressure p at depth h is proportional to the density of the seawater (ρ). The density also varies with depth, and is modelled by the equation $\rho = 1000(1 + 0.001h)$. Write a differential equation for the rate of increase of pressure with depth.

7. A rumour spreads at a rate proportional to the square root of the number of people who have already heard it, and inversely proportional to the time it has been spreading. After 5 minutes, 25 people have heard the rumour and it is spreading at the rate of 3 people per minute. Write N for the number of people who have heard the rumour and t for the time, in minutes, since the rumour started. Write a differential equation to model this situation, and explain why the model needs to be modified for small values of t.

8. A cylindrical tank has a base radius of 1.2 m. Water leaks out of the tank so that the rate at which the volume is decreasing is proportional to the height of the water remaining in the tank. Initially the height of water is 2.5 m and it is decreasing at the rate of 0.05 m per minute. Find an equation for the rate of change of volume of water in the tank.

CROSS-TOPIC REVIEW EXERCISE 2

1 Find the equation of the curve that has gradient $\frac{dy}{dx} = 3\tan x$ and passes through the point (0, 4).

2 Find $\int \frac{\sin x + \cos x}{2\cos x}\, dx$.

3 **a** Given that $y = e^{\lambda x}$, find $\frac{d^2y}{dx^2}$.

b Given that $y = e^{\lambda x}$ is a solution of the differential equation $\frac{d^2y}{dx^2} + 5\frac{dy}{dx} - 6y = 0$, find the possible values of λ.

4 The diagram below shows the graphs of $y = \sin x$ and $y = \cos x$. Find the value of the shaded area.

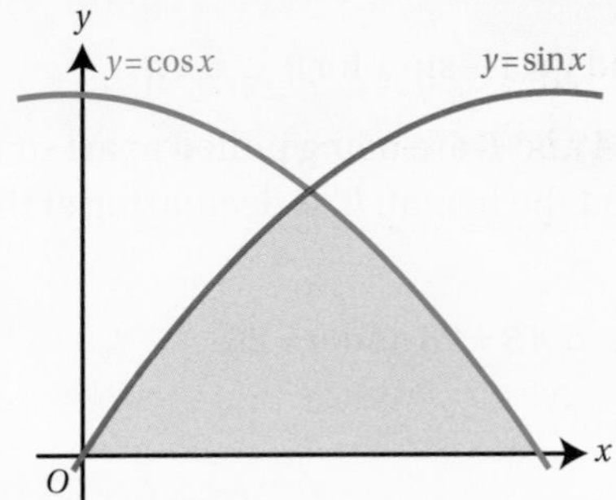

5 The region R in the diagram is enclosed between the graph of $y = \ln x$ and the x-axis between $x = 2$ and $x = 5$.

a Find the shaded area between the curve and the y-axis.

b Hence, find the exact area of R.

6 The diagram shows a part of the curve with parametric equations $x = t^2$, $y = \sin t$.

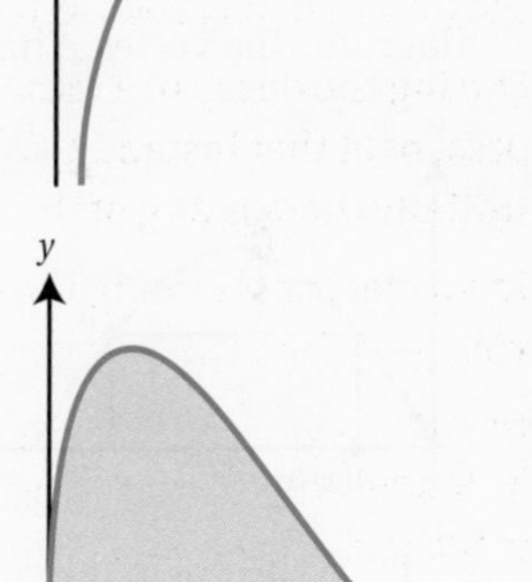

a Find the values of t at the points where the graph crosses the x-axis.

b Find the exact value of the shaded area.

c Find the Cartesian equation of the curve.

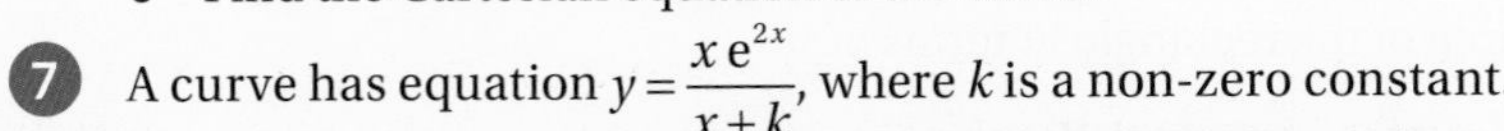

7 A curve has equation $y = \frac{x e^{2x}}{x + k}$, where k is a non-zero constant.

i Differentiate xe^{2x}, and show that $\frac{dy}{dx} = \frac{e^{2x}(2x^2 + 2kx + k)}{(x + k)^2}$.

ii Given that the curve has exactly one stationary point, find the value of k, and determine the exact coordinates of the stationary point.

© OCR, GCE Mathematics, Paper 4723, January 2008

8 By taking natural logarithms of both sides, or otherwise, find $\frac{dy}{dx}$ given that $y = x^{\sin x}$.

9 **a** Simplify $\sin[(A+B)x] - \sin[(A-B)x]$.

b Hence, or otherwise, find $\int \sin 3x \cos 5x\, dx$.

10 **a** Given that $y = \arcsin x$, express x in terms of y.

b Find $\frac{dx}{dy}$ in terms of y.

c Hence, show that $\frac{d}{dx}(\arcsin x) = \frac{1}{\sqrt{1 - x^2}}$.

11 **a** Show that $\frac{d}{dx}(\operatorname{cosec} x) = -\operatorname{cosec} x \cot x$.

b Find the coordinates of the point on the curve $y = \operatorname{cosec} x$ ($x \in [0, \pi]$), where the gradient is equal to $2\sqrt{3}$.

12 **a** Find $\frac{d}{dx}\ln y$ in terms of y and $\frac{dy}{dx}$.

b If $y = \frac{x^4}{(2+5x)\sqrt{x^2+1}}$, find and simplify an expression for $\ln y$.

c Hence, find the derivative of $y = \frac{x^4}{(2+5x)\sqrt{x^2+1}}$.

13 Find the exact area enclosed between the graphs of $y = \sin x$ and $y = 1 - \sin x$ for $0 < x < \pi$.

14 Triangle ABC is made out of an elastic piece of string. Vertices A and B are being pulled apart so that the length of the base, AB, is increasing at the rate of $3\,\text{cm}\,\text{s}^{-1}$ and the height, h, is decreasing at the rate of $2\,\text{cm}\,\text{s}^{-1}$. Initially, $AB = 20\,\text{cm}$ and $h = 30\,\text{cm}$.

a Find the rate at which the area of the triangle is changing when $AB = 26$ and $h = 26$.

b Show that $AB = 20 + 3t$, and find an expression for h in terms of t.

c Find an expression for A in terms of t.

15 A rectangle is drawn inside the region bounded by the curve $y = \sin x$ and the x-axis, as shown in the diagram. The vertex A has coordinates $(x, 0)$.

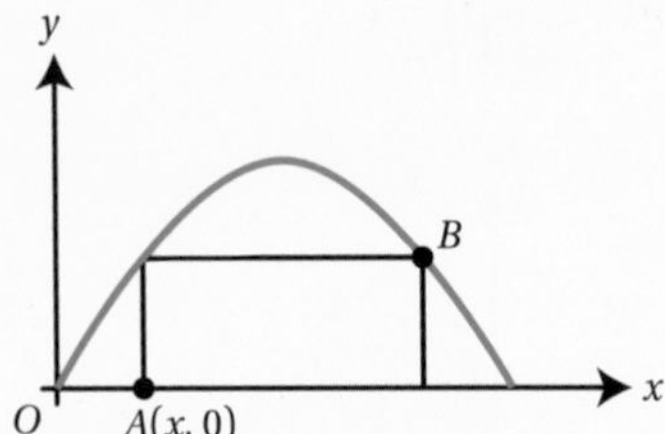

a **i** Write down the coordinates of point B.

ii Find an expression for the area of the rectangle in terms of x.

b **i** Show that the stationary point of the area satisfies the equation.

ii By sketching graphs, show that this equation has one root for $0 < x < \frac{\pi}{2}$.

iii Use the second derivative to show that the stationary point is a maximum.

c **i** The equation for the stationary point can be written as $x = \arctan\left(\frac{\pi}{2} - x\right)$. Use a suitable iterative formula, with $x_1 = 0.5$, to find the root of the equation $2\tan x = \pi - 2x$, correct to three decimal places.

ii Hence, find the maximum possible area of the rectangle.

16 Consider the infinite geometric series $1 + \cos x + \cos^2 x + \cos^3 x + \ldots$ for $0 < x < \pi$.

a Explain why the series converges.

b Show that the sum of the series is $\frac{1}{2}\operatorname{cosec}^2\frac{x}{2}$.

c Find the exact value of $\int_{\pi/3}^{\pi/2}(1 + \cos x + \cos^2 x + \cos^3 x + \ldots)\,dx$.

17 Let $I = \int_0^1 \frac{1}{4+x^2}\,dx$.

a Use the trapezium rule with four intervals of equal width to estimate the value if I.

b Using the first three non-zero terms of the binomial expansion of $\frac{1}{4+x^2}$, find another approximation for I.

You are given that $\int \frac{1}{1+x^2}\,dx = \arctan x + c$.

c Use the substitution $x = 2u$ to calculate the exact value of I. Hence determine whether method **a** or method **b** gives a better approximation.

18 **i** Sketch the graph of $y = 4k^x$, where k is a constant such that $k > 1$. State the coordinates of any points of intersection with the axes.

ii The point P on the curve $y = 4k^x$ has its y-coordinate equal to $20k^2$. Show that the x-coordinate of P may be written as $2 + \log_k 5$.

a Use the trapezium rule, with two strips each of width $\frac{1}{2}$, to find an expression for the approximate value of

$$\int_0^1 4k^x\,dx.$$

b Given that this approximate value is equal to 16, find the value of k.

© OCR, GCE Mathematics, Paper 4722, June 2009

19 **i** Express $3\cos x + 3\sin x$ in the form $R\cos(x - \alpha)$, where $R > 0$ and $0 < \alpha < \frac{1}{2}\pi$.

ii The expression $T(x)$ is defined by $T(x) = \frac{8}{3\cos x + 3\sin x}$.

a Determine a value of x for which $T(x)$ is not defined.

b Find the smallest positive value of x satisfying $T(3x) = 8^{9\sqrt{6}}$, giving your answer in an exact form.

© OCR, GCE Mathematics, Paper 4723, June 2010

20 Evaluate $\sum_{r=0}^{n} \binom{n}{r} \tan^{2r}\left(\frac{\pi}{3}\right)$.

21 **a** State an expression for $\sum_0^n x^k$.

b Hence, or otherwise, show that $1 + 2x + 3x^2 + 4x^3 + \ldots + nx^{n-1} = \frac{1-(n+1)x^n + nx^{n+1}}{(1-x)^2}$.

22 **a** Use the identity $\cos^2 x + \sin^2 x = 1$ to show that $\cos(\arcsin x) = \sqrt{1-x^2}$.

b The diagram below shows part of the curve $y = \sin x$. Write down the x-coordinate of the point P.

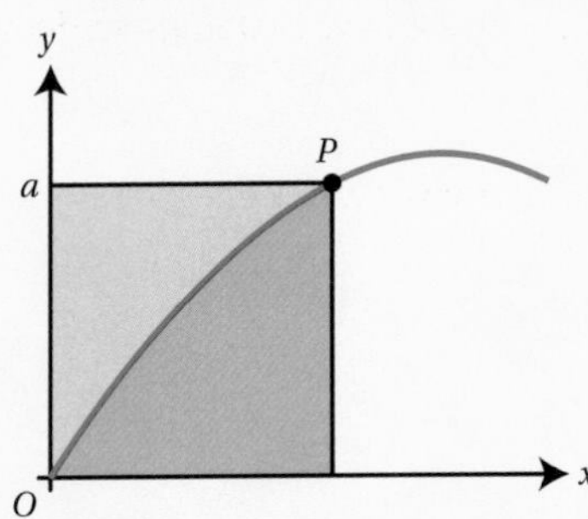

c Find the red-shaded area in terms of a, writing your answer in a form without trigonometric functions.

d By considering the blue-shaded area, find $\int_0^a \arcsin x \, dx$ for $0 < a < 1$.

23 A function is defined by $f(x) = 2x + \frac{1}{2}\sin 2x - \tan x$ for $x \in \left(-\frac{\pi}{2}, \frac{\pi}{2}\right)$.

a Find $f'(x)$.

b Show that the stationary points of $f(x)$ satisfy the equation $2\cos^4 x + \cos^2 x - 1 = 0$.

c Hence, show that the function has only one stationary point.

24 **a** Sketch the graph $y = \ln x$.

b The tangent to this graph at the point $(p, \ln p)$ passes through the origin. Find the value of p.

c For what range of values of k does $\ln x = kx$ have two solutions?

25

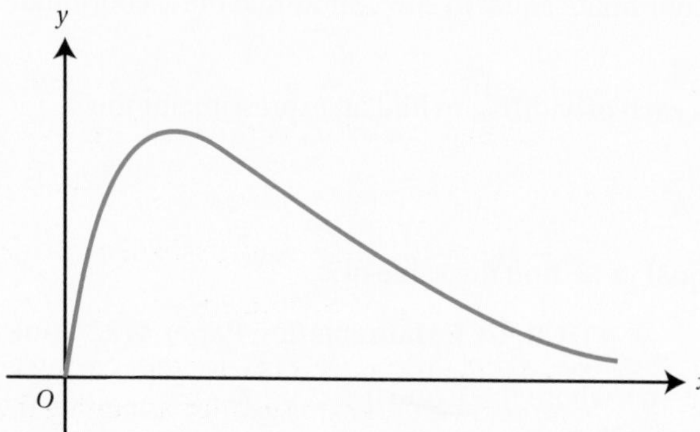

The function f is defined for the domain $x \geqslant 0$ by

$$f(x) = \frac{15x}{x^2 + 5}.$$

The diagram shows the curve with equation $y = f(x)$.

i Find the range of f.

ii The function g is defined for the domain $x \geqslant k$ by

$$g(x) = \frac{15x}{x^2 + 5}.$$

Given that g is a one-to-one function, state the least possible value of k.

iii Show that there is no point on the curve $y = g(x)$ at which the gradient is -1.

© OCR, GCE Mathematics, Paper 4723, June 2008

16 Conditional probability

In this chapter you will:

- use set notation to describe probabilities
- learn how to work with conditional probabilities in the context of Venn diagrams, two-way tables and tree diagrams
- learn a formula for conditional probability.

Before you start…

Student Book 1, Chapter 17	You should understand the basic laws of probability, including the terms 'mutually exclusive' and 'independent'.	1 In a certain village, having a car is mutually exclusive of having a motorbike. The probability of having a car is $\frac{1}{2}$. The probability of having a motorbike is $\frac{1}{3}$. What is the probability of having neither a car nor a motorbike?
GCSE	You should be able to use tree diagrams to solve problems.	2 What is the probability of a mother having two children with the same gender, assuming they are born independently?
GCSE	You should be able to find simple conditional probabilities.	3 a A bag contains ten red balls and five blue balls. One ball is taken from the bag and not replaced. A second ball is then taken. Given that the first ball is red, what is the probability that the second ball is also red? b In a group of 45 children, 30 have a pet. Out of those, 12 have a dog. Find the probability that: i a child has a dog ii a child has a dog, given that they have a pet.
Student Book 1, Chapter 1	You should understand and be able to use set notation.	4 Write out the set {prime numbers} $\cap$ {even numbers}.
Student Book 1, Chapter 17	You should understand probability distributions, including the binomial distribution.	5 What is the probability of getting four heads when six fair coins are tossed?

What is conditional probability?

What is the probability that you will become a millionaire? You could just look at data for how many millionaires there are in the world, but this is not likely to give you a very reliable answer because it depends on lots of other factors. Where you were born, what your parents do and your attitude towards risk all change the probability. You may be glad to know that the fact that you are doing Maths A Level immediately increases your probability of becoming a millionaire!

Information often changes probabilities. A probability that takes into account information is called a **conditional probability**. In reality nearly all probabilities are conditional: the probability of a patient having heart disease may change depending on their age; the probability of a defendant being guilty may change depending on their prior convictions; the probability of a football team winning may depend on the team they are playing.

Most people have a very poor intuition for conditional probabilities. In this chapter you will visualise conditional probabilities in various ways and see how you can use them to solve problems.

Focus on ...

See Focus on ... Problem solving 3 for the approach of using extreme values to evaluate possible solutions.

Section 1: Set notation and Venn diagrams

What is more likely when you roll a dice once:

- getting a prime number *and* an odd number?
- getting a prime number *or* an odd number?

The first possibility is restrictive – we have to satisfy both conditions. The second opens up many more possibilities – we can satisfy either condition. So the second must be more likely.

These are examples of two of the most common ways of combining events: intersection (in normal language 'and') and union (in normal language 'or'). These are given the following symbols.

Key point 16.1

$A \cap B$ is the **intersection** of A and B, meaning when both A and B happen.

$A \cup B$ is the **union** of A and B, meaning when either A happens, or B happens, or both happen.

A' is the **complement** of A, meaning everything that could happen other than A.

You can use Venn diagrams to illustrate these concepts:

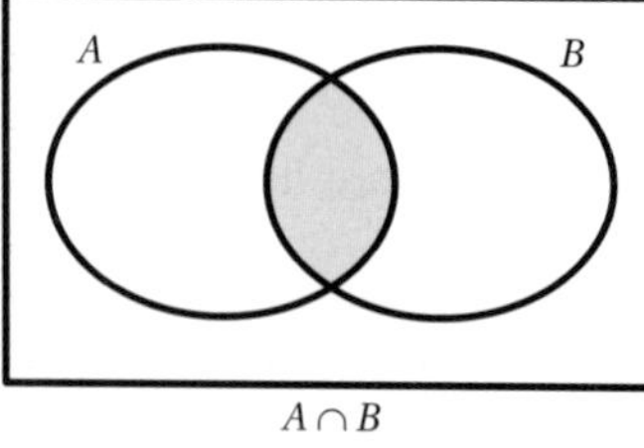

$A \cap B$

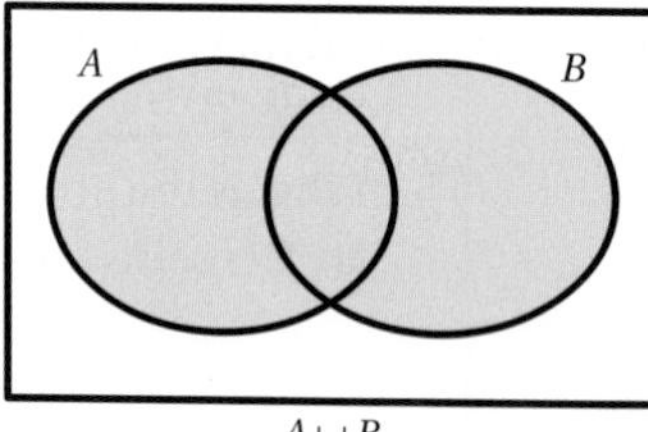

$A \cup B$

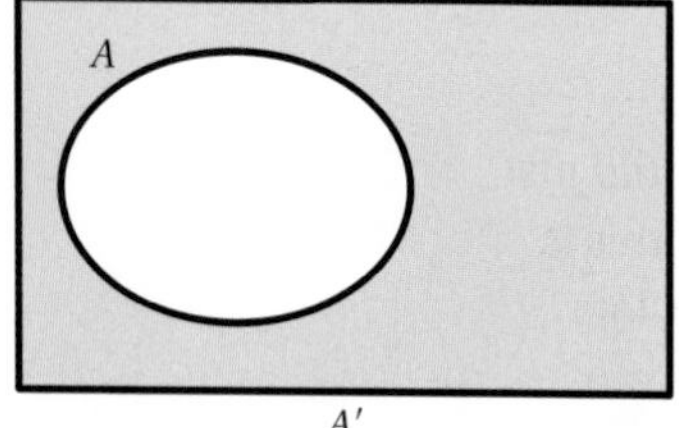

A'

Explore

If you have neither apples nor pears then you have no apples and no pears. In set notation this can be written as $(A \cup B)' = A' \cap B'$. This is one of De Morgan's laws – a description of some of the algebraic rules obeyed by sets and, hence, probability. What other similar rules can you find?

Did you know?

Why don't mathematicians just use simple words? One of the reasons for this is the ambiguity of everyday language. If you say that you play rugby or hockey some people may think this means you do not play both.

There is a very important result that comes from looking at the Venn diagrams on the previous page:

Key point 16.2

$P(A \cup B) = P(A) + P(B) - P(A \cap B)$

You can interpret this formula as saying 'if you want to count the number of ways of getting A or B, count the number of ways of getting A and add to that the number of ways of getting B. However, you have then counted the number of ways of getting both A and B twice, so you need to compensate by subtracting that number'.

Explore

This is an example of a rule called the 'inclusion–exclusion principle', which can be extended to more complicated Venn diagrams. Investigate some applications of this rule.

If there is no possibility of A and B occurring at the same time, then $P(A \cap B) = 0$. These events are **mutually exclusive**, and the formula reduces to $P(A \cup B) = P(A) + P(B)$.

WORKED EXAMPLE 16.1

A chocolate is selected randomly from a box. The probability of it containing nuts is $\frac{1}{4}$. The probability of it containing caramel is $\frac{1}{3}$. The probability of it containing both nuts and caramel is $\frac{1}{6}$. What is the probability of a randomly chosen chocolate containing either nuts or caramel or both?

$$P(\text{nuts} \cup \text{caramel}) = P(\text{nuts}) + P(\text{caramel}) - P(\text{nuts} \cap \text{caramel})$$
$$= \frac{1}{4} + \frac{1}{3} - \frac{1}{6} = \frac{5}{12}$$

Use the formula.

Venn diagrams and conditional probability

Conditional probability is the probability that an event happens given that we know that another event has already happened. For example, the probability that a randomly selected person owns a car might be 0.2. But if we know that this person has already passed the driving test, the probability that they own a car will be larger.

Venn diagrams provide a good way of thinking about conditional probability. Remember that the probability that A happens, given that B has already happened, is denoted by $P(A \mid B)$.

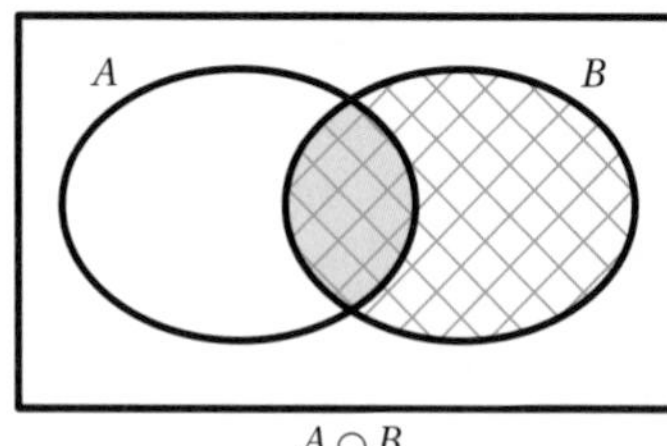

The hatched region shows B has happened. The probability of A now happening depends upon the relative probability of the shaded region compared to the hatched region. This leads to an extremely useful formula for conditional probability.

Key point 16.3

$$P(A \mid B) = \frac{P(A \cap B)}{P(B)}$$

where $P(A \mid B)$ is the probability of A given that B has happened.

WORKED EXAMPLE 16.2

The probability that a randomly chosen resident of a city in Japan is a millionaire is $\frac{1}{10\,000}$. The probability that a randomly chosen resident lives in a mansion is $\frac{1}{30\,000}$. Only 1 in 40 000 are millionaires who live in mansions. What is the probability of a randomly chosen individual being a millionaire given that they live in a mansion?

$$P(\text{millionaire} \mid \text{mansion}) = \frac{P(\text{millionaire} \cap \text{mansion})}{P(\text{mansion})}$$

Write required probability in 'given' notation and apply the formula.

$$= \frac{(1/40\,000)}{(1/30\,000)}$$

$$= \frac{3}{4}$$

WORKED EXAMPLE 16.3

You are given that $P(A) = \frac{1}{2}$, $P(B) = \frac{1}{4}$, and $P((A \cup B)') = \frac{5}{12}$.

a Find $P(A \cap B)$.

b Hence, find $P(A \mid B)$.

a

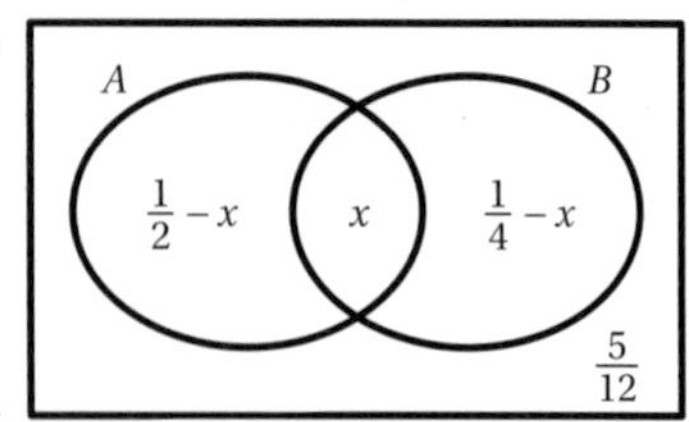

It is often a good idea to start with labelling the intersection with an unknown and writing in all the remaining information in terms of the unknown.

$$\text{So}\left(\frac{1}{2} - x\right) + x + \left(\frac{1}{4} - x\right) + \frac{5}{12} = 1$$

Using the fact that all the probabilities together sum to 1.

Continues on next page ...

$\frac{7}{6} - x = 1$ — Make it clear that you know x is $P(A \cap B)$.

$x = \frac{1}{6} = P(A \cap B)$

$P(A|B) = \frac{P(A \cap B)}{P(B)} = \frac{\frac{1}{6}}{\frac{1}{4}}$ — Use Key point 16.3.

$= \frac{2}{3}$

WORKED EXAMPLE 16.4

In a class of 32 students, 19 students have a bicycle, 21 have a mobile phone and 16 have a laptop computer. 11 have both a bike and a phone, 12 have both a phone and a laptop, and 6 have both a bike and a laptop. 2 have none of these objects.

a How many have a bike, a phone and a laptop?

b What is the probability that a randomly chosen student from the class has all three of the items, given that they have at least two of them?

a

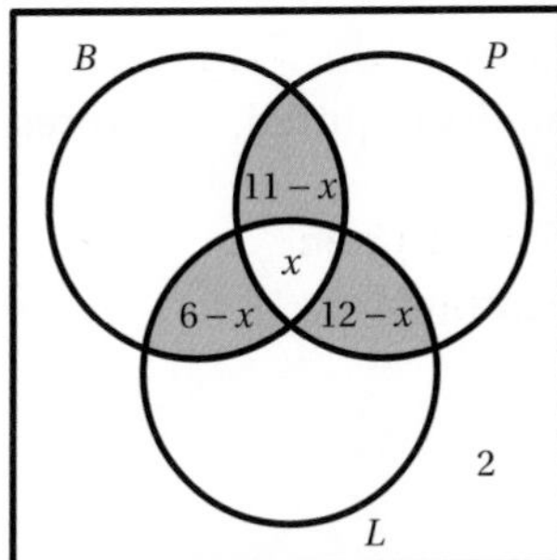

Draw a Venn diagram showing three overlapping groups, and label the size of the central region as x. Then work outwards. For example, the number who have a bicycle and a phone but not a laptop will be $11 - x$.

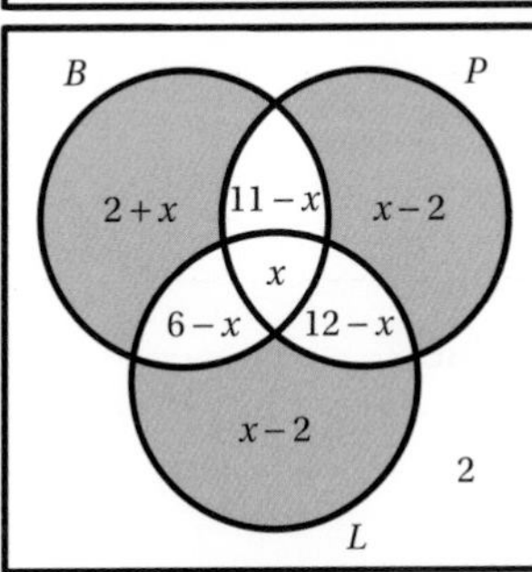

Continue working outwards. For example, the total of all the bicycle regions must be 19, so the remaining section is $19 - (11 - x) - (6 - x) - x$, which is $2 + x$.

There are two students outside B, L and P.

$(2 + x) + (11 - x) + (6 - x) + x + (x - 2)$
$+ (12 - x) + (x - 2) + 2 = 32$
$29 + x = 32$
$x = 3$

Use the fact that there are 32 students in the class to form an equation.

Therefore, three students have a bicycle, a phone and a laptop.

b There are 23 students who have at least two items and 3 with three items. So $P(3 \text{ items} \mid \text{at least 2 items}) = \frac{3}{23}$.

Use the Venn diagram to find the total number of students in overlapping regions.

Independence revisited

You will recall from Student Book 1 (Chapter 17) that events A and B are independent if $P(A \cap B) = P(A)P(B)$. The formula in Key Point 16.3 provides another, more intuitive condition.
If A and B are independent, then:

$$P(A|B) = \frac{P(A \cap B)}{P(B)} \quad \text{(from Key Point 16.3)}$$

$$= \frac{P(A)P(B)}{P(B)} \quad \text{(definition of independence)}$$

$$= P(A)$$

Tip

Notice that A and B can be swapped round, so if P(A|B) = P(A) then also P(B|A) = P(B).

This simply says that, if A and B are independent, then the probability of A happening given that B has happened is the same as the overall probability of A. In other words, having information about B does not change our knowledge about probability of A. This agrees with our intuitive understanding of 'independence'.

EXERCISE 16A

1 For each of the questions below write in mathematical notation the probability required. An expression rather than a number is required.

- **a** the probability that the outcome on a dice is prime and odd
- **b** the probability that a person is from either Senegal or Taiwan
- **c** the probability that a student studying A Levels is also studying French
- **d** the probability that a red playing card is a heart
- **e** the probability that a German person lives in Munich
- **f** the probability of someone wearing neither black nor white socks
- **g** the probability that a vegetable is a potato if it is not a cabbage
- **h** the probability that a ball drawn is red given that the ball is either red or blue.

2 **a** **i** If $P(X) = 0.3$ and $P(X \cap Y) = \frac{1}{4}$, find $P(Y | X)$.

ii If $P(Y) = 0.8$ and $P(X \cap Y) = \frac{3}{7}$, find $P(X | Y)$.

b **i** If $P(X) = 0.4$, $P(Y) = 0.7$ and $P(X \cap Y) = \frac{1}{4}$, find $P(X | Y)$.

ii If $P(X) = 0.6$, $P(Y) = 0.9$ and $P(X \cap Y) = \frac{1}{2}$, find $P(Y | X)$.

3 You may find that Venn diagrams are helpful in solving the questions below.

a **i** When a fruit pie is selected at random, $P(\text{it contains pears}) = \frac{1}{5}$ and $P(\text{it contains apples}) = \frac{1}{4}$. Ten per cent contain both apples and pears. Find $P(\text{apples} \cup \text{pears})$.

ii In a library 80% of books are classed as fiction and 70% are classed as 20th century. Half of the books are 20th century fiction. What proportion of the books are either fiction or from the 20th century?

b **i** 95% of students in a school play either football or tennis. The probability of a randomly chosen students playing football is $\frac{6}{10}$ and the probability that they play tennis is $\frac{5}{8}$. What percentage of students play both football and tennis?

ii Two in 5 students in a school study Spanish and 1 in 3 study French. Half of the school's students study either French or Spanish. What fraction of students study both French and Spanish?

c **i** 90% of students in a school have a Facebook account and 3 out of 5 have a Twitter account. One-twentieth of students have neither a Facebook nor a Twitter account. What percentage of students are on both Facebook and Twitter?

ii 25% of teams in a football league have French players and one-third have Italian players. 60% have neither French nor Italian players. What percentage of teams have both French and Italian players?

d **i** In a class of 30 students, 20 take French, 12 take German and four take neither. What is the probability that a student who takes German also takes French?

ii In a survey, 60% of like pizza and 50% like lasagne. 10% like neither pizza nor lasagne. Find the probability that a participant likes lasagne if they like pizza.

4 Simplify the following expressions where possible.

a $\mathrm{P}(x > 2 \cap x > 4)$

b $\mathrm{P}(y \leqslant 3 \cup y < 2)$

c $\mathrm{P}(a < 3 \cap a > 4)$

d $\mathrm{P}(a < 5 \cup a \geqslant 0)$

e $\mathrm{P}(\text{apple} \cup \text{fruit})$

f $\mathrm{P}(\text{apple} \cap \text{fruit})$

g $\mathrm{P}(\text{multiple of } 4 \cap \text{multiple of } 2)$

h $\mathrm{P}(\text{square} \cup \text{rectangle})$

i $\mathrm{P}(\text{blue} \cap (\text{blue} \cup \text{red}))$

j $\mathrm{P}(\text{blue} \cap (\text{blue} \cap \text{red}))$

k $\mathrm{P}(\text{rectangle} \mid \text{square})$

l $\mathrm{P}(x^2 = 9 \mid x = 2)$

5 **a** **i** $\mathrm{P}(A) = 0.4$, $\mathrm{P}(B) = 0.3$ and $\mathrm{P}(A \cap B) = 0.2$. Find $\mathrm{P}(A \cup B)$.

ii $\mathrm{P}(A) = \frac{3}{10}$, $\mathrm{P}(B) = \frac{4}{5}$ and $\mathrm{P}(A \cap B) = \frac{1}{10}$. Find $\mathrm{P}(A \cup B)$.

b **i** $\mathrm{P}(A) = \frac{2}{3}$, $\mathrm{P}(B) = \frac{1}{8}$ and $\mathrm{P}(A \cup B) = \frac{5}{8}$. Find $\mathrm{P}(A \cap B)$.

ii $\mathrm{P}(A) = 0.2$, $\mathrm{P}(B) = 0.1$ and $\mathrm{P}(A \cup B) = 0.25$. Find $\mathrm{P}(A \cap B)$.

c **i** $\mathrm{P}(A \cap B) = 20\%$, $\mathrm{P}(A \cup B) = 0.4$ and $\mathrm{P}(A) = \frac{1}{3}$. Find $\mathrm{P}(B)$.

ii $\mathrm{P}(A \cup B) = 1$, $\mathrm{P}(A \cap B) = 0$ and $\mathrm{P}(B) = 0.8$. Find $\mathrm{P}(A)$.

d **i** Find $\mathrm{P}(A \cup B)$ if $\mathrm{P}(A) = 0.4$, $\mathrm{P}(B) = 0.3$, and A and B are mutually exclusive.

ii Find $\mathrm{P}(A \cup B)$ if $\mathrm{P}(A) = 0.1$, $\mathrm{P}(B) = 0.01$, and A and B are mutually exclusive.

6 Out of 145 students in a college, 34 play football, 18 play badminton, and five play both sports.

a Draw a Venn diagram showing this information.

b How many students play neither sport?

c What is the probability that a randomly chosen student plays badminton?

d If you know that the chosen student plays football, what is the probability that they also play badminton?

7 Out of 145 students in a college, 58 study Mathematics, 47 study Economics and 72 study neither of the two subjects.

a Draw a Venn diagram to show this information.

b How many students study both subjects?

c A student tells you that she studies Mathematics. What is the probability that she studies both Mathematics and Economics?

8 **a** In a survey, 60% of participants are in favour of a new primary school and 85% are in favour of a new library. Half of all those surveyed would like both a new primary school and a new library. What percentage supported neither a new library nor a new primary school?

b What proportion of those wanting a new primary school also wanted a new library?

9 Assume that $P(A) = 0.6$, $P(B) = 0.5$ and $P(A \cup B) = 0.9$.

a By drawing a Venn diagram, or otherwise, find $P(A \cap B)$.

b Find $P(A \mid B)$.

10 Given that $P(A) = 0.2$, $P(A \cap B) = 0.1$ and $P(A \cup B) = 0.7$, find:

a $P(B)$ **b** $P(A \mid B)$

11 Events A and B satisfy $P((A \cup B)') = 0.2$, $P(A) = P(B) = 0.5$.

a Find $P(A \cap B')$. **b** Find $P(A \mid B)$.

12 An integer is chosen at random from the first one thousand positive integers. Find the probability that the integer chosen is:

a a multiple of 6

b a multiple of both 6 and 8

c a multiple of 8, given that it is a multiple of 6.

13 Denise conducts a survey about food preferences in the college. She asks students which of the three meals (spaghetti bolognese, chilli con carne, and vegetable curry) they would eat. She finds out that, of the 145 students:

- 43 would eat spaghetti bolognese
- 80 would eat vegetable curry
- 20 would eat both the bolognese and the curry
- 24 would eat both curry and chilli
- 35 would eat both chilli and bolognese
- 12 would eat all three meals.
- 10 would not eat any of the three meals.

a Draw a Venn diagram showing this information.

b How many students would eat only bolognese?

c How many students would eat chilli?

d What is the probability that a randomly selected student would eat only one of the three meals?

e Given that a student would eat only one of the three meals, what is the probability that they would eat curry?

f Find the probability that a randomly selected student would eat at least two of the three meals.

14 The probability that a person has dark hair is 0.7, the probability that they have blue eyes is 0.4 and the probability that they have both dark hair and blue eyes is 0.2.

a Draw a Venn diagram showing this information.

b Find the probability that a person has neither dark hair nor blue eyes.

c Given that a person has dark hair, find the probability that they also have blue eyes.

d Given that a person does not have dark hair, find the probability that they have blue eyes.

e Are the characteristics of having dark hair and having blue eyes independent? Explain your answer.

15 The probability that it rains on any given day is 0.45, and the probability that it is cold is 0.6. The probability that it is neither cold nor raining is 0.25.

- **a** Find the probability that it is both cold and raining.
- **b** Draw a Venn diagram showing this information.
- **c** Given that it is raining, find the probability that it is not cold.
- **d** Given that it is not cold, find the probability that it is raining.
- **e** Are the events 'it's raining' and 'it's cold' independent? Explain your answer and show any supporting calculations.

16 If $P(A \mid B) = \frac{1}{2}$ and $P(B \mid A) = \frac{1}{3}$, find $\frac{P(A \cup B)}{P(A \cap B)}$.

17 If $P(A) = P(B) = \frac{4}{5}$ and $P(A \cup B) = 1$, find $P(A \mid B)$.

18 If $P(A) = 0.8$ and $P(B) = 0.4$, find the maximum and minimum values of $P(A \mid B)$.

19
- **a** If $P(X)$ represents a probability, state the possible values that $P(X)$ can take.
- **b** Express $P(A) - P(A \cap B)$ in terms of $P(A)$ and $P(B \mid A)$.
- **c** By considering an expression for $P(A \cup B) - P(A \cap B)$, show that $P(A \cup B) \geqslant P(A \cap B)$.

Section 2: Two-way tables

Another useful way of looking at conditional probability is to use a two-way table. This lists all the possible outcomes varying along two factors.

WORKED EXAMPLE 16.5

These data show the arrival time of a random sample of 100 letters, as well as whether they were posted 1st class or 2nd class.

	Next day	Later
1st class	64	16
2nd class	12	8

On the basis of these data, find:

- **a** P(1st class and Next day)
- **b** P(Next day | 1st class)
- **c** P(1st class | Next day)

a $\frac{64}{100} = 0.64$ — There are 64 letters in the '1st class' and 'Next day' categories, out of 100 letters.

b $\frac{64}{80} = 0.8$ — There are 64 'Next day' letters out of 80 '1st class' letters.

c $\frac{64}{76} \approx 0.842$ — There are 64 '1st class' letters out of 76 'Next day' letters.

EXERCISE 16B

1 In each of the following two-way tables, find P(A | X).

a **i**

	A	B
X	12	18
Y	14	16

ii

	A	B
X	15	35
Y	12	16

b **i**

	X	Y
A	3	7
B	6	4

ii

	A	B
X	10	16
Y	15	13

c **i**

	X	Y	Z
A	6	5	4
B	8	7	2
C	10	9	0

ii

	X	Y	Z
A	3	8	9
B	5	6	2
C	7	4	1

2 The following two-way table describes the number of students in different year groups in a school.

	Year 9	Year 10	Year 11	Total
Girls		85		
Boys	88			240
Total	186		163	509

a Complete the table.

b Find the probability that a randomly selected student is a girl from Year 11.

c Find the probability that a randomly selected girl is from Year 11.

3 The following two-way table describes the additions made to coffee in a drinks machine in one day.

	Milk	No milk
Sugar	28	14
No sugar	32	16

a Find the probability of sugar being added.

b Find the probability that sugar is added if milk is added.

c Show that whether milk is added is independent of whether sugar is added.

4 The following table shows the number of returned shoes to three stores in one day.

	Store A	Store B	Store C
Returned	7	14	6
Unreturned	18	20	16

a Find P(returned).

b Find P(returned | store A).

c Find P(returned | store A′).

5 The following table shows a general two-way table.

	Q	R
S	a	b
R	c	d

Find, in terms of a, b, c and d:

a $P(Q \cap S)$ **b** $P(Q \cup S)$ **c** $P(Q)$ **d** $P(S \mid Q)$ **e** $P(S \mid Q')$

6 The following table shows the results of the three top-performing countries in the 2016 Olympics.

	Gold	Silver	Bronze
USA	46	37	38
GB	27	23	17
China	26	18	26

A random result is chosen from amongst these 258 results. Find:

a P(gold | GB) **b** P(gold) **c** P(gold $\cap$ GB) **d** P(gold $\cup$ GB)

7 A company makes three different sizes of T-shirt in three different colours. The following table shows the sales in a week.

	S	M	L
White	14	22	18
Black	24	36	33
Green	23	30	23

a Find P(S $\cap$ white).

b Find P(S $\cup$ white).

c Find P(S).

d P(S | white).

e Find P(S′ | white′).

8 The following table gives the probabilities of different midday temperatures in different air pressures in the United Kingdom based on long-term observations.

	$>$1000 hPa	$\leqslant$1000 hPa
$<$10 °C	0.08	0.12
10 °C to 20 °C	0.27	0.29
$>$20 °C	0.14	0.10

a For a randomly chosen day, find:

a P($>$1000 hPa) **b** P($\leqslant$1000 hPa $\quad >$ 20 °C) **c** P($>$1000 hPa | $\geqslant$ 10 °C)

9 James investigates two identities:

1 $P(A \mid B) + P(A \mid B') \equiv 1$ **2** $P(A' \mid B) + P(A \mid B) \equiv 1$

Use a counterexample to show that one of these identities is incorrect.

Section 3: Tree diagrams

A tree diagram is a useful way of illustrating situations where one outcome depends upon another. For example, the following diagram shows the experience of a restaurant trying to predict how many portions of chips it serves.

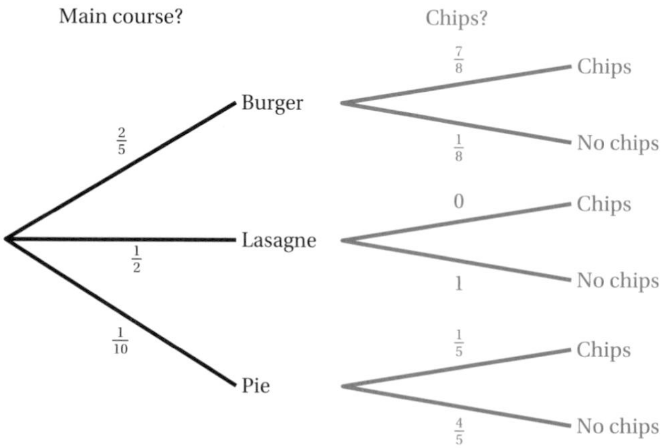

The second, red probabilities all depend on the first, so they are conditional probabilities. For example, $P(\text{chips} \mid \text{burger}) = \frac{7}{8}$.

You may already know that the probability of being on a branch is found by multiplying along the branch. For example, this means:

$$P(\text{chips} \cap \text{burger}) = P(\text{burger}) \times P(\text{chips}|\text{burger}) = \frac{2}{5} \times \frac{7}{8} = \frac{7}{20}$$

In general:

Key point 16.4

$P(A \cap B) = P(B) \times P(A \mid B)$

Tip

This is actually just a rearrangement of Key point 16.3.

If we wanted to find the overall probability of chips, we need to add different branches together:

$$P(\text{chips}) = P(\text{chips} \cap \text{burger}) + P(\text{chips} \cap \text{lasagne}) + P(\text{chips} \cap \text{pie})$$

$$= \left(\frac{2}{5} \times \frac{7}{8}\right) + \left(\frac{1}{2} \times 0\right) + \left(\frac{1}{10} \times \frac{1}{5}\right) = \frac{37}{100}$$

WORKED EXAMPLE 16.6

Laila has a test at the end of each week for History. If she revises for a particular test, Laila estimates that there is an 80% chance that she will pass. However, if she does not revise, she estimates only a 30% chance of passing.

The probability that Laila revises for any particular test is $\frac{3}{4}$. What proportion of her History tests should Laila expect to pass?

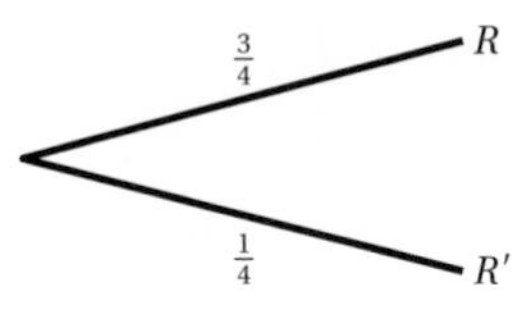

Decide which probability is not conditional. Start the tree diagram with this event.

The probability of passing the test is conditional on revision, so the revision branches have to come first.

Revise? Pass?
3/4 R: 80% P, 20% P'
1/4 R': 30% P, 70% P'

Add the conditional event.

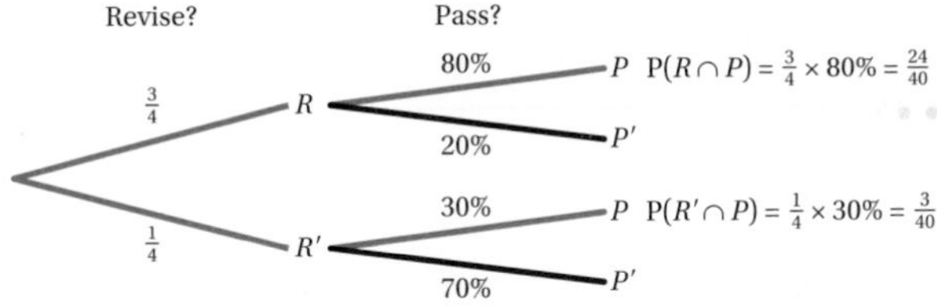

Identify which branches result in passing the test.
Multiply to find the probability at the end of each branch.

$$\text{P(passing)} = \text{P(revising} \cap \text{passing)} + \text{P(not revising} \cap \text{passing)}$$
$$= \frac{24}{40} + \frac{3}{40}$$
$$= \frac{27}{40}$$

Tip

The questions in Worked examples 16.6 and 16.7 use the terms 'chance' and 'proportion'. These are just other words for probability.

Sometimes, you can use the information found from a tree diagram to find another conditional probability.

WORKED EXAMPLE 16.7

If it is raining in the morning, there is a 90% chance that I will bring my umbrella. If it is not raining in the morning, there is only a $\frac{1}{5}$ chance of me taking my umbrella. On any given morning the probability of rain is 0.1.

a What is the probability that I take my umbrella?
b If you see me with my umbrella, what is the probability that it was raining that morning?

Continues on next page ...

a

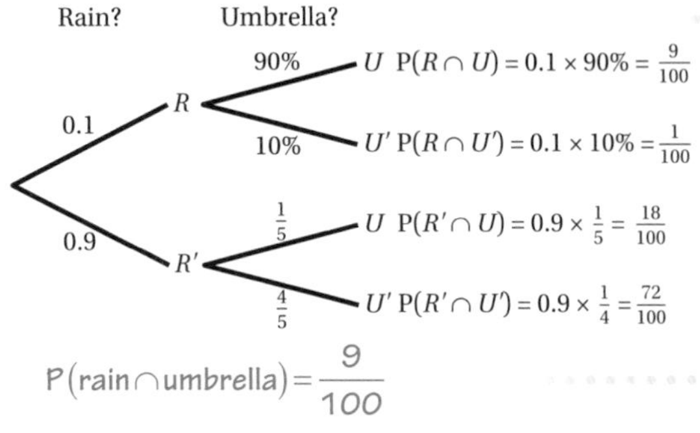

First, draw a tree diagram.

$$\text{P}(\text{rain} \cap \text{umbrella}) = \frac{9}{100}$$

$$\text{P}(\text{rain}' \cap \text{umbrella}) = \frac{18}{100}$$

$$\text{P}(\text{umbrella}) = \frac{9}{100} + \frac{18}{100} = \frac{27}{100}$$

Use the tree diagram to find relevant probabilities.

b $\text{P}(\text{rain}|\text{umbrella}) = \dfrac{\text{P}(\text{rain} \cap \text{umbrella})}{\text{P}(\text{umbrella})}$

$$= \frac{\left(\frac{9}{100}\right)}{\left(\frac{27}{100}\right)} = \frac{1}{3}$$

Since a conditional probability is required, use Key point 16.3.

In Worked example 16.7 we were given P(umbrella | rain) and found P(rain | umbrella). We can use Key point 16.4 to derive a formula for this.

Key point 16.4 says that $\text{P}(A \cap B) = \text{P}(B) \times \text{P}(A \mid B)$ but there is nothing special about A and B here. We could also have written

$$\text{P}(A \cap B) = \text{P}(A) \times \text{P}(B \mid A).$$

This leads to the following formula, which could be used to solve Worked example 16.7.

Tip

Quite often in questions like this you use the answer to the first part in the second part.

Key point 16.5

$$\text{P}(B) \times \text{P}(A \mid B) = \text{P}(A) \times \text{P}(B \mid A)$$

Focus on ...

See Focus on ... Proof 3 for the use of conditional probability and tree diagrams in analysing a claim of guilt in a legal case.

Explore

This is related to a very important theorem in modern mathematics called Bayes' theorem, named after the Reverend Thomas Bayes. It is a way of seeing how new information changes our knowledge about probabilities. Find out how this result may be used in hypothesis testing.

WORK IT OUT 16.1

The probability of an acorn landing more than 2 m from the original tree is 80%. Of those that land more than 2 m from the tree 20% germinate. Of those that land less than 2 m from the tree 5% germinate. A seed germinates. What is the probability that it landed more than 2 m from the tree?

Which is the correct solution? Can you identify the errors made in the incorrect solutions?

Solution 1

We can work out P(germinate) from a tree diagram:

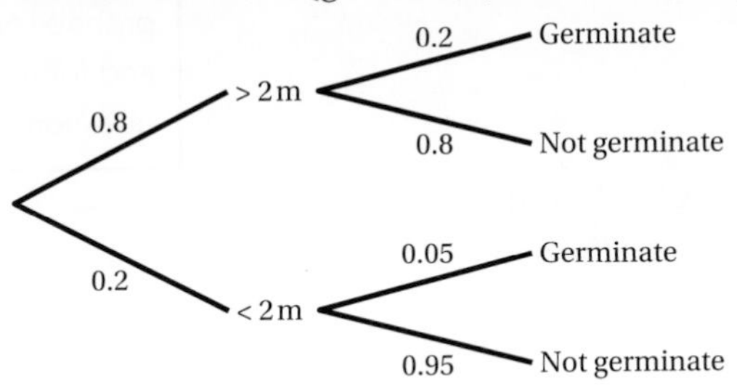

$P(> 2\text{ m}) \times P(\text{germinate} \mid > 2\text{ m}) = P(\text{germinate}) \times P(> 2\text{ m} \mid \text{germinate})$

$0.8 \times 0.2 = [0.8 \times 0.2 + 0.2 \times 0.05] \times P(>2\text{ m} \mid \text{germinate})$

So $P(> 2\text{ m} \mid \text{germinate}) = 0.16 \div 0.170 \approx 0.941$

Solution 2

$$P(>2\text{ m} \mid \text{germinate}) = \frac{P(>2\text{ m} \cap \text{germinate})}{P(\text{germinate})}$$

$$= \frac{P(>2\text{ m})P(\text{germinate})}{P(\text{germinate})} = P(>2\text{ m}) = 0.8$$

Solution 3

Using a Venn diagram:

Since $P(\text{germinate} \mid > 2\text{ m}) = 0.2$:

$$\frac{x}{0.8} = 0.2$$

So P(germinate and > 2 m) = 0.16

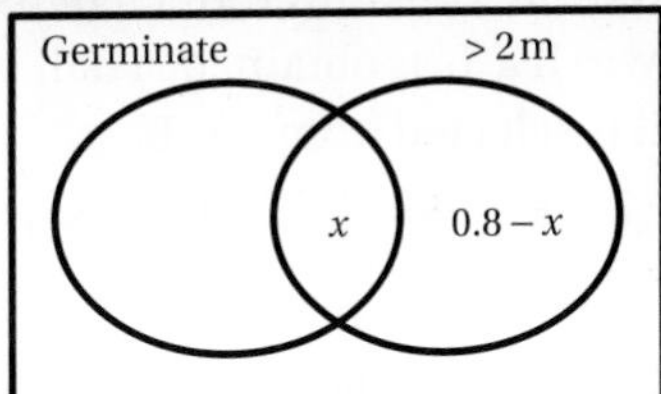

EXERCISE 16C

1 In the following questions, you may find that writing the information on a suitable tree diagram is helpful.

a **i** $P(A) = 0.4$ and $P(B \mid A) = 0.3$. Find $P(A \cap B)$.

ii $P(X) = \frac{3}{5}$ and $P(Y \mid X) = 0$. Find $P(X \cap Y)$.

b **i** $P(A) = 0.3$, $P(B) = 0.2$ and $P(B \mid A) = 0.8$. Find $P(A \cap B)$.

ii $P(A) = 0.4$, $P(B) = 0.8$ and $P(A \mid B) = 0.3$. Find $P(A \cap B)$.

c **i** $P(A) = \frac{2}{5}$, $P(B) = \frac{1}{3}$ and $P(A \mid B) = \frac{1}{4}$. Find $P(A \cup B)$.

ii $P(A) = \frac{3}{4}$, $P(B) = \frac{1}{4}$ and $P(B \mid A) = \frac{1}{3}$. Find $P(A \cup B)$.

2 A class contains six boys and eight girls. Two are picked at random. What is the probability that they are both boys?

3 A bag contains four red balls, three blue balls and two green balls. A ball is chosen at random from the bag and is not replaced. A second ball is chosen. Find the probability of choosing one green ball and one blue ball in any order.

4 $P(A) = 0.3$, $P(B \mid A) = 0.6$, and $P(B \mid A') = 0.8$.

a Illustrate this information on a tree diagram.

b Find $P(A \cap B)$.

c Find $P(A \cup B)$.

d Find $P(B)$.

5 Given that $P(X) = \frac{1}{3}$, $P(Y \mid X) = \frac{2}{9}$ and $P(Y \mid X') = \frac{1}{3}$, find:

a $P(Y')$

b $P(X' \cup Y')$

6 A factory has two machines making widgets. The older machine has larger capacity, so it makes 60% of the widgets but 6% are rejected by quality control. The newer machine has only a 3% rejection rate. Find the probability that a randomly selected widget is rejected.

7 The school tennis league consists of 12 players. Daniella has a 30% chance of winning any game against a higher-ranked player, and a 70% chance of winning any game against a lower-ranked player. If Daniella is currently in third place, find the probability that she wins her next game against a randomly selected opponent.

8 Box A contains six red balls and four green balls. Box B contains five red balls and three green balls. A standard fair cubic dice is thrown. If a '6' is obtained, a ball is selected from box A; otherwise a ball is selected from box B.

a Calculate the probability that the ball selected is red.

b Given that the ball selected is red, calculate the probability that it comes from box B.

9 Robert travels to work by train every weekday from Monday to Friday. The probability that he catches the 7.30 a.m. train on Monday is $\frac{2}{3}$. The probability that he catches the 7.30 a.m. train on any other weekday is 90%. A weekday is chosen at random.

a Find the probability that he catches the 7.30 a.m. train on that day.

b Given that he catches the 7.30 a.m. train on that day, find the probability that the chosen day is Monday.

10 Bag 1 contains six red cubes and ten blue cubes. Bag 2 contains seven red cubes and three blue cubes. Two cubes are drawn at random, the first from bag 1 and the second from bag 2.

a Find the probability that the cubes are the same colour.

b Given that the cubes selected are of different colours, find the probability that the red cube was selected from bag 1.

Elevate

See Support sheet 16 for a further example on conditional probability and tree diagrams, and for more practice questions.

11 On any day in April there is a $\frac{2}{3}$ chance of rain in the morning. If it's raining there is a $\frac{4}{5}$ chance I will remember my umbrella, but if it is not raining there is only a $\frac{2}{5}$ chance of remembering my umbrella.

a On a random day in April, what is the probability that I have my umbrella with me?

b Given that I have my umbrella with me on a day in April, what is the probability that it was raining that morning?

12 A new blood test has been devised for early detection of a disease. Studies show that the probability that the blood test correctly identifies someone with this disease is 0.95, and the probability that the blood test correctly identifies someone without that disease is 0.99. The incidence of this disease in the general population is 0.0003.

The result of the blood test on a particular patient indicates that he has the disease. What is the probability that this patient has the disease?

13 You have two coins: one is a normal fair coin with heads on one side and tails on the other. The second coin has heads on both sides. You randomly pick a coin and flip it. The result comes up heads. What is the probability that you chose the fair coin?

14 There are 36 discs in a bag. Some of them are black and the rest are white. Two are simultaneously selected at random. Given that the probability of selecting two discs of the same colour is equal to the probability of selecting two discs of different colour, how many black discs are there in the bag?

15 Prove that if A and B are independent, then so are A' and B'.

Section 4: Modelling with probability

When answering probability questions, you often need to make various assumptions about the situation you are modelling; for example, that dice are fair, that each counter is equally likely to be picked, or that the probability of rain doesn't change from one day to the next. In this section we look at some of the most common modelling assumptions and ask how justified they are, and how changing them would affect the result of our calculations.

When you first met probability, you learnt to calculate it as the number of favourable outcomes divided by the number of all possible outcomes. For example, the probability of selecting a yellow ball from a bag containing five yellow and eight green balls is $\frac{5}{13}$. This calculation assumes that each ball is equally likely to be picked.

WORKED EXAMPLE 16.8

A bag contains 12 blue counters and nine yellow counters. Two counters are picked at random without replacement.

a Find the probability that both counters are blue.
b Identify one assumption you have made in your calculation. Is this assumption justified?
c If the blue counters were slightly larger than the yellow counters, how would that change the answer in part **a**?

a P(both blue)

$= \text{P(first blue)P(second blue} \mid \text{first blue)}$

$= \frac{12}{21} \times \frac{11}{20} = \frac{11}{35}$

You can draw a tree diagram, or think in terms of conditional probabilities.

b We have assumed that each of the 21 counters is equally likely to be picked.

The probabilities $\frac{12}{21}$ and $\frac{11}{20}$ are based on the assumption that each counter is equally likely to be picked.

This assumption may be justified if all the counters are exactly the same shape and size.

c The answer would be larger because larger counters would be more likely to be picked.

Another common assumption in probability calculations is that probabilities don't change over time, for example, if you have dice that are fair today, they will also be fair tomorrow. When considering the probability of two events happening simultaneously, or one after the other, it is also sometimes appropriate to assume that they are independent.

WORKED EXAMPLE 16.9

a A simple weather model assumes that the probability that it rains on any given day is $\frac{1}{5}$, independently of any other day.
 i Find the probability that it rains on two consecutive days.
 ii Comment on the suitability of the two assumptions made in this model.

b In an improved model, the probability that it rains on the first day is still $\frac{1}{5}$, but the probability that it rains on the second day is $\frac{1}{2}$ if it rained on the first day and q if it didn't.
 i Is the probability that it rains on two consecutive days larger or smaller than for the first model?
 ii The probability that it rains on the second day is still $\frac{1}{5}$. Find the value of q.

Continues on next page ...

a **i** $\frac{1}{5}\times\frac{1}{5}=\frac{1}{25}$

The consecutive days are independent so you can just multiply the probability of rain for each.

ii The probability of rain will be different at different times of year; however, it won't change so much from one day to the next, so the assumption that the probability is $\frac{1}{5}$ on both days is reasonable.

Is it reasonable to assume that the probability of rain is the same for each day?

If it rains on one day it is more likely that it will rain the next day, so the assumption of independence is probably not suitable.

Does rain on one day make it more or less likely that it will rain the next day?

b

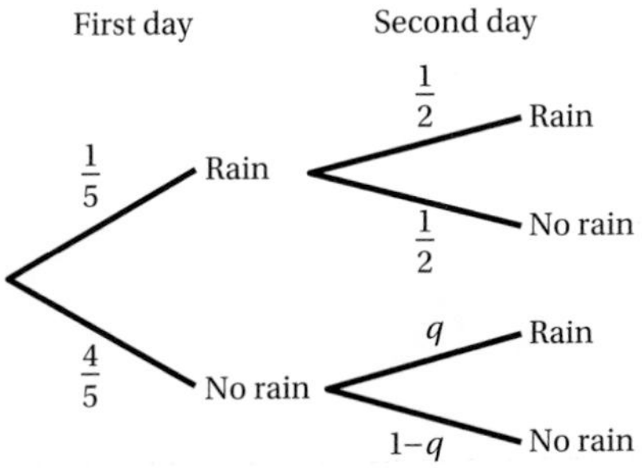

First day / Second day

- Rain ($\frac{1}{5}$)
  - Rain ($\frac{1}{2}$)
  - No rain ($\frac{1}{2}$)
- No rain ($\frac{4}{5}$)
  - Rain (q)
  - No rain ($1-q$)

This question seems a bit more complicated so draw a tree diagram.

i $P(\text{rain on both days})=\frac{1}{5}\times\frac{1}{2}=\frac{1}{10}$

This is larger than predicted by the first model.

Multiply the probabilities along the two branches.

ii P(rain on second day)

$=\left(\frac{1}{5}\times\frac{1}{2}\right)+\left(\frac{4}{5}\times q\right)$

There are two sets of branches corresponding to rain on the second day.

$\frac{1}{10}+\frac{4q}{5}=\frac{1}{5}$

This probability needs to equal $\frac{1}{5}$.

$\Rightarrow q=\frac{1}{8}$

Notice that in part **b** the probability of rain is the same on both days, but the two days are not independent: P(rain on second day) $=\frac{1}{5}$, but P(rain on second day | rain on first day) $=\frac{1}{2}$.

Rewind

In Student Book 1, Chapter 17 you learnt that to use the binomial distribution, trials must be both independent and have constant probability of success.

Focus on ...

In Focus on ... Modelling 3 you will also consider modelling assumptions when using the normal distribution.

The Mixed practice at the end of this chapter contains questions about modelling with probability.

Checklist of learning and understanding

- We can use set notation when describing probabilities:

  $A \cap B$ is the intersection of A and B, meaning when both A and B happen.

  $A \cup B$ is the union of A and B, meaning when either A happens, or B happens, or both happen.

  A' is the complement of A, meaning everything that could happen other than A.

- A Venn diagram leads to a formula relating the probabilities of the union and intersection:

  $P(A \cup B) = P(A) + P(B) - P(A \cap B)$

- $P(A \mid B)$ is the probability of A happening if B has happened. This can be visualised using Venn diagrams, two-way tables or tree diagrams.
  - We can also use the formula:

    $$P(A|B) = \frac{P(A \cap B)}{P(B)}$$

  - In a tree diagram we often rearrange this formula to get:

    $P(A \cap B) = P(A) \times P(B \mid A)$ and $P(B) \times P(A \mid B) = P(A) \times P(B \mid A)$.

Mixed practice 16

1. A drawer contains six red socks, four black socks and eight white socks. Two socks are picked at random.

   a What is the probability that two socks of the same colour are drawn?

   b What assumptions have you made in calculating the probability?

2. Out of 100 flies studied in an experiment, 24 have the gene ig9, 52 have the gene xar3 and 28 flies have neither gene.

   a Illustrate this information on a Venn diagram.

   b Find $P(\text{ig9} \cap \text{xar3})$.

   c Find $P(\text{ig9} \mid \text{xar3})$.

3. In an event, $P(X) = 0.2$, $P(A \mid X) = 0.4$ and $P(A \mid X') = 0.5$.

   a Illustrate this information on a tree diagram.

   b Find $P(A \cap X)$.

   c Find $P(A \cup X)$.

   d Find $P(A)$.

4. The number of hours spent practising for a music examination is recorded by a teacher for each of her students.

Hours practised	Male	Female
10 or fewer	4	4
11 to 20	8	12
21 or more	7	5

   a Find P(male | 10 or fewer hours practised).

   b Two different students are randomly selected for further interviews. Find the probability that both are male.

5. The probability that a student plays badminton is 0.3. The probability that a student plays neither football nor badminton is 0.5, and the probability that a student plays both sports is x.

   a Draw a Venn diagram showing this information.

   b Find the probability that a student plays badminton but not football.

   Given that a student plays football, the probability that they also play badminton is 0.5.

   c Find the probability that a student plays both badminton and football.

   d Hence, complete your Venn diagram. What is the probability that a student plays only badminton?

   e Given that a student plays only one sport, what it the probability that they play badminton?

6. Only two international airlines fly daily into an airport. Pi Air has 40 flights a day and Lambda Air has 25 flights a day. Passengers flying with Pi Air have a $\frac{1}{10}$ probability of losing their luggage, and passengers flying with Lambda Air have a $\frac{1}{4}$ probability of losing their luggage. Someone complains that their luggage has been lost. Find the probability that they travelled with Pi Air.

7. A girl walks to school every day. If it is not raining, the probability that she is late is $\frac{1}{5}$. If it is raining, the probability that she is late is $\frac{2}{3}$. The probability that it rains on a particular day is $\frac{1}{4}$. On a particular day the girl is late.

   a Find the probability that it was raining on that day.

   b Is the assumption of constant probability reasonable?

8 The table shows the number of male and female members of a vintage car club who own either a Jaguar or a Bentley. No member owns both makes of car.

	Male	Female
Jaguar	25	15
Bentley	12	**8**

One member is chosen at random from these 60 members.

i Given that this member is male, find the probability that he owns a Jaguar.

Now two members are chosen at random from the 60 members. They are chosen one at a time, without replacement.

ii Given that the first one of these members is female, find the probability that both own Jaguars.

9 A game uses an unbiased dice with faces numbered 1 to 6. The dice is thrown once. If it shows 4 or 5 or 6 then this number is the final score. If it shows 1 or 2 or 3 then the dice is thrown again and the final score is the sum of the numbers shown on the two throws.

i Find the probability that the final score is 4.

ii Given that the dice is thrown only once, find the probability that the final score is 4.

iii Given that the dice is thrown twice, find the probability that the final score is 4.

10 The probability that Thomas leaves his umbrella in any shop he visits is $\frac{1}{5}$. After visiting two shops in succession, he finds he has left his umbrella in one of them. What is the probability that he left his umbrella in the second shop?

11 **a** A large bag of sweets contains eight red and twelve yellow sweets. Two sweets are chosen at random from the bag without replacement.

i Find the probability that two red sweets are chosen.

ii What assumption is made in your calculation for part **a i**?

b A small bag contains 4 red and n yellow sweets. Two sweets are chosen without replacement from this bag. If the probability that two red sweets are chosen is $\frac{2}{15}$, show that $n = 6$.

Ayesha has one large bag and two small bags of sweets. She selects a bag at random and then picks two sweets without replacement.

c Calculate the probability that two red sweets are chosen.

d Given that two red sweets are chosen, find the probability that Ayesha selected from the large bag.

12 Two events, A and B, satisfy $\mathrm{P}(A) = \mathrm{P}(B) = k\mathrm{P}(A \cup B)$.

a Find the possible values k can take.

b Find $\mathrm{P}(A \mid B)$ in terms of k.

13 The probability that it rains during a summer's day in a certain town is 0.2. In this town, the probability that the daily maximum temperature exceeds 25 °C is 0.3 when it rains and 0.6 when it does not rain. Given that the maximum daily temperature exceeded 25 °C on a particular summer's day, find the probability that it rained on that day.

14 Given that $\mathrm{P}((A \cup B)') = 0$, $\mathrm{P}(A' \mid B) = \frac{1}{5}$ and $\mathrm{P}(A) = \frac{14}{15}$, find $\mathrm{P}(B)$.

Elevate

See Extension sheet 16 for a selection of more challenging problems.

17 The normal distribution

In this chapter you will learn:

- how to calculate probabilities for a normally distributed random variable
- that any normal distribution is related to the standard normal distribution
- how to calculate the value of the variable with a given cumulative probability
- how to find mean and standard deviation from information about probabilities
- how the normal distribution can be used as a model
- how the normal distribution can be used as an approximation to the binomial distribution.

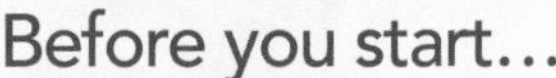

Before you start...

Student Book 1, Chapter 16	You should be able to interpret histograms.	1 What is the frequency density of a group of 60 people with masses strictly between 40 kg and 50 kg?
Chapter 16	You should be able to work with tree diagrams.	2 There is a 20% chance of it raining. If it rains, there is a 60% chance I am late. If it does not rain, there is a 25% chance I am late. What is the probability that I am late?
Chapter 16	You should be able to calculate conditional probability.	3 Two dice are rolled: one red and one blue. If the total score is 5, what is the probability that the score on the red dice is 3?
Student Book 1, Chapter 17	You should be able to use the binomial distribution.	4 The probability of rolling a 6 on a biased dice is $\frac{1}{5}$. If the dice is rolled four times, find the probability of getting exactly one 6.
GCSE	You should be able to solve simultaneous equations.	5 Solve: $x+4.72y=7.32$ $x-1.28y=0.435$

What is the normal distribution?

In Student Book 1, Chapter 17 you met discrete random variables, which you could describe by listing all possible values and their probabilities. With a continuous variable, such as height or time, listing all values is impossible. You need a different way to describe how the probability is distributed across the possible values.

In Student Book 1, Chapter 16 you used histograms to represent continuous data. On a histogram, frequency is represented by the area of a bar, and the y-axis shows frequency density. A similar idea can be used to describe the probability distribution of a continuous random variable. You can draw a curve such that the area under the curve represents probability. This curve is called the **probability density function**.

There are many situations where a variable is very likely to be close to its average value, with values farther away from the average becoming increasingly unlikely. Many such situations can be modelled using the **normal distribution**. Natural measurements, such as heights of people or masses of animals, tend to follow a normal distribution.

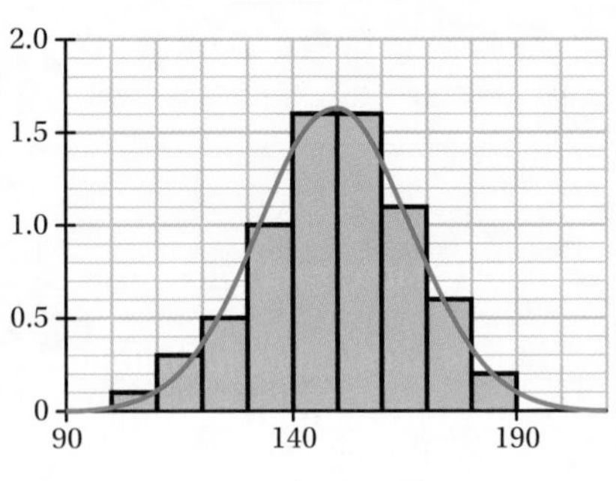

Did you know?

The normal distribution is not the only probability distribution that follows this 'bell shape'. However, there are mathematical reasons why this particular distribution is a good model for many naturally occurring measurements. You will learn more about this if you study the Statistics option in Further Maths.

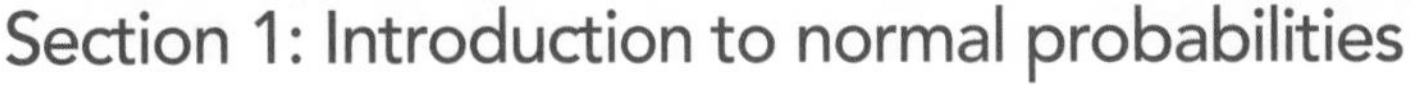

Section 1: Introduction to normal probabilities

To specify a normal distribution fully you need to know its mean (μ) and variance (σ^2). If a variable follows this distribution you use the notation $X \sim \text{N}(\mu, \sigma^2)$.

Tip

Be careful with the notation: σ^2 is the variance, so $X \sim \text{N}(10, 9)$ has standard deviation $\sigma = 3$.

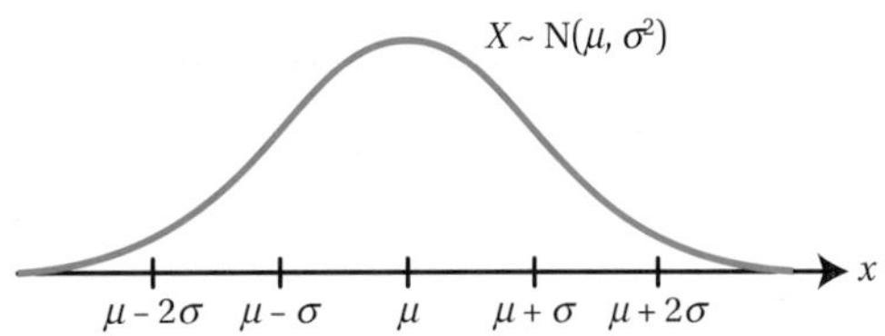

The mean corresponds to the maximum point on the graph of the probability density function, and the standard deviation affects the width of the curve. Remember that the probability corresponds to the *area* under the graph.

You know that the area under a curve can be found by integration. However, the expression for the normal distribution curve cannot be integrated exactly, so most calculators have a built-in function to find approximate probabilities.

Different calculators may have slightly different ways of finding normal probabilities. Make sure you are familiar with your model. You usually need to enter the mean and standard deviation (not variance!). Some models can find the probability between any two values. For example, to find $\text{P}(13.2 < X < 15.7)$, where $X \sim \text{N}(12.5, 16)$, you need to enter (in the correct order):

lower bound = 13.2, upper bound = 15.7, mean = 12.5, standard deviation = 4

To find $\text{P}(X < 13.8)$ you need to enter a negative number (e.g. −9999999) for the lower bound.

Some models can find only cumulative probabilities; that is, probabilities of the form $\text{P}(X < k)$. On those models, you would need to find $\text{P}(13.2 < X < 15.7)$ as $\text{P}(X < 15.7) - \text{P}(X < 13.2)$.

You should remember that, since the normal distribution is continuous, $\text{P}(X < 15.7)$ is the same as $\text{P}(X \leqslant 15.7)$.

You may find it helpful to sketch a diagram and shade the area corresponding to the probability you are trying to find.

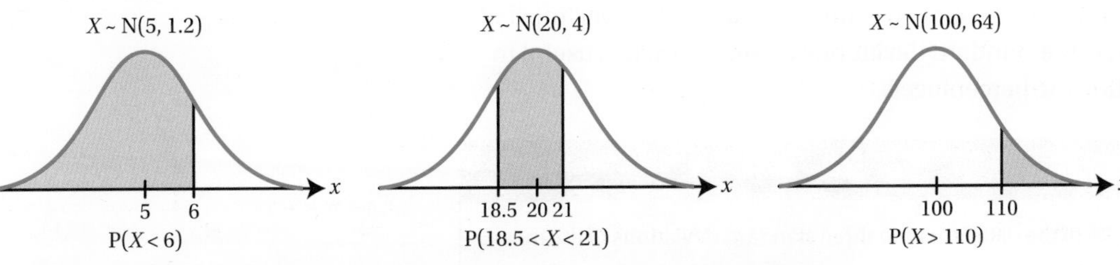

Tip

With a continuous variable, $P(X \leqslant k)$ and $P(X < k)$ mean exactly the same thing, so you don't have to worry about whether end points should be included. This is not the case for discrete variables!

The diagram can also provide a useful check, as you can see whether to expect the probability to be smaller or greater than 0.5.

WORKED EXAMPLE 17.1

The height of people in a town can be modelled by a normal distribution with mean 170 cm and standard deviation 10 cm. Give the probability that a randomly selected resident:

a is less than 165 cm tall

b is between 180 cm and 190 cm tall.

X is the 'height of a town resident' so $X \sim N(170, 100)$. — State the distribution used.

a

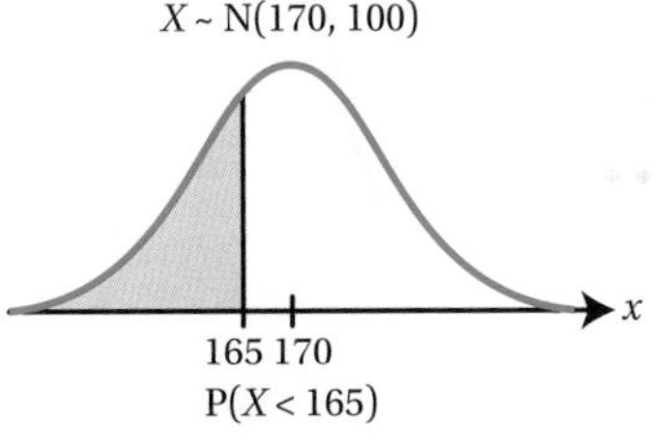

Sketch a normal distribution curve and shade the required area.

$P(X < 165) = 0.309$ (3 s.f.) (from calculator) — State the probability to be found and use the calculator.

b

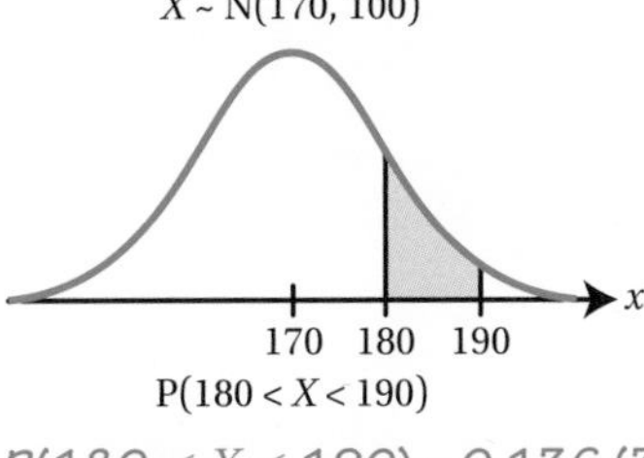

$P(180 < X < 190) = 0.136$ (3 s.f.) (from calculator)

Note that the domain of the normal probability density function is all real numbers; the x-axis is an asymptote to the graph. This means that, in theory, a normal variable could take any real value. However, most of the data lie within three standard deviations of the mean. It is useful to remember the following percentages.

Key point 17.1

Approximately 99.7% of the data lie within three standard deviations of the mean.

Approximately 95% of data lie within two standard deviations of the mean.

Approximately two-thirds of the data lie within one standard deviation of the mean.

Rewind

You met points of inflection in Chapter 12.

It turns out that the points of inflection of the normal distribution curve lie one standard deviation from the mean. This can be used to estimate the standard deviation.

PROOF 10

The curve corresponding to the normal distribution with mean zero and standard deviation σ is $y = k\mathrm{e}^{-\left(\frac{x^2}{2\sigma^2}\right)}$.

Prove that the points of inflection of $y = k\mathrm{e}^{-\left(\frac{x^2}{2\sigma^2}\right)}$ occur at $x = \pm\sigma$.

$$\frac{\mathrm{d}y}{\mathrm{d}x} = -\frac{2kx}{2\sigma^2}\mathrm{e}^{-\left(\frac{x^2}{2\sigma^2}\right)}$$

$$= -\frac{kx}{\sigma^2}\mathrm{e}^{-\left(\frac{x^2}{2\sigma^2}\right)}$$

To find a point of inflection we will use the fact that $\frac{\mathrm{d}^2y}{\mathrm{d}x^2} = 0$. Start by differentiating, using the chain rule.

$$\frac{\mathrm{d}^2y}{\mathrm{d}x^2} = -\frac{k}{\sigma^2}\mathrm{e}^{-\left(\frac{x^2}{2\sigma^2}\right)} + \left(-\frac{2x}{2\sigma^2}\right)\left(-\frac{kx}{\sigma^2}\right)\mathrm{e}^{-\left(\frac{x^2}{2\sigma^2}\right)}$$

The second derivative needs both the chain rule and the product rule.

$$= -\frac{k}{\sigma^2}\mathrm{e}^{-\left(\frac{x^2}{2\sigma^2}\right)} + \frac{kx^2}{\sigma^4}\mathrm{e}^{-\left(\frac{x^2}{2\sigma^2}\right)}$$

At a point of inflection, $\frac{\mathrm{d}^2y}{\mathrm{d}x^2} = 0$ so:

$$-\frac{k}{\sigma^2}\mathrm{e}^{-\left(\frac{x^2}{2\sigma^2}\right)} + \frac{kx^2}{\sigma^4}\mathrm{e}^{-\left(\frac{x^2}{2\sigma^2}\right)} = 0$$

Factorising:

The best way to solve complicated equations is to factorise.

$$\frac{k}{\sigma^2}\mathrm{e}^{-\left(\frac{x^2}{2\sigma^2}\right)}\left(-1 + \frac{x^2}{\sigma^2}\right) = 0$$

Since $\frac{k}{\sigma^2}\mathrm{e}^{-\left(\frac{x^2}{2\sigma^2}\right)} \neq 0$,

$$-1 + \frac{x^2}{\sigma^2} = 0$$

$$x^2 = \sigma^2$$

$$x = \pm\sigma$$

EXERCISE 17A

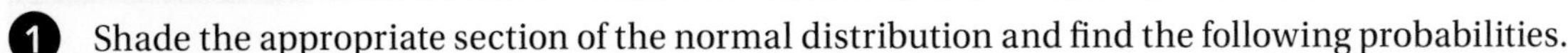

1 Shade the appropriate section of the normal distribution and find the following probabilities.

a If $X \sim N(20, 100)$:

i $P(X \leqslant 32)$ **ii** $P(X < 12)$

b If $Y \sim N(4.8, 1.44)$:

i $P(Y > 5.1)$ **ii** $P(Y \geqslant 3.4)$

c If $R \sim N(17, 2)$:

i $P(16 < R < 20)$ **ii** $P(17.4 < R < 18.2)$

d If Q has a normal distribution with mean 12 and standard deviation 3:

i $P(Q > 9.4)$ **ii** $P(Q < 14)$

e If F has a normal distribution with mean 100 and standard deviation 25:

i $P(|F - 100| < 15)$ **ii** $P(|F - 100| > 10)$

2 A normal curve has points of inflection with x-coordinates 5 and 11. Find the mean and standard deviation of this distribution.

3 The curve in diagram 1 represents a normal distribution. Copy the diagram and mark the approximate position of the points of inflection. Hence, estimate the mean and standard deviation of the normal distribution.

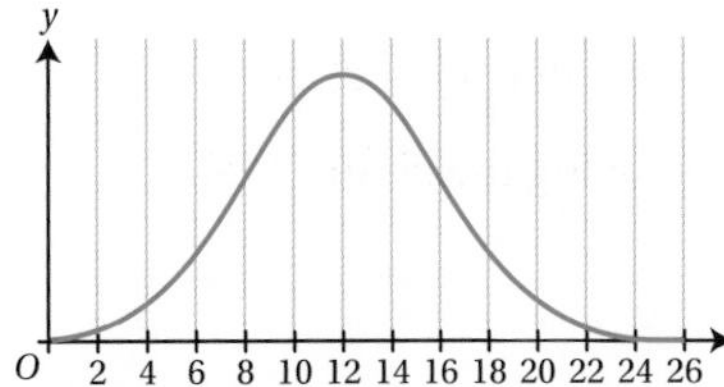

Diagram 1

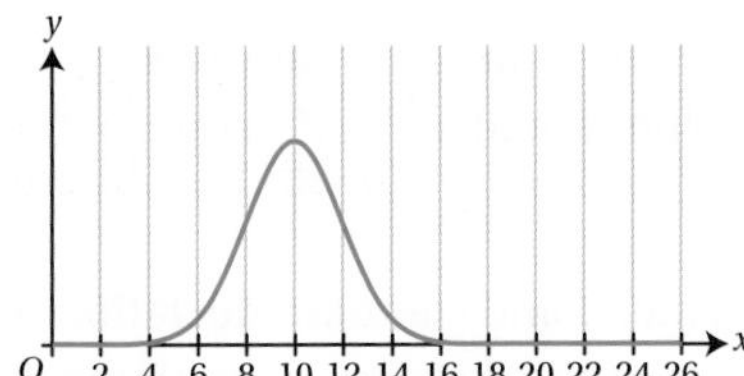

Diagram 2

4 Estimate the mean and standard deviation of the normal distribution represented by the curve in diagram 2.

Using Z-scores and the standard normal distribution

If a normally distributed random variable has mean 120, should a value of 150 be considered unusually large? The answer depends on how spread out the variable is, and this is measured by its standard deviation. If the standard deviation is 30, then a value around 150 will be quite common. However, if the standard deviation were 5, then 150 would indeed be very unusual.

It turns out that, for a normally distributed random variable, the cumulative probability $P(X \leqslant x)$ depends only on the number of standard deviations x is away from the mean. This is called the **Z-score**.

Key point 17.2

For $X \sim N(\mu, \sigma^2)$ the **Z-score** measures the number of standard deviations away from the mean:

$$z = \frac{x - \mu}{\sigma}$$

WORKED EXAMPLE 17.2

Given that $X \sim \mathrm{N}(15, 6.25)$:

a How many standard deviations is $x = 16.1$ away from the mean?

b Find the value of X that is 1.2 standard deviations below the mean.

a $z = \dfrac{x-\mu}{\sigma}$

The number of standard deviations away from the mean is measured by the Z-score.

$\sigma = \sqrt{6.25} = 2.5$

6.25 is the variance, so take its square root to get the standard deviation.

$\therefore z = \dfrac{16.1-15}{2.5} = 0.44$

16.1 is 0.44 standard deviations away from the mean.

b $z = -1.2$

Values below the mean have a negative Z-score.

$\therefore -1.2 = \dfrac{x-15}{2.5}$

$\Rightarrow x - 15 = -3$

$\Rightarrow x = 12$

Starting with a random variable $X \sim \mathrm{N}(\mu, \sigma^2)$ you can create a new random variable, Z, which takes the values equal to the Z-scores of the values of X.

It turns out that, whatever the original mean and standard deviation of X, this new random variable Z always has normal distribution with mean 0 and variance 1, called the **standard normal distribution:** $Z \sim \mathrm{N}(0, 1)$.

Key point 17.3

If $X \sim \mathrm{N}(\mu, \sigma^2)$ and $Z \sim \mathrm{N}(0, 1)$, then the probabilities of X and Z are related by:

$$\mathrm{P}(X \leqslant x) = \mathrm{P}\left(Z \leqslant \frac{x-\mu}{\sigma}\right)$$

Fast forward

This is an extremely important property of the normal distribution and needs to be used in situations when the mean and standard deviation of X are not known (see Section 3).

Did you know?

Because of their importance, cumulative probabilities of the standard normal distribution are given special notation: $\Phi(z) = \mathrm{P}(Z \leqslant z)$. Although you do not have to use this notation, you should understand what it means.

WORKED EXAMPLE 17.3

Let $X \sim \mathrm{N}(6,\ 0.5^2)$. Write the following in terms of probabilities of Z.

a $\mathrm{P}(X \leqslant 6.1)$

b $\mathrm{P}(5 < X < 7)$

a $\mathrm{P}(X \leqslant 6.1) = \mathrm{P}\left(Z \leqslant \frac{6.1-6}{0.5}\right) = \mathrm{P}(Z \leqslant 0.2)$

We are given that $x = 6.1$, so we can calculate Z.

b $\mathrm{P}(5 < X < 7) = \mathrm{P}\left(\frac{5-6}{0.5} < Z < \frac{7-6}{0.5}\right)$
$= \mathrm{P}(-2 < Z < 2)$

We now have two x values, so find the corresponding z value for each of them.

Questions on the normal distribution can be combined with other probability facts. In particular, watch out for questions that bring in conditional probability or the binomial distribution.

Rewind

The binomial distribution was covered in Student Book 1, Chapter 17. Conditional probability was covered in Chapter 16.

WORKED EXAMPLE 17.4

The masses of fish caught by a trawler follow a normal distribution with mean 4 kg and standard deviation 0.5 kg. A juvenile fish is classified as one having a mass less than 3 kg.

a What is the probability that a randomly chosen fish is a juvenile?

b If 300 fish are caught, what is the probability that there are more than ten juveniles? State any assumptions you have to make, and comment on their validity.

c Given that a fish is a juvenile, what is the probability that it has a mass more than 2.5 kg?

a Let X be 'mass of a fish' so $X \sim \mathrm{N}(4, 0.25)$.

$\mathrm{P}(X < 3) = 0.0228$ (3 s.f.) from calculator.

b Let Y be the 'number of juveniles' so that $Y \sim \mathrm{B}(300, 0.0228)$.

$\mathrm{P}(Y > 10) = 1 - \mathrm{P}(Y \leqslant 10) = 0.085$

To use the binomial distribution we need to assume that the probability of catching a juvenile does not change. This may be valid if the 300 fish are caught in a short period of time and in the same location; it may not be valid if they are caught over a period of several months. We also need to assume that one fish being a juvenile is independent of other fish. This may not be valid, as fish of similar age may stay in a group.

It is useful to write down the names of all the random variables to make it obvious which distribution you are using. Y has a binomial distribution, with the probability of 'juvenile' being the one found in part **a**. Use unrounded values in your calculations.

Continues on next page ...

c $P(X>2.5|X<3)=\frac{P(X>2.5\cap X<3)}{P(X<3)}$

This is a question about conditional probability. It is useful to write the question in terms of probability statements involving the variables defined, then use the formula.

$=\frac{P(2.5<X<3)}{P(X<3)}$

The best way to find the intersection is to think about what it means: if X is bigger than 2.5 and less than 3, it is between 2.5 and 3.

$=\frac{P(X<3)-P(X<2.5)}{P(X<3)}$

$=\frac{0.0228-0.00135}{0.0228}$

$=0.941$

It is very common in this type of question to use some of the probabilities already calculated.

EXERCISE 17B

1 Find the Z-score corresponding to the given value of X.

a i $X\sim N(12,2^2)$, $x=13$ ii $X\sim N(38,7^2)$, $x=45$

b i $X\sim N(20,9)$, $x=15$ ii $X\sim N(162,25)$, $x=160$

2 Given that $X\sim N(16,\ 2.5^2)$, write the following in terms of probabilities of the standard normal variable.

a i $P(X<20)$ ii $P(X<19.2)$

b i $P(X\geqslant 14.3)$ ii $P(X\geqslant 8.6)$

c i $P(12.5<X<16.5)$ ii $P(10.1\leqslant X\leqslant 15.5)$

3 It is found that the lifespan of a certain brand of laptop batteries follows normal distribution with mean 16 hours and standard deviation 5 hours. A particular battery has a lifespan of 10.2 hours.

a How many standard deviations below the mean is this?

b What is the probability that a randomly chosen laptop battery has a lifespan shorter than this?

4 When Ali competes in long jump competitions, the lengths of his jumps are normally distributed with mean 5.2 m and standard deviation 0.7 m.

a What is the probability that Ali will record a jump between 5 m and 5.5 m?

b Ali needs to jump 6 m to qualify for the school team.

i What is the probability that he will qualify with a single jump?

ii If he is allowed three jumps, what is the probability that he will qualify for the school team?

c What assumptions did you have to make in your answer to **b ii**? Are these likely to be met in this situation?

5 Masses of a species of cat have a normal distribution with mean 16 kg and variance 16 kg^2. Estimate the number in a sample of 2000 such cats that will have a mass above 13 kg.

6 The 400 m time of a group of athletes can be modelled by a normal distribution, with mean 60 seconds and standard deviation 2 seconds.

a Find the probability that a randomly chosen athlete will run the 400 m in under 59 seconds.

b Show that, if the binomial distribution can be used, the probability that all four athletes in a 4×400 m team run under 59 seconds is 0.9%.

c Miguel says that this means that the probability of the team breaking the school record of 3 minutes and 56 seconds is only 0.9%. Give three reasons why this is likely to be incorrect. Do you think the real value will be greater or less than 0.9%?

7 If $D \sim \text{N}(250, 400)$, find:

a $\text{P}(D > 265 \cap D < 280)$ b $\text{P}(D > 265 \mid D < 280)$ c $\text{P}(D < 242 \cup D > 256)$

8 If $Q \sim \text{N}(4, 160)$, find:

a $\text{P}(5 < |Q|)$ b $\text{P}(Q > 5 \mid 5 < |Q|)$

9 The masses of apples are normally distributed with mean mass 150 g and standard deviation 25 g. Supermarkets classify apples as 'medium' if they are between 120 g and 170 g.

a What proportion of apples are medium?

b In a bag of ten apples, what is the probability that there are at least eight medium apples?

10 The wingspans of a species of pigeon are normally distributed with mean length 60 cm and standard deviation 6 cm. A pigeon is chosen at random and its wingspan measured.

a Find the probability that its length is greater than 50 cm.

b Given that its length is greater than 50 cm, find the probability that its length is greater than 55 cm.

11 Grains of sand are believed to have a normal distribution with mean 2 mm and variance 0.25 mm^2.

a Find the probability that a randomly chosen grain of sand is larger than 1.5 mm.

b The sand is passed through a filter that blocks grains wider than 2.5 mm. The sand that passes through the filter is examined. What is the probability that a randomly chosen grain of filtered sand is larger than 1.5 mm?

12 The amount of paracetamol per tablet is believed to be normally distributed with mean 500 mg and standard deviation 160 mg. A dose of less than 300 mg is ineffective in dealing with toothache. In a trial of 20 people suffering toothache, what is the probability that two or more of them have less than the effective dose?

13 A variable has a normal distribution with a mean that is seven times its standard deviation. What is the probability of the variable taking a value less than five times the standard deviation?

14 If $X \sim \text{N}(\mu, \sigma^2)$ and $\text{P}(X \leqslant x) = k$, find $\text{P}(X \leqslant 2\mu - x)$ in terms of k.

Section 2: Inverse normal distribution

In Section 1 you saw how to find probabilities when you knew information about the variable. In real life it is often useful to work backwards from probabilities to estimate information about the data. This requires the **inverse normal distribution**.

Key point 17.4

For a given value of probability p, the inverse normal distribution gives the value of x such that $P(X \leqslant x) = p$.

Note that many textbooks use the $\Phi(z)$ notation mentioned in the previous section to write inverse normal distribution: If $P(X \leqslant x) = p$, then $\Phi^{-1}(p) = z = \frac{x - \mu}{\sigma}$.

To find inverse normal values on your calculator, you usually need to enter the value of x, the mean and the standard deviation. Make sure you know the correct order to use on your calculator.

Fast forward

You will use inverse normal distribution to find critical values for a hypothesis tests in Chapter 18.

WORKED EXAMPLE 17.5

The length of men's feet is thought to be normally distributed with mean 22 cm and variance 25 cm^2. A shoe manufacturer wants only 5% of men to be unable to find shoes large enough for them. How big should their largest shoe be?

If X is the continuous random variable 'length of a man's foot' then $X \sim N(22, 25)$.

Convert the question into mathematical terms.

You need to find the value of x such that

$P(X > x) = 0.05$

$P(X \leqslant x) = 1 - P(X > x) = 0.95$

Use the inverse normal distribution.

$\Rightarrow x = 30.2$ cm

So their largest shoe must fit a foot 30.2 cm long.

You may have to convert into a probability of the form $P(X \leqslant x)$ in order to use the calculator.

EXERCISE 17C

1 **a** The random variable X follows the normal distribution N(14, 49). Find x if:

i $P(X < x) = 0.8$ **ii** $P(X < x) = 0.46$

b The random variable X follows the normal distribution N(36.5, 10). Find x if:

i $P(X > x) = 0.9$ **ii** $P(X > x) = 0.4$

c The random variable X follows the normal distribution N(0, 12). Find x if:

i $P(|X| < x) = 0.5$ **ii** $P(|X| < x) = 0.8$

2 IQ tests are designed to have a mean of 100 and a standard deviation of 20. What IQ score is needed to be in the top 2% of IQ scores?

3 Rabbits' masses are normally distributed with an average mass of 2.6 kg and a variance of 1.44 kg^2. A vet decides that the top 20% of rabbits are obese. What is the minimum mass for an obese rabbit?

4 The amount of coffee dispensed by a machine follows the normal distribution with mean 150 mL and standard deviation 5 mL.

a Calculate the probability that the machine dispenses less than 142 mL of coffee.

b Find the value of a if 20% of cups contain more than a mL of coffee.

5. The times taken for students to complete a test are normally distributed with a mean of 32 minutes and a standard deviation of 6 minutes.
   - **a** Find the probability that a randomly chosen student completes the test in less than 35 minutes.
   - **b** 90% of students complete the test in less than t minutes. Find the value of t.
   - **c** A random sample of eight students has their completion time for the test recorded. Find the probability that exactly two of these students complete the test in less than 30 minutes.
6. An old textbook says that the range of data can be estimated as six times the standard deviation. If the data are normally distributed, what percentage of the data are within this range?
7. The time taken to do a maths question can be modelled by a normal distribution with mean 80 seconds and standard deviation 15 seconds. The probability of two randomly chosen questions both taking longer than a seconds is 0.063752. Find the value of a.
8. The concentration of salt in a cell, X, can be modelled by a normal distribution with mean μ and standard deviation 2%. Find the value of α such that $\mathrm{P}(\mu - \alpha < X < \mu + \alpha) = 0.9$.
9. For a normal distribution, find the following ratios.
   - **a** $\dfrac{\text{Median}}{\text{Mean}}$
   - **b** $\dfrac{\text{Standard deviation}}{\text{Interquartile range}}$
10. Evaluate $\Phi^{-1}(x) + \Phi^{-1}(1 - x)$, where $\Phi^{-1}(x)$ is the inverse normal distribution function for the standard normal distribution.
11. If $Z \sim \mathrm{N}(0, 1)$ and $\mathrm{P}(Z < k) = \Phi(k)$, for $k > 0$, find $\mathrm{P}(|Z| > k)$ in terms of $\Phi(k)$.
12. Most calculators have a random number generator that generates random numbers from 0 to 1. These random numbers are uniformly distributed, which means that the probability is evenly spread over all possible values. How can you use these to form random numbers drawn from a normal distribution?

Section 3: Finding unknown μ or σ

One of the main applications of statistics is to determine parameters of the population when given information about the data. But how can you use the normal distribution calculations if the mean or the standard deviation is unknown? This is where the standard normal distribution comes in useful: you can replace all the X values by their Z-scores, as they follow a known distribution, N(0, 1).

Tip

This will involve solving equations, and sometimes simultaneous equations. As the numbers are usually not 'nice', you may want to use your calculator.

WORKED EXAMPLE 17.6

Random variable X follows a normal distribution with standard deviation $\sigma = 1.2$. An experiment estimates that $\mathrm{P}(X > 3.4) = 0.2$. Estimate the mean of X, correct to two significant figures.

$\mathrm{P}(X \leqslant 3.4) = 0.8$ — You may need the probability to be in the form $\mathrm{P}(X \leqslant k)$.

If $Z = \dfrac{X - \mu}{\sigma}$, $Z \sim \mathrm{N}(0, 1)$: — Since you don't know μ, convert the probability into information about Z.

Continues on next page ...

$P(Z \leqslant z) = 0.8 \Rightarrow z = 0.8416$ — Use inverse normal distribution to find z.

$z = \frac{3.4 - \mu}{1.2} = 0.8416$ — Relate z to the given x value.

$\Rightarrow 3.4 - \mu = 1.01 \Rightarrow \mu = 2.4$

WORKED EXAMPLE 17.7

The masses of gerbils are thought to be normally distributed. If 30% of gerbils have a mass more than 65 g and 20% have a mass less than 40 g, estimate the mean and the variance of the mass of a gerbil.

If X is 'mass of a gerbil', then $X \sim \mathrm{N}(\mu, \sigma^2)$. — Convert the information into mathematical terms.

$P(X < 40) = 0.2 \ldots$ (1)

$P(X > 65) = 0.3$

$P(X \leqslant 65) = 0.7 \ldots$ (2) — If you need all the probabilities to be in the form $P(X \leqslant k)$, convert the first one.

From (1): — Use the inverse normal distribution for Z and relate it to the given X values.

$P(Z < z) = 0.2$

$\Rightarrow z = \frac{40 - \mu}{\sigma} = -0.842$

From (2):

$P(Z \leqslant z) = 0.7$

$\Rightarrow z = \frac{65 - \mu}{\sigma} = 0.524$

$40 - \mu = -0.842\sigma \ldots$ (3) — Solve the simultaneous equations.

$65 - \mu = 0.524\sigma \ldots$ (4)

(4) − (3) gives:

$25 = 1.366\sigma \Rightarrow \sigma = 18.3\text{ g, so } \sigma^2 = 335\text{ g}^2$

$\therefore \mu = 55.4\text{ g}$

WORK IT OUT 17.1

If $X \sim N(10, 25)$ and $P(X > x) = 0.75$, find the value of x.

Which is the correct solution? Can you identify the errors made in the incorrect solutions?

Solution 1	Solution 2	Solution 3
$P(X < x) = 0.25$ so, from the calculator, the corresponding Z-score is -0.674. Therefore, $\frac{x-10}{5} = -0.674$ $x - 10 = -3.37$ $x = 6.63$ (to 3 s.f.)	$\Phi^{-1}(0.75) = 0.674$ Therefore, $0.674 = \frac{x-10}{25}$ So $x - 10 = 16.9$ $x = 26.9$	$\frac{x-10}{25} = 0.75$ $x - 10 = 18.75$ $x = 28.75$

EXERCISE 17D

1 a If $X \sim N(\mu, 4)$, find μ when:

i $P(X > 4) = 0.8$ ii $P(X > 9) = 0.2$

b If $X \sim N(8, \sigma^2)$, find σ when:

i $P(X \leqslant 19) = 0.6$ ii $P(X \leqslant 0) = 0.3$

2 If $X \sim N(\mu, \sigma^2)$, find μ and σ when:

a i $P(X > 7) = 0.8$ and $P(X < 6) = 0.1$ ii $P(X > 150) = 0.3$ and $P(X < 120) = 0.4$

b i $P(X > 0.1) = 0.4$ and $P(X \geqslant 0.6) = 0.25$ ii $P(X > 700) = 0.8$ and $P(X \geqslant 400) = 0.99$

3 A manufacturer knows that his machines produce bolts whose diameters follow a normal distribution with standard deviation 0.02 cm. He takes a random sample of bolts and finds that 6% of them have diameter greater than 2 cm. Find the mean diameter of the bolts.

4 The energy of an electron can be modelled by normal distribution with mean 12 eV and standard deviation σ eV. If 20% of electrons have an energy above 15 eV, find the value of σ.

5 It is known that the heights of a certain plant follow a normal distribution. In a sample of 200 plants, 32 are less than 45 cm tall and 50 are more than 88 cm tall. Estimate the mean and the standard deviation of the heights.

6 The time taken for a computer to start is modelled by a normal distribution. It is tested 100 times and on 40 of these it takes longer than 30 seconds. On 25 of the tests it takes less than15 seconds. Estimate the mean and standard deviation of the start-up times.

7 The actual voltage of a brand of 9 V battery is thought to be normally distributed with standard deviation 0.8 V and mean $(9.2 - t)$V, where t is the time, in hours, that the battery has been used. The batteries can no longer power a lamp when they drop below 7 V. In one batch of batteries only 10% can power the lamp. Assuming that the model is correct, estimate how long the batteries have been used (assume that they were all used for the same length of time).

8 A scientist noticed that 36% of temperature measurements were 4 °C lower than the average. Assuming that the measurements follow a normal distribution, estimate the standard deviation.

9 The waiting time for a train is normally distributed with mean 10 minutes. 80% of the time the waiting time is over 8 minutes. Find the probability that a person waits over 15 minutes on exactly two out of three times they wait for the train.

10 The random variable X models the temperature in an oven in °C. It follows a normal distribution, where the mean value is the temperature set on the oven. The probability of being within 5 °C of the temperature set is 40%. Find the probability of being within 10 °C of the temperature set.

Section 4: Modelling with normal distribution

Many real-world situations can be modelled using a normal distribution, such as the heights of people, masses of gerbils or error in experimental measurements. However, you should not just assume that a variable follows a normal distribution. There are various useful checks that you can use to help you.

Focus on ...

In Focus on ... Modelling 3 you can investigate further examples of using the normal distribution as a model.

Key point 17.5

To decide whether a normal distribution is an appropriate model:

When you look at a histogram you would expect the distribution to be approximately symmetrical with only one mode and no sharp cut-off.

When you are looking at summary statistics you would expect nearly all of the data to fall within three standard deviations of the mean.

Fast forward

If you study the Statistics option of Further Mathematics, you will find out about a statistical test called the chi-squared test, which allows us to decide more precisely whether data come from a normal distribution.

WORKED EXAMPLE 17.8

For each of the following histograms, explain why the normal distribution is not a good model for the data.

a

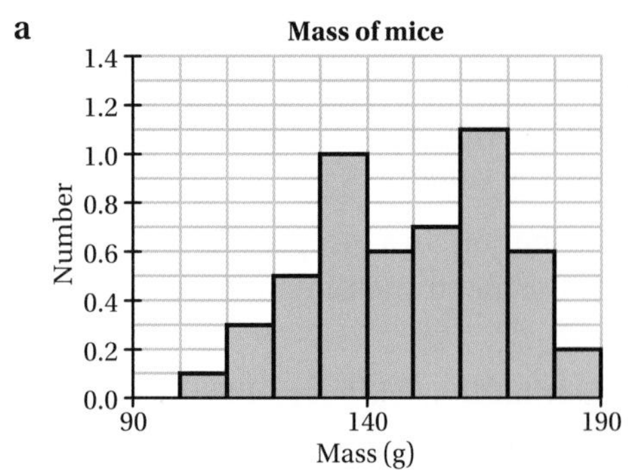

b

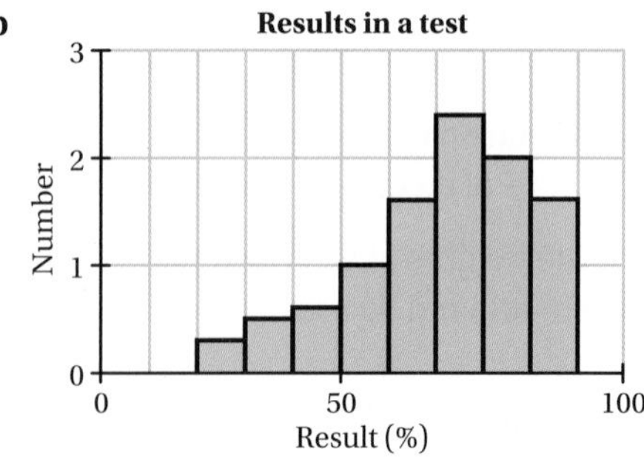

a *There appear to be two modes.*

b *These data do not seem to be symmetrical and there is a sharp cut-off at the top end because it is not possible to score over 100%.*

WORKED EXAMPLE 17.9

In a sample, it is found that the mean time taken to complete a puzzle is 42 seconds with a standard deviation of 28 seconds. Explain why the normal distribution would not be an appropriate model to predict the time taken to complete this puzzle.

There is a cut-off at zero seconds, which is 1.5 standard deviations below the mean. The normal distribution would therefore predict that a significant number of people complete the puzzle in a negative amount of time, which is not possible.

With only the mean and standard deviation provided (no graph of the distribution), consider whether virtually all the data fall within 3 standard deviations of the mean.

Many other statistical distributions can be approximated by the normal distribution. Historically, this was very important because calculations with the normal distribution were often much easier.

For example, consider these bar charts for the binomial distribution.

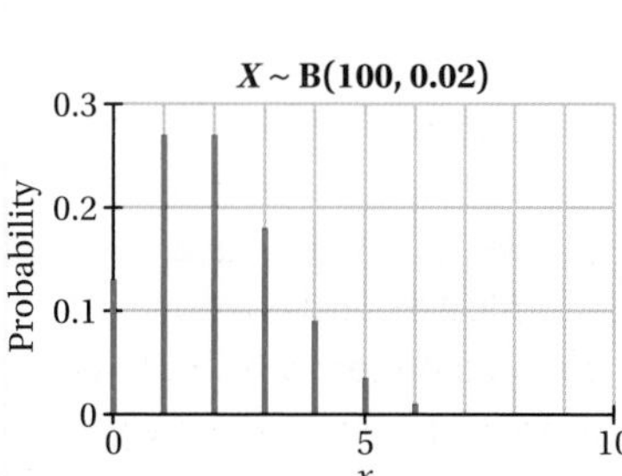

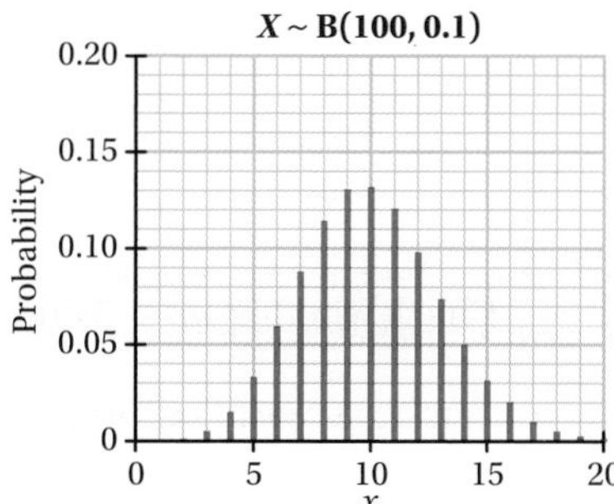

The one on the left has a sharp cut-off at 0 and is not symmetrical, but the one on the right appears to have roughly the shape of a normal distribution. It turns out that it can indeed be approximated by a normal distribution, although the proof of this is beyond the scope of this book.

Key point 17.6

If $X \sim B(n, p)$ with $np > 5$ and $nq > 5$ (where $q = 1 - p$), then X can be approximated by a normal distribution with $\mu = np$ and $\sigma^2 = npq$.

Explore

Because the binomial distribution deals with discrete variables and the normal distribution deals with continuous variables, technically we should use something called a *continuity correction*. This says that $P(X = 5)$ in the binomial distribution is equivalent to $P(4.5 < X < 5.5)$ in the normal distribution. You do not need to do this within this course, but you may want to find out about it and use it to check how good this approximation is.

WORKED EXAMPLE 17.10

A fair dice is rolled 300 times. The random variable X models the number of 6s rolled.

a Explain why X follows a binomial distribution.

b The random variable X can be approximated by a normal distribution. Find the mean and variance of this normal distribution. What properties of X make this approximation valid?

c Let Y be a random variable with the normal distribution from part **b**. Find $P(Y \leqslant 40)$.

d Find $P(X \leqslant 40)$. Explain why this is not the same as your answer to part **c**.

a There is a fixed number of rolls. The rolls are independent, with constant probability of rolling a '6'. We can classify the outcomes into '6' or 'not 6'.

Recall the conditions for when using a binomial distribution is appropriate.

b $n=300$ and $p=\frac{1}{6}$, so $np=50$ and $npq=\frac{250}{6}$.

Use the fact that $N(np, npq)$ is the approximate distribution.

So the approximate normal distribution is $N\left(50, \frac{250}{6}\right)$.

$np=50$ and $nq=250$, which are both larger than 5. This means that the binomial distribution will be reasonably symmetrical.

Check whether $np > 5$ and $nq > 5$.

c For $Y \sim N\left(50, \frac{250}{6}\right)$,

$(Y \leqslant 40) = 0.0607$ (3 s.f.)

State the distribution of Y and use the calculator to find probability.

d For $X \sim B\left(300, \frac{1}{6}\right)$,

$P(X \leqslant 40) = 0.0675$ (3 s.f.)

Use your a calculator to find the probability for the original binomial distribution.

X and Y don't have exactly the same distribution: X is discrete and Y is continuous.

The normal distribution is only an approximation to the binomial, so the probabilities won't be exactly the same.

In binomial hypothesis tests, when the value of n is large the normal approximation is useful because the exact binomial probabilities can be difficult to find.

Rewind

You met hypothesis testing using binomial distribution in Student Book 1, Chapter 18. Remember that the significance level gives the probability of incorrectly rejecting the null hypothesis.

Fast forward

You will learn more about hypothesis testing using normal distribution in the next chapter.

WORKED EXAMPLE 17.11

A survey of a random sample of 5000 people in a large city is conducted in order to test a hypothesis about the proportion of people who cycle to work. In this sample, c people cycle to work. The test conclude that there is evidence, at the 5% significance level, that this proportion is less than 0.06. Use an appropriate normal distribution to estimate the maximum possible value of c.

Let X be the number of people in a sample of 5000 who cycle to work.

Then $X \sim \text{B}(5000, p)$.

The hypotheses are:

$\text{H}_0: p = 0.06, \text{H}_1: p < 0.06$

This is a hypothesis test for the proportion of the binomial distribution. So start by stating the distribution and the hypotheses.

We need c such that:

$\text{P}(X \leqslant c) < 0.05$, where $X \sim \text{B}(5000, 0.06)$.

c is the critical value for this test. The significance level is 5%.

Approximate normal distribution:

$np = 300, npq = 282$

So $X \approx \text{N}(300, 282)$

We can use normal approximation because $np = 300 > 5$ and $nq = 4700 > 5$.

Using this normal distribution,

Use inverse normal distribution to find the value of c.

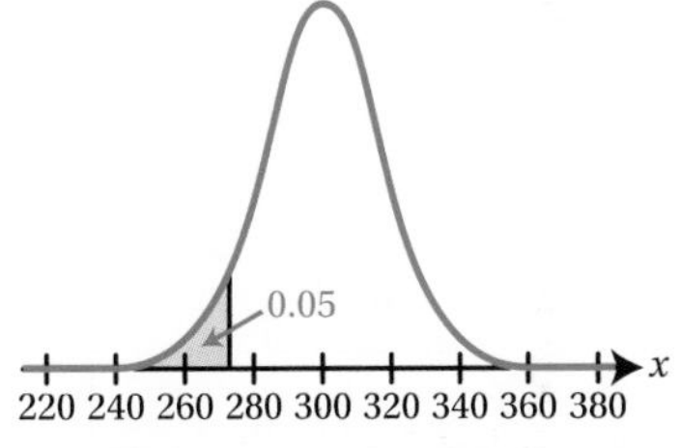

$\text{P}(X \leqslant c) < 0.05 \Rightarrow c < 272.3$

So $c \approx 272$.

c is the number of people who cycle to work, so needs to be a whole number.

EXERCISE 17E

1 For each of the following histograms, decide if the data could be modelled by a normal distribution. If it cannot, give a reason.

a

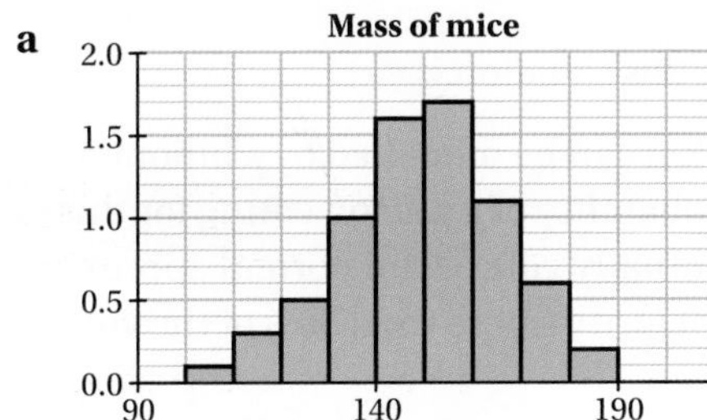

b

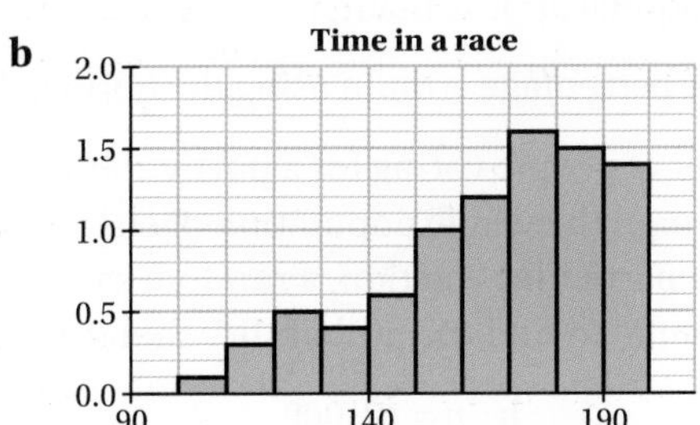

c GDP of a country

d

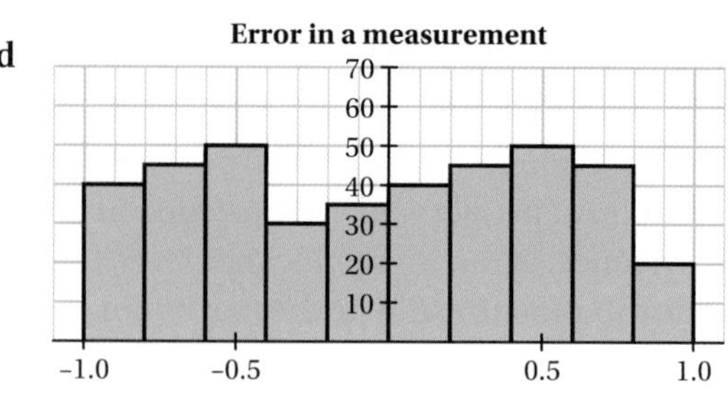

2 The mean number of children in a family in the UK is 2.4 with a standard deviation of 1.1. Use these figures to explain why a normal distribution would not be a good model of the number of children in a family in the UK.

3 A psychology student asks people to estimate the value of an angle. Her results are summarised in the histogram below.

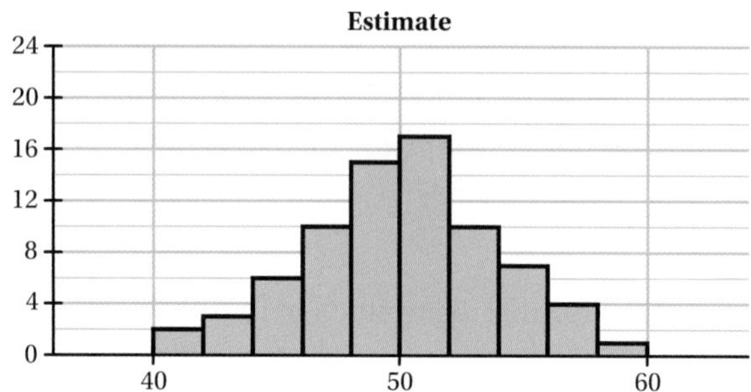

a Copy and complete the frequency table below.

Angle	40–42	42–44	44–46	46–48	48–50	50–52	52–54	54–56	56–58	58–60
Frequency	2	3	6	10			10	7	4	1

b Hence, estimate the mean and standard deviation of the data.

c What features of the graph suggest that a normal distribution might be an appropriate model?

d The student compares these data estimates to another group of 100 people. If they follow the same normal distribution, how many would you expect to estimate over 55°?

4 A fair coin is tossed 100 times.

a Find the probability that there are more than 60 heads using:

i the binomial distribution

ii the normal approximation.

b Find the percentage error in using the normal distribution in this situation.

5 The number of people voting for a particular party in an election can be modelled by a binomial distribution. In the whole population of eligible voters, the probability of a person voting for this is 0.48. In a particular election, a random sample of n voters actually vote. Use a normal approximation to the binomial to find the probability that this party wins a majority (more than 50% of the vote) if:

a $n = 100$ **b** $n = 10,000$

6 Data collected over a long period of time indicate that 23% of children contract a certain disease. Following a public awareness campaign, a doctor conducts a survey to find out whether this proportion has decreased. She uses a random sample of 3000 children and conducts a hypothesis test at the 2.5% significance level. Use an appropriate normal distribution to find the approximate critical region for this test.

7 **a** Prove that if $np > 5$ and $n(1-p) > 5$, then $n > 10$. Show, using a counterexample, that the reverse is not true.

b A binomial distribution $B(n, 0.8)$ has a probability of 0.181 of being above 100. Find the value of n.

8 The random variable $X \sim B(n, p)$ is approximated by the normal distribution $N(np, np(1-p))$. Prove using this approximation that if $np > 9$, then all values of X within three standard deviations of the mean are positive.

Checklist of learning and understanding

- The normal distribution models many physical situations. It is described completely once we know its mean (μ) and its variance (σ^2). Calculators can provide the probabilities of being in any given range.
- The following are useful values to know:
  - Approximately 99.7% of the data lie within three standard deviations of the mean.
  - Approximately 95% of data lie within two standard deviations of the mean.
  - Approximately two-thirds of the data lie within one standard deviation of the mean.
- The Z-score is the number of standard deviations above the mean that has a given cumulative probability. It is related to the original variable by the equation:

$$z = \frac{x - \mu}{\sigma}.$$

- If we know probabilities relating to a variable with a normal distribution we can deduce information about the variable using the inverse normal distribution.
- We need to use the Z-score when the mean or the standard deviation are unknown.
- If $X \sim B(n, p)$ with $np > 5$ and $nq > 5$ (where $q = 1 - p$), then X can be approximated by a normal distribution with $\mu = np$ and $\sigma^2 = npq$.

Mixed practice 17

1 a The test scores of a large group of students can be modelled by a normal distribution with mean 62 and variance 144. Find the percentage of students with scores above 80.

b What is the lowest score achieved by the top 50% of these students?

2 The masses of kittens can be modelled by a normal distribution with mean 1.2 kg and standard deviation 0.3 kg.

a Out of a group of 20 kittens, how many would be expected to have a mass of less than 1 kg?

b 30% of kittens have a mass of more than m kg. Determine the value of m.

3 The random variable X is normally distributed with a mean of 3 and standard deviation of 1.5. By sketching a normal curve, or otherwise, find the value of k such that $P(2.6 < X < k) = 0.32$.

4 The masses, M kg, of babies born at a certain hospital satisfy $M \sim N(3.2, 0.72)$. Find the value of m such that 35% of the babies have a mass between m kg and 3.2 kg, where $m < 3.2$.

5 Tennis balls are dropped from a standard height, and the height of the bounce, H cm, is measured. H is a random variable with the distribution $N(40, \sigma^2)$. It is given that $P(H < 32) = 0.2$.

i Find the value of σ.

ii 90 tennis balls are selected at random. Use an appropriate approximation to find the probability that more than 19 have $H < 32$.

© OCR, GCE Mathematics, Paper 4733, June 2010

6 The adult female of a breed of dog has average height 0.7 m with variance 0.05 m^2. If the height follows a normal distribution, find the probability that in six independently selected dogs of this breed exactly four are above 0.75 m tall.

7 Heights of trees in a forest are distributed normally with mean 26.2 m and standard deviation 5.6 m.

a Find the probability that a tree is more than 30 m tall.

b What is the probability that among 16 randomly selected trees at least two are more than 30 m tall?

8 It is known that the scores on a test can be modelled by a normal distribution $N(\mu, \sigma^2)$. 20% of the scores are above 82 and 10% of the scores are below 47.

a Show that $\mu + 0.8416\sigma = 82$.

b By writing another similar equation, find the mean and the standard deviation of the scores.

9 200 people are asked to estimate the size of an angle. 16 give an estimate that is less than 25° and 42 give an estimate that is more than 35°. Assuming that the data can be modelled by a normal distribution, estimate the mean and the standard deviation of the results.

10 The continuous random variable X has the distribution $N(\mu, \sigma^2)$.

i Each of the three following sets of probabilities is impossible. Give a reason in each case why the probabilities cannot both be correct. (You should not attempt to find μ and σ.)

a $P(X > 50) = 0.7$ and $P(X < 50) = 0.2$

b $P(X > 50) = 0.7$ and $P(X > 70) = 0.8$

c $P(X > 50) = 0.3$ and $P(X < 70) = 0.3$

ii Given that $P(X > 50) = 0.7$ and $P(X < 70) = 0.7$, find the values of μ and σ.

© OCR, GCE Mathematics, Paper 4733, January 2010

11 50% of students in a university are female. The discrete random variable X, the number of female students in a group of size n, is assumed to follow a binomial distribution.

a Explain why, if n is large, the binomial distribution can be approximated by the normal distribution, and state its parameters.

b A dancing club contains 200 students. Assuming the binomial distribution is valid, use the normal approximation to find the probability that more than 60% are female.

c Are the conditions for the binomial distribution met in this situation? Explain your answer.

12 The results of an examination have a mean of 54%, a median of 55% and a standard deviation of 12%.

a Explain why a normal distribution could be a plausible model for these data.

Grades are awarded in the following way.

- The top 20% get a distinction.
- The next 30% get a merit.
- The next 40% get a pass.
- The remaining people get a fail.

b Assuming a normal model, find the grade boundaries for this examination.

13 A company makes a large number of steel links for chains. They know that the force required to break any individual link is modelled by a normal distribution with mean 20 kN. The company tests chains consisting of four links. If any link breaks, the chain will break. A force of 18 kN is applied to all of the chains and 30% break.

a Estimate the probability of a single link breaking.

b Hence, estimate the standard deviation in the breaking strength of the links.

14 a 30% of sand from the beach Playa Gauss falls through a sieve with gaps of 1 mm, but 90% passes through a sieve with gaps of 2 mm. Assuming that the diameters of grains of sand are normally distributed, estimate the mean and standard deviation of the sand diameters.

b 80% of sand from Playa Fermat falls through a sieve with gaps of 2 mm. 40% of this filtered sand passes through a sieve with gaps of 1 mm. Assuming that the diameters of grains of sand are normally distributed, estimate the mean and standard deviation of the sand diameters.

18 Further hypothesis testing

In this chapter you will learn:

- that the sample mean is a random variable
- how the sample mean is distributed
- how to test whether the mean of a normally distributed population is different from a predicted value
- how to test whether a set of bivariate data provides evidence for significant correlation.

Before you start...

Student Book 1, Chapter 16	You should be able to interpret correlation coefficients.	1 Information on height, weight (mass), waist size and average time spent exercising per week is recorded from a random sample of adult males. Match the values of the product moment correlation coefficients with each of the sets of variables. A Height and weight B Height and time spent exercising C Waist measurement and time spent exercising 1 $r = -0.82$ 2 $r = 0.13$ 3 $r = 0.71$
Student Book 1, Chapter 18	You should be able to conduct hypothesis tests using the binomial distribution.	2 A dice is rolled ten times and four 6s are obtained. It is claimed that the dice is biased in favour of getting a 6. Test this claim at the 10% level.
Chapter 17	You should be able to perform calculations using the normal distribution.	3 $X \sim \text{N}(175, 10^2)$. Find: a $\text{P}(X < 190)$ b $\text{P}(150 < X < 185)$ c a such that $\text{P}(X > a) = 0.01$

Testing means and correlation coefficients

A cereal packet claims that it weighs (has mass of) on average 500 g. A sample of 10 packets contains a mean of 499 g of cereal. Is this evidence that the company is systematically underfilling the packets? Intuition suggests probably not. You would not expect the mean of every sample to be exactly 500 g and the result seems to be reasonably close. You may wonder how far below 500 g the mean would have to be before there was significant evidence. To answer questions like this you can use a hypothesis test.

In this chapter you will look at two different types of hypothesis tests. The first is a test to see if the mean of a sample is very different from a predicted value, such as in the previous example. To do this we first need to establish some theory about the **distribution of sample means**.

In Student Book 1, Chapter 16 you saw that correlation coefficients could be used to describe the strength of correlation, but it was not clear how big the coefficient needed to be to have significant evidence of correlation. In Section 3 you will see how hypothesis tests can be used to decide if the sample correlation coefficient provides evidence for correlation in the population.

Section 1: Distribution of the sample mean

If data follow a normal distribution then every observation is a random variable, meaning that an observation can take a different value each time. The histogram below shows samples taken from a N(10, 16) distribution.

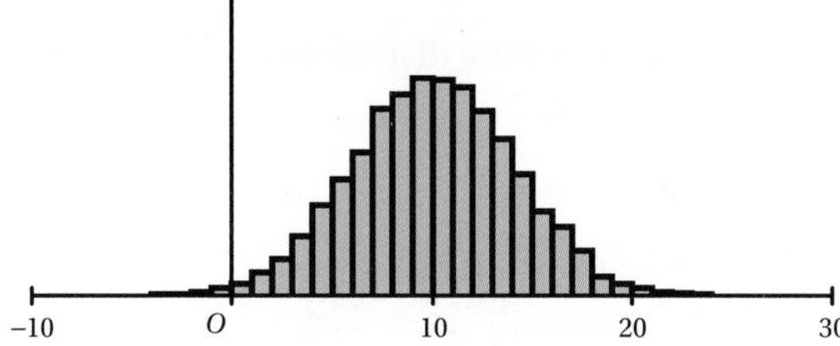

Instead of looking at a single value, you can look at a sample of n independent observations and calculate a mean. This might take a different value every time you do it, so it is also a random variable and is given the symbol $\bar{X}_n$ or simply $\bar{X}$. For the distribution above, you can take lots of samples of size 20 and create a histogram of their mean, shown in dark blue in the diagram below.

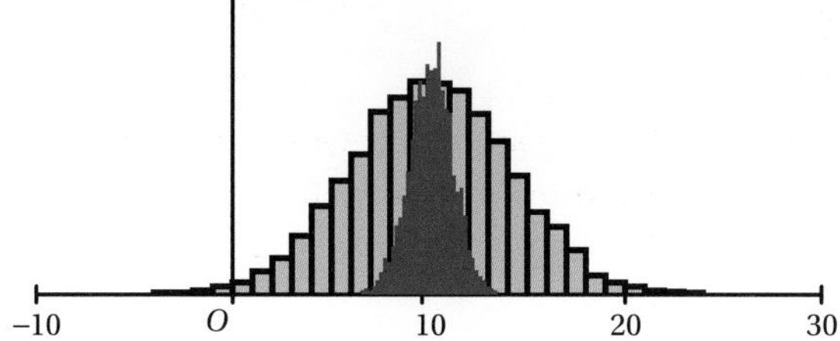

Tip

You might like to use technology to see if you can create a similar histogram.

There are two important things to note about the sample means:

- They are clustered around the same mean as the original data.
- They are less spread out.

It can be shown that the sample mean of n independent observations from a normal distribution also follows a normal distribution, with parameters relating to the original distribution and n.

Fast forward

You will find a proof for this if you study Further Mathematics, in Pure Core Student Book 1.

Key point 18.1

If the original distribution was $N(\mu, \sigma^2)$ then

$$\bar{X}_n \sim N\left(\mu, \frac{\sigma^2}{n}\right)$$

WORKED EXAMPLE 18.1

If $X \sim \text{N}(10, 16)$:

a Find $\text{P}(9 < X < 11)$.
b Find $\text{P}(9 < \bar{X}_{20} < 11)$.
c Comment on your results in parts **a** and **b**.

a $\text{P}(9 < X < 11) = 0.197$
(from calculator)

To find probabilities for a given normal distribution you can go straight to the calculator. However, it can be useful to 'sense check' your result. The required region is within less than one standard deviation away from the mean, so the result must be less than $\frac{2}{3}$.

b $\bar{X}_{20} \sim \text{N}\left(10, \frac{16}{20}\right)$

You should always write down the distribution you are using if it is not given.

So the standard deviation is $\frac{4}{\sqrt{20}} \approx 0.89$.

$\text{P}(9 < \bar{X}_{20} < 11) = 0.736$ (3 s.f.)
(from calculator)

Here the required region is within just over one standard deviation away from the mean, so the answer should be just over $\frac{2}{3}$.

c The mean of 20 observations is much more likely to be within 1 unit of the true mean (10) than a single observation is.

You probably already had some intuition that calculating a mean of several observations provides a result that is likely to be closer to the true mean than a single observation. You can now have a mathematical justification for that intuition.

EXERCISE 18A

1 Write down the distribution of the sample mean, given the original distribution.

a **i** If $X \sim \text{N}(4, 100)$, find $\bar{X}_4$.

ii If $X \sim \text{N}(20, 125)$, find $\bar{X}_5$.

b **i** If $X \sim \text{N}(0, 1)$, find $\bar{X}_{10}$.

ii If $X \sim \text{N}(0, 10)$, find $\bar{X}_4$.

2 Find the following probabilities.

a **i** If $X \sim \text{N}(4, 100)$, find $\text{P}(\bar{X}_4 < 6)$.

ii If $X \sim \text{N}(20, 125)$, find $\text{P}(\bar{X}_5 > 16)$.

b **i** If $X \sim \text{N}(0, 1)$, find $\text{P}(-0.5 < \bar{X}_{10} < 1)$.

ii If $X \sim \text{N}(0, 10)$, find $\text{P}(0 < \bar{X}_4 < 3)$.

Tip

In this exercise we will use $\bar{X}_n$ for the sample mean to emphasise the size of the sample. In later chapters, if the sample size is clearly given in the question, we will not include the subscript and simply write $\bar{X}$.

3 X is the energy (in eV) of beta particles emitted from a radioactive isotope. It is known that $X \sim N(40, 25)$. $\bar{X}_{100}$ is the mean energy of 100 beta particles.

a Stating one necessary assumption, write down the distribution of $\bar{X}_{100}$ along with its parameters.

b Find $P(39 < X < 41)$.

c Find $P(39 < \bar{X}_{100} < 41)$.

4 The mass of a breed of dog is known to follow a normal distribution with a mean of 10 kg and a standard deviation of 2.5 kg. A random sample of four dogs is taken, and each dog's mass is recorded. What is the probability that their mean mass is more than 9 kg?

5 The volume of apple juice in a carton follows a normal distribution with a mean of 152 mL and a standard deviation of 4 mL. A quality control process rejects a batch if a random sample of 16 cartons has a mean of less than 150 mL. Find the probability that a batch gets rejected.

6 Eggs are sold in boxes of six. The masses of eggs have a normal distribution with mean μ g and variance of 50 g^2. What value of μ must be chosen if the average mass of eggs in a box must be more than 75 g in at least 90% of boxes?

7 The lifetime of a light bulb, X hours, is modelled by $N(10\,000, \sigma^2)$. 5% of samples of 100 light bulbs have a mean lifetime of less than 9900 hours. Find the value of σ.

8 The length of a species of fly follows a normal distribution with mean 8 mm and standard deviation σ mm. 10% of samples of 50 flies have a mean of more than 9.2 mm. Find the value of σ.

9 The diameter of an apple has mean 8 cm and standard deviation 1 cm. A sample of n apples is chosen and their mean diameter measured.

a What is the probability that the mean diameter is between 7.9 cm and 8.1 cm if $n = 3$?

b What is the smallest value of n that must be chosen if the probability of the mean diameter being between 7.9 cm and 8.1 cm must be at least 0.3?

c By what factor must n be increased (compared to your answer in part **b**) if the probability of being between 7.9 cm and 8.1 cm is required to double to 0.6?

10 The mass of a student in a group is X kg, where X follows the $N(70, 9)$ distribution. In a sample of four students find the probability that:

a The total mass of all the students is less than 300 kg.

b The heaviest student has a mass less than 75 kg.

Section 2: Hypothesis tests for a mean

One very common decision you have to make is whether a mean is different from a predicted value. For example, you may be told that the average IQ is 100 and want to see if students in a particular school have above-average IQ. If you only have a sample from the school it is possible that the sample mean is above 100 just through chance. You can conduct a hypothesis test to see if the difference above 100 is big enough to be significant. You should take care with definitions: $\bar{X}$ is the mean of the sample that you are using to make a decision about μ, the true mean of the population.

In hypothesis testing, you assume that the conservative position – called the null hypothesis – is true and then see how likely you are to see something like the observed data. If the probability of seeing the observed data is very low, you reject the null hypothesis.

To conduct a hypothesis test you need to make some assumptions about the underlying distribution. The test you will study requires the underlying distribution to be normal with known variance.

To test the value of a population mean, μ, against a suggested value, μ_0, at significance level α:

1 Set up appropriate hypotheses, depending on the context, using one of the following.

- H_0: $\mu = \mu_0$ H_1: $\mu > \mu_0$
- H_0: $\mu = \mu_0$ H_1: $\mu < \mu_0$
- H_0: $\mu = \mu_0$ H_1: $\mu \neq \mu_0$

2 Conduct the test. Do this by:

- *either* seeing if your observed mean falls into the **acceptance region** or the **critical (rejection) region**. To do this write down the distribution of $\bar{X}$ (using Key point 18.1). Then find the regions at the ends of the distribution that have a total probability of α (the critical region). Where these regions are depends on the alternative hypothesis:

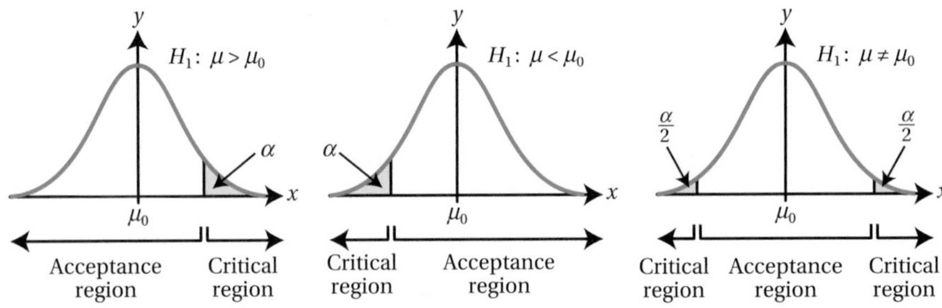

- *or* by getting your calculator to find the ***p*-value** of the observed mean. This is the probability of getting the observed value or more extreme (in the direction of the alternative hypothesis).

3 Reject the null hypothesis if the mean falls into the critical region or if the p-value is less than the significance level.

It is important that the conclusion is put in context and that it is not overly certain; you must show an appreciation that you have found only evidence rather than stating a certain conclusion.

 **Rewind**

The terminology associated with hypothesis tests was introduced in Student Book 1, Chapter 18.

 **Tip**

$\bar{X}$ is called the 'test statistic'. It is a value calculated from the sample that you use in the hypothesis.

Testing using the critical region

We will first look at the method using the critical region.

WORKED EXAMPLE 18.2

It is believed that the healthy level of testosterone in blood is normally distributed with mean 24 nmol/L and standard deviation 6 nmol/L. Following a race a sprinter gives two samples with an average of 34 nmol/L. Is this sufficiently high (at 1% significance) to suggest that the sprinter's testosterone level is above the mean?

X = level of blood testosterone in a sprinter $X \sim N(\mu, 36)$	Define the variables.
H_0: $\mu = 24$ H_1: $\mu > 24$	State the hypotheses. This is a one-tailed test because the question is looking only for evidence of high testosterone.
Under H_0, $\bar{X} \sim N\left(24, \frac{36}{2}\right)$.	State the distribution of $\bar{X}$ under H_0.
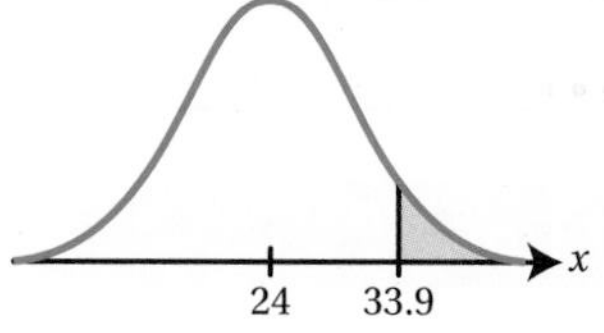	Find the critical region by sketching the normal curve and using the inverse normal distribution.
$P(X < a) = 0.99$, so $a = 33.9$. $\therefore$ Critical region: $\bar{X} > 33.9$ $34 > 33.9$	On your calculator, you probably need to enter the mean, standard deviation, and $p = 0.99$. Some calculators can find the inverse normal value for the 'right tail' (using $p = 0.01$) directly.
Therefore, as 34 nmol/L falls in the rejection region, reject the null hypothesis. There is evidence that the sprinter's testosterone level is above average.	Draw a conclusion.

Sometimes questions ask for you to find only the critical region without actually performing a test.

WORKED EXAMPLE 18.3

The temperature of a water bath is normally distributed with a mean of 60 °C and a standard deviation of 1 °C. After the water bath is serviced, the temperature is measured on five independent occasions and a test is performed at the 5% significance level to see if the temperature has changed from 60 °C. It is assumed that the standard deviation is unchanged. What range of mean temperatures would provide sufficient evidence that the temperature has changed?

X = temperature of water bath $X \sim N(\mu, 1)$	Define the variables.

Continues on next page ...

$H_0: \mu = 60$
$H_1: \mu \neq 60$

State the hypotheses. This is a two-tailed test because the question does not specify that you are looking for evidence that the bath is too warm or too cold.

$\bar{X} \sim N\left(60, \frac{1}{5}\right)$

State the distribution of $\bar{X}$ under H_0.

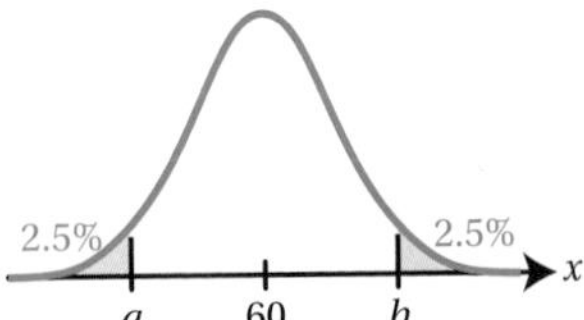

Use the inverse normal distribution to find the critical values of $\bar{X}$ for the two-tailed region. The probability of being in each tail is half of the significance level, so it is 2.5%.

$P(\bar{X} < a) = 0.025 \Rightarrow a = 59.1$
By symmetry about the mean, $b = 60.9$.

$\therefore \bar{X} < 59.1$ or $\bar{X} > 60.9$

Write down the critical region.

Testing using the p-value

Many people find the p-value method more straightforward.

Tip

Many calculators can calculate the p-value. You should check your manual to see how to do this with yours.

WORKED EXAMPLE 18.4

Standard light bulbs have a mean lifetime of 800 hours and a standard deviation of 100 hours. A low-energy light bulb manufacturer claims that the lifetimes of their low-energy bulbs have the same standard deviations but that they last longer on average. A sample of 50 low-energy light bulbs has a mean lifetime of 829.4 hours. Test the manufacturer's claim at the 5% significance level.

X = lifetime of a bulb
$X \sim N(\mu, 100^2)$

Define the variables.

$H_0: \mu = 800$
$H_1: \mu > 800$

State the hypotheses.

$\bar{X} \sim N\left(800, \frac{100^2}{50}\right)$

State the test statistic and its distribution.

p-value $= P(\bar{X} \geq 829.4)$
$= 0.0188$ (3 s.f.) (from calculator)

Use the calculator to find the p-value.

$0.0188 > 0.05$

Compare to the significance level and conclude.

Therefore, reject H_0 as there is evidence to support the manufacturer's claim that the light bulbs last longer than 800 hours on average.

WORK IT OUT 18.1

The wingspan of a species of butterfly is known to be normally distributed with mean 10 cm and standard deviation 1 cm. A scientist thinks she may have found some butterflies that belong to a different species with a different wingspan. The mean of a sample of six of these butterflies is 11.2 cm. Test the scientist's claim at the 5% significance level, assuming the wingspans are still normally distributed with standard deviation 1 cm.

Which is the correct solution? Can you identify the errors made in the incorrect solutions?

Solution 1	Solution 2	Solution 3
H_0: $\mu = 10$, H_1: $\mu \neq 10$ If $\bar{X} \sim N(10,1)$ then $P(\bar{X} > 11.2) = 0.115$ (from calculator). $0.115 > 0.05$, so accept H_0; that is, these butterflies do not belong to a different species.	H_0: $\mu = 10$, H_1: $\mu \neq 10$ If $\bar{X} \sim N\left(10, \frac{1}{6}\right)$ then $P(\bar{X} > 11.2) = 0.00164$ (from calculator). The p-value is twice this $= 0.00329$ $0.00329 < 0.05$ so reject H_0. There is evidence for a different species.	H_0: $\mu = 10$, H_1: $\mu > 10$ If the mean is 10 and the standard deviation is $\frac{1}{6}$, then the critical region is $\bar{X} > 10.3$. $11.2 > 10.3$, so the observed value lies in the critical region. Reject H_0; that is, these butterflies are from a different species.

EXERCISE 18B

1 Write null and alternative hypotheses for each of the following situations.

a **i** The average IQ in a school (μ) over a long period of time has been 102. It is thought that changing the menu in the cafeteria might have an effect upon the average IQ.

ii It is claimed that the average size of photos created by a camera (μ) is 1.2 Mb. A computer scientist believes that this figure is inaccurate.

b **i** A consumer believes that steaks sold in portions of 250 g are, on average, underweight.

ii A careers adviser believes that the average extra amount earned by people with a degree is more than the \$150 000 figure he has been told at a seminar.

c **i** The mean breaking tension of a brake cable (μ_t) does not normally exceed 3000 N. A new brand claims that it regularly does exceed this value.

ii The average time taken to match a fingerprint (μ_t) is normally more than 28 minutes. A new computer program claims to be able to do better.

2 In each of the following situations it is believed that $X \sim N(\mu, 100)$. Find the acceptance region in each of the following cases.

a **i** $H_0: \mu = 60$ $H_1: \mu \neq 60$ 5% significance $n = 16$

ii $H_0: \mu = 120$ $H_1: \mu \neq 120$ 10% significance $n = 30$

b **i** $H_0: \mu = 80$ $H_1: \mu > 80$ 1% significance $n = 18$

ii $H_0: \mu = 750$ $H_1: \mu > 750$ 2% significance $n = 45$

c **i** $H_0: \mu = 80.4$ $H_1: \mu < 80.4$ 10% significance $n = 120$

ii $H_0: \mu = 93$ $H_1: \mu < 93$ 5% significance $n = 400$

3 In each of the following situations it is believed that $X \sim N(\mu, 400)$. Find the p-value of the observed sample mean. Hence, decide the result of the test if it is conducted at the 5% significance level.

a **i** $H_0: \mu = 85$ $H_1: \mu \neq 85$ $n = 16$ $\bar{X} = 95$

ii $H_0: \mu = 144$ $H_1: \mu \neq 144$ $n = 40$ $\bar{X} = 150$

b **i** $H_0: \mu = 85$ $H_1: \mu > 85$ $n = 16$ $\bar{X} = 95$

ii $H_0: \mu = 144$ $H_1: \mu > 144$ $n = 40$ $\bar{X} = 150$

c **i** $H_0: \mu = 265$ $H_1: \mu < 265$ $n = 14$ $\bar{X} = 256.8$

ii $H_0: \mu = 377$ $H_1: \mu < 377$ $n = 100$ $\bar{X} = 374.9$

d **i** $H_0: \mu = 95$ $H_1: \mu > 95$ $n = 12$ $\bar{X} = 96.4$

ii $H_0: \mu = 184$ $H_1: \mu > 184$ $n = 50$ $\bar{X} = 183.2$

4 The average height of 18-year-olds in England is 168.8 cm and the standard deviation is 12 cm. Caroline believes that the students in her school are taller than average. To test her belief she measures the heights of a sample of 16 students from her school.

a State the hypotheses for Caroline's test.

You can assume that the heights follow the normal distribution and that the standard deviation of heights in Caroline's school is the same as the standard deviation for the whole population. The students in Caroline's school have mean height of 171.4 cm.

b Test Caroline's belief at the 5% level of significance.

5 All students in a large school are given a typing test and it is found that the times taken to type one page of text are normally distributed with mean 10.3 minutes and standard deviation 3.7 minutes. The students are given a month-long typing course and then a random sample of 20 students is asked to take the typing test again. The mean time is now 9.2 minutes. Test at the 10% significance level whether there is evidence that the time taken to type a page of text has decreased.

6 The national mean score in Mathematics GCSE is 4.73 with a standard deviation of 1.21. In a particular school the mean score of a sample of 50 students is 4.81.

a State two assumptions that are needed to perform a hypothesis test to see if the mean is better in this school than the background population.

b Assuming that these assumptions are met, test at the 5% significance level whether the school is producing better results than the national average.

7 A farmer knows from experience that the average height of apple trees is 2.7 m with standard deviation 0.7 m. He buys a new orchard and wants to test whether the average height of apple trees is different. He assumes that the standard deviation of heights is still 0.7 m.

a State the hypotheses he should use for his test.

The farmer measures the heights of 45 trees and finds their mean.

b Find the critical region for the test at the 10% level of significance.

c If the average height of the 45 trees is 2.3 m, state the conclusion of the hypothesis test.

See Support sheet 18 for a further example of testing for the mean of a normal distribution and for more practice questions.

8 A doctor has a large number of patients starting a new diet in order to become slimmer. Before the diet the masses of the patients were normally distributed with mean 82.4 kg and standard deviation 7.9 kg. The doctor assumes that the diet does not change the standard deviation of the masses. After the patients have been on the diet for a while, the doctor takes a sample of 40 patients and finds their mean mass.

a The doctor believes that the average mass of the patients has decreased following the diet. She wishes to test her belief at the 5% level of significance. Find the critical region for this test.

b State an additional assumption required in your answer to part **a**.

c The mean average mass of the 40 patients after the diet is 78.4 kg. State the conclusion of the test.

9 The school canteen sells coffee in cups claiming to contain 250 mL. It is known that the amount of coffee in a cup is normally distributed with standard deviation 6 mL. Adam believes that, on average, the cups contain less coffee than claimed. He wishes to test his belief at the 5% significance level.

a Adam measures the amount of coffee in 10 randomly chosen cups and finds the average to be 248 mL. Can he conclude that the average amount of coffee in a cup is less than 250 mL?

b Adam decides to collect a larger sample. He finds the average to be 248 mL again, but this time this is sufficient evidence to conclude that the average amount of coffee in a cup is less than 250 mL. What is the minimum sample size he must have used?

10 The null hypothesis $\mu = 30$ is tested and a value $X = 35$ is observed. Will it have a higher p-value if the alternative hypothesis is $\mu \neq 30$ or $\mu > 30$?

Section 3: Hypothesis tests for correlation coefficients

You already know that values of the correlation coefficient close to 1 or −1 represent strong positive or negative correlation, respectively.

However, values in between can be difficult to interpret, for instance, is 0.6 evidence of significant correlation? The answer depends on the number of data points and how certain you want to be.

You need to distinguish between two related values: the correlation coefficient of the sample, given the symbol r and the correlation coefficient of the underlying population, given the symbol ρ (the Greek letter 'rho'). A hypothesis test uses r to decide if there is evidence that ρ is not zero. In a two-tailed test you are looking to see if there is correlation in either direction – positive or negative – so the alternative hypothesis is $\rho \neq 0$. In a one-tailed test you are looking for correlation in just one direction, so the alternative hypothesis would be either $\rho > 0$ or $\rho < 0$.

Finding the distribution of r goes beyond the scope of this book, but the critical values can be found in tables that will be provided when needed. They are calculated assuming that both variables follow a normal distribution, and provide critical values for different numbers of data pairs n.

 **Rewind**

See Student Book 1, Chapter 16 for a reminder of the product moment correlation coefficient.

Key point 18.2

If the modulus of r is larger than the appropriate critical value, then reject the null hypothesis.

n	Level of significance for one-tailed test	
	0.05	0.025
	Level of significance for two-tailed test	
	0.1	0.05
3	0.988	0.997
4	0.900	0.950
5	0.805	0.878
6	0.729	0.811

Explore

The correlation coefficient used in this course is called the Pearson product- moment correlation coefficient. This is just one type of correlation coefficient. You could also use Spearman's rank correlation coefficient or Kendall's tau. They all have their own advantages and disadvantages.

WORKED EXAMPLE 18.5

The correlation coefficient between the mass and height of students in a sample of six students is 0.85. Test at the 5% significance level whether height and mass of students from this school are positively correlated.

H_0: $\rho = 0$
H_1: $\rho > 0$

Write down the hypotheses. You are looking only for positive correlation, so it is a one-tailed test we are performing.

n	Level of significance for one-tailed test	
	0.05	0.025
	Level of significance for two-tailed test	
	0.1	0.05
3	0.988	0.997
4	0.900	0.950
5	0.805	0.878
6	0.729	0.811

Write down the critical value from the table. $n = 6$, the test is one-tailed and the level of significance is $5\% = 0.05$.

The critical value from the table is 0.729.
$0.85 > 0.729$

Reject H_0. There is evidence that mass and height are positively correlated.

State the conclusion in context.

Did you know?

You should remember from Student Book 1 that correlation does not imply causation. There are many examples of spurious correlations. For example, there is a very strong negative correlation between the number of pirates and global warming! Can you explain this?

WORKED EXAMPLE 18.6

Twenty students were asked to give the number of hours they spent watching television each week and their results in a reading test. The correlation coefficient for their results was −0.31. Test for evidence of correlation at the 10% significance level.

H_0: $\rho = 0$
H_1: $\rho \neq 0$

Write down the hypotheses. You are not told to look for correlation in any particular direction, so it is a two-tailed test.

Continues on next page ...

n	Level of significance for one-tailed test	
	0.05	0.025
	Level of significance for two-tailed test	
	0.1	0.05
17	0.4124	0.4821
18	0.4000	0.4682
19	0.3887	0.4555
20	0.3783	0.4438

Write down the critical value from the table. $n = 20$, 0.1 level of significance

The critical value is 0.3783.

$|-0.31| < 0.3783$

Do not reject H_0. There is not significant evidence for correlation between hours watching television and results in a reading test.

State the conclusion in context.

EXERCISE 18C

A table of critical values of the correlation coefficient is given on page 545. In the examination, a relevant extract from the table will be given in each question that requires it.

1. Test each of the following sample correlation coefficients for positive correlation at 5% significance, where n is the sample size.

   a **i** $r = 0.4, n = 15$ **ii** $r = 0.3, n = 100$ **b** **i** $r = 0.3, n = 15$ **ii** $r = 0.4, n = 9$

2. Test each of the following sample correlation coefficients for correlation at 5% significance, where n is the sample size.

   a **i** $r = -0.5, n = 15$ **ii** $r = -0.3, n = 30$ **b** **i** $r = 0.25, n = 100$ **ii** $r = 0.6, n = 10$

3. Information for 20 students is used to investigate the hypothesis that there is a correlation between IQ and results in a Maths test.

   a Write down the null and alternative hypotheses for this investigation.

   b Data are collected and the p-value for the correlation coefficient is 0.00218. What is the conclusion of the hypothesis test at the 5% significance level?

4. The average speed of cars is measured at six different checkpoints at varying distances from a junction. There is a belief that, in general, cars get faster as they are further from the junction.

   a Write down the null and alternative hypotheses for this investigation.

   b The p-value of the observed data is found to be 0.084. Test the data at the 5% significance level.

5. The amount spent by a government on unemployment support is expected to be negatively correlated with the amount spent on education. Data are collected across 50 countries in 2016.

   a What is the population associated with this sample?

   b Write down appropriate null and alternative hypotheses.

   c The sample correlation coefficient is found to be –0.36. What is the conclusion of the hypothesis test at 5% significance?

6 The correlation coefficient between the amount of water used in a town on 30 summer days and the temperature is 0.85.

a Jane thinks that there is a correlation between water usage and temperature on a summer day. Write down the null and alternative hypotheses Jane should use to test her suspicion.

b Conduct the test at the 5% significance level.

c Karl says that if people use more water, the days will be warmer. Give two reasons why your hypothesis test does not support Karl's statement.

7 The level of antibodies in blood is thought to go down as the dose of a medical drug is increased.

a State appropriate null and alternative hypotheses to test this statement.

b In a sample of 65 patients the correlation coefficient between these two variables is found to be −0.34. Conduct an appropriate hypothesis test at the 1% significance level.

c What are the advantages of using a 1% significance level rather than a 5% significance level for medical tests?

8 Data are collected on the height of a cake and the temperature.

a When a hypothesis test is conducted to test for positive correlation, the p-value is 0.032. Is this evidence of positive correlation at the 5% significance level?

b If the same data were instead used to test for correlation in either direction, what would be the p-value? Is there evidence of correlation at the 5% significance level?

c If the correlation coefficient increases, does this increase or decrease the p-value found in part **a**? Justify your answer.

9 It is suspected that there is correlation between the height of a tree and the total surface area of its leaves. A random sample of n trees is measured and the correlation coefficient is found to be 0.402. What is the smallest value of n which makes this significant at 5% significance?

10 Why do critical value tables for correlation coefficients start at $n = 3$?

Checklist of learning and understanding

- The sample mean, $\bar{X}$, is a random variable.
  - If $X \sim \mathrm{N}(\mu, \sigma^2)$, then $\bar{X}_n \sim \mathrm{N}\left(\mu, \frac{\sigma^2}{n}\right)$.
- To test the value of a population mean, μ, against a suggested value, μ_0:
  - Set up appropriate hypotheses, depending on the context. Either
    - H_0: $\mu = \mu_0$ H_1: $\mu \neq \mu_0$

    or
    - H_0: $\mu = \mu_0$ H_1: $\mu > \mu_0$

    or
    - H_0: $\mu = \mu_0$ H_1: $\mu < \mu_0$
  - Then, use the distribution of $\bar{X}$ and your calculator to either find the p-value or set up the critical region for the given significance level, α.
    - If $p \leqslant \alpha$ (or if $\bar{X}$ is in the critical region), reject H_0.
- To test whether there is correlation between two variables:
  - Set up appropriate hypotheses depending on the context. Either
    - H_0: $\rho = 0$ H_1: $\rho \neq 0$

    or
    - H_0: $\rho = 0$ H_1: $\rho > 0$

    or
    - H_0: $\rho = 0$ H_1: $\rho < 0$
  - Then look up in the tables the critical value for the given significance level and sample size.
    - If the modulus of the sample correlation coefficient, r, is greater than the critical value, then reject H_0.

Mixed practice 18

1. A random sample of 20 people have their height and mass measured. Which of the following correlation coefficients is the smallest that would suggest evidence of positive correlation between height and mass using a 5% significance level?

   A −0.6 **B** 0.24 **C** 0.41 **D** 0.52

2. The breaking load of steel wire is known to be normally distributed with mean 80 N and standard deviation 4 N. Find the probability that the mean breaking load of a sample of ten such wires is between 80 N and 81 N.

3. Data are collected on HIV rates and literacy rates of 40 countries in 2016.

   a What is the population from which this sample is drawn?

   b A hypothesis test is conducted to see if there is correlation between HIV rates and literacy rates. Write down appropriate null and alternative hypotheses.

   c The p-value for the observed correlation coefficient is 0.12. What is the conclusion of the hypothesis test at the 10% significance level?

4. The mass of cakes produced by a bakery is known to be normally distributed with mean 300 g and standard deviation 40 g. A new baker is employed.

   a State appropriate null and alternative hypotheses to test if the mean mass of cakes has changed.

   b The mean mass of 12 cakes is found to be 292 g. What is the p-value of these data? What is the conclusion of the hypothesis test at the 10% significance level?

5. The results of a group of students in a test are thought to follow an $N(\mu, 25)$ distribution. The mean of a random sample of 20 students is used to test the hypothesis $\mu = 100$ against $\mu < 100$.

   Which of the following is the critical region at the 10% significance level (given to three significant figures)?

   A $\bar{X} < 91.8$ **B** $\bar{X} < 92.8$ **C** $\bar{X} < 93.6$ **D** $\bar{X} < 98.6$

6. A test is conducted to see if the time spent revising correlates with the results in a test.

   a State a distributional assumption that is required to use tables of critical values for the correlation coefficient.

   b A random sample of 25 students is surveyed. The correlation coefficient for their responses is 0.55. Conduct a hypothesis test at the 5% significance level.

7. The time taken for a full kettle to boil is known to follow a normal distribution with mean 40 seconds and standard deviation 5 seconds. After cleaning the kettle it is boiled ten times to test if the time taken to boil has decreased.

   a Stating two necessary assumptions, find the critical region for this hypothesis test at the 5% significance level.

   b The mean time is found to be 37 seconds. State the outcome of the hypothesis test.

   c Why should there be a long delay between the ten observations for this test to be valid?

8 Over a long period the number of visitors per week to a stately home was known to have the distribution $N(500, 100^2)$. After higher car parking charges were introduced, a sample of four randomly chosen weeks gave a mean number of visitors per week of 435. You should assume that the number of visitors per week is still normally distributed with variance 100^2.

i Test, at the 10% significance level, whether there is evidence that the mean number of visitors per week has fallen.

ii Explain why it is necessary to assume that the distribution of the number of visitors per week (after the introduction of higher charges) is normal in order to carry out the test.

© OCR, GCE Mathematics, Paper 4733, January 2008

9 Yukun wants to test the null hypothesis H_0: $\mu = 10$ against the alternative hypothesis H_1: $\mu > 10$. He finds the mean sample of the data, $\bar{X}$, is 11.2. His calculator tells him that the p-value of his data is 0.04. Which of the following expressions defines the p-value of his hypothesis test?

A $P(H_0 | \bar{X} = 11.2)$ **B** $P(H_0 | \bar{X} \geqslant 11.2)$ **C** $P(\bar{X} = 11.2 | H_0)$ **D** $P(\bar{X} \geqslant 11.2 | H_0)$

10 The distance an athlete jumps in a long jump is known to be normally distributed with mean 5.84 m and standard deviation 0.31 m. After a change to her technique, she looks at the average of n jumps to see if her average distance has changed at the 5% significance level.

a Write down appropriate null and alternative hypotheses for this test.

b If the jumps are still normally distributed with standard deviation 0.31 m, find the acceptance region in terms of n.

c If the mean is found to be 5.6 m, find the smallest value of n that would result in the null hypothesis being rejected.

11 The viewing figures of a long-running television series is X million. In the past it was known to follow a normal distribution with a standard deviation of 0.3 million. A producer wants to know if a new presenter has changed the viewing figures across 12 episodes. He conducts a hypothesis test, assuming the viewing figures are still normally distributed with standard deviation 0.3 million. The acceptance region is found to be $6.258 < \bar{X} < 6.542$.

a Deduce the null and alternative hypotheses.

b Find the significance level of this hypothesis test, giving your answer as a percentage to the nearest whole number.

12 The continuous random variable Y has the distribution $N(23.0, 5.0^2)$. The mean of n observations of Y is denoted by $\bar{Y}$. It is given that $P(\bar{Y} > 23.625) = 0.0228$. Find the value of n.

© OCR, GCE Mathematics, Paper 4733, January 2009

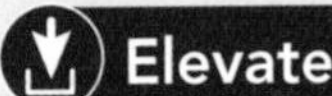

See Extension sheet 18 for some questions to make you think about appropriate significance levels in various situations.

FOCUS ON ... PROOF 3

The prosecutor's fallacy

A man is accused of robbing a jeweller's shop and stealing diamonds. The only evidence against him is a bag of diamonds found in his car during the police investigation.

The prosecution argues that the probability that the bag is found in the car if the man is innocent is 1 in 10 000 and, hence, the probability of him being guilty is 9999 in 10 000 (or 99.99%). You are going to investigate whether this is a valid argument.

Questions

1. Let p denote the probability that the man is guilty of stealing the diamonds. Without taking into account any information (such as any findings of the police investigations), estimate the value of p.

2. Denote by G the event that the man is guilty, so $P(G) = p$, and let E be the event that the evidence (in this case, the bag of diamonds) is found in his car. Then the prosecution's statement says that $P(E|G') = 0.0001$. You also need to estimate the probability of finding the evidence if he is guilty; let's assume this is quite likely, so set $P(E|G) = 0.99$.

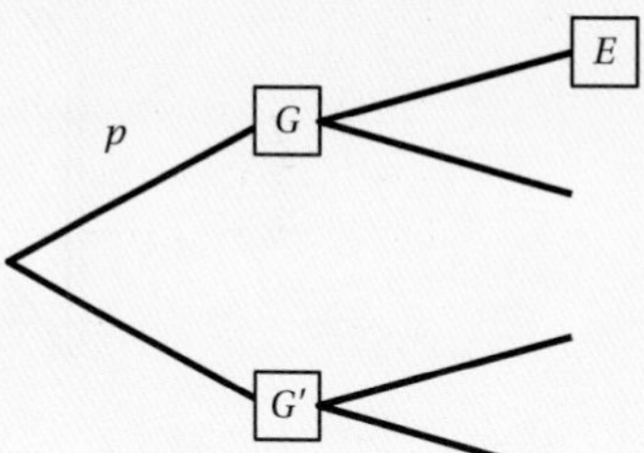

   a Complete the relevant tree diagram.

   b Using the tree diagram:

      i Find $P(E)$.

      ii Use the conditional probability formula to find $P(G|E)$ and $P(G'|E)$ in terms of p.

   c Prove that, when $p < 1/10\,000$, $P(G|E) < P(G'|E)$. What does this tell you about the prosecutor's argument?

3. Why was it reasonable to assume that p is very small? Think about what p represents.

4. How do $P(G|E)$ and $P(G'|E)$ compare to each other if p is larger (say, 0.1)?

5. Would it make sense to swap the branches on the tree diagram, so that the first 'level' has E and E'?

6. The prosecutor stated that 'the probability that the bag is found in the car if the man is innocent is 1 in 10 000'. Write this event using conditional probability notation. Hence, write down and interpret the event that has the probability of 9999 in 10 000.

7. In law, the phrase 'proof beyond reasonable doubt' is used. What do you think this means? How does this compare to mathematical proof?

FOCUS ON ... PROBLEM SOLVING 3

Using extreme values

Probability can often be counter-intuitive, and people find it difficult to evaluate their solutions. One useful strategy can be to use extreme values to make the answer more obvious.

The Monty Hall problem

The following game featured in a US television show.

You are shown three closed doors and told that one door hides a car while the other two hide goats. You will win whatever is behind the door that you choose. The show host knows which door hides the car.

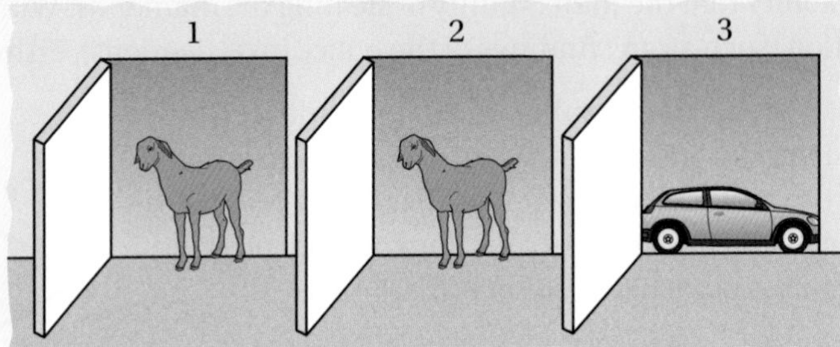

You are asked to choose a door. The host then opens one of the other two doors to reveal a goat. You are then given a choice: stick with the original door or switch to the third one. What should you do to maximise your probability of winning the car?

Most people's intuition is that it doesn't matter – there are two closed doors and the car is equally likely to be behind either of them. But this doesn't take into account the fact the host *knows* where the car is, so would never open that door.

Questions

1 Imagine that instead there are 100 doors and you initially choose Door 1. The host opens 98 of the other doors, leaving out Door 43. What would you do?

The fact that the host knew which door to leave closed gives you additional information, so the probability is no longer 'equally likely for each door'.

2 Suppose you play the game 300 times. Call the door hiding the car Door 1. Your initial choice of the door is random. If you picked Door 1 then the host can choose whether to open Door 2 or Door 3; assume he chooses randomly. If you initially picked Door 2 or 3, then the host has no choice about which one to open.

Fill in this table showing the possible outcomes, assuming the car is behind Door 1.

		You choose			
		1	**2**	**3**	
Host opens	**1**				
	2				
	3				
		100	100	100	300

Use the table to find the probability that you win the car if you switch. You should find that it is not the 0.5 intuitive probability discussed at the start of this example.

3 There are two children in the garden. One of them is a girl. What is the probability that both of them are girls?

(You may assume that both genders are equally likely and that the genders of the two children are independent of each other so, for example, they are not identical twins.)

a Which of the following arguments do you find most convincing?

i Both genders are equally likely, and the genders of the two children are independent, so the probability that the second child is also a girl is $\frac{1}{2}$.

ii The two genders are independent, so the probability of two girls is $\frac{1}{2} \times \frac{1}{2} = \frac{1}{4}$.

iii The options for the two genders are GG, BB and GB. Hence, the probability that both are girls is $\frac{1}{3}$.

iv The options for the two genders are GG, BB, GB and BG. Hence, the probability of two girls is $\frac{1}{4}$.

v You already know that one child is a girl, so there are fewer options to choose from. Hence, the probability of two girls is more than $\frac{1}{4}$.

b Now suppose there are ten children in the garden and nine of them are known to be girls. Do you think that the probability that all ten are girls is bigger or smaller than $\left(\frac{1}{2}\right)^{10}$?

c The table shows possible outcomes for two children. Fill in the probabilities and, hence, find the probability that both children are girls, given that one of them is a girl.

		First child	
		Girl	**Boy**
Second child	**Girl**		
	Boy		

FOCUS ON ... MODELLING 3

When can you use the normal distribution?

The normal distribution is commonly used as a model in many applications. However, it is important to be aware that this model isn't always suitable. This section focuses on the properties of the normal distribution, which you should consider when deciding whether to use it as a model.

WORKED EXAMPLE

The marks for a group of 1000 students on a Statistics exam are summarised in the following histogram. The mean mark is 50 and the standard deviation of the marks is 20.6.

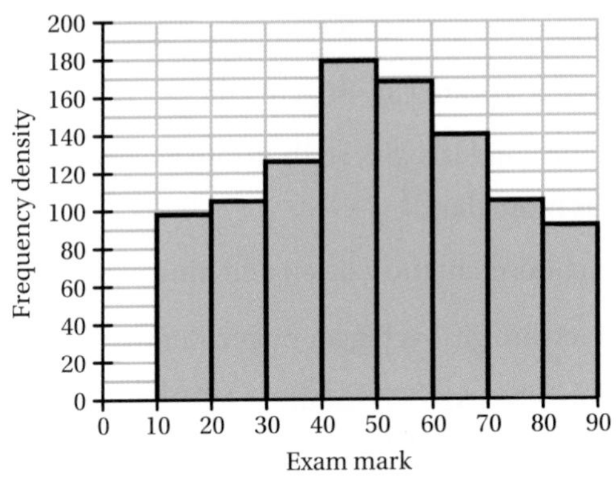

a Estimate the number of students whose marks are more than two standard deviations away from the mean.
b Hence, state, with a reason, whether a normal distribution could be used to model the distribution of the marks.

a $50 + 2 \times 20.6 = 91.2$

$50 - 2 \times 20.6 = 8.8$

No students had marks more than 2 standard deviations from the mean.

On the histogram, there are no data values below 10 or above 90.

b For the normal distribution, around 5% of the marks should be more than 2 standard deviations from the mean.

For a normal distribution, 95% of the data should be within two standard deviations of the mean.

Hence, the normal distribution does not seem to be a good model for these marks.

Questions

1 The table summarises heights of a group of 80 school children.

Height (cm)	Frequency
120–130	9
130–140	32
140–150	26
150–160	11
160–170	4

a Draw a histogram to represent the data (you may want to use technology to do this).

b Hence, explain whether a normal distribution would be a suitable model for these heights.

2 a An old textbook says that the range of the data is about six times the standard deviation. For a normal distribution, what percentage of the values is contained in this range?

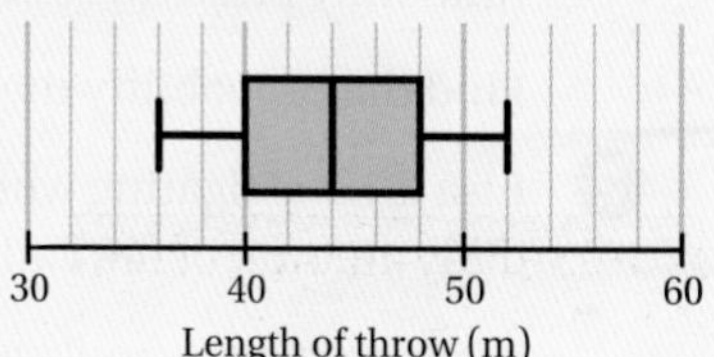

The box plot alongside summarises the results of a discus throw competition (length, measured in metres).

b Assuming the dataset follows a normal distribution, use the box plot to estimate its mean and standard deviation. Find the interquartile range for this normal distribution.

c Hence, state, with a reason, whether a normal distribution is a suitable model for the lengths of the throws.

3 The mean, median and standard deviation for two sets of data are given below. For each set of data decide, based on this information, whether a normal distribution would be a suitable model.

a mean = 231, median = 252, SD = 168

b mean = 165, median = 153, SD = 2.7

4 In social science research, subjects are often asked to rank their opinions on a five-point scale, called the Likert scale (e.g. strongly disagree, disagree, no opinion, agree, strongly agree). For the purpose of statistical analysis, these responses are sometimes translated into numbers (e.g. 'strongly disagree' = 1, 'strongly agree' = 5). Give a reason why data measured on a Likert scale should not be modelled using a normal distribution.

5 a A law firm has found that the average length of phone calls made by its employees is 5.8 minutes. Give a reason why a normal distribution may not be a suitable model for the length of phone calls.

b It is often said that many naturally occurring measurements approximately follow a normal distribution. Discuss whether a normal distribution would be an appropriate model in the following situations.

i the weight of red squirrels in a forest

ii the heights of all parents and children at a nursery school open day

iii the number of children in a family.

6 The diagram shows three cumulative frequency curves. Which curves show:

a a symmetrical distribution

b a normal distribution?

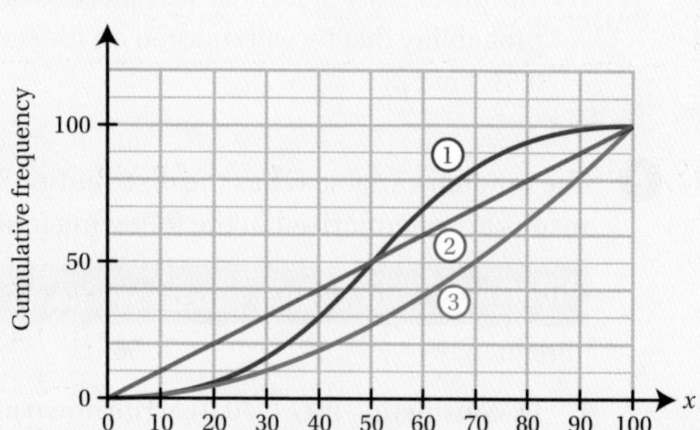

CROSS-TOPIC REVIEW EXERCISE 3

1 Asher has a large bag of sweets, half of which are red. He rolls a fair six-sided dice once. If the dice shows 1 or 2, he randomly picks two sweets from the bag. If the dice shows any other number, he randomly picks three sweets from the bag.

Find the probability that Asher picks at least one red sweet.

2 Elsa is investigating whether there is any correlation between the average daily temperature and the daily amount of rainfall.

a State suitable null and alternative hypotheses for her test.

Elsa collects the data for a random sample of 12 days and calculates that the correlation coefficient between the average temperature and the amount of rainfall is -0.52.

b Conduct the hypothesis test at the 5% level of significance. State your conclusion in context.

3 It is known that the heights of a certain type of rose bush follow a normal distribution with mean 86 cm and standard deviation 11 cm. Larkin thinks that the roses in her garden have the same standard deviation of heights, but are taller on average. She measures the heights of 12 rose bushes in her garden and finds that their mean height is 92 cm.

a State suitable hypotheses to test Larkin's belief.

b Showing your method clearly, test at the 5% level of significance whether there is evidence that Larkin's roses are taller than average.

4 The lifetime of a certain type of light bulb, T hours, is modelled by the distribution $N(620, \sigma^2)$. It is given that $P(T > 670) = 0.15$.

a Find the value of σ.

b Find the probability that, in a sample of 40 randomly selected light bulbs, at least ten last more than 670 hours.

c By considering the range of values that contains nearly all values of T, discuss whether the normal distribution is a reasonable model for the lifetime of the light bulbs.

5 Jenny and Omar are each allowed two attempts at a high jump.

i The probability that Jenny will succeed on her first attempt is 0.6. If she fails on her first attempt, the probability that she will succeed on her second attempt is 0.7. Calculate the probability that Jenny will succeed.

ii The probability that Omar will succeed on his first attempt is p. If he fails on his first attempt, the probability that he will succeed on his second attempt is also p. The probability that he succeeds is 0.51. Find p.

© OCR, GCE Mathematics, Paper 4732, January 2011

6 The random variable G has the distribution $N(\mu, \sigma^2)$. One hundred observations of G are taken. The results are summarised in the following table.

Interval	$G < 40.0$	$40.0 \leqslant G < 60.0$	$G \geqslant 60.0$
Frequency	17	58	25

i By considering $P(G < 40.0)$, write down an equation involving μ and σ^2.

ii Find a second equation involving μ and σ^2. Hence calculate values for μ and σ.

iii Explain why your answers are only estimates.

7 A dataset consists of four numbers: 1, 4, 5 and x. Find the value of x for which the standard deviation of the data is the minimum possible.

8 Two events A and B are such that $P(A) = \frac{3}{4}$, $P(B|A) = \frac{1}{5}$ and $P(B'|A') = \frac{4}{7}$. By use of a tree diagram, or otherwise, find:

a $P(A \cap B)$

b $P(B)$

c $P(A|B)$.

9 Theo repeatedly rolls a fair dice until he gets a 6.

a Show that the probability of him getting this 6 on the third roll is $\frac{25}{216}$.

b P_r is the probability of getting his first 6 on the rth roll. Find an expression for P_r in terms of r.

c Prove algebraically that $\sum_{r=1}^{r=\infty} p_r = 1$.

10 A supermarket has a large stock of eggs. 40% of the stock are from a farm called Eggzact. 12% of the stock are brown eggs from Eggzact.

An egg is chosen at random from the stock. Calculate the probability that

i this egg is brown, given that it is from Eggzact.

ii this egg is from Eggzact and is not brown.

11 The masses of bags of sugar are normally distributed with mean 150 g and standard deviation 12 g.

a Find the probability that a randomly chosen bag of sugar weighs more than 160 g.

b Find the probability that in a box of 20 bags there are at least two that weigh more than 160 g.

c Darien picks up bags of sugar from a large crate at random. What is the probability that he has to pick up exactly 4 bags before he finds one that weighs more than 160 g?

12 A random variable, X, has a normal distribution with mean 0 and standard deviation 1.

a Use your calculator to find $P(0 < X < 1)$ correct to five decimal places.

The exact value of the probability is given by $\frac{1}{\sqrt{2\pi}}\int_0^1 e^{-\frac{x^2}{2}}\, dx$.

b Use the trapezium rule with six strips to estimate the value of this integral. Give your answer correct to five decimal places.

c Find the percentage error in using the trapezium rule to estimate this probability.

13 The random variable X has normal distribution $B(n, p)$. The line graph shows the probability distribution of X.

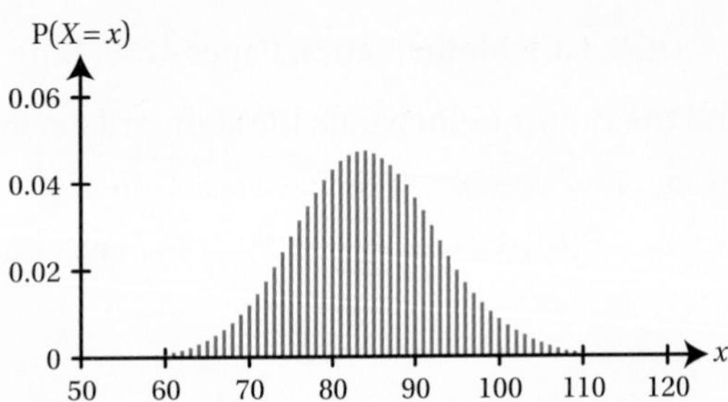

The distribution of X can be approximated by a normal distribution.

a Use the graph to estimate the mean and standard deviation of the normal distribution. Explain clearly how you arrived at your answer.

b Hence, estimate the values of n and p.

14 A student is investigating whether there is any correlation between the amount of time spent revising and marks on a test. She uses information from a sample of six tests. In order to have a larger sample, she collects data from two of her friends.

She finds that the correlation coefficient between hours spent revising and the percentage mark on the test is -0.511. She therefore suggests that there is negative correlation between the amount of time spent revising and the test marks.

a State the null and alternative hypotheses for her test.

b Test the hypotheses at the 5% level of significance and interpret the conclusion in context.

The scatter graph of her data is shown below.

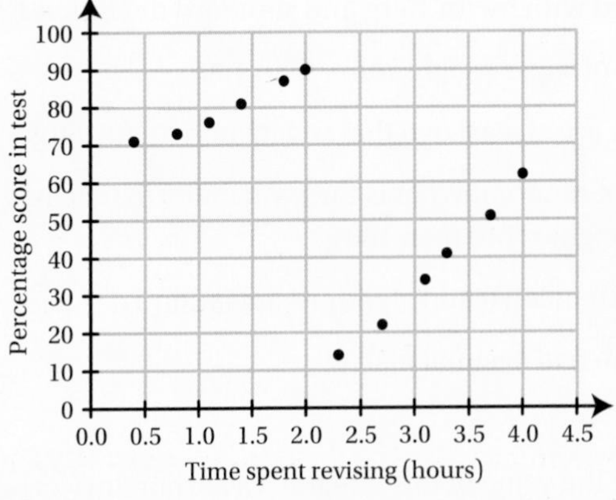

c Suggest one possible interpretation of the data and the result of the hypothesis test.

15 The continuous random variable X has the distribution $N(\mu, \sigma^2)$. The mean of a random sample of n observations of X is denoted by $\bar{X}$. It is given that $P(\bar{X} < 35.0) = 0.9772$ and $P(\bar{X} < 20.0) = 0.1587$.

Obtain a formula for s in terms of n.

Two students are discussing this question. Aidan says, 'If you were told another probability, for instance $P(\bar{X} > 32) = 0.1$, you could work out the value of s.' Binya says, 'No, the value of $P(\bar{X} > 32)$ is fixed by the information you know already.'

ii State which of Aidan and Binya is right. If you think that Aidan is right, calculate the value of σ given that $P(\bar{X} > 32) = 0.1$. If you think that Binya is right, calculate the value of $P(\bar{X} > 32)$.

© OCR, GCE Mathematics, Paper 4733, January 2013

16 Daniel and Paolo play a game with a biased coin. They take it in turns to toss the coin. There is a probability of $\frac{1}{5}$ of the coin showing a head and a probability of $\frac{4}{5}$ of it showing a tail. If the coin shows a head the player who tossed the coin wins the game. If the coin shows a tail, the other player has the next toss. Daniel plays first and the game continues until there is a winner.

a Write down the probability that Daniel wins on his first toss.

b Calculate the probability that Paolo wins on his first toss.

c Calculate the probability that Daniel wins on his second toss.

d Show that the probability of Daniel winning is $\frac{5}{9}$.

e State the probability of Paolo winning.

f They play the game with a different biased coin and find that the probability of Daniel winning is five times the probability of Paolo winning. Find the probability of this coin showing a head.

17 In a large typesetting company the time taken for a typesetter to type one page is normally distributed with mean 7.80 minutes and standard deviation 1.22 minutes. A new training scheme is introduced and, after all the typesetters have completed the training, the times taken by a random sample of 35 typesetters are recorded. The mean time for the sample is 7.24 minutes. You may assume that the population standard deviation is unchanged.

a Test, at the 1% significance level, whether the mean time to type a page has decreased.

b It is required to redesign the test so that the probability of incorrectly rejecting the null hypothesis is less than 0.01 when the sample mean is 7.50. Find the smallest sample size needed.

18 A normal distribution can be represented by a curve shown in the diagram.

The equation of the curve is $y = \frac{1}{\sqrt{8\pi}} e^{-\frac{1}{8}(x-7)^2}$.

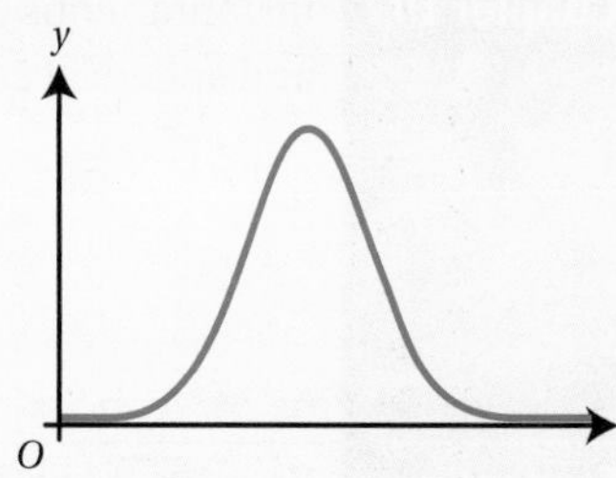

a Find the x-coordinates of the points of inflection of the curve.

Random variable X follows this normal distribution.

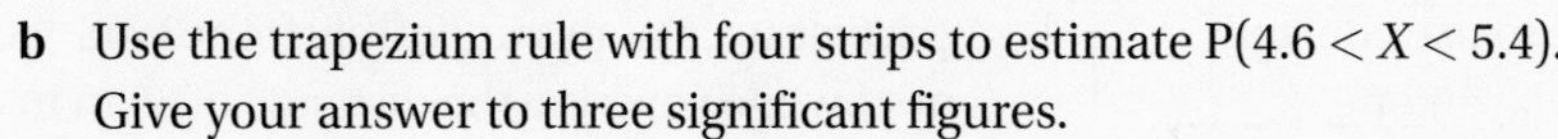

b Use the trapezium rule with four strips to estimate $P(4.6 < X < 5.4)$. Give your answer to three significant figures.

c Is it possible to tell, without doing any further calculations, whether the answer in part **b** is an over-estimate or an underestimate? Explain your answer.

19 Applications of vectors

In this chapter you will learn how to:

- use displacement, velocity and acceleration vectors to describe motion in two dimensions
- use some of the constant acceleration formulae with vectors
- use calculus to relate displacement, velocity and acceleration vectors in two dimensions when acceleration varies with time
- represent vectors in three dimensions using the base vectors **i**, **j** and **k**
- use vectors to solve geometrical problems in three dimensions.

Before you start...

Student Book 1, Chapter 12	You should be able to link displacement vectors to coordinates and perform operations with vectors.	1 Consider the points $A(2, 5)$, $B(-1, 3)$ and $C(7, -2)$. Let $\mathbf{p} = \overrightarrow{AB}$ and $\mathbf{q} = \overrightarrow{BC}$. Write in column vector form: a $\mathbf{p}$ b $\mathbf{q} - \mathbf{p}$ c $4\mathbf{q}$ d $\overrightarrow{AC}$
Student Book 1, Chapter 12	You should be able to find the magnitude and direction of a vector.	2 Find the magnitude and direction of the vector $\begin{pmatrix} -3 \\ 2 \end{pmatrix}$.
Student Book 1, Chapter 19	You should understand the concepts of displacement and distance; instantaneous and average velocity and speed; acceleration.	3 In the diagram below, positive displacement is measured to the right. A ——— 120 m ——— B ——— 180 m ——— C A particle takes 3 seconds to travel from B to C and another 7 seconds to travel from C to A. Find: a the average velocity b the average speed for the whole journey.
Student Book 1, Chapter 20	You should be able to use constant acceleration formulae in one dimension.	4 A particle accelerates uniformly from 3 m s^{-1} to 7 m s^{-1} while covering the distance of 60 m in a straight line. Find the acceleration.
Student Book 1, Chapter 19	You should be able to use calculus to work with displacement, velocity and acceleration in one dimension.	5 A particle moves in a straight line with velocity $v = 2e^t - t^2$. Find: a the acceleration when $t = 3$ b an expression for the displacement from the starting position.
Chapter 12	You should know how to work with curves defined parametrically.	6 Find the Cartesian equation of the curve with parametric equations $x = 1 - 2t^2$ and $y = 1 + t$.

Why do we need to use vectors to describe motion?

In Student Book 1, Chapters 19 and 20, you studied motion in a straight line. You saw how displacement, velocity and acceleration are related through differentiation and integration:

$$v = \frac{dx}{dt}, \ x = \int v \, dt$$

$$a = \frac{dv}{dt}, \ v = \int a \, dt$$

In the special case when the acceleration is constant, you can use the constant acceleration equations:

$$v = u + at, \quad v^2 = u^2 + 2as, \quad s = ut + \frac{1}{2}at^2, \quad s = vt - \frac{1}{2}at^2, \quad s = \frac{1}{2}(u+v)t$$

But the world is three-dimensional, and objects don't always move in a straight line. You need to be able to describe positions and motion in a plane (such as a car moving around a race track) or in space (e.g. flight paths of aeroplanes). This requires the use of vectors to describe displacement, velocity and acceleration.

Rewind

Vectors were introduced in Student Book 1, Chapter 12.

Remember that the vector $\begin{pmatrix} 2 \\ 3 \end{pmatrix}$ can also be written as $2\mathbf{i} + 3\mathbf{j}$.

Section 1: Describing motion in two dimensions

When a particle moves in two dimensions, the displacement, velocity and acceleration are vectors. The distance and speed are still scalars.

WORKED EXAMPLE 19.1

Points A, B and C have position vectors $\begin{pmatrix} 3 \\ -1 \end{pmatrix}$, $\begin{pmatrix} 1 \\ 5 \end{pmatrix}$ and $\begin{pmatrix} -2 \\ 1 \end{pmatrix}$, where the distance is measured in metres.

A particle travels along the straight lines between the points. It takes 5 seconds to travel from A to C and then another 3 seconds to travel from C to B. Find:

a the average velocity and average speed from C to B

b the final displacement of the particle from A

c the average velocity for the whole journey

d the average speed for the whole journey.

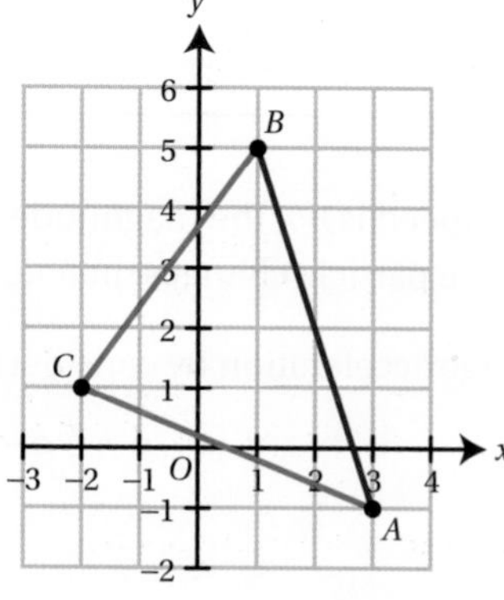

Continues on next page ...

a $\overrightarrow{CB} = \begin{pmatrix} 1 \\ 5 \end{pmatrix} - \begin{pmatrix} -2 \\ 1 \end{pmatrix} = \begin{pmatrix} 3 \\ 4 \end{pmatrix}$

Average velocity $= \dfrac{\text{Displacement}}{\text{Time}}$

The displacement is the difference between the position vectors.

Velocity $= \begin{pmatrix} 3 \\ 4 \end{pmatrix} \div 3 = \begin{pmatrix} 1 \\ 1.33 \end{pmatrix}$ m s^{-1}

$CB = \sqrt{3^2 + 4^2} = 5$

Average speed $= \dfrac{\text{Distance}}{\text{Time}}$

Speed $= \dfrac{5}{3} = 1.67$ m s^{-1}

b $\overrightarrow{AB} = \begin{pmatrix} 1 \\ 5 \end{pmatrix} - \begin{pmatrix} 3 \\ -1 \end{pmatrix} = \begin{pmatrix} -2 \\ 6 \end{pmatrix}$ m

The displacement from A to B is the difference between their position vectors. It is highlighted blue in the diagram.

c Total time $= 5 + 3 = 8$ s

Average velocity $= \dfrac{\text{Final displacement}}{\text{Time}}$

Average velocity $= \begin{pmatrix} -2 \\ 6 \end{pmatrix} \div 8 = \begin{pmatrix} -0.25 \\ 0.75 \end{pmatrix}$ m s^{-1}

d

Average speed $= \dfrac{\text{Total distance}}{\text{Time}}$

You need to add the distance from A to C to the distance from C to B. This is highlighted red in the diagram.

$\overrightarrow{AC} = \begin{pmatrix} -2 \\ 1 \end{pmatrix} - \begin{pmatrix} 3 \\ -1 \end{pmatrix} = \begin{pmatrix} -5 \\ 2 \end{pmatrix}$

The distance is the modulus of the vector between two points.

$AC = \sqrt{5^2 + 2^2} = \sqrt{29}$

$\overrightarrow{CB} = \begin{pmatrix} 1 \\ 5 \end{pmatrix} - \begin{pmatrix} -2 \\ 1 \end{pmatrix} = \begin{pmatrix} 3 \\ 4 \end{pmatrix}$

$CB = \sqrt{3^2 + 4^2} = \sqrt{25}$

Total distance $= \sqrt{29} + \sqrt{25} = 10.4$ m

You have already found that the total time is 8 s.

$\therefore$ Average speed $= \dfrac{10.4}{8} = 1.3$ m s^{-1}

Notice that the average speed is *not* the magnitude of the average velocity vector. This is because the particle changes direction during the motion.

You can calculate average acceleration by considering the change in velocity.

Tip

You should include units with the final answer, even when it is a vector.

WORKED EXAMPLE 19.2

A particle moves in a plane. It passes point A with velocity $(3\mathbf{i} - 2\mathbf{j})$ m s^{-1} and passes point B 4 seconds later with velocity $(2\mathbf{i} + 5\mathbf{j})$ m s^{-1}. Find the magnitude and direction of the average acceleration of the particle between A and B.

Average acceleration:

$= \frac{1}{4}((2\underline{i} + 5\underline{j}) - (3\underline{i} - 2\underline{j}))$

$= \left(-\frac{1}{4}\underline{i} + \frac{7}{4}\underline{j}\right)$ m s^{-2}

Average acceleration $= \frac{\text{Change in Velocity}}{\text{Time}}$

You need to find the acceleration vector first, then find its magnitude.

The magnitude is:

$|a| = \sqrt{\left(\frac{1}{4}\right)^2 + \left(\frac{7}{4}\right)^2} = 1.77$ m s^{-2}

The magnitude of a vector $p\mathbf{i} + q\mathbf{j}$ is $\sqrt{p^2 + q^2}$.

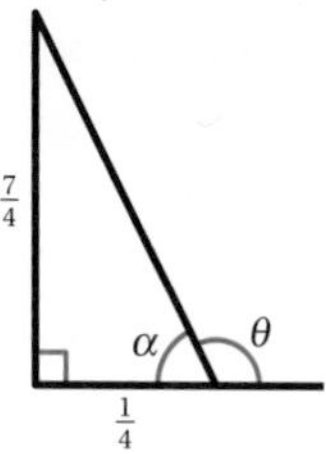

The direction is represented by the angle measured anticlockwise from the horizontal (the direction of vector **i**).

It is always a good idea to draw a diagram to see which angle you are looking for.

$\tan\alpha = \frac{\frac{7}{4}}{\frac{1}{4}} = 7$

$\alpha = 81.7$

$\therefore \theta = 180 - 81.7 = 98.3°$

The direction is 98.3° from the horizontal.

Acceleration can cause a change in the direction of the velocity as well as its magnitude (speed). This means that the object will not necessarily move in a straight line. The velocity vector gives the direction of motion.

If you know how the displacement vector varies with time, you can sometimes find the Cartesian equation of the object's path.

Rewind

The displacement vector gives the parametric equations of the object's path, with the parameter being time. See Chapter 12, Section 3 for a reminder.

Tip

The path an object follows is also called a **trajectory**.

WORKED EXAMPLE 19.3

A particle moves in a plane. At time t the particle is at a point p and its displacement from the origin, O, is given by the position vector $\overrightarrow{OP} = \begin{pmatrix} t+2 \\ 1-t^2 \end{pmatrix}$. Prove that the particle moves along a parabola; find its Cartesian equation and sketch it.

The coordinates of P are:

$x = t + 2, y = 1 - t^2$

The two components of the position vector give the x- and y-coordinates of the particle's position.

$t = x - 2 \Rightarrow y = 1 - (x - 2)^2$

$\therefore y = -x^2 + 4x - 3$

We want to find y in terms of x, so substitute t from the first equation into the second.

Continues on next page ...

Hence, the path of the particle is a parabola.

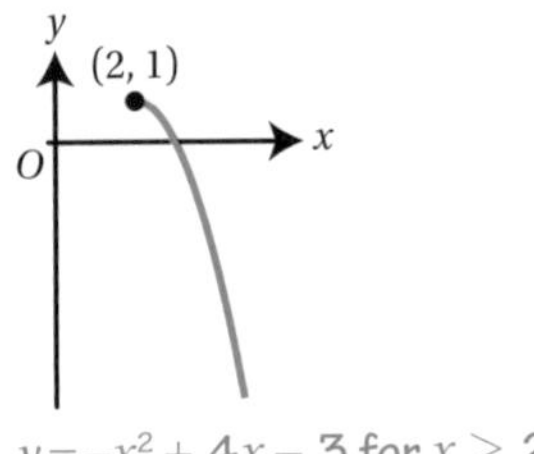

Note that, since $t \geqslant 0$, the object covers only a part of the parabola with $x \geqslant 2$.

$y = -x^2 + 4x - 3$ for $x \geqslant 2$.

We can also look at two particles moving in a plane and ask questions about the distance between them, and whether they ever meet.

Rewind

In Worked example 19.4, part **b** is an example of proof by contradiction. See Chapter 1 for a reminder.

WORKED EXAMPLE 19.4

Two particles, A and B, move in the plane. A starts from the origin and moves with constant velocity $\mathbf{v}_1 = (3\mathbf{i} - 2\mathbf{j})\text{ m s}^{-1}$.

a Write down the position vector of A in terms of t.

Particle B starts from the point with position vector $(\mathbf{i} - 5\mathbf{j})$ m and moves with constant velocity $\mathbf{v}_2 = (\mathbf{i} + 3\mathbf{j})\text{ m s}^{-1}$.

b Prove that A and B never meet.

c Find the minimum distance between the two particles.

a $\underline{a} = (3\underline{i} - 2\underline{j})t$

$= (3t)\underline{i} + (-2t)\underline{j}$

The position vector of A is its displacement from the origin, and displacement equals velocity times time.

b Position vector of B is:

$\underline{b} = (\underline{i} - 5\underline{j}) + (\underline{i} + 3\underline{j})t$

$= (t+1)\underline{i} + (3t-5)\underline{j}$

The displacement of B from its initial position is $\mathbf{v}_2 t$. So its position vector equals the initial position plus this displacement.

The particles meet when $\underline{a} = \underline{b}$:

$(3t)\underline{i} + (-2t)\underline{j} = (t+1)\underline{i} + (3t-5)\underline{j}$

$\Rightarrow \begin{cases} 3t = t+1 \\ -2t = 3t-5 \end{cases}$

We want to show that A and B are never in the same place at the same time.

So try to find the value of t when the two displacements are equal and show that this is impossible.

From the first equation:

$2t = 1 \Rightarrow t = \frac{1}{2}$

If two vectors are equal, then both components have to be equal. So we need a value of t that works in both equations.

Check in the second equation:

$-2\left(\frac{1}{2}\right) \neq 3\left(\frac{1}{2}\right) - 5$

The second equation is NOT satisfied.

Continues on next page ...

There is no t for which $\underline{a} = \underline{b}$, so the particles never meet.

There is no value of t that makes the two position vectors equal.

c At time t:

$$\overrightarrow{AB} = \underline{b} - \underline{a} = ((t+1)\underline{i} + (3t-5)\underline{j}) - ((3t)\underline{i} + (-2t)\underline{j})$$
$$= (1-2t)\underline{i} + (5t-5)\underline{j}$$

The distance between the particles is the magnitude of the displacement between them, which is found by subtracting the two position vectors.

The distance between A and B is:

$$AB = \sqrt{(1-2t)^2 + (5t-5)^2}$$

$$AB^2 = (1-4t+4t^2) + (25t^2 - 50t + 25)$$
$$= 29t^2 - 54t + 26$$

This expression has a minimum value when its square has a minimum value; so look at AB^2 to avoid having to work with the square root.

Let $y = 29t^2 - 54t + 26$.

Then $\frac{dy}{dt} = 58t - 54 = 0$ when $t = \frac{27}{29}$.

You could complete the square to find the minimum value, but the numbers aren't nice so differentiate instead.

The minimum value of y is:

$$29\left(\frac{27}{29}\right)^2 - 54\left(\frac{27}{29}\right) + 26 = 0.862$$

Don't forget that this is the minimum value for AB^2.

Hence, the minimum distance AB is

$\sqrt{0.862} = 0.928$ m

EXERCISE 19A

1 Points A, B and C have position vectors $4\mathbf{i} - 3\mathbf{j}$, $\mathbf{i} + 2\mathbf{j}$ and $-5\mathbf{i} + \mathbf{j}$, where distance is measured in metres. Find the average velocity when a particle travels:

a **i** from A to B in 3 seconds **ii** from A to C in 4 seconds

b **i** from C to B in 5 seconds **ii** from B to A in 4 seconds

c **i** from A to B in 3 seconds and then from B to C in 5 seconds

ii from C to A in 7 seconds and then from A to B in 4 seconds.

2 Find the average acceleration vector, and the magnitude of average acceleration in each of the following cases.

a **i** The velocity changes from $\begin{pmatrix} 6 \\ -2 \end{pmatrix}$ m s^{-1} to $\begin{pmatrix} 8 \\ 3 \end{pmatrix}$ m s^{-1} in 10 seconds.

ii The velocity changes from $\begin{pmatrix} -3 \\ 5 \end{pmatrix}$ m s^{-1} to $\begin{pmatrix} 1 \\ 10 \end{pmatrix}$ m s^{-1} in 8 seconds.

b **i** A particle accelerates from rest to $(4\mathbf{i} - 2\mathbf{j})$ m s^{-1} in 5 seconds.

ii A particle accelerates from rest to $(-3\mathbf{i} + 4\mathbf{j})$ m s^{-1} in 10 seconds.

3 Three points have coordinates $A(3, 5)$, $B(12, 7)$ and $C(8, 0)$.

- **a** A particle travels in a straight line from A to B in 6 seconds. Find its average velocity and average speed.
- **b** Another particle travels in a straight line from B to C in 8 seconds and then in a straight line from C to B in 5 seconds. Find its average velocity and average speed.

4 A particle moves in the plane so that its displacement from the origin (measured in metres) at time t seconds is given by the vector $\begin{pmatrix} t-3 \\ 2+t^2 \end{pmatrix}$.

- **a** Find the particle's distance from the origin when $t = 2$.
- **b** Find the Cartesian equation of the particle's trajectory.

5
- **a** An object's velocity changes from $(5\mathbf{i} - 2\mathbf{j})$ m s^{-1} to $(3\mathbf{i} + 4\mathbf{j})$ m s^{-1} in 3 seconds. Find the magnitude of its average acceleration.
- **b** The object then moves for another 10 seconds with average acceleration $(-\mathbf{i} + 0.5\mathbf{j})$ m s^{-2}. Find its direction of motion at the end of the 10 seconds.

6 A particle travels in a straight line from point P with coordinates $(-4, 7)$ to point Q with coordinates $(3, -2)$. The journey takes 12 seconds and the distance is measured in metres.

- **a** Find the average speed of the particle.

The particle then takes a further 7 seconds to travel in a straight line to point R with coordinates $(2, 5)$.

- **b** Find the displacement from P to R.
- **c** Find the average velocity of the particle for the whole journey.
- **d** Find the average speed for the whole journey from P to R. Explain why this is not equal to the magnitude of the average velocity.

7 Two particles, A and B, move in a plane. A has constant velocity $\begin{pmatrix} -3 \\ 1 \end{pmatrix}$ m s^{-1} and its initial displacement from the origin is $\begin{pmatrix} 14 \\ 0 \end{pmatrix}$ m. B starts from the origin and moves with constant velocity $\begin{pmatrix} 4 \\ 1 \end{pmatrix}$ m s^{-1}. Show that the two particles meet and find the position vector of the meeting point.

8 A particle moves in a plane so that its displacement from the origin at time $t \geqslant 0$ is given by the vector $((t-1)\mathbf{i} + (6 + 4t - t^2)\mathbf{j})$ m.

- **a** Find the distance of the particle from the origin when $t = 3$.
- **b** Sketch the trajectory of the particle.

9 An object moves with a constant velocity $(-2\mathbf{i} + \mathbf{j})$ m s^{-1}. Its initial displacement from the origin is $(3\mathbf{i} - 4\mathbf{j})$ m.

- **a** Find the Cartesian equation of the particle's trajectory.
- **b** Find the minimum distance of the particle from the origin.

10 A particle moves in a plane so that its displacement from the origin at time t seconds is $(4\cos(2t)\mathbf{i} + 2\sin(2t)\mathbf{j})$ m. Find the maximum distance of the particle from the origin.

Section 2: Constant acceleration equations

When a particle moves with constant acceleration, we can use formulae analogous to those for one-dimensional motion.

Rewind

See Student Book 1, Chapter 20 for a reminder of the constant acceleration formulae.

Key Point 19.1

Constant acceleration formulae in two dimensions:

$$\mathbf{v} = \mathbf{u} + \mathbf{a}t$$

$$\mathbf{s} = \mathbf{u}t + \frac{1}{2}\mathbf{a}t^2$$

$$\mathbf{s} = \mathbf{v}t - \frac{1}{2}\mathbf{a}t^2$$

$$\mathbf{s} = \frac{1}{2}(\mathbf{u} + \mathbf{v})t$$

Fast forward

Notice that the list in Key point 19.1 does not contain the vector version of the formula $v^2 = u^2 + 2as$. If you study the Mechanics option of Further Mathematics you will meet a way of multiplying vectors (called the scalar product) that enables us to extend this formula to two dimensions as well.

WORKED EXAMPLE 19.5

A particle starts with initial velocity $(3\mathbf{i} - \mathbf{j})$ m s^{-1} and moves with constant acceleration. After 5 seconds its velocity is $(1.5\mathbf{i} + 2\mathbf{j})$ m s^{-1}. Find its displacement and its distance from the initial position at this time.

For displacement:

$$\underline{s} = \frac{1}{2}(\underline{u} + \underline{v})t$$

You know **u**, **v** and t and want to find **s**, so use the third formula from Key point 19.1.

$$\underline{s} = \frac{1}{2}((3\underline{i} - \underline{j}) + (1.5\underline{i} + 2\underline{j})) \times 5$$

$$= 2.5(4.5\underline{i} + \underline{j})$$

$$= (11.25\underline{i} + 2.5\underline{j}) \text{ m}$$

For distance:

Distance is the magnitude of the displacement.

$$\sqrt{11.25^2 + 2.5^2} = 11.5 \text{ m}$$

If a particle does not move in a straight line, its distance from the starting point (which is measured in a straight line) is not the same as distance travelled (which is along a curve).

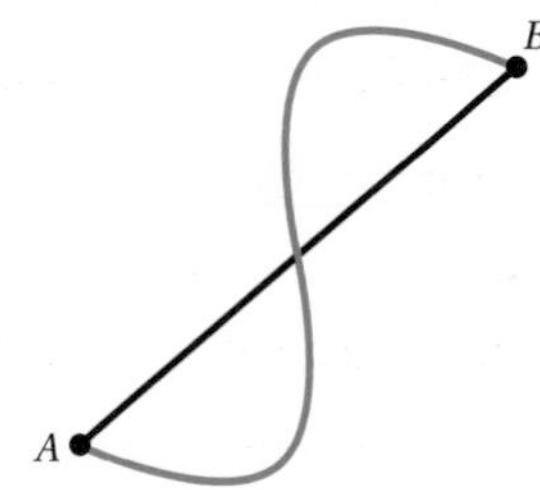

Explore

Find out how you can use calculus to calculate the length of a curve.

You need to be a little careful when solving equations with vectors. If you are comparing two sides of a vector equation, both components need to be equal.

WORKED EXAMPLE 19.6

A particle moves with constant acceleration $\begin{pmatrix}-1.5\\3\end{pmatrix}$ m s^{-2}. It is initially at the origin and its initial velocity is $\begin{pmatrix}2\\5\end{pmatrix}$ m s^{-1}. Find the time when the particle is at the point with position vector $\begin{pmatrix}1\\4\end{pmatrix}$ m.

$\underline{s}=\underline{u}t+\frac{1}{2}\underline{a}t^2$

You have **u**, **a** and **s** and want to find t, so use the second formula from Key point 19.1.

$\begin{pmatrix}1\\4\end{pmatrix}=\begin{pmatrix}2\\5\end{pmatrix}t+\frac{1}{2}\begin{pmatrix}-1.5\\3\end{pmatrix}t^2$

First component:

$1=2t-0.75t^2$

$\Leftrightarrow 0.75t^2-2t+1=0$

$t=2$ or $\frac{2}{3}$

The first component of the vectors gives a quadratic equation for t. This will give us two possible values.

Second component:

When $t=2$: $5t+\frac{1}{2}(3)t^2=16$

When $t=\frac{2}{3}$: $5t+\frac{1}{2}(3)t^2=4$

We need to check for which of these values of t the second component equals 4.

The particle is at $\begin{pmatrix}1\\4\end{pmatrix}$ when $t=\frac{2}{3}$ seconds.

WORK IT OUT 19.1

A particle moves with constant acceleration, starting from the origin. Its position vector at time t is given by $\mathbf{s}=(t^2-3t)\mathbf{i}+(2t^2-15t)\mathbf{j}$. How many times does the particle pass through the origin during the subsequent motion?

Which is the correct solution? Can you identify the errors made in the incorrect solutions?

Solution 1	Solution 2	Solution 3
You need the displacement to be zero. When $t^2-3t=0$: $t=0$ or 3. So the particle passes the origin once, when $t=3$.	You need both components of the displacement to equal zero. When $t^2-3t=0$: $t=0$ or 3. When $2t^2-15t=0$: $t=0$ or 7.5. So the particle passes the origin twice, when $t=3$ and 7.5.	You need both components of the displacement to be zero. When $t^2-3t=0$: $t=0$ or 3. When $2t^2-15t=0$: $t=0$ or 7.5. So the particle does not pass the origin again.

EXERCISE 19B

1 In each of the following questions a particle moves with constant acceleration. Time is measured in seconds and displacement in metres.

a **i** $\mathbf{u}=\begin{pmatrix}3\\-1\end{pmatrix}$, $\mathbf{a}=\begin{pmatrix}-0.6\\0.7\end{pmatrix}$. Find **v** when $t=4$.

ii $\mathbf{u}=4\mathbf{i}+2\mathbf{j}$, $\mathbf{a}=1.2\mathbf{i}-0.6\mathbf{j}$. Find **v** when $t=7$.

b **i** $\mathbf{u}=-2\mathbf{i}+0.5\mathbf{j}$, $\mathbf{a}=0.3\mathbf{i}-0.8\mathbf{j}$. Find **s** when $t=5$.

ii $\mathbf{u}=\begin{pmatrix}3\\-1\end{pmatrix}$, $\mathbf{a}=\begin{pmatrix}-0.6\\0.7\end{pmatrix}$. Find **s** when $t=3$.

c i $\mathbf{v} = 2\mathbf{i} + 5\mathbf{j}$, $\mathbf{s} = -2\mathbf{i} + \mathbf{j}$, $t = 4$. Find $\mathbf{u}$.

ii $\mathbf{v} = \begin{pmatrix} -1 \\ 3 \end{pmatrix}$, $\mathbf{s} = \begin{pmatrix} 2 \\ 2 \end{pmatrix}$, $t = 6$. Find $\mathbf{u}$.

d i $\mathbf{a} = \begin{pmatrix} -1 \\ 1 \end{pmatrix}$, $\mathbf{u} = \begin{pmatrix} 2 \\ 3 \end{pmatrix}$, $\mathbf{s} = \begin{pmatrix} 2 \\ 8 \end{pmatrix}$. Find t.

ii $\mathbf{a} = \begin{pmatrix} 2 \\ 6 \end{pmatrix}$, $\mathbf{u} = \begin{pmatrix} 2 \\ -1 \end{pmatrix}$, $\mathbf{s} = \begin{pmatrix} 48 \\ 18 \end{pmatrix}$. Find t.

2 An object moves with constant acceleration $\begin{pmatrix} 0.6 \\ -0.4 \end{pmatrix}$ m s^{-2} and initial velocity $\begin{pmatrix} 3.5 \\ 2.4 \end{pmatrix}$ m s^{-1}. Find its velocity and displacement from the initial position after 7 seconds.

3 A particle moves with constant acceleration $(3\mathbf{i} - \mathbf{j})$ m s^{-2}. It is initially at the origin and its velocity is $(2\mathbf{i} + 5\mathbf{j})$ m s^{-1}.

a Find the distance of the particle from the origin after 3 seconds.

b Find the direction of motion of the particle at this time.

4 A particle passes the origin with velocity $(2\mathbf{i} + 5\mathbf{j})$ m s^{-1} and moves with constant acceleration.

a Given that 7 seconds later its velocity is $(-12\mathbf{i} + 15.5\mathbf{j})$ m s^{-1}, find the acceleration.

b Find the time when the particle's displacement from the origin is $(-8\mathbf{i} + 32\mathbf{j})$ m.

5 An object moves with constant acceleration. When $t = 0$ it has velocity $\begin{pmatrix} -1 \\ 3 \end{pmatrix}$ m s^{-1}. When $t = 5$ its displacement from the initial position is $\begin{pmatrix} 5 \\ 7 \end{pmatrix}$ m. Find the magnitude of the acceleration.

6 A particle moves with constant acceleration. Its initial velocity is $(3\mathbf{i} - 2\mathbf{j})$ m s^{-1}. 8 seconds later, its displacement from the initial position is $(-44\mathbf{i} + 20\mathbf{j})$ m. Find its direction of motion at this time.

7 An object moves with constant acceleration and initial velocity $(5\mathbf{j})$ m s^{-1}. When its displacement from the initial position is $(12.5\mathbf{i} + 5\mathbf{j})$ m, its velocity is $(5\mathbf{i} - 3\mathbf{j})$ m s^{-1}. Find the magnitude of the acceleration.

8 A particle moves with constant acceleration $\begin{pmatrix} 3.8 \\ 2.2 \end{pmatrix}$ m s^{-2}. Given that its initial velocity is $\begin{pmatrix} -1 \\ 2 \end{pmatrix}$ m s^{-1}, find the time when its displacement from the initial position is $\begin{pmatrix} 180 \\ 130 \end{pmatrix}$ m.

9 A particle starts with initial velocity $(6\mathbf{j})$ m s^{-1} and moves with constant acceleration $(0.5\mathbf{i})$ m s^{-2}. Prove that the speed of the particle increases with time.

10 A particle moves with constant acceleration $\mathbf{a} = (-2\mathbf{i} + \mathbf{j})$ m s^{-2}. When $t = 0$ the particle is at rest, at the point with the position vector $(5\mathbf{i} + 3\mathbf{j})$ m. Find the shortest distance of the particle from the origin during the subsequent motion.

Section 3: Calculus with vectors

When the acceleration is not constant you need to use differentiation and integration to find expressions for displacement and velocity. In Student Book 1, Chapter 19 you learnt how to do that for motion in one dimension. The same principles apply to two-dimensional motion: differentiating the displacement equation gives the velocity equation, and differentiating the velocity equation gives the acceleration equation. The only difference is that those quantities are now represented by vectors.

Key Point 19.2

To differentiate or integrate a vector, differentiate or integrate each component separately.

In particular, If $\mathbf{x} = \mathrm{f}(t)\mathbf{i} + \mathrm{g}(t)\mathbf{j}$, then

$$\mathbf{v} = \frac{\mathrm{d}\mathbf{x}}{\mathrm{d}t} = \mathrm{f}'(t)\mathbf{i} + \mathrm{g}'(t)\mathbf{j}$$

and

$$\mathbf{a} = \frac{\mathrm{d}\mathbf{v}}{\mathrm{d}t} = \frac{\mathrm{d}^2\mathbf{x}}{\mathrm{d}t^2} = \mathrm{f}''(t)\mathbf{i} + \mathrm{g}''(t)\mathbf{j}$$

Tip

Some people use a dot to denote differentiation with respect to time; for example, $v = \dot{x}$ and $a = \dot{v}$.

WORKED EXAMPLE 19.7

A particle moves in two dimensions. Its displacement from the starting point, measured in metres, varies with time (measured in seconds) as:

$$\mathbf{r} = \begin{pmatrix} 2t^2 - 4 \\ 1 - t^3 \end{pmatrix}$$

Find the speed of the particle when $t = 3$.

$$\underline{v} = \frac{dr}{dt} = \begin{pmatrix} 4t \\ -3t^2 \end{pmatrix}$$

The speed is the magnitude of the velocity vector. To find the velocity, differentiate the displacement equation with respect to r.

When $t = 3$:

$$\underline{v} = \begin{pmatrix} 12 \\ -27 \end{pmatrix}$$

$$\text{Speed} = |\underline{v}| = \sqrt{12^2 + 27^2} = 29.5 \text{ m s}^{-1}$$

When using integration with vectors, the constant of integration will also be a vector.

WORKED EXAMPLE 19.8

A particle moves with acceleration $\mathbf{a} = \begin{pmatrix} 2t+1 \\ 2\sin t \end{pmatrix}$. Its initial velocity is $\begin{pmatrix} -1 \\ 3 \end{pmatrix}$.

Find the expression for the velocity at time t.

$$\underline{v} = \int \underline{a}\, dt = \int \begin{pmatrix} 2t+1 \\ 2\sin t \end{pmatrix} dt$$

To find the velocity, integrate the acceleration vector.

$$= \begin{pmatrix} t^2 + t \\ -2\cos t \end{pmatrix} + \underline{c}$$

Continues on next page ...

When $t=0$, $\underline{v}=\begin{pmatrix}-1\\3\end{pmatrix}$:

Use the initial velocity to find **c**.

$$\begin{pmatrix}-1\\3\end{pmatrix}=\begin{pmatrix}0\\-2\end{pmatrix}+\underline{c}$$

$$\Rightarrow \underline{c}=\begin{pmatrix}-1\\5\end{pmatrix}$$

So

$$\underline{v}=\begin{pmatrix}t^2+t-1\\-2\cos t+5\end{pmatrix}$$

The constant can be included within the existing vector.

Remember that, for two vectors to be equal, both components need to be equal.

WORKED EXAMPLE 19.9

A particle starts from point P with velocity $(3\mathbf{i}+\mathbf{j})\text{ m s}^{-1}$. Its acceleration is given by $\mathbf{a}=(-t\,\mathbf{i}+2t\,\mathbf{j})\text{ m s}^{-2}$. Show that the particle never returns to P.

Let $\underline{x}$ be the displacement from P at time t.

You need to find an expression for the displacement from P and show that it never equals 0 for $t>0$.

$$\underline{v}=\int(-t\,\underline{i}+2t\,\underline{j})\,dt$$

$$=-\frac{1}{2}t^2\underline{i}+t^2\underline{j}+\underline{c}$$

First integrate **a** to find **v**.

$\underline{v}=3\underline{i}+\underline{j}$ when $t=0$, so $\underline{c}=3\underline{i}+\underline{j}$.

$$\therefore \underline{v}=\left(-\frac{1}{2}t^2+3\right)\underline{i}+(t^2+1)\underline{j}$$

Use the initial velocity to find **c**.

$$\underline{x}=\int\left(-\frac{1}{2}t^2+3\right)\underline{i}+(t^2+1)\underline{j}\,dt$$

$$=\left(-\frac{1}{6}t^3+3t\right)\underline{i}+\left(\frac{1}{3}t^3+t\right)\underline{j}$$

Now integrate the velocity to find the displacement. The initial displacement is 0, so $\mathbf{c}=0$.

When $\underline{x}=\underline{0}$:

$$-\frac{1}{6}t^3+3t=0$$

$$\Leftrightarrow \frac{1}{6}t(-t^2+18)=0$$

$t=0$ or $\sqrt{18}$

You now need to check if there is any value of t (other than $t=0$) when $\mathbf{x}=0$. You need to check both components of the vector.

$t=0$ is the starting position.

When $t=\sqrt{18}$:

$$\frac{1}{3}t^3+t=19.7\neq 0$$

Hence, the displacement is never $\underline{0}$ for $t>0$, so the particle does not return to the starting point.

Forces in two dimensions

Newton's second law still applies: $\mathbf{F} = m\mathbf{a}$, where $\mathbf{F}$ and $\mathbf{a}$ are vectors and m is a scalar.

WORKED EXAMPLE 19.10

A particle of mass 2.4 kg moves under the action of a constant force, **F** N. When $t = 0$ the velocity of the particle is $\begin{pmatrix} -2 \\ 5 \end{pmatrix}$ m s^{-1} and when $t = 4$ seconds its displacement from the initial position is $\begin{pmatrix} 16 \\ -4 \end{pmatrix}$ m.

Find the vector **F**.

$\underline{u} = \begin{pmatrix} -2 \\ 5 \end{pmatrix}, t = 4, \underline{s} = \begin{pmatrix} 16 \\ -4 \end{pmatrix}, \underline{a} = ?$

You are going to find the acceleration and then use $\mathbf{F} = m\mathbf{a}$.

Use $\underline{s} = \underline{u}t + \frac{1}{2}\underline{a}t^2$:

$$\begin{pmatrix} 16 \\ -4 \end{pmatrix} = 4\begin{pmatrix} -2 \\ 5 \end{pmatrix} + \frac{1}{2}(4^2)\underline{a}$$

Since the force is constant the acceleration is also constant, so we can use the constant acceleration equations.

$$8\underline{a} = \begin{pmatrix} 16 \\ -4 \end{pmatrix} - \begin{pmatrix} -8 \\ 20 \end{pmatrix} = \begin{pmatrix} 24 \\ -24 \end{pmatrix}$$

$$\underline{a} = \begin{pmatrix} 3 \\ -3 \end{pmatrix} \text{m s}^{-2}$$

$\underline{F} = m\underline{a}$

Now use $\mathbf{F} = m\mathbf{a}$.

$$= 2.4\begin{pmatrix} 3 \\ -3 \end{pmatrix} = \begin{pmatrix} 7.2 \\ -7.2 \end{pmatrix}$$

Newton's second law ($\mathbf{F} = m\mathbf{a}$) means that the particle accelerates in the direction of the net force.

WORKED EXAMPLE 19.11

A particle moves under the action of two constant forces, $\mathbf{F}_1 = ((p+2)\mathbf{i} + p\,\mathbf{j})$ N and $\mathbf{F}_2 = ((-4p)\mathbf{i} + (2p+1)\mathbf{j})$ N. The particle's acceleration is $(4\mathbf{j})$ m s^{-2}. Find the value of p.

$\underline{F}_1 + \underline{F}_2 = (2 - 3p)\underline{i} + (3p + 1)\underline{j}$

The resultant force should be in the same direction as the acceleration.

If this is in the direction of $\underline{j}$, then

$2 - 3p = 0$

This means that the **i**-component is zero.

$\Rightarrow p = \frac{2}{3}$

If the net force changes with time you need to use integration to find an expression for the velocity. Remember that the direction of the velocity vector shows the direction of motion, whereas its magnitude gives the speed; both of these may change with time.

WORKED EXAMPLE 19.12

A particle of mass 0.5 kg starts from rest and moves under the action of the force $((4t)\mathbf{i}+(2t-2)\mathbf{j})$ N. Find the speed and direction of motion of the particle after 3 seconds.

$\underline{F}=m\underline{a}$:

$(4t)\underline{i}+(2t-2)\underline{j}=0.5\underline{a}$

$\Rightarrow \underline{a}=(8t)\underline{i}+(4t-4)\underline{j}$

You need to find the velocity, which we can do by integrating the acceleration.

Use $\mathbf{F}=m\mathbf{a}$ first.

$\underline{v}=\int(8t)\underline{i}+(4t-4)\underline{j}\,dt$

$=(4t^2)\underline{i}+(2t^2-4t)\underline{j}+\underline{c}$

$\underline{v}(0)=0\Rightarrow\underline{c}=0$

$\therefore \underline{v}=((4t^2)\underline{i}+(2t^2-4t)\underline{j})\text{ m s}^{-1}$

Remember to find **c**.

When $t=3$:

$\underline{v}=(36\underline{i}+6\underline{j})\text{ m s}^{-1}$

You can now use the given value of t to find the velocity vector.

For the speed:

$|\underline{v}|=\sqrt{36^2+6^2}=36.5\text{ m s}^{-1}$

Speed is the magnitude of the velocity vector.

For the direction:

$\tan\theta=\frac{6}{36}$

$\theta=\tan^{-1}\left(\frac{6}{36}\right)=9.46°$

The direction of motion is 9.46° above the horizontal.

The direction of motion is given by the velocity vector; its direction is determined by the angle it makes with the vector **i**.

WORK IT OUT 19.2

A particle starts from rest and moves with acceleration $\mathbf{a}=\begin{pmatrix}3\sin t\\-5\cos t\end{pmatrix}$. Find an expression for the velocity of the particle.

Which is the correct solution? Can you identify the errors made in the incorrect solutions?

Solution 1	Solution 2	Solution 3
$\mathbf{v}=\int\begin{pmatrix}3\sin t\\-5\cos t\end{pmatrix}dt.$ $=\begin{pmatrix}-3\cos t\\-5\sin t\end{pmatrix}+c$	$\mathbf{v}=\int\begin{pmatrix}3\sin t\\-5\cos t\end{pmatrix}dt$ $=\begin{pmatrix}-3\cos t\\-5\sin t\end{pmatrix}+\mathbf{c}$	$\mathbf{v}=\int\begin{pmatrix}3\sin t\\-5\cos t\end{pmatrix}dt$ $=\begin{pmatrix}-3\cos t\\-5\sin t\end{pmatrix}+\mathbf{c}$

Continues on next page ...

Initially at rest means that the speed is zero. When $t = 0$: $\mathbf{v} = \begin{pmatrix} -3 \\ 0 \end{pmatrix}$ Speed $= \sqrt{(-3)^2 + 0^2} = 3$ $c = -3$ $\therefore \mathbf{v} = \begin{pmatrix} -3\cos t - 3 \\ -5\sin t - 3 \end{pmatrix}$	Initially at rest: $\mathbf{v}(0) = \begin{pmatrix} 0 \\ 0 \end{pmatrix} = \begin{pmatrix} -3 \\ 0 \end{pmatrix} + \mathbf{c}$ $\Rightarrow \mathbf{c} = \begin{pmatrix} 3 \\ 0 \end{pmatrix}$ $\therefore \mathbf{v} = \begin{pmatrix} -3\cos t + 3 \\ -5\sin t \end{pmatrix}$	Initially at rest, so $\mathbf{c} = 0$. $\therefore \mathbf{v} = \begin{pmatrix} -3\cos t \\ -5\sin t \end{pmatrix}$

EXERCISE 19C

1 For the particles moving with the given displacements, find expressions for the velocity and acceleration vectors. Also find the speed when $t = 3$.

a **i** $\mathbf{s} = (3t - \sin(t))\mathbf{i} + (t - t^2)\mathbf{j}$ **ii** $\mathbf{s} = (e^{2t} - t)\mathbf{i} + (t^2 + e^{2t})\mathbf{j}$

b **i** $\mathbf{s} = \begin{pmatrix} 4\cos(3t) \\ 3\sin(2t) \end{pmatrix}$ **ii** $\mathbf{s} = \begin{pmatrix} 3\ln(t+1) - t \\ t^2 + \ln(t+1) \end{pmatrix}$

2 For a particle moving with the accelerations given below, find expressions for the velocity and displacement vectors. The initial displacement is zero, and the initial velocity is given in each question. Also find the distance from the starting point when $t = 3$.

a **i** $\mathbf{a} = (3 - t^2)\mathbf{i} + (2t)\mathbf{j}$, $\mathbf{v}(0) = 2\mathbf{i} + 5\mathbf{j}$ **ii** $\mathbf{a} = (t + 1)\mathbf{i} + \mathbf{j}$, $\mathbf{v}(0) = \mathbf{i} - 2\mathbf{j}$

b **i** $\mathbf{a} = \begin{pmatrix} 3e^t \\ 2e^{-t} \end{pmatrix}$, $\mathbf{v}(0) = \begin{pmatrix} -1 \\ 1 \end{pmatrix}$ **ii** $\mathbf{a} = \begin{pmatrix} 3\sin(2t) \\ 3\cos(2t) \end{pmatrix}$, $\mathbf{v}(0) = \begin{pmatrix} 0 \\ 0 \end{pmatrix}$

c **i** $\mathbf{a} = (2\cos(t))\mathbf{i} + (3\sin(t))\mathbf{j}$, $\mathbf{v}(0) = \mathbf{0}$ **ii** $\mathbf{a} = (e^{2t})\mathbf{i} + (3e^t)\mathbf{j}$, $\mathbf{v}(0) = \mathbf{0}$

3 An object of mass m kg moves under the action of the force $\mathbf{F}$ N. The object is initially at rest. Find the speed of the object at time t seconds, in the following cases.

a **i** $m = 6$, $t = 5$, $\mathbf{F} = 24\mathbf{i} + 6\mathbf{j}$ **ii** $m = 2$, $t = 10$, $\mathbf{F} = 6\mathbf{i} + 10\mathbf{j}$

b **i** $m = 0.2$, $t = 7$, $\mathbf{F} = 6\mathbf{i} - 2\mathbf{j}$ **ii** $m = 0.5$, $t = 5$, $\mathbf{F} = -3\mathbf{i} + 9\mathbf{j}$

4 A particle moves in a plane with the displacement from the starting point given by $\mathbf{s} = (e^{2t})\mathbf{i} + (t - 1)\mathbf{j}$.

a Find an expression for the velocity of the particle at time t.

b Find the speed of the particle when $t = 5$.

5 A particle moves in a plane, starting from rest. Its acceleration varies according to the equation $\mathbf{a} = \begin{pmatrix} 6t \\ \cos(2t) \end{pmatrix}$ m s^{-2}.

a Find an expression for the velocity of the particle at time t.

b Find the displacement from the initial position after 3 seconds.

6 The velocity, measured in m s^{-1}, of a particle moving in a plane is given by $\mathbf{v}(t)=(3-\sin(2t))\mathbf{i}+(2\cos(2t))\mathbf{j}$.

a Find the initial speed of the particle.

b Find the magnitude of the acceleration when $t=12$.

c Find an expression for the displacement from the initial position after t seconds.

7 A particle of mass 2.5 kg is subjected to a constant force $\mathbf{F}=(1.2\mathbf{i}+0.9\mathbf{j})$ N. The initial velocity of the particle is $(0.6\mathbf{i}-1.3\mathbf{j})$ m s^{-1}. Find the velocity of the particle after 5 seconds.

8 A particle starts from rest and moves with acceleration $((2+e^{-2t})\mathbf{i}+(4e^{-2t})\mathbf{j})$ m s^{-2}. Find its distance from the initial position after 1.2 seconds.

9 The velocity of a particle moving in a plane is given by $\mathbf{v}=\begin{pmatrix}2-3t^2\\4t-1\end{pmatrix}$ m s^{-1}. Show that the particle never returns to its initial position.

10 A particle is acted upon by two forces, $\mathbf{F}_1=((c-1)\mathbf{i}+(1-2c)\mathbf{j})$ N and $\mathbf{F}_2=((2c+1)\mathbf{i}+(c-3)\mathbf{j})$ N. The particle moves in the horizontal plane with acceleration $(3\mathbf{i})$ m s^{-2}. Find the value of c.

11 A particle of mass 0.4 kg moves in the horizontal plane under the action of three forces, $\mathbf{F}_1=(3\mathbf{i}-4\mathbf{j})$ N, $\mathbf{F}_2=(-2\mathbf{i}+4\mathbf{j})$ N and $\mathbf{F}_3=(p\mathbf{i}+q\mathbf{j})$ N. The particle moves with constant acceleration $(5\mathbf{j})$ m s^{-2}. Find the values of p and q.

12 For a particle moving in two dimensions, the displacement vector from the starting point is given by $\mathbf{s}=\begin{pmatrix}3t^3-4t\\t^4-2t^3+t\end{pmatrix}$.

a The components of the displacement vector give parametric equations of the trajectory of the particle, $x=x(t)$, $y=y(t)$. Use parametric differentiation to find the gradient of the tangent to this curve, $\frac{dy}{dx}$, when $t=3$.

b Find the velocity vector when $t=3$. What do you notice?

13 A particle moves with acceleration $\mathbf{a}=((12\cos(2t))\mathbf{i}-(12\sin(2t))\mathbf{j})$ m s^{-2}. Its initial velocity is $\mathbf{v}(0)=(6\mathbf{j})$ m s^{-1}.

a Show that the speed of the particle is constant.

b By considering the x and y components of the displacement vector, show that the particle moves in a circle.

14 A particle moves in the plane, from the initial position $\begin{pmatrix}5\\0\end{pmatrix}$ m. Its velocity, $\mathbf{v}$ m s^{-1}, at time t s is given by the equation: $\mathbf{v}(t)=\begin{pmatrix}-8t\\2\end{pmatrix}$.
Find the time when the particle is closest to the origin, and find this minimum distance.

Section 4: Vectors in three dimensions

In the previous sections you have learnt how to use vector equations to represent motion in two dimensions. But you live in a three-dimensional world, so you need to extend vector methods to be able to describe positions and various types of motion around you.

Did you know?

Although our space is three-dimensional, it turns out that many situations can be modelled as motion in two dimensions. For example, it is possible to prove that the orbit of a planet lies in a plane, so two–dimensional vectors are sufficient to describe it.

To represent positions and displacements in three-dimensional space, you need three base vectors, all perpendicular to each other. They are conventionally called **i**, **j**, **k**.

You can also show the components in a column vector: $\overrightarrow{AB} = \begin{pmatrix} 3 \\ 2 \\ 4 \end{pmatrix}$.

Each point in a three-dimensional space can be represented by a position vector, which equals its displacement from the origin. The displacement from one point to another is the difference between their position vectors.

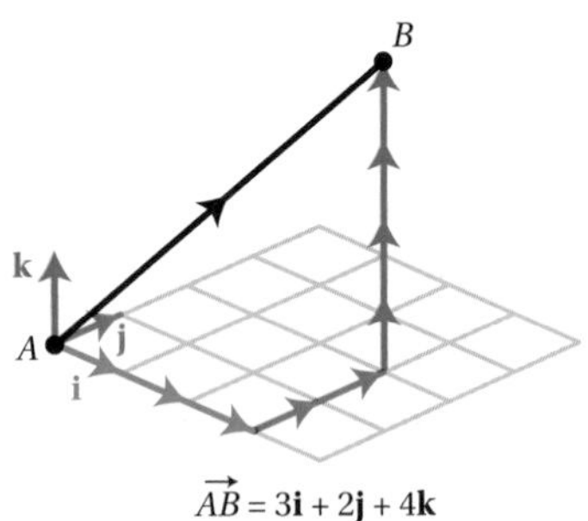

$\overrightarrow{AB} = 3\mathbf{i} + 2\mathbf{j} + 4\mathbf{k}$

WORKED EXAMPLE 19.13

Points A and B have coordinates $(3, -1, 2)$ and $(5, 0, 3)$, respectively. Write as column vectors:

a the position vectors of A and B

b the displacement vector $\overrightarrow{AB}$.

a $\underline{a} = \begin{pmatrix} 3 \\ -1 \\ 2 \end{pmatrix}$

The components of the position vectors are the coordinates of the point.

$\underline{b} = \begin{pmatrix} 5 \\ 0 \\ 3 \end{pmatrix}$

b $\overrightarrow{AB} = \underline{b} - \underline{a}$

$= \begin{pmatrix} 5 \\ 0 \\ 3 \end{pmatrix} - \begin{pmatrix} 3 \\ -1 \\ 2 \end{pmatrix} = \begin{pmatrix} 2 \\ 1 \\ 1 \end{pmatrix}$

The formula for the magnitude of a three-dimensional vector is analogous to the two-dimensional vector.

Key Point 19.3

The magnitude (modulus) of a vector $\mathbf{a}=\begin{pmatrix}a_1\\a_2\\a_3\end{pmatrix}$ is $|\mathbf{a}|=\sqrt{a_1^2+a_2^2+a_3^2}$.

The distance between points with position vectors **a** and **b** is $|\mathbf{b}-\mathbf{a}|$.

Tip

It is useful to remember that this formula comes from Pythagoras' theorem.

WORKED EXAMPLE 19.14

Points A and B have position vectors $\mathbf{a}=2\mathbf{i}-\mathbf{j}+5\mathbf{k}$ and $\mathbf{b}=5\mathbf{i}+2\mathbf{j}+3\mathbf{k}$. Find the exact distance AB.

$\overrightarrow{AB}=\underline{b}-\underline{a}$
$=(5\underline{i}+2\underline{j}+3\underline{k})-(2\underline{i}-\underline{j}+5\underline{k})$
$=3\underline{i}+3\underline{j}-2\underline{k}$

The distance is the magnitude of the displacement vector, so you need to find $\overrightarrow{AB}$ first.

$|\overrightarrow{AB}|=\sqrt{3^2+3^2+2^2}=\sqrt{22}$

Now use the formula for the magnitude.

Remember that you can use vector addition and subtraction to combine displacements.

WORKED EXAMPLE 19.15

The diagram shows points M, N, P, Q such that $\overrightarrow{MN}=3\mathbf{i}-2\mathbf{j}+6\mathbf{k}$, $\overrightarrow{NP}=\mathbf{i}+\mathbf{j}-3\mathbf{k}$ and $\overrightarrow{MQ}=-2\mathbf{j}+5\mathbf{k}$.

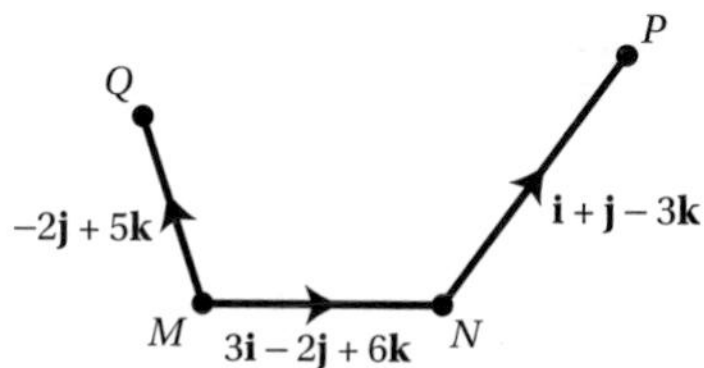

Write the following vectors in component form.

a $\overrightarrow{MP}$
b $\overrightarrow{PM}$
c $\overrightarrow{PQ}$

a $\overrightarrow{MP}=\overrightarrow{MN}+\overrightarrow{NP}$
$=(3\underline{i}-2\underline{j}+6\underline{k})+(\underline{i}+\underline{j}-3\underline{k})$
$=4\underline{i}-\underline{j}+3\underline{k}$

You can get from M to P via N.

Continues on next page ...

b $\overrightarrow{PM} = -\overrightarrow{MP} = -4\underline{i} + \underline{j} - 3\underline{k}$

Going from P to M is the reverse of going from M to P.

c $\overrightarrow{PQ} = \overrightarrow{PM} + \overrightarrow{MQ}$

$= (-4\underline{i} + \underline{j} - 3\underline{k}) + (-2\underline{j} + 5\underline{k})$

$= -4\underline{i} - \underline{j} + 2\underline{k}$

You can get from P to Q via M, using the answers from previous parts.

EXERCISE 19D

1 Write the following vectors in column vector notation (in three dimensions).

a i $4\mathbf{i}$ ii $-5\mathbf{j}$ b i $3\mathbf{i}+\mathbf{k}$ ii $2\mathbf{j}-\mathbf{k}$

2 Let $\mathbf{a} = \begin{pmatrix} 7 \\ 1 \\ 12 \end{pmatrix}$, $\mathbf{b} = \begin{pmatrix} 5 \\ -2 \\ 3 \end{pmatrix}$ and $\mathbf{c} = \begin{pmatrix} 1 \\ 1 \\ 2 \end{pmatrix}$. Find the following vectors.

a i $3\mathbf{a}$ ii $4\mathbf{b}$ b i $\mathbf{a}-\mathbf{b}$ ii $\mathbf{b}+\mathbf{c}$

c i $2\mathbf{b}+\mathbf{c}$ ii $\mathbf{a}-2\mathbf{b}$ d i $\mathbf{a}+\mathbf{b}-2\mathbf{c}$ ii $3\mathbf{a}-\mathbf{b}+\mathbf{c}$

3 Let $\mathbf{a}=\mathbf{i}+2\mathbf{j}$, $\mathbf{b}=\mathbf{i}-\mathbf{k}$ and $\mathbf{c}=2\mathbf{i}-\mathbf{j}+3\mathbf{k}$. Find the following vectors.

a i $-5\mathbf{b}$ ii $4\mathbf{a}$ b i $\mathbf{c}-\mathbf{a}$ ii $\mathbf{a}-\mathbf{b}$

c i $\mathbf{a}-\mathbf{b}+2\mathbf{c}$ ii $4\mathbf{c}-3\mathbf{b}$

4 Find the magnitude of the following vectors in three dimensions.

a $\mathbf{a} = \begin{pmatrix} 4 \\ 1 \\ 2 \end{pmatrix}$ b $\mathbf{b} = \begin{pmatrix} 1 \\ -1 \\ 0 \end{pmatrix}$ c $\mathbf{c}=2\mathbf{i}-4\mathbf{j}+\mathbf{k}$ d $\mathbf{d}=\mathbf{j}-\mathbf{k}$

5 Find the distance between the following pairs of points in three dimensions.

a i $A(1, 0, 2)$ and $B(2, 3, 5)$ ii $C(2, 1, 7)$ and $D(1, 2, 1)$

b i $P(3, -1, -5)$ and $Q(-1, -4, 2)$

ii $M(0, 0, 2)$ and $N(0, -3, 0)$

6 Find the distance between the points with the given position vectors.

a $\mathbf{a}=2\mathbf{i}+4\mathbf{j}-2\mathbf{k}$ and $\mathbf{b}=\mathbf{i}-2\mathbf{j}-6\mathbf{k}$ b $\mathbf{a} = \begin{pmatrix} 3 \\ 7 \\ -2 \end{pmatrix}$ and $\mathbf{b} = \begin{pmatrix} 1 \\ -2 \\ -5 \end{pmatrix}$

c $\mathbf{a} = \begin{pmatrix} 2 \\ 0 \\ -2 \end{pmatrix}$ and $\mathbf{b} = \begin{pmatrix} 0 \\ 0 \\ 5 \end{pmatrix}$ d $\mathbf{a}=\mathbf{i}+\mathbf{j}$ and $\mathbf{b}=\mathbf{j}-\mathbf{k}$

7 Given that $\mathbf{a}=4\mathbf{i}-2\mathbf{j}+\mathbf{k}$, find the vector $\mathbf{b}$ such that:

a $\mathbf{a}+\mathbf{b}$ is the zero vector

b $2\mathbf{a}+3\mathbf{b}$ is the zero vector

c $\mathbf{a}-\mathbf{b}=\mathbf{j}$ d $\mathbf{a}+2\mathbf{b}=3\mathbf{i}$

8 Given that $\mathbf{a}=\begin{pmatrix}-1\\1\\2\end{pmatrix}$ and $\mathbf{b}=\begin{pmatrix}5\\3\\3\end{pmatrix}$, find vector $\mathbf{x}$ such that $3\mathbf{a}+4\mathbf{x}=\mathbf{b}$.

9 Given that $\mathbf{a}=3\mathbf{i}-2\mathbf{j}+5\mathbf{k}$, $\mathbf{b}=\mathbf{i}-\mathbf{j}+2\mathbf{k}$ and $\mathbf{c}=\mathbf{i}+\mathbf{k}$, find the value of the scalar t such that $\mathbf{a}+t\mathbf{b}=\mathbf{c}$.

10 Find the possible values of the constant c such that the vector $\begin{pmatrix}2c\\c\\-c\end{pmatrix}$ has magnitude 12.

11 Let $\mathbf{a}=\begin{pmatrix}-2\\0\\-1\end{pmatrix}$ and $\mathbf{b}=\begin{pmatrix}2\\-1\\2\end{pmatrix}$. Find the possible values of λ such that $|\mathbf{a}+\lambda\mathbf{b}|=5\sqrt{2}$.

12 Points A and B are such that $\overrightarrow{OA}=\begin{pmatrix}-1\\-6\\13\end{pmatrix}$ and $\overrightarrow{OB}=\begin{pmatrix}1\\-2\\4\end{pmatrix}+t\begin{pmatrix}2\\1\\-5\end{pmatrix}$, where O is the origin. Find the possible values of t such that $AB=3$.

13 Points P and Q have position vectors $\mathbf{p}=\mathbf{i}+\mathbf{j}+3\mathbf{k}$ and $\mathbf{q}=(2+t)\mathbf{i}+(1-t)\mathbf{j}+(1+t)\mathbf{k}$. Find the value of t for which the distance PQ is the minimum possible and find this minimum distance.

Elevate

See Support sheet 19 for a further example of three, dimensional vectors and for more practice questions.

Section 5: Solving geometrical problems

This chapter concludes by reviewing how vector methods can be used to solve geometrical problems. You have already used these results:

- The position vector of the midpoint of line segment AB is $\frac{1}{2}(\mathbf{a}+\mathbf{b})$.
- If vectors $\mathbf{a}$ and $\mathbf{b}$ are parallel, then there is a scalar t such that $\mathbf{b}=t\mathbf{a}$.
- The unit vector in the same direction as $\mathbf{a}$ is $\hat{\mathbf{a}}=\frac{1}{|\mathbf{a}|}\mathbf{a}$.

Rewind

These results were introduced in Student Book 1, Chapter 12.

WORKED EXAMPLE 19.16

Points A, B, C and D have position vectors

$\mathbf{a}=\begin{pmatrix}3\\-1\\1\end{pmatrix}$, $\mathbf{b}=\begin{pmatrix}5\\0\\3\end{pmatrix}$, $\mathbf{c}=\begin{pmatrix}7\\8\\-3\end{pmatrix}$, $\mathbf{d}=\begin{pmatrix}4\\3\\-2\end{pmatrix}$. Point E is the midpoint of BC.

a Find the position vector of E.

b Show that $ABED$ is a parallelogram.

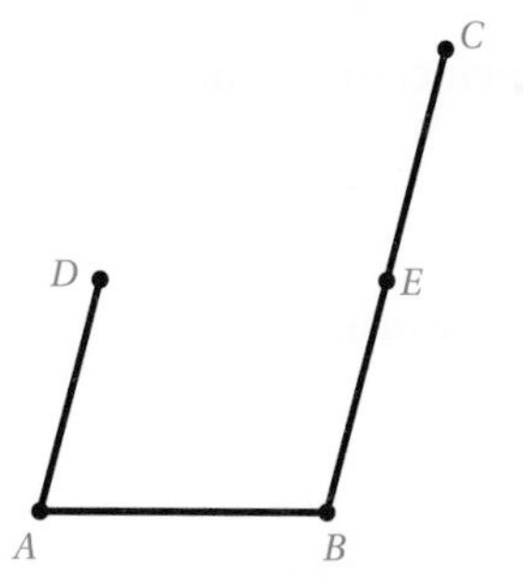

Draw a diagram to help you see what is going on.

Continues on next page ...

Tip

Vector diagrams don't have to be accurate or to scale to be useful. A two-dimensional sketch of a 3D situation is often enough to show you what's going on.

a $\underline{e} = \frac{1}{2}(\underline{b} + \underline{c})$

$= \frac{1}{2}\left(\begin{pmatrix} 5 \\ 0 \\ 3 \end{pmatrix} + \begin{pmatrix} 7 \\ 8 \\ -3 \end{pmatrix}\right)$

$= \begin{pmatrix} 6 \\ 4 \\ 0 \end{pmatrix}$

The position vector of the midpoint is the average of the two position vectors.

b $\overrightarrow{AD} = \underline{d} - \underline{a}$

$= \begin{pmatrix} 4 \\ 3 \\ -2 \end{pmatrix} - \begin{pmatrix} 3 \\ -1 \\ 1 \end{pmatrix} = \begin{pmatrix} 1 \\ 4 \\ -3 \end{pmatrix}$

$\overrightarrow{BE} = \underline{e} - \underline{b}$

$= \begin{pmatrix} 6 \\ 4 \\ 0 \end{pmatrix} - \begin{pmatrix} 5 \\ 0 \\ 3 \end{pmatrix} = \begin{pmatrix} 1 \\ 4 \\ -3 \end{pmatrix}$

$\overrightarrow{AD} = \overrightarrow{BE}$

So $ABED$ is a parallelogram.

In a parallelogram, opposite sides are equal and parallel, which means that the vectors corresponding to those sides are equal. So you need to show that $\overrightarrow{AD} = \overrightarrow{BE}$.

WORKED EXAMPLE 19.17

Given vectors $\mathbf{a} = \begin{pmatrix} 1 \\ 2 \\ 7 \end{pmatrix}$, $\mathbf{b} = \begin{pmatrix} -3 \\ 4 \\ 2 \end{pmatrix}$ and $\mathbf{c} = \begin{pmatrix} -2 \\ p \\ q \end{pmatrix}$:

a Find the values of p and q such that $\mathbf{c}$ is parallel to $\mathbf{a}$.

b Find the value of scalar m such that $\mathbf{a} + m\mathbf{b}$ is parallel to the vector $\begin{pmatrix} 0 \\ 10 \\ 23 \end{pmatrix}$.

a Write $\underline{c} = t\,\underline{a}$ for some scalar t.

Then:

$\begin{pmatrix} -2 \\ p \\ q \end{pmatrix} = t\begin{pmatrix} 1 \\ 2 \\ 7 \end{pmatrix} = \begin{pmatrix} t \\ 2t \\ 7t \end{pmatrix}$

When two vectors are parallel you can write $\mathbf{v}_1 = t\,\mathbf{v}_2$.

$\begin{cases} -2 = t \\ p = 2t \\ q = 7t \end{cases}$

If two vectors are equal, then all their components are equal.

$p = -4, q = -14$

b $\underline{a} + m\underline{b} = \begin{pmatrix} 1 \\ 2 \\ 7 \end{pmatrix} + \begin{pmatrix} -3m \\ 4m \\ 2m \end{pmatrix} = \begin{pmatrix} 1-3m \\ 2+4m \\ 7+2m \end{pmatrix}$

We can write vector $\mathbf{a} + m\mathbf{b}$ in terms of m and then use $\mathbf{a} + m\mathbf{b} = s\begin{pmatrix} 0 \\ 10 \\ 23 \end{pmatrix}$.

Continues on next page ...

Parallel to $\begin{pmatrix} 0 \\ 10 \\ 23 \end{pmatrix}$:

$$\begin{pmatrix} 1-3m \\ 2+4m \\ 7+2m \end{pmatrix} = s\begin{pmatrix} 0 \\ 10 \\ 23 \end{pmatrix}$$

$$\begin{cases} 1-3m=0 \\ 2+4m=10s \\ 7+2m=23s \end{cases}$$

$1-3m=0 \Rightarrow m=\frac{1}{3}$

You can find m from the first equation, but you need to check that all three equations are satisfied.

$2+4\left(\frac{1}{3}\right)=10s \Rightarrow s=\frac{1}{3}$

$7+2\left(\frac{1}{3}\right)=23\left(\frac{1}{3}\right)$ is correct.

$m=\frac{1}{3}$

WORKED EXAMPLE 19.18

a Find the unit vector in the same direction as $\mathbf{a}=\begin{pmatrix} 2 \\ -2 \\ 1 \end{pmatrix}$.

b Find a vector of magnitude 5 parallel to **a**.

a $|\underline{a}|=\sqrt{4+4+1}=3$

To find a unit vector, you need to divide the given vector by its magnitude (as the resulting vector will then have length 1).

$$\therefore \ \underline{\hat{a}} = \frac{1}{3}\begin{pmatrix} 2 \\ -2 \\ 1 \end{pmatrix} = \begin{pmatrix} \frac{2}{3} \\ -\frac{2}{3} \\ \frac{1}{3} \end{pmatrix}$$

b Let $\underline{b}$ be parallel to $\underline{a}$ and $|\underline{b}|=5$.
Then $\underline{b}=5\underline{\hat{a}}$.

To get a vector of magnitude 5 you need to multiply the unit vector by 5.

$$= \begin{pmatrix} \frac{10}{3} \\ -\frac{10}{3} \\ \frac{5}{3} \end{pmatrix}$$

Tip

Note that part **b** has two possible answers, as $\hat{\mathbf{b}}$ could be in the opposite direction. To get the second answer we would take the scalar to be –5 instead of 5.

You can use vectors to divide a line segment according to a given ratio.

WORKED EXAMPLE 19.19

Points A and B have position vectors **a** and **b**. Find, in terms of **a** and **b**, the position vector of the point M on AB such that $AM : MB = 2 : 3$.

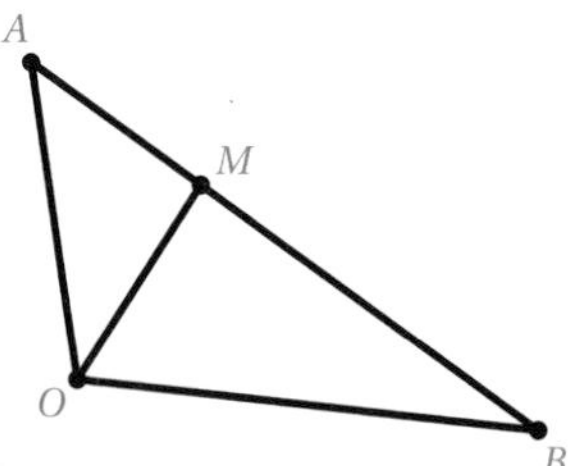

Always start by drawing a diagram. Since the question is about position vectors, include the origin.

$\overrightarrow{OM} = \overrightarrow{OA} + \overrightarrow{AM}$

$= \overrightarrow{OA} + \frac{2}{5}\overrightarrow{AB}$

You can get from O to M via either A or B. (You may want to confirm that both give you the same answer!)

$= \underline{a} + \frac{2}{5}(\underline{b} - \underline{a})$

$= \frac{3}{5}\underline{a} + \frac{2}{5}\underline{b}$

$AM : MB = 2 : 3$ means that $\overrightarrow{AM} = \frac{2}{5}\overrightarrow{AB}$.

EXERCISE 19E

1 **a** **i** Find a unit vector parallel to $\begin{pmatrix} 2 \\ 2 \\ 1 \end{pmatrix}$.

ii Find a unit vector parallel to $6\mathbf{i} + 6\mathbf{j} - 3\mathbf{k}$.

b **i** Find the unit vector in the same direction as $\mathbf{i} + \mathbf{j} - \mathbf{k}$.

ii Find the unit vector in the same direction as $\begin{pmatrix} 4 \\ -1 \\ 2\sqrt{2} \end{pmatrix}$.

2 Points A and B have position vectors $\overrightarrow{OA} = \begin{pmatrix} 3 \\ 1 \\ -2 \end{pmatrix}$ and $\overrightarrow{OB} = \begin{pmatrix} 4 \\ -2 \\ 5 \end{pmatrix}$.

a Write $\overrightarrow{AB}$ as a column vector.

b Find the position vector of the midpoint of the line segment AB.

3 Points A, B and C have position vectors $\mathbf{a} = \begin{pmatrix} 2 \\ -1 \\ 4 \end{pmatrix}$, $\mathbf{b} = \begin{pmatrix} 5 \\ 1 \\ 2 \end{pmatrix}$ and $\mathbf{c} = \begin{pmatrix} 3 \\ 1 \\ 4 \end{pmatrix}$. Find the position vector of point D such that $ABCD$ is a parallelogram.

4 Given that $\mathbf{a} = \begin{pmatrix} 2 \\ 0 \\ 2 \end{pmatrix}$ and $\mathbf{b} = \begin{pmatrix} 3 \\ 1 \\ 3 \end{pmatrix}$, find the value of the scalar p such that $\mathbf{a} + p\mathbf{b}$ is parallel to the vector $\begin{pmatrix} 3 \\ 2 \\ 3 \end{pmatrix}$.

5 Given that $\mathbf{x} = 2\mathbf{i} + 3\mathbf{j} + \mathbf{k}$ and $\mathbf{y} = 4\mathbf{i} + \mathbf{j} + 2\mathbf{k}$, find the value of the scalar λ such that $\lambda\mathbf{x} + \mathbf{y}$ is parallel to vector $\mathbf{j}$.

6 Points A and B have position vectors $\mathbf{a} = \begin{pmatrix} 2 \\ 2 \\ 1 \end{pmatrix}$ and $\mathbf{b} = \begin{pmatrix} 1 \\ -1 \\ 3 \end{pmatrix}$. Point C lies on AB so that $AC : BC = 2 : 3$. Find the position vector of C.

7 Points P and Q have position vectors $\mathbf{p} = 2\mathbf{i} - \mathbf{j} - 3\mathbf{k}$ and $\mathbf{q} = \mathbf{i} + 4\mathbf{j} - \mathbf{k}$.

a Find the position vector of the midpoint M of PQ.

b Point R lies on the line PQ such that $QR = QM$. Find the coordinates of R.

8 Given that $\mathbf{a} = \mathbf{i} - \mathbf{j} + 3\mathbf{k}$ and $\mathbf{b} = 2q\mathbf{i} + \mathbf{j} + q\mathbf{k}$, find the values of scalars p and q such that $p\mathbf{a} + \mathbf{b}$ is parallel to vector $\mathbf{i} + \mathbf{j} + 2\mathbf{k}$.

9 **a** Find a vector of magnitude 6 parallel to $\begin{pmatrix} 4 \\ -1 \\ 1 \end{pmatrix}$.

b Find a vector of magnitude 3 in the same direction as $2\mathbf{i} - \mathbf{j} + \mathbf{k}$.

10 Points A and B have position vectors $\mathbf{a}$ and $\mathbf{b}$. Point M lies on AB and $AM : MB = p : q$. Express the position vector of M in terms of $\mathbf{a}$, $\mathbf{b}$, p and q.

11 In the following diagram, O is the origin and points A and B have position vectors $\mathbf{a}$ and $\mathbf{b}$. P, Q and R are points on OA, OB and AB extended such that $OP : PA = 1 : 4$, $OQ : QB = 3 : 2$ and $AB : BR = 5 : 1$.

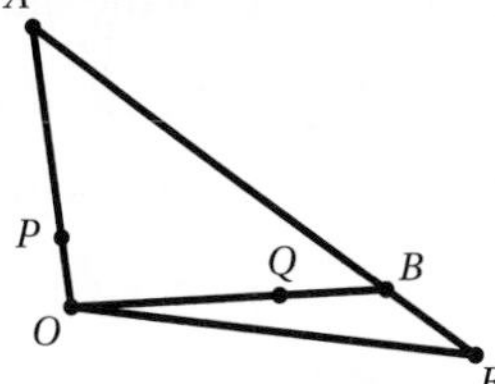

Prove that:

a PQR is a straight line

b Q is the midpoint of PR.

Checklist of learning and understanding

- Constant acceleration formulae in two dimensions:

$$\mathbf{v} = \mathbf{u} + \mathbf{a}t$$
$$\mathbf{s} = \mathbf{u}t + \frac{1}{2}\mathbf{a}t^2$$
$$\mathbf{s} = \mathbf{v}t - \frac{1}{2}\mathbf{a}t^2$$
$$\mathbf{s} = \frac{1}{2}(\mathbf{u} + \mathbf{v})t$$

- To differentiate or integrate a vector, differentiate or integrate each component separately.
- Vectors in three dimensions can be expressed in terms of **base vectors i, j, k** using **components**.
- The magnitude of a vector can be calculated using the components of the vector:

$$|\mathbf{a}| = \sqrt{a_1^2 + a_2^2 + a_3^2}$$

- The distance between the points with position vectors $\mathbf{a}$ and $\mathbf{b}$ is given by $|\mathbf{b} - \mathbf{a}|$.
- The unit vector in the same direction as $\mathbf{a}$ is $\hat{\mathbf{a}} = \frac{1}{|\mathbf{a}|} \times \mathbf{a}$.

Mixed practice 19

1. A particle of mass 6 kg moves with constant acceleration $(1.6\mathbf{i} - 0.3\mathbf{j})$ m s^{-2}.

   a Find the magnitude of the net force acting on the particle.

   When $t = 0$ the particle has velocity $(-2\mathbf{i} + 2.5\mathbf{j})$ m s^{-1}.

   b Find the speed and the direction of motion of the particle 5 seconds later.

2. Points A and B have position vectors $\mathbf{a} = \begin{pmatrix} 4 \\ 1 \\ 2 \end{pmatrix}$ and $\mathbf{b} = \begin{pmatrix} 2 \\ -1 \\ 3 \end{pmatrix}$. C is the midpoint of AB. Find the exact distance AC.

3. Points A, B and C have position vectors $\mathbf{a} = \mathbf{i} + 3\mathbf{j} - 4\mathbf{k}$, $\mathbf{b} = 3\mathbf{i} + 2\mathbf{j} + 2\mathbf{k}$ and $\mathbf{c} = -3\mathbf{i} + 3\mathbf{j} + 4\mathbf{k}$.

   a Find the position vector of the point D such that $ABCD$ is a parallelogram.

   b Prove that $ABCD$ is a rhombus.

4. A particle moves in the plane so that its position vector at time t seconds is $((3.2 - t^2)\mathbf{i} + (-4.6 + 0.2t^3)\mathbf{j})$ m. Find the speed of the particle when $t = 2.5$.

5. Points A, B and C have position vectors $\mathbf{a} = -7\mathbf{i} + 11\mathbf{j} + 9\mathbf{k}$, $\mathbf{b} = 13\mathbf{i} - 4\mathbf{j} + 14\mathbf{k}$ and $\mathbf{c} = 3\mathbf{i} + \mathbf{j} + 4\mathbf{k}$.

   a Prove that the triangle ABC is isosceles.

   b Find the position vector of point D such that the four points form a rhombus.

6. A particle of mass 0.3 kg starts from rest and moves under the action of a constant force $(6\mathbf{i} - 2\mathbf{j})$ N. Find how long it takes to reach the speed of 12 m s^{-1}.

7. A helicopter is initially hovering above the helipad. It sets off with constant acceleration $(0.3\mathbf{i} + 1.2\mathbf{j})$ m s^{-2}, where the unit vectors $\mathbf{i}$ and $\mathbf{j}$ are directed east and north, respectively. The helicopter is modelled as a particle moving in two dimensions.

   a Find the bearing on which the helicopter is travelling.

   b Find the time at which the helicopter is 300 m from its initial position.

   c Explain in everyday language the meaning of the modelling assumption that the helicopter moves in two dimensions.

8. Points P and Q have position vectors $\mathbf{p} = 4\mathbf{i} - \mathbf{j} + 11\mathbf{k}$ and $\mathbf{q} = 3\mathbf{j} - \mathbf{k}$. S is the point on the line segment PQ such that $PS : SQ = 3 : 2$. Find the exact distance of S from the origin.

9. A particle of mass 2 kg moves in the plane under the action of the force $\mathbf{F} = ((20 \sin (2t))\mathbf{i} + (30 \cos (t))\mathbf{j})$ N. The particle is initially at rest at the origin. Find the direction of motion of the particle after 5 seconds.

10. *In this question, vectors* **i** *and* **j** *point due east and north, respectively.*

    A port is located at the origin. One ship starts from the port and moves with velocity $\mathbf{v}_1 = (3\mathbf{i} + 4\mathbf{j})$ km h^{-1}.

    a Write down the position vector at time t hours.

    At the same time, a second ship starts 18 km north of the port and moves with velocity $\mathbf{v}_2 = (3\mathbf{i} - 5\mathbf{j})$ km h^{-1}.

    b Write down the position vector of the second ship at time t hours.

    c Show that, after half an hour, the distance between the two ships is 13.5 km.

d Show that the ships meet, and find the time when this happens.

e How long after the meeting are the ships 18 km apart?

11 At time $t = 0$ two aircraft have position vectors $5\mathbf{j}$ and $7\mathbf{k}$. The first moves with constant velocity $3\mathbf{i} - 4\mathbf{j} + \mathbf{k}$ and the second with constant velocity $5\mathbf{i} + 2\mathbf{j} - \mathbf{k}$.

a Write down the position vector of the first aircraft at time t.

Let d be the distance between the two aircraft at time t.

b Find an expression for d^2 in terms of t. Hence, show that the two aircraft will not collide.

c Find the minimum distance between the two aircraft.

12 A position vector of a particle at time t seconds is given by $\mathbf{s} = ((5 \cos t)\mathbf{i} + (2 \sin t)\mathbf{j})$ m.

a Find the Cartesian equation of the particle's trajectory.

b Find the maximum speed of the particle, and its position vector at the times when it has this maximum speed.

13 A particle of mass 3 kg moves on a horizontal surface under the action of the net force $\mathbf{F} = ((36e^{-t})\mathbf{i} + (-96e^{-2t})\mathbf{j})$ N.
The particle is initially at the origin and has velocity $(-6\mathbf{i} + 20\mathbf{j})$ m s^{-1}. The unit vectors **i** and **j** are directed east and north, respectively.

Find the distance of the particle from the origin at the time when it is travelling in the northerly direction.

Elevate

See Extension sheet 18 for questions on modelling rotation with vectors.

20 Projectiles

In this chapter you will learn how to:

- model projectile motion in two dimensions
- find the maximum height and the range of a projectile
- find the Cartesian equation of the trajectory of a projectile.

Before you start…

Student Book 1, Chapter 12	You should be able to find the magnitude and direction of a vector.	1 Find the magnitude and direction of the vector $\begin{pmatrix} -3 \\ 2 \end{pmatrix}$
Student Book 1, Chapter 20	You should be able to use constant acceleration formulae in one dimension.	2 A particle accelerates uniformly from 3 m s^{-1} to 7 m s^{-1} while covering a distance of 60 m in a straight line. Find the acceleration.
Chapter 19	You should be able to use constant acceleration formulae in two dimensions.	3 A particle initially has velocity $(3\mathbf{i} - 4\mathbf{j})\text{ m s}^{-1}$ and accelerates at $(\mathbf{i} + 2\mathbf{j})\text{ m s}^{-2}$. Find its velocity after 3 seconds.
Chapter 8	You should be able to use trigonometric identities and solve trigonometric equations.	4 Express $\sin x \cos x$ in terms of $\sin 2x$.
		5 Solve the equation $2\sec^2 x + \tan x - 5 = 0$ for $0° < x < 180°$.

Motion in two dimensions

In Student Book 1, Chapter 20 you used the constant acceleration formulae to analyse the motion of a particle that was projected in one dimension, either horizontally or vertically. In this chapter we extend this idea to look at projectiles moving in a two-dimensional vertical plane.

This extension enables us to model the motion of, for example, a bullet, a golf ball or water from a fountain.

Section 1: Modelling projectile motion

Consider an object projected vertically upwards at an angle. If you model the object as a particle and ignore air resistance, then the only force acting on it is gravity. If we also assume that g is constant, then the acceleration is constant with magnitude g and is directed downwards. There is no acceleration horizontally as there is no force acting in this direction.

Fast forward

You will see in Section 2 how to prove that the path of a projectile is a parabola.

Rewind

You met the particle model in Student Book 1, Chapter 19. It assumes that you can ignore an object's size and any internal motion, such as spin.

In Student Book 1 you also explored the assumption of constant g, and effects of air resistance.

Key point 20.1

In projectile motion the acceleration of the particle is $\mathbf{a} = \begin{pmatrix} 0 \\ -g \end{pmatrix} = -g\mathbf{j}$, where the vector $\mathbf{j}$ (or the y-axis) is directed vertically upwards.

Rewind

You met the constant acceleration formulae with two-dimensional vectors in Chapter 19, Section 2.

This means that the motion can be described using the constant acceleration equations in two dimensions.

WORKED EXAMPLE 20.1

A particle is projected from point O with velocity $\begin{pmatrix} 7.2 \\ 4.8 \end{pmatrix}$ m s^{-1}. Taking g to be 9.8 m s^{-2}, find:

a the speed and direction of motion of the particle after 0.8 seconds

b the distance of the particle from O at this time.

a $\underline{u} = \begin{pmatrix} 7.2 \\ 4.8 \end{pmatrix}$

You first need to find the velocity vector after 0.8 seconds. Use $\mathbf{v} = \mathbf{u} + \mathbf{a}t$.

$\underline{a} = \begin{pmatrix} 0 \\ -9.8 \end{pmatrix}$

$t = 0.8$

$\underline{v} = \underline{u} + \underline{a}t$

$= \begin{pmatrix} 7.2 \\ 4.8 \end{pmatrix} + 0.8\begin{pmatrix} 0 \\ -9.8 \end{pmatrix}$

$= \begin{pmatrix} 7.2 \\ -3.04 \end{pmatrix}$

Speed $= \sqrt{7.2^2 + 3.04^2} \approx 7.82$ m s^{-1} (2 d.p)

Speed is the magnitude of velocity.

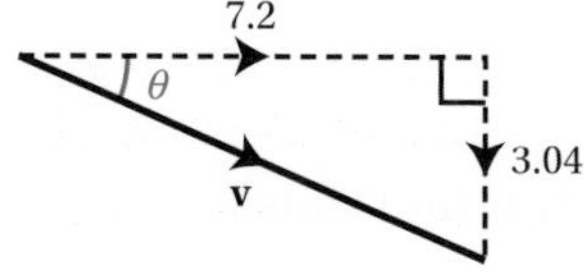

$\tan\theta = \dfrac{3.04}{7.2}$

$\Rightarrow \theta = 22.9°$

The direction of motion is 22.9° below the horizontal.

The direction of motion is the direction of the velocity vector.
Draw a diagram to make sure you are finding the correct angle.

Continues on next page ...

b $\underline{s} = \underline{u}t + \frac{1}{2}\underline{a}t^2$

$= 0.8\begin{pmatrix} 7.2 \\ 4.8 \end{pmatrix} + \frac{0.8^2}{2}\begin{pmatrix} 0 \\ -9.8 \end{pmatrix}$

$= \begin{pmatrix} 5.76 \\ 0.704 \end{pmatrix}$

Now we want the position vector.

Use $s = \mathbf{u}t + \frac{1}{2}\mathbf{a}t^2$.

Distance from the origin:

$\sqrt{5.76^2 + 0.704^2} = 5.80\text{ m (2 d.p.)}$

Distance is the magnitude of displacement.

The initial velocity may be specified by giving the speed and the angle of projection.

Key point 20.2

If a particle is projected with an initial speed u at an angle θ above the horizontal, then the components of the initial velocity are:

- horizontally: $u_x = u\cos\theta$
- vertically: $u_y = u\sin\theta$

or as a vector: $\mathbf{u} = \begin{pmatrix} u\cos\theta \\ u\sin\theta \end{pmatrix}$

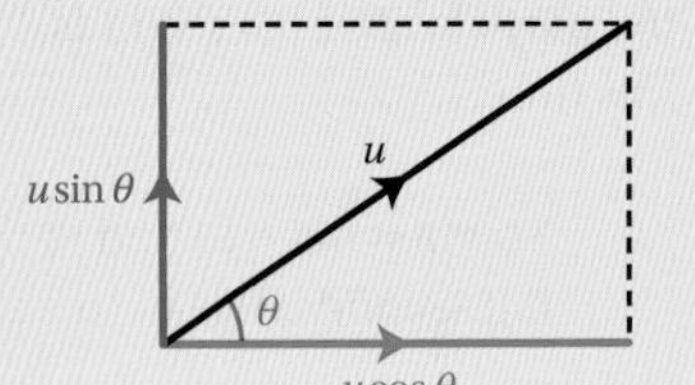

When solving problems involving projectiles, it is often useful to consider the horizontal and vertical motion separately rather than using vectors.

This means using the one-dimensional constant acceleration formulae in each direction separately. We will use x and y to denote the horizontal and vertical components of the displacement vector.

Tip

Since there is no acceleration horizontally, the horizontal component of velocity is constant throughout the motion, and so the horizontal displacement is $x = (u\cos\theta)t$.

WORKED EXAMPLE 20.2

A particle is projected from ground level with speed 12 m s^{-1} at an angle of 30° above the horizontal.

Using $g = 9.8\text{ m s}^{-2}$, find the height of the particle above horizontal ground level at the time when its horizontal displacement from the starting point is 10 m.

Horizontally:

$x = (u\cos\theta)t$

$10 = (12\cos 30°)t$

$\Rightarrow t = \frac{10}{12\cos 30°} = 0.962$

You need to find the time first, using the horizontal displacement equation.

Continues on next page ...

Vertically:

$u_y = 12 \sin 30°$

$a = -g$

$t = 0.962$

$y = u_y t + \frac{1}{2}at^2$

$= (12 \sin 30°)(0.962) + \frac{1}{2}(-9.8)(0.962)^2$

$= 1.24 \text{ m}$

Use a constant acceleration formula for the vertical direction.

If the particle is projected from a point above ground level, then the vertical displacement can be negative, corresponding to the particle falling below the starting point.

WORKED EXAMPLE 20.3

A stone is thrown from the top of a cliff that is 30 m above sea level. The initial velocity has magnitude 8 m s^{-1} and is directed at 20° above the horizontal.

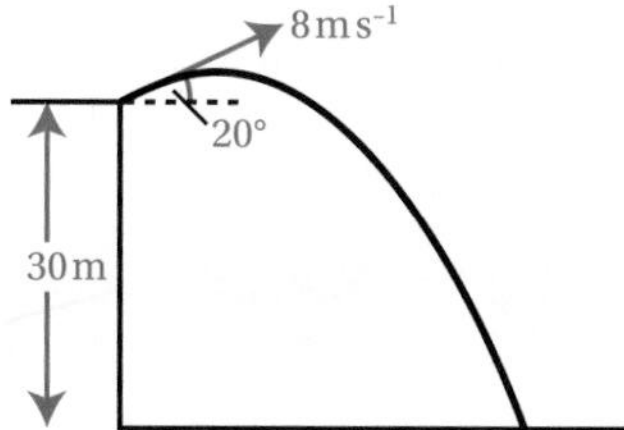

Find the speed with which the stone hits the sea.

Horizontally:

$v_x = u \cos\theta$

$= 8 \cos 20°$

$= 7.518$

The horizontal component of the velocity is constant.

Vertically:

$u_y = 8 \sin 20°$

$a = -g$

$y = -30$

Note that $y = -30$ as the stone finishes 30 m below its starting point.

$v_y^2 = u_y^2 + 2as$

$= (8 \sin 20°)^2 + 2(-9.8)(-30)$

$= 595.49$

Use $v^2 = u^2 + 2as$ to find the vertical component of the velocity.

$|\underline{v}|^2 = v_x^2 + v_y^2$

$= 7.518^2 + 595.49$

≈ 652

$\therefore |\underline{v}| = 25.5 \text{ m s}^{-1}$

Now find the magnitude of the velocity.

We are often interested in the maximum height a projectile reaches, or in how far horizontally from the starting point it lands.

Key point 20.3

- A projectile is at its maximum height when $v_y = 0$.
- For a particle projected from ground level, set $y = 0$ to find the **range** (the horizontal distance travelled before it returns to ground level).

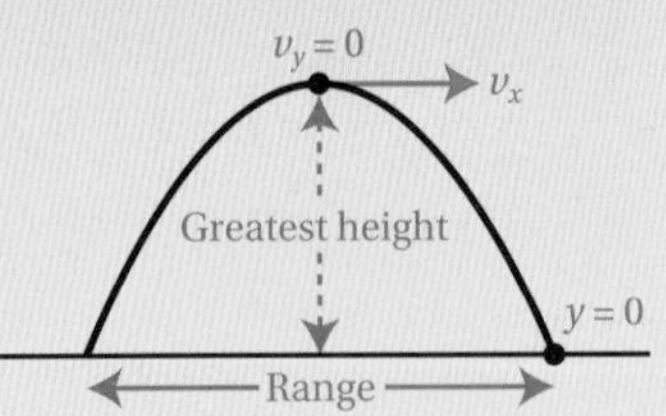

Tip

In practical problems, the ground may not be horizontal or the projectile might hit something before returning to ground level.

WORKED EXAMPLE 20.4

A particle is projected from ground level with speed u in the direction $\theta°$ above the horizontal.

a Show that the maximum height the particle reaches is $\frac{u^2 \sin^2 \theta}{2g}$.

b Given that $u = 4.5\text{ m s}^{-1}$ and $\theta = 30°$, find the range of the projectile.

c How will the answer to part **b** change if air resistance is included in the model?

a Vertically:

$u_y = u \sin\theta$

$v_y = 0$

$a = -g$

The maximum height is reached when $v_y = 0$.

Use $v^2 = u^2 + 2as$ to find the vertical displacement at this point.

$$v_y^2 = u_y^2 + 2ay$$
$$0 = (u \sin\theta)^2 + 2(-g)y$$
$$2gy = u^2 \sin^2\theta$$
$$y = \frac{u^2 \sin^2\theta}{2g}$$

b Vertically:

$u_y = 4.5 \sin 30°$

$a = -g$

$y = 0$

The projectile lands when $y = 0$. First find the time the particle lands using $s = ut + \frac{1}{2}at^2$.

$$0 = (4.5 \sin 30°)t - 4.9t^2$$
$$0 = 2.25t - 4.9t^2$$
$$t(2.25 - 4.9t) = 0$$
$$\therefore t = \frac{2.25}{4.9} = 0.459$$

$t = 0$ corresponds to the starting position, so you want the other value of t.

$$x = (u \cos\theta)t$$
$$= 4.5 \cos 30° \times 0.459$$
$$= 1.79\text{ m}$$

You can now find the horizontal distance at this time.

c The range will be smaller.

Air resistance would cause deceleration in the horizontal direction, so the projectile would travel less far.

In all of the previous examples, the particle was projected upwards at an angle. But the same equations still apply if the particle is projected downwards.

WORKED EXAMPLE 20.5

A small ball is thrown from a window 12 m above ground with the initial velocity $6\,\text{m}\,\text{s}^{-1}$ directed at 30° below the horizontal.

Find how long it takes to reach the ground.

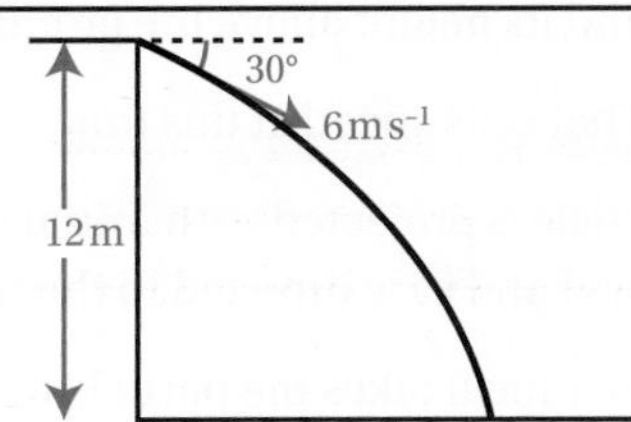

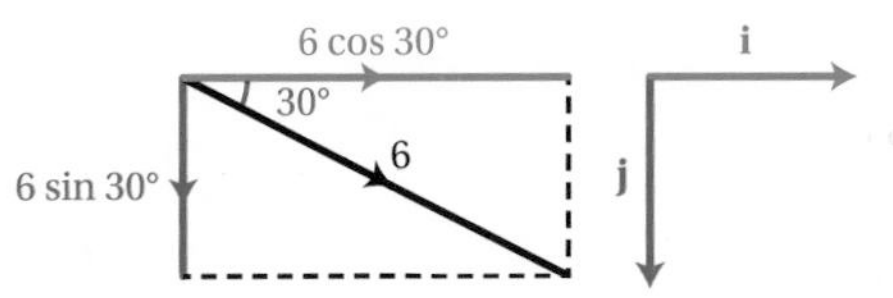

The vertical component of the initial velocity is downwards. In this case, it is easier to take the positive direction (the direction of vector **j**) to be downwards.

Vertically:

$u_y = 6\sin 30 = 3$

$a = 9.8$

$y = 12$

The displacement is measured downwards from the points of projection, so the ground is at $y = 12$. The acceleration is downwards, so is also positive.

$12 = 3t + \frac{1}{2}(9.8)t^2$

$4.9t^2 + 3t - 12 = 0$

Use $s = ut + \frac{1}{2}at^2$. In this case, the vertical displacement s is denoted by y.

$t = \frac{-3 \pm \sqrt{9 - 4 \times 4.9 \times (-12)}}{9.8}$

$= -1.90$ or 1.29

Solve the quadratic for t.

It takes 1.29 seconds.

t must be positive.

EXERCISE 20A

In this exercise use $g = 9.8\,\text{m}\,\text{s}^{-2}$ unless instructed otherwise.

1 A particle is projected from a point, P. Find its velocity vector after 2 seconds if its initial velocity is:

a **i** $(5\mathbf{i} + 21\mathbf{j})\,\text{m}\,\text{s}^{-1}$
ii $(7\mathbf{i} + 6\mathbf{j})\,\text{m}\,\text{s}^{-1}$

b **i** $(8\mathbf{i} - 3\mathbf{j})\,\text{m}\,\text{s}^{-1}$
ii $(4\mathbf{i} - 9\mathbf{j})\,\text{m}\,\text{s}^{-1}$

c **i** $14\,\text{m}\,\text{s}^{-1}$ at 40° above the horizontal
ii $25\,\text{m}\,\text{s}^{-1}$ at 65° above the horizontal

d **i** $8\,\text{m}\,\text{s}^{-1}$ at 35° below the horizontal
ii $20\,\text{m}\,\text{s}^{-1}$ at 10° below the horizontal.

2 A particle is projected from the origin. Find its position vector after 2 seconds if its initial velocity is as in question 1.

3 A small stone is projected from ground level with speed $10\,\text{m s}^{-1}$ at an angle of 25° above the horizontal.

a Find its height above the ground after 0.6 seconds.

b What is its speed at this time?

4 A particle is projected with initial velocity $(5\mathbf{i} + 2.4\mathbf{j})\,\text{m s}^{-1}$. The unit vectors **i** and **j** are directed to the right and vertically upwards. Find:

a the time it takes the particle to reach its maximum height

b the magnitude and direction of its velocity 1.5 seconds after projection.

5 A ball is projected from a point A on a horizontal plane with speed $20\,\text{m s}^{-1}$ at an angle of elevation of 50°. The ball returns to the plane at point B. Find:

a the greatest height above the plane reached by the ball

b the distance AB.

6 A particle is projected with speed $14\,\text{m s}^{-1}$ at an angle θ above the horizontal. The greatest height reached above the point of projection is 8 m.

Find, to the nearest degree, the value of θ.

7 A particle is projected from a point, O, with speed $35\,\text{m s}^{-1}$ at an angle of elevation of 30°.

Find the length of time the particle is more than 15 m above the horizontal level of O.

8 A ball is hit from a point, P, 1.5 m above the ground with speed $28\,\text{m s}^{-1}$ at an angle of elevation of 45°. The ball lands at the point Q, as shown in the diagram.

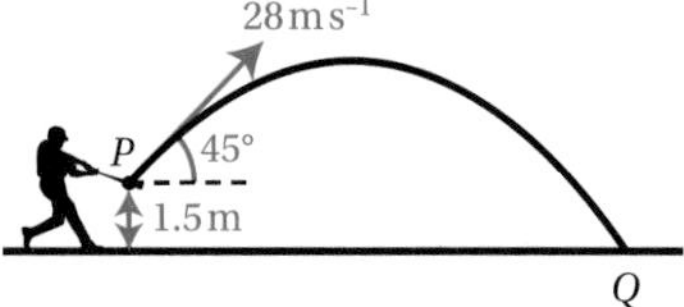

Find:

a the time taken for the ball to travel from P to Q

b the distance PQ

c the speed with which the ball hits the ground.

Elevate

See Support sheet 20 for an example of finding the angle and speed of projection and for more practice questions.

9 A ball is projected with speed $12\,\text{m}\,\text{s}^{-1}$ at an angle of 30° above the horizontal. A 1.6 m high wall is located 6 m from the point of projection. Determine whether the ball will clear the wall.

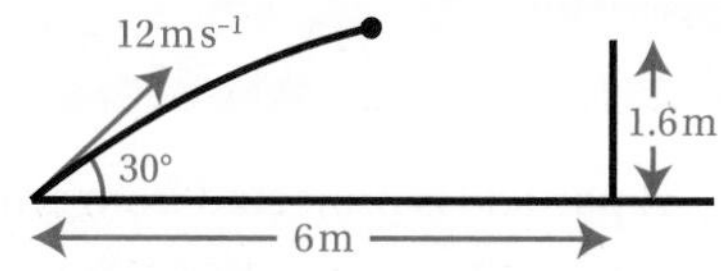

10 A ball is projected horizontally with speed $10\,\text{m}\,\text{s}^{-1}$ from the top of a 12 m tall building.

a Find the distance from the foot of the building and the point where the ball hits the ground.

A second ball is projected with speed $14\,\text{m}\,\text{s}^{-1}$ from the foot of the building.

b Find the possible angles of projection so that the second ball hits the ground at the same place as the first ball.

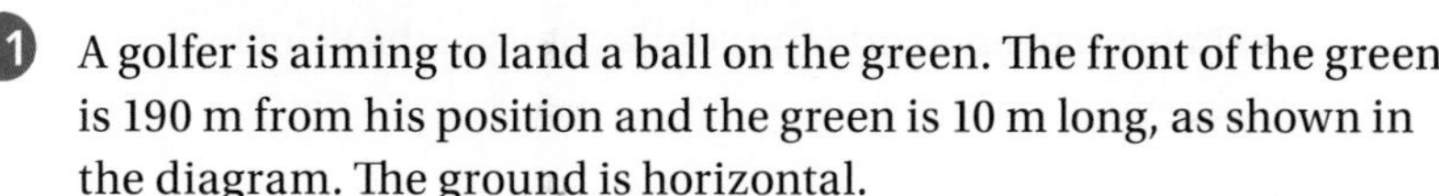

11 A golfer is aiming to land a ball on the green. The front of the green is 190 m from his position and the green is 10 m long, as shown in the diagram. The ground is horizontal.

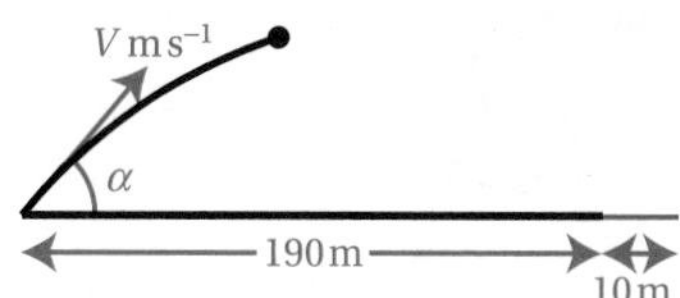

a If the golfer strikes the ball with speed $V\,\text{m}\,\text{s}^{-1}$ at an angle α above the horizontal, show that the horizontal distance travelled by the ball when it lands is $\dfrac{V^2\sin 2\alpha}{g}$.

b If $V = 50$, find the range of values of α that will result in the golfer landing the ball on the green.

12 A film director wants to include the 'human fired out of a cannon' stunt in his film. For ethical reasons, he uses a scale model of a cannon, which is one-tenth of the real size, with a toy fired out of it.

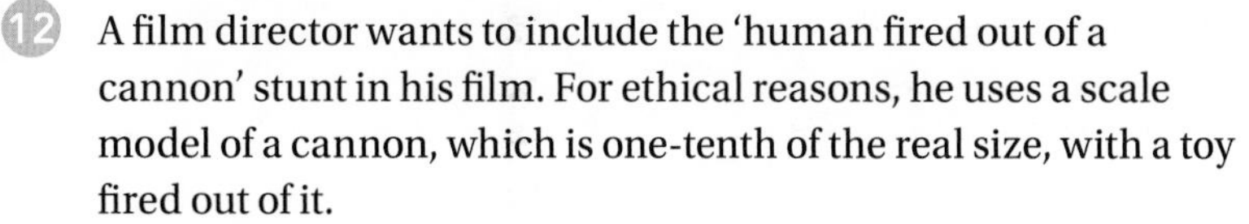

a What is the magnitude of the force of gravity that would be observed by someone watching the film?

b Does the film need to speed up or be slowed down to correct this?

Section 2: The trajectory of a projectile

So far we have only looked at how the displacement and velocity of a projectile change with time. But we can also find a relationship between the horizontal and vertical displacements. This leads to an equation describing the path, or **trajectory**, of the projectile.

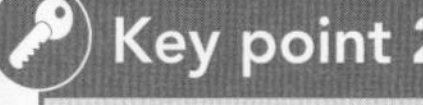

Key point 20.4

To find an equation for the trajectory of a projectile:

- Make t the subject of the $x = (u\cos\theta)t$ equation.
- Substitute this expression for t into $y = (u\sin\theta)t - \frac{1}{2}gt^2$.

Rewind

This is an example of *parametric equations*, which you met in Chapter 12. You can apply the method of eliminating t to find the Cartesian equation of the trajectory of a particle moving in two dimensions.

WORKED EXAMPLE 20.6

A particle is projected from ground level with speed 7 m s^{-1} at an angle θ above the horizontal, such that $\tan\theta = \frac{5}{12}$. Let x and y be the horizontal and vertical displacements from the point of projection, with y measured upwards, and use $g = 9.8\text{ m s}^{-2}$.

Find an expression for y in terms of x.

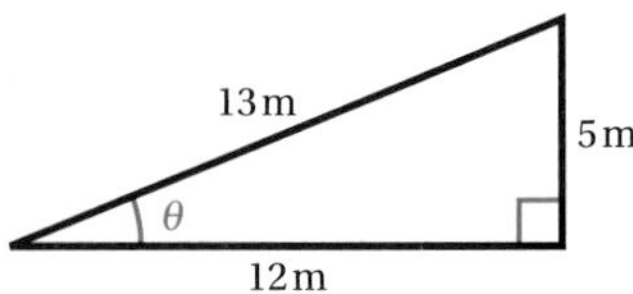

$\cos\theta = \frac{12}{13}$

$\sin\theta = \frac{5}{13}$

First you need to find the components of the velocity.

Horizontally:

$x = (u\cos\theta)t$

$x = 7\times\frac{12}{13}t$

$\Rightarrow t = \frac{13x}{84}$

Make t the subject of the horizontal equation.

Vertically:

$y = (u\sin\theta)t - \frac{1}{2}gt^2$

$= \left(7\times\frac{5}{13}\right)t - 4.9t^2$

$= \frac{35}{13}\times\frac{13x}{84} - 4.9\left(\frac{13x}{84}\right)^2$

And substitute t into the vertical equation.

$\therefore y = \frac{5}{12}x - \frac{169}{1440}x^2$

As you can see, the trajectory of a projectile is a parabola. It is important to remember that the equations we have used include gravitational acceleration, but no other force. In particular, this model of a projectile assumes no air resistance. If the air resistance is included the trajectory is no longer a parabola.

without air resistance

with air resistance

You may need to find the angle of projection in order for the particle to pass through a specific point. There will often be two possible values.

WORKED EXAMPLE 20.7

A particle is projected from a point, P, on horizontal ground, with speed $21\ \text{m s}^{-1}$ at an angle α above the horizontal. The particle passes through the point Q, which is at a horizontal distance of 12 m from P and a height of 4 m above the ground.

a Show that $2\tan^2\alpha - 15\tan\alpha + 7 = 0$.

b Find the two possible values of α.

a Horizontally:

$x = (u\cos\alpha)t$

$12 = (21\cos\alpha)t$

$t = \dfrac{4}{7\cos\alpha}$

Make t the subject of the horizontal equation.

Vertically:

$y = (u\sin\alpha)t - \dfrac{1}{2}gt^2$

$4 = (21\sin\alpha)t - \dfrac{1}{2}gt^2$

$4 = (21\sin\alpha)\left(\dfrac{4}{7\cos\alpha}\right) - \dfrac{1}{2}g\left(\dfrac{4}{7\cos\alpha}\right)^2$

And substitute t into the vertical equation.

$4 = 12\dfrac{\sin\alpha}{\cos\alpha} - \dfrac{1}{2}\times 9.8 \times \dfrac{16}{49\cos^2\alpha}$

$4 = 12\tan\alpha - \dfrac{8}{5}\sec^2\alpha$

$5 = 15\tan\alpha - 2\sec^2\alpha$

$\dfrac{\sin\alpha}{\cos\alpha} = \tan\alpha$ and $\dfrac{1}{\cos^2\alpha} = \sec^2\alpha$.

$5 = 15\tan\alpha - 2(1 + \tan^2\alpha)$

$5 = 15\tan\alpha - 2 - 2\tan^2\alpha$

$\sec^2\alpha = 1 + \tan^2\alpha$

$\therefore 2\tan^2\alpha - 15\tan\alpha + 7 = 0.$

b $(2\tan\alpha - 1)(\tan\alpha - 7) = 0$

$\tan\alpha = \dfrac{1}{2}$ or 7

$\therefore \alpha = 26.6°$ or $81.9°$

Factorise and solve for α.

Note that there are two possible trajectories that pass through Q:

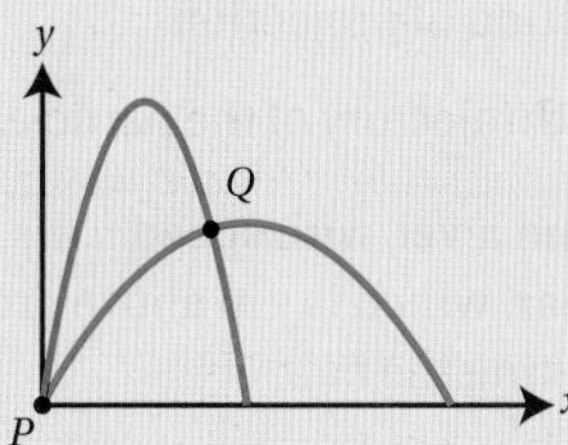

WORK IT OUT 20.1

A ball is thrown from a point, P, at ground level with speed $15\,\text{m s}^{-1}$ at an angle $\theta°$ above the horizontal. It lands at a point 12 m horizontally from P on a platform that is 4 m above the ground. The platform starts 10 m from P and is 4 m long, as shown in the diagram.

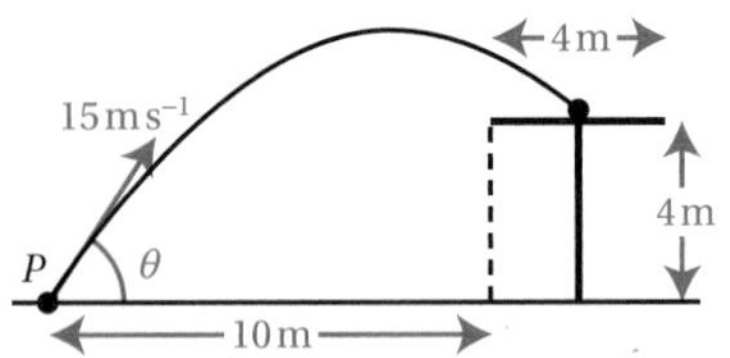

The trajectory of the ball is given by

$$y = x\tan\theta - \frac{gx^2}{2u^2}\left(1+\tan^2\theta\right)$$

Taking $g = 10\,\text{m s}^{-2}$, find the angle θ.

Which is the correct solution? Can you identify the errors made in the incorrect solutions?

Solution 1	Solution 2	Solution 3
$x=12$, $y=4$, $u=15$ and $g=10$. $4=12\tan\theta-\frac{10(12)^2}{2(15)^2}(1+\tan^2\theta)$ $4=12\tan\theta-\frac{16}{5}(1+\tan^2\theta)$ $5=15\tan\theta-4-4\tan^2\theta$ $4\tan^2\theta-15\tan\theta+9=0$ $(4\tan\theta-3)(\tan\theta-3)=0$ $\tan\theta=\frac{3}{4}$ or 3 $\theta=37°$ or $72°$ $\therefore\theta=37°$ as this is the first point of contact with the platform.	$x=12$, $y=4$, $u=15$ and $g=10$. $4=12\tan\theta-\frac{10(12)^2}{2(15)^2}(1+\tan^2\theta)$ $4=12\tan\theta-\frac{16}{5}(1+\tan^2\theta)$ $5=15\tan\theta-4-4\tan^2\theta$ $4\tan^2\theta-15\tan\theta+9=0$ $(4\tan\theta-3)(\tan\theta-3)=0$ $\tan\theta=\frac{3}{4}$ or 3 $\theta=37°$ or $72°$ $\therefore\theta=72°$ as the particle needs to be on the way down.	$x=10$, $y=4$, $u=15$ and $g=10$. $4=10\tan\theta-\frac{10(10)^2}{2(15)^2}(1+\tan^2\theta)$ $4=10\tan\theta-\frac{20}{9}(1+\tan^2\theta)$ $18=45\tan\theta-10-10\tan^2\theta$ $10\tan^2\theta-45\tan\theta+28=0$ $\tan\theta=0.746$ or 3.75 $\theta=37°$ or $75°$

EXERCISE 20B

In this exercise use $g = 9.8\,\text{m s}^{-2}$ unless instructed otherwise.

1. A particle is projected horizontally with speed $8\,\text{m s}^{-1}$ from the top of a 25 m tall cliff. Let the origin of an x–y coordinate system be located at the top of the cliff, with the y-axis pointing vertically downwards and the x-axis horizontal in the direction of projection.

   Find the Cartesian equation of the trajectory of the particle.

2. A rugby ball is kicked from ground level, with speed $u\,\text{m s}^{-1}$, at an angle of elevation of 45° towards a crossbar, which is y m above ground and x m away horizontally from the person kicking the ball.

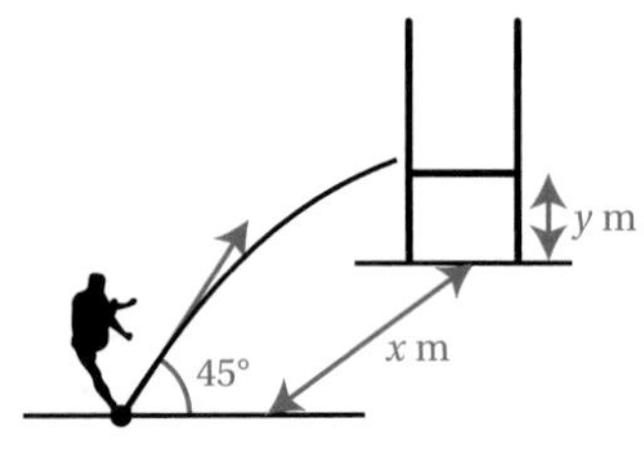

   a If the ball hits the crossbar, show that $y = x - \frac{gx^2}{u^2}$.

   b If the crossbar is 3 m high and the kick is to be taken 35 m from the posts, find the minimum velocity with which the ball must be kicked to clear the crossbar.

   c State two modelling assumptions you needed to make.

3 **a** Show that the equation of the trajectory of a particle projected at speed $u\,\text{m s}^{-1}$ at an angle of elevation θ is:

$$y = x\tan\theta - \frac{gx^2}{2u^2\cos^2\theta}$$

b An archer fires an arrow from a point 1.5 m above the ground with speed $44\,\text{m s}^{-1}$ at an angle of elevation of 7°. The target is 50 m away and the centre of the target is 1.3 m above the ground. The diameter of the target is 15 cm.

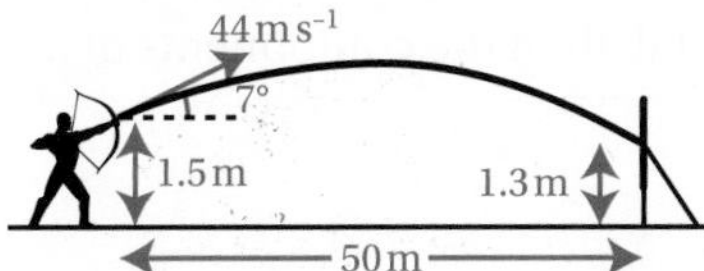

Determine whether the arrow hits the target.

4 A particle is projected from the origin with speed $V\,\text{m s}^{-1}$ at an angle of elevation α. It passes through the point with position vector $4\mathbf{i} + 8\mathbf{j}$.

a Show that $\dfrac{2g}{V^2\cos^2\alpha} = \tan\alpha - 2$

b The particle subsequently passes through the point with position vector $6\mathbf{i} + 5\mathbf{j}$.

i Show that $\tan\alpha = \dfrac{13}{3}$.

ii Find V.

5 A particle is projected from a point on horizontal ground with speed u at an angle of elevation θ. The maximum height reached by the particle is 28 m and the particle hits the ground 84 m from the point of projection.

Find u and θ.

6 A basketball player shoots at the hoop. The hoop is 3 m from the ground and the basketball player stands 6 m horizontally from the hoop. The ball is released from 2 m above the ground at an angle of α above the horizontal.

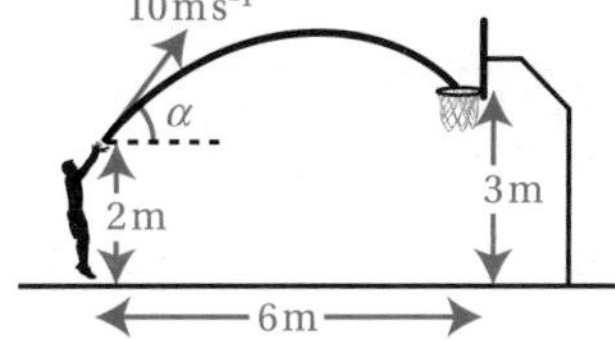

The initial speed of the ball is $10\,\text{m s}^{-1}$. Assume that the ball passes through the hoop.

a Show that $9g\tan^2\alpha - 300\tan\alpha + 50 + 9g = 0$.

b Hence, find the angle at which the ball was released, justifying your answer.

Checklist of learning and understanding

- In projectile motion the acceleration of the particle is $\mathbf{a} = \begin{pmatrix} 0 \\ -g \end{pmatrix}$ m s^{-2}, where the y-axis points vertically upwards.
- The modelling assumptions for projectile motion are:
  - the projectile is modelled as a particle
  - air resistance can be ignored
  - the value of g remains constant.
- If a particle is projected with speed u at an angle θ above the horizontal, then the components of the initial velocity are:
  - horizontally: $u_x = u\cos\theta$
  - vertically: $u_y = u\sin\theta$
- A projectile is at its maximum height when $v_y = 0$.
- For a particle projected from ground level, set $y = 0$ to find the range (the maximum horizontal distance travelled).
- To find an equation for the trajectory of a projectile:
  - Make t the subject of the $x = (u\cos\theta)t$ equation.
  - Substitute this expression for t into $y = (u\sin\theta)t - \frac{1}{2}gt^2$.

Mixed practice 20

In this exercise use $g = 9.8\,\text{m}\,\text{s}^{-2}$ unless instructed otherwise.

1 A particle is projected horizontally with a speed of $7\,\text{m}\,\text{s}^{-1}$ from a point 10 m above horizontal ground. The particle moves freely under gravity. Calculate the speed and direction of motion of the particle at the instant it hits the ground.

© OCR, GCE Mathematics, Paper 4729, June 2010

2 A particle of mass m is projected horizontally off the edge of a cliff and lands in the sea below at a distance x from the base of the cliff.

A second particle of mass $2m$ is projected horizontally from the same point at the same speed and lands in the sea at a distance y from the base of the cliff.

Which one of the following statements is true?

A $x > y$ **B** $y > x$

C $x = y$ **D** It depends on the height of the cliff.

3 A ball is thrown horizontally at $12\,\text{m}\,\text{s}^{-1}$ from the top of a 30 m tall building. Find:

a the time it takes for the ball to hit the ground below

b the distance from the bottom of the building to the point where the ball hits the ground.

4 A projectile is launched from the point O with velocity $(10\mathbf{i} + 15\mathbf{j})\,\text{m}\,\text{s}^{-1}$. After t seconds it is at the point A and is travelling with velocity $(10\mathbf{i} - 9.5\mathbf{j})\,\text{m}\,\text{s}^{-1}$. Find:

a the value of t

b the distance OA.

5 A ball is thrown from a window 5 m above the ground with velocity $(9\mathbf{i} + 8\mathbf{j})\,\text{m}\,\text{s}^{-1}$. It is caught by a child 1 m above the ground. The child stands x m from the point vertically below the window at ground level.

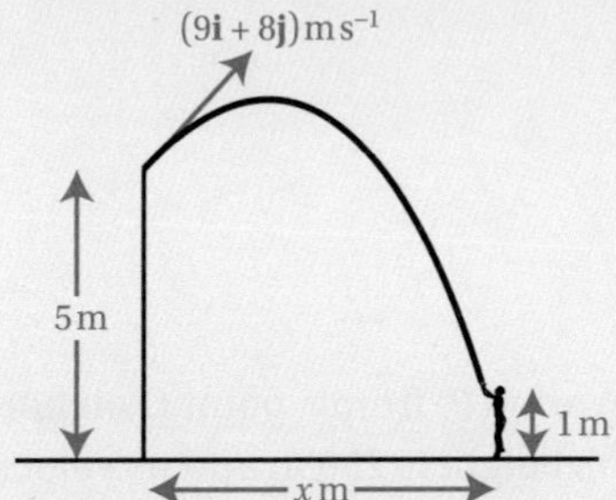

Using $g = 10\,\text{m}\,\text{s}^{-2}$, find:

a the value of x

b the speed of the ball as it is caught.

6 A particle is projected from a point, A, on a horizontal plane with speed $u\,\text{m}\,\text{s}^{-1}$ at an angle θ above the horizontal. It lands on the plane at the point B.

a i Show that $AB = \dfrac{u^2 \sin 2\theta}{g}$.

ii Hence, deduce that for fixed u, the maximum range is achieved when $\theta = 45°$.

b If $AB = \dfrac{2u^2}{3g}$ find, to the nearest degree, the two possible angles at which the particle was projected.

7 Kim stands on a bridge that passes over a river, which is 6 m below. He throws a stone with speed $15\,\text{m}\,\text{s}^{-1}$ directly at a small stationary rock, which is 8 m from the base of the bridge, as shown in the diagram.

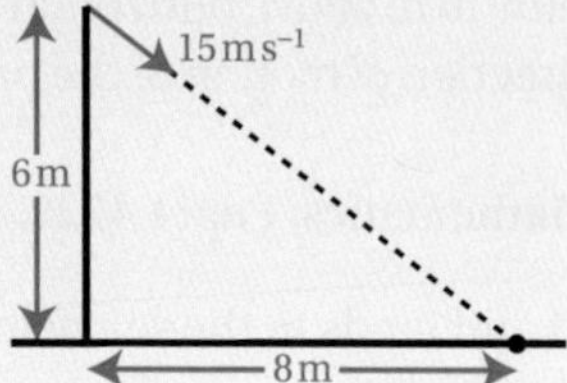

How far away from the rock does the stone land in the river?

8 A particle is projected from O with velocity $(8\mathbf{i} + 11\mathbf{j})\,\text{m}\,\text{s}^{-1}$. It passes through the point P at time t seconds.

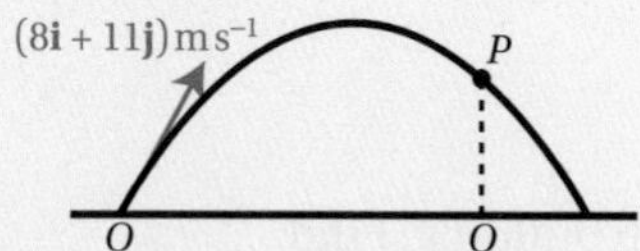

Given that $OQ = 2PQ$:

a Find the value of t.

At point R the ball has the same speed as at P.

b Find the time taken for the ball to travel from O to R.

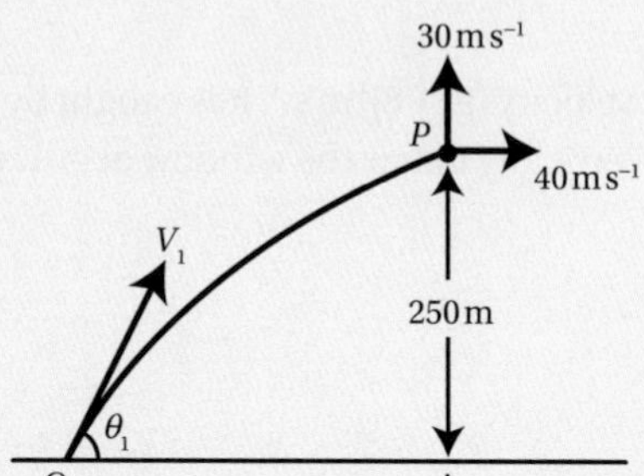

A particle P is projected with speed $V_1\,\text{m}\,\text{s}^{-1}$ at an angle of elevation θ_1 from a point O on horizontal ground. When P is vertically above a point A on the ground its height is 250 m and its velocity components are $40\,\text{m}\,\text{s}^{-1}$ horizontally and $30\,\text{m}\,\text{s}^{-1}$ vertically upwards (see diagram).

i Show that $V_1 = 86.0$ and $\theta_1 = 62.3°$, correct to 3 significant figures.

At the instant when P is vertically above A, a second particle Q is projected from O with speed $V_2\,\text{m}\,\text{s}^{-1}$ at an angle of elevation θ_2. P and Q hit the ground at the same time and at the same place.

ii Calculate the total time of flight of P and the total time of flight of Q.

iii Calculate the range of the particles and, hence, calculate V_2 and θ_2.

© OCR, GCE Mathematics, Paper 4729, January 2010

  A particle is projected from a point O with speed $v\,\text{m}\,\text{s}^{-1}$ at an angle of elevation θ above the horizontal and it moves freely under gravity. The horizontal and upward vertical displacements of the particle from O at any subsequent time, t seconds, are x m and y m, respectively.

i Express x and y in terms of θ and t and, hence, show that

$$y = x\tan\theta - \frac{4.9x^2}{v^2\cos^2\theta}.$$

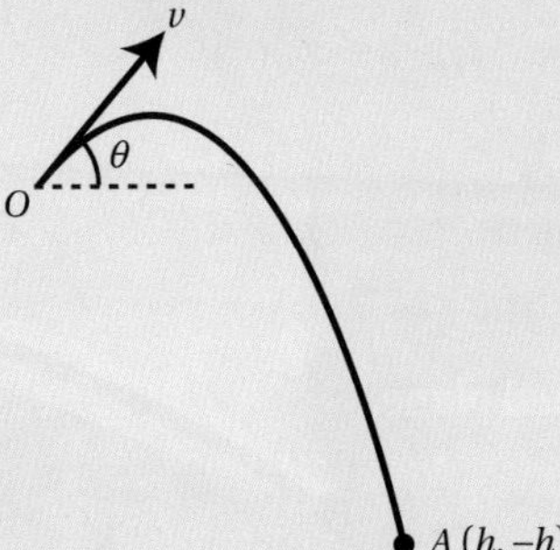

The particle subsequently passes through the point A with coordinates $(h, -h)$, as shown in the diagram. It is given that $v = 14$ and $\theta = 30°$.

ii Calculate h.

iii Calculate the direction of motion of the particle at A.

iv Calculate the speed of the particle at A.

© OCR, GCE Mathematics, Paper 4729, January 2009

11 Take g to be $10\,\text{m}\,\text{s}^{-2}$ in this question.

A particle is projected from a point 30 m above ground level with velocity $u = (3\mathbf{i} + 4\mathbf{j})\,\text{m}\,\text{s}^{-1}$, as shown in the diagram.

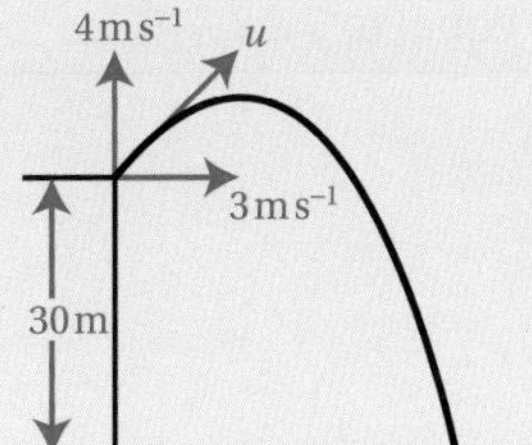

Find the distance from the point of projection at the instant the particle is moving in a direction perpendicular to its initial velocity. Give your answer to an appropriate degree of accuracy.

12 A particle P is projected horizontally with speed $15\,\text{m}\,\text{s}^{-1}$ from the top of a vertical cliff. At the same instant a particle Q is projected from the bottom of the cliff, with speed $25\,\text{m}\,\text{s}^{-1}$ at angle $\theta°$ above the horizontal. P and Q move in the same vertical plane. The height of the cliff is 60 m and the ground at the bottom of the cliff is horizontal.

i Given that the particles hit the ground simultaneously, find the value of θ and find also the distance between the points of impact with the ground.

ii Given instead that the particles collide, find the value of θ, and determine whether Q is rising or falling immediately before the collision.

© OCR, GCE Mathematics, Paper 4729, January 2012

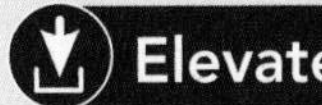

Elevate

See Extension sheet 20 for a selection of more challenging problems.

21 Forces in context

In this chapter you will learn:

- how to resolve forces in a given direction in order to calculate the resultant force
- about a model for friction
- how to determine the acceleration of a particle moving on an inclined plane.

Before you start...

Student Book 1, Chapter 18	You should be able to add vectors and find magnitudes.	1 Three horizontal forces act on a particle. In newtons, the forces are $\mathbf{F}_1 = 2\mathbf{i}$, $\mathbf{F}_2 = 3\mathbf{j}$ and $\mathbf{F}_3 = \mathbf{i} - 2\mathbf{j}$. Calculate the magnitude of the resultant force and its angle from the direction **i**.
Student Book 1, Chapter18	You should be able to find horizontal and vertical components of a vector.	2 A force of 40 N acts at an angle of 30° to the horizontal. Find the horizontal component of the force.
Student Book 1, Chapter 17	You should be able to solve problems involving motion with constant acceleration.	3 A force of 5 N acts on a particle with mass 2 kg. If the particle is initially at rest, after how many seconds will its displacement be equal to 5 m?

Improving our physical model

In Student Book 1, Chapter 18 you learnt to add and subtract forces in vector form and to determine the angle and magnitude of the resultant force. This chapter deals with more complex situations involving strings and planes in different orientations where the forces are not perpendicular. To solve these problems you will need to combine your knowledge of forces, vectors and trigonometry.

In Student Book 1 you met problems where there is a constant resistance force acting on an object. Here we shall improve our model of friction to enable us to model more real-world situations.

Section 1: Resolving forces

When considering forces acting on a moving body, it can be useful to split each force into components in two perpendicular directions. This process is called **resolving** the force.

For example, consider a force acting in the **i**–**j** plane, with magnitude 10 N at an angle of 50° anticlockwise from the direction of **i**.

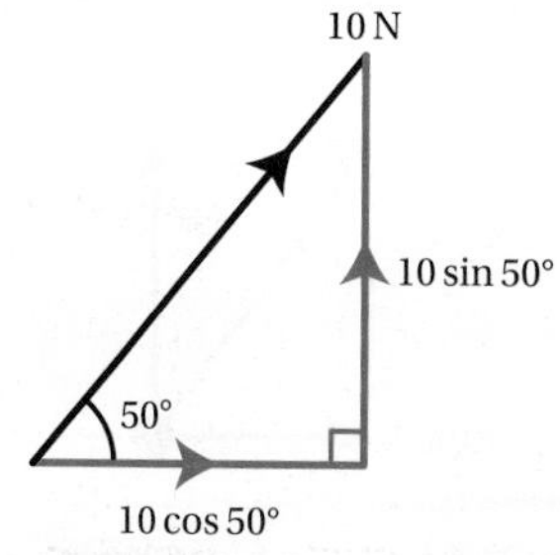

We can find the components of this force in the directions of **i** and **j**:

The component in the **i** direction is $10\cos 50° = 6.42787... = 6.43$ (3 s.f.)

The component in the **j** direction is $10\sin 50° = 7.6604... = 7.66$ (3 s.f.)

Rewind

In Student Book 1, Chapter 12, you learnt how to find the components of a vector; in Chapter 21 you learnt how to add forces given in component form.

In some situations it will be useful to resolve in directions other than **i** and **j**. For example, the force might be acting on a particle that lies on a slope making an angle of 20° with the horizontal. In that case we can resolve the force in the directions parallel and perpendicular to the slope:

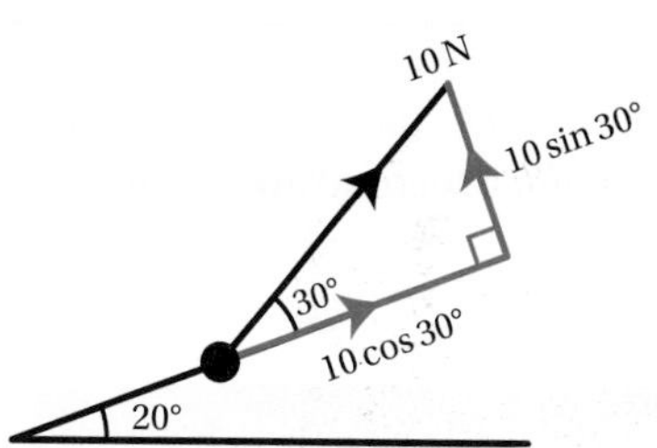

The component up the slope is $10\cos 30° = 8.66$ N.

The component perpendicular to the slope is $10\sin 30° = 5$ N.

Once all forces have been resolved you can find the resultant force.

WORKED EXAMPLE 21.1

Two forces act on a particle in the horizontal x–y plane. Force $\mathbf{F}_1$ has magnitude 6 N and acts at angle 30° to the positive x-axis. Force $\mathbf{F}_2$ has magnitude 5 N and acts in the direction of the negative x-axis. Find the magnitude and direction of the resultant force.

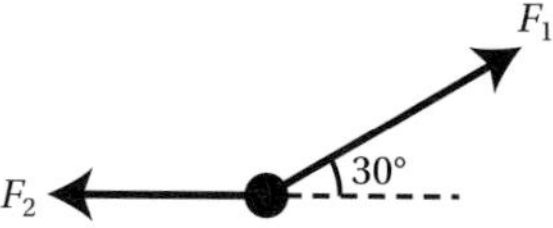

Always draw a diagram.

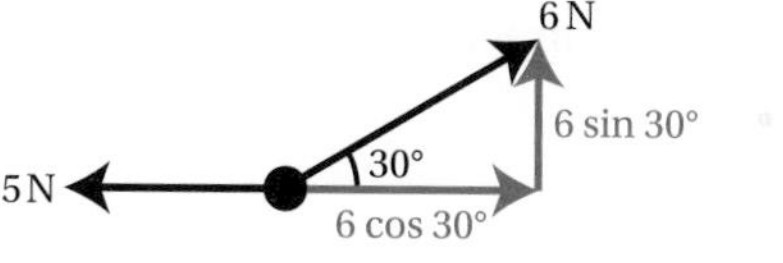

Form a right-angled triangle with the force as hypotenuse and the sides parallel to the x and y directions. In this case, since the force $\mathbf{F}_2$ is in the x direction, we need to resolve only force $\mathbf{F}_1$.

$(\rightarrow)$: $6\cos 30 - 5 = 3\sqrt{3} - 5 = -0.196$

$(\uparrow)$: $6\sin 30 = 3$

Calculate horizontal and vertical components of $\mathbf{F}_1$ and add $\mathbf{F}_2$ to the horizontal direction.
The arrow notation indicates which component we are calculating; for example, $(\rightarrow)$ indicates the component in the positive x direction.

Continues on next page ...

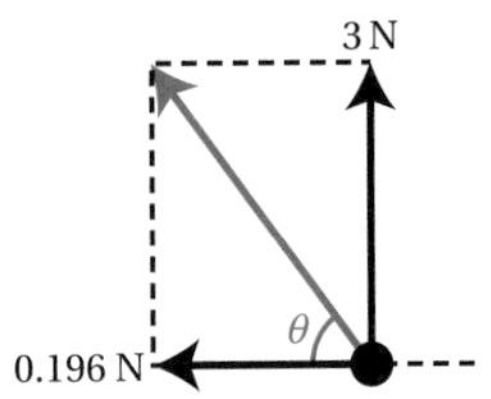

Draw another triangle showing the resultant force. This helps find its magnitude and direction. Note that -0.196 means that the force is acting in the negative x direction.

Magnitude: $\sqrt{0.196^2+3^2}=3.01\text{N}$

Direction: $\theta=\arctan\left(\frac{3}{0.196}\right)=86.3^\circ$

$180-86.3=93.7^\circ$, so the direction is 93.7° from the positive x-axis.

Once forces have been found you may have to work with them using Newton's second law ($\mathbf{F}=m\mathbf{a}$).

Rewind

You met Newton's second law in Student Book 1, Chapter 18, Section 1.

WORKED EXAMPLE 21.2

A particle with mass 5 kg moves on a horizontal (x–y) plane with constant acceleration $a\mathbf{i}$, where $a>0$, acted upon by two forces, $\mathbf{F}_1$ and $\mathbf{F}_2$, in the plane.

$\mathbf{F}_1$ has magnitude 3 N and acts at angle 30° anticlockwise from the positive x-axis.

$\mathbf{F}_2$ has magnitude 5 N and acts at acute angle θ clockwise from the positive x-axis.

a Show that $\cos\theta=\frac{\sqrt{91}}{10}$.

b Calculate the exact value of a.

a

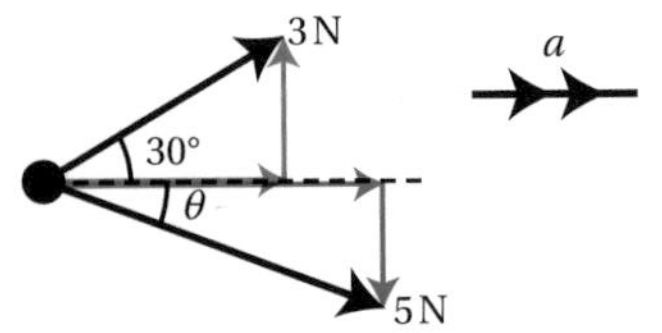

a

Always draw a diagram.

$(\uparrow): 3\sin 30^\circ - 5\sin\theta = 0$

Resolve in the y direction and set equal to zero (no acceleration, so equilibrium in this direction).

$\sin\theta=\frac{3}{5}\sin 30^\circ$

Rearrange to find $\sin\theta$.

$\sin\theta=\frac{3}{10}$

$\sin^2\theta+\cos^2\theta=1$

$\cos\theta=\sqrt{1-\sin^2\theta}$

$=\sqrt{1-\frac{9}{100}}$

$=\frac{\sqrt{91}}{10}$

Use $\sin^2\theta+\cos^2\theta=1$ to convert $\sin\theta$ into $\cos\theta$. Since the angle is acute we only need to take the positive root as $\cos\theta>0$ for acute angles.

Continues on next page ...

b $(\rightarrow)$: $3\cos 30° + 5\cos\theta = 5a$

Resolve in the x direction and use Newton's second law.

$$a = \frac{1}{5}\left(\frac{3\sqrt{3}}{2} + \frac{5\sqrt{91}}{10}\right)$$

$$= \frac{3\sqrt{3} + \sqrt{91}}{10}\ \text{ms}^{-2}$$

When an object is in contact with a surface there is a contact force between them. If the contact is smooth this contact force (also called the normal reaction force) is perpendicular to the surface.

Fast forward

In Section 2 you will learn how to find the contact force in the presence of friction.

WORKED EXAMPLE 21.3

A box of mass 18 kg moves on a smooth horizontal surface under the action of a constant force of magnitude 65 N acting at an angle of 35° above the horizontal.

a Find the magnitude of the normal contact force between the box and the surface.

b The box's speed increases from 0.6 m s^{-1} to 1.3 m s^{-1}. How far does the box travel in that time?

a

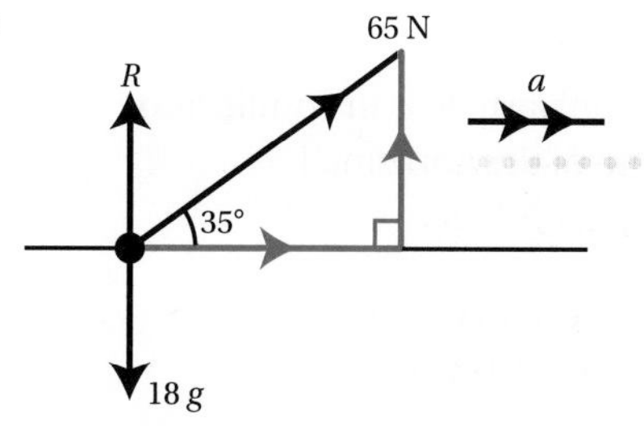

Draw a diagram showing all the forces. Don't forget the weight and the normal contact force.
The 65 N force needs to be resolved in horizontal and vertical directions.

$(\uparrow)$: $R + 65\sin 35 - 18g = 0$

$R = 139$ N (3 s.f.)

There is no acceleration in the vertical direction.

b $(\rightarrow)$: $65\cos 35 = 18a$

$a = 2.958\ldots$ m s^{-2}

Use Newton's second law in the horizontal direction to find the acceleration.

$1.3^2 = 0.6^2 + 2(2.958\ldots)s$

$s = 0.225$ m (3 s.f.)

Use $v^2 = u^2 + 2as$ to find the distance travelled.

When an object is in equilibrium, the resolved part of the net force in any direction is zero.

Fast forward

You will meet more complex equilibrium problems in Section 4.

Fast forward

In Section 4 you will see that you can also solve the following problem using a triangle of forces.

WORKED EXAMPLE 21.4

A particle of mass 4 kg is attached to the ceiling by two light inextensible strings. The strings make angles of 30° and 35° with the horizontal, as shown in the diagram.

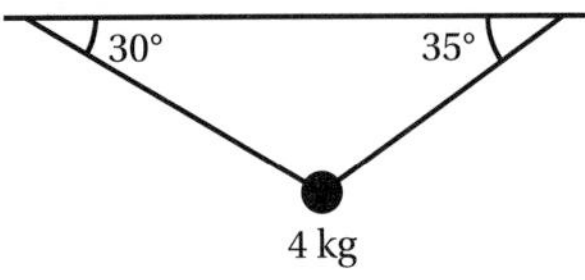

Given that the particle is in equilibrium, find the magnitude of the tension in each string.

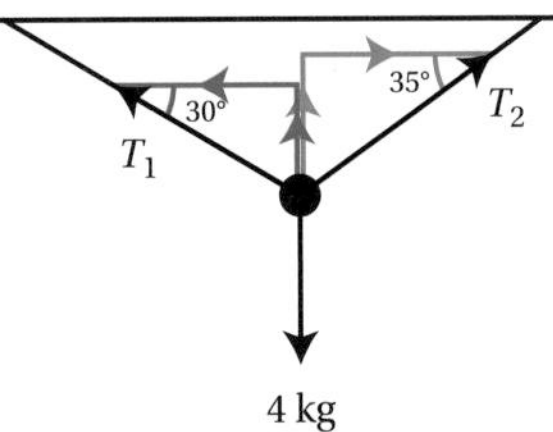

Resolve the tension forces in horizontal and vertical directions...

$(\rightarrow)$: $T_1\cos 30° - T_2\cos 35° = 0$

Since the particle is in equilibrium the sum of the horizontal components is zero...

$(\uparrow)$: $T_1\sin 30° + T_2\sin 35° - 4g = 0$

... and the sum of the vertical components is zero.

From the first equation:

$$T_2 = \frac{T_1\cos 30°}{\cos 35°}$$

These are two simultaneous equations for T_1 and T_2. The best way to solve them is to substitute T_2 from the first equation into the second.

Substitute into the second equation:

$$T_1\sin 30° + \left(\frac{T_1\cos 30°}{\cos 35°}\right)\sin 35° = 4g$$

$$\Rightarrow T_1\left(\sin 30° + \frac{\cos 30°\sin 35°}{\cos 35°}\right) = 4g$$

$$\Rightarrow T_1 = 35.4\text{ N (3 s.f.)}$$

It is best to enter the expression in the large bracket into your calculator in one go, then divide 4g by it.

$$T_2 = \frac{T_1\cos 30°}{\cos 35°} = 37.5\text{ N (3 s.f.)}$$

Use the 'unrounded' value of T_1 in this calculation.

The next example illustrates (in part **b**) how to resolve forces in a direction that is not horizontal or vertical.

Fast forward

Resolving in the direction of motion will also be used with inclined planes in Section 3.

WORKED EXAMPLE 21.5

A toy helicopter of mass 0.2 kg has its rotors set so that the force provided by the engine is given by $\mathbf{F} = a\mathbf{i} + b\mathbf{j}$, where a and b can be varied using a remote control, but the magnitude of **F** is always 3 N. The unit vector **i** is horizontal and **j** is vertical. Take $g = 9.8$ m s^{-2}.

Find the acceleration of the helicopter in the following two cases.

a the helicopter is set to fly horizontally

b the helicopter starts from rest and accelerates at 45° above the horizontal.

a

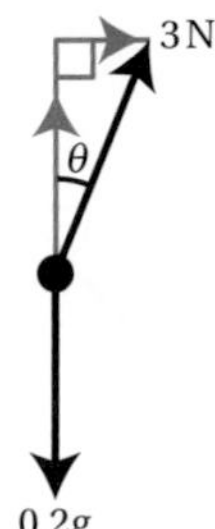

Always draw a diagram. You could define θ to be the angle the force F makes with the vertical or the horizontal. Here it is convenient to choose the vertical.

$(\uparrow)$: $3\cos\theta - 0.2g = 0$

There is no vertical acceleration.

$\cos\theta = \dfrac{1.96}{3}$

$\theta = 49.2°$

$(\rightarrow)$: $3\sin\theta = 0.2a$

Use Newton's second law in the horizontal direction.

$a = 15\sin\theta$

$= 11.4$ m s^{-2}

b Resolve in the direction of motion.

The 3 N force acts at angle ϕ above 45°:

The resultant force acts 45° above the horizontal, so choose this direction to resolve in. The net force in the perpendicular direction is zero.

(You could solve this problem by resolving horizontally and vertically. However, resolving in the direction of motion gives simpler equations.)

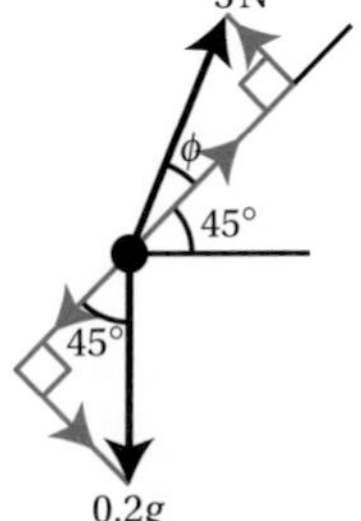

Perpendicular to movement:

$(\nwarrow)$: $3\sin\phi - 0.2g\cos 45 = 0$

$\sin\phi = \dfrac{0.2\times 9.8}{3\sqrt{2}} = 0.462$

$\phi = 27.5°$

In direction of movement:

$(\nearrow)$: $3\cos\phi - 0.2g\sin 45 = 0.2a$

$a = 6.37$ m s^{-2}

EXERCISE 21A

1 In each of the following systems, a particle on a horizontal surface is acted on by two forces, $\mathbf{F}_1$ and $\mathbf{F}_2$. Find the **i** and **j** components of the resultant force, where **j** represents due north and **i** represents due east.

a **i** $\mathbf{F}_1 = 3\mathbf{i} + 2\mathbf{j}$, $\mathbf{F}_2$ has magnitude 5 N and acts at bearing 60°.

ii $\mathbf{F}_1 = 5\mathbf{i} - 7\mathbf{j}$, $\mathbf{F}_2$ has magnitude 12 N and acts at bearing 105°.

b **i** $\mathbf{F}_1$ has magnitude 7 N and acts at bearing 15°, $\mathbf{F}_2$ has magnitude 8 N and acts at bearing 210°.

ii $\mathbf{F}_1$ has magnitude 7 N and acts at bearing 75°, $\mathbf{F}_2$ has magnitude 7 N and acts at bearing 285°.

2 A particle of mass m kg hangs at rest attached to two light inextensible strings at angles θ_1 and θ_2 from the horizontal.

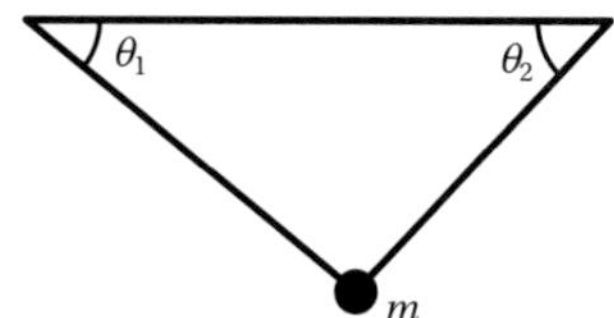

For each system, find the tension in each string.

a **i** $m = 5$ kg, $\theta_1 = 0°$, $\theta_2 = 10°$

ii $m = 8$ kg, $\theta_1 = 30°$, $\theta_2 = 30°$

b **i** $m = 15$ kg, $\theta_1 = 50°$, $\theta_2 = 70°$

ii $m = 10$ kg, $\theta_1 = 20°$, $\theta_2 = 30°$

3 Find the resultant force acting on the object in the diagram below, giving your answer in the form $a\mathbf{i} + b\mathbf{j}$.

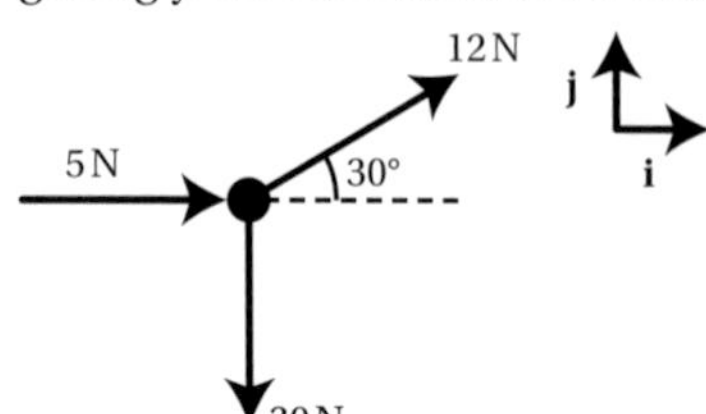

4 In the following diagram, the particle is in equilibrium.

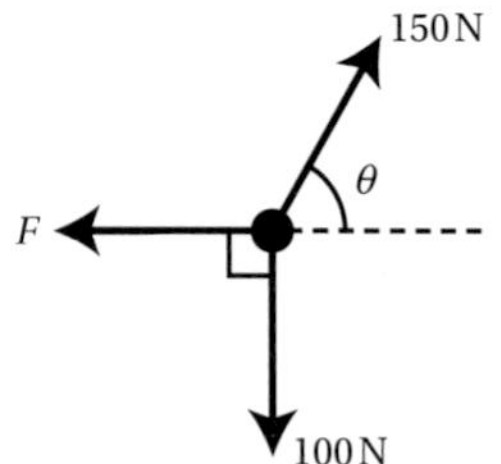

a Find the angle θ.

b Find the force F.

5 A mass of 200 g is being held in equilibrium, in the vertical plane, by a string at an angle θ to the vertical with tension T N and a horizontal force of 5 N. You may take $g = 10$ m s^{-2}.

a Show that $T\cos\theta = 2$.

b Find the value of θ.

c Find the value of T.

Tip

Remember that if a particle is in equilibrium, the resultant force is zero.

6 Three friends are pulling a 100 kg load across a smooth horizontal surface, using horizontal ropes. Alf pulls with a force of 200 N. Bert pulls with a force 150 N and is positioned at an angle 15° clockwise from Alf. Charlie pulls with force k N and is positioned at an angle 40° clockwise from Bert.

Modelling the load as a particle, and given that the load begins to move exactly towards Bert, find k and determine the initial acceleration of the load.

7 Two forces of magnitudes 8 N and 15 N act at a point, P.

a Given that the two forces are perpendicular to each other, find:

  i the angle between the resultant and the 15 N force

  ii the magnitude of the resultant force.

b If it is given instead that the resultant of the two forces acts in a direction perpendicular to the 8 N force, find:

  i the angle between the resultant and the 15 N force

  ii the magnitude of the resultant.

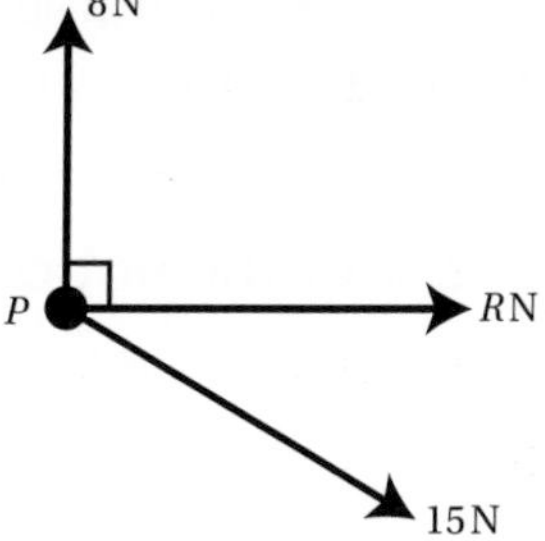

8 A particle with mass 1 kg hangs at rest suspended by two light inextensible strings. One string is at an angle of 30° to the horizontal and the other is at an angle of 45° to the horizontal.

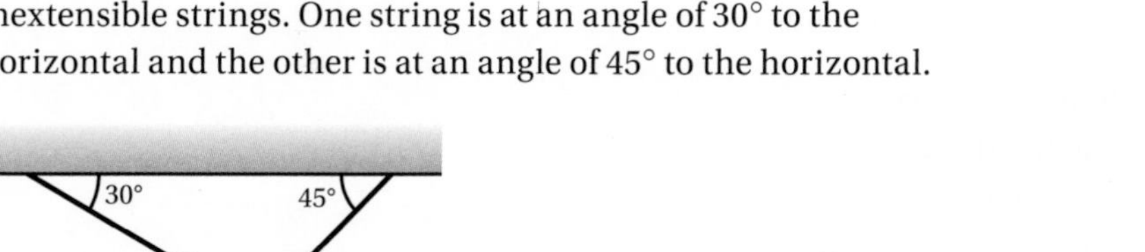

Find the tension in the two strings.

9 A small, smooth ring, R, of weight 5 N is threaded on a light, inextensible, taut string. The ends of the string are attached to fixed points A and B at the same horizontal level. A horizontal force of magnitude 4 N is applied to R. In the equilibrium position the angle ARB is a right angle, and the portion of the string attached to B makes an angle θ with the horizontal.

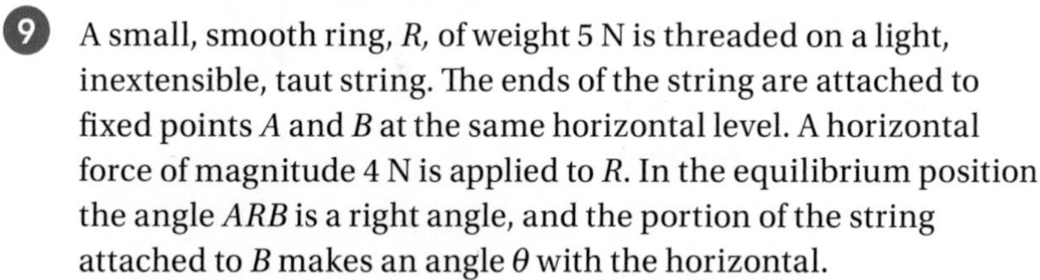

a Explain why the magnitude of the tension T is the same in each part of the string.

b Find T and θ.

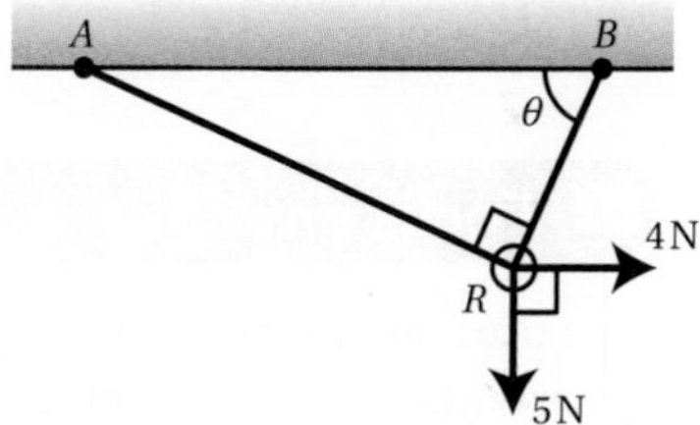

10 A light, smooth ring, R, is threaded on a light, inextensible string. One end of the string is attached to a fixed point, A. The other end of the string is threaded through a fixed smooth ring, S, directly below A, and attached to a particle of mass 2 kg. The angle SAR equals $\alpha°$.

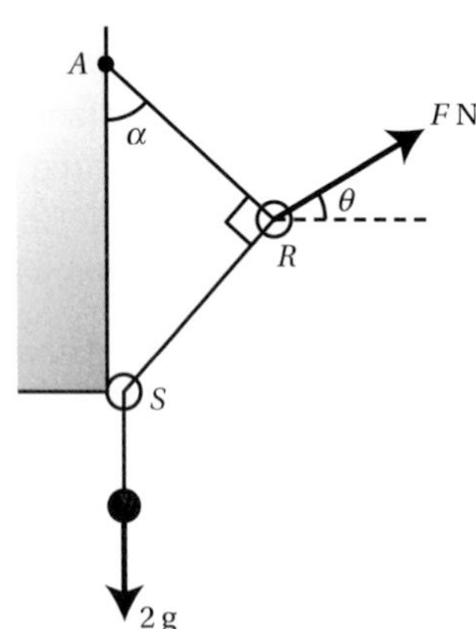

A force of magnitude F N is applied to ring R at an angle θ with the horizontal.

a Given that the string is taut, find the exact value of F required to maintain the system in equilibrium with angle $ARS = 90°$ and $\theta = 0°$.

b Given that $\angle ARS = 90°$ and the system is in equilibrium, find the relationship between θ and α.

c If ring R actually has mass 0.1 kg, find the new force, F, required to hold the system in equilibrium with angle $ARS = 90°$ and $\theta = 0°$, and determine the new value of α.

Section 2: Coefficient of friction

In Student Book 1 you met friction as a constant force opposing motion. However, the magnitude of the frictional force depends on:

- the force pushing the object into the surface
- the roughness of the object and the surface
- any external forces applied to the object.

Imagine a heavy box resting on a rough horizontal floor. You pull the box with a force P. When P is small, the box remains at rest and the frictional force exactly counter balances P.

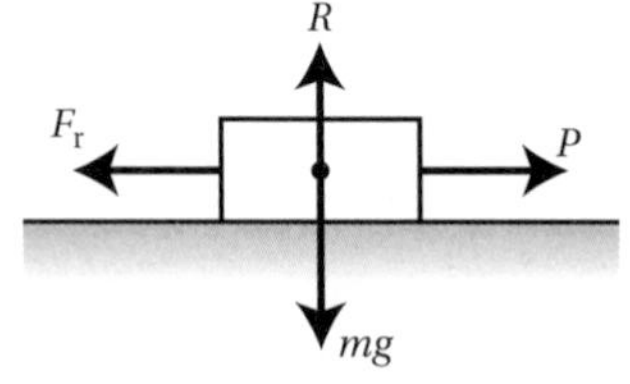

If the pulling force is strong enough, friction will be overcome and the box will start to accelerate. There must therefore be a maximum value of friction, called **limiting friction**. When friction is at its limiting value, the object is on the point of moving and is said to be in **limiting equilibrium**.

If the box is heavier it will take a larger force to move it; this suggests that the magnitude of the limiting friction depends on the magnitude of the normal contact force between the object and the surface. Similarly, a box is more difficult to move on a rough carpet than on a smooth floor.

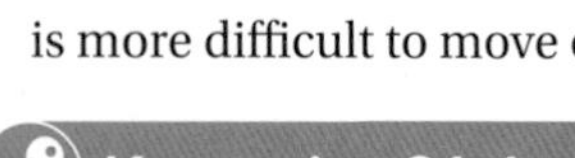

Key point 21.1

The maximum or limiting value of friction, F_{max}, is given by:

$$F_{max} = \mu R$$

where R is the normal contact force between the object and the surface, and μ is the **coefficient of friction**.

Focus on ...

Focus on ... Problem solving 3 asks you to decide whether values of certain quantities (including frictional force and μ) are reasonable in the given contexts.

The diagram at the side shows how the frictional force depends on the external (pushing or pulling) force.

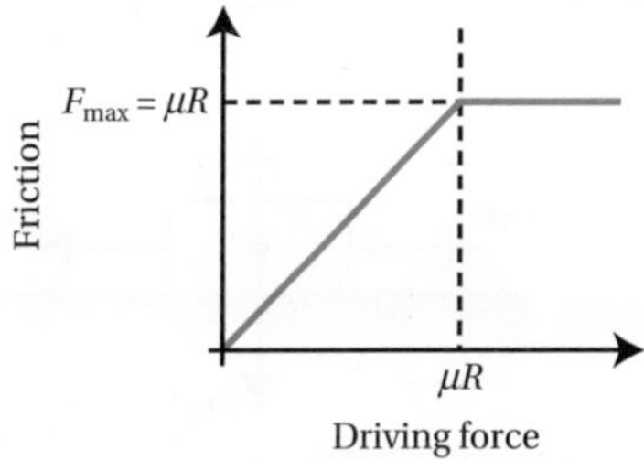

If the external force is not sufficiently strong to overcome F_{max}, the frictional force will just match it so that the object remains at rest. In this case $F_r < \mu R$.

Once the object is moving, the frictional force remains constant at F_{max}.

If more than one force is acting on an object, the frictional force will match the component of the resultant force parallel to the surface, up to the limiting value.

Key point 21.2

If the sum of all the forces on a particle, excluding friction F, is smaller than F_{max}, then:

- the particle will remain at rest
- F_r will have an equal magnitude and opposite direction to the sum of the other forces.

Explore

The coefficient of friction between the ground and a static object is in fact usually slightly higher than the coefficient of friction between the ground and a moving object; the graph above right should look more like this.

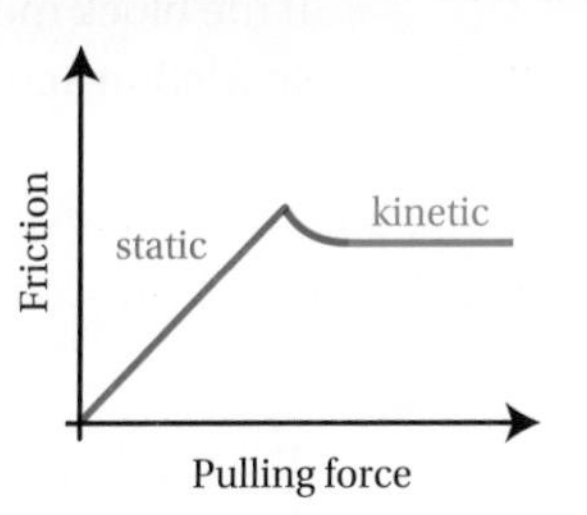

Find out more about static and dynamic (kinetic) friction.

WORKED EXAMPLE 21.6

A block of mass 10 kg lies at rest on a rough horizontal surface. Attached to opposite ends of the block are two light strings, each of which is under 5 N tension. The coefficient of friction, $\mu = 0.2$. Take $g = 9.8$ m s^{-2}.

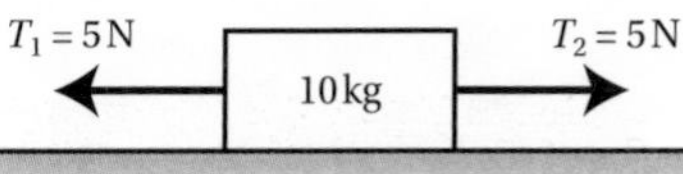

a The tension in the left string is increased to 10 N.
Show that the block remains at rest.

b The tension in the right string is then increased to 30 N.
Show that the block moves, and determine its acceleration.

Continues on next page ...

a

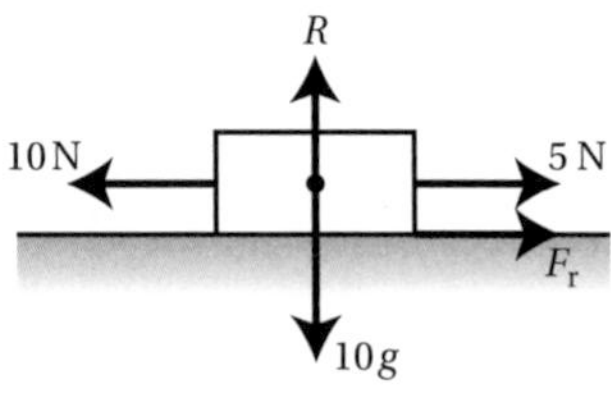

Always draw a diagram. If the block moves it will be to the left, so friction acts to the right.

$(\uparrow)$: $R - 10g = 0$

$R = 98$ N

Since any movement will be horizontal, there is no vertical acceleration.

$\therefore$ Maximum friction is $\mu R = 19.6$ N.

Calculate limiting friction μR.

Horizontal forces without friction:

$10 - 5 = 5\text{ N} < 19.6\text{ N}$

The frictional force can take the value 5 N, so the block will not move.

Friction will oppose the horizontal resultant without friction, up to a maximum of limiting friction. Since the resultant without friction is less than limiting friction, the object will not move. Friction will just balance the resultant of the other forces.

b As before $|F_r| \leqslant 19.6$.

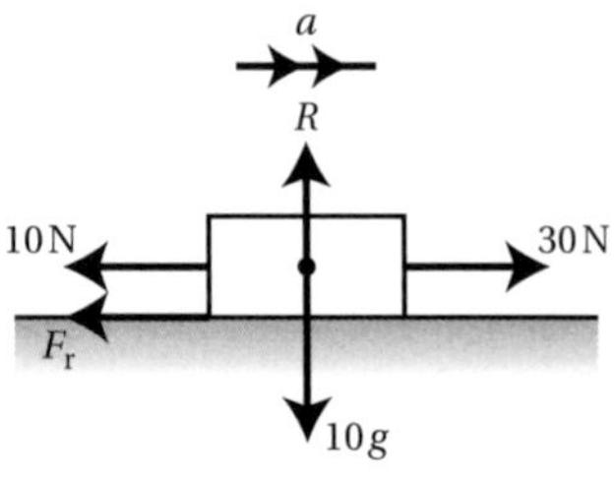

If the block moves it will now be to the right, so friction acts to the left.

Horizontal forces without friction:
$30 - 10 = 20\text{ N} > 19.6\text{ N}$

The frictional force takes the limiting value $F_r = 19.6$ N.

The resultant of the horizontal forces without friction exceeds the limiting friction, so friction takes it limiting value.

$(\rightarrow)$: $30 - 10 - 19.6 = 10a$
$a = 0.04\text{ m s}^{-2}$

Use F = ma in the horizontal direction.

Notice that the frictional force acts in different directions in part **a** and part **b** of Worked example 21.6 because it must always be in the opposite direction to that in which the object would move in the absence of friction.

Tip

In some questions you may be initially uncertain in which direction the friction acts. If you calculate a negative friction force in your answer, you have probably drawn the friction in the wrong direction. Change your diagram and adjust your equations.

Focus on ...

See Focus on ... Proof 4 for proofs of formulae for the minimum force required to move a particle on a rough surface, in various situations.

WORKED EXAMPLE 21.7

Two blocks, A and B, lie at rest on a rough horizontal surface, with block A on top of block B. The coefficient of friction between the blocks is 0.15, the mass of block A is 5 kg and the mass of block B is 8 kg. The coefficient of friction between block B and the surface is 0.3. A horizontal light, inextensible string is attached to block B, and the tension in the string is $T = 5$ N.

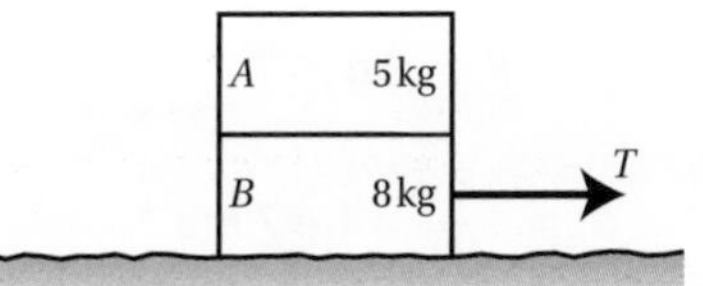

a Show that the system remains at rest.

The tension in the string is increased to 100 N and block A begins to slide on block B.

b What is the acceleration of each block?

a Treating the blocks as a single object of mass 13 kg, let frictional force between B and the surface be F_{BS}:

Since you are interested in the motion of the whole system, you can treat the two blocks as a single object.

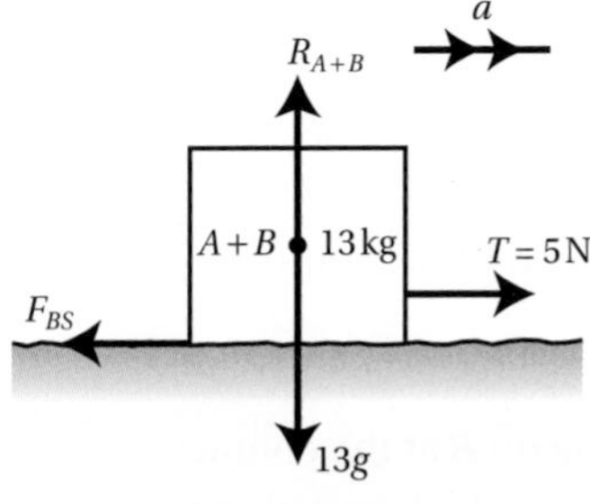

Consider horizontal and vertical components separately. Remember to include the normal reaction force in your diagram.

$(\uparrow)$: $R_{A+B} - 13g = 0$

$R_{A+B} = 13g$

There is no movement in the vertical direction, so the net force is zero.

Limiting friction: $0.3 \times 13g = 38.22$ N

Friction will oppose the tension up to a maximum of limiting friction.

The tension is less than the limiting frictional force, so $F_{BS} = 5$ N and the system remains at rest.

b 100 N exceeds the limiting friction (38.22 N) so the blocks will move, under the action of force $100 - 38.22 = 61.78$ N.

If A is sliding on B, B itself must be sliding on the floor. (There will be different frictional force between the two blocks, and between block B and the floor.)

Let the frictional force between the blocks be F_{AB}.

For the upper block, A:

Since the two blocks may move with different accelerations, consider forces for each block separately, starting with block A.

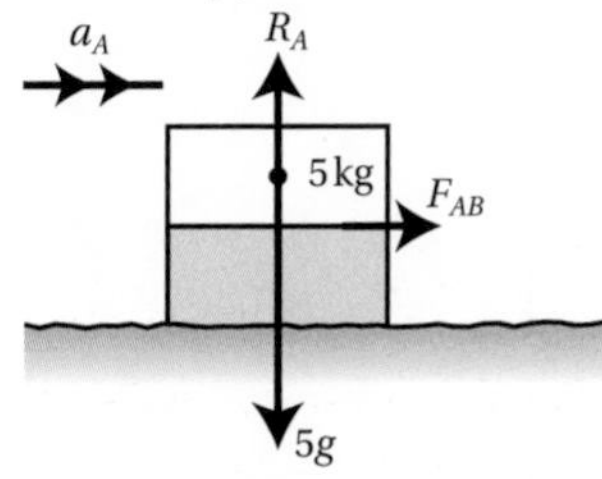

$(\uparrow)$: $R_A - 5g = 0$ (1)

$R_A = 5g$

Continues on next page ...

$F_{AB} = 0.15 \times 5g = 7.35$ N

Since the block is moving, the magnitude of the frictional force is μR_A.

$(\rightarrow)$: $F_{AB} = 5a_A$ (2)

$$a_A = \frac{7.35}{5} = 1.47 \text{ m s}^{-2}$$

For block B:

Now look at the lower block, considering vertical components first. According to Newton's third law, the normal reaction force R_A acts downwards on block B.

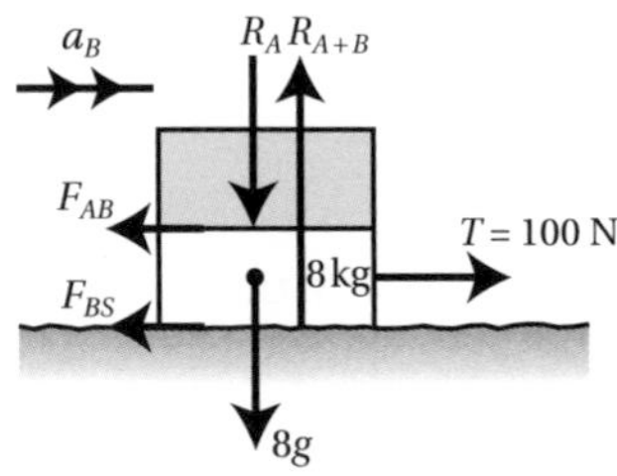

$(\uparrow)$: $R_{A+B} - 8g - R_A = 0$

Substituting for R_A from (1):

$R_{A+B} = 13g$

$F_{BS} = 0.3(13g) = 38.22$ N

The frictional force between block B and the surface is $0.3 \times R_{A+B}$.

$(\rightarrow)$: $100 - F_{AB} - F_{BS} = 8a_B$

Substituting F_{AB} from (2):

$$a_B = \frac{100 - 38.22 - 7.35}{8} = 6.80 \text{ m s}^{-2}$$

The frictional force acting on B at the contact with A equals F_{AB} from the calculation above (but acts to the left) – this follows from Newton's third law.

Did you know?

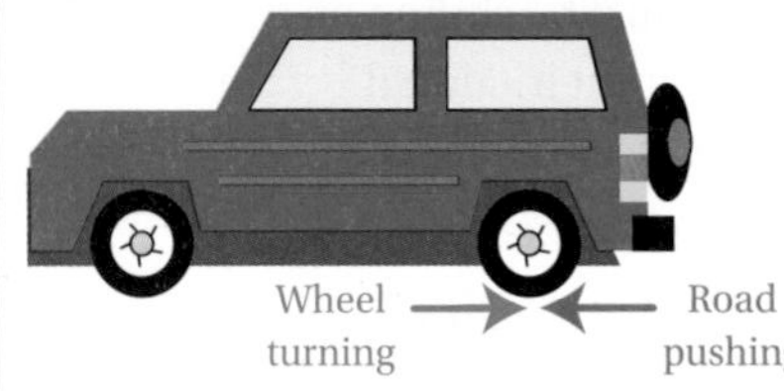

Although you may normally think of friction as a force that resists motion, it in fact enables motion in some cases. For example, you can walk only because of the friction between your feet and the ground (which is why it is so difficult to walk on ice). Friction also enables a car to move forward: as the wheels rotate, the friction force prevents slipping, and this in turn produces a forward force on the car.

It may be necessary to resolve all the forces before the direction of the frictional force can be calculated.

WORKED EXAMPLE 21.8

A particle of mass 2.3 kg rests on a rough horizontal surface and the coefficient of friction between the particle and the surface is 0.25. The unit vectors **i** and **j** are both in the horizontal plane.

Two horizontal forces act on the particle: $\mathbf{F}_1 = (3\mathbf{j} - 2\mathbf{i})$ N and $\mathbf{F}_2 = 6\mathbf{i}$ N.

a The frictional force $\mathbf{F} = (a\mathbf{i} + b\mathbf{j})$ N. Find a and b.

b A third force $\mathbf{F}_3 = -13\mathbf{i}$ N is applied. Find the new frictional force in the form $\mathbf{F} = (p\mathbf{i} + q\mathbf{j})$ N.

a $\underline{F}_1 + \underline{F}_2 = (4\underline{i} + 3\underline{j})$ N — Find the sum of all the given forces.

Sum of all the forces without friction is:

$\sqrt{4^2 + 3^2} = 5$ N

Normal reaction equals weight since there is no vertical movement: — Compare to the maximal friction.

$R = 2.3g = 22.54$ N

Limiting friction $\mu R = 5.635 > 5$

The particle will not move and the friction will counter the $4\underline{i} + 3\underline{j}$ force. — The sum of the two forces is less than maximal friction, so the particles will be in equilibrium.

$\underline{F}_r = -(4\underline{i} + 3\underline{j})$ N

b $\underline{F}_1 + \underline{F}_2 + \underline{F}_3 = (-9\underline{i} + 3\underline{j})$ N — Find the sum of the three given forces.

The magnitude is:

$\sqrt{(-9)^2 + 3^2} = 3\sqrt{10}$ N $= 9.49$ N

Limiting friction $5.635 < 9.49$ — Compare to the magnitude of the maximal friction (as found in part **a**).

The friction force has magnitude 5.635 N in the direction of $(-9\underline{i} + 3\underline{j})$. Hence, the friction force is:

$\frac{5.635}{9.49}(9\underline{i} + 3\underline{j}) = (3.44\underline{i} - 1.78\underline{j})$ N

The magnitude of the friction force is 5.635 N and its direction is opposite to the that of the $(-9\underline{i} + 3\underline{j})$ N force (which has magnitude 9.49). To change the magnitude without changing the direction, divide by 9.49 and multiply by 5.635.

The magnitude of the contact force

When an object is in contact with a rough surface, two forces act on it due to this contact:

- the normal reaction force (also called the **normal contact** force)
- the frictional force.

The resultant of these two forces is the total **contact force** between the object and the surface.

Because the two forces are perpendicular to each other, it is straightforward to find the magnitude of the resultant.

Key point 21.3

The contact force between two surfaces has two components: the normal contact force (R) and the frictional force (F_r).

The magnitude of the contact force is $\sqrt{R^2 + F_r^2}$.

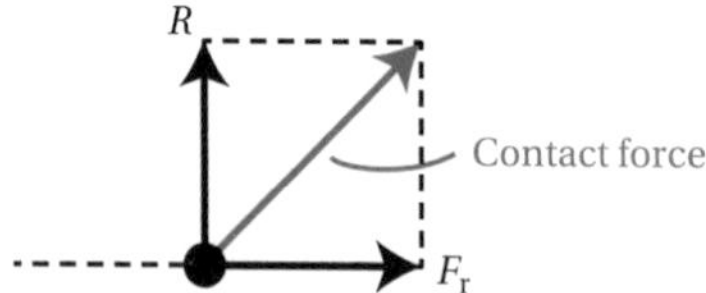

WORKED EXAMPLE 21.9

A box of mass 20 kg rests on a rough horizontal table. The coefficient of friction between the box and the table is 0.3. A force of magnitude F N is applied to the box, at an angle of 24° above the horizontal.

Given that the box is on the point of moving:

a Find the value of F.

b Find the magnitude of the contact force between the box and the table.

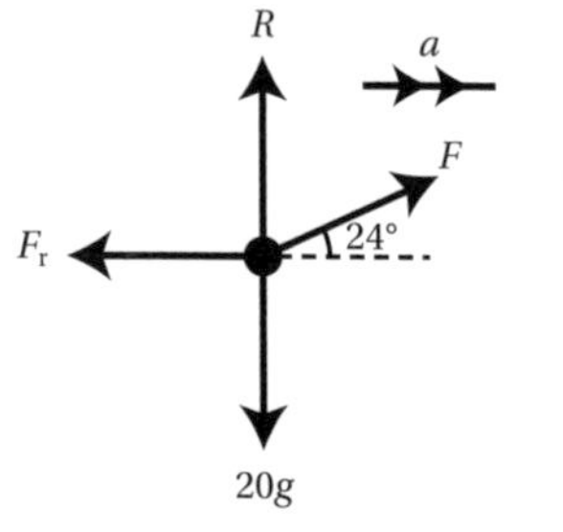

Draw a diagram showing all the forces. You need to include the weight, the normal contact force and the frictional force, as well as the force F.

a $(\rightarrow)$: $F\cos 24° - F_r = 0$

$(\uparrow)$: $R + F\sin 24° - 20g = 0$

Resolve horizontally and vertically. As the box is not moving, the net force in each direction is zero.

$F_r = 0.3R$

As the box is on the point of moving, the friction has its limiting value.

$R = 20g - F\sin 24°$

$F\cos 24° - 0.3(20g - F\sin 24°) = 0$

Since you want to find F, substitute R from the second equation into the first.

$F(\cos 24° + 0.3\sin 24°) = 6g$

$1.0356F = 58.8$

Collect the terms containing F and factorise.

$F = 56.8$ N (to 3 s.f.)

Take $g = 9.8$ m s^{-2}

Continues on next page ...

b

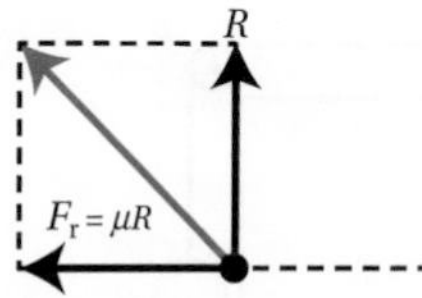

The contact force is resultant of the normal contact force and the frictional force.

$R = 20g - F\sin 24°$

$= 172.9\text{ N}$

Use the second equation from part **a** to find R.

$F_r = 0.3R = 51.9\text{ N}$

Use $F_r = \mu R$ to find the frictional force.

The magnitude of the contact force is

$\sqrt{172.9^2 + 51.9^2} = 181\text{ N} \text{ (3 s.f.)}$

EXERCISE 21B

1 In each of the following problems, a block of mass m kg is pulled along a rough horizontal surface by a light horizontal rope with tension T newtons. The acceleration is a m s^{-2}. The coefficient of friction is μ. Use $g = 10$ m s^{-2}.

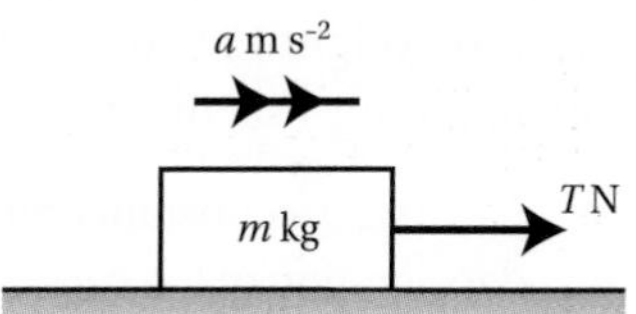

a Find μ when:

   i $m = 2, T = 5, a = 0.1$ **ii** $m = 8, T = 2, a = 0.2$

b Find a if:

   i $m = 1.1, T = 6, \mu = 0.455$ **ii** $m = 5, T = 1, \mu = 0.01$

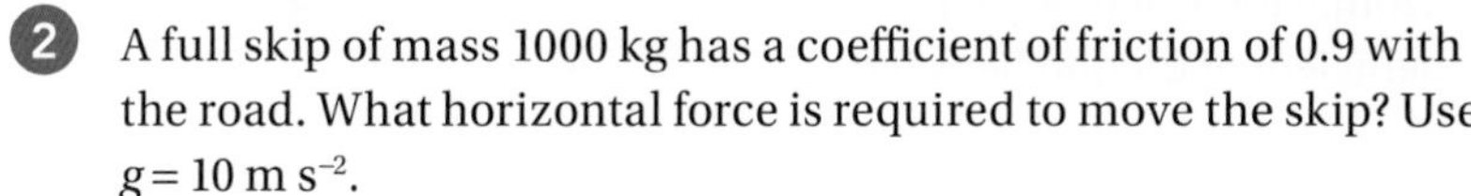

2 A full skip of mass 1000 kg has a coefficient of friction of 0.9 with the road. What horizontal force is required to move the skip? Use $g = 10$ m s^{-2}.

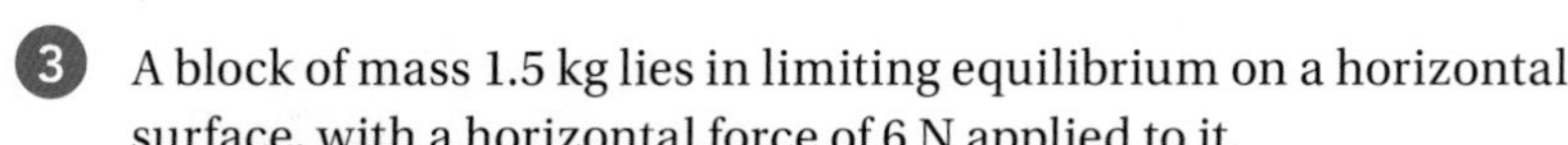

3 A block of mass 1.5 kg lies in limiting equilibrium on a horizontal surface, with a horizontal force of 6 N applied to it.

a Find the coefficient of friction between the block and the surface.

b Find the magnitude of the contact force between the block and the table.

4 A child pulls a toy box of mass 3.5 kg across a rough floor, using a light string tied to the box at one end. The tension in the string is 28 N and the string remains at an angle of 25° to the horizontal. If the coefficient of friction between the box and the floor is 0.7, what is the acceleration of the box?

5 Two particles, A and B, are connected by a light inextensible string.

Particle A, which weighs 8 N, is placed on a rough horizontal surface. The connecting string runs horizontally to a pulley, P, at the end of the surface, then vertically downward to B, which weighs 5 N. The pulley is light and free to rotate.

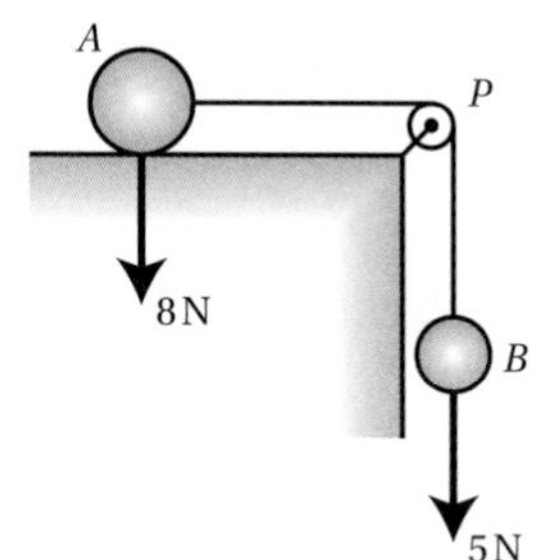

a The system is in limiting equilibrium. Calculate the coefficient of friction between A and the surface.

b A smooth ring with weight 1 N is threaded on to the string so that it lies on particle B. Calculate the downward acceleration of B.

6 Two particles, P and Q, are connected by a taut, light, inextensible string and lie at rest on a horizontal plane, with one particle at point A and the other at point B. P weighs 5 N and Q weighs 8 N. The coefficient of friction between either particle and the surface near point A is μ_A and the coefficient of friction between either particle and the surface near point B is μ_B.

When P is at A, a horizontal force of 7 N is applied to P acting in direction $\overrightarrow{QP}$, and the system is in limiting equilibrium. When P is at B, a horizontal force of 6 N is applied to P acting in direction $\overrightarrow{QP}$, and the system is once again in limiting equilibrium.

Calculate μ_A and μ_B.

Rewind

Connected particles, including pegs and pulleys, were covered in Student Book 1, Chapter 22.

7 A car of weight 12 000 N travelling at 25 m s^{-1} skids to a halt in 50 m, taking 4 seconds.

a Assuming a constant braking horizontal force, find the deceleration of the car.

b Assume that friction is the only horizontal force acting on the car and that $g = 10$ m s^{-2}. Find the coefficient of friction between the car and the road.

8 A particle of mass 5 kg rests on a rough horizontal table. The coefficient of friction between the particle and the table is 0.4. A light inextensible string, inclined at an angle 20° above the horizontal, is attached to the particle. The tension in the string is 15 N.

a Show that the particle remains at rest.

b Find the magnitude of the contact force between the particle and the table.

9 A particle of mass m lies on a rough horizontal surface. The coefficient of friction between the particle and the surface is μ. A horizontal force acts on the particle, which is in limiting equilibrium. Show that the magnitude of the contact force between the particle and the surface is $mg\sqrt{1+\mu^2}$.

10 A particle of mass 1 kg lies on a rough horizontal surface, with the coefficient of friction between surface and particle equal to 0.75.

A light inextensible string is attached to the particle and tension is applied. The string is at an angle θ above the horizontal, where $0° < \theta < 90°$.

a Given the system is in limiting equilibrium, show that the tension T in the string satisfies the equation $T = \dfrac{5.88}{\sin(\theta+\alpha)}$ for some value α, and find α.

b The string will break if $T > 6$ N. Find the range of values for θ for which the particle will be caused to move by tension in the intact string.

c Find the maximum possible acceleration for the particle.

11 In the model for friction used in this section, which of the following factors affect the frictional force of a surface acting on an object?

A the contact surface area between the surface and object

B the speed of the object

C the acceleration of the object

D lubrication between the surface and the object

Section 3: Motion on a slope

If an object is on a slope (sometimes called an inclined plane) it is often convenient to resolve forces parallel or perpendicular to the slope. We use the same technique as for all resolving problems: drawing forces as the hypotenuse of a right-angled triangle with sides parallel and perpendicular to the slope.

WORKED EXAMPLE 21.10

A block of mass 2 kg slides down a smooth slope inclined at 20° to the horizontal. Find the acceleration of the block.

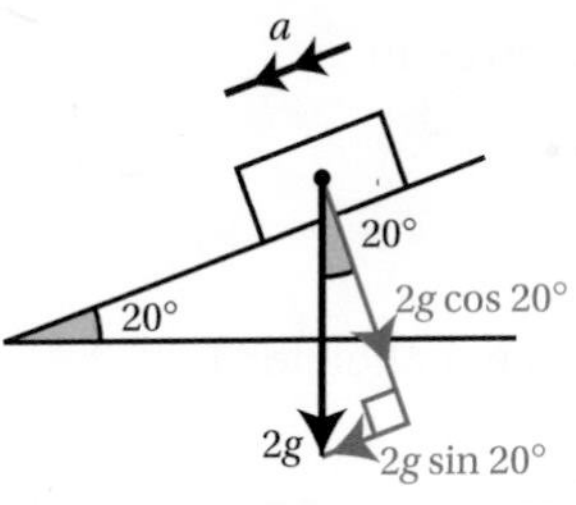

Always draw a diagram. The only force acting on the block is its weight.

Form a right-angled triangle with the force as hypotenuse and the sides parallel and perpendicular to the slope. The angle at the top of the triangle is 20°. (See text after this example for a general explanation.)

$(\swarrow)\ 2g \sin 20 = 2a$

$a = 3.35 \text{ m s}^{-2}$

Use $F = ma$ in the direction down the slope.

Weight comes up so often in inclined plane problems that it is useful to remember these general results:

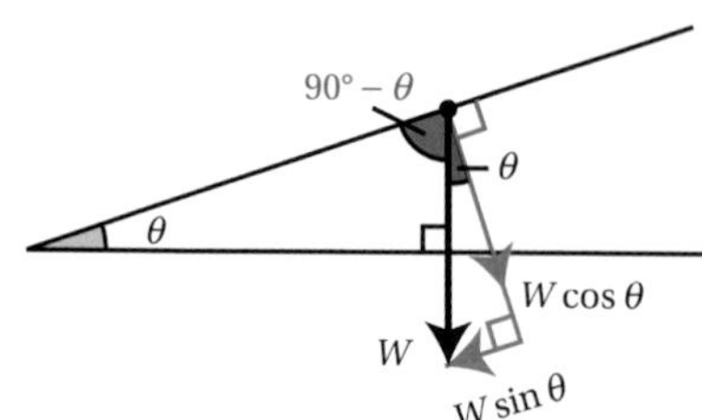

Let θ be the angle that the slope makes with the horizontal. The green angle equals $90° - \theta$ and, therefore, the blue angle is θ.

Tip

A good way of remembering this is to think about what happens when θ is zero. Then there is no component of weight parallel to the plane, and a component mg perpendicular to the plane.

Key point 21.4

The components of the weight of an object on a slope inclined at an angle θ to the horizontal are:

- down the slope: $mg \sin \theta$
- perpendicular to the slope: $mg \cos \theta$

WORKED EXAMPLE 21.11

A block with mass 3.5 kg lies on a smooth slope inclined at 15° to the horizontal, and is held in equilibrium by a string with tension T parallel to the slope.

Calculate T and the normal reaction force, R.

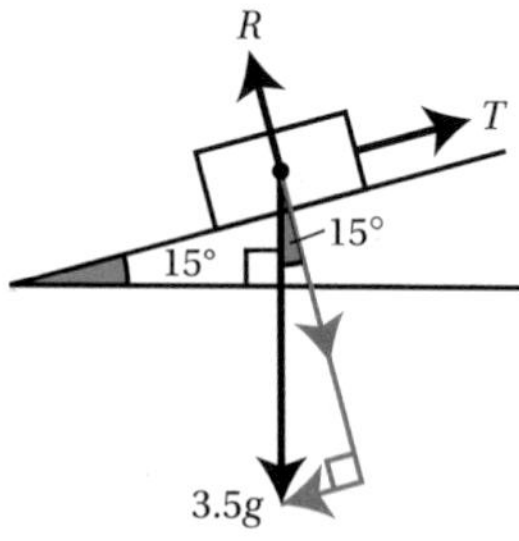

The system is in equilibrium, so the components of the resultant force parallel and perpendicular to the slope will be zero. (In fact, resolving in any direction will give a zero net force.)

Perpendicular to the slope:

($\nwarrow$): $R - 3.5g \cos 15 = 0$

$R = 3.5g \cos 15 \approx 33.1$ N

Resolving perpendicular to the slope gives an equation for R.

Parallel to the slope:

($\nearrow$): $T - 3.5g \sin 15 = 0$

$T = 3.5g \sin 15 \approx 8.88$ N

Resolving parallel to the slope gives an equation for T.

Some problems about motion on a slope also involve friction. As before, identify the direction of movement in the absence of friction, and assign the frictional force to act in the opposite direction.

WORKED EXAMPLE 21.12

A rough inclined plane makes angle θ with the horizontal. A particle, P, of mass m lies at rest on the slope.

a Given that P is on the point of slipping down the slope find, in terms of θ, the coefficient of friction between P and the slope.

b The particle is now attached to a light inextensible string. The string passes over a light pulley at the top of the slope. A particle, Q, of mass M is attached to the other end of the string and hangs freely under gravity. The particle P is on the point of moving up the slope. Show that $M = 2m\sin\theta$.

a

R

$F_r = \mu R$

θ

θ

mg

Draw a diagram: The forces acting on the particle are its weight and friction.

Without friction, the particle would move down the slope. Hence, the friction acts upslope.

Perpendicular to the slope:

$R - mg\cos\theta = 0$

$R = mg\cos\theta$

Resolve perpendicular to the slope to find R.

Down the slope:

$mg\sin\theta - F_r = 0$

But the particle is on the point of slipping, so $F_r = \mu R$

$$\mu = \frac{mg\sin\theta}{mg\cos\theta}$$

$= \tan\theta$

The particle is in equilibrium, so the component of the resultant force parallel to the slope is zero.

Since the particle is on the point of slipping, the friction is limiting.

b

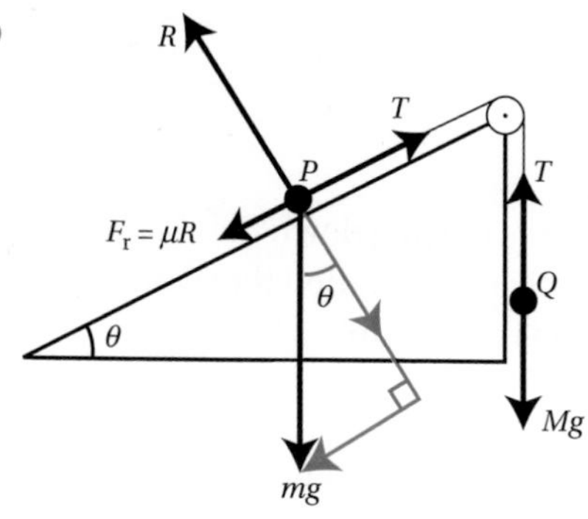

The forces acting on P now are its weight, friction, the tension in the string and the normal contact force.

Since P is on the point of moving up the slope, friction acts down the slope.

The forces acting on Q are its weight and tension.

Perpendicular to the slope:

$R = mg\cos\theta$

Consider, the contact normal forces on P first.

Down the slope:

$mg\sin\theta + \mu R = T$

$T = mg\sin\theta + \mu\, mg\cos\theta$

The particle is in limiting equilibrium again, so $F_r = \mu R$ and the net force is zero.

$= mg\sin\theta + \tan\theta(mg\cos\theta)$

Use $\mu = \tan\theta$ from part **a**.

$= mg\sin\theta + mg\sin\theta$

$= 2\,mg\sin\theta$

Use $\tan\theta\cos\theta = \sin\theta$.

Continues on next page ...

Forces on Q:

$Mg - T = 0$

$Mg = T = 2mg\sin\theta$

$M = 2m\sin\theta$

Now consider forces on Q, which is also in equilibrium.

WORKED EXAMPLE 21.13

A block, B, with mass 5 kg lies on a rough surface inclined at 15° to the horizontal. The coefficient of friction between block and surface is 0.3.

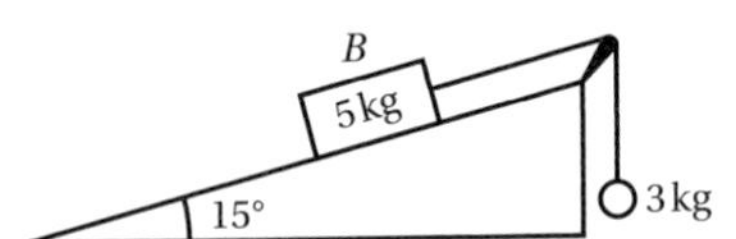

A light, inextensible string attached to the block passes over a smooth peg at the highest point of the surface (so that the length between block and peg is parallel to the slope) and is attached at its other end to a particle of mass 3 kg, which hangs freely.

The system is initially held at rest and then released. You may assume that the block does not reach the peg or the bottom of the slope, and that the particle does not reach the peg or the floor.

a Calculate the direction and magnitude of the frictional force between B and the surface.

b After the block has travelled 1 metre, the string breaks. Calculate the total distance it travels in the subsequent 10 seconds.

a

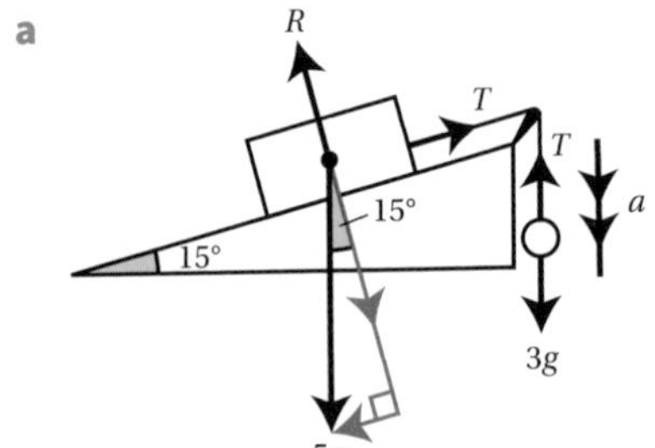

Always start by drawing a force diagram. You don't know which way the friction acts, so you will first find the direction the system would move if there was no friction.

For the block:

($\swarrow$): $5g\sin 15 - T = 5a$ (1)

For the particle:

($\uparrow$): $T - 3g = 3a$ (2)

Assume that the block is moving down the plane. If you get negative acceleration that will tell you that it is in fact moving up.

(1) + (2): $5g\sin 15 - 3g = 8a$

$a = -3.34\text{ m s}^{-2}$

Since you are interested in the direction of a, add the two equations to eliminate T.

Negative acceleration means that the block actually moves up the slope.

Net force on block without friction:

$5a = 5 \times 3.34 = 16.7\text{ N}$

Limiting friction:

$F_r = 0.3R$

You have found that, if there was no friction, the block would move up the slope. With friction, the block will move only if the sum of forces without friction is larger than the limiting friction.

Continues on next page ...

Block (↖): $R - 5g\cos 15 = 0$
$R = 47.3$ N

Resolve perpendicular to the slope to find R.

So $0.3R = 14.2$ N < 16.7 N
Hence, the block moves up the slope; the frictional force acts down the force and has magnitude 14.2 N.

Compare the limiting friction (14.2) to the sum of all the other forces without friction (16.7).

The friction is not strong enough to prevent motion up the slope.

b There are two separate phases of motion:

Phase 1: Moving up the slope with the string attached.

Phase 2: Moving up the slope without string, slowing down.

Phase 3: Possibly sliding back down the slope (or being kept still by friction).

You now know that the block initially accelerates up the slope.

When the string breaks, the block will continue to move up for a while, slow down and stop.

It then may start moving back down again, depending on whether the friction is strong enough to counteract gravity.

Phase 1:

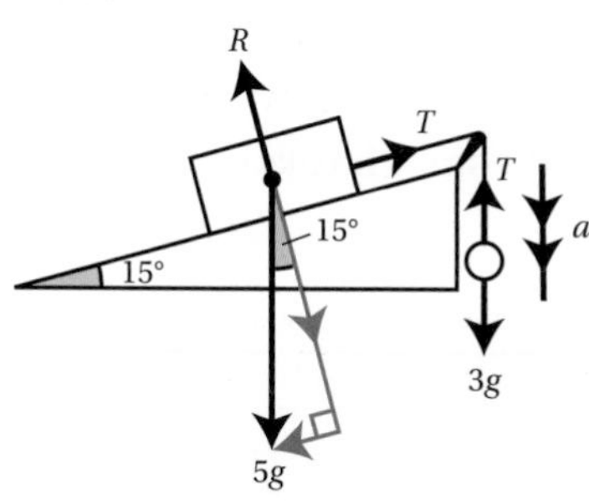

You need to know the speed of the block when the string breaks, so that you can find how far it travels before stopping. For this, you need to find the acceleration.

Particle: $3g - T = 3a$ (3)

Use '$F = ma$' for both particle and block, in the direction of motion for each one.

Block: $T - 5g\sin 15 - 14.2 = 5a$ (4)

You found in part **a** that the magnitude of the frictional force is 14.2.

(3) + (4): $3g - 5g\sin 15 - 14.2 = 8a$

$a = 0.315$ m s^{-2}

$u = 0, a = 0.315, s = 1, v = ?$

$v^2 = 0^2 + 2 \times 0.315 \times 1$

$v = 0.794$ m s^{-1}

You now need to know the speed of the block after it has travelled 1 m, using constant acceleration formula '$v^2 = u^2 + 2as$'.

Phase 2: Set $T = 0$ in (4)

$-5g\sin 15 - 14.2 = 5a$

$a = -5.38$ m s^{-2}

When the string breaks, the forces on the block are the component of gravity and friction, both with the same magnitude and direction as in equation (4).

Continues on next page ...

$u = 0.794, a = -5.38, v = 0, s = ?$

$0^2 = 0.794^2 + 2(-5.38)s$

$s = 0.0586$ m

Use a constant acceleration formula again to find the distance travelled before stopping.

$0 = 0.794 + (-5.38)t$

$t = 0.15$ s < 10 s

You also need to know whether the block takes less than 10 seconds to stop.

Phase 3: Movement after coming to rest

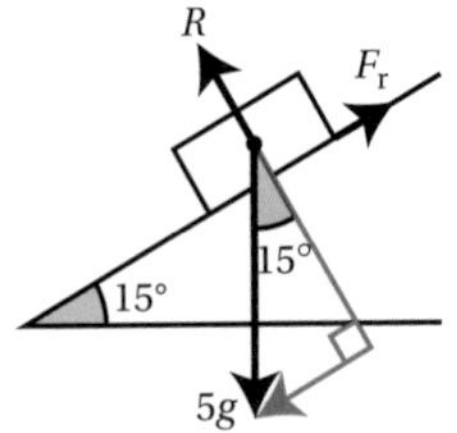

Once the block has stopped, it may or may not start to slip down the slope. You need to find out whether friction is strong enough to overcome the component of gravity pulling it down the slope.

Total force acting down the slope is $5g \sin 15 = 12.7$ N < 14.2 N.

You already know that the limiting friction is 14.2 N.

The force down the slope is less than maximal friction, so the block will remain at rest.

Total distance travelled after the string breaks is therefore equal to 0.0586 m.

The only movement after the string breaks is 0.0586 m.

EXERCISE 21C

Unless otherwise indicated, use $g = 9.8$ m s^{-2} in this exercise.

1 A particle of mass m kg is released from rest on a slope inclined at an angle θ to the horizontal, with coefficient of friction between particle and slope being μ.

For each of the following cases, determine the force of friction acting on the particle.

a **i** $m = 5, \theta = 30°, \mu = 0$ **ii** $m = 8, \theta = 45°, \mu = 0$

b **i** $m = 1, \theta = 30°, \mu = 0.8$ **ii** $m = 3, \theta = 20°, \mu = 1$

c **i** $m = 2, \theta = 60°, \mu = 0.2$ **ii** $m = 5, \theta = 45°, \mu = 0.1$

2 A particle P of mass m kg and a particle Q of mass M kg are connected by a light, inextensible string.

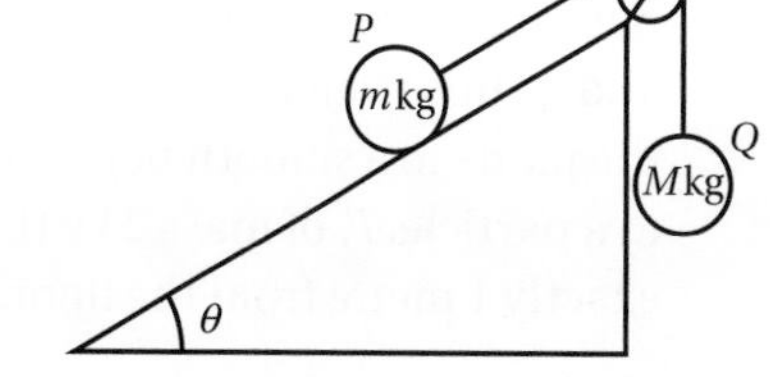

Particle P lies on a slope inclined at an angle θ to the horizontal. The string passes from P parallel to the line of greatest slope, and runs over a light pulley (which can rotate freely) at the top of the slope, then descends vertically to Q.

The coefficient of friction between P and the slope is μ.

For each of the following systems, find:

A the force of friction acting on P and its direction

B the acceleration of P when the system is released from rest.

a **i** $m = 5, M = 3, \theta = 30°, \mu = 0$

ii $m = 5, M = 3, \theta = 60°, \mu = 0$

b **i** $m = 8, M = 8, \theta = 45°, \mu = 0.2$

ii $m = 8, M = 4, \theta = 15°, \mu = 0.3$

c **i** $m = 5, M = 1, \theta = 30°, \mu = 0.7$

ii $m = 5, M = 1, \theta = 60°, \mu = 0.7$

3 A particle of mass 5 kg is projected with velocity 20 m s^{-1} up the line of steepest slope of a long smooth plane inclined at 30° to the horizontal. Using $g = 10$ m s^{-2}, calculate:

a the normal contact force between the plane and the particle

b the total distance travelled in the first 2 seconds.

4 A child of mass 30 kg is sliding down a slide at an angle of 40° to the horizontal.

a Find the normal contact force between the slide and the child.

b Find the acceleration if:

i the slide is smooth

ii there is a coefficient of friction of 0.1 between the child and the slide.

5 A block of mass 3 kg lies at rest on a rough board, with $\mu = 0.45$. If the board is slowly raised at one end, beyond what angle will the block begin to slide?

6 A particle P is projected upwards along a line of greatest slope from the foot of a surface inclined at 45° to the horizontal. The initial speed of P is 8 m s^{-1} and the coefficient of friction is 0.3. The particle P comes to instantaneous rest before it reaches the top of the inclined surface.

a Calculate the distance P moves before coming to rest.

b Calculate the time P takes before coming to rest.

c Find the time taken for P to return to its initial position from its highest point.

7 A block B of mass 1 kg lies on a smooth plane inclined at 35° to the horizontal. One end of a light, inextensible string is attached to B, and it runs from B upslope parallel to the line of greatest slope on the plane to a smooth peg. The other end of the string is attached to a particle, P, of mass 2 kg that hangs vertically below the peg exactly 1 metre from the floor.

The system is released from rest.

a Find the acceleration of B up the slope.

When P hits the floor, the string breaks.

b Assuming the initial distance between the block and the peg is sufficiently great that the block will not reach the peg, find the total distance travelled by the block when it instantaneously passes through its initial position.

Elevate

See Support sheet 18 for a further example on limiting equilibrium on a rough inclined plane, and for more practice questions.

8 A block of mass m lies on a flat, rough surface. The coefficient of friction between the block and the surface is μ. The surface is initially horizontal, and its inclination is gradually increased. When the inclination of the surface exceeds 42° to the horizontal, the block begins to move.

a Find μ.

b The inclination of the surface is increased further to 44°. Find, in terms of m, the magnitude of the contact force between the block and the surface.

9 Two small blocks, A and B, connected by a light inextensible string, lie with B above A on the line of greatest slope of a rough plane inclined at 30° to the horizontal. Block A has mass 2.5 kg and block B has mass 1.5 kg. The connecting string is 1 metre long, and block A begins 2 metres above the foot of the slope.

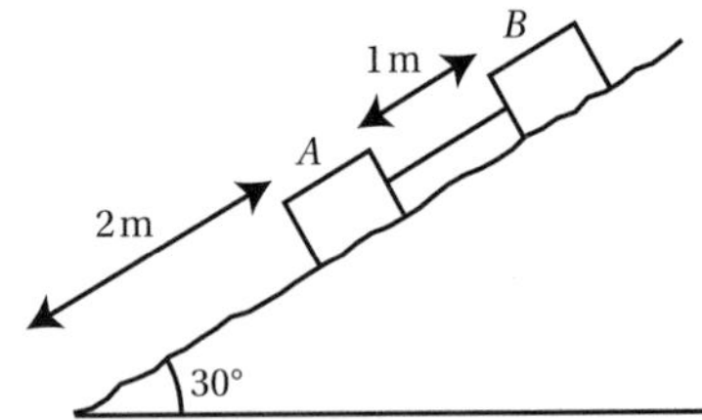

The coefficient of friction between each block and the surface is 0.15.

The system is released from rest at time $t = 0$; when block A reaches the foot of the slope, its motion stops immediately. Find the time at which B collides with A.

10 A particle P with mass 4.5 kg lies on a rough plane inclined at 30° to the horizontal. A light, inextensible string connects to P, runs parallel with the line of greatest slope of the plane to a smooth peg, then vertically downwards through a smooth, free ring R, with mass 2 kg, and then vertically upwards to attach to a fixed point S.

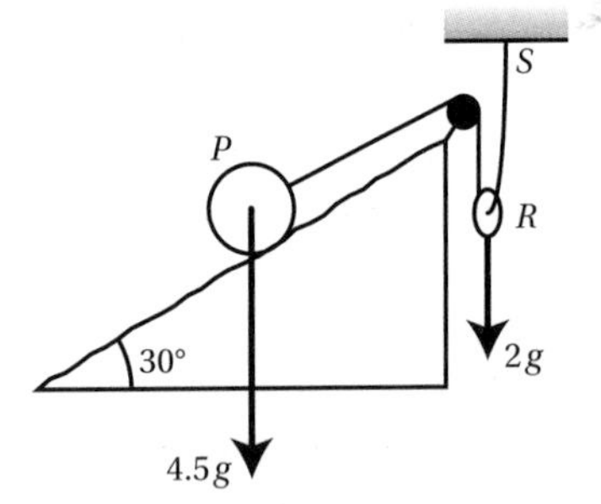

The coefficient of friction between P and the plane is 0.15.

a Let a be the acceleration of the ring when the system is released form rest. By considering the distance moved by each object, explain why the acceleration of P is $2a$.

b By considering forces on P, find an equation linking a and T with friction F.

c Find the direction and magnitude of the frictional force.

d Determine whether P will remain stationary, move up the slope or move down the slope when the system is released from rest.

11 A toy with mass 0.5 kg is placed on a rough surface inclined at 30° to the horizontal. Propulsion of the toy is achieved by directing two small fans, one on either side of the toy, set at an angle to provide a driving force for movement. The total force produced by the fans is 10 N and is directed to make the toy move up the slope.

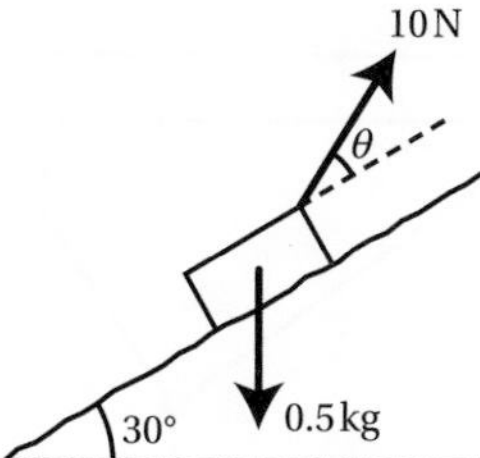

The coefficient of friction between the toy and the surface is 0.1.

a Find the acceleration of the toy up the slope if the fans are set to blow horizontally.

b Find the acceleration of the toy up the slope if the fans are set to blow parallel to the slope.

c The fans are set so that the direction of the driving force is $\theta°$ above the slope (i.e. at $(30+\theta)°$ above the horizontal, where $0° < \theta < 90°$). Find the value of θ that maximises the acceleration.

12 A block B of mass 3 kg lies on a surface inclined at 45° to the horizontal. A light, inextensible string is attached at one end to B, and runs from B up the slope parallel to the line of greatest slope on the plane to a smooth peg P. The string passes over the peg, through a smooth ring R of mass 4 kg, and is attached to a wall at W.

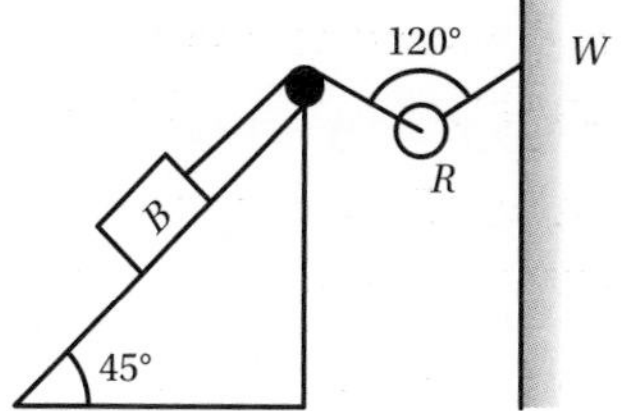

Given that the angle PRW equals 120° and the system is in equilibrium, determine the possible values for μ, the coefficient of friction between block B and the surface.

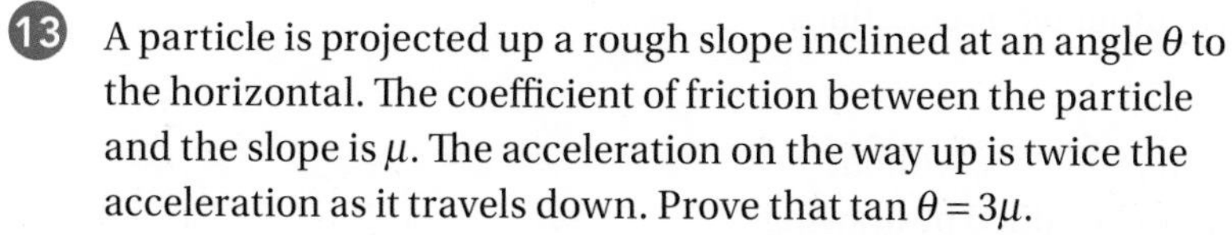

13 A particle is projected up a rough slope inclined at an angle θ to the horizontal. The coefficient of friction between the particle and the slope is μ. The acceleration on the way up is twice the acceleration as it travels down. Prove that $\tan\theta = 3\mu$.

Section 4: Further equilibrium problems

Throughout this chapter, and in Student Book 1, you solved problems about particles in equilibrium using the fact that the resultant force is zero. You usually resolved forces either horizontally and vertically, or parallel and perpendicular to a slope. However, you could look at the sum of the components of all the forces in any direction.

Key point 21.5

A particle is in equilibrium if and only if the sum of the components of all the forces in any given direction is zero.

It is often helpful to look at the components in a direction perpendicular to one of the unknown forces. You may need to calculate some additional angles.

WORKED EXAMPLE 21.14

A particle of weight 80 N is attached to two light inextensible strings, which are also attached to a horizontal ceiling. The strings are perpendicular to each other and make angles of 35° and 55° with the ceiling.

Find the tension in each string.

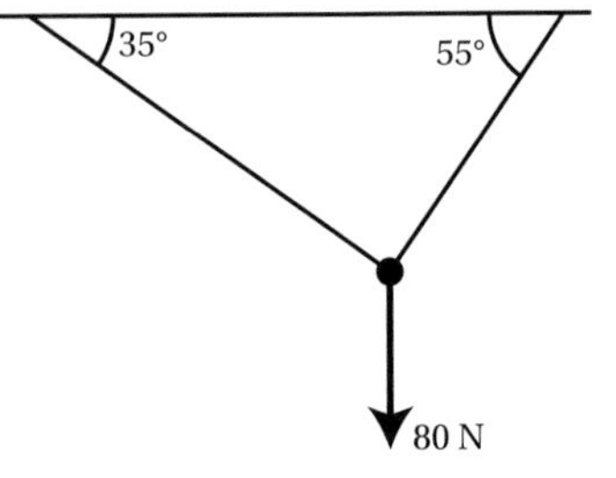

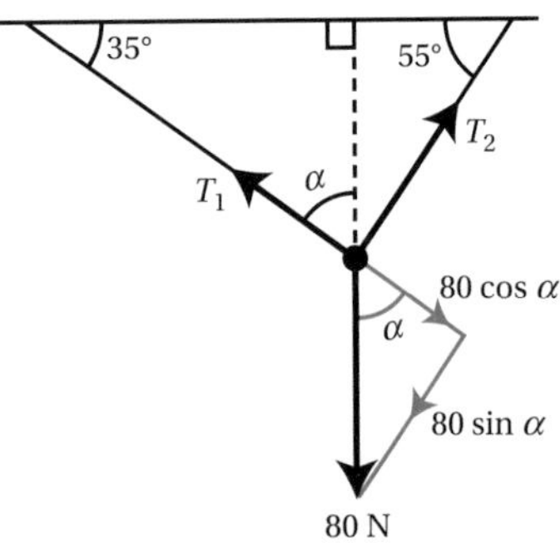

Look at the components in the direction of each string.

Since the strings are perpendicular, only the weight needs to be resolved.

Adding a perpendicular line allows you to find the angle between the weight and one of the strings.

$\alpha = 90° - 35° = 55°$

$T_1 - 80\cos 55 = 0 \Rightarrow T_1 = 45.9$ N

$T_2 - 80\sin 55 = 0 \Rightarrow T_2 = 65.5$ N

Since the particle is in equilibrium, the net force in the direction of each string is zero.

You could also solve the previous problem by resolving horizontally and vertically; you would then need to solve two simultaneous equations for T_1 and T_2.

There is an alternative way to solve equilibrium problems, without resolving any forces. Remember that vectors can be added by drawing arrows, joining the 'tail' of one vector to the 'head' of another. If the vectors add up to zero, this will result in a closed polygon.

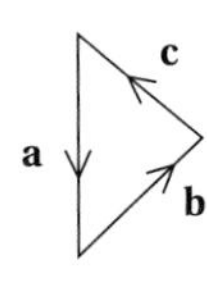

$\mathbf{a} + \mathbf{b} + \mathbf{c} = 0$

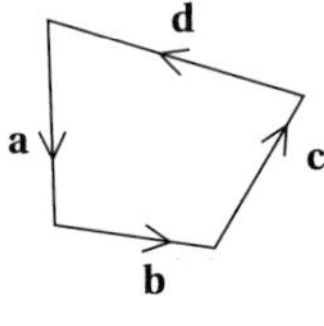

$\mathbf{a} + \mathbf{b} + \mathbf{c} + \mathbf{d} = 0$

Key point 21.6

If a particle is in equilibrium, the forces acting on it form a closed polygon.

WORKED EXAMPLE 21.15

Three forces act on a particle in the horizontal plane, as shown in the diagram. Given that the particle is in equilibrium, find, to the nearest degree, the angles between the 10 N force and each of the other two forces.

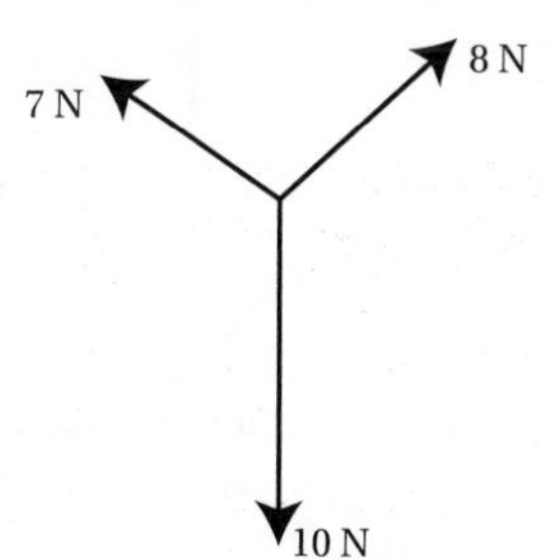

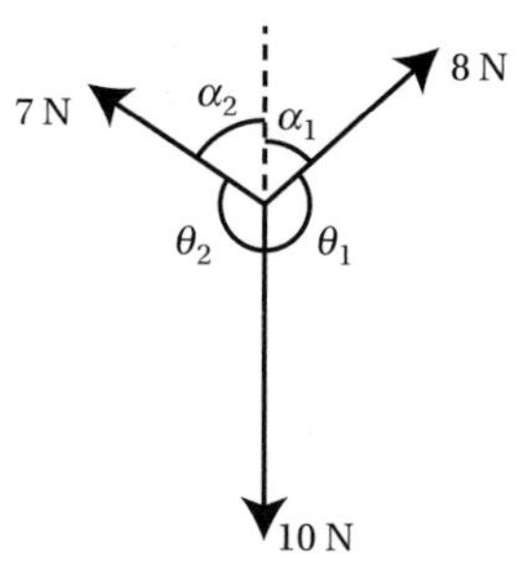

Label the angles you want to find.

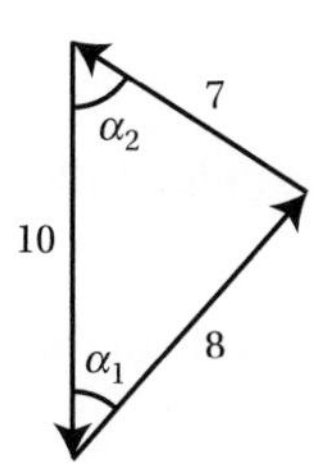

'Move' the vectors to form a triangle.

$\alpha_1 = 180° - \theta_1, \alpha_2 = 180° - \theta_2$

Relate the angles you want to find to the ones in the triangle.

$7^2 = 10^2 + 8^2 - 160\cos\alpha_1$

$\Rightarrow \cos\alpha_1 = 0.719...$

$\Rightarrow \alpha_1 = 44.0°$

$8^2 = 10^2 + 7^2 - 140\cos\alpha_2$

$\Rightarrow \cos\alpha_2 = 0.607...$

$\Rightarrow \alpha_2 = 52.6°$

You can now use the cosine rule to find the angles in the triangle.

$\theta_1 = 180° - \alpha_1 = 136°$

$\theta_2 = 180° - \alpha_2 = 127.4°$

You can now find the required angles.

EXERCISE 21D

1 In the following diagrams, the particle is in equilibrium. Find the forces and angles marked with italic letters.

a i F, θ, 10 N, 8 N

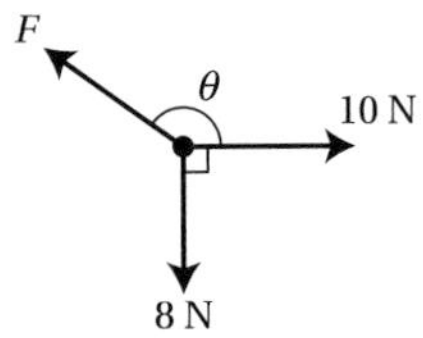

ii F, 8 N, θ, 5 N

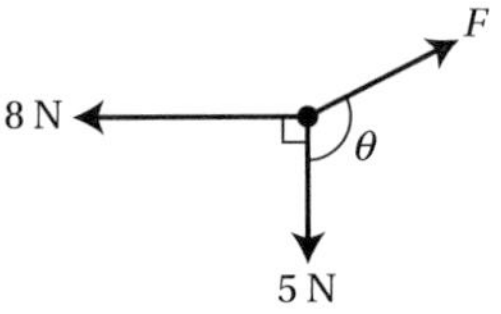

b i F_2, 130°, 80°, F_1, 12 N

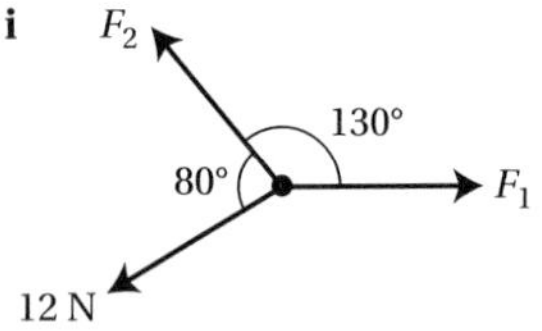

ii 10 N, 110°, 120°, F_2, F_1

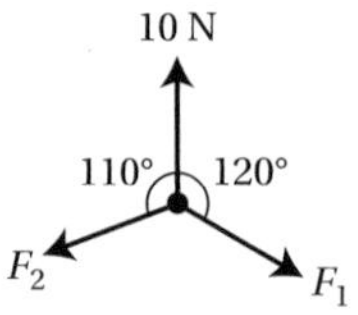

c i 13 N, 15 N, θ_2, θ_1, 26 N

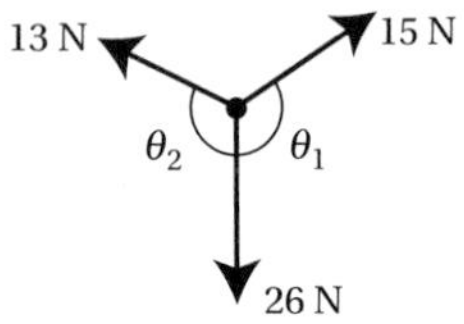

ii 9 N, θ_1, 18 N, θ_2, 12 N

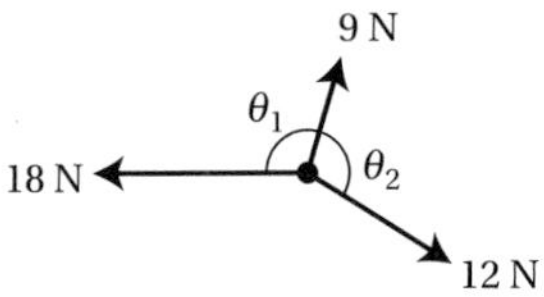

2 A particle of weight 18 N is suspended by two light inextensible strings, which make angles of 30° and 60° with the horizontal ceiling. By considering components of the forces in the directions of the strings, find the tension in each string.

3 A particle is in equilibrium under the action of three horizontal forces, each making an angle of 120° with the other two. Prove that the three forces all have equal magnitudes.

4 A box with mass 36 kg rests in limiting equilibrium on a rough inclined plane. The magnitude of the frictional force between the box and the plane is 120.7 N.

a Use a triangle of forces to find the angle that the plane makes with the horizontal.

b Find the coefficient of friction between the box and the plane.

5 Three forces, of magnitudes 17 N, 21 N and 30 N, act on a particle in equilibrium. All three forces act in the same horizontal plane. Find the angles that the 30 N force makes with the other two.

6 A particle of mass 2.4 kg hangs in equilibrium suspended by two light inextensible strings. The strings make angles α and β with the upward vertical, as shown in the diagram. The tensions in the strings are 18 N and 12 N. Find, to the nearest degree, the values of α and β.

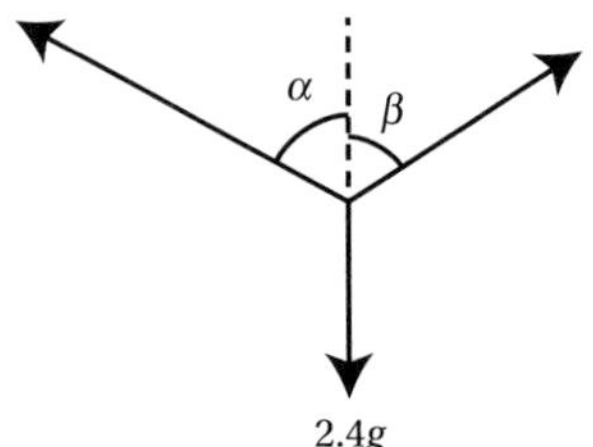

Checklist of learning and understanding

- To resolve a force in a given direction, draw a right-angled triangle with the force as the hypotenuse and the other sides of the triangle parallel and perpendicular to the direction of interest.
- When calculating motion on a slope, resolve forces parallel and perpendicular to the slope rather than vertically and horizontally. In particular, the components of weight acting on a slope inclined at an angle θ to the horizontal are:
  - down the plane: $mg \sin \theta$
  - perpendicular to the plane: $mg \cos \theta$
- The contact force between an object and a surface has two components:
  - the normal contact force, perpendicular to the surface
  - the frictional force, parallel to the surface.
- The maximum or limiting value of friction, F_{max}, between an object and a surface is given by $F_{max} = \mu R$ where R is the normal reaction force between the object and the surface, and μ is the coefficient of friction.
  - If an object is stationary and the sum of all the other forces parallel to the surface, excluding friction, is smaller than F_{max}, the object will remain at rest and the friction force, F_r will equal the sum of the other forces.
  - If the sum of all the forces parallel to the surface excluding friction, is larger than F_{max}, the object will move and $F_r = \mu R$.

Mixed practice 21

Unless otherwise indicated use $g = 9.8\ \mathrm{m\,s^{-2}}$ throughout this exercise.

1 A canal boat of mass 1500 kg is being pulled along a straight canal by two horses. Each horse has a rope with tension 600 N acting at an angle 15° to the canal.

- **a** Assuming the resistance from the water is much smaller than the tension in the ropes, find the acceleration of the boat, to three significant figures.
- **b** How will your answer change if the assumption about the resistance due to the water is wrong?

2 A block with mass 2 kg is projected up a rough slope, which makes a 35° angle with the horizontal. The coefficient of friction is 0.6.

- **a** Find the magnitude of the initial acceleration of the block.
- **b** Find the magnitude of the contact force between the block and the slope.

3 The diagram below shows two forces acting on a particle.

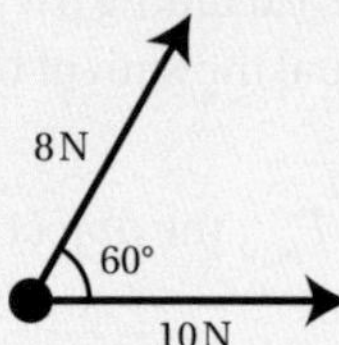

- **a** Find the component of the resultant force in the direction of the 10 N force.
- **b** The direction of the 8 N force is allowed to vary. Find the maximum and minimum value of the magnitude of the resultant force.

4 A block of mass 5 kg slides freely from rest down a smooth slope inclined at 25° to the horizontal. What is the acceleration of the block down the slope?

5 A particle is projected with an initial speed of $8\ \mathrm{m\,s^{-1}}$ across a rough horizontal surface and comes to rest 10 m from its starting point.

- **a** Calculate the coefficient of friction between the particle and the surface.
- **b** A second, identical particle is projected across the same surface and comes to rest 20 m from its starting point. Determine its initial speed.

6 A small ball, B, of mass 320 grams is suspended from point O by a light inextensible string. The string is displaced from the vertical (see diagram) and the ball is held in equilibrium by a force of 5 N. The string OB makes a $\theta°$ angle with the downward vertical.

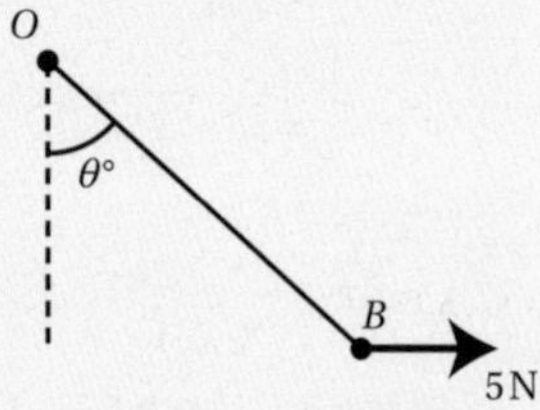

- **a** Find the tension in the string.
- **b** Find the value of θ.

7 A small box of mass 5 kg is placed on a rough slope inclined at an angle of 20° to the horizontal. It is released from rest and slides down the slope.

a Draw a diagram showing the forces acting on the box.

The slope is 1.5 m long. The box takes 4.8 seconds to reach the bottom of the slope.

b Find the acceleration of the box.

c Find the coefficient of friction between the box and the slope.

d State an assumption that you have made about the forces acting on the box.

8 In this question take $g = 9.81\text{ m s}^{-2}$.

A box of mass 4 kg is held at rest on a plane inclined at an angle of 40° to the horizontal. The box is then released and slides down the plane.

a A simple model assumes that the only forces acting on the box are its weight and the normal reaction from the plane. Show that, according to this simple model, the acceleration of the box would be 6.31 m s^{-2}, correct to three significant figures.

b In fact, the box moves down the plane with constant acceleration and travels 3.5 metres in 1.2 seconds. Using this information, find the acceleration of the box.

c Explain why the answer to part **b** is less than the answer to part **a**.

9 Three horizontal forces, of magnitudes 15 N, 11 N and 13 N, act on a particle P in the directions shown in the diagram. The angles α and β are such that $\sin\alpha = 0.28$, $\cos\alpha = 0.96$, $\sin\beta = 0.8$ and $\cos\beta = 0.6$.

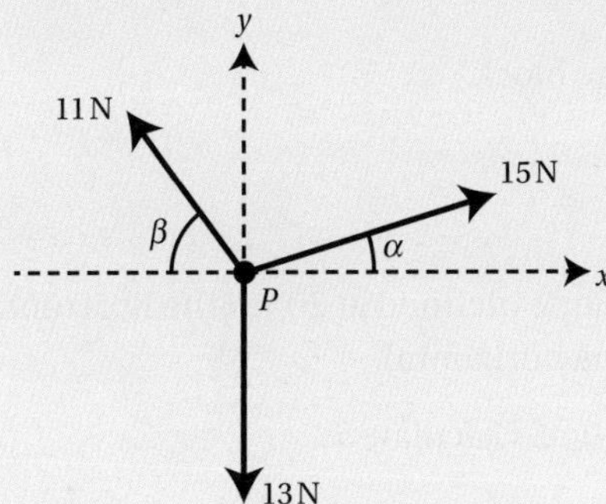

i Show that the component, in the y-direction, of the resultant of the three forces is zero.

ii Find the magnitude of the resultant of the three forces.

iii State the direction of the resultant of the three forces.

10 Two horizontal forces act at the point O. One force has magnitude 12 N and acts along a bearing of 000°. The other force has magnitude 14 N and acts along a bearing of 030° (see diagram).

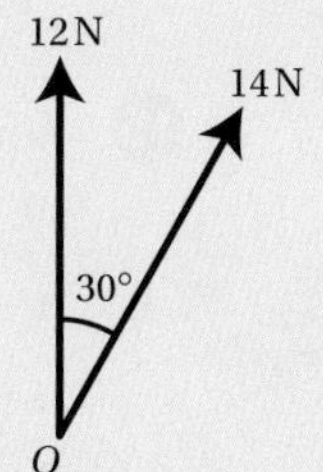

i Show that the resultant of the two forces has magnitude 25.1 N, correct to 3 significant figures.

ii Find the bearing of the line of action of the resultant.

11 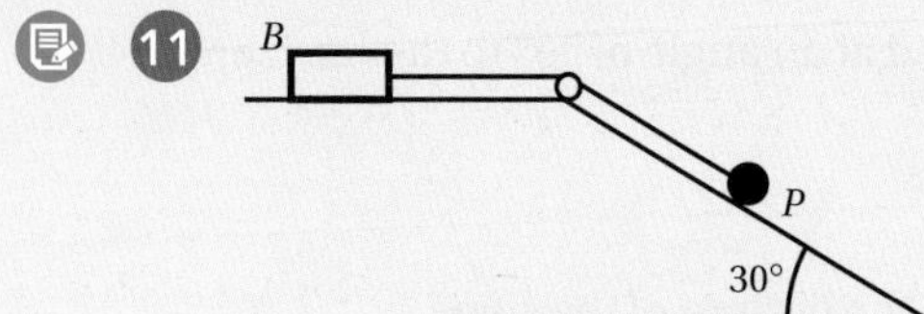

The diagram shows a small block B, of mass 3 kg, and a particle P, of mass 0.8 kg, which are attached to the ends of a light inextensible string. The string is taut and passes over a small smooth pulley. B is held at rest on a horizontal surface, and P lies on a smooth plane inclined at 30° to the horizontal. When B is released from rest it accelerates at 0.2 m s^{-2} towards the pulley.

i By considering the motion of P, show that the tension in the string is 3.76 N.

ii Calculate the coefficient of friction between B and the horizontal surface.

12 A block of mass 8 kg is held at rest on a rough horizontal surface. The coefficient of friction between the block and the surface is 0.3. A light inextensible string, which passes over a smooth peg, is attached at one end to the block and at the other end to a particle of mass 5 kg. The system is released from rest.

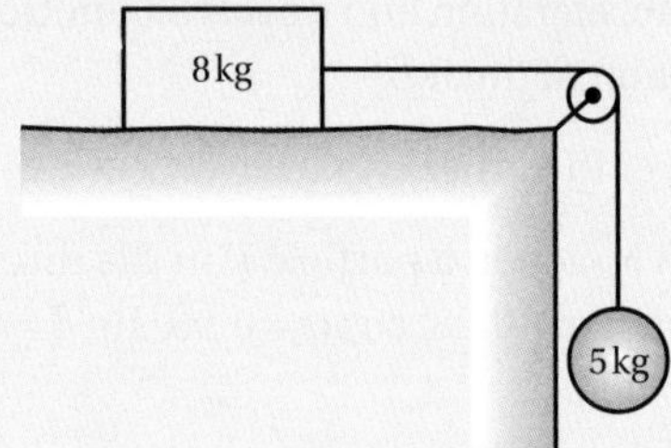

a Find the magnitude of the frictional force acting on the block.

b Find the acceleration of the block.

c Find the tension in the string.

13 A block with mass 2 kg is pulled from rest up a smooth slope inclined at 20° to the horizontal by a string with tension T, maintained at an angle of 30° to the horizontal.

a After 5 seconds, the block has moved 1 m along the slope. Calculate T.

b The block is allowed to come to rest again, then the tension is increased so that the block is about to lift off the slope. Calculate the minimum tension needed to achieve this.

14 A particle P, of mass 1 kg, is projected up a line of greatest slope of a rough plane inclined at 30° to the horizontal. The initial velocity is 8 m s^{-1} and the particle comes to instantaneous rest on the plane after travelling 4 metres.

a Calculate the frictional force acting on P, and the coefficient of friction between P and the plane.

b Determine the acceleration of P down the plane subsequent to the instant of rest.

15 A particle of mass 2.2 kg is projected with velocity 5 m s^{-1} up the line of steepest slope of a plane inclined at 20° to the horizontal.

a If the plane is smooth, determine the velocity of the particle after 10 seconds, assuming it does not reach the end of the plane.

b If the plane is rough, with coefficient of friction 0.3 between particle and plane, calculate the maximum vertical height above its starting point that the particle will reach.

16 Particle P, of mass 1 kg, is projected with speed 5 m s^{-1} down the line of steepest slope of a rough plane inclined at an angle θ to the horizontal. The coefficient of friction between the particle and the plane is 1.

Another particle, Q, of mass 2 kg, is projected down another rough plane, inclined at an angle 2θ to the horizontal. The initial speed of Q is also 5 m s^{-1} and the coefficient of friction is also 1.

The time taken for P to travel 1 m equals the time taken for Q to travel 2 m.

Show that $(4\cos\theta - 1)(\cos\theta - \sin\theta) = 2$.

17 A block of mass 12 kg is pulled in a straight line on a rough horizontal surface by a constant horizontal force of magnitude 70 newtons. Assume that there is no air resistance acting on the block.

a The acceleration of the block is 3.3 m s^{-2}. Find the coefficient of friction between the block and the surface. Give your answer correct to two significant figures.

b Explain how and why your answer to part **a** will change if you assume that air resistance does act on the block.

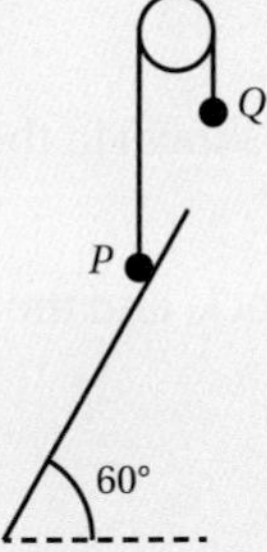

Particles P and Q, of masses 0.4 kg and 0.3 kg respectively, are attached to the ends of a light inextensible string. The string passes over a smooth fixed pulley and the sections of the string not in contact with the pulley are vertical. P rests in limiting equilibrium on a plane inclined at 60° to the horizontal (see diagram).

i a Calculate the components, parallel and perpendicular to the plane, of the contact force exerted by the plane on P.

b Find the coefficient of friction between P and the plane.

P is held stationary and a particle of mass 0.2 kg is attached to Q. With the string taut, P is released from rest.

ii Calculate the tension of the string and the acceleration of the particles.

© OCR, GCE Mathematics, Paper 4728, January 2010

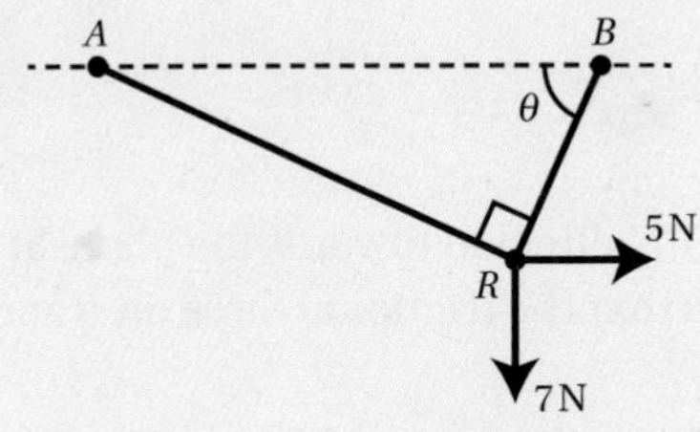

A small smooth ring R of weight 7 N is threaded on a light inextensible string. The ends of the string are attached to fixed points A and B at the same horizontal level. A horizontal force of magnitude 5 N is applied to R. The string is taut. In the equilibrium position the angle ARB is a right angle, and the portion of the string attached to B makes an angle θ with the horizontal (see diagram).

i Explain why the tension T N is the same in each part of the string.

ii By resolving horizontally and vertically for the forces acting on R, form two simultaneous equations in $T\cos\theta$ and $T\sin\theta$.

iii Hence, find T and θ.

© OCR, GCE Mathematics, Paper 4728, June 2011

20 A block of weight 14.7 N is at rest on a horizontal floor. A force of magnitude 4.9 N is applied to the block.

i The block is in limiting equilibrium when the 4.9 N force is applied horizontally. Show that the coefficient of friction is $\frac{1}{3}$.

ii

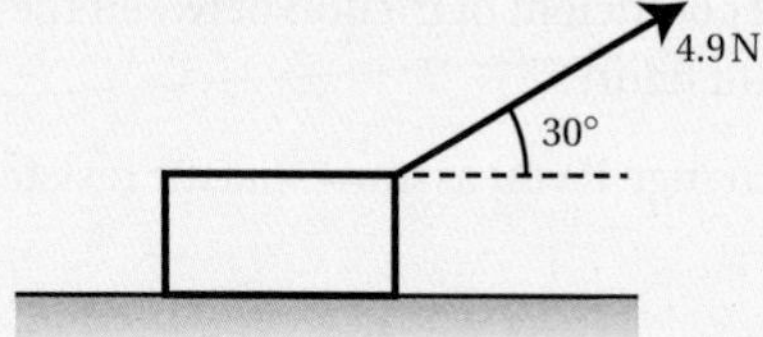

When the force of 4.9 N is applied at an angle of 30° above the horizontal, as shown in the diagram, the block moves across the floor. Calculate

a the vertical component of the contact force between the floor and the block, and the magnitude of the frictional force,

b the acceleration of the block.

iii Calculate the magnitude of the frictional force acting on the block when the 4.9 N force acts at an angle of 30° to the upward vertical, justifying your answer fully.

© OCR, GCE Mathematics, Paper 4728, January 2008

21 A block B of weight 10 N is projected down a line of greatest slope of a plane inclined at an angle of 20° to the horizontal. B travels down the plane at constant speed.

i a Find the components perpendicular and parallel to the plane of the contact force between B and the plane.

b Hence, show that the coefficient of friction is 0.364, correct to 3 significant figures.

ii

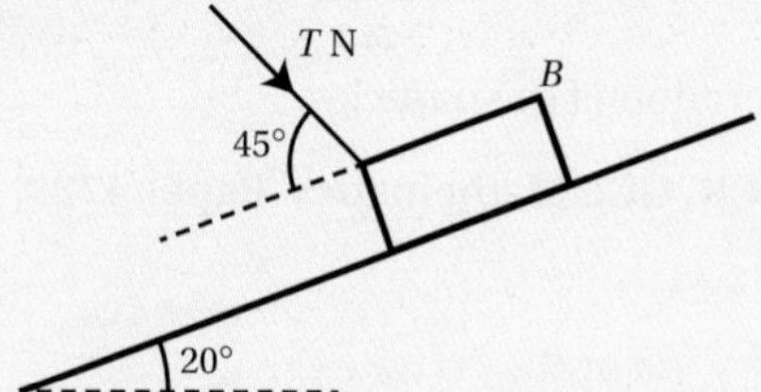

B is in limiting equilibrium when acted on by a force of T N directed towards the plane at an angle of 45° to a line of the greatest slope (see diagram). Given that the frictional force on B acts down the plane, find T.

© OCR, GCE Mathematics, Paper 4728, June 2009

22 Two right-angled triangular prisms of equal height, with angles of greatest slope 30° and 45° respectively, are positioned as shown, with a smooth peg, P, between the two highest points.

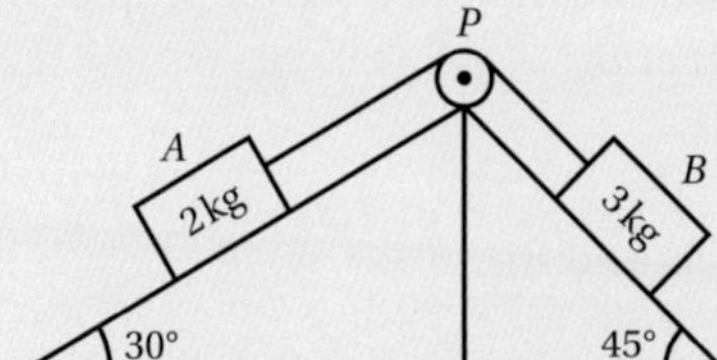

Block A, with mass 2 kg, is placed on the 30° slope and block B, with mass 3 kg, is placed on the 45° slope. The two blocks are connected by a light, inextensible string, which runs parallel to the line of greatest slope of each prism and passes over the smooth peg.

The coefficient of friction between block A and the 30° slope surface is μ, and the coefficient of friction between block B and the 45° slope surface is 2μ.

At time $t = 0$, block A is projected down the 30° slope with speed 9 m s^{-1}.

a Calculate the acceleration of block A in terms of μ.

It is determined that $\mu = 0.1$.

b Calculate whether the blocks will return to their original positions and, if so, the time at which this will occur.

  A particle P of mass 0.5 kg moves upwards along a line of greatest slope of a rough plane inclined at an angle of 40° to the horizontal. P reaches its highest point and then moves back down the plane. The coefficient of friction between P and the plane is 0.6.

i Show that the magnitude of the frictional force acting on P is 2.25 N, correct to 3 significant figures.

ii Find the acceleration of P when it is moving

a up the plane,

b down the plane.

iii When P is moving up the plane, it passes through a point A with speed 4 m s^{-1}.

a Find the length of time before P reaches its highest point.

b Find the total length of time for P to travel from the point A to its highest point and back to A.

24

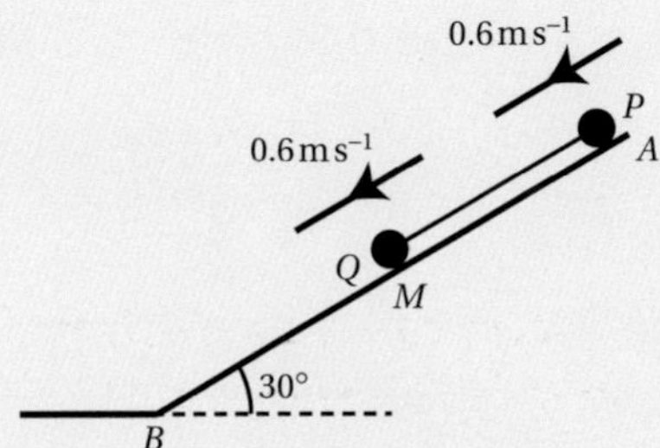

A and B are points at the upper and lower ends, respectively, of a line of greatest slope on a plane inclined at 30° to the horizontal. M is the midpoint of AB. Two particles, P and Q, joined by a taut, light inextensible string, are placed on the plane at A and M, respectively. The particles are simultaneously projected with speed 0.6 m s^{-1} down the line of greatest slope (see diagram). The particles move down the plane with acceleration 0.9 m s^{-2}. At the instant 2 s after projection, P is at M and Q is at B. The particle Q subsequently remains at rest at B.

i Find the distance AB.

The plane is rough between A and M, but smooth between M and B.

ii Calculate the speed of P when it reaches B.

P has mass 0.4 kg and Q has mass 0.3 kg.

iii By considering the motion of Q, calculate the tension in the string while both particles are moving down the plane.

iv Calculate the coefficient of friction between P and the plane between A and M.

Elevate

See Extension sheet 20 for a selection of more challenging problems.

22 Moments

In this chapter you will learn:

- how to find the turning effect of a force
- about uniform rods and laminas
- how to find the centre of mass of a non-uniform rod
- about rotational equilibrium.

Before you start…

Student Book 1, Chapter 21	You should be able to recognise types of force acting on a particle.	1 A particle is pulled across a smooth horizontal table by a string that is parallel to the table. Draw a diagram and label all the forces acting on the particle.
Student Book 1, Chapter 21	You should understand when a particle is in equilibrium.	2 Three forces act on a particle, as shown. 5N F 12N The particle is in equilibrium. Find the magnitude of F.

Modelling rotating systems

Until now you have used the particle model to analyse forces and motion. However, there are situations in which this isn't appropriate.

Consider, for example, closing a door.

A force is applied to push the door closed, but when the door moves it doesn't do so in a straight line. Instead it rotates about the hinge. In this chapter you will find out how to model situations like this.

Section 1: The turning effect of a force

To describe the motion of a rotating object you need to specify the axis of rotation. In the example of a door, this is the vertical line passing through the hinges. In this chapter you will consider only situations where the object can be modelled as one- or two-dimensional, and the axis of rotation is perpendicular to the plane in which the object lies. In that case, you can talk about the object rotating about a point in the plane.

From your experience of closing doors you probably know that it is easier to push if your hand is further away from the hinge. This is because the **moment** (the turning effect of a force) depends upon both the force applied and the distance away from the pivot point.

Key point 22.1

The moment of a force F about a point P is:

$$\text{Moment} = Fd$$

where d is the perpendicular distance of the line of action of the force from P.

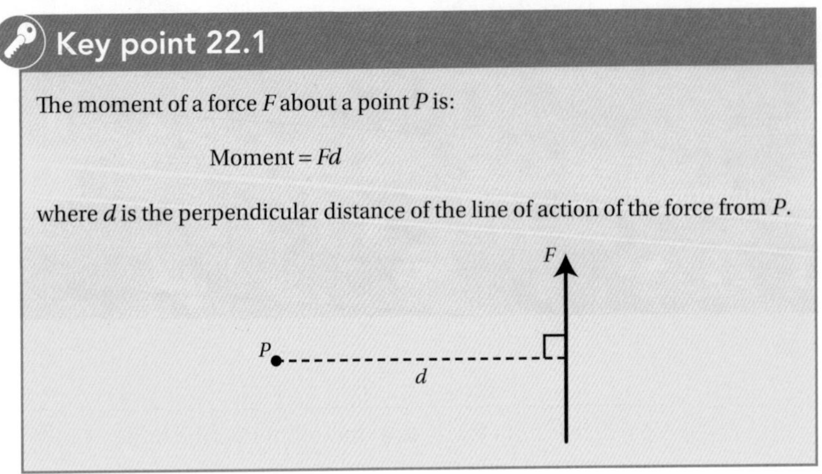

The units of moment are newton metres (N m).

The moment will either cause clockwise or anticlockwise rotation about a point.

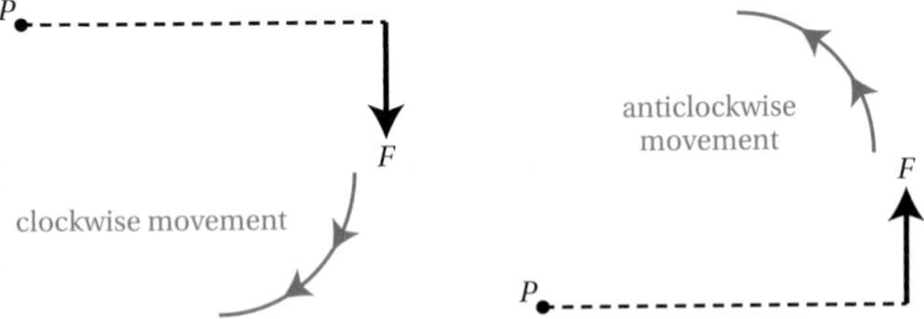

If the line of action of the force acts through P, then the moment about P will be zero (as the perpendicular distance from P is 0 m). So in this case there is no rotational effect from the force.

Many situations involving forces that cause rotation can be modelled using two basic shapes:

- a **uniform lamina**, which is a two-dimensional object (for example, in the shape of a rectangle, triangle or circle). We might use this to model objects such as a door or a book.
- a **uniform rod**, which has just one dimension. We might use this to model a see-saw, a snooker cue or a plank.

In both cases 'uniform' means that the object has the same density throughout. The key fact you need to know is where the **centre of mass** is for both of these shapes.

Key point 22.2

The centre of mass is the point at which the object's weight acts.

- For a uniform rod, this is at the midpoint.
- For a uniform rectangular lamina, this is at the intersection of its diagonals.

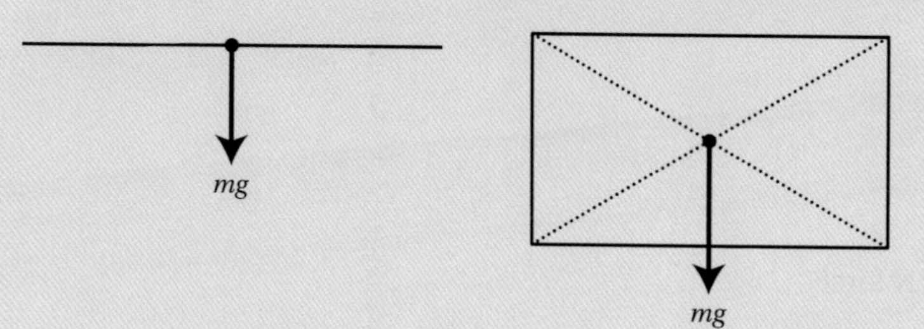

Fast forward

Although this might sound obvious, determining the centre of mass of more complex shapes can be quite difficult. You will see how to do this if you study the Mechanics option of Further Mathematics.

WORKED EXAMPLE 22.1

A uniform rod of length 6 m has weight 5 N. Point P is at one end of the rod and point Q is 5 m from P.

P ← 5 m → Q

Find the moment of its weight about the point:

a P **b** Q

a Moment $= Fd = 5 \times 3$ — The perpendicular distance from P to the centre of mass is 3 m.

P ← 3 m → ← 2 m → Q; 5 N — The weight acts at the mid point. It would cause the rod to rotate clockwise about P.

$= 15$ N m clockwise

b Moment $= Fd = 5 \times 2$ — The perpendicular distance from Q to the centre of mass is 2 m.

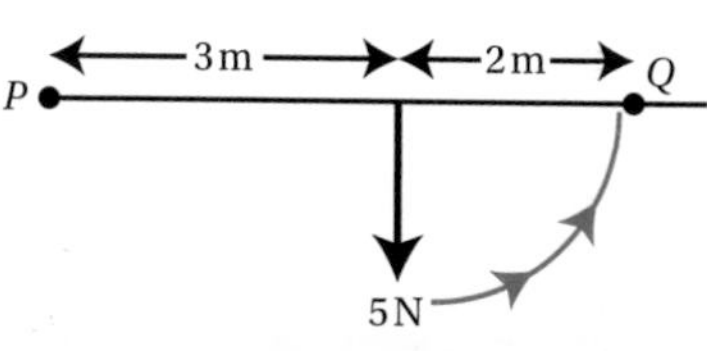

$= 10$ N m anticlockwise — The centre of mass would cause the rod to rotate anticlockwise about Q.

WORKED EXAMPLE 22.2

A uniform rectangular lamina, measuring 0.4 m by 0.6 m, has centre C and weight 8 N.

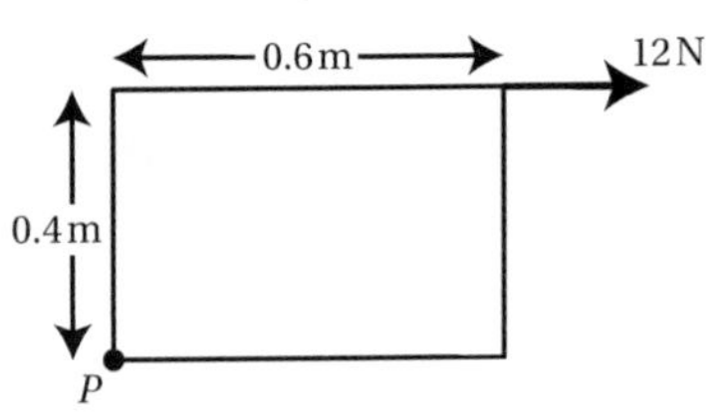

The lamina is free to rotate in a vertical plane about P.

Find the moment about P of:

a the weight **b** the 12 N force.

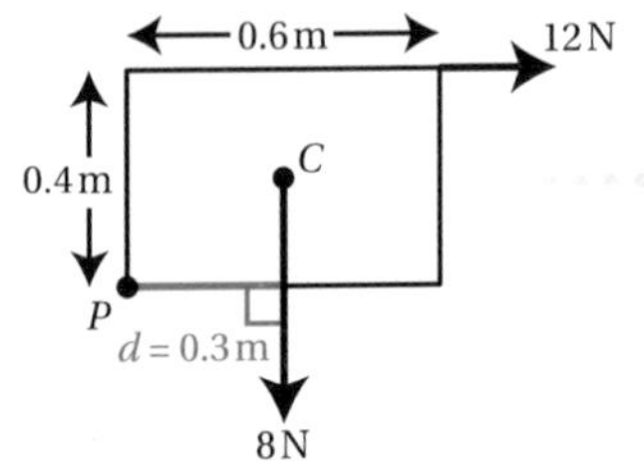

The weight acts at the centre.

a Moment $= Fd$

$= 8 \times 0.3$

$= 2.4$ N m clockwise

The perpendicular distance from P to the line of action of the weight is $d = 0.3$ m.

The rotation will be clockwise.

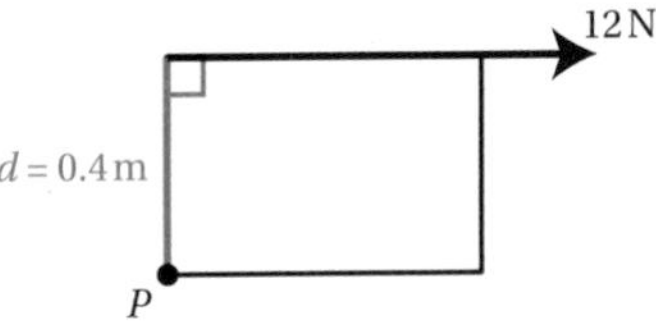

b Moment $= Fd$

$= 12 \times 0.4$

$= 4.8$ N m clockwise

The perpendicular distance from P to the line of action of the 12 N force is $d = 0.4$ m.

The rotation will be clockwise.

When several forces act on a body they combine to give an overall resultant force; this is also true of moments.

Key point 22.3

To find the resultant moment about a point, find the sum of the clockwise and anticlockwise moments separately.

The resultant moment will be the difference between the two sums (in the direction of the larger).

Focus on ...

Focus on ... Modelling 4 applies moments to the context of levers.

WORKED EXAMPLE 22.3

A uniform rod of length 8 m and weight 10 N is acted on by a 7 N and 3 N force, as shown in the diagram.

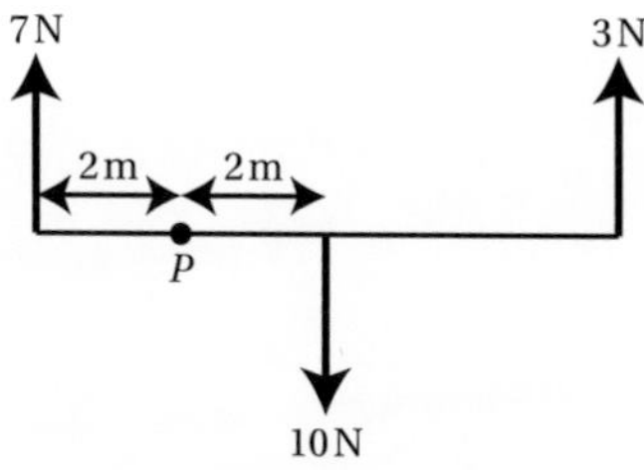

Find the resultant moment about the point P.

Moment of 7 N force $= 7 \times 2$
$= 14$ N m clockwise

Find the moment of each force in turn.

Moment of weight $= 10 \times 2$
$= 20$ N m clockwise

Moment of 3 N force $= 3 \times 6$
$= 18$ N m anticlockwise

The 3 N force is $2 + 4 = 6$ m from P.

Total clockwise moments $= 14 + 20 = 34$ N m
Total anticlockwise moments $= 18$ N m

Find the sum of the moments that act in the same direction.

Resultant moment about $P = 34 - 18 = 16$ N m clockwise.

The sum of the clockwise moments is greater.

EXERCISE 22A

Use $g = 10\text{ m s}^{-2}$ unless otherwise stated.

1 Find the moment, about the point P, of the weight of each of the following uniform rods.

a **i**

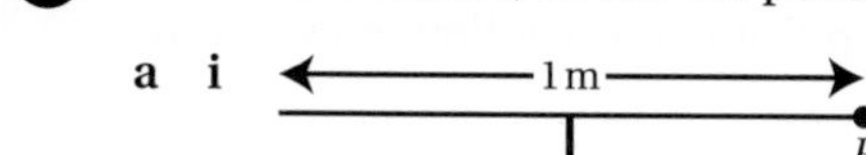

ii

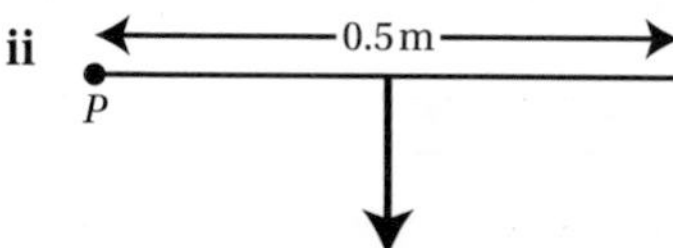

b **i**

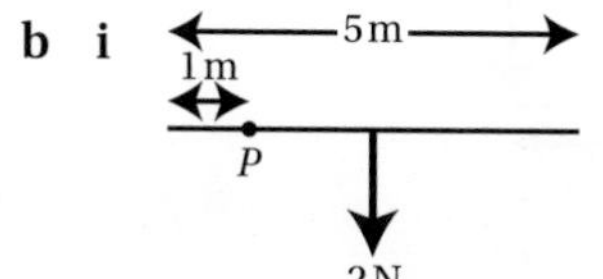

ii

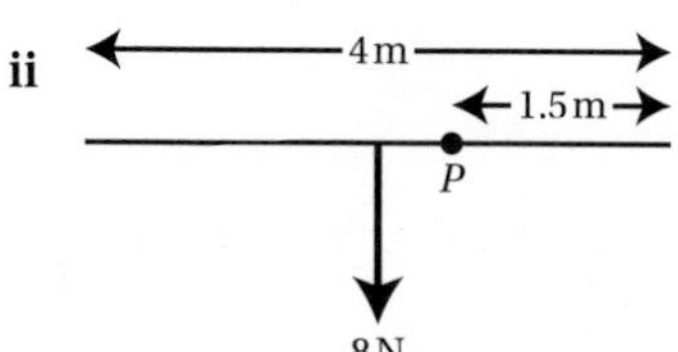

c **i**

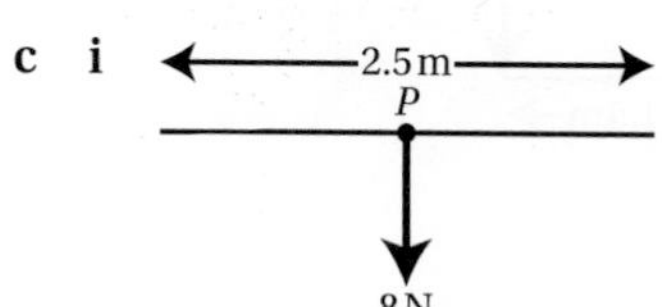

ii

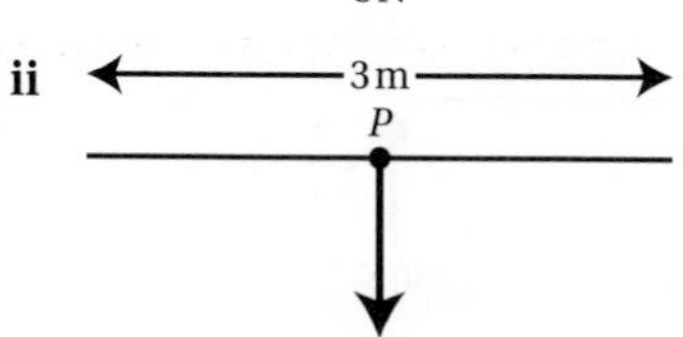

2 Find the moment, about the point P, of the weight of each of the following uniform laminas.

a i

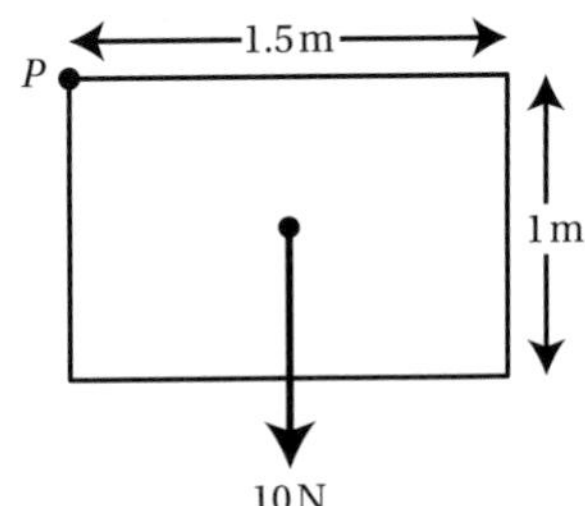

ii

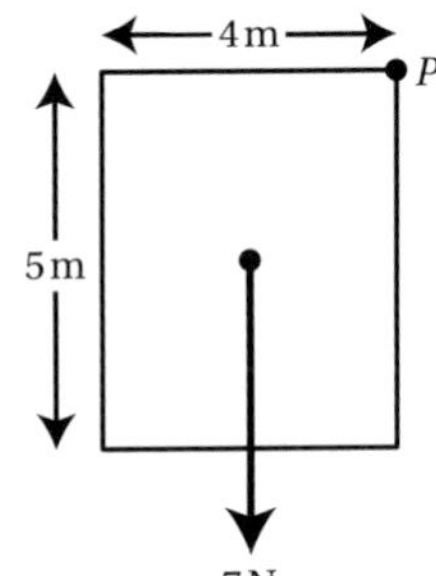

b i

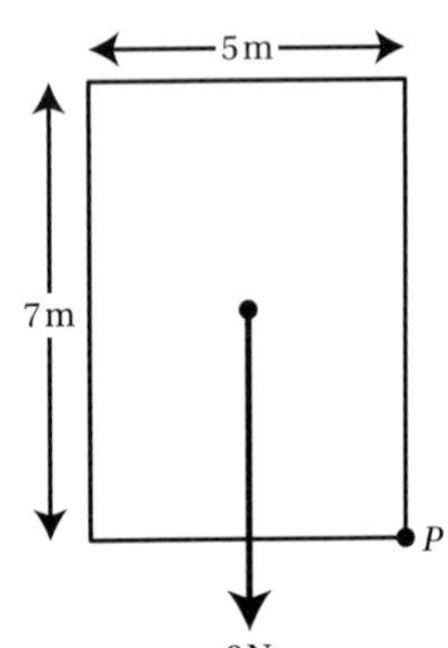

ii

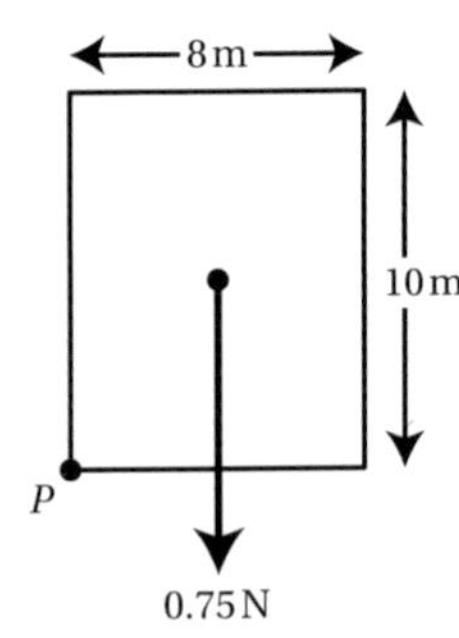

c i

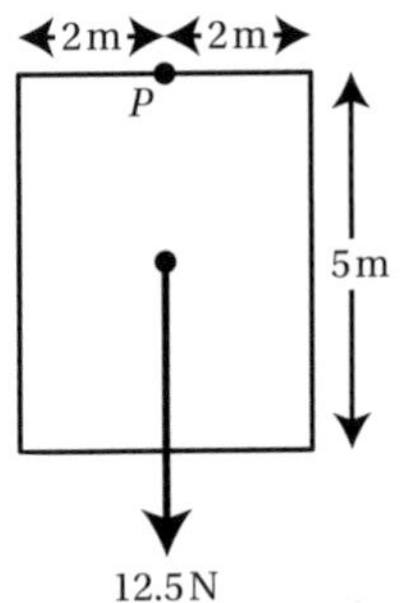

ii

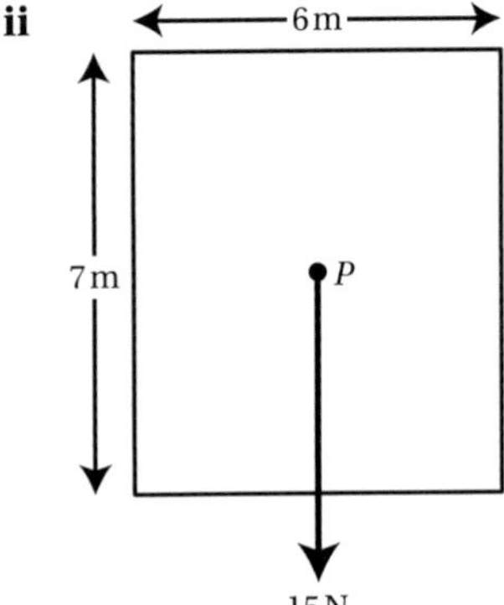

3 A 4 m long uniform rod weighs 50 N. Find the net moment about the point P in the following situations.

a i

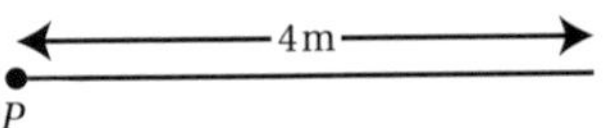

ii

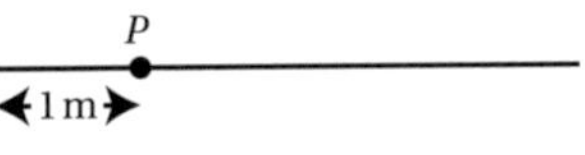

b i

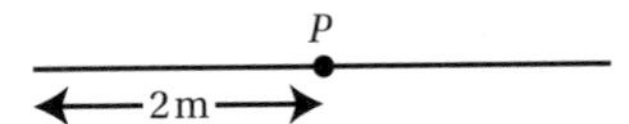

ii

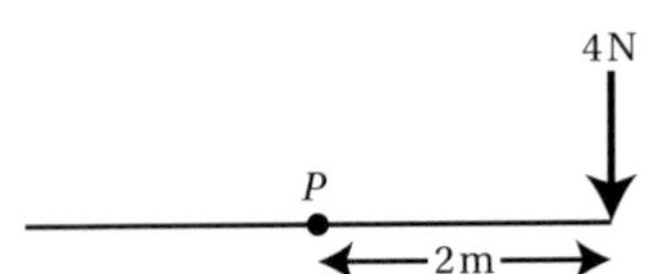

c i

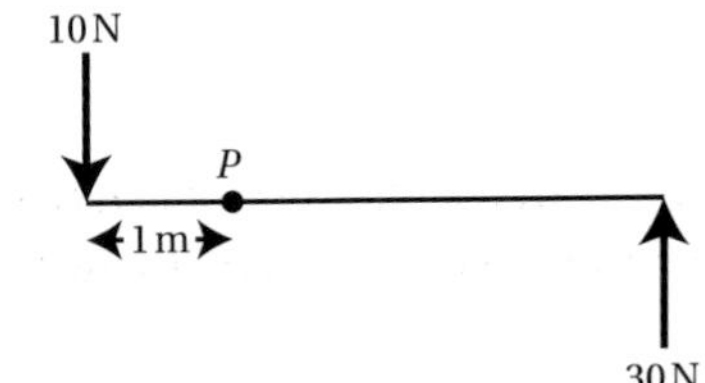

ii

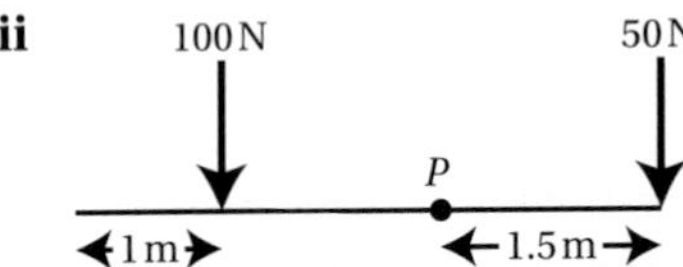

4 A 4 m by 6 m uniform rectangular lamina weighs 150 N.

Find the net moment about the point P in the following situations, given that the lamina is in a vertical plane.

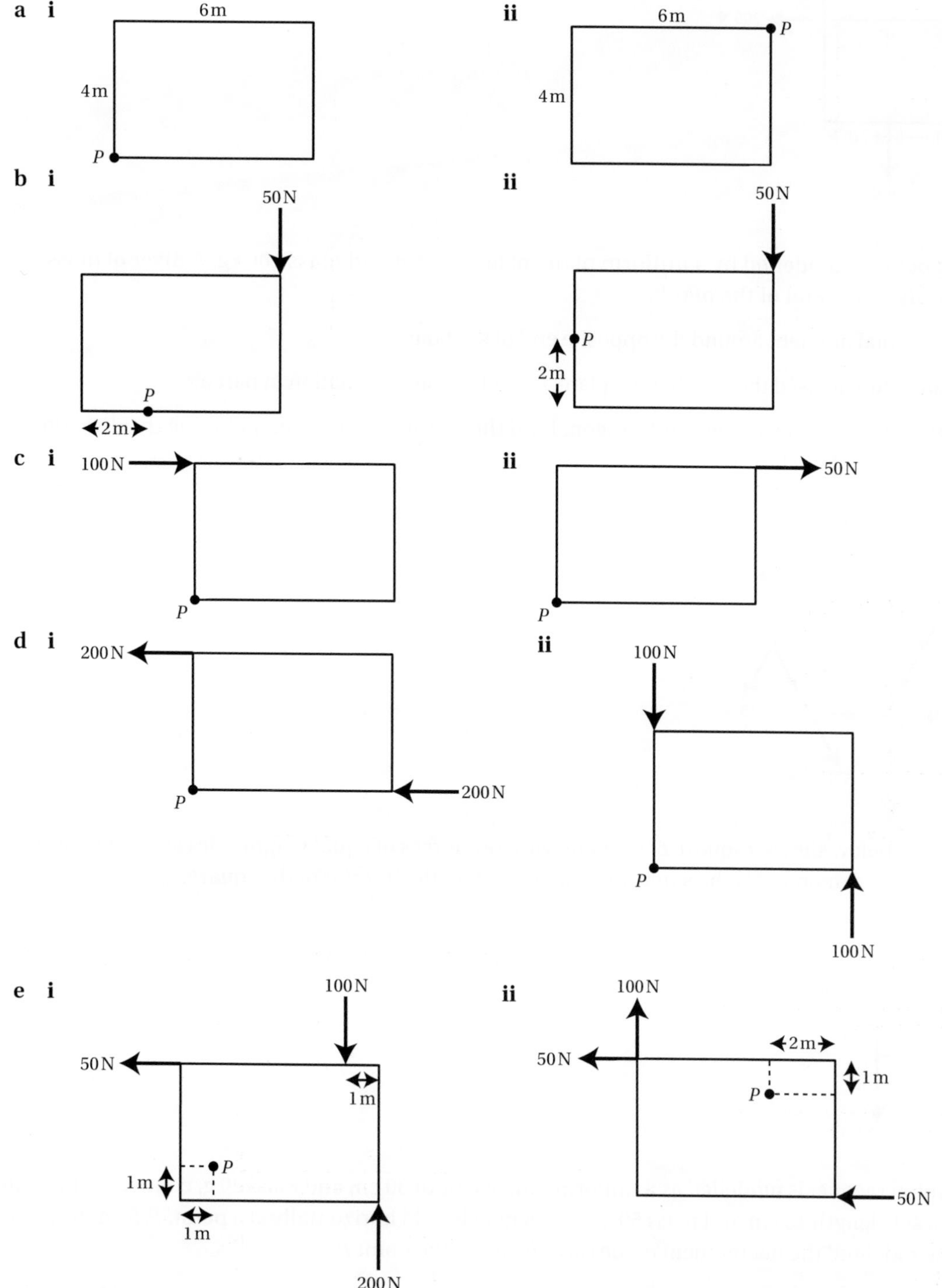

5 A steering wheel is modelled as a ring of diameter 30 cm. The driver applies two clockwise forces of 3 N tangentially at diametrically opposite sides of the steering wheel. Find the net moment about the centre of the wheel.

6 Find the resultant moment, including the direction, about the point P in the following diagram.

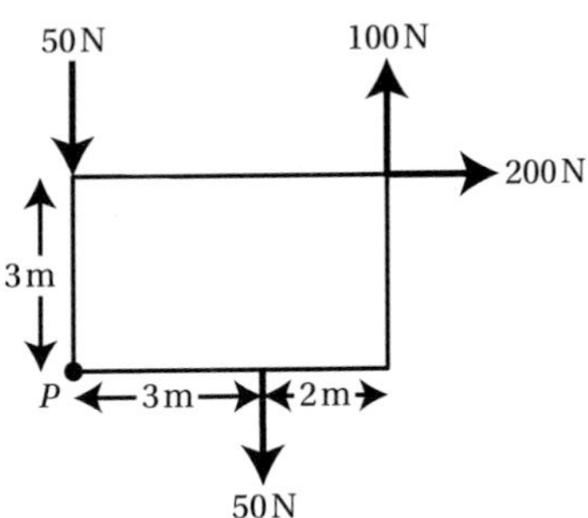

7 A diving board is modelled by a uniform plank of length 3 m and mass 100 kg. A diver of mass 70 kg stands at one end of the plank.

a Find the total moment around the opposite end of the board.

b Explain how you used the fact that the plank is rigid in your calculation in part **a**.

8 The diagram below shows a regular hexagon. Find the resultant moment, including the direction, about the centre of the hexagon.

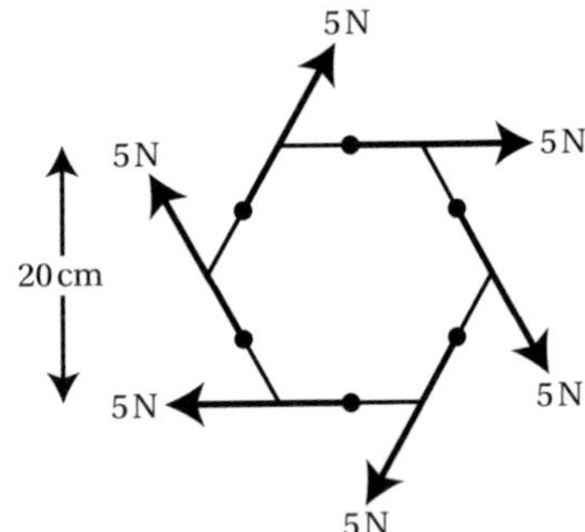

9 The diagram below shows a square of side 1 m with four forces of equal magnitudes acting at the corners. Prove that the net moment is the same about any point on the interior of the square.

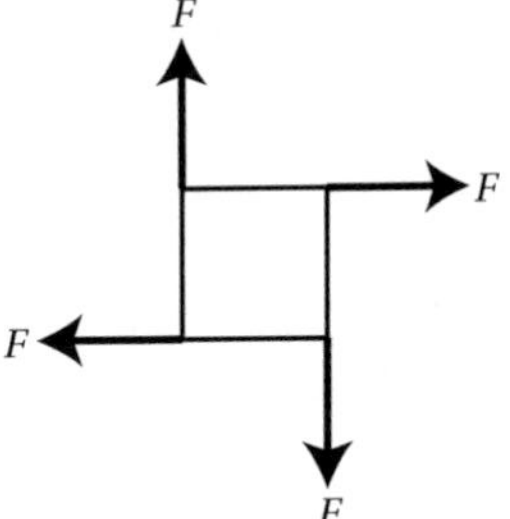

10 A badminton racquet is modelled as a uniform rod, of length 30 cm and mass 20 g, connected to a square lamina of side length 15 cm and mass 50 g. The racquet is held horizontally at a point, P, 5 cm from the end of the rod. Find the net moment of the racquet about the point P.

Section 2: Equilibrium

To maintain an object in equilibrium, there need to be additional forces acting on it to counterbalance its weight. Some common situations you will meet in this chapter are:

- smooth supports providing a normal reaction force

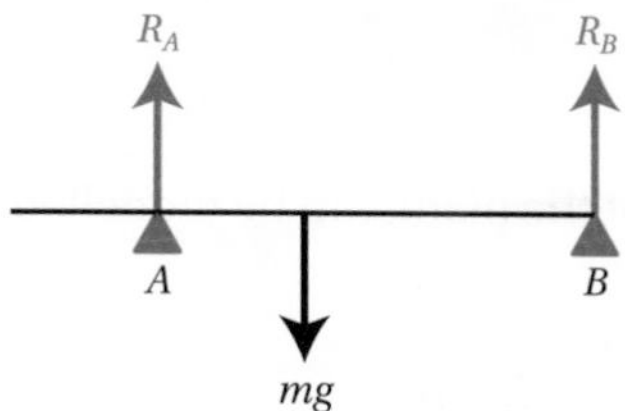

or

- light strings providing a tension.

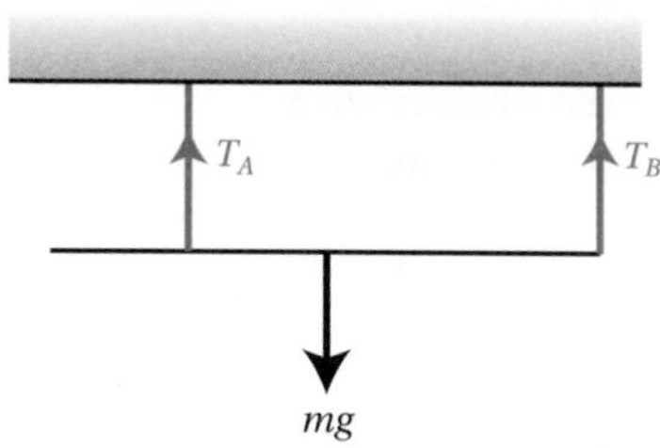

For an object to be at rest in equilibrium, you now need to add the condition that there is no rotation.

Fast forward

In Section 4 you will also see examples of a rod leaning against a wall.

Rewind

Remember from Chapter 21 that 'smooth' means there is no friction (so here the force at the support will be perpendicular to the surface of the object), and 'light' means the string has no mass.

Key point 22.4

If an object is in equilibrium, there is zero resultant force and zero resultant moment about any point.

Notice that the resultant moment will, in general, be different about different points. However, if the object is in equilibrium, the resultant moment will be zero about *any point*.

Since you have a choice of which point to take moments about, it is a good idea to choose a point where at least one force acts. The moment of that force will be zero, making the calculation simpler.

WORKED EXAMPLE 22.4

A plank of length 8 m and mass 10 kg rests in equilibrium on two identical chairs. Chair A is placed 1 m from one end of the plank, and chair B is placed at the other end, as shown in the diagram.

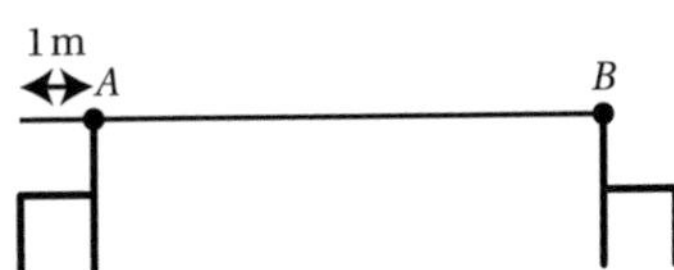

The chairs can provide a reaction force of 50 N before breaking. Assuming that the plank can be modelled as a uniform rod and $g = 9.8\,\text{m s}^{-2}$, determine if either chair will break.

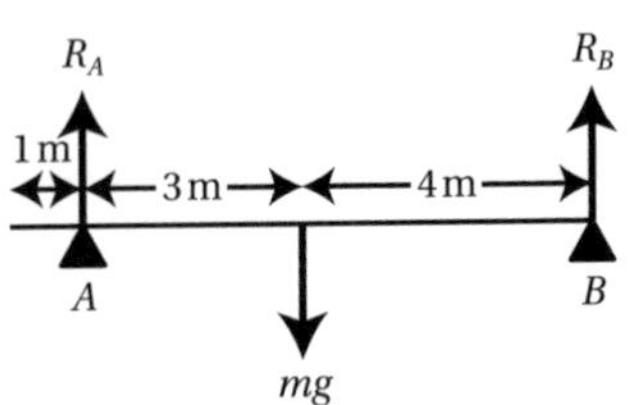

Since the plank is a uniform rod the centre of mass is 4 metres from either end, so 3 metres from A.

Taking moments around A:

$3 \times 10g = 7 \times R_B$

$R_B = \frac{30g}{7}$

$= 42\,\text{N}$

As the plank is in equilibrium, sum of clockwise moments = sum of anticlockwise moments.

Notice that taking moments about either A or B allows you to ignore one of the unknown forces. You could have chosen either point to start with.

So chair B will not break.

$42 < 50$, so doesn't break.

Vertical forces:

$R_A + R_B = mg$

Equilibrium also means that forces up = forces down.

$R_A = mg - R_B$

$= 56\,\text{N}$

This exceeds the breaking force, so chair A will break.

$56 > 50$, so does break.

WORKED EXAMPLE 22.5

A shop sign is formed from a rectangular plastic sheet, $ABCD$, of weight 40 N. It is held in equilibrium by a vertical wire at A and horizontal wires at A and C, as shown in the diagram.

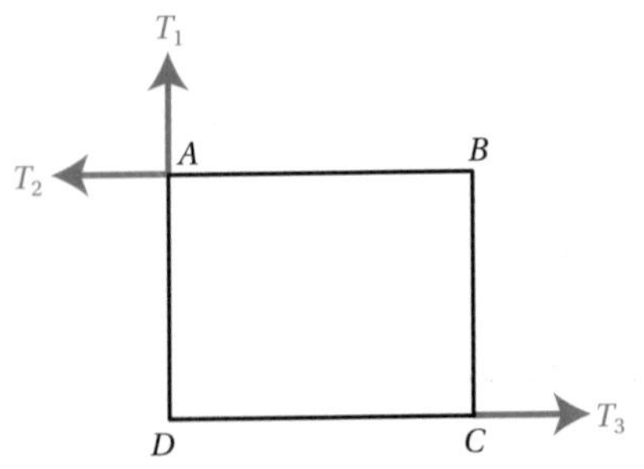

Continues on next page ...

If the sign can be modelled as a uniform lamina with $AB = 0.5$ m and $AD = 0.4$ m, find T_1, T_2 and T_3.

Take moments about A: — Moments about A eliminates two of the unknown forces.

$0.25 \times 40 = 0.4 \times T_3$

$T_3 = \frac{10}{0.4}$

$= 25$ N

— Since it is in equilibrium, sum of clockwise moments = sum of anticlockwise moments. The centre of mass is 0.25 m to the right of A.

Horizontal forces: — Forces right = forces left.

$T_3 = T_2 = 25$ N

Vertical forces: — Forces up = forces down.

$T_1 = 40$ N

WORK IT OUT 22.1

A uniform rectangular lamina, $ABCD$, of width $CD = 30$ cm and height $AD = 20$ cm, has weight 80 N and is attached to a fixed bolt at point D, about which it can rotate freely. A horizontal string is attached midway along CB under a tension of 130 N. A downward force of 20 N is applied at a point, P, which lies on AB, with $AP = x$ so that the lamina hangs in equilibrium with DC horizontal. Find the value of x.

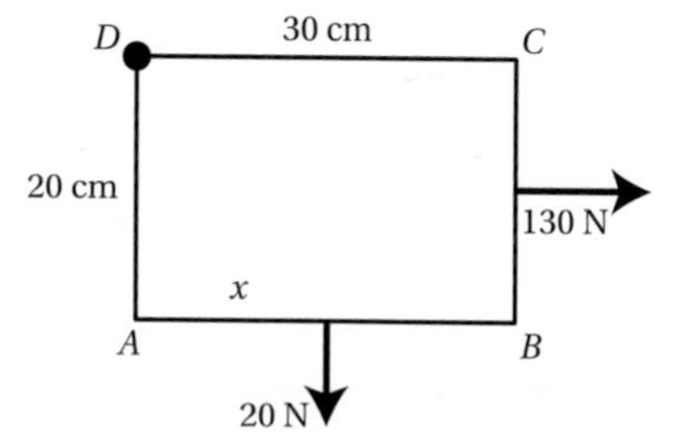

Which is the correct solution? Can you identify the errors made in the incorrect solutions?

Solution 1	Solution 2	Solution 3
Taking moments about D: Clockwise moments: $20x$ Anticlockwise moments: $130 \times 10 = 1300$ So $20x = 1300$ $x = 65$ cm	Taking moments about the centre of mass: Clockwise moments: $20(x - 15) + 100 \times 10 = 20x + 700$ Anticlockwise moments: $130 \times 15 = 1950$ So $20x + 700 = 1950$ $x = 62.5$	Taking moments about D: Clockwise moments: $20x + 80 \times 15 = 20x + 1200$ N cm Anticlockwise moments: $130 \times 10 = 1300$ N cm So $20x + 1200 = 1300$ $x = 5$

EXERCISE 22B

Use $g = 10$ m s^{-2} unless otherwise stated.

1 In each of the following diagrams, a uniform rod of length 10 metres and weight 50 N is being held in equilibrium by two vertical wires. Find the unknown values.

a **i**   **ii**

b **i**

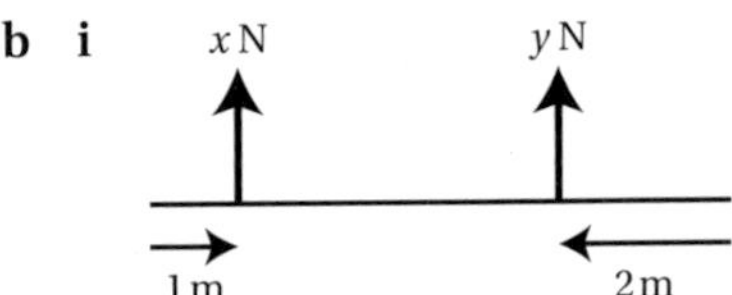

ii

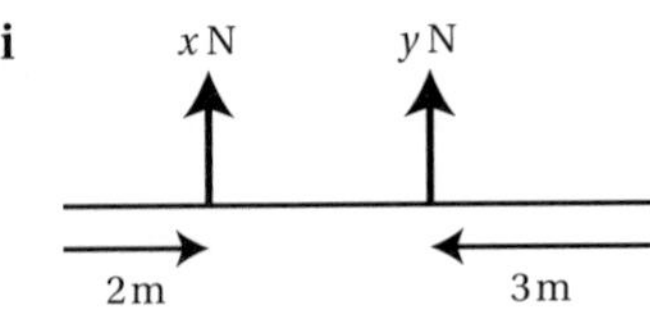

2 The following uniform rectangular lamina have a weight of 100 N and are hanging in equilibrium in a vertical plane. Find the unknown values.

a **i**

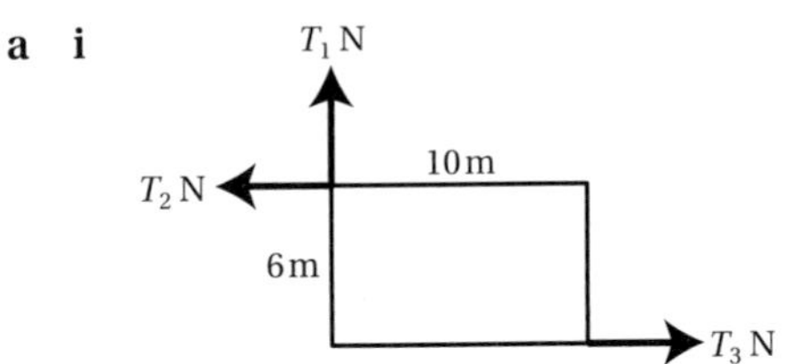

ii

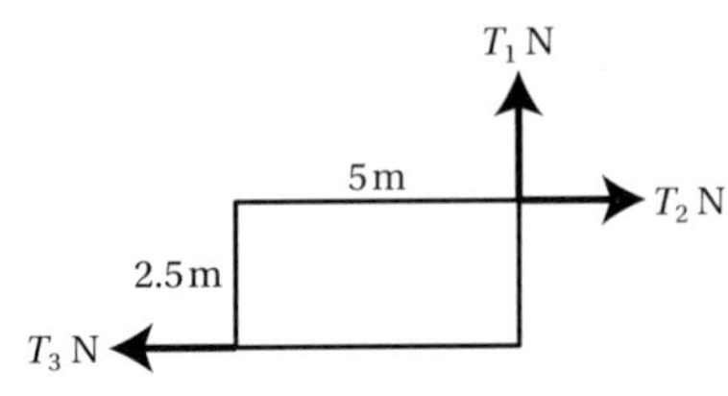

b **i**

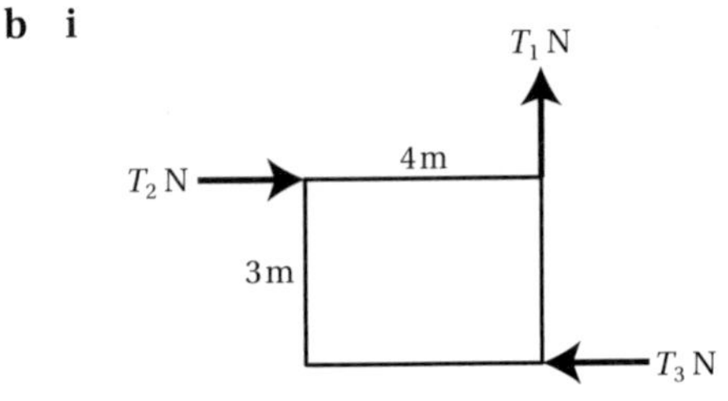

ii

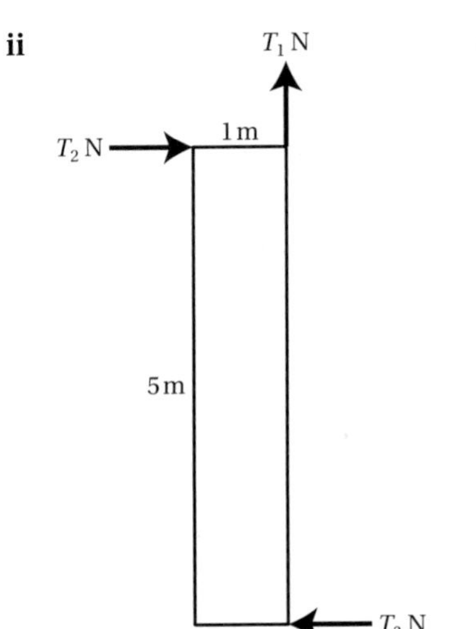

c **i**

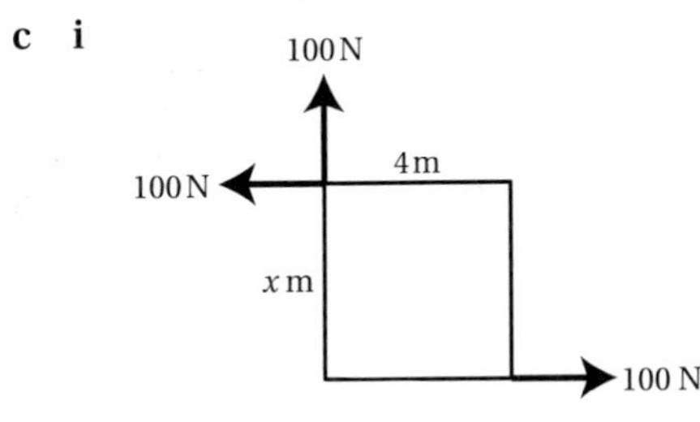

ii

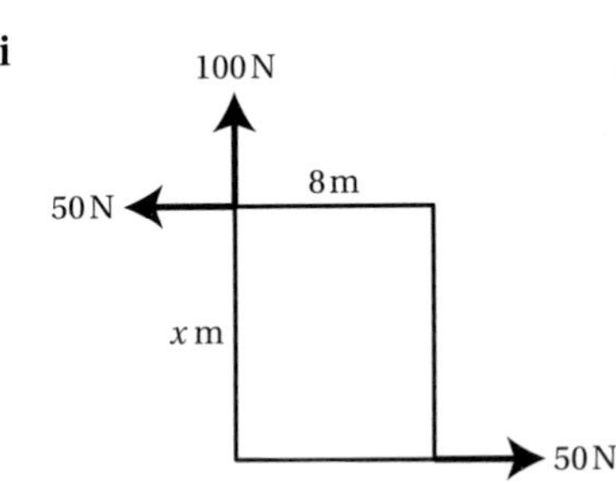

3 Two children sit on a see-saw formed from a uniform rod of length 4 m, balanced in the middle. One child, of mass 30 kg, sits on one end. How far from the other end should the other child, of mass 40 kg, sit so that the see-saw is balanced in a horizontal position?

4 A door is 120 cm wide. A perpendicular force of 80 N is applied 90 cm from the hinge but a wedge at the end of the door opposite the hinge is keeping it shut. Find the frictional force acting through the wedge.

5 In a simplified model of a crane, the arm PQ is modelled as a uniform rod of length 20 m and mass 1000 kg.

The arm is attached to the main body of the crane 5 m from P. A weight of 5000 kg is suspended 2 m from Q. A counterweight of 15 000 kg can be moved along the arm to keep the crane in equilibrium.

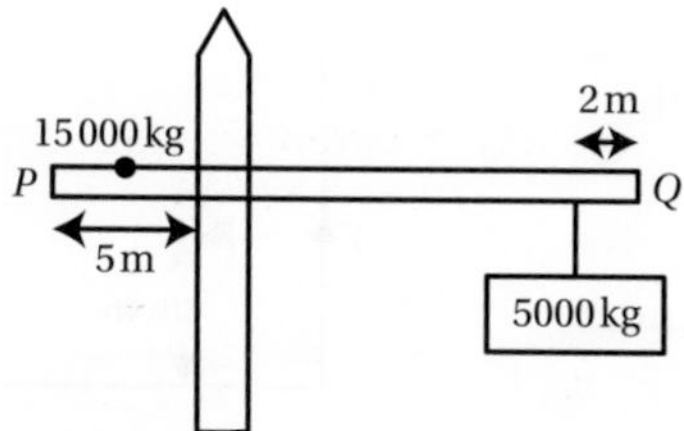

a Find at what distance from P the counterweight should be attached.

b Explain why the counterweight would not need to be placed precisely at the position found in part **a**.

6 A uniform plank, of length 3 m and mass 5 kg, rests in a horizontal equilibrium on two supports, one at the end of the plank and the other 1 m from the other end. Find the reaction force supplied by each support.

7 A uniform beam of length 2 m and mass 20 kg is suspended horizontally by wires at either end. A painter of weight 80 kg is standing 0.5 m from one end of the beam. Find the tension in each of the wires.

8 A pole vaulter holds a pole in a horizontal position, with one hand on the end and the other x cm away. The length of the pole is 4 m and its weight is 40 N.

a Find, in terms of x, the vertical forces exerted by his hands.

b State one additional assumption you have made in part **a**.

9 A spade is modelled as a uniform rod, of mass 2 kg and length 90 cm, attached to a uniform square lamina, of side 20 cm and mass 0.5 kg. A gardener holds the spade horizontally with hands 30 cm and 60 cm from the end of the rod. Find the vertical forces exerted by the gardener's hands.

10 A model for the elbow joint models the bicep muscle connecting to the horizontal forearm by a vertical tendon 4 cm from the elbow joint. A mass m is held in the hand 30 cm from the elbow joint.
If the maximum tension that can be exerted by the tendon before injury occurs is 2250 N, find the maximum mass that can be held in this way.

11 A shop sign, $ABCD$, is modelled as a uniform rectangular lamina of width 50 cm, height 40 cm and weight 60 N. It is resting on a rough support at X with a horizontal wire connected at A.

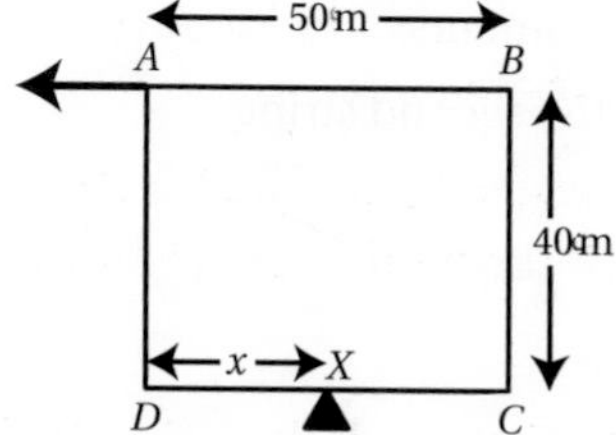

a Find, in terms of x where necessary:

i the tension in the wire

ii the normal reaction at X

iii the friction force at X

b How would your answer to part **a i** be different if a light rod rather than a wire were attached at A?

12 A door is modelled as a rectangular lamina of weight 150 N, with height 2 m and width 1.2 m, supported in equilibrium by two hinges at X and Y.

If the force at X is entirely horizontal, find the magnitude of the forces at X and Y.

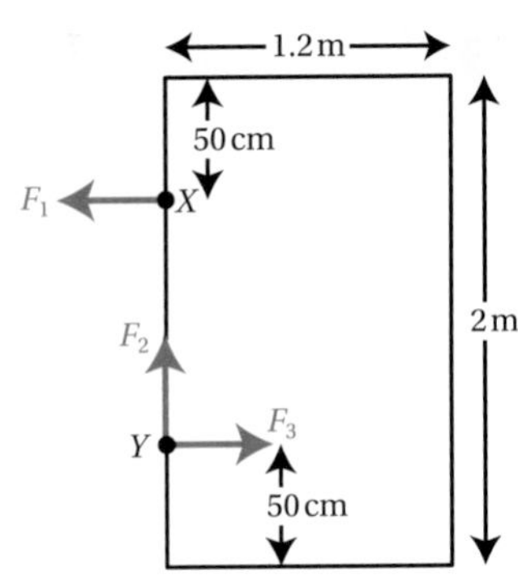

13 In the film *The Italian Job*, a coach is balancing on the edge of a cliff with gold bullion at one end and a group of people at the other. Model the coach as a uniform rod of length 4 m and mass 1500 kg, with 1000 kg of gold at the end overhanging the cliff and 500 kg of people at the other end. How much of the coach can overhang the cliff before it falls?

Section 3: Non-uniform rods

When the mass of a rod is not evenly distributed throughout its length you say that the rod is said to be **non-uniform**. This could happen, for example, if the rod varies in thickness, or if it is made out of several different materials.

The centre of mass of a non-uniform rod is not necessarily at its mid-point. You may be told the position of the centre of mass or may be able to determine it experimentally by measuring forces acting on the rod when it is in equilibrium.

WORKED EXAMPLE 22.6

A non-uniform rod of length 6 m and mass 12 kg hangs in equilibrium, supported by two light inextensible vertical strings of equal lengths attached to its ends. The tension in the first string is 88.2 N. Find the distance of the centre of mass from the end attached to the second string.

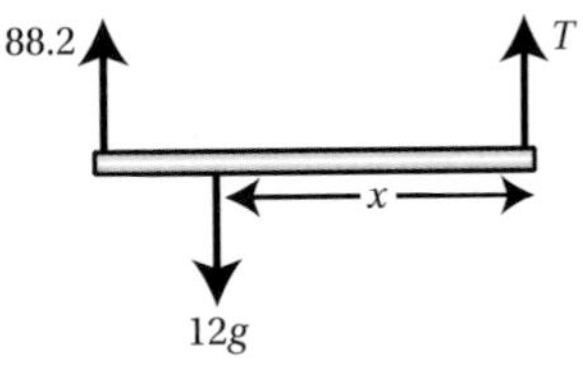

The weight acts at a distance x from the right-hand end. (This is the position of the centre of mass.)

Taking moments about the right-hand end:

$$88.2 \times 6 = 12g \times x$$

$$x = \frac{88.2 \times 6}{12 \times 9.8}$$

$$= 4.5$$

Since the plank is in equilibrium, sum of clockwise moments = sum of anticlockwise moments.

Since you don't know the force in the second string, take moments about that end.

The centre of mass is 4.5 m from the right-hand end.

If you already know the position of the centre of mass, you can use it as before to solve problems about a rod in equilibrium.

WORKED EXAMPLE 22.7

A non-uniform rod AB, of mass 10 kg and length 6 m, has its centre of mass at a point 2.5 m from end A. It rests in equilibrium on two supports located 0.3 m from each end. A particle of mass m kg is placed 1 m from the support closer to end B.

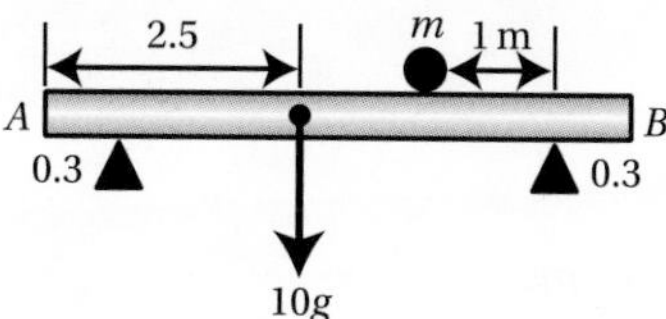

Given that the reaction forces in the two supports are equal, find the value of m.

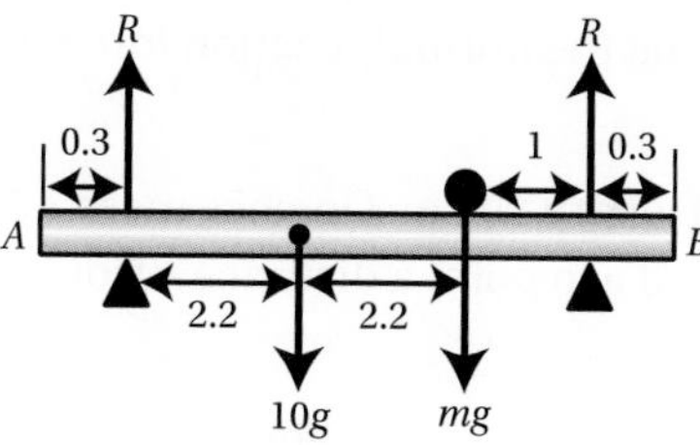

Forces on the plank:

$10 \times 9.8 + m \times 9.8 = 2R$

$\Rightarrow R = 49 + 4.9m$

Since the rod is in equilibrium, the net force is zero...

Moments about the support closer to end A:

$98 \times 2.2 + mg \times 4.4 = 5.4 \times (49 + 4.9m)$

$\Rightarrow 215.6 + 43.12m = 264.6 + 26.46m$

$\Rightarrow 16.66m = 49$

$\Rightarrow m = 2.94$

...and the net moment is zero.

You can choose to take moments either about one of the supports or about the centre of mass.

EXERCISE 22C

In this exercise, take $g = 9.8\,\mathrm{m\,s^{-2}}$.

1 A non-uniform plank AB, of length 5 m and mass 4 kg, rests in equilibrium on two supports, one at each end. The centre of mass of the plank is located 1.2 m from end A. Find the reaction force in each support.

2 A non-uniform plank of length 3 m rests in equilibrium on two supports, located 60 cm and 80 cm from each end. The reaction forces in the two supports are equal. Find the position of the centre of mass of the plank.

3 A non-uniform plank of weight 180 N and length 4 m is placed on a support at its midpoint. The plank is held in equilibrium by a downward force of magnitude 60 N acting on one end. Find the distance of the centre of mass of the plank from its midpoint.

4 A non-uniform rod is held in a horizontal position by two light inextensible strings attached to its ends. The centre of mass of the rod is located 1.5 m from one end, and the tensions in the strings are T and $3T$. Find the possible lengths of the rod.

5 A non-uniform rod AB, of mass 10 kg and length 6 m, has its centre of mass at a point 2.5 m from end A. It rests in equilibrium on two supports located 0.3 m from each end. A particle of mass m kg is placed 0.6 m from the support closer to end B.

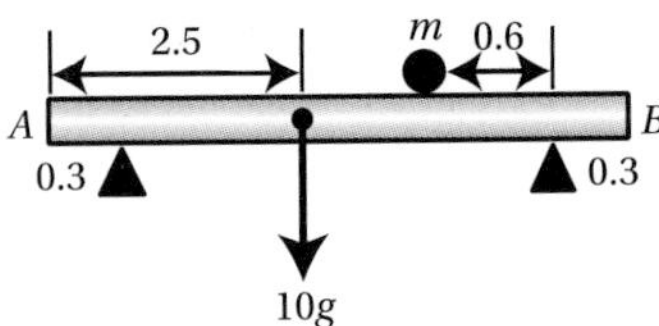

Given that the reaction forces in the two supports are equal, find the value of m.

6 A non-uniform plank of mass M and length 6 m rests on two supports, C and D, located 0.3 m from its ends. The centre of mass of the plank is 2.2 m from support C. A particle of mass $10M$ is placed on the plank at the distance x from the centre of mass, towards support D, so that the normal reaction forces in the two supports are equal. Find the distance x.

7 A snooker cue is formed by connecting end-to-end two uniform rods of length 80 cm. One has mass 1.5 kg and the other has mass 2 kg. The cue rests in equilibrium when supported at a point a distance x from the exterior end of the 2 kg section. Find the value of x.

8 A non-uniform rod has length 2 m. The rod is placed on a support at its midpoint. It is in equilibrium when a particle of weight 50 N is placed at one end and a particle of weight 30 N on the other end. The particles are then removed and the rod is then suspended by two light inextensible strings attached to its ends. When the rod is horizontal, the tension in one of the strings is 120 N. Find the two possible values for the weight of the rod.

Section 4: Further equilibrium problems

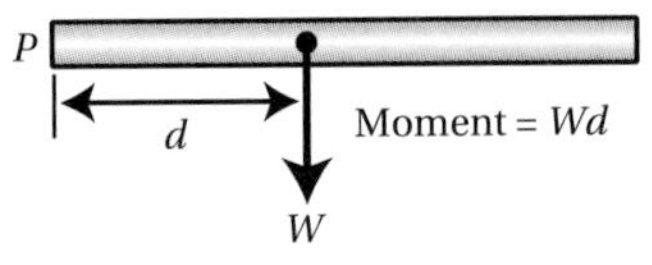

Remember that at the start of this chapter the moment about a point was defined as the force times the *perpendicular* distance from the point to the force. In all the examples with rods so far, the forces have been acting perpendicular to the rod so that the perpendicular distance was measured along the rod.

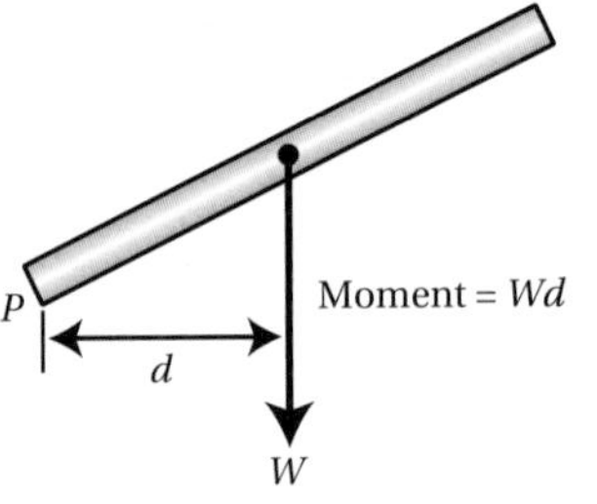

Now look at a rod that is held at an angle to the horizontal. To calculate the moment of its weight about an end point you need to use the perpendicular distance from that point to the vertical line, as shown in the diagram.

When a rod is in equilibrium, you can still use the rule that the net force is zero and the net moment about any point is zero. However, it is now possible to write three equations, because you can consider horizontal and vertical components separately.

Key point 22.5

If an object is in equilibrium, then:

- The sum of horizontal components of all the forces equals zero.
- The sum of vertical components of all the forces equals zero.
- The sum of clockwise moments equals the sum of anticlockwise moments about any point.

WORKED EXAMPLE 22.8

A uniform rod of length $2l$ and weight 50 N is held in equilibrium by four light inextensible strings, as shown in the diagram. Two of the strings are horizontal and two are vertical. The rod makes a 30° angle with the horizontal. The tension in the vertical string to the left of the diagram is 20 N. Find the tensions in the two horizontal strings.

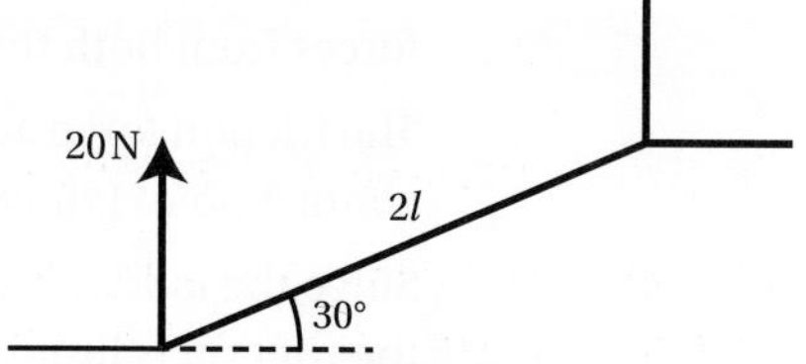

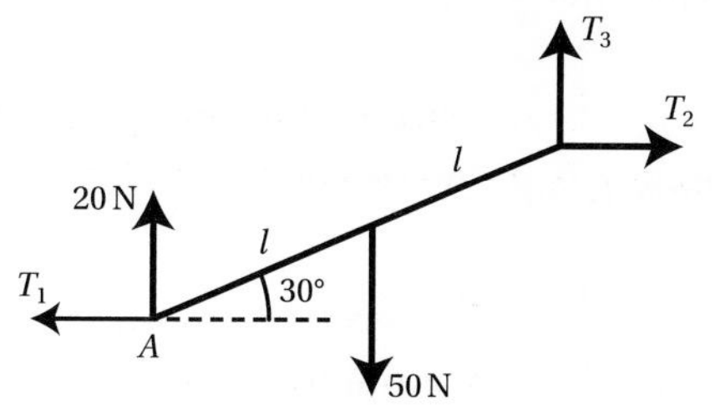

Label all four tensions and the weight on the diagram.
Since the rod is in equilibrium...

$T_1 = T_2$

...the net horizontal force is zero,

$T_3 + 20 = 50 \Rightarrow T_3 = 30$

...the net vertical force is zero,

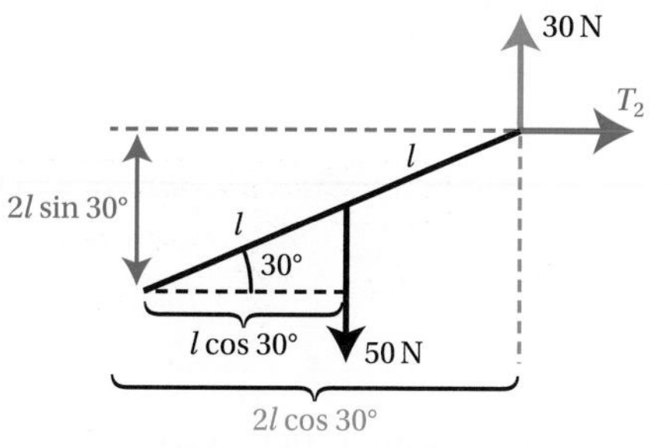

...and the net clockwise moment equals the net anticlockwise moment.

Take moments about the lower end of the rod (marked A). You need perpendicular distances from A to the line of the forces marked 50 N, 30 N and T_2.

$50 \times l \cos 30° + T_2 \times 2l \sin 30° = 30 \times 2l \cos 30°$

$\Rightarrow T_2 \times 2 \sin 30° = 30 \times 2 \cos 30° - 50 \cos 30°$

$\Rightarrow T_2 = \dfrac{10 \cos 30°}{2 \sin 30°}$

$T_1 = T_2 = 8.66$ N

When the rod is placed on the ground or against a wall, you may also need to include friction in your force diagram.

WORKED EXAMPLE 22.9

A ladder can be modelled as a uniform rod of length 4 m and mass 12 kg. The ladder is placed on rough horizontal ground and against a smooth vertical wall. The coefficient of friction between the ladder and the ground is 0.4 and the ladder is on the point of slipping. Find the angle the ladder makes with the horizontal.

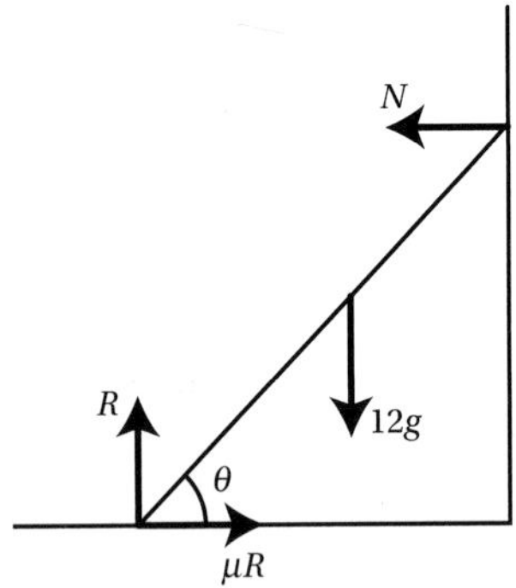

Remember to include the normal reaction forces from both the ground and the wall.

The friction force acts only at the ground contact point (since the wall is smooth).

Since the ladder is on the point of slipping, the friction is limiting (so equals μR) and directed towards the wall.

$R = 12g$ — The net vertical force is zero.

$\mu R = N$ — The net horizontal force is zero.

$$12g \times 2\cos\theta = N \times 4\sin\theta$$

$$\Rightarrow 12g \times 2\cos\theta = 12\mu g \times 4\sin\theta$$

The clockwise moments equal the anti-clockwise moments about any point. We chose the point of contact with the ground since this eliminates two forces.

$$\Rightarrow 24\cos\theta = 19.2\sin\theta$$

$$\Rightarrow \tan\theta = \frac{24}{19.2}$$

$$\theta = 51.3°$$

EXERCISE 22D

1 Find the moment of each force about the point P, stating whether it is clockwise or anticlockwise.

a i

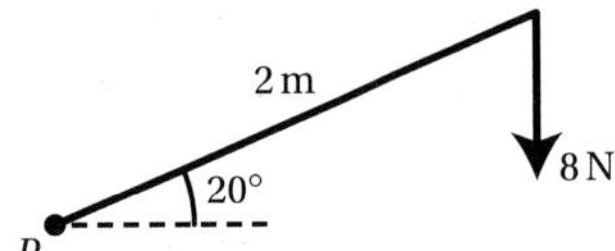

ii

P
30°
5 m
12 N

b i

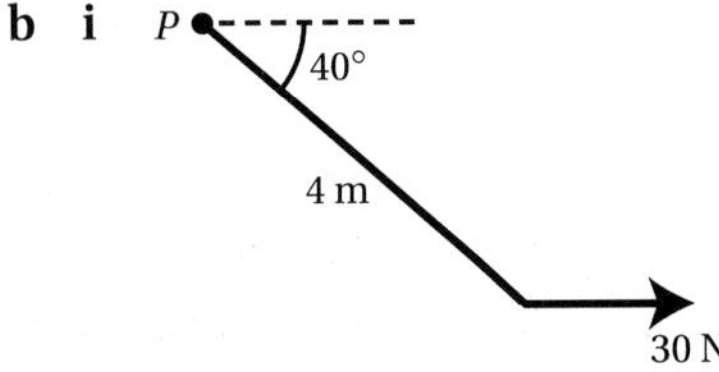

ii

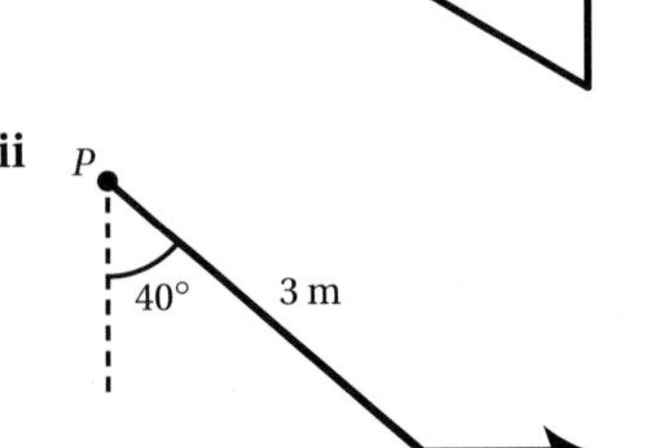

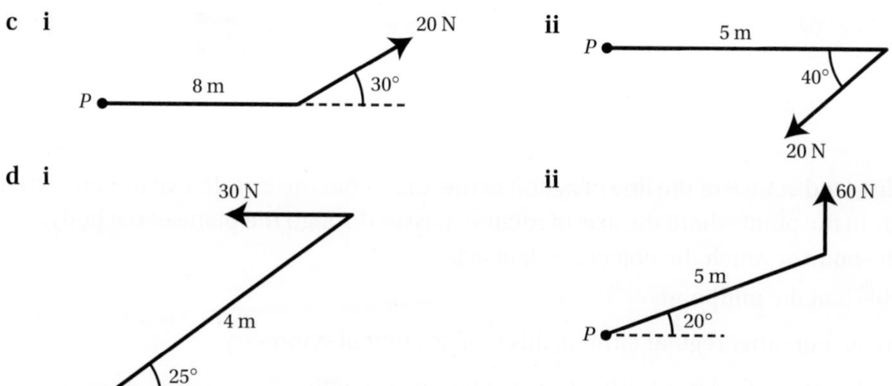

2 A uniform rod of length 5 m and weight 30 N is freely hinged at one end. The other end is attached to a light inextensible string. The rod is held in equilibrium with the string horizontal.

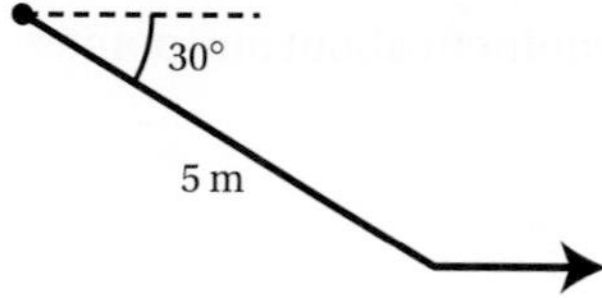

Find the tension in the string required to keep the rod at an angle of 30° to the horizontal.

3 A uniform rod of length $2l$ and weight 20 N is freely hinged at end A. End B is attached to a light inextensible string. The rod is in equilibrium with the string horizontal. The tension in the string is 4 N.

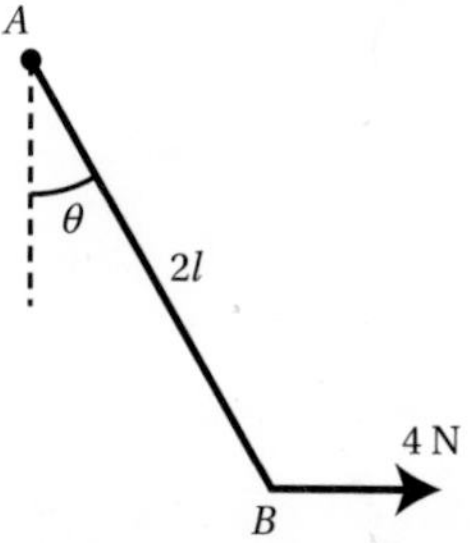

Find the angle θ that the rod makes with the vertical.

4 A uniform ladder of length 4 m and mass 30 kg rests against a smooth vertical wall. The ladder makes a 70° angle with the rough horizontal ground and is in limiting equilibrium. Find the coefficient of friction between the ladder and the ground.

5 A uniform ladder of length 5 m rests on rough horizontal ground against a rough vertical wall. The coefficient of friction between the ladder and the ground is 0.7, and the coefficient of friction between the ladder and the wall is 0.3. The equilibrium is limiting at both contact points. Find the angle the ladder makes with the horizontal.

6 A ladder of mass 12 kg rests on rough horizontal ground against a smooth vertical wall, making a 40° angle with the wall. The coefficient of friction between the ladder and the ground is 0.6. The ladder is modelled as a uniform rod of length 4 m. A man of mass 70 kg climbs up the ladder. How far can he climb before the ladder slips?

Checklist of learning and understanding

- The moment of a force F about an axis is:

  Moment $= Fd$

  where d is the *perpendicular* distance of the line of action of the force from the axis. In two dimensions, the distance is measured from the point where the axis of rotation passes through the plane of the body.
- The centre of mass is the point at which the object's weight acts.
  - For a uniform rod, this is at the midpoint.
  - For a uniform rectangular or other regular lamina, this is at its point of symmetry.
  - For a non-uniform rod, you can find its position by considering moments.
- To find the resultant moment about a point, find the sum of the clockwise and anticlockwise moments separately. The resultant moment will be the difference between the two sums (in the direction of the larger).
- If an object is in equilibrium, there is zero resultant force and zero resultant moment about any point.

Mixed practice 22

Use $g = 10\,\text{m}\,\text{s}^{-2}$ unless otherwise stated.

1 What is the resultant moment about point O on the uniform rectangular lamina of weight 10 N shown in the diagram?

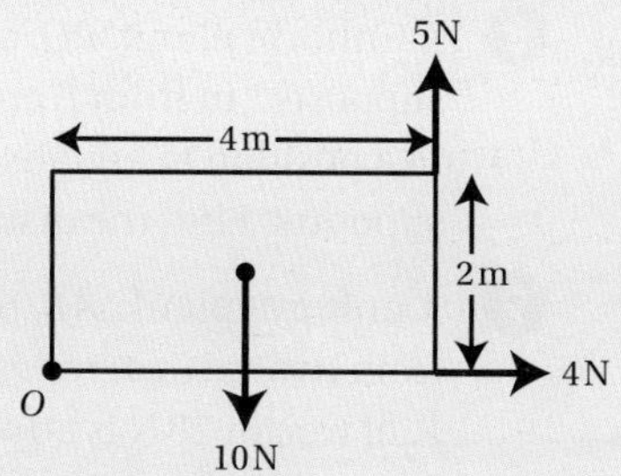

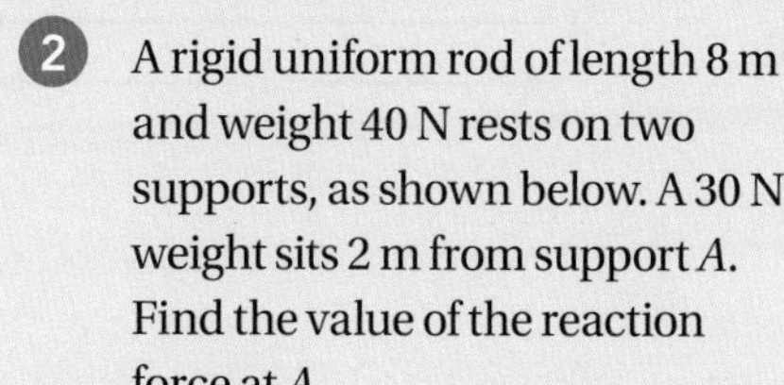

2 A rigid uniform rod of length 8 m and weight 40 N rests on two supports, as shown below. A 30 N weight sits 2 m from support A. Find the value of the reaction force at A.

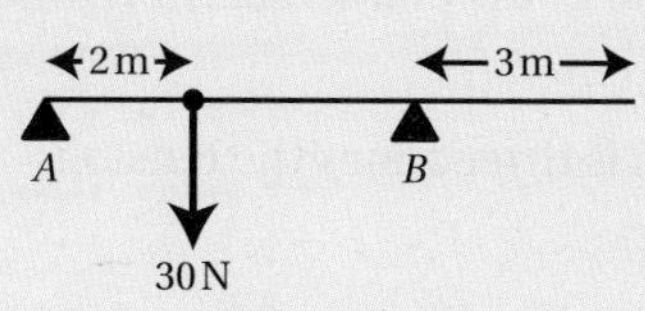

3 The diagram below shows a uniform rod of length 2 m and weight 50 N lying in equilibrium suspended from two wires. The tensions in the wires are 20 N and 30 N and are set at distance x m and $2x$ m, respectively. Find the value of x.

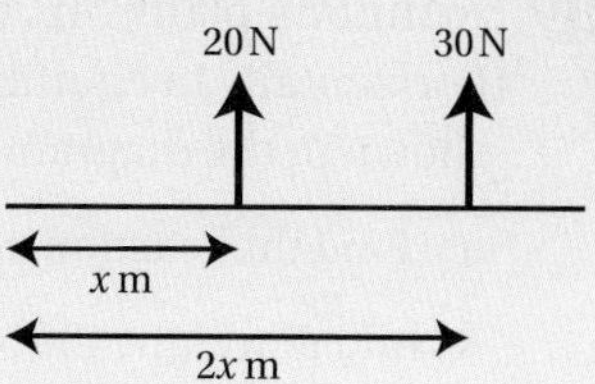

4 A non-uniform plank of length 6 m is placed on two supports, one at each end. The reaction forces in the supports are 30 N and 50 N. Find the distance of the centre of mass from the midpoint of the plank.

5 A ladder of length 3 m and weight 50 N rests on rough horizontal ground and against a smooth vertical wall. The ladder is modelled as a uniform rod, and makes an angle of $\theta°$ with the horizontal. The coefficient of friction between the ladder and the ground is 0.8. A boy of weight 400 N stands at the top of the ladder. Given that the ladder is on the point of slipping, find the value of θ.

6 A uniform rod AB of mass 10 kg and length 2.4 m rests with A on rough horizontal ground. The rod makes an angle of 60° with the horizontal and is supported by a fixed smooth peg, P. The distance AP is 1.6 m (see diagram).

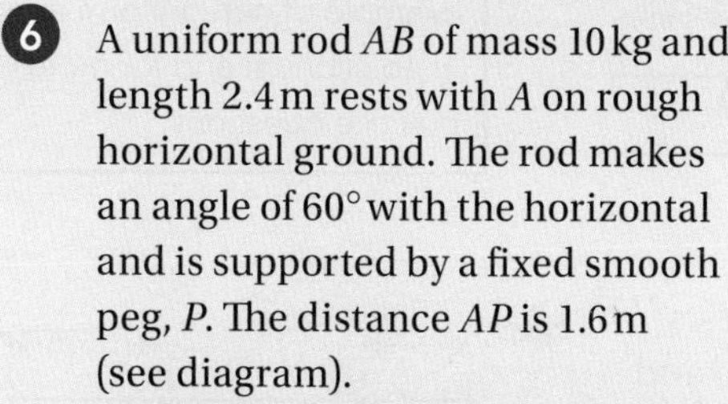

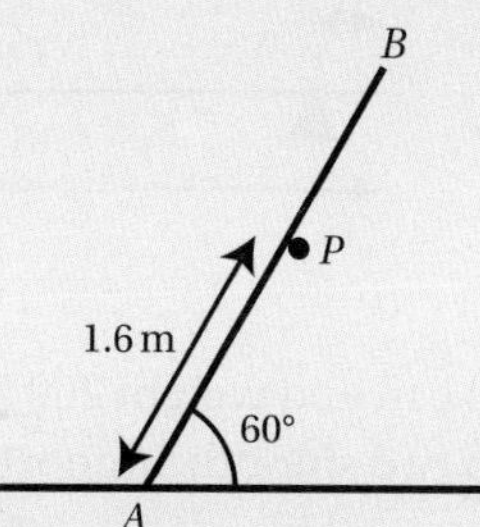

i Calculate the magnitude of the force exerted by the peg on the rod.

ii Find the least value of the coefficient of friction between the rod and the ground needed to maintain equilibrium.

Tip

The hinge is fixed in space and applies a horizontal force X and a vertical force Y to the rod.

7 An oar is modelled as a uniform rod, PQ, of length 3 m and mass 5 kg with an additional mass of 1 kg attached to end P. The oar is hung by a single wire. How far from Q must this be attached if the oar is to hang horizontally?

8 A uniform plank, PQ, of mass 10 kg and length 5 m rests on supports 1 m from P and 2 m from Q. A mass, 60 kg is placed in a position to equalise the reaction forces on the two supports. Find the distance of the mass from P.

9 A uniform plank, AB, of mass 40 kg and length 5 m hangs from two vertical ropes attached to A and C. When a particle, P, of weight 28 N is attached to B, the plank rests horizontally in equilibrium.

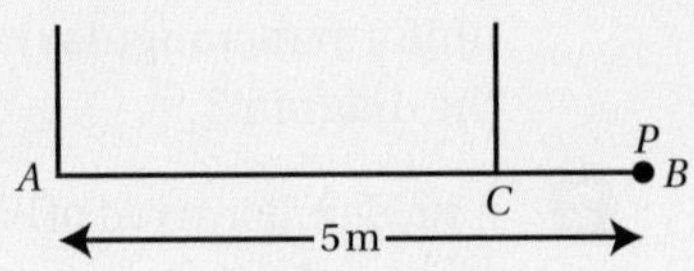

If the tension in the rope at C is three times the tension at A, find:

a the tension at C **b** the distance CB.

10 A uniform plank, AB, of length 6 m and weight 100 N rests horizontally in equilibrium on two smooth supports, as shown in the diagram.

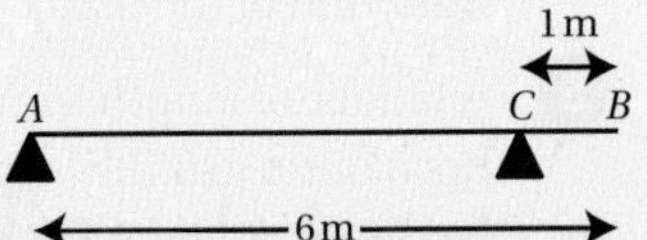

a Find the reaction at C.

A child of weight 400 N stands on the plank at D. The plank remains in equilibrium. The reactions on the plank at A and C are now equal.

b Find the distance AD.

11 A non-uniform plank has length 4 m and weight 125 N. It rests horizontally in equilibrium, as shown in the diagram.

A particle of weight W N is placed on the plank at B. The plank remains in equilibrium and the reaction at D is 139 N. The centre of mass of the plank is a distance x from A.

a Show that $7W + 250x = 820$.

The particle is now removed from B and placed at A. The rod remains in equilibrium and the reaction at D is now 43 N.

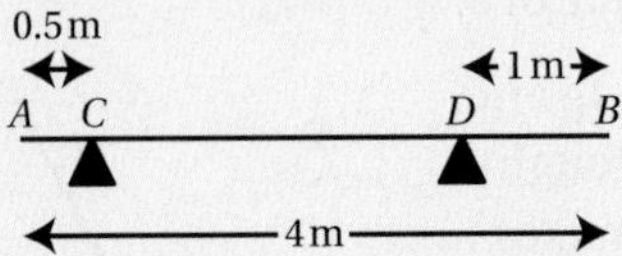

b Find W and x.

Elevate

See Support sheet 22 for an example of non-uniform rods in equilibrium and for more practice questions.

12 A uniform plank, AB, of length 6 m and weight 200 N rests horizontally in equilibrium on two smooth supports, C and D, as shown in the diagram.

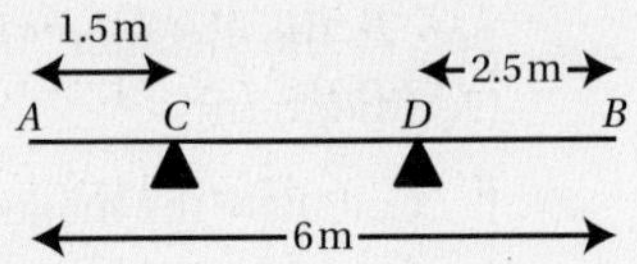

A particle of weight W N is attached to a point on the plank x m from A. The plank remains in equilibrium and the reactions at C and D are now equal.

a Show that $W = \dfrac{200}{11 - 4x}$.

b Hence, find the range of possible values of x.

Elevate

See Extension sheet 22 for some questions involving laminas formed of a rectangle and a triangle.

13 A rectangular lamina is formed by connecting two square uniform laminas of side 2 metres and masses M and m, where $M > m$.

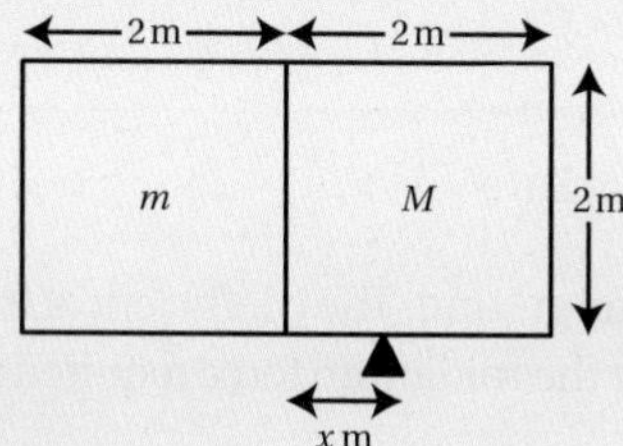

The rectangular lamina balances on a point a distance x from the line joining the two square laminas, as shown in the diagram below. Find an expression for x in terms of M and m.

14 A uniform rod of length 6 m and weight 100 N is being pushed over a fixed smooth peg (P) and a fixed support (S), with a coefficient of friction 0.6. P and S are 3 m apart. x is the length of the rod overhanging S.

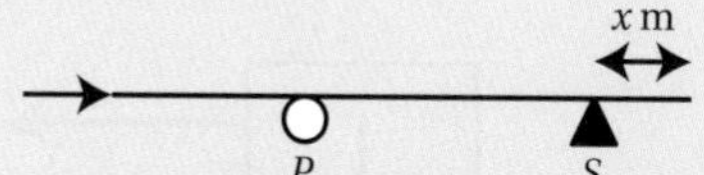

Find, as a function of x, the force required for the rod to move at a constant speed.

15 In this question take $g = 9.8\,\text{m}\,\text{s}^{-2}$.

A car with its contents is modelled by a uniform rectangular lamina (having length and height only since width will not be relevant) of mass 1200 kg and length 4 m. The wheels are located 1.5 m from the front of the car and 1 m from the rear of the car. Assume that air resistance is negligible.

a By taking moments about the rear wheel, show that the normal reaction of the ground on the front wheel is 7840 N.

b The car has front wheel drive. Given that the coefficient of friction between the front wheel and the road is 0.5, and assuming that the car has sufficient power, find the maximum acceleration of the car.

c What modelling assumptions have been made in part **b**?

16 A uniform rod AB, of weight 30 N and length 2 m, is freely hinged at A with a vertical string attached at B. The tension, T N, in the string is sufficient to maintain the rod in a horizontal equilibrium.

a Find the value of T.

b Find the magnitude and direction of the force provided by the hinge.

FOCUS ON ... PROOF 4

Overcoming friction

A block of weight W rests on rough horizontal ground. The coefficient of friction between the block and the ground is μ. You are going to derive the formulae for the minimum force required to move the block in various situations.

Questions

A horizontal force of magnitude F acts on the block

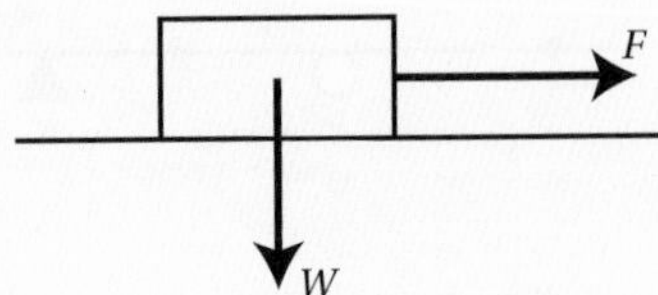

1 Find, in terms of W and μ, the minimum value of F required to move the block.

The force acts at a fixed angle θ above the horizontal

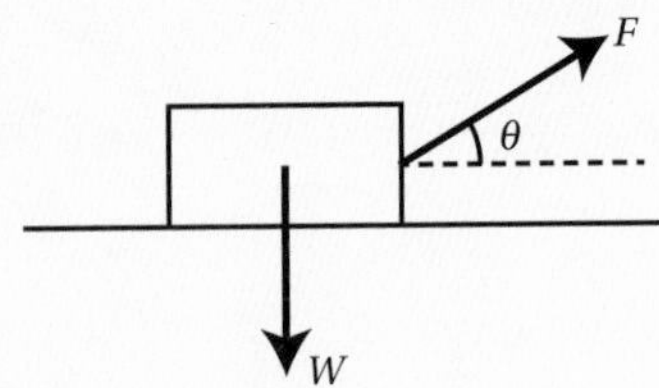

2 Prove that the minimum value of F is $\frac{\mu W \sec\theta}{1+\mu\tan\theta}$.

Both F and θ can vary

3 **a** Find the maximum value of $\cos\theta + \mu\sin\theta$ for $0° \leqslant \theta \leqslant 90°$. Hence, find the minimum magnitude of the force required to move the box. Prove that this minimum magnitude is always less than W. (In other words, however large μ is, it is always possible to move the box using a force smaller than its weight.)

b Prove that the angle at which the minimal force needs to act is $\theta = \arctan\mu$.

The force pushes the block at an angle θ below the horizontal

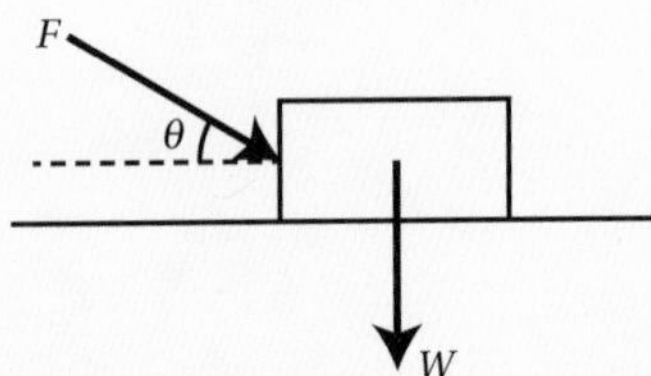

4 **a** Prove that $F(\cos\theta + \mu\sin\theta) \geqslant \mu W$.

b By considering the graph of $y = \cos\theta + \mu\sin\theta$ for $0° \leqslant \theta \leqslant 90°$, or otherwise, prove that the required magnitude of the force is minimal when the force is horizontal, and state this magnitude.

FOCUS ON ... PROBLEM SOLVING 4

Checking for reasonableness

When solving problems in real contexts answers are rarely 'nice' numbers. It can therefore be difficult to tell whether your answer is correct. However, there are still some checks you can do, such as confirming that your calculation gives correct units and making sure that the answer isn't completely unreasonable.

Below are proposed answers to some Mechanics problems. Decide which ones are obviously wrong.

1. A car's deceleration is $260\,\text{m}\,\text{s}^{-2}$.
2. The tension in the cable supporting the lift is 0.36 N.
3. The frictional force acting on the box is 30 N.
4. The stone was dropped from a height of 2.8×10^{-3} m.
5. The road is inclined at 72° to the horizontal.
6. The mass of the car is 2600 kg.
7. The coefficient of friction between the box and the floor is 36.2.
8. An athlete runs 100 m at an average speed of $32\,\text{km}\,\text{h}^{-1}$.
9. The maximum height reached by the projectile is 3600 km.
10. The two trains will meet after 0.45 seconds.
11. The coefficient of friction between the skates and the ice is 0.6.
12. The car accelerates at $47\,000\,\text{km}\,\text{h}^{-2}$.
13. The coefficient of friction between the box and the ice is 0.035.
14. The ball takes 12.3 seconds to fall from the tenth floor.
15. The journey from London to Manchester takes 18 hours.

FOCUS ON ... MODELLING 4

Modelling with moments

It is alleged that Archimedes once said:

Give me a place to stand and I will move the Earth.

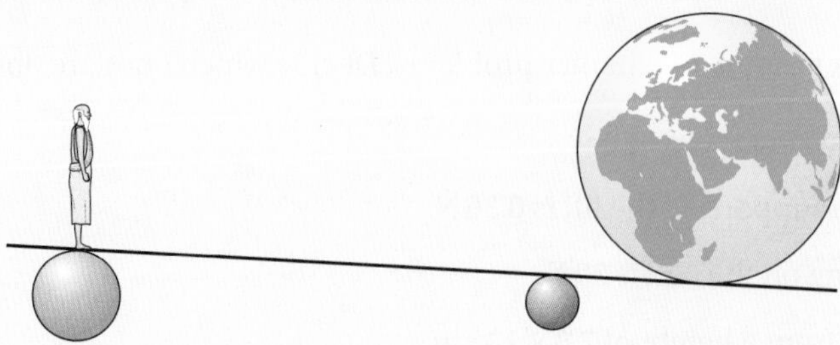

It is theoretically possible to move any weight using a long enough lever. To move the Earth, Archimedes would need to be standing on a different planet and he would also need a support for the lever.

Questions

1. Suppose the Earth is modelled as a particle of mass 6×10^{24} kg, resting on one end of the lever, and that Archimedes is a particle of mass 60 kg, sitting on the other end. The lever rests on a support 1 m from the Earth. How long would the other side of the lever need to be?
2. Other than modelling the Earth and Archimedes as particles, what other assumption did you make in your calculation?
3. Is modelling the Earth as a particle realistic? What could you change in your model to make the particle assumption reasonable? (The radius of the Earth is 6.4×10^6 m.) How does this change your answer to question 1?
4. Using the modelling assumptions from question 1, suppose Archimedes moves his end of the lever for a year, at an average speed of 6 km/h. By how much would he move the Earth?

Did you know?

The Ancient Greek mathematician Archimedes is perhaps best known for exclaiming 'Eureka!' on realising that a body submerged in water displaces its own volume of water. This idea is now commonly known as Archimedes' principle. However, his work extended well beyond this discovery and his work on levers. He designed the screw pump for raising water, compound pulleys and siege machines, and also developed the fundamentals of integral calculus 2000 years before Newton and Leibniz eventually formalised it.

CROSS-TOPIC REVIEW EXERCISE 4

1 A uniform plank of mass 12 kg and length 4.6 m rests on two supports, A and B. The support A is 0.8 m from one end of the plank and support B is 0.3 m from the other end. The plank is horizontal. A box of mass 7 kg is placed on the plank, 1.2 m from A.

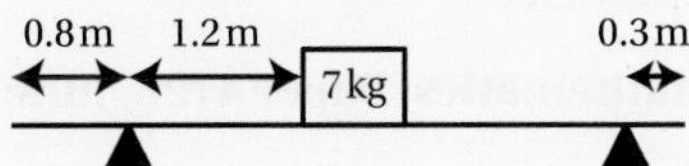

Find, in terms of g, the force acting on the plank at each support.

2 Points A and B have position vectors $\mathbf{a} = 3\mathbf{i} - \mathbf{j} + 5\mathbf{k}$ and $\mathbf{b} = 2\mathbf{j} - \mathbf{k}$.

a Find the vector $\overrightarrow{AB}$.

b Find the exact distance between the two points.

3 A particle of mass 5 kg moves on a horizontal plane. Its position, $\mathbf{r}$ m, at time t seconds is given by:

$$\mathbf{r} = \left(5t - e^{-2t}\right)\mathbf{i} + \left(e^{0.1t} + 1\right)\mathbf{j}$$

a Find an expression for the velocity of the particle at time t.

b Find the speed and the direction of motion of the particle when $t = 2$.

c Find, when $t = 2$:

i the magnitude of the acceleration

ii the magnitude of the resultant force on the particle.

4 Points M, N and P have coordinates (2, 1, –5), (5, –3, 2) and (–2, –3, 7), respectively.

a Find the coordinates of the point Q so that $MNPQ$ is a parallelogram.

b Show that $MNPQ$ is a rhombus.

c Find the coordinates of the point S on the line MN such that $NS = MN$.

5 A non-uniform plank of mass 8 kg and length 4 m rests on a support at its midpoint. A particle of mass 3 kg rests on the plank, 0.6 m to the left of the support. Given that the plank is in equilibrium, find:

a the position of its centre of mass

b the magnitude of the force acting on the plank at the support.

6

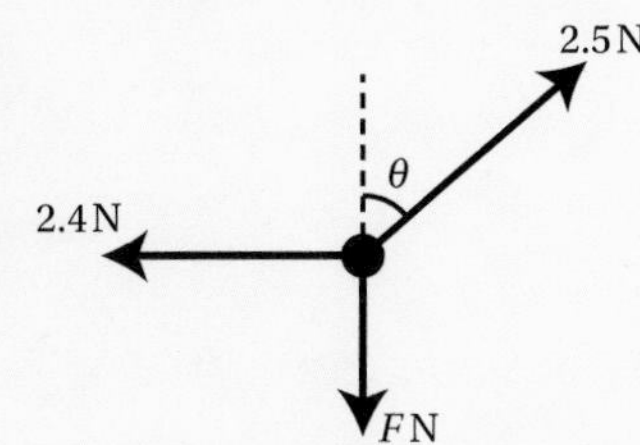

A particle rests on a smooth horizontal surface. Three horizontal forces of magnitudes 2.5 N, F N and 2.4 N act on the particle on the bearings $\theta°$, 180° and 270°, respectively (see diagram). The particle is in equilibrium.

i a Find θ and F.

The 2.4 N force suddenly ceases to act on the particle, which has mass 0.2 kg.

b Find the magnitude and direction of the acceleration of the particle.

7 The position vectors of two particles, A and B, at time t, are given by $\mathbf{r}_A = (4\cos(\pi t) + 2)\mathbf{i} + 5\mathbf{j}$ and $\mathbf{r}_B = 2\mathbf{i} + (5 - 4\sin(\pi t))\mathbf{j}$. Prove that the distance between the two particles is constant.

8 Three points have coordinates $T(-3, 1, 4)$, $U(0, 2, 3)$ and $V(5, a, b)$. Find the values of a and b so that TUV is a straight line.

9 Two small blocks, each of mass 3 kg, are connected by a light inextensible string passing over a smooth pulley. One block rests on a rough horizontal table and the other hangs freely with the string vertical. The coefficient of friction between the block and the table is 0.4.

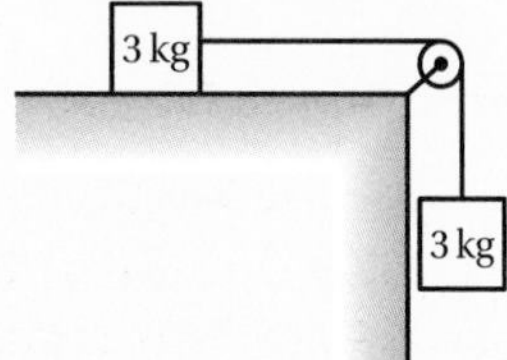

The first block is initially 1.2 m from the edge of the table when the system is released from rest.

a Find, in terms of g, the acceleration of the system.

b How long does it take for the first block to reach the edge of the table?

c Find the magnitude and direction of the force acting on the pulley from the string.

d How did you use the modelling assumption that:

i the pulley is smooth

ii the string is inextensible?

10 A uniform rectangular lamina has sides of length 68 cm and 42 cm and mass 620 grams. The lamina is freely hinged at point A and is held in equilibrium, with the longer side horizontal, by means of a light inextensible string attached to point B.

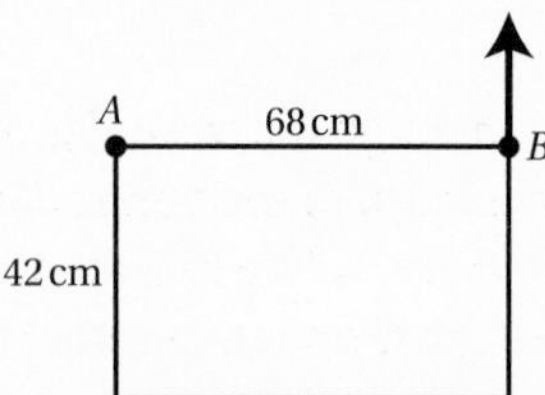

a Find the tension in the string.

b Find the magnitude and direction of the force acting on the lamina at A.

11 A non-uniform beam AB, of length 4 m and mass 5 kg, has its centre of mass at the point G of the beam where $AG = 2.5$ m. The beam is freely suspended from its end A and is held in a horizontal position by means of a wire attached to the end B. The wire makes an angle of 20° with the vertical and the tension is T N (see diagram).

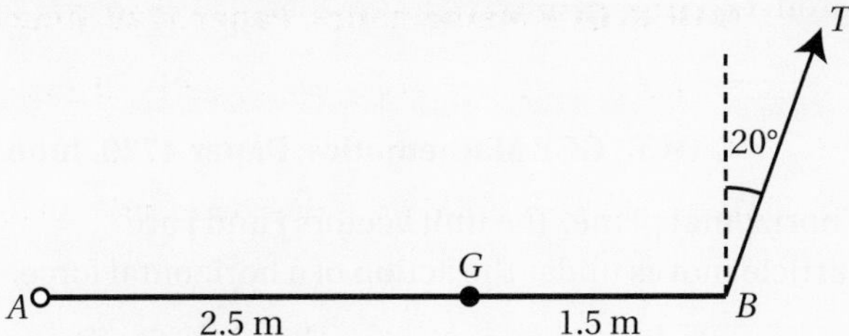

i Calculate T.

ii Calculate the magnitude and the direction of the force acting on the beam at A.

© OCR, GCE Mathematics, Paper 4729, June 2010

12 A particle P is projected with speed u m s^{-1} from the top of a smooth inclined plane of length $2d$ metres. After its projection P moves downwards along a line of greatest slope with acceleration 4 m s^{-2}. At the instant 3 s after projection P has moved half way down the plane. P reaches the foot of he plane 5 s after the instant of projection.

i Form two simultaneous equations in u and d, and hence calculate the speed of projection of P and the length of the plane.

ii Find the inclination of the plane to the horizontal.

iii Given that the contact force exerted on P by the plane has magnitude 6 N, calculate the mass of P.

© OCR, GCE Mathematics, Paper 4728, June 2013

13

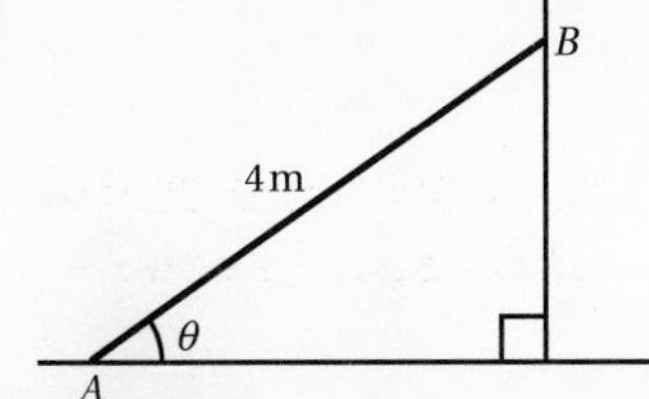

A uniform ladder AB, of weight W N and length 4 m, rests with its end A on rough horizontal ground and its end B against a smooth vertical wall. The ladder is inclined at an angle θ to the horizontal, where $\tan\theta = \frac{1}{2}$ (see diagram). A small object S of weight $2W$ N is placed on the ladder at a point C, which is 1 m from A. The coefficient of friction between the ladder and the ground is μ and the system is in limiting equilibrium.

i Show that $\mu = \dfrac{2}{3}$.

A small object of weight aW N is placed on the ladder at its midpoint, and the object S of weight $2W$ N is placed on the ladder at its lowest point A.

ii Given that the system is in equilibrium, find the set of possible values of a.

© OCR, GCE Mathematics, Paper 4729, June 2015

14 A golfer hits a ball from a point O on horizontal ground with a velocity of $35\,\text{m s}^{-1}$ at an angle θ above the horizontal. The horizontal range of the ball is R metres and the time of flight is t seconds.

a **i** Express t in terms of θ and, hence, show that $R = 125\sin 2\theta$.

The golfer hits the ball so that it lands 110 m from O.

ii Calculate the two possible values of t.

15 A particle of mass 70 kg moves on a smooth horizontal plane. The unit vectors **i** and **j** are directed east and north, respectively. The particle moves under the action of a horizontal force, $(140\pi\sin(\pi t)\mathbf{i} + 210\pi\cos(\pi t)\mathbf{j})$ N.

a The particle is initially moving with velocity $(-\mathbf{i})\,\text{m s}^{-1}$. Find the velocity of the particle at time t.

b At time $t = T$, the particle is moving due south.

i Show that $\sin(\pi t) = -\frac{\sqrt{3}}{2}$.

ii Hence, find the speed of the particle when it is moving due south.

16 The acceleration, $a\,\text{m s}^{-2}$, of a particle moving in a straight line is given by $a = -k\sqrt{v}$, where $v\,\text{m s}^{-1}$ is the velocity of the particle and k is a positive constant. When $t = 0$ the velocity of the particle is $u\,\text{m s}^{-1}$. Find an expression for v in terms of t, u and k.

17 A particle moves in a horizontal plane with acceleration $\mathbf{a} = (-3e^{t}\mathbf{i} + 5e^{-t}\mathbf{j})\,\text{m s}^{-2}$. The particle is initially at the origin and has velocity $\mathbf{v} = (3\mathbf{i} - 5\mathbf{j})\,\text{m s}^{-1}$. Prove that the particle moves in a straight line.

18 A netball player takes a shot at the hoop, 3 m above ground. The player stands 5 m from the foot of the post and releases a ball at a height of 1.5 m, as shown in the diagram. The ball is released with speed V at an angle α above horizontal.

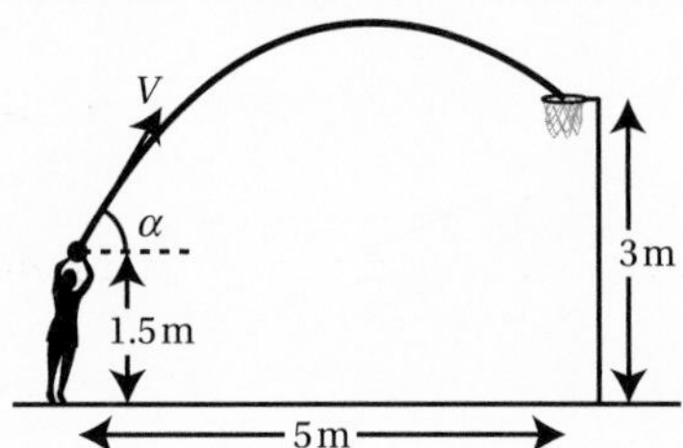

a Given that the ball passes through the hoop, show that $\frac{50g}{V^2} = 3 + 10\sin 2\alpha + 3\cos 2\alpha$.

b **i** Find the maximum value of $10\sin 2\alpha + 3\cos 2\alpha$.

ii Hence, find the minimum speed with which the ball can be released and still pass through the hoop.

PAPER 1 PRACTICE QUESTIONS

2 hours, 100 marks

1 The graph of $y = x^2 - x + 1$ is translated two units to the right. What is the equation of the resulting graph? Give your answer in the form $y = ax^2 + bx + c$. **[2 marks]**

2 A sequence is defined by $u_1 = 2$, $u_{n+1} = \frac{1}{1 - u_n}$.

a Find the first four terms of the sequence. Hence, describe the behaviour of the sequence. **[2 marks]**

b Find the value of u_{100}. **[1 mark]**

c Find $\sum_{n=1}^{100} u_n$. **[3 marks]**

3 In this question you must show detailed reasoning.

Find the exact value of $\int_0^{\frac{\pi}{2}} \cos 3x \, dx$. **[3 marks]**

4 In this question you must show detailed reasoning.

Solve the equation $\ln(x + 2) = 3 + \ln(x - 1)$.

Give your answer in terms of e. **[4 marks]**

5 Find an approximate expression for $\cos 2\theta(1 - 4\sin\theta)$ when θ is small enough to neglect the terms in θ^3 and above. **[3 marks]**

6 The triangle in the diagram has area $22\,\text{cm}^2$. The angle θ is obtuse.

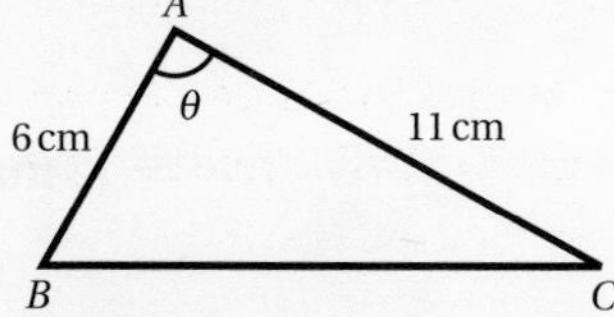

Find the length of BC, correct to one decimal place. **[6 marks]**

7 Find the equation of the normal to the curve $y = 2\mathrm{e}^{-x}$ at the point where $x = \ln 3$. Give your answer in the form $ax + by = p\ln q + c$, where a, b, c, p and q are integers. **[6 marks]**

8 The sector shown in the diagram has perimeter P.

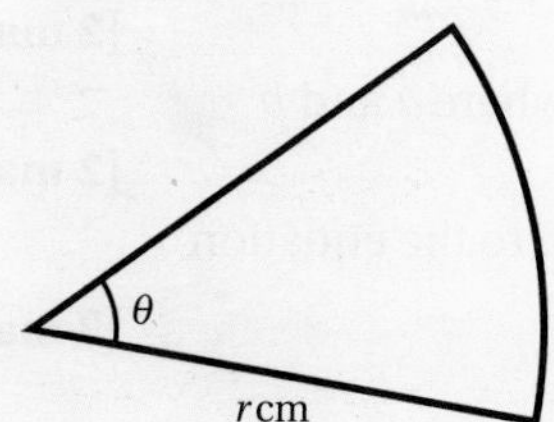

Find, in terms of P, the largest possible area of the sector. **[6 marks]**

9 **a** Express $\frac{9x + 3}{(1 + x)(2 + 5x)}$ in the form $\frac{A}{1 + x} + \frac{B}{2 + 5x}$, where A and B are integers. **[3 marks]**

b Hence, or otherwise, find the binomial expansion of $\frac{9x + 3}{(1 + x)(2 + 5x)}$ up to and including the term in x^2. **[6 marks]**

c Find the range of values of x for which the binomial expansion of $\frac{9x + 3}{(1 + x)(2 + 5x)}$ is valid. **[1 mark]**

10 **a** Three consecutive terms in an arithmetic sequence are $3e^{a}, 8, 5e^{-a}$. Find the possible values of a. **[5 marks]**

b Prove that there is no value of b for which $3e^{b}, 8, 5e^{-b}$ are consecutive terms of a geometric sequence. **[3 marks]**

11 Use a substitution to find

$$\int_{2}^{3} \frac{3x^5}{(x^3-3)^2}\,dx$$

in the form $\ln p + q$, where p and q are rational numbers. **[7 marks]**

12 The diagram shows a part of the graph with equation $y = \ln(x)\sin(x)$. The coordinates of the maximum point are (7.915, 2.065).

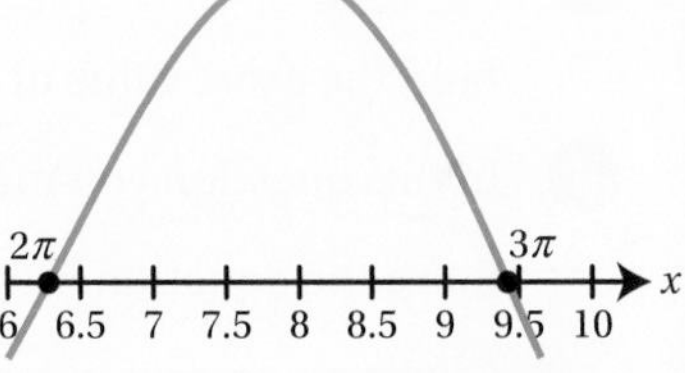

a Use the trapezium rule with four strips to find an approximate value of $\int_{2\pi}^{3\pi} \ln x \sin x\,dx$.

State whether your answer is an overestimate or an underestimate. **[4 marks]**

b Use four rectangles of equal width to find an upper bound for $\int_{2\pi}^{3\pi} \ln x \sin x\,dx$. **[4 marks]**

c Write down values of L and U such that

$$L < \int_{2\pi}^{3\pi} \ln x \sin x\,dx < U.$$

How can the difference between L and U be reduced? **[2 marks]**

13 A curve is defined by the implicit equation $x^2 - \frac{1}{2}y^2 + 2xy + 5 = 0$.

a Find an expression for $\frac{dy}{dx}$ in terms of x and y. **[5 marks]**

b Hence, prove that the curve has no tangents parallel to the y-axis. **[3 marks]**

14 Consider the equation $\ln(x-2) = \frac{1}{2}\sin x$, where x is measured in radians.

a By means of a sketch, show that this equation has only one solution. **[3 marks]**

b Show that this solution lies between 3 and 4. **[2 marks]**

c Show that the equation can be rearranged into the form $x = e^{a\sin x} + b$, where a and b are constants to be found. **[2 marks]**

d Hence, use a suitable iterative formula to find an approximate solution to the equation $\ln(x-2) = \frac{1}{2}\sin x$, correct to three decimal places. **[3 marks]**

15 The polynomial f(x) is defined by $f(x) = 9x^3 - 7x - 2$.

a Use the Factor theorem to show that $(3x+1)$ is a factor of f(x). **[2 marks]**

b Hence, express f(x) as a product of three linear factors. **[2 marks]**

c **i** Show that the equation $9\cos 2\theta \sin\theta + 5\sin\theta + 4 = 0$ can be written as $9x^3 - 7x - 2 = 0$, where $x = \sin\theta$.

ii Hence, find all solutions of the equation

$$2\cos 2\theta \sin\theta + 9\sin\theta + 3 = 0$$

in the interval $0° < \theta < 360°$, giving your solutions to the nearest degree. **[8 marks]**

PAPER 2 PRACTICE QUESTIONS

Section A

2 hours, 100 marks

1 The diagram shows the graph of the function $y = f(x)$. The graph crosses the x-axis at the points $(1, 0)$, $(3, 0)$ and $(6, 0)$. The area labelled R equals 15 and the area labelled S equals 26.

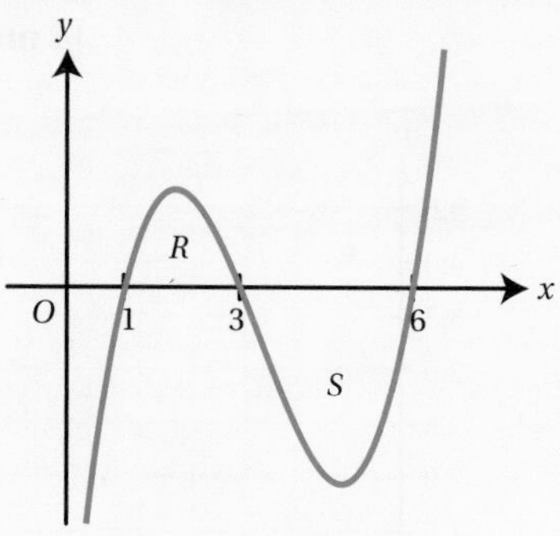

What is the value of $\int_1^6 f(x)\,dx$? **[1 mark]**

2 The largest possible domain of the function $f(x) = \ln(x^2 + x - 6)$ is $(-\infty, a) \cup (b, \infty)$. Find the values of a and b. **[2 marks]**

3 The first term of an arithmetic sequence is -4 and the 15th term is 31. Find the sum of the first 15 terms. **[3 marks]**

4 The polynomial $f(x) = 2x^3 + ax^2 + b$ gives the remainder 7 when divided by $(2x + 1)$, and $(x - 3)$ is a factor of $f(x)$. Find the values of a and b. **[5 marks]**

5 **a** Write $6x^2 - 12x + 11$ in the form $a(x - p)^2 + q$. **[3 marks]**

b A function is defined by $f(x) = 2x^3 - 6x^2 + 11x + 2$ for $x \in \mathbb{R}$.

i Prove that $f(x)$ is an increasing function. **[2 marks]**

ii Does $f(x)$ have an inverse function? Explain your answer. **[2 marks]**

iii Find the range of values of x for which $f(x)$ is convex. **[3 marks]**

6 **a** Express $\sqrt{5}\sin x + \sqrt{7}\cos x$ in the form $R\sin(x + \alpha)$, where $0 < \alpha < \frac{\pi}{2}$. Give the value of α correct to three decimal places. **[3 marks]**

b Hence, find the minimum value of $\frac{48}{2 - (\sqrt{5}\sin x + \sqrt{7}\cos x)}$.

Give your answer in the form $a + b\sqrt{3}$. **[3 marks]**

7 The diagram shows a part of the graph with equation $y = x^2 - 3\ln x - 3$.

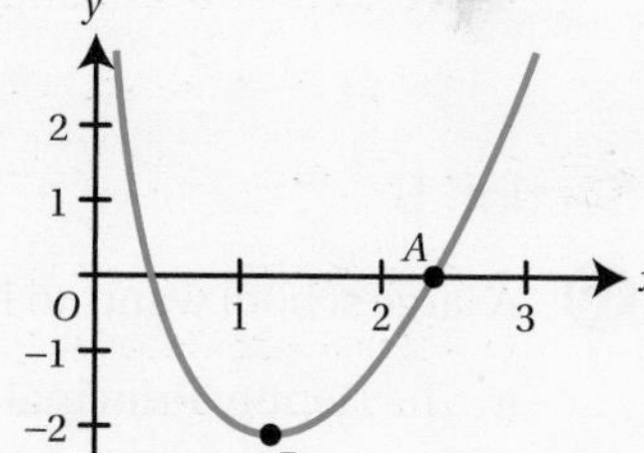

One of the roots of the equation $x^2 - 3\ln x - 3 = 0$ lies between 2 and 3.

a The Newton–Raphson method is used to find an approximation to the root at A.

i Taking the first approximation to be $x_1 = 3$, find the second approximation, x_2. Give your answer to three significant figures.

ii Illustrate the relationship between x_1 and x_2 on a copy of the diagram. **[5 marks]**

b The point B is the minimum point on the curve.

i Find the exact x-coordinate of B.

ii Explain why an iteration starting at B would not converge to a root of the equation $x^2 - 3\ln x - 3 = 0$. **[4 marks]**

8 A student is investigating the number of friends people have on a large social networking site. He collects some data on the percentage (P) of people who have n friends and plots the graph shown.

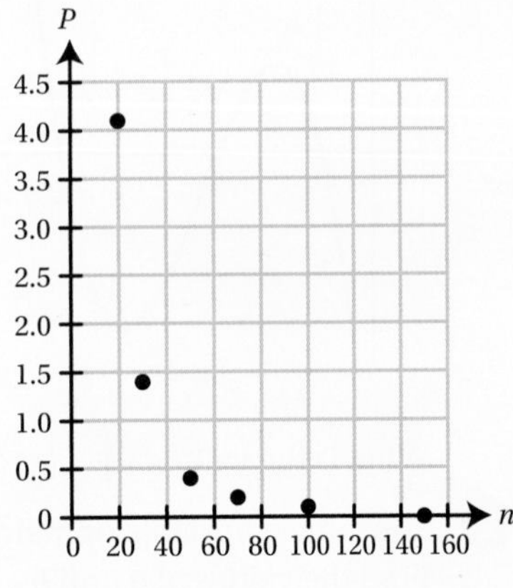

The student proposes two possible models for the relationship between n and P.

Model 1: $P = ak^{-n}$ Model 2: $P = an^{-k}$

To check which model is a better fit, he plots the graph of y against x, where $y = \log P$ and $x = \log n$.

The graph is approximately a straight line with equation $y = 1.2 - 2.6x$.

a Is model 1 or model 2 a better fit for the data? Explain your answer. **[2 marks]**

b Find the values of a and k. **[3 marks]**

9 A curve is given by parametric equations $x = \cos t$, $y = \sin 2t$, for $t \in [0, 2\pi)$. The curve crosses the x-axis at point A, and B is a maximum point on the curve.

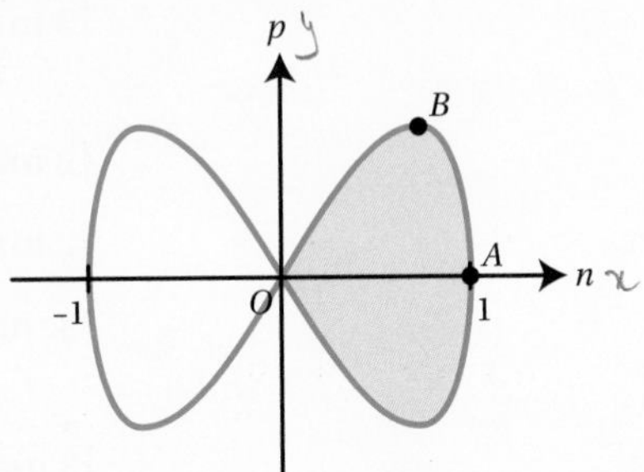

a Find the exact coordinates of B. **[4 marks]**

b i Find the values of t at the points O and A.

ii Find the shaded area. **[6 marks]**

Section B

10 A large school wants to investigate the reasons why students are late in the morning.

a The Deputy Principal selects ten classes at random, and randomly selects four pupils from each class to take part in a survey. What is the name of this sampling procedure? **[1 mark]**

The Deputy Principal thinks that there may be a correlation between how far a pupil lives from school and the number of times in a month they are late. In the sample of 40 students, the correlation coefficient is –0.25.

b A test is carried out using the following hypotheses:

$H_0: \rho = 0$

$H_1: \rho \neq 0$

Show that, at the 5% significance level, H_0 is not rejected. **[2 marks]**

c Decide, based on the test, and explaining your reasoning, whether each of the following statements is correct.

i There is no correlation between the distance a student lives from school and the number of times they are late. **[2 marks]**

ii The number of times a student is late is independent of the distance they live from school. **[2 marks]**

11 A company carried out a 'Travel to Work' survey among its employees. The two-way table below shows the number of people in the survey using different modes of transport, split by gender.

	Male	Female
Walk	6	8
Bus	23	32
Cycle	14	16
Drive	56	62

a Find P(male $\cap$ walk). **[2 marks]**

b Find P(male $\cup$ walk). **[1 mark]**

c Find P(male | walk). **[2 marks]**

d Two employees who walk to work are chosen without replacement. Find the probability that they are both male. **[2 marks]**

e Use appropriate figures from this table to provide a counterexample to the identity $P(A|B) + P(A|B') \equiv 1$ **[2 marks]**

12 There are 655 girls at a school. 312 of them describe themselves as having blonde hair.

a Use the binomial distribution to find the probability that a randomly selected group of 14 girls contains exactly 10 girls with blonde hair. **[2 marks]**

b A club contains 14 girls of whom 10 have blonde hair. Use the binomial distribution to test at 5% significance whether this is more than the expected number of girls with blonde hair. State your null and alternative hypotheses and your p-value. **[4 marks]**

c Give two reasons why the binomial distribution may not be an appropriate model for the number of girls with blonde hair in this club. **[2 marks]**

13 The distribution of the number of books, B, borrowed by members of a library follows the following distribution.

b	0	1	2	3
$P(B = b)$	0.4	0.35	0.15	a

a Find the value of a. **[1 mark]**

b Find the probability that a randomly chosen member has borrowed at least one book. **[1 mark]**

c The librarian proposes the following model for the probability of a book being overdue. If a member has borrowed b books, the probability that they have an overdue book is $\text{P(overdue)} = 1 - (0.5)^b$.

Find the probability that a randomly chosen member has an overdue book. **[3 marks]**

14 Two events, A and B, satisfy: $\text{P}(B) = \frac{7}{10}$, $\text{P}(A|B) = \frac{2}{7}$ and $P(A \cup B) = \frac{69}{70}$.

a Find $\text{P}(A)$. **[3 marks]**

b Show that A and B are not independent **[2 marks]**

15 Alex takes the bus to work every day. He keeps a record of the length of time it takes him to travel to work, over the course of several years. The mean is 25 minutes and standard deviation 2.1 minutes. The lowest value is 20 minutes and the highest value is 32 minutes.

a Give two reasons why the numerical information given supports a normal model for the data. **[2 marks]**

b Assuming that a normal model holds, find the probability that Alex takes longer than 26 minutes to travel to work. **[1 mark]**

c Stating a necessary assumption, find the probability that Alex takes more than 26 minutes to travel to work on at least three days in a 5-day week. **[4 marks]**

d After a change to the bus route, Alex times how long it takes him to travel to work every day during a 5-day week. The total time for the five days is 119 minutes. Test at the 5% significance level if his average time to travel to work has changed, assuming that it still comes from a normal distribution with standard deviation 2.1 minutes. State your null and alternative hypotheses. **[4 marks]**

e Ming takes a different bus to work. It takes her more than 30 minutes on 5% of days and less than 20 minutes on 10% of days. Assuming a normal distribution, estimate the value of the mean and variance of Ming's travel times. **[4 marks]**

PAPER 3 PRACTICE QUESTIONS

Section A

2 hours, 100 marks

1 Let a be the smallest positive solution of the equation $\cos 2x = k$, where x is in radians. Find, in terms of a, the next **two** positive solutions. **[2 marks]**

2 The diagram shows the graphs of $y = x^2$ and $y = 6 - x$.

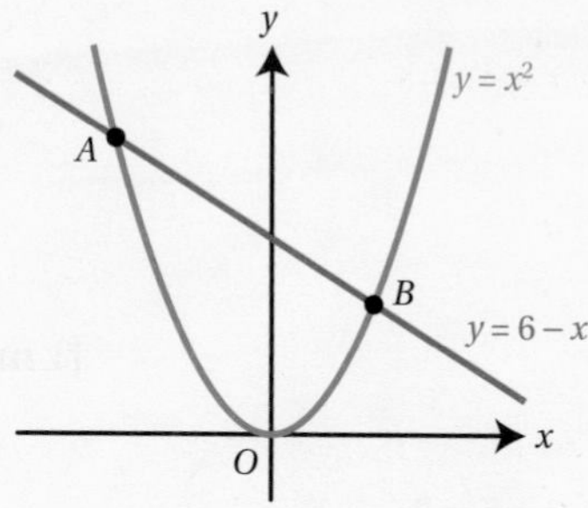

a Find the coordinates of points A and B. **[2 marks]**

b Shade the region determined by the inequalities $y \geqslant x^2$ and $y \leqslant 6 - x$. **[1 mark]**

c State the smallest integer value of x which satisfies both inequalities. **[1 mark]**

3 Points A and B have position vectors $\mathbf{a} = 3\mathbf{i} - 7\mathbf{j} + 3\mathbf{k}$ and $\mathbf{b} = \mathbf{i} - \mathbf{j} + 5\mathbf{k}$.

a Find the position vector of the midpoint of AB. **[2 marks]**

b Point C has position vector $2t\mathbf{i} + t\mathbf{j} - 3\mathbf{k}$. It is given that $CA = CB$. Find the value of t. **[3 marks]**

4 Find the exact coordinates of the point of inflection on the graph of $y = x\mathrm{e}^{-3x}$. **[5 marks]**

5 Prove by contradiction that $\log_3 5$ is an irrational number. **[4 marks]**

6 **a** Show that the equation $3\operatorname{cosec}^2\theta + 5\cot\theta = 5$ can be written in the form $a\cot^2\theta + b\cot\theta + c = 0$. State the values of the constants a, b and c. **[3 marks]**

b Hence, solve the equation $3\operatorname{cosec}^2\theta + 5\cot\theta = 5$ for $0° \leqslant \theta \leqslant 360°$, giving your answers to the nearest degree. **[4 marks]**

7 Find $\int_1^2 x^3 \ln x \,\mathrm{d}x$, giving your answer in the form $\ln p - q$. **[5 marks]**

8 The circle shown in the diagram has equation $x^2 + y^2 - 10x - 10y + 25 = 0$.

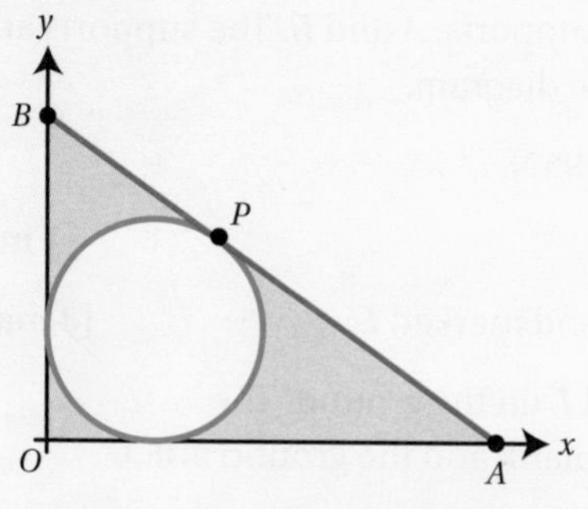

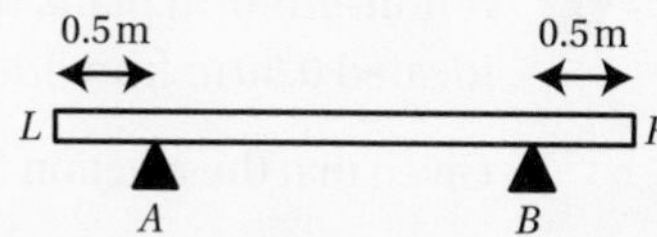

a Show that the point $P(8, 9)$ lies on the circle. **[2 marks]**

b The line AB is tangent to the circle at P. Find the area shaded in the diagram. **[5 marks]**

9 The diagram shows the curves with equations $y = 3e^x - 3$ and $y = 13 - 5e^{-x}$.

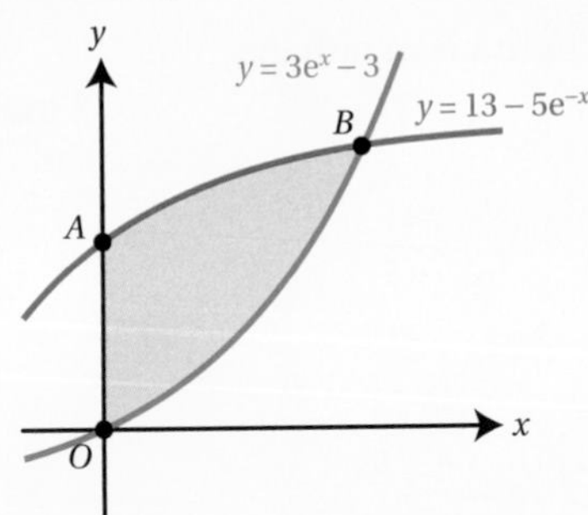

a Write down the coordinates of point A. **[1 mark]**

b The curves intersect at the point B.

i Show that the x-coordinate of B satisfies the equation $3e^{2x} - 16e^x + 5 = 0$.

ii Hence, find the exact coordinates of B. **[4 marks]**

c Find the exact value of the shaded area. **[6 marks]**

Section B

10 A cyclist moves along a straight horizontal road. The velocity–time graph of her journey is shown in the diagram.

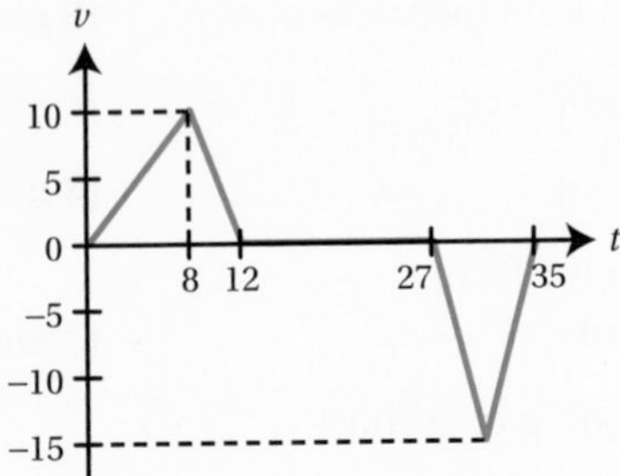

a Calculate the acceleration of the cyclist during the first 8 seconds. **[2 marks]**

b Show that the cyclist returns to the starting point after 35 seconds. **[3 marks]**

c State the average **velocity** of the cyclist for the whole journey. **[1 mark]**

11 A non-uniform plank of length 5 m and mass 16 kg rests on two supports, A and B. The supports are located 0.50 m from the ends of the plank, marked L and R on the diagram.

Given that the reaction force acting on the plank at the support A is 95 N:

a Find the reaction force acting on the plank at B. **[1 mark]**

b Find the distance of the centre of mass of the plank from the end marked L. **[3 marks]**

The plank is now placed against a smooth vertical wall, with end L on the ground. The ground is horizontal and the coefficient of friction between the plank and the ground is 0.3.

c Given that the plank is on the point of slipping, find the angle θ it makes with the horizontal. Give your answer correct to the nearest degree. **[5 marks]**

12 Four forces act on a particle in a horizontal plane, as shown in the diagram. The unit vectors **i** and **j** are directed east and north, respectively.

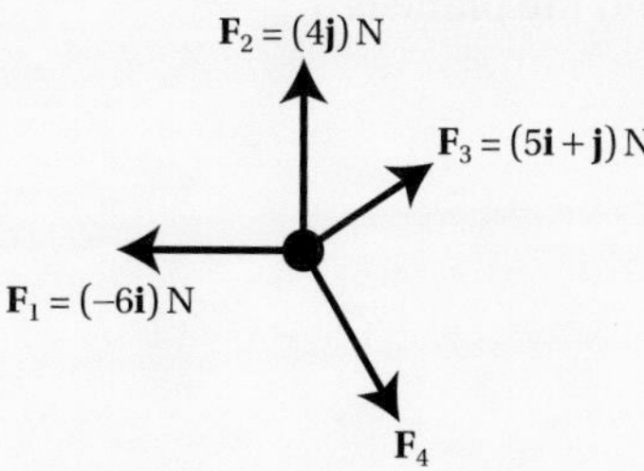

a The particle is in equilibrium. Find the force $\mathbf{F}_4$ in the form $(a\mathbf{i} + b\mathbf{j})$ N. **[2 marks]**

b The force $\mathbf{F}_4$ is suddenly removed. Given that the mass of the particle is 600 grams, find:

i the magnitude of the acceleration of the particle

ii the angle the acceleration vector makes with the direction of vector **i**. **[5 marks]**

13 A particle moves in a straight line with constant acceleration a m s^{-2}. The initial velocity of the particle is U m s^{-1}. At time T seconds, the velocity of the particle is V m s^{-1} and its displacement from the initial position is S m.

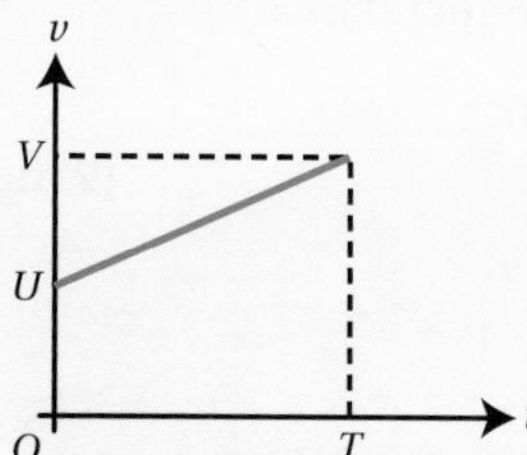

By considering the velocity–time graph shown above:

a Write down an equation relating a, T, U and V.

b Hence, show that $S = VT - \frac{1}{2}aT^2$. **[4 marks]**

14 A child kicks a ball from ground level at an angle θ above the horizontal. The speed of projection is V m s^{-1}. The ball is modelled as a particle and air resistance can be ignored.

a At time t seconds the ball's displacement from the point of projection is $(x\mathbf{i} + y\mathbf{j})$ m. Show that:

$$y = (\tan\theta)\,x - \left(\frac{g\sec^2\theta}{2V^2}\right)x^2$$ **[4 marks]**

b The angle of projection is $\theta = 52°$. The ball passes over a 2.4 m tall fence that is 8.6 m from the point of projection. Find the minimum possible value of V. **[3 marks]**

c How will the answer change if your model includes air resistance? **[1 mark]**

Two particles, P and Q, are connected by a light inextensible string, which passes over a smooth pulley. Particle P has mass m kg and lies on a rough plane. The plane is inclined at $35°$ to the horizontal, and the coefficient of friction between P and the plane is μ. Particle Q has mass 5.2 kg and hangs freely below the pulley.

The system is in equilibrium.

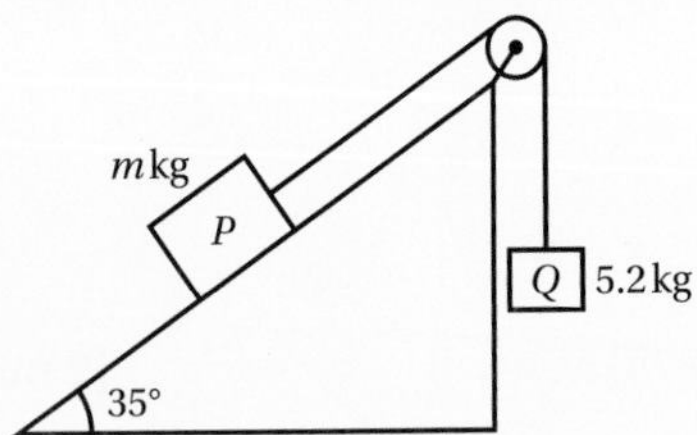

a Show that $m \leqslant \dfrac{5.2}{\sin 35° + \mu \cos 35°}$ **[5 marks]**

b Obtain another similar inequality for m. **[2 marks]**

c In the case when $\mu = 0.48$, find the range of values of m for which the system remains in equilibrium. **[2 marks]**

A particle of mass 3 kg moves in a straight line. At time t seconds the velocity of the particle is $v\,\text{m s}^{-1}$ and the force acting on the particle is F N, where $F = 36\sqrt{v}\cos(2t)$. When $t = 0$ the velocity of the particle is $16\,\text{m s}^{-1}$.

Find the velocity of the particle after 5 seconds. **[7 marks]**

working in radians

FORMULAE

The following formulae will be given on the A Level assessment papers.

Arithmetic series

$$S_n = \frac{1}{2}n(a+l) = \frac{1}{2}n\{2a+(n-1)d\}$$

Geometric series

$$S_n = \frac{a(1-r^n)}{1-r}$$

$$S_\infty = \frac{a}{1-r} \text{ for } |r|<1$$

Binomial series

$$(a+b)^n = a^n + {}^nC_1 a^{n-1}b + {}^nC_2 a^{n-2}b^2 + \ldots + {}^nC_r a^{n-r}b^r + \ldots + b^n \quad (n \in \mathbb{N})$$

where $${}^nC_r = \binom{n}{r} = \frac{n!}{r!(n-r)!}$$

$$(1+x)^n = 1 + nx + \frac{n(n-1)}{2!}x^2 + \ldots + \frac{n(n-1)\ldots(n-r+1)}{2!}x^r + \ldots \quad (|x|<1, n \in \mathbb{N})$$

Differentiation

f(x)	f′(x)
$\tan kx$	$k\sec^2 kx$
$\sec x$	$\sec x \tan x$
$\cot x$	$-\operatorname{cosec}^2 x$
$\operatorname{cosec} x$	$-\operatorname{cosec} x \cot x$

Quotient rule: $y = \frac{u}{v}$, $\frac{dy}{dx} = \frac{v\frac{du}{dx} - u\frac{dv}{dx}}{v^2}$

Differentiation from first principles

$$f'(x) = \lim_{h\to 0}\frac{f(x+h)-f(x)}{h}$$

Integration

$$\int \frac{f'(x)}{f(x)}\,dx = \ln|f(x)| + c$$

$$\int f'(x)(f(x))^n\,dx = \frac{1}{n+1}(f(x))^{n+1} + c$$

Integration by parts $\int u\frac{dv}{dx}\,dx = uv - \int v\frac{du}{dx}\,dx$

Small angle approximations

$\sin\theta \approx \theta$, $\cos\theta \approx 1 - \frac{1}{2}\theta^2$, $\tan\theta \approx \theta$, where θ is measured in radians.

Trigonometric identities

$\sin(A \pm B) = \sin A \cos B \pm \cos A \sin B$

$\cos(A \pm B) = \cos A \cos B \mp \sin A \sin B$

$\tan(A + B) = \dfrac{\tan A \pm \tan B}{1 \mp \tan A \tan B} \quad (A \pm B \neq (k + \frac{1}{2})\pi)$

Numerical methods

Trapezium rule: $\int_a^b y \, dx \approx \frac{1}{2} h\{(y_0 + y_n) + 2(y_1 + y_2 + \ldots + y_{n-1})\}$, where $h = \dfrac{b-a}{n}$

The Newton–Raphson iteration for solving $f(x) = 0$: $x_{n+1} = x_n - \dfrac{f(x_n)}{f'(x_n)}$

Probability

$P(A \cup B) = P(A) + P(B) - P(A \cap B)$

$P(A \cap B) = P(A)P(B \mid A) = P(B)P(A \mid B)$ or $P(A \mid B) = \dfrac{P(A \cap B)}{P(B)}$

Standard deviation

$$\sqrt{\frac{\Sigma(x-\bar{x})^2}{n}} = \sqrt{\frac{\Sigma x^2}{n} - \bar{x}^2} \text{ or } \sqrt{\frac{\Sigma f(x-\bar{x})^2}{\Sigma f}} = \sqrt{\frac{\Sigma fx^2}{\Sigma f} - \bar{x}^2}$$

The binomial distribution

If $X \sim B(n, p)$, then $P(X = x) = \binom{n}{x} p^x (1-p)^{n-x}$; Mean of X is np; Variance of X is $np(1-p)$.

Hypothesis test for the mean of a normal distribution

If $X \sim N(\mu, \sigma^2)$, then $\bar{X} \sim N\left(\mu, \dfrac{\sigma^2}{n}\right)$ and $\dfrac{\bar{X} - \mu}{\sigma/\sqrt{n}} \sim N(0,1)$.

Percentage points of the normal distribution

If Z has a normal distribution with mean 0 and variance 1 then, for each value of p, the table gives the value of z such that $P(Z \leqslant z) = p$.

p	0.75	0.90	0.95	0.975	0.99	0.995	0.9975	0.999	0.9995
z	0.674	1.282	1.645	1.960	2.326	2.575	2.807	3.090	3.291

Kinematics

Motion in a straight line

$v = u + at$

$s = ut + \frac{1}{2}at^2$

$s = \frac{1}{2}(u + v)t$

$v^2 = u^2 + 2as$

$s = vt - \frac{1}{2}at^2$

Motion in two dimensions

$\mathbf{v} = \mathbf{u} + \mathbf{a}t$

$\mathbf{s} = \mathbf{u}t + \frac{1}{2}\mathbf{a}t^2$

$\mathbf{s} = \frac{1}{2}(\mathbf{u} + \mathbf{v})t$

$\mathbf{s} = \mathbf{v}t - \frac{1}{2}\mathbf{a}t^2$

STATISTICS

Critical values for the product-moment correlation coefficient, r.

1-Tailed test	5%	2½%	1%	½%
2-Tailed test	10%	5%	2%	1%
n				
1	–	–	–	–
2	–	–	–	–
3	0.9877	0.9969	0.9995	0.9999
4	0.9000	0.9500	0.9800	0.9900
5	0.8054	0.8783	0.9343	0.9587
6	0.7293	0.8114	0.8822	0.9172
7	0.6694	0.7545	0.8329	0.8745
8	0.6215	0.7067	0.7887	0.8343
9	0.5822	0.6664	0.7498	0.7977
10	0.5494	0.6319	0.7155	0.7646
11	0.5214	0.6021	0.6851	0.7348
12	0.4973	0.5760	0.6581	0.7079
13	0.4762	0.5529	0.6339	0.6835
14	0.4575	0.5324	0.6120	0.6614
15	0.4409	0.5140	0.5923	0.6411
16	0.4259	0.4973	0.5742	0.6226
17	0.4124	0.4821	0.5577	0.6055
18	0.4000	0.4683	0.5425	0.5897
19	0.3887	0.4555	0.5285	0.5751
20	0.3783	0.4438	0.5155	0.5614
21	0.3687	0.4329	0.5034	0.5487
22	0.3598	0.4227	0.4921	0.5368
23	0.3515	0.4132	0.4815	0.5256
24	0.3438	0.4044	0.4716	0.5151
25	0.3365	0.3961	0.4622	0.5052
26	0.3297	0.3882	0.4534	0.4958
27	0.3233	0.3809	0.4451	0.4869
28	0.3172	0.3739	0.4372	0.4785
29	0.3115	0.3673	0.4297	0.4705
30	0.3061	0.3610	0.4226	0.4629

1-Tailed test	5%	2½%	1%	½%
2-Tailed test	10%	5%	2%	1%
n				
31	0.3009	0.3550	0.4158	0.4556
32	0.2960	0.3494	0.4093	0.4487
33	0.2913	0.3440	0.4032	0.4421
34	0.2869	0.3388	0.3972	0.4357
35	0.2826	0.3338	0.3916	0.4296
36	0.2785	0.3291	0.3862	0.4238
37	0.2746	0.3246	0.3810	0.4182
38	0.2709	0.3202	0.3760	0.4128
39	0.2673	0.3160	0.3712	0.4076
40	0.2638	0.3120	0.3665	0.4026
41	0.2605	0.3081	0.3621	0.3978
42	0.2573	0.3044	0.3578	0.3932
43	0.2542	0.3008	0.3536	0.3887
44	0.2512	0.2973	0.3496	0.3843
45	0.2483	0.2940	0.3457	0.3801
46	0.2455	0.2907	0.3420	0.3761
47	0.2429	0.2876	0.3384	0.3721
48	0.2403	0.2845	0.3348	0.3683
49	0.2377	0.2816	0.3314	0.3646
50	0.2353	0.2787	0.3281	0.3610
51	0.2329	0.2759	0.3249	0.3575
52	0.2306	0.2732	0.3218	0.3542
53	0.2284	0.2706	0.3188	0.3509
54	0.2262	0.2681	0.3158	0.3477
55	0.2241	0.2656	0.3129	0.3445
56	0.2221	0.2632	0.3102	0.3415
57	0.2201	0.2609	0.3074	0.3385
58	0.2181	0.2586	0.3048	0.3357
59	0.2162	0.2564	0.3022	0.3328
60	0.2144	0.2542	0.2997	0.3301

Answers

Chapter 1

Before you start...

1 A $\Leftrightarrow$; B $\Leftarrow$

2 e.g. 64

3 Proof

4 Proof

Exercise 1A

1 Proof

2 Proof

3 Proof

4 a Proof

b e.g. $y = x^2 + 3$

5 e.g. $x = 225°$

6 Proof

7 e.g. 0, 0, 10, 11, 12

8 a Proof

b Proof

c Proof

9 a Proof

b Proof

c Its diagonals are perpendicular (so it must be a kite).

10 a e.g. $\ln(5) = 1.61$, $\ln(2) + \ln(3) = 1.79$

b Proof

c Only when $x, y > 0$.

11 a Proof, $k = -1$

b Proof

12 Proof

Exercise 1B

1 Proof

2 Proof

3 Proof

4 Proof

5 Proof

6 Proof

7 Proof

8 Proof

9 Proof

10 Proof

11 a Proof

b Proof

c Proof

12 Proof

Exercise 1C

1 a $x = 4$ b Line 2

2 a Proof b $\Leftarrow$

3 a $x = -1$ b Line 3

4 2

5 Step 3: should say $x = 1$ or -1; Step 5: differentiating a specific value rather than the function; Step 7: second derivative $= 0$ does not imply minimum.

6 If $q = 0$ the suggested factorisation is not necessarily true. Not all coefficients were compared at line 3.

7 Line 8 does not follow from line 7.

Mixed practice 1

1 Proof

2 Proof

3 Proof

4 Line 3 does not necessarily follow from line 2. Line 5 is not equivalent to line 4.

5 C

6 Proof

7 Proof

8 Proof

9 a Proof b Proof

10 a 2: Not equivalent. 6: Missing ±. 7: Final solution may not be a solution to the original equation.

b $x+\frac{4x}{x-2}=\frac{8}{x-2}$

$\Rightarrow x(x-2)+4x=8$

$\Leftrightarrow x^2-2x+4x=8$

$\Leftrightarrow x^2+2x=8$

$\Leftrightarrow (x+1)^2=9$

$\Leftrightarrow x+1=\pm3$

$\Leftrightarrow x=2$ or -4

Check: only $x=-4$ works.

11 7

12 C

13 Proof

14 a Proof

b Proof

15 Proof

Chapter 2

Before you start...

1 a -1 **b** 6

2 a $x\in(3,6]$ **b** $x\in(-\infty,3)\cup[6,\infty)$

3 a $\left(x+\frac{5}{2}\right)^2-\frac{13}{4}$ **b** $\left(-\frac{5}{2},-\frac{13}{4}\right)$

4 $x<-1$ or $x>5$

5 a $x=\frac{1}{2}(\ln y+1)$

b $x=\frac{1}{3}(e^y-4)$

6 $x>\frac{16}{9}$

Exercise 2A

1 a Function: many-one

b Mapping

c Mapping

d Function: one-one

e Function: one-one

f Function: one-one

2 a i No **ii** No

b i Yes **ii** Yes

c i Yes **ii** Yes

Exercise 2B

1 a i Domain: $\mathbb{R}$; Range: $(0,\infty)$

ii Domain: $\mathbb{R}$; Range: $(0,\infty)$

b i Domain: $(0,\infty)$; Range: $\mathbb{R}$

ii Domain: $(0,\infty)$; Range: $\mathbb{R}$

2 a i $x\neq2$

ii $x\neq7$

b i $x\neq2$ or -4

ii $x\neq\pm3$

c i $y\geqslant1$

ii $x\geqslant-3$

d i $a>1$

ii $x<\frac{2}{5}$

e i $x\neq0$ or -1

ii $x\geqslant-1$

f i $x\geqslant0$

ii $x\geqslant-\frac{3}{2}$

3 a i $f(x)\leqslant7$ **ii** $f(x)\geqslant3$

b i $g(x)\geqslant12$ **ii** $g(x)>8$

c i $h(x)<3$, $h(x)\in\mathbb{Z}$

ii $h(x)>4$, $h(x)\in\mathbb{Z}$

d i $d(x)\leqslant-1$ or $d(x)>0$

ii $q(x)>0$

4 a i $x\in\mathbb{R}$, $f(x)\geqslant-5$

ii $x\in\mathbb{R}$, $f(x)\geqslant4$

b i $x\in\mathbb{R}$, $g(x)\leqslant5$

ii $x\in\mathbb{R}$, $g(x)\leqslant3$

c i $x\leqslant-\sqrt{5}$ or $x\geqslant\sqrt{5}$, $f(x)\geqslant0$

ii $-3\leqslant x\leqslant3$, $f(x)\geqslant0$

d i $x\leqslant2$ or $x\geqslant4$, $f(x)\geqslant0$

ii $x\leqslant-3$ or $x\geqslant1$, $f(x)\geqslant0$

5 a $2\left(x+\frac{3}{2}\right)^2-\frac{15}{2}$

b $f(x)\geqslant-\frac{15}{2}$

6 $x>-\frac{3}{2}$, $g(x)\in\mathbb{R}$

7 $x\geqslant5$

8 $x\geqslant1$, $x\neq2$, $x\neq3$

9 a

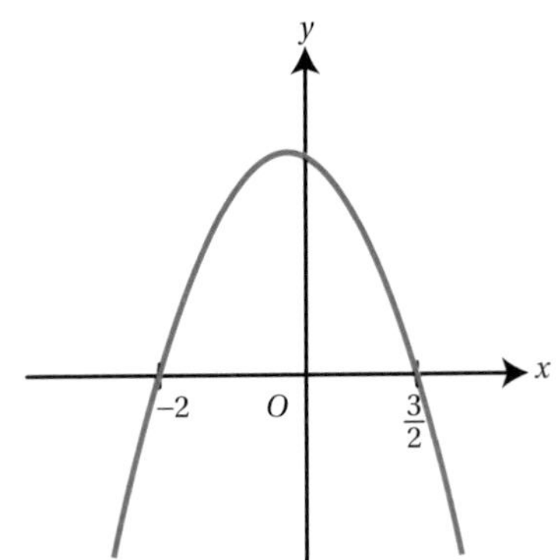

b $-2 \leqslant x \leqslant \frac{3}{2}$

10 $x < -2$ or $x > -1$

11 $x \leqslant \frac{1}{2}$ or $x > 12$

12 a i $a \leqslant x < b$ **ii** $\varnothing$

b $f(a) = \begin{cases} \ln(b-a) \text{ for } a < b \\ \text{undefined for } a \geqslant b \end{cases}$

Work it out 2.1

Answer = Solution 2

Exercise 2C

1 a i 5 **ii** 26

b i 17 **ii** 32

2 a i $3x^2 + 5$ **ii** $x^4 + 2x^2 + 2$

b i $9x + 8$ **ii** $9x^2 + 12x + 5$

3 a i $9\sqrt{a} + 17$ **ii** $y^4 - 4y^3 + 8y^2 - 8y + 5$

b i $4x - x^2$ **ii** $1 + 2x + x^2$

4 a $9y^2 + 17$ **b** $27x^2 + 36x + 17$

5 a i x^2 **ii** x^3

b i $3x - 5$ **ii** $x^2 + 5x + 6$

c i $x + 4$ **ii** $x^{\frac{2}{3}}$

d i $\ln(\ln x)$ **ii** $\ln\left(\frac{x+1}{3}\right)$

6 $x = 0, -2$

7 $x = -\frac{1}{3}$

8 a $\sqrt[3]{2x+3}$ **b** $2\sqrt[3]{x} + 3$

9 $\frac{x}{6} - \frac{1}{3}$

Work it out 2.2

Answer = Solution 1

Exercise 2D

1 a i $\frac{x-1}{3}$ **ii** $\frac{x+3}{7}$

b i $\frac{2x}{3x-2}, x \neq \frac{2}{3}$ **ii** $\frac{x}{1-2x}, x \neq \frac{1}{2}$

c i $\frac{xb-a}{x-1}, x \neq 1$ **ii** $\frac{x-1}{bx-a}, x \neq \frac{a}{b}$

d i $1 - x$ **ii** $\frac{x-2}{3}$

e i $\frac{x^2+2}{3}, x \geqslant 0$ **ii** $\frac{(2-x^2)}{5}, x \geqslant 0$

f i $\frac{1-e^x}{5}$ **ii** $\frac{e^x - 2}{2}$

g i $2\ln\left(\frac{x}{7}\right), x > 0$ **ii** $\frac{1}{10}\ln\left(\frac{x}{9}\right), x > 0$

h i $5 + \sqrt{x+19},\ x > -19$

ii $\sqrt{x+10} - 3,\ x > -1$

2 a

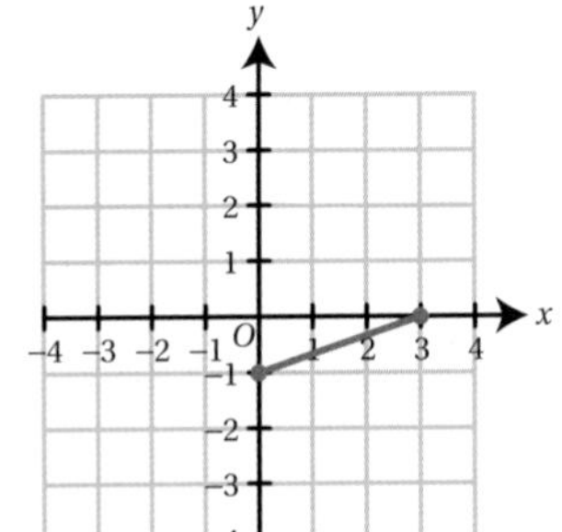

b

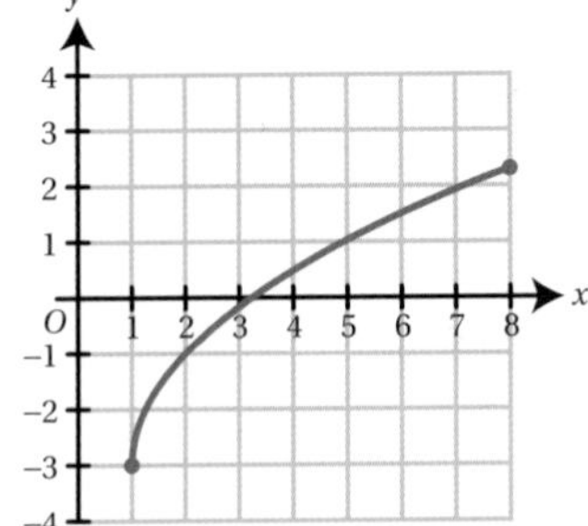

c

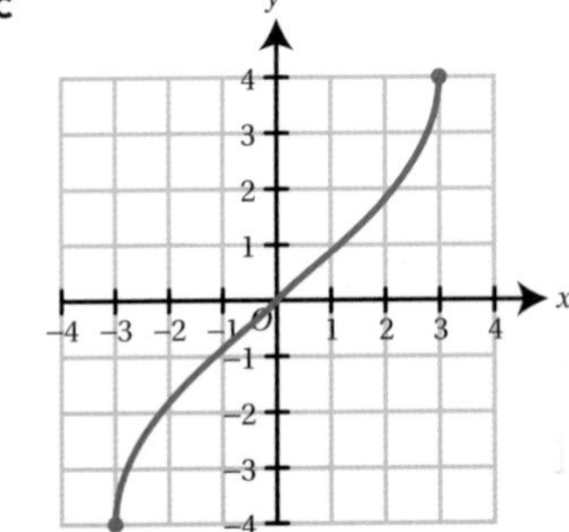

d

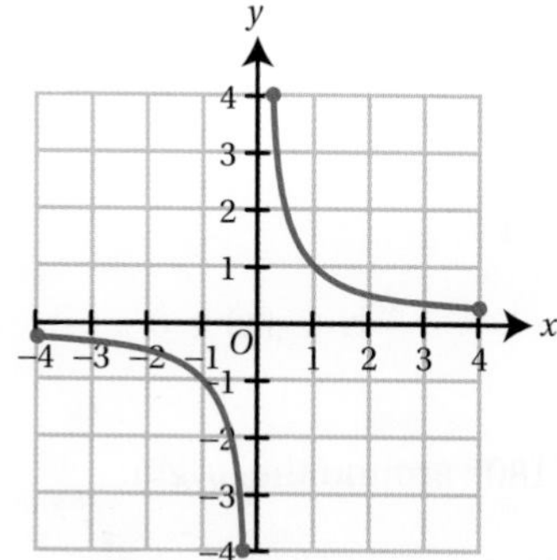

3

	$f^{-1}(x)$	f domain = f^{-1} range	f range = f^{-1} domain
a i	$\frac{2x+1}{3-x}$	$x \neq -2$	$y \neq 3$
ii	$\frac{2x+3}{x-2}$	$x \neq 2$	$y \neq 2$
b i	$\frac{1}{3}\left(\left(\frac{2-x}{3}\right)^2+1\right)$	$x \geqslant \frac{1}{3}$	$y \leqslant 2$
ii	$-4x^2+8x$	$x \leqslant 4$	$y \geqslant 1$
c i	$\frac{1}{4}(e^{x-3}+3)$	$x > \frac{3}{4}$	$y \in \mathbb{R}$
ii	$e^{(x+1)/2}-3$	$x > -3$	$y \in \mathbb{R}$
d i	$\ln\left(\frac{(3-x)}{2}\right)$	$x \in \mathbb{R}$	$y < 3$
ii	$\frac{1}{2}\left(5-\ln\left(\frac{x-1}{3}\right)\right)$	$x \in \mathbb{R}$	$y > 1$

4 a -1 **b** 1

5 -23

6 a $f^{-1}(x)=\frac{1}{2}\ln\left(\frac{x}{3}\right)$

b Domain: $x > 0$; range: $f^{-1}(x) \in \mathbb{R}$

7 $(f \circ g)^{-1}(x)=\sqrt[3]{\frac{x-3}{2}}$

8 Proof

9 a

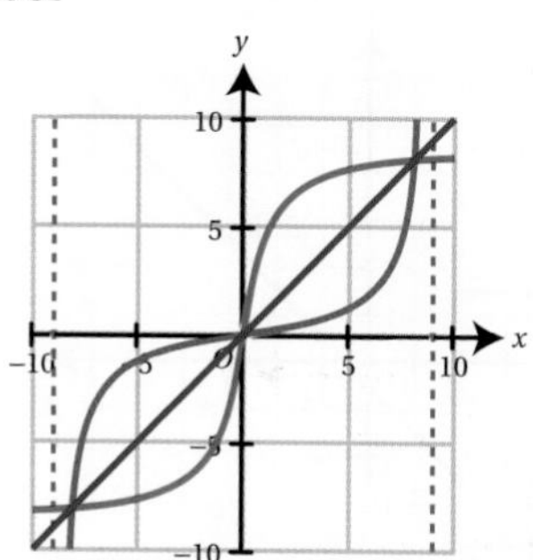

b Domain: $-9 < x < 9$; range: $f^{-1}(x) \in \mathbb{R}$

c $x=-8, 0, 8$ (Hint: Use the graph.)

10 a $\ln 3$

b Proof

11 $f^{-1}(x)=-\sqrt{\frac{9x+4}{1-x}}$

12 a $f^{-1}(x)=\frac{e^x}{3}+1$

b $(g \circ f)(x)=3x-3$; domain $x > 1$; range $g \circ f(x) > 0$

13 a

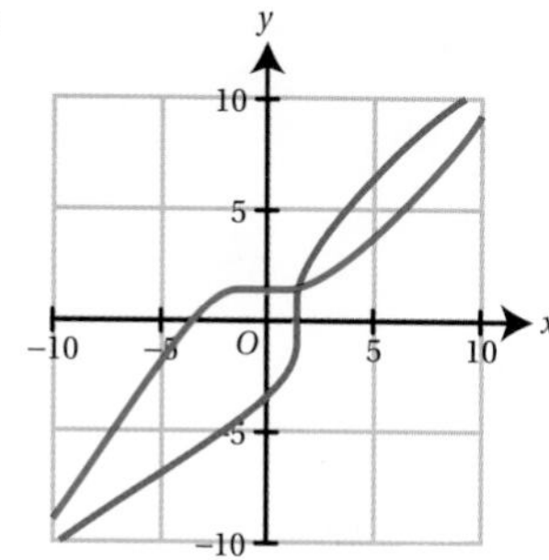

b $x=\frac{3}{2}$

Work it out 2.3

Answer = Solution 3

Exercise 2E

1 a $k=0; f^{-1}(x)=-\sqrt{x}, x \geqslant 0$

b $k=-1; f^{-1}(x)=\sqrt{x-2}-1, x > 2$

c $k=1; f^{-1}(x)=1-\sqrt{6-x}, x \leqslant 6$

d $k=-2; f^{-1}(x)=\sqrt{x+1}-2, x > -1$

2 a $x \leqslant -5$

b $x \in [-5, 2]$

c $1 \leqslant x < 3$

3 a e^x-3

b f(x) has a turning point, so is not one-to-one.

c $\ln(3)$

4 $k=-3$

5 $a \in [0, 1]$

Mixed practice 2

1 a 3^x-3, x in $\mathbb{R}$ **b** $\sqrt[3]{\ln\left(\frac{x}{3}\right)+1}, x > 0$

2 a $y=\log_2 x$ **b** $(1, 0)$

3 -1

4 a 10

b $4 - x^2$

c Reflection in the line $y = x$.

d i $\sqrt{x-1}$

ii $f_1(x) \geqslant 3$

iii $x \geqslant 10$

e $f(x) = g(3x) \to x = -4$ or $+1$ but domain of $f(x)$ is limited to $x \geqslant 3$. -4 and $+1$ are not in the domain, therefore there are no solutions.

5 i -23 **ii** 2

6 a $(x-3)^2 + 1$

b $\sqrt{x-1} + 3$ $x \geqslant 1$

7 a i 15

ii $y \in \mathbb{R}$

iii $2z + 1$

iv $\dfrac{3x+5}{x-1}$

v $4x + 3$

b $f(x)$ can be 1, which is not in the domain of g.

c i $\dfrac{x+3}{x-1}$

ii Reflection in the line $y = x$.

iii $x \neq 1$

iv $y \neq 1$

8 a $(x+2)^2 + 5$

b

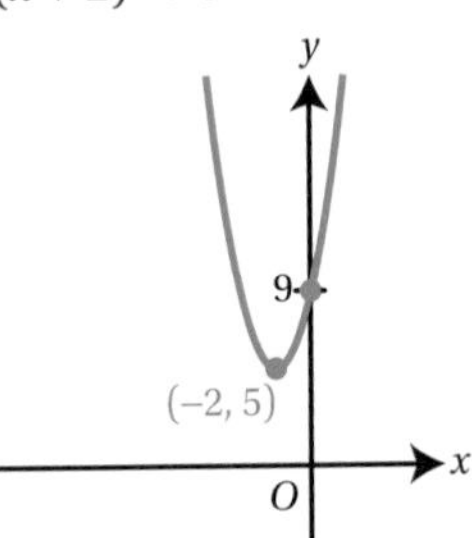

c Range of f is $y \geqslant 5$; range of g is $y > 0$.

d $y > 9$

9 i $f(x) \geqslant -9$

ii Not one-to-one.

iii Proof

iv $b < -4$

10 a $(x-3)^2 - 7$

b $y \geqslant -7$

c $\sqrt{x+7} + 3$

11 a Proof

b $f\left(\dfrac{1}{x}\right) + 2f(x) = \dfrac{2}{x} + 1$

c $\dfrac{1}{3}\left(\dfrac{4}{x} - 2x + 1\right)$

12 a $a = -2, b = 1$ **b** $fg(x) \geqslant 0$

13 a Proof

b Rotation 180° around the origin.

c Proof

d Proof

e Reflection in the y-axis.

f Proof

g Proof

Chapter 3

Before you start...

1 a

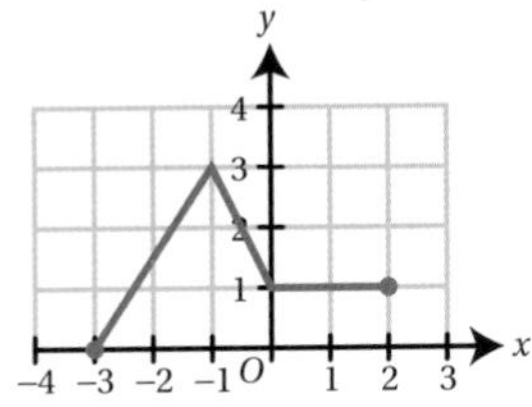

b

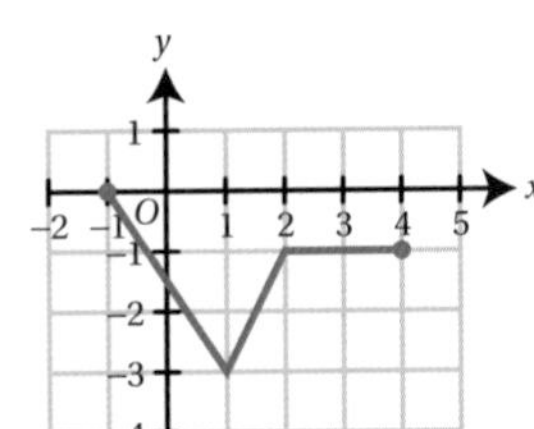

2 a $y = x^2 - 3x + 5$ **b** $y = \dfrac{x^2}{4} - \dfrac{3x}{2}$

3 a $x \in [3, \infty)$ **b** $x \in (-2, 1)$

Work it out 3.1

Answer = Solution 2

Exercise 3A

1 a i

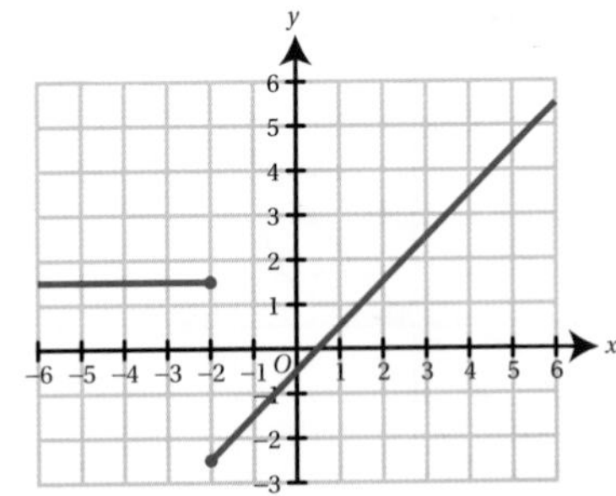

ii

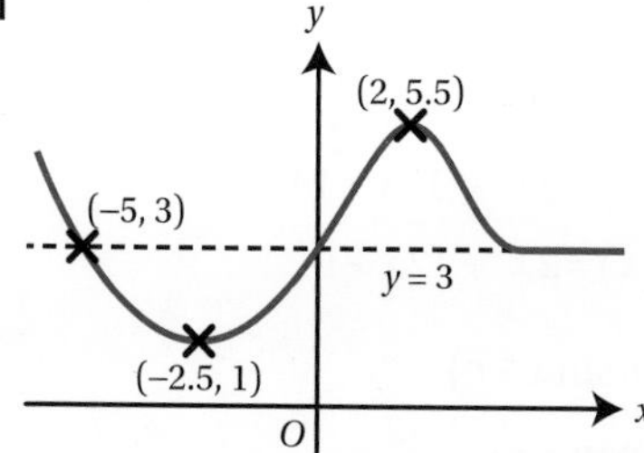

b i

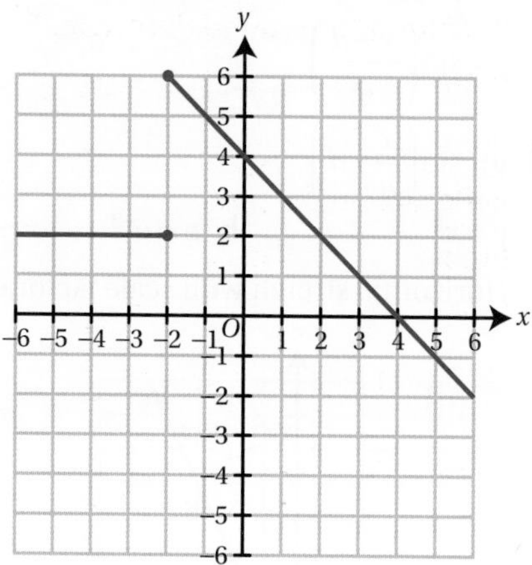

ii

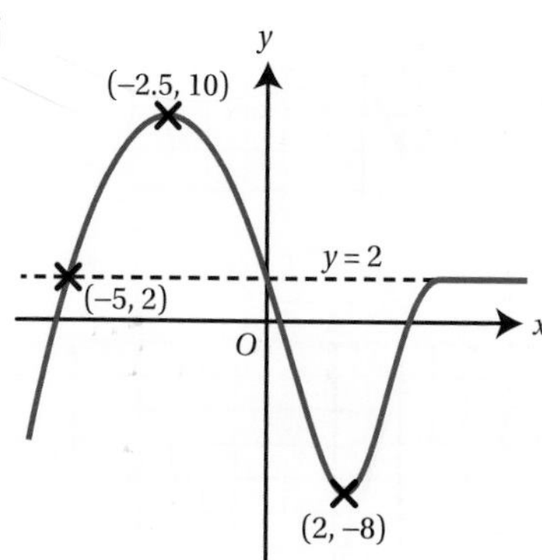

c i

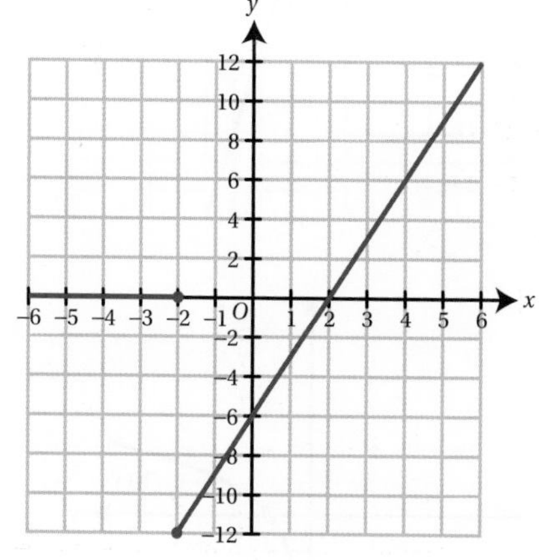

ii

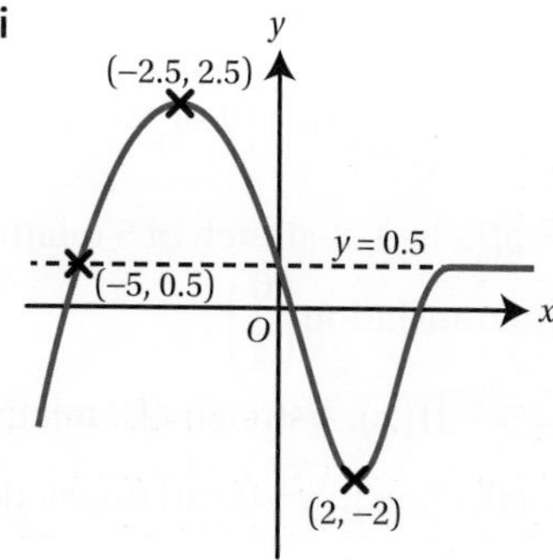

d i

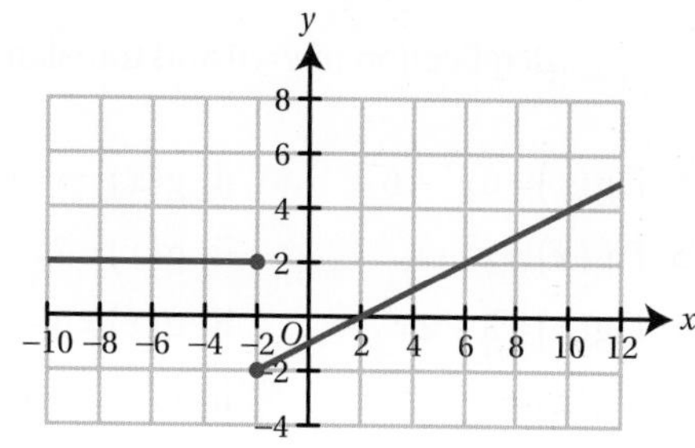

ii

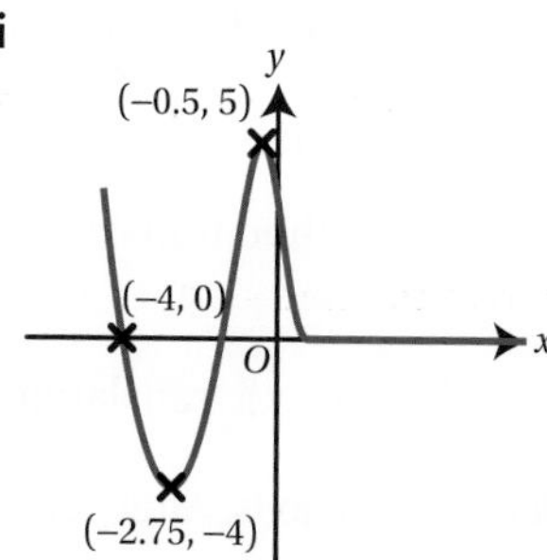

e i

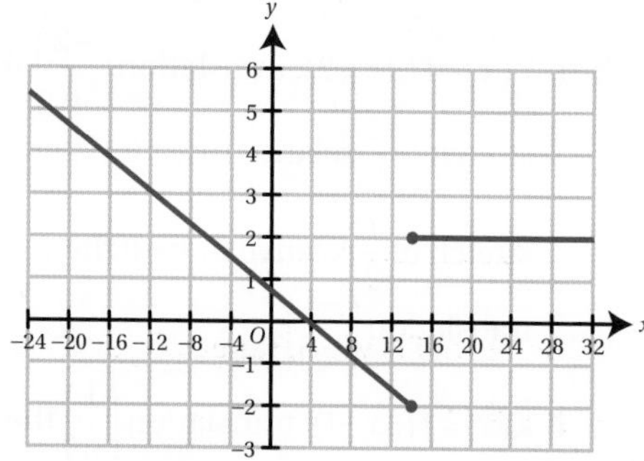

ii

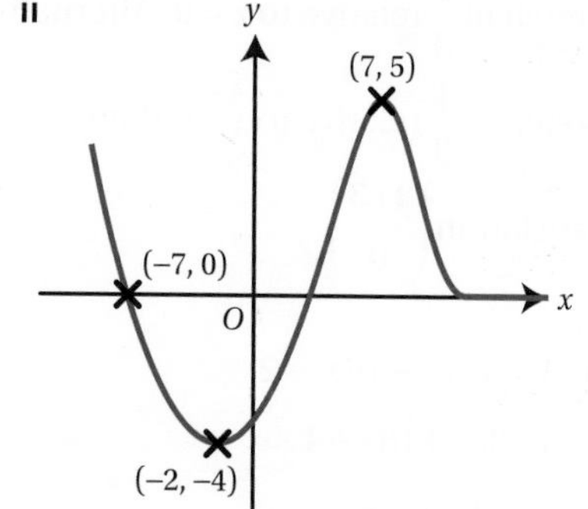

2 a i $k(x)=2f(x)-6$. A vertical stretch of 2 and translation $\begin{pmatrix}0\\-6\end{pmatrix}$ (in either order).

ii $k(x)=5f(x)+4$. A stretch of 5 relative to $y=0$ and translation $\begin{pmatrix}0\\4\end{pmatrix}$.

b i $h(x)=5-3f(x)$. A stretch of 3 relative to $y=0$, reflection in $y=0$ and translation $\begin{pmatrix}0\\5\end{pmatrix}$.

ii $h(x)=4-8f(x)$. A stretch of 8 relative to $y=0$, reflection in $y=0$ and translation $\begin{pmatrix}0\\4\end{pmatrix}$.

3 a i $g(x)=6x^2-6$ **ii** $g(x)=x^2+1$

b i $g(x)=x^2+4$ **ii** $g(x)=7x^2-4$

c i $g(x)=3-2x^2$ **ii** $g(x)=6-2x^2$

d i $g(x)=5-x^2$ **ii** $g(x)=-3-3x^2$

4 a i $g(x)=f(x+1)=f(-x-1)$: translation $\begin{pmatrix}1\\0\end{pmatrix}$ then reflection in y-axis. Alternatively, reflection in y-axis then translation $\begin{pmatrix}-1\\0\end{pmatrix}$.

ii $g(x)=f(x-3)=f(3-x)$: translation $\begin{pmatrix}-3\\0\end{pmatrix}$ then reflection in y-axis. Alternatively, reflection in y-axis then translation $\begin{pmatrix}3\\0\end{pmatrix}$.

b i $k(x)=f(2x+2)$: translation $\begin{pmatrix}-2\\0\end{pmatrix}$ then stretch of $\frac{1}{2}$ relative to $x=0$. Alternatively, stretch of $\frac{1}{2}$ relative to $x=0$ then translation $\begin{pmatrix}-1\\0\end{pmatrix}$.

ii $k(x)=f(3x-1)$: translation $\begin{pmatrix}1\\0\end{pmatrix}$ then stretch of $\frac{1}{3}$ relative to $x=0$. Alternatively, stretch of $\frac{1}{3}$ relative to $x=0$ then translation $\begin{pmatrix}1/3\\0\end{pmatrix}$.

5 a i $g(x)=32x^2-16x-2$

ii $g(x)=8x^2+16x+4$

b i $g(x)=8x^2+64x+124$

ii $g(x)=\frac{9x^2}{2}-9x+\frac{1}{2}$

c i $g(x)=2x^2-12x+14$

ii $g(x)=2x^2+12x+14$

6 a $y=p(\sin x+c)$

b $y=p\sin x+c$

c $y=\sin\left(\frac{x+d}{q}\right)$

d $y=\sin\left(\frac{x}{q}+d\right)$

7 a $y=x^2$ **b** $q=e^{-2}$

c Horizontal stretch with scale factor e^2.

8 a

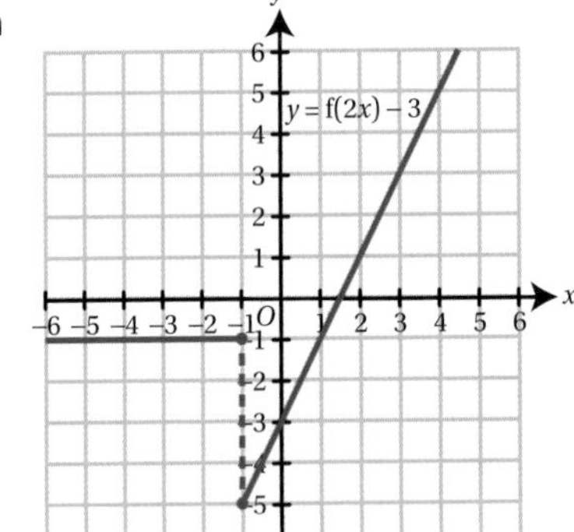

b

y = 1 − 3f(x)

9 a

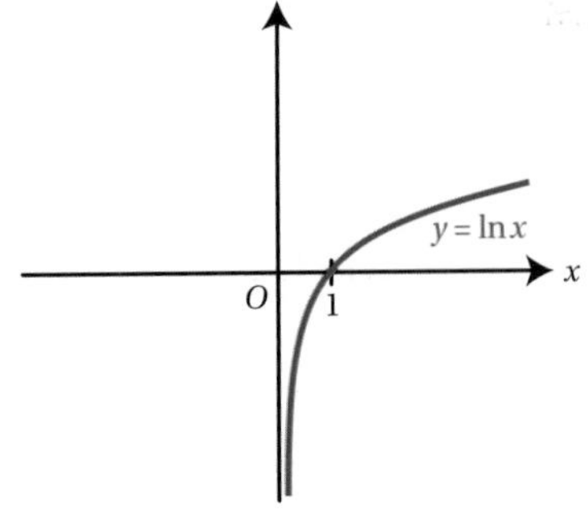

b

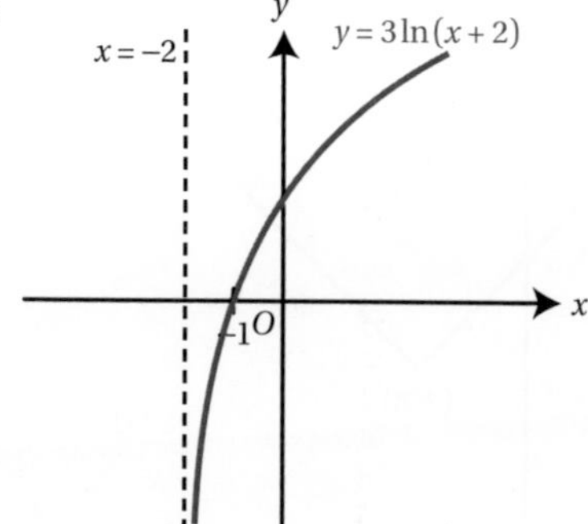

c

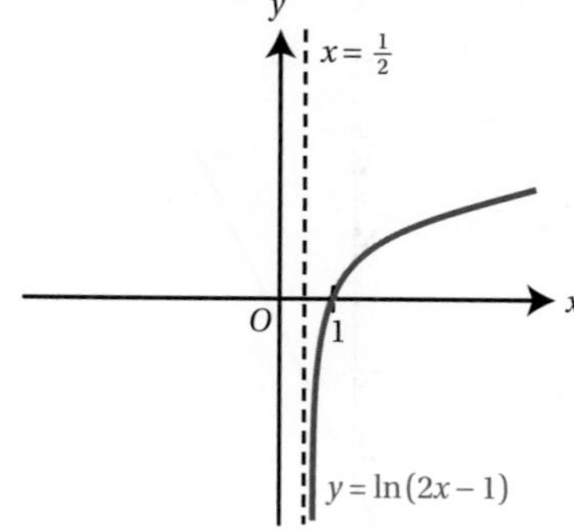

10 $y=-x^2+7x-10$

11 $a=5,\ b=4$

12 $a=2, b=3, c=-5$

13 $\mathrm{h}(x)=4^{x+1}+16x-4$

Exercise 3B

1 a i

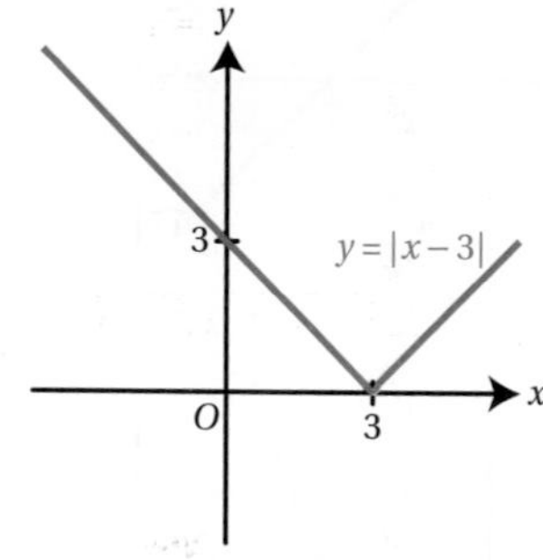

ii

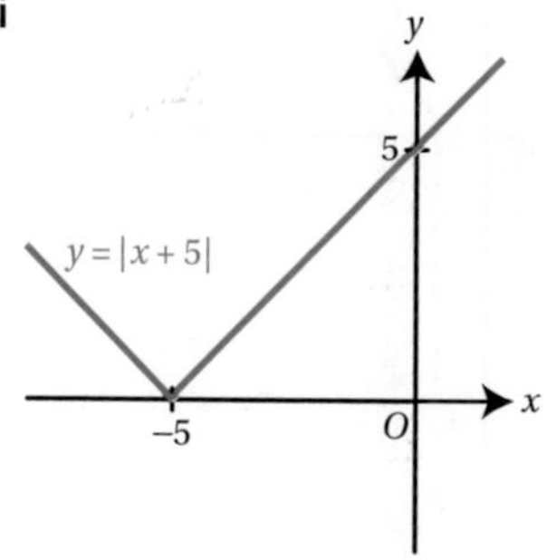

b i

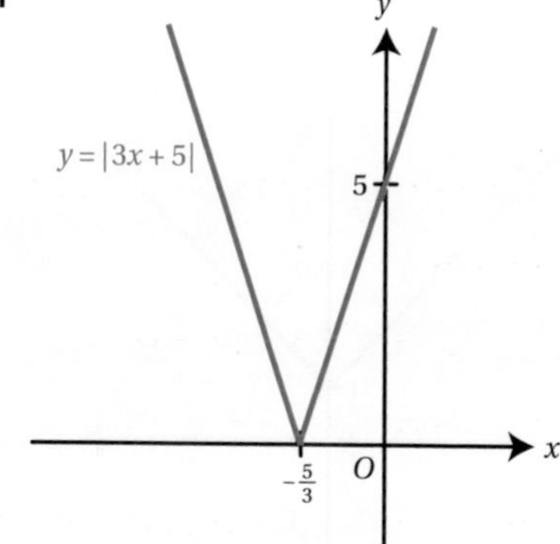

ii

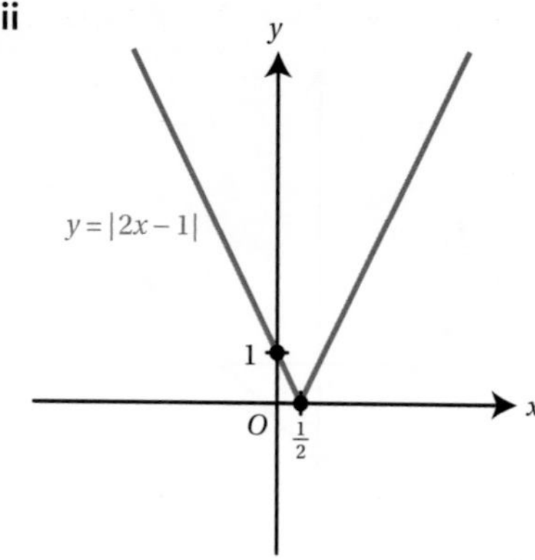

c i

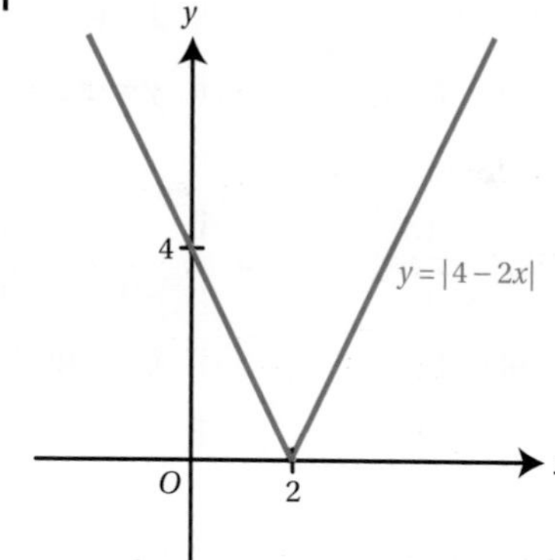

ii

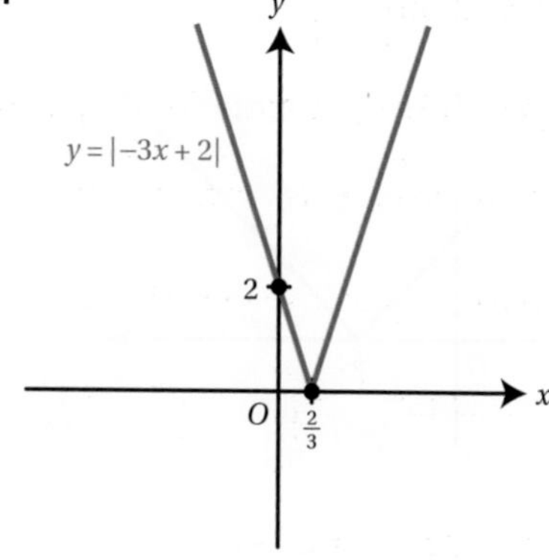

d i

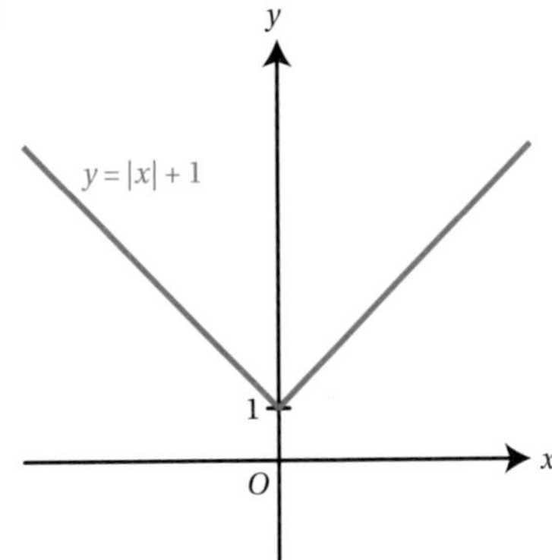

ii

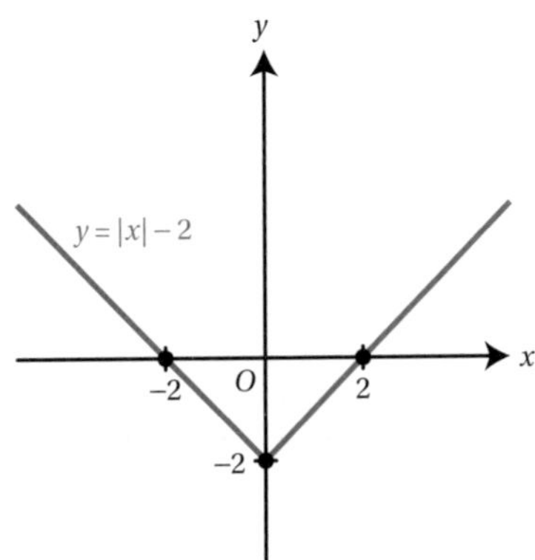

2 a i $y = |x - 4|$ **ii** $y = |x + 2|$

b i $y = |2x + 4|$ **ii** $y = |3x + 6|$

c i $y = |3x - 3|$ **ii** $y = |2x - 5|$

3 a i $-3 < x < 13$ **ii** $-7 < x < 11$

b i $-6 < x < 4$ **ii** $-9 < x < -3$

4 a i $|x - 9| \leqslant 4$ **ii** $|x - 18| \leqslant 7$

b i $|x + 2| \leqslant 12$ **ii** $|x + 7| \leqslant 9$

c i $|x - 6.5| \leqslant 3.5$ **ii** $|x - 12.5| \leqslant 7.5$

5 a

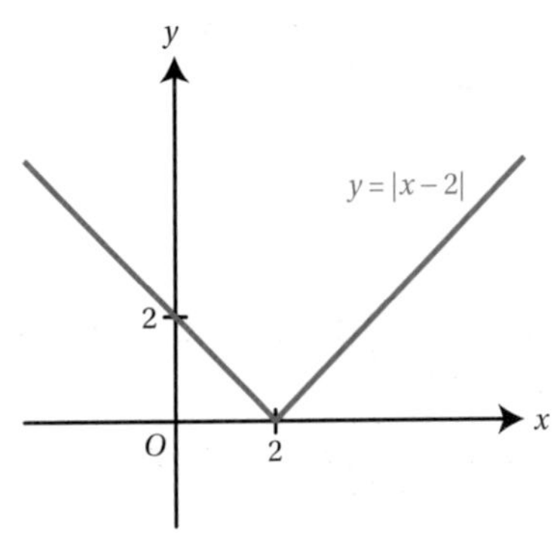

b

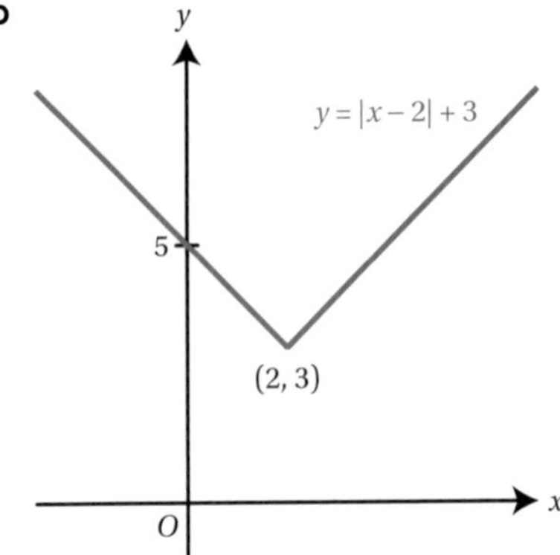

6

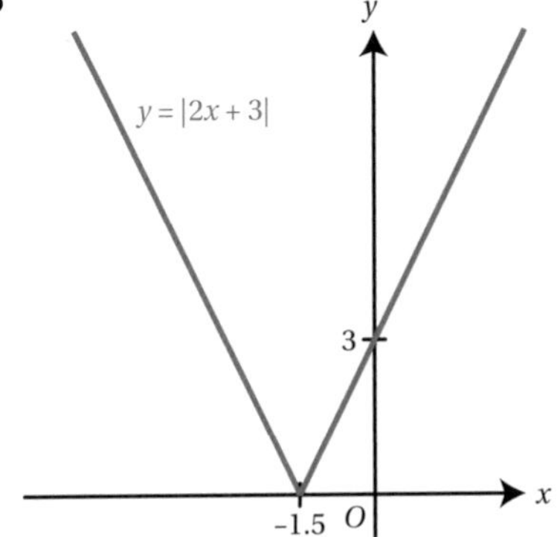

7

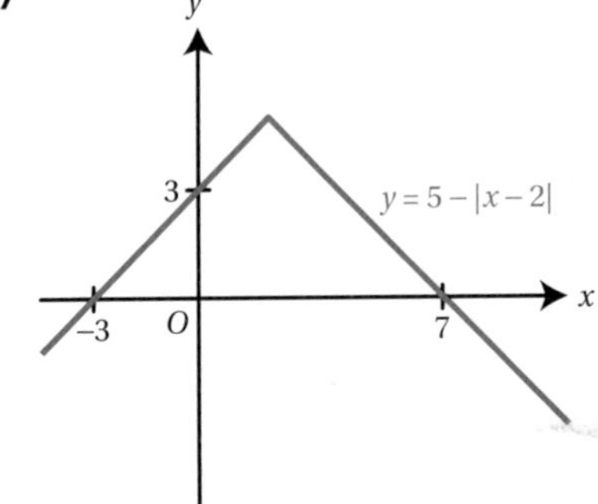

8

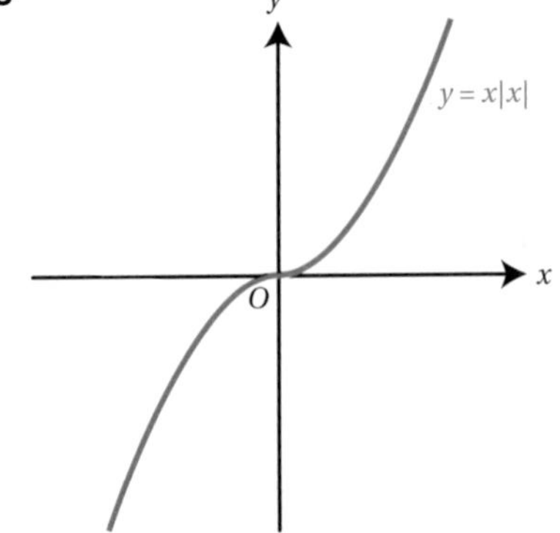

Work it out 3.2

Answer = Solution 1

Exercise 3C

1 a i $x = \pm 4$ **ii** $x = \pm 18$

b i $x = 0, 4$ **ii** $x = -1, \frac{1}{3}$

c i $x = 0, -8$ **ii** $x = 8, \frac{2}{3}$

d i $x = -2, 3$ **ii** $x = -\frac{1}{2}$

e i $x = \frac{2}{3}, 4$ **ii** $x = \frac{1}{4}, \frac{9}{2}$

f i $x = \frac{1}{2}$ **ii** $x = -1, -2$

2 a i $x \in (-\infty, -5) \cup (5, \infty)$

ii $x \in (-\infty, -2) \cup (2, \infty)$

b i $-3 < x < 3$ **ii** $-10 < x < 10$

c i $x \in \left(-\infty, -\frac{5}{2}\right] \cup \left[\frac{3}{2}, \infty\right)$ **ii** $x \in \left[\frac{-1}{3}, \frac{5}{3}\right]$

d i $\frac{4}{3} < x < 6$ **ii** $x < 1$ or $x > 5$

e i $x \in \left(-\infty, -\frac{5}{3}\right) \cup (3, \infty)$

ii $x \in \left(-\infty, \frac{3}{5}\right) \cup (5, \infty)$

f i $-\frac{4}{3} \leqslant x \leqslant 4$ **ii** $-1 \leqslant x \leqslant 1$

3 a $-\frac{4}{5}, \frac{2}{3}$ **b** $-\frac{4}{5} < x < \frac{2}{3}$

4 a $x = 1, 7$

b $x \geqslant 1$ or $x \leqslant 7$

5 a

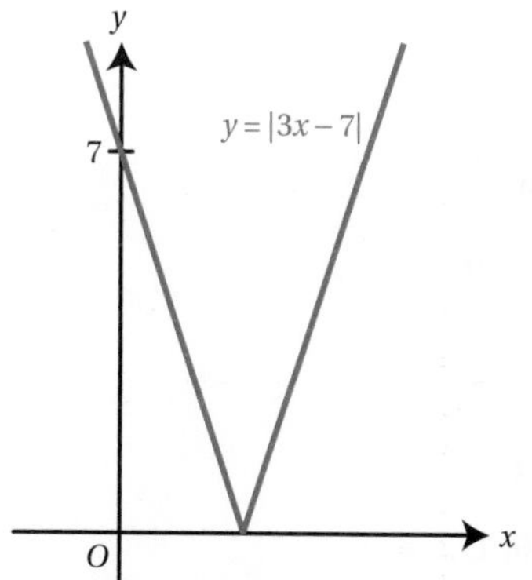

b No solutions

6 $x \in \mathbb{R}$

7 $x \leqslant 0$ or $x \geqslant \frac{2k}{3}$

8 $x \geqslant 0$

Mixed practice 3

1 a

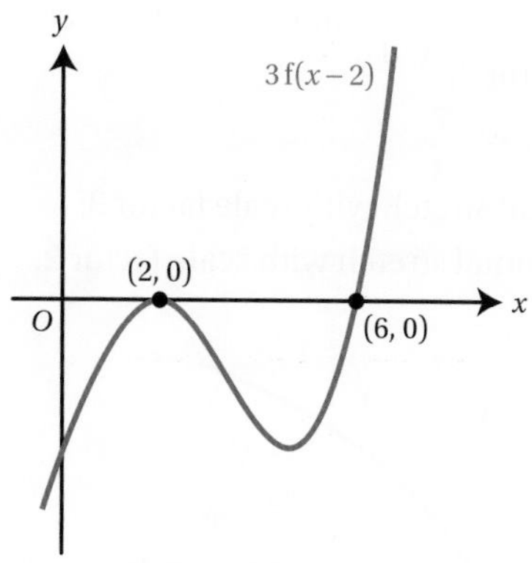

b

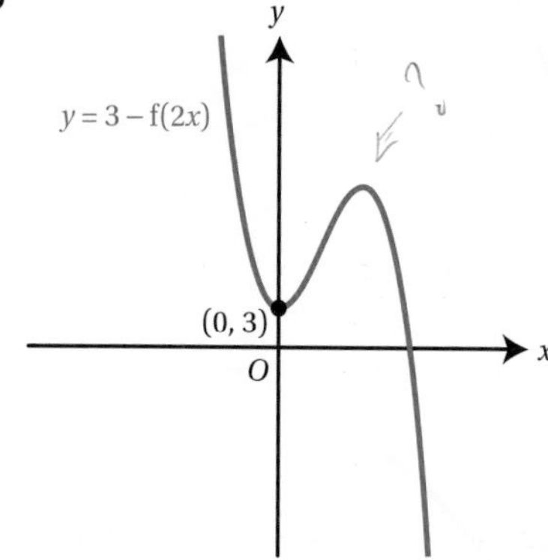

2 $y = 2x^3 - 12x^2 + 24x - 18$

3 a

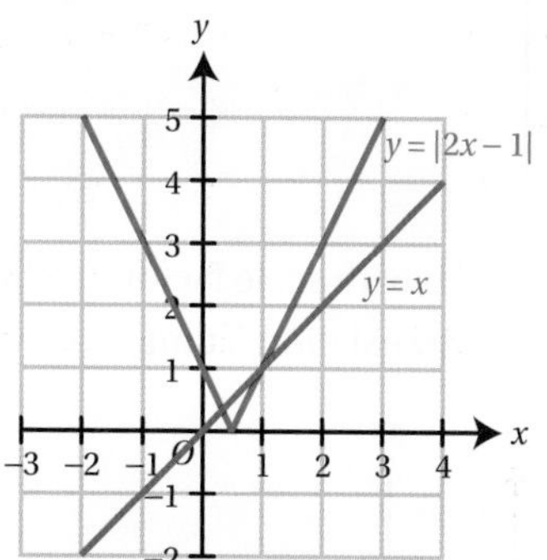

b $\frac{1}{3} < x < 1$

4 a Translation by $\begin{pmatrix} 2 \\ 0 \end{pmatrix}$ and vertical stretch with scale factor 3.

b Translation by $\begin{pmatrix} 3 \\ 0 \end{pmatrix}$ and translation by $\begin{pmatrix} 0 \\ 10 \end{pmatrix}$.

c Translation by $\begin{pmatrix} 5 \\ 10 \end{pmatrix}$ and vertical stretch with scale factor 3.

5 a $y = -\ln(x-4)$ **b** T, S, S

6 Translation by $\begin{pmatrix} -3 \\ 0 \end{pmatrix}$ and vertical stretch with scale factor 3.

7 $x < -5$ or $x > \frac{7}{3}$

8 a Vertical stretch with scale factor 3; horizontal stretch with scale factor 2.

b

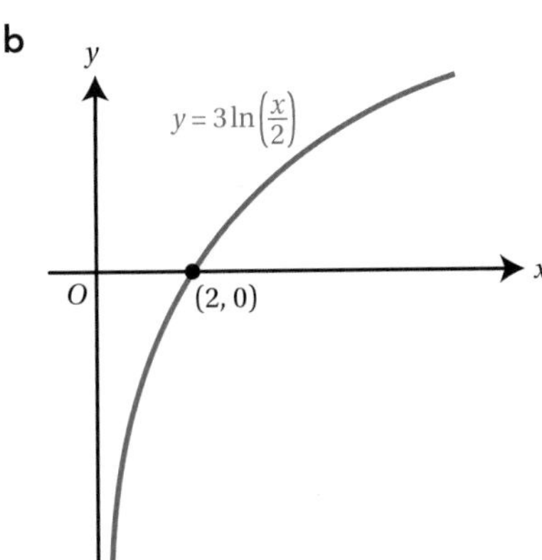

c

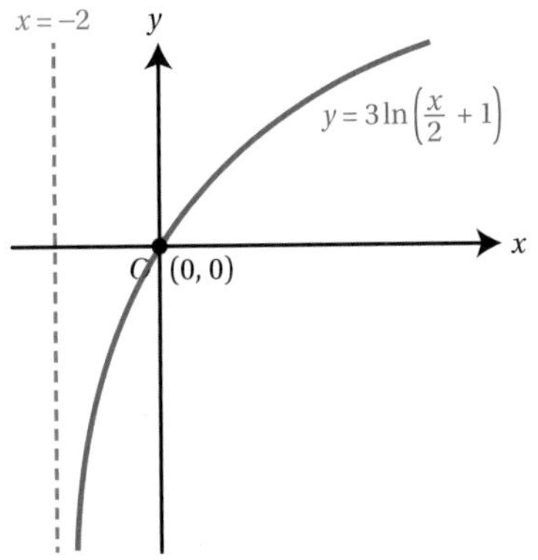

9 a Vertical stretch with scale factor 3; reflection in the x-axis; translation 5 units up.

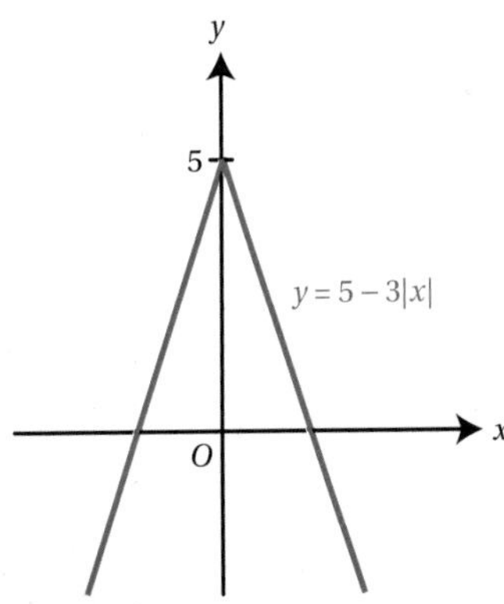

b 1.2, –0.8

c $-0.8 \leqslant x \leqslant 1.2$

10 a Translation by $\begin{pmatrix} -2 \\ 0 \end{pmatrix}$.

b

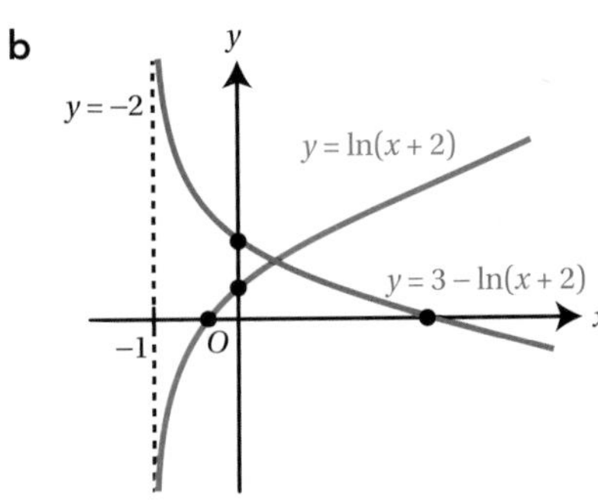

c i $\begin{pmatrix} 2 \\ 0 \end{pmatrix}$

ii $a = -1$, $b = 6$, $c = -9$, $d = -3$

11 a $y \leqslant 2$

b 2

c $0 < k \leqslant 2$

12 $x \geqslant 0$

13

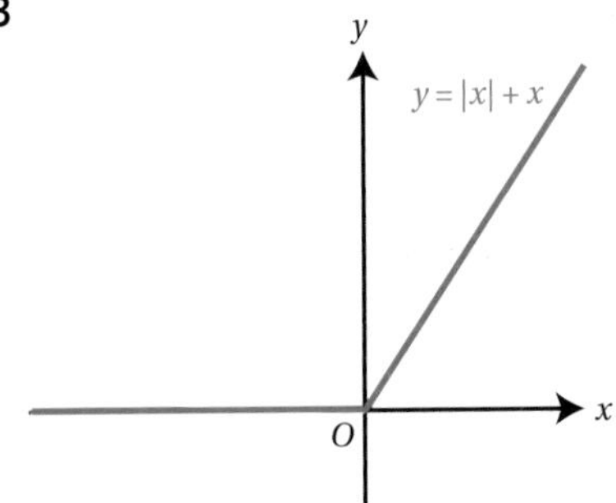

Chapter 4

Before you start...

1 a $3n - 1$

b $-4n + 19$

2 $u_2 = 10$; $u_3 = 28$

3 7

4 17

5 $a = -4$, $b = 3$

6 –3, –2, –1, 0, 1, 2, 3

Exercise 4A

1 a i 3.1, 8.1, 13.1, 18.1, 23.1

ii 10, 6.2, 2.4, –1.4, –5.2

b **i** 0, 1, 4, 13, 40

ii 1, −1, −19, −181, −1639

c **i** $1, 3, \frac{5}{3}, \frac{11}{5}, \frac{21}{11}$

ii 3, −1, 3, −1, 3

d **i** 0, 4, 8, 12, 16

ii 13, 11, 9, 7, 5

2 **a** **i** 5, 8, 11, 14, 17

ii −4.5, −3, −1.5, 0, 1.5

b **i** 0, 7, 26, 63, 124

ii 5, 20, 45, 80, 125

c **i** 3, 9, 27, 81, 243

ii $4, 2, 1, \frac{1}{2}, \frac{1}{4}$

d **i** 1, 4, 27, 256, 3125

ii 1, 0, −1, 0, 1

3 **a** **i** $u_n = n+3$ **ii** $u_n = 3n$

b **i** $u_n = n^2 + 1$ **ii** $u_n = (n+1)^2$

c **i** $u_n = 2^n$ **ii** $u_n = \left(\frac{1}{3}\right)^n$

d **i** $u_n = \frac{n}{n+1}$ **ii** $u_n = \frac{n+2}{n}$

4 **a** **i** Increases, converges to 10

ii Decreases, diverges

b **i** Periodic, period 2

ii Periodic, period 2

5 **a** 2, 8 **b** Proof

6 **a** $\frac{47}{17}$

b Converges to 3 (and oscillates)

7 $\frac{2}{5}$

8 **a** Proof **b** $\frac{1}{2}$

9 **a** $0.5, -2, -\frac{1}{3}, 0, 0.5$

b 0.5

10 **a** 2.5, 3.625

b It doesn't converge; the terms increase without limit.

Exercise 4B

1 **a** **i** 27 **ii** 39

b **i** 119 **ii** $\frac{665}{48}$

c **i** $14b$ **ii** $19p$

2 **a** **i** $\sum_{2}^{43} r$ **ii** $\sum_{3}^{30} 2r$

b **i** $\sum_{1}^{6} \frac{1}{2^{r+1}}$ **ii** $\sum_{0}^{5} \frac{2}{3^r}$

c **i** $\sum_{2}^{10} 7ar$ **ii** $\sum_{0}^{19} r^b$

3 39

4 **a** Proof **b** $\frac{3}{2}$

5 $15\ln 3$

6 **a** 0 **b** $\sqrt{3}$

Exercise 4C

1 **a** **i** $u_n = 9 + 3(n-1)$

ii $u_n = 57 + 0.2(n-1)$

b **i** $u_n = 12 - (n-1)$

ii $u_n = 18 - \frac{1}{2}(n-1)$

c **i** $u_n = 1 + 3(n-1)$

ii $u_n = 9 + 10(n-1)$

d **i** $u_n = 4 - 4(n-1)$

ii $u_n = 27 - 7(n-1)$

e **i** $u_n = -17 + 11(n-1)$

ii $u_n = -32 + 10(n-1)$

2 **a** **i** 33 **ii** 29

b **i** 100 **ii** 226

3 **a** $u_n = 5 + 8(n-1)$ **b** 50

4 121

5 25

6 17

7 $a = 2, b = -3$

8 **a** Proof **b** 456 pages

Exercise 4D

1 **a** **i** 3060 **ii** 1495

b **i** 9009 **ii** 23 798

c **i** −204 **ii** 1470

d **i** 667.5 **ii** 14.25

2 **a** **i** 13 **ii** 32

b **i** $\frac{x}{2}$ **ii** $5\sqrt{x}$

3 30

4 **a** 1, 5, 9 **b** $u_n = 4n - 3$

5 $a = 15, d = -8$

6 $a=2, d=5$

7 $a=-7, d=3$

8 Proof

9 559

10 55

11 $u_n=6n-4$

12 $\theta=20°$

13 a 71071 b 429429

14 10300

15 a $\ln x^{590}$ b e^5

16 23926

Exercise 4E

1 a i $u_n=6\times2^{n-1}$ ii $u_n=12\times\left(\frac{3}{2}\right)^{n-1}$

b i $u_n=20\times\left(\frac{1}{4}\right)^{n-1}$ ii $u_n=\left(\frac{1}{2}\right)^{n-1}$

c i $u_n=(-2)^{n-1}$ ii $u_n=5\times(-1)^{n-1}$

d i $u_n=2\times\left(\sqrt{3}\right)^{n-1}$ ii $u_n=\frac{4}{\left(\sqrt{2}\right)^{n-1}}$

e i $u_n=ax^{n-1}$ ii $u_n=3\times(2x)^{n-1}$

2 a i 13 ii 7

b i 10 ii 10

c i 10 ii 8

3 a $2\times3n^{-1}$ b 39366

4 a $a=3, r=\pm2$ b ±384

5 a $-1, 2$ b 19683, 39336

6 10

7 a Proof b 8

8 23

9 $\frac{\left(1\pm\sqrt{2}\right)}{2}$

10 $a=-2, b=4$

11 $m=7$

Exercise 4F

1 a i 17089842 ii 2303.4375

b i 514.75 ii 9.487171

c i 39368 ii 9840

d i 191.953125 or 63.984375

ii 24414062.5 or 16276041.67

2 a i $r=0.15$ ii $r=2.7$

b i $r=-1.3, 0.3$

ii $r=-0.184, -0.186$

3 a 5 b $S_n=\frac{375\left(5^n-1\right)}{4}$

4 $r=-\frac{1}{2}\pm\frac{\sqrt{147}}{6}$

5 $r=\pm\sqrt{\frac{27}{38}}=\pm0.843, a=12.9;$

$r=-0.843, a=151.27$

6 a 1.5 b 160

7 a $1+x+x^2+x^3=\frac{\left(1-x^4\right)}{(1-x)}$

b $(x-1)(x^5+x^4+x^3+x^2+x+1)$

Exercise 4G

1 a i $\frac{27}{2}$ ii $\frac{196}{3}$

b i $\frac{1}{3}$ ii $\frac{26}{33}$

c i Divergent ii Divergent

d i $\frac{25}{3}$ ii $\frac{18}{5}$

e i Divergent ii $\frac{7}{3}$

2 a i $|x|<1$ ii $|x|<1$

b i $|x|<\frac{1}{3}$ ii $|x|<\frac{1}{10}$

c i $|x|<\frac{1}{5}$ ii $|x|<\frac{1}{3}$

d i $|x|<4$ ii $|x|<12$

e i $|x|<3$ ii $|x|<\frac{4}{5}$

f i $|x|>2$ ii $|x|>\frac{1}{2}$

g i $1<x<2$ ii $0<x<4$

h i $\frac{1}{2}<x<1$ ii $x<-\frac{1}{2}$

i i $|x|<1$ ii $|x|<\frac{1}{\sqrt[3]{4}}$

3 $-\frac{54}{5}$

4 a $S_n=\frac{18\left(1-\left(\frac{-1}{3}\right)^n\right)}{\frac{4}{3}}$ b $S_\infty=\frac{27}{2}$

5 a $\frac{2}{3}$ b 9

6 $\frac{1}{8}$

7 a $|x|<\frac{3}{2}$ b 5

8 9

9 a $1<x<\frac{5}{3}$ b 7

10 a $x<0$ b $x=-3$

11 a 3 b undefined

Work it out 4.1

Answer = Solution 3

Exercise 4H

1 a £34.78 b £1194.05

2 a £60 500 b 22 years

3 a 5000×1.063^n b £6786.35

c i $5000 \times 1.063^n > 10000$ ii 12 years

4 a $f_{n+1} = 0.8f_n = 10$

b Decreases; tends to 50 in the long term.

5 a $V = £265.33$ b 235 months

6 a 12 days b Day 102

7 12 months

8 a 0.82 m b 15.3 m

c For smaller bounces, motions will be damped by physical effects such as air resistance so that the object will come to rest

9 a Proof

b $25000(1.04^n - 1)$

c Year 29

10 a 14 b 30.5%

11 a Proof

b $M_{n+1} = 1.02M_n - 5000$ c 17 years

Mixed practice 4

1 $a = 11, d = -\frac{7}{2}$

2 97.2

3 a $a = 3072, r = \frac{1}{4}$ b 4096

4 $\frac{5}{6}$

5 2

6 i 2, 5, 8; arithmetic ii 15 050

7 13th

8 $\frac{2}{3}$

9 $\frac{4\sqrt{2}}{3}$

10 a $2n - 1$ b 6 c 64

11 $n < 19$ years

12 a −3, 7 b 54

13 4.5

14 19 264

15 a $-\frac{1}{2} \leqslant k \leqslant 2$ b −2.4

16 i a 1295 b 167 400

ii 124 359

17 i Proof

ii $\frac{-1+\sqrt{5}}{2}$ iii 2

18 $d = 0, -\frac{1}{4}$

19 $\frac{-1+\sqrt{5}}{2}$

20 $\ln\left(\frac{a^{69}}{b^{138}}\right)$

21 a n b $\frac{n(n+1)}{2}$

c $\frac{n(n-1)}{2}+1$ d Proof

e 32

22 a Proof

b $150000 \times 1.06^n - \frac{500000(1.06^n - 1)}{3}$

c 40 years

Chapter 5

Before you start...

1 $(2x+1)(3x+2)$

2 $\frac{2+2x}{x(2+x)}$

3 $x^2 - 2x + 4$

4 $x - 1$

Exercise 5A

1 a i $(2x+1)(x-2)(x-3)$

ii $(3x-1)(x-1)^2$

b i $(2x-3)(x+2)(x+3)$

ii $(3x+5)(x+4)(x-4)$

2 $(2x+5)(2x+1)(x-3)$

3 $a = -2$

4 a $a = -8$

b $2(3x+1)(x-1)(2x+1)$

5 a Proof b $(2x-a)(x-a)^2$

6 Proof; $x = a$, $2a$ or $3a$

7 Proof

8 $b = \pm\sqrt{\frac{a^3}{a-1}}$

9 a $a=-23, b=-6$

b $x=-\frac{1}{2}, -\frac{1}{3}, -2, \frac{3}{5}$

10 $x=\pm 0.5, 2, -3$

Work it out 5.1

Answer = Solution 2

Exercise 5B

1 a i $2x+3$ ii $2x+4$

b i $\frac{1}{2}$ ii $\frac{1}{5}$

c i $3x+4$ ii $5x-7$

d i -1 ii -1

e i $\frac{2}{x-2}$ ii $\frac{4}{x+3}$

f i $\frac{x+1}{x+4}$ ii $\frac{x+2}{x+4}$

g i $\frac{3x+1}{4x+1}$ ii $\frac{4x-5}{3x-2}$

2 a i $2x$ ii $3x$

b i $\frac{x}{2}$ ii $5x^2$

c i $\frac{1}{6}$ ii $\frac{5}{2}$

d i $4x$ ii $2x$

e i $\frac{x+3}{x+2}$ ii $\frac{x-3}{x-1}$

3 a i 2 ii $\frac{5}{3}$

b i $\frac{2}{x+1}$ ii $\frac{3x}{5}$

c i $\frac{x}{3}$ ii $\frac{x+5}{x+1}$

d i $\frac{x}{3x+2}$ ii $\frac{5}{7x-2}$

4 a i $\frac{1}{2}x-\frac{1}{4}+\frac{\frac{1}{4}}{2x+1}$ ii $\frac{1}{2}x-\frac{3}{4}+\frac{\frac{9}{4}}{2x+3}$

b i $x+1+\frac{3}{2x+1}$ ii $x+\frac{4}{5x+3}$

5 $\frac{x+5}{x+4}$

6 $\frac{x+3}{2x^2}$

7 a $x+2$

b $x=-2$ or -1

8 $x=\pm 6$

9 Quotient: 2; remainder: 25

10 Quotient: $x-1$; remainder: 3

11 $2+\frac{3}{x+2}$

12 $x+1$

13 a Proof b $x-a$

14 $a=-1$; quotient $=x+1$

15 Proof

16 a $\frac{3ab}{2a+b}$ b Proof

Exercise 5C

1 a i $\frac{1}{x}+\frac{1}{x+2}$ ii $\frac{1}{x-3}-\frac{1}{x}$

b i $\frac{1}{x+1}+\frac{2}{x+2}$ ii $\frac{2}{x-1}+\frac{3}{x+2}$

c i $\frac{1}{x-3}-\frac{2}{x+4}$ ii $\frac{2}{x-5}-\frac{3}{x+6}$

2 a i $\frac{1}{x}+\frac{1}{x-2}-\frac{2}{x-3}$ ii $\frac{2}{x}-\frac{1}{x+2}-\frac{1}{x+1}$

b i $\frac{5}{x-1}-\frac{2}{x+1}-\frac{3}{x+2}$

ii $\frac{4}{x-3}-\frac{1}{x+4}-\frac{3}{x+1}$

3 $A=-\frac{2}{21}, B=\frac{5}{21}$

4 $\frac{1}{2(2x-1)}-\frac{1}{2(2x+1)}$

5 $\frac{1}{x}+\frac{1}{x+1}-\frac{2}{x+2}$

6 $\frac{1}{3x+1}+\frac{1}{3x-1}-\frac{2}{3x}$

7 $-\frac{1}{6(x-1)}+\frac{1}{6(x+1)}+\frac{1}{12(x-2)}-\frac{1}{12(x+2)}$

8 a Proof b $1-\frac{3}{x-1}+\frac{3}{x-2}$

9 $\frac{1}{x-a}-\frac{1}{x}$

10 $\frac{1}{x-a}+\frac{1}{x-2a}$

11 a $R=1$

b $1+\frac{1}{5(x+1)}-\frac{1}{5(x+6)}$

12 Proof

Exercise 5D

1 a i $\frac{1}{x+1}-\frac{1}{(x+1)^2}$ ii $\frac{1}{x-2}+\frac{2}{(x-2)^2}$

b i $\frac{4}{x^2}+\frac{1}{x+4}-\frac{1}{x}$ ii $-\frac{1}{x^2}-\frac{1}{x}+\frac{1}{x-1}$

c i $\frac{2}{x-1}+\frac{3}{(x+2)^2}-\frac{2}{x+2}$

ii $\frac{1}{x-2}+\frac{6}{(x-2)^2}-\frac{1}{x+1}$

2 $\frac{1}{x-2}-\frac{1}{x}-\frac{2}{x^2}$

3 $\frac{1}{x^2}-\frac{4}{x+1}+\frac{4}{x}$

4 $\frac{1}{16(x+2)}-\frac{1}{16(x-2)}+\frac{1}{4(x-2)^2}$

5 a Proof b $(2x-1)(x+1)^2$

c $\frac{2}{2x-1}-\frac{1}{x+1}+\frac{3}{(x+1)^2}$

6 a $x+2+\frac{2}{x^3+3x^2}$

b $x+2+\frac{2}{3x^2}-\frac{2}{9x}+\frac{2}{9(x+3)}$

7 a Proof

b $\frac{1}{x-1}+\frac{3-x}{(x-2)^2}$

8 $\frac{1}{x-a}+\frac{1}{(x-a)^2}-\frac{1}{x}$

Mixed practice 5

1 a x^2-x+1

b 7, 11, 13

2 a Proof

b $3(2x+3)(x-1)(x+4)$

c $x=-\frac{3}{2}, 1, -4$

d $\frac{3(x-1)}{2}$

3 $\frac{1}{x-3}-\frac{1}{x+2}$

4 $\frac{1}{x}-\frac{2}{x+3}+\frac{1}{x-3}$

5 $\frac{1}{12(3x+2)}+\frac{1}{12(3x-2)}$

6 $\frac{1}{4x}-\frac{1}{4(x+2)}-\frac{1}{2(x+2)^2}$

7 $4x+3$

8 $\frac{\sqrt{10}}{x-\sqrt{10}}-\frac{\sqrt{10}}{x+\sqrt{10}}$

9 $\frac{x+6}{x}$

10 $-\frac{3}{x-1}-\frac{1}{(x-1)^2}+\frac{4}{x-2}$

11 a $\frac{3}{(2x+3)(x+2)}$

b $\frac{6}{2x+3}-\frac{3}{x+2}$

12 a Proof

b $(x-1)(3x+1)^2$

c $x=1$ or $-\frac{1}{3}$

d $\frac{1}{2(x-1)}-\frac{3}{2(3x+1)}-\frac{2}{(3x+1)^2}$

13 a Proof

b $x=\pm 0.5, -1$

c $\frac{1}{2x-1}+\frac{1}{2x+1}-\frac{1}{x+1}$

14 a $2x+1+\frac{3x+7}{x^2+5x+6}$

b $2x+1+\frac{1}{x+2}+\frac{2}{x+3}$

15 Quotient: $x^2+\frac{x}{3}+\frac{16}{9}$; remainder: $-\frac{65}{9}$

16 a $a=35, b=6$

b $(2x+1)(3x+1)(x+2)(x+3)$

c $x=-\frac{1}{2}, -\frac{1}{3}, -2, -3$

17 a $\frac{1}{x+1}-\frac{1}{x+5}$

b $\frac{1}{(x+1)^2}+\frac{1}{(x+5)^2}+\frac{1}{2(x+5)}-\frac{1}{2(x+1)}$

18 a $1+\frac{8}{u-4}$ b $1+\frac{2}{x-2}-\frac{2}{x+2}$

19 $\frac{1}{x}+\frac{a}{x^2}+\frac{2}{x-a}$

20 $A=1, B=2, k=3$

21 $b=-2a^2$

22 0

23 Proof

24 a $R_T=\frac{R_1R_2}{R_1+R_2}$

b Proof

Chapter 6

Before you start...

1 $2x^2$

2 $16x^4-96x^3+216x^2-216x+81$

3 $\frac{1}{x-2}-\frac{2}{x}$

4 $-1<x<5$

Exercise 6A

1 a i $1-2x+3x^2; |x|<1$

ii $1-3x+6x^2; |x|<1$

b i $1+\frac{x}{3}-\frac{x^2}{9}; |x|<1$ **ii** $1+\frac{x}{4}-\frac{3x^2}{32}; |x|<1$

c i $1-x-\frac{x^2}{2}; |x|<\frac{1}{3}$ **ii** $1-\frac{3x}{2}-\frac{9x^2}{8}; |x|<\frac{1}{3}$

d i $\frac{1}{4}+\frac{x}{16}+\frac{x^2}{64}; |x|<4$

ii $\frac{1}{5}+\frac{x}{25}+\frac{x^2}{125}; |x|<5$

2 $1+x+\frac{2x^2}{3}$

3 $\frac{1}{2}-\frac{x}{48}+\frac{x^2}{576}-\frac{7x^3}{41472}$

4 a $1-4x+12x^2$

b $|x|<\frac{1}{2}$

5 a Proof **b** $|x|<9$

c i $1-\frac{x}{18}-\frac{x^2}{648}$

ii $1+\frac{x^2}{18}-\frac{x^4}{648}$

iii $3+\frac{x}{6}-\frac{x^2}{216}$

d 3.1620

6 a $1-2x-2x^2-4x^3$

b $|x|<\frac{1}{4}$

c 9.79796

d 2.44

7 4

8 a $2+\frac{1}{12}x^2-\frac{1}{288}x^4$ for $|x|<2\sqrt{2}$

b 4.05

9 a $\frac{1}{81}-\frac{1}{6561}x^4+\frac{1}{531441}x^8$

b $I=0.0361$ (The expansion is only valid for $|x|<3$).

10 -540

11 $-\frac{1}{2}$

12 $1+\frac{1}{2}x-\frac{1}{8}x^2$

Work it out 6.1

Answer = Solution 2

Exercise 6B

1 $x+2x^2+3x^3\ldots$

2 $x+x^2-\frac{x^3}{2}; |x|<\frac{1}{2}$

3 $1+2x+2x^2$

4 $1-2x+5x^2$

5 a $\frac{1}{1+x}+\frac{1}{1+2x}$

b $2-3x+5x^2$

c $|x|<\frac{1}{2}$

6 a $\frac{1}{(x+1)^2}+\frac{2}{2-x}+\frac{2}{x+1}$

b $4-\frac{7x}{2}+\frac{21x^2}{4}$

c $|x|<1$

7 $1-3x+7x^2$

> **Tip**
>
> There are several ways to do this – you could treat it as $\frac{2}{1+2x}-\frac{1}{1+x}$ or $\frac{2}{1+2x}-\frac{1}{1+x}$ or $\frac{1}{1+u}$, where $u=3x+x^2$.

8 a $\frac{\frac{1}{9}}{x-2}+\frac{-\frac{1}{9}}{x+1}+\frac{-\frac{1}{3}}{(x+1)^2}$

b $-\frac{1}{2}+\frac{3}{4}x-\frac{9}{8}x^2$

c -0.203

9 a $-\frac{89}{80}+\frac{231}{1600}x$

b $m=4, -8.9$

10 a $1-\frac{7}{2}x$

b $|x|<\frac{1}{12}$

c 3.86

11 $\frac{8}{3}$

12 No, as the expression is not defined for small values of x.

Mixed practice 6

1 $1+4x+12x^2+32x^3; |x|<\frac{1}{2}$

2 $\frac{1}{2}-\frac{x}{16}+\frac{3x^2}{256}; |x|<4$

3 $1-2x+3x^2-4x^3$

4 $1-\frac{x^2}{2}-\frac{x^4}{8}$

5 i $1+\frac{1}{3}x-\frac{1}{9}x^2$

ii a $2+\frac{4}{3}x-\frac{8}{9}x^2$ **b** $|x|<\frac{1}{2}$

6 a $2+\frac{1}{12}x-\frac{1}{288}x^2+\dots$ **b** 20.08

7 a $\frac{1}{3-x}+\frac{1}{x+2}+\frac{2}{(x+2)^2}$

b $\frac{4}{3}-\frac{23}{36}x+\frac{29}{54}x^2$ **c** $|x|<2$

8 $\frac{1}{6}-\frac{x}{36}-\frac{11x^2}{216}$; $|x|<2$

9 $a=1, b=3$ or $a=3, b=1$

10 i Proof **ii** Proof

11 a $1+x+\frac{2x^3}{3}$ **b** 1.44267

12 –270

13 $1-x+x^3$

14 a $A=1, B=-1, C=1$; $|x|<1$

b Proof

c $P=1, Q=-1, R=1$; $|x|>1$

d 0.9901

e 0.019608

15 a $mc^2+\frac{1}{2}mv^2+\frac{3m}{8c^2}v^4+\dots$

b i 0.00373% **ii** 17.5%

c Proof

Focus on … Proof 1

Arithmetic series proof 1

1 $a+(n-1)d$

2 $a+(n-2)d$

3 $2a+(n-1)d$

4 $2a+(n-1)d$

5 n

6 Divide by 2.

Geometric series proof 2

1 Multiply through by r.

2 a

3 ar^n

4 $1-r$

5 $1-r^n$

Questions

1 $1-r^n=0$, so can't divide by it on last line.
$S_n=an$

2 a $\frac{1+\sqrt{5}}{2}$

b 2

Focus on … Problem solving 1

1 45

2 n^2

3 $2n+5$

4 89

Focus on … Modelling 1

1 a i 0.333

ii 8000

iii

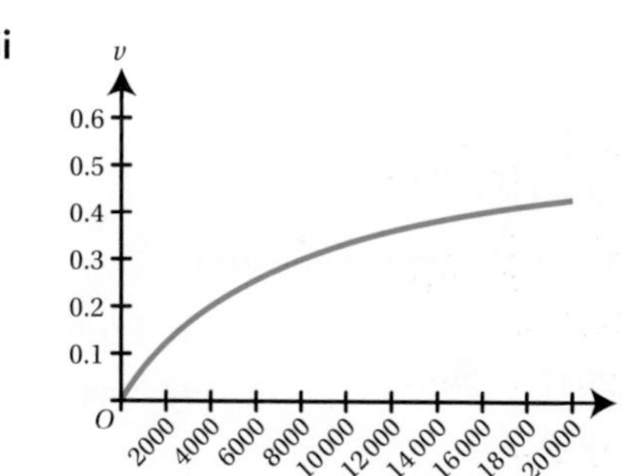

b The maximum possible rate (asymptote, can't be reached).

2 $b=2, c=1$

3 a Rational function

b Exponential function

Cross-topic review exercise 1

1 a

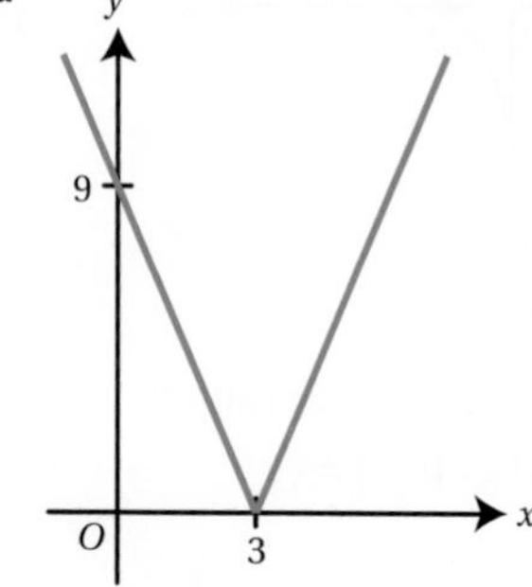

b $x = 1$ or 5

c $x < 1$ or $x > 5$

2 4

3

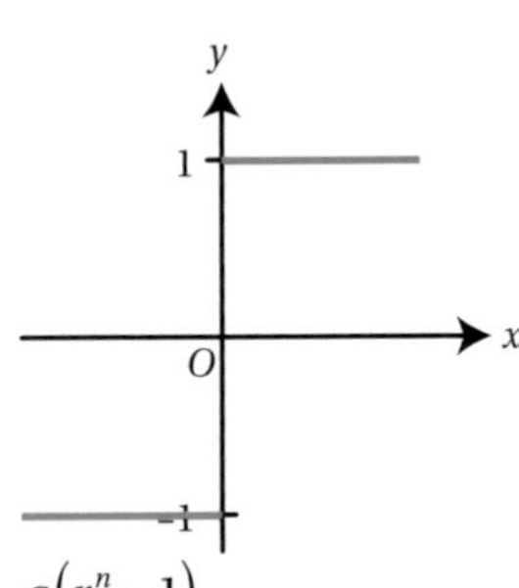

4 $\dfrac{a(r^n - 1)}{n(r-1)}$

5 $a = 4, b = -1$, or $a = -4, b = 3$

6 a i 0

ii Proof

b $\dfrac{4x}{(x-1)(3x+5)}$

7 i 0

ii $x \leqslant 7$

iii $(2-x)^3 - 1$

iv Reflection in the line $y = x$.

8 a $f(x) \geqslant 7$ **b** Proof

9 a $\dfrac{2047}{1024}$ **b** $-55\ln 2$

10 $\dfrac{3}{64}$

11 $-0.618 < x < 1.62$

12 a $A = 2, B = -5$

b Range: $y \neq 2$

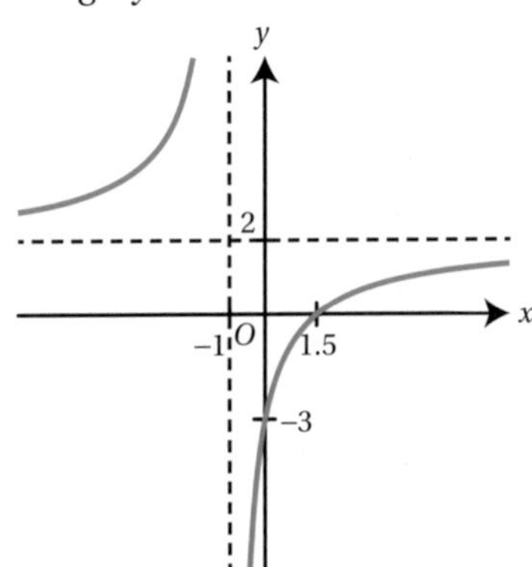

c Domain: $x < -1$ or $x \geqslant 1.5$; range: $g \circ h(x) \geqslant 0$ and $g \circ h(x) \neq \sqrt{2}$

13 a $A = 2, B = 1$

b i $2 - \dfrac{3}{2}x + \dfrac{17}{4}x^2$

ii The expansion is valid only for $|x| < 0.5$.

14 i Proof

ii Proof

iii 21

15 $mc^2 + \dfrac{1}{2}mv^2 + \dfrac{3}{8c^2}mv^4$. When v is small, this is mc^2 plus the kinetic energy.

16 $e^8 - 1$

17 a No

b 6

c −7

18 a $(-y, x)$ **b** $y = f^{-1}(-x)$

19 a Proof

b $2(x-a)\,g(x) + (x-a)^2\,g'(x) + m$

c Proof

d $f(a) = 0, f'(a) = 0$

Chapter 7

Before you start...

1 $\dfrac{\sqrt{3}}{2}$

2 $x = 30°, 150°, 210°, 330°$

3 $y = 2\cos(x - 30°)$

4 26.4°

5 $2 + 6x^2 + 18x^4$

Work it out 7.1

Answer = Solution 2

Exercise 7A

1 a i and ii

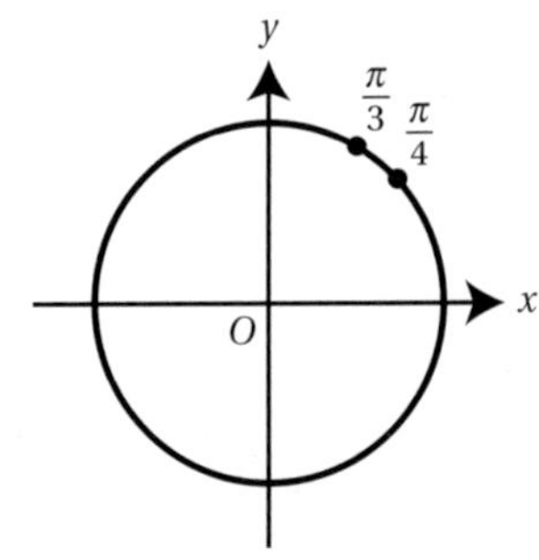

b i and ii

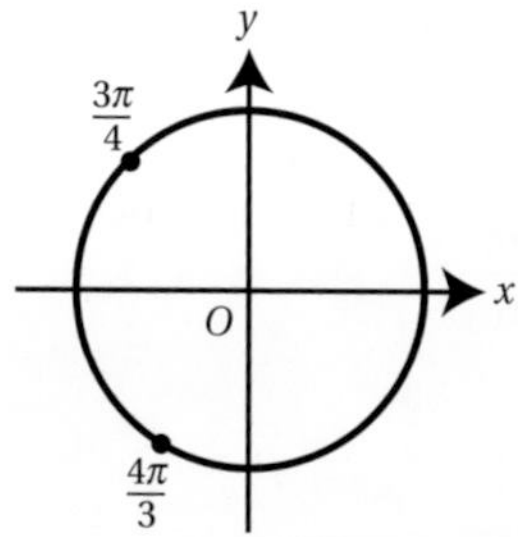

c i and ii

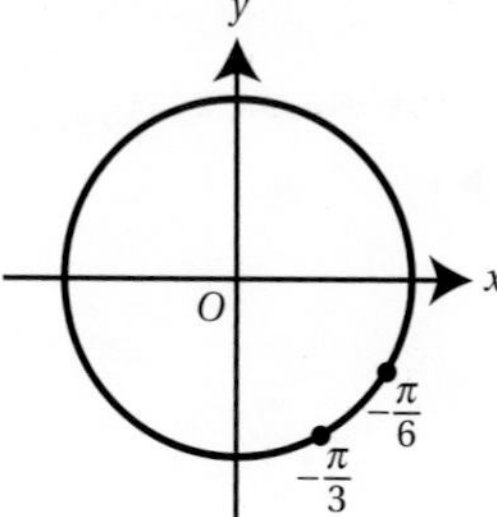

d i and ii

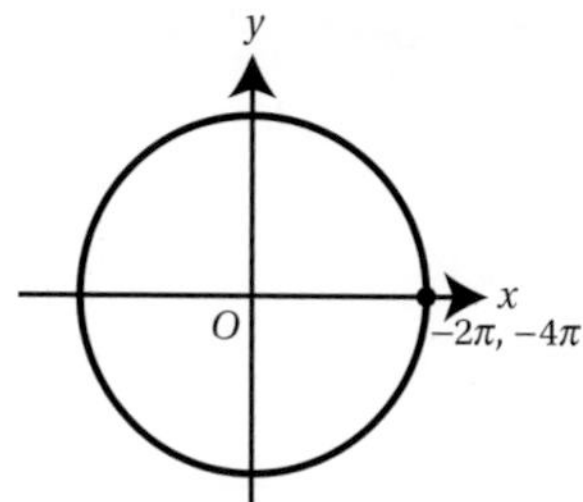

2 a i $\frac{3\pi}{4}$ **ii** $\frac{\pi}{4}$

b i $\frac{\pi}{2}$ **ii** $\frac{3\pi}{2}$

c i $\frac{2\pi}{3}$ **ii** $\frac{5\pi}{6}$

d i $\frac{5\pi}{18}$ **ii** $\frac{4\pi}{9}$

3 a i 5.585 **ii** 0.349

b i 4.712 **ii** 1.571

c i 1.134 **ii** 2.531

d i 1.745 **ii** 1.449

4 a i 60° **ii** 45°

b i 150° **ii** 120°

c i 270° **ii** 300°

d i 69.9° **ii** 265°

5 a i

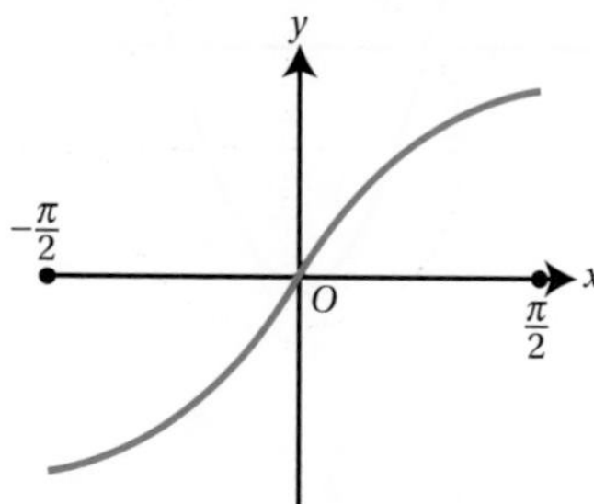

ii

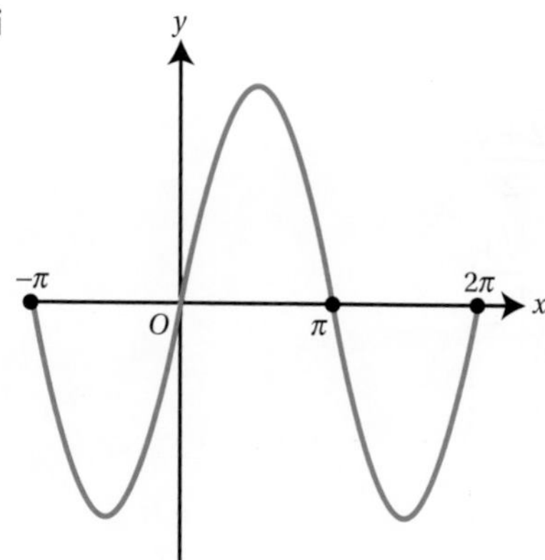

b i

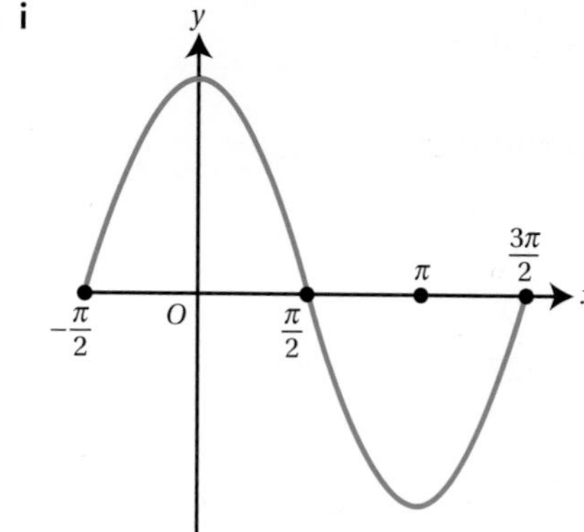

ii

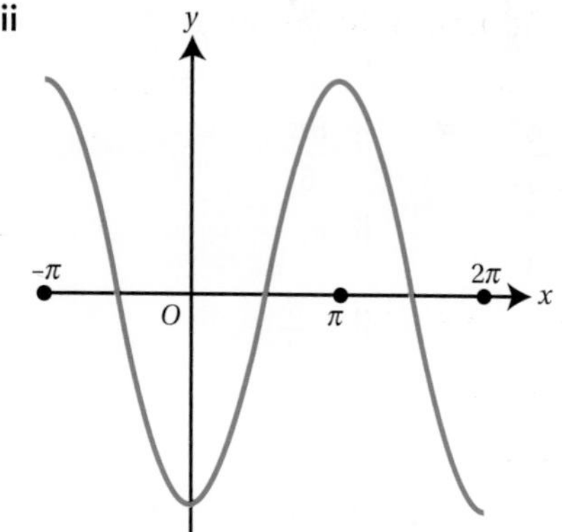

6 a 0.434 **b** 0.434

c −0.434 **d** −0.434

7 a −0.809 **b** 0.809

c 0.809 **d** −0.809

8 a 0.414 **b** −0.414

c 0.414 **d** −0.414

9 a i $-\frac{\sqrt{2}}{2}$ **ii** $-\frac{\sqrt{2}}{2}$

b i $-\frac{1}{2}$ **ii** $-\frac{\sqrt{3}}{2}$

c i −1 **ii** −1

10 a $\frac{3}{4}$

b $\frac{\sqrt{2}+\sqrt{3}}{2}$

c $\frac{1-\sqrt{3}}{2}$

11 Proof

12 Proof

13 $-2\cos x$

14 $\sin x$

Work it out 7.2

Answer = Solution 1

Work it out 7.3

Answer = Solution 3

Exercise 7B

1 a i 0.927 **ii** 0.201

b i −1.25 **ii** −0.927

2 a i $\frac{\pi}{6}$ **ii** $\frac{\pi}{6}$

b i $-\frac{\pi}{3}$ **ii** $\frac{3\pi}{4}$

c i $-\frac{\pi}{2}$ **ii** $\frac{\pi}{4}$

3 a i $\frac{\pi}{3}$ **ii** $\frac{5\pi}{6}$

b i $\frac{\pi}{3}$ **ii** π

c i $\frac{\pi}{3}$ **ii** $-\frac{\pi}{4}$

d i $-\frac{\pi}{4}$ **ii** $-\frac{\pi}{6}$

4 a 0.866 **b** −0.433 **c** 0.141

5 a i $\frac{\pi}{6}, \frac{11\pi}{6}$ **ii** $\frac{\pi}{4}, \frac{7\pi}{4}$

b i $\frac{2\pi}{3}, \frac{4\pi}{3}$ **ii** $\frac{5\pi}{6}, \frac{7\pi}{6}$

c i $\frac{\pi}{4}, \frac{3\pi}{4}$ **ii** $\frac{\pi}{3}, \frac{2\pi}{3}$

d i $\frac{\pi}{6}, \frac{7\pi}{6}$ **ii** $\frac{3\pi}{4}, \frac{7\pi}{4}$

6 a i 0.644, 5.64, 6.93, 11.9

ii 0.841, 5.44, 7.12, 11.7

b i −2.21, −0.927, 4.07, 5.36

ii −2.78, −0.358, 3.50, 5.93

c i −0.588, 2.55

ii −1.25, 1.89

d i $0, 2\pi, 4\pi$

ii $\frac{\pi}{2}, \frac{3\pi}{2}, \frac{5\pi}{2}, \frac{7\pi}{2}$

7 $-\frac{\pi}{6}, -\frac{5\pi}{6}$

8

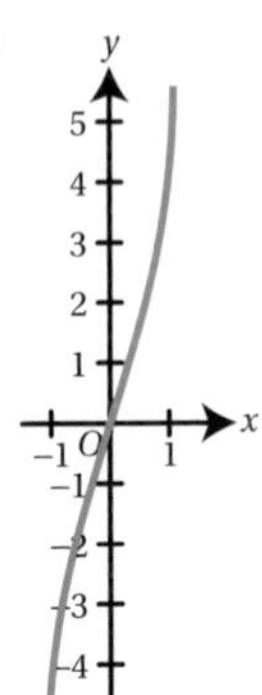

9 $\frac{\pi}{12}, \frac{\pi}{3}, \frac{7\pi}{12}, \frac{5\pi}{6}$

10 a Proof

b 1.01, 2.13

11 $0, \frac{\pi}{3}, \pi$

12 e.g. $x = 3\pi$

13 $\pm\sqrt{\frac{\pi}{6}}, \pm\sqrt{\frac{5\pi}{6}}, \pm\sqrt{\frac{13\pi}{6}}, \pm\sqrt{\frac{17\pi}{6}}$

14 a e.g. $x = 1$

b $\arcsin x = \frac{\pi}{2} - \arccos x$

c $x = 1$

Exercise 7C

1 a Amplitude = 3; period = $\frac{\pi}{2}$

b Amplitude = 1; period = 4π

c Amplitude = 1; period = $\frac{2\pi}{3}$

d Amplitude = 2; period = 2

2 a i

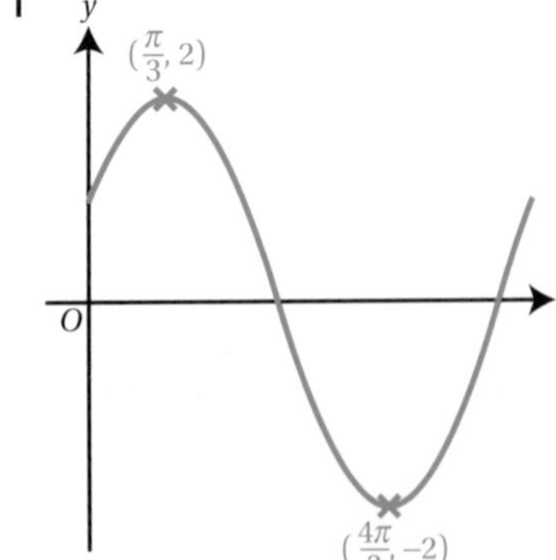

ii

b i

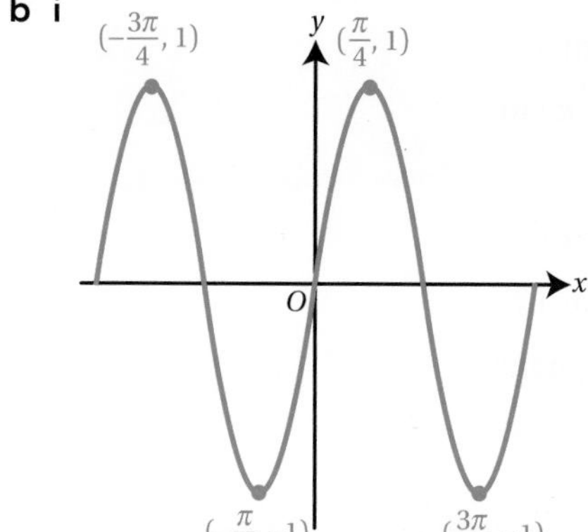

ii

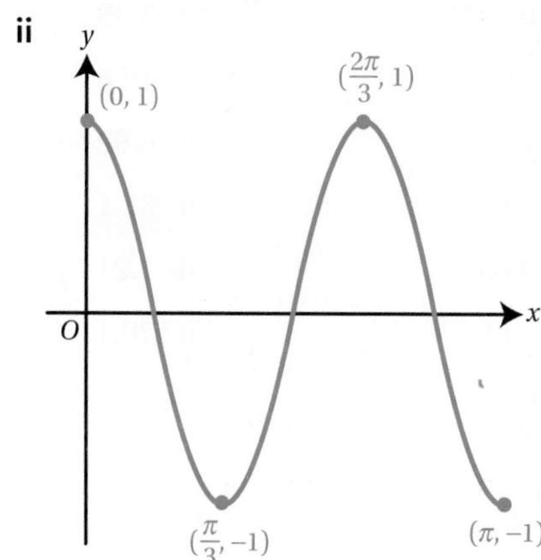

c i

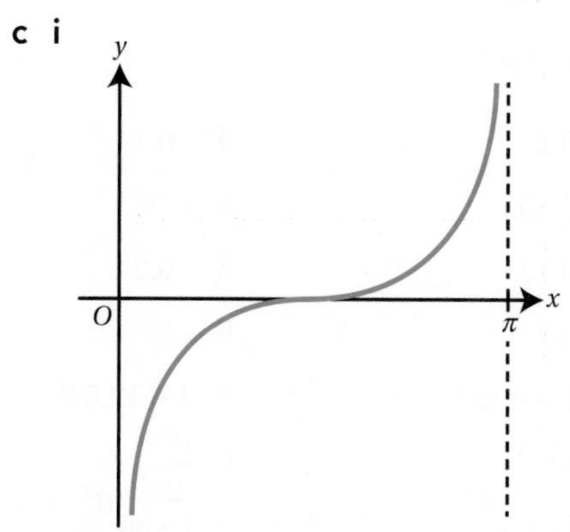

ii

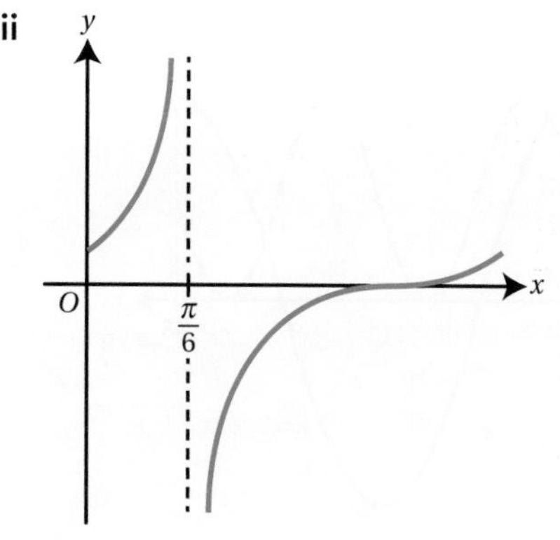

d i

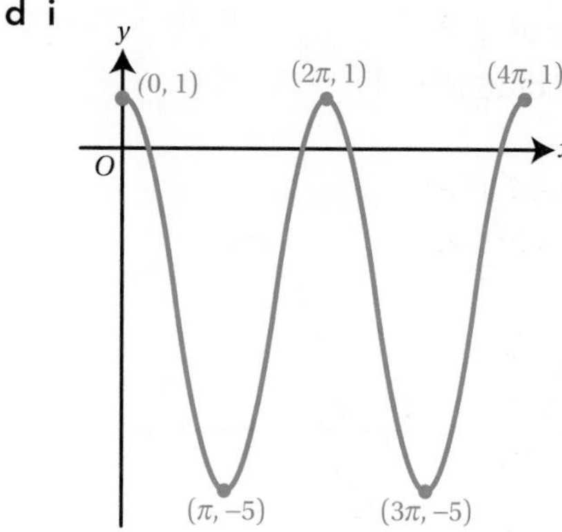

ii

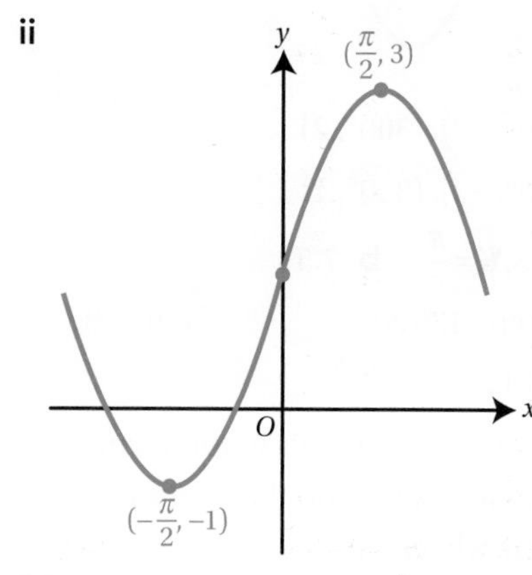

3 a 9 m, 23 m **b** 6 a.m.

4 a 4 **b** 2 s

c There is no loss of energy, for example due to air resistance, so that the amplitude of oscillation remains constant.

5 $p = 5, q = 2$

6 $a = 2, b = 20°$

7 a

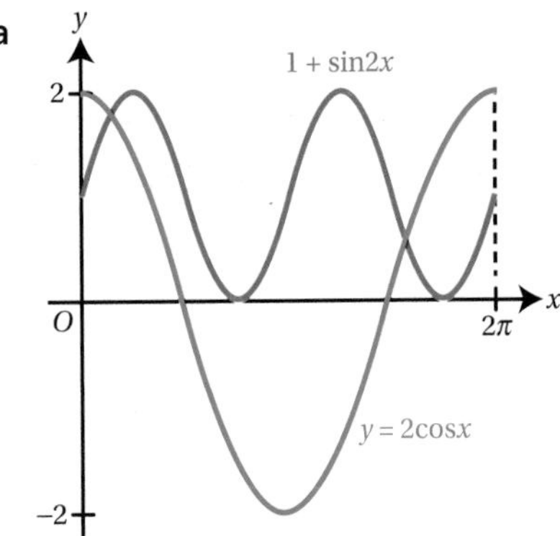

b 2 **c** 8

8 $a = 1.5; b = \frac{\pi}{6}; m = 4.5$

9 a

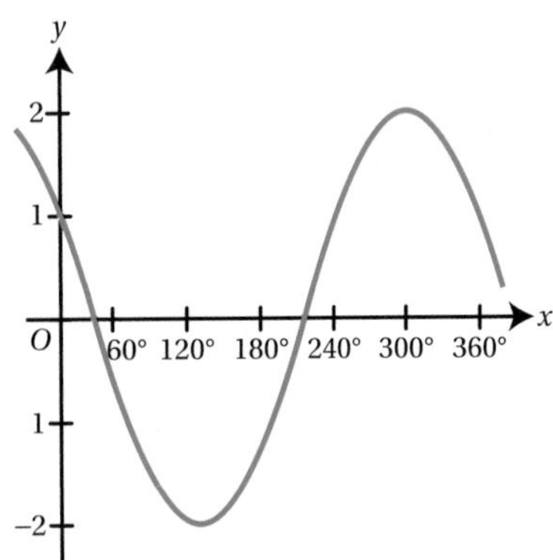

b (120°, −2), (300°, 2)

c (120°, −3), (300°, 1)

10 a $a = 5, b = \frac{\pi}{5}$ **b** 7.5 s

11 a 110 cm, 130 cm **b** 0.628 s

c 0.314s

12 a The size of the seat is ignored, and it is attached exactly on the circumference of the wheel.

b $h = 14 - 12\cos\theta$

c $\theta = \frac{\pi t}{2}$

d $h = 14 - 12\cos\left(\frac{\pi t}{2}\right)$; 1 min 20 s

Exercise 7D

1 a 7.8 cm **b** 1.8 cm

2 a 82.2 cm **b** 6.84 cm

3 a 16.25 cm^2 **b** 0.072 cm^2

4 a 463 cm^2 **b** 4.79 cm^2

5 25 cm

6 a 0.938 **b** 53.7°

7 2.53 radians

8 7.5 cm

9 0.8 radians

10 167°

11 6.69 cm

12 9.49 cm

13 48.4 cm^2

14 15.7 cm

15 31.6 cm

16 11.3 cm

17 $10 + \frac{25}{6}\pi$ cm

18 5 cm

19 5.14 cm^2

20 2 cm or 1.5 cm

21 2.54 radians

22 $\frac{6\pi}{5}$ radians

Exercise 7E

1 a i 0.935 **ii** 3.39

b i 21.7 **ii** 15.8

2 a i 1.89 **ii** 6.99

b i 52.5 **ii** 37.1

3 a i 0.0595 **ii** 1.21

b i 149 **ii** 70.1

4 Proof

5 a Proof

b 70.1°

c 3.67 cm^2

Exercise 7F

1 a i 0.2 **ii** −0.14

b i 0.955 **ii** 0.98

c i 0.12 **ii** −0.2

2 a i 2θ **ii** $-3x$

b i $1 - 4.5x^2$ **ii** $1 - 12.5\theta^2$

c i x^2 **ii** $\frac{\theta^2}{2}$

3 a i $1 - 13\frac{\theta^2}{2}$ **ii** $1 - 65\frac{\theta^2}{8}$

b **i** $1+2\theta-2\theta^2$ **ii** $1-2\theta-\frac{\theta^2}{2}$

c **i** $2-3\theta-2\theta^2$ **ii** $-3+8\theta+3\theta^2$

4 **a** $1+\theta-6\theta^2$ **b** 0.96

5 **a** $1-\frac{1}{2}\theta$ **b** $6\sqrt{2-\sqrt{3}}$

6 **a** $1+6x+12x^2$

b **i** 0.0838% **ii** 41.6%

7 **a** $\sin(x)$: 0.244; $\cos(x)$: 0.662; $\tan(x)$: 0.173

b Proof

8 $1+3\theta+\frac{17}{2}\theta^2$

9 $1-3\theta+7\theta^2$

10 $\sin\theta\approx\frac{\pi\theta}{180}$, $\cos\theta\approx1-\frac{\pi^2\theta^2}{64\,800}$

11 **a** $1+\frac{1}{2}\theta-\frac{1}{8}\theta^3$

b $\frac{\pi}{10}+\frac{\pi^2}{400}-\frac{\pi^3}{24000}\approx0.338$

12 $\frac{1}{3}-\frac{x^2}{27}$

13 $2+\frac{1}{2}\theta+\frac{\theta^2}{8}$

Mixed practice 7

1 **a** 1.4 m **b** 2.09 m

2 $\pm2.41, \pm0.730$

3 **a** $\frac{\pi}{3}$ **b** 28.9 cm^2

c 23.8 cm

4 180 cm^2

5 1.564

6 **a** 10.2 cm^2 **b** 18.8 cm

7 **i** Proof **ii** 13.8 cm

iii 24.3 cm

8 $a=5, b=\frac{\pi}{4}$

9 **a** 9.42 m; The bridge comes down to water level exactly at the edge of the bank.

b 5.05 m

c 1.50 m

10 **a** 78.5 s **b** 377 m **c** 4.8 m s^{-1}

11 **a** π

b $\left(\frac{\pi}{3},0\right),\left(\frac{5\pi}{6},0\right),\left(\frac{4\pi}{3},0\right),\left(\frac{11\pi}{6},0\right)$

c Proof

12 $1-\theta+\frac{1}{2}\theta^2$

13 **a** The quadrilateral *SATB* has four equal sides (all *r*) and a right angle, so it is a square.

b $r\sqrt{2}$

c $\frac{\pi r^2}{4}$

d $\left(\frac{\pi}{2}-1\right)r^2$

14 $-\frac{7\pi}{24}, -\frac{\pi}{24}, \frac{17\pi}{24}, \frac{23\pi}{24}$

15 5.48 cm^2

16 **i**

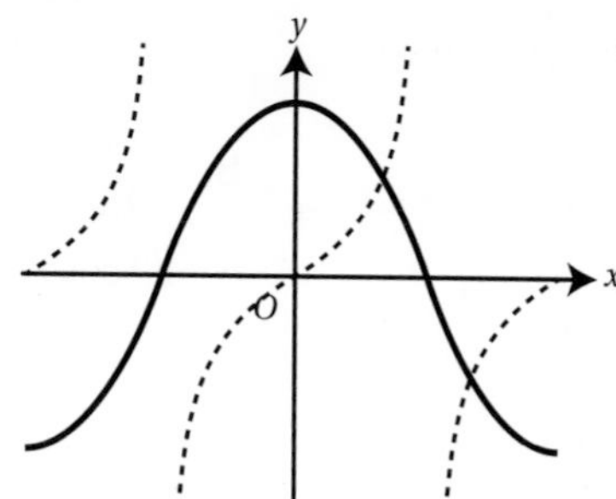

ii 2.02, 4.26

17 **a** $2+\frac{3}{4}x-\frac{9}{64}x^2$ **b** 0.843

18 $\frac{\pi}{2}, \frac{3\pi}{2}, \frac{2\pi}{3}, \frac{4\pi}{3}$

19 **a** $\frac{\pi}{2}$, right angle between a tangent and a radius.

b ABO_2P is a rectangle because there are right angles at *A* and *B*, and *AB* is parallel to PO_2.

c 24.5 cm

d 1.369

e 85.6 cm

20 **a** x

b Proof

c $\frac{1}{\sqrt{2}}$

Chapter 8

Before you start...

1 **a** $\frac{2\sqrt{2}}{3}$ **b** $2\sqrt{2}$

2 $\left(2-\frac{\pi}{2},-2\right)$

3 **a** 21.1°, 81.1°

b $\frac{\pi}{6}, \frac{5\pi}{6}, -\frac{\pi}{2}$

Exercise 8A

1 a $\frac{1}{2}\sin x+\frac{\sqrt{3}}{2}\cos x$

b $\frac{\sqrt{2}}{2}\sin x-\frac{\sqrt{2}}{2}\cos x$

c $-\frac{\sqrt{2}}{2}\sin x-\frac{\sqrt{2}}{2}\cos x$

d $-\sin x$

2 a $\frac{\sqrt{6}-\sqrt{2}}{4}$

b $\frac{\sqrt{2}+\sqrt{6}}{4}$

c $-2\sqrt{3}$

3 a $\frac{56}{65}$ b $\frac{8+3\sqrt{5}}{15}$

4 a Proof b $\sqrt{2}\cos x$

5 a $\frac{\tan\theta-1}{\tan\theta+1}$

b $-\frac{1}{2}, -\frac{1}{3}$

c 2.68, 2.82

6 a $\sin\left(x+\frac{\pi}{4}\right)$, 1, $x=\frac{\pi}{4}$

b $2\cos(x-25°)$, 2, $x=25°$

7 $\frac{\sqrt{3}}{2}+\frac{1}{2}x-\frac{\sqrt{3}}{4}x^2$

8 a Proof

b $\frac{\pi}{3}$

9 a Proof

b $\frac{\pi}{4}, \frac{3\pi}{4}, \frac{5\pi}{4}, \frac{7\pi}{4}$

Exercise 8B

1 a i $-\frac{7}{8}$ ii $\frac{1}{9}$

b i $\frac{2\sqrt{2}}{3}$ ii $\frac{4}{5}$

c i $\frac{4\sqrt{2}}{9}$ ii $\frac{24}{25}$

2 a $\frac{2-\sqrt{2}}{4}$ b $\frac{2-\sqrt{3}}{4}$

c $\frac{\sqrt{3}+2}{4}$

3 $\sqrt{2}-1$

4 a $\cos(6A)$ b $2\sin 10x$

c $3\cos b$ d $\frac{5}{2}\sin\left(\frac{2x}{3}\right)$

5 a $0, \pi, 2\pi$ b $90°$

c $-\frac{\pi}{2}, \frac{\pi}{2}, 0.305, 2.84$ d $0°, 180°, 360°$

6 a Proof b Proof

c Proof d Proof

7 0.955, −0.955, 2.19, −2.19

8 Proof

9 a $\pm\frac{\sqrt{3}}{2}$ b $\frac{\pi}{6}, \frac{5\pi}{6}$

10 a $4\cos^3 A-3\cos A$

b $\frac{3\tan A-\tan^3 A}{1-3\tan^2 A}$

11 a $8\cos^4\theta-8\cos^2\theta+1$

b $8\sin^4\theta-8\sin^2\theta+1$

12 a i Proof ii Proof

b $\frac{1-\cos x}{1+\cos x}$

13 $\frac{2a-b}{4a}$

14 a $\frac{17}{4}$ b $\frac{3}{4}$

15 a Proof b Proof

Exercise 8C

1 a $2\sqrt{13}\sin(x+0.983)$

b $\sqrt{10}\sin(x+0.322)$

2 a $2\sqrt{2}\sin(\theta-45°)$

b $2\sin(\theta-60°)$

3 a $2\sqrt{2}\cos\left(x+\frac{\pi}{6}\right)$ b $5\sqrt{2}\cos\left(x+\frac{\pi}{4}\right)$

4 a $9.22\cos(x-40.6°)$

b $13\cos(x-22.6°)$

5 a $13\sin(x+1.18)$

b Vertical stretch with scale factor 13; translation 1.18 units to the left

6 a $\sqrt{58}\sin(x-1.17)$

b $y\in\left[-\sqrt{58}, \sqrt{58}\right]$

7 a $\sqrt{41}\cos(x+0.896)$ b 0.675

8 a $2\cos\left(x-\frac{\pi}{3}\right)$

b minimum: $\left(\frac{4\pi}{3}, -2\right)$; maximum: $\left(\frac{\pi}{3}, 2\right)$

9 a 1.57, 2.50

10 $-\pi, -\frac{3\pi}{4}, 0, \frac{\pi}{4}, \pi$

Exercise 8D

1 a i 2.760 **ii** 1.480

b i −2.670 **ii** 1.212

c i 1.051 **ii** 0.5774

2 a i $\frac{2\sqrt{3}}{3}$ **ii** $\sqrt{2}$

b i $-\sqrt{2}$ **ii** $-\frac{2\sqrt{3}}{3}$

c i −1 **ii** $\frac{\sqrt{3}}{3}$

d i −1 **ii** 0

3 $\operatorname{cosec} A = \frac{5}{4}$; $\sec B = \frac{3}{\sqrt{5}}$

4 a i 1.05, 5.24 **ii** 1.23, 5.05

b i 0.730, 2.41 **ii** 0.379, 2.76

c i 0.197, 3.34 **ii** 1.11, 4.25

d i 0.615, 2.53, 3.76, 5.67

ii 0.126, 1.44, 3.27, 4.59

5 a i $-\frac{5\pi}{6}$ **ii** $-\frac{\pi}{2}$

b i $\frac{\pi}{6}, -\frac{5\pi}{6}$ **ii** $\frac{\pi}{4}, -\frac{3\pi}{4}$

c i 0 **ii** $\frac{5\pi}{6}, -\frac{5\pi}{6}$

d i $\frac{\pi}{2}, -\frac{\pi}{2}$ **ii** $-\frac{\pi}{4}, \frac{3\pi}{4}$

6 a i $\frac{5}{3}$ **ii** $\frac{\sqrt{29}}{5}$

b i $2\sqrt{6}$ **ii** $2\sqrt{2}$

c i $\frac{1}{\sqrt{10}}$ **ii** $\frac{2}{\sqrt{5}}$

d i $\pm\frac{3}{\sqrt{7}}$ **ii** $\pm\frac{2}{\sqrt{3}}$

7 Proof

8 Proof

9 Proof

10 a Proof

b 1, 2

c $\frac{\pi}{4}, \frac{5\pi}{4}$, 1.11, 4.2

11 Proof

12 Proof

13 $1+\frac{9}{2}\theta^2$

14 $\arccos\left(\frac{1}{x}\right)$

Mixed practice 8

1 a Proof **b** $\frac{\pi}{6}, \frac{5\pi}{6}, \frac{3\pi}{2}$

2 a $\frac{1}{2}\cos x - \frac{\sqrt{3}}{2}\sin x$ **b** $-2\pi, -\pi, 0, \pi, 2\pi$

3 a $AB = 2r\sin\theta$, $BC = 2r\cos\theta$

b $2r^2\sin\theta\cos\theta$

c $\frac{1}{2}r^2\sin 2\theta$

d $\frac{1}{2}$

4 a Proof **b** −1

c $1+\sqrt{2}$

5 a $a = 1.2,\ p = \frac{2\pi}{3}$

b Amplitude = 0.9; period = 3

c $y = \frac{3}{2}\sin\left(\frac{2\pi}{3}x + 0.927\right)$

d Amplitude = $\frac{3}{2}$; period = 3

e 1.06

f 0.058, 0.557

6 i

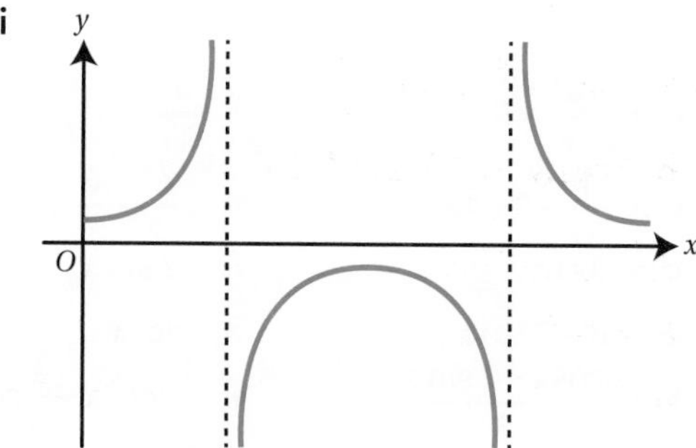

ii 1.23, 5.05

iii 1.37, 4.51

7 a Proof

b $\frac{2\pi}{3}, \frac{4\pi}{3}$

8 a $(t+1)(t^2-4t+1)$ **b** Proof

c 1

d $\tan 15° = 2-\sqrt{3}$, $\tan 75° = 2+\sqrt{3}$

9 i $\sqrt{18}\cos\left(x - \frac{1}{4}\pi\right)$

ii a $\frac{3}{4}\pi$ **b** $\frac{\pi}{36}$

10 a $2\sqrt{5}\sin\left(2x + \frac{\pi}{6}\right)$

b i $2+\frac{4}{5}\sqrt{5}$ **ii** $x = \frac{2\pi}{3}$

11 a x **b** Proof **c** $2x\sqrt{1-x^2}$

12 a i $x^2-2\sqrt{10}x+10$ **ii** Proof

iii $x=\sqrt{10}$

b Proof

c Proof

d $\sqrt{10}$

e 0.443

Chapter 9

Before you start...

1 $\ln 3+4\ln x$

2 $\frac{dy}{dx}=6x+\frac{4}{3x^3}$

3 $\frac{3}{2}$

4 $\frac{1}{2}-\frac{\sqrt{3}\pi}{200}$

Exercise 9A

1 a i $3e^x$ **ii** $\frac{2e^x}{5}$

b i $-\frac{2}{x}$ **ii** $\frac{1}{3x}$

c i $\frac{1}{5x}-3+4e^x$ **ii** $-\frac{e^x}{2}+\frac{3}{x}$

d i $3\cos x$ **ii** $-2\sin x$

e i $2+5\sin x$ **ii** $\sec^2 x$

f i $\frac{\cos x-2\sin x}{5}$ **ii** $\frac{1}{2}\sec^2 x-\frac{1}{3}\cos x$

2 a i $\frac{3}{x}$ **ii** $\frac{10}{x}$

b i $\frac{3}{x}$ **ii** $\frac{1}{x}$

c i e^3e^x **ii** $\frac{e^x}{e^3}$

d i $2x$ **ii** $3e^2x^2$

e i $3\sec^2 x$ **ii** $4\sec^2 x$

f i e^x **ii** $-\frac{1}{2}e^x$

3 $2-\frac{7}{\ln 4}$

4 $3-\frac{1}{2\ln 3}$

5 $x=\ln 3$

6 $x=3$

7 π

8 $\frac{22-\pi^2}{12}$

9 $y=3x-\ln 4+2$

10 $y=2x+2.26$

11 $x=\frac{\pi}{4},\frac{5\pi}{4}$

12 Tangent: $4x-y+1-\pi=0$;

Normal: $4x+16y-\pi-16=0$

13 $x=\frac{\pi}{3},\frac{2\pi}{3},\frac{4\pi}{3},\frac{5\pi}{3}$

14 (0.245, 4.12) local maximum;

(3.39, –4.12) local minimum

15 Proof

16 $y\geqslant 6-4\ln 4$

17 a $(4, \ln 4-2)$ local maximum

b $(\ln(2.5), 5-5\ln(2.5))$ local minimum

18 a 40 million litres

b $t=\frac{\pi}{2}$ (1.6 days), $\frac{3\pi}{2}$ (3.8 days)

Work it out 9.1

Answer = Statement 4

Exercise 9B

1 a i $5e^x+c$ **ii** $9e^x+c$

b i $\frac{2e^x}{5}+c$ **ii** $\frac{7e^x}{11}+c$

c i $\frac{e^x}{2}+\frac{3x^2}{4}+c$ **ii** $\frac{e^x}{5}+\frac{x^4}{20}+c$

d i $3\sin x+c$ **ii** $-4\cos x+c$

e i $-\frac{1}{2}\cos x-\sin x+c$ **ii** $\frac{2}{3}\sin x+\frac{1}{3}\cos x+c$

f i $\frac{2}{3}x^{\frac{3}{2}}-\cos x+c$ **ii** $\sin x+2\sqrt{x}+c$

2 a i $2\ln x+c$ **ii** $3\ln x+c$

b i $\frac{1}{2}\ln x+c$ **ii** $\frac{1}{3}\ln x+c$

c i $\frac{5}{2}\ln x+c$ **ii** $\frac{2}{3}\ln x+c$

d i $\frac{x^2}{2}-\ln x+c$ **ii** $\frac{x^3}{3}+5\ln x+c$

e i $3\ln x-\frac{2}{x}+c$ **ii** $-\frac{3}{x}-5\ln x+c$

f i $2\ln x+6\sqrt{x}+c$ **ii** $\frac{2}{3}x^{\frac{3}{2}}-4\ln x+c$

3 a i $3(e^2-1)$ **ii** $2(e^3-e^1)$

b i 2 **ii** 8

c i $4-3e+2\ln 2$ **ii** $4\ln 3-13+3e$

d i $1.5\ln 3$ **ii** $\frac{4}{3}\ln\left(\frac{5}{2}\right)$

e i 2 **ii** $\frac{9}{2}$

f i 1 ii −2

g i 0 ii 0

4 $\frac{2}{3}\ln(3)$

5 1.5

6 $\frac{1}{2}+\sqrt{3}$

7 15

8 a $-2\ln(3)$ b $2\ln(3)$

9 $y=\sin x-\cos x$

10 $\frac{1}{2}\ln|\sec x|+\frac{1}{2}x+c$

11 a $f(x)=\frac{1}{2}\ln x+c$

b $y=\frac{1}{2}\ln x-\frac{1}{2}\ln 2+7$

12 0.838

13 a Proof b $\frac{15}{2}-4\ln\left(\frac{8}{3}\right)$

14 Proof

15 $y=\ln\left|\frac{e^5}{x}\right|$

Mixed practice 9

1 $y=e^{\frac{\pi}{2}}x-\frac{\pi}{2}e^{\frac{\pi}{2}}+e^{\frac{\pi}{2}}+2$

2 $f(x)=\frac{1}{2}-\cos x$

3 $12-\frac{1}{2\ln 4}$

4 $e^{\pi}+\pi+1$

5 $\frac{21}{2}+10\ln\left(\frac{2}{5}\right)$

6 $\ln|x|+\frac{2}{5}x^{\frac{5}{2}}+c$

7 (0.245, 4.12) local maximum; (3.39, −4.12) local minimum

8 $\frac{\pi}{6},-\frac{5\pi}{6}$ local minima; $-\frac{\pi}{6},\frac{5\pi}{6}$ local maxima

9 $x+6y=36+\ln 2$

10 a i 11 000 ii $t=9.55$ h

b i $\frac{dP}{dt}=e^t-3$ ii 8.70 h

c i $\frac{d^2P}{dt^2}=e^t$ (Shows that the rate of growth increases exponentially.)

ii 9704, $\frac{d^2p}{dx^2}(\ln 3)>0$ (so a minimum point), 9704

11 $\sqrt{3}-1$

12 $\sin x-\cos x+c$

Tip

Use an identity.

Chapter 10

Before you start...

1 a $6x^2-\frac{3}{2\sqrt{x}}$

b $\frac{5}{x}-\frac{1}{x^4}$

c $5e^x$

d $4\cos x+3\sin x+2\sec^2 x$

2 a $y=-x+2,\ y=x$ b $(2, 2-\ln 4)$

3 a 3 b $\frac{3}{4}\tan x$

4 a $\frac{\sin x}{\cos^2 x}$ b $\frac{1}{\cos x}$

5 a $\frac{x^2+x-1}{-3x-1}$ b $\frac{x}{(x-1)^{3/2}}$

6 a $y=\frac{1}{2}(1+\ln x)$ b $y=-\frac{x}{x+1}$

Exercise 10A

1 a i $15(3x+4)^4$ ii $35(5x+4)^6$

b i $\frac{3}{2\sqrt{3x-2}}$ ii $\frac{1}{2\sqrt{x+1}}$

c i $\frac{1}{(3-x)^2}$ ii $-\frac{4}{(2x+3)^3}$

d i $10e^{10x+1}$ ii $-3e^{4-3x}$

e i $4\cos 4x$ ii $-3\sin(3x+\pi)$

f i $-\frac{1}{5-x}$ ii $-\frac{2}{3-2x}$

2 a i $7(2x-3)(x^2-3x+1)^6$ ii $15x^2(x^3+1)^4$

b i $(2x-2)e^{x^2-2x}$ ii $-3x^2e^{4-x^3}$

c i $-6e^x(2e^x+1)^{-4}$ ii $20e^x(2-5e^x)^{-5}$

d i $6x\cos(3x^2+1)$

ii $-(2x+2)\sin(x^2+2x)$

e i $-3\sin x\cos^2 x$ ii $4\cos x\sin^3 x$

f i $\frac{2-15x^2}{2x-5x^3}$ ii $\frac{8x}{4x^2-1}$

g i $\frac{16}{x}(4\ln x-1)^3$ ii $-\frac{5}{x}(\ln x+3)^{-6}$

h i $\frac{3x}{\sqrt{3x^2+1}}$ ii $-\frac{2x}{\sqrt{5-2x^2}}$

3 a i $10(2x+3)^4$ **ii** $32(4x-1)^7$

b i $4(5-x)^{-5}$ **ii** $7(1-x)^{-8}$

c i $4\sin(1-4x)$ **ii** $\sin(2-x)$

d i $\dfrac{5}{5x+2}$ **ii** $\dfrac{1}{x-4}$

e i $-3\operatorname{cosec}^2 3x$

ii $-5\operatorname{cosec} 5x\cot 5x$

f i $2\sec(2x+1)\tan(2x+1)$

ii $-\sec^2(1-x)$

4 a i $6\sec^2 3x\tan 3x$

ii $4\tan 2x\sec^2 2x$

b i $6\sin 3x\cos 3x\, e^{\sin^2 3x}$

ii $\dfrac{2\ln 2x}{x}e^{(\ln 2x)^2}$

c i $-16\sin 2x\cos 2x(1-2\sin^2 2x)$

ii $-24\sin 3x(4\cos 3x+1)$

d i $\dfrac{6\sin 2x}{1-3\cos 2x}$ **ii** $\dfrac{5\sin 5x}{2-\cos 5x}$

5 $y=66x-11$

6 $y=\dfrac{27\sqrt{2}}{8}x-\dfrac{77}{12}$

7 7

8 $(0,-216), (\sqrt{2},0), (-\sqrt{2},0)$

9 a $-\sqrt{3}\,\text{m s}^{-1}$ **b** $\dfrac{1}{3}\,\text{m s}^{-2}$

10 $(0,-1), (1,0)$

11 $\left(\dfrac{\pi}{2},e\right),\left(\dfrac{3\pi}{2},e^{-1}\right)$

12 $\left(6,-\dfrac{1}{9}\right)$

13 492 or 493

14 a $-2\operatorname{cosec}^2 x\cot x$ **b** $-\dfrac{\pi}{4},\dfrac{3\pi}{4}$

15 a Left post **b** Proof

c $\sqrt[3]{2}+\dfrac{1}{\sqrt[3]{4}}=\dfrac{3\sqrt[3]{2}}{2}$

16 a $0,\dfrac{\pi}{3},\pi,\dfrac{5\pi}{3},2\pi$

b (0.568, 0.369), (2.21, –1.76), (4.08, 1.76), (5.72, –0.369)

c

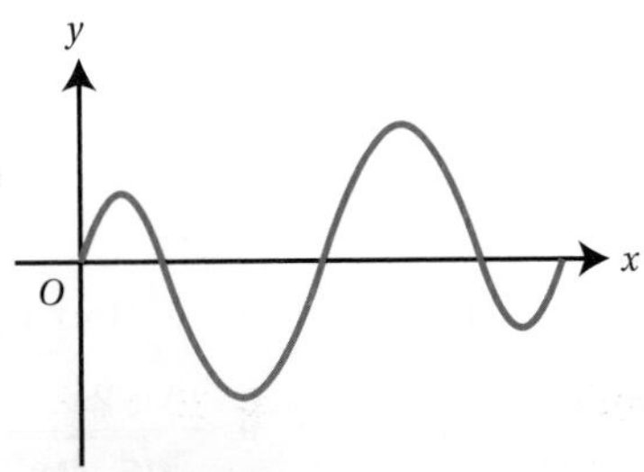

Work it out 10.1

Answer = Solution 2

Exercise 10B

1 a i $2x\cos x-x^2\sin x$

ii $-x^{-2}\sin x+x^{-1}\cos x$

b i $-2x^{-3}\ln x+x^{-3}$ **ii** $\ln x+1$

c i $3x^2\sqrt{2x+1}+x^3(2x+1)^{-\frac{1}{2}}$

ii $-x^{-2}\sqrt{4x}+2x^{-1}(4x)^{-\frac{1}{2}}$

d i $2e^{2x}\tan x+e^{2x}\sec^2 x$

ii $e^{x+1}\sec 3x+3e^{x+1}\sec 3x\tan 3x$

2 a i $3(x+1)^3(x-2)^4(3x-1)$

ii $(x-3)^6(x+5)^3(11x+23)$

b i $(2x-1)^3(1-3x)^2(-42x+17)$

ii $(1-x)^4(4x+1)(-28x+3)$

3 $(6x^2+4x+3)e^{2x}$

4 $(9x^2+12x+2)e^{3x}$

5 $x=-\dfrac{1}{2},2$

6 $x=3,-\dfrac{1}{3},\dfrac{7}{4}$

7 $e^x(1+x)\cos(xe^x)$

8 a $\ln x+1$ **b** $x\ln x-x+c$

9 $\left(\dfrac{3\pi}{4},-\dfrac{\sqrt{2}}{2}e^{-\frac{3\pi}{4}}\right)$

10 $a=4, b=5$

11 a $y=e^{\ln x^x}$ **b** $(\ln x+1)x^x$ **c** $(e^{-1}, e^{-e^{-1}})$

12 a $\dfrac{qa+pb}{p+q}$

b

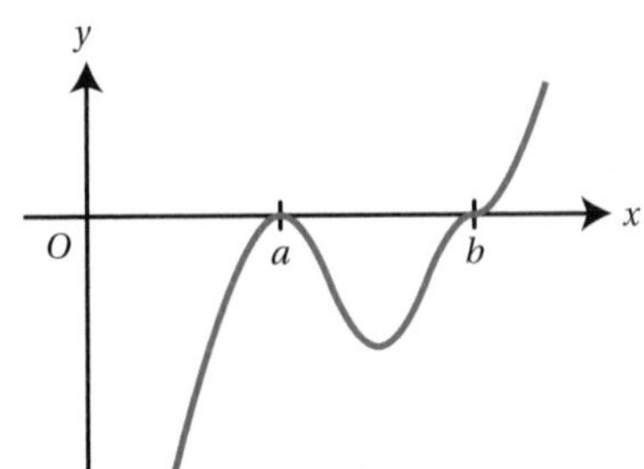

c q is odd.

Work it out 10.2

Answer = All solutions are correct.

Exercise 10C

1 a i $\frac{2}{(x+1)^2}$ ii $\frac{-5}{(x-3)^2}$

b i $\frac{x(2x+1)^{-\frac{1}{2}}-(2x+1)^{\frac{1}{2}}}{x^2}$

ii $\frac{2x(x-1)^{\frac{1}{2}}-\frac{1}{2}x^2(x-1)^{-\frac{1}{2}}}{x-1}$

c i $\frac{2(x^2-x-2)}{(x^2+2)^2}$ ii $-\frac{x^2+2x+4}{(1+x)^2}$

d i $\frac{1-\ln 3x}{x^2}$ ii $\frac{1-2\ln 2x}{x^3}$

2 $y=\frac{\pi^2}{4}x+\frac{16-\pi^4}{8\pi}$

3 (0, 0), (1, 1)

4 $a=-1$

5 $\left(e, \frac{1}{e}\right)$, local max

6 $x\in(0, 2), x\neq 1$

7 $a=3, b=4, p=\frac{3}{2}$

8 Proof

Exercise 10D

1 a i $\frac{2}{3}$ ii $\frac{1}{2}$

b i 0 ii −1

c i −1 ii 5

d i −1 ii $-\frac{1}{2}$

2 a i $\frac{2x}{y^2}$ ii $-\frac{2x^3}{3y}$

b i $\frac{y(8x-y)}{2x(y-2x)}$ ii $\frac{y}{2y-x}$

c i $\frac{1-2y}{2x-4y-1}$ ii $\frac{y}{2y-x}$

d i $\frac{y(2x-e^y)}{xye^y-4}$ ii $\frac{\cos x-3\sin y}{3x\cos y-2\sin y}$

3 a (3, 2), (−3, −2)

b $(\sqrt{2}, 4\sqrt{2}), (-\sqrt{2}, -4\sqrt{2})$

4 a i 3 ln 3 ii 25 ln 5

b i $4\ln\left(\frac{1}{2}\right)$ ii $3\ln\left(\frac{1}{3}\right)$

c i $\frac{3\ln 2}{8}$ ii 4 ln 4

d i −3 ln 3 ii $-\frac{\ln 5}{5}$

5 2

6 a Proof b $6x+5y-13=0$

7 a Proof b $6x-5y-22=0$?

8 4

9 $17x-8y+6=0$

10 $x=2$?

11 $\frac{y2^y}{1-xy2^y\ln 2}$

12 $(2, e^4)$

13 a $y=3x-4$ b Proof

c (1, −1)

Exercise 10E

1 a $x=y^2$ b $\frac{dy}{dx}=\frac{1}{2y}=\frac{1}{2\sqrt{x}}$

2 a Proof b 3710 (3 s.f.)

3 a Proof b $\frac{1}{3}$

4 a $f^{-1}(x)=a^x$ b Proof

5 a $\frac{dt}{dr}=\frac{\pi r^2}{8}$ b $r=\sqrt[3]{125+\frac{24}{\pi}t}$

6 a Proof b Proof

c $2+\sqrt{2}$

7 a cos y b $\frac{1}{\sqrt{1-x^2}}$

8 Proof

Mixed practice 10

1 a $5e^{5x}$ b $\frac{3}{2\sqrt{3x+2}}$

c $5e^{5x}\sqrt{3x+2}+\frac{3e^{5x}}{2\sqrt{3x+2}}$

2 $\frac{16}{225}$

3 $15\ln 5-20$ m s^{-1}

4 a Proof b $\frac{1}{4}$

5 $\frac{729}{80}$

6 i $3x^2(x+1)^5+5x^3(x+1)^4$

ii $6x^3(3x^4+1)^{-\frac{1}{2}}$

7 $\frac{5}{2}$

8 $(3, 3e^{-3})$

9 a $k=\ln a$ b Proof

10 9 ln 3

11 a 3 seconds b 30 m s^{-1}

12 a $x=\frac{1}{2}$ b (0, 0), (1, −1)

c (0, 0) local min; (1, −1) local max

d

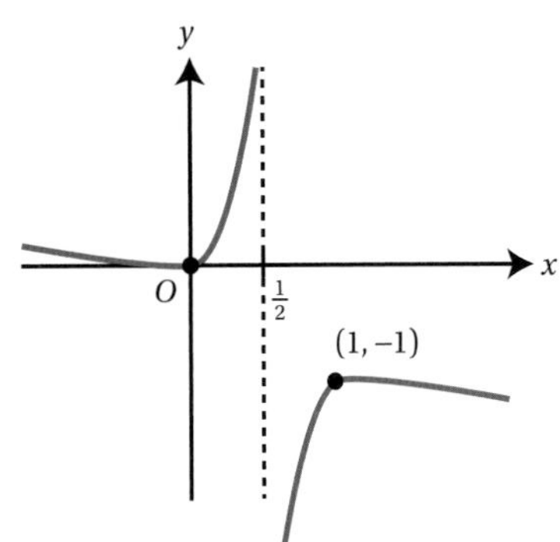

13 a Proof **b** $y-2=-2\sqrt{3}\left(x-\frac{\pi}{6}\right)$

14 a $g'(x)=3+\frac{1}{x}>0$. Proof **b** $\frac{1}{4}$

15 i $\frac{6y-3x^2}{3y^2-6x}$ **ii** Proof

iii $a=3; \frac{dy}{dx}=-1$

16 a (2, 4), (−2, −4) **b** Proof

c (2, 4) local max; (−2, −4) local min

17 a $\sec^2 x=\tan^2 x+1$ **b** Proof

c $y-\frac{\pi}{6}=-\frac{4}{3}\left(x-\frac{1}{\sqrt{3}}\right)$

18 a $A=1, B=3$

b (4, 0.272)

c $\frac{4}{3}$

Chapter 11

Before you start...

1 a $\frac{4}{3}x^3+3\ln x+c$ **b** $-5\cos(x)+c$

2 a $4e^x$ **b** $4e-4$

3 a $4\cos(4x)$ **b** $\frac{2x}{x^2+1}$

4 0.8, −0.8

5 $\frac{4}{x-1}-\frac{4}{x+2}-\frac{12}{(x+2)^2}$

Work it out 11.1

Answer = Solution 2 and 3 are

Exercise 11A

1 a i $(x+3)^5+c$ **ii** $\frac{x-2^6}{6}+c$

b i $\frac{1}{32}(4x-5)^8+c$ **ii** $2\left(\frac{1}{8}x+1\right)^4+c$

c i $-\frac{8}{7}\left(3-\frac{1}{2}x\right)^7+c$ **ii** $-\frac{1}{9}(4-x)^9+c$

d i $\frac{1}{3}(2x-1)^{\frac{3}{2}}+c$ **ii** $-\frac{4}{5}(2-5x)^{\frac{7}{4}}+c$

e i $4\left(2+\frac{x}{3}\right)^{\frac{3}{4}}+c$ **ii** $2(4-3x)^{-1}+c$

2 a i $e^{3x}+c$ **ii** $\frac{1}{2}e^{2x+5}+c$

b i $6e^{\frac{2x-1}{3}}+c$ **ii** $2e^{\frac{1}{2}x}+c$

c i $2e^{-3x}+c$ **ii** $-\frac{1}{4}e^{-4x}+c$

d i $8e^{-\frac{x}{4}}+c$ **ii** $-\frac{3}{2}e^{-\frac{2}{3}x}+c$

3 a i $\ln|x+4|+c$ **ii** $\ln|5x-2|+c$

b i $\frac{2}{3}\ln|3x+4|+c$ **ii** $-4\ln|2x-5|+c$

c i $-\frac{3}{4}\ln|1-4x|+c$ **ii** $-\frac{1}{2}\ln|7-2x|+c$

d i $x+3\ln|5-x|+c$ **ii** $3x-\ln|3-x|+c$

4 a $\operatorname{cosec} x+c$ **b** $\tan 3x+c$

c $\frac{1}{3}\cos(2-3x)+c$ **d** $-4\cot\left(\frac{1}{4}x\right)+c$

e $\frac{1}{2}\sin 4x+c$ **f** $2\sec\frac{x}{2}+c$

5 $\frac{1}{5}$

6 $\frac{3}{2}\left(e^{-2}-e^{-8}\right)$

7 18

8 0.492

Exercise 11B

1 a i $\frac{1}{4}\left(x^2+3\right)^4+c$ **ii** $\frac{1}{6}\left(x^2-1\right)^6+c$

b i $\frac{1}{15}\left(3x^2-15x+4\right)^5+c$

ii $\frac{1}{12}\left(x^3+3x^2-5\right)^4+c$

c i $\ln|x^2+3|+c$ **ii** $\ln|x^3-4x+5|+c$

d i $\frac{1}{2}\ln|x^2+8x-3|+c$

ii $\frac{1}{3}\ln|x^3+3x^2-15x+1|+c$

e i $\sqrt{x^2+2}+c$ **ii** $-\frac{1}{3(x^3-4)}+c$

f i $-\frac{2}{3}\cos^6 x+c$ **ii** $\frac{1}{8}\sin^4 2x+c$

g **i** $\frac{1}{4}\tan^4 x+c$ **ii** $-\frac{1}{5}\cot^5 x+c$

h **i** $\frac{1}{2}e^{3x^2-1}+c$ **ii** $\frac{3}{2}e^{x^2}+c$

i **i** $\frac{1}{2}\ln\left|e^{2x+3}+4\right|+c$ **ii** $\frac{1}{4}\ln|3+4\sin x|+c$

2 $-e^{\cos x}+c$

3 e^5-e^{-1}

4 $\ln k=\ln 8$, so $k=8$.

5 $-\frac{1}{12\sin^4 3x}+c$

6 $-\frac{1}{10}\operatorname{cosec}^5 2x+c$

Exercise 11C

1 **a** **i** $\frac{2}{5}(x+1)^{5/2}-\frac{2}{3}(x+1)^{3/2}+c$

ii $\frac{2}{7}(x-2)^{7/2}+\frac{8}{5}(x-2)^{5/2}+\frac{8}{3}(x-2)^{3/2}+c$

b **i** $\frac{2}{9}(x-5)^9+\frac{5}{4}(x-5)^8+c$

ii $\frac{1}{7}(x+3)^7-\frac{1}{2}(x+3)^6+c$

2 **a** **i** $2\ln\left|\sqrt{x}+1\right|+c$ **ii** $\frac{1}{2}\ln\left|3+4\sqrt{x}\right|+c$

b **i** $\ln|\ln x|+c$ **ii** $-\frac{1}{2(\ln x)^2}+c$

3 **a** **i** $\frac{1}{24}(2x-1)^6+\frac{1}{20}(2x-1)^5+c$

ii $\frac{1}{125}(3x+2)^7-\frac{1}{3}(3x+2)^6+c$

b **i** $\frac{2}{125}(x-3)^{\frac{5}{2}}+2(x-3)^{\frac{3}{2}}+c$

ii $\frac{2}{75}(5x-6)^{5/2}+\frac{22}{75}(5x-6)^{3/2}+c$

c **i** $\frac{2}{5}(x-5)^{\frac{5}{2}}+\frac{20}{3}(x-5)^{\frac{3}{2}}+50\sqrt{x-5}+c$

ii $-\frac{1}{(2x-3)}-\frac{13}{2(2x-3)^2}+c$

4 **a** **i** 2732.8 **ii** 1.8

b **i** $\frac{1}{6}$ **ii** $\frac{1}{3}$

c **i** $9-8\ln 2$ **ii** $-\frac{76}{15}-12\ln 3+12\ln 5$

5 $\frac{2}{3}(x-2)^{3/2}+4(x-2)^{1/2}+c$

6 **a** Proof **b** $\ln|x^2+x+1|+c$

7 $\left(\frac{1}{4}\right)\tan\left(\ln x^2\right)+c$

8 $2\sqrt{3}-2$, so $a=2$, $b=3$, $c=-2$

9 $\frac{\pi}{12}$

Exercise 11D

1 **a** **i** $\frac{1}{2}x\sin 2x+\frac{1}{4}\cos 2x+c$

ii $-2x\cos\left(\frac{x}{2}\right)+4\sin\left(\frac{x}{2}\right)+c$

b **i** $-2x\,e^{-2x}-e^{-2x}+c$

ii $\frac{1}{4}x\,e^{4x}-\frac{1}{16}e^{4x}+c$

c **i** $x^2\ln 5x-\frac{1}{2}x^2+c$

ii $\frac{1}{2}x^2\ln x-\frac{1}{4}x^2+c$

d **i** $\frac{1}{8}x^4\ln x-\frac{1}{32}x^4+c$

ii $\frac{1}{2}x^6\ln 2x-\frac{1}{12}x^6+c$

2 1

3 $\left(e^3-1\right)\ln 2+\frac{2}{3}e^3+\frac{1}{3}$

Exercise 11E

1 **a** $\frac{1}{3}x^2\sin 3x+\frac{2}{9}x\cos 3x-\frac{2}{27}\sin 3x+c$

b $-x^2\cos x+2x\sin x+2\cos x+c$

c $x^2e^{\frac{x}{4}}-8x\,e^{\frac{x}{4}}+32\,e^{\frac{x}{4}}+c$

d $x(\ln x)^2-2x\ln x+2x+c$

2 **a** $2x\ln(3x)-2x+c$

b $x\ln(2x+1)-x+\frac{1}{2}\ln(2x+1)+c$

3 **a** $\frac{\pi}{2}-1$ **b** $\frac{1}{2}(1-\ln 2)$

4 Proof

5 $-\frac{2}{3}x\,e^{-3x}-\frac{2}{9}e^{-3x}+c$

6 $\frac{5e^6+1}{36}$

7 **a** Proof

b $x\tan x-\ln|\sec x|+c$

8 e^2+1

9 **a** Proof

b $\left(\frac{e^x}{2}\right)(\sin x+\cos x)+c$

Work it out 11.2

Answer = They are all correct, with different values for c:

$\frac{1}{2}\sin^2 x = -\frac{1}{2}\cos^2 x + \frac{1}{2} = -\frac{1}{4}\cos 2x + \frac{1}{4}$

Exercise 11F

1 a $\frac{1}{3}\sec 3x + c$ **b** $-\cot x + c$

c $-\frac{1}{4}\cos 4x + c$

d $\frac{1}{2}(-3\cot 2x + \operatorname{cosec} 2x) + c$

e $\sin x + \cos x + c$

2 a $\frac{1}{3}\sin^3 x - \frac{1}{5}\sin^5 x + c$ **b** $-\frac{1}{\sin x} - \sin x + c$

c $-\frac{1}{4}e^{\cos 2x} + c$ **d** $\frac{1}{15}\tan^5 3x + c$

e $-\frac{1}{4}\sqrt{1+\cos 4x} + c$

3 a i $x - \frac{1}{2}\sin 2x + c$ **ii** $\frac{1}{2}\left(\frac{1}{6}\sin 6x + x\right) + c$

b i $4\tan\left(\frac{x}{2}\right) - 2x + c$ **ii** $\frac{1}{3}\tan 3x - x + c$

4 a i $\frac{\pi}{2}$ **ii** $\frac{9\pi}{8} - 1$

b i $1 - \ln 2$ **ii** $6\sqrt{3} - 2\pi$

5 a i $\ln 2$ **ii** $2 - 2\ln 2$

b i $\frac{\pi}{9} - \frac{1}{2\sqrt{3}}$

ii $\frac{1}{4}\left(24\sqrt{7} - 4\sqrt{15}\right) - \ln\left(8 + 3\sqrt{7}\right) + \ln\left(4 + \sqrt{15}\right)$

c i $\frac{1}{2}x\sqrt{1-x^2} - \sin^{-1} x$

ii $\frac{1}{2}x\sqrt{36-x^2} + 18\sin^{-1}\frac{x}{6}$

6 $\frac{1}{2}x - \frac{3}{4}\sin\left(\frac{2x}{3}\right) + c$

7 a Proof **b** $\frac{1}{2}\tan^2 x - \ln|\sec x| + c$

8 $k = 3$

9 a Proof **b** $-\frac{2}{3}\cos^3 x + \cos x + c$

10 $2\arcsin(\sqrt{x}) + c$

11 $\arctan x + c$

12 a Proof **b** 4

13 a $y = \sqrt{25 - x^2}$ **b** Proof

Exercise 11G

1 a $\frac{3}{2}\ln|x^2 - 4| + c$

b $2\ln|x^2 - 3x + 1| + c$

c No **d** $\frac{5}{2}\ln|x^2 + 1| + c$

e No **f** $\frac{1}{3}\ln|x^3 - 9x| + c$

g $6\ln|x^3 + 2| + c$

2 a $\frac{1}{6}(2x-3)^3 + c$ **b** $-\frac{1}{5}\ln|2 - 5x| + c$

c $\frac{1}{3}\ln|x - 1| + c$ **d** $x - \ln|x| + c$

3 a i $3\ln|x - 10| + 2\ln|x - 3| + c$

ii $2\ln|x + 1| - \ln|x - 3| + c$

b i $\frac{1}{2}\ln|x-1| - \frac{1}{2}\ln|x+1| + c$

ii $\frac{1}{2}\ln|x-1| + \frac{1}{2}\ln|x+1| + c$

c i $3\ln|x - 2| - \ln|1 - x| + c$

ii $-\ln|1 - x| - 2\ln|1 + x| + c$

d i $5\ln|x+3| + \ln|x| - \frac{3}{x} + c$

ii $2\ln|x-2| + 2\ln|x| + \frac{1}{x} + c$

e i $\ln(x-1) - \frac{2}{x-1} - \ln(x+3) + c$

ii $\ln(x+1) - \frac{1}{x+1} - \ln(x-2) + c$

4 a i $x - \ln|x + 2| + c$

ii $2x + 5\ln|x - 1| + c$

b i $\frac{1}{2}x^2 + 3x + 11\ln|x-3| + c$

ii $\frac{1}{2}x^2 - 3x + 14\ln|x+5| + c$

5 c $\ln|x - 2| - \ln|x + 2| + c$

e $2\ln|x| + 3\ln|x - 3| - \ln|x + 3| + c$

6 a $\frac{1}{x-2} - \frac{1}{x+3}$ **b** $\ln\left|\frac{x-2}{x+3}\right| + c$

7 $-\ln 3$

8 $3 - 3\ln\left(\frac{7}{4}\right)$

9 a $\frac{1}{2-x} + \frac{2}{x+1}$ **b** 8

10 $\ln\left(\frac{4}{9}\right) + \frac{1}{2}$

Mixed practice 11

1 $\frac{\pi}{2}$

2 $\frac{1}{2}x\sin 2x+\frac{1}{4}\cos 2x+c$

3 6.36

4 $\frac{\sqrt{3}}{4}$

5 a $-\frac{1}{3}\ln|1-3x|+c$

b $-\frac{1}{2}(2x+3)^{-1}+c$

6 $\frac{1}{6}$

7 $x\ln x-x+c$

8 a $\frac{e^{-2x}}{e^{-2x}-3}$ or $\frac{1}{1-3e^{2x}}$ b $\frac{1}{2}\ln\left|\frac{1}{e^{-2x}-3}\right|+c$

9 $\arcsin\left(\frac{x}{2}\right)+c$

10 a $\frac{2}{x-1}-\frac{1}{x+2}$ b $\ln\left(\frac{7}{4}\right)$

11 $\ln|\ln x|+c$

12 $\frac{8}{3}\left(\frac{1}{2}x-1\right)^{\frac{3}{2}}+8\left(\frac{1}{2}x-1\right)^{\frac{1}{2}}+c$

13 i $x\tan x-\ln|\sec x|+c$

ii $x\tan x-\ln|\sec x|-\frac{1}{2}x^2+c$

14 $\ln|x-2|-\frac{5}{x-2}+c$

15 $\frac{e-1}{e+1}$

16 a $\frac{9\pi}{2}$ b Proof

17 a $x+c$

b $\ln|\sin x+\cos x|+c$

c $\frac{1}{2}(x-\ln|\sin x+\cos x|)+c$

18 $6+4\ln 4$ m

Chapter 12

Before you start...

1 a Proof b Proof

2 Proof

3 Proof

4 a Proof b Proof

c Proof

Work it out 12.1

Answer = Solutions 2 and 3 are correct.

Exercise 12A

1 a i Decreasing, convex

ii Concave

iii Increasing, convex

b i Increasing

ii Increasing, concave

iii Increasing, convex

2 a

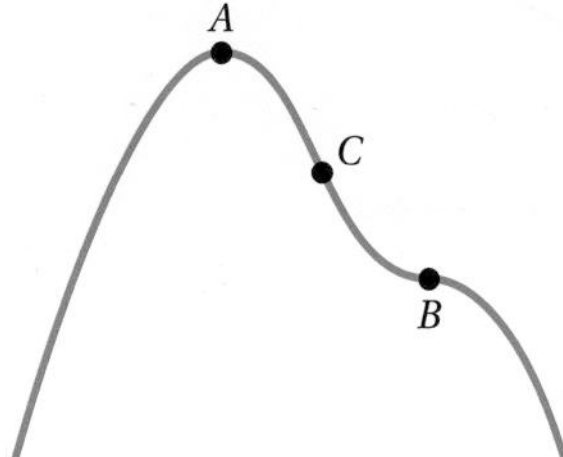

b

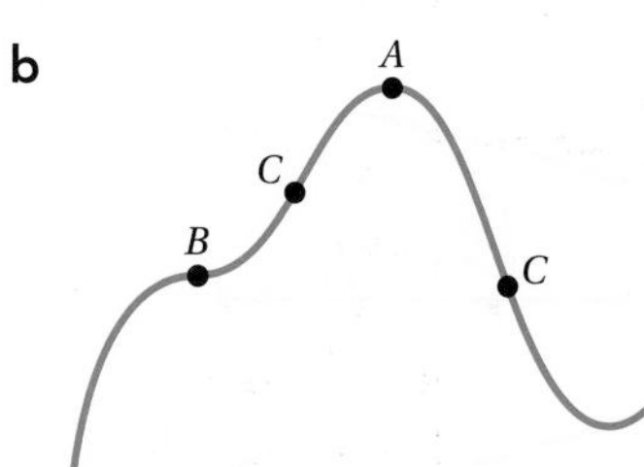

3

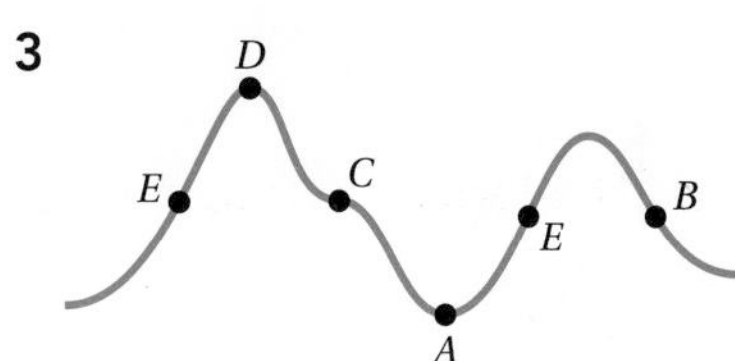

4 $(\ln 2, 2-(\ln 2)^2)$

5 $(1,4), (-1,-10)$

6 Proof

7 $x<-3$ or $x>2$

8 $\left(\frac{\pi}{2},\frac{\pi}{2}\right), \left(\frac{3\pi}{2},\frac{3\pi}{2}\right)$

9 Proof

10 Minimum point

11 Proof

12 $\frac{1}{9}$

13 $2-\sqrt{2}<x<2+\sqrt{2}$

14

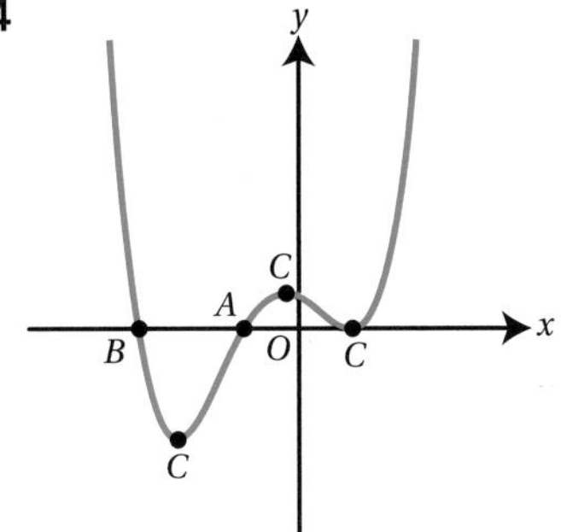

Exercise 12B

1 a i

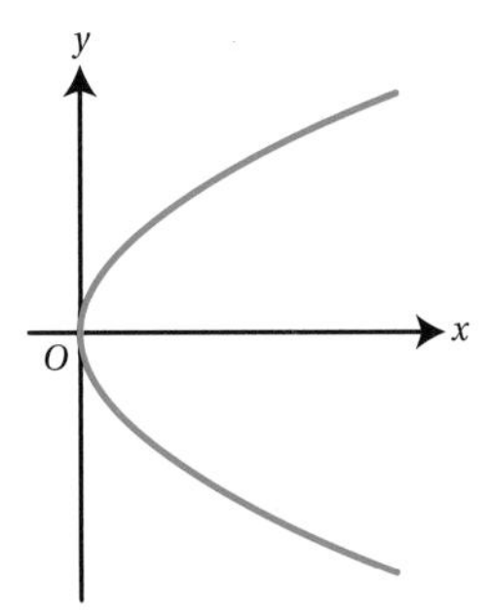

ii

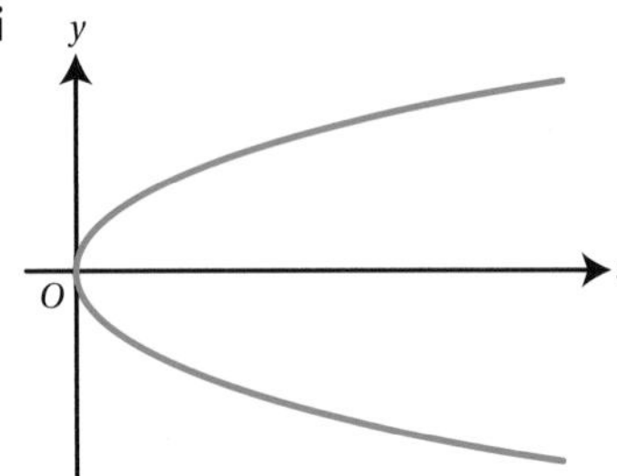

b i

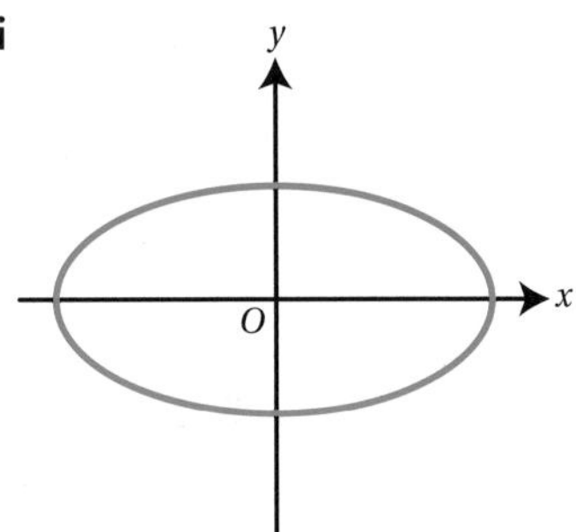

ii

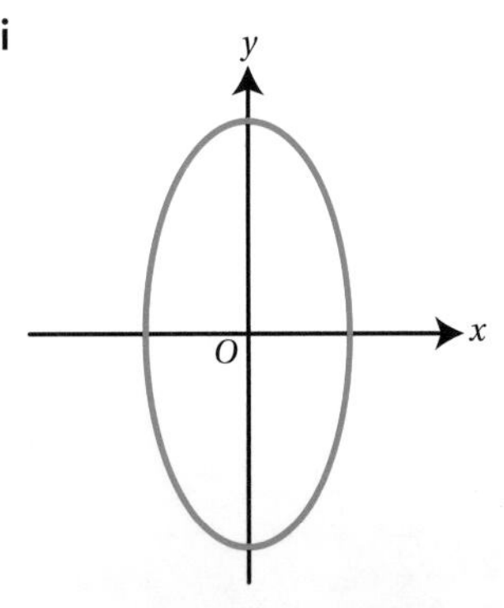

c i

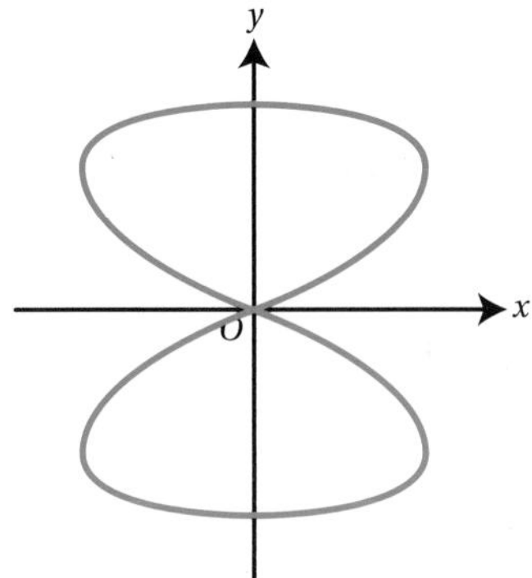

ii

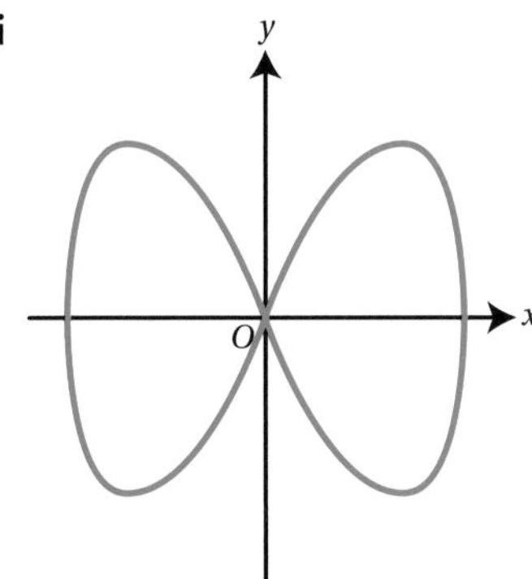

2 a i -1 **ii** 2

b i -2 **ii** -3

c i 2.50 **ii** $\pi/3$

3 a i $x=5t+1, y=12t+1$

ii $x=t-2, y=\dfrac{24-6t}{11}$

b i $x=t-1, y=4t^2-8t+4$

ii $x=t+1, y=-2t^2-4t$

c i $x=3\cos t, y=\dfrac{3}{2}\sin t$

ii $x=\dfrac{1}{2}\cos t, y=2\sin t$

d i $x=3+5t, y=-1+3t$

ii $x=1+t, y=1-6t$

4 a i $4x=3y^2$ **ii** $x=5(2-y)^2$

b i $x^3=8y^2$ **ii** $125x^2=4y^3$

c i $x^2+y^2=25$ **ii** $9x^2+y^2=36$

d i $x=4y^2-2$ **ii** $9x=9-2y^2$

e i $y^2-x^2=1$ **ii** $4x^2-9y^2=36$

5 a 4.4 m **b** 8.57 m

6 a $2-\dfrac{1}{\sqrt{3}}$

b 2; the distance along the line.

c $\sqrt{3}y-x=2\sqrt{3}-1$

7 a Proof; 25; 1.1 weeks **b** 41.7, 8.3

8 a 61.9

b $D(S+160) = 19\,300$

c 20

Work it out 12.2

Answer = Solution 2

Exercise 12C

1 a i $\frac{2}{3t}$ **ii** $-\frac{1}{10t}$

b i $\frac{\sin\theta}{4\sin(2\theta)}$ **ii** $-\frac{3\cos\theta}{2\sin(2\theta)}$

c i $\sin\theta$ **ii** $\frac{2}{3}\operatorname{cosec}\theta$

2 a i $-\frac{1}{3}$ **ii** $-\frac{1}{20}$

b i $-\frac{3}{2}$ **ii** $+\frac{5}{9}$

c i $\frac{3}{4}$ **ii** $-\sqrt{3}$

3 $y = -6x + 17$

4 $y = -1$

5 $\frac{9}{4e}$

6 a $y = 16x - 225$ **b** $\left(-\frac{1}{16}, -256\right)$

7 $(27, -18)$

8 Proof

9 Proof

10 a $(2a + aq^2, 0)$ **b** Proof

11 a 1.5, 7.5, 13.5, 19.5

b between 8.6 and 11.6 months

c Proof; the rate of change of the number of rats as the number of snakes increases.

Exercise 12D

1 a i 45 **ii** $\frac{112}{3}$

b i $4 - \ln 5$ **ii** $6 - 4\ln 2$

c i 6 **ii** $4\pi - 8$

2 a $(1, 0), (16, 0)$ **b** -22.5

3 a 0 and $\ln 2$ **b** $\ln 2 - \frac{5}{8}$

4 a 3 **b** $\frac{80}{9} - 2\ln 3$

c $x^2 - y^2 = 4$

Exercise 12E

1 a i $144x^3$ **ii** $6x^2(x^3 + 1)$

b i $-6x\sin(3x^2)$ **ii** $2x\sec^2(x^2 + 1)$

2 a i 50 **ii** -12

b i -6 **ii** 1

c i $\pm\frac{1}{3}$ **ii** -2

3 a i 22 **ii** 38

b i 45 **ii** 176

c i 0.24 **ii** 0.00667

4 $113\text{ cm}^2\text{ s}^{-1}$

5 2 cm s^{-1}

6 $768\pi\text{ cm}^3\text{ s}^{-1}$

7 $75\text{ cm}^2\text{ s}^{-1}$

8 2 cm s^{-1}

9 $160\pi\text{ cm}^3\text{ s}^{-1}$

10 19.1 units s^{-1}

Work it out 12.3

Answer = Solution 3

Exercise 12F

1 a i $\frac{32}{3}$ **ii** $\frac{1}{6}$

b i 9 **ii** $\frac{1}{3}$

c i $\frac{9}{8}$ **ii** $\frac{1}{3}$

d i $\frac{15}{4} - 4\ln 2$ **ii** $12 - 5\ln 5$

2 a i 9.13 **ii** 2.50

b i 0.828 **ii** 41.3

c i 2.35 **ii** 5.38

3 2

4 $\frac{32}{3}$

5 $e^2 - \frac{11}{3}$

6 Proof

7 6

8 $e^2 - 3$

9 $12 - 5\ln 5$

10 $\frac{37}{2}$

11 $m = 4$

12 Proof

Mixed practice 12

1 $x=2, y=-\frac{2}{3}$

2 a $t=1$ **b** $y-1=-\frac{1}{6}(x-3)$

3 36

4 a 6 **b** $\frac{22}{3}$

5 i $-2, 1$ **ii** 4.5

6 25

7 a (0, 0) minimum; (0.8, 0.082) maximum

b Proof

8 $\frac{1024}{5}$

9 a $0, \frac{\pi}{3}, \pi$ **b** $\frac{9}{4}$

10 a Proof **b** 4

11 3

12 Proof

13 a $100h-\frac{1}{2}h^2$ **b** Proof **c** 6

14 i Proof **ii** $2x+y=2xy+2$

15 a $\frac{\pi}{4}$ and $\frac{5\pi}{4}$ seconds **b** 1.93 m

16 Proof

17 a $0, \frac{\pi}{2}$ **b** 2.5π; 10π

18

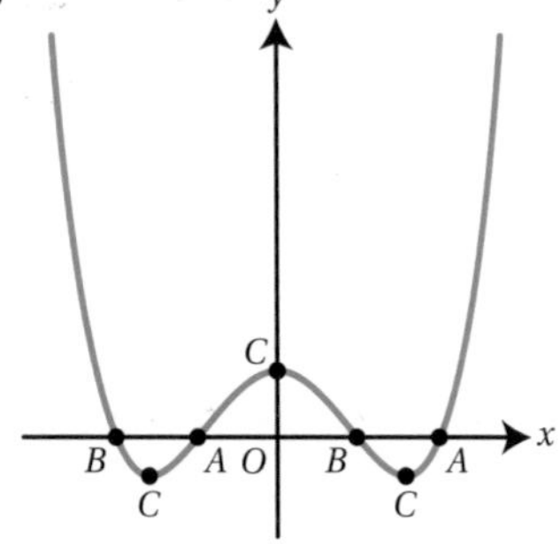

19 a Proof

b $(-a, 0)$ and $(3a, 8a^2)$

c $\frac{64}{3}a^3$ **d** $\frac{15}{16}$

Chapter 13

Before you start...

1 $2\ln\left|\frac{2+x}{2-x}\right|+c$

2 a $2\ln|x^2+3|+c$ **b** $\frac{1}{3}x^3\ln x-\frac{1}{9}x^3+c$

3 $\frac{1}{2}\tan 2x-x+c$

4 $\frac{dV}{dt}=20\pi r^2\sqrt{r}$

5 $v=3+5e^t$

6 27 N downwards

Exercise 13A

1 a i $y=-\frac{3}{2}\cos 2x+c$ **ii** $y=12\sin\left(\frac{x}{3}\right)+c$

b i $y=\frac{1}{3}e^{2x}+c$ **ii** $y=8e^{\frac{x}{2}}+c$

c i $y=3\tan x+c$ **ii** $y=\tan x-x+c$

d i $y=\frac{1}{4}x^4\ln x-\frac{1}{16}x^4+c$ **ii** $y=\sec x+c$

2 a i $y=\frac{4}{3}\sqrt{3x+9}-2$ **ii** $y=-2\sqrt{4-x}+3$

b i $y=\ln|x^2+1|-\ln 2$

ii $y=\frac{1}{4}x^2+\frac{1}{2}\ln|x|+\frac{3}{4}$

c i $y=-2e^{-3x}+2$ **ii** $y=-2e^{1-2x}+2$

d i $y=-\frac{1}{4x^2}-\frac{\ln|x|}{2x^2}+c$ **ii** $y=\frac{1}{2}\sec^2 x-4$

Work it out 13.1

Answer = Solution 2

Exercise 13B

1 a i $y=\pm\frac{2}{3}x^{\frac{3}{2}}$ **ii** $y=\frac{1}{1-2x^2}$

b i $y=2x^4$ **ii** $y=3e-x^3$

2 a i $\sin y=\frac{1}{2}-\cos x$

ii $\tan y=\tan x-\sqrt{3}$

b i $\ln|y|=\frac{1}{3}x^3$ **ii** $-\frac{1}{y}=\ln|x|-2$

c i $e^{-2y}=-4e^x+5$ **ii** $e^y=e^x+e^2-1$

3 a i $y=\pm\sqrt{x^3+c}$ **ii** $y=-\frac{1}{x^2+c}$

b i $y=\arcsin(\ln|x|+c)$

ii $y=\arctan(\ln|x-2|+c)$

c i $y=Ae^x(x-1)-3$ **ii** $y=\frac{A}{1-x}$

4 $y=e^{-(1-x)^2}$

5 $H=10$

6 Proof

7 $y=\frac{2cx^4+2}{1-cx^4}$

8 $k=3$

Exercise 13C

1 a i $\frac{dN}{dt} = 5N$ ii $\frac{dM}{dt} = -3M$

b i $\frac{dv}{dt} = \frac{kv}{\sqrt{t}}$ ii $\frac{dN}{dt} = k\sqrt{N}\sqrt[3]{t}$

c i $\frac{dr}{dt} = \frac{k}{2\pi\sqrt{r}}$ ii $\frac{dr}{dt} = -\frac{0.2}{\pi r^2}$

2 a Proof

b $N = 700\,e^{0.2t} = 38\,200$

3 a Proof b 3.47 s

4 a Proof b $v = \frac{8}{1+2t}$; 1.5 s

5 a When $t = 0$, $\frac{dN}{dt} = 1.6 > 0$; decreases from 5.7 years.

b $N = 2e^{0.8t - 0.07t^2}$ c 19 665

d It will decay to zero.

6 a $\frac{dQ}{dP}$ is the rate of change. 'Proportional to Q and inversely proportional to P' means that $\frac{dQ}{dP} = \varepsilon\frac{Q}{P}$, so $\frac{1}{Q}\frac{dQ}{dP} = \frac{\varepsilon}{P}$. Here ε is negative because demand decreases as price increases, so the rate of change $\frac{dQ}{dP}$ is negative.

b $Q = AP^{\varepsilon}$

c i

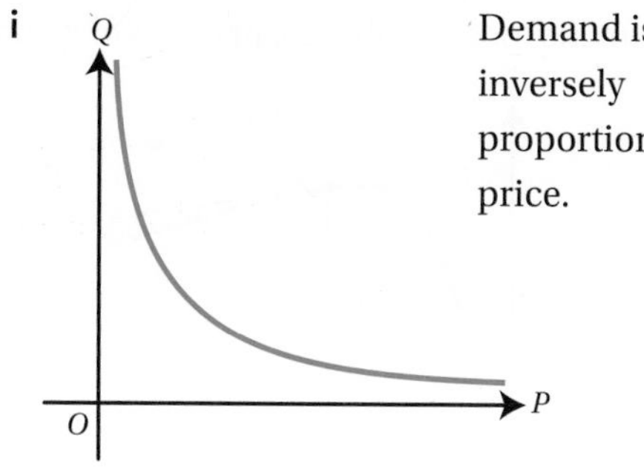

Demand is inversely proportional to price.

ii

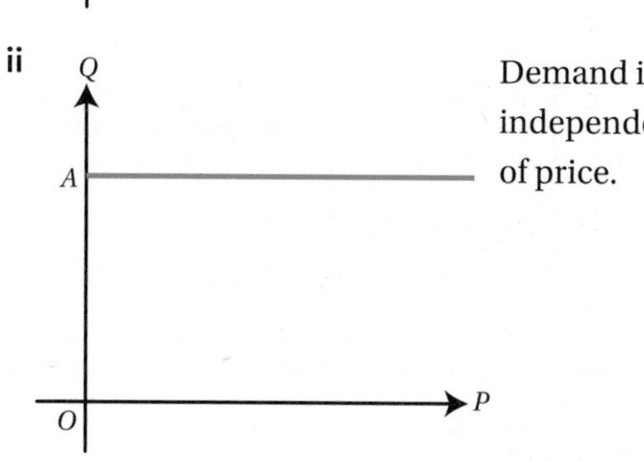

Demand is independent of price.

7 a Proof

b $\theta = 19 - 14e^{-0.3t}$; 11 minutes

8 a $v = 5 - 5e^{-0.8t}$

b The velocity approaches $5\,\text{m}\,\text{s}^{-1}$.

9 a Proof b 2.1 seconds

10 a Proof b $v = 10\,e^{-0.3t}$

c $x = \frac{100}{3}(1 - e^{-0.3t})$; it approaches $\frac{100}{3}$ m.

11 a $x > 1, 0 < y < 1$

b $\frac{y(x-1)}{x(1-y)}$ c Proof

Mixed practice 13

1 $y = 3 + e^{x^2}$

2 $y = \arctan\left(\sin x + \frac{1}{2}\right)$

3 $A = 6, B = 4$

4 i $\tan y = x + \frac{1}{4}\sin 4x + c$ ii $y = 1.05$

5 a Proof b 34.7 months

c Not suitable, as it predicts indefinite growth.

d $N = 250e^{\left\{0.04\left(\frac{t+15}{\pi\sin(\frac{t}{b}\pi)}\right)\right\}}$

6 a $Q = KP^{\varepsilon}$

b Demand is inversely proportional to the root of the price.

c Luxury goods; the demand increases with price.

7 a $h = 10 - \frac{20}{(t+2)}$

b It will never fill, as $h < 10$ for all t.

8 a Proof

b $C = 2, k = 4.9$

c The velocity increases, but tends to $2\,\text{m}\,\text{s}^{-1}$ as t increases.

9 i $\frac{d\theta}{dt} = k(160 - \theta)$ ii 96 °C

10 a Decrease in size due to, for example, competition for food.

b $N = \frac{3e^{1.2t}}{1 + e^{1.2t}}$

c Increases with the limit of 3.

11 Proof

12 a $\frac{dv}{dx} = -\frac{8e^{-4x}}{v}$ b Proof

c $x = \frac{1}{2}\ln(4t+1)$; $v = \frac{2}{4t+1}$

Chapter 14

Before you start...

1 a $e^{\frac{x}{3}}-2$ b $x=\frac{1}{2}\sqrt{x^2+12}$

c $x=\arctan\left(\frac{x}{3}\right)$

2 a $6x\tan x+3x^2\sec^2 x$

b $\frac{x-2x\ln x}{x^4}$ c $6xe^{3x^2}-\frac{1}{x}$

3 1, 3, −3, −33

Exercise 14A

1 a Exact solution b Can't rearrange

c Exact solution d Exact solution

e Can't rearrange f Exact solution

g Can't rearrange h Can't rearrange

2 a 2 and 3 b 0 and 1

c 1 and 2 d −2 and −1

3 a i Proof ii Proof

b i Proof ii Proof

4 a i Proof ii Proof

b i Proof ii Proof

c i Proof ii Proof

d i Proof ii Proof

5 a, b Proof

6 a Proof b $k=2$

7 a Proof

b i $f(2)=-6$, $f(3)=11$

ii $f(x)$ is not continuous (has an asymptote) at $x=2.5$.

8 a i

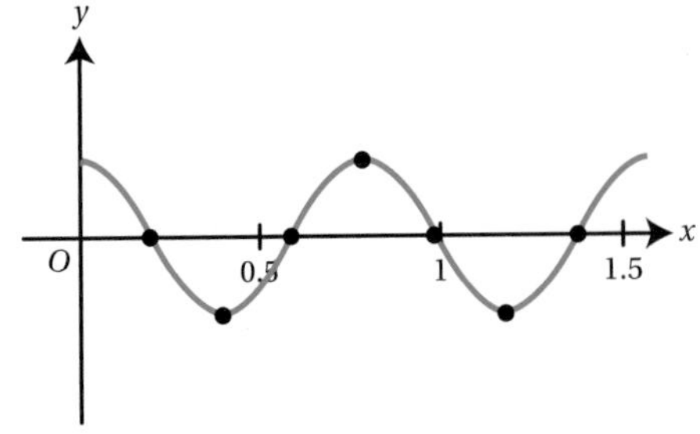

ii Two

b i $g(0)=g\left(\frac{\pi}{4}\right)=1$

ii $g(x)$ changes sign twice.

iii Use, for example, $x=0, \frac{\pi}{8}, \frac{\pi}{4}$.

Exercise 14B

1 a i 2.257 ii 0.5

b i 3.611 ii 0.995

2 a i 1.31 ii −0.347

b i 1.78 ii 11.6

3 −0.7

4 a Proof b 1.32, 1.29

5 6.5904, 6.5915

6 a Proof b 3.23

c Proof

7 a Proof b 1.327

8 0.407

Exercise 14C

1 a i $x_1=4$; x_0 close to stationary point

ii $x_1=4$; x_0 close to stationary point

b i $x_1=3.7$; on the other side of an asymptote

ii $x_1=-4.52$; outside the domain

2 a $x=0$ and $\frac{1}{3}$ b Proof

c It may be close to a stationary point.

3 $x=3$; the tangent crosses the x-axis further away from the root, so subsequent values of x_n increase.

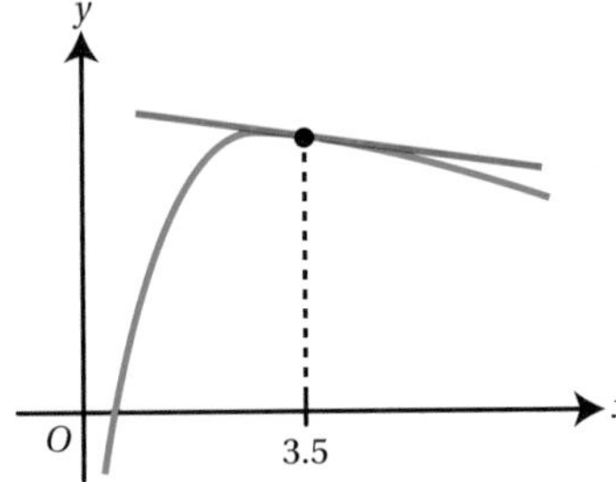

4 a (0, −2), (2, 2)

b i $x=\alpha$ ii Doesn't converge

c $x_0>2$

5 a $0, \frac{\pi}{2}, \frac{3\pi}{2}, \frac{5\pi}{2}$

b $x_1=3.55$

c x_1 on the far side of a discontinuity and a turning point.

6 a −2 and −1, −1 and 1, 1 and 2

b (−1, 5), (1, −3)

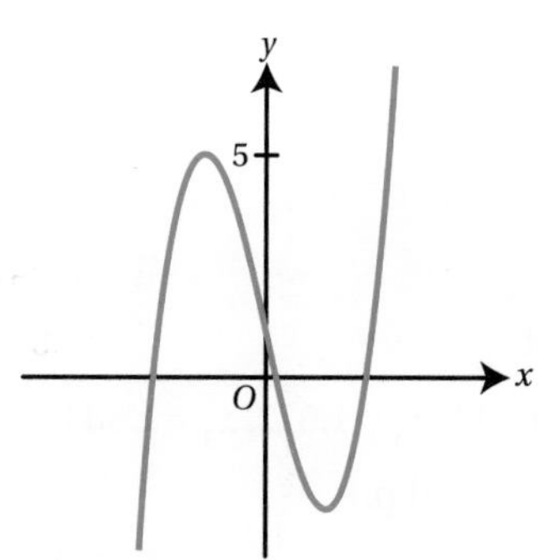

c (−1.68,0)

d It will converge to *a*.

e 0.168

7 a (1, 1.5)

b

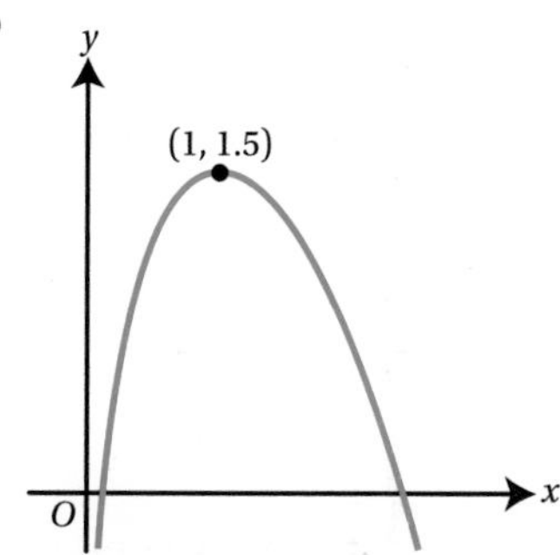

c 2 and 3

d $x_1 = -0.29$, which is outside of the domain of f(x).

e $x_0 > 1$

8 a i Proof ii Proof

iii Proof iv Proof

b i $1.311 < x_0 < 1.83$ ii $0 < x_0 < 0.869$

iii $0 < x_0 < 0.978$ iv $4.30 < x_0 < \frac{3\pi}{2}$

9 a Proof

b $x_0 > 1, x_0 \neq \sqrt{5}$

c

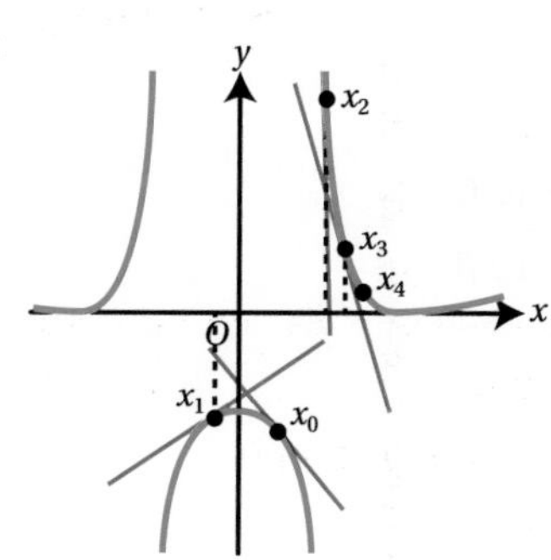

10 a

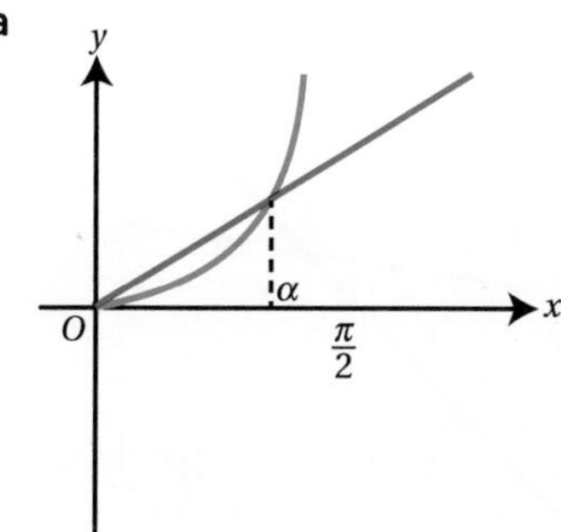

b Proof

c

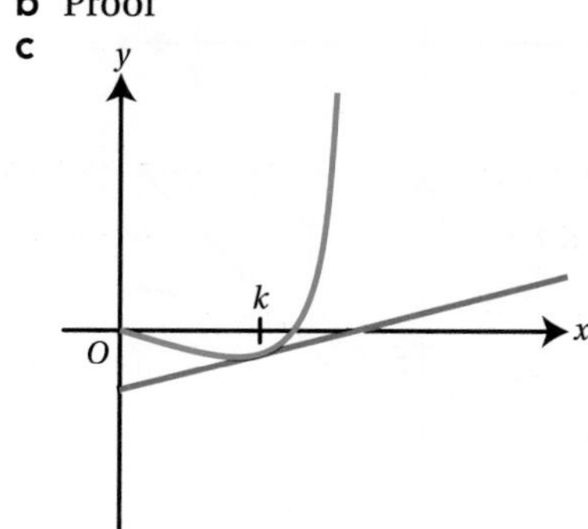

d Doesn't converge, or converges to another root (in a different interval).

Exercise 14D

1 a i 3, 3.219, 3.305, 3.337, 3.349

ii 4, 2.982, 2.949, 2.948, 2.948

b i −1,0, −0.250, −0.200, −0.211

ii 1, 0.540, 0.997, 0.546, 0.996

c i 0.5, 1.057, 0.938, 1.056, 0.940

ii 1, 1.364, 1.052, 1.329, 1.089

2 a i 0.70 ii 0.95

b i 4.51 ii 0.41

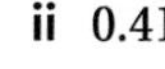

3 a

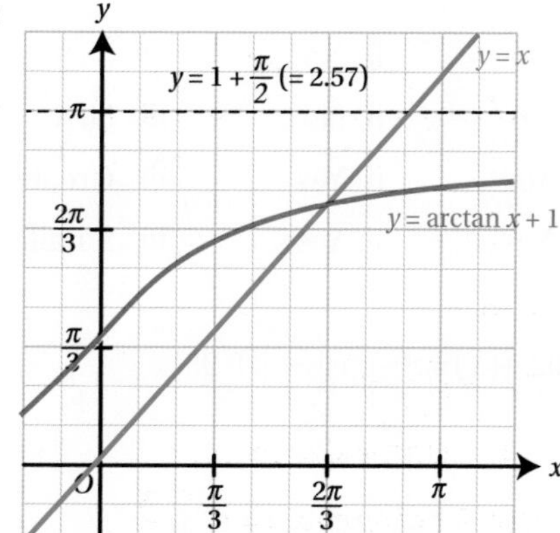

b

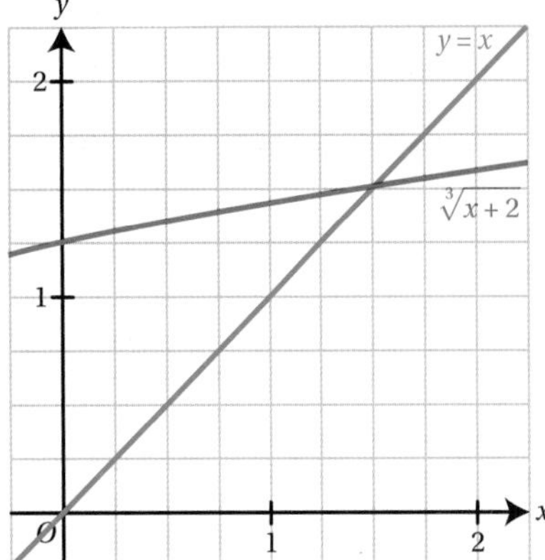

c

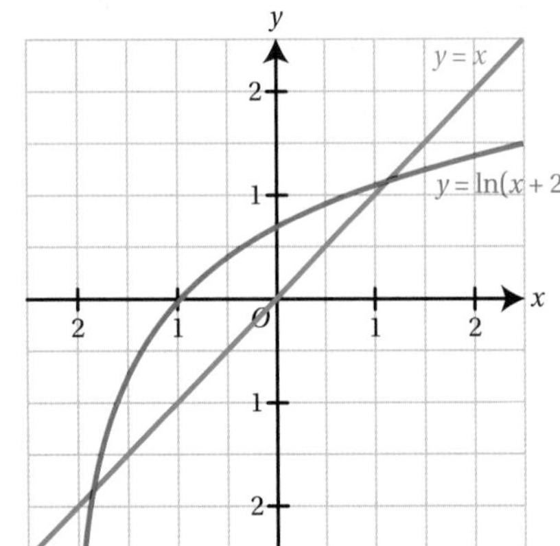

d

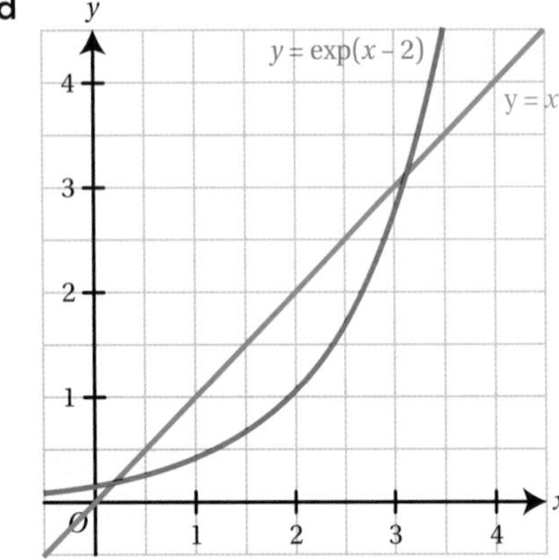

a	**i** No	**ii** No	**iii** N/A
b	**i** No	**ii** No	**iii** N/A
c	**i** Yes	**ii** Yes	**iii** Greater root
d	**i** Yes	**ii** Yes	**iii** Smaller root

4 2.58

5 0.9502; $f(x)=x-\cos\left(\frac{x}{3}\right)$, 0.95

6 0.892

7 a −0.8041, −0.8780

b $a=4, b=3, c=5$

8 x_3

9 a Proof

b $x_2=1.611, x_3=1.572, x_4=1.584$

c $x=1.58$ (2 d.p.)

10 a Proof **b** 5.24

c $3+\sqrt{5}$; 0.0751%

11 a

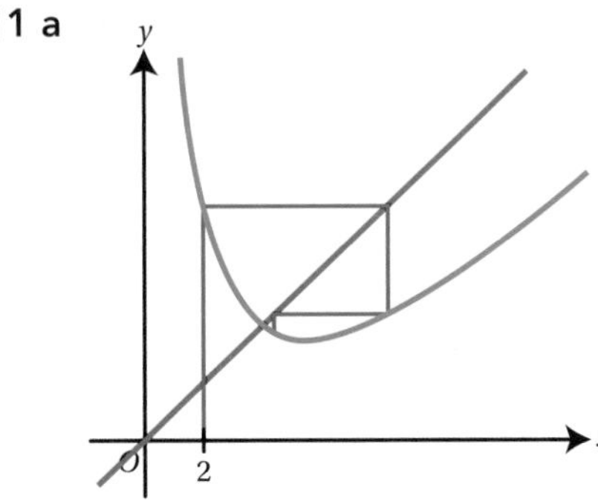

b Proof

Exercise 14E

1 a Diverges (increases without a limit)

b Diverges (decreases without a limit)

c Converges to 1.54 (and oscillates)

d Converges to −0.397 (decreases)

e Oscillates between 1 and 2.

f Converges (increases to 4.536.)

g Undefined after x_4.

2 a Converges

b Converges

c Converges to B

d Converges to A

e Converges to C

f Converges to B

g Diverges

3 a i $x=\sin^{-1}\left(\frac{x}{3}\right)$ **ii** $x=\tan^{-1}\left(\frac{x}{5}\right)$

b i $x=e^x+3$ **ii** $x=\ln x+2$

c i $x=\left(\frac{x}{3}\right)^2+1$ **ii** $x=\left(\frac{x}{2}\right)^3-5$

d i $x=\sqrt{\frac{x+1}{3}}$ **ii** $x=\sqrt{7x-1}$

4 a i $a=2, b=-\frac{1}{2}$ **ii** $a=2, b=-6$

b i $a=4, b=-1$ **ii** $a=2, b=1, c=2$

c i $a=\frac{1}{2}, b=-\frac{5}{2}$ **ii** $c=\frac{1}{3}, d=\frac{2}{3}$

d i $a=1, b=2$ **ii** $a=3, b=1$

5 a Proof **b** Proof

c Proof

6 a α **b** γ

7 a Converges to P

b Converges to P

c Converges to S

8 a $g(x)=x-\frac{f(x)}{f'(x)}$

b $g'(x)=\frac{f(x)f''(x)}{f'(x)^2}$, so $g'(a)=0$

9 a Proof

b $x<-2\ln 2$; the positive root.

10 a Proof **b** β

c $c=1, k=15, m=-3; \alpha=0.067$

11 a 0 and $\frac{k-1}{k}$ **b** $2-k$

c $1<k<3$

Mixed practice 14

1 a Proof **b** 0.248

2 a Proof **b** Proof **c** 2.77

3 a Two solutions;

b Proof **c** 1.13

4 a Proof **b** Proof

c 2.065

5 i 2.877 **ii** $2x^3+5x-62=0$

6 a Proof **b** $x_1=1.5$

c x_1 is on the other side of the asymptote.

d −1.365

7 a Proof **b** 1.895

8 a Proof **b** 0.7105; 1.122

9 33

10 i 5.24 **ii** Proof

iii 1.31 **iv** $f'(\ln 36)=0$

11 a Proof **b** Proof

c $x=\pi+\tan^{-1}\left(\frac{x}{2}\right)$; 4.275

Chapter 15

Before you start...

1 7.5

2

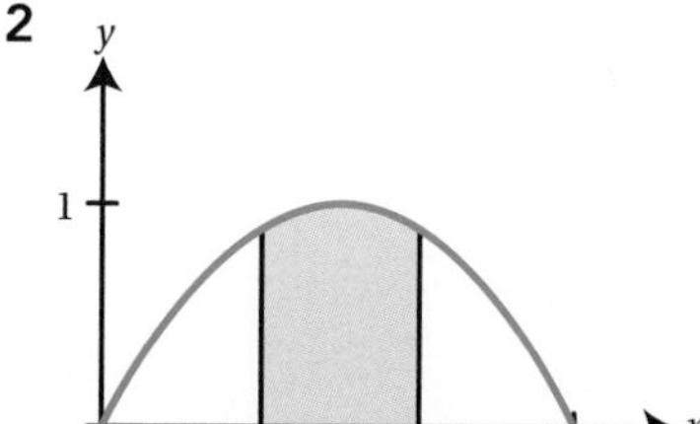

3 63 m

Work it out 15.1

Answer = Solution 2

Exercise 15A

1 a i

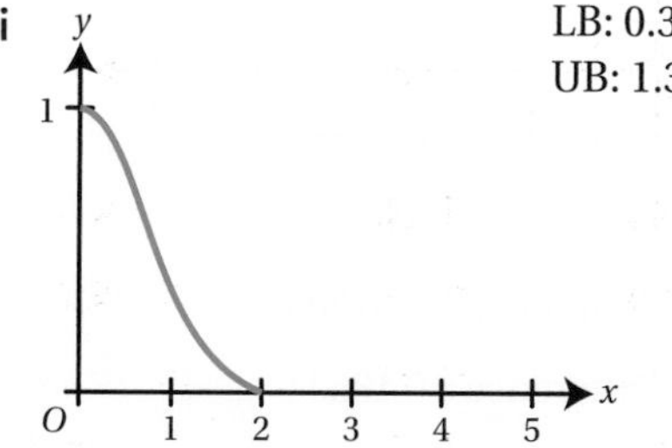

LB: 0.386;
UB: 1.39

ii

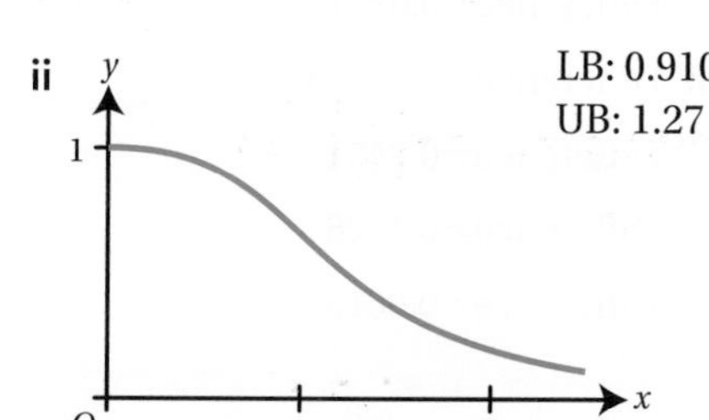

LB: 0.910;
UB: 1.27

b i

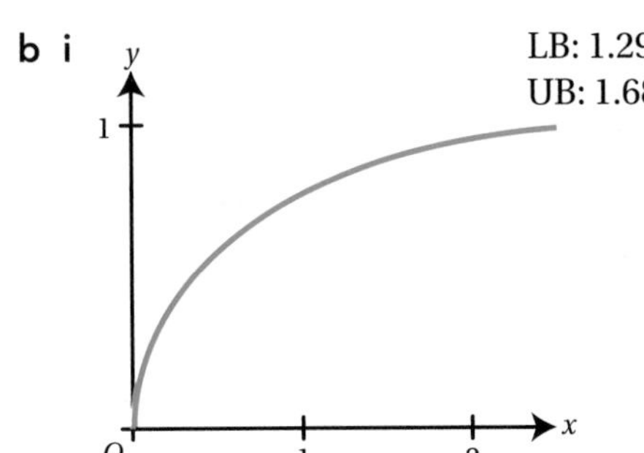

LB: 1.29;
UB: 1.68

ii

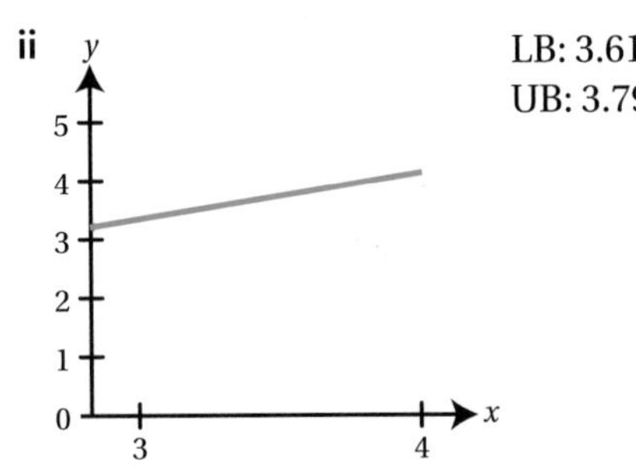

LB: 3.61;
UB: 3.79

c i

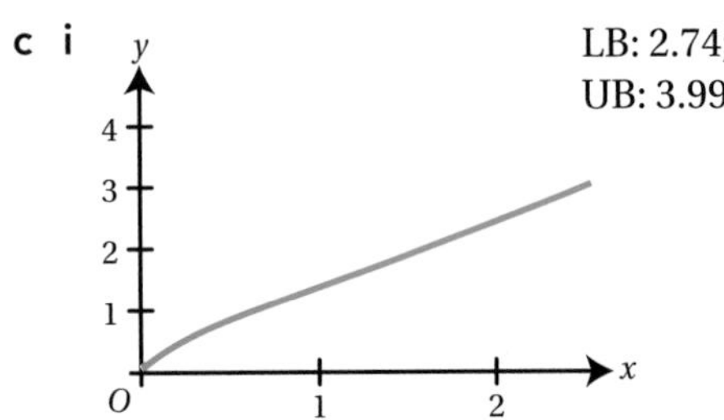

LB: 2.74;
UB: 3.99

ii

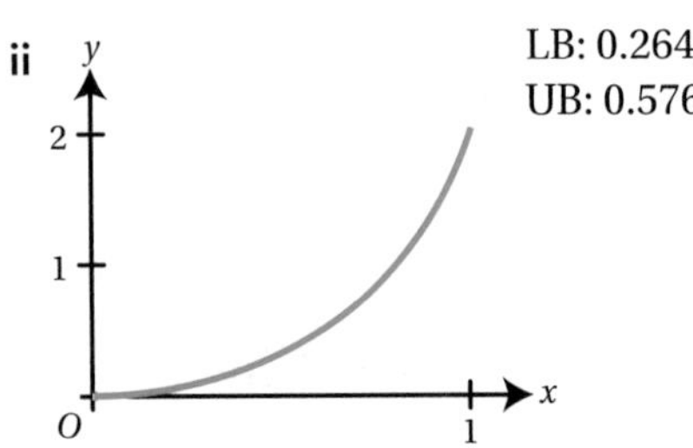

LB: 0.264;
UB: 0.576

2 a i Difference = 0.07221

ii Difference = 0.03610

iii Difference = 0.01805

b i Difference = 0.18631

ii Difference = 0.09315

iii Difference = 0.04658

c i Difference = 0.2451

ii Difference = 0.1226

iii Difference = 0.0613

d i Difference = 0.03156

ii Difference = 0.01578

iii Difference = 0.00789

e In general, doubling the number of rectangles from 10 to 20 or from 20 to 40 halves the difference between the upper and lower bounds.

3 LB: 1.83; UB: 2.33

4 a LB: 2.89; UB: 4.97

b By using more rectangles.

5 a

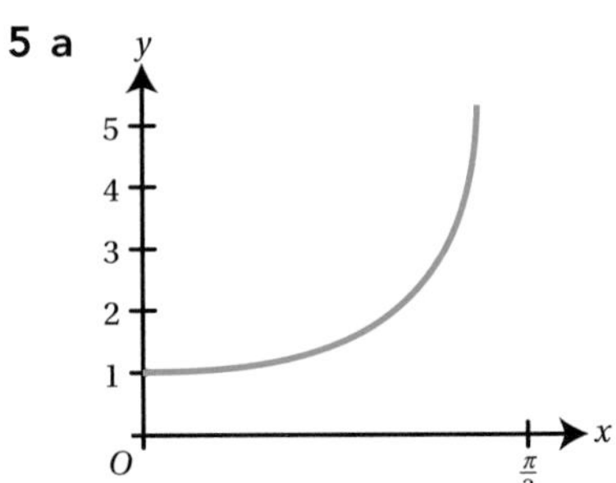

b 1.35

c Decrease

6 a $\left(\frac{\pi}{2}, 1\right)$ **b** 2.01

Work it out 15.2

Answer = Solution 3

Exercise 15B

1 a i 0.886 **ii** 1.09

b i 1.46 **ii** 3.70

c i 3.38 **ii** 0.455

2 a,b See table in Worked solutions.

c Usually error decreases by a factor of 3 to 4.

3 a Approximation 1.26

b $2\left(\sqrt{5}-\sqrt{2}\right)$

c $\frac{\pi}{2}$

d Approximation 0.609

e $3\ln(6.75)-3$

f Exact integral

$$\ln\left(\frac{\operatorname{cosec}(0.5)+\cot(0.5)}{\operatorname{cosec}(2)+\cot(2)}\right)^2 \approx 3.62.$$

4 a

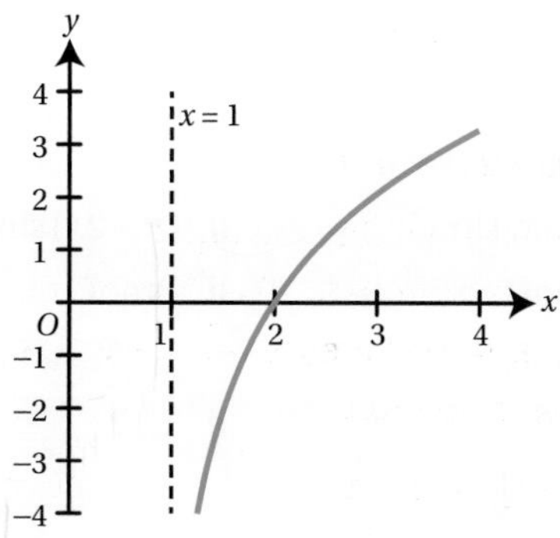

b 3.86

c Concave curve: underestimate

5 a 1.98

b Use more trapezia; exact integration is possible.

6 a $\sqrt{\frac{\pi}{2}}$ **b** 0.957

c Concave curve: underestimate

7 10.2 m

8 a $p=\pi^2, q=4\pi^2$ **b** 22.3 m

Mixed practice 15

1 18.1

2 a 1650

b Concave curve: underestimate

c By using more intervals.

3 $L=4.14$, $U=5.20$

4 i 1.313 **ii** 0.518

iii Use more rectangles.

5 26.7

6 2.50

7 a $t=0, \frac{\pi}{3}, \frac{2\pi}{3}, \pi, \frac{4\pi}{3}, \frac{5\pi}{3}$ and 2π

b 1.05

8 $K=\left(\frac{2542}{17}\right)^5$

9 a

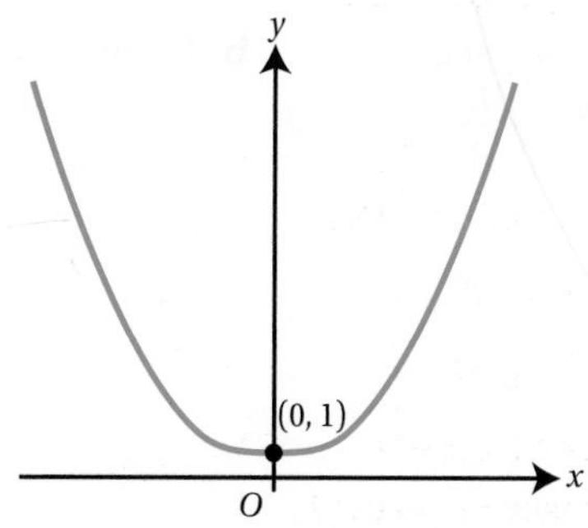

b 2.09

10 4.35 m s^{-1}

Focus on … Proof 2

Questions

1 Yes, by varying the base (or hypotenuse) accordingly.

2 Yes

3 Proof

Focus on … Problem solving 2

1 a i Tends to 1500.

ii Stays at 1000.

iii Dies out after 48 years.

b i Same as in part **a**.

ii Proof

iii Proof

c Proof

2 Increases with α, decreases with β.

3 a i 500, 1500

ii 1000

iii No solutions

b $0.16-0.0008k$

c $x=\frac{0.4\pm\sqrt{0.16-0.0008k}}{0.0004}$

4 a $(\alpha-1)^2-4\beta k$ **b** Proof

5 Investigation

6 Investigation

Focus on … Modelling 2

1 $\frac{dN}{dt}=0.0343N$

2 $\frac{dm}{dt}=-0.005m$

3 $\frac{dV}{dt}=-0.0032V^2$

4 $\frac{dT}{dt}=-0.0263(T-24)$

5 $\frac{dT}{dx} = -kx$

6 $\frac{dp}{dh} = 1000k(1+0.001h)$

7 $\frac{dN}{dt} = \frac{3\sqrt{N}}{t}$; this model predicts infinite initial rate of growth.

8 $\frac{dV}{dt} = -0.0905h$ or $-0.002V$

Cross-topic review exercise 2

1 $y = 3\ln|\sec x| + 4$

2 $\frac{1}{2}\ln|\sec x| + \frac{x}{2} + c$

3 a $\frac{d^2y}{dx^2} = \lambda^2 e^{\lambda x}$

b $\lambda = -6, 1$

4 $2 - \sqrt{2}$

5 a 3

b $5\ln 5 - 2\ln 2 - 3$

6 a $0, \pi^2$

b 2π

c $y = \sin\sqrt{x}$

7 i Proof　ii $(-1, -e^{-2})$

8 $x^{\sin x}\left(\cos x \ln|x| + \frac{\sin x}{x}\right)$

9 a $2\sin Bx\cos Ax$

b $\frac{1}{4}\cos 2x - \frac{1}{16}\cos 8x + c$

10 a $x = \sin y$　b $\frac{dx}{dy} = \cos y$

c Proof

11 a Proof　b $\left(\frac{5\pi}{6}, 2\right)$

12 a $\frac{1}{y}\frac{dy}{dx}$

b $4\ln x - \ln(2+5x) - \frac{1}{2}\ln(x^2+1)$

c $\left(\frac{4}{x} - \frac{5}{2+5x} + \frac{x}{x^2+1}\right)\left(\frac{x^4}{(2+5x)\sqrt{x^2+1}}\right)$

13 $2\sqrt{3} - \frac{2\pi}{3}$

14 a $13\,\text{cm}^2\,\text{s}^{-1}$

b Proof; $h = 30 - 2t$

c $A = 300 + 25t - 3t^2$

15 a i $(\pi - x, \sin x)$　ii $(\pi - 2x)\sin x$

b i Proof　ii Proof

iii Proof

c i 0.710　ii 1.12

16 a $|\cos x| < 1$ for $0 < x < \pi$.

b Proof

c $\sqrt{3} - 1$

17 a 0.23141　b 0.23229

c 0.23182; trapezium rule is better.

18 i

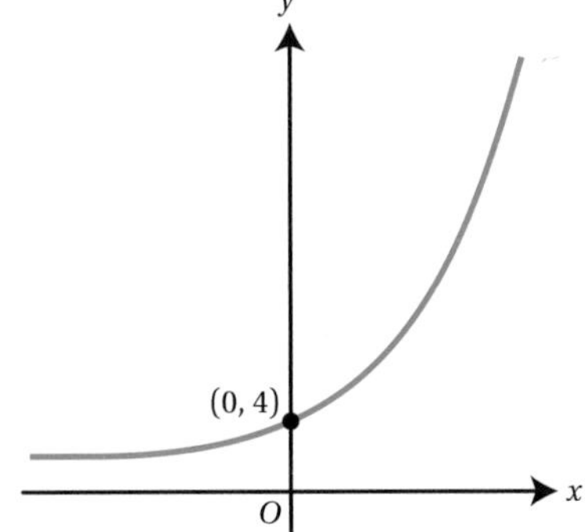

ii Proof

iii $1 + 2k^{\frac{1}{2}} + k$

iv 9

19 i $\sqrt{18}\cos(x - \frac{\pi}{4})$

ii a $\frac{3\pi}{4}$　b $x = \frac{\pi}{36}$

20 4^n

21 a $\frac{1-x^{n+1}}{1-x}$　b Proof

22 a Proof　b $\arcsin a$

c $1 - \sqrt{1-a^2}$

d $a\arcsin a + \sqrt{1-a^2} - 1$

23 a $2 + \cos 2x - \sec^2 x$　b Proof

c Proof, $x = \pm\frac{\pi}{4}$

24 a

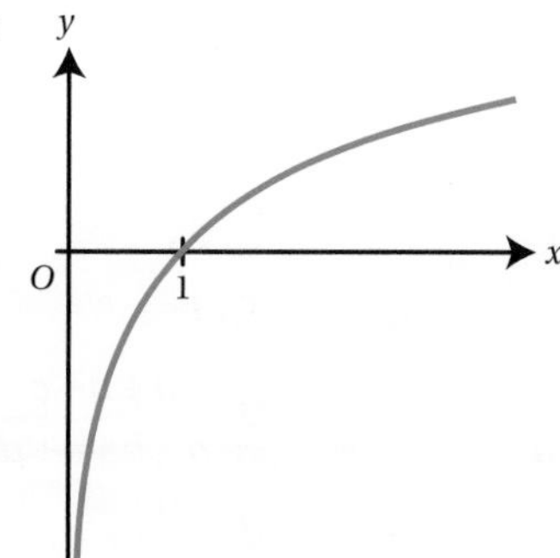

b e **c** $0<k<\frac{1}{e}$

25 i $0\leqslant x\leqslant\frac{3}{2}\sqrt{5}$ **ii** $\sqrt{5}$ **iii** Proof

Chapter 16

Before you start...

1 $\frac{1}{6}$

2 $\frac{1}{2}$

3 a $\frac{9}{14}$ **b i** $\frac{12}{45}$ **ii** $\frac{12}{30}$

4 $\{2\}$

5 $\frac{15}{64}$

Exercise 16A

1 a $P(\text{prime}\cap\text{odd})$

b $P(\text{Senegal}\cup\text{Taiwan})$

c $P(\text{French}\mid\text{A Levels})$

d $P(\text{heart}\mid\text{red})$

e $P(\text{lives in Munich}\mid\text{German})$

f $P(\text{not black}\cap\text{not white})$

g $P(\text{potato}\mid\text{not cabbage})$

h $P(\text{red}\mid\text{red}\cup\text{blue})$

2 a i $\frac{5}{6}$ **ii** $\frac{15}{28}$

b i $\frac{5}{14}$ **ii** $\frac{5}{6}$

3 a i $\frac{7}{20}$ **ii** All (100%)

b i 27.5% **ii** $\frac{7}{30}$

c i 55% **ii** 18.3%

d i 0.5 **ii** 1/3

4 a $P(x>4)$ **b** $P(y\leqslant 3)$

c 0 **d** $P(a\in \mathbb{R})$

e P(fruit) **f** P(apple)

g P(multiple of 4) **h** P(rectangle)

i P(blue) **j** $P(\text{blue}\cap\text{red})$

k 1 **l** 0

5 a i 0.5 **ii** 1

b i $\frac{1}{6}$ **ii** 0.05

c i $\frac{4}{15}$ **ii** 0.2

d i 0.7 **ii** 0.11

6 a

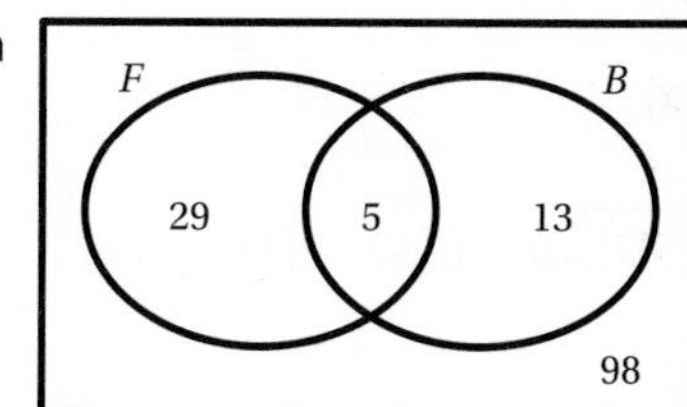

b 98

c $\frac{18}{145}$

d $\frac{5}{34}$

7 a

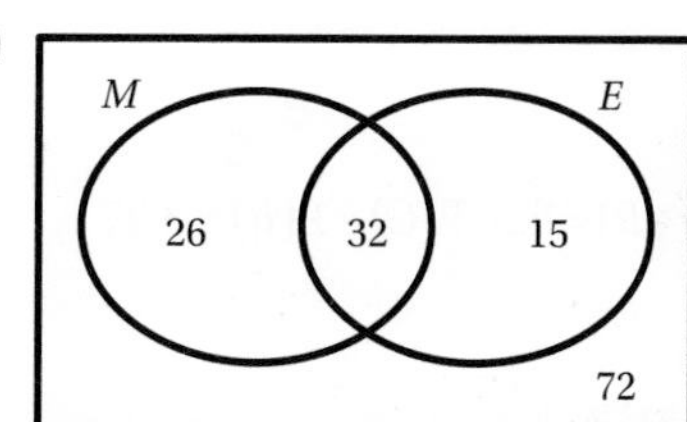

b 32

c $\frac{16}{29}$

8 a 5% **b** $\frac{5}{6}$

9 a 0.2 **b** 0.4

10 a 0.6 **b** $\frac{1}{6}$

11 a 0.3 **b** 0.4

12 a 0.166 **b** 0.041

c 0.247

13 a

B C V

0, 23, 32, 12, 8, 12, 48, 10

b 0
c 79
d $\frac{16}{29}$
e $\frac{3}{5}$
f $\frac{11}{29}$

14 a

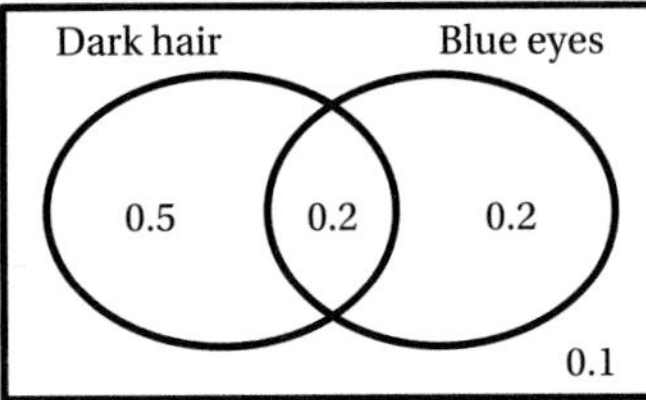

b 0.1
c $\frac{2}{7}$
d $\frac{2}{3}$
e No: $P(B \cap D) = 0.2$, $P(B) \times P(D) = 0.28$

15 a 0.3

b

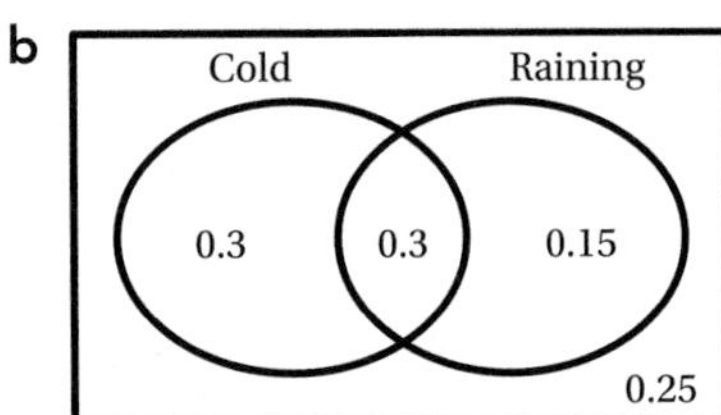

c $\frac{1}{3}$
d $\frac{3}{8}$
e No: $P(C \cap R) = 0.3$, $P(C) \times P(R) = 0.27$

16 4

17 0.75

18 0.5 to 1

19 a $0 \leqslant P(X) \leqslant 1$

b $P(A) - P(B|A)P(A)$

c Proof

Exercise 16B

1 a i 0.4
ii 0.3
b i $\frac{1}{3}$
ii $\frac{5}{13}$ or 0.385
c i 0.25
ii 0.2

2 a

	Year 9	Year 10	Year 11	Total
Girls	98	85	86	269
Boys	88	75	77	240
Total	186	160	163	509

b $\frac{86}{509}$
c $\frac{86}{269}$

3 a $\frac{7}{15}$
b $\frac{7}{15}$
c Proof

4 a $\frac{1}{3}$
b $\frac{7}{25}$
c $\frac{5}{14}$

5 a $\frac{a}{a+b+c+d}$
b $\frac{a+b+c}{a+b+c+d}$
c $\frac{a+c}{a+b+c+d}$
d $\frac{a}{a+c}$
e $\frac{b}{b+d}$

6 a $\frac{27}{67}$
b $\frac{99}{258}$
c $\frac{27}{258}$
d $\frac{139}{258}$

7 a $\frac{14}{223}$
b $\frac{101}{223}$
c $\frac{61}{223}$
d $\frac{7}{27}$
e $\frac{122}{169}$

8 a 0.49
b 0.1
c 0.5125

9 For example, playing cards in a deck with A = diamonds and B = red.

Work it out 16.1

Answer = Solution 1

Exercise 16C

1 a i 0.12
ii 0
b i 0.24
ii 0.24
c i $\frac{13}{20}$
ii $\frac{3}{4}$

2 0.165

3 0.167

4 a

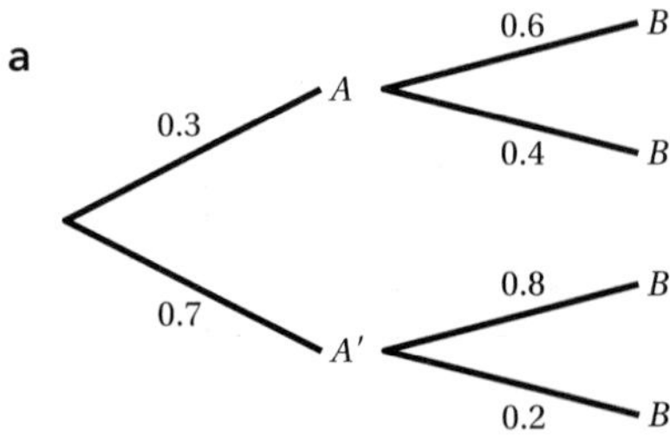

b 0.18
c 0.86
d 0.74

5 a $\frac{19}{27}$ b $\frac{25}{27}$

6 0.048

7 0.627

8 a 0.621 b 0.839

9 a 0.853 b 0.156

10 a 0.45 b $\frac{9}{44}$

11 a $\frac{2}{3}$ b $\frac{4}{5}$

12 0.0277

13 $\frac{1}{3}$

14 15 or 21

15 Proof

Mixed practice 16

1 0.320

2 a

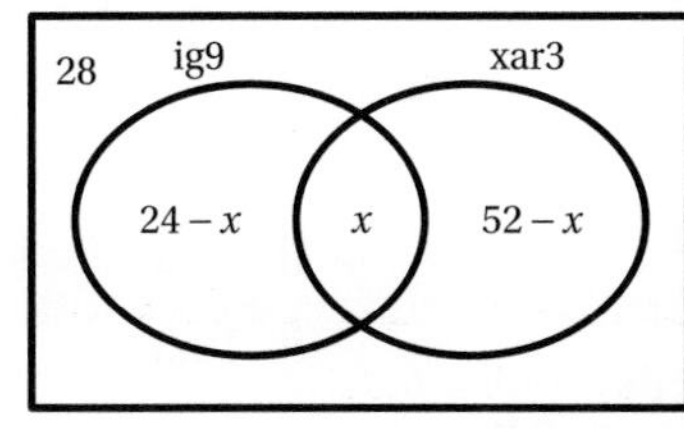

b 0.04 c $\frac{1}{13}$

3 a

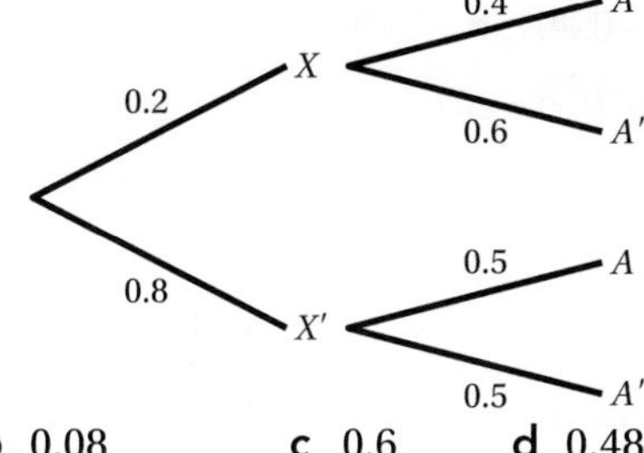

b 0.08 c 0.6 d 0.48

4 a 0.5 b 0.219

5 a

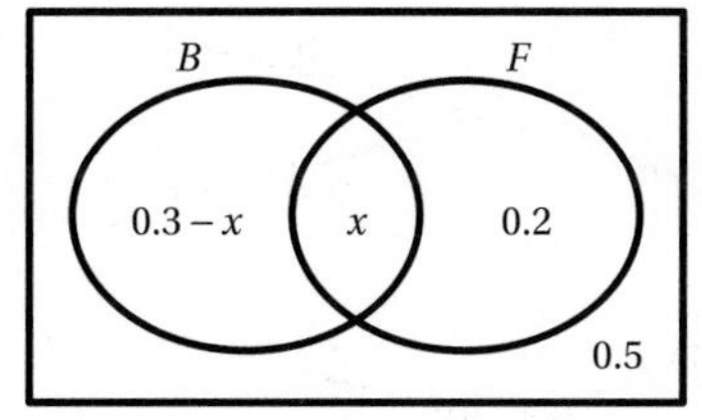

b $0.3-x$ c 0.2

d 0.1

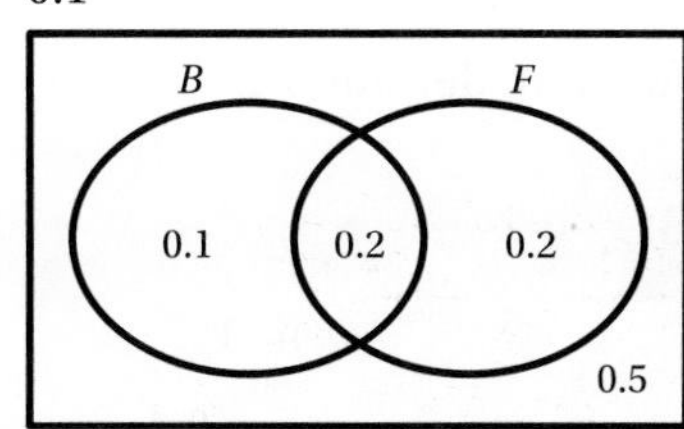

e $\frac{1}{3}$

6 $\frac{16}{41}$

7 $\frac{10}{19}$

8 i $\frac{25}{37}$ ii 0.431

9 i $\frac{1}{4}$ ii $\frac{1}{3}$ iii $\frac{1}{6}$

10 $\frac{4}{9}$

11 a $\frac{14}{95}$

b Proof c 0.138 d 0.356

12 a $0.5 \leqslant k \leqslant 1$ b $2-\frac{1}{k}$

13 0.111

14 $\frac{1}{3}$

Chapter 17

Before you start...

1 6 people/kg

2 32%

3 25%

4 41%

5 $x = 1.90; y = 1.15$

Exercise 17A

1 a i 0.885 ii 0.212

b i 0.401 ii 0.878

c i 0.743 ii 0.191

d i 0.807 ii 0.748

e i 0.451 ii 0.689

2 Mean: 8, Standard deviation: 3

3 Mean: 12, standard deviation: 4

4 Mean: 10, standard deviation: 2

Exercise 17B

1 a i 0.5 ii 1

b i −1.67 ii −0.4

2 a i $P(Z<1.6)$ ii $P(Z<1.28)$

b i $P(Z\geqslant -0.68)$ ii $P(Z\geqslant -2.96)$

c i $P(-1.4<Z<0.2)$

ii $P(-2.36\leqslant Z\leqslant -0.2)$

3 a 1.16 b 0.123

4 a 0.278

b i 0.127 ii 0.334

c Assumes that they are independent, but Ali might be getting tired.

5 1547

6 a 0.309 b Proof

c Best athletes likely to be chosen for the team; not independent as will depend on the weather / track / how well other athletes are doing; all four going under 59 seconds is a sufficient but not necessary condition.

7 a 0.160 b 0.171

c 0.727

8 a 0.707 b 0.663

9 a 67.3% b 0.314

10 a 0.952 b 0.838

11 a 0.841 b 0.811

12 0.640

13 0.0228

14 $1-k$

Exercise 17C

1 a i 19.9 ii 13.3

b i 32.4 ii 37.3

c i 2.34 ii 4.44

2 141

3 3.61 kg

4 a 0.0548 b 154.2

5 a 0.691 b 39.7

c 0.240

6 99.7%

7 90

8 3.29

Tip

Did you try sketching a graph? What is the probability of being below $\mu+\alpha$?

9 a 1 b 0.741

10 0

11 $2\Phi(k)-1$

12 Investigation

Work it out 17.1

Answer = Solution 1

Exercise 17D

1 a i 5.68  ii 7.32

b i 43.4 ii 15.3

2 a i $\mu=8.91, \sigma=2.27$

ii $\mu=130, \sigma=38.6$

b i $\mu=-0.201, \sigma=1.19$

ii $\mu=870, \sigma=202$

3 1.97 cm

4 3.56

5 $\mu=70.6, \sigma=25.8$

6 $\mu=25.9, \sigma=16.2$

7 3.23 hours

8 11.2

9 9.22×10^{-4}

10 70.6%

Exercise 17E

1 a Yes

b No, not symmetrical.

c No, two modes.

d No, not a characteristic bell curve.

2 Three standard deviations below the mean would be –0.9 children, so the normal model would predict impossible results.

3 a 15; 17

b Mean: 50.1, standard deviation: 3.87

c Symmetric, bell-shaped curve

d About 10 students

4 a i 0.0176 ii 0.0228

b 29.3%

5 a 0.344 b 3.12×10^{-5}

6 $X \leqslant 645$

7 a Proof b 120

8 Proof

Mixed practice 17

1 a 6.68% b 62

2 a 5 b 1.36kg

3 3.85

4 2.32

5 i 9.51 ii accept 0.338, 0.346 or 0.396

6 0.149

7 a 0.249 b 0.935

8 a Proof b 68.1, 16.5

9 $\mu = 31.4, \sigma = 4.52$

10 i a Probabilities don't add up to 1.

b $P(X > 70)$ must be the smaller one.

c $P(X > 70) = 0.7$, but this should be the smaller one.

ii 60, 19.1

11 a It is roughly symmetric. Mean $\frac{n}{2}$, Variance $\frac{n}{4}$.

b 0.234%

c No, probably not independent.

12 a Within 3 standard deviations of the mean are scores from 18% to 90%, which are all possible. The mean is about the same as the median, suggesting a symmetrical distribution.

b Distinction: 64.1%, Merit: 54%, Pass: 38.6%

13 a 0.0853 b 1.46

14 a $\mu = 1.29, \sigma = 0.554$

b $\mu = 1.36, \sigma = 0.764$

Chapter 18

Before you start...

1 A3; B2; C1

2 $p = 0.0697 < 0.10$, reject H_0.

3 a 0.9332 b 0.8351

c 198.3

Exercise 18A

1 a i N(4, 25) ii N(20, 25)

b i N(0, 0.1) ii N(0, 2.5)

2 a i 0.655 ii 0.788

b i 0.942 ii 0.471

3 a N(40, 0.25), assuming independence of emissions.

b 0.159

c 0.955

4 0.788

5 0.0228

6 78.7 g

7 608

8 6.62

9 a 0.138 b 15

c 4.73

10 a 0.9996 b 0.822

Work it out 18.1

Answer = Solution 2

Exercise 18B

1 a i $H_0: \mu = 102; H_1: \mu \neq 102$

ii $H_0: \mu = 1.2; H_1: \mu \neq 1.2$

b i $H_0: \mu = 250; H_1: \mu < 250$

ii $H_0: \mu = 150\,000; H_1: \mu > 150\,000$

c i $H_0: \mu_T = 3000; H_1: \mu_T > 3000$

ii $H_0: \mu = 28; H_1: \mu < 28$

2 a i $55.1 < \overline{X} < 64.9$ **ii** $117 < \overline{X} < 123$

b i $\overline{X} < 85.5$ **ii** $\overline{X} < 753$

c i $\overline{X} > 79.2$ **ii** $\overline{X} > 92.2$

3 a i 0.0455, reject H_0.

ii 0.0578, do not reject H_0.

b i 0.0228, reject H_0.

ii 0.0288, reject H_0.

c i 0.0625, do not reject H_0.

ii 0.147, do not reject H_0.

d i 0.404*t*, do not reject H_0.

ii 0.611, do not reject H_0.

4 a $H_0: \mu = 168.8$, $H_1: \mu > 168.8$

b $p = 0.193$, do not reject H_0.

5 $p = 0.0918$, reject H_0.

6 a The scores of students in the school follow a normal distribution. The standard deviation is still 1.21.

b $p = 0.320$, do not reject H_0.

7 a $H_0: \mu = 2.7$; $H_1: \mu \neq 2.7$

b $\overline{X} < 2.53$ or $\overline{X} > 2.87$

c Reject H_0.

8 a $\overline{X} < 80.3$

b The weights follow a normal distribution.

c Reject H_0.

9 a No ($p = 0.146$) **b** 25

10 Higher p-value if $\mu \neq 30$, as you have the probability from both tails.

Exercise 18C

1 a i Significant evidence

ii Significant evidence

b i No significant evidence

ii No significant evidence

2 a i No significant evidence

ii No significant evidence

b i Significant evidence

ii Significant evidence

3 a $H_0: \rho = 0$; $H_1: \rho \neq 0$

b Reject H_0.

4 a $H_0: \rho = 0$; $H_1: \rho > 0$

b Do not reject H_0.

5 a All countries in 2016.

b $H_0: \rho = 0$; $H_1: \rho < 0$

c Reject H_0.

6 a $H_0: \rho = 0$; $H_1: \rho \neq 0$

b Reject H_0.

c No, correlation does not imply causation and the test was not for positive correlation.

7 a $H_0: \rho = 0$; $H_1: \rho < 0$

b Reject H_0.

c Less likely to get a false positive, which would result in a useless drug being used.

8 a Significant evidence

b $p = 0.064$; no significant evidence

c Decrease

9 25

10 When $n = 2$ the correlation coefficient is always 1 or −1.

Mixed practice 18

1 C

2 0.285

3 a All countries in 2016.

b $H_0: \rho = 0$; $H_1: \rho \neq 0$

c Do not reject H_0.

4 a $H_0: \mu = 300$; $H_1: \mu \neq 300$

b 0.244; do not reject H_0.

5 D

6 a Both variables must be normally distributed.

b Reject H_0.

7 a Still normally distributed. Still standard deviation 5 seconds. $\overline{X} < 37.4$.

b Reject H_0.

c They would not be independent – the water needs to cool down to the original temperature.

8 $p = 0.0968$; reject H_0; Sufficient evidence that the mean number of visitor has fallen.

9 D

Tip

Many people think that p-values are a direct measure of how likely H_0 is to be true. Make sure you do not fall into this trap.

10 a H_0: $\mu=5.84$; H_1: $\mu\neq5.84$

b $5.84-\frac{0.608}{\sqrt{n}}<\bar{X}<5.84+\frac{0.608}{\sqrt{n}}$ c 7

11 a H_0: $\mu=6.4$; H_1: $\mu\neq6.4$ b 10%

12 256

Focus on… Proof 3

1 Very small ($<$1 in 1 000 000)

2 a

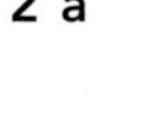

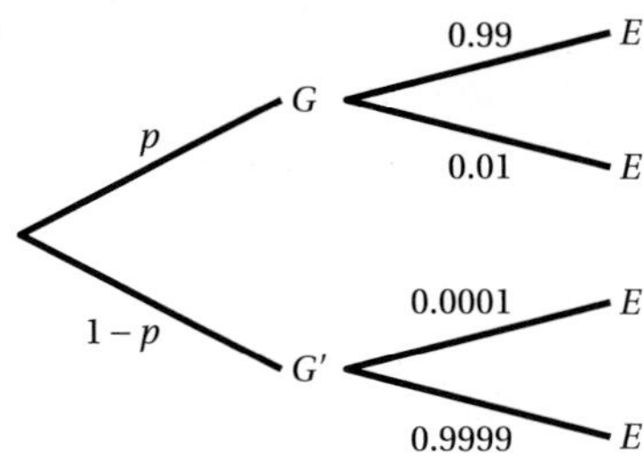

b i $0.0001+0.9899p$

ii $P(G|E)=\frac{9900p}{1+9899p}$; $P(G'|E)=\frac{1-p}{1+9899p}$.

c The argument is flawed.

3 p is the probability of an arbitrary person being guilty.

4 The relative likelihood is reversed.

5 No, because he is either guilty or not, irrespective of whether evidence has been found.

6 $P(E\,|\,G')=0.0001$; $P(E'\,|\,G')=0.9999$

7 In legal matters, some alternative explanation may still have non-zero probability, so some doubt remains. Mathematical proof can be absolute.

Focus on … Problem solving 3

1 Investigation

2

		You choose			
		1	2	3	
Host opens	1	0	0	0	0
	2	50	0	100	150
	3	50	100	0	150
		100	100	100	300

P(win if switch) $=\frac{200}{300}=\frac{2}{3}$.

3 a Proof

b Larger, because we already know that there are 9 girls.

c

		First child	
		girl	boy
Second child	girl	¼	¼
	boy	¼	¼

P(two girls | at least one girl) $=\frac{1}{3}$.

Focus on … Modelling 3

1 a

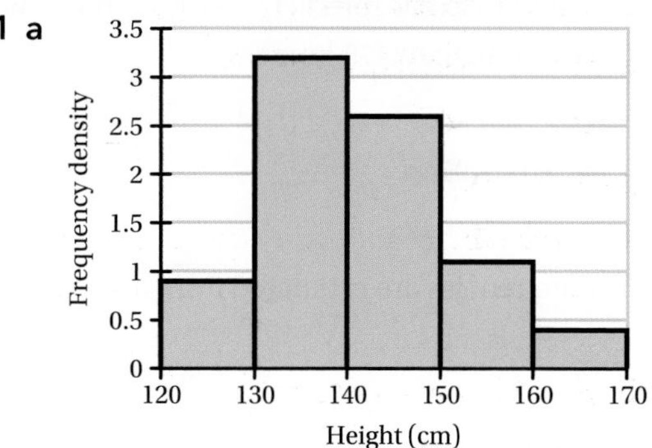

b No, not symmetrical

2 a 99.7%

b Mean ≈ 44, SD ≈ 5.93; IQR ≈ 8

c It could be a suitable model (the IQR of the data is 8 and the box plot looks symmetrical.)

3 a Yes   b No

4 It is discrete, but the normal distribution is continuous.

5 a It is likely that the distribution would not be symmetrical, as the minimum possible length of a phone call is 0 (cannot be less than 0), but the maximum can be more than 11.6 minutes.

b i Yes

ii No; bimodal

iii No; discrete

6 a Curves 1 and 2   b Curve 1

Cross-topic review exercise 3

1 $\frac{5}{6}$

2 a $H_0: \rho=0$, $H_1: \rho \neq 0$

b Do not reject H_0; there is no significant evidence of correlation between temperature and rainfall.

3 a $H_0: \mu=86$; $H_1: \mu>86$.

b There is evidence that they're taller ($p=0.0294<0.05$)

4 a 48.2 b 0.0672

c Not reasonable; predicts nearly all bulbs will last more than 475 hours.

5 i 0.88 ii 0.3

6 i $40=\mu-0.954\sigma$

ii $\mu=51.7, \sigma=12.3$

iii Frequencies are estimated from a sample.

7 $3\frac{1}{3}$

8 a $\frac{3}{20}$ b $\frac{9}{35}$

c $\frac{7}{12}$

9 a Proof b $\frac{1}{6}\left(\frac{5}{6}\right)^{r-1}$

c Proof

10 i 0.3 ii 0.28

11 a 0.202 b 0.934

c 0.103

12 a 0.34134 b 0.34078

c 0.164%

13 a $\mu \approx 83.5, \sigma \approx 8.5$

b $p \approx 0.03, n \approx 2780$ (a range of answers is acceptable)

14 a $H_0: \rho=0$, $H_1: \rho<0$

b Reject H_0. Significant evidence of negative correlation; as the amount of time increases the test marks decrease.

c The two sections of the scatter graph represent two different students; for each student there is positive correlation, but one student got better marks despite spending less time on revision.

15 i $\sigma=5\sqrt{n}$

ii Binya is right; $P(\bar{X}>32)=0.0808$

16 a $\frac{1}{5}$ b $\frac{4}{25}$

c $\frac{16}{125}$ d Proof

e $\frac{4}{9}$ f 0.8

17 a Reject H_0, sufficient evidence that the mean time has decreased ($z=-2.72, p=0.0033$)

b 90

18 a $x=5$ or 9. b 0.0968

c No, because some of the trapezia are above and some below the curve.

Chapter 19

Before you start...

1 a $\begin{pmatrix}-3\\-2\end{pmatrix}$ b $\begin{pmatrix}11\\-3\end{pmatrix}$

c $\begin{pmatrix}32\\-20\end{pmatrix}$ d $\begin{pmatrix}5\\-7\end{pmatrix}$

2 $\sqrt{13}$; 146° from horizontal

3 a -12 m s^{-1} b 48 m s^{-1}

4 0.333 m s^{-2}

5 a 34.2 b $x=2e^t-\frac{1}{3}t^3-2$

6 $x=-1+4y-2y^2$

Exercise 19A

1 a i $(-\mathbf{i}+1.67\mathbf{j})\text{ m s}^{-1}$

ii $(-2.25\mathbf{i}+\mathbf{j})\text{ m s}^{-1}$

b i $(1.2\mathbf{i}+0.25\mathbf{j})\text{ m s}^{-1}$

ii $(0.75\mathbf{i}-1.25\mathbf{j})\text{ m s}^{-1}$

c i $(-1.13\mathbf{i}+0.5\mathbf{j})\text{ m s}^{-1}$

ii $(0.545\mathbf{i}+0.091\mathbf{j})\text{ m s}^{-1}$

2 a i $(0.2\mathbf{i}+0.5\mathbf{j})\text{ m s}^{-2}$; 0.539 m s^{-2}

ii $(0.5\mathbf{i}+0.625\mathbf{j})\text{ m s}^{-2}$; 0.800 m s^{-2}

b i $(0.8\mathbf{i}-0.4\mathbf{j})\text{ m s}^{-2}$; 0.894 m s^{-2}

ii $(-0.3\mathbf{i}+0.4\mathbf{j})\text{ m s}^{-2}$; 0.5 m s^{-2}

3 a $(1.5\mathbf{i}+0.33\mathbf{j})\text{ m s}^{-1}$; 1.54 m s^{-1}

b $(0\mathbf{i}+0\mathbf{j})\text{ m s}^{-1}$; 1.24 m s^{-1}

4 a 6.08 m b $y=x^2+6x+11$

5 a 2.11 m s^{-2}

b 128° from horizontal

6 a 0.95 m s^{-1} b $(6\mathbf{i}-2\mathbf{j})$ m

c $(0.316\mathbf{i}-0.105\mathbf{j})\text{ m s}^{-1}$

d 0.972 m s^{-1}; the particle changes direction during the motion

7 $\begin{pmatrix}8\\2\end{pmatrix}$ m

8 a 9.22 m

b

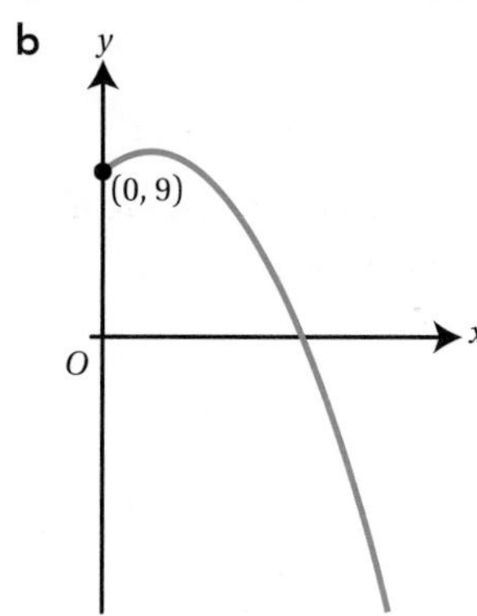

9 a $x+2y=-5$ b $\sqrt{5}=2.24$ m

10 4 m

Work it out 19.1

Answer = Solution 3

Exercise 19B

1 a i $\begin{pmatrix}0.6\\1.8\end{pmatrix}\text{ m s}^{-1}$

ii $(12.4\mathbf{i}-2.2\mathbf{j})\text{ m s}^{-1}$

b i $(-6.25\mathbf{i}-7.5\mathbf{j})$ m ii $(6.3\mathbf{i}+0.15\mathbf{j})$ m

c i $(-3\mathbf{i}-4.5\mathbf{j})\text{ m s}^{-1}$

ii $(1.67\mathbf{i}-2.33\mathbf{j})\text{ m s}^{-1}$

d i 2 s ii 6 s

2 $\mathbf{v}=(7.7\mathbf{i}-0.4\mathbf{j})\text{ m s}^{-1}$, $\mathbf{s}=(39.2\mathbf{i}+7\mathbf{j})$ m

3 a 22.1 m

b 10.3° from horizontal

4 a $(-2\mathbf{i}+1.5\mathbf{j})\text{ m s}^{-2}$ b 4 s

5 1.02 m s^{-2}

6 153° from horizontal

7 1.89 m s^{-2}

8 10 s

9 Proof

10 4.92 m

Work it out 19.2

Answer = Solution 2

Exercise 19C

1 a i $\mathbf{v}=(3-\cos t)\mathbf{i}+(1-2t)\mathbf{j}$, $\mathbf{a}=(\sin t)\mathbf{i}-2\mathbf{j}$, $v(3)=6.40$

ii $\mathbf{v}=(2e^{2t}-1)\mathbf{i}+(2t+2e^{2t})\mathbf{j}$, $\mathbf{a}=(4e^{2t})\mathbf{i}+(2+4e^{2t})\mathbf{j}$, $v(3)=1145$

b i $\mathbf{v}=(-12\sin(3t))\mathbf{i}+(6\cos(2t))\mathbf{j}$, $\mathbf{a}=(-36\cos(3t))\mathbf{i}-(12\sin(2t))\mathbf{j}$, $v(3)=7.59$

ii $\mathbf{v}=\left(\frac{3}{t+1}-1\right)\mathbf{i}+\left(2t+\frac{1}{t+1}\right)\mathbf{j}$,

$\mathbf{a}=\left(-\frac{3}{(t+1)^2}\right)\mathbf{i}+\left(2-\frac{1}{(t+1)^2}\right)\mathbf{j}$, $v(3)=6.25$

2 a i $\mathbf{v}=\left(3t-\frac{1}{3}t^3+2\right)\mathbf{i}+(t^2+5)\mathbf{j}$,

$\mathbf{s}=\left(\frac{3}{2}t^2-\frac{1}{12}t^4+2t\right)\mathbf{i}+\left(\frac{1}{3}t^3+5t\right)\mathbf{j}$, $|\mathbf{s}(3)|=27.2$

ii $\mathbf{v}=\left(\frac{1}{2}t^2+t+1\right)\mathbf{i}+(t-2)\mathbf{j}$,

$\mathbf{s}=\left(\frac{1}{6}t^3+\frac{1}{2}t^2+t\right)\mathbf{i}+\left(\frac{1}{2}t^2-2t\right)\mathbf{j}$, $|\mathbf{s}(3)|=12.1$

b i $\mathbf{v}=(3e^t-4)\mathbf{i}+(-2e^{-t}+3)\mathbf{j}$, $\mathbf{s}=(3e^t-4t-3)\mathbf{i}+(2e^{-t}+3t-2)\mathbf{j}$, $|\mathbf{s}(3)|=45.8$

ii $\mathbf{v}=\left(-\frac{3}{2}\cos(2t)+\frac{3}{2}\right)\mathbf{i}+\left(\frac{3}{2}\sin(2t)\right)\mathbf{j}$,

$\mathbf{s}=\left(-\frac{3}{4}\sin(2t)+\frac{3}{2}t\right)\mathbf{i}+\left(-\frac{3}{4}\cos(2t)+\frac{3}{4}\right)\mathbf{j}$,

$|\mathbf{s}(3)|=4.71$

c i $\mathbf{v}=(2\sin t)\mathbf{i}+(-3\cos t+3)\mathbf{j}$, $\mathbf{s}=(-2\cos t+2)\mathbf{i}+(-3\sin t+3t)\mathbf{j}$, $|\mathbf{s}(3)|=9.46$

ii $\mathbf{v}=\left(\frac{1}{2}e^{2t}-\frac{1}{2}\right)\mathbf{i}+(3e^t-3)\mathbf{j}$,

$\mathbf{s}=\left(\frac{1}{4}e^{2t}-\frac{1}{2}t-\frac{1}{4}\right)\mathbf{i}+(3e^{3t}-3t-3)\mathbf{j}$,

$|\mathbf{s}(3)|=24\,300$

3 a i 20.6 m s^{-1} ii 58.3 m s^{-1}

b i 221 m s^{-1} ii 94.9 m s^{-1}

4 a $\mathbf{v}=(2e^{2t})\mathbf{i}+\mathbf{j}$ b $44\,053\text{ m s}^{-1}$

5 a $\mathbf{v}=\begin{pmatrix}3t^2\\\frac{1}{2}\sin(2t)\end{pmatrix}$ b $\begin{pmatrix}27\\0.00996\end{pmatrix}$ m

6 a 3.61 m s^{-1} b 3.72 m s^{-2}

c $\left(3t+\frac{1}{2}\cos(2t)-\frac{1}{2}\right)\mathbf{i}+(\sin(2t))\mathbf{j}$

7 $(3\mathbf{i}+0.5\mathbf{j})\ \text{m s}^{-1}$

8 2.35 m

9 Proof

10 4

11 $p=-1, q=2$

12 a $\frac{5}{7}$ b $\begin{pmatrix}77\\55\end{pmatrix}$

13 a Proof b Proof

14 1.06 s, 2.18 m

Exercise 19D

1 a i $\begin{pmatrix}4\\0\\0\end{pmatrix}$ ii $\begin{pmatrix}0\\-5\\0\end{pmatrix}$

b i $\begin{pmatrix}3\\0\\1\end{pmatrix}$ ii $\begin{pmatrix}0\\2\\-1\end{pmatrix}$

2 a i $\begin{pmatrix}21\\3\\36\end{pmatrix}$ ii $\begin{pmatrix}20\\-8\\12\end{pmatrix}$

b i $\begin{pmatrix}2\\3\\9\end{pmatrix}$ ii $\begin{pmatrix}6\\-1\\5\end{pmatrix}$

c i $\begin{pmatrix}11\\-3\\8\end{pmatrix}$ ii $\begin{pmatrix}-3\\5\\6\end{pmatrix}$

d i $\begin{pmatrix}10\\-3\\11\end{pmatrix}$ ii $\begin{pmatrix}17\\6\\35\end{pmatrix}$

3 a i $-5\mathbf{i}+5\mathbf{k}$ ii $4\mathbf{i}+8\mathbf{j}$

b i $\mathbf{i}-3\mathbf{j}+3\mathbf{k}$ ii $2\mathbf{j}+\mathbf{k}$

c i $4\mathbf{i}+7\mathbf{k}$ ii $5\mathbf{i}-4\mathbf{j}+15\mathbf{k}$

4 a $|\mathbf{a}|=\sqrt{21}$ b $|\mathbf{b}|=\sqrt{2}$

c $|\mathbf{c}|=\sqrt{21}$ d $|\mathbf{d}|=\sqrt{2}$

5 a i $\sqrt{19}$ ii $\sqrt{38}$

b i $\sqrt{74}$ ii $\sqrt{13}$

6 a $\sqrt{53}$ b $\sqrt{94}$

c $\sqrt{53}$ d $\sqrt{2}$

7 a $-4\mathbf{i}+2\mathbf{j}-\mathbf{k}$ b $-\frac{8}{3}\mathbf{i}+\frac{4}{3}\mathbf{j}-\frac{2}{3}\mathbf{k}$

c $4\mathbf{i}-3\mathbf{j}+\mathbf{k}$ d $-\frac{1}{2}\mathbf{i}+\mathbf{j}-\frac{1}{2}\mathbf{k}$

8 $\begin{pmatrix}2\\0\\-\frac{3}{4}\end{pmatrix}$

9 -2

10 $\pm2\sqrt{6}$

11 $3, -\frac{5}{3}$

12 $-2, -\frac{23}{15}$

13 $t=\frac{1}{3}; d=\sqrt{\frac{14}{3}}$

Exercise 19E

1 a i $\frac{1}{3}\begin{pmatrix}2\\2\\1\end{pmatrix}$ ii $\frac{1}{3}\begin{pmatrix}2\\2\\-1\end{pmatrix}$

b i $\frac{1}{\sqrt{3}}\begin{pmatrix}1\\1\\-1\end{pmatrix}$ ii $\frac{1}{5}\begin{pmatrix}4\\-1\\2\sqrt{2}\end{pmatrix}$

2 a $\begin{pmatrix}1\\-3\\7\end{pmatrix}$ b $\begin{pmatrix}3.5\\-0.5\\1.5\end{pmatrix}$

3 $\begin{pmatrix}0\\-1\\6\end{pmatrix}$

4 $-\frac{4}{3}$

5 -2

6 $\begin{pmatrix}1.6\\0.8\\1.8\end{pmatrix}$

7 a $\frac{3}{2}\mathbf{i}+\frac{3}{2}\mathbf{j}-2\mathbf{k}$ b $\left(\frac{1}{2},\frac{13}{2},0\right)$

8 $p=\frac{3}{8}, q=\frac{1}{8}$

9 a $\begin{pmatrix}4\sqrt{2}\\-\sqrt{2}\\\sqrt{2}\end{pmatrix}$ b $\begin{pmatrix}\sqrt{6}\\-\sqrt{1.5}\\\sqrt{1.5}\end{pmatrix}$

10 $\mathbf{m}=\frac{q}{p+q}\mathbf{a}+\frac{p}{p+q}\mathbf{b}$

11 a Proof b Proof

Mixed practice 19

1 a 9.77 N

b 6.08 m s^{-1}; 9.46° from the horizontal

2 $\frac{3}{2}$

3 a $-5\mathbf{i}+4\mathbf{j}-2\mathbf{k}$ b Proof

4 6.25 m s^{-1}

5 a Proof b $3\mathbf{i}+6\mathbf{j}+19\mathbf{k}$

6 0.569 s

7 a 14° b 22 s

c It stays at a constant height

8 $\frac{\sqrt{474}}{5}$

9 57.4° below the horizontal

10 a $\begin{pmatrix} 3t \\ 4t \end{pmatrix}$ b $\begin{pmatrix} 3t \\ 18-5t \end{pmatrix}$

c Proof d $t=2$

e 2 hours

11 a $(3t)\mathbf{i}+(5-4t)\mathbf{j}+t\mathbf{k}$

b $d^2=44t^2-88t+74$ c $\sqrt{30}$ km, or 5.48 km

12 a $4x^2+25y^2=100$

b 5 m s^{-1} when $\mathbf{s}=\pm 2\mathbf{j}$

13 8.96 m

Chapter 20

Before you start...

1 $\sqrt{13}$ at 146° from vector **i**

2 0.333 m s^{-2}

3 $(6\mathbf{i}+2\mathbf{j})$ m s^{-1}

4 $\frac{1}{2}\sin 2x$

5 45°, 124°

Exercise 20A

1 a i $(5\mathbf{i}+1.4\mathbf{j})$ m s^{-1} ii $(7\mathbf{i}-13.6\mathbf{j})$ m s^{-1}

b i $(8\mathbf{i}-22.6\mathbf{j})$ m s^{-1} ii $(4\mathbf{i}-28.6\mathbf{j})$ m s^{-1}

c i $(10.7\mathbf{i}-10.6\mathbf{j})$ m s^{-1} ii $(10.6\mathbf{i}+3.1\mathbf{j})$ m s^{-1}

d i $(6.6\mathbf{i}-24.2\mathbf{j})$ m s^{-1} ii $(19.7\mathbf{i}-23.1\mathbf{j})$ m s^{-1}

2 a i $10\mathbf{i}+22\mathbf{j}$ ii $14\mathbf{i}-7.6\mathbf{j}$

b i $16\mathbf{i}-26\mathbf{j}$ ii $8\mathbf{i}-38\mathbf{j}$

c i $21.4\mathbf{i}-1.6\mathbf{j}$ ii $21.2\mathbf{i}+26\mathbf{j}$

d i $13\mathbf{i}-29\mathbf{j}$ ii $39.4\mathbf{i}-27\mathbf{j}$

3 a 0.772 m b 9.21 m s^{-1}

4 a 0.245 s

b 13.3 m s^{-1}; 67.9° below the horizontal.

5 a 12.0 m b 40.2 m

6 63°

7 0.714 s

8 a 4.12 s b 81.5 m

c 28.5 m s^{-1}

9 Yes; height is 1.8 m at that point.

10 a 15.6 m b 25.7° or 64.3°

11 a Proof

b $24.1° < a < 25.8°$ or $64.2° < \alpha < 65.9°$.

12 a Ten-times that of normal.

b Slowed down.

Work it out 20.1

Answer = Solution 2

Exercise 20B

1 $y=-\frac{49}{640}x^2$

2 a Proof b 19.4 m s^{-1}

c No air resistance; rugby ball is a particle (we ignore its size).

3 a Proof b Yes

4 a Proof

b i Proof ii 12.9 m s^{-1}

5 $u=29.3$ m s^{-1}, $\theta=53.1°$.

6 a Proof

b 28.8° or 70.7°; it must be falling when it goes through the hoop.

Mixed practice 20

1 15.7 m s^{-1}, 63.4° below the horizontal

2 C

3 a 2.47 s b 29.7 m

4 a 2.5 s b 25.9 m

5 a 18 m b 15 m s^{-1}

6 a i, ii Proof b 21°, 69°

7 1.76 m

8 a 1.43 s b 0.816 s

9 i Proof

ii $t_P = 15.5$ s, $t_Q = 10.8$ s

iii 622 m, 78.2 m s^{-1}, 42.8°

10 i Proof ii 47.3 m

iii 68.8° below horizontal iv 33.5 m s^{-1}

11 2 m

12 i 43.3°, 11.2 m ii 53.1°, falling

Chapter 21

Before you start...

1 $\mathbf{F} = 3\mathbf{i} + \mathbf{j}$; magnitude 3.16 N; angle 18.4° from direction **i**

2 34.6 N

3 2 seconds

Exercise 21A

1 a i $7.33\mathbf{i} + 4.5\mathbf{j}$ ii $16.6\mathbf{i} - 10.1\mathbf{j}$

b i $-2.19\mathbf{i} - 0.167\mathbf{j}$ ii $3.62\mathbf{j}$

2 a i $T_1 = 278$ N, $T_2 = 282$ N

ii $T_1 = T_2 = 78.4$ N

b i $T_1 = 58.1$ N, $T_2 = 109$ N

ii $T_1 = 111$ N, $T_2 = 120$ N

3 $15.4\mathbf{i} - 24\mathbf{j}$

4 a 41.8° b 112 N

5 a Proof b 68.2° c 5.39

6 $k = 80.5$ N, $a = 4.05$ m s^{-2}

7 a i 28.1° ii 17 N

b i 32.2° ii 12.7 N

8 7.17 N, 8.79 N

9 a They are two parts of the same string.

b 4.53 N, 83.7°

10 a $19.6\sqrt{2}$ N b $\theta° = S\hat{A}R - 45°$

c $F = 27.7$ N, $SAR = 43°$

Exercise 21B

1 a i 0.24 ii 0.005

b i 0.9 ii 0.1

2 9000 N

3 a 0.408 b 15.9 N

4 2.75 m s^{-2}

5 a 0.625 b $\frac{g}{14}$ m s^{-2}

6 $\mu_A = \frac{1}{3}$, $\mu_B = \frac{2}{3}$

7 a 6.25 m s^{-2} b 0.625

8 a Proof b 46.4 N

9 Proof

10 a $\alpha = \tan^{-1}\left(\frac{4}{3}\right) = 53.1°$

b $25.4° < t < 48.3°$ c 0.15 m s^{-2}

11 c and d only.

Exercise 21C

1 a i 0 N ii 0 N

b i 4.9 N ii 10.1 N

c i 1.96 N ii 3.46 N

2 a i A: 0 N; B: 0.613 m s^{-2} up the slope

ii A: 0 N; B: 1.63 m s^{-2} down the slope

b i A: 11.1 N up the slope; B: 0.742 m s^{-2} up the slope

ii A: 18.9 N up the slope; B: 0 m s^{-2}

c i A: 14.7 N up the slope; B: 0 m s^{-2}

ii A: 17.2 N up the slope; B: 2.58 m s^{-2} down the slope

3 a 43.3 N b 30 m

4 a 225 N

b i 6.30 m s^{-2} ii 5.55 m s^{-2}

5 24.2°

6 a 3.55 m b 0.888 s c 1.21 s

7 a 4.66 m s^{-2} b 3.66 m

8 a 0.9 b 9.49 m

9 0.78 seconds

10 a Proof

b $T - 0.9g\sqrt{2} - F = 2a_R$

c Up the slope with magnitude 1.87 N

d Down the slope, with acceleration 0.267 m s^{-2}

11 a 10.6 m s^{-2} b 14.3 m s^{-2}

c 5.71°

12 $\mu \geqslant 0.47$

13 Proof.

Exercise 21D

1 a i $F = 12.8$ N, $\theta = 141°$

ii $F = 9.43$ N, $\theta = 122°$

b i $F_1 = 15.4$ N, $F_2 = 7.83$ N

ii $F_1 = 12.3$ N, $F_2 = 11.3$ N

c i $\theta_1 = 160°, \theta_2 = 157°$

ii $\theta_1 = 144°, \theta_2 = 63°$

2 9 N, 15.6 N

3 Proof

4 a 20° **b** 0.364

5 137° and 147°

6 $\alpha = 30°, \beta = 49°$

Mixed practice 21

1 a $0.773\,\text{m s}^{-2}$

b Acceleration would be less

2 a $10.4\,\text{m s}^{-2}$ **b** 18.8 N

3 a 14 N **b** 18 N, 2 N.

4 $4.14\,\text{m s}^{-2}$

5 a 0.327 **b** $11.3\,\text{m s}^{-1}$

6 a 5.90 N **b** 57.9°

7 a

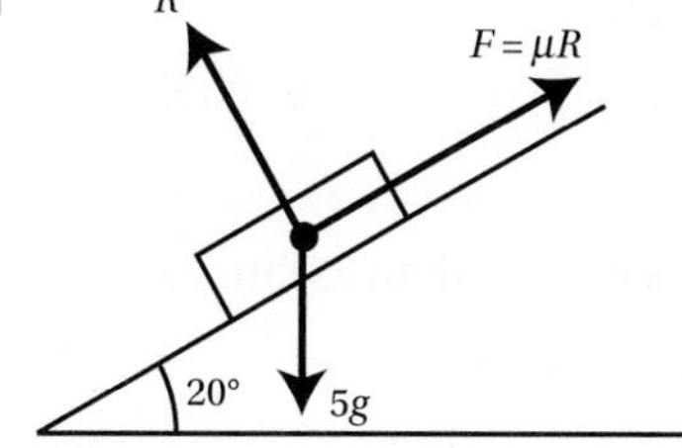

b $0.13\,\text{m s}^{-2}$

c 0.35

d No air resistance force acting; no other forces acting on the box; no turning effect (due to forces).

8 a Proof

b $4.86\,\text{m s}^{-2}$

c The acceleration is reduced because of air resistance or the fact that there is friction.

9 i Proof **ii** 7.8 N

iii To the right

10 i Proof **ii** 016.2°

11 i Proof **ii** 0.107

12 a 23.5 N **b** $1.96\,\text{m s}^{-2}$

c 39.2 N

13 a 6.97 N **b** 106 N

14 a 3.1 N, 0.365 **b** $1.8\,\text{m s}^{-2}$

15 a $28.5\,\text{m s}^{-1}$ directed down the slope.

b 0.699 m

16 Proof

17 a 0.26

b Less friction, so a smaller coefficient of friction.

18 i a 0.849 N, 0.49 N **b** 1.73

ii 4.36 N, $1.09\,\text{m s}^{-2}$

19 i Because the ring is smooth.

ii $T\cos\theta + 5 = T\sin\theta$, $T\cos\theta + T\sin\theta = 7$

iii 6.08 N. 80.5°

20 i Proof

ii a 12.25 N, 4.08 N **b** $0.107\,\text{m s}^{-2}$

iii 2.45 N

21 i a 9.40 N, 3.42 N **b** Proof

ii 15.2 N

22 a $a = 1.96\left(\mu\left(\sqrt{3} + 3\sqrt{2}\right) - 1 + 1.5\sqrt{2}\right)$ (in direction of A moving upslope)

b Yes; 7.51 seconds after the start of movement.

23 i Proof

ii a $10.8\,\text{m s}^{-2}$ **b** $1.79\,\text{m s}^{-2}$

iii a 0.370 **b** 1.28 s

24 i 6 m **ii** $5.93\,\text{m s}^{-1}$

iii 1.2 N **iv** 0.825

Chapter 22

Before you start...

1

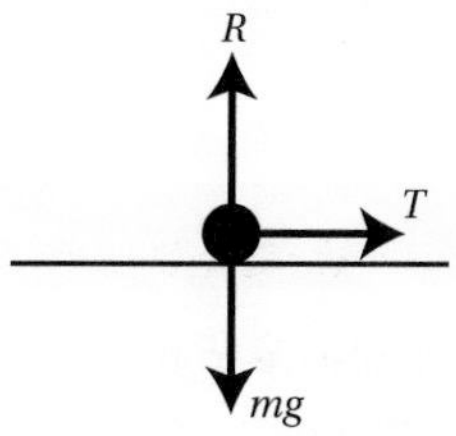

2 7 N

Exercise 22A

1 a i 1.5 N m anticlockwise

ii 1 N m clockwise

b i 3 N m clockwise

ii 4 N m anticlockwise

c i 0 N m   ii 0 N m

2 a i 7.5 N m clockwise

ii 14 N m anticlockwise

b i 15 N m anticlockwise

ii 3 N m clockwise

c i 0 N m

ii 0 N m

3 a i 100 N m clockwise

ii 50 N m clockwise

b i 0   ii 8 N m clockwise

c i 50 N m anticlockwise

ii 100 N m anticlockwise

4 a i 450 N m clockwise

ii 450 N m anticlockwise

b i 350 N m clockwise

ii 750 N m clockwise

c i 850 N m clockwise

ii 650 N m clockwise

d i 350 N m anticlockwise

ii 150 N m anticlockwise

e i 450 N m anticlockwise

ii 350 N m clockwise

5 0.9 N m clockwise

6 250 N m clockwise

7 a 3600 N m

b Since there is no bending, the diver is 3 m from the other end.

8 3 N m

9 Proof

Tip

Write a general point (x, y) relative to the bottom left corner of the square.

10 0.183 N m

Work it out 22.1

Answer = Solution 3

Exercise 22B

1 a i $x=9, y=10$ ii $x=5.5, y=40$

b i $x=21.4, y=28.6$ ii $x=20, y=30$

2 a i $T_1=100, T_2=T_3=83.3$

ii $T_1=100, T_2=T_3=100$

b i $T_1=100, T_2=T_3=66.7$

ii $T_1=100, T_2=T_3=10$

c i $x=2$ ii $x=8$

3 0.5 m

4 60 N

5 a 0.333 m

b The crane attachment would be able to handle some net moment.

6 37.5 N, 12.5 N

7 300 N, 700 N

8 a $\frac{80}{x}$ and $\frac{80}{x}-40$.

b That the pole is straight.

9 21.7 N, 3.3 N

10 30 kg

11 a $1.5(25-x)$ b 60 N

c $1.5(25-x)$

d x could be greater than 25 cm.

12 At X: 90 N; at Y: 175 N

13 1.67 m

Exercise 22C

1 9.41 N, 29.8 N

2 80 cm from each support

3 66.7 cm

4 2 m or 6 m

5 2.38 kg

6 55 cm

7 74.3 cm

8 220 N and 260 N

Exercise 22D

1 a i 15 N m clockwise

ii 52 N m anticlockwise

b i 77 N m anticlockwise

ii 115 N m anticlockwise

c i 80 N m anticlockwise

ii 64 N m clockwise

d i 51 N m anticlockwise

ii 282 N m anticlockwise

2 26.0 N

3 21.8°

4 0.182

5 29.4°

6 3.01 m

Mixed practice 22

1 0 N m

2 26 N

3 0.625 m

4 75 cm

5 49.7°

6 i 36.8 N ii 0.400

7 1.75 m

8 1.92 m

9 a 315 N b 1.44 m

10 a 60 N b 2.375 m

11 a Proof

b $W=60$ N, $x=1.6$ m

12 a Proof b $0 \leqslant x < \frac{11}{4}$

13 $\frac{M-m}{M+m}$

14 $20x$

15 a Proof b 3.27 m s^{-2}

c There are no resistive forces other than the friction.

16 a 15 N b 15 N upwards.

Focus on… Proof 4

1 μW

2 Proof

3 a $\sqrt{1+\mu^2}$; $F_{min} = \frac{\mu}{\sqrt{1+\mu^2}} Ws$

b Proof

4 a Proof b Proof

Focus on … Problem solving 4

The answers that are clearly wrong are: 1, 2, 4, 5, 7, 9, 10, and 11.

Focus on … Modelling 4

1 10^{23} m

2 The gravitational acceleration on Archimedes' planet is also 9.8 m s^{-2}.

3 We need the support to be further away from the point where the Earth is resting on the lever. If this distance is increased to d m, the length of the other end would need to be $d \times 10^{23}$ m.

4 5×10^{-16} m

Cross-topic review exercise 4

1 7.54g N, 9.49g N

2 a $-3i+3j-6\kappa$

b $3\sqrt{6}$

3 a $v=(5+2e^{-2t})\mathbf{i}+(0.1e0.1t)^{j}$

b 5.27 m s^{-1}, 1.4° above horizontal

c i 0.54 m s^{-2} ii 2.7 N

4 a (−5, 1, 0) b Proof

c (8, −7, 9)

5 a 0.225 m to the right of the support

b 107.8 N

6 i 73.3°, 0.7 N

ii 12 m s^{-2}, bearing 090°

7 Proof

8 $a=\frac{11}{3}, b=\frac{4}{3}$

9 a 0.3 m s^{-2} b 0.904 s

c 29.1 N, 45° below the horizontal (to the left)

d i The tension is the same on both sides.

ii The two blocks have the same speed and acceleration.

10 i 3.04 N **ii** 3.04 N up

11 i 32.6 N

ii 21.5 N, 31.2° to left of vertical

12 i $u = 14\text{ m s}^{-1}, 2d = 120\text{ m}$ **ii** 24.1°

iii 0.671 kg

13 i Proof **ii** $a \leqslant 3$

14 i $t = \frac{50}{7}\sin\theta$, Proof **ii** 3.66 s, 6.13 s

15 a $(1 - 2\cos(\pi t))\mathbf{i} + (3\sin(\pi t))\mathbf{j}\text{ m s}^{-1}$

b i Proof

ii $\frac{3\sqrt{3}}{2}\text{ m s}^{-1}$

16 $v = \left(\sqrt{u} - \frac{1}{2}kt\right)^2$

17 Proof

18 a Proof

b i $\sqrt{109}$ **ii** 6.04 m s^{-1}

Paper 1 practice questions

1 $y = x^2 - 5x + 7$

2 a 2, −1, 0.5, 2; periodic with period 3.

b 2 **c** 51.5

3 $-\frac{1}{3}$

4 $\frac{e^3 + 2}{e^3 - 1}$

5 $1 - 4\theta - 2\theta^2$

6 16.0 cm

7 $9x - 6y = 9\ln 3 - 4$

8 $\frac{P^2}{16}$

9 a $A = 2, B = -1$

b $2 - 3.5x + \frac{29}{4}x^2$

c $|x| < \frac{2}{5}$.

10 a ln 5 or −ln 3 **b** Proof

11 $p = \frac{24}{5}, q = \frac{19}{40}$.

12 a 3.902; under-estimate

b 5.524

c $L = 3.902, U = 5.524$, use more rectangles and trapezia.

13 a $\frac{2x + 2y}{y - 2x}$ **b** Proof

14 a Proof **b** Proof

c $a = \frac{1}{2}, b = 2$ **d** 3.048

15 a Proof

b $(3x + 1)(x - 1)(3x + 2)$

c i Proof

ii 90°, 199°, 222°, 318°, 341°

Paper 2 practice questions

1 −11

2 −3, 2

3 202.5

4 $a = -7, b = 9$

5 a $6(x - 1)^2 + 5$

b i Proof

ii Yes; it is increasing and therefore one-to-one.

iii $x > 1$

6 a $\sqrt{12}\sin(x + 0.869)$

b $-12 + 12\sqrt{3}$

7 a i 2.46

ii

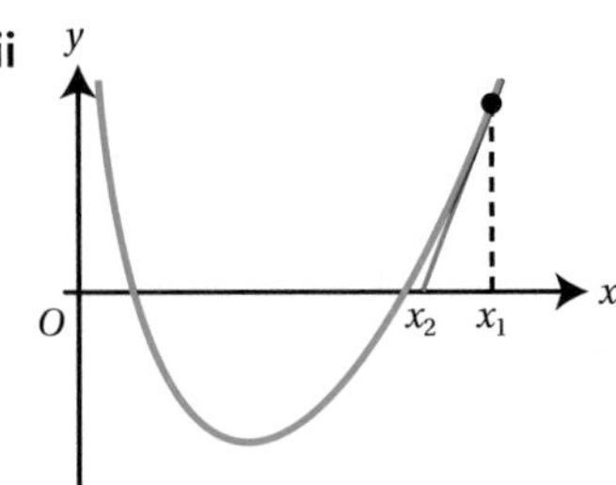

b i $\sqrt{\frac{3}{2}}$

ii The tangent does not cross the x-axis.

8 a Model 2; taking logs gives $\log a - kx$ which is of the form $y = 1.2 - 2.6x$

b $a = 16, k = 2.6$

9 a $\left(\frac{\sqrt{2}}{2}, 1\right)$

b i 0 at A, $\frac{\pi}{2}$ at O

ii $\frac{4}{3}$

10 a Cluster sampling

b $|r| < 0.3120$

c i No – we can only say that *this sample* does not provide significant evidence of correlation.

ii No – there may be a non-linear relationship.

11 a $\frac{6}{217}$ b $\frac{107}{217}$

c 0.429 d 0.165

e For example, P(Male | Walk) + P(Male | Walk') = 0.887

12 a 4.53%

b H_0: $p = \frac{312}{655}$; H_1: $p > \frac{312}{655}$; p-value = 6.42%. Do not reject H_0: this is not significantly above the expected number.

c May not be independent; club not representative of whole school.

13 a 0.1 b 0.6

c 0.375

14 a $\frac{17}{35}$ b Proof

15 a Mean is around middle of range. Range is about 6 standard deviations.

b 0.317

c 0.186, assuming independence.

d H_0: $\mu = 25$; H_1: $\mu \neq 25$; p-value = 20.1%. Do not reject H_0. No significant change in the mean travel time.

e $\mu = 24.4$ min, $\sigma^2 = 11.7$ min^2

Paper 3 practice questions

1 $\pi - a$, $\pi + a$.

2 a (2, 4), (−3, 9)

b

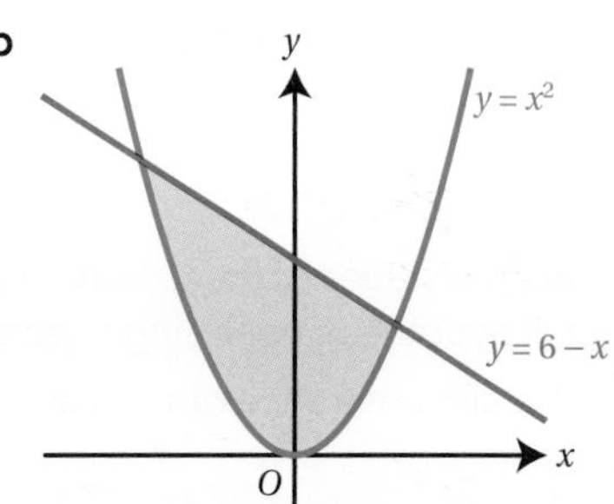

c −3

3 a $2\mathbf{i} - 4\mathbf{j} + 4\mathbf{k}$

b −7

4 $\left(\frac{2}{3}, \frac{2}{3}e^{-2}\right)$

5 Proof

6 a $a = 3$, $b = 5$, $c = -2$

b 72°, 153°, 252°, 333°

7 $\ln 16 - \frac{15}{16}$.

8 a Proof b $150 - 25\pi$

9 a (0, 8)

b i Proof ii (ln 5, 12)

c $16 \ln 5 - 16$

10 a 1.25 m s^{-2} b Proof

c 0 m s^{-1}

11 a 61.8 N b 2.08 m

c 54°

12 a $(\mathbf{i} - 5\mathbf{j})$ N

b i 8.50 m s^{-2} ii 101°

13 a $a = \frac{V - U}{T}$ b Proof

14 a Proof b 10.5 m s^{-1}

c V would need to be larger.

15 a Proof

b $m \leqslant \frac{5.2}{\sin 35° - \mu \cos 35°}$

c $5.4 \leqslant m \leqslant 29$

16 5.61 m s^{-1}

Glossary

Absolute value: See 'modulus'

Acceptance region:The values of the observed data that lead to the null hypothesis not being rejected

Arc: The part of the circumference of a circle between two points

Arithmetic sequence/progression: A sequence that has a common difference between each term: to get from one term to the next you add the common difference (which may be negative)

Arithmetic series: The sum of the terms of an arithmetic sequence

Boundary condition: The value of a function, y, at given input value, x

Cartesian equation: An equation involving just x and y

Centre of mass: The point at which the object's weight acts

Chain rule: A rule for differentiating composite functions: if $y = \mathrm{f}(u)$ where $u = \mathrm{g}(x)$, so that $y = \mathrm{f}(\mathrm{g}(x))$ then $\frac{\mathrm{d}y}{\mathrm{d}x} = \frac{\mathrm{d}y}{\mathrm{d}u} \times \frac{\mathrm{d}u}{\mathrm{d}x}$

Chord: A straight line segment whose endpoints both lie on the circumference of a circle

Cobweb diagram: A diagram that shows successive terms of an iterative sequence oscillating either side of a value to which the sequence is converging

Coefficient of friction: A constant, denoted by μ, that measures the roughness of the surface a particle is moving over

Complement: For a set *A*, the complement is everything that could happen other than *A*, written in set notation as *A*′

Composite function: A function that results from applying a function to the output of another function

Compound angle identities: Identities that express the sine, cosine or tangent of the sum and difference of angles in terms of trigonometric functions of the individual angles

Concave curve: A curve that curves downwards. It has $\frac{\mathrm{d}^2y}{\mathrm{d}x^2} < 0$

Conditional probability: A probability that takes into account information about events that have previously occurred

Continuous function: A function whose graph can be drawn without taking the pen off the paper

Convergent sequence: A sequence converges when the terms approach a limiting value

Convex curve: A curve that curves upwards. It has $\frac{\mathrm{d}^2y}{\mathrm{d}x^2} > 0$

Critical region: The values of the observed data that lead to the null hypothesis being rejected

Decreasing sequence: A sequence where each term is smaller than the previous one

Differential equation: An equation involving a derivative, for example $\frac{\mathrm{d}y}{\mathrm{d}x} = 3x^2$

Distribution of the sample mean: If a random variable, X, is normally distributed, $X \sim N(\mu, \sigma^2)$, then the sample mean, $\bar{X}$ is also normal, and $\bar{X} \sim \mathrm{N}\left(\mu, \frac{\sigma^2}{n}\right)$

Divergent sequence: A sequence diverges when the terms increase or decrease without limit

Domain: The set of allowed input values of a function.

Double angle identities: Identities that express the sine, cosine or tangent of twice the value of an angle in terms of trigonometric functions of the angle

Explicit function: A function expressed in the form $y = \mathrm{f}(x)$

Family of solutions: The set of solutions to a given differential equation obtained by varying the constant of integration

Finite sequence: Has a finite number of terms.

Fixed-point iteration: A method of creating a sequence that gets closer to a root of an equation of the form $x = \mathrm{g}(x)$. A starting guess, x_1, generates a sequence $x_{n+1} = \mathrm{g}(x_n)$. If this sequence converges to a limit, then this limit is a solution of the equation

Function: A mapping where there is only one y value for each x value

General solution: The solution to a differential equation that includes the constant of integration

Geometric sequence/progression: A sequence that has a common ratio between each term: to get from one term to the next you multiply by the common ratio

Geometric series: The sum of the terms of a geometric sequence

Horizontal line test: A function is one-to-one if any horizontal line will cross its graph at most once

Image: The image of an x value is the y value it is mapped to

Implicit function: A function not expressed in the form $y = \mathrm{f}(x)$

Increasing sequence: A sequence where each term is larger than the previous one

Infinite sequence: Continues for ever, so it is not possible to list all of the terms.

Initial condition: The value of a function, y, at given input value, x

Integration by parts: A method of integrating the product of two functions: $\int u\frac{\mathrm{d}v}{\mathrm{d}x}\mathrm{d}x = uv - \int v\frac{\mathrm{d}u}{\mathrm{d}x}\mathrm{d}x$

Integration by substitution: A method of integration whereby the variable of integration is changed

Intersection: The intersection of events A and B means when both A and B happen, written in set notation as $A \cap B$

Inverse function: A function, denoted by f^{-1}, that reverses the effect of another function

Inverse normal distribution: For a given value of probability p the inverse normal distribution gives the value of x such that $\mathrm{P}(X \leqslant x) = p$

Inverse trigonometric function: The inverse function of the sine, cosine or tangent functions (denoted by, for example, $\sin^{-1}$ or arcsin)

Limit: The value to which a sequence converges

Limiting equilibrium: When friction is at its limiting value and an object subjected to a driving force is on the point of moving

Limiting friction: The maximum value of friction before an object starts to move under the action of a force

Lower bound: The lower bound on a definite integral is a value that is definitely smaller than the integral. Found by underestimating the area under the curve

Major arc: The longer arc between two points on the circumference of a circle

Major sector: The larger part of the circle bounded by two radii and an arc

Many-to-one: A function is many-to-one if there are some y values that come from more than one x value

Mapping: Any rule that assigns to each input value (x) one or more output values (y)

Minor arc: The shorter arc between two points on the circumference of a circle

Minor sector: The smaller part of the circle bounded by two radii and an arc

Modulus: An operation that leaves positive numbers alone but makes negative numbers positive. $|x|$ denotes the modulus of number x. Also known as absolute value

Moment: The turning effect of a force. The moment of a force F about a point P is moment = Fd, where d is the perpendicular distance of the line of action of the force from P

Mutually exclusive: If there is no possibility of A and B occurring at the same time, then the events are mutually exclusive, written in set notation as $\mathrm{P}(A \cap B) = 0$

Newton–Raphson method: An iterative method for finding the numerical solution to an equation which uses the tangent to the graph of $\mathrm{f}(x)$ to suggest where to look for the root. Given an approximate root x_0 of the equation $\mathrm{f}(x) = 0$, a better approximation is $x_1 = x_0 - \frac{\mathrm{f}(x_0)}{\mathrm{f}'(x_0)}$.

Non-uniform rod: A rod whose mass is not evenly distributed throughout its length; the centre of mass may not be at the midpoint

Normal distribution: A symmetrical distribution of values where a variable is very likely to be close to its average value, with values further away from the average becoming increasingly unlikely

One-to-many: A mapping where a single input corresponds to more than one output (so is not a function)

One-to-one: A function is one-to-one if every y-value corresponds to only one x-value

Ordinates: The y-values to be substituted into the trapezium rule formula for numerical integration

Parameter: The third variable in parametric equations (usually denoted by t or θ), on which both x and y depend

Parametric equation: An equation in which both x and y are expressed in terms of a third variable, usually denoted by t or θ

Partial fractions: Two or more algebraic fractions which add together to give a more complicated fraction

Particular solution: A specific solution to a differential equation that does not depend on any unknown constants

Periodic sequence: A sequence where the terms start repeating after a while: $u_{n+k} = u_n$ for some number k (the period of the sequence)

Point of inflection: A point at which a curve changes from convex to concave (or vice versa). At a point of inflection $\frac{d^2y}{dx^2}=0$ and the second derivative changes sign.

Position-to-term rule: A rule that generates any term of the sequence from a formula (the nth term formula)

Probability density function: A curve such that the area under the curve represents probability

Product rule: A rule for differentiating the products of two functions: if $y=f(x)g(x)$ then $\frac{dy}{dx}=f'(x)g(x)+f(x)g'(x)$

Proof by contradiction: A method of proof that starts with the opposite of the statement you are trying to prove, and shows that this results in an impossible conclusion

p-value: The probability of getting the observed data or more extreme if the null hypothesis is true

Quotient: For polynomial division, this is 'how many times' a polynomial divides into a higher order polynomial, usually expressed as another, lower order polynomial. Q(x) is usually used to represent the quotient.

Quotient rule: A rule for differentiation the quotients of two functions: if $y=\frac{f(x)}{g(x)}$ then $\frac{dy}{dx}=\frac{f'(x)g(x)-f(x)g'(x)}{[g(x)]^2}$

Radian: The angle subtended at the centre of a circle by an arc equal in length to the radius. There are 2π radians in a complete rotation

Range: The set of all possible outputs of a function

Rational function: A fraction where both the denominator and numerator are polynomials

Reciprocal trigonometric functions: The cosecant, secant and cotangent functions: $\operatorname{cosec} x=\frac{1}{\sin x}$, $\sec x=\frac{1}{\cos x}$ and $\cot x=\frac{1}{\tan x}$

Rejection region: See 'critical region'

Remainder: If a given polynomial does not divide exactly by a lower order polynomial, the remainder is what is 'left over'. The remainder is usually represented with the variable r.

Resolve (forces): A force is resolved when it is split into two (often perpendicular) components

Sector: A part of a circle bounded by two radii and an arc

Segment: A segment of a circle is the region bounded by a chord and the arc subtended by the chord

Separation of variables: A method used to solve a differential equation that is in the form $\frac{dy}{dx}=f(x)g(y)$

Series: The sum of the terms of a sequence

Sigma notation: A shorthand way to describe a series $\sum_{r=1}^{r=n} f(r)$, where r is a placeholder that increases by 1 with each new term

Small angle approximation: For small θ, measured in radians, $\sin\theta\approx\theta$, $\cos\theta\approx 1-\frac{1}{2}\theta^2$, and $\tan\theta\approx\theta$

Smooth: A surface with no friction: $\mu=0$

Staircase diagram: A diagram that shows successive terms of an iterative sequence all increasing (or all decreasing)

Standard normal distribution: A random variable Z that has normal distribution with mean 0 and variance 1: $Z\sim N(0, 1)$

Subtended: The angle at the centre of a circle between radii to the end of an arc is the angle subtended by the arc

Sum to infinity: The limiting value of a geometric series. Exists only when $|r|<1$, denoted by S_∞

Term-to-term rule: A rule that generates the next term of a sequence from the previous term(s)

Trajectory: The path of a projectile

Trapezium rule: A method of approximating a definite integral using n equal intervals with end-points $x_0, x_1, \ldots x_n$:

$\int_a^b f(x)dx\approx\frac{h}{2}[y_0+y_n+2(y_1+y_2+\ldots+y_{n-1})]$, where $y_i=f(x_i)$ and $h=\frac{b-a}{n}$

Uniform lamina: A two-dimensional object which has constant mass per unit area

Uniform rod: A one-dimensional shape with constant mass per unit length

Union: The union of events A and B means when either A happens, or B happens, or both happen, written in set notation as $A\cup B$

Upper bound: The upper bound on a definite integral is a value that the integral is definitely smaller than. Found by overestimating the area under the curve

Vertical line test: A mapping is a function if any vertical line will cross its graph at most once

Z-score: The number of standard deviations a value is away from the mean: $z=\frac{x-\mu}{\sigma}$

Index

Acknowledgements

The authors and publishers acknowledge the following sources of copyright material and are grateful for the permissions granted. While every effort has been made, it has not always been possible to identify the sources of all the material used, or to trace all copyright holders. If any omissions are brought to our notice, we will be happy to include the appropriate acknowledgements on reprinting.

Thanks to the following for permission to reproduce images:

Cover image: huskyomega/Getty Images

Back cover: Fabian Oefner www.fabianoefner.com

dunlin/Getty Images; Hulton Archive/Stringer/Getty Images; litu92458/Getty Images; Photograph by Patrick Murphy/Getty Images; David Soanes Photography/Getty Images; Bettmann/Contributor/Getty Images; Esben_H/Getty Images; Stefan Swalander/EyeEm/Getty Images; Hulton Archive/Stringer/Getty Images; Thai Yuan Lim/EyeEm/Getty Images; Dave Porter Peterborough UK/Getty Images; Elli Thor Magnusson/Getty Images; Kalawin/Getty Images; vili45/Getty Images; Mark Tipple/Getty Images; Graiki/Getty Images; Vico Collective/Michael Shay/Getty Images; Rafe Swan/Getty Images; shank_ali/Getty Images; Hulton Archive/Stringer/Getty Images; Wikipedia; James Aiken/EyeEm/Getty Images; Jack Andersen/Getty Images; Bettmann/Contributor/Getty Images; Shoji Fujita/Getty Images; BSIP/UIG /Getty Images; Iryna Rieber/EyeEm/Getty Images; Ed Freeman/Getty Images; Yoshinori Kuwahara/Getty Images; Peter Beavis/Getty Images; Stock Montage/Getty Images.